Contents in Brief

Contents

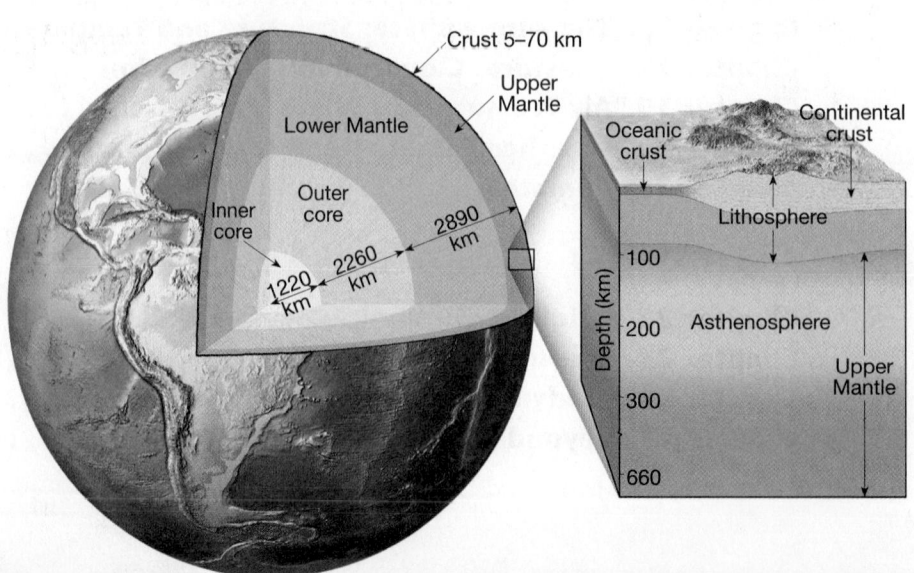

Unit 2 Sculpturing Earth's Surface

Unit 3 Forces Within

Unit 4 Historical Geology

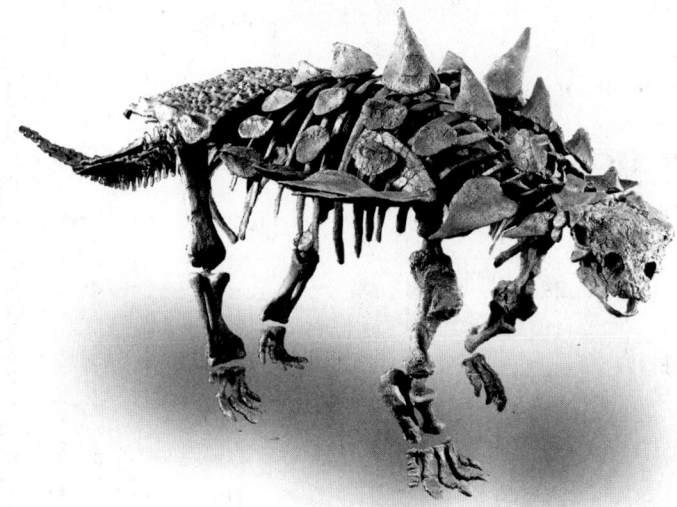

Unit 5 Oceanography

Unit 6 Meteorology

Unit 7 Astronomy

Skills and Reference Handbook

Labs and Activities

Quick Lab
Introduce and reinforce key lesson content using simple materials.

Exploration Lab
Practice and develop science methods.

Application Lab
Apply concepts in a real-world context.

Problem-Solving Activity
Apply science content in a new situation.

Features

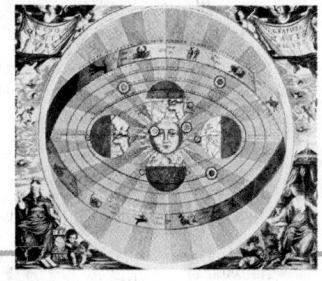

How the Earth Works

MAP★MASTER™
Skills Activity

GEODe EARTH SCIENCE

This engaging CD-ROM takes you on an audiovisual tour of the key concepts in the text. Through the wonder of animation, you can actually see in just a few seconds the dynamic processes that occur on Earth over millions of years. To be sure that you understand what you've learned, you'll work with a number of interesting interactive exercises to test your knowledge of each topic.

LEARNING FOR THE 21st CENTURY

The Partnership for 21st Century Skills is the leading advocacy organization focused on infusing skills for the 21st century into education. The organization brings together the business community, education leaders, and policy makers to define a powerful vision for 21st century education to ensure every child's success as citizens and workers by providing tools and resources to help facilitate and drive change.

Today's students will spend their adult lives in a multitasking, multifaceted, technology-driven, diverse, vibrant world—and they must arrive equipped to do so. The goal of 21st Century Learning is to bridge the gap between how students live and how they learn. A way to bridge the gap is summarized in the diagram below and explained on the following page.

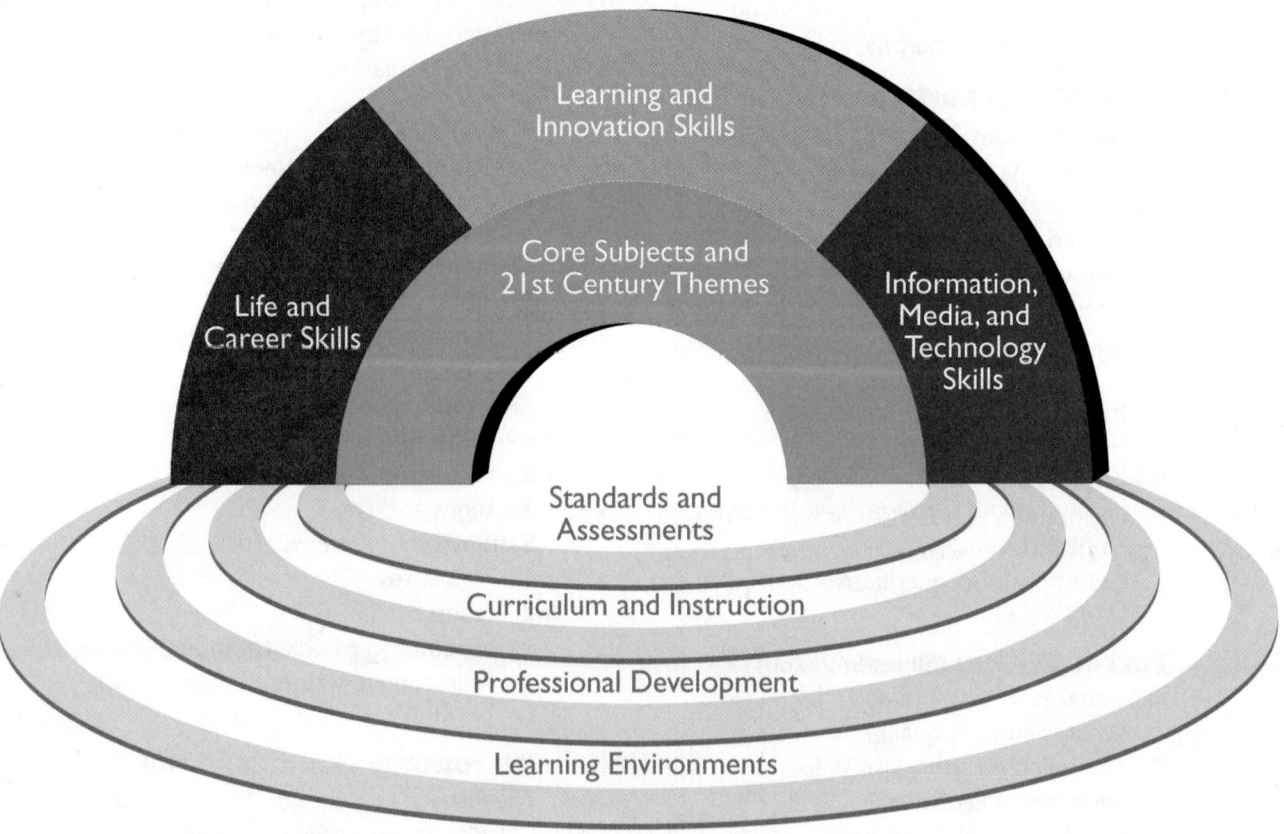

The arches of the rainbow represent student outcomes. These are the skills, knowledge, and expertise students will need to master to succeed in work and life in the 21st century. The pools at the base of the rainbow represent the 21st Century Support Systems that must be present in order for students to master the skills described in the rainbow.

CORE SUBJECTS AND THE 21st CENTURY THEMES

Let's start with the green section of the rainbow: **Core Subjects and 21st Century Themes.** Today's students will still need to master core subjects such as English (reading or language arts), world languages, arts, mathematics, economics, sciences, geography, history, government, and civics. However, they can move beyond basic competence to higher levels of understanding if schools weave into those subjects such themes as global awareness; financial, economic, business, and entrepreneurial literacy; civic literacy; and health literacy.

LEARNING AND INNOVATION SKILLS

The yellow section, **Learning and Innovation Skills,** prepares students for increasingly complex life and work environments. Skills such as *creativity and innovation* allow students to implement, analyze, refine, and evaluate new ideas. *Critical thinking and problem-solving* skills allow students to make their way through the multistep process required to find solutions—be they conventional or innovative—to non-familiar problems. *Communication and collaboration* skills will be key to success in today's global, interconnected, multicultural world.

INFORMATION, MEDIA, AND TECHNOLOGY

The 21st century is a technology- and media-suffused environment that requires mastery of the skills in the blue section—**Information, Media, and Technology Skills.** These skills include *information literacy, media literacy,* and *ICT (information, communications, and technology) literacy.* Students must learn to access, evaluate, and use information from a wide variety of sources. They will need to know how to recognize, understand, and create media messages. In order to function in the new knowledge economy, today's students will need to use digital devices, communication and networking tools, and social networks professionally as well as personally.

LIFE AND CAREER SKILLS

The ultimate goal is to prepare students for success beyond the classroom with **Life and Career Skills.** This is a globally competitive information age with complex life and work environments. These environments require such skills as flexibility and adaptability, initiative and self-direction, social and cross-cultural skills, productivity and accountability, and leadership and responsibility.

Careers in Earth and Space Science

The career opportunities available in Earth and space science are far reaching—from exploring distant galaxies to investigating deep inside Earth. Here are a few of these exciting careers.

Meteorologist

Meteorologists study how the physical characteristics, processes, and movements of the atmosphere affect the environment. They use this information to forecast the weather and study the patterns of weather change, such as droughts and global warming.

Educational requirements Four-year college degree, majoring in meteorology or atmospheric science

Seismologist

Seismologists are Earth scientists who investigate earthquakes. They determine the location and size of earthquakes and use seismic waves to study Earth's interior. Some seismologists help the building industry design earthquake-proof structures.

Educational requirements Four-year college degree, majoring in geology, geophysics, or mathematics

Surveying Technician

Helping to measure and map Earth's surface are the responsibilities of surveying technicians. They assist land surveyors who measure distances, directions, and contours on, above, or below Earth's surface. Surveying technicians use surveying instruments to collect data and then enter the data into computers.

Educational requirements Two-year junior or community college program, one to three years of technical school

Go Online
PHSchool.com

For: Career links
Visit: PHSchool.com
Web Code: ccb-3000

Commercial Diver

Just about anywhere there is water, there is a need for commercial divers. Their work ranges from operating submersibles to helping map the ocean floor. They may perform underwater surveys or carry out underwater rescue and salvage operations.

Educational requirements High-school diploma, diving-school certification or naval training

Archaeologist

Archaeologists excavate, preserve, study, and classify objects and structures from past cultures. In order to interpret what they see at a particular site, archaeologists must be able to identify different types of soil and notice the smallest of changes in soil characteristics.

Educational requirements Master's degree in anthropology or archaeology

Astronomer

Astronomers use the laws of physics and mathematics to study the universe. They may specialize to investigate the moon, sun, planets, stars, or galaxies, such as the Andromeda Galaxy shown in the photo at the left. They also may use what they know about astronomy to help develop satellites and spacecraft.

Educational requirements Doctoral degree in physics, astrophysics, or space physics

CHAPTER 1 Introduction to Earth Science

21st Century Learning

Creativity and Intellectual Curiosity

What science subject interests you?

The subject of earth science includes many different topics, such as the study of rocks, water, weather, Earth's movements, and the solar system. Scientists, including earth scientists, study what they are most interested in. What topic of earth science most interests you? What questions would you like answered? Why are you interested in this particular topic? Write about your interest in a blog or in your notes.

Exploration Lab

Determining Latitude and Longitude

Earth as a System

Earth's Place in the Universe

This photograph shows British Columbia's Mount Robson, the highest point in the Canadian Rockies.

Chapter Preview

Inquiry › Activity

Developing Your Observation Skills

Procedure
Look at the photograph on this page. Have you ever seen anything like it?

Think About It

1. Observing What features can you identify in the photograph?

2. Inferring Where do you think this photograph came from?

3. Designing Experiments If you were an Earth scientist, how could you use this photograph in your work?

1.1 What Is Earth Science?

Reading Focus

Key Concepts

- What is the study of Earth science?
- How did Earth and the solar system form?

Vocabulary

- Earth science
- geology
- oceanography
- meteorology
- astronomy

Reading Strategy

Categorizing As you read about the different branches of Earth science, fill in the column with the name of each branch and list some of the things that are studied.

geology	a. _____ ?
b. _____ ?	c. _____ ?
d. _____ ?	e. _____ ?
f. _____ ?	g. _____ ?

The spectacular eruption of a volcano, the magnificent scenery of a rocky coast, and the destruction created by a hurricane are all subjects for Earth science. The study of Earth science deals with many fascinating and practical questions about our environment. What forces produced the mountains shown on page 1? Why does our daily weather change? Is our climate changing? How old is Earth? How is Earth related to the other planets in the solar system? What causes ocean tides? What was the Ice Age like? Will there be another?

Understanding Earth is not an easy task because our planet is always changing. Earth is a dynamic planet with a long and complex history.

Overview of Earth Science

Earth science is the name for the group of sciences that deals with Earth and its neighbors in space. Earth science includes many subdivisions of geology such as geochemistry, geophysics, geobiology and paleontology, as well as oceanography, meteorology, and astronomy.

Units 1 through 4 focus on the science of **geology,** a word that means "study of Earth." Geology is divided into two broad areas—physical geology and historical geology.

Physical geology includes the examination of the materials that make up Earth and the possible explanations for the many processes that shape our planet. Processes below the surface create earthquakes, build mountains, and produce volcanoes. Processes at the surface break rock apart and create

Figure 1 Scientists called paleontologists study fossils, which are signs of life in the distant past, to find out how life forms have changed through time.
Posing Questions *What questions do you have about this fossil?*

different landforms. Erosion by water, wind, and ice results in different landscapes. You will learn that rocks and minerals form in response to Earth's internal and external processes. Understanding the origin of rocks and minerals is an important part of understanding Earth.

In contrast to physical geology, the aim of historical geology is to understand Earth's long history. Historical geology tries to establish a timeline of the vast number of physical and biological changes that have occurred in the past. See Figure 1. We study physical geology before historical geology because we must first understand how Earth works before we try to unravel its past.

 **Reading Checkpoint** *What are the two main areas of geology?*

Unit 5 is devoted to **oceanography.** Oceanography integrates the sciences of chemistry, physics, geology, and biology. Oceanographers study the composition and movements of seawater, as well as coastal processes, seafloor topography, and marine life. See Figure 2.

Unit 6 examines the composition of Earth's atmosphere. The combined effects of Earth's motions and energy from the sun cause the atmosphere to produce different weather conditions. This, in turn, creates the basic pattern of global climates. **Meteorology** is the study of the atmosphere and the processes that produce weather and climate. Like oceanography, meteorology also involves other branches of science.

Unit 7 demonstrates that understanding Earth requires an understanding of Earth's position in the universe. The science of **astronomy,** the study of the universe, is useful in probing the origins of our own environment. All objects in space, including Earth, are subject to the same physical laws. Learning about the other members of our solar system and the universe beyond helps us to understand Earth.

Throughout its long existence, Earth has been changing. In fact, it is changing as you read this page and will continue to do so. Sometimes the changes are rapid and violent, such as when tornadoes, landslides, or volcanic eruptions occur. Many changes, however, take place so gradually that they go unnoticed during a lifetime.

Formation of Earth

Earth is one of several planets that revolve around the sun. Our solar system has an orderly nature. Scientists understand that Earth and the other planets formed during the same time span and from the same material as the sun. ⬤**The nebular hypothesis suggests that the bodies of our solar system evolved from an enormous rotating cloud called the solar nebula. It was made up mostly of hydrogen and helium, with a small percentage of heavier elements.** Figure 3 on page 4 summarizes some key points of this hypothesis.

Figure 2 Oceanographers study all aspects of the ocean—the chemistry of its waters, the geology of its seafloor, the physics of its interactions with the atmosphere, and the biology of its organisms.

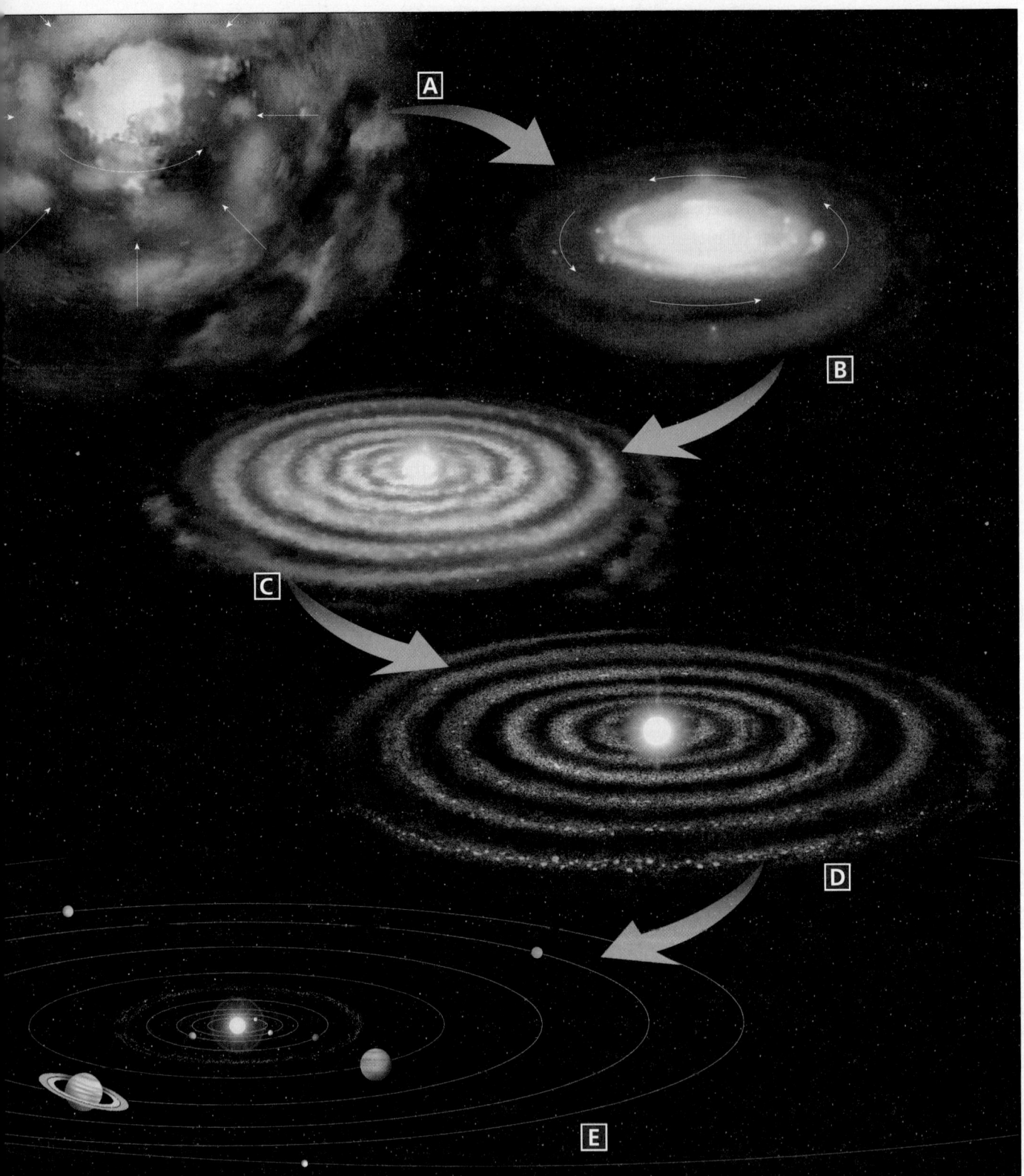

Figure 3 Formation of the Solar System According to the Nebular Hypothesis A Our solar system began as an enormous cloud of dust and gases made up mostly of hydrogen and helium with a small percentage of heavier elements. **B** This cloud, called a nebula, started to rotate and collapse toward the center of the cloud. Heat was generated at the center, which eventually formed the sun. **C** Cooling of the nebula caused rocky and metallic materials to form tiny solid particles. **D** Repeated collisions of these particles resulted in the formation of asteroid-sized bodies. **E** These asteroids eventually combined to form the four inner planets—Mercury, Venus, Earth, and Mars. The lighter materials and gases combined farther away from the center to form the four outer planets—Jupiter, Saturn, Uranus, and Neptune.

High temperatures and weak fields of gravity characterized the inner planets. As a result, the inner planets were not able to hold onto the lighter gases of the nebular cloud. The lightest gases, hydrogen and helium, were whisked away toward the heavier planets by the solar wind. Earth, Mars, and Venus were able to retain some heavier gases including water vapor and carbon dioxide. The materials that formed the outer planets contained mostly hydrogen and helium, but also high percentages of water, carbon dioxide, ammonia, and methane, in addition to rock and metal cores. Because of their large size, the outer planets' gravity was strong enough to hold all of these gases.

Layers Form on Earth Shortly after Earth formed, the decay of radioactive elements, combined with heat released by colliding particles, produced some melting of its interior. This allowed the denser elements, mostly iron and nickel, to sink to Earth's center because of gravity. The less dense, rocky components floated outward, toward the surface. This sinking and floating is believed to still be occurring, but on a much smaller scale. As a result of this process, Earth's interior is not made of uniform materials. It consists of layers of materials that have different properties.

 *Why does Earth have layers?*

An important result of this process is that gaseous materials were allowed to escape from Earth's interior, just as gases escape today during volcanic eruptions. In this way, an atmosphere gradually formed along with the ocean. It was composed mainly of gases that were released from within the planet.

Section 1.1 Assessment

Reviewing Concepts
1. What are the sciences that are included in Earth science?
2. What topics are included in the study of physical geology?
3. Explain how physical geology differs from historical geology.
4. Describe the nebular hypothesis.

Critical Thinking
5. **Forming Conclusions** Explain why Earth is called a dynamic planet.

6. **Inferring** Would meteorology be a useful science to apply to the study of planets such as Mercury and Mars? Explain.
7. **Hypothesizing** Suppose that as Earth formed, all lighter elements were released to surrounding space. How might this affect the structure of Earth today?

Connecting Concepts

Summarizing Earth science is composed of many different areas of study. Why is it important to include all of these areas in the study of Earth and the solar system?

Earth's Place in the Universe

For centuries, people who have gazed at the night sky have wondered about the nature of the universe, Earth's place within it, and whether or not we are alone. Today many exciting discoveries in astronomy are beginning to provide answers about the origin of the universe, the formation and evolution of stars, and how Earth came into existence.

The realization that the universe is immense and orderly began in the early 1900s. Edwin Hubble and other scientists demonstrated that the Milky Way galaxy is one of hundreds of billions of galaxies, each of which contains billions of stars. Evidence supports that Earth, its materials, and all living things are the result of the Big Bang theory. The universe began between 13 and 14 billion years ago as a dense, hot, massive amount of material exploded with violent force. See Figure 4. Within about one second, the temperature of the expanding universe cooled to approximately 10 billion degrees. Basic atomic particles called protons and neutrons began to appear. After a few minutes, atoms of the simplest elements—hydrogen and helium—had formed. The initial conversion of energy to matter in the young universe was completed.

During the first billion years or so, matter (essentially hydrogen and helium) in the expanding universe clumped together to form enormous clouds that eventually collapsed to become galaxies and clusters of galaxies. Inside these collapsing clouds, smaller concentrations of matter formed into stars. One of the billions of galaxies to form was the Milky Way.

During the life of most stars, energy produced as hydrogen nuclei (protons) fuses with other hydrogen nuclei to form helium. During this process, called nuclear fusion, matter is converted to energy. Stars begin to die when their nuclear fuel is used up. Massive stars often have explosive deaths. During these events, called supernovas, nuclear fusion produces atoms such as oxygen, carbon, and iron. These atoms may become the materials that make up future generations of stars. From the debris scattered during the death of a preexisting star, our sun, and the solar system formed

Our star, the sun, is at the very least a second-generation star. Along with the planets in our solar system, the sun began forming nearly 5 billion years ago from a large interstellar cloud called a nebula. This nebula consisted of dust particles and gases enriched in heavy elements from supernova explosions. Gravitational energy caused the nebula to contract, rotate, and flatten. Inside, smaller concentrations of matter began condensing to form the planets. At the center of the nebula there was sufficient pressure and heat to initiate hydrogen nuclear fusion, and our sun was born.

It has been said that all life on Earth is related to the stars. This is true because the atoms in our bodies and the atoms that make up everything on Earth, owe their origin to a supernova event that occurred billions of years ago, trillions of kilometers away.

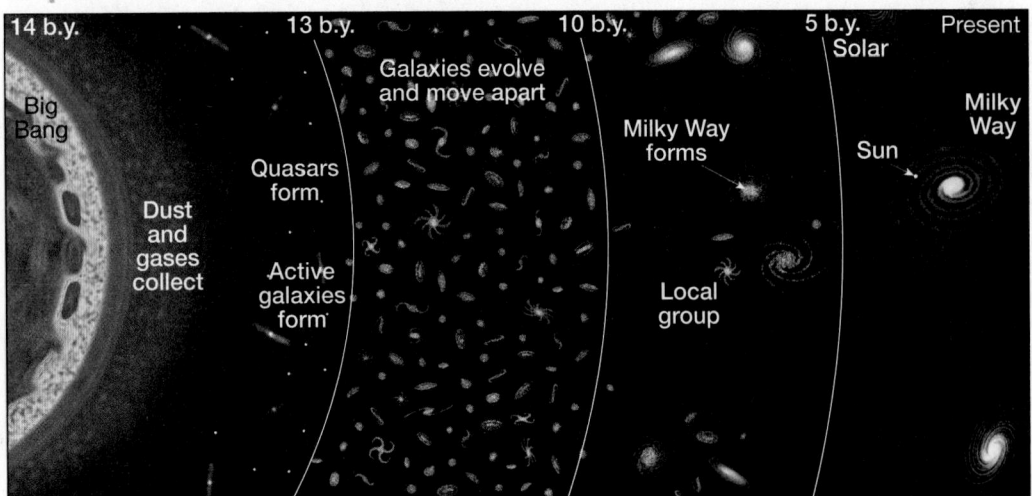

Figure 4 Big Bang Theory Between 13 and 14 billion years ago, a huge explosion sent all of the universe's matter flying outward at great speed. After a few billion years, the material cooled and condensed into the first stars and galaxies. About 5 billion years ago, our solar system began forming in a galaxy that is now called the Milky Way galaxy.

1.2 A View of Earth

Key Concepts

- What are the four major spheres into which Earth is divided?
- What defines the three main parts of the solid Earth?
- What theory explains the position of continents and the occurrence of volcanoes and earthquakes?

Vocabulary

- hydrosphere
- atmosphere
- geosphere
- biosphere
- core
- mantle
- crust

Reading Strategy

Predicting Before you read, predict the meaning of the vocabulary words. After you read, revise your definition if your prediction was incorrect.

Vocabulary Term	Before You Read	After You Read
hydrosphere	a. ___?___	b. ___?___
atmosphere	c. ___?___	d. ___?___
geosphere	e. ___?___	f. ___?___
biosphere	g. ___?___	h. ___?___
core	i. ___?___	j. ___?___
mantle	k. ___?___	l. ___?___
crust	m. ___?___	n. ___?___

A view such as the one in Figure 5A provided the *Apollo 8* astronauts with a unique view of our home. Seen from space, Earth is breathtaking in its beauty. Such an image reminds us that our home is, after all, a planet—small, self-contained, and in some ways even fragile.

If you look closely at Earth from space, you may see that it is much more than rock and soil. The swirling clouds and the vast global ocean emphasize the importance of water on our planet.

Earth's Major Spheres

The view of Earth shown in Figure 5B should help you see why the physical environment is traditionally divided into three major spheres: the water portion of our planet, the **hydrosphere**; Earth's gaseous envelope, the **atmosphere**; and the **geosphere**.

Our environment is characterized by the continuous interactions of air and rock, rock and water, and water and air. The **biosphere**, which is made up of all the life forms on Earth, interacts with all three of these physical spheres. **Earth can be thought of as consisting of four major spheres: the hydrosphere, atmosphere, geosphere, and biosphere.**

Figure 5 A View that greeted the *Apollo 8* astronauts as their spacecraft emerged from behind the moon. **B** Africa and Arabia are prominent in this image of Earth taken from *Apollo 17*. The tan areas are desert regions. The bands of clouds over central Africa are associated with rainforests. Antarctica, which is covered by glacial ice, is visible at the south pole. The dark blue oceans and white swirling clouds remind us of the importance of oceans and the atmosphere.

Hydrosphere Water is what makes Earth unique. All of the water on Earth makes up the hydrosphere. The portion of the hydrosphere that controls frozen water is often referred to as the *cryosphere*. Continually on the move, water evaporates from the oceans to the atmosphere, falls back to Earth as rain, and runs back to the ocean. The oceans account for approximately 97 percent of the water on Earth. The remaining 3 percent is fresh water and is present in groundwater, streams, lakes, and glaciers. These freshwater sources are responsible for sustaining life and creating many of Earth's varied landforms.

The properties of water and its distribution are major factors that affect life on Earth. Living things require liquid water. Fortunately, much of Earth has temperatures at which water remains in the liquid state. The availability of water also helps to determine where many organisms, including humans, can live. For example, fewer people live in desert areas than in areas where water is abundant.

Atmosphere A life-sustaining, thin, gaseous envelope called the atmosphere surrounds Earth. It reaches beyond 100 kilometers above Earth, yet 90 percent occurs within just 16 kilometers of Earth's surface. This thin blanket of air is an important part of Earth. It provides the air that we breathe. It protects us from the sun's intense heat and dangerous radiation. The energy exchanges between space, the atmosphere, and Earth's surface produce weather and climate.

Geosphere Lying beneath both the atmosphere and the ocean is the geosphere. **Because the geosphere is not uniform, it is divided into three main parts based on differences in composition—the core, the mantle, and the crust.** Figure 6A shows the dense or heavy inner sphere that is the core; the less dense mantle; and the lighter, thin crust. The crust is not uniform in thickness. It is thinnest beneath the oceans and thickest beneath the continents. Figure 6B shows that the crust and uppermost mantle make up a rigid outer layer called the lithosphere. Beneath the lithosphere, the rocks become partially molten, or melted. They are able to slowly flow because of the uneven distribution of heat deep within Earth. This region is called the asthenosphere. Beneath the asthenosphere, the rock becomes more dense. This region of Earth is called the lower mantle.

Figure 6 A On this diagram, the inner core, outer core, and mantle are drawn to scale but the thickness of the crust is exaggerated by about 5 times. **B** There are two types of crust—oceanic and continental. The lithosphere is made up of the crust and upper mantle. Below the lithosphere are the asthenosphere and the lower mantle.

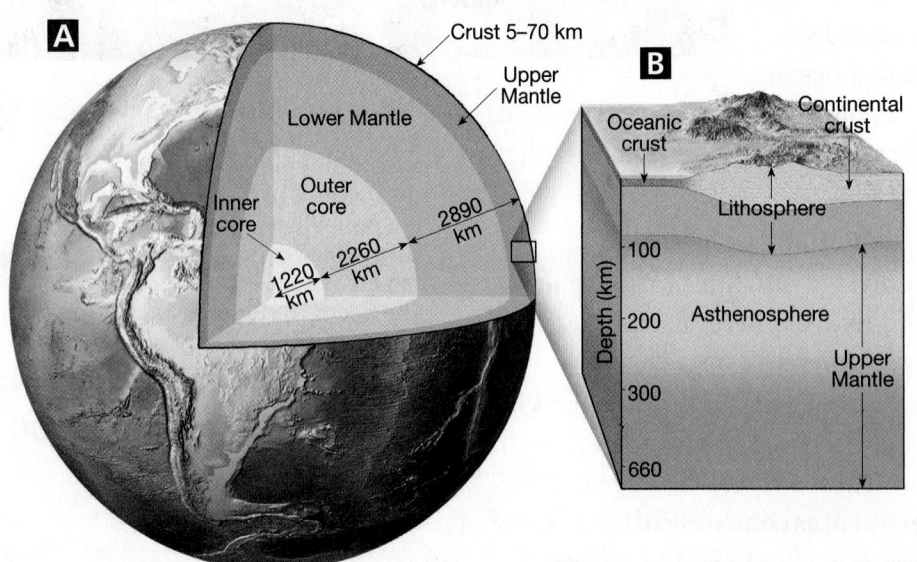

Biosphere The biosphere includes all life on Earth. It is concentrated in a zone that extends from the ocean floor upward for several kilometers into the atmosphere. Plants and animals depend on the physical environment for life. However, organisms do more than just respond to their physical environment. Through countless interactions, organisms help maintain and alter their physical environment. Without life, the makeup and nature of the solid Earth, hydrosphere, and atmosphere would be very different.

 *What are Earth's four major spheres?*

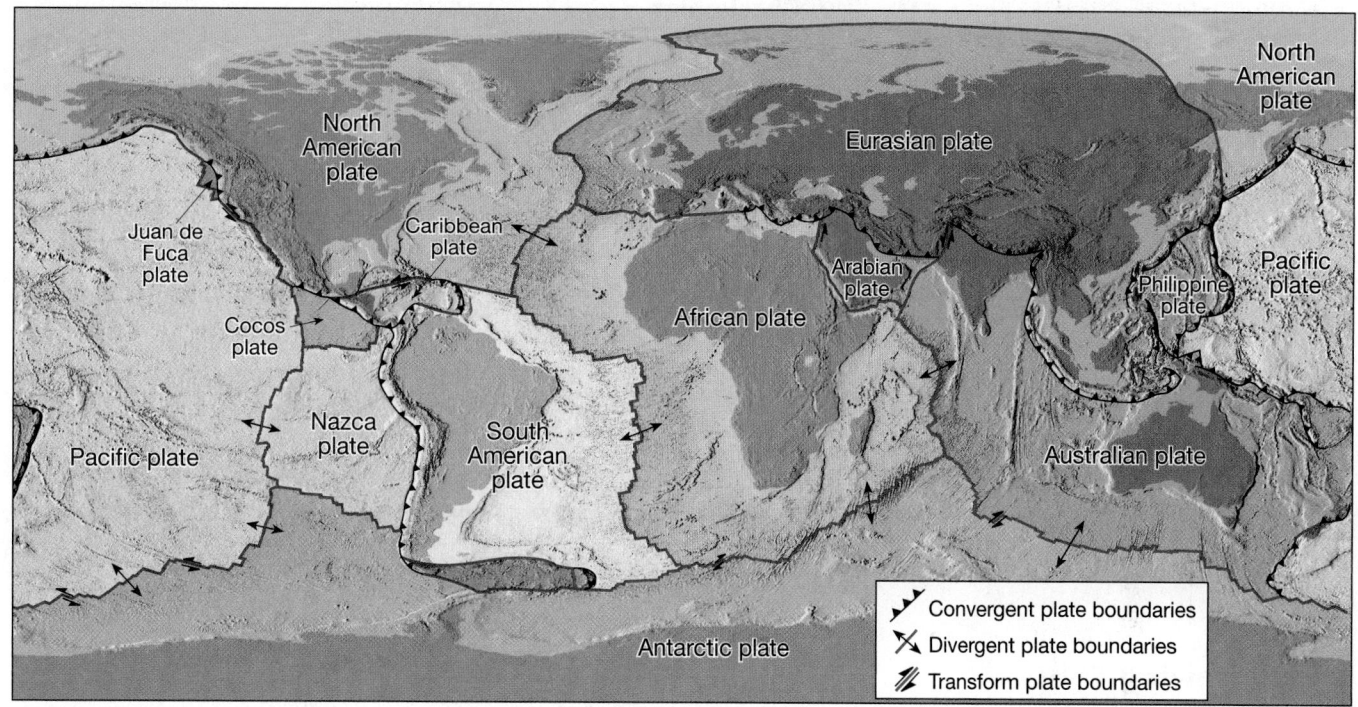

Plate Tectonics

You have read that Earth is a dynamic planet. If we could go back in time a billion years or more, we would find a planet with a surface that was dramatically different from what it is today. Such prominent features as the Grand Canyon, the Rocky Mountains, and the Appalachian Mountains did not exist. We would find that the continents had different shapes and were located in different positions from those of today.

There are two types of forces affecting Earth's surface. *Destructive forces* such as weathering and erosion work to wear away high points and flatten out the surface. *Constructive forces* such as mountain building and volcanism build up the surface by raising the land and depositing new material in the form of lava. These constructive forces depend on Earth's internal heat for their source of energy.

Figure 7 Plate Tectonics There are currently 7 major plates recognized and numerous smaller plates.
Relating Cause and Effect
What is the relationship between mountain chains and plate boundaries?

Within the last several decades, a great deal has been learned about the workings of Earth. In fact, this period is called a revolution in our knowledge about Earth. This revolution began in the early part of the twentieth century with the idea that the continents had moved about the face of the Earth. This idea contradicted the accepted view that the continents and ocean basins are stationary features on the face of Earth. Few scientists believed this new idea. More than 50 years passed before enough data were gathered to transform this hypothesis into a widely accepted theory. **The theory that finally emerged, called plate tectonics, provided geologists with a model to explain how earthquakes and volcanic eruptions occur and how continents move.**

 **Reading Checkpoint** — *What is the difference between destructive forces and constructive forces?*

According to the plate tectonics model, Earth's lithosphere is broken into several individual sections called plates. Figure 7 on page 9 shows their current position. These plates move slowly and continuously across the surface. This motion is driven by the result of an unequal distribution of heat within Earth. Ultimately, this movement of Earth's lithospheric plates generates earthquakes, volcanic activity, and the deformation of large masses of rock into mountains. You will learn more about the powerful effects of plate tectonics in Chapter 9.

Section 1.2 Assessment

Reviewing Concepts

1. Which of Earth's spheres do each of these features belong: lake, meadow, canyon, cloud?
2. What are the three main parts of the geosphere?
3. Why is the solid Earth layered?
4. The plate tectonics theory explains the existence and occurrence of what features?
5. What sort of energy allows the tectonic plates to move?
6. Describe an example of how water moves through the hydrosphere.

Critical Thinking

7. **Inferring** Using the definitions of spheres as they occur on Earth, what spheres do you think are present on Venus?
8. **Applying Concepts** Describe a situation in which two or more of Earth's spheres are interacting.
9. **Classifying** Choose an Earth science branch. List how some of its studies relate to Earth's spheres.

Connecting Concepts

Earth's Spheres You learned in Section 1.1 that Earth is a dynamic planet. Explain how features in each of Earth's spheres are changing over time.

1.3 Representing Earth's Surface

Reading Focus

Key Concepts

- What lines on a globe are used to indicate location?
- What problems do mapmakers face when making maps?
- How do topographic maps differ from other maps?

Vocabulary

- latitude
- longitude
- topographic map
- contour line
- contour interval

Reading Strategy

Monitoring Your Understanding Preview the Key Concepts, topic headings, vocabulary, and figures in this section. List two things you expect to learn. After reading, state what you learned about each item you listed.

What I Expect to Learn	What I Learned
a. _____?_____	b. _____?_____
c. _____?_____	d. _____?_____

Determining Location

Long ago, people had to rely on maps made by travelers and explorers. During the twentieth century, photographs of the land surface taken from airplanes became important in mapmaking. Later, satellite images provided even more accurate data about Earth's surface. In addition to accurate data, mapmakers need a way of precisely describing the location of features on Earth's surface. Mapmakers use a global grid to help determine location.

Global Grid Scientists use two special Earth measurements to describe location. The distance around Earth is measured in degrees. **Latitude is the distance north or south of the equator, measured in degrees. Longitude is the distance east or west of the prime meridian, measured in degrees.** Earth is 360 degrees in circumference. Lines of latitude are east-west circles around the globe. All points on the circle have the same latitude. The line of latitude around the middle of the globe, at 0 degrees (°), is the equator. Lines of longitude run north and south. The prime meridian marks 0° of longitude as shown in Figure 8.

Figure 8 Global Grid

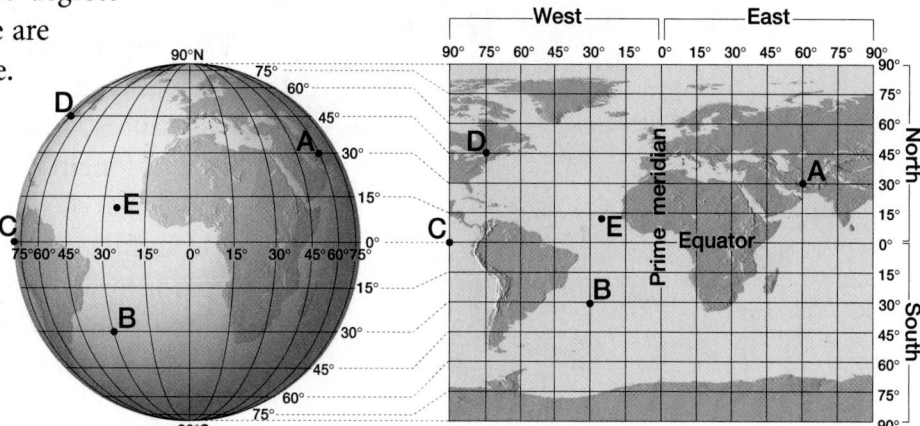

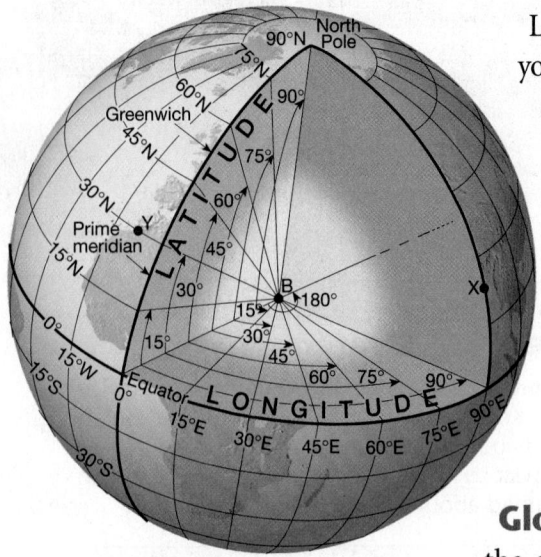

Figure 9 Measuring Latitude and Longitude

Figure 10 Mercator Map To make a Mercator map, mapmakers have to carve an image of Earth's surface into slices and then stretch the slices into rectangles. Stretching the slices enlarges parts of the map. The enlargement becomes greater toward the north and south poles. **Observing** *What areas on the map appear larger than they should?*

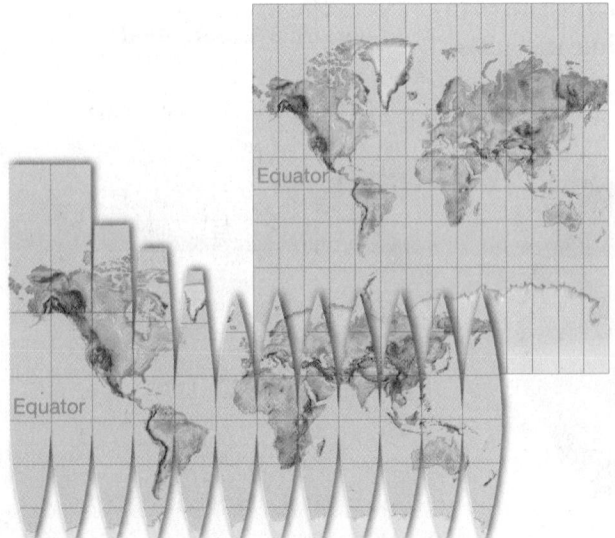

Lines of latitude and longitude form a global grid. This grid allows you to state the absolute location of any place on Earth. For example, Savannah, Georgia, is located at 32° north latitude and 81° west longitude.

The equator divides Earth in two. Each half is called a hemisphere. The equator divides Earth into northern and southern hemispheres. The prime meridian and the 180° meridian divide Earth into eastern and western hemispheres.

 **Reading Checkpoint** *How does the global grid divide Earth?*

Globes As people explored Earth, they collected information about the shapes and sizes of islands, continents, and bodies of water. Mapmakers wanted to present this information accurately. The best way was to put the information on a model, or globe, with the same round shape as Earth itself. By using an accurate shape for Earth, mapmakers could show the continents and oceans of Earth much as they really are. The only difference would be the scale, or relative size.

But there is a problem with globes. Try making a globe large enough to show the streets in your community. The globe might have to be larger than your school building! A globe can't be complete enough to be useful for finding directions and at the same time small enough to be convenient for everyday use.

Maps and Mapping

A map is a flat representation of Earth's surface. But Earth is round. Can all of Earth's features be accurately represented on a flat surface without distorting them? The answer is no. **No matter what kind of map is made, some portion of the surface will always look either too small, too big, or out of place. Mapmakers have, however, found ways to limit the distortion of shape, size, distance, and direction.**

The Mercator Projection In 1569, a mapmaker named Gerardus Mercator created a map to help sailors navigate around Earth. On this map, the lines of longitude are parallel, making this grid rectangular, as shown on the map in Figure 10. The map was useful because, although the sizes and distances were distorted, it showed directions accurately. Today, more than 400 years later, many seagoing navigators still use the Mercator projection map.

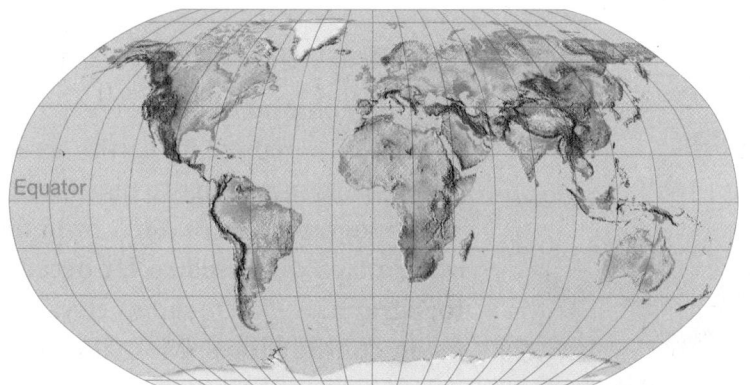

Figure 11 Robinson Projection Map
Compare this map to the Mercator projection.
Comparing and Contrasting *How do the shapes in the continents differ between these maps? Are there any other differences?*

Different Projection Maps for Different Purposes

The best projection is always determined by its intended use. Robinson projection maps show most distances, sizes, and shapes accurately. However, a Robinson projection has distortions, especially in areas around the edges of the map. You can see this in Figure 11.

Conic projection maps are made by wrapping a cone of paper around a globe at a particular line of latitude, as shown in Figure 12. Various points and lines are projected onto the paper. There is almost no distortion along the line of latitude that's in contact with the cone, but there can be much distortion in areas away from this latitude. Because accuracy is great over a small area, these maps are used to make road and weather maps.

Gnomonic projections, as shown in Figure 13, are made by placing a piece of paper on a globe so that it touches a single point on the globe's surface. Various points and lines are then projected onto the paper. Although distances and directions are distorted on these maps, they are useful to sailors and navigators because they show with great accuracy the shortest distance between two points.

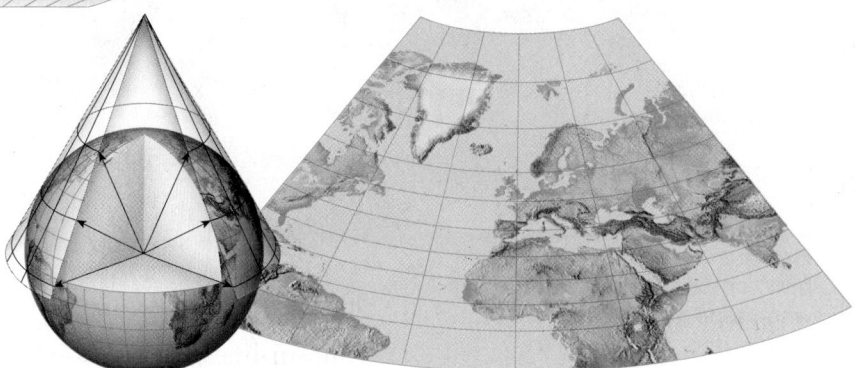

Figure 12 Conic Projection Map Because there is little distortion over small areas, conic projections are used to make road maps and weather maps.

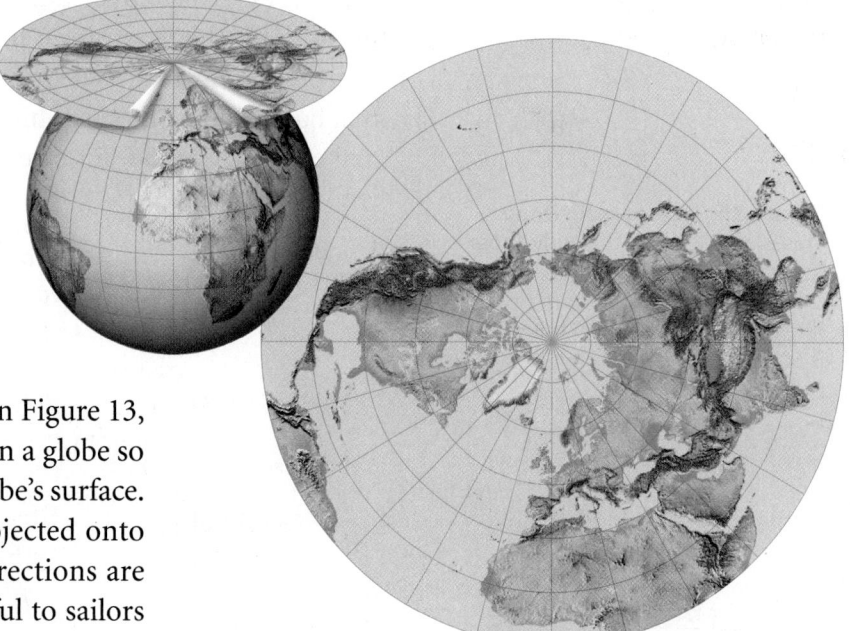

Figure 13 Gnomonic Projection Map Gnomonic projections allow sailors to accurately determine distance and direction across the oceans.

What major problem must mapmakers overcome?

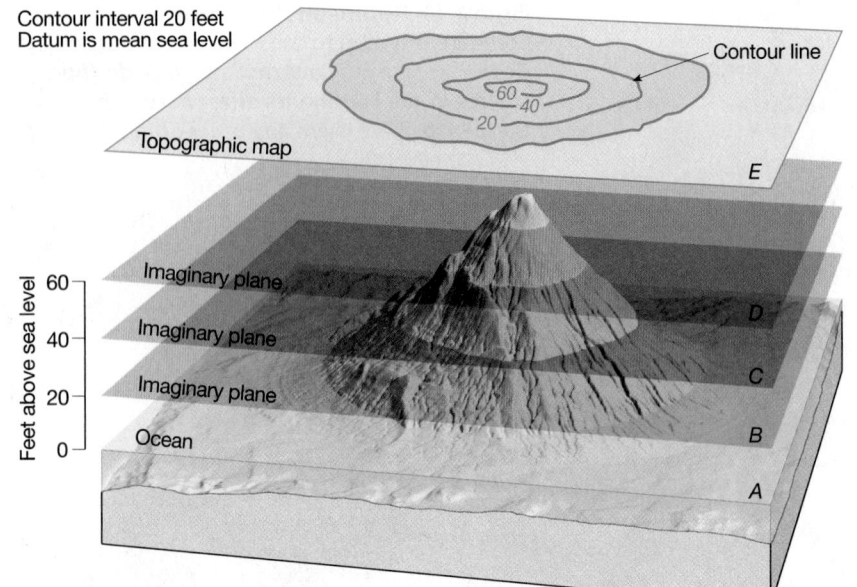
Contour interval 20 feet
Datum is mean sea level

Contour line

Topographic map

60
40
20

E

Feet above sea level
60
40
20
0

Imaginary plane

Imaginary plane

Imaginary plane

Ocean

D

C

B

A

Figure 14 This illustration shows how contour lines are determined when topographic maps are constructed.

Go Online
active art

For: Topographic map activity
Visit: PHSchool.com
Web Code: czp-1013

Figure 15 Topographic Map
This is a portion of the Holy Cross, Colorado, topographic map. Contour lines are shown in brown. The contour interval on this map is 50 feet.

Topographic Maps

A **topographic map,** like the one shown in Figure 15, represents Earth's three-dimensional surface in two dimensions. **Topographic maps differ from the other maps discussed so far because topographic maps show elevation using contour lines.** Most also show the presence of bodies of water, roads, government and public buildings, political boundaries, and place names. These maps are important for geologists, hikers, campers and anyone else interested in the three-dimensional lay of the land.

Contour Lines The elevation of the land is indicated by using contour lines. Every position along a single contour line is the same elevation. Adjacent contour lines represent a change in elevation. Every fifth line is bold and labeled with the elevation. It is called an index contour. The **contour interval** tells you the difference in elevation between adjacent lines. The steepness of an area can be determined by examining a map. Lines that are closer together indicate a steeper slope, while lines farther apart indicate a gentler slope. You can see this relationship on the illustration in Figure 14. Contour lines that form a circle represent a hill. A depression is represented by circular contours that have hachure marks, which are small lines on the circle that point to the center. Contour lines never touch or intersect, except where there is a vertical cliff.

Reading Checkpoint   *How do topographic maps indicate changes in elevation?*

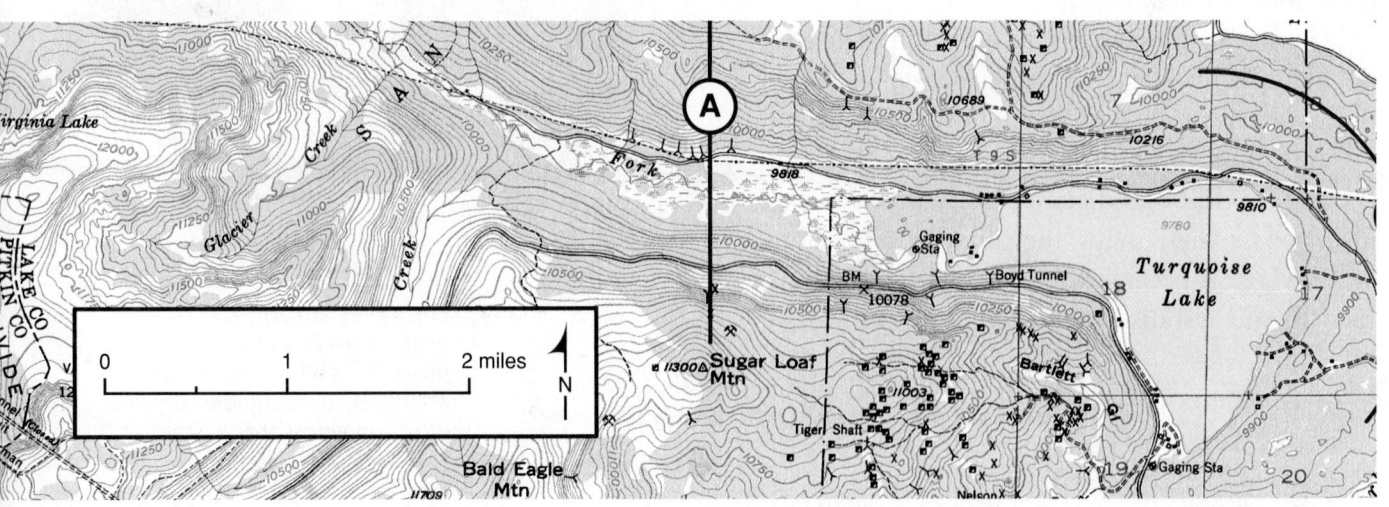

Scale A map represents a certain amount of area on Earth's surface. So it is necessary to be able to determine distances on the map and relate them to the real world. Suppose you want to build a scale model of a boat that is 20 feet long. If your model is a 1/5-scale model, then it is 4 feet long. Expressed as a ratio, the scale of your model is 1:5. This means that 1 foot on the model equals 5 feet on the boat.

In a similar way, a map is drawn to scale where a certain distance on the map is equal to a certain distance at the surface. Because maps model Earth's surface, the ratio of the map scale must be larger than that of the model boat. Look at the scale on the map in Figure 16. The ratio reads 1:24,000. This means that 1 unit on the map is equal to 24,000 units on the ground. Because the ratio has no units, it may stand for anything. We usually use inches or centimeters for our units. If the 1 stands for 1 centimeter on the map, how many kilometers does the 24,000 stand for on the ground?

Another scale provided on a map is a bar scale. See Figure 15. This allows you to use a ruler to measure the distance on the map and then line the ruler up to the bar to determine the distance represented.

Geologic Maps It is often desirable to know the type and age of the rocks that are exposed, or crop out, at the surface. This kind of map is shown in Figure 16. **A map that shows the type and age of exposed rocks is called a geologic map.** Once individual rock formations are identified and mapped, each rock formation is assigned a color and sometimes a pattern. A key provides the information needed to learn what formations are present on the map.

Go Online

For: Links on mapping
Visit: www.SciLinks.org
Web Code: cjn-1013

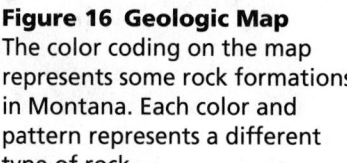

Figure 16 Geologic Map
The color coding on the map represents some rock formations in Montana. Each color and pattern represents a different type of rock.

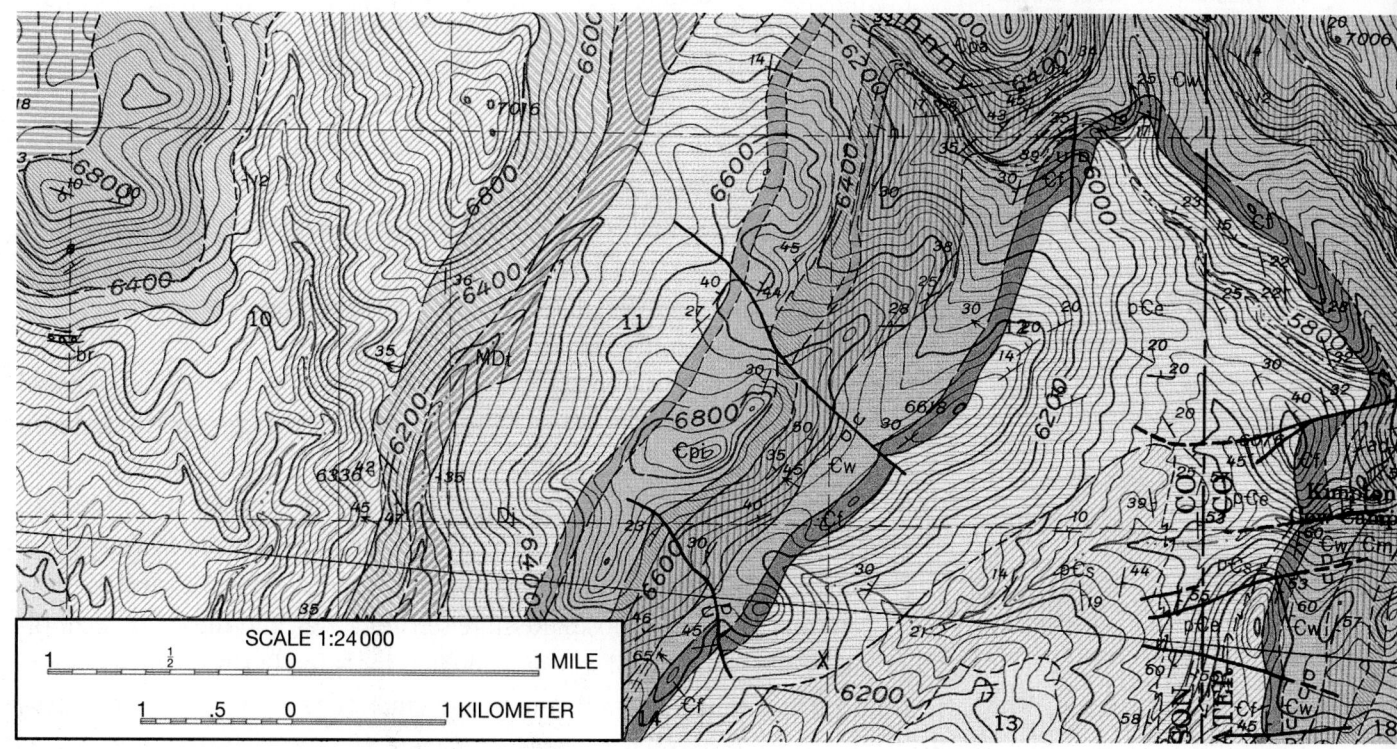

Figure 17 Satellite Image of the Mississippi River Delta
Moving sediment (light blue) indicates current patterns. Red shows vegetation.

Go Online
PLANETDIARY

For: Links on GPS
Visit: PHSchool.com
Web Code: czd-1013

Satellites and Information Technology

Today's technology provides us with the ability to more precisely analyze Earth's physical properties. Scientists now use satellites and computers to send and receive data. These data are converted into usable forms such as images and accurate maps.

The process of collecting data about Earth from a distance, such as from orbiting satellites, is called remote sensing. Satellites use remote sensing to produce views of Earth that scientists use to study rivers, oceans, fires, pollution, natural resources, and many other topics. How might a scientist use the image shown in Figure 17?

We can use this technology in our daily lives too. For example, Global Positioning Systems (GPS) can provide maps in our cars to help us reach our destinations. GPS consists of an instrument that receives signals to compute the user's latitude and longitude as well as speed, direction, and elevation. GPS is an important tool for navigation by ships and airplanes. Scientists use GPS to track wildlife, study earthquakes, measure erosion, and many other purposes. Remote sensing, GPS, and the other technologies described in Table 1 are valuable tools for Earth scientists. Some people, however, worry that these information technologies can also have negative effects, such as loss of privacy.

Table 1 Technology and Earth Science	
Type of Equipment	**Capabilities**
Weather Satellites	• These monitor atmospheric temperature and humidity, ground and surface seawater temperature, cloud cover, and water-ice boundaries. • They can help locate sources of distress signals. • They are able to scan Earth's surface in one 24-hour period.
Navigation Satellites	• These assist ships and submarines to determine their exact location at any time.
Landsat Satellites	• The first Landsat satellite was launched in 1972. Landsat 7 was launched in 1999. • They provide data on Earth's landmasses, coastal boundaries, and coral reefs. • Pictures taken are transmitted to ground stations around the world. • They orbit Earth every 99 minutes and complete 14 orbits per day. • Total coverage of Earth is achieved in 16 days.
Global Positioning System (GPS)	• This system combines satellite information with computer technology to provide location information in three dimensions: latitude, longitude, and altitude. • Three satellite signals are detected by a receiver. The distance from the satellites to the receiver is calculated, and the location is determined using the triangulation method. A fourth signal is then used to mathematically determine exact position.
Very Long Baseline Interferometry (VLBI)	• VLBI utilizes a large network of antennas around the world to receive radio waves from space objects such as quasars. • In Earth science, VLBI is used in geodesy, or the measurement of the geosphere. • Using the arrival times of radio waves from quasars, the position of radio telescopes on Earth are determined to within millimeters of their position. • Small changes in the telescope positions allow scientists to study tectonic plate motions and other movements of Earth's crust with great precision and accuracy.

Section 1.3 Assessment

Reviewing Concepts

1. Describe the two sets of lines that are used on globes and some maps.

2. What happens to the images on the globe when they are transferred to a flat surface?

3. What is the purpose of contour lines on topographic maps?

4. What two lines mark zero degrees on the globe? In which directions do these lines run?

5. Why is the Mercator projection map still in use today?

6. What types of advanced technology are used in mapmaking today?

Critical Thinking

7. **Applying Concepts** Why are there so many different types of maps?

8. **Drawing Conclusions** How can data from VLBI be used in mapmaking today?

9. **Conceptualizing** An area on a topographic map has the following contour line configuration: First, the lines are fairly widely spaced. Then they are closely spaced. Finally, they are circular. Describe the topography represented by these lines.

Math Practice

Use the bar scale on Figure 15 to answer the following question.

10. Determine the distance along the shoreline of Turquoise Lake from the gaging station on the west shore to the gaging station on the south shore. Record your answer in miles.

1.4 Earth System Science

Reading Focus

Key Concepts

- How is Earth a system?
- What is a system?
- Where does the energy come from that powers Earth's systems?
- How do humans affect Earth's systems?
- What makes a resource renewable or nonrenewable?

Vocabulary

- system

Reading Strategy

Outlining As you read, make an outline of the most important ideas in this section. Begin with the section title, then list the green headings as the next step of the outline. Outline further as needed.

> **I. Earth System Science**
>   A. What is a System?
>   1. _____?_____
>   2. _____?_____
>   B. _____?_____

As we study Earth, we see that it is a dynamic planet with many separate but interactive parts or spheres. Earth scientists are studying how these spheres are interconnected. **This way of looking at Earth is called Earth system science. Its aim is to understand Earth as a system made up of numerous interacting parts, or subsystems.** Instead of studying only one branch of science, such as geology, chemistry, or biology, Earth system science tries to put together what we know from our study of all of these branches. Using this type of approach, we hope to eventually understand and solve many of our global environmental problems.

 **Reading Checkpoint** *What is Earth system science?*

What Is a System?

Most of us hear and use the term system frequently. You might use your city's transportation system to get to school. A news report might inform us of an approaching weather system. We know that Earth is just a small part of the much larger solar system.

A system can be any size group of interacting parts that form a complex whole. Most natural systems are driven by sources of energy that move matter and/or energy from one place to another. A simple analogy is a car's cooling system. It contains a liquid (usually water and antifreeze) that is driven from the engine to the radiator and back again. The role of this system is to transfer the heat generated by combustion in the engine to the radiator, where moving air removes the heat from the system.

This kind of system is called a closed system. Here energy moves freely in and out of the system, but no matter enters or leaves the system. In the case of the car's cooling system, the matter is the liquid. By contrast, most natural systems are open systems. Here both energy and matter flow into and out of the system. In a river system, for example, the amount of water flowing in the channel can vary a great deal. At one time or place, the river may be fuller than it is at another time or place.

Earth as a System

The Earth system is powered by energy from two sources. **One source is the sun, which drives external processes that occur in the atmosphere, hydrosphere, and at Earth's surface.** Weather and climate, ocean circulation, and erosional processes are driven by energy from the sun. **Earth's interior is the second source of energy.** There is heat that remains from the time Earth formed. There is also heat continuously generated by the decay of radioactive elements. These sources power the internal processes that produce volcanoes, earthquakes, and mountains.

The parts of the Earth system are linked so that a change in one part can produce changes in any or all of the other parts. For example, when a volcano erupts, lava may flow out at the surface and block a nearby valley. This new obstruction influences the region's drainage system by creating a lake or causing streams to change course. Volcanic ash and gases that can be discharged during an eruption might be blown high into the atmosphere and influence the amount of solar energy that can reach Earth's surface. The result could be a drop in air temperatures over the entire hemisphere.

Reading Checkpoint *How do we know that Earth's systems are connected?*

Over time, soil will develop on the lava or ash-covered surface and, as shown in Figure 18, plants and animals will reestablish themselves. This soil will reflect the interactions among many parts of the Earth system—the original volcanic material, the type and rate of weathering, and the impact of biological activity. Of course, there would also

Figure 18 When Mount St. Helens erupted in May 1980, the area shown here was buried by a volcanic mudflow. Now, plants are reestablished and new soil is forming.

be significant changes in the biosphere. Some organisms and their habitats would be eliminated by the lava and ash, while new settings for life, such as the lake, would be created. The potential climate change could also have an effect on some life-forms.

The Earth system is characterized by processes that occur over areas that range in size from millimeters to thousands of kilometers. Time scales for Earth's processes range from milliseconds to billions of years. Despite this great range in distance and time, many processes are connected. A change in one component can influence the entire system.

Humans are also part of the Earth system. **Our actions produce changes in all of the other parts of the Earth system.** When we burn gasoline and coal, build breakwaters along a shoreline, dispose of our wastes, and clear the land, we cause other parts of the Earth system to respond, often in unforeseen ways. Throughout this book, you will learn about many of Earth's subsystems, such as the hydrologic (water) system, the tectonic (mountain-building) system, and the climate system. Remember that these components and we humans are all part of the complex interacting whole we call the Earth system.

People and the Environment

Environment refers to everything that surrounds and influences an organism. Some of these things are biological and social. Others are nonliving such as water, air, soil and rock as well as conditions such as temperature, humidity, and sunlight. These nonliving factors make up our physical environment. Because studying the Earth sciences leads to an understanding of the physical environment, most of Earth science can be characterized as environmental science.

 **Reading Checkpoint** *What are examples of nonliving factors?*

Today the term *environmental science* is usually used for things that focus on the relationships between people and the natural environment. For example, we can dramatically influence natural processes. A river flooding is natural, but the size and frequency of flooding can be changed by human activities such as clearing forests, building cities, and constructing dams. Unfortunately, natural systems do not always adjust to artificial changes in ways we can anticipate. An alteration to the environment that was intended to benefit society may also have some negative effects, as shown in Figure 19.

Resources Resources are an important focus of the Earth sciences. They include water and soil, metallic and nonmetallic minerals, and energy. Together they form the foundation of modern civilization. The Earth sciences deal not only with the formation and occurrence of

Figure 19 The Aswan Dam in Egypt provides water for generating electricity and for irrigating crops. But the dam also flooded historic sites and prevented the annual floods that helped keep soils in the Nile River Valley fertile.

these vital resources but also with maintaining supplies and the environmental impact of their mining and use.

Resources are commonly divided into two broad categories—renewable resources and nonrenewable resources. **Renewable resources can be replenished over relatively short time spans.** Common examples are plants and animals for food, natural fibers for clothing, and forest products for lumber and paper. Energy from flowing water, wind, and the sun are also considered renewable resources.

Important metals such as iron, aluminum, and copper plus our most important fuels of oil, natural gas, and coal are classified as nonrenewable resources. **Although these and other resources continue to form, the processes that create them are so slow that it takes millions of years for significant deposits to accumulate.** Earth contains limited quantities of these materials. Although some nonrenewable resources, such as aluminum, can be used over and over again, others, such as oil, cannot. When the present supplies are exhausted, there will be no more.

Reading Checkpoint *How do renewable and nonrenewable resources differ?*

Go Online
NSTA SciLINKS

For: Links on environmental decision-making
Visit: www.SciLinks.org
Web Code: cjn-1014

Population Figure 20 shows that the population of Earth is growing rapidly. Although it took until the beginning of the nineteenth century for the population to reach 1 billion, just 130 years were needed for the population to double to 2 billion. Between 1930 and 1975, the figure doubled again to 4 billion, and by about 2010, as many as 7 billion people may inhabit Earth. Clearly, as population grows, so does the demand for resources. However, the rate of mineral and energy resource usage has increased more rapidly than the overall growth of the population.

How long will the remaining supplies of basic resources last? How long can we sustain the rising standard of living in today's industrialized countries and still provide for the growing needs of developing regions? How much environmental deterioration are we willing to accept to obtain basic resources? Can alternatives be found? If we are to cope with the increasing demand on resources and a growing world population, it is important that we have some understanding of our present and potential resources.

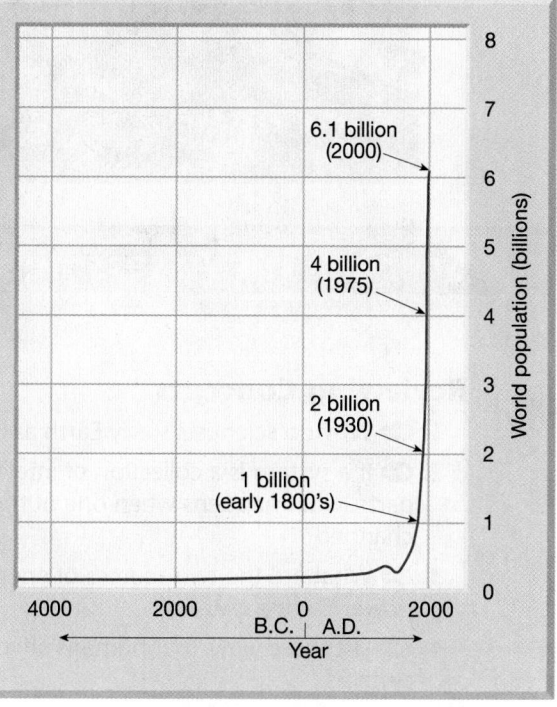

Figure 20 Growth of World Population

Environmental Problems

In addition to the search for mineral and energy resources, the Earth sciences must also deal with environmental problems. Some of these problems are local, some are regional, and still others are global. Humans can cause problems, such as the one shown in Figure 21. **Significant**

Figure 21 Air pollution in the Chinese city of Guangzhou. Air quality problems affect many cities. **Interpreting Photographs** *What may have contributed to this air pollution problem?*

threats to the environment include air pollution, acid rain, ozone depletion, and global warming. The loss of fertile soils to erosion, the disposal of toxic wastes, and the contamination and depletion of water resources are also of considerable concern. The list continues to grow.

People must cope with the many natural hazards that exist such as the one shown in Figure 22. Earthquakes, landslides, floods, hurricanes, and drought are some of the many risks. Of course, environmental hazards are simply natural processes. They become hazards only when people try to live where these processes occur.

It is clear that as world population continues to grow, pressures on the environment will increase as well. Therefore, an understanding of Earth is essential for the location and recovery of basic resources. It is also essential for dealing with the human impact on the environment and minimizing the effects of natural hazards. Knowledge about Earth and how it works is necessary to our survival and well being. Earth is the only suitable habitat we have, and its resources are limited.

Figure 22 The damage here was caused by a landslide that was triggered by an earthquake.

Section 1.4 Assessment

Reviewing Concepts

1. Why do scientists study Earth as a system?
2. If a system is a collection of interacting parts, what happens when one of the parts is changed?
3. What are the two sources of energy that power Earth's systems?
4. List three ways that humans affect Earth's systems.
5. Large numbers of tiny ocean organisms die every day, fall to the ocean floor, are buried, and are eventually converted to oil and natural gas. Why are these two fuels considered nonrenewable?

Critical Thinking

6. **Applying Concepts** Describe the parts of a tree in terms of it being a system.
7. **Evaluating** Is it possible for humans to have no effect on any of Earth's systems? Explain.
8. **Applying Concepts** How can scientists help to prevent a natural process from becoming an environmental hazard?

Connecting Concepts

City Planning In Section 1.3, you learned about Landsat satellite imaging. How can data from Landsat help city planners determine where and where not to build?

1.5 What Is Scientific Inquiry?

Reading Focus

Key Concepts
- What is a hypothesis?
- What is a theory?

Vocabulary
- hypothesis
- theory

Reading Strategy
Comparing and Contrasting Complete the Venn diagram by listing the ways hypothesis and theory are alike and how they differ.

hypothesis   theory

All science is based on two assumptions. First, the natural world behaves in a consistent and predictable manner. Second, through careful, systematic study, we can understand and explain the natural world's behavior. We can use this knowledge to predict what should or should not be expected. For example, by knowing how oil deposits form, geologists can predict where oil will be found.

Scientists approach their study of the natural world with certain habits of mind. These include curiosity, honesty, openness to new ideas, and skepticism. Skepticism is a willingness to question an idea unless that idea is supported with firm evidence. Scientists also use a range of skills and methods, including methods to ensure safety in the laboratory. You can learn more about these skills, methods, and safety procedures in the Skills Handbook on pages 728–733.

Hypothesis

The development of new scientific knowledge begins as scientists collect data through observation and measurement. **Once data have been gathered, scientists try to explain how or why things happen in the manner observed. Scientists do this by stating a possible explanation called a scientific hypothesis.** Sometimes more than one hypothesis is developed to explain a given set of observations. Just because a hypothesis is stated doesn't mean that it is correct.

Before a hypothesis can be accepted by the scientific community, it must be tested and analyzed. If a hypothesis can't be tested, it is not scientifically useful. Hypotheses that fail rigorous testing are discarded. One example of a discarded hypothesis is the Earth-centered model of the universe.

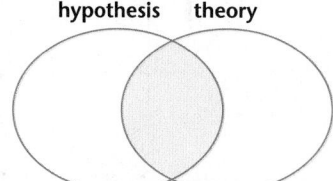

For: Links on scientific methods
Visit: www.SciLinks.org
Web Code: cjn-1015

Theory

When a hypothesis has survived extensive testing and when competing hypotheses have been eliminated, a hypothesis may become a scientific theory. ⊖**A scientific theory is well tested and widely accepted by the scientific community and best explains certain observable facts.** For example, the theory of plate tectonics provides the framework for understanding the origin of continents and ocean basins, plus the occurrence of mountains, earthquakes, and volcanoes.

Theories differ from laws. A scientific law is a statement that summarizes a pattern found in nature. Similar to theories, laws are based on repeatable observations and are widely accepted. However, unlike theories, laws describe relationships but do not explain why the relationships exist.

Scientific Methods

The process of gathering facts through observations and formulating scientific hypotheses and theories is called the scientific method. There is no set path that scientists must follow in order to gain scientific knowledge. However, many scientific investigations involve the following steps: (1) the collection of scientific facts through observation and measurement, (2) the development of one or more working hypotheses or models to explain these facts, (3) development of observations and experiments to test the hypotheses, and (4) the acceptance, modification, or rejection of the hypothesis based on extensive testing.

Section 1.5 Assessment

Reviewing Concepts

1. ⊖ You have just come up with an explanation to a question that has bothered you for some time. What must you do to have your explanation become a hypothesis?

2. ⊖ What is the difference between a scientific theory and a hypothesis?

3. According to the scientific community, how does the natural world behave?

4. What happens if more than one hypothesis is put forward to explain the same observations?

5. When is a model useful in scientific investigations?

Thinking Critically

6. **Applying Concepts** Why do most scientists follow a set order of steps when carrying out a scientific investigation?

7. **Designing Experiments** While carrying out an investigation, a scientist observes some unexpected results. What are the scientist's next steps?

8. **Understanding Concepts** Why is it necessary to use careful and systematic methods when carrying out scientific investigations?

Writing in Science

Explanatory Paragraph It took a long time for the scientific community to accept the theory of plate tectonics. Write a paragraph suggesting how the use of proper scientific methods helped the theory gain acceptance.

understanding EARTH

Studying Earth From Space

Scientific facts are gathered in many ways, such as laboratory studies, field observations, and field measurements. Satellite images like the one in Figure 23 are another useful source of data. Such images provide perspectives that are difficult to get from more traditional sources. The high-tech instruments aboard many satellites enable scientists to gather information from remote regions where data are otherwise scarce.

The image in Figure 23 makes use of the Advanced Spaceborne Thermal Emission and Reflection Radiometer (ASTER). Because different materials reflect and give off energy in different ways, ASTER can provide detailed information about the composition of Earth's surface. Figure 23 is a three-dimensional view looking north over Death Valley, California. The data have been computer enhanced to exaggerate the color variations that highlight differences in types of surface materials.

Figure 23 This satellite shows detailed information about the composition of surface materials in Death Valley, California. It was produced by superimposing nighttime thermal infrared data, acquired on April 7, 2000, over topographic data from the U.S. Geological survey. (Image courtesy of NASA)

Salt deposits on the floor of Death Valley appear in shades of yellow, green, purple, and pink. These indicate the presence of carbonate, sulfate, and chloride minerals. The Panamint Mountains to the west and the Black Mountains to the east are made up of sedimentary limestones, sandstones, shales, and metamorphic rocks. The bright red areas are dominated by the mineral quartz, found in sandstone; the green areas are limestone. In the lower center of the image is Badwater, the lowest point in North America.

Determining Latitude and Longitude

Using maps and globes to find places and features on Earth's surface is an essential skill required of all Earth scientists. The grid that is formed by lines of latitude and longitude form the basis for locating points on Earth. Latitude lines indicate north-south distance and longitude lines indicate east-west distance. Degrees are used to mark latitude and longitude distances on Earth's surface. Degrees can be divided into sixty equal parts called minutes (') and a minute of angle can be divided into sixty parts, called seconds ("). Thus, 31°10′20″ means 31 degrees, 10 minutes, and 20 seconds. This exercise will introduce you to the systems used for determining location on Earth.

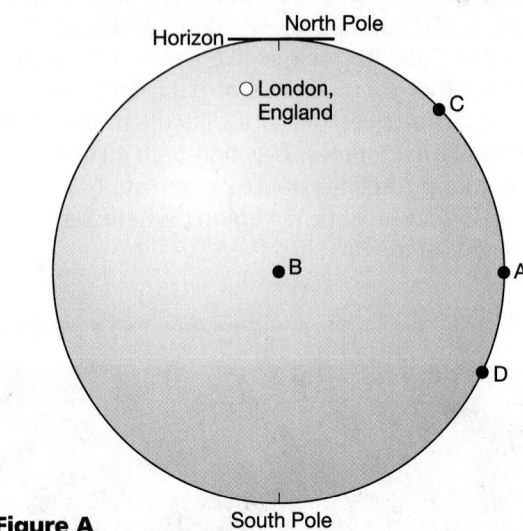

Figure A

Problem
How are latitude and longitude calculated and how do they indicate a particular location's position on the globe?

Materials

- globe
- protractor
- ruler
- compass or round object for tracing
- pencil
- world map

Skills
Interpreting, Measuring, Inferring

Procedure

Part A: Determining Latitude

1. Figure A represents Earth, with point B its center. Draw this figure on a separate piece of paper. Locate the equator on the globe. Sketch and label the equator on your diagram. Label the Northern Hemisphere and Southern Hemisphere on your diagram.

2. On your diagram, make an angle by drawing a line from point A on the equator to point B (the center of Earth). Then extend the line from point B to point C in the Northern Hemisphere. The angle you have drawn (∠ABC) is 45°. By definition of latitude, point C is located at 45° N latitude.

3. Draw a line on your figure through point C that is also parallel to the equator. What is the latitude at all points on this line? Record this number on the line.

4. Using a protractor, measure ∠ABD on your paper. Then draw a line parallel to the equator that also goes through point D. Label the line with its proper latitude.

5. How many degrees of latitude separate the latitude lines (or parallels) on the globe that you are using? Record this on your paper.

6. Refer to Figure B. Determine the latitude for each point A–F. Be sure to indicate whether it is north or south of the equator and include the word "latitude." Record these numbers on your paper.

7. Use a globe or map to locate the cities listed below. On your paper, record their latitude to the nearest degree.
   A. Moscow, Russia
   B. Durban, South Africa
   C. Your home city

8. Use the globe or map to give the name of a city or feature that is equally as far south of the equator as your home city is north.

Part B: Determining Longitude

9. Locate the prime meridian on Figure C. Sketch and label it on your diagram. Label the Eastern and Western Hemispheres.

10. How many degrees of longitude separate each meridian on your globe? Record this on your paper.

11. Refer to Figure C. Determine the longitude for each point A–F. Be sure to indicate whether it is east or west of the Prime Meridian. Record these numbers on your paper.

12. Use the globe or map to give the name of a city or feature that is equally as far east of the prime meridian as your home city is west.

Analyze and Conclude

1. **Applying Concepts** What is the maximum number of 1 degree longitude or latitude lines that can be drawn on a globe?

2. **Comparing and Contrasting** How are longitude and latitude lines the same and how are they different?

3. **Thinking Critically** Amelia Earhart, her flight engineer, and her plane are believed to have been lost somewhere over the Pacific Ocean. It is now thought that the coordinates that she was given for her fuel stop at Howley Island in the Pacific Ocean were wrong. Knowing what you do about how latitude and longitude coordinates are written, why would a wrong number have been so catastrophic for her?

Go Further Use reference books or the Internet to research the number of time zones on Earth. Find out how many there are and draw their boundaries on the figure you created for this lab. What time zone do you live in? What time zone is the location that you chose in question 12? What is the time difference between these two locations?

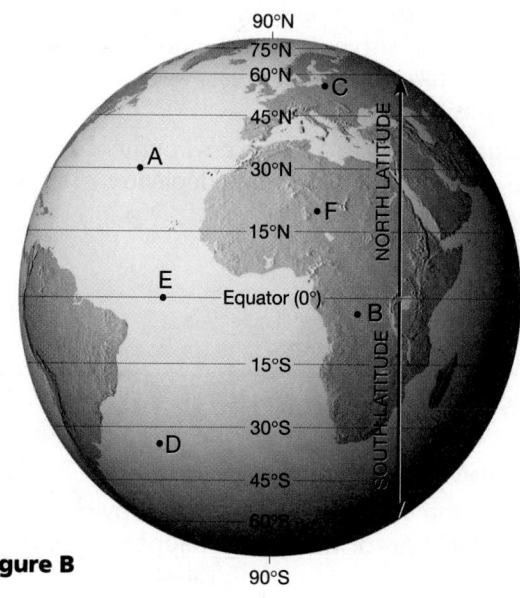

Figure B

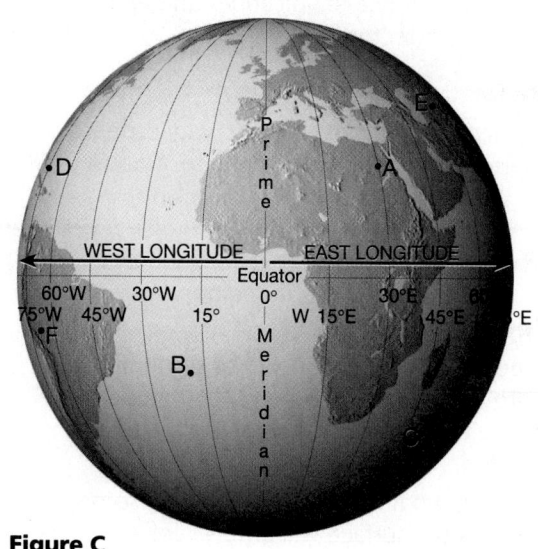

Figure C

Study Guide

1.1 What Is Earth Science?

🌐 Key Concepts

- Earth science is the name for the group of sciences that deals with Earth and its neighbors in space.
- The nebular hypothesis suggests that the bodies of our solar system evolved from an enormous rotating cloud called the solar nebula. It was made up mostly of hydrogen and helium, with a small percentage of heavier elements.

Vocabulary

Earth science, *p. 2;* geology, *p. 2;* oceanography, *p. 3;* meteorology, *p. 3;* astronomy, *p. 3*

1.2 A View of Earth

🌐 Key Concepts

- Earth can be thought of as consisting of four major spheres: the hydrosphere, atmosphere, geosphere, and biosphere.
- Because the geosphere is not uniform, it is divided into three main parts based on differences in composition—the core, the mantle, and the crust.
- The model that explains the position of continents and the occurrence of volcanoes and earthquakes is called plate tectonics.

Vocabulary

hydrosphere, *p. 7* atmosphere, *p. 7;* geosphere, *p. 7;* biosphere, *p. 7;* core, *p. 8;* mantle, *p. 8;* crust, *p. 8*

1.3 Representing Earth's Surface

🌐 Key Concepts

- Latitude is the distance north or south of the equator, measured in degrees. Longitude is the distance east or west of the prime meridian, measured in degrees.
- No matter what kind of map is made, some portion of the surface will always look either too small, too big, or out of place. Mapmakers have, however, found ways to limit the distortion of shape, size, distance, and direction.
- Topographic maps differ from other maps because topographic maps show elevation.

- The elevation of the land is indicated by using contour lines.
- A map that shows the type and age of exposed rock is called a geologic map.
- Today's technology provides us with the ability to more precisely analyze Earth's physical properties.

Vocabulary

latitude, *p. 11;* longitude, *p. 11;* topographic map, *p. 14;* contour line, *p. 14;* contour interval, *p. 14*

1.4 Earth System Science

🌐 Key Concepts

- Earth system science aims to study Earth as a system made up of numerous interacting parts, or subsystems.
- A system can be any size group of interacting parts that form a complex whole.
- The sun drives external processes that occur in the atmosphere, hydrosphere, and at Earth's surface. Earth's interior is also a source of energy.
- Our actions produce changes in all other parts of the Earth system.
- Renewable resources can be replenished over relatively short time spans. Nonrenewable resources form over such a long period of time that it takes millions of years for significant deposits to accumulate.
- Significant threats to the environment include air pollution, acid rain, ozone depletion, and global warming.

Vocabulary

system, *p. 18*

1.5 What Is Scientific Inquiry?

🌐 Key Concepts

- A hypothesis is a statement made by scientists to explain how or why things happen in the manner observed.
- A scientific theory is well tested and widely accepted by the scientific community and best explains certain observable facts.

Vocabulary

hypothesis, *p. 23;* theory, *p. 24*

Assessment

Reviewing Content

Choose the letter that best answers the question or completes the statement.

1. The science that deals with the study of the atmosphere is
   a. oceanography.
   b. meteorology.
   c. geology.
   d. astronomy.

2. What caused Earth to develop layers as it cooled?
   a. differences in density
   b. the magnetic field
   c. the speed of rotation
   d. escaping gases

3. What drives the process of plate tectonics, the currently accepted explanation for the movement of drifting continents?
   a. gravity
   b. ocean currents
   c. unequal heat distribution
   d. earthquakes

4. Lines of latitude describe position
   a. north or south of the equator.
   b. east or west of the equator.
   c. north or south of the prime meridian.
   d. east or west of the prime meridian.

5. The Robinson map projection is considered very useful because
   a. all of the continents are the same size.
   b. most distances, sizes, and shapes are accurate.
   c. it shows landmasses in three dimensions.
   d. features along latitude lines are accurate.

6. Which of the following types of map would best show the three dimensions of Earth's surface?
   a. road map
   b. topographic map
   c. political map
   d. tectonic map

7. Which type of technology can scientists use to monitor coral reef development?
   a. Landsat satellites   b. VLBI
   c. computer imaging   d. weather satellites

8. What makes a hypothesis scientifically useful?
   a. Many people think it is a good idea.
   b. It can be tested.
   c. It contains numerical data.
   d. It applies directly to Earth science.

9. The theory that Earth's lithosphere is broken into large sections that move is called
   a. biosphere.
   b. global positioning.
   c. nebular.
   d. plate tectonics.

10. On a topographic map, contour lines that are closer together indicate
    a. forest.
    b. a steeper slope.
    c. a mountain top.
    d. roads.

Understanding Concepts

11. Briefly list the events that led to the formation of the solar system.

12. Which of Earth's spheres do mountains, lakes, trees, clouds, ice, and snow represent?

13. List the four parts of the geosphere indicated at the letters in the figure below.

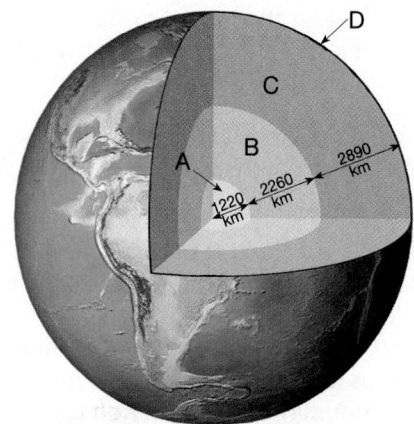

14. The Mercator projection map shows Earth's features on a grid. Why is this map useful to sailors?

15. Why is the contour interval included on a topographic map?

16. What type of satellite is used to monitor cloud cover and air temperature?

17. What happens to matter and energy in a closed system?

18. What types of factors make up our nonliving environment?

19. What are the two sources of energy for the Earth system?

20. What requirements must be satisfied in order for a resource to be considered renewable?

21. List at least four processes that could be regarded as natural hazards.

22. Briefly describe the four steps that most scientific investigations follow.

Critical Thinking

23. **Comparing and Contrasting** How is a scientific hypothesis different from a scientific theory?

24. **Applying Concepts** If oceans cover nearly 71 percent of Earth's surface, why is it important to conserve water?

25. **Inferring** Explain the following statement: If Earth had no atmosphere, our planet would be lifeless.

26. **Hypothesizing** Predict what the effect will be on some of Earth's systems if a forest is cut down for lumber.

27. **Comparing and Contrasting** As part of the Great Plains of the United States, the state of Kansas has relatively flat topography. On the other hand, portions of the state of Colorado are mountainous. Describe how the contour interval and the contour lines might vary on topographic maps of these two states.

Math Skills

Use the map scale to answer Questions 28 and 29.

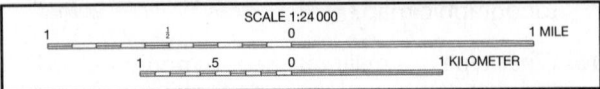

28. **Using Graphs** Approximately how many miles is 1 kilometer equal to?

29. **Calculating** If 1 kilometer is equal to 1 centimeter on the map, what is the distance in km between two cities that are 7.5 cm apart?

30. **Calculating** Recall that Earth is divided into 360 degrees. If you travel to a location that is 90 degrees starting from the prime meridian, how far around the globe have you gone? What about a location that is 120 degrees from the prime meridian?

Map Skills

Use the topographic map in Figure 15 on page 14 to answer Questions 31–33.

31. **Reading Maps** About how wide is Turquoise Lake at its widest point from east to west?

32. **Reading Maps** What is the elevation of Sugar Loaf Mountain?

33. **Reading Maps** How does the land on the east side of Turquoise Lake differ from the land on the southwest side of the lake? How do you know?

Concepts in Action

34. **Applying Concepts** List at least three examples of how you can influence one or more of Earth's major spheres.

35. **Applying Concepts** A local company wants to open a new limestone quarry. Explain what type of map they should use to determine if limestone is present in your area.

36. **Classifying** The planet Mars has been in the news recently. Based on the information that has been reported, list and explain the spheres that are present or might have been present on Mars.

37. **Writing in Science** You are given the opportunity to address the city council about the proposed construction of a dam on the river in your community. Prepare a list of questions about the project that you would like to ask the city council and the dam engineers before deciding whether or not you would support the project.

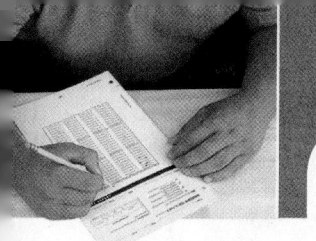

Standardized Test Prep

Test-Taking Tip

Narrowing the Choices

If, after reading all the answer choices, you are not sure which one is correct, eliminate those answers that you know are wrong. In the question below, read the descriptions provided in I, II, and III. Eliminate any of these that you know to be wrong. Then carefully read the answer choices and choose the one that matches up with your decision above.

Which of these statements is(are) true of geologic maps?

   I. They show the location and extent of different rock formations.
   II. They indicate the age of each rock formation.
   III. They never indicate the topography of the land.

   (A) I only
   (B) I and II
   (C) I, II and III
   (D) II only

(Answer: B)

Choose the letter that best answers the question or completes the statement.

1. The _____ strongly influences the other three "spheres" because without life their makeup and nature would be much different.
   (A) atmosphere
   (B) hydrosphere
   (C) geosphere
   (D) biosphere

2. The science that includes the study of the composition and movements of water, as well as coastal processes, the seafloor, and marine life is _____.
   (A) geology
   (B) oceanography
   (C) meteorology
   (D) astronomy

3. Which of these situations is(are) an example of an open system?
   I. a car's cooling system
   II. a boiling teakettle
   III. a loaf of bread in a sealed plastic bag.
   IV. your digestive system
   (A) I only
   (B) II & IV
   (C) I & III
   (D) I, II, III & IV

Use the figure below to answer Questions 4, 5, and 6.

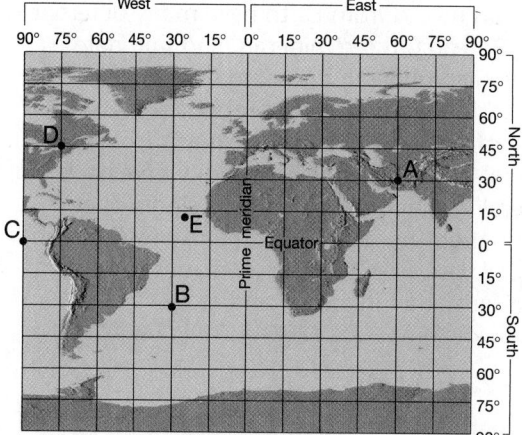

4. What is the latitude and longitude for point A on the map?

5. Locate the state of Florida on the map. What is the approximate location of its southernmost point?

6. Why does the continent of Antarctica appear to be stretched out?

7. The three principal layers of Earth are differentiated by their density. List these three layers by increasing density.

What are minerals used for?

Minerals mined from Earth have many different uses. Research three minerals, and find data about each mineral, including its chemical composition and physical properties. Identify some of the products that are made from each mineral. Also, list some countries where each mineral is mined. Next, create a single-page information sheet or Web page to present each mineral. Use both tables and images to present the information in a clear and attractive way.

Exploration Lab

Mineral Identification

Earth Materials
↳ Minerals

The large reddish-orange crystals are crystals of wulfenite. Wulfenite is one of more than 3800 minerals found on Earth.

Chapter Preview

Inquiry Activity

How Are a Group of Minerals Alike and Different?

Procedure

1. Obtain the mineral samples from your teacher. Examine them closely.

2. Make a data table to record at least three ways that the samples are alike.

3. Now record at least three ways that the samples differ.

4. Classify the minerals into two groups based on your observations. Give reasons for your classification scheme.

5. Put on safety goggles. Gently strike each sample with a hammer and observe the pieces of each sample. If necessary, use these results to reclassify the minerals into two groups.

Think About It

1. **Observing** What kinds of characteristics did you observe in all of the samples?

2. **Contrasting** How did the samples differ?

3. **Formulating Hypotheses** Each of the minerals you just observed belongs to a different group. Design a scheme for how these minerals might be classified into four different groups.

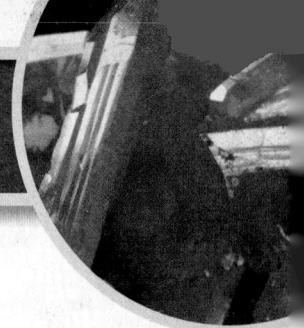

2.1 Matter

Reading Focus

Key Concepts

- What is an element?
- What particles make up atoms?
- What are isotopes?
- What are compounds and why do they form?
- How do chemical bonds differ?

Vocabulary

- element
- atomic number
- energy level
- isotope
- mass number
- compound
- chemical bond
- ion
- ionic bond
- covalent bond
- metallic bond

Reading Strategy

Comparing and Contrasting Copy the graphic organizer. As you read, complete the organizer to compare and contrast protons, neutrons, and electrons.

Protons	Electrons	Neutrons
	Differences	
	Similarities	

You and everything else in the universe are made of matter. Matter is anything that has volume and mass. On Earth, matter usually exists in one of three states—solid, liquid, or gas. A solid is a type of matter that has a definite shape and a definite volume. Rocks and minerals are solids. A liquid is matter that has a definite volume, but not a definite shape. Earth's oceans, rivers, and lakes are liquids. A gas is matter that has neither a definite shape nor a definite volume. Most of Earth's atmosphere is composed of the gases nitrogen and oxygen. Though matter can be classified by its physical state: solid, liquid, or gas, it is more useful to look at its chemical composition and structure. Each of Earth's nearly 4000 minerals is a unique substance. The building blocks of minerals are **elements.**

Elements and the Periodic Table

The names of many elements are probably very familiar to you. Many common metals are elements, such as copper, iron, silver, and gold. **An element is a substance that cannot be broken down into simpler substances by chemical or physical means.** There are more than 112 known elements, and new elements continue to be discovered. Of these, 95 occur naturally; the others are produced in laboratories.

The elements have been organized by their properties in a document called the periodic table, which is shown in Figure 1 on pages 36 and 37. You see from the table that the name of each element is represented by a symbol consisting of one, two, or three letters. Symbols provide a shorthand way of representing an element. Each element is

Go Online

For: Links on the periodic table
Visit: www.SciLinks.org
Web Code: cjn-1021

also known by its atomic number, which is shown above each symbol on the table. Look at the block for sulfur, element 16, and gold, element 79. Sulfur and gold are minerals made of one element. Most elements are not stable enough to exist in pure form in nature. Thus, most minerals are combinations of elements.

The rows in the periodic table are called periods. The number of elements in a period varies. Period 1, for example, contains only two elements. These elements are hydrogen (H) and helium (He). Period 2 contains the elements lithium (Li) through neon (Ne). Periods 4 and 5 each contain 18 elements while Period 6 includes 32 elements.

The columns in the periodic table are called groups. Note that there are 18 groups in the periodic table shown on pages 36 and 37. Elements within a group have similar properties.

Of the known elements, only eight make up most of Earth's continental crust. These eight elements are listed in Table 1. Notice that six of the eight elements in Table 1 are classified as metals. Metals have specific properties such as the ability to be shaped and drawn into wire. Metals are also good conductors of heat and electricity. They combine in thousands of ways to form compounds, the building blocks of most Earth materials. To understand how elements form compounds we need to review their building blocks which are atoms.

Table 1 Relative Abundance of the Most Common Elements in Earth's Continental Crust	
Element	Approximate Percentage by Weight
Oxygen (O)	46.6
Silicon (Si)	27.7
Aluminum (Al)	8.1
Iron (Fe)	5.0
Calcium (Ca)	3.6
Sodium (Na)	2.8
Potassium (K)	2.6
Magnesium (Mg)	2.1
All others	1.7

Source: Data from Brian Mason.

Atoms

As you might already know, all elements are made of atoms. ⬤**An atom is the smallest particle of matter that contains the characteristics of an element.**

The central region of an atom is called the nucleus. The nucleus contains protons and neutrons. Protons are dense particles with positive electrical charges. Neutrons are equally dense particles that have no electrical charge. Electrons, which are small particles with little mass and negative electrical charges, surround an atom's nucleus.

Protons and Neutrons A proton has about the same mass as a neutron. Hydrogen atoms have only a single proton in their nuclei. Other atoms contain more than 100 protons. The number of protons in the nucleus of an atom is called the **atomic number.** All atoms with six protons, for example, are carbon atoms. The atomic number of carbon is 6. Likewise, every atom with eight protons is an oxygen atom. The atomic number of oxygen is 8.

Atoms have the same number of protons and electrons. Carbon atoms have six protons and therefore six electrons. Oxygen atoms have eight protons in their nuclei and have eight electrons surrounding the nucleus.

Figure 1

Legend:

Nonmetals	Metals	Metalloids	
C	Li	B	Solid
Br	Hg		Liquid
H			Gas
Uuo	Tc		Not found in nature

1
1A

1
H
Hydrogen
1.0079

2
2A

3	4
Li	**Be**
Lithium	Beryllium
6.941	9.0122

11	12
Na	**Mg**
Sodium	Magnesium
22.990	24.305

3 **3B**	**4** **4B**	**5** **5B**	**6** **6B**	**7** **7B**	**8**	**8B**	**9**
21 **Sc** Scandium 44.956	22 **Ti** Titanium 47.90	23 **V** Vanadium 50.941	24 **Cr** Chromium 51.996	25 **Mn** Manganese 54.938	26 **Fe** Iron 55.847		27 **Co** Cobalt 58.933

Row 4:

19	20	21	22	23	24	25	26	27
K Potassium 39.098	**Ca** Calcium 40.08	**Sc** Scandium 44.956	**Ti** Titanium 47.90	**V** Vanadium 50.941	**Cr** Chromium 51.996	**Mn** Manganese 54.938	**Fe** Iron 55.847	**Co** Cobalt 58.933

Row 5:

37	38	39	40	41	42	43	44	45
Rb Rubidium 85.468	**Sr** Strontium 87.62	**Y** Yttrium 88.906	**Zr** Zirconium 91.22	**Nb** Niobium 92.906	**Mo** Molybdenum 95.94	**Tc** Technetium (98)	**Ru** Ruthenium 101.07	**Rh** Rhodium 102.91

Row 6:

55	56	71	72	73	74	75	76	77
Cs Cesium 132.91	**Ba** Barium 137.33	**Lu** Lutetium 174.97	**Hf** Hafnium 178.49	**Ta** Tantalum 180.95	**W** Tungsten 183.85	**Re** Rhenium 186.21	**Os** Osmium 190.2	**Ir** Iridium 192.22

Row 7:

87	88	103	104	105	106	107	108	109
Fr Francium (223)	**Ra** Radium (226)	**Lr** Lawrencium (262)	**Rf** Rutherfordium (261)	**Db** Dubnium (262)	**Sg** Seaborgium (263)	**Bh** Bohrium (264)	**Hs** Hassium (265)	**Mt** Meitnerium (268)

Lanthanide Series

57	58	59	60	61	62
La Lanthanum 138.91	**Ce** Cerium 140.12	**Pr** Praseodymium 140.91	**Nd** Neodymium 144.24	**Pm** Promethium (145)	**Sm** Samarium 150.4

Actinide Series

89	90	91	92	93	94
Ac Actinium (227)	**Th** Thorium 232.04	**Pa** Protactinium 231.04	**U** Uranium 238.03	**Np** Neptunium (237)	**Pu** Plutonium (244)

Metals—elements that are good conductors of heat and electric current

Nonmetals—elements that are poor conductors of heat and electric current

Metalloids—elements with properties that are somewhat similar to metals and nonmetals

Atomic number — 6							18
Element symbol — **C**							**8A**
Element name — Carbon							2 **He** Helium 4.0026
Atomic mass — 12.011							

Periodic table legend:
- Atomic number → 6
- Element symbol → C
- Element name → Carbon
- Atomic mass → 12.011

	13 **3A**	14 **4A**	15 **5A**	16 **6A**	17 **7A**	18 **8A**
						2 **He** Helium 4.0026
	5 **B** Boron 10.81	6 **C** Carbon 12.011	7 **N** Nitrogen 14.007	8 **O** Oxygen 15.999	9 **F** Fluorine 18.998	10 **Ne** Neon 20.179
	13 **Al** Aluminum 26.982	14 **Si** Silicon 28.086	15 **P** Phosphorus 30.974	16 **S** Sulfur 32.06	17 **Cl** Chlorine 35.453	18 **Ar** Argon 39.948

10	11 **1B**	12 **2B**						
28 **Ni** Nickel 58.71	29 **Cu** Copper 63.546	30 **Zn** Zinc 65.38	31 **Ga** Gallium 69.72	32 **Ge** Germanium 72.59	33 **As** Arsenic 74.922	34 **Se** Selenium 78.96	35 **Br** Bromine 79.904	36 **Kr** Krypton 83.80
46 **Pd** Palladium 106.4	47 **Ag** Silver 107.87	48 **Cd** Cadmium 112.41	49 **In** Indium 114.82	50 **Sn** Tin 118.69	51 **Sb** Antimony 121.75	52 **Te** Tellurium 127.60	53 **I** Iodine 126.90	54 **Xe** Xenon 131.30
78 **Pt** Platinum 195.09	79 **Au** Gold 196.97	80 **Hg** Mercury 200.59	81 **Tl** Thallium 204.37	82 **Pb** Lead 207.2	83 **Bi** Bismuth 208.98	84 **Po** Polonium (209)	85 **At** Astatine (210)	86 **Rn** Radon (222)
110 **Ds** Darmstadtium (269)	111 **Rg** Roentgenium (272)	112 **Cn** Copernicium (277)	113 *Uut Ununtrium (284)	114 *Uuq Ununquadium (289)	115 *Uup Ununpentium (288)	116 *Uuh Ununhexium (293)		118 *Uuo Ununoctium (299)

*Name not officially assigned

63 **Eu** Europium 151.96	64 **Gd** Gadolinium 157.25	65 **Tb** Terbium 158.93	66 **Dy** Dysprosium 162.50	67 **Ho** Holmium 164.93	68 **Er** Erbium 167.26	69 **Tm** Thulium 168.93	70 **Yb** Ytterbium 173.04

95 **Am** Americium (243)	96 **Cm** Curium (247)	97 **Bk** Berkelium (247)	98 **Cf** Californium (251)	99 **Es** Einsteinium (252)	100 **Fm** Fermium (257)	101 **Md** Mendelevium (258)	102 **No** Nobelium (259)

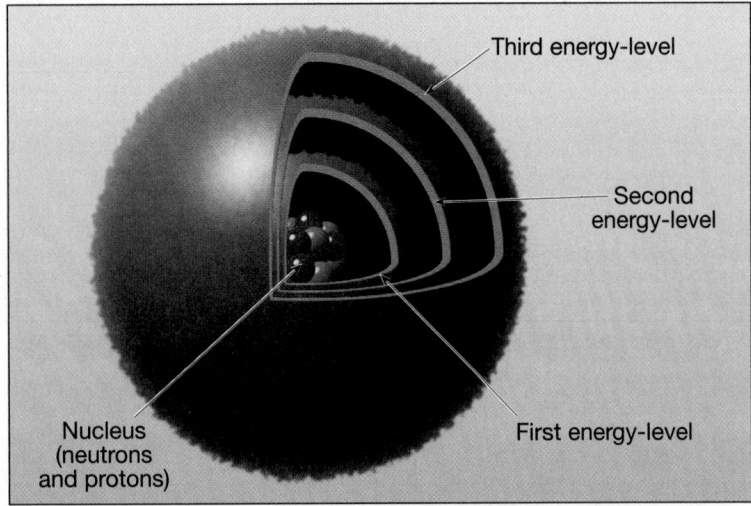

Third energy-level

Second energy-level

First energy-level

Nucleus (neutrons and protons)

Figure 2 Model of an Atom
The electrons that move about an atom's nucleus occupy distinct regions called energy levels.

Electrons An electron is the smallest of the three fundamental particles in an atom. An electron has a mass of about 1/1836 the mass of a proton or a neutron. Electrons move about the nucleus so rapidly that they create a sphere-shaped negative zone. You can picture moving electrons by imagining a cloud of negative charges surrounding the nucleus, as shown in Figure 2.

Electrons are located in regions called **energy levels.** Each energy level contains a certain number of electrons. Interactions among electrons in the outermost energy levels explains how atoms form compounds, as you will find out later in the chapter.

 **Reading Checkpoint** *How are electrons, protons, and neutrons alike and how are they different?*

Isotopes

Atoms of the same element always have the same number of protons. For example, every carbon atom has 6 protons. Carbon is element number 6 on the periodic table. But the number of neutrons for atoms of the same element can vary. **Atoms with the same number of protons but different numbers of neutrons are isotopes of an element.** Isotopes of the same element are labeled using a convention called the mass number and with the element's name or symbol. The **mass number** of an atom is the total mass of the atom (protons plus neutrons) expressed in atomic mass units. The proton and the neutron each have a mass that is slightly larger than the atomic mass unit. Recall that the mass of an electron is so small that the number of electrons has no effect on the mass number of an atom.

Carbon has 15 different isotopes. Models for three of these are shown in Figure 3. Carbon-12 makes up almost 99 percent of all carbon on Earth. Carbon-12 has 6 protons and 6 neutrons. Carbon-13 makes up much of the remaining naturally occurring carbon atoms on Earth. Carbon-13 has 6 protons and 7 neutrons. Though only traces of carbon-14 are found in nature, the presence of this isotope is often used to determine the age of once-living things. Carbon-14 has 6 protons and 8 neutrons

The nuclei of most atoms are stable. However, many elements have atoms whose nuclei are unstable. Such atoms disintegrate through a process called radioactive decay. Radioactive decay occurs because the forces that hold the nucleus together are not strong enough.

During radioactive decay, unstable atoms radiate energy and particles. Some of this energy powers the movements of Earth's crust and upper mantle. The rates at which unstable atoms decay are measurable. Therefore certain radioactive atoms can be used to determine the ages of fossils, rocks, and minerals.

 **Reading Checkpoint** *What are isotopes?*

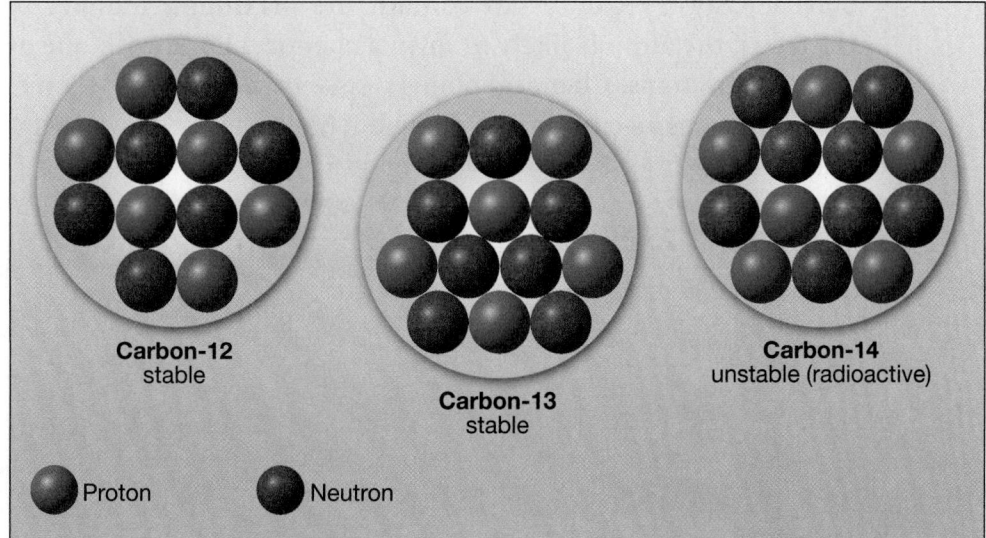

Carbon-12
stable

Carbon-13
stable

Carbon-14
unstable (radioactive)

● Proton   ● Neutron

Figure 3 Nuclei of Isotopes of Carbon Carbon has many isotopes. Of these, three occur in nature.
Comparing and Contrasting *How are the nuclei of these isotopes the same, and how do they differ?*

Why Atoms Bond

Most elements exist combined with other elements to form substances with properties that are different from the elements themselves. Sodium is often found combined with the element chlorine as the mineral halite. Lead is found in the mineral galena, which is made up of the element lead combined with the element sulfur. Chemical combinations of the atoms of elements are called **compounds.** **⬭A compound is a substance that consists of two or more elements that are chemically combined in specific proportions.** Compounds form when atoms are more stable (exist at a lower energy state) in a combined form. The chemical process, called bonding, centers around the electron arrangements of atoms. Thus, when atoms combine with others to form compounds, they gain, lose, or share electrons.

Scientists have discovered that the most stable elements are found on the right side of the periodic table in Group 8A (18). These elements have a very low reactivity and exist in nature as single atoms. Scientists explain why atoms form compounds by considering how an atom undergoes changes to its electron structure to be more like atoms in Group 8A.

Look at Figure 4. It shows the shorthand way of representing the number of electrons in the outer energy level. Recall that electrons move about the nucleus of an atom in a region called an electron cloud. Within this cloud, only a certain number of electrons can occupy each energy level. For example, a maximum of two electrons can occupy the first energy level. From Figure 4, you see that helium (He) is shown with two electrons. A maximum of eight electrons can be found in the second energy level. You also see from the figure that neon (Ne) is shown with eight electrons. ◐ **When an atom's outermost energy level does not contain the maximum number of electrons, the atom is likely to form a chemical bond with one or more other atoms. Chemical bonds** can be thought of as the forces that hold atoms together in a compound. The principal types of chemical bonds are ionic bonds, covalent bonds, or metallic bonds.

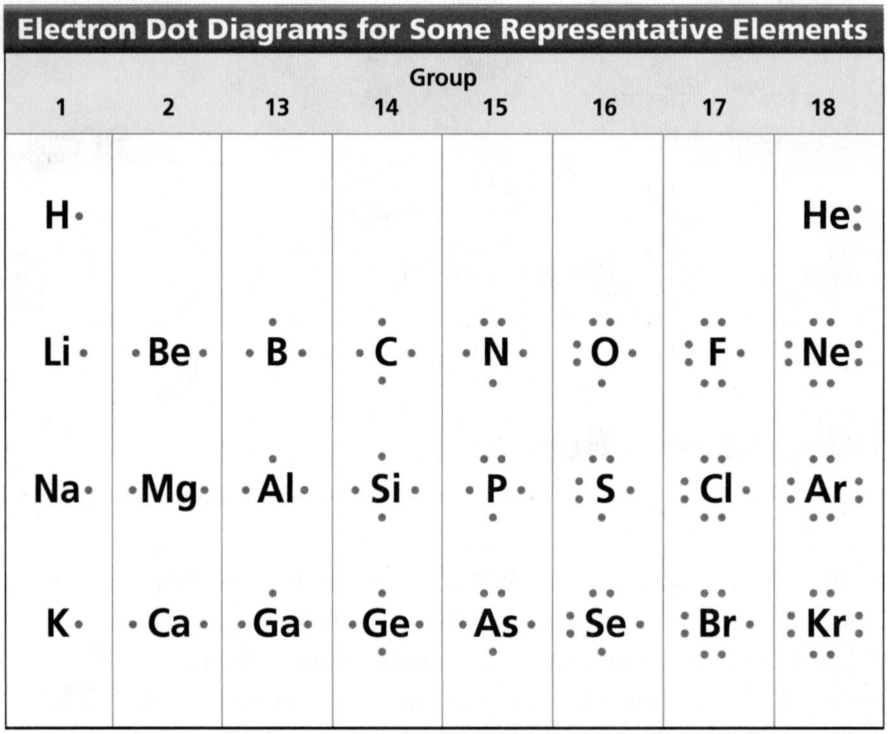

Figure 4 In an electron dot diagram, each dot represents an electron in the atom's outer energy level. These electrons are sometimes called valence electrons.
Observing *How many electrons do sodium and chlorine have in their outer energy levels?*

Electron Dot Diagrams for Some Representative Elements

Group							
1	2	13	14	15	16	17	18
H·							He:
Li·	·Be·	·B·	·C·	·N·	:O·	:F·	:Ne:
Na·	·Mg·	·Al·	·Si·	·P·	:S·	:Cl·	:Ar:
K·	·Ca·	·Ga·	·Ge·	·As·	:Se·	:Br·	:Kr:

Types of Chemical Bonds

Ionic Bonds An atom that gains electrons becomes negatively charged. This happens because the atom now has more electrons than protons. An atom that loses electrons becomes positively charged. This happens because the atom now has more protons than electrons. An atom that has an electrical charge because of a gain or loss of one or more electrons is called an **ion.** Oppositely charged ions attract each other to form crystalline compounds. ◐ **Ionic bonds form between positive and negative ions.**

Some common compounds on Earth have both a chemical name and a mineral name. For example, table salt has a chemical name, sodium chloride, and a mineral name, halite. Salt forms when sodium (Na) reacts with chlorine (Cl) as shown in Figure 5A. Sodium is very unstable and reactive. Sodium atoms lose one electron and become positive ions. Chlorine atoms gain one electron and become negative ions. These oppositely charged ions are attracted to each other and form the compound called sodium chloride.

The properties of a compound are different from the properties of the elements in the compound. Sodium is a soft, silvery metal that reacts vigorously with water. If you held it in your hand, sodium could burn your skin. Chlorine is a green poisonous gas. Chemically combined these atoms produce table salt, the familiar crystalline solid that is essential to health.

Reading Checkpoint   *What happens when two or more atoms react?*

Formation of Sodium Chloride

Figure 5 A When sodium metal comes in contact with chlorine gas, a violent reaction occurs. **B** Sodium atoms transfer one electron to the outer energy levels of chlorine atoms. Both ions now have filled outer energy levels **C** The positive and negative ions formed attract each other to form a crystalline solid with a rigid structure.

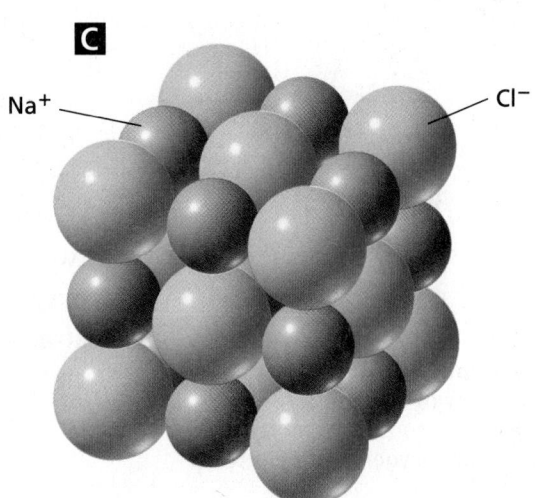

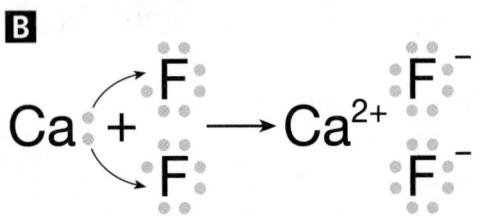

Figure 6 Ionic Compound A Fluorite is an ionic compound that forms when calcium reacts with fluorine. **B** The dots shown with the element's symbol represent the electrons in the outermost levels of the ions.
Explaining *Explain what happens to the electrons in calcium atoms and fluorine atoms when fluorite forms.*

Compounds that contain ionic bonds are called ionic compounds. Figure 6 shows calcium fluoride, a common ionic compound. Our model for ionic bonding suggests that one calcium atom transfers two electrons from its outermost energy level to two atoms of fluorine. This transfer gives all atoms the right numbers of electrons in their outer energy levels. The compound that forms is known as the mineral fluorite.

Ionic compounds are rigid solids with high melting and boiling points. These compounds are poor conductors of electricity in their solid states. When melted, however, many ionic compounds are good conductors of electricity. Most ionic compounds consist of elements from groups 1 and 2 on the periodic table reacting with elements from groups 16 and 17 of the table.

 **Reading Checkpoint** *How do ionic bonds form, and what are some properties of ionic compounds?*

Covalent Bonds ◯ **Covalent bonds form when atoms share electrons.** Compounds with covalent bonds are called covalent compounds. Figure 7 shows silicon dioxide, one of the most common covalent compounds on Earth. Silicon dioxide forms when one silicon atom and two oxygen atoms share electrons in their outermost energy levels. Silicon dioxide is also known as the mineral quartz.

The bonding in covalent compounds results in properties that differ from those of ionic compounds. Unlike ionic compounds, many covalent compounds have low melting and boiling points. For example, water, a covalent compound, boils at 100°C at standard pressure. Sodium chloride, an ionic compound, boils at 1413°C at standard pressure. Covalent compounds also are poor conductors of electricity, even when melted.

The smallest particle of a covalent compound that shows the properties of that compound is a molecule. A molecule is a neutral group of atoms joined by one or more covalent bonds. Water, for example, consists of molecules. These molecules are made of two hydrogen atoms covalently-bonded to one oxygen atom. The many gases that make up Earth's atmosphere, including hydrogen, oxygen, nitrogen, and carbon dioxide, also consist of molecules.

Figure 7 Covalent Compounds A Quartz is a covalent compound that forms when silicon and oxygen atoms bond. **B** Water consists of molecules formed when hydrogen and oxygen share electrons.

Metallic Bonds Metals are malleable, which means that they can be easily shaped. You've observed this property when you wrapped aluminum foil around food or crushed an aluminum can. Metals are also ductile, meaning that they can be drawn into thin wires without breaking. The wiring in your school or home is probably made of the metal copper. Metals are excellent conductors of electricity.

🔑**Metallic bonds form when electrons are shared by metal ions.** Figure 8 shows a model for this kind of bond. The sharing of an electron pool gives metals their characteristic properties. Using the model you can see how an electrical current is easily carried through the pool of electrons. Later in this chapter, you will learn about some metals that are classified as minerals.

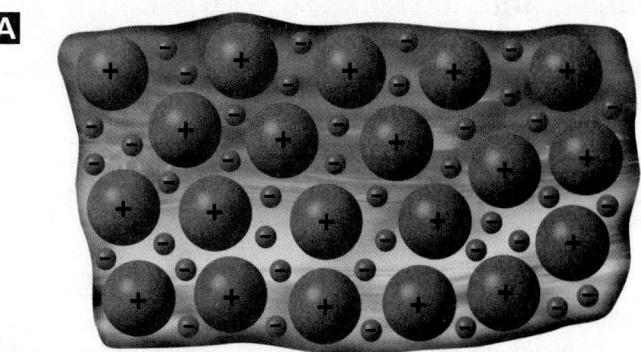

Figure 8 Metallic Bonds A Metals form bonds with one another by sharing electrons. **B** Such bonds give metals, such as this copper, their characteristic properties. Metals can be easily formed and shaped.

Section 2.1 Assessment

Reviewing Concepts

1. 🔑 What is an element?
2. 🔑 What kinds of particles make up atoms?
3. 🔑 What are isotopes?
4. 🔑 What are compounds and why do they form?
5. 🔑 Contrast ionic, covalent, and metallic bonds.

Critical Thinking

6. **Comparing and Contrasting** Compare and contrast solids, liquids, and gases.
7. **Applying Concepts** What elements in Table 1 are metals?
8. **Applying Concepts** A magnesium atom needs two electrons to fill its outermost energy level. A chlorine atom needs one electron to fill its outermost shell. If magnesium reacts with chlorine, what type of bond will most likely form? Explain.
9. **Applying Concepts** Which elements in the periodic table might combine with oxygen to form compounds similar to magnesium dioxide (MgO_2)?

Math Practice

10. The isotopes of carbon have from 2 to 16 neutrons. Use this information to make a table that shows the 15 isotopes of carbon and the atomic number and mass number of each.

2.2 Minerals

Reading Focus

Key Concepts

- What are five characteristics of a mineral?
- What processes result in the formation of minerals?
- How can minerals be classified?
- What are some of the major groups of minerals?

Vocabulary

- mineral
- silicate
- silicon-oxygen tetrahedron

Reading Strategy

Previewing Copy the organizer below. Skim the material on mineral groups on pages 47 to 49. Place each group name into one of the ovals in the organizer. As you read this section, complete the organizer with characteristics and examples of each major mineral group.

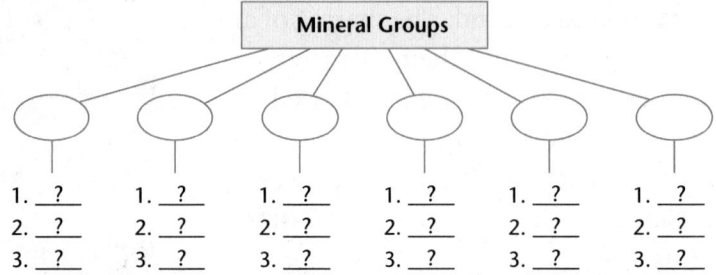

Mineral Groups

1. ?	1. ?	1. ?	1. ?	1. ?	1. ?
2. ?	2. ?	2. ?	2. ?	2. ?	2. ?
3. ?	3. ?	3. ?	3. ?	3. ?	3. ?

A

B

Look at the salt shaker in Figure 9B. This system is made up of the metal cap, glass container, and salt grains. Each component is made of elements or compounds that either are minerals or that are obtained from minerals. In fact, practically every manufactured product that you might use in a typical day contains materials obtained from minerals. What other minerals do you probably use regularly? The lead in your pencils actually contains a soft black mineral called graphite. Most body powders and many kinds of make-up contain finely ground bits of the mineral talc. Your dentist's drill bits contain tiny pieces of the mineral diamond. It is hard enough to drill through your tooth enamel. The mineral quartz is the main ingredient in the windows in your school and the drinking glasses in your family's kitchen. What do all of these minerals have in common? How do they differ?

Figure 9 A Table salt is the mineral halite. **B** The glass container is made from the mineral quartz. Bauxite contains minerals that provide aluminum for the cap.

Minerals

A mineral in Earth science is different from the minerals in foods. ⬦A **mineral is a naturally occurring, inorganic solid with an orderly crystalline structure and a definite chemical composition.** For an Earth material to be considered a mineral, it must have the following characteristics:

1. **Naturally occurring** A mineral forms by natural geologic processes. Therefore, synthetic gems, such as synthetic diamonds and rubies, are not considered minerals.

2. **Solid substance** Minerals are solids within the temperature ranges that are normal for Earth's surface.

3. **Orderly crystalline structure** Minerals are crystalline substances which means that their atoms or ions are arranged in an orderly and repetitive manner. You saw this orderly type of packing in Figure 5 for halite (NaCl). The gemstone opal is not a mineral even though it contains the same elements as quartz. Opal does not have an orderly internal structure.

4. **Definite chemical composition** Most minerals are chemical compounds made of two or more elements. A few, such as gold and silver, consist of only a single element (native form). The common mineral quartz consists of two oxygen atoms for every silicon atom. Thus the chemical formula for quartz would be SiO_2.

5. **Generally considered inorganic** Most minerals are inorganic crystalline solids found in nature. Table salt (halite) is one such mineral. However, sugar, another crystalline solid is not considered a mineral because it is classified as an organic compound. Sugar comes from sugar beets or sugar cane. We say "generally inorganic" because many marine animals secrete inorganic compounds, such as calcium carbonate (calcite). This compound is found in their shells and in coral reefs. Most geologists consider this form of calcium carbonate a mineral.

How Minerals Form

Minerals form nearly everywhere on Earth under different conditions. For example, minerals called silicates often form deep in the crust or mantle where temperatures and pressures are very high. Most of the minerals known as carbonates form in warm, shallow ocean waters. Most clay minerals form at or near Earth's surface when existing minerals are exposed to weathering. Still other minerals form when rocks are subjected to changes in pressure or temperature. ⬦**There are four major processes by which minerals form: crystallization from magma, precipitation, changes in pressure and temperature, and formation from hydrothermal solutions.**

Feldspar

Quartz

Muscovite

Hornblende

Figure 10 These minerals often form as the result of crystallization from magma.

For: Links on Minerals
Visit: PHSchool.com
Web Code: (czd-1022)

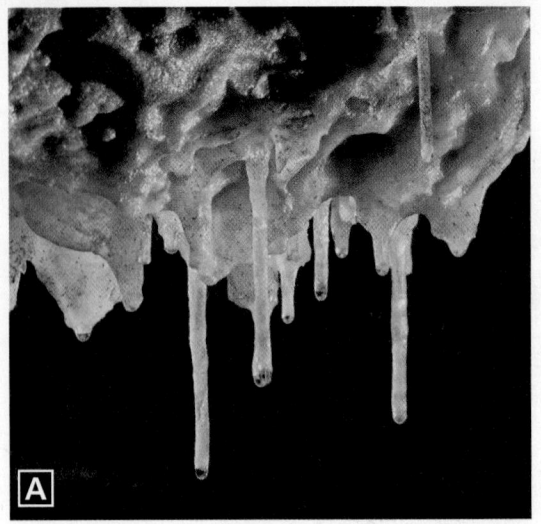

5 cm

Figure 11 A This limestone cave formation is an obvious example of precipitation. **B** Halite and calcite are also formed by precipitation.

Crystallization from Magma Magma is molten rock. It forms deep within Earth. As magma cools, elements combine to form minerals such as those shown in Figure 10 on page 45. The first minerals to crystallize from magma are usually those rich in iron, calcium, and magnesium. As minerals continue to form, the composition of the magma changes. Minerals rich in sodium, potassium, and aluminum then form.

Precipitation The water in Earth's lakes, rivers, ponds, oceans, and beneath its surface contains many dissolved substances. If this water evaporates, some of the dissolved substances can react to form minerals. Changes in water temperature may also cause dissolved material to precipitate out of a body of water. The minerals are left behind, or precipitated, out of the water. Two common minerals that form in this way are shown in Figure 11.

Pressure and Temperature Some minerals, including talc and muscovite, form when existing minerals are subjected to changes in pressure and temperature. An increase in pressure can cause a mineral to recrystallize while still solid. The atoms are simply rearranged to form more compact minerals. Changes in temperature can also cause certain minerals to become unstable. Under these conditions, new minerals form, which are stable at the new temperature.

Hydrothermal Solutions A hydrothermal solution is a very hot mixture of water and dissolved substances. Hydrothermal solutions have temperatures between about 100°C and 300°C. When these solutions come into contact with existing minerals, chemical reactions take place to form new minerals. Also, when such solutions cool, some of the elements in them combine to form minerals such as quartz and pyrite. The sulfur minerals in the sample shown in Figure 12 formed from thermal solutions.

Figure 12 Bornite (blue and purple) and chalcopyrite (gold) are sulfur minerals that form from thermal solutions.

Reading Checkpoint *Describe what happens when a mineral is subjected to changes in pressure or temperature.*

Mineral Groups

Over 3800 minerals have been named, and several new ones are identified each year. You will be studying only the most abundant minerals. **Common minerals, together with the thousands of others that form on Earth, can be classified into groups based on their composition.** Some of the more common mineral groups include the silicates, the carbonates, the oxides, the sulfates and sulfides, the halides, and the native elements. First, you will learn about the most common groups of minerals on Earth—the **silicates.**

Silicates If you look again at Table 1, you can see that the two most abundant elements in Earth's crust are silicon and oxygen. **Silicon and oxygen combine to form a structure called the silicon-oxygen tetrahedron.** This structure is shown in Figure 13. The tetrahedron, which consists of one silicon atom and four oxygen atoms, provides the framework of every silicate mineral. Except for a few silicate minerals, such as pure quartz (SiO_2), most silicates also contain one or more other elements.

Silicon-oxygen tetrahedra can join in a variety of ways, as you can see in Figure 14 on the next page. The silicon-oxygen bonds are very strong. Some minerals, such as olivine, are made of millions of single tetrahedra. In minerals such as augite, the tetrahedra join to form single chains. Double chains are formed in minerals such as hornblende. Micas are silicates in which the tetrahedra join to form sheets. Three-dimensional network structures are found in silicates such as quartz and feldspar. As you will see, the internal structure of a mineral affects its properties.

 **Reading Checkpoint** *What is the silicon-oxygen tetrahedron, and in how many ways can it combine?*

Figure 13 A The silicon-oxygen tetrahedron is made of one silicon atom and four oxygen atoms. The rods represent chemical bonds between silicon and the oxygen atoms. **B** Quartz is the most common silicate mineral. A typical piece of quartz like this contains millions of silicon-oxygen tetrahedra.

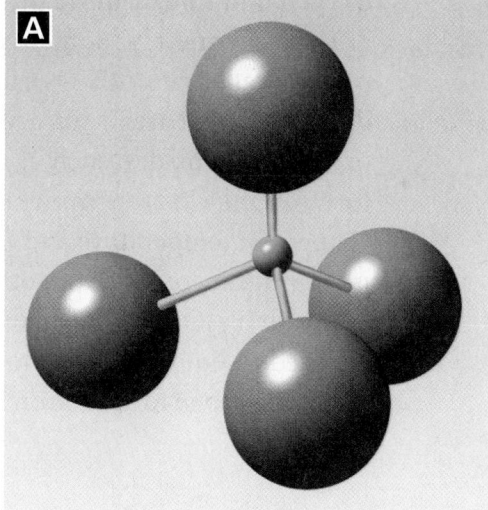

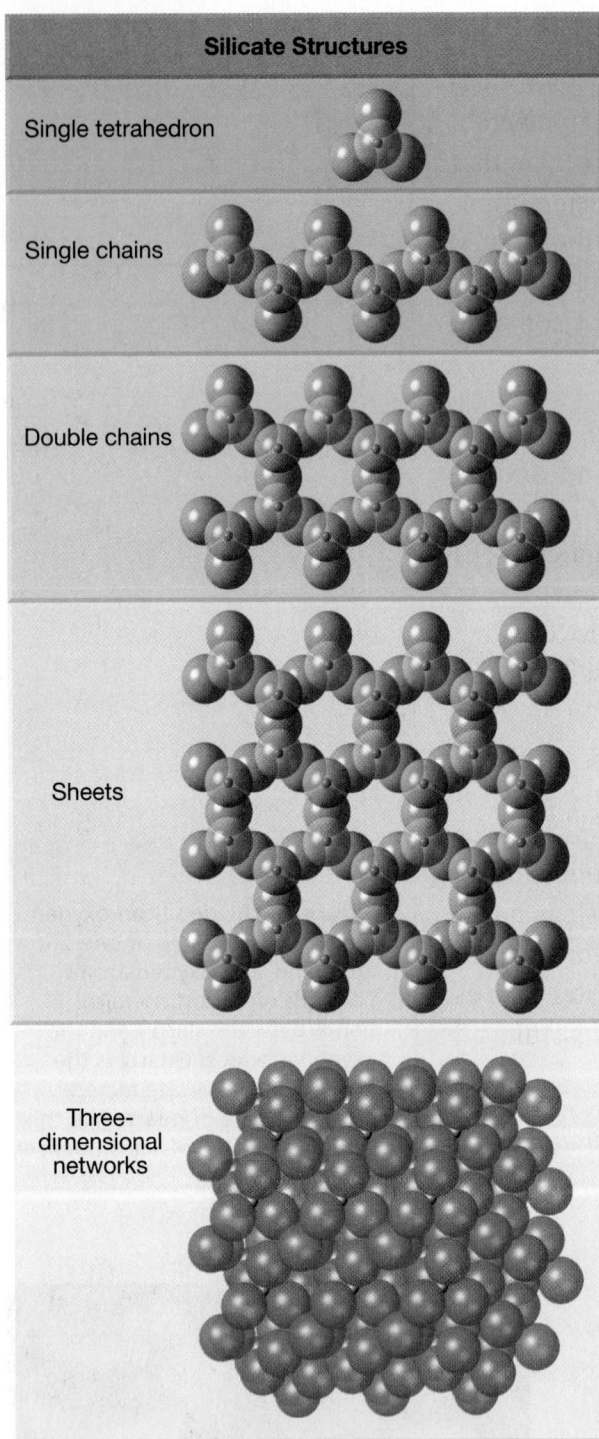

Figure 14 Silicon-oxygen tetrahedra can form chains, sheets, and three-dimensional networks.
Formulating Hypotheses *What type of chemical bond is formed by silicon atoms in an SiO$_4$ tetrahedron?*

Recall that most silicate minerals crystallize from magma as it cools. This cooling can occur at or near Earth's surface, where temperatures and pressures are relatively low. The formation of silicates can also occur at great depths, where temperatures and pressures are high. The place of formation and the chemical composition of the magma determine which silicate minerals will form. For example, the silicate olivine crystallizes at temperatures of about 1200°C. Quartz crystallizes at about 700°C.

Some silicate minerals form at Earth's surface when existing minerals are exposed to weathering. Clay minerals, which are silicates, form this way. Other silicate minerals form under the extreme pressures that occur with mountain building. Therefore, silicate minerals can often provide scientists with clues about the conditions in which the minerals formed.

Carbonates Carbonates are the second most common mineral group. **Carbonates are minerals that contain the elements carbon, oxygen, and one or more other metallic elements.** Calcite (CaCO$_3$) is the most common carbonate mineral. Dolomite is another carbonate mineral that contains magnesium and calcium. Both limestone and marble are rocks composed of carbonate minerals. Both types of rock are used in building and construction.

Oxides **Oxides are minerals that contain oxygen and one or more other elements, which are usually metals.** Some oxides, including the mineral called rutile (TiO$_2$), form as magma cools deep beneath Earth's surface. Rutile is titanium oxide. Other oxides, such as corundum (Al$_2$O$_3$), form when existing minerals are subjected to changes in temperature and pressure. Corundum is aluminum oxide. Still other oxides, such as hematite (Fe$_2$O$_3$), form when existing minerals are exposed to liquid water or to moisture in the air. Hematite is one form of iron oxide.

Sulfates and Sulfides

Sulfates and sulfides are minerals that contain the element sulfur. Sulfates, including anhydrite ($CaSO_4$) and gypsum ($CaSO_4 \cdot 2H_2O$), form when mineral-rich waters evaporate. Sulfides, which include the minerals galena (PbS), sphalerite (ZnS), and pyrite (FeS_2), often form from thermal, or hot-water, solutions. Figure 15 shows two of these sulfides.

Halides

Halides are minerals that contain a halogen ion plus one or more other elements. Halogens are elements from Group 7A of the periodic table. This group includes the elements fluorine (F) and chlorine (Cl). The mineral halite (NaCl), table salt, is a common halide. Fluorite (CaF_2) is also a common halide and is used in making steel. It forms when salt water evaporates.

Native Elements

Native elements are minerals that only contain one element or type of atom. You are probably familiar with many native elements, such as gold (Au), silver (Ag), copper (Cu), sulfur (S), and carbon (C). Native forms of carbon are diamond and graphite. Some native elements form from hydrothermal solutions.

Figure 15 Sulfides A Galena is a sulfide mineral that can be mined for its lead. **B** Pyrite, another sulfide, is often called fool's gold.
Inferring *What element do you think pyrite is generally mined for?*

Section 2.2 Assessment

Reviewing Concepts

1. What are five characteristics of a mineral?
2. Describe four processes that result in the formation of minerals.
3. How can minerals be classified?
4. Name the major groups of minerals, and give at least two examples of minerals in each group.

Critical Thinking

5. **Comparing and Contrasting** Compare and contrast sulfates and sulfides.
6. **Formulating Conclusions** When hit with a hammer, quartz shows an uneven breakage pattern. Using Figure 14, what can you suggest about its structure?
7. **Applying Concepts** To which mineral group does each of the following minerals belong: bornite (Cu_5FeS_4), cuprite (Cu_2O), magnesite ($MgCO_3$), and barite ($BaSO_4$)?

Writing in Science

Explanatory Paragraph Coal forms from ancient plant matter that has been compressed over time. Do you think coal is a mineral? Write a paragraph that explains your reasoning.

2.3 Properties of Minerals

Reading Focus

Key Concepts

- What properties can be used to identify minerals?
- What is the Mohs scale?
- What are some distinctive properties of minerals?

Vocabulary

- ◆ streak
- ◆ luster
- ◆ crystal form
- ◆ hardness
- ◆ Mohs scale
- ◆ cleavage
- ◆ fracture
- ◆ density

Reading Strategy

Outlining Before you read, make an outline of this section, following the format below. Use the green headings as the main topics. As you read, add supporting details.

I. **Properties of Minerals**
  A. **Color**
    1. _____
    2. _____
  B. **Luster**
    1. _____
    2. _____

As you can see from the photographs in this chapter, minerals occur in different colors and shapes. Now you will learn that minerals vary in the way they reflect light and in the way in which they break. You will also find out that some minerals are harder than others and that some minerals smell like rotten eggs. All of these characteristics, or properties, of minerals can be used to identify them.

Color

One of the first things you might notice about a mineral is its color. While color is unique to some minerals, this property is often not useful in identifying many minerals. **Small amounts of different elements can give the same mineral different colors.** You can see examples of this in Figure 16.

Figure 16 Small amounts of different elements give these sapphires their distinct colors. **Observing** *Why is color often not a useful property in mineral identification?*

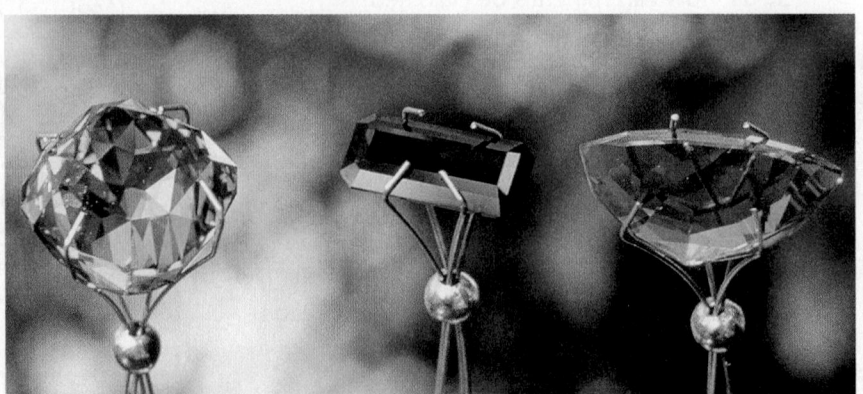

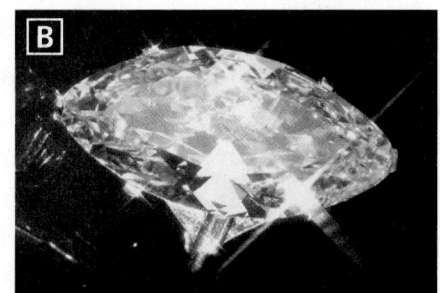

Figure 17 A The mineral copper has a metallic luster. **B** The brilliant luster of diamond is also known as an adamantine luster.

Streak

⊂⊃ **Streak is the color of a mineral in its powdered form.** Streak is obtained by rubbing a mineral across a streak plate, a piece of unglazed porcelain. While the color of a mineral may vary from sample to sample, the streak usually doesn't. Therefore, streak can be a good indicator. Streak can also help to see the difference between minerals with metallic lusters and minerals with nonmetallic lusters. Metallic minerals generally have a dense, dark streak. Minerals with nonmetallic lusters do not have such streaks.

Luster

⊂⊃ **Luster is used to describe how light is reflected from the surface of a mineral.** Minerals that have the appearance of metals, regardless of their color, are said to have a metallic luster. The piece of copper shown in Figure 17A has a metallic luster. Minerals with a nonmetallic luster are described by many adjectives. These include vitreous or glassy, like the quartz crystals in Figure 13B. Other lusters include pearly, silky, and earthy. Diamond has an adamantine, or brilliant, luster. Some minerals appear *somewhat* metallic and are said to have a sub-metallic luster.

Crystal Form

⊂⊃ **Crystal form is the visible expression of a mineral's internal arrangement of atoms.** Every mineral has a crystal form based on one of six distinct crystal systems. All the minerals that belong to a given crystal system have crystals of the same shape. For example, the fluorite in Figure 18 belongs to the cubic crystal system. Quartz has hexagonal (six-sided) crystals and belongs to the hexagonal crystal system.

Usually, when a mineral forms slowly and without space restrictions, it will develop into a crystal with well-formed faces—sides, top, and bottom. Most of the time, however, minerals compete for space. This crowding results in an intergrown mass of small crystals. None of these crystals shows its crystal form.

Go Online
active art

For: Crystal System activity
Visit: PHSchool.com
Web Code: czp-1022

Figure 18 Crystal Form
Fluorite often forms cubic crystals.

Reading Checkpoint) *What two conditions produce crystals with well-defined faces?*

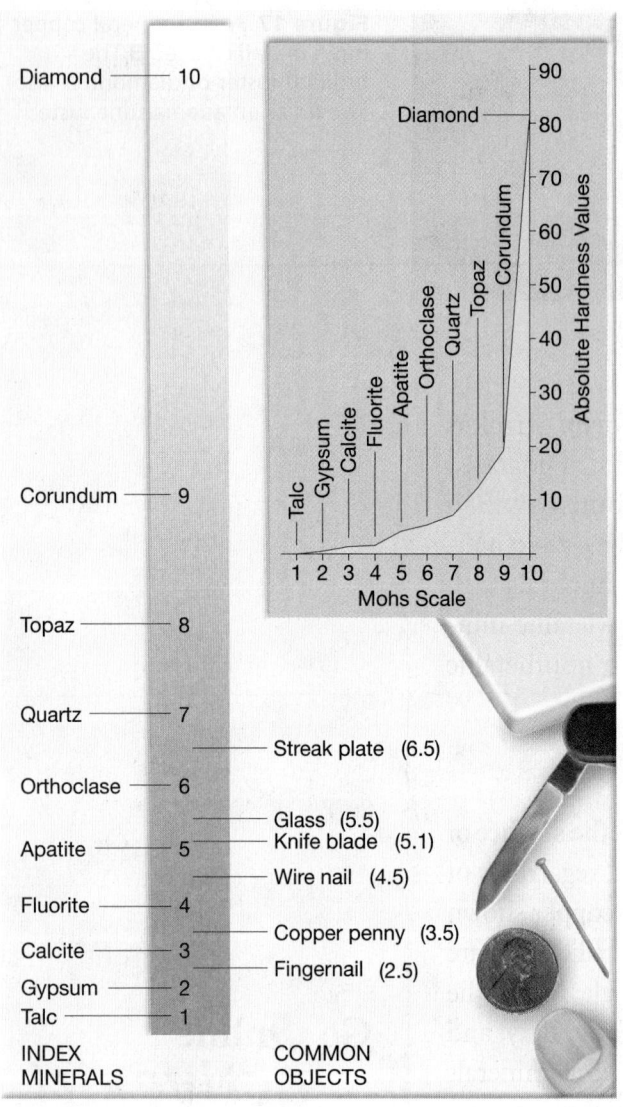

Figure 19 Mohs Scale of Hardness Common objects can be used with the Mohs scale to determine mineral hardness. **Using Tables and Graphs** *A mineral has a hardness of 4.2. Which common items on the chart will that mineral scratch?*

Hardness

One of the most useful properties to identify a mineral is hardness. **Hardness** is a measure of the resistance of a mineral to being scratched. You can find this property by rubbing the mineral against another mineral of known hardness. One will scratch the other, unless they have the same hardness.

Geologists use a standard hardness scale called the Mohs scale. **The Mohs scale consists of 10 minerals arranged from 10 (hardest) to 1 (softest).** See Figure 19. Any mineral of unknown hardness can be rubbed against these to determine its hardness. Other objects can also be used to determine hardness. Your fingernail, for example, has a hardness of 2.5. A copper penny has a hardness of 3.5. A piece of glass has a hardness of about 5.5. Look again at Figure 19. The mineral gypsum, which has a Mohs hardness of 2, can be easily scratched by your fingernail. The mineral calcite, which resembles gypsum, has a hardness of 3. Calcite cannot be scratched by your fingernail. Calcite, which can resemble the mineral quartz, cannot scratch glass, because its hardness is less than 5.5. Quartz, the hardest of the common minerals with a Mohs hardness of 7, will scratch a glass plate. Diamond, the hardest mineral on Earth, can scratch anything.

 **Reading Checkpoint** *Describe three or four of the most useful properties for identifying unknown minerals.*

Cleavage

In the atomic structure of a mineral, some bonds are weaker than others. These weak bonds are places where a mineral will break when it is stressed. **Cleavage is the tendency of a mineral to cleave, or break, along flat, even surfaces.**

Minerals called micas show the simplest type of cleavage. Because the micas have weak bonds in one direction, they cleave to form thin, flat sheets, as shown in Figure 20A. Look again at Figure 14. Can you see the relationship between mica's internal structure and the cleavage it shows? Mica, and all other silicates, tend to cleave between the silicon-oxygen structures rather than across them. This is because the silicon-oxygen bonds are strong. The micas' sheet structure causes them to cleave into flat plates. Quartz has equally strong silicon-oxygen bonds in all directions. Therefore, quartz has no cleavage but fractures instead.

Some minerals have cleavage in more than one direction. Look again at Figure 11. Halite (11A) has three directions of cleavage. The cleavage planes of halite meet at 90-degree angles. Calcite (11B) also has three directions of cleavage. The cleavage planes of calcite, however, meet at 75-degree angles.

Fracture

**Minerals that do not show cleavage when broken are said to fracture. Fracture** is the uneven breakage of a mineral. For example, quartz shows a curvy and glassy fracture. Like cleavage, there are different kinds of fracture. Minerals that break into smooth, curved surfaces like the quartz in Figure 20B have a conchoidal fracture. Other minerals, such as asbestos, break into splinters or fibers. Many minerals have an irregular fracture.

 **Reading Checkpoint** *How are cleavage and fracture different?*

Density

**Density is a property of all matter that is the ratio of an object's mass to its volume.** Density is a ratio and can be expressed using the following equation.

$$Density\ (D) = \frac{mass\,(m)}{Volume\,(V)}$$

Density is expressed using derived units with a unit of mass over a unit of volume. For example, the density of copper is 8.96 g/cm^3 (grams per cubic centimeter). Therefore, any sample of pure copper with a volume of one cubic centimeter will have a mass of 8.96 grams.

Many common minerals have densities between 2 and 5 g/cm^3. Some metallic minerals have densities that are often greater than rock-forming minerals. Galena, the ore of lead, has a density around 7.5 g/cm^3. The density of gold is 19.3 g/cm^3. The density of a pure mineral is a constant value. Thus, density can be used to determine the purity or identity of some minerals.

Figure 20 A Mica has cleavage in one direction and therefore cleaves into thin sheets. **B** The bonds in quartz are very strong in all directions, causing quartz to display conchoidal fracture.

For: Links on mineral identification
Visit: www.SciLinks.org
Web Code: cjn-1023

Table 2 Some Common Minerals and Their Properties					
Name	Chemical Formula and Mineral Group	Common Color(s)	Density (g/cm³)	Hardness	Comments
Quartz	SiO_2 silicates	colorless, milky white, pink, brown	2.65	7	glassy luster; conchoidal fractures
Orthoclase feldspar	$KAlSi_3O_8$ silicates	white to pink	2.57	6	cleaves in two directions at 90°
Plagioclase feldspar	$(Na,Ca)AlSi_3O_8$ silicates	white to gray	2.69*	6	cleaves in two directions at 90°; striations common
Galena	PbS sulfides	metallic silver	7.5*	2.5	cleaves in three directions at 90°; lead gray streak
Pyrite	FeS_2 sulfides	brassy yellow	5.02	6–6.5	fractures; forms cubic crystals; greenish-black streak
Sulfur	S native elements	yellow	2.07*	1.5–2.5	fractures; yellow streak smells like rotten eggs
Fluorite	CaF_2 halides	colorless, purple	3.18	4	perfect cleavage in three directions; glassy luster
Olivine	$(Mg,Fe)_2SiO_4$ silicates	green, yellowish-green	3.82*	6.5–7	fractures; glassy luster; often has granular texture
Calcite	$CaCO_3$ carbonates	colorless, gray	2.71	3	bubbles with HCl; cleaves in three directions
Talc	$Mg_3Si_4O_{10}(OH)_2$ silicates	pale green, gray, white	2.75*	1	pearly luster; feels greasy; cleaves in one direction
Gypsum	$CaSO_4 \cdot 2H_2O$ sulfates	colorless, white, gray	2.32	2	glassy or pearly luster; cleaves in three directions
Muscovite mica	$KAl_3Si_3O_{10}(OH)_2$ silicates	colorless in thin sheets to brown	2.82*	2–2.5	silky to pearly luster; cleaves in one direction to form flexible sheets

* Average density of the mineral

Figure 21 Calcite shows the property of double refraction.

Distinctive Properties of Minerals

Some minerals can be recognized by other distinctive properties. Talc and graphite, for example, both have distinctive feels. Talc feels soapy. Graphite feels greasy. Metallic minerals, such as gold, silver, and copper, are easily shaped. Some minerals, such as magnetite and hematite, are magnetic. Magnetite will attract paper clips and small nails. When a piece of transparent calcite is placed over printed material, the lines appear doubled, as Figure 21 shows. This property is called double refraction. Streaks of a few minerals that contain sulfur smell like rotten eggs. A droplet of hydrochloric acid will cause carbonate minerals, such as calcite, to fizz.

A mineral's properties depend on the elements that compose the mineral (its composition) and its structure (how its atoms are arranged). Table 2 lists some of the more common minerals and their properties. You will use this table to identify minerals in the lab on pages 58 and 59.

Table 2 Some Common Minerals and Their Properties, *continued*					
Name	**Chemical Formula and Mineral Group**	**Common Color(s)**	**Density (g/cm³)**	**Hardness**	**Comments**
Biotite mica	$K(Mg,Fe)_3(AlSi_3O_{10})(OH)_2$ silicates	dark green to brown to black	3.0*	2.5–3	perfect cleavage in one direction to form flexible sheets
Halite	$NaCl$ halides	colorless, white	2.16	2.5	has a salty taste; dissolves in water; cleaves in three directions
Augite	$(Ca, Na)(Mg, Fe, Al)(Si, Al)_2O_6$ silicates	dark green to black	3.3*	5–6	glassy luster; cleaves in two directions; crystals have 8-sided cross section
Hornblende	$(Ca, Na)_{2-3}(Mg, Fe, Al)_5Si_6(Si, Al)_2O_{22}(OH)_2$ silicates	dark green to black	3.2*	5–6	glassy luster; cleaves in two directions; crystals have 6-sided cross section
Hematite	Fe_2O_3 oxides	reddish brown to black	5.26	5.5–6.5	metallic luster in crystals; dull luster in earthy variety; dark red streak; weakly magnetic
Dolomite	$CaMg(CO_3)_2$ carbonates	pink, colorless, white, gray	2.85	3.5–4	does not react to HCl as quickly as calcite; cleaves in three directions
Magnetite	Fe_3O_4 oxides	black	5.18	6	metallic luster; black streak; strongly magnetic
Copper	Cu native elements	copper-red on fresh surface	8.9	2.5–3	metallic luster; fractures; can be easily shaped
Graphite	C native elements	black to gray	2.3	1–2	black to gray streak; marks paper; feels slippery

Section 2.3 Assessment

Reviewing Concepts

1. 🔵 Describe five common properties of minerals that can be used to identify them.

2. 🔵 How is the Mohs scale used?

3. 🔵 What are some unique properties that can be used to identify minerals?

Critical Thinking

4. **Applying Concepts** What kind of luster do the minerals shown in Figure 15 have? Explain your choice.

5. **Applying Concepts** Hornblende is a double-chain silicate. How many planes of cleavage do you think hornblende has when it breaks? Explain your answer.

6. **Applying Concepts** A mineral scratches a piece of fluorite but cannot be scratched by a piece of glass. What is this mineral's hardness?

Connecting Concepts

Mineral Properties Choose one of the minerals pictured in this chapter. Find out to which mineral system it belongs as well as its luster, streak, hardness, specific gravity, and whether it cleaves or fractures. Also note any unique properties of the mineral.

Gemstones

Precious stones have been prized by people since ancient times. Unfortunately, much misinformation exists about the nature of gems and the minerals of which they are composed. Part of the misinformation stems from the ancient practice of grouping precious stones by color rather than mineral makeup.

For example, the more common red spinels were often passed off to royalty as rubies, which are more valuable gems. Even today, when modern techniques of mineral identification are commonplace, yellow quartz is frequently sold as topaz.

What's In a Name?

Compounding the confusion is the fact that many gems have names that are different from their mineral names. For example, diamond is composed of the mineral of the same name, whereas sapphire is a form of corundum, an aluminum oxide-rich mineral. Although pure aluminum oxide is colorless, a tiny amount of a foreign element can produce a vividly colored gemstone. Therefore, depending on the impurity, sapphires of nearly every color exist. Pure aluminum oxide with trace amounts of titanium and iron produce the most prized blue sapphires. If the mineral corundum contains enough chromium, it exhibits a brilliant red color, and the gem is called ruby. Large gem-quality rubies are much rarer than diamonds and thus command a very high price.

If the specimen is not suitable as a gem, it simply goes by the mineral name corundum. Although common corundum is not a gemstone, it does have value as an abrasive material. Whereas two gems—rubies and sapphires—are composed of the mineral corundum, quartz is the parent mineral of more than a dozen gems. Table 3 lists some well-known gemstones and their mineral names.

Figure 22 Emerald is the dark green variety of the mineral beryl. More common blue-green beryl is aquamarine.

Precious or Semiprecious?

What makes a gem a gem instead of just another mineral? Basically, certain mineral specimens, when cut and polished, possess beauty of such quality that they can command a price that makes the process of producing the gem profitable. Gemstones can be divided into two categories: precious and semiprecious. A *precious* gem has beauty, durability, size, and rarity, whereas a *semiprecious* gem usually has only one or two of these qualities. The gems that have traditionally enjoyed the highest esteem are diamonds, rubies, sapphires, emeralds, and some varieties of opal. All other gemstones are classified as semiprecious. It should be noted, however, that large, high-quality specimens of semiprecious stones can often command a very high price.

Obviously, beauty is the most important quality that a gem can possess. Today we prefer translucent stones with evenly tinted colors. The most favored hues appear to be red, blue, green, purple, rose,

Figure 23 A diamond in the rough looks very different from the brilliant, multi-faceted gem it can become.

and yellow. The most prized stones are deep red rubies, blue sapphires, grass-green emeralds, and canary-yellow diamonds. Colorless gems are generally less than desirable except in the case of diamonds that display "flashes of color" known as brilliance.

Notice in figure 23 that gemstones in the "rough" are dull and would be passed over by most people as "just another mineral." Gemstones must be cut and polished by experienced artisans before their true beauty can be displayed.

The durability of a gem depends on its hardness—that is, its resistance to abrasion by objects normally encountered in everyday living. For good durability, gems should be as hard or harder than quartz, as defined by the Mohs scale of hardness. One notable exception is opal, which is comparatively soft (hardness 5 to 6.5) and brittle. Opal's esteem comes from its fire, which is a display of a variety of brilliant colors including greens, blues, and reds.

It seems to be human nature to treasure that which is rare. In the case of gemstones, large, high-quality specimens are much rarer than smaller stones. Thus, large rubies, diamonds, and emeralds, which are rare in addition to being beautiful and durable, command the very highest prices.

Table 3 Some Important Gemstones

Gem	Mineral Name	Prized Hues
Precious		
Diamond	Diamond	Colorless, yellows
Emerald	Beryl	Greens
Opal	Opal	Brilliant hues
Ruby	Corundum	Reds
Sapphire	Corundum	Blues
Semiprecious		
Alexandrite	Chrysoberyl	Variable
Amethyst	Quartz	Purples
Aquamarine	Beryl	Blue-greens
Cat's-eye	Chrysoberyl	Yellows
Chalcedony	Quartz (agate)	Banded
Citrine	Quartz	Yellows
Garnet	Garnet	Reds, greens
Jade	Jadeite or nephrite	Greens
Moonstone	Feldspar	Transparent blues
Peridot	Olivine	Olive greens
Smoky quartz	Quartz	Browns
Spinel	Spinel	Reds
Topaz	Topaz	Purples, reds
Tourmaline	Tourmaline	Reds, blue-greens
Turquoise	Turquoise	Blues
Zircon	Zircon	Reds

Mineral Identification

Most minerals can be easily identified by using the properties discussed in this chapter. In this lab, you will use what you have learned about mineral properties and the table on pages 54 and 55 to identify some common rock-forming minerals. In the next chapter, you will learn about rocks, which are mixtures of one or more minerals. Being able to identify minerals will enable you to understand more about the processes that form and change the rocks at and beneath Earth's surface.

Problem
How can you use simple tests and tools to identify common minerals?

Materials
- mineral samples
- hand lens
- streak plate
- copper penny
- steel knife blade
- glass plate
- piece of quartz
- dilute hydrochloric acid
- magnet
- hammer
- 50 mL graduated cylinder
- tap water
- balance
- thin thread
- scissors
- paper or cloth towels
- Table 2 on pages 54–55

Skills
Observing, Comparing and Contrasting, Measuring

Procedure

Part A: Color and Luster

1. Examine each mineral sample with and without the hand lens. Examine both the central part of each mineral as well as the edges of the samples.

2. Record the color and luster of each sample in a data table like the one shown on the next page.

Part B: Streak and Hardness

3. To determine the streak of a mineral, gently drag it across the streak plate and observe the color of the powdered mineral. If a mineral is harder than the streak plate (H = 7), it will not produce a streak.

4. Record the streak color for each mineral in your data table.

5. Use your fingernail, the penny, the glass plate, the knife blade, and the piece of quartz to test the hardness of each mineral. Remember that if a mineral scratches an object, the mineral is harder than the object. If an object scratches a mineral, the mineral is softer than the object.

6. Record the hardness values for each sample in your data table.

Part C: Cleavage and Fracture

7. With your goggles on and everyone out of your way, gently strike one of the mineral samples with a hammer.

8. Observe the broken mineral pieces. Does the mineral cleave or fracture? Remember that cleavage is breakage along flat, even surfaces and fracture is uneven breakage. Record your observations in your data table.

9. Repeat Steps 7 and 8 for the other minerals.

Data Table										
Mineral Number	Color	Luster	Streak	Relative Hardness	Cleavage/ Fracture	Density				Other Properties
						m	V_1	V_2	d	
1										
2										
3										
4										
5										
6										
7										
8										

Part D: Density

10. Using a balance, determine the mass of your mineral sample. Record the mass in the first column under Density.

11. Cut a piece of thread about 20 cm long. Tie a small piece of your mineral sample to one end of the thread.

12. Securely tie the other end of the thread to a pencil or pen.

13. Fill the graduated cylinder about half full with water. Record the volume of the water in the second column under Density.

14. Lower the mineral into the graduated cylinder. Read the volume of the water now. Record the volume in the third column under Density.

15. Calculate the density of the mineral using the following equation:

$$\frac{mass_1}{volume_2 - volume_1}$$

Record this value in the fourth column.

Part E: Other Properties

16. Use the magnet to determine if any of the minerals are magnetic. Record your observations in the data table.

17. Place the transparent minerals over a word on this page to see if any have the property of double refraction. If a mineral has this property, you will see two sets of the word. Record your observations.

18. Compare the feel of the minerals. In the data table, note any differences.

19. Carefully place one or two drops of dilute hydrochloric acid on each mineral. Record your observations. When you are finished with this test, wash the minerals well with tap water to rinse away the acid.

Analyze and Conclude

1. **Identifying** Use your data and Table 2 to identify each of the minerals tested.

2. **Evaluating** Which of the properties did you find most useful? Least useful? Give reasons for your answers.

3. **Comparing and Contrasting** In general, how did the minerals with metallic luster differ from those with non-metallic luster?

4. **Classifying** Classify your minerals into at least three groups based on your observations. How does your classification scheme differ from those of at least two other students?

Go Further Obtain some rock samples from your teacher or collect some of your own. Use the hand lens to try to identify the minerals in each rock. Make a table in which to record your observations. Compare your table to the information presented in Chapter 3.

Study Guide

2.1 Matter

Key Concepts

- An element contains only one type of atom. Therefore, an element cannot be broken down, chemically or physically, into a simpler substance.

- An atom is a submicroscopic particle made of even smaller components called protons, neutrons, and electrons.

- Atoms with the same number of protons but different numbers of neutrons are isotopes of an element.

- A compound is a substance that consists of two or more elements. Compounds form when electrons are transferred or shared to form bonds.

- When an atom's outermost energy level does not contain the maximum number of electrons, the atom is likely to form a chemical bond with one or more other atoms.

- Ionic bonds form between positive and negative ions. Covalent bonds form when atoms share electrons. Metallic bonds form when electrons are shared by metal ions.

Vocabulary

element, *p. 34*; atomic number, *p. 35*; energy level, *p. 38*; isotope, *p. 38*; mass number, *p. 38*; compound, *p. 39*; chemical bond, *p. 40*; ion, *p. 40*; ionic bond, *p. 40*; covalent bond, *p. 42*; metallic bond, *p. 43*

2.2 Minerals

Key Concepts

- A mineral is a naturally occurring, inorganic solid with an orderly internal structure and a definite chemical composition.

- There are four major processes by which minerals form: crystallization from magma, precipitation, changes in pressure and temperature, and formation from hydrothermal solutions.

- Common minerals, together with the thousands of others that form on Earth, can be classified into groups based on their composition.

- Silicates are the most common minerals on Earth and are made of millions of silicon-oxygen tetrahedra. Carbonates contain carbon, oxygen, and one or more other elements. Oxides contain oxygen and one or more other elements, usually metals. Sulfates and sulfides are minerals that contain sulfur. Halides contain a halogen ion plus one or more other elements. Native elements are minerals that only contain one element or type of atom.

Vocabulary

mineral, *p. 45*; silicate, *p. 47*; silicon-oxygen tetrahedron, *p. 47*

2.3 Properties of Minerals

Key Concepts

- Small amounts of different elements can give the same mineral many different colors.

- Streak is the color of a mineral in its powdered form.

- Luster describes how light is reflected from the surface of a mineral.

- Crystal form is the visual expression of a mineral's internal arrangement of atoms.

- The Mohs scale is a scale that can be used to determine a mineral's hardness.

- Cleavage is the tendency of a mineral to cleave, or break along flat, even surfaces; fracture is uneven breakage.

- Density is a property of all matter that is the ratio of an object's mass to its volume.

- Some minerals can be recognized by other distinctive properties.

Vocabulary

streak, *p. 51*; luster, *p. 51*; crystal form, *p. 51*; hardness, *p. 52*; Mohs scale, *p. 52*; cleavage, *p. 52*; fracture, *p. 53*; density, *p. 53*

Thinking Visually

Observing Use what you have learned about minerals and Table 2 to list as many properties as possible of the mineral below.

Reviewing Content

Choose the letter that best answers the question or completes the statement.

1. Which of the following is neutrally charged?
   a. an ion
   b. a compound
   c. an electron
   d. a proton

2. Atoms combine when
   a. their outer electron shells are filled.
   b. their electrons are shared or transferred.
   c. the number of protons and neutrons is the same.
   d. the number of electrons and protons is the same.

3. Compounds with low boiling points have
   a. metallic bonds.
   b. ionic bonds.
   c. covalent bonds.
   d. no chemical bonds.

4. Minerals that form from magma form as the result of
   a. crystallization.
   b. evaporation.
   c. precipitation.
   d. condensation.

5. The mineral barite ($BaSO_4$) is a(n)
   a. oxide.
   b. silicate.
   c. carbonate.
   d. sulfate.

6. Color is often not a useful identification property because
   a. some minerals are colorless.
   b. the same mineral can be different colors.
   c. different minerals can be different colors.
   d. some minerals are single elements.

7. What is a mineral's streak?
   a. the resistance to being scratched
   b. the color of the mineral in powder form
   c. the way in which the mineral reflects light
   d. the way the mineral reacts to hydrochloric acid

8. A particular mineral breaks like a piece of glass does. Which of these describes the breakage?
   a. cleavage
   b. hardness
   c. metallic luster
   d. fracture

9. Mineral properties depend on composition and
   a. structure.
   b. luster.
   c. cleavage.
   d. streak.

Understanding Concepts

10. Name the three types of particles found in an atom and explain how they differ.

11. Compare and contrast ionic and covalent bonds.

12. What are five characteristics of a mineral?

13. Explain three ways in which new minerals can form from existing minerals.

14. Contrast the composition of minerals in each of the mineral groups discussed in the chapter.

15. How is cleavage related to a mineral's atomic structure?

16. Give examples of four minerals that can be identified by unique properties. Describe each property.

Use this diagram to answer Questions 17–21.

A

$$Mg \; \overset{\cdot \cdot}{\underset{}{\cdot}} \; + \; \overset{\cdot \cdot}{\underset{\cdot \cdot}{O}} \overset{\cdot \cdot}{\cdot} \; \longrightarrow \; Mg^{2+} \; \overset{\cdot \cdot}{\underset{\cdot \cdot}{\cdot O \cdot}}{}^{2-}$$

B

$$\overset{\cdot \cdot}{\underset{\cdot \cdot}{\cdot Cl}} \overset{\cdot \cdot}{\underset{\cdot \cdot}{Cl \cdot}}$$

17. Briefly describe the kind of bond that is formed when two atoms shown in **A** bond.

18. Describe the kind of bond that forms when the atoms shown in **B** bond.

19. Is the atom on the left in **A** an ion? Explain your answer.

20. Use the periodic table to determine the atomic number of the atom on the left side of **A**. What group is this element in?

21. The atoms in **B** contain 17 protons. Are these atoms ions when they bond with each other? Can these atoms form ions when they react with other elements? Explain your answers.

Critical Thinking

22. Comparing and Contrasting Three atoms have the same atomic number but different mass numbers. What can you say about the atoms?

23. Predicting Potassium metal in group 1 of the periodic table is very reactive. When placed in chlorine gas, potassium reacts to form a halide compound. Using Figure 4 and the periodic table propose the formula and name for the compound.

24. Formulating Hypotheses Why do you think metals can easily be rolled into thin sheets and drawn into wires? (*Hint:* Think about the arrangement of electrons in metals.)

25. Explaining Explain the processes that result in the formation of silicate minerals.

26. Formulating Hypotheses A mineral forms deep beneath the surface. It reaches Earth's surface during mountain building. Describe two things that might happen to this mineral at the surface.

27. Applying Concepts Classify the following minerals based on their chemical formulas.

a. $NaCO_3$ b. PbS
c. $FeCr_2O_4$ d. CaF_2

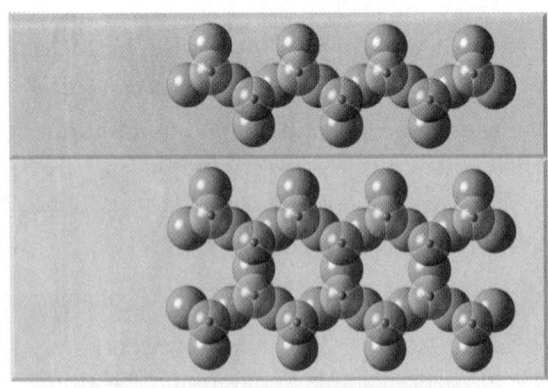

Use the diagrams to answer Questions 28–31.

28. Identifying What is the basic structural unit in these two diagrams?

29. Classifying What are the names given to these two silicate structures?

30. Applying Concepts How do these two structures affect mineral breakage?

31. Formulating Hypotheses Which of the two structures is more complex? Explain your choice.

Concepts in Action

32. Applying Concepts Your friend shows you a crystal that he thinks is a diamond. Without asking an expert, how could you tell if the crystal is really a diamond?

33. Hypothesizing Which two minerals discussed in this chapter would be useful as abrasives? Which could be used as a lubricant? Which might be used in sparkly eye shadows?

34. Calculating Gold has a density of 19.3 g/cm^3. What would be the mass of a gold brick that is 30 cm long, 8 cm wide, and 4 cm tall?

Performance-Based Assessment

Applying Concepts Go on a scavenger hunt around your school or home to find at least 20 items that are minerals, that contain minerals, or that were obtained from minerals. Make a poster that shows what you found and display it for the class.

Standardized Test Prep

Choose the letter that best answers the question or completes the statement.

1. The central region of an atom includes
  (A) only neutrons.
  (B) only electrons.
  (C) electrons and protons.
  (D) neutrons and protons.

2. Protons in an atom
  (A) make up the atom's electron cloud.
  (B) are equal in number to the atom's neutrons.
  (C) determine the kind of element.
  (D) are NOT used to determine atomic mass.

3. If the atomic number of an element is 6 and its mass number is 14, how many neutrons are in the atom's nucleus?
  (A) 0   (B) 6
  (C) 8   (D) 20

Use the graph to answer Questions 4–6.

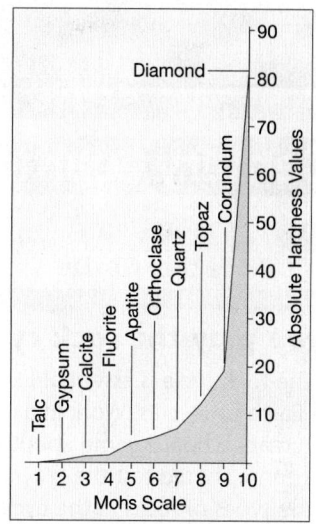

4. What does this graph show?

5. How does talc's hardness on the Mohs scale compare with its absolute hardness?

6. Describe the relationship between Mohs hardness and absolute hardness.

Answer the following questions in complete sentences.

7. How do the isotopes of an element differ?

8. Define a mineral.

Columns of rock called hoodoos dot Bryce Canyon National Park.

21st Century Learning

Interpersonal and Collaborative Skills

How can you play the rock cycle?

Knowledge of the rock cycle is essential to understanding Earth processes. Work in a small group to create a board game about the rock cycle. The game should test the players' knowledge of the types of rocks in the cycle as well as some of the key events in the rock cycle. When the game is done, exchange games with another group to play and provide feedback. Use the feedback to improve your game.

Quick Lab
Observing Some of the Effects of Pressure on Mineral Grains

Exploration Lab
Earth's Atmosphere

Earth as a System
The Carbon Cycle

GEODe
EARTH SCIENCE

Earth Materials
↳ Rock Cycle
Igneous Rocks
Sedimentary Rocks
Metamorphic Rocks

Chapter Preview

Inquiry > Activity

What Are Some Similarities and Differences Among Rocks?

Procedure

1. Your teacher will provide you with six rock samples. Examine them closely.

2. Record at least three ways in which the rocks are alike.

3. Now determine and record at least three ways in which the rocks differ.

4. Classify the rock samples into three groups based on your observations. Give reasons for your groupings.

Think About It

1. **Comparing and Contrasting** How are the rock samples similar? How do they differ?

2. **Comparing and Contrasting** How does your classification scheme compare with the classification schemes of at least two other students? How do they differ?

3. **Formulating Hypotheses** Each of the rocks used in this activity belongs to one of the three major groups of rocks. Hypothesize what makes one group of rocks different from the others.

3.1 The Rock Cycle

Reading Focus

Key Concepts

- What is a rock?
- What are the three major types of rocks?
- How do igneous, sedimentary, and metamorphic rocks differ?
- What is the rock cycle?
- What powers Earth's rock cycle?

Vocabulary

- rock
- igneous rock
- sedimentary rock
- metamorphic rock
- rock cycle
- magma
- lava
- weathering
- sediments

Reading Strategy

Building Vocabulary Copy and expand the table to include each vocabulary term. As you read, write down the definition for each term.

Term	Definition
rock	a. _____?_____
igneous rock	b. _____?_____
sedimentary rock	c. _____?_____
sediments	d. _____?_____

Figure 1 A Obsidian and **B** pumice are two examples of rocks that do not have a crystalline structure.

5 cm

A

5 cm

B

Why do we study rocks? All Earth processes such as volcanic eruptions, mountain building, weathering, erosion, and even earthquakes involve rocks and minerals. Rocks contain clues about the environments in which they were formed. For example, if a rock contains shell fragments, it was probably formed in a shallow ocean environment. The locations of volcanic rocks tell a story of volcanic activity on Earth through time. Thus, you can see that a basic knowledge of rocks is essential to understanding the Earth.

Rocks

A rock is any solid mass of mineral or mineral-like matter that occurs naturally as part of our planet. A few rocks are composed of just one mineral. However, most rocks, like granite, occur as solid mixtures of minerals. A characteristic of rock is that each of the component minerals retains their properties in the mixture. A few rocks are composed of nonmineral matter. Coal is considered a rock even though it consists of organic material. Obsidian and pumice, shown in Figure 1, are volcanic rocks that do not have a crystalline structure.

Rocks are classified into three groups based on how they were formed. The three major types of rocks are igneous rocks, sedimentary rocks, and metamorphic rocks. Before examining each group, you will look at a model for the rock cycle, which is the process that shows the relationships between the rock groups.

Reading Checkpoint **What are the three types of rocks?**

The Rock Cycle

Earth is a system. It consists of many interacting parts that form a complex whole. ◯**Interactions among Earth's water, air, and land can cause rocks to change from one type to another. The continuous processes that cause rocks to change make up the rock cycle.** Most changes in the rock cycle take place over long periods of time.

Figure 2 shows some key events in the rock cycle. Refer to the figure throughout this section as you examine how rock might change over time. Look at Figures 2A and 2B. **Magma** is molten material that forms deep beneath Earth's surface. ◯**When magma cools and hardens beneath the surface or as the result of a volcanic eruption, igneous rock forms.** Magma that reaches the surface is called **lava**.

Go ◯nline
active art

For: Rock Cycle activity
Visit: PHSchool.com
Web Code: czp-1031

Rock Cycle

Figure 2 The rock cycle consists of many processes that change Earth's rocks.
Formulating Hypotheses *Can a sedimentary rock become an igneous rock without changing first to a metamorphic rock? Explain.*

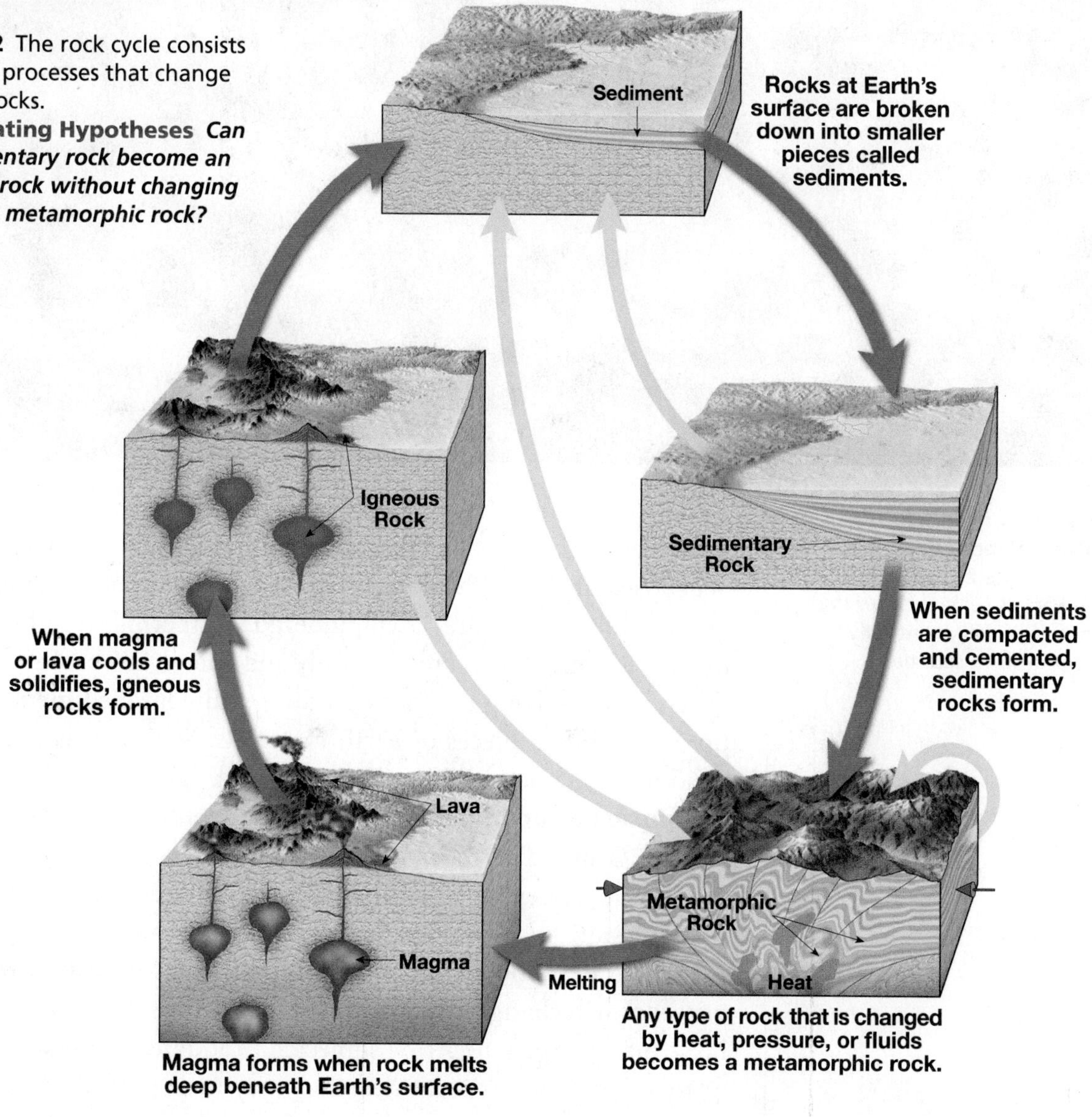

Rocks at Earth's surface are broken down into smaller pieces called sediments.

Sediment

Igneous Rock

Sedimentary Rock

When sediments are compacted and cemented, sedimentary rocks form.

When magma or lava cools and solidifies, igneous rocks form.

Lava

Magma

Metamorphic Rock

Melting

Heat

Any type of rock that is changed by heat, pressure, or fluids becomes a metamorphic rock.

Magma forms when rock melts deep beneath Earth's surface.

Figure 3 El Capitan in Yosemite National Park This granite was once buried deep beneath Earth's surface. Now that it is exposed, it will eventually weather and form sediments.

What will happen if an igneous rock that formed deep within Earth is exposed at the surface? Any rock at Earth's surface, including the granite shown in Figure 3, will undergo weathering. **Weathering** is a process in which rocks are physically and chemically broken down by water, air, and living things to produce sediment. **Sediment** is made up of weathered pieces of earth materials. Sediment is moved and deposited by water, gravity, glaciers, or wind. **Eventually, sediment is compacted and cemented to form sedimentary rock, as shown in Figure 2C and 2D.**

If the sedimentary rocks become buried deep within Earth, they will be subjected to increases in pressure and/or temperature. **Under extreme pressure and temperature conditions, sedimentary rock will change into metamorphic rock, as shown in Figure 2E.** If the metamorphic rocks are subjected to additional pressure changes or to still higher temperatures, they may melt to form magma. The magma will eventually crystallize to form igneous rock once again.

Alternate Paths

The purple arrows in Figure 2 show only one way in which an igneous rock might form and change. Other paths are just as likely to be taken as an igneous rock goes through the rock cycle. The blue arrows show a few of these alternate paths.

Suppose, for example, that an igneous rock remained deeply buried. Eventually, the rock could be subjected to strong forces and high temperatures such as those associated with mountain building. Then, the igneous rock could change into one or more kinds of metamorphic rock. If the temperatures and pressures were high enough, the igneous rock could melt and recrystallize to form new igneous rock.

Metamorphic and sedimentary rocks, as well as sediment, do not always remain buried. Often, overlying rocks are stripped away, exposing the rock that was once buried. When this happens, the rocks weather to form sediments that eventually become sedimentary rocks. However, if the sedimentary rocks become buried again, metamorphic rocks, like those used for the roof tiles in Figure 4, will form.

Where does the energy that drives Earth's rock cycle come from? **Processes driven by heat from Earth's interior are responsible for forming both igneous and metamorphic rocks. Weathering and the movement of weathered materials are external processes powered by energy from the sun and by gravity. Processes on and near Earth's surface produce sedimentary rocks.**

Figure 4 The roof on this house is made of slate. Slate is a metamorphic rock that forms from the sedimentary rock shale. **Explaining** *How can shale become slate?*

Section 3.1 Assessment

Reviewing Concepts

1. What is a rock?
2. What are the three major types of rocks?
3. How do igneous, sedimentary, and metamorphic rocks differ?
4. What is the rock cycle?
5. What powers Earth's rock cycle?

Critical Thinking

6. **Comparing and Contrasting** Compare and contrast igneous and metamorphic rocks.

7. **Applying Concepts** How might a sedimentary rock become an igneous rock?

8. **Applying Concepts** List in order the processes that could change one sedimentary rock into another sedimentary rock.

Writing in Science

Writing to Persuade Coral reefs are made of calcium carbonate that is secreted by the corals and algae that make up the reefs. Over time, this calcium carbonate accumulates to form limestone. Use what you know about minerals and rocks to write a paragraph explaining whether or not you think that this limestone is a rock.

3.2 Igneous Rocks

Reading Focus

Key Concepts

- How are intrusive and extrusive igneous rocks alike and different?
- How does the rate of cooling affect an igneous rock's texture?
- How are igneous rocks classified according to composition?

Vocabulary

- intrusive igneous rock
- extrusive igneous rock
- porphyritic texture
- granitic composition
- basaltic composition
- andesitic composition
- ultramafic

Reading Strategy

Outlining Copy the outline and complete it as you read. Include points about how each of these rocks form, some of the characteristics of each rock type, and some examples of each.

I. Igneous Rocks
  A. Intrusive Rocks
    1. ____?____
    2. ____?____
  B. Extrusive Rocks
    1. ____?____
    2. ____?____

Recall from the discussion of the rock cycle that igneous rocks form when magma or lava cools and hardens. When the red hot lava shown in Figure 5 cools, a dark-colored igneous rock called basalt will form. If this melted material had stayed deep beneath Earth's surface, a very different kind of igneous rock would have been produced as the material cooled. Different kinds of igneous rocks form when magma and lava cool and harden.

Go Online
PLANETDIARY

For: Links on Extrusive Igneous Rocks
Visit: PHSchool.com
Web Code: czd-1032

Figure 5 Basaltic Lava
Lava from this Hawaiian volcano flows easily over Earth's surface. When the lava cools and hardens, the igneous rock called basalt will form.

Formation of Igneous Rocks

The word *igneous* comes from the Latin word *ignis,* which means "fire." Perhaps that is why people often associate igneous rock with fiery volcanic eruptions like the one shown in Figure 5. Igneous rock also forms deep beneath Earth's surface.

A

B

Intrusive Igneous Rocks ⊂**Rocks that form when magma hardens beneath Earth's surface are called intrusive igneous rocks.** That is because they *intrude* into the existing rocks. We would never see these deep rocks were it not for erosion stripping away the overlying rock.

Magma consists mainly of the elements silicon and oxygen, plus aluminum, iron, calcium, sodium, potassium, and magnesium. Magma also contains some gases, including water vapor. These gases are kept within the magma by the pressure of the surrounding rocks. Because magma is less dense than the surrounding rocks, it slowly works its way toward the surface. As magma rises, it cools, allowing elements to combine and form minerals. Gradually, the minerals grow in size, forming a solid mass of interlocking crystals. Granite, shown in Figure 6A, is a common intrusive igneous rock.

Extrusive Igneous Rocks You know that when magma reaches Earth's surface, it is called lava. Lava is similar to magma, except that in lava, most of the gases have escaped. ⊂**When lava hardens, the rocks that form are called extrusive igneous rocks.** That is because they are *extruded* onto the surface. The rhyolite shown in Figure 6B is an extrusive igneous rock.

Figure 6 A Granite is an intrusive igneous rock that forms when magma cools slowly beneath Earth's surface. **B** Rhyolite is an extrusive igneous rock that forms when lava cools quickly at Earth's surface.

Q *How are magma and lava the same, and how are they different?*

A Magma and lava are both terms used to describe melted rock. The composition of magma and lava can be the same. However, magma is melted material beneath Earth's surface. Lava is melted material at Earth's surface.

Q *Native Americans used obsidian for making arrowheads and cutting tools. Is this the only material they used?*

A No. Native Americans used whatever materials were locally available to make tools, including any hard dense rock material that could be shaped. This includes materials such as the metamorphic rocks slate and quartzite, sedimentary deposits made of silica called jasper, chert, opal, flint, and even jade. Some of these deposits occur in only a few areas. That helps anthropologists reconstruct trade routes between different Native American groups.

Figure 7 This sample of andesite displays igneous rock with a porphyritic texture.
Describing *Describe how this rock probably formed.*

Classification of Igneous Rocks

A quick glance at the two rocks in Figure 6 tells you that they are different. The granite contains large mineral grains. Only a few of the mineral grains in the sample of rhyolite can be seen with the unaided eye. **Texture and composition are two characteristics used to classify igneous rocks.** Texture describes the appearance of an igneous rock based on its size, shape, and the arrangement of its interlocking crystals. The composition classes of igneous rocks are based on the proportions of light and dark minerals in the rock.

Coarse-Grained Texture The rate of cooling strongly affects the textures of igneous rocks. If magma cools very slowly, few centers of crystal growth develop. Slow cooling also allows charged atoms, or ions, to move large distances within the magma. **Slow cooling results in the formation of large crystals.** Igneous rocks with large crystals exhibit a coarse-grained texture.

Fine-Grained Texture If cooling of magma or lava occurs rapidly, the ions in the melted material lose their motion and quickly combine. This results in a large number of tiny crystals that all compete for the available ions. **Rapid cooling of magma or lava results in rocks with small, interconnected mineral grains.** Igneous rocks with small grains are said to have a fine-grained texture.

Glassy Texture When lava spews onto Earth's surface, there may not be enough time for the ions in the lava to arrange themselves into a network of crystals. So the solids produced this way are made of randomly distributed ions. Such rocks have a glassy texture. The obsidian and pumice shown in Figure 1 on page 66 are igneous rocks with glassy textures.

Porphyritic Texture A large body of magma located deep within Earth may take tens of thousands of years to harden. Minerals that crystallize from the magma do not form at the same rate or at the same time. It is possible for some crystals to become quite large before others even start to form. The resulting rock can have large crystals, called phenocrysts, surrounded by fine-grained minerals. Rocks with very different-size minerals experience different rates of cooling. These rocks have a **porphyritic texture.** The igneous rock shown in Figure 7 has a porphyritic texture.

Reading Checkpoint *How does the rate of cooling of magma or lava affect the texture of igneous rocks?*

Granitic Composition Igneous rocks in which the light-colored silicate minerals quartz and feldspar are the main minerals are said to have a **granitic composition.** In addition to quartz and feldspar, most granitic rocks contain about 10 percent dark silicate minerals. These dark minerals are often biotite mica and amphibole. Granitic rocks contain about 70 percent silica. Rhyolite is an extrusive granitic rock.

Intrusive granitic rocks make up much of the continental crust. Plate movements push crustal rock deep beneath the surface, where it melts and then cools, forming granite. Uplift and erosion later expose this rock at the surface. You will learn how these huge masses of granite rock form in Chapter 10.

Basaltic Composition Rocks that contain many dark silicate minerals and plagioclase feldspar have a **basaltic composition.** Basaltic rocks are rich in the elements magnesium and iron. Because of their iron content, basaltic rocks are typically darker and denser than granitic rocks. The most common basaltic rock is basalt, shown in Figure 8. Gabbro is an intrusive igneous rock with a basaltic composition.

Basaltic igneous rocks make up Earth's ocean floor. As tectonic plates move apart, magma with a basaltic composition erupts through the gap between the plates and hardens to form the ocean floor. You will learn about this process in Chapter 9.

Other Compositional Groups Rocks with a composition between granitic and basaltic rocks have an **andesitic composition.** This group of igneous rocks is named after the common volcanic rock andesite. Andesitic rocks contain at least 25 percent dark silicate minerals—mainly amphibole, pyroxene, and biotite mica. The other dominant mineral in andesitic rocks is plagioclase feldspar.

Certain volcanoes are made up of rocks with andesitic composition. As you will learn in Chapter 10, these volcanoes form where tectonic plates collide. In this type of collision between plates, the dense basaltic rock of the ocean floor sinks back into the mantle beneath less dense continental crust.

Another important igneous rock is peridotite. This rock contains mostly the minerals olivine and pyroxene. Because peridotite is composed almost entirely of dark silicate minerals, its chemical composition is referred to as **ultramafic.** Although ultramafic rocks are rare at Earth's surface, much of the upper mantle is thought to be made of peridotite.

Figure 8 Basalt is an igneous rock made mostly of dark-colored silicate minerals.
Describing *Describe the texture of this igneous rock.*

To summarize, igneous rocks form when magma or lava cools and hardens. Intrusive rocks form when magma cools and hardens deep within Earth. Extrusive rocks form when lava cools and hardens on Earth's surface. Igneous rocks can be classified according to texture and composition. A general classification scheme based on texture and mineral composition is shown in Table 1.

Table 1 Classification of Major Igneous Rocks

Chemical Composition			Granitic	Andesitic	Basaltic	Ultramafic
Dominant Minerals			Quartz Potassium feldspar Sodium-rich plagioclase feldspar	Amphibole Sodium- and calcium-rich plagioclase feldspar	Pyroxene Calcium-rich plagioclase feldspar	Olivine Pyroxene
T E X T U R E	Coarse-grained		Granite	Diorite	Gabbro	Peridotite
	Fine-grained		Rhyolite	Andesite	Basalt	Komatiite (rare)
	Porphyritic		"Porphyritic" precedes any of the above names whenever there are appreciable phenocrysts.			Uncommon
	Glassy		Obsidian (compact glass) Pumice (frothy glass)			
Rock Color (based on % of dark minerals)			0% to 25%	25% to 45%	45% to 85%	85% to 100%

Section 3.2 Assessment

Reviewing Concepts

1. Compare and contrast the formation of intrusive and extrusive igneous rocks.

2. How do coarse-grained igneous rocks form?

3. How are igneous rocks classified according to composition?

4. How do fine-grained igneous rocks form?

5. How do igneous rocks with glassy textures form?

Critical Thinking

6. **Contrasting** Contrast basalt and granite in terms of how each forms, the texture of each rock, the color of each rock, and each rock's composition.

7. **Formulating Hypotheses** The extrusive igneous rock pumice contains many small holes. Hypothesize how these holes might form.

Writing in Science

Explanatory Paragraph Write a paragraph to explain how one of the igneous rocks pictured in this chapter may have formed.

3.3 Sedimentary Rocks

Reading Focus

Key Concepts

- Describe the major processes involved in the formation of sedimentary rocks.
- What are clastic sedimentary rocks?
- What are chemical sedimentary rocks?
- What features are unique to some sedimentary rocks?

Vocabulary

- erosion
- deposition
- compaction
- cementation
- clastic sedimentary rock
- chemical sedimentary rock

Reading Strategy

Outlining Copy this outline beneath the outline you made for Section 3.2. Complete this outline as you read. Include points about how each of these rocks form, some of the characteristics of each rock type, and some examples of each.

> II. Sedimentary Rocks
>   A. Clastic Rocks
>   1. ___?___
>   2. ___?___
>   B. Chemical Rocks
>   1. ___?___
>   2. ___?___

All sedimentary rocks begin to form when existing rocks are broken down into sediments. Sediments, which consist mainly of weathered rock debris, are often transported to other places. When sediments are dropped, they eventually become compacted and cemented to form sedimentary rocks. The structures shown in Figure 9 are made of the sedimentary rock called sandstone. It is only one of many types of sedimentary rocks.

Figure 9 Sedimentary Rocks in Canyonlands National Park, Utah The rocks shown here formed when sand and other sediments were deposited and cemented. Weathering processes created this arch.

Formation of Sedimentary Rocks

The word *sedimentary* comes from the Latin word *sedimentum,* which means "settling." Sedimentary rocks form when solids settle out of a fluid such as water or air. The rocks shown in Figure 10 formed when sediments were dropped by moving water. The sediments eventually became cemented to form rocks. Several major processes contribute to the formation of sedimentary rocks.

Weathering, Erosion, and Deposition Recall that weathering is any process that breaks rocks into sediments. Weathering is often the first step in the formation of sedimentary rocks. Chemical weathering takes place when the minerals in rocks change into new substances. Weathering also takes place when physical forces break rocks into smaller pieces. Living things, too, can cause chemical and physical weathering.

Weathered sediments don't usually remain in place. Instead, water, wind, ice, or gravity carries them away. **Erosion involves weathering and the removal of rock. When an agent of erosion—water, wind, ice, or gravity—loses energy, it drops the sediments. This process is called deposition.** Sediments are deposited according to size. The largest sediments, such as the rounded pebbles in the conglomerate in Figure 10A, are deposited first. Smaller sediments, like the pieces of sand that make up the sandstone in Figure 10B, are dropped later. Some sediments are so small that they are carried great distances before being deposited.

Compaction and Cementation After sediments are deposited, they often become lithified, or turned to rock. **Compaction** and **cementation** change sediments into sedimentary rock. **Compaction is a process that squeezes, or compacts, sediments.** Compaction is caused by the weight of sediments. During compaction, much of the water in the sediments is driven out.

Cementation takes place when dissolved minerals are deposited in the tiny spaces among the sediments. Much of the cement in the conglomerate shown in Figure 10A can be seen with the unaided eye. The cement holding the sand grains together in the sandstone in Figure 10B, however, is microscopic.

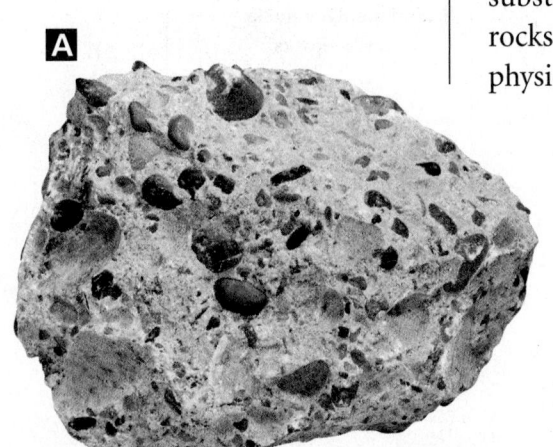

Figure 10 Although these two rocks appear quite different, both formed when sediments were dropped by moving water. **A** Conglomerate is made of rounded pebbles cemented together. **B** Sandstone is made of sand grains cemented together.

 **Reading Checkpoint** *Briefly describe the five major processes involved in the formation of sedimentary rocks.*

Classification of Sedimentary Rocks

Just like igneous rocks, sedimentary rocks can be classified into two main groups according to the way they form. The first group includes rocks that are made of weathered bits of rocks and minerals. These rocks are called **clastic sedimentary rocks.** The second group forms when dissolved minerals precipitate from water solutions. These rocks are called **chemical sedimentary rocks.**

Clastic Sedimentary Rocks Many different minerals are found in clastic rocks. The most common are the clay minerals and quartz. This is because clay minerals, like those that make up much of the shale in Figure 11A, are the most abundant products of chemical weathering. Quartz, which is a major mineral in the breccia shown in Figure 11B, is a common sedimentary mineral for a different reason. It is very durable and resistant to chemical weathering.

Clastic sedimentary rocks can be grouped according to the size of the sediments in the rocks. When rounded, gravel-size or larger particles make up most of the rock, the rock is called conglomerate. If the particles are angular, the rock is called breccia. Sandstone is the name given to rocks when most of the sediments are sand-size grains. Shale, the most common sedimentary rock, is made of very fine-grained sediment. Siltstone is another fine-grained rock.

Reading Checkpoint *Describe the major types of clastic sedimentary rocks.*

Chemical and Biochemical Sedimentary Rocks

Chemical sedimentary rocks form when dissolved substances precipitate, or separate, from water solution. This precipitation generally occurs when the water evaporates or boils off leaving a solid product. Examples of this type of chemical rock are some limestones, rock salt, chert, flint, and rock gypsum.

Figure 11 A Shale and **B** breccia are common clastic sedimentary rocks. This sample of shale contains plant fossils.
Formulating Hypotheses *How do you think this breccia might have formed?*

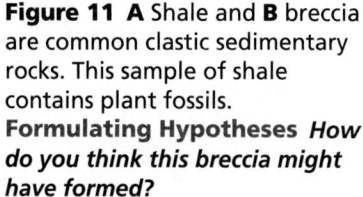

For: Links on sedimentary rocks
Visit: www.SciLinks.org
Web Code: cjn-1034

Figure 12 This biochemical rock, called coquina, is a type of limestone that is made of hundreds of shell fragments.

About 90 percent of limestones are formed from biochemical sediments. Such sediments are the shells and skeletal remains of organisms that settle to the ocean floor. The coquina in Figure 12 is one obvious example. You can actually see the shells cemented together. Another biochemical rock is chalk, the material used to write on a chalkboard.

Features of Some Sedimentary Rocks

Sedimentary rocks, like other types of rocks, are used to unravel what may have happened in Earth's long history. **The many unique features of sedimentary rocks are clues to how, when, and where the rocks formed.** Each layer of a sedimentary rock, for example, records a period of sediment deposition. In undisturbed rocks, the oldest layers are found at the bottom. The youngest layers are found at the top of the rocks. Ripple marks like the ones shown in Figure 13A may indicate that the rock formed along a beach or stream bed. The mud cracks in Figure 13B formed when wet mud or clay dried and shrank, leaving a rock record of a dry environment.

Fossils, which are the traces or remains of ancient life, are unique to some sedimentary rocks. Fossils can be used to help answer many questions about the rocks that contain them. For example, did the rock form on land or in the ocean? Was the climate hot or cold, rainy or dry? Did the rock form hundreds, thousands, millions, or billions of years ago? Fossils also play a key role in matching up rocks from different places that are the same age.

To summarize, sedimentary rocks are rocks that form as the result of four major processes. *Weathering* produces particles called sediments. Wind, water, ice, and gravity *erode* and *deposit* these sediments. Over time, the sediments are *compacted and cemented* to form rocks. Sedimentary rocks can be classified according to how they form. A general classification scheme based on a rock's formation, texture, and composition is shown in Table 2.

Figure 13 A Ripple marks and **B** mud cracks are features of sedimentary rocks that can be used to learn about the environments in which the rocks formed.

A

B

Table 2 Classification of Major Sedimentary Rocks

Clastic Sedimentary Rocks			Chemical Sedimentary Rocks		
Texture (grain size)	**Sediment Name**	**Rock Name**	**Composition**	**Texture** (grain size)	**Rock Name**
Coarse (over 2 mm)	Gravel (rounded fragments)	Conglomerate	Calcite, $CaCO_3$	Fine to coarse crystalline	Crystalline Limestone
	Gravel (angular fragments)	Breccia			Travertine
Medium (1/16 to 2 mm)	Sand	Sandstone		Visible shells and shell fragments loosely cemented	Coquina
Fine (1/16 to 1/256 mm)	Mud	Siltstone		Various size shells and shell fragments cemented with calcite cement	Fossiliferous Limestone
Very fine (less than 1/256 mm)	Mud	Shale		Microscopic shells and clay	Chalk
			Quartz, SiO_2	Very fine crystalline	Chert (light colored) Flint (dark colored)
			Gypsum $CaSO_4 \cdot 2H_2O$	Fine to coarse crystalline	Rock Gypsum
			Halite, NaCl	Fine to coarse crystalline	Rock Salt
			Altered plant fragments	Fine-grained organic matter	Bituminous Coal

(Coquina, Fossiliferous Limestone, and Chalk are grouped as **Biochemical Limestone**.)

Section 3.3 Assessment

Reviewing Concepts

1. 🔵 Contrast weathering, erosion, and deposition.

2. 🔵 Name four clastic sedimentary rocks and explain how these rocks form.

3. 🔵 Name four chemical sedimentary rocks and explain how these rocks form.

4. 🔵 Explain how three different features of sedimentary rocks can be used to determine how, where, or when the rocks formed.

5. What is compaction?

6. Where do the cements that hold sediments together come from?

Critical Thinking

7. **Applying Concepts** Briefly describe how the rock shown in Figure 12 may have formed.

8. **Predicting** Which type of sediments do you think would undergo more compaction—grains of sand or grains of clay? Explain your choice.

9. **Formulating Conclusions** Suppose you found a sedimentary rock in which ripple marks were pointing toward the ground. What could you conclude about the rock?

Connecting ⊂ Concepts

Sedimentary Rocks Choose one of the sedimentary rocks pictured in this section. Find out how the rock is useful to people.

amorphic Rocks

Key Concepts

- Where does most metamorphism take place?

- How is contact metamorphism different from regional metamorphism?

- What are three agents of metamorphism, and what kinds of changes does each cause?

- What are foliated metamorphic rocks, and how do they form?

- How are metamorphic rocks classified?

Vocabulary

- metamorphism
- contact metamorphism
- regional metamorphism
- hydrothermal solution
- foliated metamorphic rock
- nonfoliated metamorphic rock

Reading Strategy

Outlining Copy this outline beneath the outline you made for Section 3.3. Complete it as you read. Include points about how each of these rocks form, some of the characteristics of each rock type, and some examples of each.

```
III. Metamorphic Rocks
    A. Foliated Rocks
        1. ____?____
        2. ____?____
    B. Nonfoliated Rocks
        1. ____?____
        2. ____?____
```

Figure 14 Deformed Rock
Intense pressures metamorphosed these rocks by causing them to fold as well as change composition.

Recall that metamorphic rocks form when existing rocks are changed by heat and pressure. **Metamorphism** is a very appropriate name for this process because it means *to change form*. Rocks produced during metamorphism often look much different from the original rocks, or parent rocks. The folds in the rocks shown in Figure 14 formed when the parent rocks were subjected to intense forces. These highly folded metamorphic rocks may also develop a different composition than the parent rocks had.

Formation of Metamorphic Rocks

Most metamorphic changes occur at elevated temperatures and pressures. These conditions are found a few kilometers below Earth's surface and extend into the upper mantle. Most metamorphism occurs in one of two settings—contact metamorphism or regional metamorphism.

Contact Metamorphism When magma intrudes—forces its way into—rock, contact metamorphism may take place. 🔑**During contact metamorphism, hot magma moves into rock.** Contact metamorphism often produces what is described as low-grade metamorphism. Such changes in rocks are minor. Marble, like that used to make the statue in Figure 15, is a common contact metamorphic rock. Marble often forms when magma intrudes a limestone body.

Regional Metamorphism During mountain building, large areas of rocks are subjected to extreme pressures and temperatures. The intense changes produced during this process are described as high-grade metamorphism. 🔑**Regional metamorphism results in large-scale deformation and high-grade metamorphism.** The rocks shown in Figure 14 on page 80 were changed as the result of regional metamorphism.

Figure 15 Statue Carved from Marble Marble is a common metamorphic rock that forms as the result of contact metamorphism of limestone.

Agents of Metamorphism

🔑**The agents of metamorphism are heat, pressure, and hydrothermal solutions.** During metamorphism, rocks are usually subjected to all three of these agents at the same time. However, the effect of each agent varies greatly from one situation to another.

Heat The most important agent of metamorphism is heat. Heat provides the energy needed to drive chemical reactions. Some of these reactions cause existing minerals to recrystallize. Other reactions cause new minerals to form. The heat for metamorphism comes mainly from two sources—magma and the change in temperature with depth. Magma essentially "bakes" any rocks that are in contact with it. Heat also comes from the gradual increase in temperature with depth. In the upper crust, this increase averages between 20°C and 30°C per kilometer.

When buried to a depth of about 8 kilometers, clay minerals are exposed to temperatures of 150°C to 200°C. These minerals become unstable and recrystallize to form new minerals that are stable at these temperatures, such as chlorite and muscovite. In contrast, silicate minerals are stable at these temperatures. Therefore, it takes higher temperatures to change silicate minerals.

Reading Checkpoint *Compare and contrast contact and regional metamorphism.*

Q *How hot is it deep in the crust?*

A The deeper a person goes beneath Earth's surface, the hotter it gets. The deepest mine in the world is the Western Deep Levels mine in South Africa, which is about 4 kilometers deep. Here, the temperature of the surrounding rock is so hot that it can scorch human skin. In fact, miners in this mine often work in groups of two. One miner mines the rock, and the other operates a large fan that keeps the worker cool.

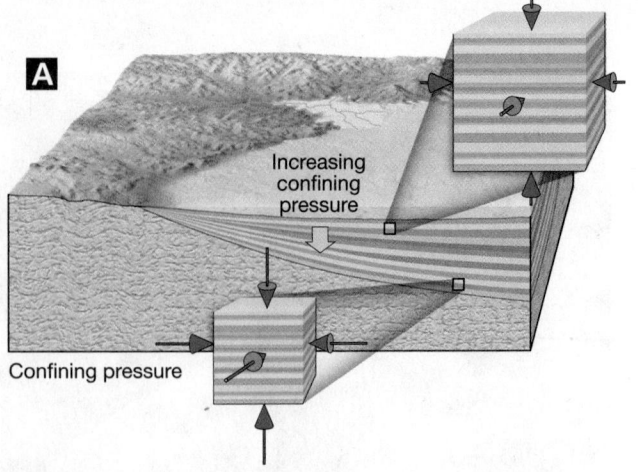

A

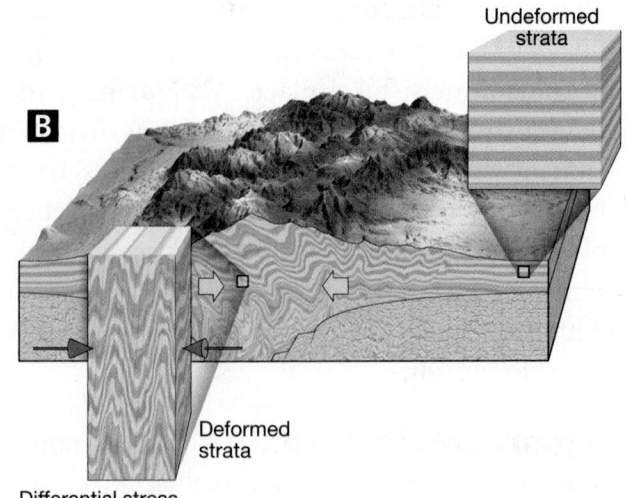

B

Undeformed strata

Increasing confining pressure

Confining pressure

Deformed strata

Differential stress

Figure 16 Pressure (Stress) As a Metamorphic Agent
A Forces in all directions are applied equally to buried rocks.
B During mountain building, rocks subjected to differential stress are shortened in the direction that pressure is applied.

Figure 17 Imagine the tremendous amounts of pressure that caused these rocks to fold.

Pressure (Stress) Pressure, like temperature, also increases with depth. Like the water pressure you might have experienced at the bottom of a swimming pool, pressure on rocks within Earth is applied in all directions. See Figure 16. Pressure on rocks causes the spaces between mineral grains to close. The result is a more compact rock with a greater density. This pressure also may cause minerals to recrystallize into new minerals.

Increases in temperature and pressure cause rocks to flow rather than fracture. Under these conditions, mineral grains tend to flatten and elongate.

≡Quick Lab

Observing Some of the Effects of Pressure on Mineral Grains

Materials

soft modeling clay; 2 pieces of waxed paper (each 20 cm × 20 cm); 20–30 small, round, elongated plastic beads; small plastic knife

Procedure

1. Use the clay to form a ball about the size of a golf ball. Randomly place all of the beads into this model rock.

2. Make a sketch of the rock. Label the sketch *Before*.

3. Sandwich the model rock between the two pieces of waxed paper. Use your weight to apply pressure to the model rock.

4. Remove the waxed paper and observe your "metamorphosed" rock.

5. Draw a top view of your rock and label it *After*. Include arrows to show the directions from which you applied pressure.

6. Make a cut through your model rock. Sketch this view of the rock.

Analyze and Conclude

1. **Comparing and Contrasting** How did the *Before* sketch of your model rock compare with the *After* sketch?

2. **Drawing Conclusions** How does pressure affect the mineral grains in a rock?

3. **Inferring** Was pressure the only agent of change that affected your rock? Explain.

During mountain building, horizontal forces caused by the collision of tectonic plates metamorphose large parts of the crust. This often produces intricately folded rocks like those in Figure 17.

Reactions in Solution Water solutions containing other substances that readily change to gases at the surface play an important role in some types of metamorphism. Solutions that surround mineral grains aid in recrystallization by making it easier for ions to move. When solutions increase in temperature reactions among substances can occur at a faster rate. When these hot, water-based solutions escape from a mass of magma, they are called **hydrothermal solutions.** These hot fluids also promote recrystallization by dissolving original minerals and then depositing new ones. As a result of contact with hydrothermal solutions, a change in a rock's overall composition may occur.

Classification of Metamorphic Rocks

Like igneous rocks, metamorphic rocks can be classified by texture and composition. ◉ **The texture of metamorphic rocks can be foliated or nonfoliated.**

Foliated Metamorphic Rocks When rocks undergo contact metamorphism, they become more compact and thus more dense. A common example is the metamorphic rock slate. Slate forms when shale is subjected to temperatures and pressures only slightly greater than those at which the shale formed. The pressure on the shale causes the microscopic clay minerals to become more compact. The increase in pressure also causes the clay minerals to align in a similar direction.

Under more extreme conditions, certain minerals will recrystallize. Some minerals recrystallize with a preferred orientation, which is at right angles to the direction of the force. The resulting alignment usually gives the rock a layered or banded appearance. This rock is called a **foliated metamorphic rock.** Gneiss, the metamorphic rock shown in Figure 18, is a foliated rock. Another foliated metamorphic rock is schist.

Nonfoliated Metamorphic Rocks A metamorphic rock that does not have a banded texture is called a **nonfoliated metamorphic rock.** Most nonfoliated rocks contain only one mineral. Marble, for example, is a nonfoliated rock made of calcite. When its parent rock, limestone, is metamorphosed, the calcite crystals combine to form the larger interlocking crystals seen in marble. A sample of marble is shown in Figure 19. Quartzite and anthracite are other nonfoliated metamorphic rocks.

 **Reading Checkpoint** *Contrast foliated and nonfoliated metamorphic rocks.*

Figure 18 Gneiss is a foliated metamorphic rock.
Inferring *In which directions was pressure exerted on this rock?*

Go Online
NSTA SciLINKS

For: Links on metamorphic rocks
Visit: www.SciLinks.org
Web Code: cjn-1033

Figure 19 Marble is a nonfoliated metamorphic rock.

To summarize, metamorphic rocks form when existing rocks are changed by heat, pressure, or hydrothermal solution. Contact metamorphism is often caused when hot magma intrudes a body of rock. Changes during this type of metamorphism are minor. Regional metamorphism is associated with mountain building. Such metamorphic changes can be extreme. Metamorphic rocks can be classified by texture as foliated or nonfoliated, as shown in Table 3.

Table 3 Classification of Major Metamorphic Rocks

Rock Name			Texture		Grain Size	Comments	Parent Rock
Slate	Increasing	Metamorphism	Foliated		Very fine	Smooth dull surfaces	Shale, mudstone, or siltstone
Phyllite					Fine	Breaks along wavy surfaces, glossy sheen	Slate
Schist					Medium to Coarse	Micaceous minerals dominate	Phyllite
Gneiss					Medium to Coarse	Banding of minerals	Schist, granite, or volcanic rocks
Marble			Nonfoliated		Medium to coarse	Interlocking calcite or dolomite grains	Limestone, dolostone
Quartzite					Medium to coarse	Fused quartz grains, massive, very hard	Quartz sandstone
Anthracite					Fine	Shiny black organic rock that fractures	Bituminous coal

Section 3.4 Assessment

Reviewing Concepts

1. Where does most metamorphism take place?
2. Compare and contrast contact metamorphism and regional metamorphism.
3. Name the agents of metamorphism and explain how each changes a rock.
4. What are foliated rocks, and how do they form?
5. How are metamorphic rocks classified?

Critical Thinking

6. **Applying Concepts** What is the major difference between igneous and metamorphic rocks?

7. **Predicting** What type of metamorphism—contact or regional—would result in a schist? Explain your choice.
8. **Formulating Conclusions** Why can the composition of gneiss vary but overall texture cannot?

Writing in Science

Explanatory Paragraph Write a short paragraph that explains the major differences and similarities among the three major rock groups.

The Carbon Cycle

Carbon moves among Earth's major spheres by way of the carbon cycle. The carbon cycle is one of Earth's biogeochemical cycles. A biogeochemical cycle is a cycle in which matter and energy move through the Earth system in a series of steps. These steps in the carbon cycle have different flow characteristics: Some steps involve chemical changes, as when wood is burned, releasing carbon dioxide gas (CO_2). Other steps involve the movement of materials containing carbon. For example, during a volcanic eruption, carbon dioxide gas is released into the atmosphere. Some steps involve the life processes of living things.

At each step in the cycle, carbon is stored for varying lengths of time in different reservoirs, or parts of the Earth system. These reservoirs include the atmosphere, oceans, biomass, fossil fuels, and carbonate rocks. For example, carbon may be part of an organism's biomass for the short span of the organism's lifetime. But the carbon that makes up coal may remain in Earth for millions of years.

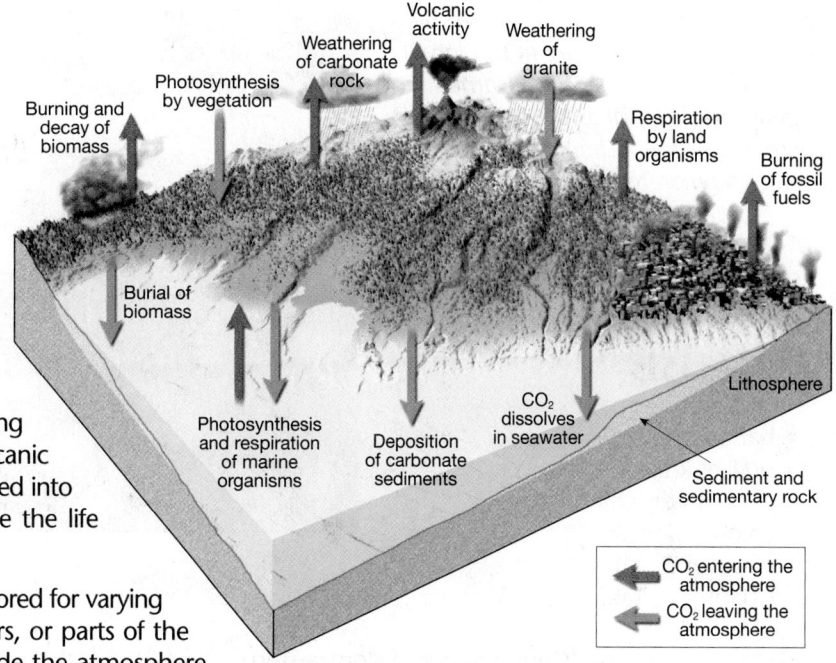

Figure 20 The Carbon Cycle

Carbon Dioxide on the Move

In the atmosphere, carbon is found mainly as carbon dioxide. The source of most CO_2 in the atmosphere is thought to be from volcanic activity early in Earth's history. Carbon dioxide moves into and out of the atmosphere by way of photosynthesis, respiration, organic decay, and combustion of organic material.

In photosynthesis, carbon dioxide gas is taken up by plants. Carbon thus becomes part of the compounds, called hydrocarbons, that make up living things. As a result, the biomass of all living organisms on Earth forms a major reservoir of carbon. Respiration, organic decay, and combustion release carbon from this reservoir back into the atmosphere as carbon dioxide.

Carbon and Fossil Fuels

The remains of once living things form another major reservoir of carbon. Some carbon from decayed organic matter is deposited as sediment. Over long periods of time, this carbon becomes buried. Under the right conditions, some of these carbon-rich deposits are changed to fossil fuels, such as coal. When fossil fuels are burned, carbon dioxide is released.

The Role of Marine Animals

Chemical weathering of certain rocks produce bicarbonate ions that dissolve in water. Rivers and streams carry these ions to the ocean. Here, some organisms extract this substance to produce shells and skeletons made of calcite ($CaCO_3$). When the organisms die, these hard parts settle to the ocean floor and become the sedimentary rock called limestone. If this rock is then exposed at the surface and subjected to chemical weathering, CO_2 is also produced. Use Figure 20 to follow the carbon cycle.

Rock Identification

Most rocks can be easily identified by texture and composition. In this lab, you will use what you have learned about rocks as well as the information on minerals from Chapter 2 to identify some common rocks.

Problem How can you use composition and texture to identify common rocks?

Materials
- rock samples
- hand lens
- pocket knife
- dilute hydrochloric acid
- colored pencils
- Chapter 2, Table 4 and Chapter 3, Tables 1, 2, 3

Skills Observing, Comparing and Contrasting, Measuring

Procedure

1. On a separate sheet of paper, make a copy of the data table shown below. Add any other columns that you think might be useful.

2. Examine each rock specimen with and without the hand lens. Determine and record the overall color of each rock.

3. Try to identify all of the minerals in each rock, using the information in Chapter 2 Table 4. Record your observations.

	Data Table					
Rock	Overall Color	Composition	Texture	Sketch	Rock Type	Rock Name
1.						
2.						
3.						
4.						
5.						

4. Determine and record the presence of any organic matter in any of the samples.

5. Observe the relationships among the minerals in each rock to determine texture. Refer to Chapter 3 Tables 1, 2, and 3 if necessary. Record your observations.

6. Note and record any other unique observations of the samples.

7. In your data table, make and color a detailed sketch of each sample.

8. Identify each sample as being an igneous rock, a sedimentary rock, or a metamorphic rock.

9. Name each sample. Use the photographs in this chapter and Tables 1, 2, and 3 if necessary.

3. **Applying Concepts** Match the metamorphic rocks with their probable parent rocks.

4. **Applying Concepts** Choose two pairs of rocks used in this investigation. Write a brief description for each pair that explains how one rock can be changed into the other. Refer to the diagram of the rock cycle on page 67.

Go Further Obtain permission to collect some local rock samples from a park or nearby road. Use what you have learned about rocks and minerals to identify the rocks. Then write a brief history of each sample to explain how it formed and how it has changed since being formed.

Analyze and Conclude

1. **Evaluating** Which of the rock identification characteristics did you find most useful? Which of the characteristics did you find least useful? Give reasons for your answers.

2. **Comparing and Contrasting** How did identifying rocks compare with the mineral identification lab you did in Chapter 2? How is identifying rocks different from identifying the minerals that compose the rocks?

Study Guide

3.1 The Rock Cycle

Key Concepts

- A rock is any solid mass of mineral or mineral-like matter that occurs naturally.
- The three major types of rocks are igneous, sedimentary, and metamorphic.
- Interactions among Earth's water, air, and land can cause rocks to change from one type to another. The continuous processes that cause rocks to change make up the rock cycle.
- When magma cools and hardens beneath the surface or as the result of a volcanic eruption, igneous rock forms.
- Eventually sediments are compacted and cemented to form sedimentary rocks.
- Under extreme pressure and temperature conditions, sedimentary rock will change into metamorphic rock.
- Heat from Earth's interior and energy from the sun power the rock cycle.

Vocabulary

rock, *p. 66;* igneous rock, *p. 66;* sedimentary rock, *p. 66;* metamorphic rock, *p. 66;* rock cycle, *p. 67;* magma, *p. 67;* lava, *p. 67;* weathering, *p. 68;* sediments, *p. 68*

3.2 Igneous Rocks

Key Concepts

- Rocks that form when magma hardens beneath Earth's surface are called intrusive igneous rocks.
- When lava hardens, the rocks that form are called extrusive igneous rocks.
- Texture and composition are two characteristics used to classify igneous rocks.
- Slow cooling results in the formation of large crystals.
- Rapid cooling of magma or lava results in rocks with small, interconnected mineral grains.

Vocabulary

intrusive igneous rock, *p. 71;* extrusive igneous rock, *p. 71;* porphyritic texture, *p. 72;* granitic composition, *p. 73;* basaltic composition, *p. 73;* andesitic composition, *p. 73;* ultramafic, *p. 73*

3.3 Sedimentary Rocks

Key Concepts

- Erosion involves weathering and the removal of rock. When an agent of erosion—water, wind, ice, or gravity—loses energy, it drops the sediments. This process is called deposition.
- Compaction is a process that squeezes, or compacts, sediments.
- Cementation takes place when dissolved minerals are deposited in the tiny spaces among the sediments.
- Just like igneous rocks, sedimentary rocks can be classified into two main groups according to the way they form.
- The many unique features of sedimentary rocks are clues to how, when, and where the rocks formed.

Vocabulary

erosion, *p. 76;* deposition, *p. 76;* compaction, *p. 76;* cementation, *p. 76;* clastic sedimentary rock, *p. 77;* chemical sedimentary rock, *p. 77*

3.4 Metamorphic Rocks

Key Concepts

- Most metamorphic changes occur at elevated temperatures and pressures. These conditions are found a few kilometers below Earth's surface and extend into the upper mantle.
- During contact metamorphism, hot magma moves into rock.
- Regional metamorphism results in large-scale deformation and high-grade metamorphism.
- The agents of metamorphism are heat, pressure, and hydrothermal solutions.
- Metamorphic rocks can be classified by texture as foliated or nonfoliated.

Vocabulary

metamorphism, *p. 80;* contact metamorphism, *p. 81;* regional metamorphism, *p. 81;* hydrothermal solution, *p. 83;* foliated metamorphic rock, *p. 83;* nonfoliated metamorphic rock, *p. 83*

Assessment

Reviewing Content

Choose the letter that best answers the question or completes the statement.

1. Which of the following is NOT one of the three major types of rocks?
   a. anthracite   b. igneous
   c. metamorphic   d. sedimentary

2. Which of the following forms as the direct result of surface processes?
   a. metamorphic slate
   b. igneous basalt
   c. magma
   d. intrusive granite

3. Which of the following would NOT be a major process in the formation of sedimentary rocks?
   a. erosion   b. melting
   c. deposition   d. compaction

4. The formation of igneous rocks is powered by
   a. the sun.   b. the rock cycle.
   c. erosion.   d. Earth's internal heat.

5. A fine-grained igneous rock forms
   a. deep within Earth.
   b. from magma.
   c. as the result of slow cooling.
   d. as the result of quick cooling.

6. Cementation often occurs directly after Earth materials are
   a. eroded.   b. weathered.
   c. intruded.   d. deposited.

7. Ripple marks likely indicate that the rock formed
   a. underground.   b. under a glacier.
   c. in water.   d. from magma.

8. A major process in the formation of clastic sedimentary rocks is
   a. contact with magma.
   b. cementation.
   c. hardening.
   d. foliation.

9. Metamorphic rocks that have a banded appearance due to the alignment of minerals are called
   a. foliated.   b. nonfoliated.
   c. clastic.   d. glassy.

10. Which rock is made of the smallest sediments?
    a. shale   b. conglomerate
    c. breccia   d. sandstone

Understanding Concepts

11. Use what you have learned about the rock cycle to explain the following statement: One rock is the raw material for another rock.

12. Which igneous rock forms when basaltic lava hardens? When basaltic magma hardens?

13. A rock has a porphyritic texture. What can you conclude about the rock?

14. How are granite and rhyolite the same, and how do they differ?

15. Explain the two main types of weathering.

16. What are the most common minerals in clastic rocks? Why?

17. Distinguish between regional and contact metamorphism.

18. How could you easily distinguish a black and white gneiss from a similar-colored granite?

Use the following diagram to answer Questions 19–22.

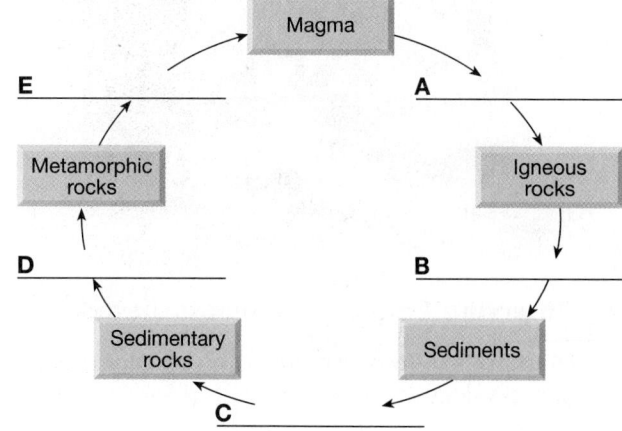

19. What process occurs at point A?

20. What three processes can occur at point B?

21. Name two processes that occur at point C.

22. What two processes occur at points D and E?

Assessment *continued*

Critical Thinking

23. Synthesizing Is it possible for two different types of igneous rocks to have the same composition and the same texture? Explain.

24. Comparing and Contrasting Compare and contrast the two types of sedimentary rocks and give at least two examples of each type.

25. Formulating Hypotheses Think about the sediments that compose both conglomerate and breccia. What one sedimentary process makes these two rocks different? Explain.

26. Comparing and Contrasting Compare and contrast the effects of heat and pressure in the formation of metamorphic rocks.

27. Explaining Explain all of the processes that might change a sandstone into a quartzite.

28. Synthesizing In what ways do metamorphic rocks differ from the sedimentary and igneous rocks from which they form?

Use the photograph to answer Questions 29–33.

29. Observing Describe the texture of the rock.

30. Identifying To which of the three major groups of rocks does the rock belong?

31. Classifying Classify the rock as specifically as possible.

32. Formulating Hypotheses Briefly describe how this rock formed.

33. Applying Concepts Explain how this rock might become an igneous rock.

Concepts in Action

34. Applying Concepts Your friend shows you a rock with distinct layers. How can you and your friend determine if the rock is a sedimentary rock or a metamorphic rock?

35. Applying Concepts Name two rocks discussed in this chapter that might be used as flooring, countertops, or facades on museums and government buildings. Name two rocks that might be used for monuments and statues.

36. Calculating Each year, roughly 9100 kilograms of rock, sand, and gravel are mined for each person in the United States. Calculate how many kilograms of rock, sand, and gravel have been mined for you thus far in your life. Then calculate how much will be mined when you are 75 years old.

37. Writing in Science Suppose you're a writer for the school newspaper. You have been asked to do a story on one of the rocks described in this chapter. Pick a rock and write a short, newspaper-type story. Include facts about the rock—its texture, mineral composition, and how it formed. Also describe how the rock might change into a rock in each of the other two categories of rocks. Be creative, but scientifically accurate.

Performance-Based Assessment

Applying Concepts Go on field trip around your house, neighborhood, and community to find at least 10 items that are made from rocks or show ways in which rocks are used. Make a poster that shows what you found and display it for the class.

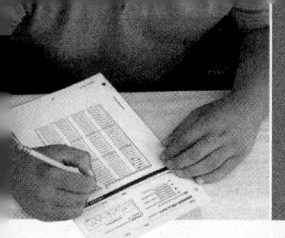

Standardized Test Prep

Test-Taking Tip

Using Visuals

Sometimes an answer to a test question requires that you interpret a drawing, a table, or a photograph. When this occurs, carefully study the visual before you read the questions pertaining to it. Refer to the visual again as you read each of the questions to which it pertains.

Use the photographs to answer Questions 1–9.

Choose the letter that best answers the question or completes the statement.

1. Which of the rocks has a fine-grained texture?
(A) A
(B) B
(C) C
(D) D

2. Which rock cooled the fastest?
(A) A
(B) B
(C) C
(D) D

3. Which of the rocks formed deep beneath the surface?
(A) only A
(B) only B
(C) both A and D
(D) both B and C

4. Which of the following best describes the texture of the rock labeled D?
(A) porphyritic
(B) glassy
(C) fine-grained
(D) coarse-grained

Write one or two complete sentences to answer each of the following questions.

5. What kinds of conditions produced the rock labeled A?

6. How and where did the rock labeled B form?

7. Compare and contrast the rocks labeled A and D.

8. How is the rock labeled C different from the other rocks shown?

9. Describe the conditions that led to the formation of the rock labeled D.

10. Use what you have learned about rocks to describe the color and texture of the rock below. What type of rock is this? How did it form?

4 Earth's Resources

Once a mountain, the Bingham Canyon copper mine in Utah is now the world's largest open-pit mine.

21st Century Learning

Problem Identification, Formulation, and Solution

Which energy source is best?

Energy resources warm your home, fuel the family car, and run your computer. Identify the different sources of energy used in the United States, and find out the percentage of total energy used by each source. Determine why some sources are used more than others and whether this could create an energy shortage in the future. Propose some possible solutions to this problem, and create a class presentation summarizing your findings.

Application Lab

Finding the Product that Best Conserves Resources

Chapter Preview

Inquiry Activity

How Can You Determine the Resources You Use?

Procedure

1. List three objects that you are using now or objects that are around you.

2. Observe the objects. Try to determine which resources they might contain. List possible resources for each object.

3. Your teacher will list several objects chosen by students on the board, along with the resources students believe they contain. Use these objects to answer the following questions.

Think About It

1. **Observing and Analyzing** How did you determine the resources that might be in each object?

2. **Designing Experiments** How could you actually test each object to determine what resources it contains?

4.1 Energy and Mineral Resources

Reading Focus

Key Concepts

- What is the difference between renewable and nonrenewable resources?
- Which energy resources are fossil fuels?
- Which energy resources might replace dwindling petroleum supplies in the future?
- What processes concentrate minerals into deposits sufficiently large enough to mine?
- How are nonmetallic mineral resources used?

Vocabulary

- renewable resource
- nonrenewable resource
- fossil fuel
- ore

Reading Strategy

Monitoring Your Understanding Copy this table onto a separate piece of paper before you read this section. List what you know about energy and mineral resources in the first column and what you'd like to know in the second column. After you read, list what you have learned in the last column.

Energy and Mineral Resources		
What I Know	What I Would Like to Know	What I Learned
a. _____?_____	c. _____?_____	e. _____?_____
b. _____?_____	d. _____?_____	f. _____?_____

Figure 1 Mineral resources went into the construction of every building in this New York skyline. Energy resources keep the lights on, too.

Mineral and energy resources are the raw materials for most of the things we use. Mineral resources are used to produce everything from cars to computers to basketballs. Energy resources warm your home, fuel the family car, and light the skyline in Figure 1.

Renewable and Nonrenewable Resources

There are two categories of resources—renewable and nonrenewable. **A renewable resource can be replenished over fairly short time spans such as months, years, or decades.** Common examples are plants and animals for food, natural fibers for clothing, and trees for lumber and paper. Energy from flowing water, wind, and the sun are also renewable resources.

By contrast, a nonrenewable resource takes millions of years to form and accumulate. When the present supply of nonrenewable resources run out, there won't be any more. Fuels such as coal, oil, and natural gas are nonrenewable. So are important metals such as iron, copper, uranium, and gold.

Earth's population is growing fast which increases the demand for resources. Because of a rising standard of living, the rate of mineral and energy resource use has climbed faster than population growth. For example, 6 percent of the world's population lives in the United States, yet we use 30 percent of the world's annual production

Average Heat Value

- Anthracite 12,700 Btu/lb
- Bituminous coal 13,100 Btu/lb
- Subbituminous coal 9500 Btu/lb
- Lignite 6700 Btu/lb

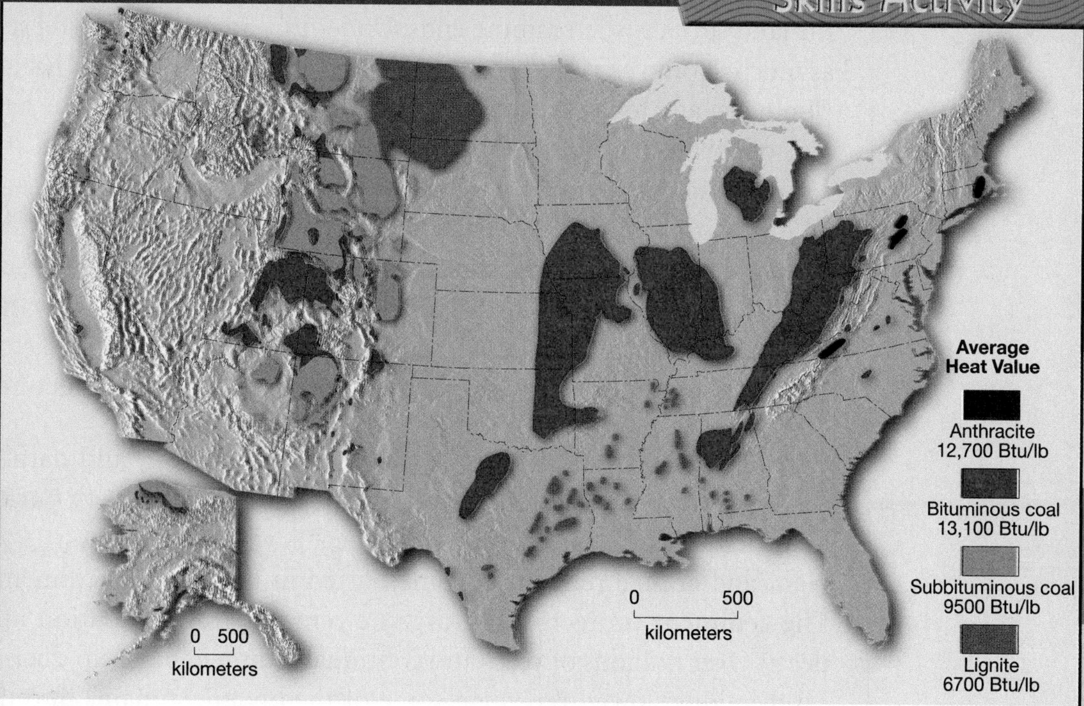

Figure 2

Location This map shows the location of major coal deposits in the United States. **Identify** Which type of coal is most plentiful? **Locate** Where are the anthracite deposits in the U.S. located?

of mineral and energy resources. How long can existing resources provide for the needs of a growing population?

Fossil Fuels

Nearly 90 percent of the energy used in the United States comes from fossil fuels. A **fossil fuel** is any hydrocarbon that may be used as a source of energy. ⟣ **Fossil fuels include coal, oil, and natural gas.**

Coal Coal forms when heat and pressure transform plant material over millions of years. Coal passes through four stages of development. The first stage, peat, is partially decayed plant material that sometimes look like soil. Peat then becomes lignite, which is a sedimentary rock that is often called brown coal. Continued heat and pressure transforms lignite into bituminous coal, or soft coal. Bituminous coal is another sedimentary rock. Coal's last stage of development is a metamorphic rock called anthracite or hard coal. As coal develops from peat to bituminous, it becomes harder and releases more heat when burned.

Power plants primarily use coal to generate electricity. In fact, electric power plants use more than 70 percent of the coal mined today. The world has enormous coal reserves. Figure 2 shows coal fields in the United States.

Go Online

NSTA *SciLINKS*

For: Links on fossil fuels
Visit: www.SciLinks.org
Web Code: cjn-1041

Although coal is plentiful, its recovery and use present problems. Surface mining scars the land. Today, all U.S. surface mines must restore the land surface when mining ends. Underground mining doesn't scar as much. However, it has been costly in terms of human life and health. Mining is safer today because of federal safety regulations. Yet, the hazards of collapsing roofs and gas explosions remain.

Burning coal—much of which is high in sulfur—also creates air pollution problems. When coal burns, the sulfur becomes sulfur oxides in the air. A series of chemical reactions turns the sulfur oxides into sulfuric acid, which falls to Earth as acid precipitation—rain or snow that is more acidic than normal. Acid precipitation can have harmful effects on forests and aquatic ecosystems, as well as metal and stone structures.

Petroleum and Natural Gas Petroleum (oil) and natural gas form from the remains of plants and animals that were buried in ancient seas. Petroleum formation begins when large quantities of plant and animal remains become buried in ocean-floor sediments. The sediment protects these organic remains from oxidation and decay. Over millions of years and continual sediment build up, chemical reactions slowly transform some of the organic remains into the liquid and gaseous hydrocarbons we call petroleum and natural gas.

These materials are gradually squeezed from the compacting, mud-rich sediment layers. The oil and gas then move into nearby permeable beds such as sandstone. The oil and gas are squeezed out of the sedimentary rock layers along with water. However, oil and natural gas are less dense than water, so they migrate upward through the water-filled spaces of the enclosing rocks. If nothing stops this migration, the fluids will eventually reach the surface.

Sometimes an oil trap—a geologic structure that allows large amounts of fluids to accumulate—stops upward movement of oil and gas. Several geologic structures may act as oil traps, but all have two things in common. First, an oil trap has a permeable reservoir rock that allows oil and gas to collect in large quantities. Second, an oil trap has a cap rock that is nearly impenetrable and so keeps the oil and gas from escaping to the surface. One structure that acts as an oil trap is an anticline. An anticline is an uparched series of sedimentary rock layers, as shown in Figure 3.

When a drill punctures the cap rock, pressure is released, and the oil and gas move toward the drill hole. Then a pump lifts the petroleum out.

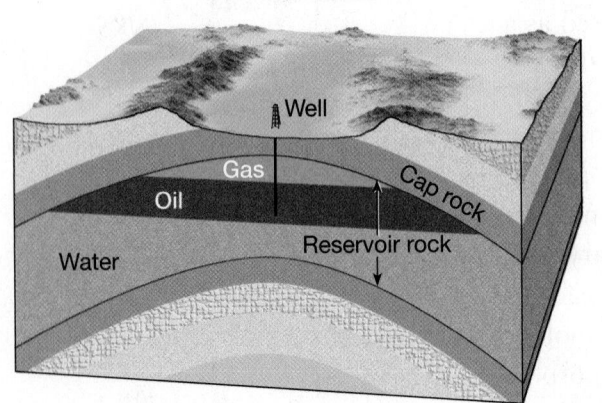

Figure 3 Anticlines are common oil traps. The reservoir rock contains water, oil, and gas. The fluids collect at the top of the arch with less dense oil and gas on top.
Interpreting Diagrams *Why is the water located beneath the oil and gas?*

 **Reading Checkpoint** *What two features must an oil trap have?*

Tar Sands and Oil Shale

In the years to come, world petroleum supplies will dwindle. 🗨 **Some energy experts believe that fuels derived from tar sands and oil shales could become good substitutes for dwindling petroleum supplies.**

Tar Sands Tar sands are usually mixtures of clay and sand combined with water and varying amounts of a black, thick tar called bitumen. Deposits occur in sands and sandstones, as the name suggests, but also in shales and limestones. The oil in these deposits is similar to heavy crude oils pumped from wells. The oil in tar sands, however, is much more resistant to flow and cannot be pumped out easily. The Canadian province of Alberta (Figure 4) has the largest tar sand deposits, which accounts for about 15 percent of Canada's oil production.

Currently, tar sands are mined at the surface, much like the strip mining of coal. The excavated material is then heated with pressurized steam until the bitumen softens and rises. The material is processed to remove impurities, add hydrogen, and refine into oil. However, extracting and refining tar sand requires a lot of energy—nearly half as much as the end product yields.

Obtaining oil from tar sand has significant environmental drawbacks. Mining tar sand causes substantial land disturbance. Processing also requires large amounts of water. When processing is completed, contaminated water and sediment accumulate in toxic disposal ponds.

Only about 10 percent of Alberta's tar sands can be economically recovered by surface mining. In the future, other methods may be used to obtain the more deeply buried material, reduce the environmental impacts, and make mining tar sands more economical.

 **Reading Checkpoint** *What are some environmental drawbacks to mining tar sands?*

Figure 4 Tar Sand Deposits In North America, the largest tar sand deposits occur in the Canadian province of Alberta. They contain an estimated reserve of 35 billion barrels of oil.

Oil Shale Oil shale is a rock that contains a waxy mixture of hydrocarbons called kerogen. Oil shale can be mined and heated to vaporize the kerogen. The kerogen vapor is processed to remove impurities, and then refined.

Roughly half of the world's oil shale supply is in the Green River Formation of Colorado, Utah, and Wyoming. See Figure 5 on page 98. The oil shales are part of sedimentary layers that accumulated at the bottom of two extremely large, shallow lakes 57 to 36 million years ago.

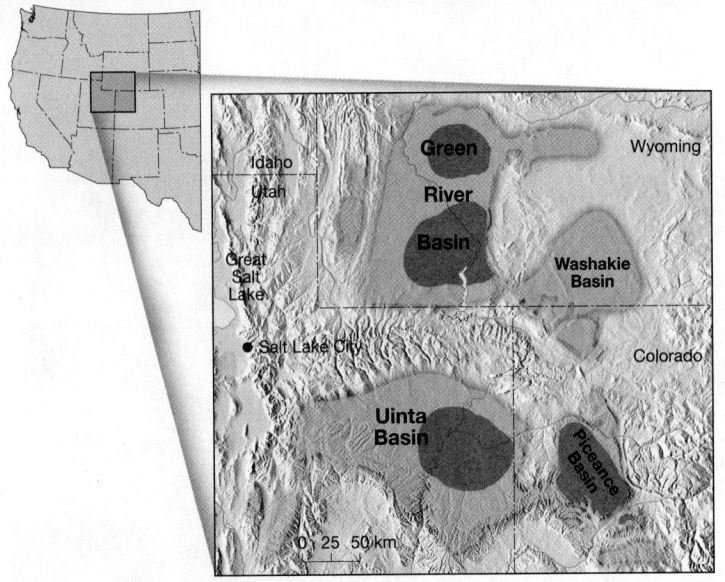

Figure 5 Distribution of Oil Shale in the Green River Formation The areas in red are the richest deposits.
Posing Questions *How might the mining and processing of oil shale become more economically attractive?*

Some people see oil shale as a partial solution to dwindling fuel supplies. However, the heat energy in oil shale is only about one-eighth that in crude oil because oil shale contains large amounts of minerals. This mineral material adds costs to the mining, processing, and waste disposal of oil shale. The processing of it requires large amounts of water, which is scarce in the semi-arid region where the shales are found. Current technology makes mining oil shale an unprofitable solution.

Formation of Mineral Deposits

Practically every manufactured product contains substances that come from minerals. Mineral resources are deposits of useful minerals that can be extracted. Mineral reserves are deposits from which minerals can be extracted profitably. **Ore** is a useful metallic mineral that can be mined at a profit.

There are also known deposits that are not yet economically or technologically recoverable. These deposits, as well as deposits that are believed to exist, are also considered mineral resources.

The natural concentration of many minerals is rather small. A deposit containing a valuable mineral is worthless if the cost of extracting it exceeds the value of the material that is recovered. For example, copper makes up about 0.0135 percent of Earth's crust. However, for a material to be considered a copper ore, it must contain a concentration of about 50 times this amount.

Geologists have established that the occurrences of valuable mineral resources are closely related to Earth's rock cycle. The rock cycle includes the formation of igneous, sedimentary, and metamorphic rock as well as the processes of weathering and erosion. **Some of the most important mineral deposits form through igneous processes and from hydrothermal solutions.**

Mineral Resources and Igneous Processes

Igneous processes produce important deposits of metallic minerals, such as gold, silver, copper, mercury, lead, platinum, and nickel. For example, as a large body of magma cools, heavy minerals crystallize early and settle to the bottom of the magma chamber. Chromite (chromium ore), magnetite, and platinum sometimes form this way. Such deposits produced layers of chromite at Montana's Stillwater Complex. Another deposit is found in the Bushveld Complex in South Africa. This deposit contains over 70 percent of the world's known platinum reserves.

Hydrothermal Solutions Hydrothermal (hot-water) solutions generate some of the best-known and most important ore deposits. Examples of hydrothermal deposits include the gold deposits of the Homestake Mine in South Dakota; the lead, zinc, and silver ores near Coeur D'Alene, Idaho; the silver deposits of the Comstock Lode in Nevada; and the copper ores of Michigan's Keweenaw Peninsula.

Most hydrothermal deposits form from hot, metal-rich fluids that are left during the late stages of the movement and cooling of magma. Figure 6 shows how these deposits form. As the magma cools and becomes solid, liquids and various metal ions collect near the top of the magma chamber. These ion-rich solutions can move great distances through the surrounding rock. Some of this fluid moves through fractures in rock or between rock layers. The fluid cools in these openings and the metallic ions separate out of the solution to produce vein deposits, like those shown in Figure 7. Many of the most productive gold, silver, and mercury deposits occur as hydrothermal vein deposits.

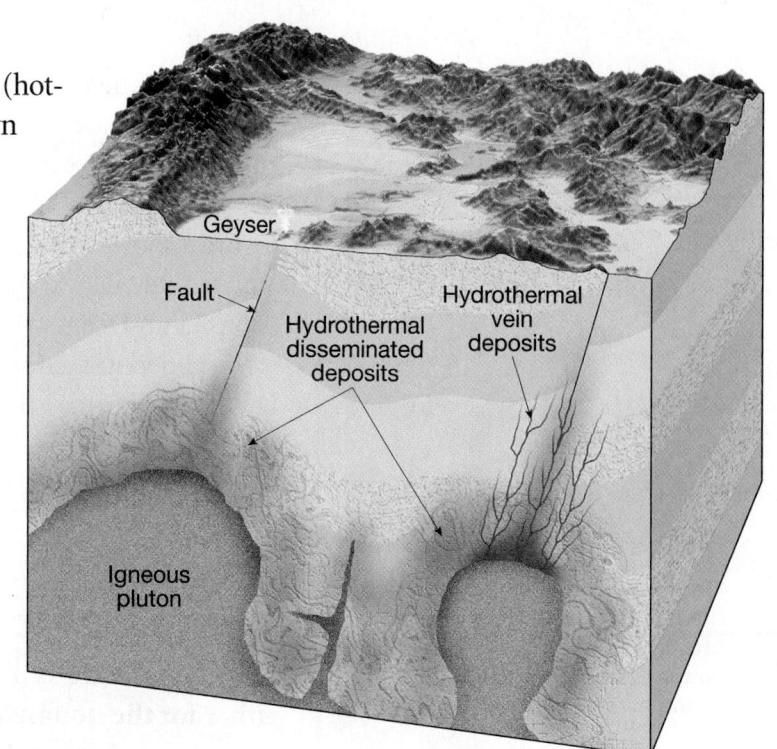

Figure 6 Mineral-rich hot water seeps into rock fractures, cools, and leaves behind vein deposits.

Placer Deposits Placer deposits are formed when eroded heavy minerals settle quickly from moving water while less dense particles remain suspended and continue to move. This settling is a means of sorting in which like-size grains are deposited together due to the density of the particles. Placer deposits usually involve minerals that are not only heavy but also durable and chemically resistant. Common sites of accumulation include point bars on the inside of bends in streams, as well as cracks, depressions, and other streambed irregularities.

Figure 7 Light veins of quartz lace a body of darker gneiss in Washington's North Cascades National Park.

Figure 8 Placer deposits led to the California gold rush. Here, a prospector in 1850 swirls his gold pan, separating sand and mud from flecks of gold.

Q *How big was the largest gold nugget ever discovered?*

A The largest gold nugget ever discovered was the Welcome Stranger Nugget found in 1869 as a placer deposit in the gold-mining region of Victoria, Australia. It weighed a massive 2520 troy ounces (210 pounds, or 95 kilograms) and, at today's gold prices, was worth over $700,000. The largest gold nugget known to remain in existence today is the Hand of Faith Nugget, which was found in 1975 near Wedderburn, Victoria, Australia. It was found with a metal detector and weighs 875 troy ounces (73 pounds, or 33 kilograms). Sold in 1982, it is now on display in the Golden Nugget Casino in Las Vegas, Nevada.

Gold is the best-known placer deposit. In 1848, placer deposits of gold were discovered in California, sparking the famous California gold rush. Early prospectors searched rivers by using a flat pan to wash away the sand and gravel and concentrate the gold "dust" at the bottom. Figure 8 shows this common method. Years later, similar deposits created a gold rush to Alaska. Sometimes prospectors follow the placer deposits upstream. This method may lead prospectors to the original mineral deposit. Miners found the gold-bearing veins of the Mother Lode in California's Sierra Nevadas by following placer deposits.

 **Reading Checkpoint** *What are mineral resources?*

Nonmetallic Mineral Resources

⊙**Nonmetallic mineral resources are extracted and processed either for the nonmetallic elements they contain or for their physical and chemical properties.** People often do not realize the importance of nonmetallic minerals because they see only the products that resulted from their use and not the minerals used to make the products.

Examples of nonmetallic minerals include the fluorite and limestone that are part of the steelmaking process and the fertilizers needed to grow food, as shown in Table 1.

Nonmetallic mineral resources are divided into two broad groups—building materials and industrial minerals. For example, natural aggregate (crushed stone, sand, and gravel), is an important material used in nearly all building construction.

Some substances, however, have many uses in both construction and industry. Limestone is a good example. As a building material, it is used as crushed rock and building stone. It is also an ingredient in cement. As an industrial mineral, limestone is an ingredient in the manufacture of steel. Farmers also use it to neutralize acidic soils.

Many nonmetallic resources are used for their specific chemical elements or compounds. These resources are important in the manufacture of chemicals and fertilizers. In other cases, their importance is related to their physical properties. Examples include abrasive minerals such as corundum and garnet.

Although industrial minerals are useful, they have drawbacks. Most industrial minerals are not nearly as abundant as building materials. Manufacturers must also transport nonmetallic minerals long distances, adding to their cost. Unlike most building materials, which need a minimum of processing before use, many industrial minerals require considerable processing to extract the desired substance at the proper degree of purity.

Table 1 Occurrences and Uses of Nonmetallic Minerals

Mineral	Uses	Geological Occurrences
Apatite	Phosphorus fertilizers	Sedimentary deposits
Asbestos (chrysotile)	Incombustible fibers	Metamorphic alteration
Calcite	Aggregate; steelmaking; soil conditioning; chemicals; cement; building stone	Sedimentary deposits
Clay minerals (kaolinite)	Ceramics; china	Residual product of weathering
Corundum	Gemstones; abrasives	Metamorphic deposits
Diamond	Gemstones; abrasives	Kimberlite pipes; placers
Fluorite	Steelmaking; aluminum refining; glass; chemicals	Hydrothermal deposits
Garnet	Abrasives; gemstones	Metamorphic deposits
Graphite	Pencil lead; lubricant; refractories	Metamorphic deposits
Gypsum	Plaster of Paris	Evaporite deposits
Halite	Table salt; chemicals; ice control	Evaporite deposits, salt domes
Muscovite	Insulator in electrical applications	Pegmatites
Quartz	Primary ingredient in glass	Igneous intrusions, sedimentary deposits
Sulfur	Chemicals; fertilizer manufacture	Sedimentary deposits, hydrothermal deposits
Sylvite	Potassium fertilizers	Evaporite deposits
Talc	Powder used in paints, cosmetics, etc.	Metamorphic deposits

Section 4.1 Assessment

Reviewing Concepts

1. What is the difference between a renewable and a nonrenewable resource?
2. What are the three major fossil fuels?
3. What are tar sands and oil shale?
4. How do hydrothermal deposits form?
5. What are the two broad categories of nonmetallic mineral resources?
6. Compare and contrast the formation of coal with that of petroleum and natural gas.

Critical Thinking

7. **Drawing Conclusions** Why isn't the use of tar sands more widespread in the United States?
8. **Applying Concepts** Explain how following placer deposits upstream would help prospectors find the original deposit.

Writing in Science

Compare-Contrast Paragraph Write a paragraph describing the difference in the use of nonmetallic building minerals and nonmetallic industrial minerals.

4.2 Alternate Energy Sources

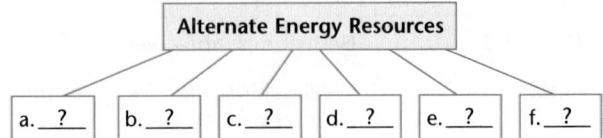

Reading Focus

Key Concepts

- What are the advantages of using solar energy?

- How do nuclear power plants use nuclear fission to produce energy?

- What is wind power's potential for providing energy in the future?

- How do hydroelectric power, geothermal energy, and tidal power contribute to our energy resources?

Vocabulary

- hydroelectric power
- geothermal energy

Reading Strategy

Previewing Skim the section and start a concept map for the various alternate energy resources.

```
        Alternate Energy Resources

a. __?__  b. __?__  c. __?__  d. __?__  e. __?__  f. __?__
```

Figure 9 Solar One is a solar installation used to generate electricity in the Mojave Desert near Barstow, California.

There's no doubt that we live in the age of fossil fuels. These nonrenewable resources supply nearly 90 percent of the world's energy. But that can't last forever. At the present rates of consumption, the amount of recoverable fossil fuels may last only another 170 years. As the world population soars, the rate of consumption will climb as well. This will leave fossil fuel reserves in even shorter supply. In the meantime, the burning of huge quantities of fossil fuels will continue to damage the environment. Our growing demand for energy along with our need for a healthy environment will likely lead to a greater reliance on alternate energy sources.

Solar Energy

Solar energy is by far Earth's most abundant energy resource. Every second, the total energy Earth receives from the sun amounts to more than 10,000 times the total amount of energy used by all human societies in a day. Solar energy also far exceeds the amount of Earth's internal energy, or geothermal energy, that is available at or near the surface. Solar energy technologies use the sun's rays to supply heat or electricity. **Solar energy has two advantages: the "fuel" is free, and it's nonpolluting.** The simplest and perhaps most widely used solar energy systems are passive solar collectors such as south-facing windows. As sunlight passes through the glass, objects in the room absorb its heat. These objects radiate the heat, which warms the air.

More elaborate systems for home heating use an active solar collector. These roof-mounted devices are usually large, blackened boxes covered with glass or plastic. The heat they collect can be transferred by circulating air or liquids through piping. Solar collectors are also used to heat water for domestic and commercial needs.

There are a few drawbacks to solar energy. While the energy collected is free, the necessary equipment and installation is not. A supplemental heating unit is also needed on cloudy days, in the winter, or at night when solar energy is unavailable. However, solar energy is economical in many parts of the United States. It will become even more cost effective as the prices of other fuels increase.

Research is currently underway to improve the technologies for collecting sunlight. Scientists are examining a way to use mirrors to track the sun and keep its rays focused on a receiving tower. Figure 9 shows a solar collection facility with 2000 mirrors. This facility heats water in pressurized panels to over 500°C by focusing solar energy on a central tower. The superheated water is then transferred to turbines, which turn electrical generators. Another type of collector, shown in Figure 10, uses photovoltaic (solar) cells. They convert the sun's energy directly into electricity.

Figure 10 Solar cells convert sunlight directly into electricity. This array of solar panels is near Sacramento, California. **Applying Concepts** *What characteristics would you look for if you were searching for a location for a new solar plant?*

 **Reading Checkpoint** *What are the two main advantages of using solar energy?*

Nuclear Energy

Nuclear power meets about 7 percent of the energy demand of the United States. The fuel for nuclear plants, like the one in Figure 11, comes from radioactive materials that release energy through nuclear fission. **In nuclear fission, the nuclei of heavy atoms such as uranium-235 are bombarded with neutrons. The uranium nuclei then split into smaller nuclei and emit neutrons and heat energy.** The neutrons that are emitted then bombard the nuclei of adjacent uranium atoms, producing a chain reaction. If there is enough fissionable material and if the reaction continues in an uncontrolled manner, fission releases an enormous amount of energy as an atomic explosion.

Figure 11 Diablo Canyon Nuclear Plant Near San Luis Obispo, California Reactors are in the dome-shaped buildings. You can see cooling water being released to the ocean. **Analyzing** *The siting of this plant was controversial because it is close to faults. Why would that be a cause for concern?*

In a nuclear power plant, however, the fission reaction is controlled by moving neutron-absorbing rods into or out of the nuclear reactor. The result is a controlled nuclear chain reaction that releases great amounts of heat. The energy drives steam turbines that turn electrical generators, as in most conventional power plants.

For: Links on Radioactivity
Visit: PHSchool.com
Web Code: cuc-1042

At one time, energy experts thought nuclear power would be the cheap, clean energy source that would replace fossil fuels. But several obstacles have slowed its development. First, the cost of building safe nuclear facilities has increased. Second, there are hazards associated with the disposal of nuclear wastes. Third, there is concern over the possibility of a serious accident that could allow radioactive materials to escape. The 1979 accident at Three Mile Island in Pennsylvania made this concern a reality. A malfunction in the equipment led the plant operators to think there was too much water in the primary system. Instead there was not enough water. This confusion allowed the reactor core to lie uncovered for hours. Although there was little danger to the public, the malfunction resulted in substantial damage to the reactor.

Unfortunately, the 1986 accident at Chernobyl in Ukraine was far more serious. In this case, the reactor went out of control. Two small explosions lifted the roof of the structure, and pieces of uranium spread over the surrounding area. A fire followed the explosion. During the 10 days that it took to put out the fire, the atmosphere carried high levels of radioactive material as far away as Norway. Eighteen people died within six weeks of the accident. Thousands more faced an increased risk of death from cancers associated with the fallout.

 **Reading Checkpoint**   *What is nuclear fission?*

Wind Energy

According to one estimate, if just the winds of North and South Dakota could be harnessed, they would provide 80 percent of the electrical energy used in the United States. Wind is not a new energy source. People have used it for centuries to power sailing ships and windmills for grinding grains.

Following the "energy crisis" brought about by the oil embargo of the 1970s, interest in wind power and other alternative forms of energy grew. In 1980, the federal government started a program to develop wind-power systems, such as the one shown in Figure 12. The U.S. Department of Energy set up experimental wind farms in mountain passes with strong, steady winds. One of these facilities, at Altamont Pass near San Francisco, now operates more than 7000 wind turbines. In the year 2000, wind supplied a little less than one percent of California's electricity.

👄 **Some experts estimate that in the next 50 to 60 years, wind power could meet between 5 to 10 percent of the country's demand for electricity.** Islands and other isolated regions that must import fuel for generating power are major candidates for wind energy expansion.

The future for wind power looks promising, but there are difficulties. The need for technical advances, noise pollution, and the cost of large tracts of land in populated areas are obstacles to development.

For: Links on wind
Visit: www.SciLinks.org
Web Code: cjn-1042

Figure 12 These wind turbines are operating near Palm Springs, California.

Figure 13 Glen Canyon Dam and Lake Powell on the Colorado River As dam operators release water in the reservoir, it passes through machinery that drives turbines and produces electricity.

Hydroelectric Power

Like wind, moving water has been an energy source for centuries. The mechanical energy that waterwheels produce has powered mills and other machinery. Today, the power that falling water generates, known as **hydroelectric power,** drives turbines that produce electricity. In the United States, hydroelectric power plants produce about 5 percent of the country's electricity. Large dams, like the one in Figure 13, are responsible for most of it. The dams allow for a controlled flow of water. ⬤ **The water held in a reservoir behind a dam is a form of stored energy that can be released through the dam to produce electric power.**

Although water power is a renewable resource, hydroelectric dams have finite lifetimes. Rivers deposit sediment behind the dam. Eventually, the sediment fills the reservoir. When this happens, the dam can no longer produce power. This process takes 50 to 300 years, depending on the amount of material the river carries. An example is Egypt's Aswan High Dam on the Nile River, which was completed in the 1960s. It is estimated that half the reservoir will be filled with sediment by 2025.

The availability of suitable sites is an important limiting factor in the development of hydroelectric power plants. A good site must provide a significant height for the water to fall. It also must have a high rate of flow. There are hydroelectric dams in many parts of the United States, with the greatest concentration in the Southeast and the Pacific Northwest. Most of the best U.S. sites have already been developed. This limits future expansion of hydroelectric power.

Geothermal Energy

Geothermal energy is harnessed by tapping natural underground reservoirs of steam and hot water. ⬤ **Hot water is used directly for heating and to turn turbines to generate electric power.** The reservoirs of steam and hot water occur where subsurface temperatures are high due to relatively recent volcanic activity.

Figure 14 The Geysers is the world's largest electricity-generating geothermal facility. Most of the steam wells are about 3,000 meters deep.

Q *Is power from ocean waves a practical alternative energy source?*

A It's being seriously explored now. In November 2000, the world's first commercial wave power station opened on the Scottish island of Islay. It provides power for the United Kingdom. The 500-kilowatt power station uses an oscillating water column, in which incoming waves push air up and down inside a concrete tube that is partly under the ocean's surface. Air rushing in and out of the top of the tube drives a turbine to produce electricity. If the facility succeeds, it could open the door for wave power to become a significant contributor of renewable energy in some coastal areas.

In the United States, areas in several western states use hot water from geothermal sources for heat. The first commercial geothermal power plant in the United States was built in 1960 at The Geysers, shown in Figure 14. The Geysers is an important source of electrical power for nearby San Francisco and Oakland. Although production in the plant has declined, it remains the world's premier geothermal field. It continues to provide electrical power with little environmental impact. Geothermal development is now also occurring in Nevada, Utah, and the Imperial Valley of California.

Geothermal power is clean but not inexhaustible. When hot fluids are pumped from volcanically heated reservoirs, the reservoir often cannot be recharged. The steam and hot water from individual wells usually lasts no more than 10 to 15 years. Engineers must drill more wells to maintain power production. Eventually, the field is depleted.

As with other alternative methods of power production, geothermal sources are not expected to provide a high percentage of the world's growing energy needs. Nevertheless, in regions where people can develop its potential, its use will no doubt grow.

 **Reading Checkpoint** *In what two ways is geothermal energy used?*

Tidal Power

Several methods of generating electrical energy from the oceans have been proposed, yet the ocean's energy potential still remains largely untapped. The development of tidal power is one example of energy production from the ocean.

Tides have been a power source for hundreds of years. Beginning in the 12th century, tides drove water wheels that powered gristmills and sawmills. During the seventeenth and eighteenth centuries, a tidal mill produced much of Boston's flour. But today's energy demands require more sophisticated ways of using the force created by the continual rise and fall of the ocean.

Tidal power is harnessed by constructing a dam across the mouth of a bay or an estuary in coastal areas with a large tidal range. The strong in-and-out flow that results drives turbines and electric generators. An example of this type of dam is shown in Figure 15.

The largest tidal power plant ever constructed is at the mouth of France's Rance River. This tidal plant went into operation in 1966. It produces enough power to satisfy the needs of Brittany—a region of 27,000 square kilometers—and parts of other regions. Much smaller experimental facilities have been built near Murmansk in Russia, near Taliang in China, and on an arm of the Bay of Fundy in Canada.

Tidal power development isn't economical if the tidal range is less than eight meters or if a narrow, enclosed bay isn't available. Although the tides will never provide a high portion of the world's ever-increasing energy needs, it is an important source at certain sites.

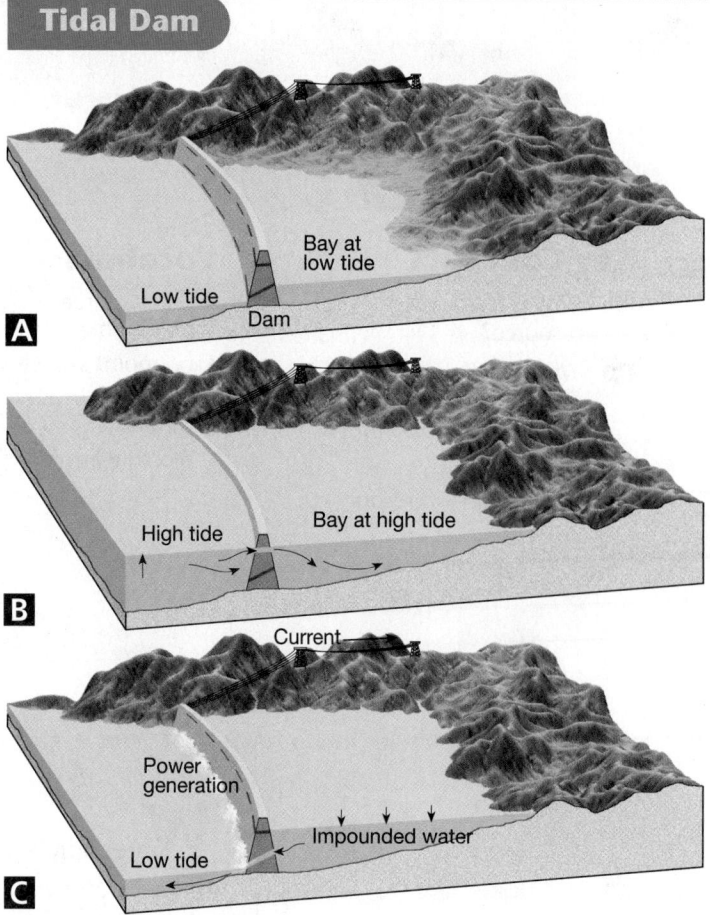

Tidal Dam

A

B

C

Figure 15 A At low tide, water is at its lowest level on either side of the dam. **B** At high tide, water flows through a high tunnel. **C** At low tide, water drives turbines as it flows back to sea through a low tunnel.
Analyzing Concepts *Why is a large tidal range (difference in water level between high and low tide) needed to produce power?*

Section 4.2 Assessment

Reviewing Concepts

1. What are the advantages and drawbacks of using solar energy?
2. How do nuclear power plants produce energy?
3. What percentage of our energy might be met by wind power over the next 60 years?
4. What are the advantages and drawbacks of hydroelectric power, geothermal energy, and tidal power?

Critical Thinking

5. **Predicting** Why will the interest in alternate energy sources probably grow in the future?
6. **Classifying** Identify solar, nuclear, and wind power as renewable or nonrenewable energy sources. Explain your answers.

 **Writing in Science**

Explain a Concept Write a letter to a family member explaining how tidal power works.

4.3 Water, Air, and Land Resources

Reading Focus

Key Concepts

- Why is fresh water a vital resource?
- Why is the chemical composition of the atmosphere important?
- What are Earth's important land resources?

Vocabulary

- point source pollution
- nonpoint source pollution
- runoff
- global warming

Reading Strategy

Building Vocabulary Copy the table below. As you read, add definitions and examples to complete the table.

Definitions	Examples
point source pollution: Pollution that can be traced to a location	factory pipes, sewer pipes
nonpoint source pollution: a. ___?___	b. ___?___
runoff: c. ___?___	d. ___?___
greenhouse gas: e. ___?___	f. ___?___

Water, air, and land resources are essential for life. You need clean air and water every day. What's more, soil provides nutrients that allow plants—the basis of our own food supply—to grow. How do people use—and sometimes misuse—these vital resources?

The Water Planet

Figure 16 shows Earth's most prominent feature—water. Water covers nearly 71 percent of Earth's surface. However, most of this water is saltwater, not fresh water. Oceans have important functions. Their currents help regulate and moderate Earth's climate. They are also a vital part of the water cycle, and a habitat for marine organisms. Fresh water, however, is what people need in order to live. **Each day, people use fresh water for drinking, cooking, bathing, and growing food.** While fresh water is extremely important, Earth's reserves are relatively small. Less than one percent of the water on the planet is usable fresh water.

Freshwater Pollution Pollution has contaminated many freshwater supplies. In general, there are two types of water pollution sources—point sources and nonpoint sources. **Point source pollution** is pollution that comes from a known and specific location, such as the factory pipes in Figure 17. Other examples include a leaking landfill or storage tank.

Figure 16 Oceans cover almost three fourths of Earth's surface, making Earth a unique planet.

Nonpoint source pollution is pollution that does not have a specific point of origin. **Runoff,** the water that flows over the land rather than seeping into the ground, often carries nonpoint source pollution. Runoff can carry waste oil from streets. It can wash sediment from construction sites or pesticides off farm fields and lawns. Water filtering through piles of waste rock from coal mines can carry sulfuric acid into rivers or lakes. This contaminated water can kill fish and other aquatic life.

As you can see in Table 2, water pollution has adverse health effects. Pollutants can damage the body's major organs and systems, cause birth defects, lead to infectious diseases, and cause certain types of cancers. Contaminated fresh water can sicken or kill aquatic organisms and disrupt ecosystems. What's more, fish and other aquatic life that live in contaminated waters often concentrate poisons in their flesh. As a result, it is dangerous to eat fish taken from some polluted waters.

 **Reading Checkpoint** *What is the difference between a point and nonpoint water pollution source?*

Figure 17 Pollution from point sources, such as these factory pipes, is easy to locate and control.

Table 2 Major Types of Water Pollution			
Type	**Examples**	**Sources**	**Effects**
Disease organisms	Bacteria, viruses	Wastes from people and animals	Typhoid, cholera, dysentery, infectious hepatitis
Wastes that remove oxygen from water	Animal manure and plant debris that bacteria decompose	Sewage, animal feedlots	Great amounts of bacteria can remove oxygen from water, killing fish
Inorganic chemicals	Acids, toxic metals	Industrial effluent, urban runoff, household cleaners	Poisons fresh water and can sicken those who drink it
Organic chemicals	Oil, gasoline, plastic, pesticides, detergent	Farm and yard runoff, industrial waste, household cleaners	Some cancers, disorders of nervous and reproductive systems
Plant fertilizer	Water soluble compounds with nitrate, phosphorus ions	Sewage, manure, farm and garden runoff	Spurs rapid growth of algae that decay and deplete water's oxygen; fish die
Sediment	Soil	Erosion	Disrupts aquatic food webs, clogs lakes and reservoirs, reduces photosynthesis of aquatic plants
Radioactive substances	Radon, uranium, radioactive iodine	Nuclear power plants, uranium ore mining and processing	Some cancers, birth defects, genetic mutations

Figure 18 Cars, trucks, and buses are the biggest source of air pollution. Laws that control motor vehicle emissions have helped make the air cleaner in many areas.

Primary Pollutants

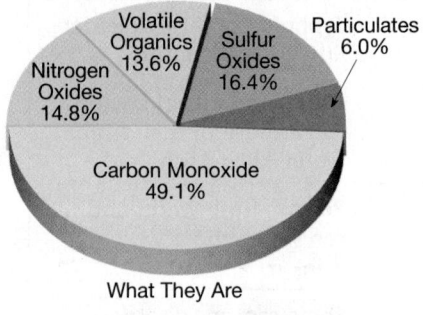

Volatile Organics 13.6%
Sulfur Oxides 16.4%
Particulates 6.0%
Nitrogen Oxides 14.8%
Carbon Monoxide 49.1%

What They Are

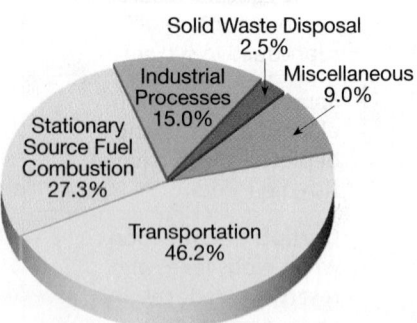

Solid Waste Disposal 2.5%
Industrial Processes 15.0%
Miscellaneous 9.0%
Stationary Source Fuel Combustion 27.3%
Transportation 46.2%

Where They Come From

Figure 19 Major Primary Pollutants and Their Sources Percentages are calculated on the basis of weight.
Using Graphs *What are the three major primary pollutants? What is the major source of air pollution?*

Earth's Blanket of Air

Earth's atmosphere is a blanket of nitrogen, oxygen, water vapor and other gases.  **The chemical composition of the atmosphere helps maintain life on Earth.** First and foremost, people and other animals could not live without the oxygen in Earth's atmosphere. But the atmosphere is also part of several other cycles, such as the carbon cycle, that make vital nutrients available to living things.

The atmosphere also makes life on land possible by shielding Earth from harmful solar radiation. There is a layer of protective ozone high in the air. Ozone is a three-atom form of oxygen that protects Earth from 95 percent of the sun's harmful ultraviolet (UV) radiation.

Certain greenhouse gases in the atmosphere—such as carbon dioxide, methane, and water vapor—help maintain a warm temperature near Earth's surface. When solar energy hits Earth, the Earth gives off some of this energy as heat. The gases absorb the heat Earth emits, keeping the atmosphere warm enough for life as we know it.

Reading Checkpoint *What is the role of ozone in the atmosphere?*

Pollution in the Air Pollution can change the chemical composition of the atmosphere and disrupt its natural cycles and functions. Fossil-fuel combustion is the major source of air pollution. Most of this pollution comes from motor vehicles and coal or oil-burning power plants. Motor vehicles, like those in Figure 18, release carbon monoxide, nitrogen oxide, soot, and other pollutants. Some of the pollutants react to form smog. Power plants release sulfur dioxide and nitrogen oxides. These pollutants combine with water vapor in the air to create acid precipitation. Figure 19 shows the primary air pollutants and the sources of those pollutants.

The burning of fossil fuels also produces carbon dioxide, an important greenhouse gas. The amount of carbon dioxide in the atmosphere has increased since industrialization began in the nineteenth century. This increase has altered the carbon cycle and contributed to the unnatural warming of the lower atmosphere, known as **global warming.** Global warming could lead to enormous changes in Earth's environment. These changes could include the melting of glaciers, which would contribute to a rise in sea level and in the flooding of coastal areas.

Chlorofluorocarbons (CFCs) once used in air conditioners and plastic foam production destroy ozone in the stratosphere layer of the atmosphere. Researchers say that a significant loss of ozone could result in an increased incidence of health problems like cataracts and skin cancers because more of the sun's UV radiation would reach Earth's surface.

Air pollution is a major public health problem. It can cause coughing, wheezing, headaches, as well as lung, eye, and throat irritation. Long-term health effects include asthma, bronchitis, emphysema, and lung cancer. The U.S. Environmental Protection Agency estimates that as many as 200,000 deaths each year are associated with outdoor air pollution.

Land Resources

Earth's land provides soil and forests, as well as mineral and energy resources. How do land resources impact your daily life? Soil is needed to grow the food you eat. Forests provide lumber for your home, wood for furniture, and pulp for paper. Petroleum provides energy and is in the plastic of your computer and CD boxes. Minerals such as zinc, copper, and nickel make up the coins in your pocket. Removing and using resources from Earth's crust can take a heavy environmental toll.

Damage to Land Resources There are an estimated 500,000 mines in the United States. Mines are essential because they produce many of the mineral resources we need. But mining tears up Earth's surface and destroys vegetation, as you can see in Figure 20. It can also cause soil erosion and create pollution that contaminates surrounding soil and water and destroys ecosystems.

Agriculture has many impacts on the land as well. Today, farmers can produce more food per hectare from their land. Extensive irrigation also has allowed many dry areas to be farmed for the first time. But heavy pumping for irrigation of dry areas is depleting the groundwater. And over time, irrigation causes salinization, or the build-up of salts in soil. When irrigation water on the soil evaporates, it leaves behind a salty crust. Eventually, the soil becomes useless for plant growth.

Go Online

NSTA *SciLINKS*

For: Links on environmental toxins
Visit: www.SciLinks.org
Web Code: cjn-1043

Figure 20 Surface mining destroys vegetation, soil, and the contours of Earth's surface. However, laws now require mine owners to restore the surface after mining operations cease.

MAP MASTER™
Skills Activity

Virgin Forests 1620–1992

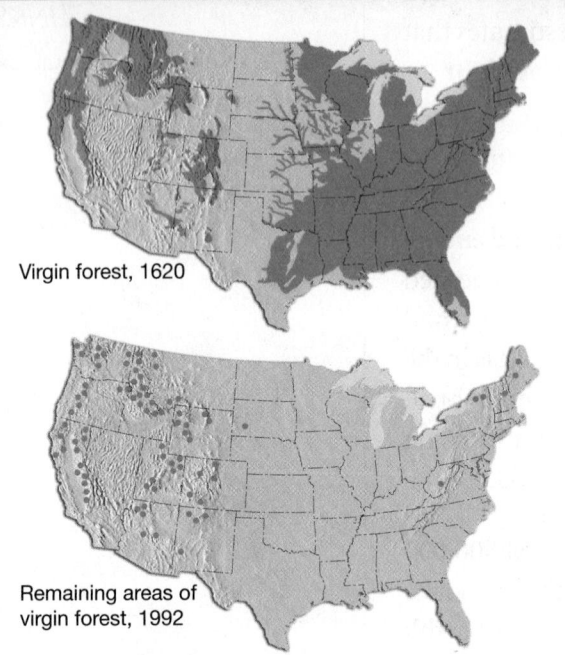

Virgin forest, 1620

Remaining areas of
virgin forest, 1992

Figure 21

Location These maps compare the location of virgin forests in the contiguous 48 states of the U.S. in 1620 and in 1992. **Identifying Effects** How has the amount of virgin forest changed? How has the location of virgin forest changed?

Trees must be cut to supply our need for paper and lumber. But the removal of forests, especially through clear-cutting, can damage land. Clear-cutting is the removal of all trees in an area of forest. Cleared areas are susceptible to soil erosion. Forest removal also destroys ecosystems and wildlife habitat. The United States actually has more hectares of forest today than it did a century ago. That's because much of the virgin forest (forest that had never been cut down) that was cut long ago has regrown as second-growth forest. The forest is not as diverse as the virgin forest—it does not contain as much variety of plant species. Some forestland has also become tree plantations, with even fewer species. As you see in Figure 21, the United States has lost most of its virgin forest during the last few centuries.

Finally, land serves as a disposal site. You may have seen landfills and other waste facilities. When disposal is done correctly, there is minimal impact on land. But many old landfills leak harmful wastes that get into soil and underground water. The same is true of buried drums of chemicals, which were often disposed of illegally. Waste is inevitable. But there is a need for ways to reduce it and make the disposal safer.

Section 4.3 Assessment

Reviewing Concepts

1. ◯ Why is fresh water a vital resource?
2. ◯ Why is the chemical composition of Earth's atmosphere important?
3. What is the difference between point source pollution and nonpoint source pollution?
4. ◯ What do Earth's land resources provide?

Critical Thinking

5. **Applying Concepts** How would Earth be different if there were no greenhouse gases?
6. **Classifying** Which of the following is a nonpoint source pollution of water: rainwater pouring from an eroded bank into a river, a boat emptying a waste tank into a lake, or a sewage plant sending sewage into a river through a pipe?
7. **Relating Cause and Effect** How would the removal of sulfur from coal affect the type of air pollution in a local area? Explain your answer.

Connecting Concepts

Write a brief paragraph that connects the following: waste of paper, loss of species diversity of forests, and the increase in second-growth forest area.

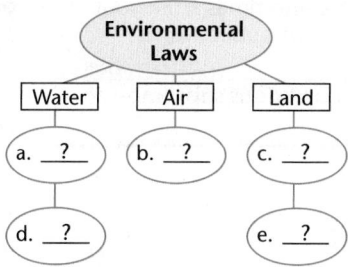

4.4 Protecting Resources

Reading Focus

Key Concepts
- When were the first laws passed to deal with water pollution?
- What was the most important law passed to deal with air pollution?
- What is involved in protecting land resources?

Vocabulary
- conservation
- compost
- recycling

Reading Strategy

Summarizing After reading this section, complete the concept map below to organize what you know about the major laws that help keep water, air, and land resources clean.

Environmental Laws
- Water
  - a. ?
    - d. ?
- Air
  - b. ?
- Land
  - c. ?
    - e. ?

Each year, Americans throw out about 30 million cell phones, 18 million computers, 8 million TV sets, and enough tires to circle the Earth about three times. With just 6 percent of the world's population, Americans use about one third of the world's resources—and produce about one third of the world's garbage.

This high rate of consumption squanders resources, many of which are nonrenewable. The manufacture and disposal of these products uses enormous amounts of energy and creates pollution, as shown in Figure 22. Is there a way to have the products and services we want and still protect resources and create less pollution?

Many people think conservation and pollution prevention are the answer. **Conservation** is the careful use of resources. Pollution prevention means stopping pollution from entering the environment.

Between the late 1940s and 1970, a number of serious pollution problems got the public's attention. Severe air pollution events killed hundreds and sickened thousands in the United States and elsewhere. In the late 1960s, many beaches closed due to pollution. An oil spill off the California coast killed wildlife. Then in 1969, Americans watched news reports of Ohio's polluted Cuyahoga River catching fire and burning for days.

Figure 22 Strict laws have helped curb air pollution, though it remains a problem.

Table 3 How You Can Prevent Water Pollution

- Never pour household chemicals (paints, thinners, cleaners, pesticides, waste oil) down the drain or into the toilet.
- Never dump toxic chemicals in the gutter or onto the ground.
- Don't put items that contain hazardous substances, such as batteries or old computer monitors, into the trash.
- Find out about hazardous waste collection sites and times from your local sanitation or public works department.
- Avoid using hazardous substances in the first place.

Go Online
PLANETDIARY

For: Links on Oil Spills
Visit: PHSchool.com
Web Code: cuc-1044

Figure 23 Air Sampler

Keeping Water Clean and Safe

Both the public and government officials became increasingly concerned about pollution. **Starting in the 1970s, the federal government passed several laws to prevent or decrease pollution and protect resources.**

America's polluted rivers and lakes got early attention. In 1972, the U.S. Congress passed the Clean Water Act (CWA). Among other provisions, the law requires industries to reduce or eliminate point source pollution into surface waters. It also led to a huge increase in the number of sewage treatment plants, which eliminated the discharge of raw sewage into many lakes, rivers, and bays. There are still water pollution problems. But because of the CWA, the percentage of U.S. surface waters safe for fishing and swimming increased from 36 percent to 62 percent between 1972 and the end of the 1990s.

The Safe Drinking Water Act of 1974 helped protect drinking resources. It set maximum contaminant levels for a number of pollutants that could harm the health of people. Public water resources are cleaner today because of this law. See Table 3 for ways that individuals can help conserve water and keep it clean.

 Reading Checkpoint   *What did the Clean Water Act do?*

Protecting the Air

As lawmakers were tackling water pollution in the 1970s, air pollution was also on the agenda. **In 1970, Congress passed the Clean Air Act, the nation's most important air pollution law.** It established National Ambient Air Quality Standards (NAAQS) for six "criteria" pollutants known to cause health problems—carbon monoxide, ozone, lead, sulfur dioxide, nitrogen oxides, and particulates (fine particles). Air monitors, such as the one in Figure 23, sample the air. If the maximum permissible level of pollutants in the air is exceeded, local authorities must come up with plans to bring these levels down. Between 1970 and 2001, the emissions of the six criteria pollutants regulated under the Clean Air Act decreased 24 percent. Over the same time span, energy consumption increased 42 percent and the U.S. population grew by 39 percent.

Today, power plants and motor vehicles use pollution control devices to reduce or eliminate certain byproducts of fossil fuel combustion. Power plants are also more likely to use low-sulfur coal. These controls cut down on emissions of sulfur and nitrogen oxides that often produce acid rain.

Increased use of clean, alternate energy sources such as solar, wind, and hydroelectric power, can also help clear the air. These energy sources don't create air or water pollution, and they're based on renewable resources.

Cars with electric and hybrid (combination of electric and either natural gas, gasoline, or diesel) motors produce fewer or no tailpipe emissions. Several of these lower-emissions models are now available. Some of the hybrid models are also very efficient and get high gas mileage. When a car can go farther on a tank of gas, it uses less fuel and creates less pollution.

Energy conservation is an important air pollution control strategy. Fossil-fuel combustion produces most of the electricity in the United States. If we can use less electricity we would have to burn less fossil fuel. Less fossil-fuel combustion means less air pollution. You can see several energy conservation tips in Table 4.

 **Reading Checkpoint** *What did the Clean Air Act do?*

Caring for Land Resources

🔑 **Protecting land resources involves preventing pollution and managing land resources wisely.** Farmers, loggers, manufacturers, and individuals can all take steps to care for land resources.

Farmers now use many soil conservation practices to prevent the loss of topsoil and preserve soil fertility. In contour plowing, farmers plow across the contour of hillsides. This method of farming decreases water runoff that washes away topsoil. Another conservation method is strip cropping—crops with different nutrient requirements are planted in adjacent rows. Strip cropping helps preserve the fertility of soil.

Selective cutting conserves forest resources. In this method of logging, some trees in an area of a forest are cut, while other trees remain. This practice preserves topsoil as well as the forest habitat. Clear-cutting, on the other hand, removes whole areas of forest and destroys habitats and contributes to the erosion of topsoil.

Some farmers and gardeners now use less pesticides and inorganic fertilizers to decrease chemicals in soil and on crops. Natural fertilizers such as compost or animal manure have replaced inorganic commercial fertilizers on some fields. **Compost** is partly decomposed organic material that is used as fertilizer. Integrated Pest Management (IPM) uses natural predators or mechanical processes (such as vacuuming pests off leaves) to decrease the number of pests. Pesticide use is a last resort.

Table 4 How You Can Save Energy
• Recycle when possible.
• Let the sun in on bright winter days using solar energy to warm rooms.
• Use energy-saving fluorescent bulbs instead of incandescent bulbs where you can.
• Turn off lights when you leave a room. Turn off the radio, TV, or computer when you're not using them.
• Walk or ride a bike when you can.
• When buying electric products, look for the Energy Star sticker which denotes energy-saving products.

Go Online

For: Links on emerging technologies
Visit: www.SciLinks.org
Web Code: cjn-1044

Figure 24 Recycling saves resources, reduces energy consumption, and prevents pollution.

Some laws reduce the possibility of toxic substances getting into the soil. Since 1977, sanitary landfills have largely replaced open dumps and old-style landfills. Sanitary landfills have plastic or clay liners that prevent wastes from leaking into the surrounding soil or groundwater. The Resource Conservation and Recovery Act (RCRA) of 1976 has decreased the illegal and unsafe dumping of hazardous waste. The law requires companies to store, transport, and dispose of hazardous waste according to strict guidelines. The 1980 Comprehensive Environmental Response, Compensation, and Liability Act (Superfund) mandates the cleaning up of abandoned hazardous waste sites that are a danger to the public or the environment.

 **Reading Checkpoint** *What is the RCRA and what does it do?*

Creating less waste by using fewer products and recycling products also helps preserve land resources. **Recycling** is the collecting and processing of used items so they can be made into new products, as Figure 24 shows. By conserving resources and producing less waste, everyone can contribute to a cleaner, healthier future.

Section 4.4 Assessment

Reviewing Concepts

1. When were the first laws passed to deal with water pollution?

2. Identify the most important air pollution control law.

3. What are National Ambient Air Quality Standards?

4. How does selective cutting of forests conserve topsoil?

5. How can gardeners care for land resources?

Critical Thinking

6. **Applying Concepts** How can turning off lights when you're not using them help decrease air pollution?

7. **Relating Cause and Effect** Explain how the Superfund law helps prevent pollution from entering underground water sources.

Writing in Science

Explanatory Paragraph Write a brief paragraph explaining how recycling your aluminum soda cans helps conserve resources and energy.

Bingham Canyon, Utah: The Largest Open-Pit Mine

This huge pit is where a mountain once stood. It's Bingham Canyon copper mine, the largest open-pit mine in the world. The mine, southwest of Salt Lake City, Utah, is 4 kilometers across and covers almost 8 square kilometers. It's so deep—900 meters—that if a steel tower were built at the bottom, it would have to be three times taller than France's Eiffel Tower to reach the pit's rim.

Figure 25 Aerial view of Utah's Bingham Canyon copper mine, the largest open-pit copper mine on Earth.

The pit began in the late 1800s as an underground silver and lead mine. Miners later discovered copper. There are similar deposits at several sites in the American Southwest and in a belt from southern Alaska to northern Chile.

The ore at Bingham Canyon formed after magma was intruded to shallow depths. After this, shattering created extensive fractures in the rock. Hydrothermal solutions penetrated these cracks, and ore minerals formed from the solutions.

Although the percentage of copper in the rock is small, the total volume of copper is huge. Ever since open-pit operations started in 1906, some 5 billion tons of material have been removed, yielding more than 1.2 million tons of copper. Miners have also recovered significant amounts of gold, silver, and molybdenum.

The ore body is far from exhausted. The mine's owners plan to remove and process an additional 3 billion tons of material. This mining operation has generated most of Utah's mineral production for more than 80 years. People have called it the "richest hole on Earth."

Like many older mines, the Bingham pit was unregulated during most of its history. Development occurred before today's awareness of the environmental impacts of mining and prior to effective environmental laws. Today, problems of groundwater and surface water contamination, air pollution, and land reclamation are receiving long overdue attention at Bingham Canyon.

Finding the Product that Best Conserves Resources

When you buy a product, you usually consider factors such as price, brand name, quality, and how much is in the package. But do you consider the amount of resources the package uses? Many products come in packages of different types and materials. You might buy a larger pack if you use a lot, or a tiny pack if you like the convenience of individual servings. But how much cardboard, plastic, or glass are you using—or wasting—depending on your choice? How about the trees, petroleum, and other resources needed to make those packages? In this lab, you will compare three sets of packages that hold the same amount of juice to determine how your decisions about packaging affect the use of resources.

Problem
Which packaging conserves resources the best?

Materials
- 1 1.89-L (64 fl. oz) cardboard juice carton
- 1 946-mL (32 fl. oz) cardboard juice carton
- 1 240-mL (8 fl. oz) cardboard juice carton
- scissors
- metric ruler

CAUTION Be careful when using scissors.

Skills
Observing, Measuring, Calculating, Comparing and Contrasting, Relating Cause and Effect, Drawing Conclusions

Procedure

Part A: Determine the Amount of Material in Each Package

1. Work in groups of three or four. Use scissors to cut apart the three cartons your teacher gives your group. Then spread each one out as you see here.

2. Measure the dimensions of the cartons with the ruler.

3. Calculate the area of each carton on a separate sheet of paper. Use these equations:
   - Area of a rectangle:
     $A = l \times w$
     (l = length; w = width)
   - Area of a square:
     $A = s^2$
     (s = length of a side of the square)

Data Table			
	Area of Cardboard in One Carton	Number of Cartons Needed to Hold 1.89 L	Area of Cardboard to Hold 1.89 L
1.89 L		1	
946 mL		2	
240 mL		8	

4. Copy the data table above on a separate sheet of paper. Then record the data you calculated.

Part B: Compare the Amount of Material in the Packages

5. On a separate sheet of paper, calculate how much more cardboard is used when you buy 1.89 L of juice in the two 946-mL cartons instead of one 1.89-L carton.

Use this procedure:

a) Subtract the area of material in the 1.89-L carton from the area of material in the two 946-mL cartons.

b) Divide the answer you get in part a by the area of material in the 1.89-L carton.

c) Multiply the answer you get in part b by 100. This is how much more material is in the two containers, expressed as a percentage.

6. Repeat this procedure for the material in eight small containers.

Analyze and Conclude

1. **Comparing and Contrasting** Based on your data, does buying the juice in one large carton or in an 8-pack of small individual cartons use more cardboard? How does buying the juice in two medium-size cartons compare.

2. **Relating Cause and Effect** How does buying the juice in several cartons instead of one large carton impact the use of resources?

3. **Drawing Conclusions** Suppose you have determined which set of cardboard cartons uses the least resources. Then you find out that the same size carton of juice comes in plastic and glass as well as cardboard. How would you decide which of these containers would be the best choice, in terms of saving resources?

Go Further

Use the process of engineering design to design packaging for an everyday product. The packaging must conserve materials and be recyclable. Write a paragraph that describes your packaging design and explains why you think it is the best solution within the given constraints.

Study Guide

4.1 Energy and Mineral Resources

Key Concepts

- A renewable resource can be replenished over fairly short time spans, whereas a nonrenewable resource takes millions of years to form and accumulate.
- Fossil fuels include coal, oil, and natural gas.
- Some energy experts believe that fuels derived from tar sands and oil shales could become good substitutes for dwindling petroleum supplies.
- Some of the most important mineral deposits form through igneous processes and from hydrothermal solutions.
- Nonmetallic mineral resources are extracted and processed either for the nonmetallic elements they contain or for their physical and chemical properties.

Vocabulary

renewable resources, *p. 94;* nonrenewable resource, *p. 94;* fossil fuel, *p. 95;* ore, *p. 98*

4.2 Alternate Energy Sources

Key Concepts

- Solar energy has two advantages: the "fuel" is free, and it's non-polluting.
- In nuclear fission, the nuclei of heavy atoms such as uranium-235 are bombarded with neutrons. The uranium nuclei then split into smaller nuclei and emit neutrons and heat energy.
- Some experts estimate that in the next 50 to 60 years, wind power could provide between 5 to 10 percent of the country's demand for electricity.
- The water held in a reservoir behind a dam is a form of stored energy that can be released through the dam to produce electric power.
- Hot water is used directly for heating and to turn turbines to generate electric power.

- Tidal power is harnessed by constructing a dam across the mouth of a bay or an estuary in coastal areas with a large tidal range. The strong in-and-out flow that results drives turbines and electric generators.

Vocabulary

hydroelectric power, *p. 105;* geothermal energy, *p. 105*

4.3 Water, Air, and Land Resources

Key Concepts

- Each day, people use fresh water for drinking, cooking, bathing, and growing food.
- The chemical composition of the atmosphere helps maintain life on Earth.
- Earth's land provides soil and forests, as well as mineral and energy resources.

Vocabulary

point source pollution, *p. 108;* nonpoint source pollution, *p. 109;* runoff, *p. 109;* global warming, *p. 110*

4.4 Protecting Resources

Key Concepts

- Starting in the 1970s, the federal government passed several laws to prevent or decrease pollution and protect resources.
- In 1970, Congress passed the Clean Air Act, the nation's most important air pollution law.
- Protecting land resources involves preventing pollution and managing land resources wisely.

Vocabulary

conservation, *p. 113;* compost, *p. 115;* recycling, *p. 116*

Reviewing Content

Choose the letter that best answers the question or completes the statement.

1. Nonrenewable resources are those that
   a. will never run out.
   b. take one or two decades to replace.
   c. have finite supplies.
   d. are contaminated by pollution.

2. Which of the following is a fossil fuel?
   a. uranium
   b. coal
   c. wood
   d. ozone

3. Petroleum and natural gas form from
   a. the remains of plants and animals buried in seas long ago.
   b. the decay of radioactive sediments underground.
   c. plant material that collected millions of years ago in swamps.
   d. heating and cooling of magma in underground chambers.

4. Hydroelectric power produces electricity using
   a. the sun's rays.
   b. wind.
   c. moving water.
   d. storms.

5. Which of the following substances is a fuel used in nuclear power plants?
   a. sulfur dioxide
   b. uranium
   c. petroleum
   d. carbon dioxide

6. Point source pollution comes from sources that are
   a. basically unknown.
   b. directly identifiable.
   c. very small.
   d. dumped illegally.

7. An unnatural warming of the atmosphere near Earth's surface is called
   a. solar wind.
   b. ozone accumulation.
   c. acid precipitation.
   d. global warming.

8. The careful use of resources is
   a. conservation.
   b. recycling.
   c. composting.
   d. deposition.

9. The Clean Air Act
   a. makes all air pollution illegal.
   b. limits greenhouse gases in outdoor air.
   c. limits nonpoint source pollution.
   d. set limits on certain pollutants in outdoor air.

10. What type of pollution did the Clean Water Act succeed in limiting?
    a. carbon dioxide
    b. sewage
    c. solid waste
    d. acid precipitation

Understanding Concepts

11. What are the three major types of fossil fuels?

12. What is a major negative impact of the use of fossil fuels?

13. What is the difference between a mineral resource and an ore?

14. Briefly explain how active solar collectors work.

15. Why do hydroelectric dams have limited lifetimes?

16. Explain why fresh water is a vital resource.

17. How can farmers help protect land resources?

18. When were some of the earliest laws passed to deal with water pollution? Why were they passed at that time?

19. Explain why an anticline might be a good place to search for petroleum and natural gas.

20. What are three things that you can do to prevent water pollution?

21. What are three things that you can do to save energy?

Assessment *continued*

Critical Thinking

22. Applying Concepts Some people predict that tar sands and oil shale will one day supply much of our energy needs. Are tar sands and oil shale a good long-term energy solution? Explain.

23. Relating Cause and Effect What effect can recycling paper have on the use of resources and the creation of pollution?

24. Inferring How might an increased use of alternate energy sources such as wind and solar radiation affect the lifetime of fossil fuel resources?

25. Summarizing Describe how a hydrothermal solution can produce a vein deposit of ore.

26. Comparing and Contrasting What is the difference between how electricity is produced with tides and how it's produced in a nuclear power plant?

Analyzing Data

Use the diagram below to answer Questions 27–29.

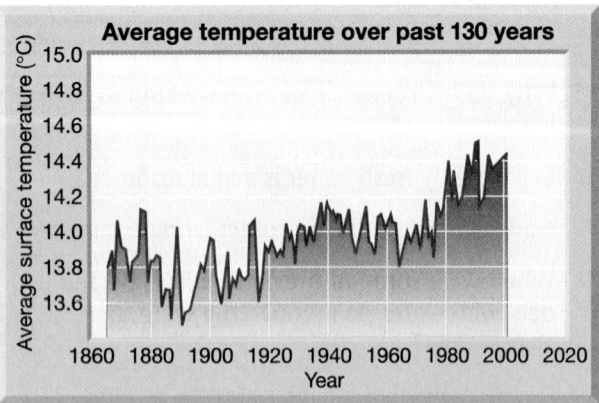

Average temperature over past 130 years

27. Interpreting Graphs What does this graph show?

28. Using Graphs What is the general temperature trend during the time period shown on the graph? What was the average temperature in 2000?

29. Drawing Conclusions How would you expect the graph to be different between 1700 and 1800, before the start of widespread industrialization? Explain.

Concepts in Action

30. Classifying Limestone is a nonmetallic mineral that has several uses: as a stone used for structures; as a substance used to neutralize acidic soils; as an ingredient in the manufacture of steel. Should limestone be classified as an industrial mineral or a building mineral? Explain.

31. Analyzing Concepts The factors in favor of the use of solar power include the fact that the fuel it uses is free, it's renewable, and it doesn't create pollution. Identify drawbacks of the use of solar power.

32. Summarizing What is the effect of the destruction of ozone on human life?

33. Connecting Concepts What is the relationship between petroleum production, the increased use of hybrid cars, and the level of air pollutants regulated by the Clean Air Act that are in the air?

Performance-Based Assessment

Drawing Conclusions Locate an electric power plant that is in or close to your community. Find out which method it uses to produce electricity. Take into consideration the way the plant produces power, its location, the pollution it produces, and the number of people it serves. Write a short essay on the plant's impact on the environment and on your community in general.

Standardized Test Prep

Choose the letter that best answers the question or completes the statement, or write a brief answer to the question.

1. Which one of the substances listed below is a fossil fuel?
(A) uranium
(B) petroleum
(C) carbon dioxide
(D) granite

2. Recycling is an important way to reduce resource consumption because
(A) reducing waste is better than recycling it.
(B) it decreases the use of new resources to make products.
(C) recycling is not a new way to save resources.
(D) curbside pick-up makes recycling more convenient in many communities.

Answer Questions 3–5 using the line graph below, which shows U.S. energy consumption between 1970 and 2000, and projected consumption between 2000 and 2020.

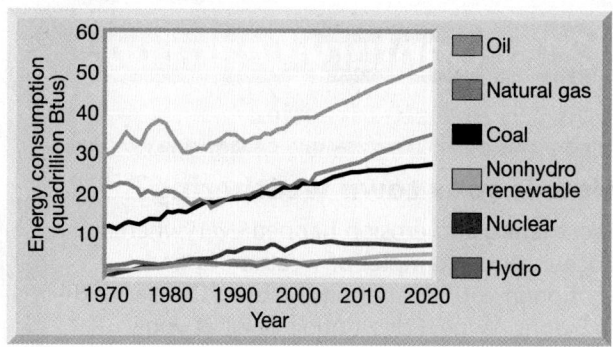

3. Which fuel source had the highest rate of consumption during this period?
(A) coal
(B) nuclear
(C) oil
(D) hydroelectric

4. Which renewable energy source is most widely used?
(A) solar
(B) hydroelectric
(C) natural gas
(D) nuclear

5. Look at the part of the graph that shows projections for U.S. energy consumption between 2000 and 2020. Explain why this pattern of consumption is, or is not, a good long-term energy strategy.

6. Explain how air pollutants can change the chemical composition of the atmosphere and how that affects Earth.

CHAPTER 5

Weathering, Soil, and Mass Movements

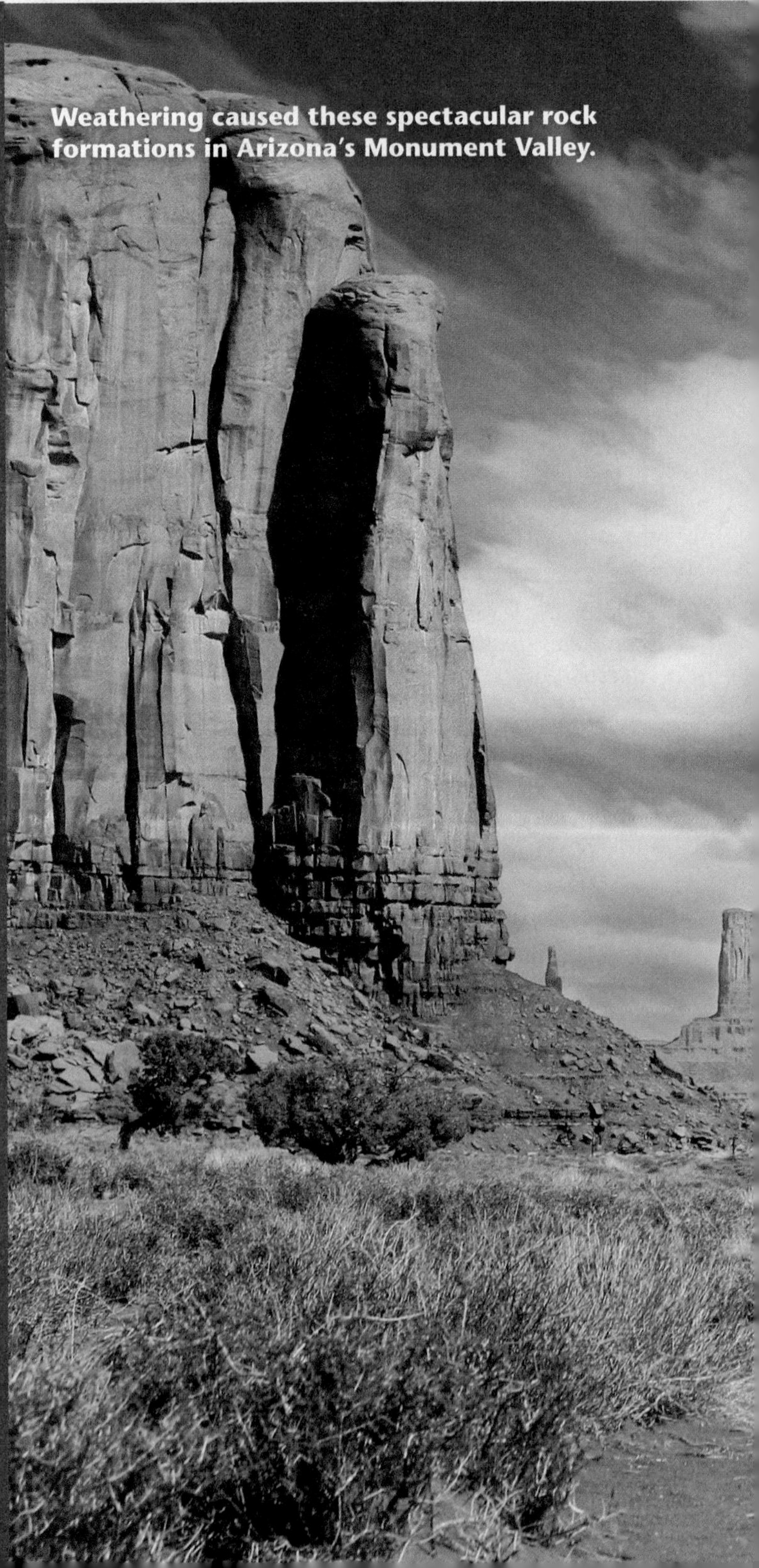

Weathering caused these spectacular rock formations in Arizona's Monument Valley.

21st Century Learning

Self-Direction

How is your town weathering?

Weathering and erosion happen everywhere. Locate some examples of weathering and erosion in your community, and visit these locations. Write a description of what you see and take some photos. Then research the possible causes of the erosion. Create a multimedia presentation that summarizes your findings.

Exploration Lab

Effect of Temperature on Chemical Weathering

How Earth Works

Soil

GEODe EARTH SCIENCE

Sculpturing Earth's Surface
↳ External vs Internal Process

Earth Materials
↳ Sedimentary Rocks

Chapter Preview

Inquiry › Activity

What Causes Weathering?

Procedure

1. Fill a 1-L plastic container about half full of rocks. Add enough water to barely cover the rocks.

2. Place a tight-fitting lid on the container and shake the container vigorously 100 times.

3. Hold a strainer over a clear glass jar. Pour the water and rocks into the strainer.

4. Use a hand lens to observe the bottom and sides of the empty container. Then use the hand lens to observe the water in the glass jar.

Think About It

1. **Observing** What did you see on the bottom or sides of the empty container during Step 4? How did shaking the rock-and-water mixture change the appearance of the water?

2. **Predicting** How do you think your observations would change if you put the rocks and water back in the container and repeated Steps 2 through 4 several more times?

3. **Predicting** Suppose you found a stream where water ran over a rock ledge into a pool. What would you expect to find at the bottom of the pool?

5.1 Weathering

Reading Focus

Key Concepts

- What is mechanical weathering?
- What is chemical weathering?
- What factors affect the rate of weathering?

Vocabulary

- mechanical weathering
- frost wedging
- talus
- exfoliation
- chemical weathering

Reading Strategy

Building Vocabulary Copy the table. As you read the section, define each vocabulary term.

Vocabulary Term	Definition
Mechanical weathering	a. _____?_____
Frost wedging	b. _____?_____
Talus	c. _____?_____
Exfoliation	d. _____?_____
Chemical weathering	e. _____?_____

Figure 1 Weathering Ice, rain, and wind are slowly breaking down the rock in this mountain. The rock fragments accumulate in sloped deposits at the base of the mountain.

Earth's surface is constantly changing. Internal forces gradually raise some parts of the surface through mountain building and volcanic activity. At the same time, external processes continually break rock apart and move the debris to lower elevations, as shown in Figure 1. The breaking down and changing of rocks at or near Earth's surface is called weathering. Weathering is a basic part of the rock cycle and a key process in the Earth system. There are two types of weathering—mechanical and chemical. Though these processes are different, they are at work at the same time.

Mechanical Weathering

Mechanical weathering occurs when physical forces break rock into smaller and smaller pieces without changing the rock's mineral composition. Each piece has the same characteristics as the original rock. Breaking a rock into smaller pieces increases the total surface area of the rock. Look at Figure 2. When rock is broken apart, more surface area is exposed to chemical weathering. In nature, three physical processes are especially important causes of mechanical weathering: frost wedging, unloading, and biological activity.

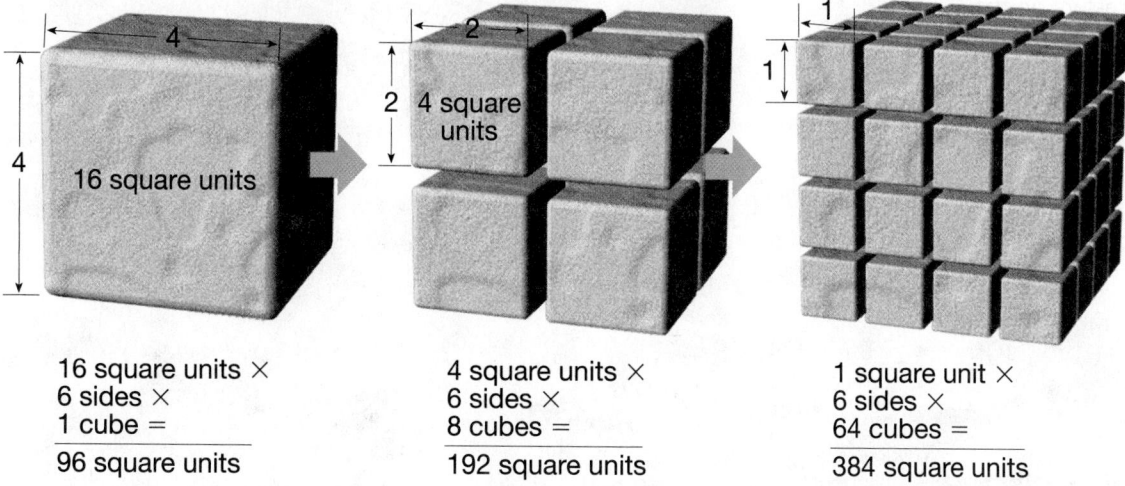

16 square units ×
6 sides ×
1 cube =
_____
96 square units

4 square units ×
6 sides ×
8 cubes =
_____
192 square units

1 square unit ×
6 sides ×
64 cubes =
_____
384 square units

Frost Wedging When liquid water freezes, it expands by about 9 percent, exerting a tremendous outward force. This force is great enough to burst water pipes during the winter. In nature, water works its way into every crack in rock. When water freezes and expands, it enlarges the cracks. After many freeze-thaw cycles, the rock breaks into pieces. This process, which is shown in Figure 3, is called **frost wedging.** Frost wedging is most common in mountainous regions in the middle latitudes. Here daily freezing and thawing often occur. Sections of rock that are wedged loose may tumble into large piles called **talus,** which typically form at the base of steep, rocky cliffs.

 Reading Checkpoint

Explain how water can cause mechanical weathering.

Figure 2 By breaking a rock into smaller pieces, mechanical weathering increases the rock's surface area that can be exposed to chemical weathering.
Calculating *Calculate the total surface area if each of the 64 cubes shown in the right diagram were broken into 8 equal-sized cubes.*

Figure 3 Frost Wedging Rainwater entered cracks in this boulder. Each time the water froze, it expanded. Eventually, the boulder split.

Figure 4 Unloading and Exfoliation A Uplift and erosion expose a buried mass of igneous rock. Reduced pressure on the rock, called unloading, causes the outer rock layers to expand. They separate from the rest of the rock mass. This process is called exfoliation. **B** The granite layers of Half Dome in Yosemite National Park, California, are undergoing exfoliation.

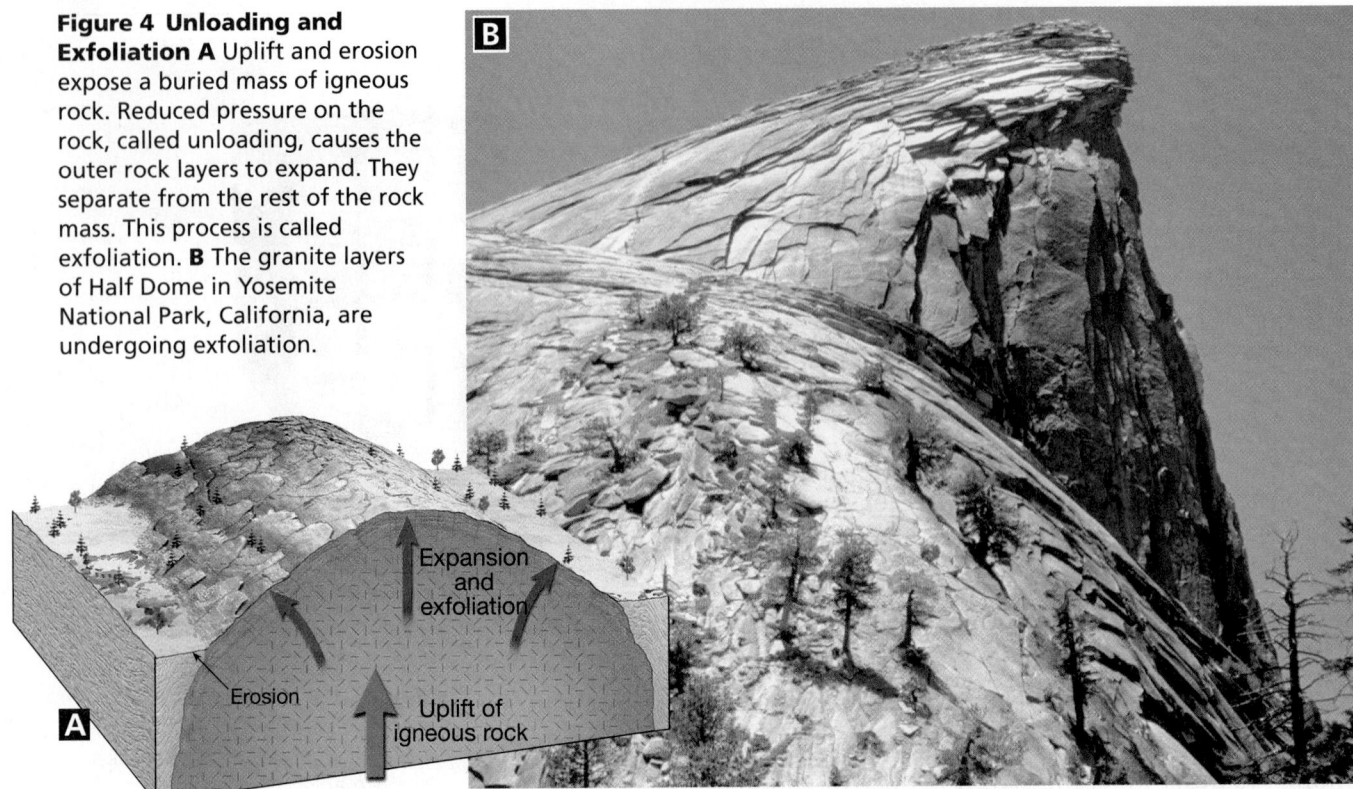

Figure 5 The roots of this tree are causing mechanical weathering by widening the cracks in the rock.

Unloading Large masses of igneous rock may be exposed through uplift and erosion of overlying rocks. When that happens, the pressure exerted on the igneous rock is reduced. This is known as unloading. As illustrated in Figure 4A, unloading causes the outer layers of the rock to expand more than the rock below. Slabs of outer rock separate like the layers of an onion and break loose in a process called **exfoliation.** Exfoliation is especially common in rock masses made of granite. It often produces large, dome-shaped rock formations. Figure 4B shows one of these formations. Other important exfoliation domes are Stone Mountain, Georgia, and Liberty Cap also in Yosemite National Park.

A striking example of the weathering effects of unloading is shown in deep underground mining. Newly cut mine tunnels suddenly reduce the pressure on the surrounding rock. As a result, large rock slabs sometimes explode off the walls of the tunnels.

Biological Activity The activities of organisms, including plants, burrowing animals, and humans, can also cause mechanical weathering. As Figure 5 shows, plant roots grow into cracks in rock, wedging the rock apart as they grow. Burrowing animals move rocks to the surface, where weathering is more rapid. Decaying organisms produce compounds called acids that cause chemical weathering.

Humans accelerate mechanical weathering through deforestation and blasting in search of minerals or in the creation of new roads.

Chemical Weathering

 **Chemical weathering is the transformation of rock into one or more new compounds.** The new compounds remain mostly unchanged as long as the environment in which they formed does not change. You can contrast chemical weathering and mechanical weathering with a sheet of paper. Tearing the paper into small pieces is like mechanical weathering of rock. Burning the paper, which changes it into carbon dioxide and water, is like chemical weathering.

Water Water is the most important agent of chemical weathering. Water promotes chemical weathering by absorbing gases from the atmosphere and the ground. These dissolved substances then chemically react with various minerals. Oxygen dissolved in water reacts easily with certain minerals, forming oxides. For example, iron-rich minerals get a yellow to reddish-brown coating of iron oxide when they react with oxygen. Iron oxide is the rust that forms when iron-containing objects are exposed to water. Figure 6A shows this rust on barrels.

Water absorbs carbon dioxide when rain falls through the atmosphere. Water that seeps through the ground also picks up carbon dioxide from decaying organic matter. The carbon dioxide dissolved in water forms carbonic acid. This is the weak acid in carbonated soft drinks. Carbonic acid reacts with many common minerals.

Reading Checkpoint *How are water, oxygen, and carbon dioxide involved in chemical weathering?*

Figure 6 A Oxygen reacted with the iron in these barrels, forming iron oxide, or rust. **B** This granite gravestone, placed in 1868, shows little evidence of chemical weathering. **C** The inscription date (1872) on this marble gravestone is nearly illegible due to chemical weathering.

Figure 7 One Effect of Acid Precipitation Acid precipitation contributed to the chemical weathering of this stone building facade in Leipzig, Germany.

Water in the atmosphere also absorbs sulfur oxides and nitrogen oxides. These oxides are produced by the burning of coal and petroleum. Through a series of chemical reactions, these pollutants are converted into acids that are the major cause of acid precipitation. Acid precipitation accelerates the chemical weathering of stone monuments and structures, such as the one shown in Figure 7.

Chemical Weathering of Granite To illustrate how chemical weathering can change the properties of rock, let's consider granite. Recall that granite consists mainly of the minerals feldspar and quartz. When granite is exposed to water containing carbonic acid, the feldspar is converted mostly to clay minerals. Quartz, in contrast, is much more resistant to carbonic acid and remains unchanged. As the feldspar slowly changes to clay, the quartz grains are released from the granite. Rivers transport some of this weathered debris to the sea. The tiny clay particles may be carried far from shore. The quartz grains are deposited near the shore where they become the main component of beaches and sand dunes.

Chemical Weathering of Silicate Minerals Recall that silicate minerals make up most of Earth's crust and are composed largely of just eight elements. When silicate minerals undergo chemical weathering, the sodium, calcium, potassium, and magnesium they contain dissolve and are carried away by groundwater. Iron reacts with oxygen, producing iron oxide. The three remaining elements are aluminum, silicon, and oxygen. These elements usually combine with water and produce clay minerals. See Table 1 for a list of products of weathering.

Spheroidal Weathering Chemical weathering can change the physical shape of rock as well as its chemical composition. For example, when water enters along the joints in a rock, it weathers the corners and edges most rapidly. These parts of the rock have a greater surface area than the faces have. As a result, the corners and edges become more rounded. The rock takes on a spherical shape, as shown in Figure 8A. This process is called spheroidal weathering.

Table 1 Products of Weathering

Mineral	Residual Products	Materials in Solution
Quartz	Quartz grains	Silica
Feldspars	Clay minerals	Silica K^+, Na^+, Ca^{2+}
Amphibole (hornblende)	Clay minerals Limonite Hematite	Silica Ca^{2+}, Mg^{2+}
Olivine	Limonite Hematite	Silica Mg^{2+}

As Figure 8B shows, spheroidal weathering sometimes causes the outer layers of a rock to separate from the rock's main body. This can happen when the minerals in the rock turn to clay, which swells by adding water. The swelling exerts a force that causes the layers to break loose and fall off. This allows chemical weathering to penetrate deeper into the boulder. Although the effects of this type of spheroidal weathering resemble exfoliation, the two processes are different. Spheroidal weathering is a form of chemical weathering. Exfoliation is caused by unloading. The layers that separate from the rock are not chemically changed.

Rate of Weathering

Mechanical weathering affects the rate of chemical weathering. By breaking rock into smaller pieces, mechanical weathering accelerates chemical weathering by increasing the surface area of exposed rock. **Two other factors that affect the rate of weathering are rock characteristics and climate.**

Rock Characteristics Physical characteristics of rock, such as cracks, are important in weathering because they influence the ability of water to penetrate rock. However, a rock's mineral composition also dramatically affects its rate of weathering. You can see this by visiting a cemetery and comparing old gravestones made from different rock types. Gravestones made of granite, like the one in Figure 6B on page 129, are relatively resistant to chemical weathering. You can easily read the inscriptions on a granite gravestone that is over 100 years old. In contrast, marble gravestones undergo much more rapid chemical weathering, as shown in Figure 6C on page 129. Marble is composed of calcite (calcium carbonate), which easily dissolves even in weak acids.

Figure 8 Spheroidal Weathering A The edges of these granite rocks in California's Joshua Tree National Monument were rounded through spheroidal weathering. **B** Spheroidal weathering has caused the outer layers of this rock to loosen and separate.

Silicates are the most abundant mineral group. Silicates weather in the same sequence as their order of crystallization. Olivine crystallizes first and weathers most rapidly. Quartz, which crystallizes last, is the most resistant to weathering.

Climate Climatic factors, especially temperature and moisture, have a strong effect on the rate of weathering. For example, these factors control the frequency of freeze-thaw cycles, which affect the amount of frost wedging. Temperature and moisture also affect the rate of chemical weathering. They influence the kind of vegetation and how much is present. Regions with lush vegetation generally have a thick layer of soil rich in decaying organic matter that releases acids into the water.

The climate most favorable for chemical weathering has high temperatures and abundant moisture. So, chemical weathering is very slow in arid regions. It is also slow in polar regions because the low temperatures there keep moisture locked up as ice.

Differential Weathering Different parts of a rock mass often weather at different rates. This process, called differential weathering, has several causes. Differences in mineral composition are one cause. More resistant rock protrudes as pinnacles, or high peaks, such as those shown in Figure 9. Another cause is the variations in the number and spacing of cracks in different parts of a rock mass.

Figure 9 These boldly sculpted pinnacles in Bryce Canyon National Park show differential weathering. **Drawing Conclusions** *In which parts of these formations is weathering happening most rapidly?*

Section 5.1 Assessment

Reviewing Concepts

1. What happens to a rock's mineral composition during mechanical weathering?
2. What is unloading? How does it contribute to weathering?
3. How does chemical weathering affect the compounds in rock?
4. Name two rock characteristics and two climatic factors that affect the rate of weathering.

Critical Thinking

5. **Using Analogies** Think about the following processes: dissolving a piece of rock salt in a pan of water and grinding a peach pit in a garbage disposal. Which process is more like mechanical weathering, and which is more like chemical weathering?

6. **Applying Concepts** The level of carbon dioxide in the atmosphere is increasing. How might this affect the rate of chemical weathering of Earth's surface rocks? Explain your reasoning.

Math Practice

7. Suppose frost wedging splits a spherical rock 2 m in diameter into two equal-sized hemispheres. Calculate the total surface area of the original rock and of the two hemispheres. (The area of a circle $= \pi r^2$, and the surface area of a sphere $= 4\pi r^2$, where r is the radius.)

5.2 Soil

Reading Focus

Key Concepts

- What are the major components of soil?
- What are the most important factors in soil formation?
- How does soil vary with depth?
- What are three common types of soil?
- How do human activities affect the rate of soil erosion?

Vocabulary

- regolith
- soil
- soil horizon
- soil profile
- pedalfer
- pedocal
- laterite

Reading Strategy

Comparing and Contrasting Copy the table. After you read, compare the three types of soils by completing the table.

Soil Type	Where It's Found
Pedalfer	a. _____?_____
Pedocal	b. _____?_____
Laterite	c. _____?_____

Soil, an important product of weathering, covers most land surfaces. Along with air and water, it is one of our most important resources. All life depends on a dozen or so elements that come from Earth's crust. Once weathering and other processes create soil, plants absorb the elements and make them available to animals, including humans.

Characteristics of Soil

Weathering produces a layer of rock and mineral fragments called **regolith,** which covers nearly all of Earth's land surface. **Soil is the part of the regolith that supports the growth of plants.** Three important characteristics of soil are its composition, texture, and structure.

Soil Composition **Soil has four major components: mineral matter, or broken-down rock; organic matter, or humus, which is the decayed remains of organisms; water; and air.** The proportions of these components vary in different soils. Figure 10 shows that in a good-quality surface soil, mineral matter and organic matter make up half the total volume. The organic matter in soil, or humus, consists of the decayed remains of animal and plant life. The other half consists of pore spaces where air and water circulate.

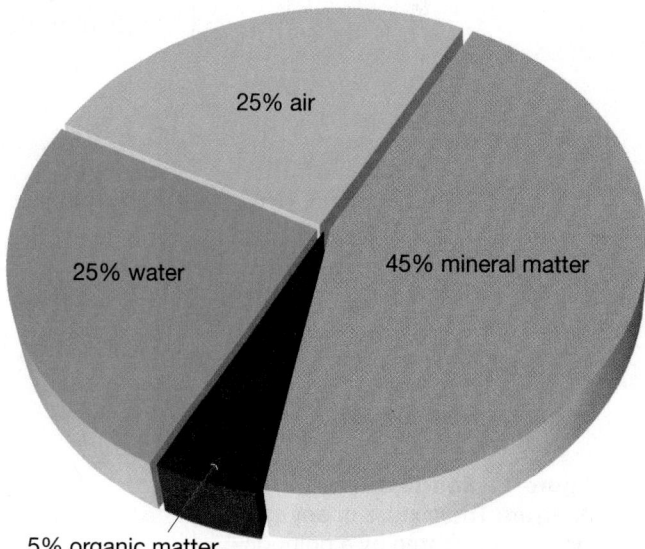

25% air

25% water

45% mineral matter

5% organic matter

Figure 10 Composition by Volume of Good-Quality Soil Using Graphs *What percentage of this soil consists of water and mineral matter?*

The percentage of organic matter in soil varies greatly. Certain bog soils are composed almost entirely of organic matter. Desert soils may contain only a tiny amount. In most soils, organic matter or humus is an essential component. It is an important source of plant nutrients and increases the soil's ability to retain water. Poor soils can be enriched with the addition of humus.

The water and air components of soil are also vital for plant growth. Soil water provides the moisture needed for chemical reactions that sustain life. Soil water provides nutrients in a form that plants can use. Air is the source of the carbon dioxide plants use to produce sugar during photosynthesis.

Soil Texture Most soils contain particles of different sizes. Soil texture refers to the proportions of different particle sizes. To classify soil texture, the U.S. Department of Agriculture has established categories based on the percentages of clay, silt, and sand in soil. The diagram in Figure 11 shows how the percentages differ for each category. For example, point A, near the left-center part of the diagram, represents a soil composed of 40 percent clay, 10 percent silt, and 50 percent sand. Such a soil is called a sandy clay. In soils called loam, which occupy the central part of the diagram, neither clay, silt, nor sand is dominant.

Texture strongly influences a soil's ability to support plant life. Sandy soils may drain and dry out too quickly, while clay-rich soils drain very slowly. Plant roots often have difficulty penetrating soils that contain a high percentage of clay and silt. Loam soils are usually best for plant growth. They retain water better and store more nutrients than do soils composed mainly of clay or sand.

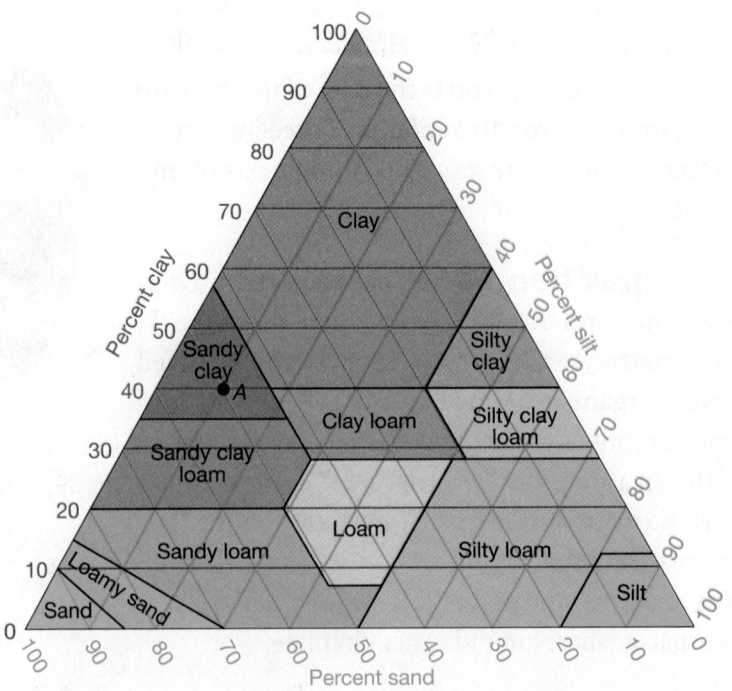

Figure 11 Soil-Texture Diagram The texture of any soil can be represented by a point on this diagram.
Interpreting Diagrams *What type of soil consists of 10 percent clay, 60 percent silt, and 30 percent sand?*

Soil Structure Soil particles usually form clumps that give soils a particular structure. Soil structure determines how easily a soil can be cultivated and how susceptible it is to erosion. Soil structure also affects the ease with which water can penetrate the soil. This, in turn, influences the movement of nutrients to plant roots.

Soil Formation

Soil forms through the complex interaction of several factors.  **The most important factors in soil formation are parent material, time, climate, organisms, and slope.** Although these factors all interact, we'll examine them separately.

Go Online
NSTA SciLINKS

For: Links on soil
Visit: www.SciLinks.org
Web Code: cjn-2052

Figure 12 Parent Materials and Soils

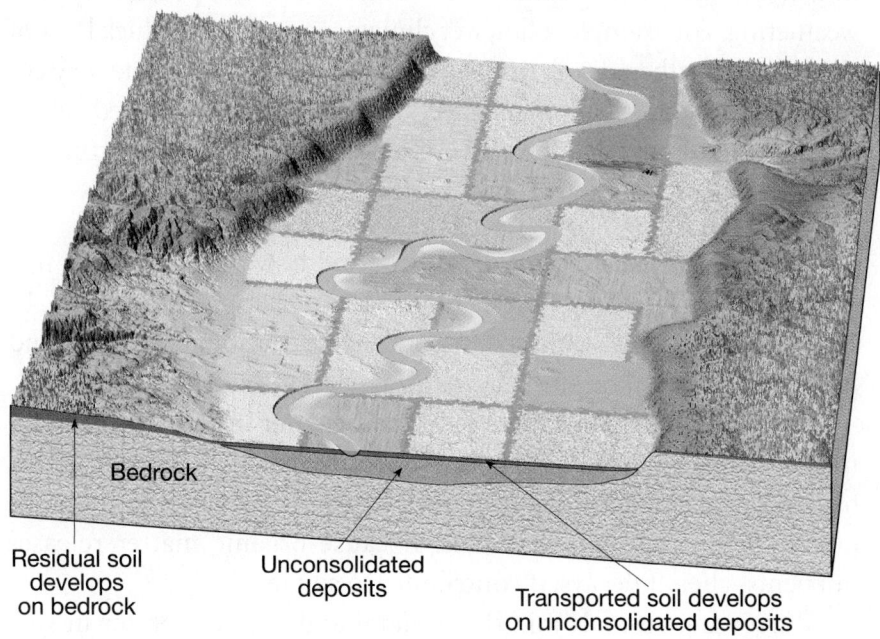

Bedrock

Residual soil develops on bedrock

Unconsolidated deposits

Transported soil develops on unconsolidated deposits

Parent Material The source of the mineral matter in soil is known as the parent material. Notice in Figure 12 that parent material may be either bedrock or unconsolidated deposits, such as those in a river valley. The soil that forms on bedrock is called residual soil. The soil that forms on unconsolidated deposits is called transported soil. Its parent material was moved from another location by gravity, water, wind, or ice.

 **Reading Checkpoint** *What is the difference between residual soil and transported soil?*

The nature of the parent material influences soils in two ways. First, it affects the rate of weathering and the rate of soil formation. Because unconsolidated deposits are already partly weathered, they provide more surface area for chemical weathering. Therefore, transported soil usually develops more rapidly than residual soil develops. Second, the chemical makeup of the parent material affects the soil's fertility. Fertility influences the types of plants the soil can support.

Time The longer a soil has been forming, the thicker it becomes. The parent material largely determines the characteristics of young soils. As weathering continues, however, the influence of the parent material can be overshadowed by the other factors, especially climate.

Climate Climate has the greatest effect on soil formation. Variations in temperature and precipitation influence the rate, depth, and type of weathering. For example, a hot, wet climate may produce a thick layer of chemically weathered soil. In the same amount of time, a cold, dry climate might produce only a thin layer of mechanically weathered debris. The amount of precipitation also influences soil fertility by affecting the rate at which nutrients are removed from the soil.

Organisms The types of organisms and how many there are in a soil have a major impact on its physical and chemical properties. In fact, scientists name some soils—such as prairie soil, forest soil, and tundra soil—based on the soils' natural vegetation.

Plants are the main source of organic matter in soil. Animals and microorganisms also contribute. Microorganisms, including fungi, bacteria, and single-celled protozoans, play an active role in decomposing dead plants and animals. Because organic matter releases nutrients when it decays, it contributes to soil fertility.

Burrowing animals mix the mineral and organic matter in soil. Earthworms, for example, mix soil as they burrow through it and feed on the organic matter it contains. The holes made by burrowing animals also help water and air to penetrate into soil.

Some bacteria also aid soil fertility. In the nitrogen cycle, these bacteria convert nitrogen gas into nitrogen compounds that plants can use. Organisms require nitrogen in order to make amino acids, the building blocks of proteins. Nitrogen gas is common in the atmosphere. But most living things cannot use nitrogen gas in their cells.

Look at Figure 13 to follow the steps in the nitrogen cycle. Certain types of bacteria take up nitrogen from the atmosphere and produce ammonia. Ammonia provides nitrogen in a form plants can use. These nitrogen-fixing bacteria live both in soil and in the roots of legumes. (Legumes are plants such as peanuts, beans, and clover that have nitrogen-fixing bacteria in nodules on their roots.) But most ammonia is

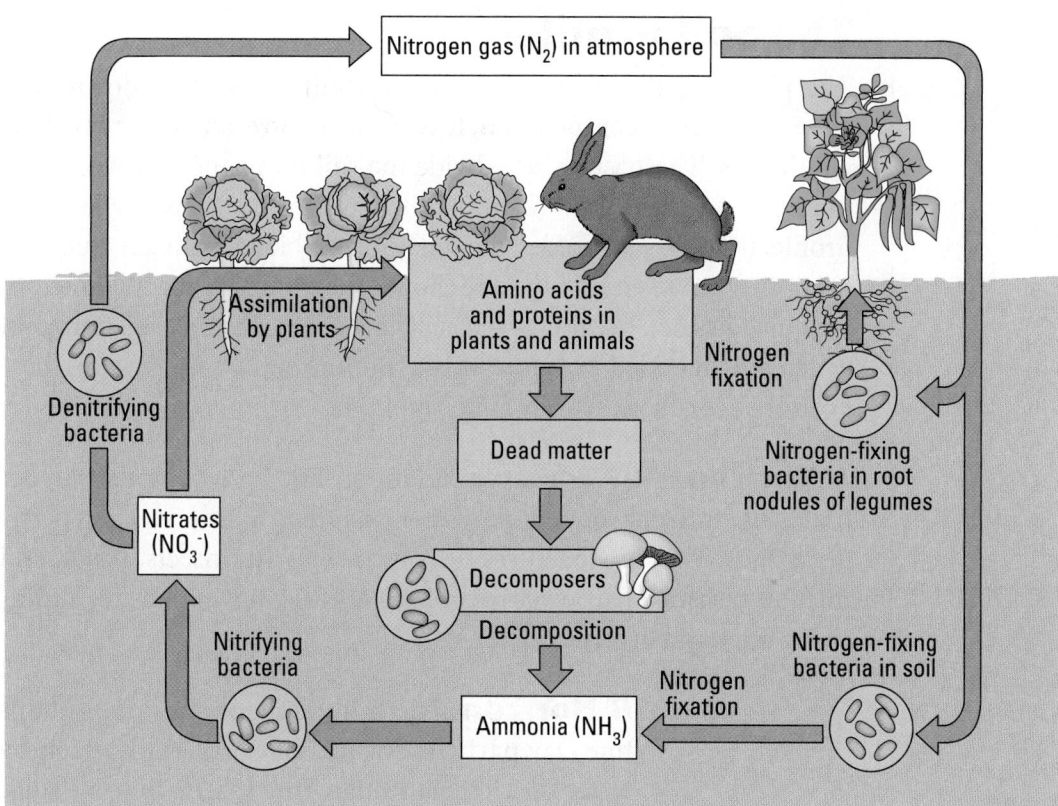

consumed by other bacteria, called nitrifying bacteria. Nitrifying bacteria produce compounds called nitrites and nitrates, which are made up of nitrogen and oxygen. Nitrate is the most common source of nitrogen for plants.

Another type of soil bacteria, called denitrifying bacteria, continues the cycle. These bacteria break down nitrates and release nitrogen gas into the atmosphere.

Slope The slope of the land can vary greatly over short distances. Such variations can result in very different soil types. Many of the differences are related to the amount of erosion and the water content of the soil.

On steep slopes, erosion is accelerated. Little water can soak in, so the soil generally holds too little moisture for vigorous plant growth. As a result, soils are usually thin or nonexistent on steep slopes. In contrast, flat areas have little erosion and poor drainage. The waterlogged soils that form in flat areas are typically thick and dark. The dark color results from large amounts of organic matter.

The direction a slope faces also affects soil formation. In the temperate zone of the Northern Hemisphere, south-facing slopes receive much more sunlight than do north-facing slopes. Consequently, soils on south-facing slopes are usually warmer and drier.

Reading Checkpoint *Explain how the slope of the land affects soil thickness.*

Figure 13 The Nitrogen Cycle
As part of the nitrogen cycle, certain bacteria in soil and plant roots absorb nitrogen gas and produce compounds containing nitrogen that plants can use.
Predicting *How would planting legumes in a field affect the soil's fertility?*

Go Online
active art

For: Soil Layers activity
Visit: PHSchool.com
Web Code: czp-2051

The Soil Profile

The processes that form soil operate from the surface downward. 🔵 **Soil varies in composition, texture, structure, and color at different depths.** These variations divide the soil into zones known as **soil horizons.** A vertical section through all of the soil horizons is called a **soil profile.** In some soil profiles, the soil horizons blend gradually from one to another. In others, like the one shown in Figure 14A, the soil horizons are quite distinct. Mature soils usually have three distinct soil horizons, which are identified in Figure 14B. From the surface downward, these horizons are called the A, B, and C horizons.

A Horizon The A horizon is commonly known as topsoil. Its upper part consists mostly of organic matter, including loose leaves and partly decomposed plant structures. It is teeming with insects, fungi, and microorganisms. The lower part of the A horizon is a mixture of mineral matter and organic matter.

B Horizon The B horizon, or subsoil, contains fine clay particles washed out of the A horizon by water that filters through pore spaces. In some soils, the clay that accumulates in the B horizon forms a compact, impenetrable layer called hardpan. The B horizon is the lower limit of most plant roots and burrowing animals.

C Horizon Between the B horizon and the unaltered parent material is the C horizon, which contains partially weathered parent material. While the A and B horizons barely resemble the parent material, the C horizon does.

Figure 14 Soil Profiles A The A, B, and C horizons have different characteristics. **B** Three soil horizons are visible in this soil. **Interpreting Photographs** *Using the diagram in B as a guide, identify the soil horizons in A.*

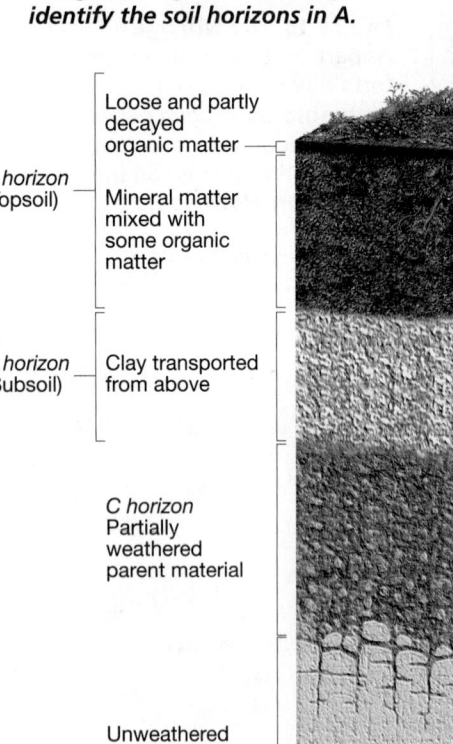

A horizon (Topsoil)
— Loose and partly decayed organic matter
— Mineral matter mixed with some organic matter

B horizon (Subsoil)
— Clay transported from above

C horizon Partially weathered parent material

Unweathered parent material

A

B

Soil Types

Recall that climate is the most important factor in soil formation. Climate also has a major effect on the type of soil that forms. ⬤ **Three common types of soil are pedalfer, pedocal, and laterite.**

Pedalfer Pedalfers usually forms in temperate areas that receive more than 63 cm of rain each year. This soil type is present in much of the eastern half of the United States, most often in forested areas. The B horizon in pedalfers contains large amounts of iron oxide and aluminum-rich clays, giving it a brown to red-brown color.

Pedocal Pedocals are found in the drier western United States in areas that have grasses and brush vegetation. Because chemical weathering is slower in dry climates, pedocals generally contains less clay than pedalfers. Pedocals contain abundant calcite, or calcium carbonate, and are typically a light gray-brown.

Figure 15 The Temple at Angkor Wat, Cambodia This temple was constructed of laterite bricks between 1113 and 1150.

Laterite Laterites form in hot, wet tropical areas. Chemical weathering is intense under such conditions. So laterites are usually deeper than soils that develop over a similar period in temperate areas. The large quantity of water that filters through these soils removes most of the calcite and silica. Iron oxide and aluminum oxide are left behind. The iron oxide gives laterite a distinctive orange or red color.

When dried, laterite becomes very hard and practically waterproof. For centuries, people in portions of South and Southeast Asia have made bricks by digging up laterite, shaping it, and allowing it to harden in the sun. Ancient structures built of laterite bricks, such as the one shown in Figure 15, are well preserved even today.

Figure 16 Clearing a Tropical Rain Forest in Borneo The laterite soil cannot support agriculture for more than a few years.

Plants that die in a tropical rain forest decompose rapidly because bacterial activity is high in hot and wet climates. As a result, laterite contains almost no organic matter. The roots of living rain forest plants quickly absorb the nutrients released during decomposition. So, even though the vegetation may be dense, the soil itself contains few available nutrients. Most of the nutrients in a tropical rain forest are present in the plants themselves.

Today, large areas of tropical rain forest are being cleared for timber and to provide land for agriculture, as shown in Figure 16. However, laterite is one of the poorest soils for agriculture. Because laterite contains little organic matter and few nutrients, it cannot nourish crops. The nutrients it does have are soon washed out by the plentiful rainwater that filters through the soil. In only a few years, the soil in a freshly cleared area may be completely useless for growing crops. Without trees or crop plants to anchor the soil and shield the ground from the full force of heavy rains, the soil erodes quickly.

 **Reading Checkpoint** *Why is the soil in a tropical rain forest poorly suited for agriculture?*

Soil Erosion

Soils are just a tiny fraction of all Earth materials, yet they are a vital resource. Because soils are necessary for the growth of rooted plants, they are the foundation of the human life-support system. However, soils are among our most abused resources. The loss of fertile topsoil is a growing problem as human activities disturb more of Earth's surface.

Figure 17 Soil Erosion by Raindrops A raindrop can splash soil particles more than a meter away from where it strikes the soil.

How Water Erodes Soil Soil erosion is a natural part of the constant recycling of Earth materials known as the rock cycle. Water, wind, and other agents move soil from one place to another. Every time it rains, raindrops strike the soil surface with surprising force. As Figure 17 shows, each drop acts like a tiny bomb, blasting soil particles off the surface. Water flowing across the surface then carries away the dislodged particles. Because thin sheets of water move the soil particles, this process is called sheet erosion.

After flowing as a thin sheet for a short distance, the water forms tiny streams called rills. As more water enters the rills, they erode the soil further, creating trenches known as gullies, like those shown in Figure 18. Although most dislodged soil particles do not move far during each rainfall, large quantities eventually make their way downslope to a stream. The stream transports these soil particles, which are now called sediment, and eventually deposits them.

Rates of Erosion In the past, soil eroded more slowly than it does today because more land was covered by trees, grasses, and other plants. ⊙ However, human activities that remove natural vegetation, such as farming, logging, and construction, have greatly accelerated erosion. Without plants, soil is more easily carried away by wind and water.

Scientists can estimate the rate of erosion due to water by measuring the amount of sediment in rivers. These estimates indicate that before humans appeared, rivers carried about 9 trillion kg of sediment to the oceans each year. In contrast, the amount of sediment currently transported to the sea by rivers is about 24 trillion kg per year.

Wind generally erodes soil much more slowly than water does. During a prolonged drought, however, strong winds can remove large quantities of soil from unprotected fields. That's exactly what happened during the 1930s in the part of the Great Plains that came to be known as the Dust Bowl.

The rate of soil erosion depends on soil characteristics and on factors such as climate, slope, and type of vegetation. In many regions, including about one-third of the world's croplands, soil is eroding faster than it is being formed. This results in lower productivity, poorer crop quality, and a threatened world food supply.

Figure 18 Gullies The unprotected soil in this field in southern Colombia is deeply eroded.

 **Reading Checkpoint** *How do human activities affect rates of erosion?*

Sediment Deposition Another problem caused by excessive soil erosion is the deposition of sediment. Rivers that accumulate sediment must be dredged to remain open for shipping. As sediment settles in reservoirs, they become less useful for storing water, controlling floods, and generating electricity.

Some sediments are contaminated with agricultural pesticides. When these chemicals enter a river or lake, they endanger organisms that live in or use the water, including humans. Sediments also contain soil nutrients, which may come from natural processes and from added fertilizers. Excessive nutrient levels in lakes stimulate the growth of algae and plants. This can accelerate a process that eventually leads to the early death of the lake.

Controlling Erosion Although we cannot completely eliminate soil erosion, we can significantly slow it by using soil conservation measures. You have seen how a misunderstanding of the composition of rain forest soil has led to the destruction of millions of acres leaving only severely leached, unproductive land. Conservation measures include steps taken to preserve environments and protect the land. These measures include planting rows of trees called windbreaks, terracing hillsides, plowing along the contours of hills, and rotating crops. Preserving fertile soil is essential to feeding the world's rapidly growing population.

Section 5.2 Assessment

Reviewing Concepts

1. List the four major components of soil.
2. How does climate affect soil formation?
3. Describe the contents of the three soil horizons found in most mature soils.
4. What climates are usually associated with pedalfer, pedocal, and laterite?
5. How can an activity such as road construction affect the rate of soil erosion?

Critical Thinking

6. **Relating Cause and Effect** A gardener notices that rain showers usually produce long-lasting puddles on the soil in her garden. Is it more likely that the soil contains too much sand or too much clay? Explain.

7. **Predicting** Which activity would cause more sediment to be deposited in a river that flows through a gently sloping valley—cultivating the valley or cultivating the hills that surround the valley? Explain.

Connecting Concepts

Weathering and Soil Using what you learned about chemical weathering in Section 5.1, explain why the soils formed in a hot, wet climate and a cold, dry climate are different.

5.3 Mass Movements

Reading Focus

Key Concepts

- What is mass movement?
- What factors trigger mass movements?
- How do geologists classify mass movements?

Vocabulary

- mass movement
- rockfall
- rockslide
- slump
- mudflow
- earthflow
- creep

Reading Strategy

Previewing Copy the table. Before you read the section, rewrite the green topic headings as *what* questions. As you read, write an answer to each question.

Question	Answer
a. _____?_____	b. _____?_____
c. _____?_____	d. _____?_____

Earth's land surface consists of slopes, some steep and others very gradual. While most slopes appear stable, they are always changing. The force of gravity causes material to move downslope. **The transfer of rock and soil downslope due to gravity is called mass movement.** Some types of mass movement are so slow that you cannot see them. Others, such as landslides like the one illustrated in Figure 19, are very sudden.

The combined actions of weathering and mass movement produce most landforms. Once weathering weakens and breaks rock apart, mass movement moves the debris downslope. There a stream usually carries it away. Stream valleys are the most common of Earth's landforms.

Q *Are snow avalanches a type of mass movement?*

A Yes. These thundering downslope movements of snow and ice can also transport large quantities of rock, soil, and trees. About 10,000 snow avalanches occur each year in the mountainous western United States. Besides damaging buildings and roads at the bottom of slopes, they are especially dangerous to skiers. In an average year, snow avalanches claim between 15 and 25 lives in the United States and Canada. Snow avalanches are a growing problem as more people participate in winter sports and recreation.

Figure 19 Landslide This home in Pacific Palisades, California, was destroyed by a landslide triggered by the January 1994 Northridge earthquake.

Figure 20 Mudflow In October 1998, heavy rains from Hurricane Mitch led to massive mudflows in Central America.
Formulating Hypotheses *What human activities before the rains might have contributed to the mudflows?*

Triggers of Mass Movements

Gravity is the force behind mass movements. Several factors make slopes more susceptible to the pull of gravity. **Among the factors that commonly trigger mass movements are saturation of surface materials with water, oversteepening of slopes, removal of vegetation, and earthquakes.**

Water Heavy rains and rapid melting of snow can trigger mass movement by saturating surface materials with water. This was the case when torrential downpours associated with Hurricane Mitch caused devastating mudflows, as shown in Figure 20. When the pores in sediment become filled with water, the particles slide past one another more easily. You can demonstrate this effect with sand. If you add water until the sand becomes slightly moist, the sand grains will stick together. However, if you add enough water to fill all the pores between the sand grains, the sand-water mixture will ooze downhill. Clay also becomes very slick when it is wet.

Oversteepened Slopes Loose soil particles can maintain a relatively stable slope up to a certain angle. That angle ranges from about 25 to 40 degrees, depending on the size and shape of the particles. If the steepness of a slope exceeds the stable angle, mass movements become more likely. Such slopes are said to be oversteepened. An oversteepened slope can result when a stream undercuts a valley wall or waves pound against the base of a cliff. People may also create oversteepened slopes by excavating during the construction of roads and buildings.

Reading Checkpoint *How do oversteepened slopes trigger mass movements?*

Removal of Vegetation Plants make slopes more stable because their root systems bind soil and regolith together. When plants are removed by forest fires or by human activities such as logging or farming, the likelihood of mass movement increases. An example that illustrates the stabilizing effect of plants occurred several decades ago on steep slopes near Menton, France. Farmers replaced olive trees, which have deep roots, with carnations, a more profitable but shallow-rooted crop. Planting carnations made the slopes less stable. A landslide on one of the slopes killed 11 people.

Earthquakes Earthquakes are one of the most dramatic triggers of mass movements. An earthquake and its aftershocks can dislodge enormous amounts of rock and unconsolidated material. In many areas, these mass movements cause more damage than the ground vibrations themselves. The landslide shown in Figure 19 was triggered by an earthquake.

Types of Mass Movements

Geologists classify mass movements based on the kind of material that moves, how it moves, and the speed of movement. We'll consider five basic types of mass movement: rockfalls, slides, slumps, flows, and creep.

Rockfalls A **rockfall** occurs when rocks or rock fragments fall freely through the air. This type of mass movement is common on slopes that are too steep for loose material to remain on the surface. Many rockfalls result from the mechanical weathering of rock caused by freeze-thaw cycles or plant roots. Rockfalls sometimes trigger other mass movements.

Slides In a slide, a block of material moves suddenly along a flat, inclined surface. Slides that include segments of bedrock are called **rockslides.** They often occur in high mountain areas such as the Andes, Alps, and Canadian Rockies. Rockslides are among the fastest mass movements, reaching speeds of over 200 km per hour. Some rockslides, such as the one shown in Figure 21, are triggered by rain or melting snow.

Figure 21 Rockslide The scar on the side of this mountain in northwestern Wyoming was made by an enormous rockslide that happened more than 75 years ago. The debris in the slide formed a dam 70 m high across the Gros Ventre River.

Figure 22 Slump Heavy rains triggered this slump in Santa Barbara, California. Notice the crescent-shaped cliff just above the slump.

Slumps A **slump** is the downward movement of a block of material along a curved surface. The material in a slump usually does not travel very fast or very far. As the block moves, its upper surface sometimes tilts backward. Slumps leave a crescent-shaped cliff just above the slump, which you can see in Figure 22. They are common on oversteepened slopes where the soil contains thick accumulations of clay.

Flows Flows are mass movements of material containing a large amount of water, which move downslope as a thick fluid. Flows that move quickly, called **mudflows,** are common in semiarid mountainous regions, such as parts of southern California. In these regions, protective vegetation is sparse. A heavy downpour or rapid snowmelt can flood canyons with a mixture of soil, rock, and water. The mixture may have the consistency of wet concrete. It follows the contours of the canyon, taking large boulders and trees along with it. As you saw in Figure 20, mudflows in populated areas are very dangerous and destructive. In 1988, a massive mudflow triggered by the eruption of Nevado del Ruiz, a volcano in Colombia, killed 25,000 people.

Earthflows are flows that move relatively slowly—from about a millimeter per day to several meters per day. Their movement may continue for years. Earthflows occur most often on hillsides in wet regions. When water saturates the soil and regolith on a hillside, the material breaks away, forming a tongue-shaped mass like the one shown in Figure 23. Earthflows range in size from a few meters long and less than 1 m deep to over 1 km long and more than 10 m deep.

 **Reading Checkpoint** *How do mudflows differ from earthflows?*

Figure 23 Earthflow This small, tongue-shaped mass movement occurred on a newly formed slope along a recently built highway. **Comparing and Contrasting** *Which other type of mass movement looks most similar to an earthflow?*

Creep The slowest type of mass movement is **creep**, which usually travels only a few millimeters or centimeters per year. One factor that contributes to creep is alternating between freezing and thawing, as Figure 24A shows. Freezing expands the water in soil, lifting soil particles at right angles to the slope. Thawing causes contraction, which allows the particles to fall back to a slightly lower level. Each freeze-thaw cycle moves the particles a short distance downhill.

Because creep is so slow, you cannot observe it directly as it happens. However, the effects of creep are easy to recognize. As Figure 24B shows, creep causes structures that were once vertical to tilt downhill. Creep can also displace fences and crack walls and underground pipes.

Figure 24 Creep A Repeated expansion and contraction of the soil on a slope results in a gradual downhill movement of the soil. **B** Years of creep have caused these gravestones to tilt. **Inferring** *In which direction is creep occurring in this photograph?*

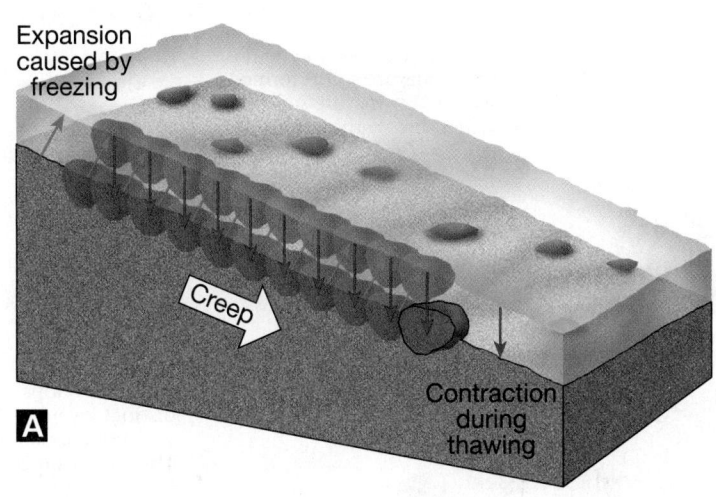

Expansion caused by freezing

Creep

Contraction during thawing

A

B

Section 5.3 Assessment

Reviewing Concepts

1. What is mass movement?
2. How does water trigger mass movements?
3. How does a rockfall differ from a rockslide?
4. What is the slowest type of mass movement?

Critical Thinking

5. **Applying Concepts** When highway engineers build a road in a mountainous area, they insert drainage pipes into the slopes alongside the road. Explain why.

6. **Making Judgments** Which mass movement—a slump, a mudflow, or an earthflow—poses the greatest risk to human life? Explain your reasoning.

Writing in Science

Explanatory Paragraph Explain how people can make mass movements more likely. Include two examples in your explanatory paragraph.

Soil

On the surface of the Earth, **soil** is the thin layer of loose material in which plants grow. Soil consists partly of mineral particles, and partly of **organic matter** derived from living plants and animals and their remains. Other key components of soil are water and air. Complex natural processes build soil over many thousands of years. The process begins when rock is broken down by weathering. Next, plants take root in the weathered rock. Then, organic material in the soil, called **humus,** is formed from decaying vegetation and animals. Different types of soil occur because of variations in climate, types of vegetation, and types of rock. In large countries like Russia, there is a wide variety of soil types.

SOIL FORMATION
Typically, the first step in soil building is the development of **regolith,** or weathered rock. Next, immature soil is formed as organic material begins to decay. Finally, mature soil supports abundant life both above and below the surface.

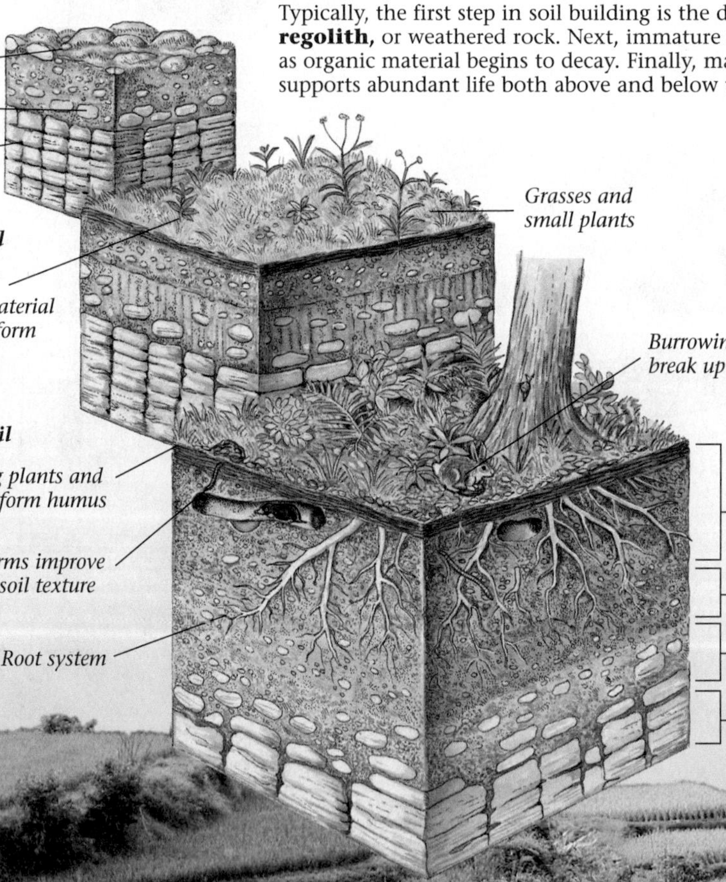

1. Regolith

Moss and lichen

Rock fragments

Bedrock

2. Immature soil

A layer of
organic material
begins to form

*Grasses and
small plants*

*Burrowing animals
break up the soil*

SOIL HORIZONS
As soil develops, distinct layers, called **soil horizons,** appear. The A horizon is topsoil that is rich in minerals and organic matter. The B horizon is poorer in humus but rich in minerals washed down from above. Further below lie the C horizon of weathered rock and, below that, unweathered bedrock.

3. Mature soil

*Decaying plants and
animals form humus*

*Worms improve
the soil texture*

Root system

A horizon
Topsoil

B horizon
Subsoil

C horizon
Rock fragments

Bedrock

CREEP
In a process called **creep,** soil moves gradually and constantly downhill because of gravity. Trees on a slope often show the effects of this process. Terrace farming is an agricultural method used to slow the process of creep.

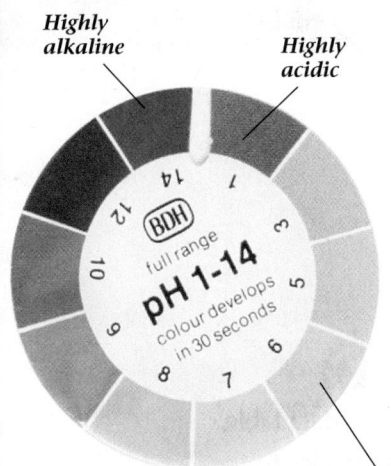

Highly alkaline

Highly acidic

Neutral

SOIL pH
The pH scale measures acidity or alkalinity on a scale of 0 to 14. When a chemical solution called an indicator is added to a soil sample, the indicator changes color, showing the soil's pH. Most plants thrive only in soils with a pH between 5 and 9.

Clay soil

Silty soil

SOIL TEXTURE
Soil texture depends on the size and nature of soil particles. Clay soils have the smallest grains, silty soils have medium-sized grains, and sandy soils have the largest grains. **Loam,** a mixture of clay, silt, and sand, is the best soil for agriculture.

Sandy soil

Wildflowers

Grass

Snail

Slug

Decomposing leaf

Roots

Spodosol is a sandy soil found in northern coniferous forests.

LIFE IN THE SOIL
Soil is home to a vast array of life, including microorganisms, ants, termites, worms, and rodents. Fungi and bacteria convert dead plant and animal matter into chemicals that enrich the soil. Burrowing creatures improve the soil by mixing it.

Aridisols, found in deserts, have high concentrations of salts

ASSESSMENT

1. **Key Terms** Define **(a)** soil, **(b)** organic matter, **(c)** humus, **(d)** regolith, **(e)** soil horizon, **(f)** creep, **(g)** loam.

2. **Physical Processes** Describe the three stages of soil formation.

3. **Physical Characteristics** How do various types of soil differ from one another?

4. **Natural Resources** What soil characteristics are most beneficial for agriculture?

5. **Critical Thinking Making Comparisons** Study the cross-sections of spodosol and aridisol. **(a)** How are they alike? **(b)** How do they differ? **(c)** Do research to learn more about their different characteristics.

SOIL CLASSIFICATION
Some experts recognize thousands of different soil types. The U.S. Department of Agriculture has devised a comprehensive soil classification system for categorizing soils. Each type of soil can be identified by the characteristics of its horizons.

Effect of Temperature on Chemical Weathering

Water is the most important agent of chemical weathering. One way water promotes chemical weathering is by reacting with the minerals in rocks. In this lab, you will model the effect of temperature on chemical weathering by measuring the rate at which antacid tablets dissolve in water at different temperatures. These tablets contain calcium carbonate, the mineral found in rocks such as limestone and marble.

Problem
How does temperature affect the rate of chemical weathering?

Materials
- 250-mL beaker
- thermometer
- hot water (40–50°C)
- ice
- 5 antacid tablets
- stopwatch
- graph paper

Skills
Measuring, Using Tables and Graphs, Drawing Conclusions, Inferring

Procedure

1. On a sheet of paper, copy the data table.

2. Add a mixture of hot water and ice to the beaker. Use the thermometer to measure the temperature of the mixture. Add either more hot water or more ice until the temperature is between 0°C and 10°C. The total volume of the mixture should be about 200 mL.

3. When the temperature is within the correct range, remove any remaining ice from the beaker. Record the starting temperature of the water in your data table. Remove the thermometer from the beaker.

4. Drop an antacid tablet into the beaker. Start the stopwatch as soon as the tablet enters the water. Stop the stopwatch when the tablet has completely dissolved and no traces of the tablet are visible. (Don't wait for the bubbling to stop.) Record the time in your data table.

5. Place the thermometer in the beaker and wait for the temperature of the water to stabilize. Record the final temperature of the water in your data table.

Data Table			
Starting Temperature (°C)	Dissolving Time(s)	Final Temperature (°C)	Average Temperature (°C)

6. Calculate the average temperature by adding the starting and final temperatures and dividing by 2. Record the result in your data table.

7. Repeat Steps 2 through 6 four more times, once at each of the following temperature ranges: 10–20°C, 20–30°C, 30–40°C, and 40–50°C. Adjust the relative amounts of hot water and ice to produce the correct water temperatures. The total volume of water and ice should always be about 200 mL.

8. On graph paper, make a graph with average temperature on the x-axis and dissolving time on the y-axis. Plot your data on the graph. Draw a smooth curve through the data points.

Analyze and Conclude

1. **Analyzing Data** At which temperature did the antacid tablet dissolve most rapidly?

2. **Analyzing Data** At which temperature did the antacid tablet dissolve most slowly?

3. **Drawing Conclusions** What is the relationship between temperature and the rate at which antacid tablets react with water?

4. **Formulating Hypotheses** Based on your observations, form a hypothesis about the relationship between temperature and the rate of chemical weathering.

5. **Designing Experiments** How could you test your hypothesis?

6. **Predicting** What would your results have been if you had ground each tablet into a fine powder before dropping it into the water? Would your conclusion be the same or different? Explain.

7. **Inferring** Would a limestone building weather more rapidly in Homer, Alaska, or in Honolulu, Hawaii? (Both cities receive about the same amount of precipitation in an average year.) Explain your reasoning.

8. **Communicating** Write a lab report in which you explain your procedures in this lab and discuss whether or not your data supported your hypotheses. In your report, identify the manipulated variable and the responding variable in this experiment.

Go Further Look for signs of chemical weathering on old stone buildings in your community. Consult your local library or historical society to find out when the buildings were constructed and what type of stone they are made of.

Study Guide

5.1 Weathering

Key Concepts

- Mechanical weathering occurs when physical forces break rock into smaller and smaller pieces without changing the rock's mineral composition.
- In nature, three physical processes are especially important causes of mechanical weathering: frost wedging, unloading, and biological activity.
- Chemical weathering is the transformation of rock into one or more new compounds.
- Two factors that affect the rate of weathering are rock characteristics and climate.

Vocabulary

mechanical weathering, *p. 126;* frost wedging, *p. 127;* talus, *p. 127;* exfoliation, *p. 128;* chemical weathering, *p. 129*

5.2 Soil

Key Concepts

- Soil is the part of the regolith that supports the growth of plants.
- Soil has four major components: mineral matter, or broken down rock; organic matter, or humus, which is the decayed remains of organisms; water; and air.
- The most important factors in soil formation are parent material, time, climate, organisms, and slope.
- Soil varies in composition, texture, structure, and color at different depths.
- Three common types of soil are pedalfer, pedocal, and laterite.
- Human activities that remove natural vegetation, such as farming, logging, and construction, have greatly accelerated erosion.

Vocabulary

regolith, *p. 133;* soil, *p. 133;* soil horizon, *p. 138;* soil profile, *p. 138;* pedalfer, *p. 139;* pedocal, *p. 139;* laterite, *p. 139*

5.3 Mass Movements

Key Concepts

- The transfer of rock and soil downslope due to gravity is called mass movement.
- Among the factors that commonly trigger mass movements are saturation of surface materials with water, oversteepening of slopes, removal of vegetation, and earthquakes.
- Geologists classify mass movements based on the kind of material that moves, how it moves, and the speed of movement.

Vocabulary

mass movement, *p. 143;* rockfall, *p. 145;* rockslide, *p. 145;* slump, *p. 146;* mudflow, *p. 146;* earthflow, *p. 146;* creep, *p. 147*

Reviewing Content

Choose the letter that best answers the question or completes the statement.

1. The breaking down and changing of rocks at or near Earth's surface is called
   a. mass movement.   b. sheet erosion.
   c. weathering.   d. uplift.

2. Which of the following is NOT a cause of mechanical weathering?
   a. dissolving   b. frost wedging
   c. unloading   d. burrowing

3. In which type of climate does chemical weathering occur most rapidly?
   a. cold, dry   b. cold, wet
   c. warm, dry   d. warm, wet

4. Organic matter in soil is also called
   a. regolith.   b. humus.
   c. talus.   d. loam.

5. A soil's texture is determined by its
   a. water content.
   b. mineral composition.
   c. thickness.
   d. particle sizes.

6. In soils with distinct soil horizons, the topmost zone is the
   a. parent material. b. A horizon.
   c. B horizon.   d. C horizon.

7. Human activities that remove plants covering the soil cause soil erosion to
   a. decrease.
   b. stay the same.
   c. increase.
   d. increase briefly, then stop.

8. Which of the following does NOT usually trigger mass movements?
   a. growth of native vegetation on slopes
   b. formation of oversteepened slopes
   c. saturation of surface materials with water
   d. vibration of the ground during an earthquake

9. When a block of material moves downward along a curved surface, the process is called
   a. a rockslide.   b. a rockfall.
   c. a slump.   d. an earthflow.

10. Which of the following best describes a mudflow?
    a. movement too slow to be observed directly
    b. material moving downslope as a thick fluid
    c. material falling freely through the air
    d. sudden movement along a flat, inclined surface

Understanding Concepts

11. What happens to the total surface area of the cubes in the process shown below? What type of weathering does this process represent?

12. What is exfoliation? Give an example of a feature produced by exfoliation.

13. How does mechanical weathering promote chemical weathering?

14. How is carbonic acid formed in nature? What happens when this acid reacts with feldspar?

15. Which factor has the greatest effect on soil formation? Explain.

16. How does slope affect the formation of soil?

17. Describe the major characteristics of A, B, and C horizons.

18. Distinguish between pedalfer and pedocal.

19. List three negative effects of soil erosion.

20. Explain how weathering and mass movement together produce most landforms.

21. What is the force behind mass movements? What other factors can trigger mass movements?

22. Distinguish between rockfalls and rockslides.

23. Distinguish between mudflows and earthflows.

24. How do freezing and thawing contribute to creep?

Critical Thinking

25. Inferring Roads in northern states such as Maine and Michigan need to be repaired more often than roads in southern states such as Florida and Louisiana. What form of mechanical weathering could account for this?

26. Comparing and Contrasting How do the effects of mechanical weathering on rock differ from the effects of chemical weathering?

27. Predicting Granite and marble are exposed at the surface in a hot, wet region. Which of the rocks will weather more rapidly? Why?

28. Applying Concepts Heat speeds up most chemical reactions. Why then does chemical weathering happen slowly in a hot desert?

29. Making Judgments Do you think that soil erosion is an artificial byproduct of careless land use by humans? Explain.

Analyzing Data

Use the diagram below to answer Questions 30–32.

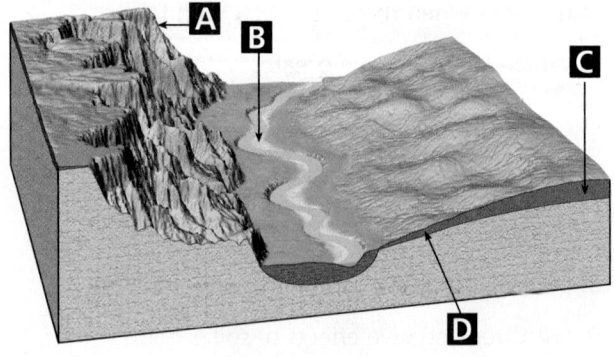

30. Comparing and Contrasting Compare the thickness of the soil in the areas labeled A and B.

31. Interpreting Diagrams What name is given to the soil that develops in the area labeled B? In the area labeled C?

32. Inferring Why is the soil in the area labeled D thinner than the soil in the area labeled C?

Concepts in Action

33. Using Analogies Explain how the following scenario is analogous to weathering: One evening you place a sealed jar full of water in a freezer. The next morning, the water has turned to ice and the jar is cracked.

34. Applying Concepts A committee has been established to design a stone memorial commemorating 100 soldiers who died in battle. The committee decides to use a large block of marble for the memorial. Considering only the memorial's durability, would it be better to use the whole block as a single memorial for all 100 soldiers or to divide it into 100 blocks of equal size, one for each soldier?

35. Classifying How would you determine the texture of the soil in your area?

36. Making Judgments Should a homeowner in a dry, mountainous area remove all vegetation from surrounding slopes to reduce fire danger? Explain why or why not.

37. Writing in Science Write a paragraph describing one type of mass movement. Include a specific example of a time when such a mass movement made the news.

Performance-Based Assessment

Observing Look for places in your community where people have taken specific actions to reduce erosion. Such places may include sites where buildings are being constructed or roads are being built or repaired. Make a list of each action and explain how it is intended to reduce erosion.

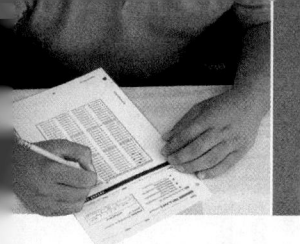

Standardized Test Prep

Watch for Qualifiers
The words *best* and *least* are examples of qualifiers. If a question contains a qualifier, more than one answer will contain correct information. However, only one answer will be complete and correct for the question asked. Look at the question below. Eliminate any answers that are clearly incorrect. Then choose the remaining answer that offers the best explanation for the question asked.

Which mass movement is LEAST dangerous to people walking below a slope?
(A) rockslide
(B) rockfall
(C) creep
(D) mudflow

(Answer: C)

Choose the letter that best answers the question or completes the statement.

1. Which of the following best describes regolith?
  (A) a soil that contains large amounts of iron oxide and aluminum-rich clays
  (B) a mixture of mineral matter, organic matter, water, and air
  (C) a large pile of rock fragments at the base of a steep cliff
  (D) the layer of rock and mineral fragments that covers nearly all of Earth's land surface

2. In which mass movement do rock fragments fall freely through the air?
  (A) rockslide
  (B) rockfall
  (C) slump
  (D) earthflow

Use the diagram below to answer Questions 3 and 4.

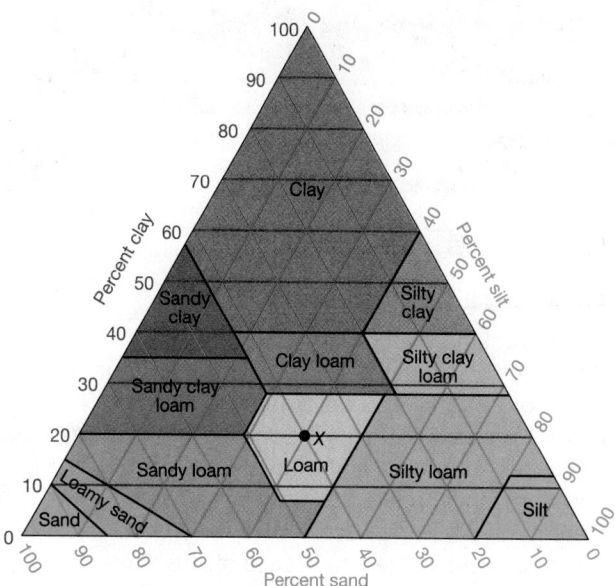

3. What are the percentages of clay, silt, and sand in the soil at the point labeled X?
  (A) 60 percent clay, 80 percent silt, and 60 percent sand
  (B) 0 percent clay, 40 percent silt, and 60 percent sand
  (C) 20 percent clay, 40 percent silt, and 40 percent sand
  (D) 50 percent clay, 40 percent silt, and 10 percent sand

4. The name given to soil that contains 60 percent clay, 20 percent silt, and 20 percent sand is
  (A) clay.   (B) loam.
  (C) silty clay loam.   (D) sandy loam.

Answer the following questions in complete sentences.

5. How does the surface area of an exposed rock affect its rate of weathering?

6. What role does acid precipitation play in weathering?

7. When a tropical rain forest is cleared, why does the soil usually become useless for growing crops after only a few years?

8. Explain how water can trigger an earthflow.

CHAPTER 6

Running Water and Groundwater

21st Century Learning

Health Literacy

How safe is your water?

Clean drinking water is key to good health. Research the source of drinking water in your local community, and determine how the water is treated and what tests are done before it reaches your tap. Next, find a news story about an illness related to drinking water. Determine what measures could have been taken to prevent the occurrence of this illness, and present your findings to the class in the form of a report, making sure to cite your sources.

Exploration Lab
Investigating the Permeability of Soils

People and the Environment
The Ogallala Aquifer—How Long Will the Water Last?

GEODe EARTH SCIENCE
Sculpturing Earth's Surface
↳ Hydrologic Cycle
Running Water
Groundwater

This photograph shows Lost Yak Rapids on Chile's Rio Bio Bio.

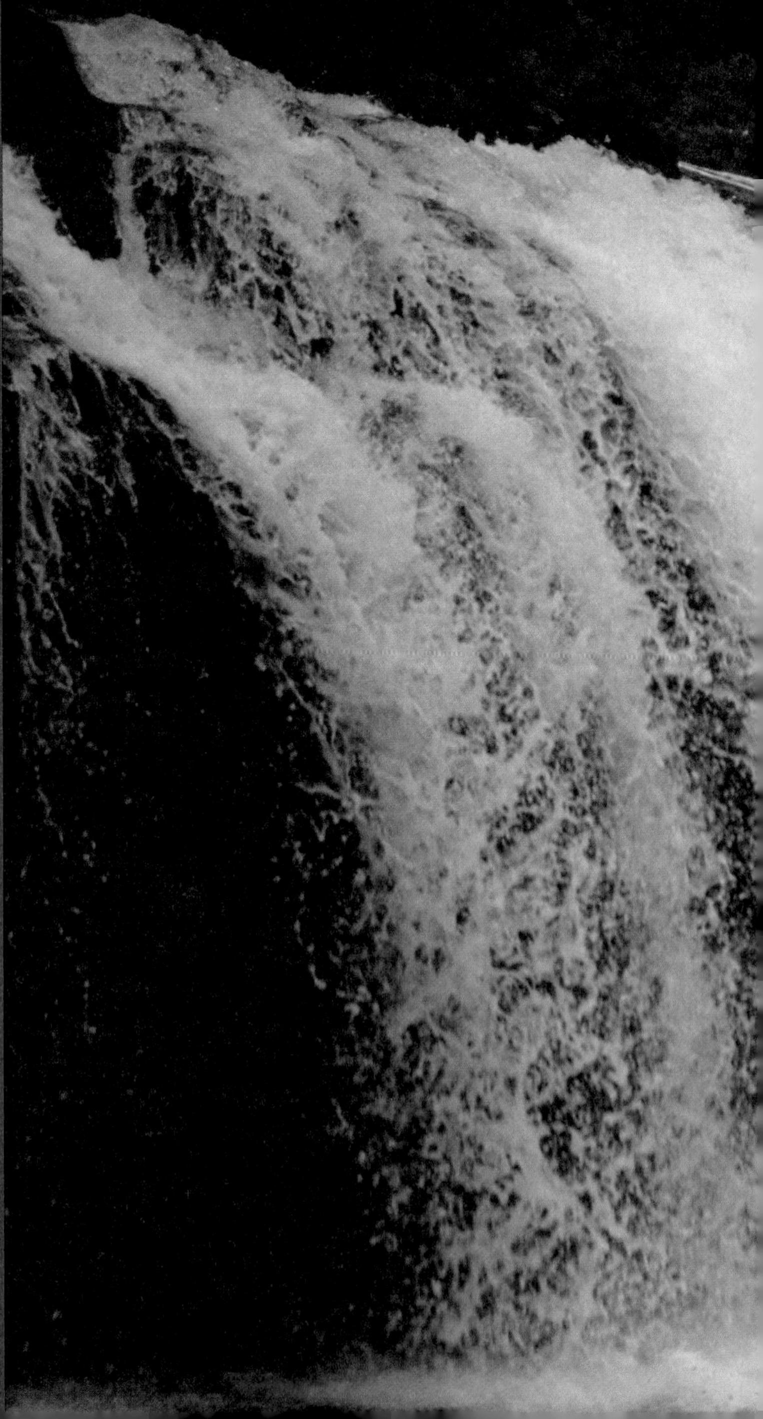

Chapter Preview

Inquiry ⟩ Activity

How Do Local Bodies of Water Affect Your Community?

Procedure

1. Identify an important body of water in or near your community. It could be a river, lake, dam reservoir, stream, ocean, or estuary.

2. List the ways the people of your community use this body of water.

3. Observe and record the ways this body of water has affected (or still affects) the local landscape.

Think About it

1. **Classifying** Is the body of water used for recreation (boating, swimming, fishing), for industry and business (transportation or waste disposal for factories and power plants), for drinking water, or a combination of these purposes?

2. **Inferring** If your community uses this body of water as a source of drinking water, how might that affect other possible uses of the water?

3. **Drawing Conclusions** Has this body of water shaped the landscape in the area? How?

6.1 Running Water

Reading Focus

Key Concepts

- What is the water cycle?
- What does it mean to say Earth's water cycle is balanced?
- What is the most important factor in determining the power of a stream to erode and transport material?
- How do gradient and discharge change between a stream's source and its mouth?
- What is a stream's base level?

Vocabulary

- water cycle
- infiltration
- transpiration
- gradient
- stream channel
- discharge
- tributary
- base level
- meander

Reading Strategy

Building Vocabulary Copy the table. As you read the section, define in your own words each vocabulary term listed in the table.

Vocabulary Term	Definition
Water cycle	?
Infiltration	?
Transpiration	?

Water is everywhere on Earth—oceans, glaciers, rivers, lakes, air, soil, and living tissue. All of these reservoirs make up Earth's hydrosphere. Most of it—about 97.2 percent—is stored in oceans, as Figure 1 shows. Ice sheets and glaciers account for another 2.15 percent, leaving only 0.65 percent to be divided among lakes, streams, groundwater, and the atmosphere. The water found in glaciers, ice sheets, lakes, streams, groundwater, and the atmosphere may seem like a tiny percent of Earth's water, but the actual quantities are great.

The Water Cycle

Water constantly moves among the oceans, the atmosphere, the solid Earth, and the biosphere. This unending circulation of Earth's water supply is the water cycle. This cycle is possible because water readily changes from one state of matter—solid, liquid, or gas—to another at temperatures and pressures common on Earth's surface.

The water cycle, shown in Figure 2, is a gigantic worldwide system powered by energy from the sun and by gravity. Water evaporates into the atmosphere from the ocean, and to a lesser extent from the continents. Winds transport this moisture-rich air until conditions cause the moisture to condense into clouds. Precipitation—rain and snow— then falls to Earth. Precipitation that falls into oceans has completed

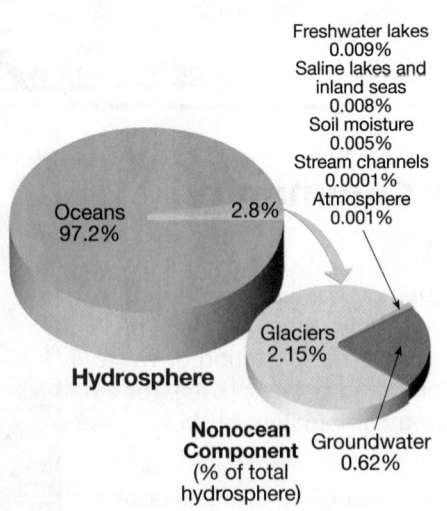

Figure 1 Distribution of Earth's Water
Using Graphs *What percentage of Earth's water is not held in its oceans?*

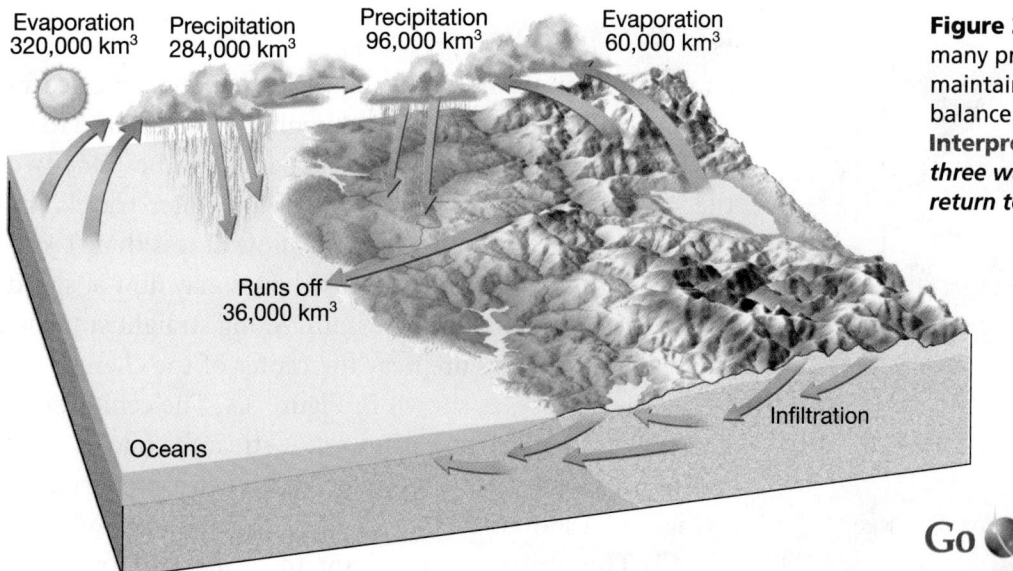

Evaporation
320,000 km³

Precipitation
284,000 km³

Precipitation
96,000 km³

Evaporation
60,000 km³

Runs off
36,000 km³

Oceans

Infiltration

Figure 2 The Water Cycle The many processes of the water cycle maintain Earth's overall water balance.
Interpreting Diagrams *In which three ways does precipitation return to oceans?*

Go **O**nline
active art

For: Water Cycle activity
Visit: PHSchool.com
Web Code: czp-2061

one full cycle and is ready to begin another. However, water that falls on land must make its way back to the ocean to complete the full cycle.

What happens to precipitation that falls on land? Some of it slowly soaks into the ground through infiltration. **Infiltration** is the movement of surface water into rock or soil through cracks and pore spaces. The water gradually moves through the land and actually seeps into lakes, streams, or the ocean. When the rate of rainfall exceeds Earth's ability to absorb it, the excess water flows over the surface into lakes and streams in a process called runoff. Much of that runoff returns to the atmosphere because of evaporation from the soil, lakes, and streams. Plants also absorb water and release it into the atmosphere through **transpiration.**

When precipitation falls in very cold areas—at high elevations or high latitudes—the water may not immediately soak in, run off, or evaporate. Instead, it may become part of a glacier. Glaciers store large amounts of water on land. If present-day glaciers were to melt and release all their water, ocean levels would rise by several dozen meters.

 Reading Checkpoint   *What is infiltration?*

Earth's Water Balance

Even with all these processes occurring, Earth's water cycle is balanced. **Balance in the water cycle means the average annual precipitation over Earth equals the amount of water that evaporates.** There are local imbalances. For example, precipitation exceeds evaporation over continents. Over oceans, evaporation exceeds precipitation. However, the fact that the level of world oceans is not changing very much indicates the system is balanced.

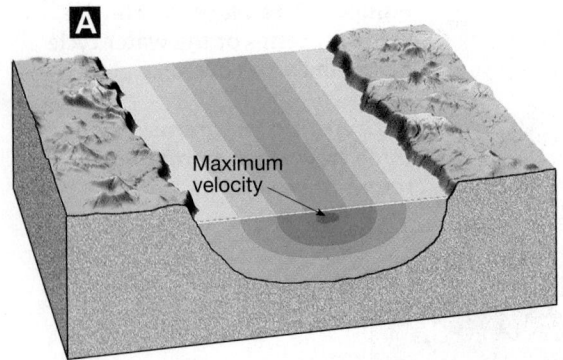

A

Maximum velocity

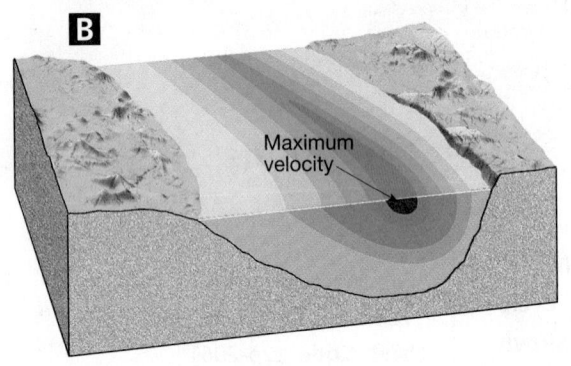

B

Maximum velocity

Figure 3 A Along straight stretches, stream velocity is highest at the center of the channel. **B** When a stream curves, its zone of maximum speed shifts toward the outer bank.
Interpreting Diagrams *How does velocity change with depth in the middle of the stream?*

Streamflow

Gravity influences the way water makes its way to the oceans. Streams and rivers carry water downhill from the land to the sea. The time this journey takes depends on the velocity of the stream. Velocity is the distance that water travels in a period of time. Some slow streams flow at less than 1 kilometer per hour, whereas a few rapid ones may flow at speeds that exceed 30 kilometers per hour. Along straight stretches, the highest velocities are near the center of the channel just below the surface, as shown in Figure 3A. The center of the channel is where friction is lowest. A stream's zone of maximum speed shifts toward its outer bank when a stream curves, as Figure 3B shows.

🔑 **The ability of a stream to erode and transport materials depends largely on its velocity.** Even slight changes in velocity greatly change the amount of sediment that water can transport. Several factors determine the velocity of a stream. They include its gradient; the shape, size, and roughness of its channel; and its discharge.

Gradient Gradient is the slope or steepness of a stream channel. Gradient is usually expressed as the vertical drop of a stream over a certain distance. Portions of the Mississippi River have very low gradients of 10 centimeters per kilometer or less. By contrast, some mountain streams tumble downhill at a rate of more than 40 meters per kilometer. This mountain stream's gradient is 400 times steeper than that of the lower Mississippi. Gradient varies over a stream's length and between streams. The steeper the gradient, the more energy the stream has as it flows downhill. Compare the steep and gentle gradients in Figure 4.

Figure 4 This cross section along the length of a stream shows a steeper gradient upstream, and a gentler gradient downstream.

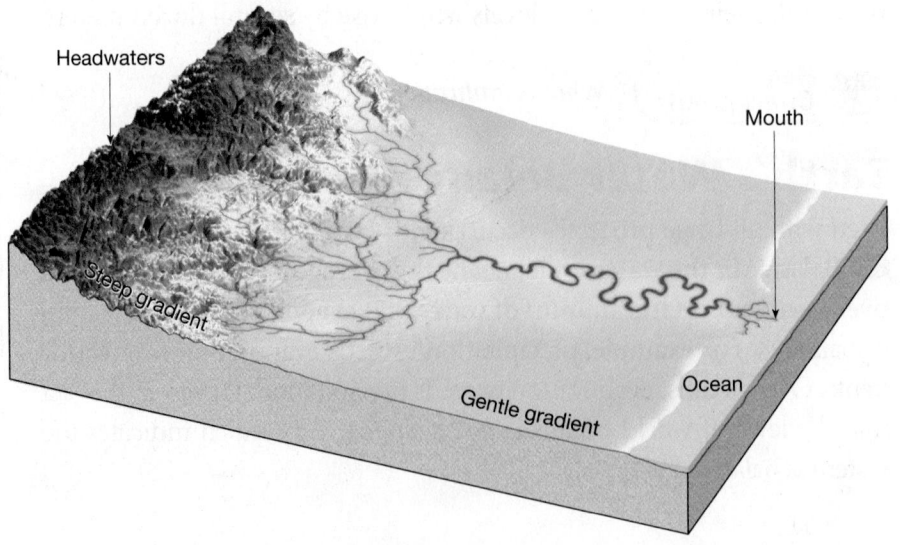

Headwaters

Mouth

Steep gradient

Gentle gradient

Ocean

Channel Characteristics A **stream channel** is the course the water in a stream follows. As the water flows, it encounters friction from the sides and the bottom of its channel. This friction slows its forward movement. The shape, size, and roughness of the channel affect the amount of friction. For example, an irregular channel filled with boulders creates enough turbulence to slow the stream significantly. Water in a smooth channel flows more easily. Larger channels also have more efficient water flow because a smaller proportion of water is in contact with the channel surfaces.

Discharge The **discharge** of a stream is the volume of water flowing past a certain point in a given unit of time. Discharge is usually measured in cubic meters per second. Table 1 lists the world's largest rivers in terms of discharge. The discharges of most rivers change with rainfall and snowmelt. The size and velocity of the stream also changes when discharge changes. The stream channel widens and deepens to handle additional water. As the size of the channel increases, there is less friction and the water flows more swiftly .

Building urban centers around a stream channel can also affect discharge. For example, the magnitude and frequency of floods can increase. The construction of streets, parking lots, and buildings covers soil that once soaked up water. Less water soaks into the ground and runoff increases, especially at times of heavy rainfall. Also, because less water soaks into the ground, the dry season flow of streams is reduced greatly. Urbanization is just one example of how humans can interfere with the normal flow of streams.

 **Reading Checkpoint** *What factors determine the velocity of a stream?*

Table 1 World's Largest Rivers Ranked by Discharge			
Rank	River	Country	Average Discharge m^3/s
1	Amazon	Brazil	212,400
2	Congo	Zaire	39,650
3	Yangtze	China	21,800
4	Brahmaputra	Bangladesh	19,800
5	Ganges	India	18,700
6	Yenisei	Russia	17,400
7	Mississippi	United States	17,300
8	Orinoco	Venezuela	17,000
9	Lena	Russia	15,500
10	Parana	Argentina	14,900

Changes from Upstream to Downstream

One useful way to study a stream is to look at its profile. A profile is a cross-sectional view of a stream from its source, or headwaters, to its mouth—the point downstream where the river empties into another body of water. In Figures 4 and 5, you can see that the most obvious feature of a typical stream profile is a decreasing gradient or slope from its headwaters to its mouth.

While gradient decreases between a stream's headwaters and mouth, discharge increases. The amount of discharge increases because more and more tributaries enter the main channel as it moves downstream. A **tributary** is a stream that empties into another stream. In most humid regions, the groundwater supply adds even more water. As the river moves downstream, its width, depth, and velocity change with the increased volume of water it carries.

The observed increase in the average velocity of the water downstream contradicts what people may think about mountain streams. Most people believe that mountain streams are swift and lowland rivers are slow. Although a mountain stream may look like a violent, gushing flow of water, its average velocity is often less than the average velocity of a river near its mouth.

The difference in velocity is mostly due to the great efficiency of the larger downstream channel. In the headwaters area where the gradient may be steep, water often flows in a small channel over many boulders. The small channel and rough bed increase friction. This increase in friction scatters the water in all directions and slows its movement. However, downstream the channel is usually smoother so that it offers less resistance to flow. The width and depth of the channel also increase toward the mouth to handle the greater discharge. These factors permit the water to flow more rapidly.

 **Reading Checkpoint** *What is a stream profile?*

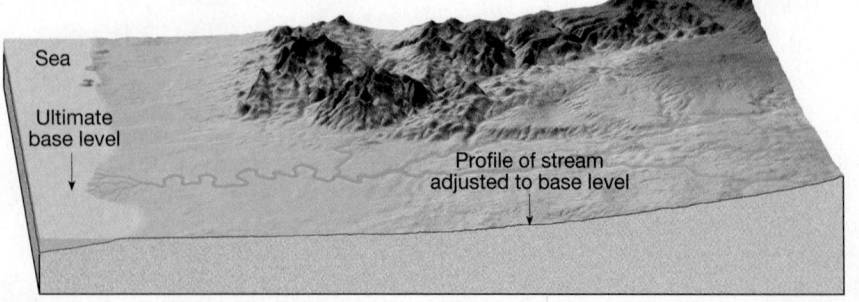

Figure 5 Sea level is the ultimate base level of any stream.

Sea

Ultimate base level

Profile of stream adjusted to base level

Base Level

Streams can't erode their channels endlessly. There is a lower limit to how deep a stream can erode. **Base level is the lowest point to which a stream can erode its channel.** The base level is the level at which the mouth of a stream enters the ocean, a lake, or another stream.

Figure 6 A river in a broad, flat-floored valley near base level often has a channel with many meanders. **Inferring** *Is the river in this picture close to or high above its base level?*

There are two types of base level—ultimate base level and temporary base level. As Figure 5 shows, sea level is the ultimate base level because it's the lowest level that stream erosion can lower the land. Temporary base levels include lakes, resistant layers of rock, and main streams that act as base level for their tributaries. For example, when a stream enters a lake, its velocity quickly approaches zero. Its ability to erode ceases. The lake prevents the stream from eroding below its level at any point upstream from the lake. However, because the outlet of the lake can cut downward and drain the lake, the lake is only a temporary obstacle to the stream's ability to erode its channel.

A stream in a broad, flat-bottomed valley that is near its base level often develops a course with many bends called **meanders,** as shown in Figure 6. If base level dropped or the land was uplifted the river, which is now considerably above base level, would have excess energy and would downcut its channel. The result could be incised meanders—a winding river in a steep, narrow valley, as shown in Figure 7.

Figure 7 When land is gradually uplifted, a meandering river adjusts to being higher above base level by downcutting. The result can be a landscape with incised meanders, such as these in Utah's Canyonlands National Park.

For: Links on river systems
Visit: www.SciLinks.org
Web Code: cjn-2062

Section 6.1 Assessment

Reviewing Concepts

1. What is the water cycle?
2. How is Earth's water cycle balanced?
3. Where is most of Earth's water located?
4. What part does infiltration play in the water cycle?
5. What factor most influences the power of a stream to erode and transport material?
6. How do gradient and discharge change between a stream's headwaters and its mouth?
7. How might lowering base level affect stream erosion?

Critical Thinking

8. **Relating Cause and Effect** What would happen if evaporation exceeded precipitation over the continents and oceans?
9. **Comparing and Contrasting** How does the development of urban areas along streams and rivers affect discharge during periods of heavy rainfall?

Math ▷ Practice

10. A stream that is 27 kilometers long drops 90 meters in elevation from its headwaters to its mouth. What is the stream's gradient?

6.2 The Work of Streams

treams are Earth's most important agents of erosion. They can downcut or erode their channels. They can also transport enormous amounts of sediment. Most of the sediment a stream carries comes from weathering. Weathering produces huge amounts of material that are delivered to the stream by sheet flow, mass movements, and groundwater. Eventually, streams drop much of this material to create many different depositional features.

Erosion

Streams generally erode their channels lifting loose particles by abrasion, grinding, and by dissolving soluble material. When the flow of water is turbulent enough, it can dislodge loose particles from the channel and lift them into the moving water. In this manner, the force of running water rapidly erodes some streambeds and banks. The stronger the current is, the more erosional power it has and the more effectively the water will pick up particles.

Sand and gravel carried in a stream can erode solid rock channels like sandpaper grinds down wood. Moreover, pebbles caught in swirling stream currents can act like cutting tools and bore circular "potholes" into the channel floor.

 **Reading Checkpoint** *What are three ways that streams erode their channels?*

Sediment Transport

Streams transport sediment in three ways.
1. in solution (dissolved load)
2. in suspension (suspended load)
3. scooting or rolling along the bottom (bed load)

Dissolved Load Most of the dissolved load enters streams through groundwater. Some of this load also enters by dissolving rock along the stream's course. The amount of material the stream carries in solution changes depending on climate and the geologic setting. Usually the dissolved load is expressed as parts of dissolved material per million parts of water (parts per million, or ppm). Some rivers may have a dissolved load of 1000 ppm or more. However, the average figure for the world's rivers is estimated at 115 to 120 ppm. Streams supply almost 4 billion metric tons of dissolved substances to the oceans each year.

Suspended Load Most streams carry the largest part of their load in suspension. The visible cloud of sediment suspended in the water is the most obvious portion of a stream's load. Streams usually carry only sand, silt, and clay this way. However, streams also transport larger particles during a flood because water velocity increases. The total amount of material a stream carries in suspension increases dramatically during floods, as shown in Figure 8.

Bed Load Bed load is that part of a stream's load of solid material that is made up of sediment too large to be carried in suspension. These larger, coarser particles move along the bottom, or bed, of the stream channel. The suspended and dissolved loads are always moving. But the bed load moves only when the force of the water is great enough to move the larger particles. The grinding action of the bed load is very important in eroding the stream channel.

Figure 8 During this 1997 flood, the suspended load in the muddy Ohio River is clearly visible. The greatest erosion and sediment transport occur during floods. **Applying Concepts** *What other types of load might account for the muddiness of the river?*

Competence and Capacity The ability of streams to carry a load is determined by two factors: the stream's competence and its capacity. Competence of a stream measures the largest particles it can transport. A stream's competence increases with its velocity. In fact, the competence of a stream increases four times when the velocity doubles.

The **capacity** of a stream is the maximum load it can carry. Capacity is directly related to a stream's discharge. The greater the volume of water in a stream is, the greater its capacity is for carrying sediment.

Figure 9

Movement This map shows the growth of the Mississippi River delta over the past 5,000 to 6,000 years. As you can see, the river has built a series of sub-deltas, one after the other. The numbers indicate the order in which they were deposited.
Locating In which overall direction has the Mississippi River built its delta over the past few thousand years?
Locating How has the growth of the delta changed the location of the mouth of the Mississippi River in relation to New Orleans?

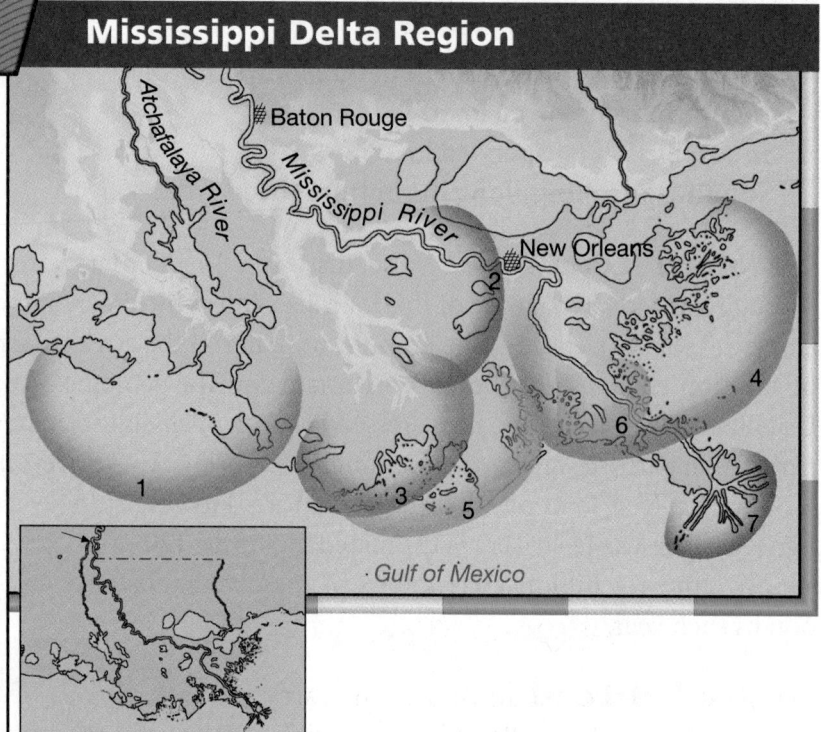

Deposition

Whenever a stream slows down, the situation reverses. As a stream's velocity decreases, its competence decreases and sediment begins to drop out, largest particles first. Each particle size has a critical settling velocity. 🔑 **Deposition occurs as streamflow drops below the critical settling velocity of a certain particle size. The sediment in that category begins to settle out.** Stream transport separates solid particles of various sizes, large to small. This process is called sorting. It explains why particles of similar size are deposited together.

The sorted material deposited by as stream is called **alluvium**. Many different depositional features are made of alluvium. Some occur within stream channels. Some occur on the valley floor next to the channel. And others occur at the mouth of a stream.

Deltas When a stream enters the relatively still waters of an ocean or lake, its velocity drops. As a result, the stream deposits sediment and forms a delta. A **delta** is an accumulation of sediment formed where a stream enters a lake or ocean. As a delta grows outward, the stream's gradient lessens and the water slows down. The channel becomes choked with sediment settling out of the slow-moving water. As a result, the river changes direction as it seeks a shorter route to base level. The main channel often divides into several smaller channels called distributaries as shown in sub-delta 7 in Figure 9. These shifting channels act in the opposite way of tributaries.

Rather than carrying water into the main channel like tributaries, distributaries carry water away. After many shifts of the channel, a delta may grow into a triangular shape, like the Greek letter delta (Δ). However, not all deltas have this idealized shape. Differences in the shapes of shorelines and variations in the strength of waves and currents result in different shapes of deltas.

Natural Levees Some rivers occupy valleys with broad, flat floors. Successive floods over many years can build natural levees along them. A **natural levee** is a ridge made up mostly of coarse sediments that parallels some streams. A natural levee forms when a stream repeatedly overflows its banks. Its velocity rapidly decreases, and it leaves coarse sediment deposits in strips that border the channel. As the water spreads out over the valley, less sediment is deposited. This uneven distribution of material produces the gentle slope of the natural levee.

Stream Valleys

Narrow Valleys The Yellowstone River, shown in Figure 10, is an excellent example of a narrow valley. ⬤ **A narrow V-shaped valley shows that the stream's primary work has been downcutting toward base level.** Rapids and waterfalls are the most prominent features of a narrow valley. Both rapids and waterfalls occur where the stream profile drops rapidly. The variations in the erosion of the underlying bedrock cause these rapid drops.

Wide Valleys Once a stream has cut its channel closer to base level, downward erosion becomes less dominant. More of the stream's energy is directed from side to side. The result is a widening of the valley as the river cuts away first at one bank and then at the other.

The side-to-side cutting of a stream eventually produces a flat valley floor, or **floodplain.** A floodplain is appropriately named because during a flood the river overflows its banks and floods the plain.

Streams that flow on floodplains move in meanders. Once a bend in a channel begins to form, it grows larger. Most of the erosion occurs on the outside of the meander—often called the cut bank—where velocity and turbulence are greatest. Much of the debris the stream removes at the cut bank moves downstream where it is deposited as point bars. Point bars form in zones of decreased velocity on the insides of meanders. In this way, meanders move side to side by eroding the outside of bends and depositing on the inside.

Figure 10 The Yellowstone River is an example of a V-shaped valley. The rapids and waterfall show that the river is vigorously downcutting the channel.

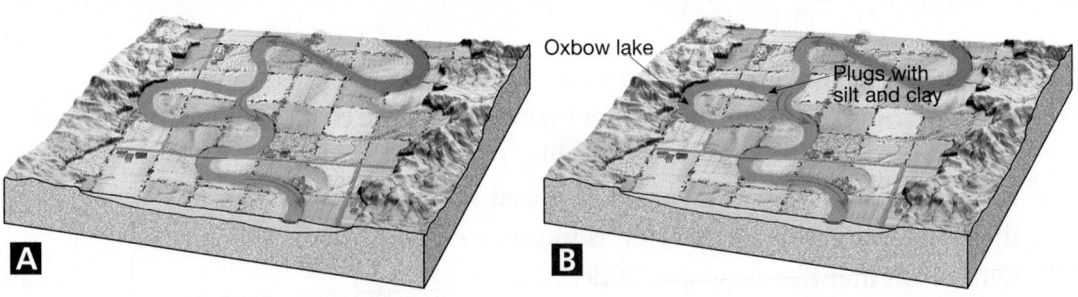

Figure 11 A One meander has overtaken the next, forming a ring of water on the floodplain. **B** After deposits of sediment cut off the ring, an oxbow lake forms.

Erosion is more effective on the downstream side of a meander because of the slope of the channel. The bends gradually travel down the valley. Sometimes the downstream movement of a meander slows when it reaches a more resistant portion of the floodplain. This resistance allows the next meander upstream to overtake it, as shown in Figure 11. Gradually the neck of land between the meanders is narrowed. Eventually the river may erode through the narrow neck of land to the next loop. The new, shorter channel segment is called a cutoff and, because of its shape, the abandoned bend is called an oxbow lake. Such a situation is shown in the bottom portion of Figure 6 on page 163.

Floods and Flood Control

A **flood** occurs when the discharge of a stream becomes so great that it exceeds the capacity of its channel and overflows its banks. Floods are the most common and most destructive of all natural geologic hazards. **Most floods are caused by rapid spring snow melt or storms that bring heavy rains over a large region.** Heavy rains caused the devastating floods in the upper Mississippi River Valley during the summer of 1993, as shown in Figure 12.

Unlike far-reaching regional floods, flash floods are more limited in extent. However, flash floods occur with little warning, and they can be deadly as walls of water sweep through river valleys. Several factors

MAP MASTER Skills Activity

Mississippi River Flooding

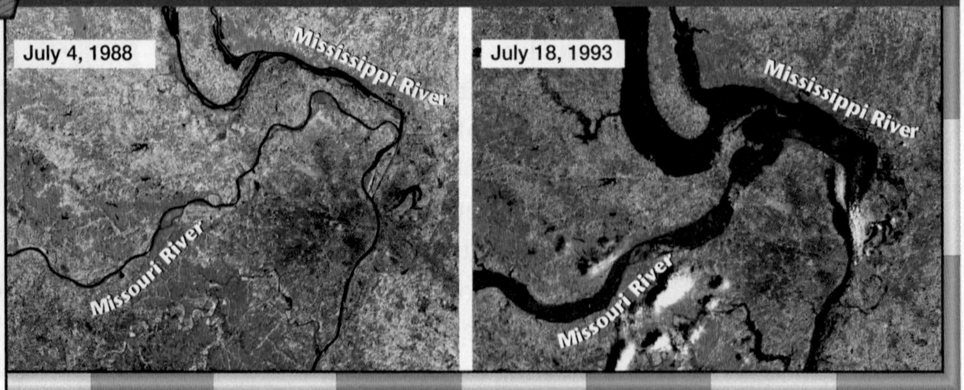

Figure 12

Region These satellite images show the confluence of the Missouri and Mississippi rivers. The first photo shows the rivers during normal flow.
Interpreting Photographs What does the second satellite image show? How do you know?

July 4, 1988

Mississippi River

Missouri River

July 18, 1993

Mississippi River

Missouri River

influence flash floods: rainfall intensity and duration, surface conditions, and topography. As you have learned, many urban areas are susceptible to flash floods. Mountainous areas are also susceptible because steep slopes can send runoff into narrow canyons.

Human interference with the stream system can worsen or even cause floods. A prime example is the failure of a dam or an artificial levee. These structures are designed to contain floods of a certain size. If that size is exceeded, water can then spill over or break through a dam or levee and rush downstream causing a disastrous flood.

There are several flood control strategies. 🡒 **Measures to control flooding include artificial levees, flood control dams, and placing limits on floodplain development.**

Artificial Levees
Artificial levees are earthen mounds built on the banks of a river. These levees increase the volume of water a channel can hold. When levees confine a river during periods of high water, the river often deposits material in its channel as the discharge diminishes. This discharge is sediment that would have been dropped on the floodplain. Because the stream cannot deposit material outside of its channel the bottom of the channel is gradually built up. When the channel is built up, it takes less water to overflow the levee. As a result, people may have to raise the height of the levee periodically to protect the floodplain behind it. Moreover, many artificial levees are not built to withstand periods of extreme flooding. For example, there were many levee failures in the Midwest during the summer of 1993 when the upper Mississippi experienced record flooding.

Flood-Control Dam
Flood-control dams store floodwater and then let it out slowly. Since the 1920s, thousands of dams have been built on nearly every major river in the United States. Many dams have other non-flood related functions, such as providing water for irrigation and for hydroelectric power generation.

Although dams may reduce flooding and provide other benefits, building dams has consequences. For example, dams trap sediment. Deltas and floodplains downstream can erode because silt no longer replenishes them during floods. Built up sediment behind a dam means the volume of the stored water will gradually diminish. This build-up reduces the effectiveness of the dam for flood control. Large dams also cause ecological damage to river environments.

Limiting Development
Today many scientists and engineers advocate sound floodplain management instead of building structures. That often means preserving floodplains in their natural state. Minimizing development on floodplains allows them to absorb floodwaters with little harm to homes and businesses.

Q *Sometimes a major flood is described as a 100-year flood. What does that mean?*

A The phrase "100-year flood" is misleading because it makes people believe that such an event happens only once every 100 years. In truth, a huge flood can happen any year. The phrase "100-year flood" is really a statistical designation. It indicates that there is a 1-in-100 chance that a flood this size will happen during any year. Perhaps a better term would be the "1-in-100 chance flood."

For: Links on Floods
Visit: PHSchool.com
Web Code: cuc-1062

Drainage Basins

Every stream has a drainage basin, also called a watershed. 🔑 **A drainage basin is the land area that contributes water to a stream.** An imaginary line called a **divide** separates the drainage basins of one stream from another. Divides range in scale from a ridge separating two small gullies on a hillside to a continental divide, which splits continents into enormous drainage basins. The Mississippi River has the largest drainage basin in North America. The river and its tributaries collect water from an area of more than 3.2 million square kilometers.

Figure 13 Mississippi River Drainage Basin Divides are the boundaries that separate drainage basins from each other.

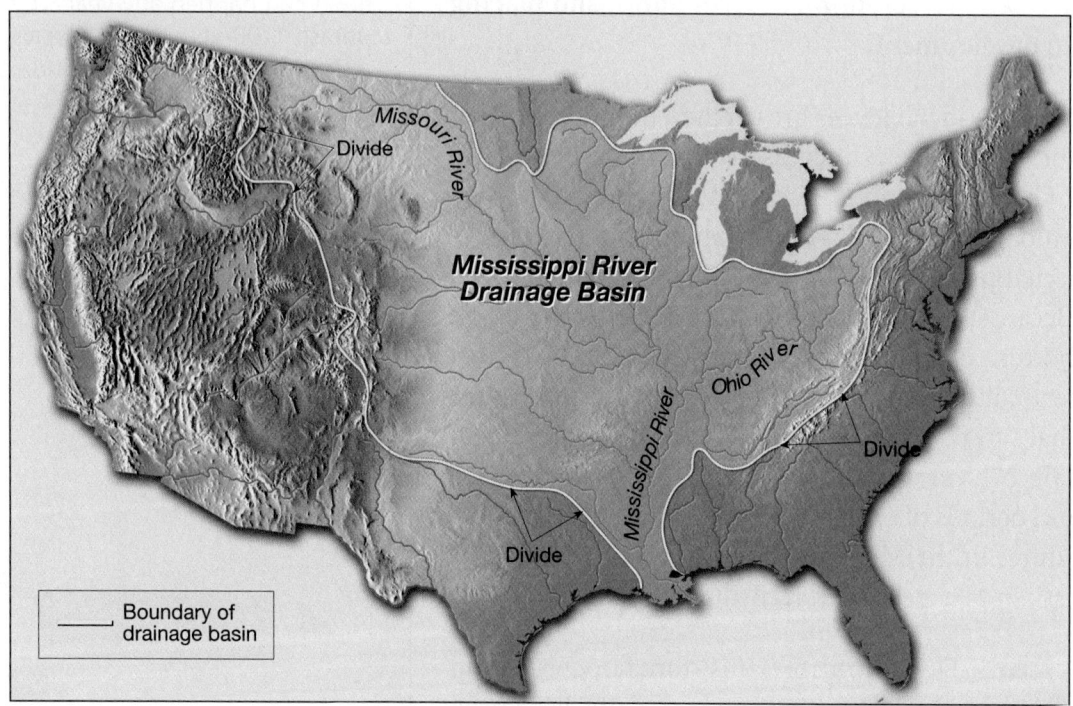

Section 6.2 Assessment

Reviewing Concepts

1. 🔑 How do streams erode their channels?
2. 🔑 What causes floods?
3. 🔑 What is the relationship between a stream and a drainage basin?
4. 🔑 How do streams transport sediments?

Critical Thinking

5. **Analyzing Concepts** How does urban development interfere with the natural function of floodplains?

6. **Summarizing** Explain the formation of one of the landforms that streams create by deposition.

Descriptive Paragraph Use library sources or the Internet to research the causes of a recent major flood. Write a paragraph that tells the name of the flood, when it happened, where it happened, and the conditions that led to the flood itself.

6.3 Water Beneath the Surface

Reading Focus

Key Concepts

- Where is groundwater and how does it move?
- How do springs form?
- What are some environmental threats to groundwater supplies?
- How and where do most caverns form?
- What landforms are common in an area of karst topography?

Vocabulary

- zone of saturation
- groundwater
- water table
- porosity
- permeability
- aquifer
- spring
- geyser
- well
- artesian well
- cavern
- travertine
- karst topography
- sinkhole

Reading Strategy

Previewing Copy the table below. Before you read the section, rewrite the green topic headings as how, why, and what questions. As you read, write an answer to each question.

Question	Answer
How does water move underground?	

The ground beneath your feet isn't as solid as you might think. It includes countless tiny pore spaces between grains of soil and sediment. It also contains narrow joints and fractures in bedrock. Together these spaces add up to an immense volume of tiny openings where water collects underground and moves.

Underground water in wells and springs provides water for cities, crops, livestock, and industry. In the United States, it is the drinking water for more than 50 percent of the population. It also provides 40 percent of the irrigation water and more than 25 percent of industry's needs.

Distribution and Movement of Water Underground

When rain falls, some of the water runs off, some evaporates, and the rest soaks into the ground to become subsurface water. The amount of water that ends up underground in an area depends on the steepness of slopes, the nature of surface materials, the intensity of rainfall, and the type and amount of vegetation.

Distribution Some of the water soaks into the ground, but it does not travel far. Molecular attraction holds it in place as a surface film on soil particles. This near-surface zone is called the belt of soil moisture. Roots, voids left by decayed roots, and animal and worm burrows crisscross this zone. These features help rainwater seep into soil.

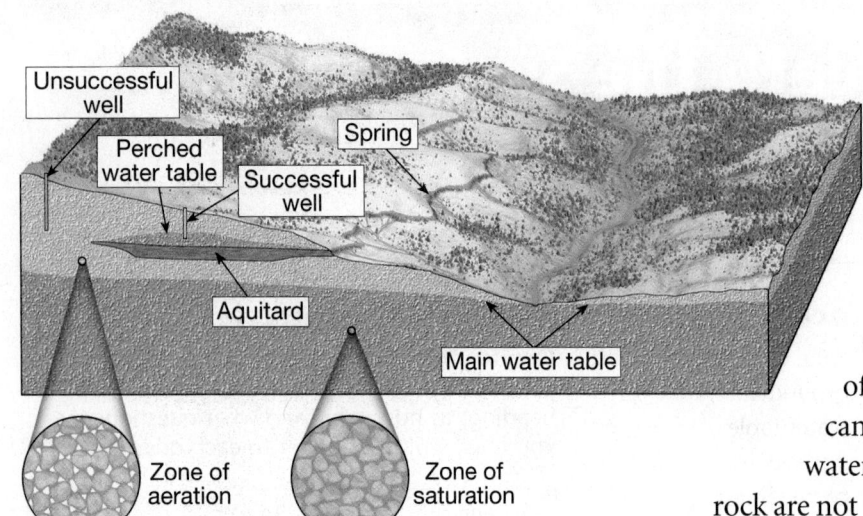

Figure 14 This diagram shows the relative positions of many features associated with subsurface water.
Applying Concepts *What is the source of the spring in the center of the illustration?*

Figure 15 A spring flows from a valley wall into a stream.

Much of the water in soil seeps downward until it reaches the zone of saturation. The zone of saturation is the area where water fills all of the open spaces in sediment and rock. Groundwater is the water within this zone. The upper limit of the zone of saturation is the **water table,** as you can see in Figure 14. The area above the water table where the soil, sediment, and rock are not saturated is the zone of aeration. Wells cannot pump water from this zone. The water clings too tightly to the rocks and soil. Only below the water table—where water pressure is great enough to allow water to enter wells—can water be pumped.

Movement The flow and storage of groundwater vary depending on the subsurface material. The amount of groundwater that can be stored depends on porosity. **Porosity** is the percentage of the total volume of rock or sediment that consists of pore spaces. Spaces between sedimentary particles form pore spaces. Joints, faults, and cavities also are formed by the dissolving of soluble rocks such as limestone.

Rock or sediment may be very porous and still block water's movement. The **permeability** of a material is its ability to release a fluid. Groundwater moves by twisting and turning through interconnected small openings. The groundwater moves more slowly when the pore spaces are smaller. If the spaces between particles are too small, water cannot move at all. For example, clay has high porosity. But clay is impermeable because its pore spaces are so small that water can't move through them.

Impermeable layers that get in the way or prevent water movement are aquitards. Larger particles, such as sand, have larger pore spaces. Water moves through them easily. Permeable rock layers or sediments that transmit groundwater freely are **aquifers.** Aquifers are important because they are the source of well water.

Springs

A spring forms whenever the water table intersects the ground surface. A **spring** is a flow of groundwater that emerges naturally at the ground surface, as shown in Figure 15. Springs form when an aquitard blocks downward movement of groundwater and forces it to move laterally.

Hot Springs A hot spring is 6°C to 9°C warmer than the mean annual air temperature where the spring occurs. There are more than 1000 hot springs in the United States.

Temperatures in deep mines and oil wells usually rise with an increase in depth at an average of 2°C per 100 meters. So when groundwater circulates at great depths, it becomes heated. If it rises to the surface, the water may emerge as a hot spring. This process heats many hot springs in the eastern United States. However, more than 95 percent of the hot springs in the United States are in the West. The source of heat for most of these hot springs is cooling igneous rock. In some places, hot acidic groundwater mixes with minerals from adjacent rock to form thick, bubbling mineral springs called mudpots.

Geysers A **geyser** is an intermittent hot spring or fountain in which a column of water shoots up with great force at various intervals. Geysers often shoot up columns of water 30 to 60 meters. After the jet of water stops, a column of steam rushes out—usually with a thundering roar. Perhaps the most famous geyser in the world is Old Faithful in Yellowstone National Park. It erupts about once each hour.

Geysers occur where extensive underground chambers exist within hot igneous rocks. Follow the formation of a geyser in Figure 16. As relatively cool groundwater enters the chambers, the surrounding rock heats it. The weight of the overlying water creates great pressure at the bottom of the chamber. This pressure prevents the water from boiling at the normal surface temperature of 100°C. However, the heat makes the water expand, and it forces some of the water out at the surface. This loss of water reduces the pressure in the chamber. The boiling point drops. Some of the water deep within the chamber then turns to steam and makes the geyser erupt. Following the eruption, cool groundwater again seeps into the chamber. Then the cycle begins again.

 **Reading Checkpoint** *What is a geyser?*

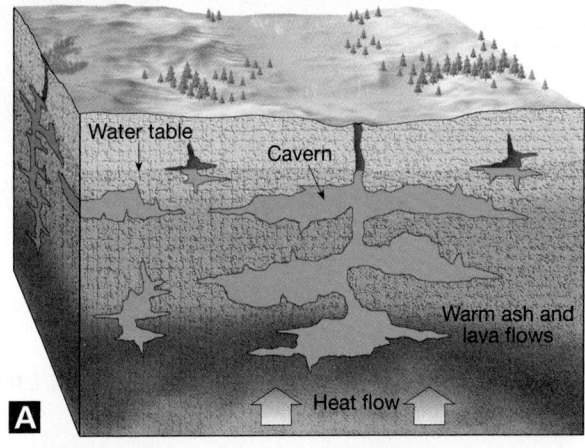

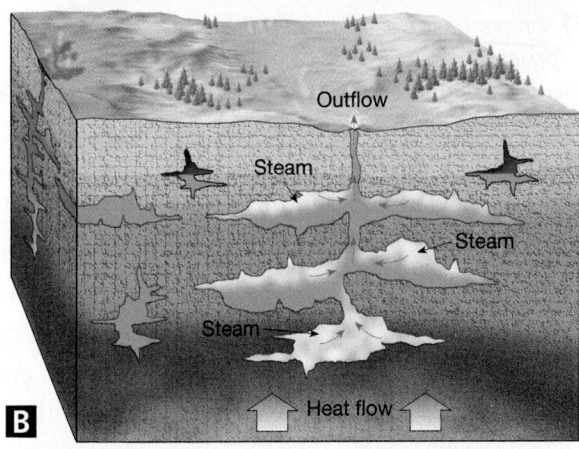

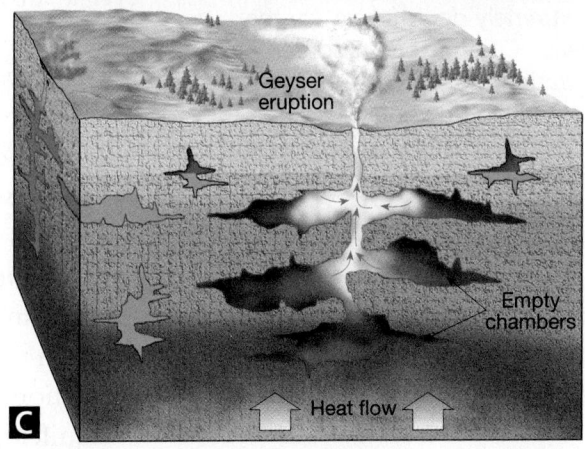

Figure 16 A Groundwater enters underground caverns and fractures in hot igneous rock where it is heated to near its boiling point. **B** Heating causes the water to expand, with some being forced out at the surface. The loss of water reduces the pressure on the remaining water, thus reducing its boiling temperature. Some of the water flashes to steam. **C** The rapidly expanding steam forces the hot water out of the chambers to produce a geyser. The empty chambers fill again, and the cycle starts anew.

Figure 17 A cone of depression in the water table often forms around a pumping well. If heavy pumping lowers the water table, some wells may be left dry.

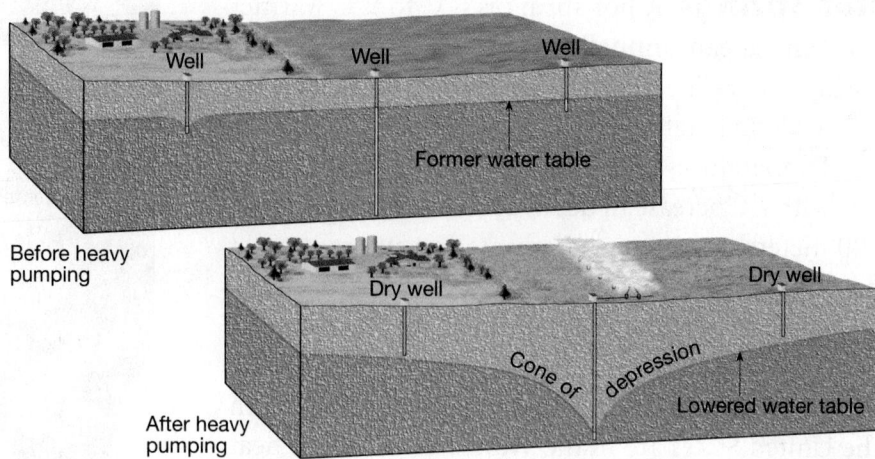

Before heavy pumping

Well · Well · Well · Former water table

After heavy pumping

Dry well · Dry well · Cone of depression · Lowered water table

Q *I have heard people say that supplies of groundwater can be located using a forked stick. Can this actually be done?*

A What you describe is a practice called "water dowsing." In the classic method, a person holding a forked stick walks back and forth over an area. When water is detected, the bottom of the "Y" is supposed to be attracted downward.

Geologists and engineers are extremely doubtful, to say the least. Case histories and demonstrations may seem convincing, but when dowsing is exposed to scientific scrutiny, it fails. Most "successful" examples of water dowsing occur in places where water would be hard to miss. In a region of adequate rainfall and favorable geology, it is difficult to drill and *not* find water!

For: Links on aquifers
Visit: www.SciLinks.org
Web Code: cjn-2064

Wells

A **well** is a hole bored into the zone of saturation. Irrigation for agriculture is by far the single greatest use of well water in the United States—more than 65 percent of groundwater used annually. Industrial uses of groundwater rank a distant second, followed by the amount used by homes.

The level of the water table may change considerably during a year. The level can drop during the dry season and rise following periods of rain. To ensure a continuous water supply, a well must penetrate far below the water table. The water table around the well drops whenever a substantial amount of water is withdrawn from a well. This effect is called drawdown, and it decreases with an increase in distance from the well. The result of a drawdown is a cone of depression in the water table. This cone of depression is shown in Figure 17. For most small domestic wells, the cone of depression is tiny. However, when wells are used for irrigation or industry, a very wide and steep cone of depression can result.

Water must be pumped out of most wells. However, water rises on its own in some wells, sometimes overflowing the surface. In an **artesian well,** groundwater rises on its own under pressure. For such a situation to occur, two conditions must exist. First, water must be in an aquifer that is tilted so that one end is exposed at the surface, where it can receive water. Second, there must be aquitards both above and below the aquifer to stop the water from escaping. The pressure created by the weight of the water above forces the water to rise when a well taps the aquifer.

 **Reading Checkpoint** *How does an artesian well differ from most wells?*

Environmental Problems Associated with Groundwater

As with many valuable natural resources, groundwater is being threatened at an increasing rate. **Overuse and contamination threatens groundwater supplies in some areas.**

Treating Groundwater as a Nonrenewable Resource

Groundwater seems like an endlessly renewable resource. However, supplies are finite. In some regions, the amount of water available to recharge an aquifer is much less than the amount being withdrawn.

The High Plains provides one example of severe groundwater depletion. In some parts of the region, intense irrigation has gone on for a long time. Even if pumping were to stop now, it could take thousands of years for the groundwater to be fully replenished.

The ground may sink when water is pumped from wells faster than natural processes can replace it. As water is withdrawn, the ground subsides because the weight of the overburden packs relatively loose sediment grains more tightly together.

This type of subsidence is extreme in the San Joaquin Valley of California, as shown in Figure 18. Land subsidence due to groundwater withdrawal for irrigation began there in the mid-1920s. It exceeded eight meters by 1970. During a drought in 1976 and 1977, heavy groundwater pumping led the ground to sink even more. Land subsidence affected more than 13,400 square kilometers of irrigable land—one half the entire valley.

Groundwater Contamination

The pollution of groundwater is a serious matter, particularly in areas where aquifers provide much of the water supply. Common sources of groundwater pollution are sewage from septic tanks, farm wastes, and inadequate or broken sewers.

If sewage water that is contaminated with bacteria enters the groundwater system, it may become purified through natural processes. The harmful bacteria can be mechanically filtered by the sediment through which the water passes, destroyed by chemical oxidation, and/or assimilated by other organisms. For purification to occur, however, the aquifer must be of the correct composition.

For example, extremely permeable aquifers have such large openings that contaminated groundwater may travel long distances without being cleansed. In this case, the water flows too quickly and is not in contact with the surrounding material long enough for purification to occur. This is the problem at Well 1 in Figure 19A.

 **Reading Checkpoint** *What are some common sources of groundwater pollution?*

Figure 18 The marks on the utility pole indicate the level of the surrounding land in years past. Between 1925 and 1975 this part of the San Joaquin Valley sank almost 9 meters because of the withdrawal of groundwater and the resulting compaction of sediments.

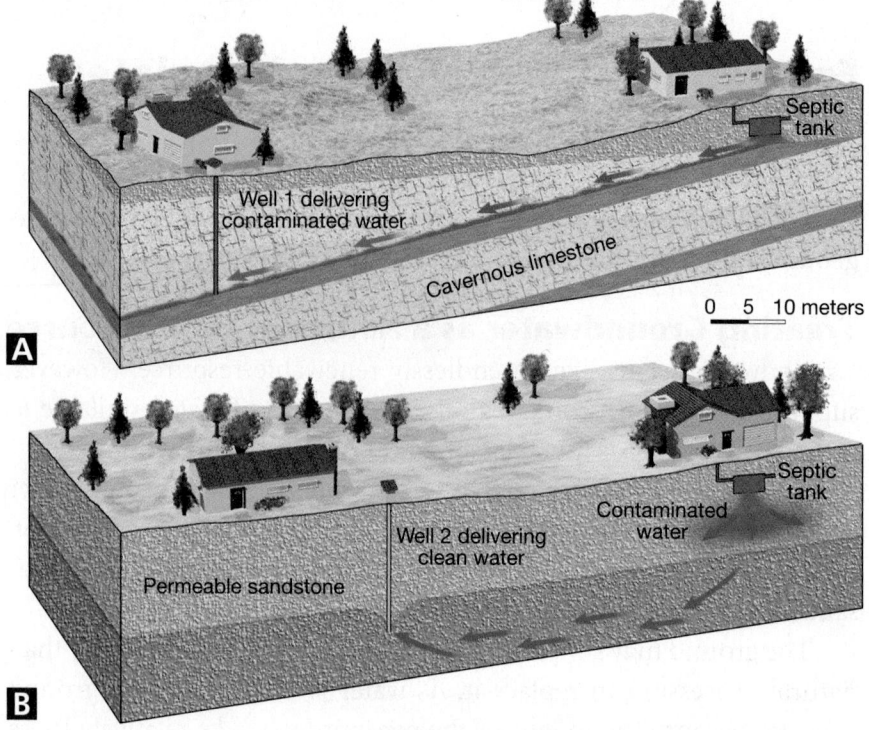

Figure 19 A Although the contaminated water has traveled more than 100 meters before reaching Well 1, the water moves too quickly through the cavernous limestone to be purified. **B** As the discharge from the septic tank percolates through the permeable sandstone, it is purified in a short distance.

Figure 20 Agricultural chemicals sprayed on farm fields can seep into soil and contaminate underground water supplies.

Figure 21 If landfills leak, harmful waste buried in them can escape into groundwater.

However, when the aquifer is composed of sand or permeable sandstone, the water can sometimes be purified after traveling only a few dozen meters through it. The openings between sand grains are large enough to permit water movement, yet the movement of the water is slow enough to allow enough time for its purification. This is the case at Well 2 in Figure 19B.

Other sources and types of contamination also threaten supplies, as you can see in Figures 20 and 21. These include fertilizers that are spread across the land, pesticides, and highway salt. In addition, chemicals and industrial materials—some hazardous—may leak from pipelines, storage tanks, landfills, and holding ponds. As rainwater oozes through the refuse, it may dissolve contaminants. If this material reaches the water table, it will mix with and contaminate groundwater. In coastal areas, heavy use can deplete aquifers, causing underground saltwater to enter wells.

Once the source of the problem has been identified and eliminated, the most common practice is to abandon the water supply. Abandoning the water supply allows the pollutants to flush out gradually. It's the least costly and easiest solution, but the aquifer must stay unused for years. To speed up this process, engineers sometimes pump out and treat polluted water. The aquifer then recharges naturally, or the treated water is pumped back in. This process can be risky, because there is no way to be sure that treatment has removed all the pollution. Prevention remains the most effective solution to groundwater contamination.

Some substances in groundwater are natural. Ions of substances (from adjacent rock) such as calcium and iron make some water "hard." Hard water forms scum with soap instead of suds. It can also deposit residue that clogs pipes. But hard water is generally not a health risk.

Caverns

The most spectacular results of groundwater's ability to erode rock are limestone caverns. Soluble rocks, especially limestone, underlie millions of square kilometers of Earth's surface. Limestone is nearly insoluble in pure water. But water containing small quantities of carbonic acid dissolves it easily. Most natural water contains the weak acid because rainwater dissolves carbon dioxide from the air and decaying plants. Therefore, when groundwater comes in contact with limestone, the carbonic acid reacts with calcite in the rocks. Calcium bicarbonate forms. As groundwater carries away calcium carbonate in solution, it slowly erodes rock. A **cavern** is a naturally formed underground chamber, such as the one you see in Figure 22. There are thousands of caverns in the United States. Most are fairly small, but some have spectacular dimensions. Carlsbad Caverns in southeastern New Mexico is a famous example. One chamber has an area equivalent to 14 football fields, and it is high enough to fit the U.S. Capitol building inside it.

Figure 22 The dissolving action of groundwater creates caverns. These dripstone features are in Three Fingers Cave in New Mexico.

⬤ **Erosion forms most caverns at or below the water table in the zone of saturation.** Here, acidic groundwater follows lines of weakness in the rock, such as joints and bedding planes. As time passes, the dissolving process slowly creates cavities and enlarges them into caverns. Material the groundwater dissolves eventually flows into streams and then the ocean.

The features that produce the greatest curiosity for most cavern visitors are depositional stone formations. These formations give some caverns a wonderland appearance. They form from seemingly endless dripping of water over great spans of time. The calcium carbonate that is left behind produces the limestone we call **travertine.** These cave deposits are commonly called dripstone.

Although the formation of caverns takes place in the zone of saturation, the deposition of dripstone features is not possible until the caverns are above the water table in the zone of aeration. The formation of caverns in the zone of aeration commonly occurs as nearby streams cut their valleys deeper. As the elevation of the stream drops, the water table also lowers, leaving the caverns high and largely dry.

Figure 23 Soda straw stalactites in Great Basin National Park's Lehman Caves.
Relating Cause and Effect *What part do these drops of water play in the formation of the stalactites?*

Go Online

NSTA *SciLINKS*

For: Links on sinkholes
Visit: www.SciLinks.org
Web Code: cjn-2065

Dripstone Features Perhaps the most familiar dripstone features are stalactites. Stalactites are icicle-like stone pendants that hang from the ceiling of a cavern. They form when water seeps through cracks in the cavern ceiling. When water reaches air in the cave, some of the dissolved carbon dioxide escapes from the drop and calcite begins to separate out. Deposition occurs as a ring around the edge of the water drops. As drops fall, each one leaves a tiny trace of calcite behind. This calcite creates a hollow limestone tube called a soda straw, as shown in Figure 23. Often the hollow tube becomes plugged or its supply of water increases. When a stalactite becomes plugged or the water supply increases, the water flows and deposits along the outside of the tube. As deposition continues, the stalactite takes on the more common conical shape.

Stalagmites are formations that develop on the floor of a cavern and reach up toward the ceiling. The water supplying the calcite for stalagmite growth falls from the ceiling and splatters over the surface of the cavern floor. As a result, stalagmites do not have a central tube. They are usually more massive and more rounded on their upper ends than stalactites. Given enough time, a downward-growing stalactite and an upward-growing stalagmite may join to form a column.

 **Reading Checkpoint** *What is a dripstone deposit?*

Karst Topography

Many areas of the world have landscapes that have been shaped largely by the dissolving power of groundwater. These areas are said to have **karst topography.** This term comes from the *Krs* region of Slovenia, where such topography is strikingly developed. In the United States, karst landscapes occur in many areas that are underlain by limestone. These areas include parts of Kentucky, Tennessee, Alabama, southern Indiana, and central northern Florida.

🔑 **Karst areas typically have irregular terrain, with many depressions called sinkholes.** A **sinkhole** is a depression produced in a region where groundwater has removed soluble rock. In the limestone areas of Florida, Kentucky, and southern Indiana, there are tens of thousands of these depressions. They vary in depth from just a meter or two to more than 50 meters.

Sinkholes commonly form in one of two ways. Some develop gradually over many years without any physical disturbance to the rock. In these situations, downward-seeping rainwater containing carbon dioxide dissolves limestone below the soil. These depressions are fairly shallow and have gentle slopes. Sinkholes can also form suddenly when the roof of a cavern collapses. The depressions created in this way are steep-sided and deep. When they form in populated areas, they may be a serious geologic hazard, as shown in Figure 24.

In addition to a surface pockmarked by sinkholes, karst regions usually show a striking lack of surface drainage (streams). Following a rainfall, runoff is quickly funneled below ground through sinkholes. It then flows through caverns until it finally reaches the water table. Where streams do exist at the surface, their paths are usually short. The names of such streams often give a clue to their fate. In the Mammoth Cave area of Kentucky, for example, there is Sinking Creek, Little Sinking Creek, and Sinking Branch. Some sinkholes become plugged with clay and debris, creating small lakes or ponds.

Figure 24 This small sinkhole formed suddenly in 1991 when the roof of a cavern collapsed. It destroyed this home in Frostproof, Florida.

Section 6.3 Assessment

Reviewing Concepts

1. Where is groundwater located under the surface?
2. How does water move underground?
3. What are some environmental threats to groundwater supplies?
4. How and where do most caverns form?
5. What landforms are common in an area of karst topography?

Critical Thinking

6. **Comparing and Contrasting** What is the difference between stalactites and stalagmites?

7. **Analyzing Concepts** How is groundwater a nonrenewable resource?
8. **Analyzing Concepts** Explain why caverns form in the zone of saturation, while dripstone features form in the zone of aeration?

Writing in Science

Relating Cause and Effect Write a paragraph that connects these three concepts: land subsidence, extensive farming in dry regions, and water conservation.

The Ogallala Aquifer— How Long Will the Water Last?

The High Plains extend from the western Dakotas south to Texas. Despite being a land of little rain, this is one of the most important agricultural regions in the United States. The reason is a vast supply of groundwater that makes irrigation possible throughout most of the region. The source of most of this water is the Ogallala Formation, the largest aquifer in the United States.

Geologically, the Ogallala Formation consists of a number of sandy and gravelly rock layers. The sediments came from the erosion of the Rocky Mountains and were carried eastward by sluggish streams. Erosion has removed much of the formation from eastern Colorado, severing the Ogallala's connection to the Rockies.

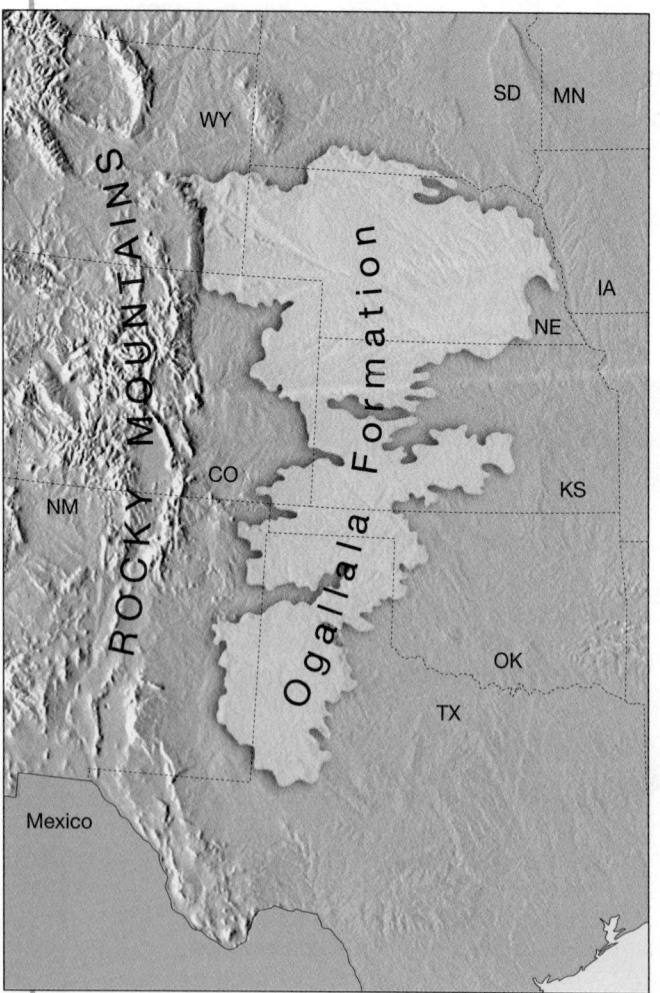

Mexico

The Ogallala Formation, the largest aquifer in the United States, averages 60 meters thick. However, in some places it is as thick as 180 meters. Groundwater in the aquifer originally traveled downslope from the Rocky Mountains and from surface precipitation that soaked into the ground over thousands of years. Because of its high porosity and great size, the Ogallala Formation accumulated a large amount of groundwater—enough to fill Lake Huron! Today, with the connection between the aquifer and the Rockies gone (erosion has removed much of the formation in eastern Colorado), all of the Ogallala's recharge must come from the meager rainfall of the Plains.

In the late 1800s, people first started to use the Ogallala for irrigation. However, the capacity of pumps available at the time limited water withdrawal. Then in the 1920s, large-capacity irrigation pumps were invented. High Plains' farmers began tapping the Ogallala for irrigation. Today, there are nearly 170,000 wells irrigating more than 65,000 square kilometers of land.

The increase in irrigation has caused a drastic drop in the Ogallala's water table, especially in the High Plains. Declines in the water table of 3 to 15 meters are common. In places, however, the water table is now 60 meters below its original level.

Although the decline in the water table has slowed in parts of the southern High Plains, substantial pumping continues—often in excess of recharge. The future of irrigated farming here is clearly in jeopardy.

The southern High Plains will return sooner or later to dry-land farming. The transition will come sooner and with fewer ecological and economic crises if the agricultural industry is weaned gradually from its dependence on groundwater irrigation. If nothing is done until all the accessible water in the Ogallala aquifer has been removed, the transition will be ecologically dangerous and economically dreadful.*

*National Research Council. *Solid-Earth Sciences and Society.* Washington, DC: National Academy Press, 1993, p. 148.

Figure 25 The Ogallala Formation underlies about 450,000 square kilometers of the High Plains, making it the largest aquifer in the United States.

Investigating the Permeability of Soils

The permeability of soils affects the way groundwater moves—or if it moves at all. Some soils are highly permeable, while others are not. In this lab, you will determine the permeability of various soils, and draw conclusions about their effect on the movement of water underground.

Problem
How does the permeability of soil affect its ability to move water?

Materials
- 100 mL graduated cylinder
- beaker
- small funnel
- 3 pieces of cotton
- samples of coarse sand, fine sand, and soil
- clock or watch with a second hand

Skills
Observing, Measuring, Comparing and Contrasting, Analyzing Data, Interpreting Data

Procedure

1. Place a small, clean piece of cotton in the neck of the funnel. Fill the funnel above the cotton with coarse sand. Fill the funnel about two-thirds of the way.

2. **Measure** Pour water into the graduated cylinder until it reaches the 50 mL mark.

3. With the bottom of the funnel over the beaker, pour the water from the graduated cylinder slowly into the sand in the funnel.

4. **Measure** In a data table like the one shown, keep track of the time from the second you start to pour the water into the funnel. Measure the amount of time that it takes the water to drain through the funnel filled with coarse sand. Using the graduated cylinder, measure the amount of water recovered in the beaker.

5. Record in the data table the time it takes for the water to drain through the sand.

6. Empty and clean the measuring cylinder, funnel, and beaker.

7. Repeat Steps 1 through 7, first using fine sand and then using soil.

Analyze and Conclude

1. **Comparing and Contrasting** Of the three materials you tested, which has the greatest permeability? The least permeability?

2. **Analyzing Data** Why were different amounts of water recovered in the beaker for each material tested?

3. **Interpreting Data** What effect would the differences you observed in this lab have on the movement of groundwater through different soils?

4. **Controlling Variables** What factors might affect the accuracy of your results in this experiment? How would repeating each test several times affect your measurements?

Data Table		
	Time Needed for Water to Drain Through Funnel	Water Collected in Beaker (mL)
Coarse Sand		
Fine Sand		
Soil		

Study Guide

6.1 Running Water

Key Concepts

- Water constantly moves among the oceans, the atmosphere, the solid Earth, and the biosphere. This unending circulation of Earth's water supply is the water cycle

- Balance in the water cycle means the average annual precipitation over Earth equals the amount of water that evaporates.

- The ability of a stream to erode and transport materials depends largely on its velocity.

- While gradient decreases between a stream's headwaters and mouth, discharge increases.

- Base level is the lowest point to which a stream can erode its channel.

Vocabulary

water cycle, *p. 158*; infiltration, *p. 159*; transpiration, *p. 159*; gradient, *p. 160*; stream channel, *p. 161*; discharge, *p. 161*; tributary, *p. 162*; meander, *p. 163*

6.2 The Work of Streams

Key Concepts

- Streams generally erode their channels by dissolving soluble material, by lifting loose particles, and by abrasion, or grinding.

- Streams transport their load of sediment in three ways: (1) in solution (dissolved load), (2) in suspension (suspended load), and (3) scooting or rolling along the bottom (bed load).

- Deposition occurs as streamflow drops below the critical settling velocity of a certain particle size.

- There are two general types of stream valleys: narrow V-shaped valleys and wide valleys with flat floors.

- Most floods are caused by rapid spring snow melt and storms that bring heavy rains over a large region.

- Measures to control flooding include the construction of artificial levees, building flood control dams, and placing limits on floodplain development.

- A drainage basin is the land area that contributes water to a stream.

Vocabulary

bed load, *p. 165*; capacity, *p. 165*; delta, *p. 166*; natural levee, *p. 167*; floodplain, *p. 167*; flood, *p. 168*; drainage basin, *p. 170*; divide, *p. 170*

6.3 Water Beneath the Surface

Key Concepts

- Much of the water in soil seeps downward until it reaches the zone of saturation. The zone of saturation is the area where water fills all of the open spaces in sediment and rock. Groundwater is the water within this zone.

- Groundwater moves by twisting and turning through interconnected small openings. The groundwater moves more slowly when the pore spaces are smaller.

- A spring forms whenever the water table intersects the ground surface.

- Overuse and contamination threatens groundwater supplies in some areas.

- Erosion forms most caverns at or below the water table in the zone of saturation.

- Karst areas typically have irregular terrain, with many depressions called sinkholes.

Vocabulary

zone of saturation, *p. 172*; groundwater, *p. 172*; water table, *p. 172*; porosity, *p. 172*; permeability, *p. 172*; aquifer, *p. 172*; spring, *p. 172*; geyser; *p. 173*; well, *p. 174*; artesian well; *p. 174*; cavern, *p. 177*; travertine, *p. 177*; karst topography, *p. 178*; sinkhole, *p. 178*

Assessment

Reviewing Content

Choose the letter that best answers the question or completes the statement.

1. The energy for the water cycle comes from the
   a. ocean.
   b. sun.
   c. atmosphere.
   d. soil.

2. How does water move from plants to the atmosphere?
   a. infiltration
   b. precipitation
   c. transpiration
   d. condensation

3. By what process do streams and rivers move material?
   a. weathering   **b.** infiltration
   c. mass wasting   **d.** erosion

4. A river's discharge is generally greatest
   a. at its source.
   b. on its floodplain.
   c. at its mouth.
   d. at the sides of its channel.

5. When do streams and rivers deposit sediment?
   a. when their velocity decreases
   b. when they are in the midst of flooding
   c. when their velocity increases
   d. when they plunge over waterfalls

6. A stream's drainage basin (or watershed) is all the water that
   a. flows into it.
   b. infiltrates from it into the ground.
   c. is removed from it for drinking water.
   d. is within 100 kilometers of its channel.

7. What is a stream's bed load?
   a. material that moves along its bottom
   b. material that is carried in solution
   c. material that floats on its surface
   d. material that is carried in suspension

8. Where is groundwater located?
   a. zone of aeration
   b. zone of reduction
   c. zone of saturation
   d. zone of distribution

9. Water in an artesian well
   a. dries up after a short amount of time.
   b. rises on its own under pressure.
   c. has been contaminated by saltwater.
   d. is heated by cooling igneous rocks.

10. Caverns form when rocks such as limestone are dissolved by a mixture of water and
   a. carbonic acid.
   b. sulfur dioxide.
   c. nitrogen.
   d. ammonia.

11. Which of these landforms is characteristic of an area with karst topography?
   a. mountains
   b. canyons
   c. sinkholes
   d. drumlins

Understanding Concepts

12. Write a list of numbered statements that summarize the major steps in the water cycle.

13. How does a stream's gradient affect its velocity?

14. Why does a stream's base level affect how it downcuts its channel?

15. Which type of stream valley is formed primarily by downcutting?

16. What are the main causes of floods?

17. What is the relationship between a spring and the water table?

18. Why are leaking landfills and septic tanks of concern to people who use groundwater?

19. How do stalactites form?

20. What type of rock is often associated with the formation of caverns and karst topography?

21. How do dripstone columns form?

Critical Thinking

22. Analyzing Concepts Why must Earth's water cycle be balanced in order for the system to work?

23. Relating Cause and Effect How would a reduction in friction in a stream channel affect the stream's velocity?

24. Applying Concepts A stream's discharge decreases. Explain how this affects the stream's capacity.

25. Summarizing Briefly explain how a material can be porous but also impermeable.

26. Drawing Conclusions The bedrock under a region is primarily a very hard rock that doesn't easily erode. The area is also very arid. Is it likely that this area has a karst landscape? Explain your answer.

Analyzing Data

Use the graph below to answer Questions 27–30.

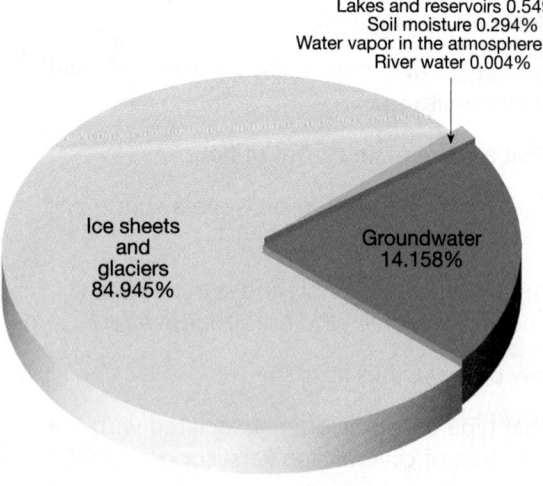

Lakes and reservoirs 0.549%
Soil moisture 0.294%
Water vapor in the atmosphere 0.049%
River water 0.004%

Ice sheets and glaciers 84.945%

Groundwater 14.158%

27. Using Graphs Where is the greatest percentage of Earth's fresh water located?

28. Calculating What percentage of Earth's fresh water is held in rivers, lakes, and reservoirs?

29. Calculating Oceans hold about 97 percent of Earth's water. The rest of the water is fresh. What percentage of Earth's water is freshwater that people can use for drinking, cooking, and growing crops?

30. Drawing Conclusions Taking into account your answer to Question #29 above, explain why many people think of Earth's supply of fresh water as a resource that must be protected.

Concepts in Action

31. Applying Concepts A person drills a well into an area where there is a known aquifer underground. But the well doesn't produce water. What might be the cause of the problem? What does this person need to know about the water table in this area to solve the problem?

32. Predicting Erosion reduces the size of pebbles on the bottom of a stream channel. Which of the following would be most affected: the stream's competence, velocity, or discharge? Explain your answer.

33. Connecting Concepts Explain what deltas and natural levees have in common.

34. Writing in Science Imagine you live in a town that floods often. The people in your community want to take measures to decrease the amount of flooding and property damage. The community has identified three choices: a set of natural levees, a flood control dam, or clearing development from the river floodplain. Write a letter to the editor supporting one of these choices.

Performance-Based Assessment

Drawing Diagrams Draw a graphic organizer that shows the major steps of the water cycle. Label each step.

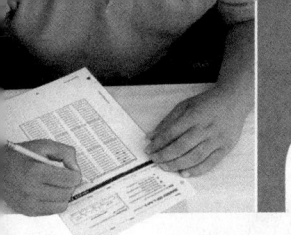

Standardized Test Prep

Test-Taking Tip

Evaluating and Revising
Frequently, a scientifically accurate answer choice may not answer the question that is being asked. Keep these tips in mind.

- Verify what the question is asking.

- Determine if an answer choice is a true statement or not.

- Determine if a true answer choice actually answers the question.

- Be cautious with inserted or deleted words that make a false statement seem accurate.

Practice using these tips in Question 3.

Choose the letter that best answers the question or completes the statement, or write a brief answer to the question.

1. Which of these processes of the water cycle is a direct effect of the sun's energy?
   (A) formation of precipitation
   (B) runoff of water over soil
   (C) evaporation
   (D) seeping of water into soil

2. Which factor is most important in determining the erosive power of a stream?
   (A) stream discharge
   (B) dissolved load
   (C) stream velocity
   (D) channel width

3. Rejuvenation causes streams to resume downcutting their channels because
   (A) the stream's greatest velocity is at its bottom.
   (B) the stream's bed load helps erode the stream's bottom.
   (C) natural levees restrict the lateral movement of stream waters.
   (D) uplift creates a new base level for the stream.

4. When a soil is impermeable, it
   (A) allows water to flow freely through it.
   (B) has no water in it at all.
   (C) does not allow water to pass through it.
   (D) has large pore spaces.

5. Which of these features is a landform associated with karst topography?
   (A) sinkholes
   (B) streams
   (C) natural levees
   (D) deltas

6. What are the major environmental problems associated with the use of groundwater?

7. What is a cone of depression and how does it form?

8. Which of the following drawings shows a feature of stream deposition?

 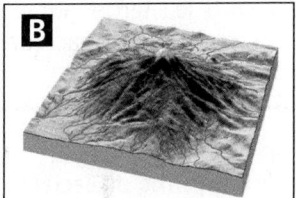

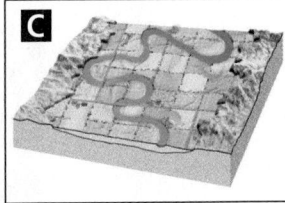 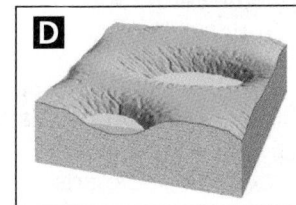

CHAPTER 7

Glaciers, Deserts, and Wind

21st Century Learning

Information and Media Literacy

Are melting glaciers due to climate change?

Scientists think that one sign of climate change is that many glaciers are retreating. Search the Web for three articles about the retreat of a glacier. One article should be a news article, the second should be from a popular science magazine, and the third should be from a scientific journal. Write a report comparing and contrasting each of the articles. Determine each article's target audience, why it was written, and what each article has that the others do not.

Exploration Lab
Interpreting a Glacial Landscape

How the Earth Works
Erosion

GEODe EARTH SCIENCE
Sculpturing Earth's Surface
↳ Glaciers
Deserts

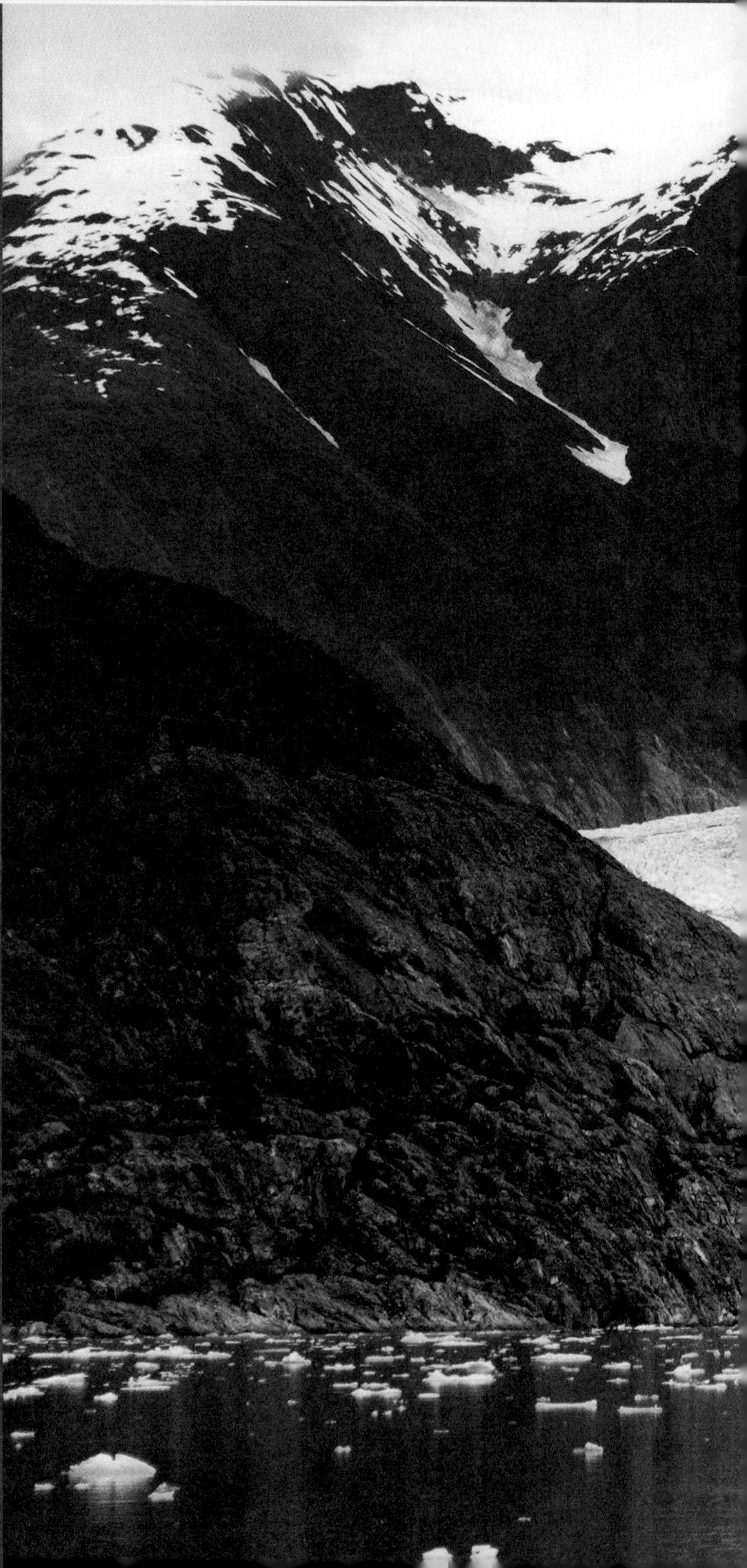

Chapter Preview

Inquiry > Activity

How Does Pressure Affect Ice Crystals?

Procedure

1. Obtain a beaker full of ice crystals, either by collecting snow outside or by scraping ice crystals from the inside surfaces of a freezer. Use a magnifying glass to observe the loose crystals. Sketch their appearance in your science notebook.

2. Use your hands to mold a snowball from the crystals. Then squeeze the snowball as hard as you can, making the snowball compact.

3. Use a table knife to cut the snowball in half. Observe the compressed crystals with your magnifying glass and sketch them.

Think About It

1. Drawing Conclusions How did the ice crystals change after you squeezed them? Describe how pressure seems to affect ice crystals.

2. Predicting The raw material for glaciers is snow. Predict how snowflakes will change under the increasing pressure of overlying snow.

This fjord at Tracy Arm, Alaska, formed as a glacier carved the valley that became submerged as sea level rose.

7.1 Glaciers

Reading Focus

Key Concepts

- What are the two types of glaciers?
- How do glaciers move?
- What distinguishes the various types of glacial drift?
- What landscape features do glaciers form?
- Describe the causes of the most recent ice age.

Vocabulary

- ice age
- glacier
- snowline
- valley glacier
- ice sheet
- glacial trough
- till
- stratified drift
- moraine

Reading Strategy

Building Vocabulary Draw a table similar to the one below that includes all the vocabulary terms listed for the section. As you read the section, define each vocabulary term in your own words.

Vocabulary Term	Definition
Glacier	a. _____?_____
Ice Sheet	b. _____?_____
Moraine	c. _____?_____
Till	d. _____?_____

Figure 1 Valley Glacier A glacier in Alaska's Chugach Mountains slowly advances down this valley.

Climate is a major factor in the processes that shape Earth's surface. In this section, you will see the strong link between climate and geology in studying how glaciers shape the land.

Types of Glaciers

As recently as 15,000 years ago, Earth was coming out of an ice age. An **ice age** is a period of time when much of Earth's land is covered in glaciers. A **glacier** is a thick ice mass that moves slowly over the land surface. About 15,000 years ago, up to 30 percent of Earth's land was covered by glaciers. In some areas, the glaciers were thousands of meters thick and covered entire continents. These massive glaciers shaped places like Cape Cod, Long Island, and the Great Lakes. Today glaciers still cover nearly 10 percent of Earth's land area. In these regions they continue to sculpt the landscape.

Glaciers originate on land in places where more snow falls than melts. The **snowline** is the lowest elevation in a particular area that remains covered in snow all year. At the poles, the snowline occurs at sea level. Closer to the equator, the snowline is near the top of tall mountains. Instead of completely melting away, snow above the snowline accumulates and compacts. The compressed snow first recrystallizes into coarse grains of ice. Further pressure from added snow above changes the coarse grains into interlocking crystals of glacial ice.

A glacier appears to be motionless, but it's not. Sit beside a glacier for an hour and you may hear a sporadic chorus of creaks, cracks, and groans as gravity pulls the mass of ice slowly downhill. Just like running water, groundwater, wind, and waves, glaciers are dynamic agents of erosion. They accumulate, transport, and deposit sediment. Thus, glaciers are an important part of the rock cycle.

Valley Glaciers Thousands of small glaciers exist in high mountains worldwide. These glaciers advance only a few centimeters to meters each day. **Valley glaciers** are ice masses that slowly advance down valleys that were originally occupied by streams. 🔑 **A valley glacier is a stream of ice that flows between steep rock walls from the top of a mountain valley.** Like rivers, valley glaciers can be long or short, wide or narrow, single or with branching tributaries. Figure 1 shows a valley glacier in Alaska.

Ice Sheets Ice sheets are enormous ice masses that flow in all directions from one or more centers and cover everything but the highest land. 🔑 **Ice sheets are sometimes called continental glaciers because they cover large regions, such as Antarctica and Greenland. They are huge compared to valley glaciers.** Ice sheets covered much of North America during the recent ice age. Figure 2 shows the two remaining ice sheets, which combined cover almost 10 percent of Earth's land area. One ice sheet covers about 80 percent of Greenland. It averages nearly 1500 meters thick, and in places it rises to 3000 meters above sea level.

The huge Antarctic Ice Sheet in the Southern Hemisphere is nearly 4300 meters thick in places. This glacier accounts for 80 percent of the world's ice, and it holds nearly two-thirds of Earth's fresh water. If it melted, sea level could rise 60 to 70 meters and many coastal cities would flood.

Go Online

For: Links on glaciers
Visit: www.SciLinks.org
Web Code: cjn-2071

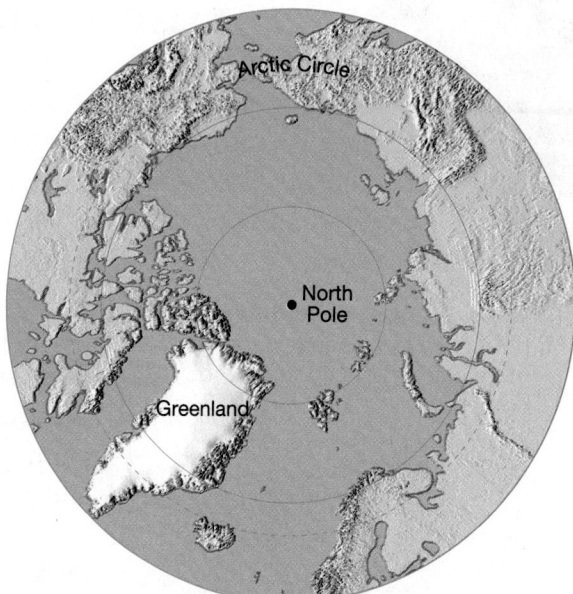

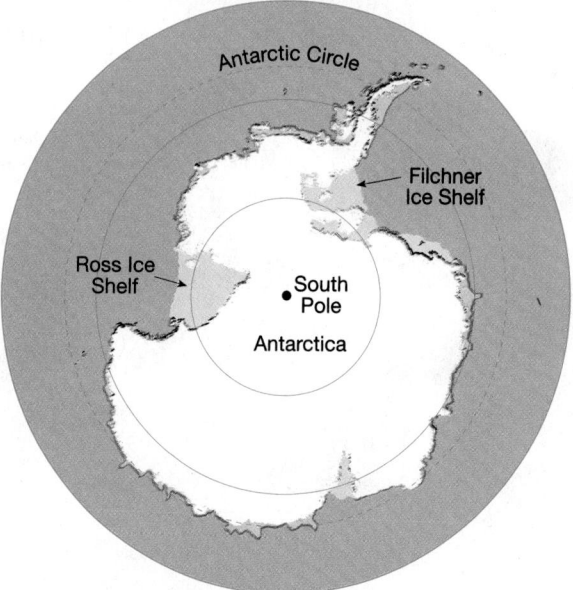

Figure 2 The only present-day ice sheets are those covering Greenland and Antarctica.

Reading Checkpoint *Where do ice sheets exist on Earth today?*

How Glaciers Move

You might wonder how a glacier, which is solid, can move.  **The movement of glaciers is referred to as flow. Glacial flow happens in two ways: plastic flow and basal slip.** Plastic flow involves movement within the ice. Under high enough pressure, the normally brittle ice begins to distort and change shape—a property known as plasticity. The weight of overlying ice exerts pressure on the ice below, causing it to flow. Plastic flow begins at about 50 meters below the glacier surface. Basal slip is the second cause of glacial movement. In basal slip, liquid water and mud at the bottom of the glacier reduce the friction between the glacier and the ground. The reduced friction and gravity causes the entire ice mass to slip and slide downhill.

The upper 50 meters of a glacier is not under enough pressure to have plastic flow. This layer of a glacier, called the zone of fracture, is brittle. The zone of fracture rides on the flowing ice below and experiences tension when the glacier moves over irregular terrain. This tension results in gaping cracks called crevasses. Crevasses are often hidden by snow, as shown in Figure 3, and make travel across glaciers dangerous.

Figure 3 Crevasses like this one in Pakistan can extend 50 meters into a glacier's brittle surface ice.

Rates of Glacial Movement Different glaciers move at different speeds. Some flow so slowly that trees and other vegetation grow in the debris on their surface. Other glaciers can advance several meters per day. Some glaciers alternate between periods of rapid movement and periods of relatively little movement.

Budget of a Glacier Glaciers constantly gain and lose ice. Glaciers gain when snow accumulates and becomes ice at the head of the glacier in the zone of accumulation, shown in Figure 4. Here new snowfall thickens the glacier and promotes movement downhill. The area of the glacier below the snowline is called the zone of wastage. Here, the glacier loses mass as ice and any new snow melts away.

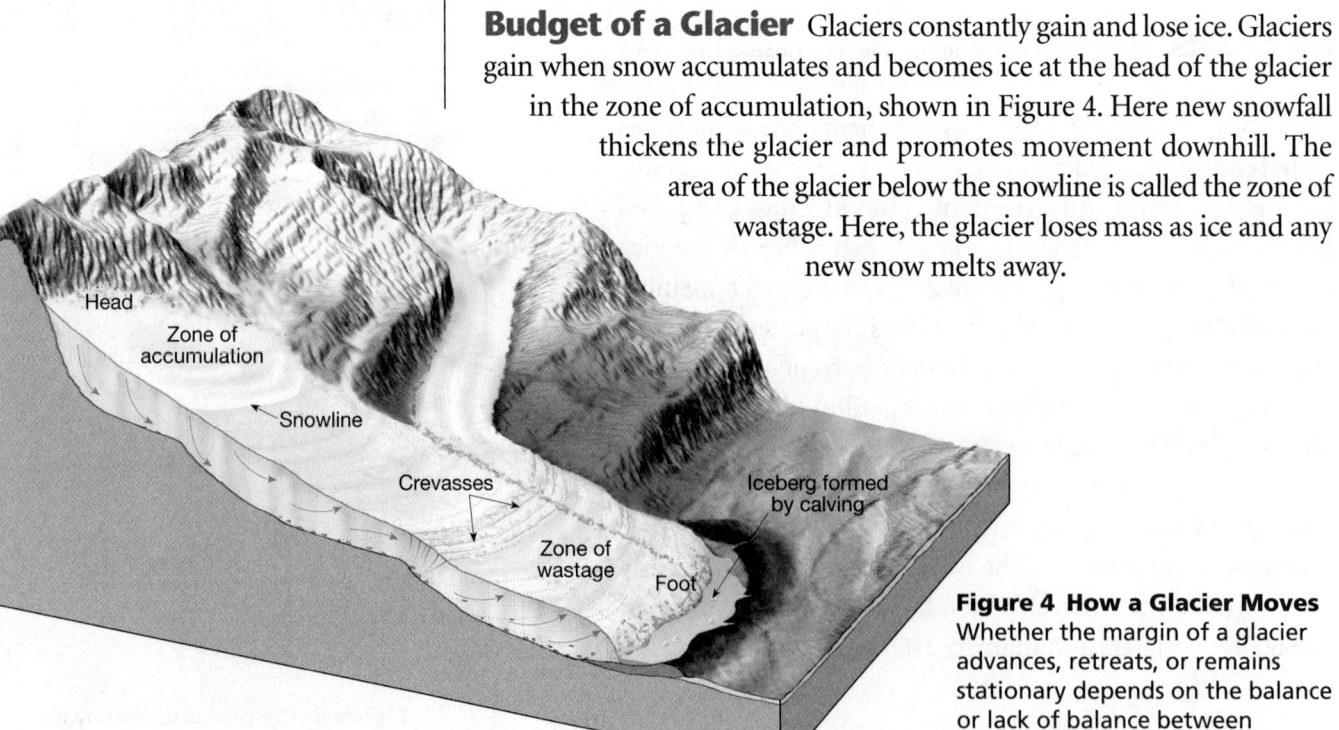

Figure 4 How a Glacier Moves Whether the margin of a glacier advances, retreats, or remains stationary depends on the balance or lack of balance between accumulation and wastage.

Whether the foot of a glacier advances, retreats, or stays in place depends on the glacier's budget. ⬤ **The glacial budget is the balance or lack of balance between accumulation at the head of a glacier and loss, or wastage, at the foot.** If more ice builds up in the zone of accumulation than is lost from the zone of wastage, then the glacier advances. The glacier retreats when it loses ice faster than it gains ice. If a glacier gains ice at the same rate as it loses ice, the foot of the glacier remains stationary. Whether the foot of a glacier advances, retreats, or remains stationary, the ice within the glacier continues to flow downhill. In the case of a receding glacier, the ice still flows downhill, but not rapidly enough to offset wastage.

In addition to melting, a glacier loses ice when large pieces break off at its foot. This process is called calving. Calving occurs where glaciers meet the ocean, and the pieces that break off into the ocean are called icebergs. Because icebergs are just slightly less dense than seawater, they float low in the water. Only about 10 percent of their mass is visible above the surface, as shown in Figure 5. The Greenland Ice Sheet calves thousands of icebergs each year. Many drift southward into the North Atlantic where they are navigational hazards.

Reading Checkpoint *What causes a glacier to retreat?*

Figure 5 Calving A Ice calves from the front of the Perito Moreno Glacier in Patagonia, Argentina. **B** Only 10 percent of an iceberg's mass is visible above the surface.

Go Online
PLANETDIARY

For: Links on Glaciers
Visit: PHSchool.com
Web Code: czd-2071

Figure 6 Glacial Abrasion A glacier smoothed and polished these rock surfaces in Canada's Hudson Bay. Rock fragments embedded in the glacier carved the scratches and grooves.

Glacial Erosion

Glaciers are nature's bulldozers. Their ice scrapes, scours, and tears rock from valley floors and walls. Glaciers then carry the rock fragments down the valley. Some of these rock fragments may become embedded in the bedrock under the weight of the glacier. The rest of the rock fragments drop at the glacier's foot, where the ice melts. Glaciers can carry rocks as big as buses over long distances. **Many landscapes were changed by the widespread glaciers of the recent ice age.**

How Glaciers Erode Glaciers mainly erode the land in two ways: plucking and abrasion. Plucking occurs when rocks and sediments from the bedrock become embedded in the ice as the glacier flows past them. Some of these rocks are plucked from the bedrock once they have been loosened by repeated cycles of water melting and freezing. When water freezes in cracks in the bedrock, it expands to pry the rock apart.

Abrasion occurs as the glacial ice and its load of rock fragments slide over bedrock. The fragments act like sandpaper to smooth and polish the rock surface below. Some of the bedrock and some of the rock carried by the glacier is pulverized into rock flour. So much rock flour may be produced that streams of meltwater leaving the glacier often have the grayish appearance of skim milk. When the bottom of a glacier contains large rock fragments, long scratches and grooves may be gouged in the bedrock, as shown in Figure 6. These grooves, or striations, provide valuable clues to the direction of past glacial movement. By mapping the striations over large areas, geologists often can reconstruct the direction in which the ice flowed.

The rate of glacial erosion is highly variable. Differences in these rates are mainly controlled by four factors: 1) rate of glacial movement; 2) thickness of the ice; 3) shape, abundance, and hardness of the rock fragments in the ice at the base of the glacier; and 4) the type of surface below the glacier. The highest rates of erosion result when glaciers that are very thick flow very quickly, carrying lots of hard rocks over a much softer bedrock.

How do glaciers cause erosion?

Landforms Created by Glacial Erosion

Erosion by valley glaciers produces many spectacular features in mountainous areas. 🔑 **Glaciers produce a variety of erosional landscape features, such as glacial troughs, hanging valleys, cirques, arêtes, and horns.** Compare and contrast the mountain setting before, during, and after glaciation as shown is Figure 7.

Glaciated Valleys Before glaciation, alpine valleys are usually V-shaped as a result of erosion by mountain streams. However, in mountain regions that have been glaciated, the valleys are no longer narrow. As a glacier moves down a valley once occupied by a stream, the glacier widens, deepens, and straightens the valley. The once narrow V-shaped valley is changed into a U-shaped valley, which is also called a **glacial trough.**

The amount of glacial erosion depends in part on the thickness of the ice. Main glaciers cut glacial troughs that are deeper than those carved by smaller side glaciers. When the ice recedes, the valleys of the smaller side glaciers are left standing higher than the main glacial trough. These higher valleys are called hanging valleys. Rivers flowing from hanging valleys sometimes produce spectacular waterfalls, such as those in Yosemite National Park, California.

 **Reading Checkpoint** *What is a glacial trough?*

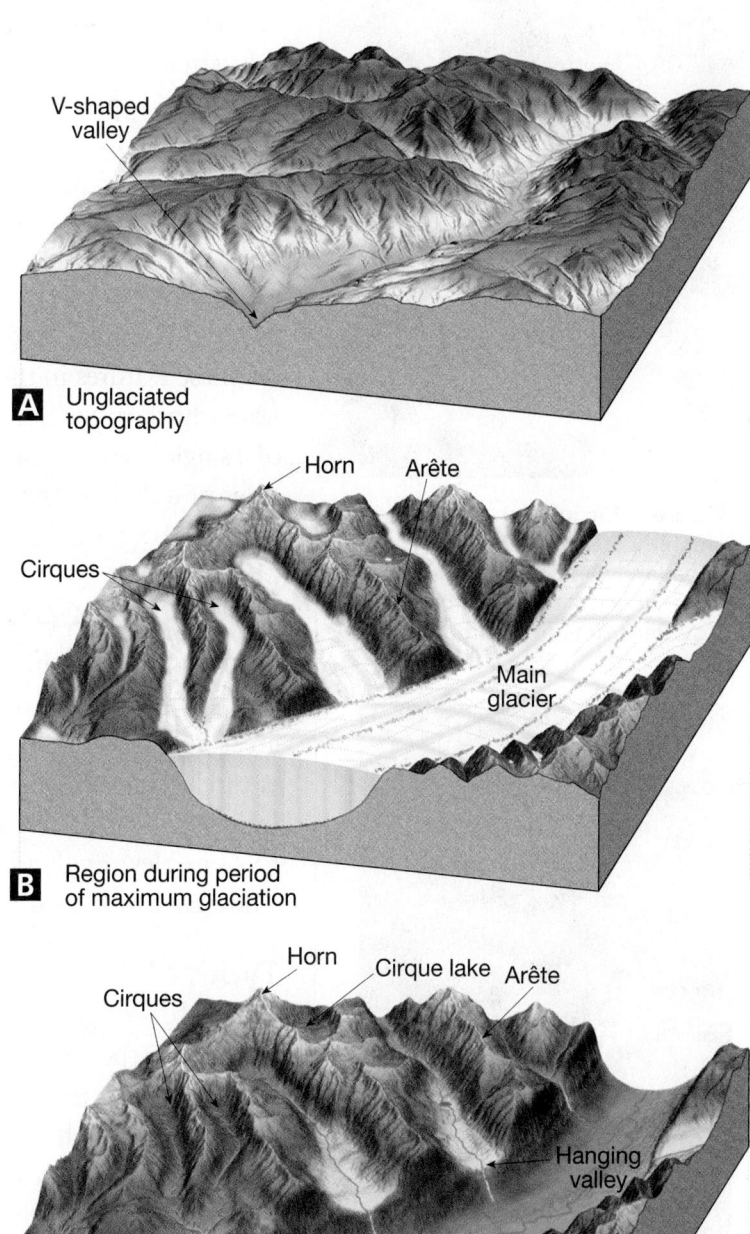

A Unglaciated topography

B Region during period of maximum glaciation

C Glaciated topography

Figure 7 Erosional Landforms Formed by Valley Glaciers
A Before glaciation, stream erosion formed a network of V-shaped valleys. **B** shows what the valley glaciers looked like in this mountainous region. **C** reveals the modified landscape and its features.
Predicting *What will happen to the glacial trough as the stream continues to flow through it?*

Figure 8 Cirque Natural amphitheaters like this one in Canada's Yukon Territory result from the plucking action of ice in a glacier's zone of accumulation.

Figure 9 Glacial till is an unsorted mixture of many different sediment sizes. A close look often reveals cobbles that have been scratched as they were dragged along by the glacier.

Cirques A cirque is a bowl-shaped depression at the head of a glacial valley that is surrounded on three sides by steep rock walls, as shown in Figure 8. Cirques begin as irregularities in the mountainside. Glaciers carve cirques by plucking rock from along the sides and the bottom. The glaciers then act as conveyor belts that carry away the debris. Sometimes the melting glacier leaves a small lake in the cirque basin.

Arêtes and Horns Valley glaciers also create snaking, sharp-edged ridges called arêtes and sharp pyramid-like peaks called horns. You can see these features in the Alps and the northern Rockies. Horns like the Matterhorn in Switzerland form where several cirques erode the sides of a single high mountain. Arêtes form where cirques occur on opposite sides of a divide. As these cirques grow, the divide separating them is reduced to a narrow, sharp ridge.

Glacial Deposition

Glaciers transport huge loads of debris as they slowly advance across the land and deposit their loads where they melt. For example, in many areas once covered by the ice sheets of the recent ice age, the bedrock is rarely exposed because glacial deposits that are dozens—or even hundreds—of meters thick completely cover the terrain. Rocky pastures in New England, wheat fields in the Dakota plains, and rolling Midwest farmland are all landscapes resulting from glacial deposition.

Types of Glacial Drift The term glacial drift applies to all of the rock debris of glacial origin, no matter how, where, or in what form they were deposited. There are two types of glacial drift: till and stratified drift. **Till** is material deposited directly by the glacier. It is deposited as the glacier melts and drops its load of rock debris. Unlike moving water and wind, ice cannot sort the rock debris it carries. Therefore, till deposits are usually unsorted mixtures made up of many particle sizes. Notice the unsorted till in Figure 9.

Stratified drift is rock debris laid down by glacial meltwater. Stratified drift contains particles that are sorted according to size and mass. Stratified drift often consists of sand and gravel. Finer sediments remain suspended and are carried far from the glacier.

Rocks that are transported by a glacier and which differ from the underlying bedrock are called erratics. Erratics can range in size from small pebbles to huge boulders. Geologists can sometimes reconstruct the path of a long-gone glacier by tracing erratics back to their source.

 **Reading Checkpoint** *What is glacial drift?*

Moraines, Outwash Plains, and Kettles

Glaciers are responsible for a variety of depositional features, including moraines, outwash plains, kettles, drumlins, and eskers.

When glaciers melt, they leave layers or ridges of till called **moraines.** These widespread glacial features come in several varieties.

Lateral Moraines The sides of a valley glacier gather large amounts of debris from the valley walls. Lateral moraines are ridges that form along the sides of glacial valleys from rock fragments that fall from the valley walls along the edge of the glacier. Medial moraines are formed when two valley glaciers join to form a single ice stream. Observe the medial and lateral moraines in Figure 10. The till that was once carried along the edges of each glacier joins to form a dark stripe of debris within the newly enlarged glacier.

End Moraines and Ground Moraines Although the ice within a glacier continues to flow downhill, the glacier can appear to remain stationary for long periods of time. This means that the glacier is at an equilibrium, where the snow and ice build up in the zone of accumulation at the same rate that snow and ice melt in the zone of wastage. A glacier acts as a conveyor belt to carry rock debris to the foot of the glacier. When the ice there melts, it deposits the debris and forms a ridge called an end moraine. The longer the glacier's foot remains stationary, the larger the end moraine grows.

Ground moraines form when glaciers begin to recede. The glacier foot continues to deliver and deposit rock debris as the ice melts away. However, instead of forming a ridge, the retreating glacier creates a rock-strewn, gently rolling plain. This ground moraine fills in low spots and clogs old stream channels. Ground moraine can thus result in poorly drained swamp lands.

Figure 10 The dark stripes running down the length of this glacier are medial moraines. They formed from lateral moraines that merged when valley glaciers flowed together.

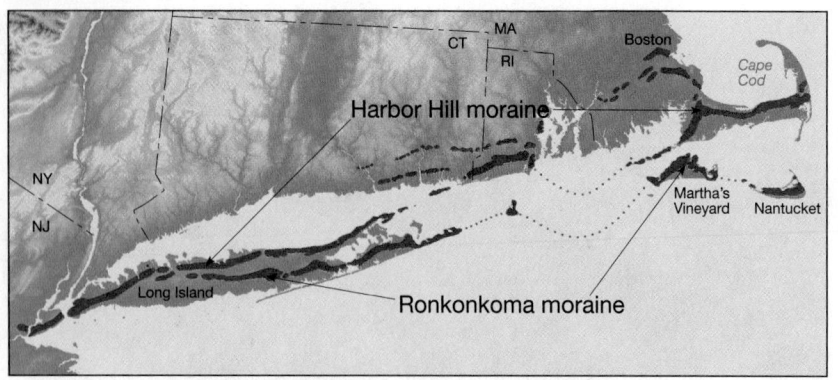

Figure 11 Ice Sheet Moraines
Long Island, Cape Cod, Martha's Vineyard, and Nantucket are remnant of end moraines deposited by ice sheets.

Terminal and Recessional Moraines

Glaciers can cycle many times between equilibrium, during which they are stationary, and retreat before the glacier melts completely. A glacier forms a new end moraine during a stationary period, then another ground moraine during a retreat. The farthest end moraine is the terminal end moraine. The end moraines that form when the ice front occasionally becomes stationary in this cycle are recessional end moraines.

End moraines that formed in the recent ice age are prominent in the landscapes of the Midwest and Northeast. New York's Long Island is part of a series of end moraines stretching from eastern Pennsylvania to Cape Cod, Massachusetts. Figure 11 shows the locations of these end moraines that form part of the Northeast coast.

Outwash Plains

An outwash plain begins to form as streams of fast-moving meltwater emerge from the bases of a glacier. This water is often so choked with rock flour that it looks like milk. Once it leaves the glacier, the water slows and drops the rock debris in a broad, ramp-like deposit downstream from the end moraine. This wide, gently-sloping apron of rock debris is called an outwash plain.

Kettles and Kettle Lakes

You can often find depressions and small lakes within end moraines and outwash plains, as shown in Figure 12. Kettles form when blocks of stagnant ice become buried in drift and eventually melt. This melting leaves pits in the glacial rock material. If these pits, or kettles, fill up with water, they are known as kettle lakes. A well-known example of a kettle lake is Walden Pond near Concord, Massachusetts. Thousands of kettles and kettle lakes dot the landscape of the Upper Midwest in Wisconsin and Minnesota.

Drumlins and Eskers

Moraines are not the only landforms deposited by glaciers. Some landscapes have many elongated parallel hills made of till, called drumlins. Other areas have narrow winding ridges made mainly of stratified drift, called eskers. If you know what to look for, the signs of a once-glaciated landscape are unmistakable—especially from an airplane.

Drumlins are streamlined hills composed of till. Drumlins are taller and steeper on one end, and they range in height from 15 to 60 meters and average 0.4 to 0.8 kilometer long. The steep side of the hill faces the direction the ice came from, and the gentler slope points in the direction

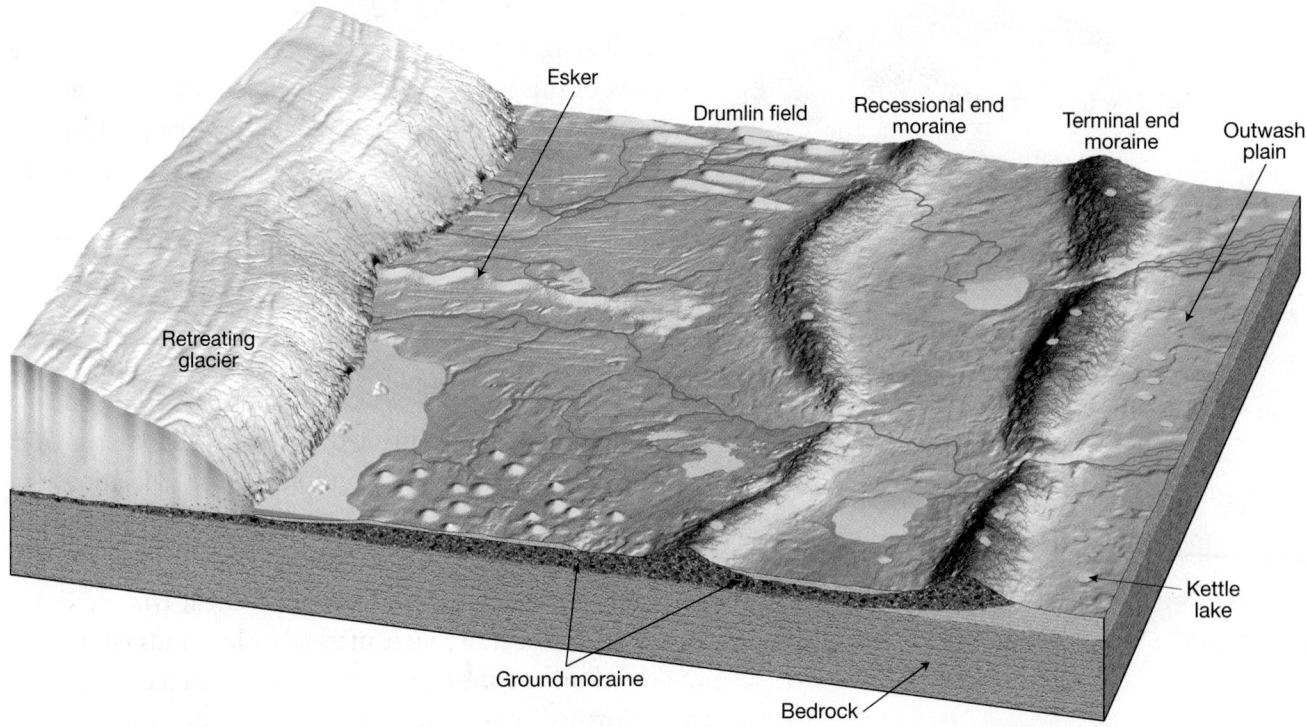

Esker

Drumlin field

Recessional end moraine

Terminal end moraine

Outwash plain

Retreating glacier

Kettle lake

Ground moraine

Bedrock

the ice moved. In areas covered by ice sheets during the recent ice age, drumlins can occur in clusters called drumlin fields. Near Rochester, New York, one cluster contains nearly 10,000 drumlins. Their streamlined shapes show that they were molded by active glaciers.

Eskers are snake-like ridges composed of sand and gravel that were deposited by streams once flowing in tunnels beneath glaciers. They can be several meters high and many kilometers long. Many eskers are mined for the sand and gravel they contain.

 **Reading Checkpoint** *What depositional features do glaciers form?*

Glaciers of the Ice Age

Thousands of years ago, continental ice sheets and alpine glaciers covered a lot more land than they do today. People once thought that glacial deposits had drifted in on icebergs or that they swept across the landscape in a catastrophic flood. However, scientific field investigations during the nineteenth century provided convincing evidence that an extensive ice age explained these deposits and many other features.

The most recent ice age is actually a series of glacial advances and retreats, which began two to three million years ago. **Continental glaciers repeatedly formed, spread, and melted as Earth's climate cooled and warmed. Each cycle of glaciation, or episode, lasted about 100,000 years.** Many of the glacial episodes occurred while wooly mammoths and saber-toothed cats roamed the landscape.

Figure 12 Glacial Deposition The terminal end moraine marks the farthest extent of the glacier. Recessional moraines occur where a retreating glacier temporarily becomes stationary.
Inferring *If the glacier were completely melted away, how would you be able to tell in which direction the glacier retreated?*

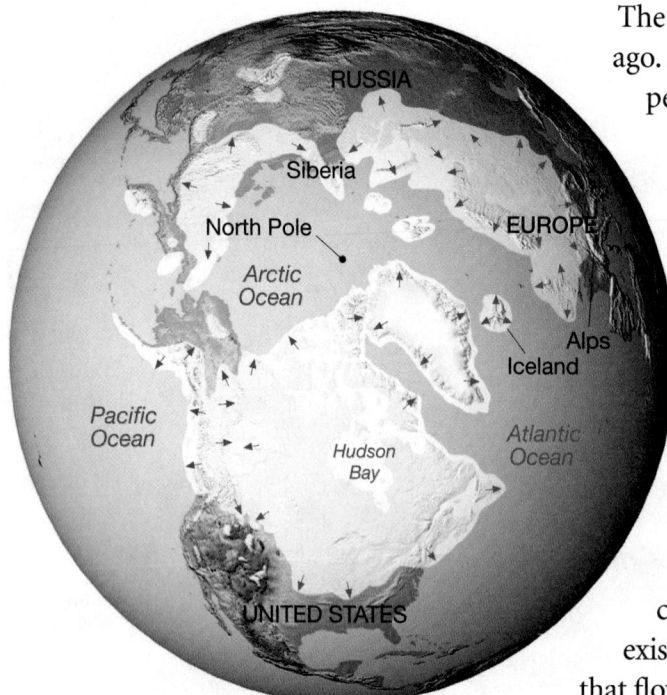

Figure 13 During the ice age, ice sheets covered large areas in the Northern Hemisphere. So much ice formed that sea level was more than 100 meters lower than it is today. (The map shows modern coastlines.)

The most recent ice age began two to three million years ago. Although the glaciers are in retreat right now, at the peak of this ice age, glaciers covered almost 30 percent of Earth's land. Glaciers covered large portions of North America, Europe, and Siberia, as shown in Figure 13. The Northern Hemisphere had twice as much ice as did the Southern Hemisphere, where glaciation was mostly confined to Antarctica.

Ice Age Effects on Drainage The ice sheets greatly affected the drainage patterns over large regions. For example, before glaciation, the Missouri River flowed northward toward Hudson Bay in Canada. The Mississippi River flowed through central Illinois. Furthermore, the Great Lakes did not exist. Their locations were marked by lowlands with rivers that flowed toward the east. During the recent ice age, glacial erosion transformed these lowlands into wide, deep basins that filled with water and eventually became the Great Lakes.

The formation and growth of ice sheets triggered changes in climates beyond the glacial margins. Regions that are arid today became cooler and wetter. This change in climate resulted in the formation of lakes in such areas as the Basin and Range region of Nevada and Utah. One of these lakes was ancient Lake Bonneville, which covered much of western Utah. The Great Salt Lake is all that remains of this glacial lake.

Section 7.1 Assessment

Reviewing Concepts

1. What are the two basic types of glaciers? Where is each type found?

2. Describe how glaciers move. Which property or properties of ice allow this movement?

3. How does glacial till differ from stratified drift? Describe one glacial feature made of each type of glacial drift.

4. Name three glacial features formed by erosion and three that are formed by deposition. What does each feature look like?

Critical Thinking

5. **Comparing and Contrasting** Compare and contrast advancing and retreating glaciers.

6. **Inferring** The snowline at the poles is sea level. Close to the equator, the snowline occurs high up on the tallest mountains. What is the relationship between the distance from the equator and snowline?

Math Practice

7. A glacier advances 20 meters over a period of about two months. What is its approximate rate of advance per day?

7.2 Deserts

Reading Focus

Key Concepts
- What roles do mechanical and chemical weathering play in deserts?
- How does running water affect deserts?

Reading Strategy

Summarizing Write each blue heading in the section on a sheet of paper. Write a brief summary of the text for each heading.

Vocabulary
- alluvial fan
- playa lake

Weathering	
?	
?	

The Role of Water	
?	
?	

If you live in a humid region, visiting an arid region, or desert, might seem like going to an alien planet. In humid regions, the hills are rounded and the slopes are curved. By contrast, arid regions, or deserts, often have angular rocks and surfaces covered in pebbles or sand, shown in Figure 14. Despite these differences, each of these features was shaped by the same processes of weathering and erosion.

Desert features reveal the effects of weathering and agents of erosion, such as water, on areas that have little ground cover and moisture. These factors combine to produce a variety of landscapes.

Figure 14 Desert landscapes, such as California's Death Valley, have relatively few plants when compared to more humid climates.

Weathering in Deserts

In humid regions, well-developed soils support an almost continuous cover of vegetation. This covering greatly reduces mechanical weathering, which means that chemical weathering is dominant here. In deserts, chemical weathering can create clays and thin soils over long time spans. Many iron-bearing silicate minerals oxidize, producing the rust-colored stain that tints some desert landscapes. **Although chemical weathering occurs in deserts, mechanical weathering is far more dominant in shaping desert landscapes.** A combination of a lack of moisture, fewer plants, and the resulting scarcity of organic acids from decaying plants, means that the minerals in the rock debris remain unchanged. It is these same factors that allow mechanical weathering agents to break down and transport rock debris easily.

 **Reading Checkpoint** *Why do deserts experience less chemical weathering than humid regions?*

Figure 15 Desert Streams
A Most of the time stream channels in deserts remain dry.
B This is the same stream shortly after a heavy rain shower. Desert streams can cause a large amount of erosion in a short time.
Predicting *How long will the water flow in this stream?*

Water in Deserts

Water is a powerful erosive agent in deserts, partially because the sands are loose and exposed due to a lack of vegetation. Although scarce in deserts, water can rapidly change and shape the landscape, especially after it rains. **In deserts, water collects in streams and rivers that can deposit alluvial fans, form playa lakes, and even carve steep-walled valleys, or canyons, through the desert.**

Desert Streams In the desert, there are bridges with no water beneath them and dips in the road crossing empty stream channels. Deserts receive very little rain during the year. In some years, these channels may remain completely dry. But after a rain, streams may carry water for a few hours or a few days. In the western states, dry channels are called *washes* or *arroyos*.

Desert streams are known for dangerous flash flooding after heavy rains. Heavy showers can release so much rain that the soil cannot absorb it. Without vegetation, water quickly runs off the land, as shown in Figure 15. The floods end as quickly as they start but the amount of erosion caused during a single short-lived rain event is impressive. By contrast, in humid regions, a flood on a river such as the Mississippi can take days to reach its crest and days to subside.

 **Reading Checkpoint** *How do floods differ between deserts and humid regions?*

Alluvial Fans Because deserts typically lack permanent streams, they have interior drainage. This means that many desert streams do not reach the ocean. When the occasional torrents of water produced by sporadic rains move down the mountain canyons, they are heavily loaded with sediment. Emerging from the confines of the canyon, the runoff spreads over the gentler slopes at the base of the mountains and quickly loses speed. Consequently, most of its load is dumped within a short distance. The result is a cone of debris known as an **alluvial fan**, which forms at the mouth of a canyon, as shown in Figure 16.

In the United States, the dry Basin and Range Province is an excellent example of interior drainage. The region includes southern Oregon, all of Nevada, western Utah, southeastern California, southern Arizona and New Mexico, and far west Texas. The Basin and Range contains more than 200 relatively small mountain ranges that rise 900 to 1500 meters above the basins that separate them. Alluvial fans are very common here.

Figure 16 Alluvial Fans Over the years, alluvial fans enlarge and merge with fans from adjacent canyons to produce an apron of sediment along the mountain front. These features are common in mountainous deserts, such as in Death Valley, California.

Figure 17 Playa Lakes and Playas A The water in playa lakes may be less than a meter deep and very rich in minerals. **B** Playas can be identified by their cracked lake bed surface and salt crusts left behind by the evaporated water.

Q *I heard that deserts are expanding. Is that true?*

A Yes. The problem is called desertification, and it refers to the alteration of land to desert-like conditions as the result of human activities. It commonly takes place on the margins of deserts. It is triggered when the modest natural vegetation in marginal areas is removed by plowing or grazing. When droughts occur, the lack of vegetation allows heavy soil erosion to remove any remnants of fertile soil. Desertification is particularly serious in the region south of the Sahara Desert known as the Sahel.

Playas Lakes and Playas On the rare occasions of abundant rainfall, or snowmelt in the mountains, streams may flow across the alluvial fans to the center of the basin, converting the basin floor into a shallow **playa lake**, as shown in Figure 17A. Playa lakes last only a few days or weeks, before evaporation and infiltration remove the water. The dry, flat lake bed that remains is called a *playa.*

Some permanent streams do manage to cross arid regions. The Colorado and Nile Rivers begin in well-watered mountains with huge water supplies. The rivers are full enough at the beginning to survive their desert crossings. The Nile River, for example, leaves the lakes and mountains of central Africa and covers almost 3000 kilometers of the Sahara without a single tributary adding to its flow. In humid regions, however, rivers generally gain water from both incoming tributaries and groundwater.

Section 7.2 Assessment

Reviewing Concepts

1. ⬤ How are desert streams different from streams in humid locations?

2. ⬤ How do weathering processes affect deserts?

3. Why is erosion by running water important in deserts?

4. How does a river survive crossing an arid region?

Critical Thinking

5. **Comparing and Contrasting** Compare and contrast the Nile River with the Mississippi River. Which factor is most responsible for their differences?

6. **Applying Concepts** Explain how evaporation affects drainage systems in desert areas.

Writing in Science

Describe how a desert stream might start to flow and the features its waters may create in the desert. Make sure to use the terms learned in this section.

7.3 Landscapes Shaped by Wind

Key Concepts

- What are two ways in which wind causes erosion?
- What types of landforms are deposited by wind?
- How do sand dunes differ?

Vocabulary

- deflation
- desert pavement
- loess
- dune

Reading Strategy

Outlining Before you read, make an outline of this section. Use the green headings as the main topics and the blue headings as subtopics. As you read, add supporting details.

Landscapes Shaped by Wind
I. Wind Erosion
A. Deflation
B. Abrasion
II. _____?_____
A. _____?_____

Wind Erosion

Compared with running water, wind does not do nearly as much erosional work on the land, even in deserts. But wind is still an important force. The wind can be very erosive to exposed sands and soils in any climate. However, in deserts, the soils are driest and generally have less vegetation to hold soil in place. Therefore, wind does its most effective erosional work in deserts.

Strong winds pick up, transport, and deposit great quantities of fine sediment. Farmers of the Great Plains experienced the power of wind erosion during the 1930s. After they plowed the natural vegetation from this semi-arid region, a severe drought set in. The land was left exposed to wind erosion. Vast dust storms swept away the exposed, fertile topsoil. The area became known as the Dust Bowl.

Wind erodes land surfaces in two ways: deflation and abrasion. **Deflation** occurs when the wind lifts and removes loose particles such as clay and silt. Coarser sand particles roll or skip along the surface in a process called saltation. In the Dust Bowl, deflation lowered the land by a meter or more in only a few years, as shown in Figure 18.

Deflation also results in shallow depressions called blowouts. You can see thousands of blowouts in the Great Plains. They range from small dimples less than 1 meter deep and 3 meters wide to depressions more than 45 meters deep and several kilometers across.

Figure 18 The mounds in this photo show the level of the land before deflation removed the topsoil. The mounds are 1.2 meters tall and are anchored by vegetation. The photo shows soil loss in the Dust Bowl.
Applying Concepts *How did farmers contribute to ruining the land during the Dust Bowl?*

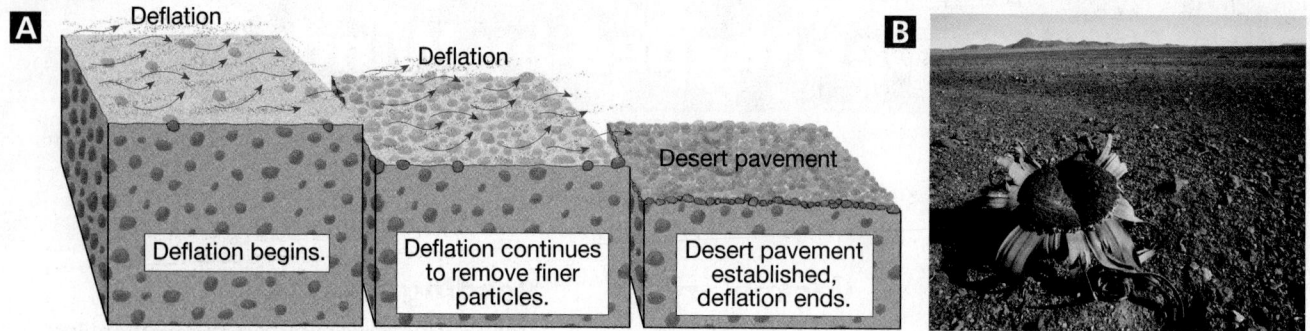

A Deflation

Deflation begins.

Deflation

Deflation continues to remove finer particles.

Desert pavement

Desert pavement established, deflation ends.

B

Figure 19 Deflation A These cross sections show how deflation removes the sand and silt of the desert surface until only coarser particles remain. These coarser particles concentrate into a tightly packed layer called desert pavement. **B** Desert pavement like this in southern Africa protects the surface from further deflation.
Predicting *What will happen if a vehicle disturbs this desert pavement?*

In portions of many deserts, the surface is characterized by a layer of coarse pebbles and cobbles that are too large to be moved by the wind. Deflation creates this kind of stony surface layer, called **desert pavement**, when it removes all the sand and silt and leaves only coarser particles. See Figure 19. The remaining surface of coarse pebbles and cobbles protects the soils and sands below it from further deflation—unless vehicles or animals break it up. If something does disturb the surface, the wind is able to erode the unprotected soils and sands again.

The second form of wind erosion is abrasion. Abrasion happens when windblown sand cuts and polishes exposed rock surfaces. Blowing sand can grind away at boulders and smaller rocks, sometimes sandblasting them into odd shapes. Abrasion is often credited for features such as balanced rocks that stand high atop narrow pedestals or the detailing on tall pinnacles. However, these features are not the results of abrasion. Sand rarely travels more than a meter above the surface, so the wind's sandblasting effect is limited in a vertical extent. However, in some areas, telephone poles have been cut through near the base.

Reading Checkpoint *What is deflation?*

Wind Deposits

 The wind can create landforms when it deposits its sediments, especially in deserts and along coasts. Both layers of loess and sand dunes are landscape features deposited by wind. These layers of silt and mounds of sand are striking features in some parts of the world.

Loess Windblown silt can build up, forming thick deposits called **loess.** The thickest and most extensive deposits of loess on Earth occur in western and northern China. The wind transported the silt from nearby deserts. This fine, buff-colored sediment gives the Yellow River its name. You also can find loess in the United States. See Figure 20. Strong winds sweeping across glacial sediments formed loess deposits in portions of the Midwest and the Columbia Plateau in the Pacific Northwest. Loess forms fertile soils, which support many crops and lush vegetation.

Figure 20 This loess bluff near the Mississippi River in southern Illinois is about 3 meters high.

Figure 21 Sand slides down the steeper face of a dune in New Mexico's White Sands National Monument. Wind blows sand up the opposite, windward, face of the dune, then it drops down this sheltered side. Slippage along the steep side results in migration of the dune in the direction the wind blows.

Figure 22 These cross-beds are found in Utah.

Sand Dunes Sand particles fall to the ground when wind speed falls and the energy available for transport diminishes, as happens at an obstruction. ◖**Wind can deposit sand in mounds or ridges called dunes when it encounters an obstruction.** Dunes can begin near obstructions as small as a clump of vegetation or a rock. Once the sand starts to mound up it serves as its own obstruction, and it traps more and more sand. With enough sand and long periods of steady wind, the mound of sand becomes a dune.

Dunes often are steeper on the sheltered side and more gently sloping on the side facing the wind. Wind blows sand grains up the gentler, windward side. Once the sand blows over the crest of the dune, the wind slows and the sand drops out. The sheltered side of the dune becomes steeper, and the sand eventually slides down the slope, as shown in Figure 21. In this way, the dune tends to migrate in the direction toward which the wind blows.

As sand is deposited on the sheltered side of the dune, it forms layers that slope in the direction toward which the wind is blowing. These sloping layers are called cross-beds. When the dunes are eventually buried under other layers of sediment and become sedimentary rock, the cross-beds remain as a record of their origin, as shown in Figure 22.

Reading Checkpoint *How do obstructions help to form dunes?*

For: Links on wind erosion
Visit: www.SciLinks.org
Web Code: cjn-2073

Types of Sand Dunes

Dunes are not just random heaps of sand. They occur in a variety of consistent forms worldwide. 👄 **The shape of a sand dune depends on the wind direction and speed, how much sand is available, and the amount of vegetation.** Figure 23 shows six different types of dunes.

Barchan Dunes Solitary sand dunes shaped like crescents are called barchan dunes. These form on flat, hard ground where vegetation and the supply of sand are limited. Barchan dunes move slowly and only reach heights of about 30 meters. If the wind direction is constant, barchan dunes remain symmetrical. One tip of the dune can grow larger than the other if the wind direction varies somewhat.

Transverse Dunes If prevailing winds are steady, sand is plentiful, and vegetation is sparse, dunes form in a series of long ridges. They are called transverse dunes because these ridges are perpendicular to the direction of the wind. Transverse dunes are typical in many coastal areas.

Figure 23 Wind strength and direction, the supply of sand, and vegetation cover are factors that affect the formation of sand dunes.
Classifying *Which type of sand dune forms in coastal areas with some vegetation and strong onshore winds?*

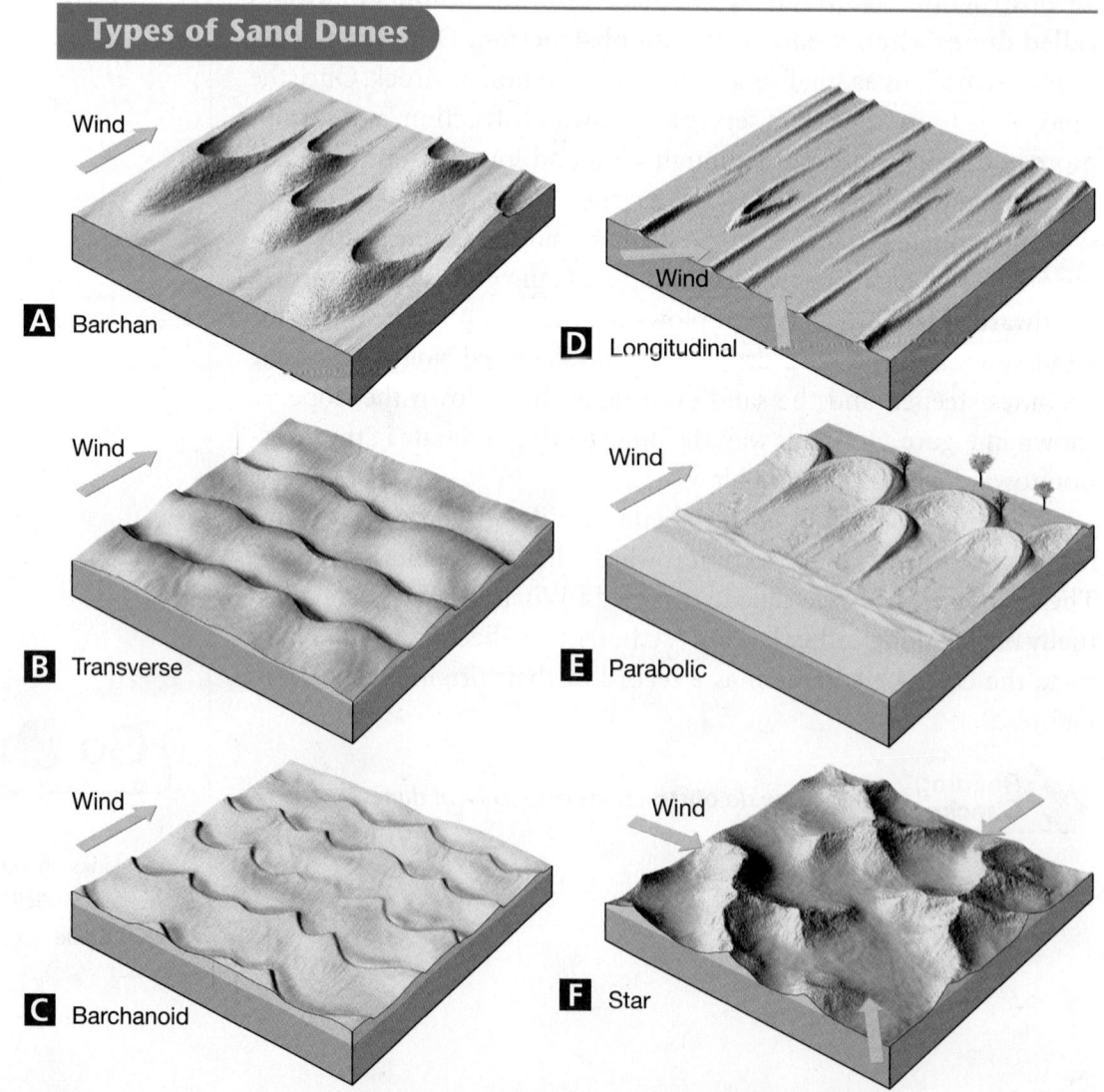

Types of Sand Dunes

A Barchan

B Transverse

C Barchanoid

D Longitudinal

E Parabolic

F Star

They also comprise the "sand seas" found in parts of the Sahara and Arabian deserts. Transverse dunes in both of these deserts reach heights of 200 meters, measure 1 to 3 kilometers across, and extend for distances of 100 kilometers or more.

Barchanoid Dunes A common dune form that is intermediate between a barchan and transverse dune is the barchanoid dune. These scalloped rows of sand form at right angles to the wind. The rows resemble a series of barchans that have been positioned side by side. You can see them at White Sands National Monument in New Mexico.

Longitudinal Dunes Longitudinal dunes are long ridges of sand that form parallel to the prevailing wind. These dunes occur where sand supplies are moderate and the prevailing wind direction varies slightly. In portions of North Africa, Arabia, and central Australia, longitudinal dunes can reach nearly 100 meters high and extend for more than 100 kilometers.

Parabolic Dunes Parabolic dunes look like backward barchans. Their tips point into the wind instead of away from it. They form where some vegetation covers the sand. Parabolic dunes often form along the coast where strong onshore winds and abundant sand are available.

Star Dunes Star dunes are isolated hills of sand mostly found in parts of the Sahara and Arabian deserts. Their bases resemble stars and they usually have three or four sharp ridges that meet in the middle. Star dunes develop in areas of variable wind direction, and they sometimes reach heights of 90 meters.

Q *Aren't deserts mostly covered with sand dunes?*

A Many people think a desert is covered in drifting sand dunes. Some deserts do have striking sand dunes. But sand dunes worldwide represent only a small percentage of the total desert area. Dunes cover only one-tenth of the world's largest desert, the Sahara, and only one-third of the world's sandiest desert, the Arabian, is covered in dunes.

Section 7.3 Assessment

Reviewing Concepts

1. How does deflation lower the surface of the desert?
2. What would you expect to see in areas subject to abrasion?
3. What was the Dust Bowl, and why did it occur?
4. How does a dune help itself to grow?
5. What factors determine the shape of sand dunes?

Critical Thinking

6. **Comparing and Contrasting** Compare and contrast loess and sand dunes.
7. **Designing Experiments** Describe how you would conduct an experiment to determine the wind speed necessary to suspend sand, silt, and clay particles.

Connecting Concepts

Which dune type would you expect to travel the least? Explain your answer.

Erosion

Erosion is the process by which weathered sediment is carried away. Rock material can be moved by streams and rivers, waves, glacial ice, or wind. The number of fragments that are moved and the distance that they travel are affected by factors such as the size and mass of the particles and the speed at which the eroding agent is moving. Erosion affects the landscapes of all of the regions of the world.

WATER FLOWING
As water flows from highlands to the sea, sharp descents result in rapids and waterfalls. Flowing water is an important agent of erosion.

Sand dunes

Rock arch

Wash

Rock fragments collect in wash

SAND DUNES
A dune begins to form where a plant or other obstacle slows the wind, which drops its load of sand. As the sand piles up, it creates an ever-growing barrier to the wind, causing more sand to be dropped. Eventually the dune crest may collapse like an ocean wave.

EROSION IN ARID LANDS
When rare torrential rain comes to arid areas, entire mountainsides may be swept clean of boulders, rock fragments, sand, and clay. Flash floods move eroded material down washes—the valleys of streams that are usually dry.

SEAS OF SAND
The huge amounts of sand that comprise some deserts started out as rock that was weathered to form fine particles. The finer the particle, the farther it can be transported by agents of erosion.

EROSION BY GLACIAL ICE

Huge masses of ice that move downhill are called **glaciers.** Over thousands or millions of years, they can scour mountainsides and dramatically change the shapes of valleys.

1. Before glaciation
A narrow, V-shaped river valley is surrounded by rounded mountains.

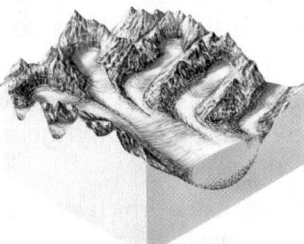

2. During glaciation
Moving ice erodes mountaintops and carves wider valleys.

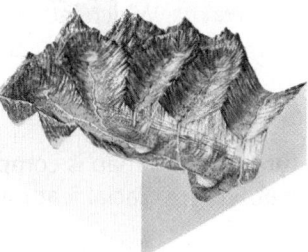

3. After glaciation
The result is a U-shaped valley with rugged, sharp peaks above.

STREAM EROSION

Streams erode their banks and beds, continually widening and deepening them. In some cases, a canyon may result. A **canyon,** such as this one in Utah, is a deep valley with steep sides that have been eroded by river water.

WAVE ACTION

Coastlines are constantly eroded by waves. Waves are formed by winds blowing over water. Cracked and soft rocks are eroded away first, forming arches. If the arch roof collapses, a **sea stack** results.

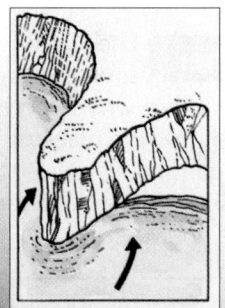

1. Waves curve around headland.

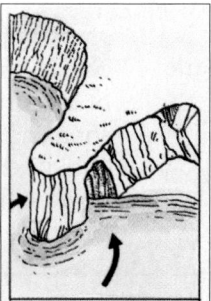

2. An arch forms.

3. A sea stack results.

Sea stack off the British Isles

ASSESSMENT

1. **Key Terms** Define (a) erosion, (b) wash, (c) glacier, (d) canyon, (e) sea stack.

2. **Environmental Change** How does water gradually reshape the land?

3. **Physical Characteristics** What are some major physical characteristics of an arid landscape eroded by wind and rain?

4. **Physical Processes** Analyze the three diagrams of glacial erosion. How can glaciers change the shapes of mountain valleys?

5. **Critical Thinking** **Analyzing Causes and Effects** How can erosion on farmlands cause a reduction in agricultural production?

Interpreting a Glacial Landscape

Topographic maps are valuable tools geologists use to interpret landscapes. Especially in the field—when your view can be limited—these maps not only help you determine your location, they can offer a bigger landscape picture than what is actually visible. See how well you can do at identifying glacial features on the map and interpreting them to reconstruct geologic history.

Problem How can a topographic map allow you to interpret a glacially formed landscape?

Materials
- topographic map
- piece of blank paper
- pencil

Skills Graphing, Inferring, Drawing Conclusions

Procedure

1. Following line A on the map, sketch a topographic profile of the Lake Fork Valley onto the grid below.

2. Place the straight edge of your blank paper along the line and mark in pencil where it meets every fifth contour line (the darker guide contours).

3. Be sure to write the elevation of every fifth contour line along the *y*-axis of the profile grid.

Analyze and Conclude

1. **Analyzing Data** How can you tell from your profile that the valley was formed by a glacier?

2. **Drawing Conclusions** Use the map to help you describe the direction the glacier flowed through this valley. How can you tell?

3. **Interpreting Diagrams** Which letter arrow points to cirques? You can refer to Figure 7 in your textbook for help.

4. **Interpreting Diagrams** Which letter arrows point to hanging valleys?

5. **Interpreting Diagrams** Which letter arrows point to arêtes?

6. **Interpreting Diagrams** Name a peak on the map that is a horn.

7. **Inferring** Feature E on the map is composed of glacial till. What type of glacial feature is E, and how did it form?

8. **Applying Concepts** Explain how Turquoise Lake formed.

Go Further Use library or Internet sources to research a glacier of interest. Find out whether it is growing or shrinking and how the glacier is used by people and other organisms. Give a short presentation on your findings to the class. Include visual aids to help make your points.

SOUTH   NORTH

Sugar Loaf Mountain   Bear Lake

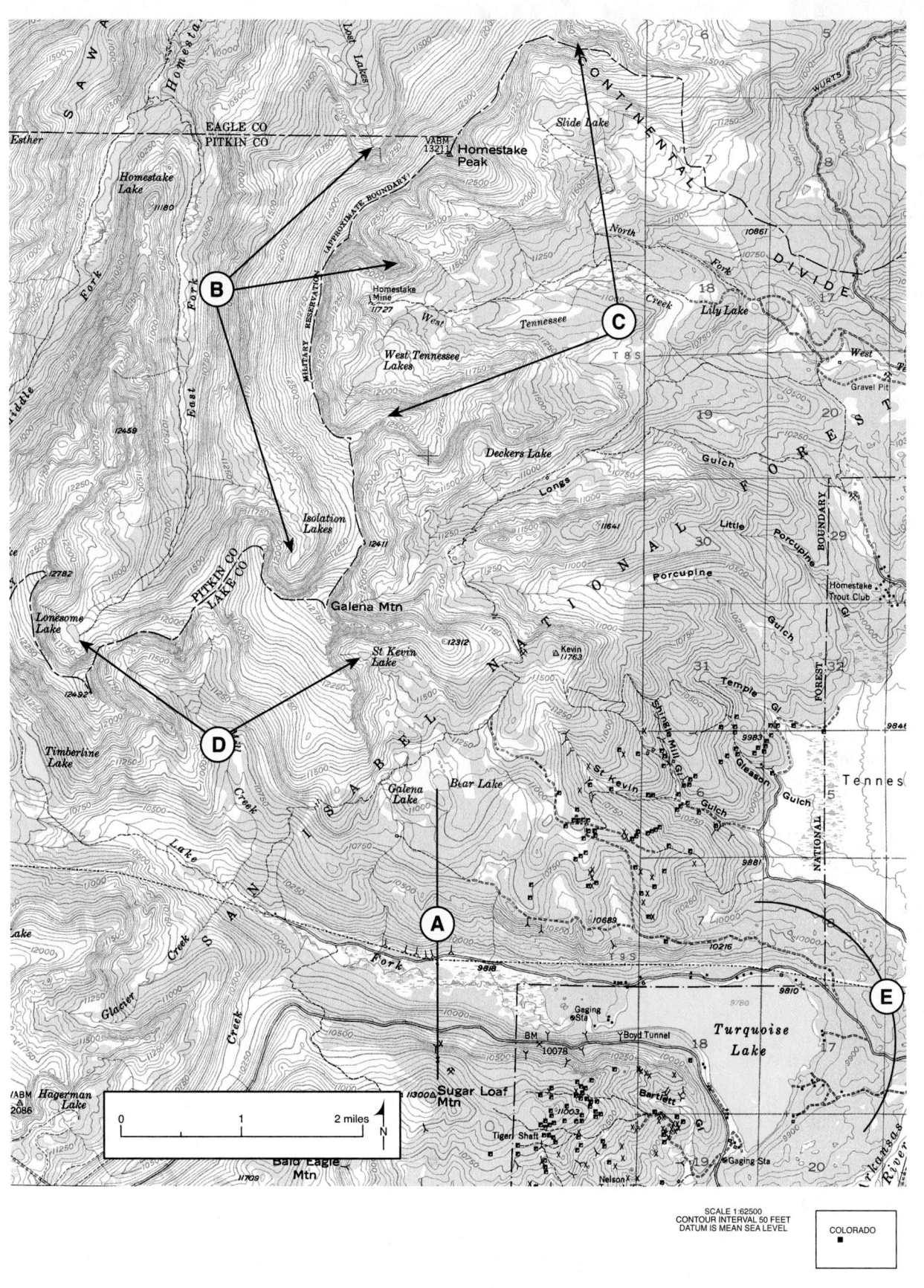

Study Guide

7.1 Glaciers

Key Concepts

- A valley glacier is a stream of ice that flows between steep rock walls from the top of a mountain valley.

- Ice sheets are sometimes called continental glaciers because they cover large regions, such as Antarctica and Greenland. They are huge compared to valley glaciers.

- The movement of glaciers is referred to as flow. Glacial flow happens in two ways: plastic flow and basal slip.

- The glacial budget is the balance or lack of balance between the build up in the zone of accumulation and loss in the zone of wastage.

- Many landscapes were changed by the widespread glaciers of the recent ice age.

- Glaciers produce a variety of erosional landscape features, such as glacial troughs, hanging valleys, cirques, arêtes, and horns.

- Glaciers are responsible for a variety of depositional landscape features, including moraines, outwash plains, kettles, drumlins, and eskers.

- Continental glaciers repeatedly formed, spread, and melted as Earth's climate cooled and warmed. Each cycle of glaciation, or episode, lasted about 100,000 years.

Vocabulary

ice age, *p. 188;* glacier, *p. 188;* snowline, *p. 189;* valley glacier, *p. 189;* ice sheet, *p. 189;* glacial trough, *p. 193;* till, *p. 194;* stratified drift, *p. 194;* moraine, *p. 195*

7.2 Deserts

Key Concepts

- Although chemical weathering occurs in deserts, mechanical weathering is far more dominant in shaping desert landscapes.

- In deserts, water collects in streams and rivers that can deposit alluvial fans, form playa lakes, and even carve steep-walled valleys, or canyons, through the desert.

Vocabulary

alluvial fan, *p. 201;* playa lake, *p. 202*

7.3 Landscapes Shaped by Wind

Key Concepts

- Wind erodes land surfaces in two ways: deflation and abrasion.

- The wind can create landforms when it deposits its sediments, especially in deserts and along coasts. Layers of loess and sand dunes are landscape features deposited by wind.

- Wind can deposit sand in mounds or ridges called dunes when it encounters an obstruction.

- The shape of a sand dune depends on the wind direction and speed, how much sand is available, and the amount of vegetation.

Vocabulary

deflation, *p. 203;* desert pavement, *p. 204;* loess, *p. 204;* dune, *p. 205*

Reviewing Content

Choose the letter that best answers the question or completes the statement.

1. Icebergs are produced when large pieces of ice break from the foot of a glacier during a process called
   a. plucking.
   b. deflation.
   c. calving.
   d. abrasion.

2. What type of dune forms at right angles to the wind when there is abundant sand, a lack of vegetation, and a constant wind direction?
   a. barchan
   b. transverse
   c. longitudinal
   d. parabolic

3. Which area was NOT covered in ice sheets at the peak of the most recent ice age?
   a. Siberia
   b. Europe
   c. North Africa
   d. Antarctica

4. All rock debris of glacial origin is called
   a. till.
   b. glacial drift.
   c. stratified drift.
   d. outwash.

5. What term is used to describe a dry channel in a desert?
   a. playa lake
   b. wash
   c. alluvial fan
   d. playa

6. The two major ways that glaciers erode land are abrasion and
   a. plucking.
   b. tension.
   c. deflation.
   d. slipping.

7. The most noticeable result of deflation in some places are shallow depressions called
   a. sinkholes.
   b. blowouts.
   c. loess.
   d. kettles.

8. In which of these places do extensive yellow loess deposits occur?
   a. Canada
   b. Cambodia
   c. China
   d. Australia

9. Which of the following is NOT a feature associated with valley glaciers?
   a. horn
   b. cirque
   c. arête
   d. arroyo

10. The broad, ramp-like surface of stratified drift built adjacent to the downstream edge of most end moraines is a (an)
    a. kettle.
    b. drumlin.
    c. outwash plain.
    d. terminal moraine.

Understanding Concepts

11. Why is the uppermost 50 m of a glacier called the zone of fracture?

12. How do the erosional processes of plucking and abrasion work?

Use the diagram below to answer Question 13.

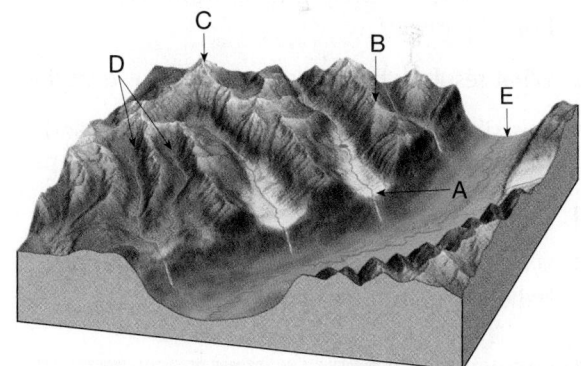

13. The area in the diagram was eroded by valley glaciers. For each feature listed below, write the letter of that feature in the diagram.
    a) cirque
    b) glacial trough
    c) hanging valley
    d) horn
    e) arête

Assessment *continued*

14. Describe each type of moraine:
    a) end moraine
    b) lateral moraine
    c) ground moraine

15. For each feature listed below, write the letter of that feature in the diagram.

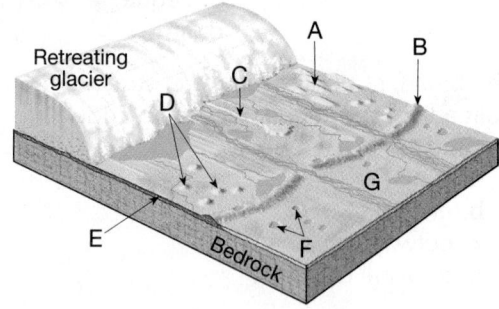

Retreating glacier

Bedrock

a) drumlin
b) outwash plain
c) esker
d) end moraine

16. Describe how sand dunes migrate.

17. How does the transport of sediment by glaciers differ from transport by water?

18. How do desert streams differ from those in humid regions?

19. What results when desert pavement is disturbed?

20. Describe the relative importance of wind and running water in eroding the desert landscape.

21. How is it possible for ice to flow?

22. Why do crevasses only extend 50 meters or so beneath the surface of a glacier?

Critical Thinking

23. **Relating Cause and Effect** Explain how a glacier's budget determines whether it advances, retreats, or remains stationary.

24. **Comparing and Contrasting** In what ways are the erosional actions of wind, water, and glaciers similar? How are they different?

25. **Inferring** Explain why glacial erratics will usually be made of rocks that differ from the bedrock in the area where they are found.

Analyzing Data

Use the graph below to answer Questions 26–28.

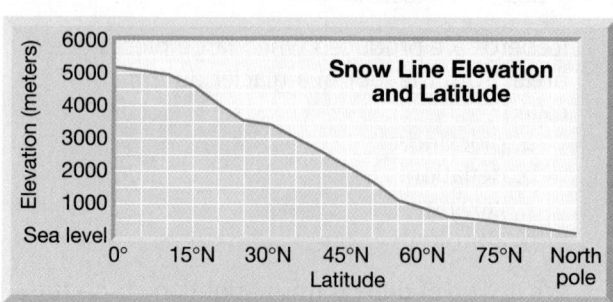

26. **Inferring** What is the minimum elevation required for year-round snow on a mountain located on the equator?

27. **Inferring** Suppose a 2000-meter tall mountain was located at 75 degrees north of the equator. What percentage of its height would have year-round snow?

28. **Drawing Conclusions** Write a statement that summarizes the information in the graph.

Concepts in Action

29. **Using Models** Explain how you would model each type of sand dune using a fan, a pan full of sand, and some playing cards.

30. **Classifying** Which types of landscape features described in this chapter resulted from erosion? Which types resulted from deposition?

31. **Writing in Science** Write a paragraph that summarizes the role of climate in the development of the landscapes discussed in this chapter.

Performance-Based Assessment

Researching Eskers are one glacial feature that people have transformed into a resource. Find out why glacial sediments are useful, who mines them, how they mine them, and the extent of their commercial value. Explain whether glacial deposits are considered renewable or nonrenewable resources.

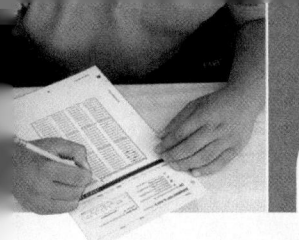

Standardized Test Prep

Test-Taking Tip

Avoiding Careless Mistakes
Students often make mistakes when they fail to read a test question and the possible answers carefully. Read the question carefully and underline key words that may change the meaning of the question, such as *not, except,* or *excluding.* After choosing an answer, reread the question to check your selection.

Choose the letter that best answers the question or completes the statement.

1. Which of the following is NOT associated with water?
   (A) desert stream
   (B) kettle
   (C) hanging valley
   (D) blowout

   (Answer: D)

2. Which of the following statements about ice sheets is NOT true?
   (A) They cover 30 percent of Earth's land surface.
   (B) They form where more snow accumulates than melts.
   (C) They are also called continental glaciers.
   (D) They can flow.

3. Which is NOT true of loess?
   (A) Loess is a blanket of silt covering the landscape.
   (B) The Yellow River in China is named for the loess that it transports.
   (C) Wind carries and deposits the sediments that comprise loess.
   (D) There are no loess deposits in the United States.

4. Under which of the following conditions will star dunes form?
   (A) in areas where the direction of the wind changes
   (B) in areas where the wind direction changes slightly and the sand supplies are moderate
   (C) in areas with steady winds, and limited vegetation and supplies of sand
   (D) along shores with strong onshore winds, lots of sand, and some vegetation

5. When a stream emerges from a mountain canyon, the stream slope is greatly reduced. As a result the sediment is deposited within a short distance and forms a (an)
   (A) playa lake.
   (B) alluvial fan.
   (C) sinkhole.
   (D) arête.

Answer the following questions in complete sentences.

6. Name the five basic types of moraines. How are they similar? How are they different?

7. Glaciers are solid, but they are a basic part of Earth's water cycle. Are glaciers a part of solid Earth or part of Earth's hydrosphere? Explain your answer.

8. What role do glaciers play in Earth's rock cycle?

CHAPTER 8

Earthquakes and Earth's Interior

21st Century Learning

Communication Skills

What can you find out about earthquakes?

Geologists present earthquake data on the United States Geological Service's (USGS) Web site. Visit the site and find the map with recent earthquakes. Click on an earthquake and read the description. Determine which pieces of information are intended for the general public and which are for scientists. Then, write a report explaining how you made decisions in categorizing the information.

Quick Lab
Measuring the Distance to Epicenters

Exploration Lab
Locating an Earthquake

How the Earth Works
Effects of Earthquakes

GEODe EARTH SCIENCE Forces Within
↳ Earthquakes

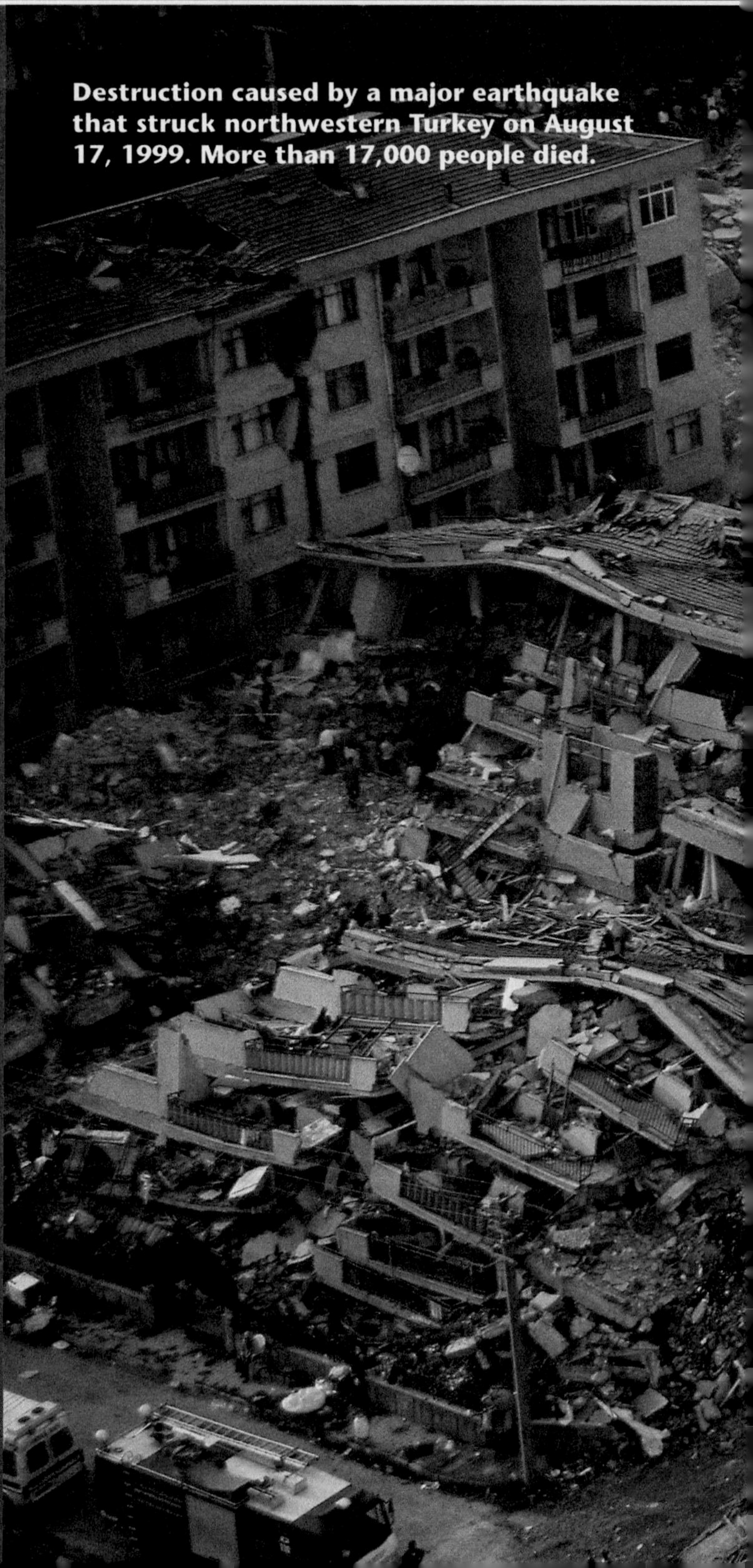

Destruction caused by a major earthquake that struck northwestern Turkey on August 17, 1999. More than 17,000 people died.

Chapter Preview

Inquiry Activity

How Can Buildings Be Made Earthquake-Safe?

Procedure

1. Construct a model of a one-story brick building using two thin pieces of cardboard as the floor and roof. Use sugar cubes as bricks and peanut butter, frosting, or double-sided tape to hold the bricks together.

2. Construct a second building. Make this building a two-story structure.

3. To test how well your buildings stand up to a simulated earthquake, place the one-story building on a table or desk. Then either drop a large book on the table, or gently shake the edge of the table. Record your observations.

4. Repeat Step 3 with the two-story model building. Record your observations.

5. Construct a third building using small pieces of window screen as reinforcement. This building should be a one-story structure. Spread a thin layer of peanut butter or frosting on the inside of the walls and carefully attach pieces of screen to each of the inside walls. Use extra peanut butter or frosting to reinforce the inside corners.

6. Repeat Step 3 with the reinforced building. Record your observations.

Think About It

1. Observing What happened to each building during the simulated earthquakes?

2. Comparing and Contrasting Compare the amount of earthquake damage in the three model buildings.

8.1 What Is an Earthquake?

Key Concepts

- What is a fault?
- What is the cause of earthquakes?

Vocabulary

- earthquake
- fault
- focus
- seismic waves
- epicenter
- elastic rebound
- aftershock

Reading Strategy

Building Vocabulary Copy the table below. Then as you read the section, write a definition for each vocabulary term in your own words.

Vocabulary	Definition
earthquake	a. _____?_____
fault	b. _____?_____
focus	c. _____?_____
seismic waves	d. _____?_____

Each year, more than 30,000 earthquakes occur worldwide that are strong enough to be felt. Most of these earthquakes are minor and do very little damage. Generally, only about 100 major earthquakes take place each year. Most of these occur in remote regions. However, if a large earthquake occurs near a city, the earthquake can be very destructive, as shown in Figure 1.

Earthquakes

An **earthquake** is the vibration of Earth produced by the rapid release of energy within the lithosphere. Earthquakes are caused by slippage along a break in the lithosphere, called a **fault**. **Faults are fractures in Earth where movement has occurred.**

Focus and Epicenter The point within Earth where an earthquake starts is called the **focus.** The focus of an earthquake is located along a fault beneath the surface. The energy released by the earthquake travels in all directions from the focus in the form of **seismic waves.** These waves are similar to the waves produced when a stone is dropped into a calm pond.

When you see a news report about an earthquake, the reporter always mentions the place on Earth's surface where the earthquake was centered. The **epicenter** is the location on the surface directly above the focus, as shown in Figure 1.

Figure 1 The focus of each earthquake is the place within Earth where the earthquake originated. The surface location directly above the focus is called the epicenter.
Predicting *Where do you think the damage from an earthquake is usually greatest?*

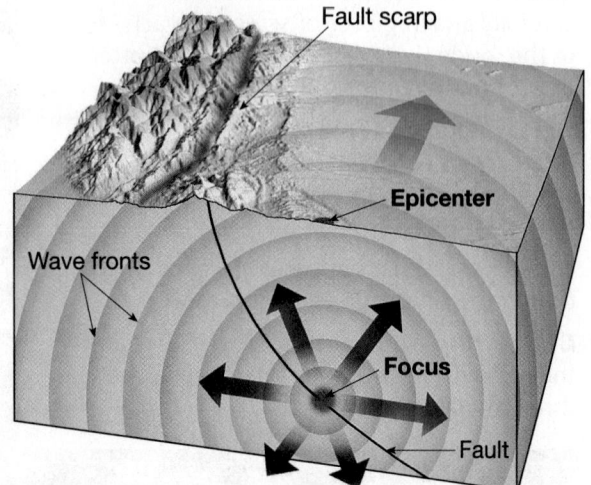

Faults and Change to Earth's Surface The movement that occurs along faults during earthquakes is a major factor in changing Earth's surface. The land along a fault can shift up to tens of meters in just one earthquake. Over time, this movement can push up coastlines, mountains, and plateaus.

The crust can move vertically or horizontally as a result of fault movements. If the crust moves up vertically, geologists say that it has been uplifted. Vertical movement can produce a sharp-edged ridge called a fault scarp. If the crust moves horizontally, they say it has been offset or displaced. Figure 2 shows the effect of horizontal displacement.

The San Andreas Fault The San Andreas fault system in California is one of the most studied in the world. The fault extends about 1300 kilometers through the state and into the Pacific Ocean. Studies have shown that displacement has often occurred along segments of the fault that are 100 to 200 kilometers long. Each fault segment behaves a bit differently than the others. Some parts of the fault show a slow, gradual movement known as fault creep. Other segments regularly slip and produce small earthquakes. However, some segments stay locked for hundreds of years before they break and cause great earthquakes.

One great earthquake on the San Andreas fault was the 1906 San Francisco earthquake. During this earthquake, the land on the western side of the fault moved as much as 4.7 meters relative to the land on the eastern side of the fault.

 **Reading Checkpoint** *What fault was involved in the 1906 San Francisco earthquake?*

Figure 2 Slippage along the Imperial fault caused an offset in this orange grove east of Calexico, California. The black arrows show the direction of fault movement.

The Cause of Earthquakes

Before the great San Francisco earthquake, scientists did not understand what causes earthquakes. Measurements and studies after the 1906 earthquake led to the development of a hypothesis that explains how earthquakes occur. **According to the elastic rebound hypothesis, most earthquakes are produced by the rapid release of energy stored in rock that has been subjected to great forces. When the strength of the rock is exceeded, it suddenly breaks, releasing some of its stored energy as seismic waves.** Earthquakes occur when the frictional forces on the fault surfaces are overcome.

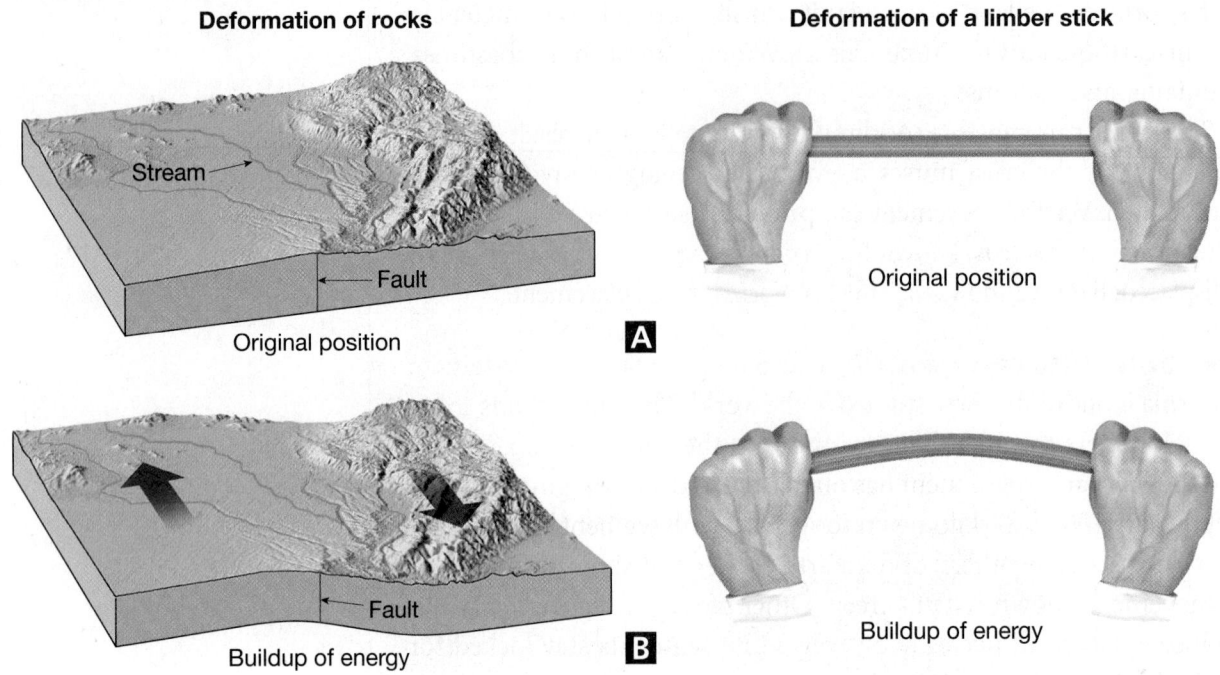

Deformation of rocks

Stream

Fault

Original position

A

Fault

Buildup of energy

B

Deformation of a limber stick

Original position

Buildup of energy

Figure 3 Rock bends as it is stressed, storing elastic energy. Once the rock is strained beyond its breaking point, it ruptures and releases the stored energy in the form of seismic waves.
Predicting *How do you think the temperature of rock would affect its ability to bend or break?*

Deformation of Rocks

Forces inside Earth slowly deform the rock that makes up Earth's crust, causing the rock to change its shape, or bend. As rocks bend, they store elastic energy, just as a wooden stick does when it is bent. Elastic energy is the same kind of energy that is stored when you stretch a rubber band. As shown in Figure 3, deformation bends the rock on both sides of a fault.

Elastic Rebound

What happens to the elastic energy stored in rock? Again, think about bending a wooden stick. If you let go of one end, the stick springs back to its original shape. At the same time, the stick's stored elastic energy is released. But if you continue to apply force to the stick, it eventually snaps, also releasing the stored energy.

As you can see in Figure 3, something similar happens in the rock along a fault. Stored elastic energy builds up as the rock is deformed. Then, suddenly, the resistance caused by internal friction that holds the rocks together is overcome. The rocks slip at their weakest point—the focus of an earthquake. This movement exerts force farther along the fault, where additional slippage occurs until most of the stored elastic energy is released. The tendency for the deformed rock along a fault to spring back after an earthquake is called **elastic rebound.** Elastic rebound is similar to what happens when you release a stretched rubber band. But most of the energy released as a result of elastic rebound causes the movement along a fault that takes place during an earthquake.

 **Reading Checkpoint** *What is elastic rebound?*

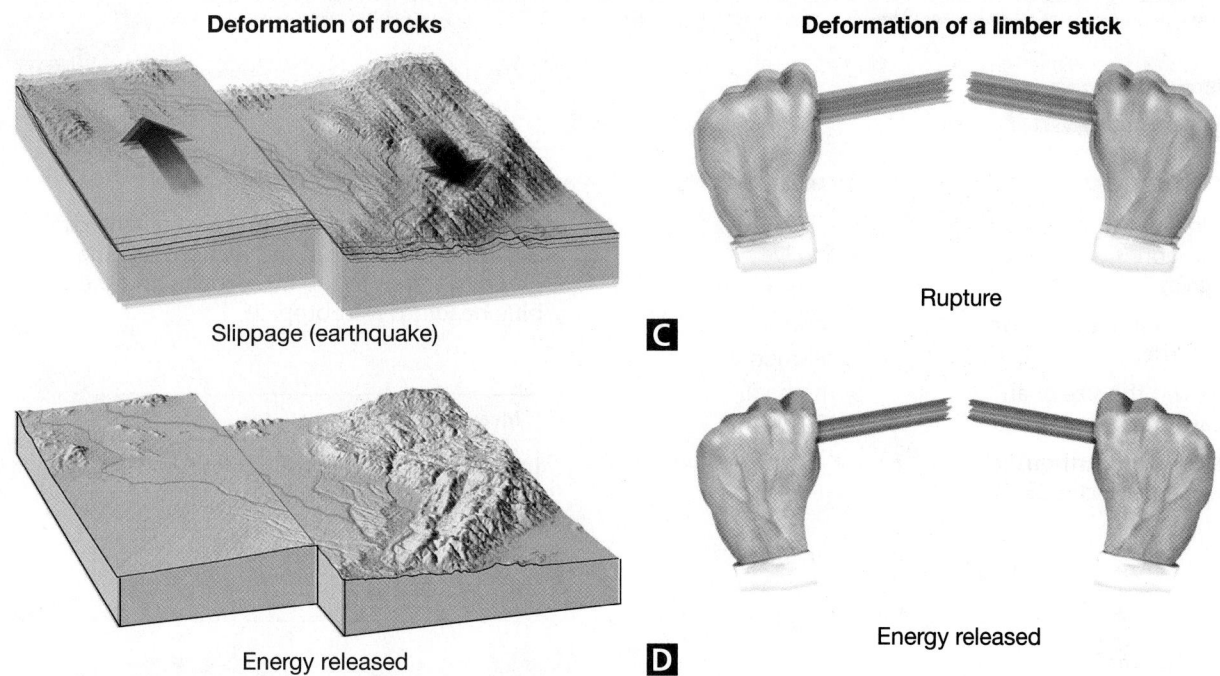

Deformation of rocks

Slippage (earthquake)

Energy released

Deformation of a limber stick

Rupture

C

Energy released

D

Aftershocks and Foreshocks Even a great earthquake like the 1906 San Francisco earthquake usually does not release all the elastic energy stored in the rock along a fault. Aftershocks and foreshocks also release some of a fault's stored elastic energy. An **aftershock** is an earthquake that occurs sometime soon after a major earthquake. Aftershocks may occur hours or even weeks after the major earthquake. Although usually much weaker than the main earthquake, an aftershock can still damage structures already weakened by the main quake. Small earthquakes called foreshocks sometimes come before a major earthquake. Foreshocks can happen days or even years before the major quake.

Go Online

SCiLINKS

For: Links on earthquakes
Visit: www.SciLinks.org
Web Code: cjn-3081

Section 8.1 Assessment

Reviewing Concepts

1. What is a fault?
2. Describe the cause of earthquakes.
3. What is an earthquake?
4. What are two ways in which deformation affects rock?
5. What are foreshocks and aftershocks?

Critical Thinking

6. **Connecting Concepts** How are an earthquake's fault, focus, and epicenter related?

7. **Explaining** What is meant by elastic rebound?
8. **Making Judgments** Why do most earthquakes cause little damage and loss of life?

Math Practice

9. In 25 years, how much movement will result from a fault that slowly slips 1.5 centimeters per year?

8.2 Measuring Earthquakes

Key Concepts

- What are the two categories of seismic waves?
- How are seismic waves recorded?
- How is the size of an earthquake measured?
- How is an earthquake epicenter located?

Vocabulary

- ◆ P wave
- ◆ S wave
- ◆ surface wave
- ◆ seismograph
- ◆ seismogram
- ◆ moment magnitude

Reading Strategy

Outlining As you read, make an outline of the important ideas in this section. Use the green headings as the main topics and the blue headings as subtopics.

Measuring Earthquakes
I. Seismic Waves
A. P Waves
B. _____?_____
C. _____?_____
II. _____?_____

In 2003, a powerful earthquake shook the Alaska wilderness south of Fairbanks along the Denali fault. The earthquake was so strong that it rippled the water in ponds and lakes thousands of kilometers away in Louisiana and Texas. What carries the energy released in an earthquake over such vast distances? The answer is seismic waves.

After an earthquake, Earth vibrates like a bell that has been struck with a hammer. Seismic waves transmit the energy of these vibrations from particle to particle through the materials that make up the lithosphere, mantle, and core.

Seismic Waves

Earthquakes produce two main types of seismic waves—body waves and surface waves. These seismic waves differ in their type of wave motion, their behavior as they travel through Earth, and their speed. The waves that travel through Earth's interior are called body waves. There are two types of body waves: P waves and S waves.

P Waves **P waves** are push-pull waves that push (or compress) and pull (or expand) particles in the direction the waves travel. P waves, shown in Figure 4, are also known as compressional waves. P waves travel faster than S waves. P waves can travel through both liquids and solids.

S Waves **S waves** shake particles at right angles to the waves' direction of travel. Their motion can be modeled by fastening one end of a rope and shaking the other end, as in Figure 4. S waves are also called transverse waves. S waves travel more slowly than P waves. S waves can travel through solids, but not liquids.

Surface Waves When body waves reach the surface, they produce **surface waves**. Surface waves travel more slowly than body waves. Surface waves move up-and-down as well as side-to-side. Surface waves are usually much larger than body waves, so surface waves are the most destructive seismic waves.

For: Seismic Waves activity
Visit: PHSchool.com
Web Code: czp-3081

Figure 4 Each type of seismic wave has characteristic motions.

Seismic Waves

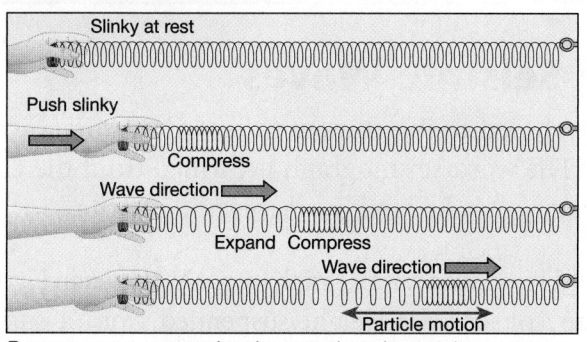

A P waves are compressional waves that alternately compress and expand the material through which they pass.

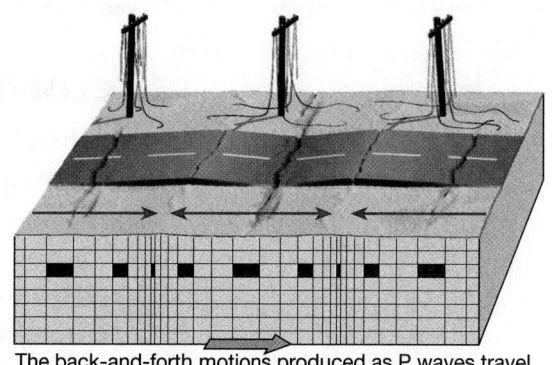

B The back-and-forth motions produced as P waves travel along the surface can cause the ground to buckle and fracture.

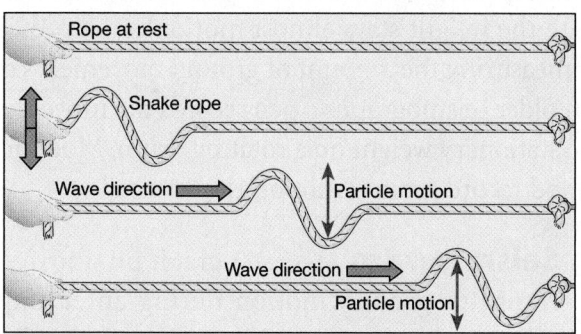

C S waves are transverse waves which cause material to shake at right angles to the direction of wave motion.

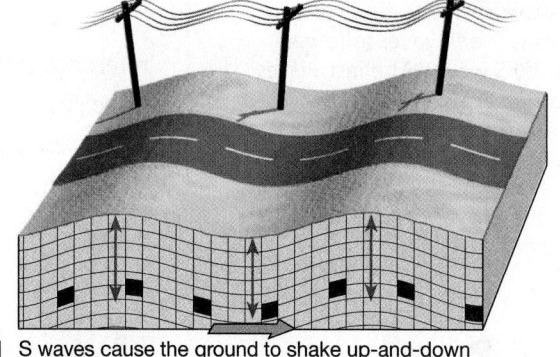

D S waves cause the ground to shake up-and-down and sideways.

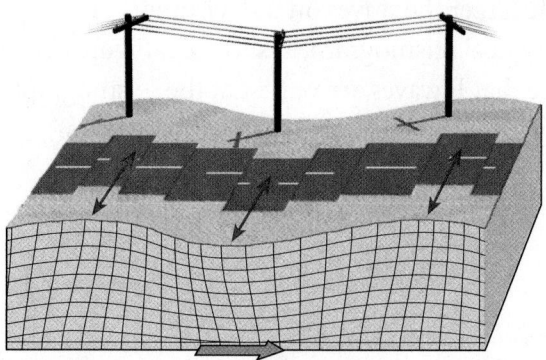

E One type of surface wave moves the ground from side to side and can damage the foundations of buildings.

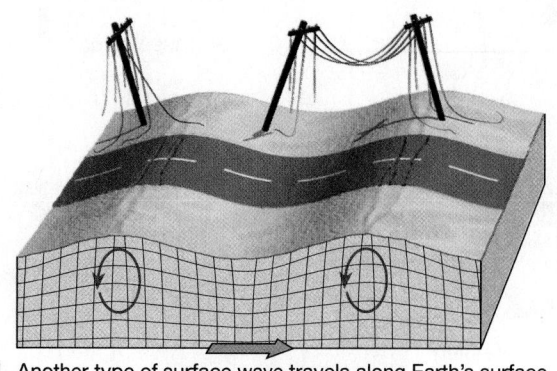

F Another type of surface wave travels along Earth's surface much like rolling ocean waves.

Figure 5 The seismograph (*seismos* = shake, *graph* = write) amplifies and records ground motion.

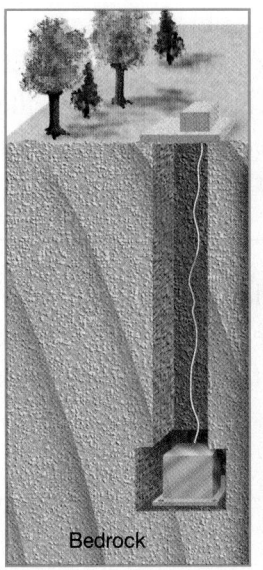

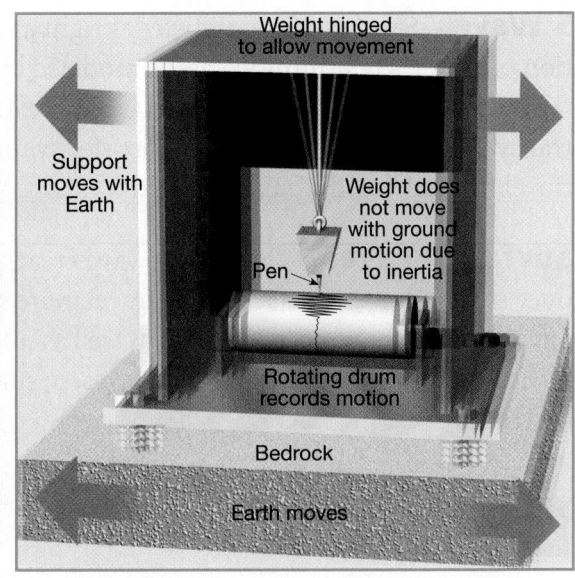

Recording Seismic Waves

Scientists have developed an instrument to record seismic waves—the seismograph. The word seismograph is formed from the Greek words *seismos,* meaning "shake" and *graph,* meaning "write."

Seismographs How does a seismograph work? As shown in Figure 5, a **seismograph** can consist of a weight suspended from a support attached to bedrock. When seismic waves reach the seismograph, the inertia of the weight keeps it almost stationary while Earth and the support vibrate. Because the weight stays almost motionless, it provides a reference point for measuring the amount of ground movement caused by seismic waves. In older seismographs a pen records the movement of Earth relative to the stationary weight on a rotating drum. Modern seismographs amplify and record ground motion electronically.

Figure 6 Typical Seismogram The first wave to arrive is the P wave, followed later by S waves. The last waves recorded are the surface waves. **Measuring** *What is the time interval in minutes between the arrival of the first P wave and the arrival of the first S wave?*

Seismogram A seismograph produces a time record of ground motion during an earthquake called a **seismogram.** A seismogram shows all three types of seismic waves. The stronger the earthquake, the larger the waves on the seismogram. By reading a typical seismogram, as shown in Figure 6, you can see that P waves arrive first at the seismograph, followed by S waves, and then surface waves.

✓ **Reading Checkpoint** *What is a seismogram?*

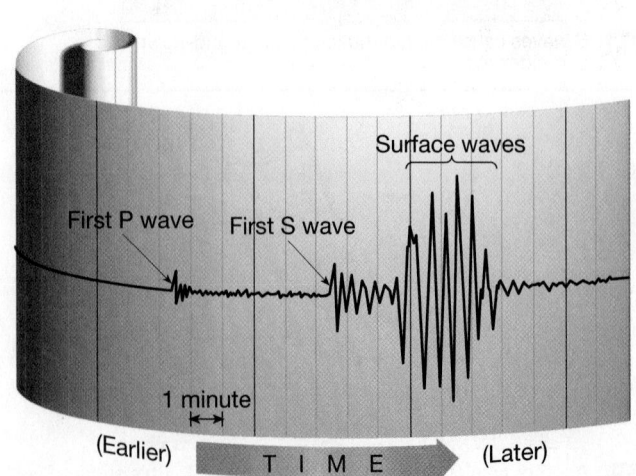

Measuring Earthquakes

Intensity is a measure of the amount of earthquake shaking at a given location based on the amount of damage. Magnitude (abbreviated as "M") is a measure of the size of seismic waves or the amount of energy released at the source of the earthquake. **The Richter scale and the moment magnitude scale measure earthquake magnitude. The Modified Mercalli scale is based on earthquake intensity.**

Richter Scale A familiar but outdated scale for measuring the magnitude of earthquakes is the Richter scale. The Richter scale is based on the height of the largest seismic wave (P, S, or surface wave) recorded on a seismogram. A tenfold increase in wave height equals an increase of 1 on the magnitude scale. For example, the amount of ground shaking for a M5.0 earthquake is 10 times greater than the shaking produced by an earthquake of M4.0 on the Richter scale.

Seismic waves weaken as the distance between the earthquake focus and the seismograph increases. The Richter scale is only useful for small, shallow earthquakes within about 500 kilometers of the epicenter. News reports often use the Richter scale in reporting earthquake magnitudes. Scientists, however, no longer use it routinely.

Moment Magnitude Scientists today use a more precise means of measuring earthquakes. It is called the moment magnitude scale. Moment magnitude is the most widely used measurement for earthquakes because it is the only magnitude scale that estimates the energy released by earthquakes. The **moment magnitude** is derived from the amount of displacement that occurs along a fault. The moment magnitude is calculated using several factors in addition to seismographic data. These factors include the average amount of movement along the fault, the area of the surface break, and the strength of the broken rock. Together these factors provide a measure of how much energy rock can store before it suddenly slips and releases this energy during an earthquake. The table describes the incidence of earthquakes of different magnitudes. During the last 100 years, there were only a few earthquakes with magnitudes of 9.0 or greater. These rare but extremely powerful earthquakes all occurred on faults located around or near the Pacific basin. Three of these earthquakes are listed in Table 2 on page 229.

 **Reading Checkpoint** *What is moment magnitude?*

Table 1 Earthquake Magnitudes		
Moment Magnitudes	**Effects Near Epicenter**	**Number per Year**
< 2.0	Generally not felt	> 600,000
2.0–2.9	Potentially perceptible	> 300,000
3.0–3.9	Rarely felt	> 100,000
4.0–4.9	Can be strongly felt	13,500
5.0–5.9	Can be damaging shocks	1,400
6.0–6.9	Destructive in built-up areas	110
7.0–7.9	Major earthquakes; serious damage	12
8.0 and above	Great earthquakes; destroy communities near epicenter	0–1

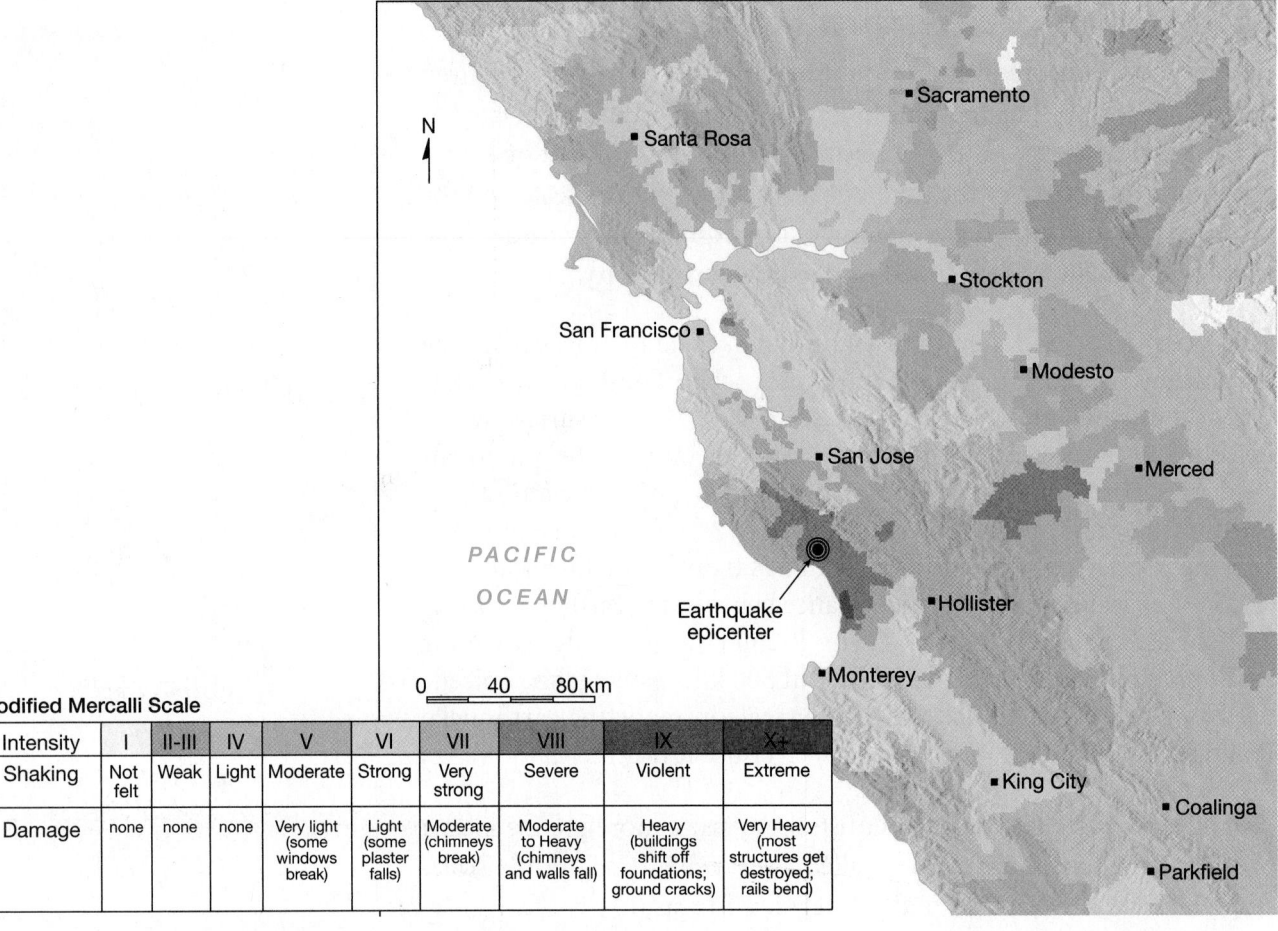

Modified Mercalli Scale

Intensity	I	II–III	IV	V	VI	VII	VIII	IX	X+
Shaking	Not felt	Weak	Light	Moderate	Strong	Very strong	Severe	Violent	Extreme
Damage	none	none	none	Very light (some windows break)	Light (some plaster falls)	Moderate (chimneys break)	Moderate to Heavy (chimneys and walls fall)	Heavy (buildings shift off foundations; ground cracks)	Very Heavy (most structures get destroyed; rails bend)

Figure 7 The magnitude-6.9 Loma Prieta earthquake struck the northern San Andreas fault near Santa Cruz, California, in 1989.

Modified Mercalli Scale Another scale used to rate earthquakes is the Modified Mercalli scale. This scale rates an earthquake's intensity in terms of the earthquake's effects at different locations. The scale has 12 steps, expressed as Roman numerals. An earthquake that can barely be felt is rated I. An earthquake that causes near total destruction is rated XII. The same earthquake can receive different Mercalli scale ratings at different locations. For example, an earthquake might be rated VIII (severe damage) near the epicenter, but only IV (light damage) 50 kilometers away. The map in Figure 7 uses the Mercalli scale to show areas affected by different levels of shaking from a major California earthquake.

Locating an Earthquake

The difference in speeds of P and S waves provides a way to locate the epicenter. The movement of these two types of seismic waves is like a race between two cars. The winning car is faster than the losing car. The P wave always wins the race, arriving ahead of the S wave. The longer the race, the greater the difference will be between the arrival times of the P and S waves at the finish line (the seismic station). The greater the interval between the arrival of the first P wave and the first S wave, the greater the distance to the earthquake epicenter.

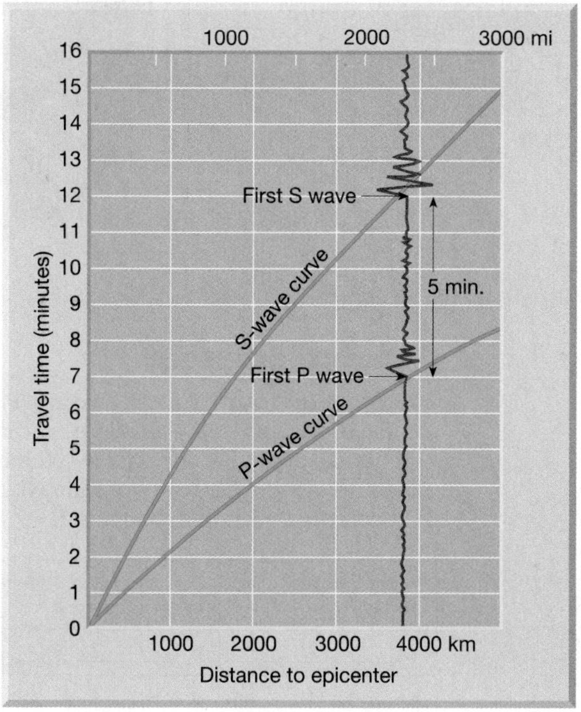

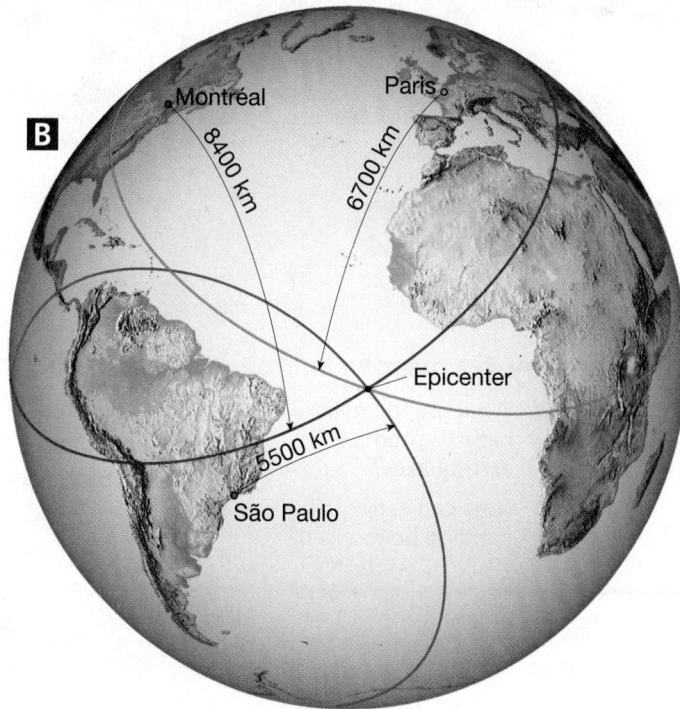

Figure 8 graph labels: Travel time (minutes), Distance to epicenter, First S wave, First P wave, S-wave curve, P-wave curve, 5 min., 1000, 2000, 3000 mi, 1000 2000 3000 4000 km

Globe labels: Montréal, Paris, 8400 km, 6700 km, Epicenter, 5500 km, São Paulo

The difference in arrival times of P waves and S waves can be shown on a travel-time graph like the one in Figure 8. 👁 **A travel-time graph, data from seismograms made at three or more locations, and a globe can be used to determine an earthquake's epicenter.** First, using the travel-time graph, you determine the distance from each seismic station to the earthquake. Then, on a globe showing each seismic station, as in Figure 8, you draw circles at the correct scale for the distance from each station to the epicenter. The radius of each circle equals the distance to the earthquake from that station. In Figure 8, you can see that the point where the three circles intersect is the epicenter of the earthquake.

Figure 8 Locating an Earthquake A The distance to the epicenter. The difference in arrival times of the first P wave and the first S wave on the travel-time graph is 5 minutes. So the epicenter is roughly 3800 kilometers away. **B** The point where the circles intersect is the epicenter.
Reading Graphs *What is the difference in arrival times between P waves and S waves for a seismic station that is 2000 km from an epicenter?*

Section 8.2 Assessment

Reviewing Concepts

1. 👁 List the two categories of seismic waves.
2. 👁 Describe how scientists detect and record seismic waves.
3. 👁 Describe the three different ways to measure the size of an earthquake.
4. 👁 Briefly describe how the epicenter of an earthquake is located.

Critical Thinking

5. **Comparing and Contrasting** Describe the differences in speed and mode of travel between primary waves and secondary waves.

6. **Applying Concepts** How does a seismograph measure an earthquake?

Writing in Science

Descriptive Paragraph Write a paragraph describing in your own words what would occur in an earthquake with a moment magnitude of 6.0.

8.3 Earthquake Hazards

Key Concepts

- What are the major hazards produced by earthquakes?
- How can earthquake damage be reduced?

Vocabulary

- liquefaction
- tsunami
- seismic gap

Reading Strategy

Monitoring Your Understanding Preview the Key Concepts, topic headings, vocabulary, and figures in this section. List two things you expect to learn. After reading, state what you learned about each item you listed.

What I Expect To Learn	What I Learned
a. _____?_____	b. _____?_____
c. _____?_____	d. _____?_____

The Prince William Sound earthquake that struck Alaska in 1964 was the most violent earthquake to jar North America in the 20th century. The earthquake was felt throughout Alaska. It had a moment magnitude of 9.2 and lasted 3 to 4 minutes. The quake left 131 people dead and thousands homeless. The state's economy was also badly damaged because the quake affected major ports and towns.

Causes of Earthquake Damage

An earthquake as powerful as the 1964 Alaska earthquake can cause catastrophic damage. But even less powerful earthquakes also pose serious hazards. ● **Earthquake-related hazards include seismic shaking, liquefaction, landslides and mudflows, and tsunamis.**

A

Figure 9 Earthquake Damage
A A magnitude-7.6 earthquake in northern Pakistan in 2005 destroyed mountain villages and killed more than 70,000 people.
B During a 1985 earthquake in Mexico, the soil beneath this toppled building liquified.
C A landslide triggered by an earthquake in 2001 buried this neighborhood in El Salvador.

Seismic Shaking The ground vibrations caused by seismic waves, called seismic shaking, are the most obvious earthquake hazard. Seismic waves interact to jolt and twist structures. Buildings made of unreinforced brick may collapse. Wood-frame buildings may remain intact, but still can be jolted off their foundations.

Seismic shaking is generally strongest close to an epicenter. Yet strong seismic shaking can occur in areas of loose soil or filled land relatively far from an epicenter. The filled soil magnifies the effects of seismic waves. Structures in such areas can experience severe damage.

Liquefaction Where soil and rock are saturated with water, earthquakes can cause a process called **liquefaction.** When liquefaction occurs, what had been stable soil suddenly turns into liquid. The liquid cannot support buildings or other structures. Buildings and bridges may settle and collapse. Underground storage tanks and sewer lines may float toward the surface.

Landslides and Mudflows Earthquakes can trigger different types of mass movement. These destructive events can quickly bury entire towns under millions of tons of debris.

Earthquakes often cause loose rock and soil on slopes to move. The result is a landslide. Most landslides occur on steep slopes where sediment is loose or where the rocks are highly fractured.

In areas where the water content of soil is high, an earthquake can start a mudflow. During a mudflow, a mixture of soil and water slides rapidly downhill.

 **Reading Checkpoint** *What is liquefaction?*

Table 2 Major Earthquakes		
Year	**Location**	**Magnitude†**
*1906	San Francisco, California	7.8
1923	Tokyo, Japan	7.9
1960	Southern Chile	9.5
*1964	Alaska	9.2
*1971	San Fernando, California	6.5
1985	Mexico City	8.1
*1989	Loma Prieta, California	6.9
*1994	Northridge, California	6.7
1999	Izmit, Turkey	7.4
1999	Chi Chi, Taiwan	7.6
2004	Indian Ocean near Indonesia	9.3

* U.S. earthquakes

† Widely differing magnitudes have been estimated for some earthquakes. When available, moment magnitudes are used.

B

C

Figure 10 Indian Ocean Tsunami, 2004 A surge of water rushes inland as a tsunami strikes the coast of Thailand. On average, only one or two destructive tsunamis occur worldwide every year. Only about one tsunami in every 10 years causes major damage and loss of life.

Tsunamis A **tsunami** is a wave formed when the ocean floor shifts suddenly during an earthquake. For example, in 2004 a magnitude-9.3 earthquake west of the island of Sumatra in the Indian Ocean produced devastating tsunamis. Without warning, the huge waves struck coastal areas of Indonesia, Sri Lanka, Thailand, and several other countries, killing nearly 300,000 people.

How do these giant waves form? A tsunami can occur when an earthquake pushes up a slab of ocean floor along a fault. An underwater landslide or volcanic eruption can also trigger a tsunami. Once formed, a tsunami resembles the ripples created when you drop a pebble in a pond. Surprisingly, a tsunami on the open ocean is usually less than 1 meter high. This wave races across the ocean at hundreds of kilometers per hour. However, as the wave enters shallower water near shore, the wave slows down and water begins to pile up. As you can see in Figure 11, a tsunami can strike the shore as a huge wave that sweeps inland causing great destruction. Tsunamis range from a few meters to more than 30 meters high.

A tsunami warning system alerts people in coastal areas around the Pacific Ocean. After the deadly 2004 tsunami, a similar system was planned for the Indian and Atlantic oceans. Scientists use devices that measure wave height to detect a tsunami. Tsunami warnings allow sufficient time to evacuate all but the area closest to the epicenter.

Figure 11 How a Tsunami Forms Movement of the ocean floor causes a tsunami. The speed of a tsunami is related to the ocean depth. As waves slow down in shallow water, they can grow in height until they topple and hit shore with tremendous force.

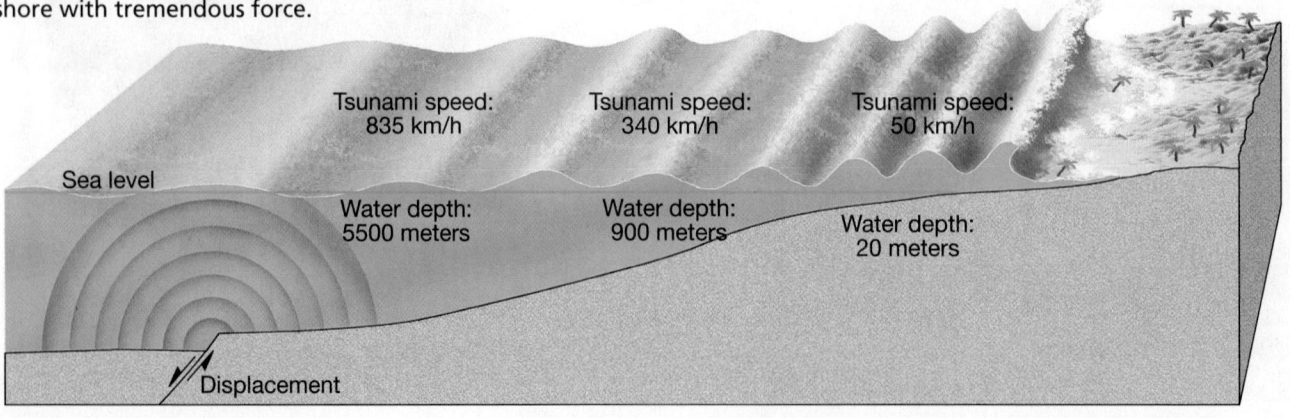

Tsunami speed: 835 km/h
Tsunami speed: 340 km/h
Tsunami speed: 50 km/h
Sea level
Water depth: 5500 meters
Water depth: 900 meters
Water depth: 20 meters
Displacement

Reducing Earthquake Damage

Earthquake damage depends on several factors. Two important factors are the strength and duration of seismic shaking and the materials and design of structures.  **Earthquake damage and loss of life can be reduced by determining the earthquake risk for an area, building earthquake-resistant structures, and following earthquake safety precautions.**

Assessing Earthquake Risk How can people reduce damage from earthquakes? First, it is important to know the risk of earthquakes in a region. As you can see in Figure 12, the distribution of earthquakes forms a pattern. Scientists have found that earthquakes are most frequent along the boundaries of Earth's tectonic plates.

Scientists use several methods to determine earthquake risk. They study historical records of earthquakes. They use devices to measure uplift, subsidence, and strain in the rocks near active faults. They also study "seismic gaps." A **seismic gap** is an area along a fault where there has not been any earthquake activity for a long period of time. Scientists hypothesize that the buildup of strain along a seismic gap will eventually lead to an earthquake. Considering all these data, scientists are studying ways to estimate the probability that an earthquake will occur in an area within the next 30 to 100 years.

Scientists also look for warning signs that an earthquake is about to strike. In addition to monitoring fault movements, they measure water levels and pressure in wells, radon gas emissions, and small changes in the electromagnetic properties of rocks. But efforts at short-term prediction of earthquakes have not yet been successful.

> **Reading Checkpoint** *What is a seismic gap?*

Figure 12 The map shows the distribution of the 14,229 earthquakes with magnitudes equal to or greater than 5 from 1980 to 1990. **Observing** *Where do you find most of the earthquakes—in the interiors of the continents or at the edges?*

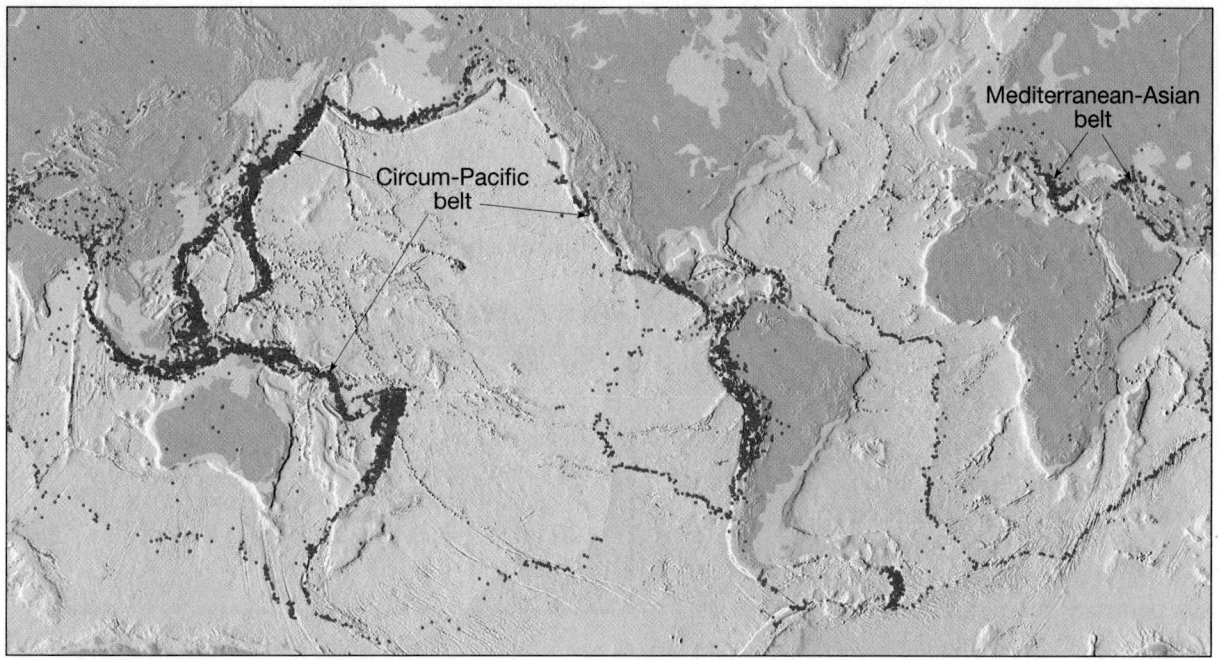

Seismic-Safe Design Many cities in earthquake-prone regions have building codes that set standards for earthquake-resistant structures. Steel frames can be reinforced with cross-braces. Buildings can be mounted on large rubber and steel pads, called base-isolators, which absorb the energy of seismic waves. Wood-frame homes can be reinforced and bolted to their foundations. People can "retrofit" or reinforce older buildings to make them more earthquake resistant.

Utility lines must also be protected. To prevent fires or explosions in gas mains, flexible pipes and automatic shut-off valves can be installed. Flexible joints in water mains can prevent loss of water pressure needed to fight fires. Much of the damage after the 1906 San Francisco earthquake resulted from fires. The fires could not be put out because water mains had broken.

Earthquake Safety Knowing what to do during an earthquake can reduce your risk of injury. The basic rule is to "drop, cover, and hold." Indoors, crouch beneath a sturdy table or desk and hold onto it. If no desk or table is nearby, crouch against an inner wall away from the outside of a building. Cover your head and neck with your arms. Avoid windows, mirrors, and furniture that might topple.

If you are outdoors when an earthquake strikes, move to an open area. Avoid vehicles, power lines, trees, and buildings. Sit down to avoid being thrown down. The danger does not end once an earthquake has stopped because an aftershock could cause weakened structures to collapse.

Figure 13 Strong, diagonal beams called cross-braces have been installed in this building to improve the structure's ability to withstand seismic waves.

Go Online
NSTA SCILINKS

For: Links on predicting earthquakes
Visit: www.SciLinks.org
Web Code: cjn-3082

Section 8.3 Assessment

Reviewing Concepts

1. Describe five hazards caused by earthquakes.
2. Explain how earthquake-related damage can be reduced.
3. What is a tsunami?
4. What is a seismic gap?

Critical Thinking

5. **Making Judgments** A builder in Alaska has a choice of two sites for a building: one is on filled land next to the ocean, and the other is inland on solid ground. Both sites are the same distance from an active fault. Which site should the builder choose? Explain.

6. **Predicting** In an earthquake-prone area, it has been many years since the last earthquake along a fault. Should residents be concerned about a future earthquake? Explain.

Connecting Concepts

Earthquakes In Section 8.1, you learned about the elastic energy stored in rocks before an earthquake and the elastic rebound hypothesis. How could this information be used to try to predict earthquakes?

8.4 Earth's Layered Structure

Reading Focus

Key Concepts

- What are Earth's layers based on composition?
- What are Earth's layers based on physical properties?
- How did scientists determine Earth's structure and composition?

Vocabulary

- crust
- mantle
- lithosphere
- asthenosphere
- outer core
- inner core
- Moho

Reading Strategy

Sequencing Copy the flowchart. After you read, complete the sequence of layers in Earth's interior.

Earth's Internal Structure

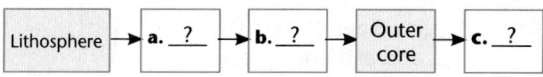

Compared to the planets we see in the night sky, Earth's interior is close by. But we can't reach it. The deepest well has drilled only 12 kilometers into Earth's crust. With such limited access, how do we know what Earth's interior is like? Most knowledge of the interior comes from the study of seismic waves that travel through Earth.

Layers Defined by Composition

If Earth's materials had the same properties throughout, seismic waves would spread through it in straight lines at constant speed. However, this is not the case. Seismic waves reaching seismographs located farther from an earthquake travel at faster average speeds than those recorded at locations closer to the event. This general increase in speed with depth is due to increased pressure, which changes the elastic properties of deeply buried rock. As a result, the paths of seismic waves through Earth are refracted, or bent, as they travel. Figure 14 shows this bending. **Earth's interior consists of three major layers defined by their chemical composition—the crust, mantle, and core.**

Crust The **crust,** the thin, rocky outer layer of Earth, is divided into oceanic and continental crust. The oceanic crust is roughly 7 kilometers thick and composed of the igneous rocks basalt and gabbro. The continental crust is 8–75 kilometers thick, but averages a thickness of 40 kilometers. It consists of many rock types. The average composition of the continental crust is granitic rock called granodiorite. Continental rocks have an average density of about 2.7 g/cm^3 and some are over 4 billion years old. The rocks of the oceanic crust are younger (180 million years or less) and have an average density of about 3.0 g/cm^3.

Figure 14 The arrows show only a few of the many possible paths that seismic waves take through Earth.
Inferring *What causes the wave paths to change?*

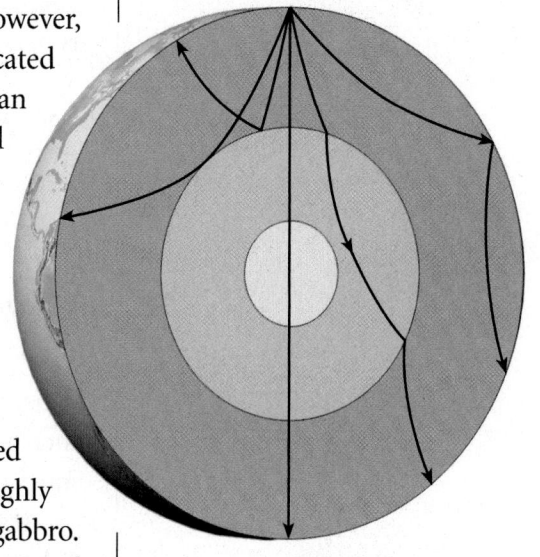

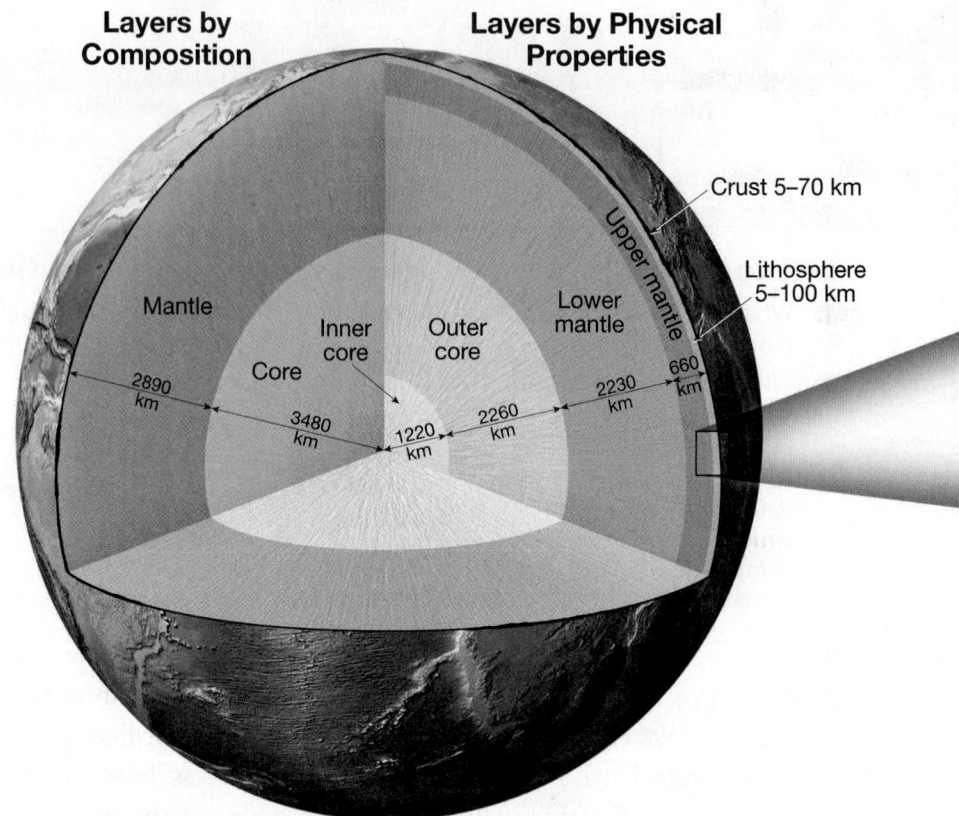

Figure 15 Earth's Layered Structure Based on composition, Earth is made up of the crust, mantle, and core. Based on physical properties, Earth is made up of the lithosphere, asthenosphere, lower mantle, outer core, and inner core. The block diagram shows the relationship between the crust, lithosphere, and asthenosphere. *Inferring **Which part of Earth has the highest density? Explain.***

Mantle Over 82 percent of Earth's volume is contained in the **mantle**—a solid, rocky shell that extends to a depth of 2890 kilometers. The boundary between the crust and mantle represents a change in chemical composition. A common rock type in the uppermost mantle is peridotite, which has a density of about 3.4 g/cm^3.

Core The core is a sphere composed mostly of an iron-nickel alloy. At the extreme pressures found in the center of the core, the iron-rich material has an average density of 13 g/cm^3 (13 times denser than water).

Layers Defined by Physical Properties

Earth's interior has a gradual increase in temperature, pressure, and density with depth. When a substance is heated, the transfer of energy increases the vibrations of particles. If the temperature exceeds the melting point, the forces between particles are overcome and melting begins.

If temperature were the only factor that determined whether a substance melted, our planet would be a molten ball covered with a thin, solid outer shell. Fortunately, pressure also increases with depth and increases rock strength. Depending on the physical environment (temperature and pressure), a material may behave like a brittle solid, a putty, or a liquid. 🔵 **Earth can be divided into layers based on physical properties—the lithosphere, the asthenosphere, lower mantle, the outer core, and the inner core.**

Lithosphere and Asthenosphere

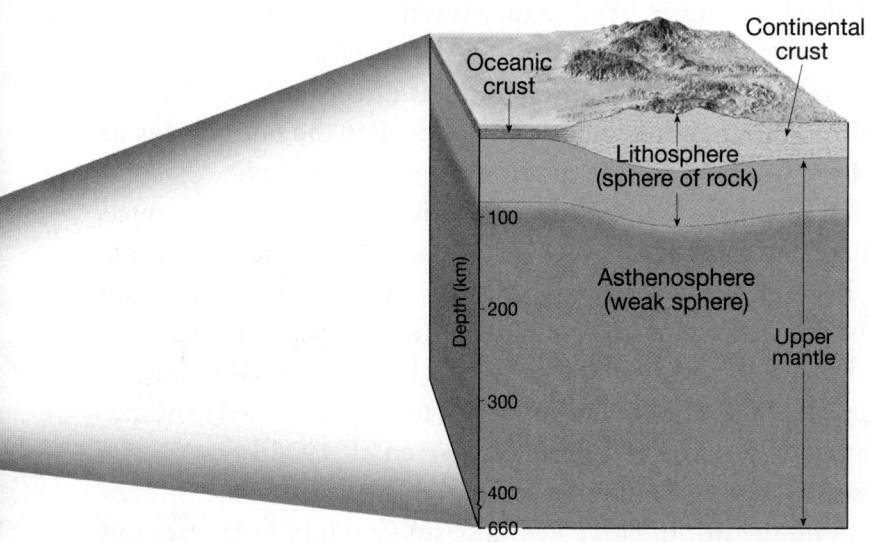

Lithosphere Earth's outermost layer consists of the crust and uppermost mantle and forms a relatively cool, rigid shell called the **lithosphere**. This layer averages about 100 kilometers in thickness.

Athenosphere Beneath the lithosphere lies a soft, comparatively weak layer known as the **asthenosphere.** Within the asthenosphere, the rocks are close enough to their melting temperatures that they are easily deformed. Thus, the asthenosphere is weak because it is near its melting point, just as hot wax is weaker than cold wax. The lower lithosphere and asthenosphere are both part of the upper mantle.

Lower Mantle From a depth of about 660 kilometers down to near the base of the mantle lies a more rigid layer called the lower mantle. Despite their strength, the rocks of the lower mantle are still very hot and capable of gradual flow.

Inner and Outer Core The core, which is composed mostly of an iron-nickel alloy, is divided into two regions with different physical properties. The **outer core** is a liquid layer 2260 kilometers thick. The flow of metallic iron within this zone generates Earth's magnetic field. Just as there is a magnetic field around a bar magnet, an immense magnetic field surrounds Earth, as shown in Figure 16. The poles of the magnetized needle on a compass align themselves with Earth's magnetic field.

The **inner core** is a sphere having a radius of 1220 kilometers. Despite its higher temperatures, the materials in the inner core is compressed into a solid state by the immense pressure.

Figure 16 Earth's Magnetic Field Movements in Earth's liquid outer core produce the planet's magnetic field. As a result, a compass needle points to one of the magnetic poles.

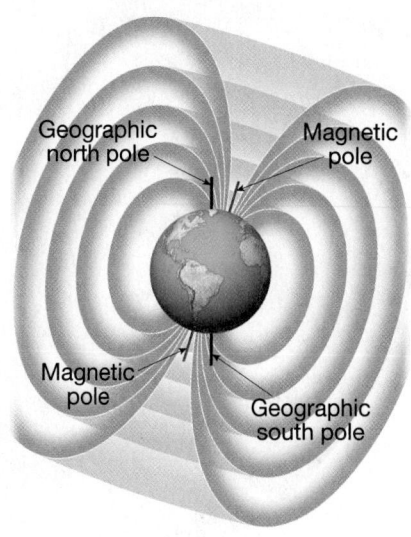

 **Reading Checkpoint** *Why is the inner core solid?*

Discovering Earth's Layers

Recall that seismic waves bend as they travel through Earth and that this information helped scientists to infer the planet's layered structure. 👁 **During the twentieth century, studies of the paths of P and S waves through Earth helped scientists identify the boundaries of Earth's layers and determine that the outer core is liquid.**

In 1909, a Croatian seismologist, Andrija Mohorovičić, presented the first evidence of layering within Earth's mantle. By studying seismic records, he found that the velocity of seismic waves increased abruptly about 50 kilometers below eastern Europe. This boundary separates the crust from the underlying mantle and is now known as the Mohorovičić discontinuity. The name of the boundary is usually shortened to **Moho.**

Another boundary had been discovered in 1906 between the mantle and outer core. Seismic waves from even small earthquakes can travel around the world. This is why a seismograph in Antarctica can record earthquakes in California or Italy. However, it was observed that P waves were bent around the liquid outer core beyond about 100 degrees away from an earthquake. The outer core also causes P waves that travel through the core to arrive several minutes later than expected. This region, where bent P waves arrive, is sometimes called the shadow zone.

The bent wave paths can be explained if the core is composed of material that is different from the overlying mantle. The P waves bend around the core in a way similar to sound waves being bent around the corner of a building. For example, you can hear people talking from around the side of a building even if you cannot see them. In this way, rather than actually stopping the P waves in the shadow zone, the outer core bends them, as you can see modeled in Figure 17. It was further shown that S waves could not travel through the outer core. Therefore, geologists concluded that this layer is liquid.

 **Reading Checkpoint** *What is the Moho?*

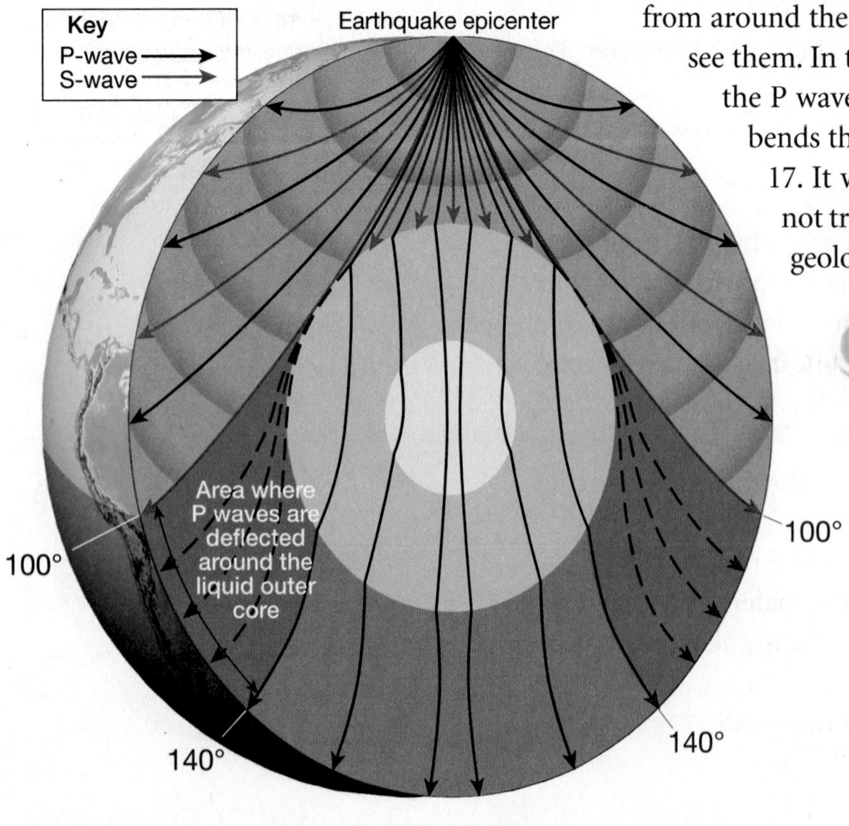

Figure 17 Earth's Interior Showing P and S Wave Paths The change in physical properties at the mantle-core boundary causes the wave paths to bend sharply.

Key
P-wave ➞
S-wave ➞

Earthquake epicenter

Area where P waves are deflected around the liquid outer core

100°   100°

140°   140°

Discovering Earth's Composition

🔑 **To determine the composition of Earth's layers, scientists studied seismic data, rock samples from the crust and mantle, meteorites, and high-pressure experiments on Earth materials.** Scientists obtain data on the seismic properties of rocks by performing high-pressure experiments. Small samples of rock and metal are squeezed and heated to the same conditions found in Earth's deep interior. Scientists then measure the speeds of P and S waves through the samples.

Seismic data and rock samples from drilling indicate that the continental crust is mostly made of low-density granitic rocks. Until the late 1960s, scientists had only seismic evidence they could use to determine the composition of oceanic crust. The development of deep-sea drilling technology made it possible to obtain rock samples from the ocean floor. The crust of the ocean floor has a basaltic composition.

The composition of the rocks of the mantle and core is known from more indirect data. Some of the lava that reaches Earth's surface comes from the partially melted asthenosphere within the mantle. In the laboratory, experiments show that partially melting the rock called peridotite produces a substance that is similar to the lava that erupts during volcanic activity of islands such as Hawaii.

Surprisingly, meteorites that collide with Earth provide evidence of Earth's inner composition. Meteorites are assumed to be composed of the original material from which Earth was formed. Their composition ranges from metallic meteorites made of iron and nickel to stony meteorites composed of dense rock similar to peridotite. Because Earth's crust contains a smaller percentage of iron than do meteorites, geologists believe that the dense iron, and other dense metals, sank toward Earth's center during the planet's formation.

Section 8.4 Assessment

Reviewing Concepts

1. 🔑 Describe Earth's layers based on composition.

2. 🔑 List Earth's layers based on physical properties, and their characteristics, in order from Earth's center to the surface.

3. 🔑 What evidence led scientists to conclude that Earth's outer core is liquid? Explain.

Critical Thinking

4. **Comparing and Contrasting** Compare the physical properties of the asthenosphere and the lithosphere.

5. **Inferring** Why are meteorites considered important clues to the composition of Earth's interior?

Writing in Science

Creative Writing Write a short fictional story about a trip to Earth's core. Make sure the details about the layers of Earth's interior are scientifically accurate.

How the Earth Works

Effects of Earthquakes

An **earthquake** is a shaking of the ground caused by sudden movements in the Earth's lithosphere. The biggest quakes are set off by the movement of tectonic plates. Some plates slide past one another gently. However, others get stuck, and the forces pushing the plates build up. The stress mounts until the plates suddenly shift their positions and cause the Earth to shake. Most earthquakes last less than one minute. Even so, the effects of an earthquake can be devastating and long-lasting.

TSUNAMI
In 1755, an earthquake in Lisbon, Portugal, caused a tsunami, as illustrated in this painting. A **tsunami** is a huge sea wave that is set off by an undersea earthquake or volcanic eruption. When tsunamis break on shore, they often devastate coastal areas. Tsunamis can race at speeds of about 450 miles per hour and may reach heights of about 100 feet (30.5 m).

LANDSLIDE
In January 2001, an earthquake struck El Salvador. It caused the landslide that left these Salvadoran women homeless. A **landslide** is a sudden drop of a mass of land down a mountainside or hillside. Emergency relief workers from around the world often rush to the site of an earthquake disaster like the one that occurred in El Salvador.

INFRASTRUCTURE DAMAGE

When an earthquake occurred in Los Angeles in 1994, underground gas and water lines burst, causing fires and floods. Earthquakes often cause tremendous damage to the **infrastructure**—the network of services that supports a community. Infrastructure includes power utilities, water supplies, and transportation and communication facilities.

AVALANCHE

Earthquakes may trigger an **avalanche**—a sudden fall of a mass of ice and snow. In 1970, a severe earthquake off the coast of Peru caused a disastrous slide of snow and rock that killed some 18,000 people in the valley below.

WHEN THE EARTH CRACKS

Most people killed or injured by an earthquake are hit by debris from buildings. Additional damage can be caused by **aftershocks**—tremors that can occur hours, days, or even months after an earthquake. The scene above shows the city of Anchorage, Alaska, after a major earthquake. Extensive ground tremors caused the street to break up as the soil below it collapsed. Buildings and cars were dropped more than 10 feet (3 m) below street level.

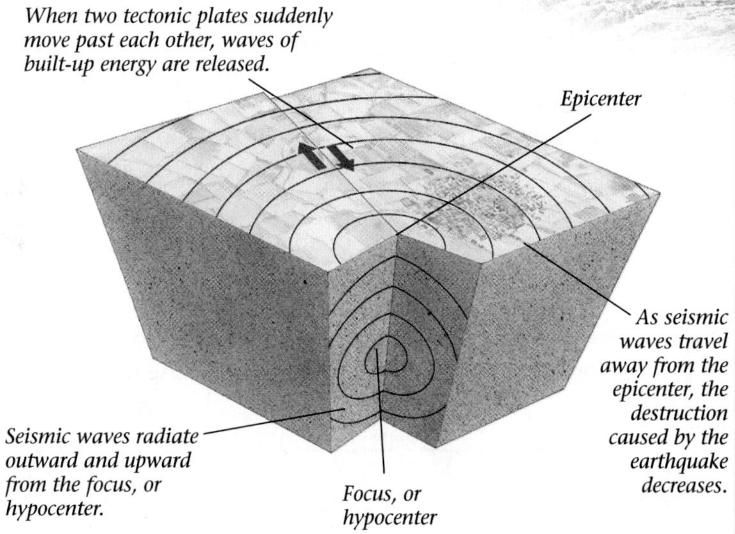

When two tectonic plates suddenly move past each other, waves of built-up energy are released.

Epicenter

As seismic waves travel away from the epicenter, the destruction caused by the earthquake decreases.

Seismic waves radiate outward and upward from the focus, or hypocenter.

Focus, or hypocenter

SEISMIC WAVES

As tectonic forces build, rock beneath the surface bends until it finally breaks. The tectonic plates suddenly move, causing **seismic waves,** or vibrations, to travel through the ground. The waves radiate outward from an underground area called the focus, or hypocenter. Damage is usually greatest near the **epicenter,** the point on the surface directly above the focus.

ASSESSMENT

1. **Key Terms** Define **(a)** earthquake, **(b)** tsunami, **(c)** landslide, **(d)** infrastructure, **(e)** avalanche, **(f)** aftershock, **(g)** seismic wave, **(h)** epicenter.

2. **Physical Processes** What physical processes cause an earthquake?

3. **Environmental Change** How can an earthquake cause changes to the physical characteristics of a place?

4. **Natural Hazards** **(a)** How can an earthquake change the human characteristics of a place? **(b)** How does the international community respond to a devastating earthquake?

5. **Critical Thinking Solving Problems** What can a community do to reduce the amount of earthquake damage that might occur in the future?

Locating an Earthquake

To locate an epicenter, records from three different seismographs are needed. Ideally, this activity should be done using a globe. When projected onto a flat map, the circles showing distances to the epicenter become distorted. For this reason, the method used here is an approximation.

Problem How can you determine the location of an earthquake's epicenter?

Materials
- pencil
- drawing compass
- world map or atlas
- photocopy of map on page 241

Skills Measuring, Interpreting Maps, Interpreting Graphs

Procedure

1. These three seismograms recorded the same earthquake, in New York City, Seattle, and Mexico City. Use the travel-time graph to determine the distance that each station is from the epicenter. Record your answers in a data table like the one shown.

2. Refer to a world map or atlas for the locations of the three seismic stations. Place a small dot showing the location of each of the three stations on the photocopy of the map on the next page. Neatly label each city on the map.

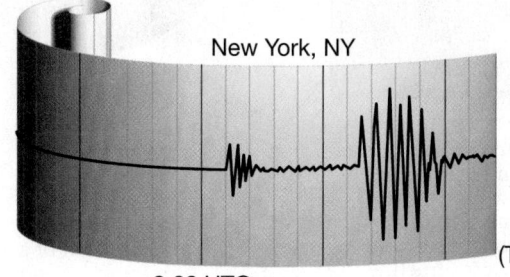

New York, NY

(Time marks in minutes)

9:00 UTC

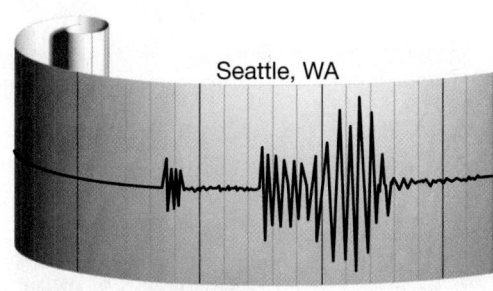

Seattle, WA

9:00 UTC

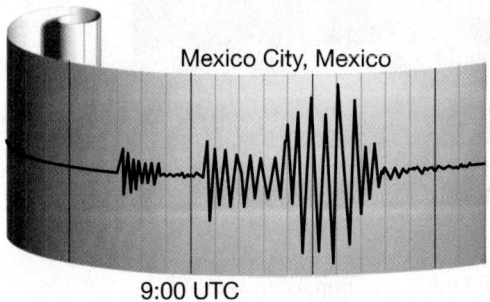

Mexico City, Mexico

9:00 UTC

Data Table			
	New York	Seattle	Mexico City
Elapsed time between first P and first S waves			
Distance from epicenter in miles			.

3. On the map, use a drawing compass to draw a circle around each of the three stations. The radius of the circle, in miles, should be equal to each station's distance from the epicenter. Use the scale on the map to set the distance on the drawing compass for each station. **CAUTION:** *Use care when handling the drawing compass.*

Analyze and Conclude

1. Using Graphs How far from the epicenter are the three cities located?

2. Calculating What would the distances from the epicenter to the cities be in kilometers?

3. Interpreting Maps What is the approximate latitude and longitude of the epicenter of the earthquake that was recorded by the three stations?

4. Drawing Conclusions On the New York seismogram the first P wave was recorded at 9:01 UTC. UTC is the international standard on which most countries base their time. At what time (UTC) did the earthquake actually occur? Explain.

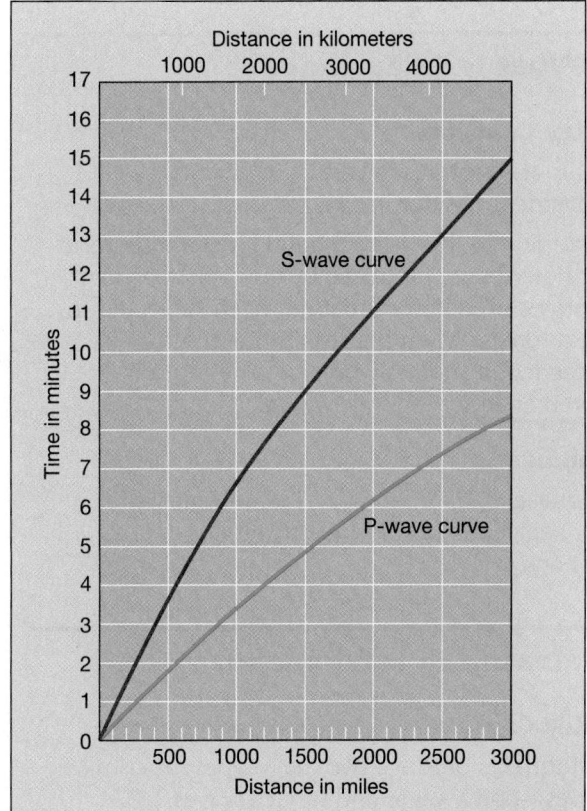

Go Further Use the Internet or the library to find the locations of recent earthquake epicenters. Make a data table displaying the location, date, and magnitude of ten recent earthquakes. Report your findings to the class.

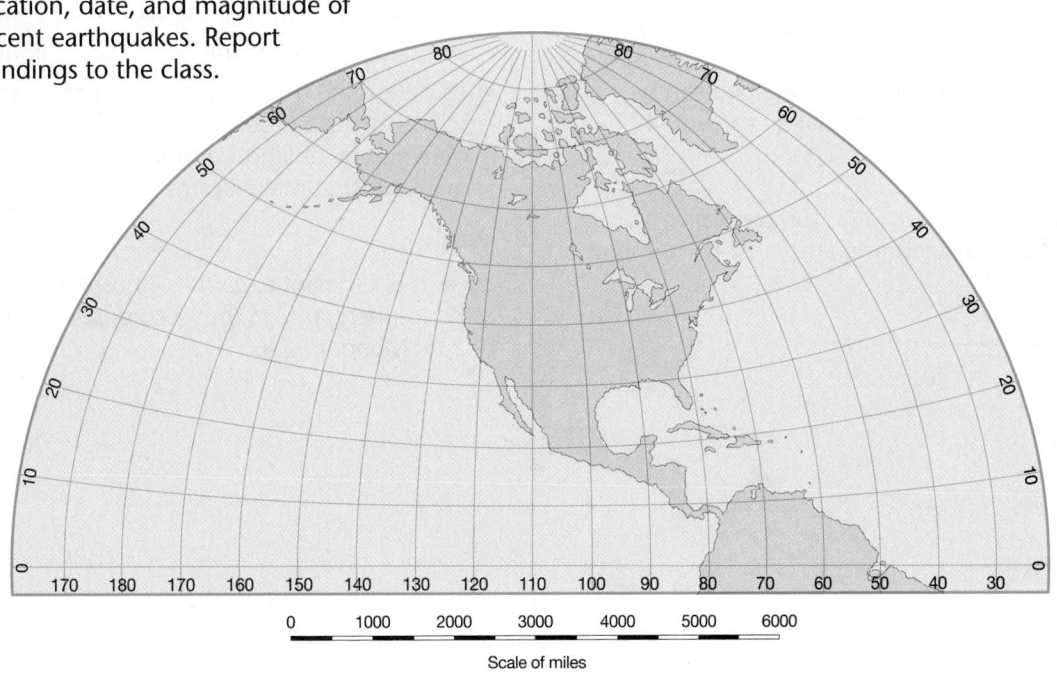

Study Guide

8.1 What Is an Earthquake?

Key Concepts

- Faults are fractures in Earth along which movement has occurred.

- According to the elastic rebound hypothesis, most earthquakes are produced by the rapid release of energy stored in rock that has been subjected to great forces. When the strength of the rock is exceeded, it suddenly breaks, releasing some of its stored energy as seismic waves.

Vocabulary

earthquake, *p. 218;* focus, *p. 218;* seismic waves, *p. 218;* epicenter, *p. 219;* elastic rebound, *p. 220;* aftershock, *p. 221*

8.2 Measuring Earthquakes

Key Concepts

- Earthquakes produce two main types of seismic waves—body waves and surface waves.

- Scientists have developed an instrument to record seismic waves—the seismograph.

- The Richter scale and the moment magnitude scale measure earthquake magnitude. The Modified Mercalli scale is based on earthquake intensity.

- A travel-time graph, data from seismograms made at three or more locations, and a globe can be used to determine an earthquake's epicenter.

Vocabulary

P wave, *p. 222;* S wave, *p. 223;* surface wave, *p. 223;* seismograph, *p. 224;* seismogram, *p. 224;* moment magnitude, *p. 225*

8.3 Earthquake Hazards

Key Concepts

- Earthquake-related hazards include: seismic shaking, liquefaction, landslides and mudflows, and tsunamis.

- Earthquake damage and loss of life can be reduced by determining the earthquake risk for an area, building earthquake-resistant structures, and following earthquake safety precautions.

Vocabulary

liquefaction, *p. 229;* tsunami, *p. 230;* seismic gap, *p. 231*

8.4 Earth's Layered Structure

Key Concepts

- Earth's interior consists of three major layers defined by their chemical composition—the crust, the mantle, and the core.

- Earth can be divided into layers based on physical properties—the lithosphere, the asthenosphere, the mantle, the outer core, and the inner core.

- During the twentieth century, studies of the paths of P waves and S waves through Earth helped scientists establish the boundaries of Earth's layers and determine that the outer core is liquid.

- To determine the composition of Earth's layers, scientists studied seismic data, rock samples obtained by drilling, samples of lava rock, and the materials that make up meteorites.

Vocabulary

crust, *p. 233;* mantle, *p. 234;* lithosphere, *p. 235;* asthenosphere, *p. 235;* outer core, *p. 235;* inner core, *p. 235;* Moho, *p. 236*

Reviewing Content

Choose the letter that best answers the question or completes the statement.

1. Approximately how many earthquakes are strong enough to be felt each year worldwide?
   - **a.** 500
   - **b.** 1000
   - **c.** 10,000
   - **d.** 30,000

2. What is the location on the surface directly above the earthquake focus called?
   - **a.** epicenter
   - **b.** fault
   - **c.** magnitude
   - **d.** Moho

3. The rigid layer of Earth that includes the entire crust and the uppermost part of the mantle is called the
   - **a.** asthenosphere.
   - **b.** mesosphere.
   - **c.** lithosphere.
   - **d.** Moho.

4. The instrument that records earthquakes is called
   - **a.** a seismogram.
   - **b.** a seismologist.
   - **c.** seismology.
   - **d.** a seismograph.

5. Look at the map on page 231. Which region has the most earthquake activity?
   - **a.** central Europe
   - **b.** the edge of the Pacific Ocean
   - **c.** eastern North America
   - **d.** central Africa

6. What material do scientists believe makes up a large part of the upper mantle?
   - **a.** basalt
   - **b.** granite
   - **c.** iron
   - **d.** peridotite

7. The point at which an earthquake begins is called
   - **a.** a foreshock.
   - **b.** the epicenter.
   - **c.** the focus.
   - **d.** the Moho.

8. In areas where soil is saturated with water, earthquakes can turn stable soil into a fluid during a process called
   - **a.** faulting.
   - **b.** liquefaction.
   - **c.** tsunamis.
   - **d.** subsidence.

9. To find the epicenter of an earthquake, what is the minimum number of seismic stations that are needed?
   - **a.** three
   - **b.** nine
   - **c.** five
   - **d.** two

10. What scale do scientists today most often use to express the magnitude of an earthquake?
    - **a.** Richter scale
    - **b.** moment magnitude
    - **c.** tsunami scale
    - **d.** Moho scale

Understanding Concepts

Use the diagram below to answer Questions 11 and 12.

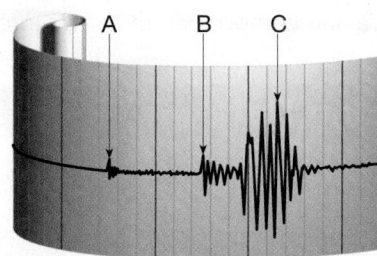

11. The diagram shows a typical recording of an earthquake. What is the record called?

12. Identify the waves recorded at A, B, and C on the diagram.

13. What is the elastic rebound hypothesis?

14. What type of seismic wave causes the greatest destruction to buildings?

15. In addition to the damage caused directly by seismic shaking, list four other types of destructive events that can be triggered by earthquakes.

16. Describe the composition and physical properties of the crust.

17. What is liquefaction and how can earthquakes cause liquefaction to occur?

18. List the major differences between P waves and S waves.

19. How much more ground shaking occurs in an earthquake that measures 4.2 on the Richter scale compared with an earthquake that measures 6.2 on the Richter scale?

20. What are two factors that can determine the amount of destruction that results from an earthquake?

Assessment *continued*

Critical Thinking

21. **Applying Concepts** Give two reasons why an earthquake with a moderate magnitude might cause more extensive damage than an earthquake with a high magnitude.

22. **Comparing and Contrasting** How are the moment magnitude scale and the Richter scale different?

23. **Inferring** How did scientists determine the structure and composition of Earth's interior?

Analyzing Data

Use the diagram below to answer Questions 24–26.

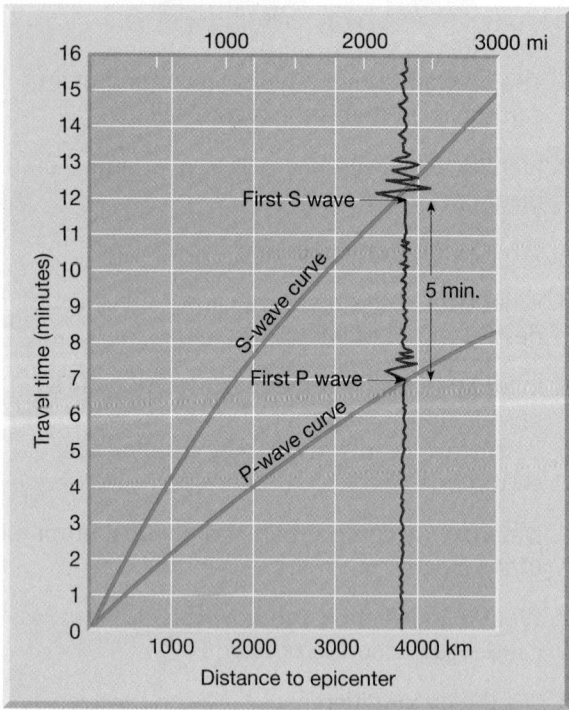

24. **Using Graphs** Determine the distance between an earthquake and seismic station if the first S wave arrives three minutes after the first P wave.

25. **Using Graphs** If a seismic station is 2500 kilometers from the earthquake's epicenter, approximately when will the first P wave be received? When will the first S wave be received?

26. **Calculating** What is the difference in the travel-times of the first P wave and the first S wave if the seismic station is 1000 kilometers from the earthquake epicenter?

Concepts in Action

27. **Applying Concepts** Why is the moment magnitude the most commonly used scale by scientists for measuring earthquakes?

28. **Relating Cause and Effect** Describe a tsunami from the event that produces it to the time that it reaches a coastline.

29. **Inferring** A magnitude 6 earthquake has an intensity of V on the Mercalli scale 10 km from the epicenter. But the same earthquake has an intensity of VII on the Mercalli scale 25 km from the epicenter. What might explain this difference?

30. **Writing in Science** Research a recent earthquake and write about the earthquake damage in the style of a newspaper article.

Performance-Based Assessment

Designing an Experiment Design a model seismograph to record simulated earthquakes. When your model is completed, test it for the class. Then determine how your seismograph design could be improved or changed if it doesn't work well.

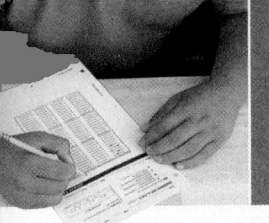

Standardized Test Prep

Use the diagram below to answer Questions 4–6.

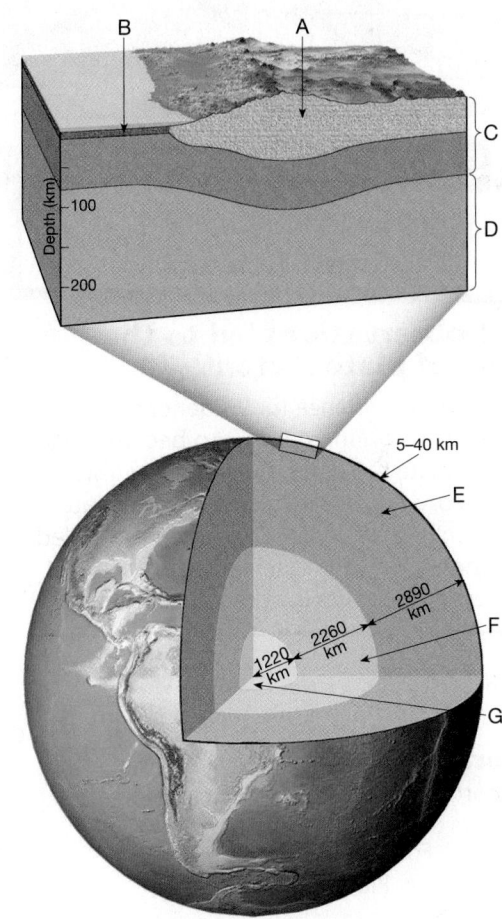

Test-Taking Tip

Narrowing the Choices
If, after reading all the answer choices, you are not sure which one is correct, eliminate those answers that you know are wrong. In the question below, first eliminate the choices you know are wrong. For example, answer choice C can be eliminated because the asthenophere, although it is solid, is not cool. Then focus on the remaining choices.

Which answer best describes the characteristics of the asthenosphere?

(A) liquid and metallic
(B) extremely hot but solid
(C) cool and solid
(D) solid but weak and able to flow slowly

(Answer: D)

Choose the letter that best answers the question or completes the statement.

1. What property that is different for P and S waves provides a method for locating the epicenter of an earthquake?
(A) magnitude
(B) foci
(C) modes of travel
(D) speed

2. Movements that follow a major earthquake often generate smaller earthquakes called
(A) aftershocks.
(B) foreshocks.
(C) surface waves.
(D) landslides.

3. An earthquake in the ocean floor can cause a destructive sea wave called a
(A) P wave.
(B) S wave.
(C) Moho.
(D) tsunami.

4. What layer of Earth's interior is labeled F in the diagram? Describe this layer.

5. What layer is labeled A in the diagram? What type of rock makes up this layer?

6. In the diagram, which letters would indicate layers that form the lithosphere? Describe the layers.

7. Describe the composition (mineral/rock makeup) of Earth's crust, mantle, and core. How did scientists determine the composition of each layer?

8. Explain the conditions that cause earthquakes.

CHAPTER 9

Plate Tectonics

21st Century Learning

Critical Thinking and Systems Thinking

What observations led to the theory of plate tectonics?

It took a lot of evidence for Wegener's hypothesis of continental drift to become the theory of plate tectonics. Research the history of the theory of plate tectonics. Then, create a concept map that details the evidence that led to the theory. Be sure to include the names of any relevant scientists in your concept map.

Quick Lab
Charting the Age of the Atlantic Ocean

Exploration Lab
Paleomagnetism and the Ocean Floor

GEODe Forces Within
EARTH SCIENCE ↳ Plate Tectonics

In this composite satellite image, two distinct pieces of Earth's crust—Africa and the Arabian peninsula—meet beneath the Red Sea.

Chapter Preview

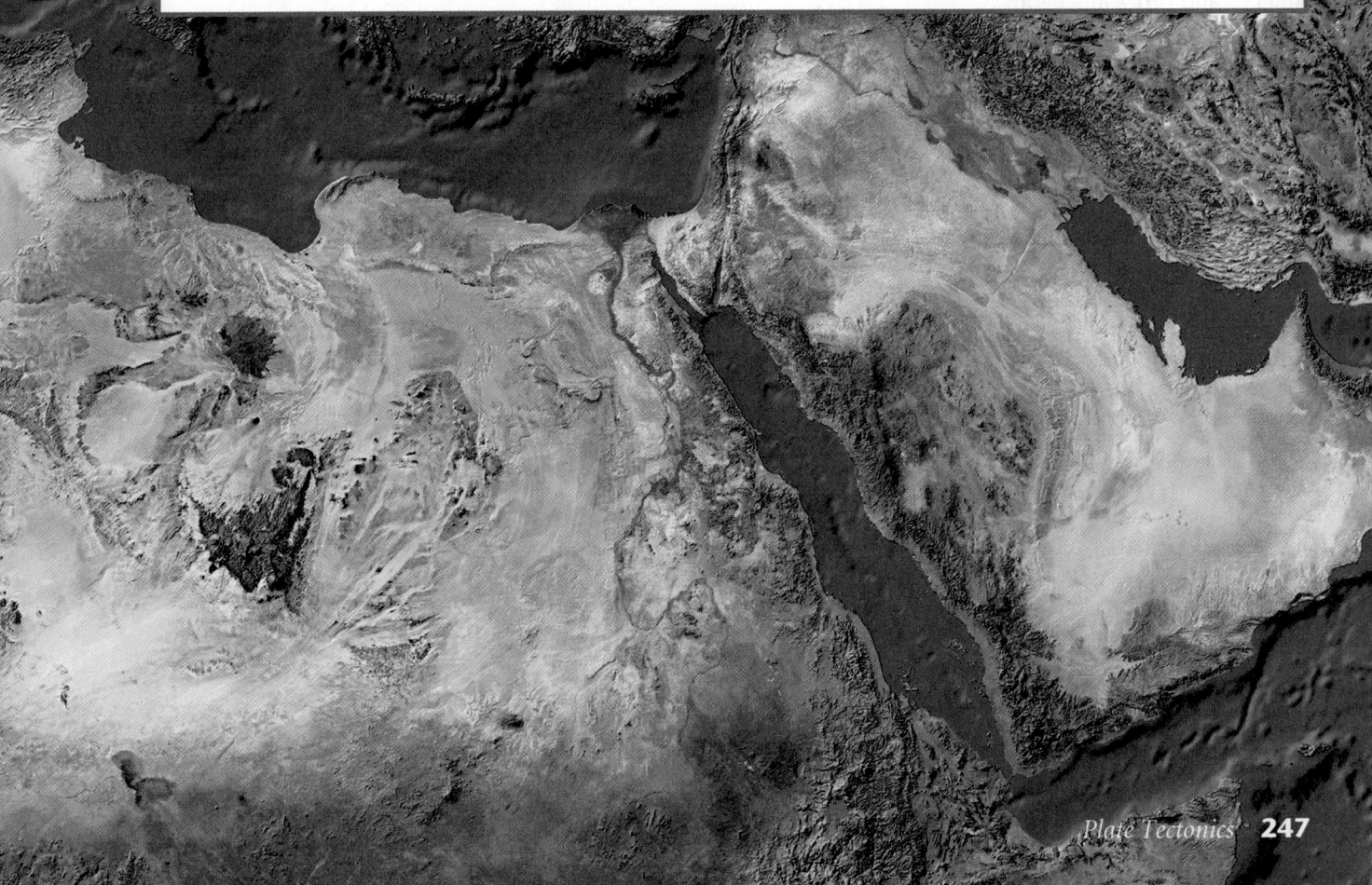

Inquiry > Activity

How Do the Continents Fit Together?

Procedure

1. Get a copy of a world map from your teacher. Cut out the continents along their coastlines. **CAUTION:** *Be careful when using scissors.*

2. Try to fit together the pieces into one large landmass. Look for a "best-fit" configuration.

3. Compare your large landmass with those of other students. Did anyone come up with a landmass that was very different from the others?

Think About It

1. **Observing** From your continental reconstruction, where did the continents fit together well? Where did problems occur?

2. **Developing Hypotheses** Use your observations to develop a hypothesis on how to get a better fit of the continents. How could the overlaps and large gaps be explained? (*Hint:* What if the outline of the coasts was not the same as the boundaries of the continents themselves?)

9.1 Continental Drift

Reading Focus

Key Concepts
- What is the hypothesis of continental drift?
- What evidence supported continental drift?
- Why was Wegener's hypothesis rejected?

Vocabulary
- continental drift
- Pangaea

Reading Strategy

Summarizing Copy the table. Fill it in as you read to summarize the evidence of continental drift.

Hypothesis	Evidence
Continental Drift	a. continental puzzle
	b. _____?_____
	c. _____?_____
	d. _____?_____

More than 300 years ago, mapmakers produced world maps that accurately showed the shapes of the continents. Looking at these maps, people noticed that some continents fit together like pieces of a jigsaw puzzle. Few people thought much about this observation until the early twentieth century. Then, scientists began to look again at the fit of the continents and think about what it might mean.

Figure 1 A Curious Fit This map shows the best fit of South America and Africa at a depth of about 900 meters. Areas of overlap appear in brown.

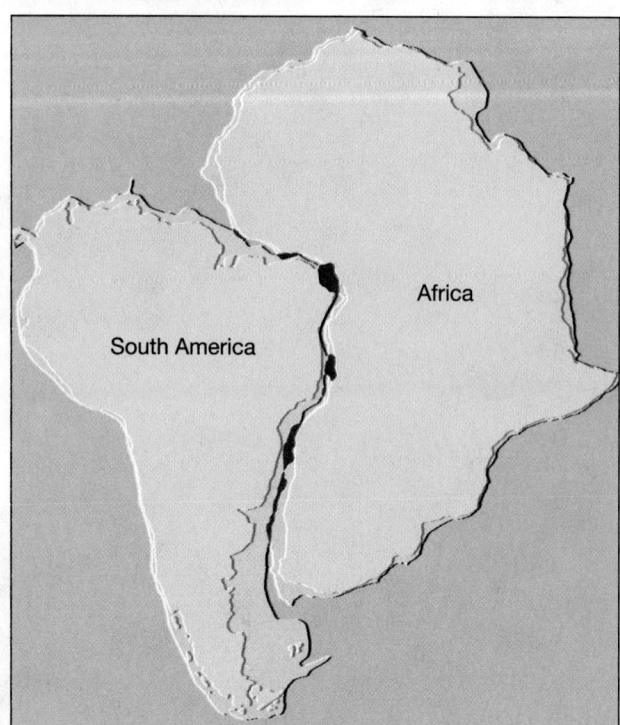

South America

Africa

The Continental Puzzle

A German scientist, Alfred Wegener, also noticed the similarity between the coastlines on opposite sides of the South Atlantic Ocean. As you can see in Figure 1, the shapes of South America and Africa are an approximate fit. In 1915, Wegener proposed his radical hypothesis of **continental drift.** **According to Wegener's hypothesis of continental drift, the continents had once been joined to form a single supercontinent.** He called this supercontinent **Pangaea,** meaning *all land*.

Wegener also hypothesized that about 200 million years ago Pangaea began breaking into smaller continents. The continents then drifted slowly to their present positions.

Evidence for Continental Drift

Wegener presented a variety of evidence to support the hypothesis of continental drift. His evidence included similar fossils, types of rock, and traces of glaciation on widely separated landmasses.

Matching Fossils  **Fossil evidence for continental drift includes several fossil organisms found on different landmasses.** Wegener reasoned that these organisms could not have crossed the vast oceans presently separating the continents. An example is *Mesosaurus*, a reptile whose fossil remains are limited to eastern South America and southern Africa, as shown in Figure 2. Scientists think that *Mesosaurus* lived in freshwater lakes and shallow bays. It could not have swum across the vast, salty Atlantic Ocean. Therefore, Wegener argued, South America and Africa must have been joined.

The distribution of other types of fossils also supported Wegener's hypothesis. For example, fossils of *Glossopteris*, a small plant, are found today in South America, southern Africa, and India. Yet the characteristics of *Glossopteris* seeds make it very unlikely that the seeds could have blown or floated long distances across the oceans. Fossils of the land reptile *Lystrosaurus* show a similar pattern of distribution.

In Wegener's time, the idea of land bridges was the accepted explanation for similar fossils being found on different landmasses. However, if land bridges did exist between South America and Africa, their remnants should still lie below sea level. But no signs of such land bridges have ever been found in the Atlantic Ocean.

> **Reading Checkpoint** *How does the distribution of Mesosaurus fossils provide evidence for continental drift?*

Q *If all the continents were once joined as Pangaea, what did the rest of Earth look like?*

A When all the continents were together, there must also have been one huge ocean surrounding them. This ocean is called *Panthalassa* (*pan* = all, *thalassa* = sea). Today all that remains of Panthalassa is the Pacific Ocean, which has been decreasing in size since the breakup of Pangaea.

Figure 2 Fossil Evidence Fossils of *Mesosaurus* have been found on both sides of the South Atlantic and nowhere else in the world. Fossil remains of this and other organisms on the continents of Africa and South America appear to link these landmasses at some time in Earth's history.

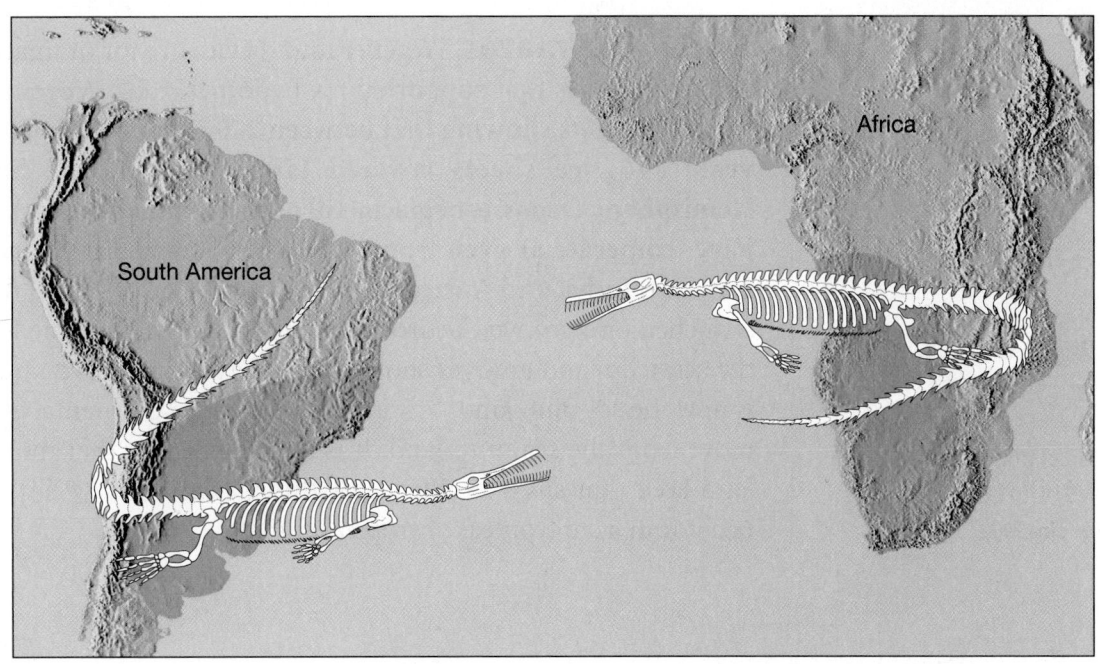

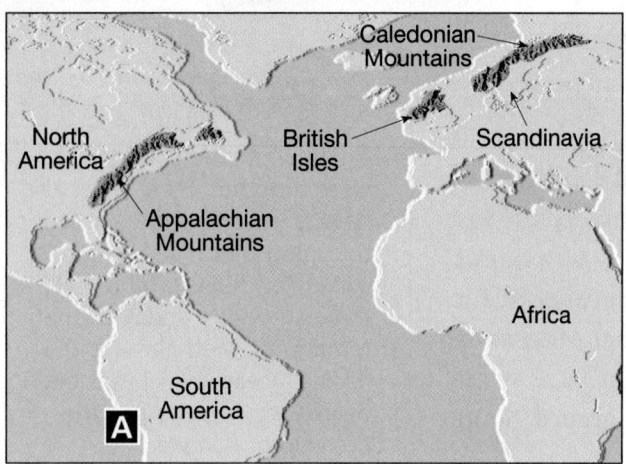

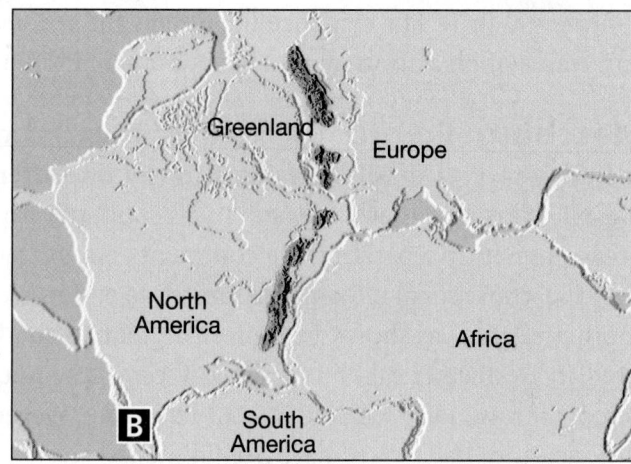

Figure 3 **A** The Appalachian Mountains run along the eastern side of North America and end off the coast of Newfoundland. Mountains that are similar in age and structure are found in the British Isles and Scandinavia. **B** When these landmasses were united as Pangaea, these ancient mountain chains formed a nearly continuous belt.

Rock Types   Anyone who has worked a jigsaw puzzle knows that the pieces must fit together to form a complete picture. The picture in the continental drift puzzle is one of matching rock types and mountain belts. If the continents were once part of Pangaea, the rocks found in a particular region on one continent should closely match in age and type those in adjacent positions on the adjoining continent.

Matching types of rock in several mountain belts that today are separated by oceans provide evidence for continental drift. For example, the Appalachian mountain belt in eastern North America ends off the coast of Newfoundland, as shown in Figure 3A. Mountains of the same age with similar rocks and structures are found in the British Isles and Scandinavia. When these landmasses are fitted together as in Figure 3B, the mountain chains form a nearly continuous belt.

Ancient Climates   Wegener found evidence for dramatic global climate changes that supported his hypothesis. **Wegener found glacial deposits showing that between 220 million and 300 million years ago, ice sheets covered large areas of the Southern Hemisphere. Deposits of glacial till occurred at latitudes that today have temperate or even tropical climates: southern Africa, South America, India, and Australia.** Below these beds of glacial debris lay scratched and grooved bedrock carved by the ice. In some locations, the scratches and grooves showed that the ice had moved from what is now the sea onto land. It is unusual for large continental glaciers to move from the sea onto land. It is also interesting that much of the land area that shows evidence of this glaciation now lies near the equator in a subtropical or tropical climate.

Could Earth have been cold enough to allow the formation of continental glaciers in what is now a tropical region? Wegener rejected this idea because, during this same time period, large tropical swamps existed in the Northern Hemisphere. The lush vegetation of these swamps eventually became the major coal fields of the eastern United States, Europe, and Siberia.

Wegener thought there was a better explanation for the ancient climate evidence he observed. Thinking of the landmasses as a supercontinent, with South Africa centered over the South Pole, would create the conditions necessary to form large areas of glacial ice over much of the Southern Hemisphere. The supercontinent idea would also place the northern landmasses nearer the tropics and account for their vast coal deposits, as shown in Figure 4.

 **Reading Checkpoint** *Summarize the climate evidence for continental drift.*

Glacier Evidence

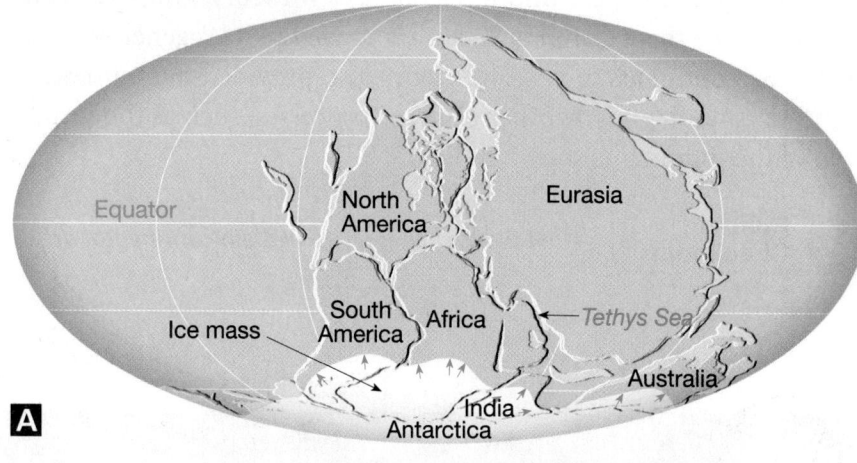

A

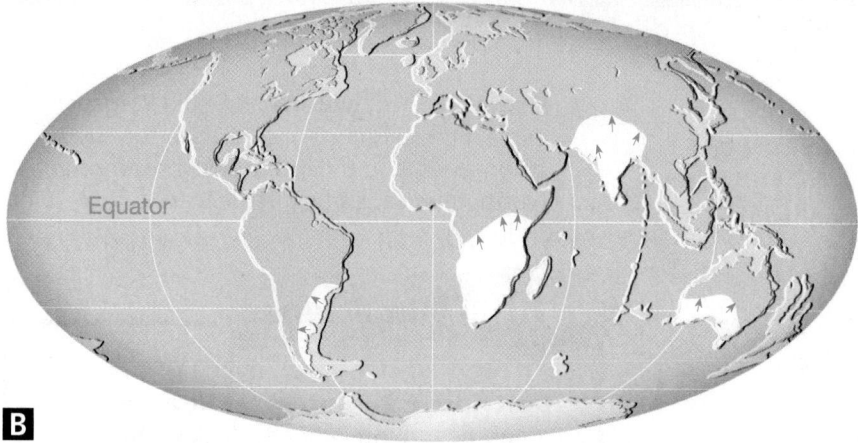

B

≡Quick⟩Lab

Charting the Age of the Atlantic Ocean

Procedure

1. The distance between two locations across the Atlantic Ocean, one in South America and one in Africa, is approximately 4300 km.

2. Assume that these two locations were once joined as part of Pangaea.

Analyze and Conclude

1. **Calculating** If the two landmasses moved away from each other at a rate of 3.3 cm per year, how long did it take these two locations to move to their current positions?

Figure 4 A The area of Pangaea covered by glacial ice 300 million years ago. **B** The continents as they are today. The white areas indicate where evidence of the old ice sheets exists.
Interpreting Diagrams *Where were the continents located when the glaciers formed?*

Rejection of Wegener's Hypothesis

Wegener's hypothesis faced a great deal of criticism from other scientists. **The main objection to Wegener's hypothesis was that he could not describe a mechanism capable of moving the continents.** Wegener proposed that the tidal influence of the Moon was strong enough to give the continents a westward motion. However, physicists quickly responded that tidal friction great enough to move the continents would stop Earth's rotation.

Wegener also proposed that the larger and sturdier continents broke through the oceanic crust, much like ice-breakers cut through ice. However, there was no evidence to suggest that the ocean floor was weak enough to permit passage of the continents without the ocean floors being broken and deformed in the process.

Most scientists in Wegener's day rejected his hypothesis. However, a few geologists continued to search for evidence of continental drift.

During the years that followed Wegener's hypothesis, major strides in technology enabled scientists to map the ocean floor. Extensive data on earthquake activity and Earth's magnetic field also became available. By 1967, these findings led to a new theory, known as plate tectonics. The theory of plate tectonics proved that Wegener was correct—the continents move. The theory also provided the framework for understanding many other geologic processes, such as the formation of the mountains shown in Figure 5.

Figure 5 Today, scientists know that plate movements helped to push up mountain ranges such as the Canadian Rockies in Banff National Park, Alberta, Canada.

Reading Checkpoint *How did Wegener try to explain continental drift?*

Section 9.1 Assessment

Reviewing Concepts

1. What is the hypothesis of continental drift?

2. List the evidence that supported the hypothesis of continental drift.

3. Why did scientists reject Wegener's continental drift hypothesis?

4. What was Pangaea?

Critical Thinking

5. Applying Concepts How does the occurrence of the same plant fossils in South America and Africa support continental drift? Explain.

6. Drawing Conclusions How did Wegener explain the existence of glaciers in the southern landmasses, and the lush tropical swamps in North America, Europe, and Siberia?

Writing in Science

Descriptive Paragraph Write a paragraph describing Pangaea. Include the location and climate of Pangaea. Use the equator as your reference for position.

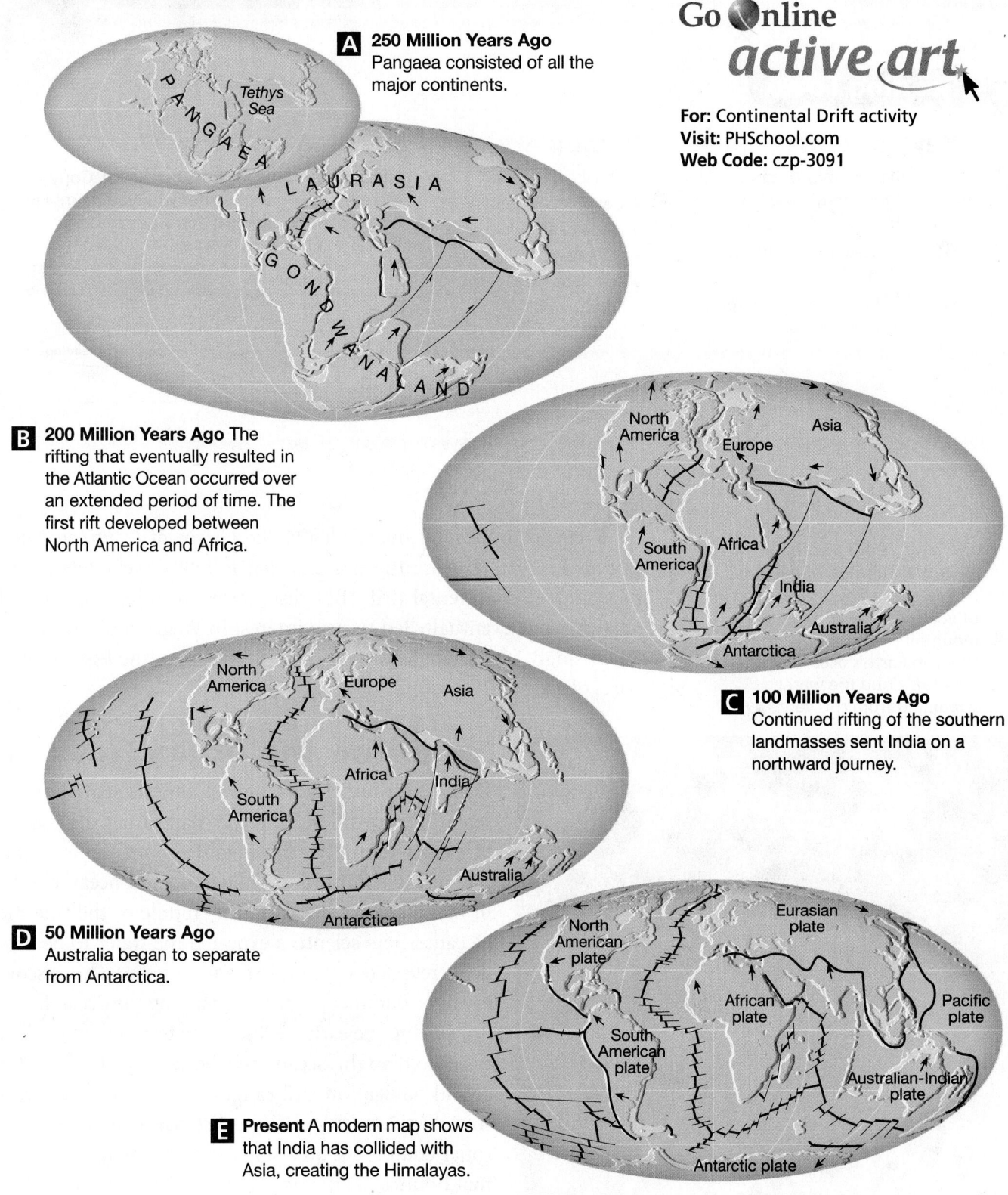

A **250 Million Years Ago**
Pangaea consisted of all the major continents.

Go Online
active art

For: Continental Drift activity
Visit: PHSchool.com
Web Code: czp-3091

B **200 Million Years Ago** The rifting that eventually resulted in the Atlantic Ocean occurred over an extended period of time. The first rift developed between North America and Africa.

C **100 Million Years Ago**
Continued rifting of the southern landmasses sent India on a northward journey.

D **50 Million Years Ago**
Australia began to separate from Antarctica.

E **Present** A modern map shows that India has collided with Asia, creating the Himalayas.

Figure 6 Pangaea broke up gradually over a period of 200 million years.

9.2 Sea-Floor Spreading

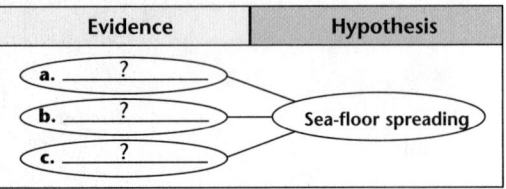

Reading Focus

Key Concepts

- What are mid-ocean ridges and deep-ocean trenches?
- What occurs during sea-floor spreading?
- What is the evidence for sea-floor spreading?

Vocabulary

- sonar
- deep-ocean trench
- mid-ocean ridge
- rift valley
- sea-floor spreading
- subduction
- paleomagnetism

Reading Strategy

Identifying Supporting Evidence Copy the graphic organizer. After you read, complete it to show the evidence that supported the hypothesis of sea-floor spreading.

Evidence	Hypothesis
a. ____ ?	
b. ____ ?	Sea-floor spreading
c. ____ ?	

Figure 7 This hot-water vent on the ocean floor is evidence of volcanic activity along the mountain range that winds through Earth's oceans. Dissolved minerals cloud the water streaming from this vent.

Wegener published his book *On the Origin of Continents and Oceans* in 1915. During the decades that followed, very few scientists studied continental drift. But discoveries in other branches of Earth science eventually led to new interest in Wegener's hypothesis. Surprisingly, important new data came from one of the least-known parts of Earth—the ocean floor.

Exploring the Ocean Floor

During the mid-1800s, several nations sent ships on scientific expeditions to gather data about the oceans. Scientists wanted to know more about the topography of the ocean floor. They measured ocean depths in many areas. Data from the middle of the Atlantic Ocean, where scientists expected the water to be very deep, revealed large undersea mountains. This discovery helped to fuel interest in mapping the ocean floor.

During the early 1900s, a new technology made it easier to map the ocean floor. **Sonar,** which stands for **so**und **na**vigation and **r**anging, is a system that uses sound waves to calculate the distance to an object. The sonar equipment on a ship sends out pulses of sound that bounce off the ocean floor. The equipment then measures how quickly the sound waves return to the ship. The deeper the water, the longer it takes the sound waves to return to the ship.

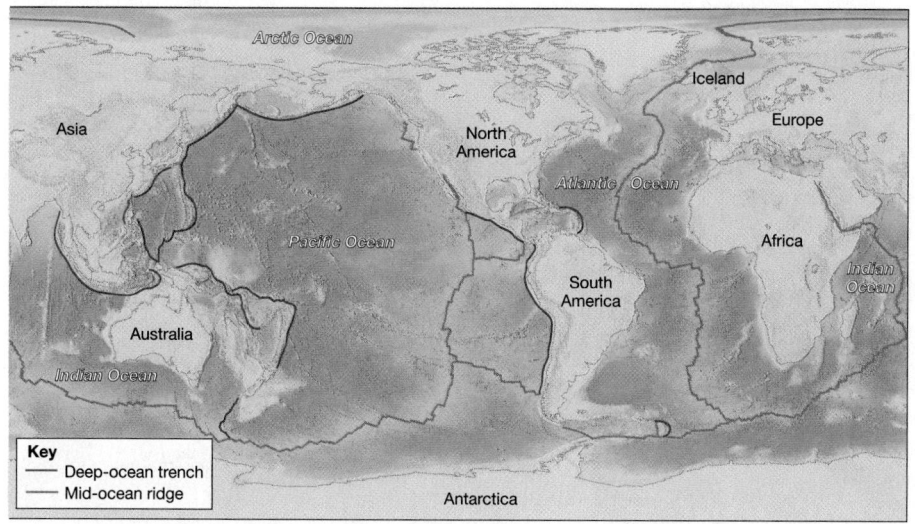

Figure 8 Deep trenches and mountainous mid-ocean ridges are major features of Earth's ocean basins.
Observing *Which ocean has the most trenches?*

Deep-Ocean Trenches

As scientists mapped the ocean floor, they found long, curved valleys along the edges of some ocean basins called deep-ocean **trenches**. Trenches form the deepest parts of Earth's oceans. For example, the Marianas Trench in the Pacific Ocean is over 11 kilometers deep. Most trenches occur around the edges of the Pacific Ocean, although others occur in the Indian and Atlantic oceans.

Mid-Ocean Ridges

By the late 1950s, scientists had constructed a more complete map of Earth's ocean floor. The map showed that the mountain range in the middle of the Atlantic Ocean was not an isolated feature. Instead, it formed a **mid-ocean ridge**, a long chain of mountains extending the length of the ocean. **Earth's mid-ocean ridge system forms the longest feature on Earth's surface. The system winds more than 70,000 kilometers through all the major ocean basins like the seam on a baseball.** The term *ridge* may be misleading. These features are not narrow like a typical ridge. They range from 1,000 to 4,000 kilometers wide. In a few places, such as Iceland, the mid-ocean ridge rises above the surface.

Often, a deep, central valley runs down the center of a *ridge*. Called a **rift valley**, the central valley of a mid-ocean ridge resembles a long canyon. Some parts of the ridge system lack a rift valley.

 **Reading Checkpoint** *What are mid-ocean ridges?*

For: Links on mid-ocean ridges
Visit: PHSchool.com
Web Code: cfd-3092

Composition of the Ocean Floor

Earth's ocean floors are made of igneous rocks of basaltic composition. Recall that basalt forms when lava reaches the surface and hardens to form solid rock. Most of the ocean floor is covered with a thick layer of sediment. Scientists found that the sediment layer became thinner closer to mid-ocean ridges, and that along the ridge there was no sediment.

Figure 9 A spreading center in the Red Sea is slowly causing the sea to become wider.

The Process of Sea-Floor Spreading

The new map of the ocean floor aroused the curiosity of many scientists. One geologist, Harry Hess, thought that the mid-ocean ridges and deep-ocean trenches might help to explain how the ocean floor was formed. In 1963, Hess published his hypothesis of sea-floor spreading. 🔑 **In the process of sea-floor spreading, new ocean floor forms along Earth's mid-ocean ridges, slowly moves outward across ocean basins, and finally sinks back into the mantle beneath deep-ocean trenches.** During **sea-floor spreading**, new oceanic lithosphere is formed, and the ocean floor gets wider. Today, the Atlantic Ocean is thousands of kilometers wide. Millions of years ago, the Atlantic would have been a narrow sea, like the Red Sea, shown in Figure 9.

Eruptions Along Mid-Ocean Ridges How did the mid-ocean ridges form? Scientists found evidence that the mid-ocean ridges formed as the result of volcanic activity. As shown in Figure 10, fractures along the central valley of a mid-ocean ridge fill with magma that wells up from the hot mantle below. (Recall that magma is molten rock that forms in the upper mantle and rises through the crust). Gradually, the magma cools to produce new slivers of ocean floor. Spreading and upwelling of magma continuously adds new ocean floor.

The process can also begin on land when a rift valley forms and splits a continental landmass. Over millions of years, the rift valley widens to form a new ocean basin like the Red Sea, shown in Figure 9.

Movement of the Ocean Floor As new ocean floor is added along mid-ocean ridges, the older ocean floor moves outward and away from the ridge on both sides. Rates of sea-floor spreading average about 5 centimeters per year. These rates are slow on a human time scale. But they are fast enough that all of Earth's ocean basins could have been formed within the last 200 million years.

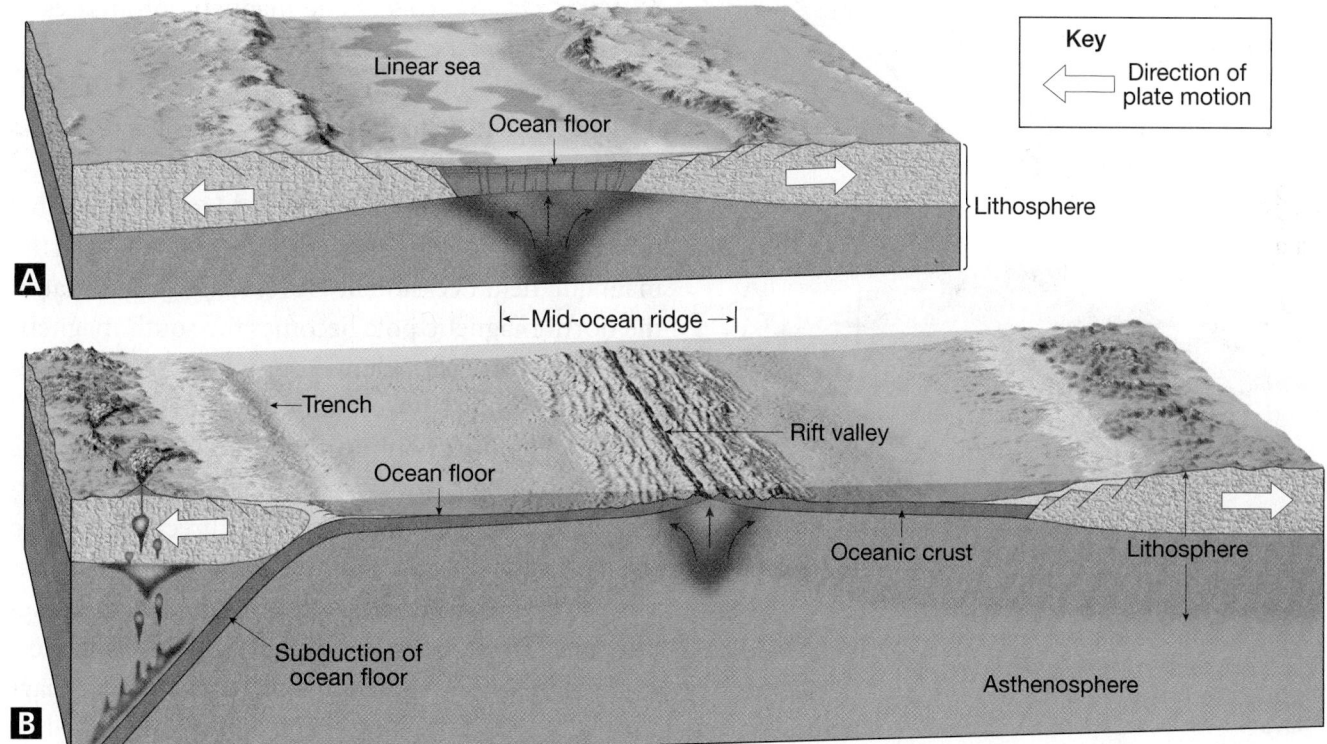

Key

⬅ Direction of plate motion

Linear sea

Ocean floor

Lithosphere

A

|← Mid-ocean ridge →|

← Trench

Rift valley

Ocean floor

Oceanic crust

Lithosphere

Subduction of ocean floor

Asthenosphere

B

Figure 10 The process of sea-floor spreading produces the ocean floor.
A A linear sea forms along a spreading center. **B** Over millions of years a mid-ocean ridge develops, the ocean basin becomes wider, and ocean floor is subducted beneath deep-ocean trenches.
Relating Cause and Effect *What process adds new material to the ocean floor?*

Subduction at Deep-Ocean Trenches Although new ocean floor is constantly being added at the mid-ocean ridges, our planet is not growing larger. Earth's total surface area remains the same. How can that be? To accommodate newly created lithosphere, older portions of the ocean floor return to the mantle. In the process of **subduction**, ocean floor returns to the mantle as it sinks beneath a deep ocean trench. The areas where subduction occurs, shown in Figure 10, are called subduction zones.

 **Reading Checkpoint** *What happens during subduction?*

Evidence for Sea-Floor Spreading

Hess's hypothesis got the attention of geologists. Sea-floor spreading explained the formation and destruction of ocean floor and how ocean basins could grow wider or close up. But what evidence was there to support Hess's hypothesis? ⚫ **Evidence for sea-floor spreading included magnetic stripes in ocean-floor rock, earthquake patterns, and measurements of the ages of ocean floor rocks.**

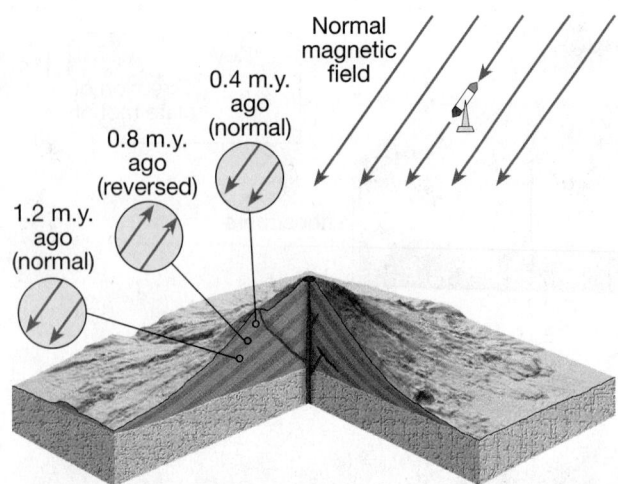

Figure 11 Paleomagnetism in Lava As lava cools, it becomes magnetized parallel to the magnetic field present at that time. When the polarity reverses, a record of the magnetism is preserved in the sequence of lava flows.

Figure 12 A As new material is added to the ocean floor at the oceanic ridges, it is magnetized according to Earth's existing magnetic field. **B** This process records each reversal of Earth's magnetic field. **C** New rock is added in strips of equal size and polarity on both sides of the ridge.
Applying Concepts *Why are the magnetized strips about equal width on either side of the ridge?*

Magnetic Strips   The magnetic properties of the rock that makes up the ocean floor provided evidence for sea-floor spreading. To understand this evidence, you need to understand how some rocks can become magnetized.

Recall that Earth's magnetic field is much like that of a bar magnet. Geophysicists learned that Earth's magnetic field occasionally reverses *polarity*. That is, the north magnetic pole becomes the south magnetic pole, and vice versa. Scientists graphed these reversals of polarity going back millions of years. When Earth's magnetic field lines up in the same direction as the present magnetic field, it is said to have *normal polarity*. When the magnetic field lines up in the opposite direction, it is said to have *reverse polarity*.

As certain rocks form, they acquire the polarity that Earth's magnetic field has at the time. These rocks possess **paleomagnetism**. How does a rock become magnetized? Many igneous rocks contain magnetite, an iron-rich mineral. As the rock cools and hardens, the iron-rich mineral grains become magnetized in the same direction as the existing magnetic field. You can see this process in Figure 11. Once the rock has formed, its polarity remains frozen unless the rock is reheated above a certain temperature. But what if the rock is moved or if the magnetic pole changes its position? The rock's paleomagnetism does not change.

Scientists collected data on the paleomagnetism of the basalt that makes up the ocean floor. Ships towed instruments called magnetometers across the ocean floor. The data revealed a pattern of alternating strips of magnetized rock. Strips of rock with normal polarity alternated with strips of rock having reverse polarity. Scientists inferred that as new basalt forms along the mid-ocean ridges, it becomes magnetized according to the polarity of Earth's magnetic field at the time. The matching pattern of strips on both sides of a ridge, shown in Figure 12, is evidence that sea-floor spreading occurs.

Reading Checkpoint   *What is paleomagnetism?*

A Period of Normal Polarity

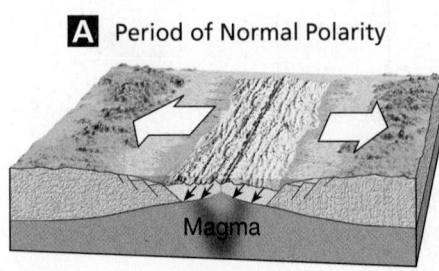

B Period of Reverse Polarity

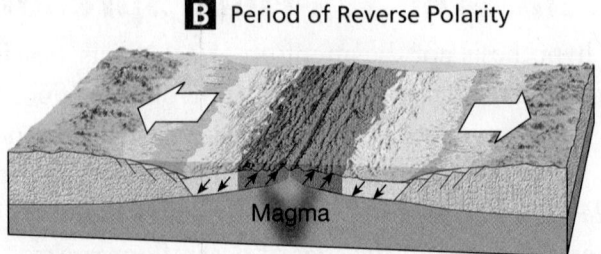

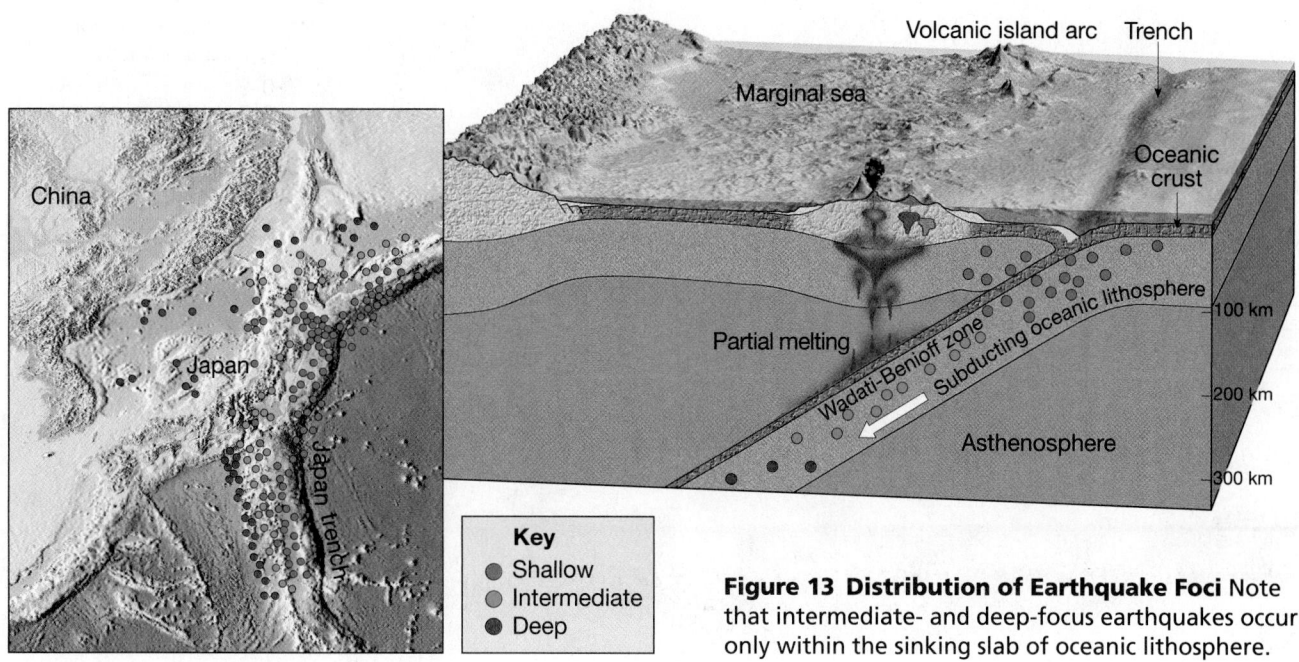

Volcanic island arc   Trench

Marginal sea

Oceanic crust

Wadati-Benioff zone

Subducting oceanic lithosphere

Partial melting

Asthenosphere

—100 km

—200 km

—300 km

China

Japan

Japan trench

Key
- Shallow
- Intermediate
- Deep

Figure 13 Distribution of Earthquake Foci Note that intermediate- and deep-focus earthquakes occur only within the sinking slab of oceanic lithosphere.

Earthquake Patterns

More evidence for sea-floor spreading came from studies of the depth at which certain earthquakes occur. Scientists knew that there were many earthquakes in subduction zones. Two scientists, Kiyoo Wadati and Hugo Benioff, found a pattern when they plotted the depth of earthquakes in relation to their distance from deep-ocean trenches.

Shallow-focus earthquakes occur in and around a trench. Wadati and Benioff observed that intermediate-focus and deep-focus earthquakes occur in a belt about 50 kilometers thick. This belt extends through the lithosphere and deep into the asthenosphere. As you can see in Figure 13, the deeper the earthquake, the farther away its focus is from the deep-ocean trench. No earthquakes have been recorded below about 700 kilometers. At this depth the subducting slab of ocean floor has been heated enough to soften.

Scientists considered the pattern of earthquakes in Wadati-Benioff zones in relation to sea-floor spreading. The pattern was what scientists expected would result from subduction of the ocean floor. These data convinced scientists that slabs of ocean floor return to the mantle in subduction zones.

C Period of Normal Polarity

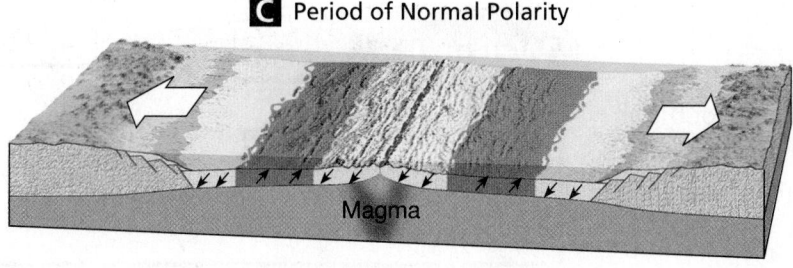

Magma

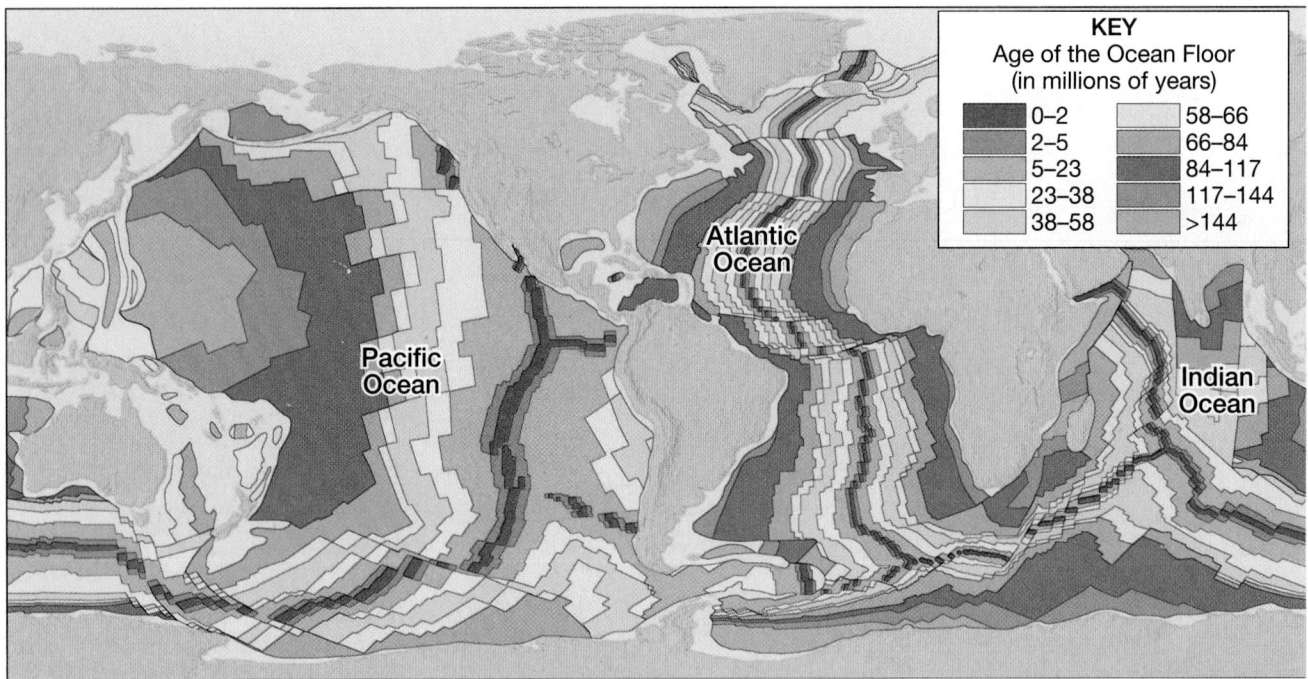

KEY
Age of the Ocean Floor
(in millions of years)

0–2		58–66
2–5		66–84
5–23		84–117
23–38		117–144
38–58		>144

Atlantic Ocean

Pacific Ocean

Indian Ocean

Figure 14 As the map shows, the youngest parts of the ocean floor lie along the mid-ocean ridges. The oldest parts of the ocean floor are found along the outer edges of ocean basins.

The Age of the Ocean Floor   Drilling into sediment on the ocean floor and the crust beneath it provided some of the best evidence for sea-floor spreading. Beginning in 1968, the drilling ship *Glomar Challenger* collected data on both sides of mid-ocean ridges.

The data confirmed what the sea-floor spreading hypothesis predicted. The ocean floor is youngest along the central valley of the mid-ocean ridge. The ocean floor is oldest in subduction zones or near the edges of continents far from the ridge. The data also confirmed that none of the ocean floor is more than about 180 million years old. Older oceanic rock would have returned to the mantle through subduction.

Section 9.2 Assessment

Reviewing Concepts

1. ⬡ Describe mid-ocean ridges and deep-ocean trenches.
2. ⬡ Explain what occurs during sea-floor spreading.
3. ⬡ List the evidence for sea-floor spreading.
4. What is a Wadati-Benioff zone?

Critical Thinking

5. **Inferring** Why are the oldest parts of the ocean floor less than 200 million years old?

6. **Applying Concepts** How do strips of magnetized rock on the ocean floor provide evidence of sea-floor spreading?
7. **Relating Cause and Effect** Would earthquakes occur at a depth of over 700 kilometers? Why or why not?

Writing in Science

Explanatory Paragraph Write a paragraph explaining how scientists learned the age of the ocean floor and how these data supported sea-floor spreading.

9.3 Theory of Plate Tectonics

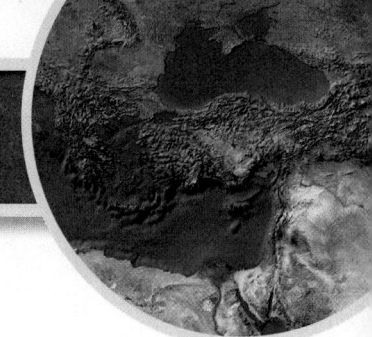

Reading Focus

Key Concepts
- What is the theory of plate tectonics?
- What are the three types of plate boundaries?

Vocabulary
- plate
- plate tectonics
- divergent boundary
- convergent boundary
- transform fault boundary
- continental volcanic arc
- volcanic island arc

Reading Strategy
Comparing and Contrasting Copy the table. After you read, compare the three types of plate boundaries by completing the table.

Boundary Type	Relative Plate Motion
convergent	a. _____?_____
divergent	b. _____?_____
transform fault	c. _____?_____

During the 1960s, scientists realized that sea-floor spreading explained part of Alfred Wegener's idea of continental drift. It explained how ocean basins could open and close. Canadian geologist J. Tuzo Wilson combined the evidence for sea-floor spreading with other observations. Wilson and other scientists soon developed a new theory that led to a revolution in geology.

Earth's Moving Plates

Wilson suggested that the lithosphere is broken into several huge pieces, called **plates.** Deep faults, like the cracks in the shell of a hard-boiled egg, separate the different plates. **In the theory of plate tectonics, Earth's lithospheric plates move slowly relative to each other, driven by convection currents in the mantle.** The plates, shown in Figure 15 on pages 262–263, generally are made up of both oceanic lithosphere and continental lithosphere.

Causes of Plate Motion Wegener had failed to explain how the lithosphere could move. The theory of plate tectonics identified a force that could set Earth's outer shell in motion. According to Wilson, convection currents within Earth drive plate motion. Hot material deep in the mantle moves upward by convection. At the same time, cooler, denser slabs of oceanic lithosphere sink into the mantle.

Effects of Plate Motion Plate motion averages about 5 centimeters per year. That's about as fast as your fingernails grow. The results of plate motion include earthquakes, volcanoes, and mountain building.

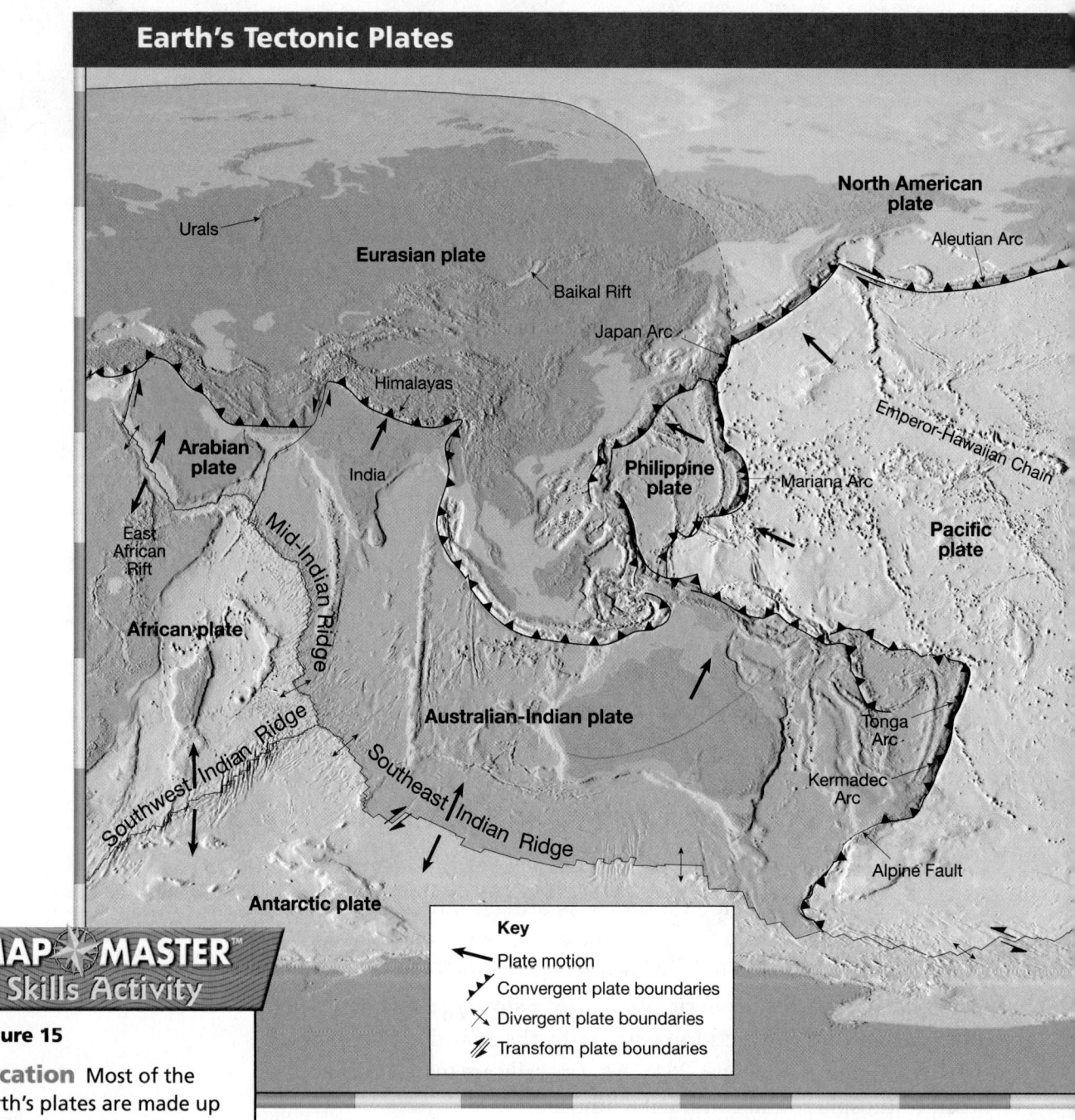

Earth's Tectonic Plates

North American plate

Aleutian Arc

Urals

Eurasian plate

Baikal Rift

Japan Arc

Himalayas

Arabian plate

India

Philippine plate

Mariana Arc

Emperor-Hawaiian Chain

East African Rift

Mid-Indian Ridge

Pacific plate

African plate

Southwest Indian Ridge

Australian-Indian plate

Southeast Indian Ridge

Tonga Arc

Kermadec Arc

Alpine Fault

Antarctic plate

Key

→ Plate motion
Convergent plate boundaries
Divergent plate boundaries
Transform plate boundaries

MAP MASTER™
Skills Activity

Figure 15

Location Most of the Earth's plates are made up of both oceanic and continental lithosphere.
Locate Find a major plate that includes an entire continent plus a large area of seafloor. Locate two examples of a divergent boundary, a convergent boundary, and a transform fault boundary.

Types of Plate Boundaries
Interactions among individual plates occur along plate boundaries. The three types of plate boundaries are convergent, divergent, and transform fault boundaries. Each plate contains a combination of each of the three types.

Divergent boundaries are found where two of Earth's plates move apart. Oceanic lithosphere is created at divergent boundaries—think of how sea-floor spreading adds rock to the ocean floor.

Convergent boundaries form where two plates move together. Lithosphere can be destroyed at convergent boundaries—think about how oceanic lithosphere sinks into the mantle during subduction.

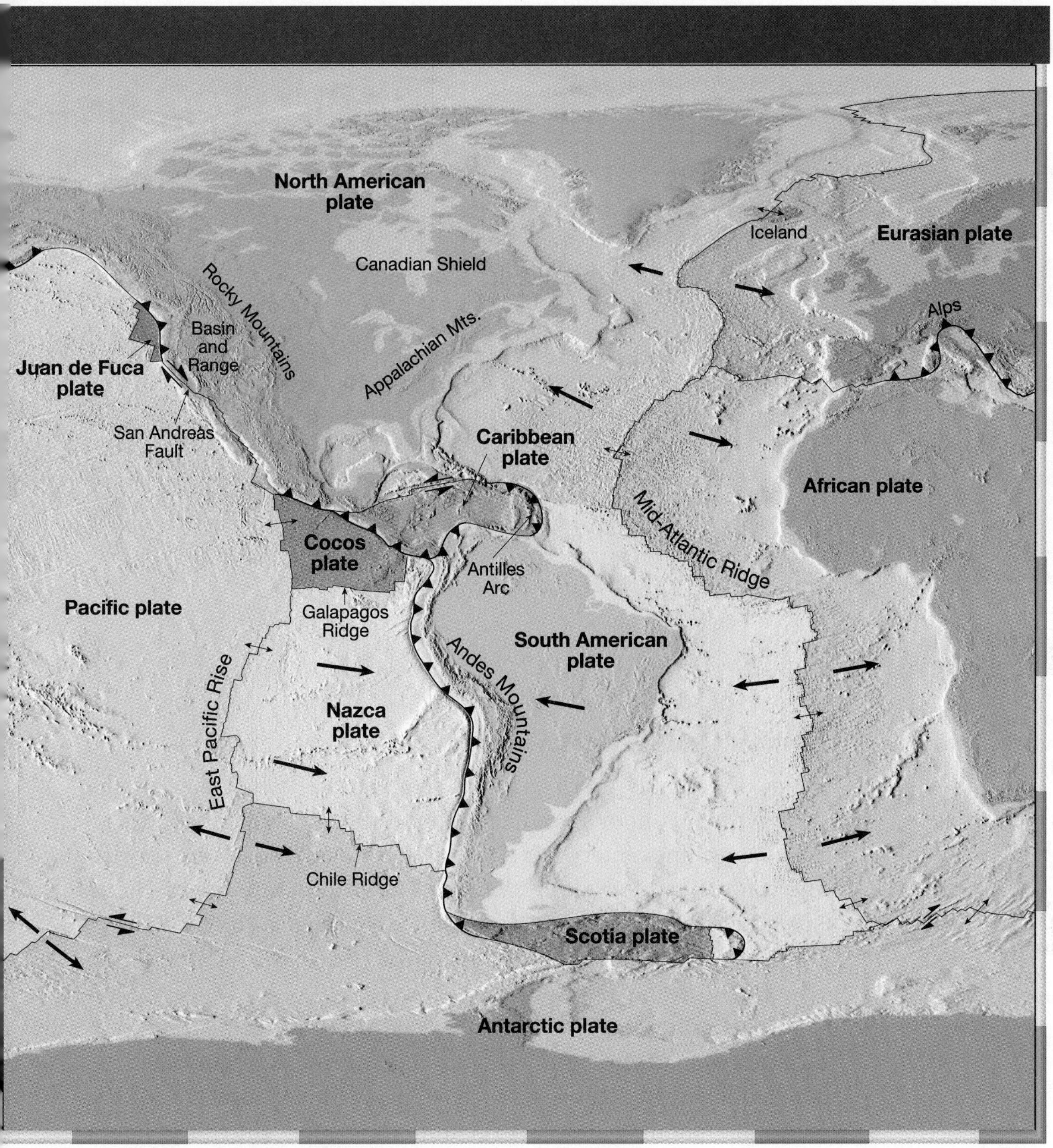

![Map of tectonic plates showing North American plate, Eurasian plate, African plate, South American plate, Pacific plate, Nazca plate, Cocos plate, Juan de Fuca plate, Caribbean plate, Scotia plate, and Antarctic plate, with labeled features including Rocky Mountains, Canadian Shield, Appalachian Mts., Basin and Range, San Andreas Fault, Iceland, Alps, Mid-Atlantic Ridge, Galapagos Ridge, Antilles Arc, Andes Mountains, East Pacific Rise, and Chile Ridge]

Transform fault boundaries occur where two plates grind past each other. Along transform boundaries, lithosphere is neither created nor destroyed.

Plates may shrink or grow in area, depending on the locations of convergent and divergent boundaries. For example, you can see in Figure 15 that the Philippine plate is subducting beneath Asia, but has no ridges as boundaries to create new lithosphere. As a result, the plate is getting smaller because of subduction.

Reading Checkpoint

What is a transform fault boundary?

A Continental crust · Upwarping

B Rift valley

C Nile River · Arabian Peninsula · Red Sea · AFRICA · Afar Lowlands · Gulf of Aden · Indian Ocean · Rift valleys · Lake Victoria · Mt. Kenya · Mt. Kilimanjaro · Lake Tanganyika · Lake Nyasa

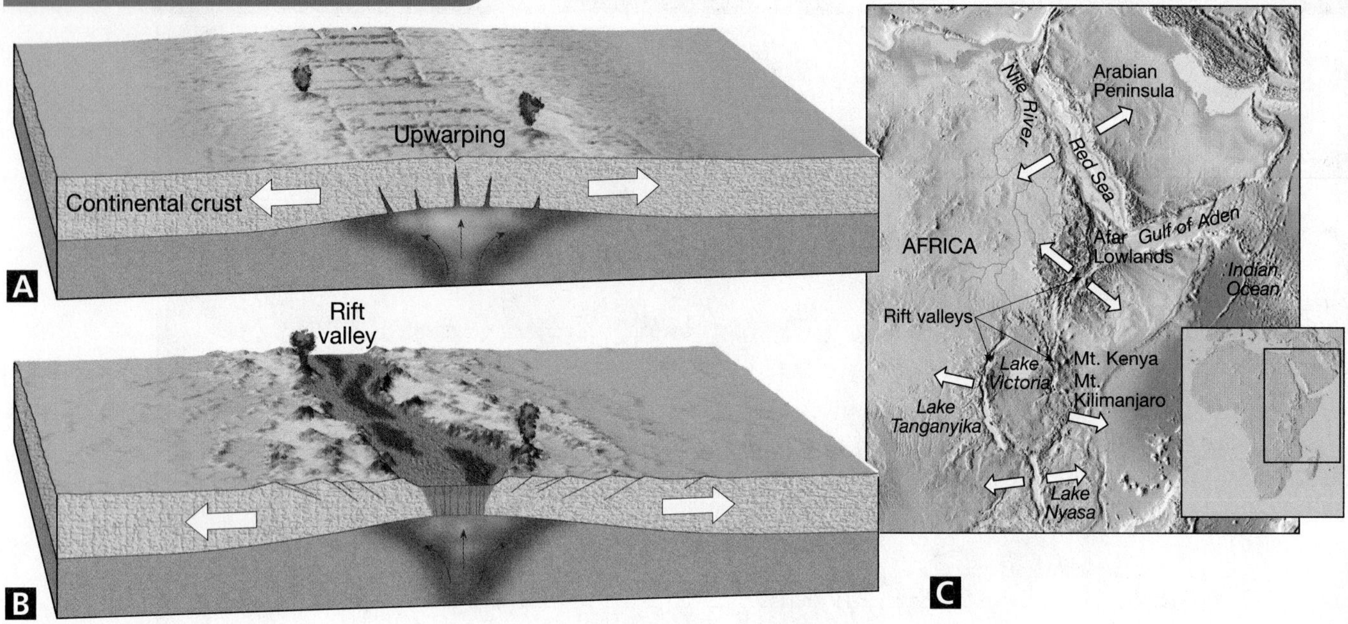

Figure 16 The East African rift valleys may represent the initial stages of the breakup of a continent along a spreading center. **A** Rising hot rock forces the crust upward, causing numerous cracks in the rigid lithosphere. **B** As the crust is pulled apart, large slabs of rock sink, causing a rift zone. **C** Further spreading causes a narrow sea like the Red Sea.
Relating Cause and Effect
What causes the continental crust to stretch and break?

Divergent Boundaries

Along divergent boundaries, plates move apart. Because they are the areas where sea-floor spreading begins, divergent boundaries are also called spreading centers. **Most divergent boundaries are spreading centers located along the crests of mid-ocean ridges. Some spreading centers, however, occur on the continents.** You can think of these plate boundaries as *constructive* plate margins because this is where new oceanic lithosphere is produced.

When a spreading center forms on land, the process can literally split a continent apart. As shown in Figure 16A, the process begins when the forces of plate motion begin to stretch part of the lithosphere. At the same time, plumes of hot rock rise from the mantle. The rising plumes bend the crust upward, weakening and fracturing it. The fractures allow magma to reach the surface. The result is the floor of a new rift valley, as shown in Figure 16B.

Examples of active rift valleys include the Rhine Valley in northwestern Europe and the Great Rift Valley in East Africa. The Great Rift Valley, shown in Figure 16C, may represent the first stage in the breakup of the African continent. If the sides of the rift valley continue to move apart, the rift could eventually become a narrow sea similar to the Red Sea.

 **Reading Checkpoint**   *How do rift valleys begin to form?*

Convergent Boundaries

At convergent boundaries, plates collide and interact, producing features including trenches, volcanoes, and mountain ranges. Along convergent boundaries, older portions of oceanic plates return to the mantle. As a result, Earth's total surface area can remain the same, even though new lithosphere is constantly being added at mid-ocean ridges.

Because lithosphere is "destroyed" at convergent boundaries, they are also called *destructive* plate margins. As two plates slowly converge, the leading edge of one is bent downward, allowing it to slide beneath the other. At destructive plate margins, oceanic crust is subducted into the mantle.

The type of lithosphere involved and the forces acting on it determine what happens at convergent boundaries. Convergent boundaries can form between two pieces of oceanic lithosphere, between oceanic lithosphere and continental lithosphere, or between two pieces of continental lithosphere.

Oceanic-Continental When the leading edge of continental lithosphere converges with oceanic lithosphere, the less dense continental lithosphere remains floating. The denser oceanic slab sinks into the asthenosphere. When a descending plate reaches a depth of about 100 to 150 kilometers, some of the asthenosphere above the descending plate melts. The newly formed magma, being less dense than the rocks of the mantle, rises. Eventually, some of this magma may reach the surface and cause volcanic eruptions.

A **continental volcanic arc** is a range of volcanic mountains produced in part by the subduction of oceanic lithosphere. As shown in Figure 17, the volcanoes of the Andes in South America are the product of magma formed during subduction of the Nazca plate.

Figure 17 Oceanic-Continental Convergent Boundary Oceanic lithosphere is subducted beneath a continental plate.
Inferring *Why doesn't volcanic activity occur closer to the trench?*

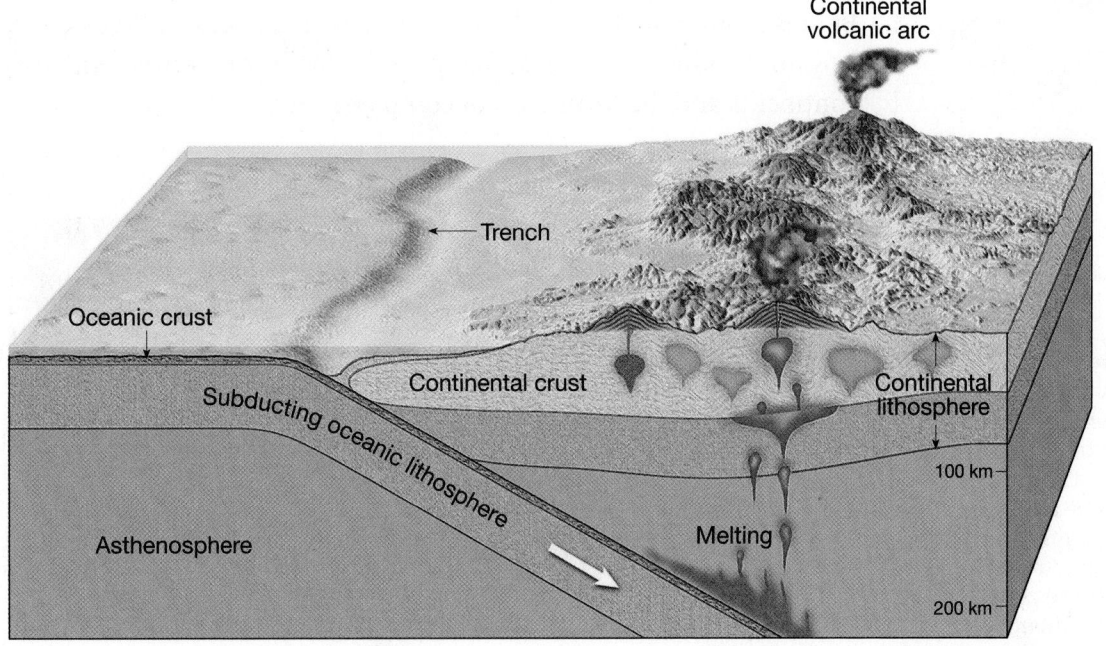

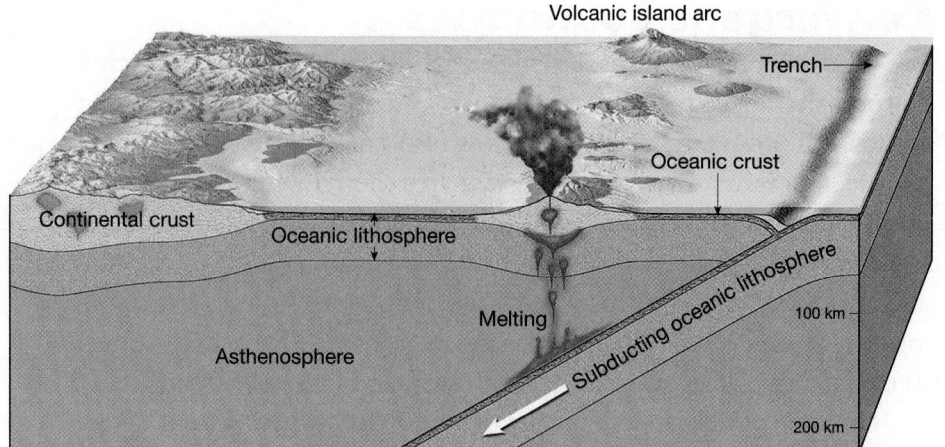

Figure 18 Oceanic-Oceanic Convergent Boundary One oceanic plate is subducted beneath another oceanic plate, forming a volcanic island arc. **Predicting** *What would happen to the volcanic activity if the subduction stopped?*

Oceanic-Oceanic When two oceanic slabs converge, one descends beneath the other. This causes volcanic activity similar to what occurs at an oceanic-continental boundary. However, the volcanoes form on the ocean floor instead of on a continent, as shown in Figure 18. If this activity continues, it will eventually build a chain of volcanic structures that become islands. This newly formed land consisting of an arc-shaped chain of small volcanic islands is called a **volcanic island arc.** The islands of Java and Sumatra in the Indian Ocean are an example of a volcanic island arc. Next to these islands is the Java trench, where one of the most powerful earthquakes ever recorded occurred in 2004.

Continental-Continental When oceanic lithosphere is subducted beneath continental lithosphere, a continental volcanic arc develops along the margin of the continent. However, if the subducting plate also contains continental lithosphere, the subduction eventually brings the two continents together, as shown in Figure 19. Because continental lithosphere is less dense than oceanic lithosphere, it is not subducted. Instead, the result is a collision between the two continents and the formation of complex mountains.

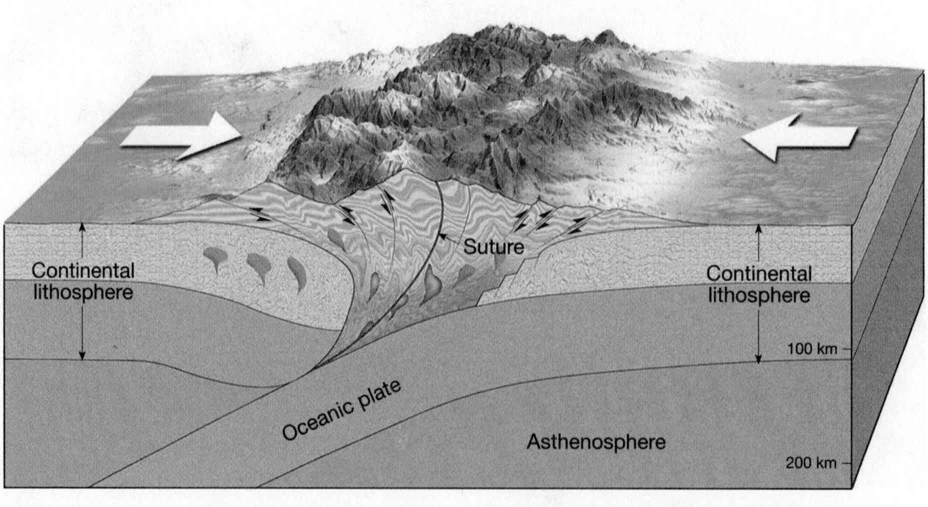

Figure 19 Continental-Continental Convergent Boundary Continental lithosphere cannot be subducted, because it floats. The collision of two continental plates forms mountain ranges. The suture (red line) represents the zone where the two plates meet.

Before continents collide, they are separated by an ocean basin. As the continents move toward each other, the seafloor between them is subducted beneath one of the plates. When the continents collide, the collision folds and deforms the sediments along the margin as if they were placed in a giant vise. A new mountain range forms that is composed of deformed and metamorphosed sedimentary rocks, fragments of the volcanic arc, and possibly slivers of oceanic crust.

This kind of collision occurred when the subcontinent of India rammed into Asia and produced the Himalayas, as shown in Figure 20. During this collision, the continental crust buckled and fractured. Several other major mountain systems, including the Alps, Appalachians, and Urals, were also formed by this process.

 **Reading Checkpoint**   ***What caused the Himalayas to form?***

Figure 20 A The leading edge of the plate carrying India is subducted beneath the Eurasian plate. **B** The landmasses collide and push up the crust. **C** India's collision with Asia continues today.

Collision of India and Asia

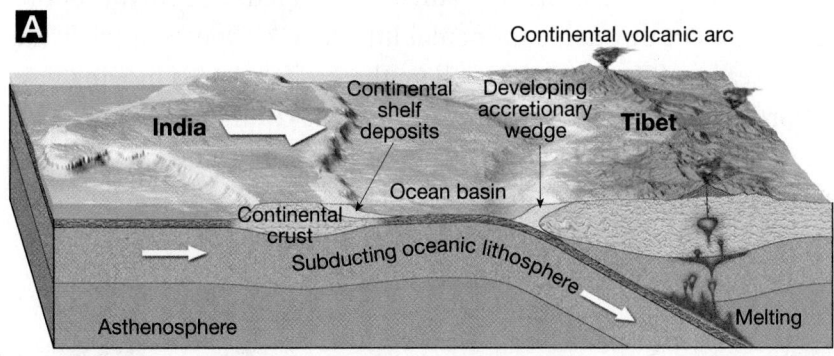

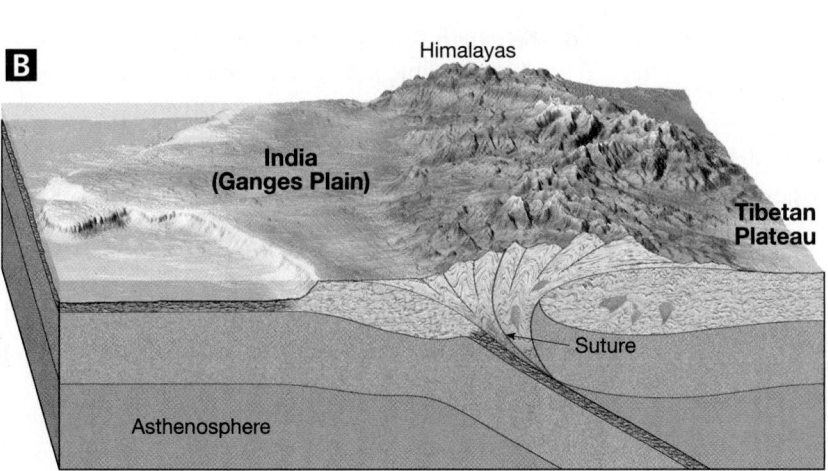

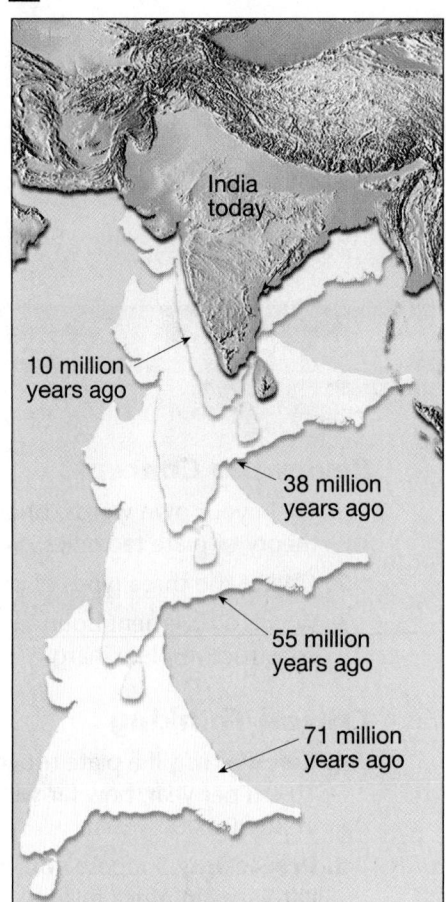

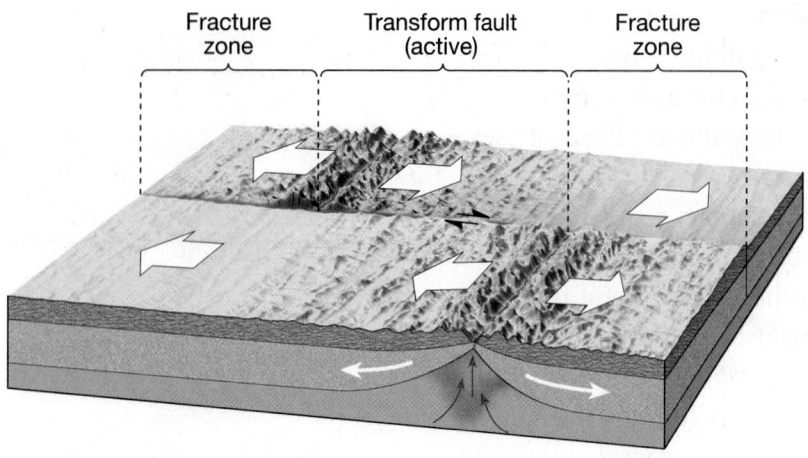
Fracture zone   Transform fault (active)   Fracture zone

Figure 21 A transform fault boundary offsets segments of a divergent boundary at an oceanic ridge.

Transform Fault Boundaries

The third type of plate boundary is the transform fault boundary. Pieces of lithosphere move past each other horizontally along a transform fault boundary. (Transform fault is another term for a strike-slip fault). **At a transform fault boundary, plates grind past each other without destroying the lithosphere.** Most transform faults join two segments of a mid-ocean ridge, as shown in Figure 21. These faults occur about every 100 kilometers along the ridge axis. Active transform faults lie between the two offset ridge segments. The seafloor produced at one ridge axis moves in a direction opposite to that of seafloor produced at the next ridge segment. Between the ridge segments, these slabs of oceanic crust are grinding past each other along a transform fault.

Although most transform faults are located within the ocean basins, a few cut through continental lithosphere. One example is the San Andreas fault in California, where the Pacific plate is moving past the North American plate. If this movement continues, that part of California west of the fault zone will become an island off the west coast of the United States and Canada. It could eventually reach Alaska. However, a more immediate concern is the earthquake activity triggered by movements along this fault system.

Section 9.3 Assessment

Reviewing Concepts

1. In your own words, briefly explain the theory of plate tectonics.
2. List the three types of plate boundaries.
3. Why is a divergent boundary considered a constructive plate margin?

Critical Thinking

4. **Calculating** If a plate moves at a rate of 10 cm per year, how far will the plate move in 20,000,000 years?
5. **Predicting** Suppose you could view the Great Rift Valley in Africa millions of years from now. How might the region have changed?

6. **Relating Cause and Effect** What forms when oceanic lithosphere collides with continental lithosphere at a convergent boundary? Explain.

Writing in Science

Descriptive Paragraph A series of deep-ocean trenches rings the Pacific Ocean. Write a paragraph that describes how the Pacific Ocean might change over millions of years, based on the theory of plate tectonics.

Plate Tectonics into the Future

Two geologists, Robert Dietz and John Holden, used present-day plate movements to predict the locations of landmasses in the future. The map below shows where they predict Earth's landmasses will be 50 million years from now if plate movements remain at their present rates.

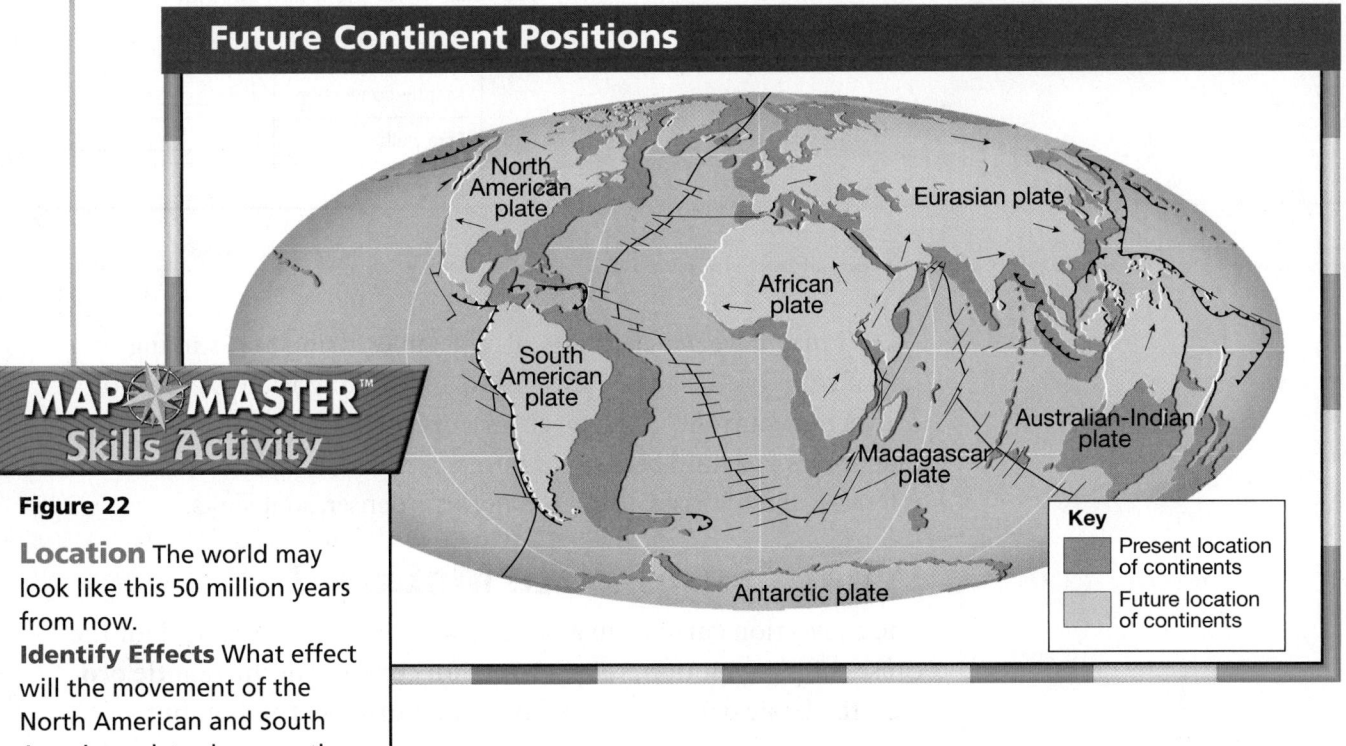

Future Continent Positions

Key
- Present location of continents
- Future location of continents

MAP MASTER™
Skills Activity

Figure 22

Location The world may look like this 50 million years from now.
Identify Effects What effect will the movement of the North American and South American plates have on the Atlantic Ocean?

L.A. on the Move

In North America, the Baja Peninsula and the portion of southern California that lies west of the San Andreas Fault will have slid past the North American plate. If this northward motion takes place, Los Angeles and San Francisco will pass each other in about 12 million years.

New Sea in Africa

Major changes are seen in Africa, where a new sea will emerge as East Africa is ripped away from the mainland. In addition, the African plate will collide with the Eurasian plate, perhaps creating the next major mountain-building stage on Earth. Meanwhile, the Arabian Peninsula will move away from Africa, allowing the Red Sea to widen.

Atlantic Ocean Grows

In other parts of the world, Australia will be located across the equator and, along with New Guinea, will be on a collision course with Asia. Meanwhile, North and South America will begin to separate, while the Atlantic and Indian oceans will continue to grow as the Pacific Ocean shrinks.

These projections, although interesting, must be viewed critically. Many assumptions must be correct for these events to occur. We can be sure that large changes in the shapes and positions of continents will occur for millions of years to come.

9.4 Mechanisms of Plate Motion

Reading Focus

Key Concepts
- What causes plate motions?
- What are the mechanisms of plate motions?

Vocabulary
- convection current
- slab-pull
- ridge-push
- mantle plume

Reading Strategy

Identifying Main Ideas Copy the table. As you read, write the main ideas for each topic.

Topic	Main Idea
Mantle convection	a. _____?_____
Slab pull	b. _____?_____
Ridge push	c. _____?_____

You may have watched bits of vegetables rising and sinking in a pot of soup on the stove. This rising and sinking is an example of a convection current. A **convection current** is the continuous flow that occurs in a fluid because of differences in density. Warm material is less dense, so it rises. Cooler material is denser, so it sinks.

What Causes Plate Motions?

The convection currents in a pot of soup can serve as a model for the causes of plate motion. **Convection currents in the mantle provide the basic driving forces for plate motions.** The hot, but solid, rock of the mantle behaves in a plastic way over geologic times—that is, it can flow slowly. The main heat source for mantle convection is energy released by radioactive isotopes in the mantle, such as uranium, thorium, and potassium. Another source is heat from the core. Since most of the heat comes from within the mantle, a bowl of soup in a microwave oven is a better analogy for this process than a pot on a stove.

But how does mantle convection produce plate motions? The plates are simply the top part of mantle convection currents. The weakness of the asthenosphere allows the stiff lithosphere above to slide across it. At the "top" of these convection currents, ocean plates cool and become denser than the mantle rock beneath them. As a result, an ocean plate will begin to subduct beneath another plate. The greater density of the cold ocean plate causes it to sink all the way down to the base of the mantle. Rock from the lower mantle rises into the upper mantle and reaches the surface at mid-ocean ridges, where new ocean floor is formed. This cyclic flow of mantle rock, which may take a half-billion years, is called whole-mantle convection, shown in Figure 23.

Plate Motion Mechanisms

 The sinking of cold ocean lithosphere directly drives the motions of mantle convection through slab-pull and ridge-push. Some scientists think mantle plumes are involved in the upward flow of rock in the mantle. In **slab-pull,** the force of gravity pulls old ocean lithosphere, which is relatively cold and dense, down into the deep mantle. In **ridge-push,** the stiff ocean lithosphere slides down the asthenosphere that is elevated near mid-ocean ridges. This downward slide is the result of gravity acting on the cool and dense ocean lithosphere. Acting together, ridge-push and slab-pull move ocean lithosphere from mid-ocean ridges toward subduction zones and then down into the mantle.

Because Earth is not growing or shrinking in size, the downward flow of subducted ocean lithosphere must equal the upward flow of rock back toward the surface. Scientists are debating how this happens. Some scientists think that most upwelling of mantle rock occurs in the form of hot-spot mantle plumes. A **mantle plume** is a rising column of hot, solid mantle rock. Other scientists do not think that large mantle plumes exist. They think that rock replaces sinking ocean lithosphere through a slow, broad rise of rock throughout the mantle. Most scientists think both processes are involved.

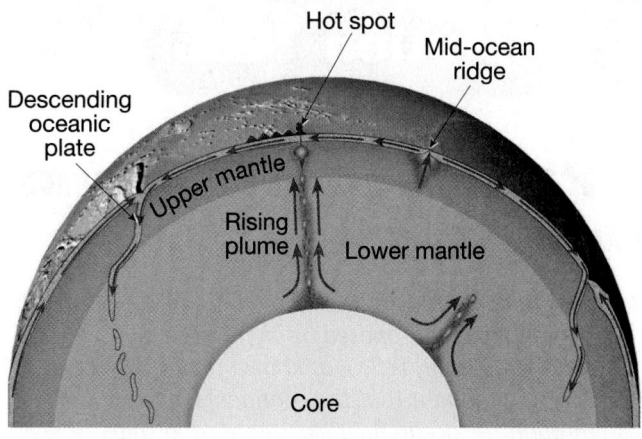

Figure 23 Whole Mantle Convection In the whole-mantle convection model, cold oceanic lithosphere descends into the mantle. Hot mantle plumes transfer heat toward the surface.

Reading Checkpoint *What is a mantle plume?*

Section 9.4 Assessment

Reviewing Concepts

1.  How are plate motions connected with motions within the rest of Earth's mantle?

2. How are the forces of slab-pull and ridge-push related to plate motions?

3. What is the ultimate source of heat that moves the plates?

Critical Thinking

4. **Predicting** If Earth did not form with very much uranium, thorium, or potassium, how might it have been different than it is today?

5. **Inferring** What characteristic of old, oceanic lithosphere in a subduction zone contributes to slab-pull? Explain.

Connecting ⊂ Concepts

Convection Currents Review Section 9.2. Use what you learned about sea-floor spreading and about the role of convection currents in plate tectonics to write the "life story" of a plate made up of oceanic lithosphere.

Paleomagnetism and the Ocean Floor

When Wegener proposed his hypothesis of continental drift, little was known about the ocean floor. He thought that the continents plowed through the ocean floor like icebreaking ships plowing through ice. Later studies of the oceans provided one of the keys to the plate tectonic theory. In this lab, you will observe how the magnetic rocks on the ocean floor can be used to understand plate tectonics.

Problem How are the paleomagnetic patterns on the ocean floor used to determine the rate of sea-floor spreading?

Materials
- pencil
- metric ruler
- calculator
- photocopy of diagrams on page 273

Skills Measuring, Interpreting Diagrams, Calculating

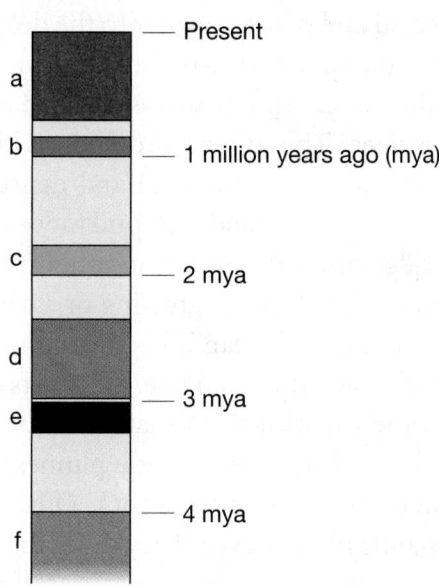

a
b — 1 million years ago (mya)
— Present
c — 2 mya
d
e — 3 mya
f — 4 mya

Procedure

1. Scientists have reconstructed Earth's magnetic polarity reversals over the past several million years. A record of these reversals is shown above. Periods of normal polarity, when a compass would have pointed north as it does today, are shown in color. Periods of reverse polarity are shown in white. Record the number of times Earth's magnetic field has had reversed polarity in the last 4 million years.

2. The three diagrams on the next page illustrate the magnetic polarity reversals across sections of the mid-ocean ridges in the Pacific, South Atlantic, and North Atlantic oceans. Periods of normal polarity are shown in color and match the colors in the illustration above. Observe that the patterns of polarity in the rock match on either side of the ridge for each ocean basin.

3. On the photocopy of the three ocean-floor diagrams, identify and mark the periods of normal polarity with the letters *a–f*. Begin at the rift valley and label along both sides of each ridge. (*Hint:* The left side of the South Atlantic has already been done and can act as a guide.)

4. Using the South Atlantic as an example, label the beginning of the normal polarity period c, "2 million years ago," on the left sides of the Pacific and North Atlantic diagrams.

5. Using the distance scale shown with the ocean floor diagrams, determine which ocean basin has spread the greatest distance during the last 2 million years. (Measure from the center of the rift valley.)

6. Refer to the distance scale. Notice that the left side of the South Atlantic basin has spread approximately 39 kilometers from the center of the rift valley in 2 million years.

Analyze and Conclude

1. **Analyzing Data** How many kilometers has the left side of the Pacific basin spread in 2 million years?

2. **Analyzing Data** How many kilometers has the left side of the North Atlantic basin spread in 2 million years?

3. **Inferring** How many kilometers has each ocean basin opened in the past 2 million years?

4. **Calculating** If both the distance that each ocean basin has opened and the time it took to open that distance are known, the rate of sea-floor spreading can be calculated. Determine the rate of sea-floor spreading for the South Atlantic Ocean basin in centimeters per year. (*Hint:* To determine the rate of spreading in centimeters per year for each ocean basin, first convert the distance from kilometers to centimeters and then divide this distance by the time, 2 million years.)

5. **Calculating** Determine the rate of sea-floor spreading for the North Atlantic and Pacific Ocean basins.

6. **Drawing Conclusions** Which ocean basin is spreading the fastest? The slowest?

7. **Inferring** Do ocean basins spread uniformly over the entire basin? Explain.

Go Further Use the library or the Internet to research the spreading rates for other divergent plate boundaries on Earth. Where is the fastest spreading rate? The slowest spreading rate?

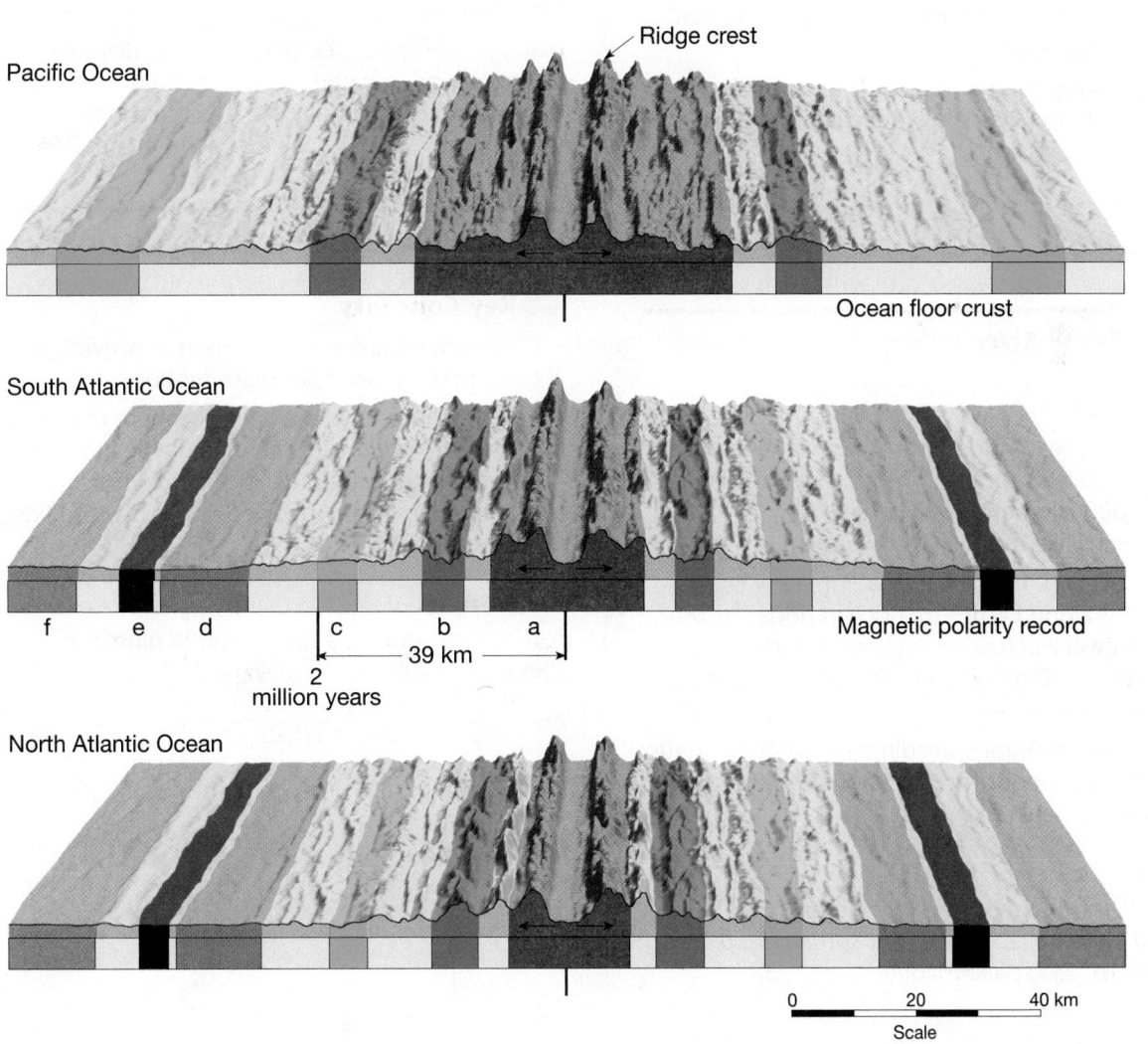

Pacific Ocean
Ridge crest
Ocean floor crust

South Atlantic Ocean
f   e   d   c   b   a
39 km
2 million years
Magnetic polarity record

North Atlantic Ocean
0   20   40 km
Scale

Study Guide

9.1 Continental Drift

Key Concepts

- According to Wegener's hypothesis of continental drift, the continents were once joined to form a single supercontinent.

- Fossil evidence for continental drift includes several fossil organisms found on different landmasses.

- Matching types of rock in several mountain belts that today are separated by oceans provide evidence for continental drift.

- Wegener found glacial deposits showing that between 220 million and 300 million years ago, ice sheets covered large areas of the Southern Hemisphere. Deposits of glacial till occurred at latitudes that today have temperate or even tropical climates: southern Africa, South America, India, and Australia.

- The main objection to Wegener's hypothesis was that he could not describe a mechanism capable of moving the continents.

Vocabulary

continental drift, *p. 248;* Pangaea, *p. 248*

9.2 Sea-Floor Spreading

Key Concepts

- Earth's mid-ocean ridge system forms the longest feature on Earth's surface. The system winds more than 70,000 kilometers through all the major ocean basins like the seam on a baseball.

- In the process of sea-floor spreading, new ocean floor forms along Earth's mid-ocean ridges, slowly moves outward across ocean basins, and finally sinks back into the mantle beneath deep-ocean trenches.

- Evidence for sea-floor spreading included magnetic stripes in ocean-floor rock, earthquake patterns, and measurements of the age of the ocean floor.

Vocabulary

sonar, *p. 254;* trench, *p. 255;* mid-ocean ridge, *p. 255;* rift valley, *p. 255;* sea-floor spreading, *p. 256;* subduction, *p. 257;* paleomagnetism, *p. 258*

9.3 Theory of Plate Tectonics

Key Concepts

- In the theory of plate tectonics, Earth's lithospheric plates move slowly relative to each other, driven by convection currents in the mantle.

- Most divergent boundaries are spreading centers located along the crests of mid-ocean ridges. Some spreading centers, however, occur on the continents.

- At convergent boundaries, plates collide and interact, producing features including trenches, volcanoes, and mountain ranges.

- At a transform fault boundary, plates grind past each other without destroying the lithosphere.

Vocabulary

plate, *p. 261;* plate tectonics, *p. 261;* divergent boundary, *p. 262;* convergent boundary, *p. 262;* transform fault boundary, *p. 263;* continental volcanic arc, *p. 265;* volcanic island arc, *p. 266*

9.4 Mechanisms of Plate Motion

Key Concepts

- Convection currents in the mantle provide the basic driving forces for plate motions.

- The sinking of cold ocean lithosphere directly drives the motions of mantle convection through slab pull and ridge push. Some scientists think mantle plumes are involved in the upward flow of rock in the mantle.

Vocabulary

convection current, *p. 270;* mantle plume, *p. 270;* slab-pull, *p. 271;* ridge-push, *p. 271*

Reviewing Content

Choose the letter that best answers the question or completes the statement.

1. What is the weaker, hotter zone beneath the lithosphere that allows for motion of Earth's rigid outer shell?
   a. crust
   b. asthenosphere
   c. outer core
   d. inner core

2. Alfred Wegener is best known for what hypothesis?
   a. plate tectonics
   b. sea-floor spreading
   c. continental drift
   d. subduction

3. What is the name given by Wegener to the supercontinent he proposed existed before the current continents?
   a. Euroamerica
   b. Atlantis
   c. Pangaea
   d. Panamerica

4. Support for Harry Hess's hypothesis of sea-floor spreading did NOT include
   a. magnetic stripes in ocean floor rock.
   b. granitic rock in the ocean floor.
   c. earthquake patterns in subduction zones.
   d. the age of the ocean floor rock.

5. Most of Earth's earthquakes, volcanoes, and mountain building occur
   a. in the center of continents.
   b. in the Himalayas.
   c. at plate boundaries.
   d. at volcanic island arcs.

6. Complex mountain systems such as the Himalayas are the result of
   a. oceanic-oceanic convergence.
   b. oceanic-continental convergence.
   c. continental volcanic arcs.
   d. continental-continental convergence.

7. Which of the following mountain ranges was NOT the result of continental-continental convergence?
   a. Himalayas
   b. Alps
   c. Appalachians
   d. Andes

8. What is the type of plate boundary where two plates move together, causing one of the slabs of lithosphere to descend into the mantle beneath an overriding plate?
   a. oceanic-continental convergent
   b. divergent
   c. transform fault
   d. continental-continental convergent

9. Most deep-focus earthquakes occur near
   a. rift valleys.
   b. trenches.
   c. mid-ocean ridges.
   d. transform fault boundaries.

10. One of the main objections to Wegener's hypothesis of continental drift was that he was unable to provide an acceptable
    a. rate of continental drift.
    b. date of continental drift.
    c. mechanism for continental drift.
    d. direction of continental drift.

Understanding Concepts

11. Describe the process of sea-floor spreading.

12. What are the three types of convergent plate boundaries?

13. How were earthquake patterns used to provide evidence of sea-floor spreading?

14. Briefly explain the theory of plate tectonics.

15. What type of plate boundary is shown? What types of lithosphere are involved?

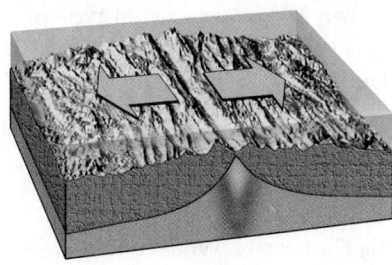

16. At what location is most lithosphere created? At what location is most lithosphere destroyed?

17. At what types of plate boundaries do subduction zones form?

Assessment *continued*

Critical Thinking

18. Drawing Conclusions In the Atlantic Ocean basin, where is the oldest oceanic lithosphere found?

19. Summarizing Describe the evidence that supported the hypothesis of continental drift.

20. Relating Cause and Effect Explain how changes in the polarity of Earth's magnetic field provided one type of evidence for the hypothesis of sea-floor spreading.

21. Inferring Why did the discovery of *Mesosaurus*, in both South America and Africa but nowhere else, support the hypothesis of continental drift?

22. Comparing and Contrasting What is the difference between the collision of an oceanic plate with a continental plate and the collision of two continental plates?

Analyzing Data

Use the diagram below to answer Questions 23–25.

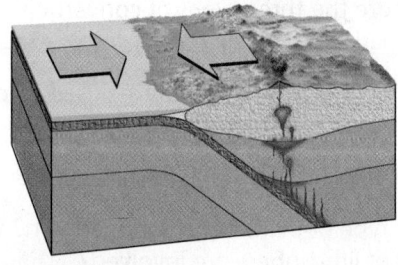

23. Interpreting Diagrams What type of boundary is shown? What types of lithosphere are involved?

24. Inferring What process occurs as the slab of oceanic lithosphere descends beneath the other plate?

25. Applying Concepts What pattern would the foci of earthquakes form if they were plotted in the diagram?

Concepts in Action

26. Predicting How would the age of a rock sample obtained by drilling in the ocean floor near a mid-ocean ridge compare with the age of a rock sample from the ocean floor near a trench? Explain.

27. Classifying What type of plate boundary is formed when two plates grind past each other? Give an example of this type of boundary.

28. Formulating Hypotheses Form a hypothesis to explain what you think would happen if the direction of motion between India and Asia changed and India began to move in a southward direction.

29. Calculating How much wider would the Atlantic Ocean become in 10 million years if the spreading rate at the Mid-Atlantic Ridge were 2.5 cm/yr? Give your answer in kilometers.

30. Writing in Science Write a paragraph explaining why earthquakes are less likely in the middle of the North American plate than they are along the edges of the plate.

Performance-Based Assessment

Classifying Use a world map to choose ten different locations around the world. Then use Figure 15 on pages 262–263 to find the plate boundary nearest each location. Classify each boundary.

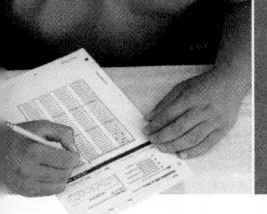

Standardized Test Prep

Choose the letter that best answers the question or completes the statement.

1. Which one of the following was NOT used as support of Wegener's continental drift hypothesis?
  (A) fossil evidence
  (B) paleomagnetism
  (C) the fit of South America and Africa
  (D) ancient climates

2. At what type of plate boundary do plates move apart, resulting in the upwelling of material from the mantle to create new seafloor?
  (A) divergent
  (B) convergent
  (C) transform fault
  (D) subduction

Use the diagram below to answer Questions 3 and 4.

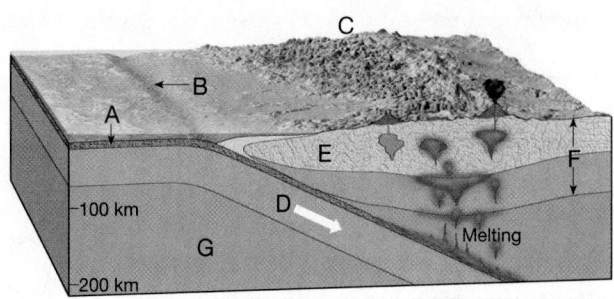

3. What feature is labeled F?
  (A) a continental volcanic arc
  (B) a subduction zone
  (C) continental lithosphere
  (D) an ocean ridge

4. The process occurring at the location labeled D is
  (A) oceanic lithosphere being created.
  (B) continental lithosphere being created.
  (C) a continental-continental collision occurring.
  (D) oceanic lithosphere being subducted.

Answer the following questions in complete sentences.

5. How does the age of the ocean lithosphere and deepest sediment in an ocean basin change with increasing distance from the oceanic ridge?

6. Why is Earth not getting larger even though new lithosphere is constantly being added at the oceanic ridges?

7. Describe two events that occur on Earth that you would not expect to find on Mars because of the lack of plate movements there.

8. At some time in the distant future, Earth's interior will cool to the point that plate movement will stop. Describe how Earth would be different from that point onward.

21st Century Learning

Civic Literacy

What are the best ways to evacuate from a volcano?

Scientists are trying to figure out how to predict a volcanic eruption far enough in advance to evacuate an area before it becomes endangered. Research the Web for articles about five recent evacuations due to volcanic eruptions. Use the articles to build a database on evacuations. Create a table that has the date, the volcano's name, the number of people evacuated, the number of deaths, and any other relevant information. Summarize the difficulties the local authorities encountered while evacuating people. Present your data to the class and answer questions.

Quick Lab
Why are some volcanoes explosive?

Exploration Lab
Melting Temperatures of Rocks

How the Earth Works
Effects of Volcanoes

GEODe
Forces Within
↳ Igneous Activity

Mount Etna, on the island of Sicily in Italy, is one of Earth's most active volcanoes.

Chapter Preview

Inquiry Activity

Where Are Volcanoes Located?

Procedure

1. Use the Internet and library resources to locate at least 15 active volcanoes and 10 historical volcanic eruptions.

2. Plot the locations of these volcanoes on a copy of a world map or on an overlay for a world atlas.

3. Neatly label the volcanoes on the map or overlay.

4. Compare your volcano map with the map of the worldwide distribution of earthquakes in Figure 12 on page 231 and the map of plate boundaries in Figure 15 on pages 262–263.

Think About It

1. **Observing** What is the relationship between the locations of the volcanoes you plotted and the earthquake epicenters and plate boundaries on the maps?

2. **Inferring** If there have been numerous volcanic eruptions in an area, would the area be a likely place for earthquakes to occur? Explain your answer.

3. **Predicting** Use your volcano map to predict if a volcanic eruption would be likely or not likely in each of the following areas: eastern coast of North America, Spain, eastern coast of South America, Italy, and Japan.

10.1 Volcanoes and Plate Tectonics

Reading Focus

Key Concepts

- How does magma form?
- What is the relationship between plate boundaries and volcanic activity?

Vocabulary

- decompression melting
- Ring of Fire
- intraplate volcanism
- hot spot

Reading Strategy

Outlining After you read, make an outline of the most important ideas in the section.

Volcanoes and Plate Tectonics
I. Origin of Magma
A. Heat
B. _____?_____
II. _____?_____

Figure 1 Tungurahua volcano in Ecuador erupted violently in 2006.

Starting in 1999, the 5000-meter-high Tungurahua volcano in Ecuador began to erupt. It spewed glowing chunks of lava, volcanic ash, and gases into the sky. Then in August 2006, streams of hot gas and rock exploded down the volcano's sides. Villagers fled as ash blanketed their farms and homes.

Tungurahua volcano is one of more than 800 active volcanoes on Earth. The process leading to a volcanic eruption begins deep beneath the surface where magma forms.

Origin of Magma

Recall that magma is molten rock beneath Earth's surface. Magma is a complex mixture that contains partly melted mineral crystals, dissolved gases, and water. **Magma forms in the crust and upper mantle when solid rock partially melts. The formation of magma depends on several factors, including heat, pressure, and water content.**

Heat What source of heat is sufficient to melt rock? At a depth of 100 kilometers, the temperature of the mantle ranges between 1400°C and 1600°C. At these temperatures, the solid rock of the lower crust and upper mantle is near, but not quite at, its melting point. The additional heat needed to produce magma comes from three sources. First, friction generates heat as huge slabs of lithosphere slide past each other in subduction zones. Second, the mantle itself heats these subducting slabs. Third, hot mantle rock can rise and intrude into the cooler lithosphere, heating it.

Pressure You have learned that pressure increases with depth inside Earth. Increasing pressure raises the melting point of rock deep beneath the surface. Decreasing pressure, in contrast, lowers rock's melting point. When pressure drops enough, **decompression melting** occurs. For example, this process takes place as hot yet solid mantle rock rises because it is less dense than the surrounding rock. As the rock rises, pressure on the rock decreases. As you can see in Figure 2, this decrease in pressure lowers the rock's melting point, forming pockets of magma.

Water Content The water content of rock also lowers the rock's melting temperature. Because of this, "wet" rock deep beneath the surface melts at a much lower temperature than does "dry" rock of the same composition and under the same pressure. Laboratory studies have shown that the melting point of basalt can be lowered by up to 100°C by adding only 0.1 percent water.

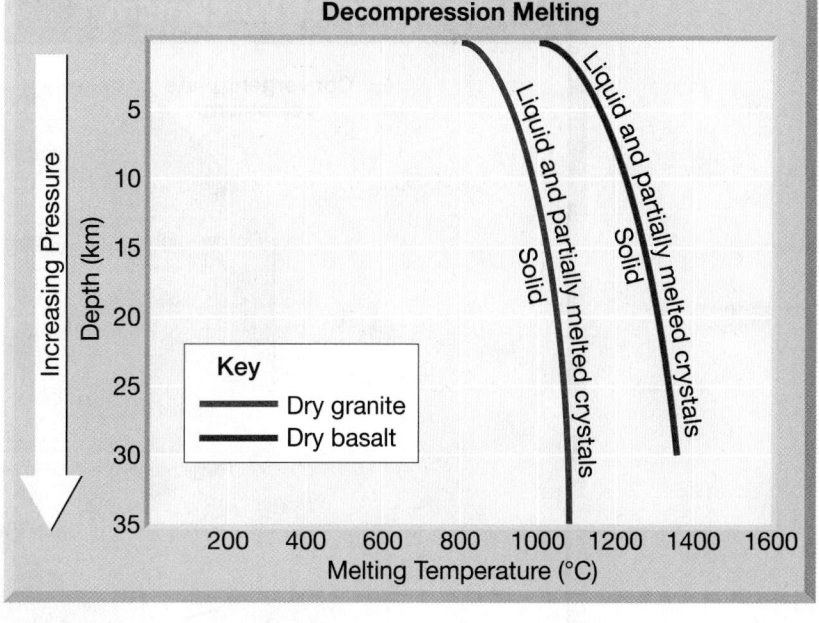

Figure 2 For granite and basalt that are "dry" (have a low water content), decompression melting occurs as pressure decreases near the surface.
Reading Graphs *What is the melting temperature of basalt at a depth of 7 km?*

 **Reading Checkpoint** *How does higher water content affect rock's melting point?*

Volcanoes and Plate Boundaries

Fortunately, magma only reaches the surface in certain areas. What determines where volcanoes form? **Most volcanoes form along divergent and convergent plate boundaries. Some volcanoes form far from plate boundaries above "hot spots" in the crust.** Figure 3 on pages 282–283 shows types of volcanic activity in relation to plate boundaries.

Divergent Boundary Volcanism At divergent boundaries, volcanic activity occurs where the plates pull apart. Mantle rock rises to fill the gap between the plates. As the rock rises, decompression melting occurs. This forms magma, which erupts along the axis of the spreading center.

Although most spreading centers are located along mid-ocean ridges, some are not. The Great Rift Valley in East Africa is an area where continental crust is being pulled apart along a divergent boundary. Mount Kilimanjaro in Tanzania is one of many volcanoes that have formed near the rift valley.

For: Links on predicting volcanic activity
Visit: www.SciLinks.org
Web Code: cjn-3103

Three Types of Volcanism

Convergent plate volcanism

Volcanic island arc · Trench · Oceanic crust · Marginal sea · Continental crust · Mantle rock melts · Water driven from plate · Subducting oceanic lithosphere · Asthenosphere

Intraplate volcanism

Oceanic crust · Hot spot · Hawaii · Decompression melting · Rising mantle plume

Convergent plate volcanism

Continental volcanic arc · Trench · Oceanic crust · Subducting oceanic lithosphere · Continental crust · Mantle rock melts · Water driven from plate

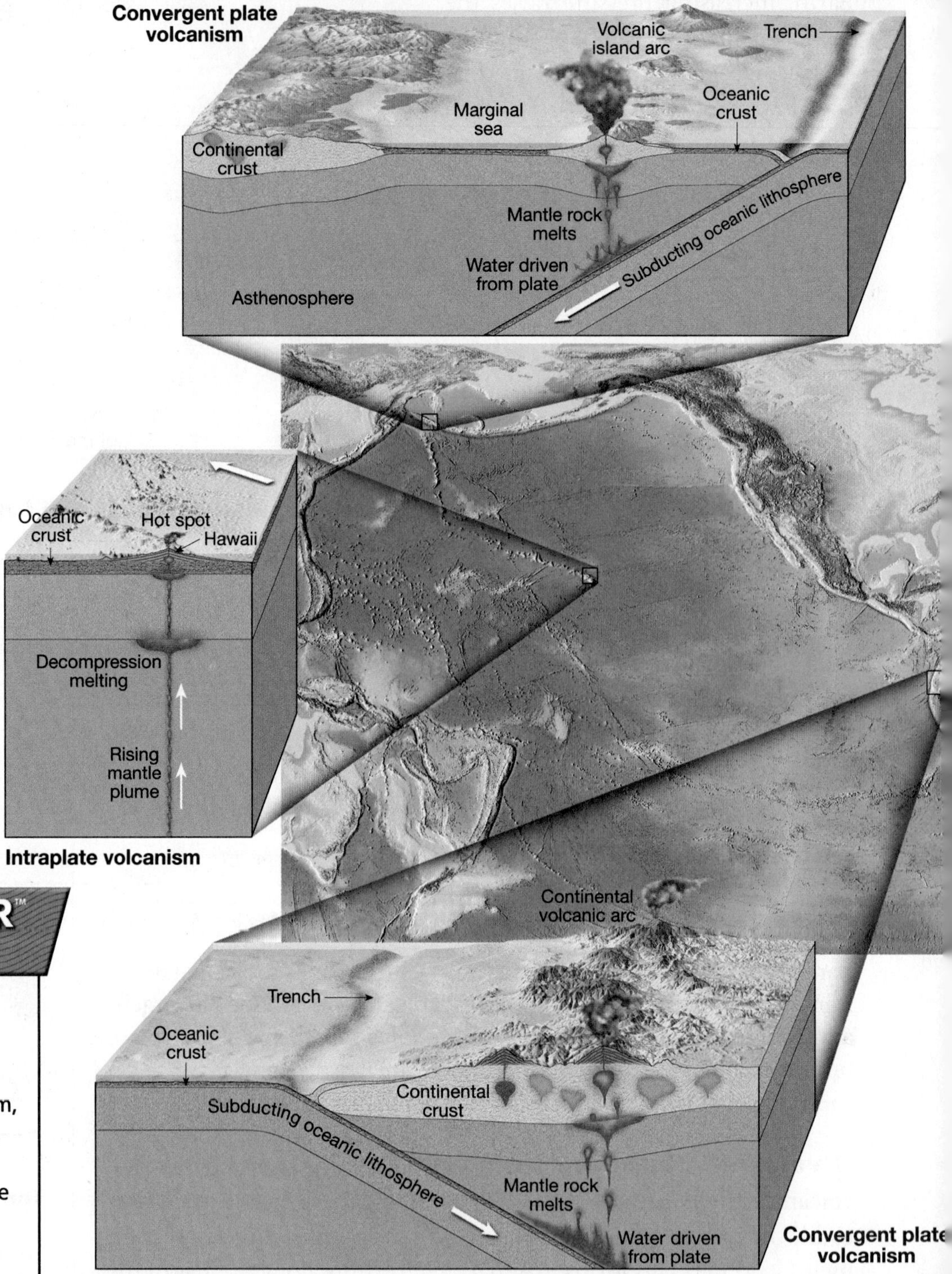

MAP MASTER™ Skills Activity

Figure 3

Regions The three types of volcanism are convergent plate volcanism, divergent plate volcanism, and intraplate volcanism. Two of these occur at plate boundaries. The third occurs in the interiors of plates.

Classifying Which type of volcanism involves the destruction of slabs of lithosphere? Explain.

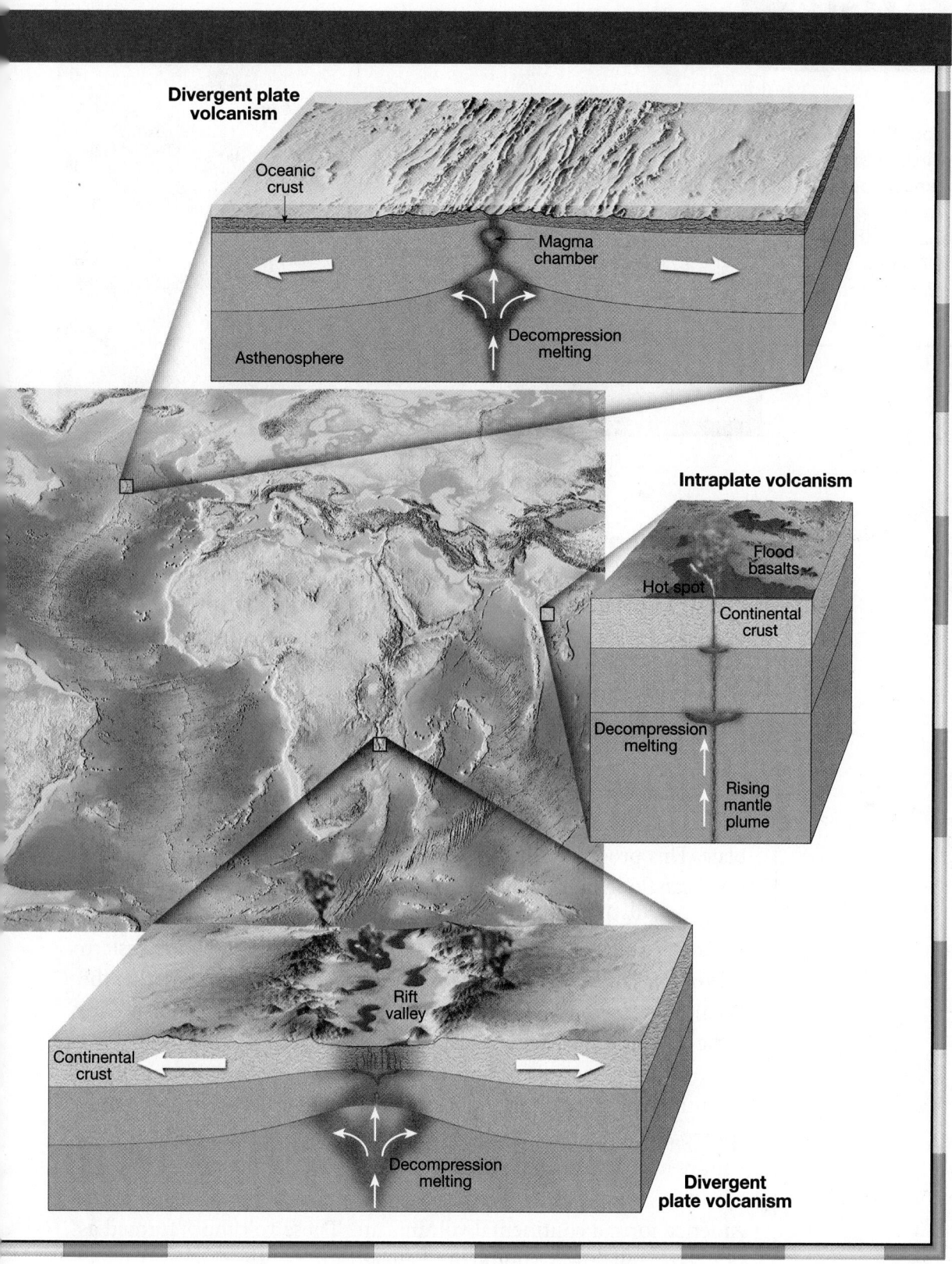

Divergent plate volcanism

Oceanic crust

Magma chamber

Asthenosphere

Decompression melting

Intraplate volcanism

Flood basalts

Hot spot

Continental crust

Decompression melting

Rising mantle plume

Rift valley

Continental crust

Decompression melting

Divergent plate volcanism

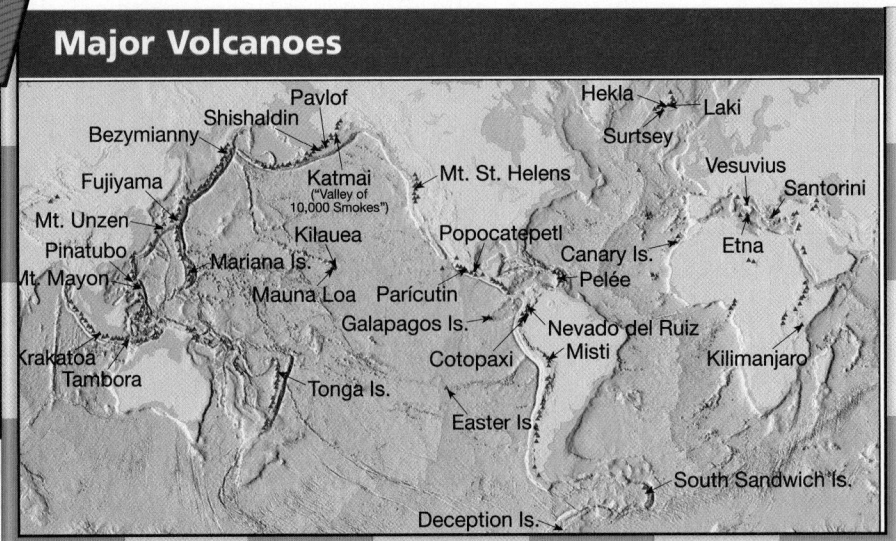

Major Volcanoes

Figure 4

Location Note the volcanoes encircling the Pacific basin, known as the Ring of Fire. **Inferring** How are the volcanoes in the middle of the Atlantic Ocean related to a plate boundary?

Convergent Boundary Volcanism Volcanoes form at convergent plate boundaries where slabs of oceanic crust are pushed down into the mantle. As a slab sinks deeper into the mantle, the increase in temperature and pressure drives water from the oceanic crust. Once the sinking slab reaches a depth of about 100 to 150 kilometers, this water reduces the melting point of hot mantle rock low enough for melting to begin. The magma formed slowly migrates upward, forming volcanoes.

Volcanoes form at convergent boundaries where two oceanic plates meet and oceanic lithosphere is subducted beneath another oceanic plate. This process results in the formation of a chain of volcanoes on the ocean floor. Eventually, these volcanic mountains grow large enough to rise above the surface and are called volcanic island arcs. Several volcanic island arcs, such as the Mariana islands, lie along the eastern side of the Pacific Ocean. Together with other volcanoes bordering the Pacific, they form the Ring of Fire, shown in Figure 4. The **Ring of Fire** is the long belt of volcanoes that circles much of the Pacific Ocean.

Volcanism may also occur at convergent plate boundaries where a continental plate meets an oceanic plate and slabs of oceanic lithosphere are subducted under continental lithosphere. The result is a continental volcanic arc. The process is basically the same as for an island arc. Tungurahua and the other volcanoes of the Andes in South America form a continental volcanic arc. These volcanoes formed as the Nazca plate was subducted beneath the South American plate. Tungurahua volcano in Ecuador, shown in Figure 4, also formed through this process.

For: Links on Volcanoes
Visit: PHSchool.com
Web Code: cuc-1101

 **Reading Checkpoint** *What process formed the volcanoes of the Andes?*

Intraplate Volcanism Kilauea volcano in Hawaii is Earth's most active volcano. But Kilauea is in the middle of the Pacific plate, thousands of kilometers from a plate boundary. Another volcanic region, centered on the hot springs and geysers of Yellowstone National Park, is in the middle of the North American plate. Both Kilauea and Yellowstone are examples of **intraplate volcanism**—volcanic activity that occurs within a plate.

Most intraplate volcanism occurs where a mass of hotter-than-normal mantle material, called a mantle plume, rises toward the surface. Once the plume nears the top of the mantle, decompression melting forms magma. The result may be a small volcanic region a few hundred kilometers across called a **hot spot.** More than 40 hot spots are known. Most of these hot spots have lasted for millions of years.

The volcanic mountains that make up the Hawaiian Islands have formed as the Pacific plate moves over a hot spot. As shown in Figure 5, the age of each volcano indicates the time when it was over the hot spot. Kauai is the oldest of the major islands in the Hawaiian chain. Its volcanoes are not likely to erupt again. The more recently formed island of Hawaii has two active volcanoes—Mauna Loa and Kilauea.

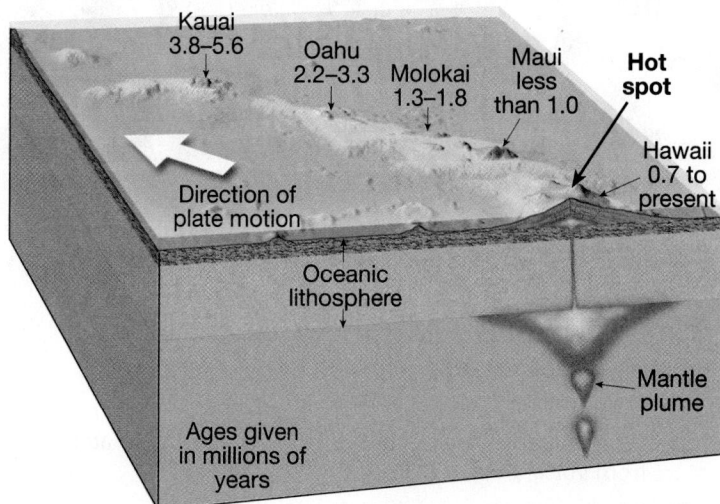

Figure 5 Intraplate Volcano An eruption of Hawaii's Kilauea volcano. The Hawaiian hot spot activity is currently centered beneath Kilauea and is an example of intraplate volcanic activity.

Section 10.1 Assessment

Reviewing Concepts

1. What three factors affect how magma forms?
2. How are the locations of volcanoes related to plate boundaries?
3. What causes intraplate volcanism?
4. What is the Ring of Fire?
5. How is magma formed through decompression melting?

Critical Thinking

6. **Applying Concepts** Describe how an island arc forms at a convergent boundary.

7. **Inferring** Geologists have found ancient deposits of lava and volcanic ash extending southwest from the Yellowstone hot spot to Nevada. What can you infer from this observation?

Writing in Science

Convection Currents Recall what you learned about convection currents in Chapter 9. Explain how convection currents could affect the depth at which molten rocks are found.

10.2 The Nature of Volcanic Eruptions

Reading Focus

Key Concepts

- What determines the type of volcanic eruption?
- What materials are ejected from volcanoes?
- What are the three main types of volcanoes?
- What other landforms are associated with volcanic eruptions?

Vocabulary

- ◆ viscosity
- ◆ vent
- ◆ pyroclastic material
- ◆ volcano
- ◆ crater
- ◆ shield volcano
- ◆ cinder cone
- ◆ composite cone
- ◆ caldera
- ◆ volcanic neck
- ◆ lava plateau
- ◆ lahar

Reading Strategy

Previewing Copy the table. Before you read the section, rewrite the green topic headings as questions. As you read, write the answers to the questions.

The Nature of Volcanic Eruptions	
What factors affect an eruption?	a. _____?_____

On May 18, 1980, Mount St. Helens erupted with tremendous force. The blast blew out the entire north side of the volcano. The eruption ejected nearly a cubic kilometer of ash and other debris. Why do volcanoes like Mount St. Helens erupt explosively, while others like Kilauea in Hawaii are relatively quiet?

Factors Affecting Eruptions

The primary factors that determine whether a volcano erupts explosively or quietly include characteristics of the magma and the amount of dissolved gases in the magma. Magma that has reached the surface is called lava. Lava cools and hardens to form solid rock.

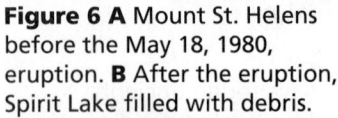

Figure 6 A Mount St. Helens before the May 18, 1980, eruption. **B** After the eruption, Spirit Lake filled with debris.

A

B
Spirit Lake

Table 1 Magma Composition					
Composition	Silica Content	Viscosity	Gas Content	Tendency to Form Pyroclastics (ejected rock fragments)	Volcanic Landform
Basaltic	Least (about 50%)	Least	Least (1–2%)	Least	Shield volcanoes Basalt plateaus Cinder cones
Andesitic	Intermediate (about 60%)	Intermediate	Intermediate (3–4%)	Intermediate	Composite cones
Granitic	Most (about 70%)	Greatest	Most (4–6%)	Greatest	Pyroclastic flows Volcanic domes

Viscosity Magma's viscosity—whether the magma is thick and sticky or thin and runny—affects the type of eruption that occurs. **Viscosity** is a substance's resistance to flow. For example, maple syrup is more viscous than water, so it flows more slowly. Magma from an explosive eruption may be thousands of times more viscous than magma that erupts quietly. The temperature and chemical composition of magma determine the magma's viscosity.

The effect of temperature on viscosity is easy to see. If you heat maple syrup, it becomes more fluid and less viscous. In the same way, the viscosity of lava is strongly affected by temperature. As a lava flow cools and begins to harden, its viscosity increases. The lava flow slows down and eventually halts.

The chemical composition of magma has a more important effect on the type of eruption. In general, the more silica in magma, the greater its viscosity. Because of their high silica content, rhyolitic lavas are very viscous and erupt explosively. Basaltic lavas, which contain less silica, are less viscous and tend to erupt quietly.

Dissolved Gases During explosive eruptions, the gases trapped in magma provide the force to propel molten rock out of the **vent,** an opening to the surface. These gases are mostly water vapor and carbon dioxide. As magma moves nearer the surface, the pressure in the upper part of the magma is greatly reduced. The reduced pressure allows dissolved gases to be released suddenly.

Very fluid basaltic magma allows the expanding gases to bubble upward and escape relatively easily. Therefore, eruptions of fluid basaltic lava, such as those that occur in Hawaii, are relatively quiet. But highly viscous magma slows the upward movement of expanding gases. The gases collect in bubbles and pockets that increase in size until they eject the magma from the volcano in an explosive eruption.

 **Reading Checkpoint** *What causes the dissolved gases in magma to be released?*

Why are some volcanoes explosive?

Procedure

1. Obtain two bottles of noncarbonated water and two bottles of club soda.

2. Open one bottle of the noncarbonated water and one bottle of the club soda. Record your observations.

3. Gently shake each of the remaining unopened bottles. **CAUTION:** *Wear safety goggles and point the bottles away from everyone.*

4. Carefully open each bottle over a sink or outside. Record your observations.

Analyze and Conclude

1. **Observing** What happened when the bottles were opened?

2. **Inferring** Which bottle represents lava with the most dissolved gas?

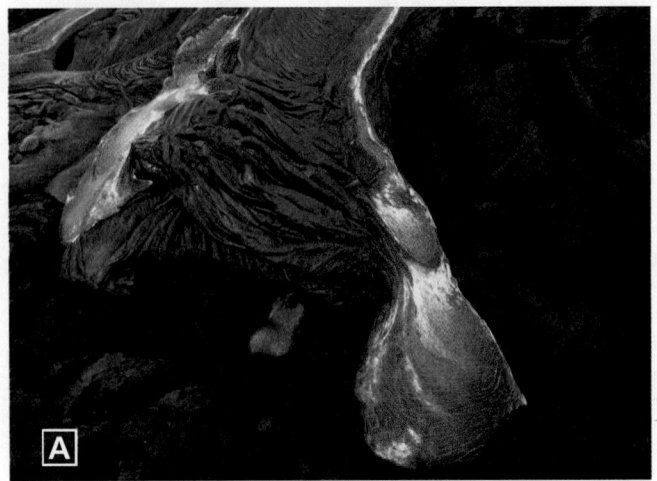

Figure 7 Lava Flows, Mount Kilauea, Hawaii Pahoehoe **(A)** is hotter and faster moving than aa. **(B)**
Drawing Conclusions *Which type of lava is more viscous?*

Volcanic Material

Lava may appear to be the main material produced by a volcano, but this is not always the case. Just as often, explosive eruptions eject huge quantities of broken rock, lava bombs, fine ash, and dust. **Depending on the type of eruption, volcanoes may produce lava flows or eject pyroclastic materials, or both. All volcanic eruptions also emit large amounts of gases.**

Lava Flows Silica content and temperature affect the characteristics of lava flows. Hot basaltic lavas are usually very fluid because of their low silica content. Flow rates of 10 to 300 meters per hour are common. In contrast, the movement of silica-rich, rhyolitic lava is often too slow to be visible.

Temperature differences produce two types of basaltic lava: pahoehoe and aa. Pahoehoe (pah HOH ee hoh ee) is hotter, fast-moving basaltic lava. Pahoehoe forms a relatively smooth skin that wrinkles as the still-molten subsurface lava continues to flow. Pahoehoe resembles the braids in twisted ropes, as shown in Figure 7. Aa (AH ah) is cooler, slower-moving basaltic lava. Aa forms a surface of rough, jagged blocks with sharp, spiny projections.

Gases Magmas contain varied amounts of dissolved gases held under pressure in the molten rock, just as carbon dioxide is held in soft drinks. As with soft drinks, as soon as the pressure is reduced, the gases begin to escape. The gaseous portion of most magmas is only about 1 to 6 percent of the total weight. The percentage may be small, but the actual quantity of emitted gas can exceed thousands of tons each day. Samples taken during a Hawaiian eruption consisted of about 70 percent water vapor, 15 percent carbon dioxide, 5 percent nitrogen, 5 percent sulfur, and lesser amounts of chlorine, hydrogen, and argon. Sulfur compounds are easily recognized because they smell like rotten eggs and readily form sulfuric acid, a natural source of air pollution.

For: Links on volcanic eruptions
Visit: www.SciLinks.org
Web Code: cjn-3101

Pyroclastic Materials Particles produced in volcanic eruptions are called **pyroclastic materials**. When basaltic lava is extruded, dissolved gases propel blobs of lava to great heights. Some of this ejected material may land near the vent and build a cone-shaped structure. The wind will carry smaller particles great distances. Viscous rhyolitic magmas are highly charged with gases. As the gases expand, pulverized rock and lava fragments are blown from the vent.

The fragments ejected during eruptions range in size from very fine dust and volcanic ash (less than 2 millimeters) to pieces that weigh several tons. Particles that range in size from small beads to walnuts (2–64 millimeters) are called lapilli, or cinders. Particles larger than 64 millimeters in diameter are called blocks when they are made of hardened lava and bombs when they are ejected as glowing lava.

 **Reading Checkpoint** *What is a volcanic bomb?*

Types of Volcanoes

Volcanic landforms come in a wide variety of shapes and sizes. Each structure has a unique eruptive history. **The three main volcanic types are shield volcanoes, cinder cones, and composite cones.**

Anatomy of a Volcano Volcanic activity often begins when a fissure, or crack, develops in the crust as magma is forced toward the surface. The magma collects in a pocket beneath the surface called the magma chamber. The gas-rich magma rises from the magma chamber, travels through a circular pipe, and reaches the surface at a vent, as shown in Figure 8. Repeated eruptions of lava or pyroclastic material eventually build a mountain called a **volcano.** Located at the summit of many volcanoes is a steep-walled depression called a **crater.**

The form of a volcano is largely determined by the composition of the magma. As you will see, fluid lavas tend to produce broad structures with gentle slopes. More viscous, silica-rich lavas produce cones with moderate to steep slopes.

Go Online
active art

For: Composite volcano eruption activity
Visit: PHSchool.com
Web Code: czp-3102

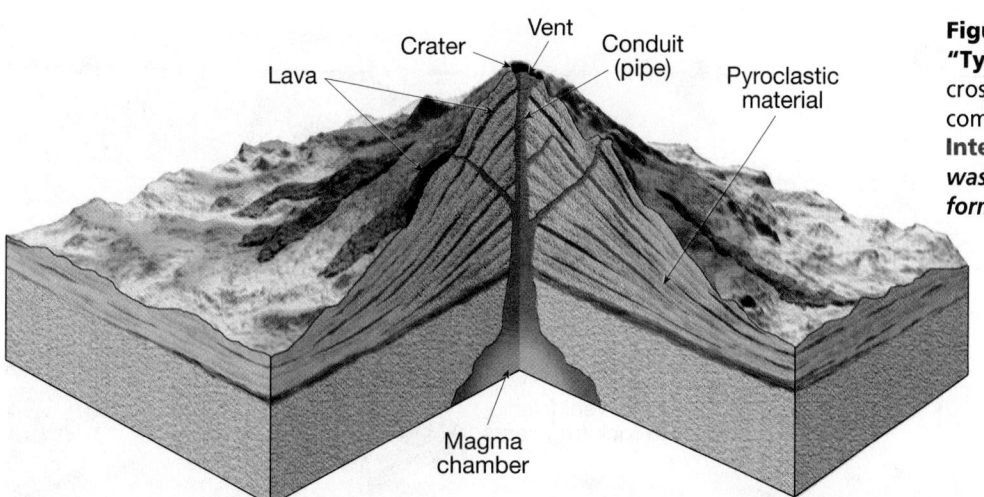

Lava — Crater — Vent — Conduit (pipe) — Pyroclastic material — Magma chamber

Figure 8 Anatomy of a "Typical" Volcano This cross section shows a typical composite cone.
Interpreting Diagrams *How was the volcano in the diagram formed?*

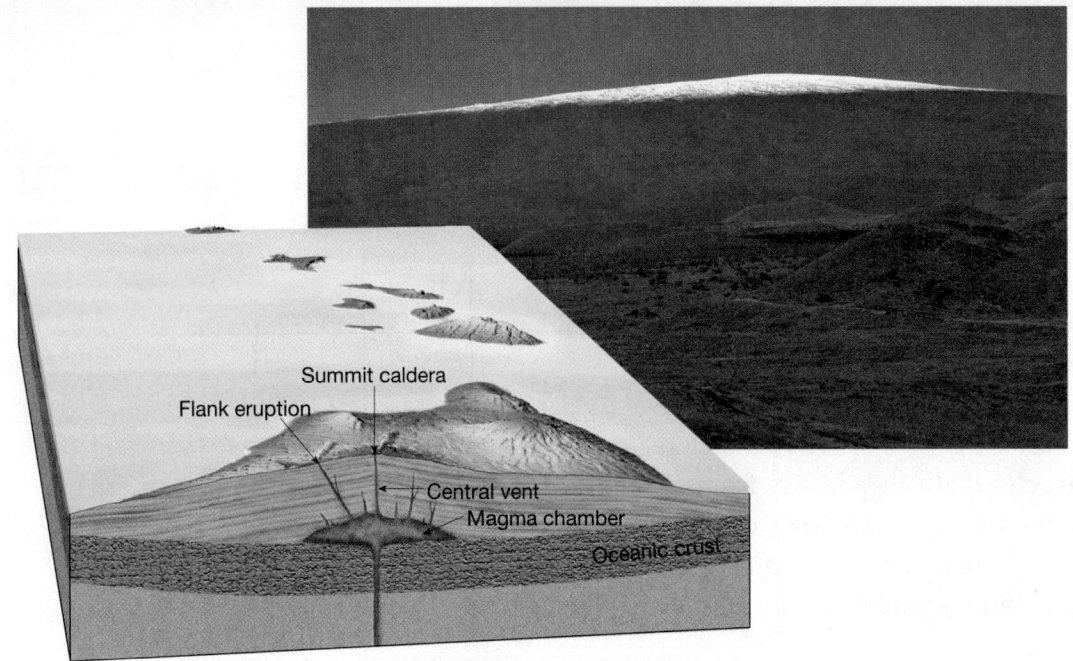

Figure 9 Shield Volcanoes
Shield volcanoes like Mauna Loa and Mauna Kea in Hawaii are built mainly of fluid basaltic lava flows. These broad, slightly domed structures are the largest volcanoes on Earth.

Labels in figure: Summit caldera, Flank eruption, Central vent, Magma chamber, Oceanic crust

Shield Volcanoes Shield volcanoes are produced by the accumulation of fluid basaltic lavas. Shield volcanoes have the shape of a broad, slightly domed structure that resembles a warrior's shield, as shown in Figure 9. Most shield volcanoes have grown up from the deep-ocean floor to form islands. Examples of shield volcanoes include those in the Hawaiian Islands and Iceland.

Cinder Cones Ejected lava fragments that harden in the air build a **cinder cone.** The fragments range in size from fine ash to bombs but consist mostly of lapilli, or cinders. Cinder cones are usually a product of relatively gas-rich basaltic or rhyolitic magma. Occasionally, cinder cones produce lava flows.

The shape of a cinder cone is determined by the steep-sided slope that forms as loose pyroclastic material builds up around the vent. Cinder cones are usually the product of a single eruption that sometimes lasts only a few weeks and rarely more than a few years. Once the eruption ends, the magma in the pipe connecting the vent to the magma chamber solidifies, and the volcano never erupts again. As shown in Figure 11, cinder cones are relatively small.

Figure 10 Cinder Cones
A A typical cinder cone has steep slopes of 30–40 degrees. **B** Many cinder cones, like this one near Flagstaff, Arizona, are located in volcanic fields. Others form on the sides of larger volcanoes.
Inferring *What feature is shown in the lower part of the photograph?*

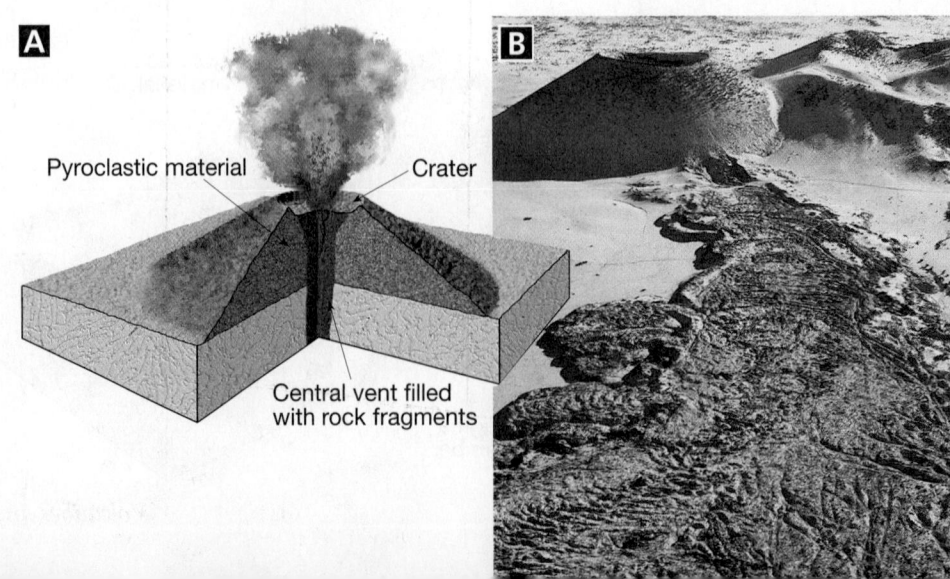

Labels in figure: Pyroclastic material, Crater, Central vent filled with rock fragments

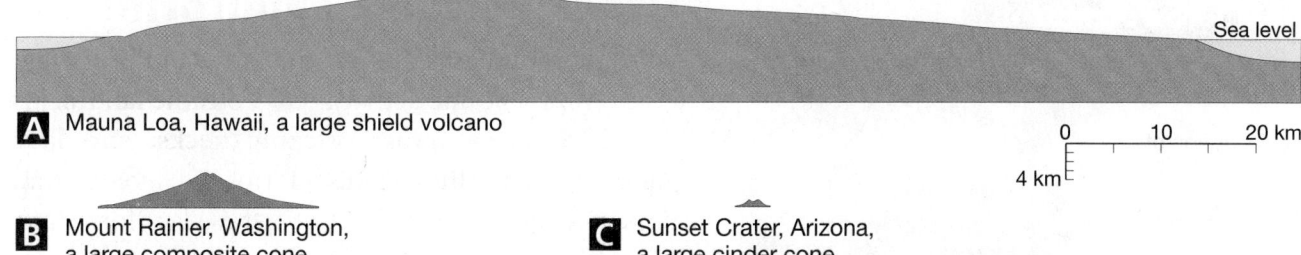

A Mauna Loa, Hawaii, a large shield volcano

0   10   20 km
4 km

B Mount Rainier, Washington, a large composite cone

C Sunset Crater, Arizona, a large cinder cone

Figure 11 Comparing Volcanic Landforms Cinder cones and composite cones are small in comparison with a large shield volcano like Mauna Loa in Hawaii.

Composite Cones Earth's most beautiful and potentially dangerous volcanoes are composite cones, or stratovolcanoes. A **composite cone** is a large, nearly symmetrical volcanic mountain composed of layers of both lava and pyroclastic deposits. For the most part, composite cones are the product of gas-rich magma having an andesitic composition. The silica-rich magmas typical of composite cones generate viscous lavas that can travel only short distances. Composite cones may generate the most explosive eruptions, ejecting huge quantities of pyroclastic material.

Most composite cones are located in a relatively narrow zone that rims the Pacific Ocean, the Ring of Fire. The Ring of Fire includes the large cones of the Andes in South America and the Cascade Range of the western United States and Canada. The Cascade Range includes Mount St. Helens, Mount Rainier, and Mount Shasta, shown in Figure 12. The most active regions in the Ring of Fire are located along volcanic island arcs next to deep ocean trenches. This nearly continuous chain of volcanoes stretches from the Aleutian Islands to Japan, the Philippines, and New Zealand.

Figure 12 Composite Cone Mount Shasta, California, is one of the largest composite cones in the Cascade Range. Shastina is the smaller cone that formed on the left flank of Mt. Shasta.

Volcanoes and Other Igneous Activity **291**

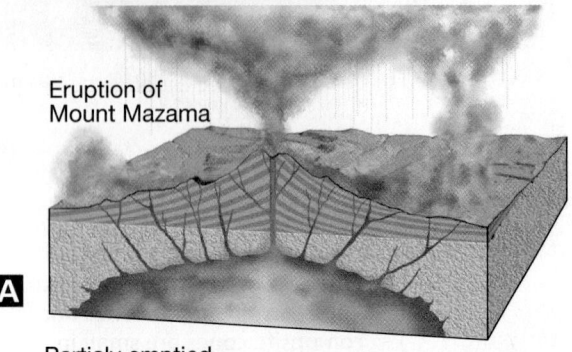

Eruption of
Mount Mazama

A

Partialy emptied
magma chamber

B

Collapse of
Mount Mazama

C

Formation of Crater Lake and Wizard Island

D

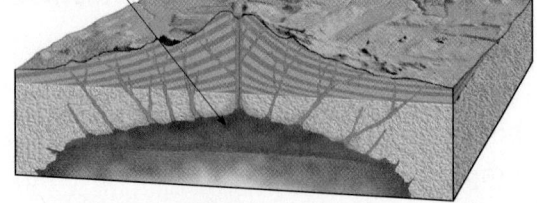
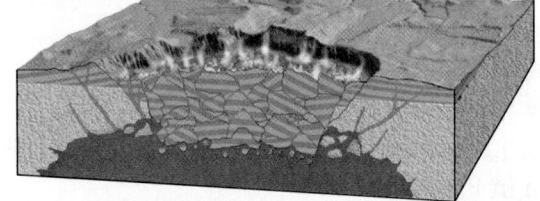
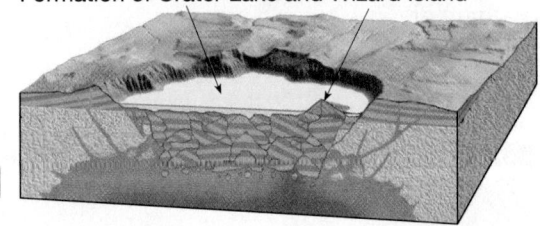

Other Volcanic Landforms

Volcanic mountains are not the only landforms that result from volcanic activity. ◯━**Volcanic landforms also include calderas, volcanic necks, and lava plateaus.** Each of these features forms in a different way. Long after eruptions have ended, these landforms can provide evidence of volcanic activity.

Calderas One spectacular reminder of what can happen when a volcano's activity ends is the caldera. A caldera is a depression in a volcanic mountain. Most calderas form in one of two ways: by the collapse of the top of a composite volcano after an explosive eruption, or from the collapse of the top of a shield volcano after the magma chamber is drained.

Crater Lake in Oregon occupies a caldera. This caldera formed about 7000 years ago when a composite cone, Mount Mazama, erupted violently, as shown in Figure 13. The eruption of Mount Mazama partly emptied the magma chamber. The roof of the magma chamber collapsed, forming a huge depression that became Crater Lake. A later eruption produced Wizard Island, the small cinder cone in the lake.

There are several other large calderas in the United States. In Hawaii, the vast "crater" atop Mount Haleakala on the island of Maui is, in fact, a caldera. In the Yellowstone caldera in Wyoming and the Valles caldera in northern New Mexico, hot springs are evidence of past, and perhaps future, volcanic activity.

Figure 13 Crater Lake in Oregon occupies a caldera about 10 kilometers in diameter that formed about 7000 years ago.

E

Volcanic Necks Another volcanic landform that provides evidence of past volcanic activity is the volcanic neck. A **volcanic neck** is a landform made of magma that hardened in a volcano's pipe and later was exposed by erosion. Recall that a volcano's pipe connects the magma chamber with the surface. When a volcano's activity ends, magma remaining in the pipe hardens to form igneous rock.

Weathering and erosion act constantly to wear away volcanoes. For example, cinder cones are easily eroded because they are made up of loose materials. But the rock in a volcano's pipe is more resistant to erosion, so it is left standing above the surrounding land after most of the cone has been eroded. Ship Rock, shown in Figure 14, is a volcanic neck in New Mexico.

Figure 14 Volcanic Neck Ship Rock, New Mexico, is a volcanic neck. Ship Rock consists of igneous rock that crystallized in the pipe of a volcano that then was eroded away.

Lava Plateaus If you visited the Columbia River gorge in Washington state, you would see huge cliffs made up of layers of dark, volcanic rock. These layers of rock are part of the Columbia plateau, a huge lava plateau that covers parts of Washington, Oregon, and Idaho. A lava plateau is a volcanic landform produced by repeated eruptions of very fluid, basaltic lava. As shown in Figure 15, the lava that forms a lava plateau erupts through long cracks called fissures. Instead of building a cone, the lava spreads out over a wide area.

The Columbia plateau is nearly 1.6 kilometers thick. The plateau formed over hundreds of thousands of years as a series of lava flows, some 50 meters thick, buried the landscape. Another major lava plateau is the Deccan plateau in India.

 **Reading Checkpoint**   *What is a volcanic neck?*

Figure 15 Lava Plateau Lava erupting from a fissure forms fluid lava flows called flood basalts that build up in layers to form a lava plateau. These dark-colored basalt flows are near Idaho Falls, Idaho.

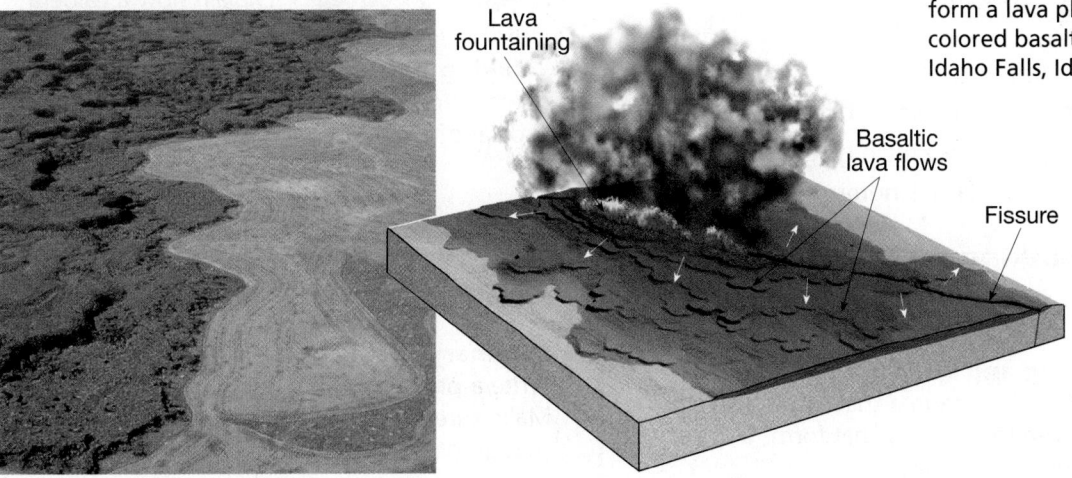

Lava fountaining

Basaltic lava flows

Fissure

Volcanic Hazards

Throughout history, people often have settled near volcanoes because rich volcanic soils are good for farming. They may not realize that an active or dormant volcano can erupt at any time, even centuries after the last eruption. 🔑 **Volcano hazards include lava flows, volcanic ash, pyroclastic flows, and mudflows.**

Lava flows are a major volcanic hazard. For example, the frequent lava flows from Mount Kilauea in Hawaii sometimes destroy homes and other structures in their path.

Active composite volcanoes, like those in the Cascade Range of the Pacific Northwest, are among the most dangerous volcanoes. A composite volcano can eject huge quantities of volcanic ash, burying widespread areas under thick ash deposits. Ash from the eruption of Mount Vesuvius completely buried the Roman city of Pompeii.

An explosive eruption can also release a *pyroclastic flow*, a scorching mixture of glowing volcanic particles and gases that sweeps rapidly down a volcano's flanks. In 1902, a pyroclastic flow from Mount Pelée on the the island of Martinique in the Caribbean killed 29,000 people.

Composite volcanoes may also produce mudflows called lahars. A **lahar** occurs when water-soaked volcanic ash and rock slide rapidly downhill. Ice and snow melted by an eruption or by heavy rains can trigger a lahar. In 1985, a lahar caused by the eruption of Nevada del Ruiz in Colombia killed 23,000 people.

Volcanoes usually give some warning that an eruption is near. For example, seismographs can detect the small earthquakes caused by movement of magma beneath the surface. Gases and ash released by a volcano may also signal an approaching eruption.

Section 10.2 Assessment

Reviewing Concepts

1. 🔑 What factors determine the type of volcanic eruption?
2. 🔑 List the materials ejected from volcanoes.
3. 🔑 Describe the three main types of volcanoes.
4. 🔑 List three volcanic landforms.

Critical Thinking

5. **Relating Cause and Effect** What propels magma out of a volcano during an eruption?
6. **Comparing and Contrasting** Compare and contrast the magma that forms a shield volcano with the magma that forms a composite cone.

7. **Applying Concepts** Explain how a caldera forms.
8. **Making Judgments** Should a resort hotel be built on the side of an active composite volcano? Explain.

Writing in Science

Summary Research a volcanic eruption. Write a paragraph describing the eruption. Make sure to classify the type of volcano that erupted.

10.3 Intrusive Igneous Activity

Reading Focus

Key Concepts

- What are the different types of plutons, and how are they classified?
- What is a batholith?

Vocabulary

- ◆ pluton
- ◆ sill
- ◆ laccolith
- ◆ dike
- ◆ batholith

Reading Strategy

Comparing and Contrasting After you read, compare the types of intrusive igneous features by completing the table.

Types of Intrusive Igneous Features	Description
Sill	a. _____?_____
Laccolith	b. _____?_____
Dike	c. _____?_____

Volcanic rock that formed from hardened lava covers large parts of Earth's surface. But you may be surprised to learn that most magma cools and hardens deep within Earth. This magma forms the roots of mountain ranges and a variety of landscape features.

Recall that magma rises through the crust toward the surface. As it rises, the magma may rise through fractures in the rock or force its way between rock layers. The magma may form thin sheets a few centimeters thick or collect in vast pools that can be many kilometers wide and several kilometers thick.

Classifying Plutons

The structures that result from the cooling and hardening of magma beneath Earth's surface are called **plutons.** The word *pluton* is derived from *Pluto*, the name of the Roman god of the underworld. Plutons form in continental crust wherever magma slowly crystallizes and forms intrusive igneous rock. Over millions of years, uplift and erosion can expose plutons at the surface.

There are several types of plutons. **Types of plutons include sills, laccoliths, and dikes. Geologists classify plutons and other bodies of intrusive igneous rock according to their size, shape, and relationship to surrounding rock layers.**

Figure 16 Dike This dike in the Grand Canyon in Arizona is an igneous intrusion that cuts across layers of sandstone.

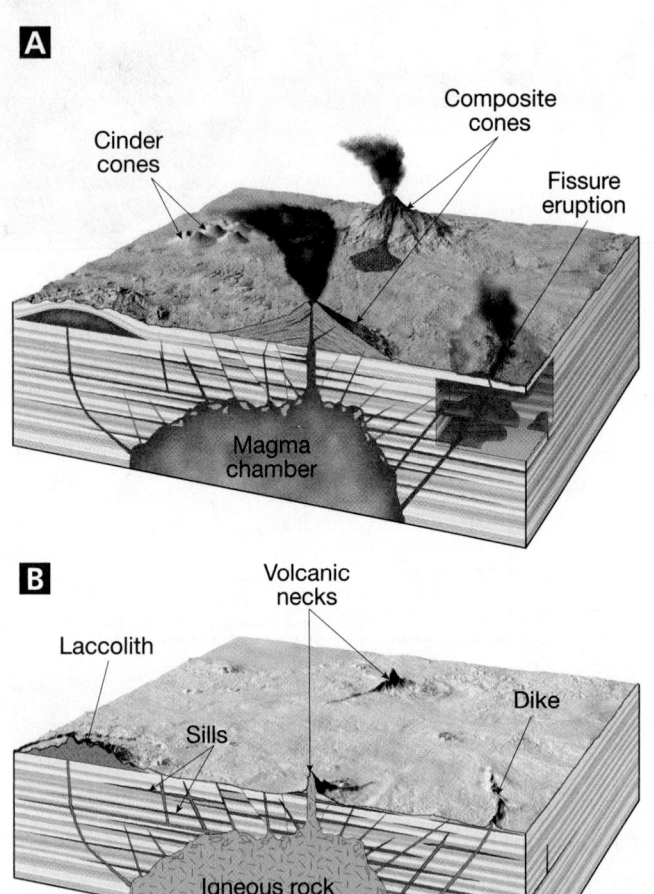

A

Cinder cones

Composite cones

Fissure eruption

Magma chamber

B

Volcanic necks

Laccolith

Sills

Dike

Igneous rock

Figure 17 Sills, Laccoliths, and Dikes
A Plutons form as magma intrudes into cracks in rock or between rock layers. **B** Erosion later exposes the plutons. A sill forms a horizontal band, laccoliths push overlying layers upward, and dikes cut across rock layers.
Inferring *How could you determine if a horizontal igneous rock layer was a lava flow or a sill?*

Sill

Sills and Laccoliths Sills and laccoliths are plutons that form when magma intrudes between rock layers close to the surface. Sills and laccoliths differ in shape and often differ in composition. A **sill** is a pluton that forms where magma flows between parallel layers of sedimentary rock. Horizontal sills, like the one shown in Figure 17, are the most common.

Sills form only at shallow depths, where the pressure exerted by the weight of overlying rock layers is low. Why is this? For a sill to form, the magma must lift the overlying rock to a height equal to the thickness of the sill. You might think that this would require a great deal of energy. But forcing the magma between rock layers often requires less energy than forcing the magma up to the surface.

A **laccolith** is a lens-shaped pluton that has pushed the overlying rock layers upward. Like sills, laccoliths form when magma intrudes between sedimentary rock layers close to the surface. But the magma that forms laccoliths has higher viscosity than the magma that forms sills. For this reason, the magma collects in a mass that bulges upward instead of spreading out in an even layer.

Dikes Some plutons form when magma from a large magma chamber moves into fractures in the surrounding rocks. A **dike** is a pluton that forms when magma moves into fractures that cut across rock layers. Dikes are sheetlike structures that can range in thickness from less than a centimeter to more than a kilometer. Most dikes, however, are a few meters thick and extend laterally for no more than a few kilometers.

Reading Checkpoint *What is a laccolith?*

Batholiths

Batholiths are the largest bodies of intrusive igneous rocks.  **A batholith is a body of intrusive igneous rock that has a surface exposure of more than 100 square kilometers.** Much larger than a pluton, a batholith can be hundreds of kilometers long and tens of kilometers across. Gravity studies and seismic evidence indicate that batholiths are also very thick, possibly extending dozens of kilometers into the crust. A body of igneous rock similar to a batholith, but having an area of less than 100 square kilometers, is called a stock.

How are batholiths formed? Batholiths form from many individual plutons that begin as blobs of magma deep beneath the surface. The plutons slowly rise through the crust. They clump together, forming a huge irregular mass. But this mass of magma never erupts to the surface. Instead, it cools slowly deep underground, forming granitic rock. Over millions of years, uplift and erosion gradually expose the batholith at the surface.

Batholiths form the core of many of Earth's great mountain ranges. For example, the Idaho batholith forms part of the northern Rocky Mountains. This batholith has an area of more than 40,000 square kilometers. The Sierra Nevada in California, shown in Figure 18, is also formed from a huge batholith. An even larger batholith makes up the coastal mountains of British Columbia in Canada.

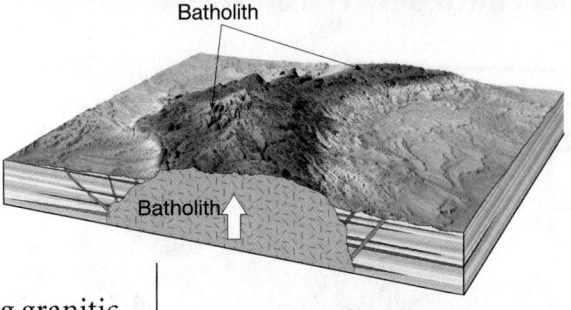

Figure 18 Batholiths Mount Whitney in California makes up just a tiny portion of the Sierra Nevada batholith, a huge structure that extends for approximately 400 kilometers.

Section 10.3 Assessment

Reviewing Concepts

1. List three different types of plutons.
2. How are plutons classified?
3. Write a definition of *batholith* in your own words.
4. Explain how a laccolith forms.

Critical Thinking

5. **Comparing and Contrasting** Describe the difference between a sill and a dike.

6. **Inferring** What can you infer about the origin of mountain ranges made of granitic rock, such as the Sierra Nevada? Explain.

Connecting Concepts

Igneous Rocks Recall what you learned about the texture of igneous rocks in Chapter 3. Predict how the texture of the rock in a batholith would compare with the texture of the rock in a sill. Explain.

How the Earth Works

Effects of Volcanoes

A **volcano** is an opening in the Earth's crust from which **lava,** or molten rock, escapes to the surface. The impact of powerful volcanic eruptions is both immediate and long-lasting. Hot rocks are flung out in all directions. Huge clouds of scorching ash and fiery gases billow high into the sky. As a result, the landscape and even the weather can be changed. Soil may become more fertile when enriched with nutrients from volcanic ash. Islands, mountains, and other landforms may be created from the material emitted by volcanoes.

The Giant's Causeway in Northern Ireland

DRAMATIC ROCK FORMATIONS
Lava flows can form amazing rock formations. **Columnar rocks** are volcanic rocks that split into columns as the lava cools. The Devil's Tower in Wyoming (below) is one example of a columnar rock. Another example is the Giant's Causeway (left). This rock formation in Northern Ireland is the result of a lava flow that erupted millions of years ago.

The Devil's Tower in Wyoming

DUST AND GAS
Composite cones, like Mount St. Helens in Washington (right), spit clouds of ash and fumes into the sky. The debris can completely cover human communities. Another hazard is that volcanic gases may be deadly poisons.

ERUPTING LAVA
Red-hot lava is hurled into the air during an eruption of a volcano on Stromboli, an island off the coast of southern Italy. The Stromboli volcano is one of only a few volcanoes to display continuous eruptive activity over a period of more than a few years.

AFFECTING THE WORLD'S WEATHER

Powerful eruptions emit gas and dust that can rise high into the atmosphere and travel around the world. Volcanic material can reduce average temperatures in parts of the world by filtering out some of the sunlight that warms the Earth.

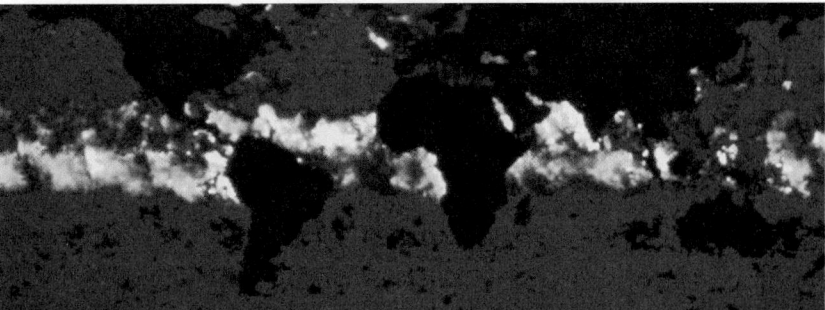

A satellite image shows the global spread of emissions from the 1991 eruptions of Mount Pinatubo in the Philippines.

A STRING OF ISLANDS

The Hawaiian Islands are the tops of volcanic mountains. They have developed over millions of years above a hot spot in Earth's mantle and have erupted great amounts of lava. As the Pacific Plate moves over the stationary plume, it carries older islands in the chain to the northwest. Today, active volcanoes are found on the island of Hawaii and the newly forming island of Loihi.

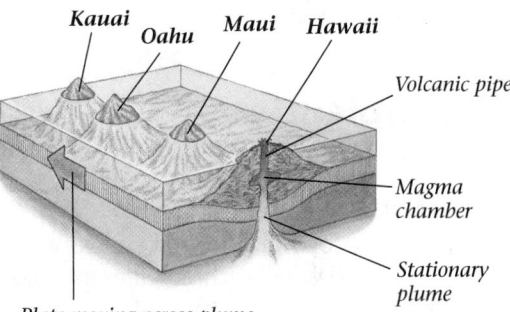

Kauai Oahu Maui Hawaii

Volcanic pipe

Magma chamber

Stationary plume

Plate moving across plume

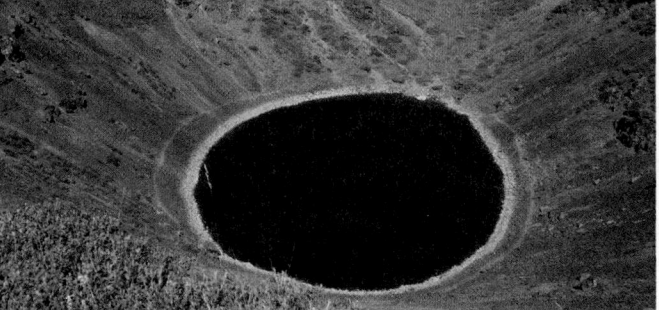

A crater lake in Iceland

A CRATER LAKE

A **crater lake** is a body of water that occupies a bowl-shaped depression around the opening of an extinct or dormant volcano. An eruption can hurl the water out of the crater. The water can then mix with hot rock and debris and race downhill in a deadly mudslide.

LIFE RETURNS TO THE LAVA

In time, plant life grows on lava. Lichen and moss often appear first. Grass and larger plants slowly follow. The upper surface of the rock is gradually weathered, and the roots of plants help break down the rock to form soil. After many generations, the land may become lush and fertile again.

A few lichens find a home on the lava.

ASSESSMENT

1. **Key Terms** Define **(a)** volcano, **(b)** lava, **(c)** columnar rock, **(d)** plume, **(e)** crater lake.

2. **Natural Resources** How can soil become more fertile as a result of volcanic eruptions?

3. **Environmental Change (a)** How can volcanic activity create new landforms? **(b)** How can explosive volcanic eruptions affect the atmosphere and weather around the world?

4. **Natural Hazards** What are some of the ways in which a volcanic eruption can devastate nearby human settlements?

5. **Critical Thinking Sequencing** Study the diagram of the Hawaiian Islands and the caption that accompanies it. **(a)** Which island on the diagram is probably the oldest? Why do you think so? **(b)** What will happen to the volcanoes on the island of Hawaii as a result of plate movement?

Plants take root in the beginnings of topsoil.

Melting Temperatures of Rocks

Measurements of temperatures in wells and mines have shown that Earth's internal temperatures increase with depth. Recall that this rate of temperature increase is called the geothermal gradient. Although the geothermal gradient varies from place to place, it is possible to calculate an average. In this lab, you will investigate Earth's internal temperatures and the temperatures at which rocks melt. You will also investigate the effect of water on the melting temperatures of rock.

Problem How can rocks melt to form magma in the crust and uppermost mantle?

Materials
- photocopy of Temperature Curves graph
- colored pencils (three different colors)
- ruler

Skills Analyzing Data, Graphing, Calculating

Procedure

1. Obtain a photocopy of the Temperature Curves graph on page 301. You will use it to plot the average temperature gradient for Earth's interior. Plot the temperature gradient on graph paper labeled like the graph shown.

2. Plot the temperature values from Table 1 on your graph. Then draw a single best-fit line through the points with a colored pencil. Extend your line from the surface to 200 kilometers. Label the line "Temperature Gradient."

3. The melting temperature of a rock changes as pressure increases deeper within Earth. The approximate melting points of the igneous rocks, granite and basalt, under various pressures (depths) have been determined in the laboratory and are shown in Table 2. Granite and basalt were used because they are common materials in the upper layer of Earth. Plot the melting temperatures from Table 2 on the same graph you made above. Use a different colored pencil to plot each set of points and draw the best-fit lines.

4. Label the two lines "Melting Curve for Wet Granite" and "Melting Curve for Basalt."

Table 1 Idealized Internal Temperatures of Earth

Depth (kilometers)	Temperature (°C)
0	20
25	600
50	1000
75	1250
100	1400
150	1700
200	1800

Table 2 Melting Temperatures of Granite (with water) and Basalt at Various Depths Within Earth

Granite (with water)		Basalt	
Depth (km)	Melting Temperature (°C)	Depth (km)	Melting Temperature (°C)
0	950	0	1100
5	700	25	1160
10	660	50	1250
20	625	100	1400
40	600	150	1600

Analyze and Conclude

1. **Using Graphs** Does the rate of increase of Earth's internal temperature stay the same or change with increasing depth?

2. **Using Graphs** Is the rate of temperature increase greater from the surface to 100 kilometers or below 100 kilometers?

3. **Interpreting Data** What is the temperature at 100 kilometers below the surface?

4. **Calculating** Use the data and your graph to calculate the average temperature gradient for the upper 100 kilometers of Earth in °C/100 kilometers and in °C/kilometer.

5. **Drawing Conclusions** Based on your data, at approximately what depth within Earth would wet granite reach its melting temperature and begin to form magma? Explain.

6. **Drawing Conclusions** Based on your data, at what depth will basalt have reached its melting temperature and begin to form magma?

Go Further What is the name of the layer within Earth's upper mantle that is below about 100 kilometers? Why do scientists theorize that this zone is capable of "flowing" more easily than other mantle rock, allowing the lithosphere to move across it?

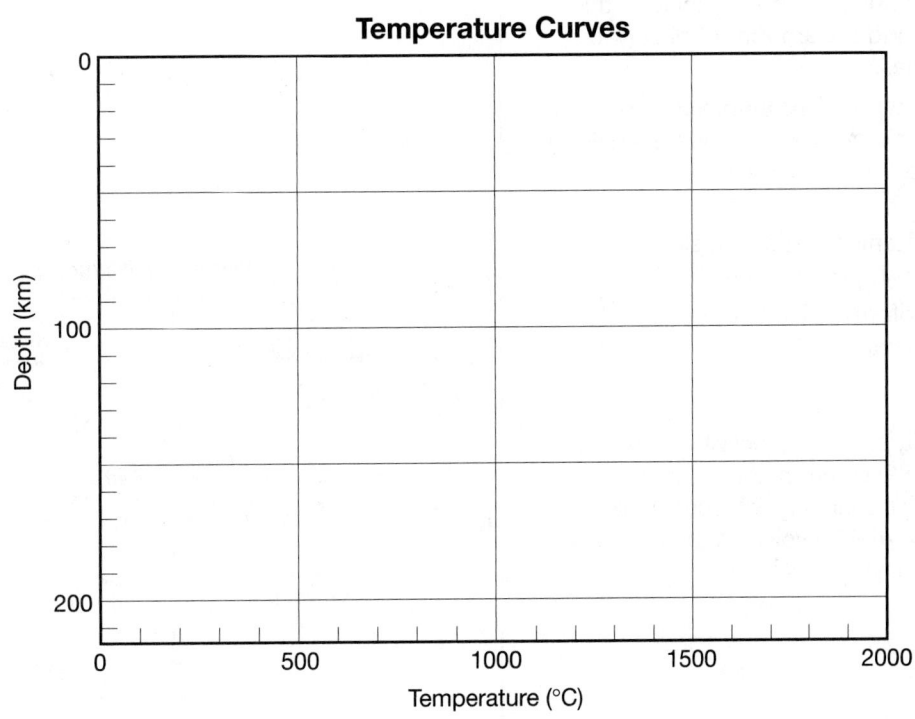

Temperature Curves

Study Guide

10.1 The Nature of Volcanic Eruptions

Key Concepts

- Magma forms in the crust and upper mantle when solid rock partially melts. The formation of magma depends on several factors, including heat, pressure, and water content.

- Most volcanoes form along convergent and divergent plate boundaries. Some volcanoes form far from plate boundaries above "hot spots" in the crust.

Vocabulary

decompression melting, *p. 281*; Ring of Fire, *p. 284*; intraplate volcanism, *p. 285*; hot spot, *p. 285*

10.2 Intrusive Igneous Activity

Key Concepts

- The primary factors that determine whether a volcano erupts explosively or quietly include the magma's viscosity and the amount of dissolved gases in the magma.

- Depending on the type of eruption, volcanoes may produce lava flows or eject pyroclastic materials, or both. All volcanic eruptions also emit large amounts of gases.

- The three main volcanic types are shield volcanoes, cinder cones, and composite cones.

- Other volcanic landforms include calderas, volcanic necks, and lava plateaus.

Vocabulary

viscosity, *p. 287*; vent, *p. 287*; pyroclastic material, *p. 289*; volcano, *p. 289*; crater, *p. 289*; shield volcano, *p. 290*; cinder cone, *p. 290*; composite cone, *p. 291*; caldera, *p. 292*; volcanic neck, *p. 293*; lava plateau, *p. 293*; lahar, *p. 294*

10.3 Plate Tectonics and Igneous Activity

Key Concepts

- Types of plutons include sills, laccoliths, and dikes. Geologists classify plutons and other bodies of intrusive igneous rock according to their size, shape, and relationship to surrounding rock layers.

- A batholith is a body of intrusive igneous rock that has a surface exposure of more than 100 square kilometers.

Vocabulary

pluton, *p. 295*; sill, *p. 296*; laccolith, *p. 296*; dike, *p. 296*; batholith, *p. 297*

Thinking Visually

Web Diagram Copy the web diagram below and use information from the chapter to complete it.

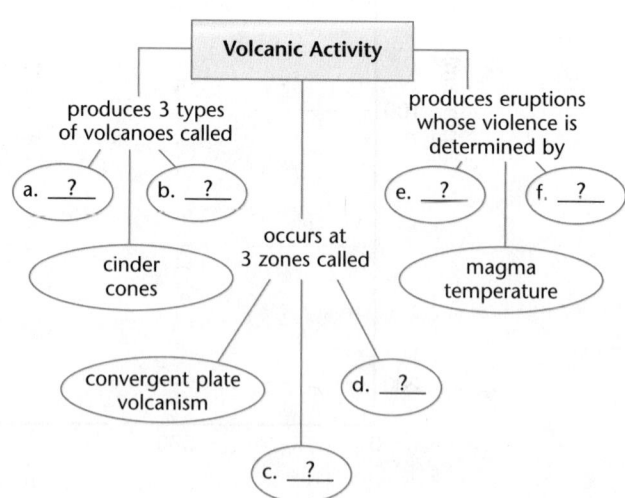

Assessment

Reviewing Content

Choose the letter that best answers the question or completes the statement.

1. Underground igneous rock bodies are called
   a. lava flows.
   b. plutons.
   c. volcanoes.
   d. calderas.

2. The greatest volume of volcanic material is produced by
   a. eruptions of cinder cones.
   b. eruptions of composite cones.
   c. eruptions along ocean ridges.
   d. eruptions of shield volcanoes.

3. The most explosive type of volcanic activity is associated with
   a. cinder cones.
   b. sills.
   c. composite cones.
   d. shield volcanoes.

4. A magma's viscosity is directly related to its
   a. depth.
   b. age.
   c. color.
   d. silica content.

5. What are the pulverized rock, lava, ash, and other fragments ejected from the vent of a volcano called?
   a. sills
   b. craters
   c. pahoehoes
   d. pyroclastic material

6. Which type of volcano consists of layers of lava flows and pyroclastic material?
   a. composite cone
   b. cinder cone
   c. shield volcano
   d. laccolith

7. The hotter of two types of basaltic lava commonly forms
   a. aa flows.
   b. pahoehoe flows.
   c. pyroclastic flows.
   d. lapilli flows.

8. What is the very large depression at the top of some volcanoes called?
   a. a vent
   b. a lava plateau
   c. a volcanic neck
   d. a caldera

9. When silica-rich magma is extruded, ash, hot gases, and larger fragments propelled from the vent at high speeds may produce which of the following?
   a. a lava plateau
   b. a lahar
   c. a pahoehoe flow
   d. a pyroclastic flow

10. What feature may form in an intraplate area over a rising plume of hot mantle material?
    a. a hot spot
    b. a dike
    c. a subduction zone
    d. an ocean ridge

Understanding Concepts

11. What is a volcanic neck, and how does it form?

12. Describe the Ring of Fire.

13. The Hawaiian Islands and Yellowstone National Park are associated with which of the three types of volcanism?

14. What is the chain of volcanoes called that forms at a convergent boundary between a subducting oceanic plate and a continental plate? What type of volcano commonly forms?

15. Explain how scientists think most magma is formed.

Use the diagram below to answer Questions 16 and 17.

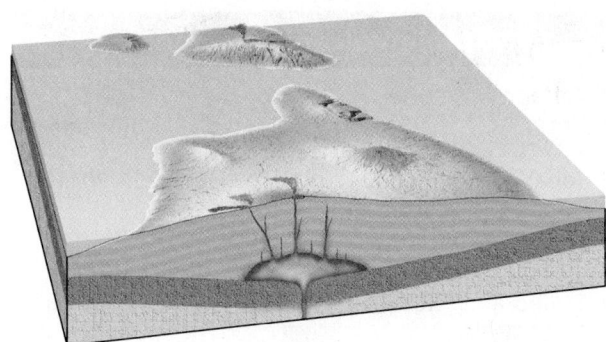

16. Identify the type of volcano shown in the diagram.

17. What types of eruptions are commonly associated with this type of volcano?

18. How do hot spots form?

19. How are pyroclastic materials classified?

20. What is viscosity, and how does it affect volcanic eruptions?

21. Give an example of each of the three types of volcanoes.

22. How do dikes form?

Critical Thinking

23. Applying Concepts How might a laccolith be detected at Earth's surface before being exposed by erosion?

24. Inferring Why is a volcano fed by a highly viscous magma likely to be a greater threat to people than a volcano fed by very fluid magma?

25. Comparing and Contrasting Compare pahoehoe lava flows and aa lava flows.

26. Relating Cause and Effect What is a lahar? Explain why a lahar can occur on a volcano without an eruption.

27. Drawing Conclusions Why are cinder cones usually small?

Analyzing Data

Use the data table below to answer Questions 28–31.

Notable Volcanic Eruptions

Volcano	Date	Volume Ejected	Height of Plume
Toba	74,000 years ago	2800 km³	50–80 km
Vesuvius	A.D. 79	4 km³	32 km
Tambora	1815	150 km³	44 km
Krakatau	1883	21 km³	36 km
Mount St. Helens	1980	1 km³	19 km
Mount Pinatubo	1991	5 km³	35 km

28. Interpreting Data Which volcanic eruption listed in the data table ejected the greatest volume of pyroclastic material?

29. Calculating How many times larger than the volume of material ejected in 1883 by the eruption of Krakatau was the volume of material ejected by the eruption of Tambora in 1815?

30. Forming Hypotheses Develop a hypothesis to explain why the eruption of Mount Vesuvius in A.D. 79 was more deadly than the eruption of Mount Pinatubo in 1991, even though the eruptions were approximately the same size.

31. Calculating Calculate how much higher the plume of volcanic debris during the eruption of Tambora in 1815 was than the plume from the 1980 eruption of Mount St. Helens. Calculate the difference in kilometers and as a percent.

Concepts in Action

32. Hypothesizing Large volcanic eruptions eject large amounts of gas, dust, and ash into the atmosphere. This volcanic material can affect the world's climate by blocking incoming solar radiation. An eruption from what type of volcano is most likely to cause global climate changes? Explain your answer.

33. Classifying On the side of a composite cone you see a large area where there are no trees, and the ground surface looks disturbed. What possible volcanic feature or event could have caused this?

34. Applying Concepts Would you be safer from a violent, explosive eruption while vacationing in Arizona near a cinder cone or while skiing in the Andes Mountains of South America? Explain.

35. Writing in Science Write a paragraph describing what an eruption of a nearby composite cone might be like.

Performance-Based Assessment

Making a Poster Make a poster illustrating the internal and external features that are typical of a composite cone. Include on your poster copies of photographs of some classic composite cones. Also explain some of the possible dangers associated with living near a composite cone.

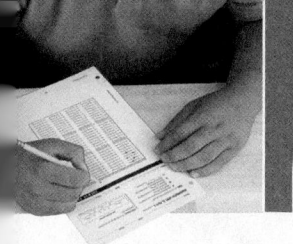

Standardized Test Prep

Choose the letter that best answers the question or completes the statement.

1. Which of the following is NOT a factor that determines if a volcano erupts explosively or quietly?
  (A) temperature of the magma
  (B) size of the volcanic cone
  (C) the magma's composition
  (D) amount of dissolved gases in the magma

2. How does an increase in pressure affect a rock's melting temperature?
  (A) The melting temperature increases.
  (B) The melting temperature decreases.
  (C) The melting temperature is stabilized.
  (D) It has no effect on the melting temperature.

Use the diagram below to answer Questions 3 and 4.

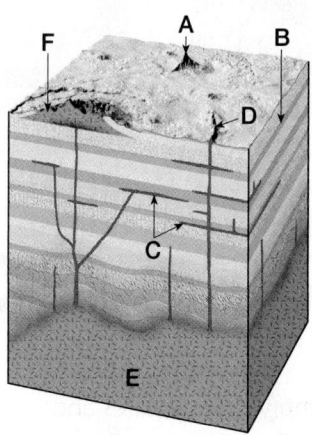

3. What intrusive igneous feature in the diagram is labeled C?
  (A) a dike
  (B) a sill
  (C) a batholith
  (D) a laccolith

4. If the feature labeled E extended for over 100 square kilometers after being exposed by erosion, what would it be classified as?
  (A) a dike
  (B) a stock
  (C) a laccolith
  (D) a batholith

Answer the following questions in complete sentences.

5. Briefly describe the relative sizes and shapes of the three types of volcanoes.

6. Explain how a volcanic eruption is affected by magma composition, magma temperature, and the amount of dissolved gases in the magma.

7. Most volcanic eruptions occur at tectonic plate boundaries, but some occur within a tectonic plate, far from plate boundaries.

   Part A Explain the tectonic setting of volcanoes that occur at plate boundaries.

   Part B Explain how volcanoes form in areas that are not associated with a plate boundary. Give an example.

CHAPTER 11 Mountain Building

How were the Rocky Mountains formed?

Research the formation of the Rocky Mountains. Identify the key dates and processes in the development of the range. Prepare an explanation, in your own words and with diagrams, of how the Rocky Mountains were formed. Assume that your readers know as much about geology as you do, and be sure to include relevant technical terms. Create a report or Web page to share your findings.

Exploration Lab
Investigating Anticlines and Synclines

People and the Environment
The San Andreas Fault System

Problem Solving
Rates of Mountain Building

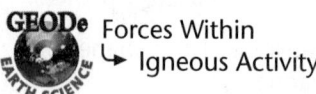 **GEODe** Forces Within
↳ Igneous Activity

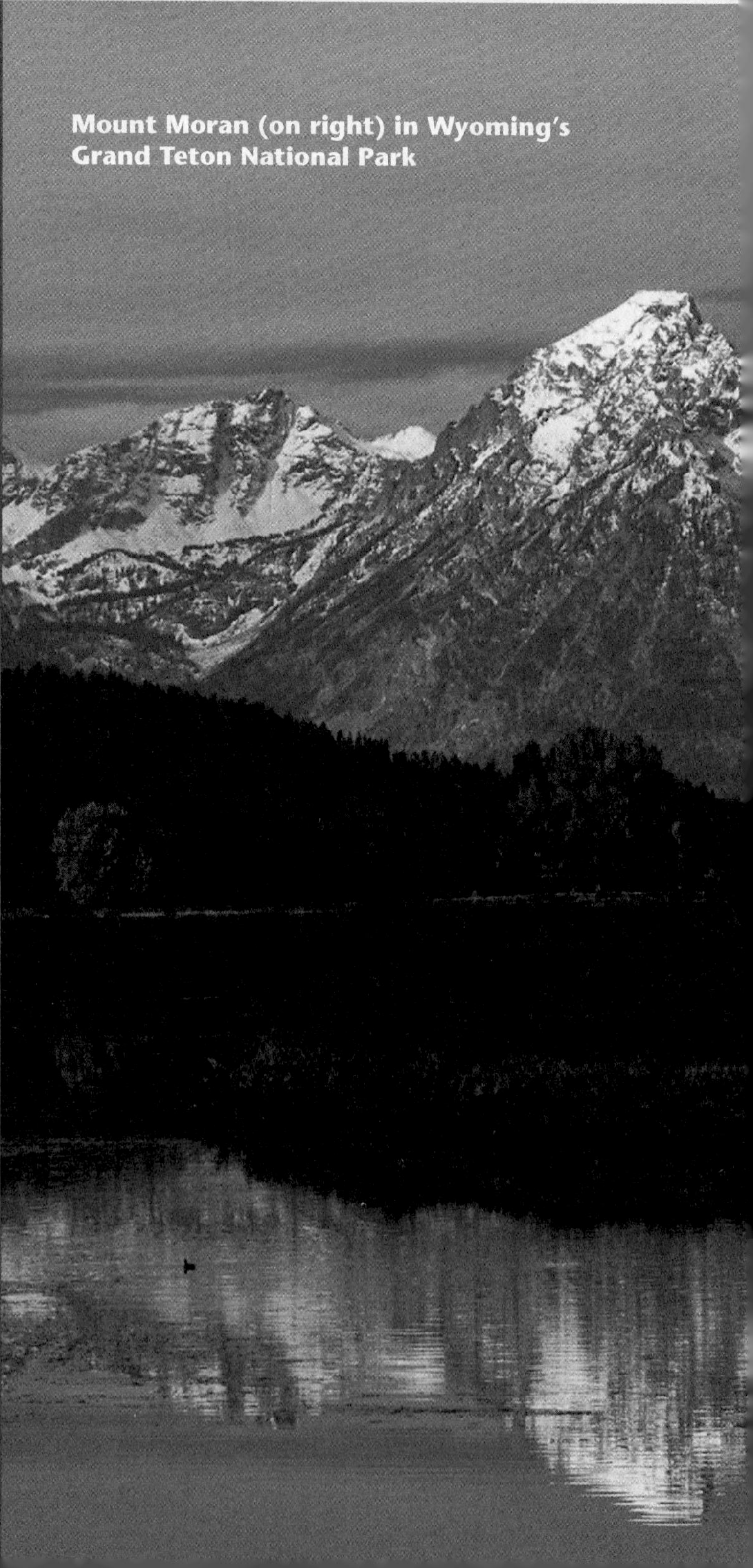

Mount Moran (on right) in Wyoming's Grand Teton National Park

Chapter Preview

Inquiry > Activity

Can You Model How Rocks Deform?

Procedure

1. Take a large, thick rubber band and stretch it out a few centimeters. Then let it relax. **CAUTION:** *Be sure to hold on to both ends of the rubber band so it does not snap your fingers. Record your observations.*

2. Take a chunk of plastic putty. Pull on the ends of the piece of putty rapidly. Record your observations.

3. Now take the chunk of plastic putty, and work it gently until it is warm and flexible. Slowly stretch it. Record your observations.

4. Take a straight, thin wooden stick about 25 centimeters long, and gently bend the ends of the stick until it breaks. **CAUTION:** *Be sure to wear safety goggles when bending the stick. Record your observations.*

Think About It

1. **Observing** Describe how the rubber band, plastic putty, and wooden stick behaved when you deformed them.

2. **Observing** Which item or items returned to the original shape and size after the force was removed?

3. **Drawing Conclusions** Which item was the easiest to deform? The hardest to deform?

4. **Inferring** Under what conditions do you think rocks are easier to bend? Under what conditions to you think rocks will break?

11.1 Forces in Earth's Crust

Reading Focus

Key Concepts

- What factors affect the deformation of a rock?
- What are the types of stresses that affect rocks?
- How does isostasy affect Earth's crust?

Vocabulary

- ◆ deformation
- ◆ stress
- ◆ strain
- ◆ isostasy
- ◆ isostatic adjustment

Reading Strategy

Previewing Copy the table below. Before you read, rewrite the green topic headings as how, why, or what questions. As you read, write an answer to each question.

Forces in Earth's Crust	
What causes deformation of rock?	a. _____?

Earth has only 14 mountains higher than 8,000 meters. Four of these peaks are in Pakistan's Karakoram Range, shown in Figure 1. What causes such huge mountains to form? Over millions of years, mountains form where plate motion and other forces uplift the crust. At the same time, weathering and erosion shape the crust into spectacular mountain peaks. The process begins when plate motions produce forces in rock that cause it to bend or break.

Deformation of Rock

Every body of rock, no matter how strong, has a point at which it will bend or break. **Deformation** is any change in the original shape and/or size of a rock body. In Earth's crust, most deformation occurs along plate margins. Plate motions and interactions at plate boundaries produce forces that can deform rock.

Deformation occurs because of stress in a body of rock. **Stress** is the force per unit area acting on a solid. When rocks are under stresses greater than their own strength, they begin to deform, usually by folding, flowing, or fracturing. The change in shape or volume of a body of rock as a result of stress is called **strain.** How can rock masses be bent into folds without being broken? When stress is gradually applied, rocks first respond by deforming elastically. A change that results from elastic deformation can be reversed. Like a rubber band, the rock will return to almost its original size and shape once the force is removed. Once the elastic limit or strength of a rock is surpassed, it either flows or fractures. The factors that affect the deformation of rock include temperature, pressure, rock type, and time.

Figure 1 Mountain Ranges
This peak is in the Karakoram Range in Pakistan, part of the Himalayas.

Temperature and Pressure Rocks deform permanently in two ways: brittle deformation and ductile deformation. Rocks near the surface, where temperatures and pressures are low, usually behave like brittle solids and fracture once their strength is exceeded. This type of deformation is called brittle failure or brittle deformation. You know that glass objects, wooden pencils, china plates, and even our bones show brittle failure once their strength is exceeded.

At depth, where temperatures and pressures are high, rocks become ductile. Ductile deformation is a type of solid-state flow that produces a change in the size and shape of an object without fracturing the object. Ductile materials include modeling clay, bee's wax, caramel candy, and most metals. For example, a copper penny placed on a railroad track will be flattened and deformed without breaking by the force applied by a passing train. Ductile deformation of a rock is somewhat similar to the deformation of a flattened penny.

Rock Type The mineral composition and texture of a rock also greatly affect how it will deform. Rocks like granite and basalt that are composed of minerals with strong internal molecular bonds usually fail by brittle fracture. Sedimentary rocks that are weakly cemented or metamorphic rocks that contain zones of weakness—such as foliation—are more likely to deform by ductile flow. Rocks that are weak and most likely become ductile when under stress include rock salt, gypsum, and shale. Limestone, schist, and marble are of intermediate strength and may also become ductile.

Time Small stresses applied over long time spans eventually cause the deformation of rock. You can see the effects of time on deformation in everyday settings. For example, marble benches have been known to sag under their own weight over a span of a hundred years or so. Forces that are unable to deform rock when first applied may cause rock to flow if the force is maintained over a long period of time.

 **Reading Checkpoint** *What is brittle deformation?*

Types of Stress

Plate motions cause different types of stress in the rocks of the lithosphere. **The three types of stress that cause deformation of rocks are tensional stress, compressional stress, and shear stress.** Look at Figure 2. When rocks are squeezed or shortened the stress is compressional. Tensional stress is caused by rocks being pulled in opposite directions. Shear stress causes a body of rock to be distorted.

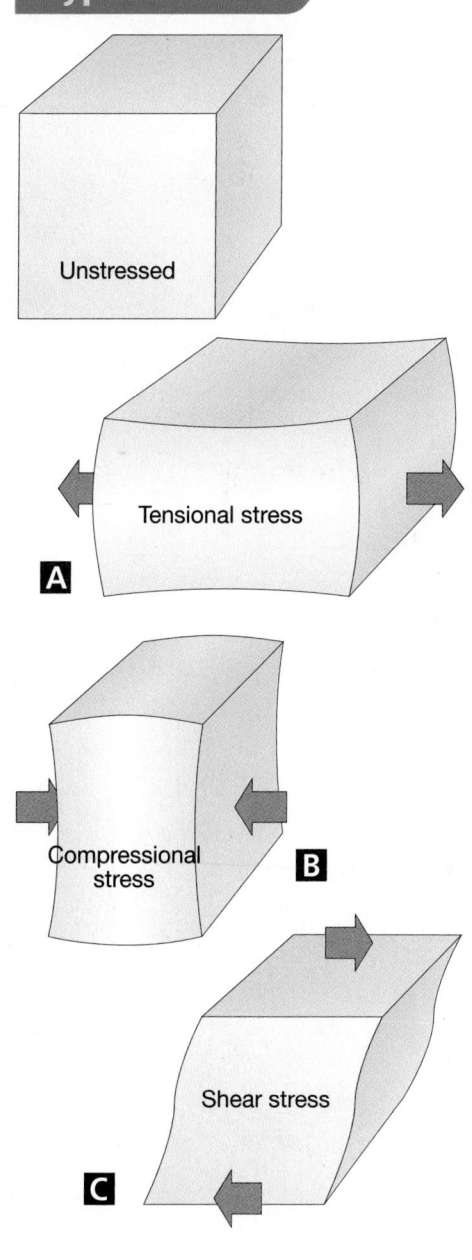

Figure 2 Undeformed material is changed as it undergoes different types of stress. The arrows show the direction of maximum stress. **A** Tensional stress causes a material to be stretched or to undergo extension. **B** Compressional stress causes a material to shorten. **C** Shear stress causes a material to be distorted with no change in volume.

Types of Stress

Unstressed

Tensional stress

A

Compressional stress

B

Shear stress

C

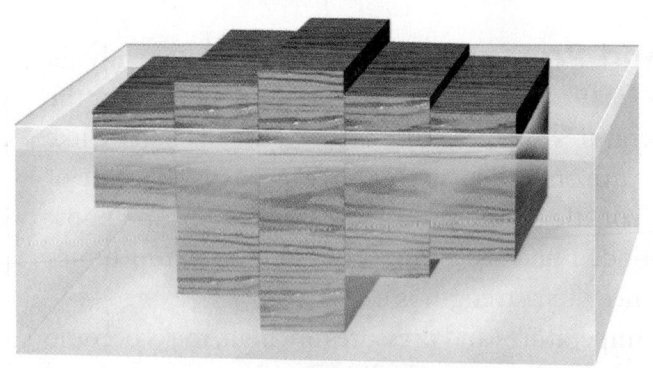

Figure 3 Isostatic Adjustment
This drawing illustrates how wooden blocks of different thicknesses float in water. In a similar manner, thick sections of crustal material float higher than thinner crustal slabs. **Inferring** *Would a denser wooden block float at a higher or lower level?*

Principle of Isostasy

In addition to the horizontal movements of lithospheric plates, there are also gradual up-and-down motions of the crust. Much of this vertical movement occurs along plate margins and is linked to mountain building. But, the up-and-down motions also occur in the interiors of continents far from plate boundaries.

What Is Isostasy? Earth's crust floats on top of the denser and more flexible rocks of the mantle. The concept of a floating crust in gravitational balance is called **isostasy** (*iso* = equal and *stasis* = standing). One way to understand the concept of isostasy is to think about a series of wooden blocks of different heights floating in water, as shown in Figure 3. Note that the thicker wooden blocks float higher than the thinner blocks. In a similar way, many mountain belts stand high above the surface because they have less dense "roots" that extend deep into the denser mantle. The denser mantle supports the mountains from below.

What would happen if another small block of wood were placed on top of one of the blocks in Figure 3? The combined block would sink until a new gravitational balance was reached. However, the top of the combined block would actually be higher than before, and the bottom would be lower. This process of establishing a new level of gravitational balance is called **isostatic adjustment.**

 *What is isostatic adjustment?*

Isostatic Adjustment for Mountains Applying the concept of isostasy, we should expect that when weight is added to the crust, the crust responds by subsiding. Also when weight is removed, the crust will rebound. Evidence of crustal subsidence followed by crustal rebound is provided by the continental ice sheets that covered parts of North America during the ice age. The added weight of a 3-kilometer-thick mass of ice depressed Earth's crust by hundreds of meters. In the 8000 years since the last ice sheet melted, uplift of as much as 330 meters has occurred in Canada's Hudson Bay region, where the ice was thickest.

Isostatic Adjustment in Mountains

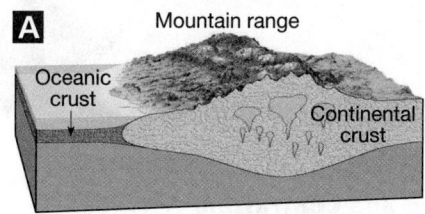

A When mountains are young, the continental crust is thickest.

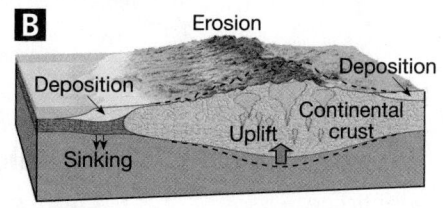

B As erosion lowers the mountains, the crust rises in response to the reduced load.

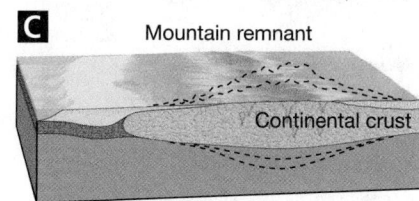

C Erosion and uplift continue until the mountains reach "normal" crustal thickness.

Isostatic adjustment can account for considerable vertical movement. Most mountain building causes the crust to shorten and thicken. **Because of isostasy, deformed and thickened crust will undergo regional uplift both during mountain building and for a long period afterward.** As the crust rises, the processes of erosion increase, and the deformed rock layers are carved into a mountainous landscape.

As erosion lowers the summits of mountains, the crust will rise in response to the reduced load, as shown in Figure 4. The processes of uplifting and erosion will continue until the mountain block reaches "normal" crustal thickness. When this occurs, the mountains will be eroded to near sea level, and the once deeply buried interior of the mountain will be exposed at the surface. This process allows igneous batholiths, which form within the cores of mountains, to be exposed at the surface.

Figure 4 This sequence illustrates how the combined effect of erosion and isostatic adjustment results in a thinning of the crust in mountainous regions.

Section 11.1 Assessment

Reviewing Concepts

1. List four factors that affect how a rock deforms.
2. Describe the different types of stress.
3. Explain the role of isostasy in vertical movements of the crust.

Critical Thinking

4. **Applying Concepts** What is the difference between brittle deformation and ductile deformation? Use examples of brittle and ductile materials in your answer.
5. **Predicting** Would rock in the lower mantle undergo brittle deformation or ductile deformation? Explain.

6. **Relating Cause and Effect** Geologists find an area in which the crust has been stretched and thinned. Which type of stress produced this effect? Explain.
7. **Interpreting Illustrations** In figure 4B above, what process leads to uplift due to isostatic adjustment? Explain.

Connecting Concepts

Compressional Stress Review the types of plate boundaries in Chapter 9. At which type of boundary would compressional stress be the dominant force?

11.2 Folds, Faults, and Mountains

Reading Focus

Key Concepts
- What are the different types of folds?
- What are the major types of faults?
- What are the major types of mountains?
- How are landforms such as domes, basins, and plateaus formed?

Vocabulary
- anticline
- syncline
- monocline
- normal fault
- reverse fault
- thrust fault
- orogenesis
- folded mountain
- graben
- horst
- fault-block mountain

Reading Strategy
Comparing and Contrasting After you read the section, compare types of faults by completing the table below.

Type of Fault	Description
Normal Fault	a. ____?____
b. ____?____	c. ____?____
d. ____?____	e. ____?____
f. ____?____	g. ____?____

How can rock bend like a piece of ribbon or a soft, cooked noodle? Over millions of years, stress forces can cause rock to fold. You can clearly see the results in Mount Kidd in the Canadian Rockies, shown in Figure 1. Before Mount Kidd formed, the rocks that make up the mountain were flat, sedimentary layers on the bottom of a shallow sea. Stress slowly folded the layers into dramatic zigzags of solid rock.

Folds

During mountain building, compressional stresses often bend flat-lying sedimentary and volcanic rocks into wavelike ripples called folds. Folds in sedimentary strata are much like those that would form if you were to hold the ends of a sheet of paper and then push them together. Folds in rock come in a wide variety of sizes and shapes. The three main types of folds are anticlines, synclines, and monoclines.

Anticlines and Synclines The two most common types of folds are anticlines and synclines. An **anticline** is usually formed by the upfolding, or arching, of rock layers, as shown in Figure 6. Often found in association with anticlines are downfolds, or troughs, called **synclines.** Notice in Figure 6 that the limb, or side, of an anticline is also a limb of the adjacent syncline.

Figure 5 Folded Mountains Folded sedimentary layers are exposed in the northern Rocky Mountains on the face of Mount Kidd, Alberta, Canada.

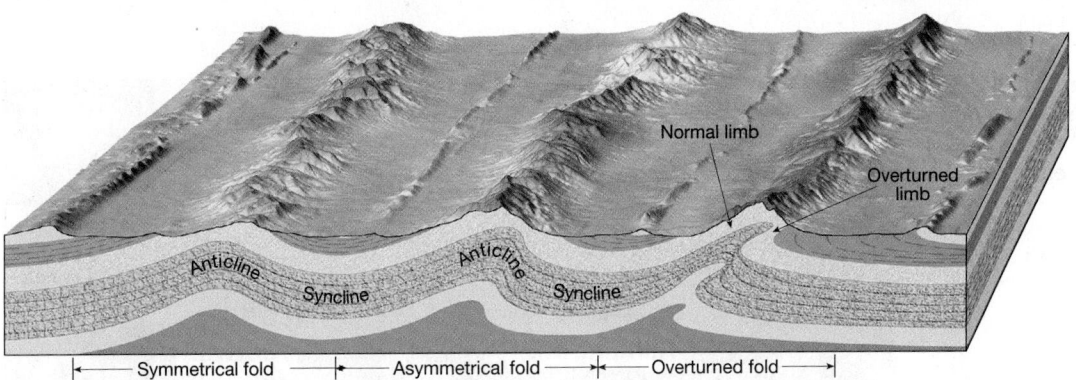

The angle that a fold or fault makes with the horizontal is called the *dip* of the fold or fault. (Flat rock layers would have a dip of 0°. A vertical fold or fault would have a dip of 90°.) In the symmetrical fold shown in Figure 6, both limbs of the anticline have the same, low-angle dip. In the asymmetrical fold, one limb has a much steeper dip than the other. In the overturned fold, one limb has been tilted beyond the vertical.

Monoclines   Folds are generally closely associated with faults. Examples of this close association are broad, regional features called monoclines. **Monoclines** are large, step-like folds in otherwise horizontal sedimentary strata. Monoclines seem to occur as sedimentary layers have been folded over a large faulted block of underlying rock. Monoclines are prominent features of the Colorado Plateau in Colorado, New Mexico, Utah, and Arizona, as shown in Figure 7.

Figure 6 Anticlines and Synclines The upfolded or arched structures are anticlines. The downfolds or troughs are synclines. Notice that the limb of an anticline is also the limb of the adjacent syncline.

Reading Checkpoint   *What is a syncline?*

Figure 7 Monocline A Monocline located near Mexican Hat, Utah. **B** This monocline consists of bent sedimentary beds that were deformed by faulting in the bedrock below.

Hanging wall   Footwall

Faults

Recall that faults are fractures in the crust along which movement has taken place. Small faults can be recognized in road cuts where sedimentary beds have been offset a few meters, as shown in Figure 8.

The rock surface that is immediately above the fault is called the hanging wall, and the rock surface below the fault is called the footwall. ◯**The major types of faults are normal faults, reverse faults, thrust faults, and strike-slip faults.**

Normal faults occur due to tensional stress, and reverse and thrust faults result from compressional stress. Compressional forces generally produce folds as well as faults. These compressional forces result in a thickening and shortening of the rocks. Shearing stresses produce strike-slip faults. Faults are classified according to the type of movement that occurs along the fault.

Normal Faults A **normal fault** occurs when the hanging wall block moves down relative to the footwall block. Most normal faults have steep dips of about 60°, as shown in Figure 9A on the next page. These dips often flatten out with depth. The movement in normal faults is mainly in a vertical direction, with some horizontal movement. Because of the downward motion of the hanging wall block, normal faults result in the lengthening, or extension, of the crust.

Reverse Faults and Thrust Faults A **reverse fault** is a fault in which the hanging wall block moves up relative to the footwall block. Reverse faults are high-angle faults with dips greater than 45°. **Thrust faults** are reverse faults with dips of less than 45°. Because the hanging wall block moves up and over the footwall block, reverse and thrust faults result in a shortening of the crust, as shown in Figure 9B and 9C.

Four Types of Faults

Footwall Hanging wall

A Normal fault (tensional)

Hanging wall Footwall

B Reverse fault (compressional)

Hanging wall Footwall

C Thrust fault (compressional)

D Strike-slip fault (shear)

Most high-angle reverse faults are small. They cause only local displacements in regions dominated by other types of faulting. Thrust faults, on the other hand, exist at all scales. In the Alps, northern Rockies, Himalayas, and Appalachians, thrust faults have displaced rock layers as far as 50 kilometers. The result of this large-scale movement is that older rocks end up on top of younger rocks.

Strike-Slip Faults   Faults in which the movement is horizontal and parallel to the trend, or strike, of the fault surface are called **strike-slip faults,** as shown in Figure 9D. Because of their large size and linear nature, many strike-slip faults produce a trace that is visible over a great distance. Rather than a single fracture, large strike-slip faults usually consist of a zone of roughly parallel fractures. The zone may be up to several kilometers wide. The most recent movement, however, is often along a section only a few meters wide, which may offset features such as stream channels. Crushed and broken rocks produced during faulting are more easily eroded, often producing linear valleys or troughs that mark strike-slip faults. The San Andreas fault in California and the Great Glen fault in Scotland are well-known strike-slip faults.

 **Reading Checkpoint** *What are the major types of faults?*

Figure 9 A Normal fault **B** Reverse fault **C** Thrust fault **D** Strike-slip fault
Interpreting Diagrams *Which type of fault would cause extension in an area?*

Q *How do you determine which side of a fault has moved?*

A For the fault shown in Figure 8, did the left side move down, or did the right side move up? Since the surface at the top of the photo has been eroded flat, either side could have moved, or both sides could have moved, with one side moving more than the other. That's why geologists talk about *relative* motion across faults. In this case, the left side moved down *relative* to the right side, and the right side moved up *relative* to the left side.

Types of Mountains

Folding and faulting produce many, but not all of Earth's mountains. In general, mountains are classified by the processes that formed them. **The major types of mountains include volcanic mountains, folded mountains, fault-block mountains, and dome mountains.** Geologists refer to the collection of processes involved in mountain building as **orogenesis**. The term is derived from the Greek *oros* meaning "mountain" and *-geny* meaning "born."

Earth's mountains do not occur at random. Several mountains of similar shape, age, and structure form a group called a mountain range. For example, the Sangre de Cristo range extends from north to south in Colorado and New Mexico. A group of different mountain ranges in the same region form a mountain system. The Sangre de Cristo and West Elk ranges are both part of the Rocky Mountains system.

Mountain ranges and systems occur in long mountain belts that stretch along the edges of continents. The Rocky Mountains and the Andes are part of a mountain belt that extends along the western sides North and South America.

Volcanic Mountains Recall from Chapter 10 that volcanic mountains form along plate boundaries and at hot spots. In addition, igneous activity forms rock deep in the crust that can be uplifted as a result of plate motions and isostatic adjustment.

Folded Mountains Mountains that are formed primarily by folding are called folded mountains. Compressional stress is the major factor that forms **folded mountains**. In Figure 10, you can see how compressional stresses helped to form the Alps in Europe.

Figure 10 Folded mountains, such as the Alps, shown here, form where compressional forces squeeze the crust.

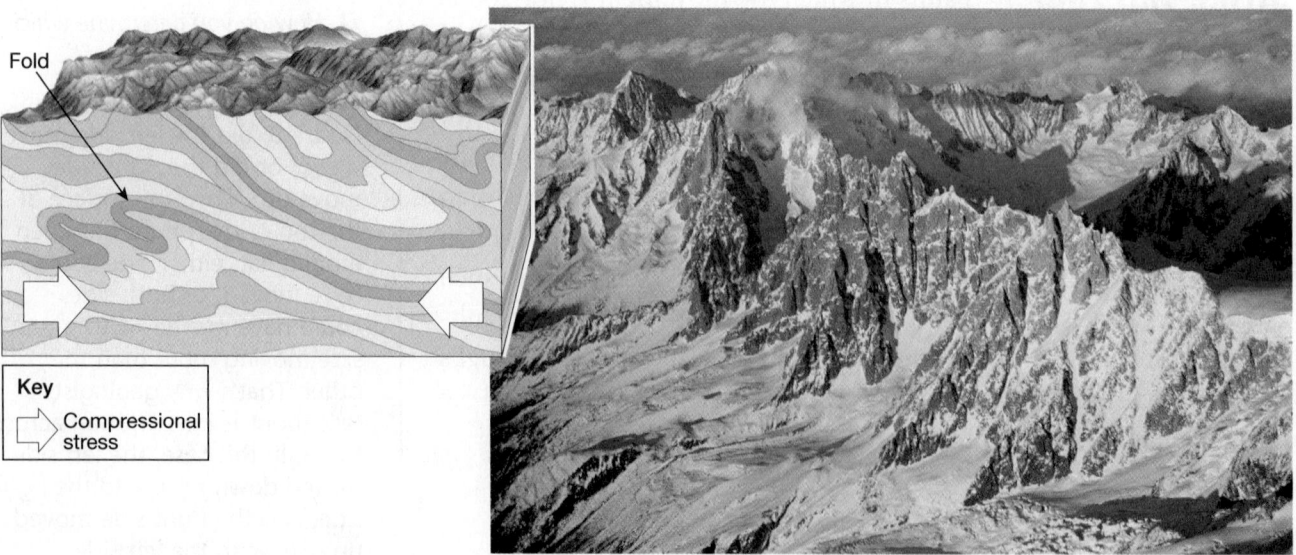

Fold

Key

⇨ Compressional stress

Thrust faulting is also important in the formation of folded mountains, which are often called fold-and-thrust belts. Folded mountains often contain numerous stacked thrust faults that have displaced the folded rock layers many kilometers horizontally. The Appalachian Mountains, the northern Rocky Mountains, and the Alps in Europe are examples of folded mountain ranges.

Fault-Block Mountains Another type of mountain forms as the result of movement along normal faults. Most normal faults are small and have displacements of only a meter or so. Others extend for tens of kilometers where they may outline the boundary of a mountain front. Large-scale normal faults are associated with fault-block mountains. **Fault-block mountains** form as large blocks of crust are uplifted and tilted along normal faults.

Normal faulting occurs where tensional stresses cause the crust to be stretched or extended. As the crust is stretched, a block called a **graben,** which is bounded by normal faults, drops down. *Graben* is the German word for ditch or trench. Grabens produce an elongated valley bordered by relatively uplifted structures called **horsts.** The Basin and Range region of Nevada, Utah, and California, shown in Figure 11, is made of elongated grabens. Above the grabens, tilted fault-blocks or horsts produce parallel rows of fault-block mountains.

In the western United States, other examples of fault-block mountains include the Teton Range of Wyoming and the Sierra Nevada of California. Both are faulted along their eastern flanks, which were uplifted as the blocks tilted downward to the west. These steep mountain fronts were produced over a period of 5 million to 10 million years by many episodes of faulting. Each faulting event produced just a few meters of displacement.

 **Reading Checkpoint** *What is a horst?*

Figure 11 Fault-Block Mountains **A** Part of the Basin and Range region of Nevada, California, and Utah **B** Here, tensional stresses have elongated and fractured the crust into numerous blocks. Movement along these fractures has tilted the blocks producing parallel mountain ranges called fault-block mountains.

Plateaus, Domes, and Basins

Mountains are not the only landforms that result from forces in Earth's crust. 👁 **Up-and-down movements of the crust can produce a variety of landforms, including plateaus, domes, and basins.**

Many of the factors that contribute to the development of mountains also help to create these landforms. Within the crust, these factors include plate motions, folding and faulting, igneous activity, and isostatic adjustment. Another factor works on the surface. Weather and climate affect the rates of weathering and erosion and the production of sediment. Because of isostasy, the weight of sediment added to or eroded from an area contributes to vertical movement of the crust.

The overall effect of these factors is that certain areas of crust may rise or sink relative to other areas. Where the crust bends downward, geologists say that the crust has been *downwarped*. Where the crust bows upward, they say it has been *upwarped*.

Plateaus A plateau is a landform with a relatively high elevation and more-or-less level surface. To form a plateau, a broad area of the crust is uplifted vertically. The Colorado Plateau in the southwestern United States is made up of sandstone and other sedimentary rocks. These rocks were laid down in horizontal layers hundreds of millions of years ago. Before being uplifted more than 2 kilometers, the area was covered by a shallow sea. Geologists are still trying to determine what caused the uplift of the Colorado Plateau. One hypothesis is that a subducting plate, sliding from west to east beneath the North American plate, scraped off the bottom of the lithosphere. This allowed the overlying rock to rise, forming the Colorado Plateau.

Domes Broad upwarping in the rock underlying an area may deform the overlying sedimentary layers. When upwarping produces a roughly circular structure, the feature is called a dome. Domes, like the one in Figure 12, often have the shape of an elongated oval. You can think of the upwarped layers that make up a dome as a large fold. Look at the cross section in Figure 12. You can see that the layers that make up the sides of the dome bend upward as in an anticline.

The Black Hills of western South Dakota are a well-known example of a dome. Geologists think that the Black Hills began to form about 60 million years ago when tectonic forces caused upwarping of the North American plate in the region. Uplift and erosion stripped away layers of sedimentary rock. This exposed crystalline igneous and metamorphic rocks that today form the core of the Black Hills. As you can see in Figure 12, the younger sedimentary layers form rings around the older rocks near the center of the Black Hills.

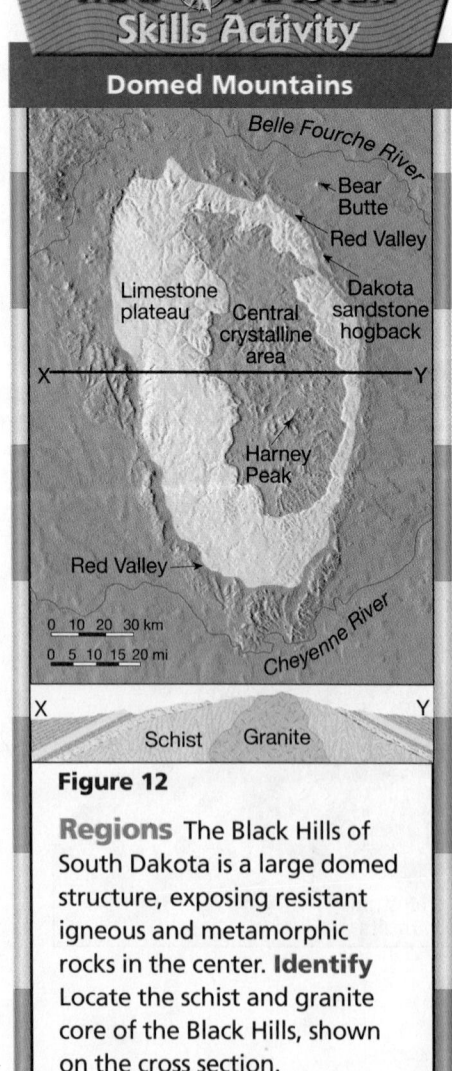

MAP ✦ MASTER™
Skills Activity

Domed Mountains

Belle Fourche River

Bear Butte
Red Valley
Limestone plateau
Central crystalline area
Dakota sandstone hogback
X ——————— Y
Harney Peak
Red Valley →
Cheyenne River

0 10 20 30 km
0 5 10 15 20 mi

X ——————— Y
Schist Granite

Figure 12

Regions The Black Hills of South Dakota is a large domed structure, exposing resistant igneous and metamorphic rocks in the center. **Identify** Locate the schist and granite core of the Black Hills, shown on the cross section.

Reading Checkpoint *What is a dome?*

Sedimentary Basins Downwarped structures that have a roughly circular shape are called *basins*. The central United States contains a number of basins, including the Michigan basin, shown in Figure 13. Sedimentary basins can form in several ways. During mountain building, plate motions can cause the crust to bend downward and form a basin. If the basin sinks below sea level, it may become a shallow sea. Over time, sediments such as sand and the skeletons of ocean organisms are laid down, forming layers of sedimentary rock.

Basins may also form along the edges of continents where thick layers of sediment build up. The weight of the sediment downwarps the crust to form a basin.

When forces in the crust uplift the sedimentary layers, the rock that fills the basin is exposed at the surface. As you can see in Figure 13, a geologic map of a basin looks somewhat like a bull's-eye. The oldest rocks are around the edges of the basin and the youngest rocks are near the center.

The plate motions that help to form sedimentary basins can also destroy them. For example, when two continental plates collide, the ocean basin between them closes up. Sedimentary rock in the basin becomes part of the landmass formed by the collision.

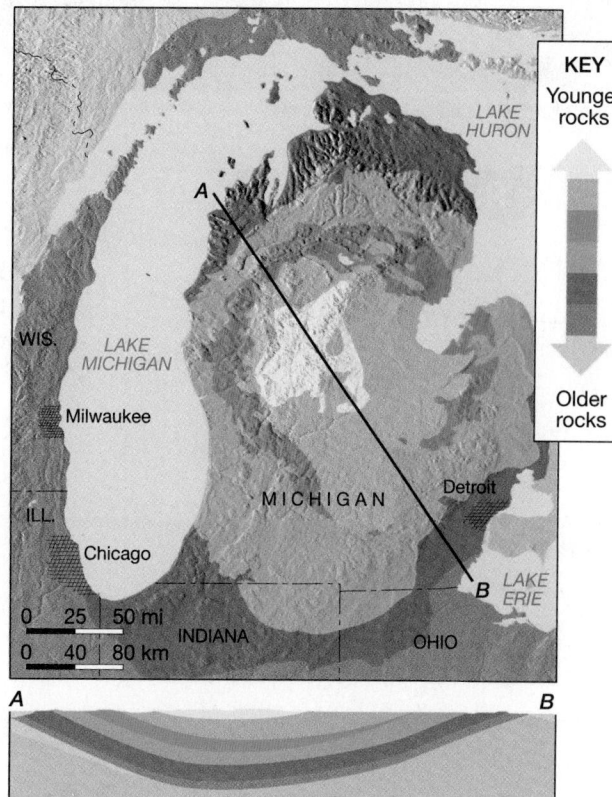

Figure 13 Erosion has exposed the layers of sedimentary rock deposited in the bowl-shaped Michigan basin. **Applying Concepts** *Should the Michigan basin be described as an anticline or a syncline? Explain.*

Section 11.2 Assessment

Reviewing Concepts

1. ⬤ List the three main types of folds.
2. ⬤ Describe the four main types of faults in terms of the motion along each type.
3. ⬤ List the major types of mountains.
4. ⬤ Define plateau, dome, and basin in your own words.
5. What is a graben? In what type of mountains are grabens most commonly found?

Critical Thinking

6. **Applying Concepts** How would you classify a mountain range made up of numerous thrust faults?
7. **Comparing and Contrasting** Compare domes and basins.

Writing in Science

Descriptive Paragraph Write a paragraph describing a trip across a fault-block mountain. Describe the types of rocks and structures you might observe.

11.3 Mountains and Plates

Reading Focus

Key Concepts

- What mountains form along convergent plate boundaries?
- What mountains form along divergent plate boundaries?
- How do mountains form away from plate boundaries?
- How does accretion affect continents and mountain building?

Vocabulary

- accretionary wedge
- accretion
- terrane

Reading Strategy

Outlining As you read, make an outline of the important ideas in this section. Use the green topic headings as the main topics and the blue headings as subtopics.

I. **Mountains and Plates**
   A. Convergent Boundary Mountains
      1. Ocean-Ocean Convergence
      2. a. _____?_____
      3. b. _____?_____
   B. Divergent Boundary Mountains

Mountain building still occurs in many places worldwide. For example, the jagged spires of the Teton Range in Wyoming began to form about a million years ago and are still rising. In contrast, older mountain ranges, such as the Appalachians in the eastern United States, are deeply eroded.

Many hypotheses have been proposed to explain mountain formation. One early proposal incorrectly suggested that mountains are wrinkles in Earth's crust, produced as the planet cooled from a semi-molten state.

Figure 14 Young Mountains The Teton Range in Wyoming is an example of a relatively young mountain range.

Convergent Boundary Mountains

With the development of the theory of plate tectonics, a widely accepted model for mountain building became available. Most mountain building occurs at convergent plate boundaries. Colliding plates produce the compressional forces that fold, fault, and metamorphose the thick layers of sediments deposited at the edges of landmasses. The partial melting of mantle rock also provides a source of magma that intrudes into and further deforms these deposits.

Ocean-Ocean Convergence

The convergence of two oceanic plates mainly produces volcanic mountains. Recall from Chapter 10 that this process occurs where oceanic plates converge in a subduction zone, as shown in Figure 15. The result of this collision is the formation of a volcanic island arc on the ocean floor.

Volcanic island arcs form along the subduction zones around a shrinking ocean basin. For example, many island arcs have formed along the trenches that ring the Pacific Ocean. The Philippines are one example of a volcanic island arc.

Ocean-Continental Convergence

The convergence of an oceanic plate and a continental plate produces volcanic mountains and folded mountains. As shown in Figure 16, these mountains develop in two belts that are roughly parallel to the edge of a continent.

Recall from Chapter 10 that a continental volcanic arc forms when an oceanic plate is subducted beneath a continental plate. The belt of mountains that results is made up of volcanoes and intrusive igneous rocks mixed with metamorphic rocks. One example is the Andes of South America. The Andes formed through the subduction of the Nazca Plate beneath the South American plate.

Another process forms a belt of coastal mountains made up of folded and faulted rocks. How do these mountains form? During subduction, sediment is eroded from the land and scraped from the subducting plate. This sediment becomes stuck against the landward side of a trench. Along with scraps of oceanic crust, the sediment forms an **accretionary wedge**. A long period of subduction can build an accretionary wedge that stands above sea level. California's Coast Ranges formed by this process.

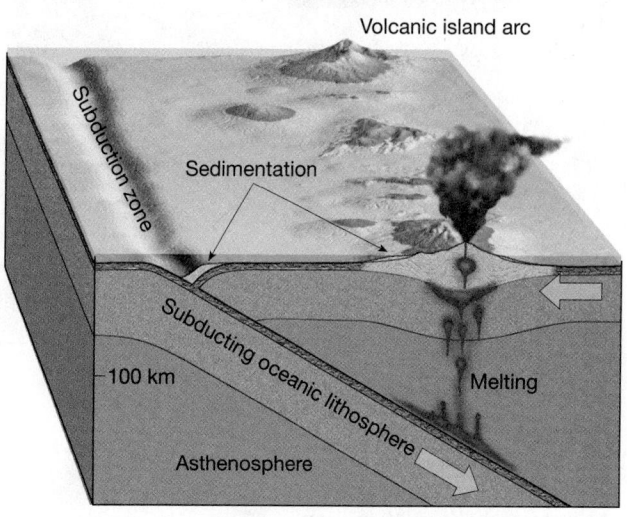

Ocean-Ocean Convergence

Volcanic island arc · Subduction zone · Sedimentation · Subducting oceanic lithosphere · 100 km · Melting · Asthenosphere

Figure 15 Subduction along a convergent boundary results in the development of volcanic mountains.

Go Online

NSTA SciLINKS

For: Links on mountain building
Visit: www.SciLinks.org
Web Code: cjn-3113

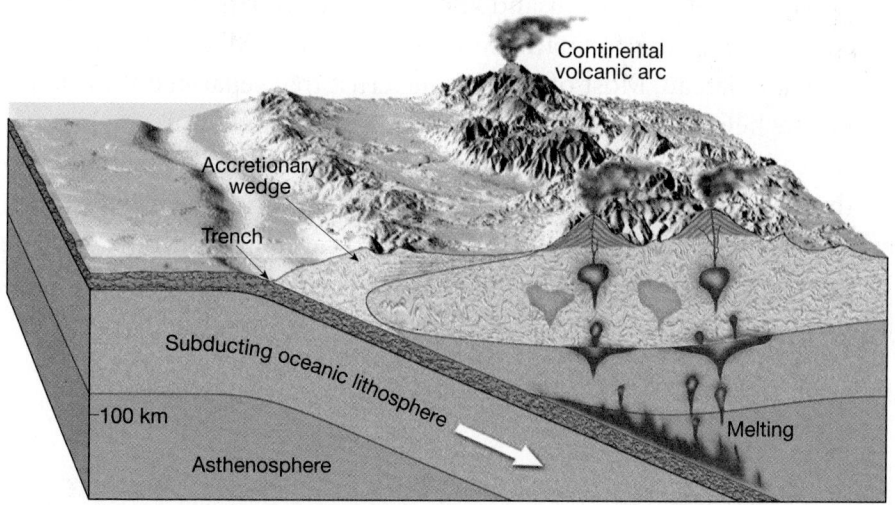

Continental volcanic arc · Accretionary wedge · Trench · Subducting oceanic lithosphere · 100 km · Asthenosphere · Melting

Figure 16 Ocean-Continental Convergence Plate convergence produces a subduction zone and a continental volcanic arc. Continued convergence and igneous activity further deforms the crust and forms a roughly parallel folded mountain belt. **Observing** *What type of mountains result from the partial melting?*

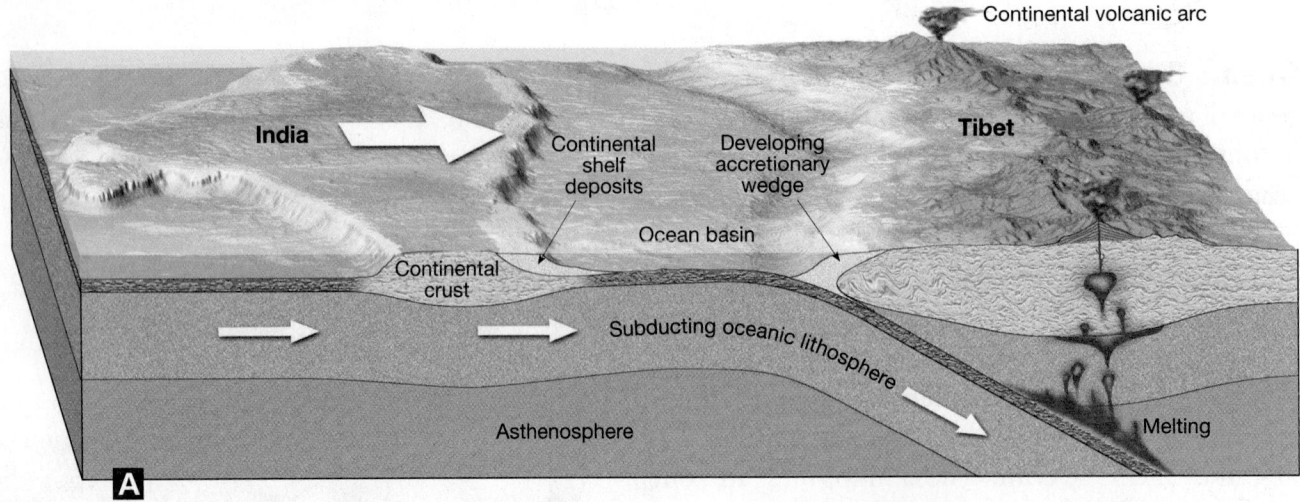

Continental volcanic arc

India

Continental shelf deposits

Developing accretionary wedge

Tibet

Ocean basin

Continental crust

Subducting oceanic lithosphere

Asthenosphere

Melting

A

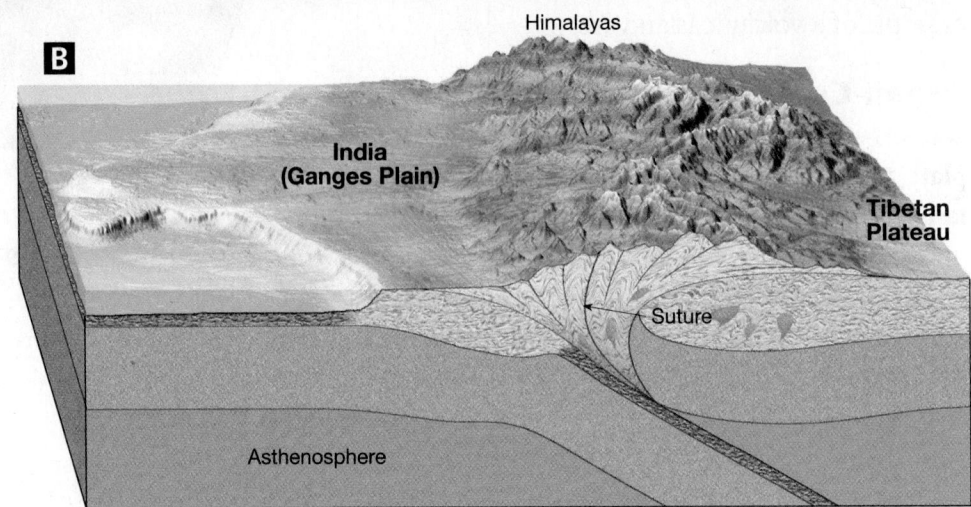

B

Himalayas

India (Ganges Plain)

Tibetan Plateau

Suture

Asthenosphere

Figure 17 Continent-Continent Convergence
The collision of India and Asia started about 45 million years ago and produced the Himalayas. **A** Converging plates collide at a subduction zone, producing a continental volcanic arc. **B** The two landmasses collided, deforming and elevating the mountain range.

Continent-Continent Convergence

At a convergent boundary, a collision between two plates carrying continental crust will form folded mountains. The reason for this is that continental crust is not dense enough, compared with the denser rock of the mantle, to be subducted. An example of such a collision began about 45 million years ago when India collided with the Eurasian plate, as shown in Figure 17. Before this event, India was part of Antarctica. It slowly moved a few thousand kilometers due north. The result of the collision was the formation of the Himalaya Mountains and the Tibetan Plateau. Most of the oceanic crust that separated these landmasses before the collision was subducted, but some was caught up in the collision zone, along with the sediment along the shoreline. Today these sedimentary rocks and slivers of oceanic crust are elevated high above sea level. The closing up of the ocean between India and the Eurasian plate is an example of how plate motions can destroy a sedimentary basin.

Reading Checkpoint *Why can't continental crust be subducted?*

Divergent Boundary Mountains

Most mountains are formed at convergent boundaries, but some are formed at divergent boundaries, usually on the ocean floor. These mountains form a chain that curves along the ocean floor at the ocean ridges. This mountain chain is over 70,000 kilometers long and rises to 2000 to 3000 meters above the ocean floor. ☞**The mountains that form along ocean ridges at divergent plate boundaries are fault-block mountains made of volcanic rock.** The mountains are elevated because of isostasy. Rock at the ridge is hotter and less dense, so it rises higher than older, colder oceanic crust.

Non-Boundary Mountains

Some mountains occur well away from plate boundaries. ☞ **Volcanic mountains at hot spots, as well as some upwarped mountains and fault-block mountains, can form far from plate boundaries.** The Hawaiian Islands are a well-known example of volcanic mountains at a hot spot. Mountains formed by upwarping and faulting include the southern Rocky Mountains and the mountains of the Basin and Range region.

The southern Rockies began to form about 60 million years ago with the subduction of an oceanic plate more than 1600 kilometers away. At first, compressional forces deformed the crust. Then the subducting plate separated from the lithosphere above. This allowed hot rock to upwell from the mantle, pushing up the crust and forming the southern Rockies. As the crust bent upward, tensional forces stretched and fractured it, forming the fault-block mountains of the Basin and Range region, as shown on page 332.

Problem-Solving Activity

Rates of Mountain Building

The mighty Himalayas between India and Tibet are the tallest mountains on Earth, rising to more than 8 kilometers. These mountains are still rising at about 1 centimeter per year. Mount Everest is the tallest peak with an elevation of 8848 meters above sea level. The Himalayas formed as a result of India colliding with the Eurasian plate.

1. **Calculating** If you assume that the Himalayas will continue to be uplifted at the current rate of 1 centimeter per year, how long will it take the mountains to rise another 500 meters?

2. **Calculating** Assuming a rate of uplift of 1 centimeter per year, how much higher could the Himalayas be in one million years?

3. **Applying Concepts** If the convergence of tectonic plates is causing the Himalayas to rise in elevation, what common surface processes are working to decrease their elevations?

4. **Predicting** Will the Himalayas continue to rise in elevation indefinitely? Explain your answer.

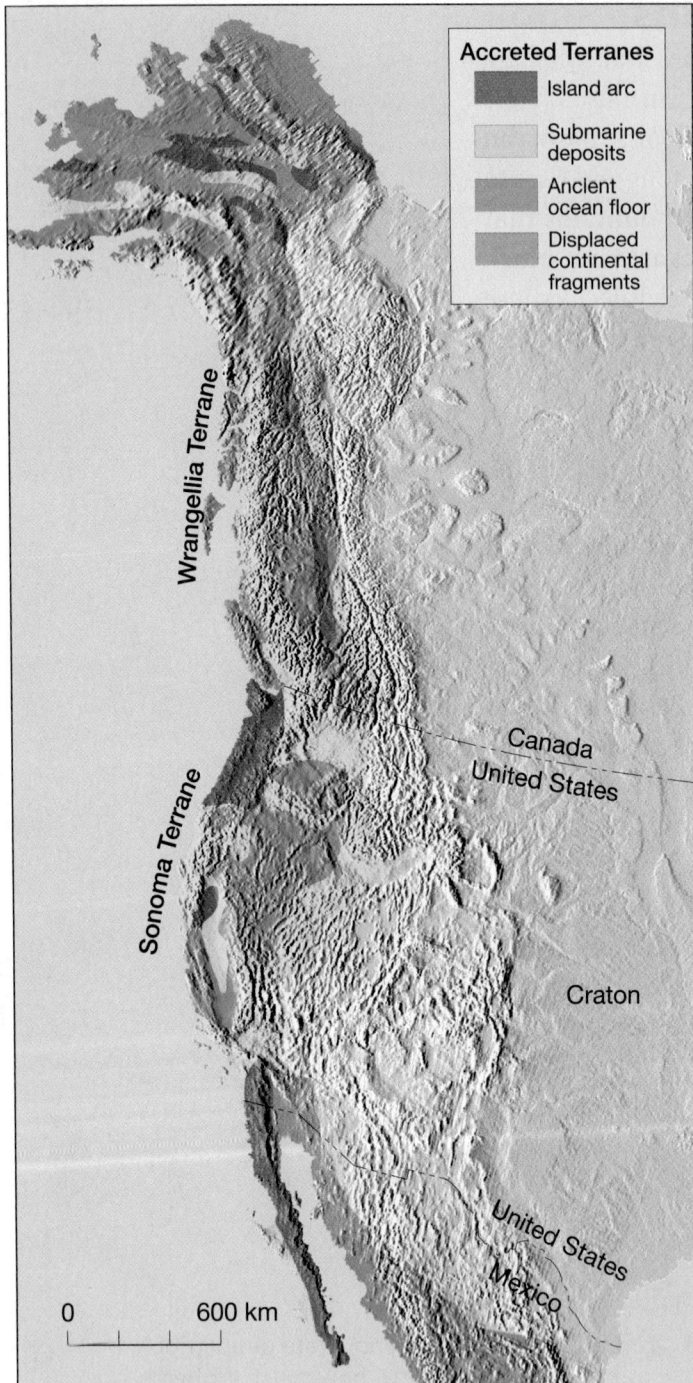

Figure 18 Accretion in Western North America These terranes are thought to have been added to western North America during the past 200 million years.
Interpreting Maps *What do the areas in blue represent?*

Map labels: Wrangellia Terrane, Sonoma Terrane, Canada / United States, Craton, United States / Mexico

Legend: **Accreted Terranes** — Island arc, Submarine deposits, Ancient ocean floor, Displaced continental fragments

Scale: 0 — 600 km

Continental Accretion

You may be surprised to learn that the size and shape of a continent changes over time. Some of these changes occur when continents collide or split apart. Geologists have studied another process in which smaller fragments of crust collide and merge with continents. **The process of accretion enlarges continental landmasses and forms mountains along the edges of continents.**

When fragments of crust collide with a continental plate, they become stuck to or embedded into the continent through **accretion.** Many of the mountainous regions rimming the Pacific have been produced through collision and accretion.

Terranes Geologists refer to accreted crustal blocks as terranes. A **terrane** is any crustal fragment that has a geologic history distinct from that of the adjoining terranes. Terranes come in many shapes and sizes. Some are no larger than volcanic islands, while others are immense, such as the one making up the entire Indian subcontinent. Before their accretion to a continental block, some of the fragments may have been microcontinents similar to the present-day island of Madagascar, located in the Indian Ocean east of Africa. Many others were island arcs like Japan and the Philippines. As you can see in Figure 18, much of western North America is made up of terranes added to the continent by accretion.

How does the process of accretion work? As oceanic plates move, they carry the embedded volcanic island arcs and microcontinents along with them. Eventually a collision between the crustal fragment and the continent occurs. Relatively small crustal pieces are peeled from the oceanic plate at a subduction zone, and thin sheets of the crustal fragment are thrust onto the continental block. This newly added material increases the width and thickness of the continental crust. The material may later be displaced farther inland by the addition of other fragments.

Reading Checkpoint   *What is a terrane?*

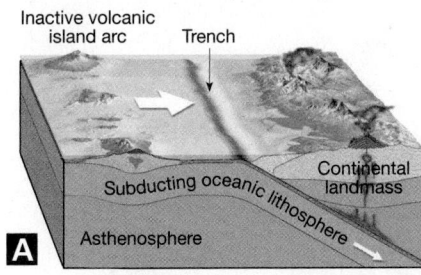

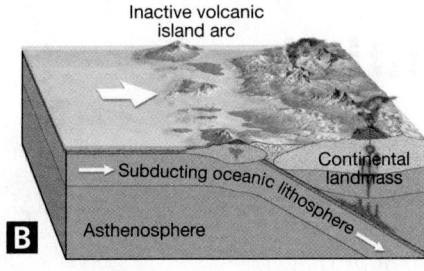

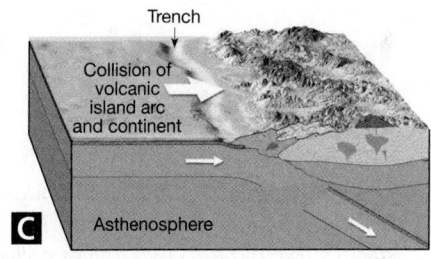

Mountains From Accretion The accretion of larger crustal fragments, such as a mature island arc, may result in a mountain range. These mountain ranges are much smaller than the ones that result from a continent–continent collision. Because of its buoyancy, or ability to float, an island arc will not subduct beneath the continental plate. Instead, it will plow into the continent and deform both blocks, as shown in Figure 19.

The idea that mountain building occurs in connection with the accretion of crustal fragments to a continental mass came mainly from studies in western North America. Areas in the mountains of Alaska and western Canada were found to contain rocks, fossils, and structures that were different from those in surrounding areas. These areas have been accreted to the western margin of North America.

Figure 19 This sequence illustrates the collision of an inactive volcanic island arc with the margin of a continental plate. The island arc becomes accreted onto the continental plate.

Section 11.3 Assessment

Reviewing Concepts

1. What types of mountains are associated with convergent plate boundaries?

2. What mountains are associated with divergent plate boundaries?

3. List three types of mountains that can form far from a plate boundary?

4. Describe the process that can enlarge a continent and form mountains along the continent's edge.

Critical Thinking

5. **Comparing and Contrasting** Compare mountain building along an ocean-continent convergent boundary and a continent-continent convergent boundary.

6. **Drawing Conclusions** How does the theory of plate tectonics help explain the existence of marine fossils in sedimentary rocks on top of the Himalayas?

7. **Inferring** A geologist collects rock samples as she travels inland from the Alaska coast. First, she finds rock from an island arc, then rock from oceanic crust, then rock from a microcontinent. What can she infer about the origin of the land in this area? Explain.

Creative Writing Describe a trip through a mountain range like the Andes that has formed at an ocean-continent convergent boundary.

Investigating Anticlines and Synclines

The axial plane of a fold is an imaginary plane drawn through the long axis of a fold. The axial plane divides the fold into two halves called limbs as shown in Figure 1. In a symmetrical fold, the limbs are mirror images of each other and move away at the same angle. In an asymmetrical fold, the limbs dip or tilt at different angles. Folds do not continue forever. Where the fold axis dips and is no longer horizontal, the fold is said to be plunging, as shown in Figure 2. A geologic principle known as the principle of superposition states that in most situations with layered rocks, the oldest rocks are at the bottom of the sequence.

Problem How are rocks oriented in anticlines and synclines?

Materials
- pencil
- protractor
- tracing paper

Skills Observing, Measuring, Classifying, Interpreting Diagrams

Procedure

1. Study the two diagrams, labeled Fold A and Fold B in Figures 3 and 4.

2. Use a protractor to measure the angles of the rock layers in both limbs of Fold A. Repeat your measurements for both limbs of Fold B. For consistency, measure the angles on both folds at the surface between layers 3 and 4.

3. Use Figures 3 and 4 and Figure 6 on page 313 to determine what types of folds are shown by Fold A and Fold B.

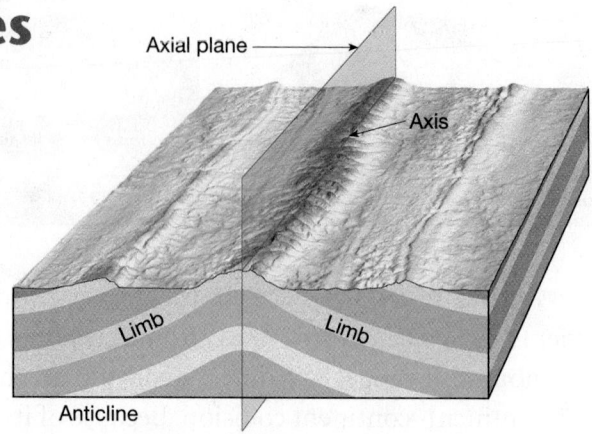

Figure 1 Horizontal Axis

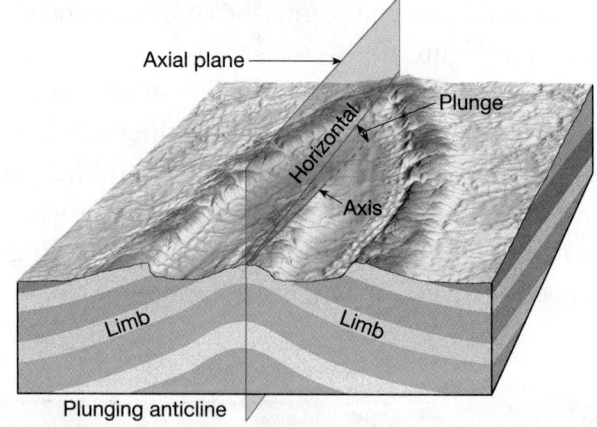

Figure 2 Plunging Axis

4. Anticlines and synclines are linear features caused by compressional stresses. Two other types of folds—domes and basins—are often nearly circular and result from vertical displacement. Uplift produces domes like those shown in Figure 3 on the next page. A basin is a downwarped structure, as shown in Figure 4.

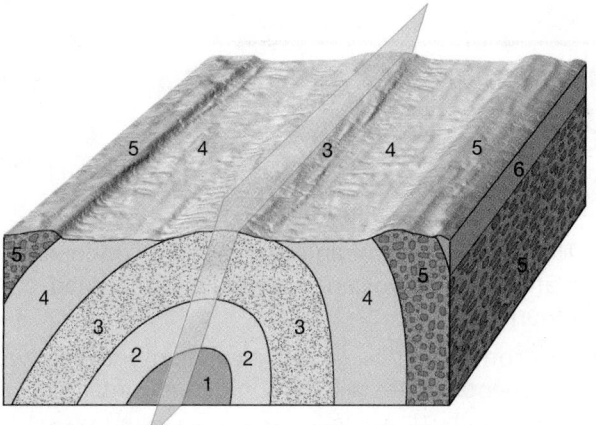

Figure 3 Fold A

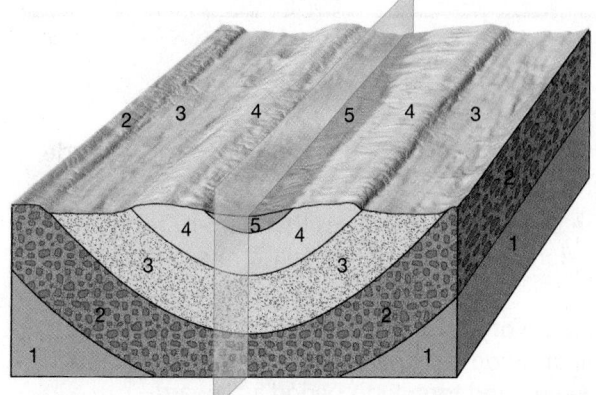

Figure 4 Fold B

5. Use tracing paper to make a copy of the blank block diagram shown below. Complete all three sides of the diagram to show an eroded fold consistent with the rock layer shown on the right side of the block.

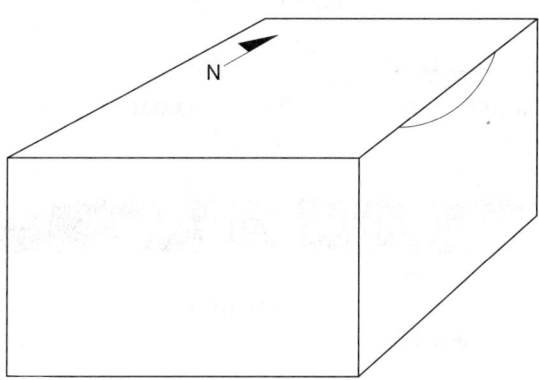

Analyze and Conclude

1. Interpreting Diagrams What type of fold is shown by Fold A? In what direction do the limbs dip or tilt from the axial plane?

2. Interpreting Diagrams What type of fold is shown by Fold B? In what direction do the limbs dip or tilt from the axial plane?

3. Drawing Conclusions In Fold A, which rock layer is the oldest shown? Which rock layer is the youngest shown?

4. Measuring In Fold A, at what angle are the rock layers in both limbs dipping or tilted?

5. Drawing Conclusions In Fold B, which rock layer is the oldest shown? Which rock layer is the youngest shown?

6. Measuring In Fold B, at what angle are the rock layers in both limbs dipping or tilted?

7. Classifying What type of fold did you draw in the blank block diagram on your tracing paper?

8. Observing Is Fold A symmetrical or asymmetrical? Is Fold B symmetrical or asymmetrical?

9. Observing Is Fold A plunging or nonplunging? Is Fold B plunging or nonplunging?

10. Applying Concepts If you walk away from the axis on an eroded anticline, do the rocks get older or younger? How do the ages of the rocks change as you walk away from the axis in a syncline?

Go Further Use library or Internet sources to research the geologic terms "strike" and "dip." Draw a block diagram showing rocks layers that illustrate these terms. Give a presentation to the class, and explain the terms using your diagram as a visual aid.

Study Guide

11.1 Forces in Earth's Crust

Key Concepts

- The factors that affect deformation of rock include temperature, pressure, rock type, and time.
- The three types of stresses that deform rocks are tensional stress, compressional stress, and shear stress.
- Because of isostasy, deformed and thickened crust will undergo regional uplift both during mountain building and for a long period afterward.

Vocabulary

deformation, *p. 308;* stress, *p. 308;* strain, *p. 308;* isostasy, *p. 310;* isostatic adjustment, *p. 310*

11.2 Folds, Faults, and Mountains

Key Concepts

- The three main types of folds are anticlines, synclines, and monoclines.
- The major types of faults are normal faults, reverse faults, thrust faults, and strike-slip faults.
- The major types of mountains include volcanic mountains, folded mountains, fault-block mountains, and dome mountains.
- Up and down movements of the crust can produce a variety of landforms, including plateaus, domes, and basins.

Vocabulary

anticline, *p. 312;* syncline, *p. 312;* monocline, *p. 313;* normal fault, *p. 314;* reverse fault, *p. 314;* thrust fault, *p. 314;* strike-slip fault, *p. 315;* orogenesis, *p. 316;* folded mountains, *p. 316;* fault-block mountain, *p. 317;* graben, *p. 317;* horst, *p. 317*

11.3 Mountains and Plates

Key Concepts

- The convergence of two oceanic plates mainly produces volcanic mountains.
- The convergence of an oceanic and a continental plate produces volcanic mountains and folded mountains.
- At a convergent boundary, a collision between two continental plates will form folded mountains.
- The mountains that form along ocean ridges at divergent plate boundaries are fault-block mountains made of volcanic rock.
- Volcanic mountains at hot spots, as well as some upwarped mountains and fault-block mountains, can form far from plate boundaries.
- The process of accretion enlarges continental landmasses and forms mountains along the edges of continents.

Vocabulary

accretionary wedge, *p. 321;* accretion, *p. 324;* terrane, *p. 324*

Thinking Visually

Concept Map Copy the concept map onto a sheet of paper. Use information from the chapter to complete it.

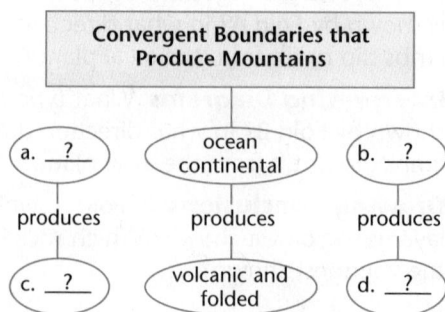

Assessment

Reviewing Content

Choose the letter that best answers the question or completes the statement.

1. Which one of the following is NOT a form of rock deformation?
   - **a.** elastic deformation
   - **b.** ductile deformation
   - **c.** brittle deformation
   - **d.** oblique deformation

2. The two most common types of folds are
   - **a.** anticlines and synclines.
   - **b.** basins and terranes.
   - **c.** fault-blocks and synclines.
   - **d.** thrusts and anticlines.

3. Orogenesis refers to those processes that produce
   - **a.** spreading centers.
   - **b.** earthquakes.
   - **c.** mountains.
   - **d.** subduction zones.

4. Which one of the following is NOT a factor that affects how a rock deforms?
   - **a.** time
   - **b.** age of the rock
   - **c.** rock type
   - **d.** temperature

5. The rock surface immediately above a fault surface is commonly called the
   - **a.** anticline.
   - **b.** foot wall.
   - **c.** hanging wall.
   - **d.** syncline.

6. Folding is usually the result of what type of stress?
   - **a.** tensional stress
   - **b.** compressional stress
   - **c.** shear stress
   - **d.** faulting

7. The collision and joining of crustal fragments to a continent is called
   - **a.** subduction.
   - **b.** isostasy.
   - **c.** accretion.
   - **d.** extension.

8. The San Andreas Fault is a
   - **a.** normal fault.
   - **b.** strike-slip fault.
   - **c.** reverse fault.
   - **d.** thrust fault.

9. What type of mountains form at convergent boundaries where two oceanic plates meet?
   - **a.** volcanic mountains
   - **b.** upwarped mountains
   - **c.** folded mountains
   - **d.** fault-block mountains

10. Because of isostasy, the erosion of rock from a mountain range would at first cause the mountains to
    - **a.** sink lower.
    - **b.** maintain the same elevation.
    - **c.** float higher on the mantle below.
    - **d.** develop normal faults.

Understanding Concepts

11. How does tensional stress deform a body of rock?

12. What is ductile deformation?

13. How is a syncline different from an anticline?

14. What types of faults are most commonly associated with fault-block mountains?

15. Define graben.

16. What types of faults are most commonly formed by compressional stress?

Use the diagram below to answer Questions 17–18.

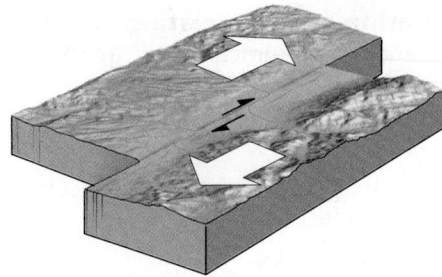

17. What type of fault is shown in the diagram?

18. What type of stress formed the fault shown in the diagram?

19. In the plate tectonics theory, what type of plate boundary is associated with the formation of the Himalayas and Appalachians?

20. What is an accretionary wedge? Briefly describe its formation.

21. Define terrane.

22. Describe folded mountains. Give an example of folded mountains.

23. How do volcanic mountains form at locations that are not near plate boundaries? Give an example.

24. How do the ages of rock layers change as you go outward from the center of an eroded dome?

25. What type of stress is most common at divergent boundaries? What type of mountains are most often found at this type of boundary? Give an example.

Critical Thinking

26. Applying Concepts How would a period of major erosion affect the isostatic adjustment of a mountain range?

27. Comparing and Contrasting Compare normal faults and reverse faults.

28. Predicting What would most likely happen if a continental fragment the size of Greenland was carried by an oceanic plate into a subduction zone along the margin of a continental plate?

29. Inferring Why don't anticlines always appear as hills, even though the rocks beneath the surface are folded upward?

30. Comparing and Contrasting How are a dome and a basin similar? How are they different?

Analyzing Data

Use the diagram below to answer Questions 31–34.

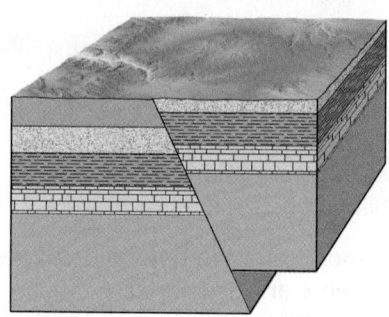

31. Inferring What is the block on the right side of the fault called?

32. Observing Describe the movement along the fault.

33. Interpreting Diagrams What type of fault is shown in the diagram?

34. Drawing Conclusions What type of stress was responsible for forming this fault?

Concepts in Action

35. Designing an Experiment Put together an experiment that models the isostatic adjustment that results from a continent-continent collision and the erosion that takes place on the resulting mountain range.

36. Hypothesizing Explain how a slice of ocean crust could be found on top of a peak in the Himalayas.

37. Writing in Science Write a paragraph briefly describing the development of volcanic mountains at an oceanic-oceanic convergent boundary.

Performance-Based Assessment

Classifying Use a world map or an atlas and Figure 15 in Chapter 9 to classify the following mountains or mountain ranges: Mount Baker in Washington State, the Zagros Mountains in Iran, Mount Fuji in Japan, and the mountains in western Egypt.

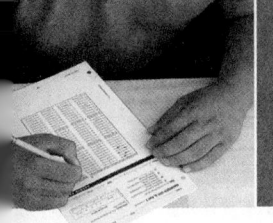

Standardized Test Prep

Test-Taking Tip

Avoiding Careless Mistakes
Students often make mistakes when they fail to examine a test question and possible answers thoroughly. Always read a question carefully and underline key words, such as NOT, EXCEPT, or EXCLUDING. After choosing an answer, reread the question to check your selection.

Which of the following is NOT caused by compressional stresses?

    (A) thrust faults
    (B) anticlines
    (C) reverse faults
    (D) normal faults

(Answer: D)

Choose the letter that best answers the question or completes the statement.

1. A fracture with horizontal displacement parallel to its surface trend is called a
    (A) joint.
    (B) normal fault.
    (C) strike-slip fault.
    (D) reverse fault.

2. Compared to the elevation of a thin piece of continental crust in isostatic balance, the highest elevation of a thick piece of crust will be
    (A) the same.
    (B) higher.
    (C) lower.
    (D) older.

3. The removal of material by erosion will cause the crust to
    (A) subduct.
    (B) fold.
    (C) rise.
    (D) subside.

4. Which of the following are NOT generally associated with convergent margins?
    (A) volcanic mountains
    (B) folded mountains
    (C) thrust faulted mountains
    (D) fault-block mountains

Use the diagram below to answer Questions 5–6.

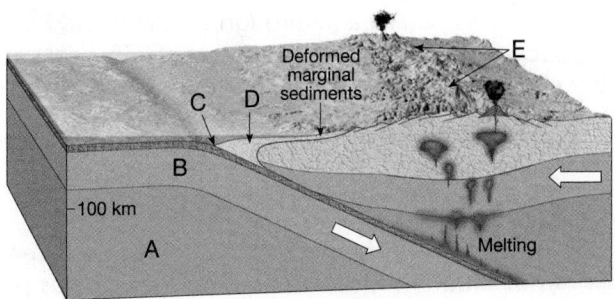

5. What feature is illustrated at the area labeled D in the diagram?
    (A) accretionary wedge
    (B) subducting continental lithosphere
    (C) ocean trench
    (D) continental volcanic arc

6. What types of mountains can form at the type of plate boundary illustrated in the diagram?
    (A) dome mountains and volcanic mountains
    (B) volcanic mountains and fault-block mountains
    (C) volcanic mountains and folded mountains
    (D) folded mountains and upwarped mountains

7. Describe the concept of isostasy.

8. Briefly describe what grabens and horsts are and how they form.

9. What type of tectonic settings are grabens and horsts commonly associated with? Give an example of an area where these structures are found.

Mountain Building Away From Plate Margins

In the American West, extending from the Front Range of the southern Rocky Mountains across the Colorado Plateau and through the Basin and Range Province, the topography consists of lofty peaks and elevated plateaus. According to the plate tectonics model, you would expect mountain belts to be produced along continental margins and convergent plate boundaries. But this mountainous region extends inland almost 1600 kilometers, far from the nearest plate boundary.

The Laramide Orogeny

The portion of the Rocky Mountains that extends from southern Montana to New Mexico was produced about 60 million years ago by a period of uplift known as the Laramide Orogeny.

The event that may have triggered the Laramide Orogeny started with the nearly horizontal subduction of the Farallon plate eastward beneath North America. As the diagrams show, this plate extended inland as far as the Black Hills of South Dakota. As the subducted slab scraped beneath the continent, compressional forces started a period of tectonic activity. About 65 million years ago, the Farallon plate stopped subducting beneath California because North America moved westward over the midocean ridge that separated the Farallon and Pacific plates. As the relatively cool Farallon plate gradually separated from the lithosphere above, it was replaced by hot rock that upwelled from the asthenosphere. Hot asthenospheric rock provided the buoyancy to raise the southern Rockies, as well as the Colorado Plateau and the Basin and Range Province.

Basin and Range

In the southern Rockies, this event uplifted large blocks of ancient basement rocks along high-angle faults. This produced mountains separated by large basins. The upwelling that is associated with the Basin and Range Province started about 50 million years ago and remains active today. Here the buoyancy of the warm material caused upwarping and rifting that elongated the overlying crust by 200 to 300 kilometers. The lower crust is ductile and easily stretched. The upper crust, on the other hand, is brittle and deforms by faulting. The extension and faulting broke the uplifted crust, causing individual blocks to shift. The high portions of these tilted blocks make up the mountain ranges. Low areas form the basins, now partially filled with sediment.

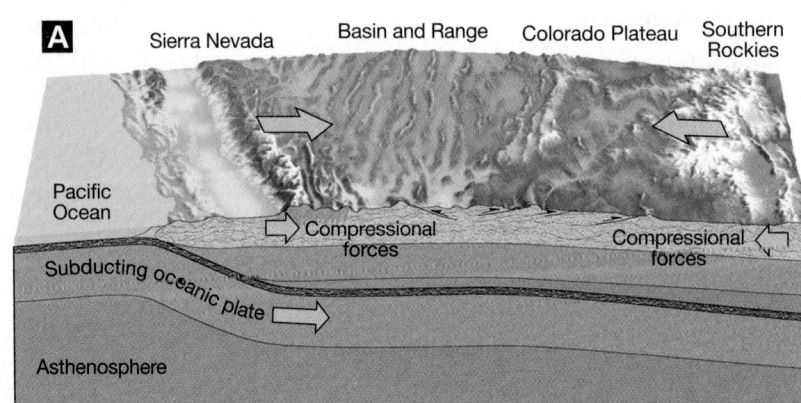

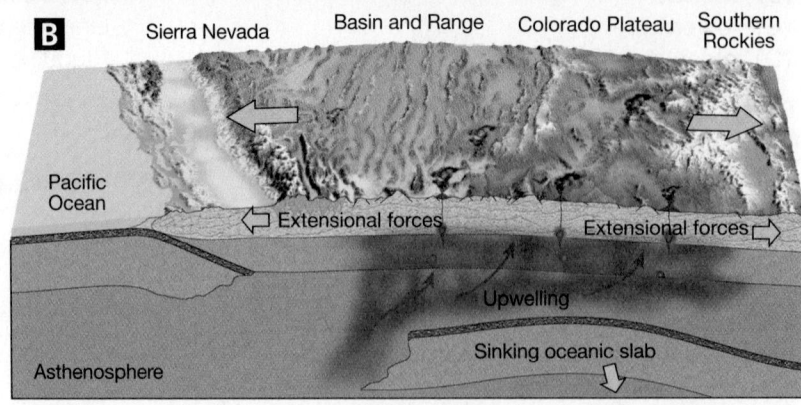

A Nearly horizontal subduction of an oceanic plate initiated a period of tectonic activity. **B** Sinking of this oceanic slab allowed for upwelling of hot mantle material that buoyantly raised the crust.

Damaging Earthquakes East of the Rockies

When you think of earthquakes, you probably think of California and Japan. However, six major earthquakes have occurred in the central and eastern United States since colonial times. Three of these had estimated moment magnitudes of 7.3, 7.0, and 7.5, and they were centered near the Mississippi River Valley in southeastern Missouri. Occurring on December 16, 1811, January 23, 1812, and February 7, 1812, these earthquakes, plus numerous smaller tremors, destroyed the town of New Madrid, Missouri, triggered massive landslides, and caused damage over a six-state area. The course of the Mississippi River was altered, and Tennessee's Reelfoot Lake was enlarged. Chimneys toppled in Cincinnati, Ohio, and Richmond, Virginia, while Boston residents, located 1770 kilometers away, felt the tremor.

Damage to Charleston, South Carolina, caused by the August 31, 1886 earthquake.

Memphis, Tennessee, the largest population center in the New Madrid area today, is located on unconsolidated floodplain deposits. Therefore, buildings are more susceptible to damage than similar structures built on bedrock. It has been estimated that if earthquakes the size of New Madrid events were to strike in the next decade, they would result in casualties in the thousands and damages in tens of billions of dollars.

Damaging earthquakes that occurred in Aurora, Illinois (1909), and Valentine, Texas (1931), remind us that other areas in the central United States are vulnerable.

The greatest historical earthquake in the eastern states occurred August 31, 1886, in Charleston, South Carolina. The event, which spanned 1 minute, caused 60 deaths, numerous injuries, and great economic loss within 200 kilometers of Charleston. Within 8 minutes, effects were felt as far away as Chicago and St. Louis, where strong vibrations shook the upper floors of buildings, causing people to rush outdoors. In Charleston alone, over 100 buildings were destroyed, and 90 percent of the remaining structures were damaged. It was difficult to find a chimney still standing as the photograph shows.

Numerous other strong earthquakes have been recorded in the eastern United States. New England and adjacent areas have experienced sizable shocks since colonial times. The first reported earthquake in the Northeast took place in Plymouth, Massachusetts, in 1683, and was followed in 1755 by the destructive Cambridge, Massachusetts, earthquake. Moreover, ever since records have been kept, New York State alone has experienced over 300 earthquakes large enough to be felt.

Earthquakes in the central and eastern United States occur far less frequently than in California. Yet history indicates that the East is vulnerable. Further, these shocks east of the Rockies have generally produced structural damage over a larger area than counterparts of similar magnitude in California. The reason is that the underlying bedrock in the central and eastern United States is older and more rigid. As a result, seismic waves are able to travel greater distances with less weakening than in the western United States. It is estimated that for earthquakes of similar magnitude, the region of maximum ground motion in the East may be up to 10 times larger than in the West. Therefore, the higher rate of earthquake occurrence in the western United States is balanced somewhat by the fact that central and eastern U.S. quakes can damage larger areas.

CHAPTER

12 Geologic Time

Exploration Lab
Fossil Occurrence and the Age of Rocks

Understanding Earth
Dating With Tree Rings

 GEODe
EARTH SCIENCE

Geologic Time
↳ Relative Dating
Radiometric Dating
Geologic Time Scale

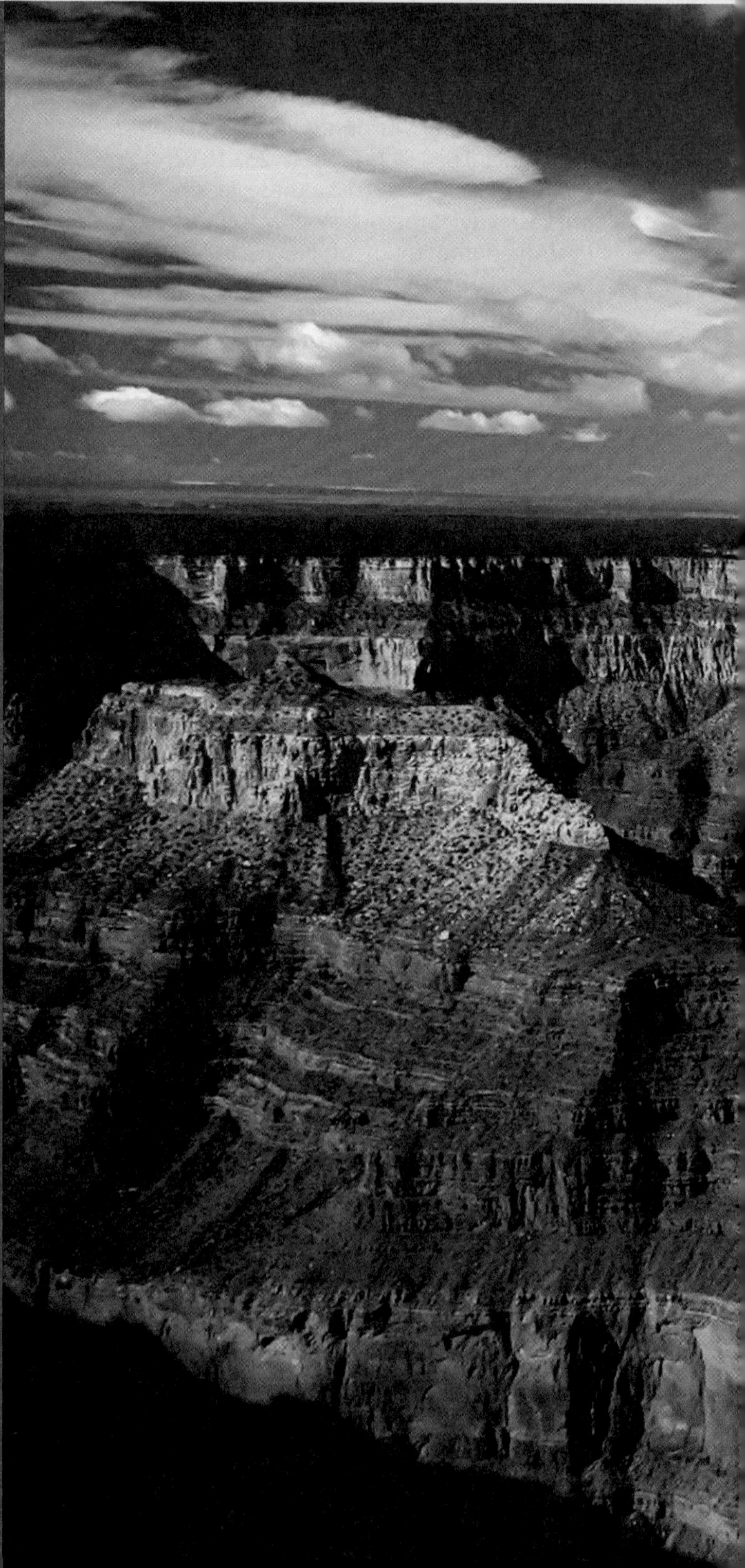

Chapter Preview

The rock layers exposed in Arizona's Grand Canyon contain clues to hundreds of millions of years of Earth history.

Inquiry Activity

What Can Become a Fossil?

Procedure

1. Your teacher will give you some samples of different organic materials. Organic material comes from a living thing.

2. Using a magnifying glass and microscope, examine each sample carefully.

3. Separate those items that you think have a good chance of becoming a fossil.

Think About It

1. **Observing and Inferring** What characteristics do the samples have that led you to select them as possible candidates for fossilization?

2. **Hypothesizing** What do you think needs to happen to these samples in order for them to become fossilized?

3. **Designing Experiments** Outline an experiment to test your answers to Questions 1 and 2.

12.1 Discovering Earth's History

Reading Focus

Key Concepts

- What are three main ideas of the science of geology?
- What are the key principles of relative dating?
- How do geologists interpret the rock record?

Vocabulary

- uniformitarianism
- relative dating
- law of superposition
- principle of original horizontality
- principle of cross-cutting relationships
- unconformity
- correlation

Reading Strategy

Identifying Main Ideas Copy and expand the table below. As you read, fill in the first column with a main idea and add details that support it in the second column.

Main Idea	Details
1. _____a. ?_____	_____b. ?_____
2. _____c. ?_____	_____d. ?_____
3. _____e. ?_____	_____f. ?_____

Figure 1 Exploring the Grand Canyon A John Wesley Powell, pioneering geologist and the second director of the U.S. Geological Survey **B** Start of the expedition from Green River station

In 1869, Major John Wesley Powell led a scientific expedition down the Colorado River and through the Grand Canyon. Powell and his crew traveled by boat through the canyon. They marveled at the canyon's huge walls made up of colorful sedimentary rocks. A veteran of the Civil War, Powell was also a geologist. To him, the walls of the Grand Canyon provided evidence of Earth's long history.

Before the 1800s, most scientists thought that Earth was only a few thousand years old. By John Wesley Powell's time, developments in the science of geology had led many scientists to change their ideas about Earth's age and history. Geologic time grew from thousands to many millions of years.

Studying Earth's History

For John Wesley Powell, and for geologists today, one goal of geology is to interpret Earth's history. Geologists do this by studying the rocks of the crust—especially sedimentary rocks. Together, these rocks make up the rock record of Earth's past. In studying Earth's history, geologists make use of three main ideas:

- the rock record provides evidence of geological events and life forms of the past;
- processes observed on Earth in the present also acted in the past;
- Earth is very old and has changed over geologic time.

Scientists in Europe and the British Isles began to develop these ideas during the 1700s, as they observed the landscapes around them. They wondered about the processes that formed mountains and the rock beneath the land surface. They noticed that sedimentary rocks were laid down in layers, and thought about how much time it must have taken for these layers to form.

In the late 1700s, James Hutton, a Scottish physician and gentleman farmer, published his *Theory of the Earth*. In this work, Hutton put forth the fundamental principle of **uniformitarianism,** which simply states that the physical, chemical, and biological laws that operate today have also operated in the geologic past. Uniformitarianism means that the forces and processes that we observe today have been at work for a very long time. To understand the geologic past, we must first understand present-day processes and their results.

Today, scientists understand that these same processes may not always have had the same relative importance or operated at precisely the same rate. Moreover, some important geologic processes are not currently observable, but evidence that they occur is well established. For example, we know that Earth has been hit by large meteorites even though we have no human witnesses. Such events altered Earth's crust, modified its climate, and strongly influenced life on the planet.

The acceptance of uniformitarianism meant the acceptance of a very long history for Earth. It is important to remember that although many features of our physical landscape may seem to be unchanging over our lifetimes, they are still changing, but on time scales of hundreds, thousands, or even millions of years.

 **Reading Checkpoint** **What is uniformitarianism?**

Relative Dating—Key Principles

During the 1800s, the geologists that followed William Hutton worked to interpret Earth's rock record. By studying layers of rock exposed at the surface, they inferred the order in which the layers had formed. The method that geologists used to place rocks in chronological order is called **relative dating**. Relative dating identifies which rock units formed first, second, third, and so on.

 🔑 **In relative dating, geologists follow several principles: the law of superposition, the principle of original horizontality, and the principle of cross-cutting relationships.** These principles help geologists determine the sequence in which events occurred, but not how long ago they occurred.

For: Links on relative dating
Visit: www.SciLinks.org
Web Code: cjn-4122

Kaibab Limestone

Toroweap Formation

Coconino Sandstone

Hermit Shale

Supai Group

Younger

A   **B**

Figure 2 Ordering the Grand Canyon's History The law of superposition can be applied to the layers exposed in the Grand Canyon. **Interpreting Illustrations** *Which layer is the oldest? The youngest?*

Law of Superposition Nicolaus Steno, a Danish anatomist, geologist, and priest (1636–1686), made observations that are the basis of relative dating. Based on his observations, Steno developed the **law of superposition.** The law of superposition states that in an undeformed sequence of sedimentary rocks, each layer is older than the one above it and younger than the one below it. Although it may seem obvious that a rock layer could not be deposited unless it had something older beneath it for support, it was not until 1669 that Steno stated the principle. This rule also applies to other surface-deposited materials, such as lava flows and layers of ash from volcanic eruptions. Applying the law of superposition to the layers exposed in the upper portion of the Grand Canyon, shown in Figure 2, you can easily place the layers in their proper order.

Figure 3 Disturbed Rock Layers Rock layers that are folded or tilted must have been moved into that position by crustal disturbances after their deposition. These folded layers are exposed in the Namib Desert (southwestern Africa).

Principle of Original Horizontality

Steno also developed the **principle of original horizontality.** The principle of original horizontality states that layers of sediment are generally deposited in a horizontal position. If you see rock layers that are flat, it means they haven't been disturbed and they are still in their original horizontal position. The layers in the Grand Canyon, shown on pages 334–335 and in Figure 2, clearly demonstrate this. However, the rock layers shown in Figure 3 have been tilted and bent. This tilting means they must have been moved into this position sometime after their deposition.

Reading Checkpoint

To what rock type can the law of superposition and the principle of original horizontality be best applied?

Principle of Cross-Cutting Relationships

Later geologists developed another principle used in relative dating. The **principle of cross-cutting relationships** states that when a fault cuts through rock layers, or when magma intrudes other rocks and hardens, then the fault or intrusion is younger than the rocks around it. For example, in Figure 4 you can see that Fault A occurred after the sandstone layer was deposited because it "broke" the layer. However, Fault A occurred before the conglomerate was laid down, because that layer is unbroken. Because they cut through the surrounding layers, the faults and dikes must have formed after those layers were deposited.

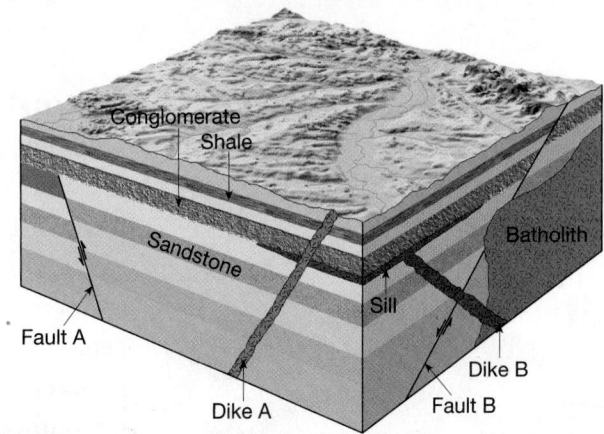

Figure 4 Cross-cutting Relationships An intrusive rock body is younger than the rocks it intrudes. A fault is younger than the rock layers it cuts.
Interpreting Diagrams *What are the relative ages of the batholith, dike B, dike A, and the sill?*

Reading the Rock Record

As they apply Steno's principles, geologists interpret, or "read," other geologic features to reconstruct Earth's history. Geologists also determine how the rocks in one area are related to similar rocks in other places. **Methods that geologists use to interpret the rock record include the study of inclusions and unconformities. Geologists also correlate rock layers at different locations.** By studying rocks from many different places worldwide, geologists can construct a model of the rock record. Such a model is called a *geologic column*. It is made up of rocks arranged according to their relative ages. The oldest rocks are at the bottom of the column, while the youngest rocks are at the top.

Inclusions Sometimes the study of inclusions can help the relative dating process. Inclusions are pieces of one rock unit that are contained within another. The rock unit next to the one containing the inclusions must have been there first in order to provide the rock fragments. Therefore, the rock unit containing inclusions is the younger of the two. Figure 5 provides an example. The photograph in Figure 5 shows inclusions of igneous rock within a layer of sedimentary rock. How did the inclusions get there? The inclusions indicate that the sedimentary layer was deposited on top of a weathered igneous mass. The sedimentary layer must be younger than the igneous rock because the sedimentary layer contains pieces of the igneous rock. We know the layer was not intruded upon by magma from below that later hardened, because the igneous rock shows signs of weathering.

Figure 5 Inclusions Inclusions made of older igneous rock can be found within younger sedimentary rock layers on top of the weathered igneous rock.

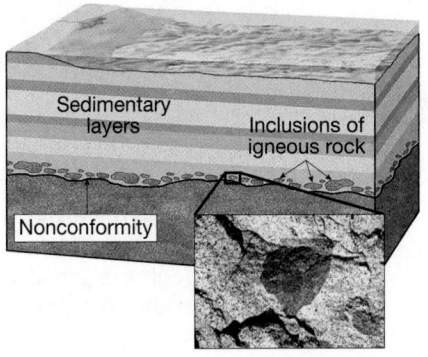

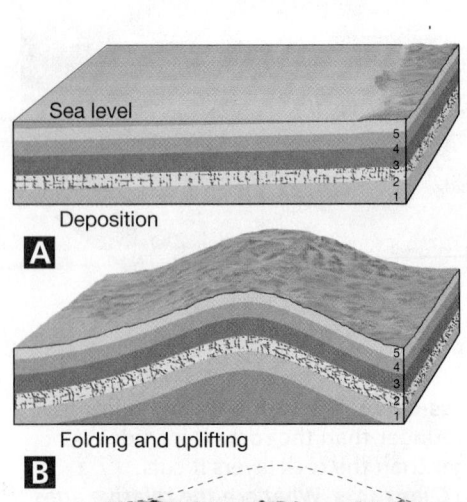

Sea level

Deposition

A

Folding and uplifting

B

Erosion

C

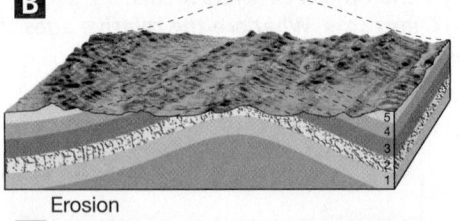

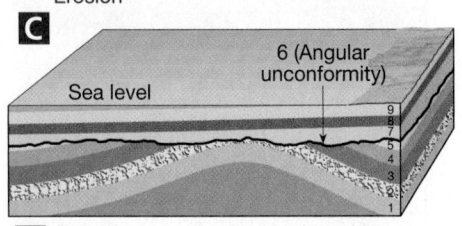

Sea level

6 (Angular unconformity)

D Subsidence and renewed deposition

Figure 6 Formation of an Angular Unconformity
An angular unconformity, (labeled as "6" in the diagram above) represents an extended period during which deformation and erosion occurred. The numbers show the sequence of geologic events.

Unconformities Throughout Earth's history, the deposition of sediment has been interrupted again and again. Nowhere is Earth's rock record complete. A surface that represents a break in the rock record is termed an **unconformity**. An unconformity indicates a long period during which deposition stopped, erosion removed previously formed rocks, and then deposition resumed. Unconformities help geologists identify what intervals of time are not represented in the rock record. There are three basic types of unconformities: angular unconformities, disconformities, and nonconformities.

In an angular unconformity, layers of sedimentary rock form over older sedimentary rock layers that are tilted or folded. Figure 6 shows the process that produces an angular unconformity.

In a disconformity, two sedimentary rock layers are separated by an erosional surface. Because the rocks on both sides of the unconformity are of the same type, disconformities can be difficult to recognize. Figure 7 shows disconformities in the Grand Canyon.

In a nonconformity, an erosional surface separates older metamorphic or igneous rocks from younger sedimentary rocks. Figure 7 shows a nonconformity in the Grand Canyon.

Correlating Rock Layers Interpreting unconformities helps geologists read the rock record in one location. Geologists use **correlation** to match rocks of similar age in different locations. Geologists often correlate layers by noting the position of a distinctive rock layer in a sequence of layers. They may find the distinctive layer in another location. If they do, then they can infer that the same layer once covered both locations.

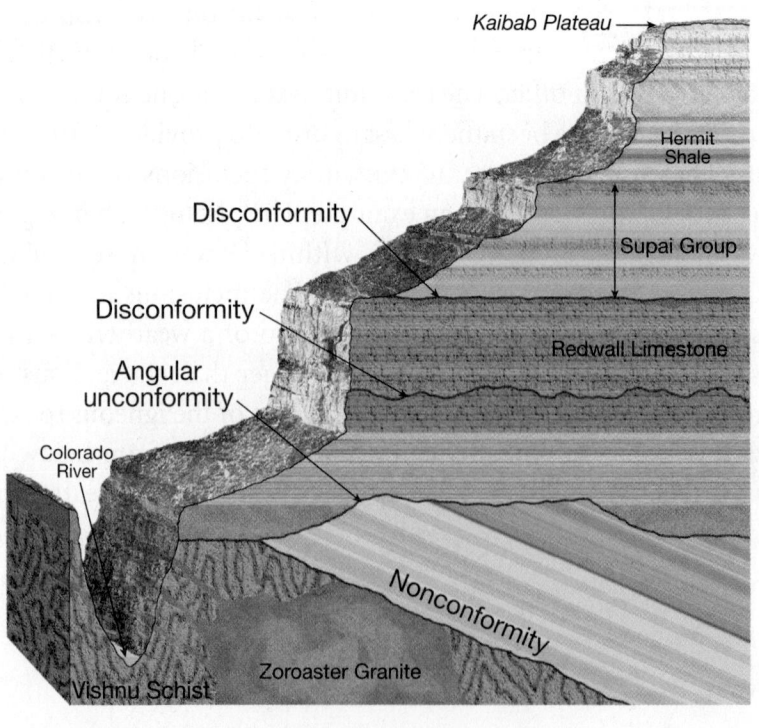

Kaibab Plateau

Hermit Shale

Supai Group

Redwall Limestone

Disconformity

Disconformity

Angular unconformity

Colorado River

Nonconformity

Zoroaster Granite

Vishnu Schist

Figure 7 Unconformities in the Grand Canyon This cross section through the Grand Canyon illustrates the three basic types of unconformities.

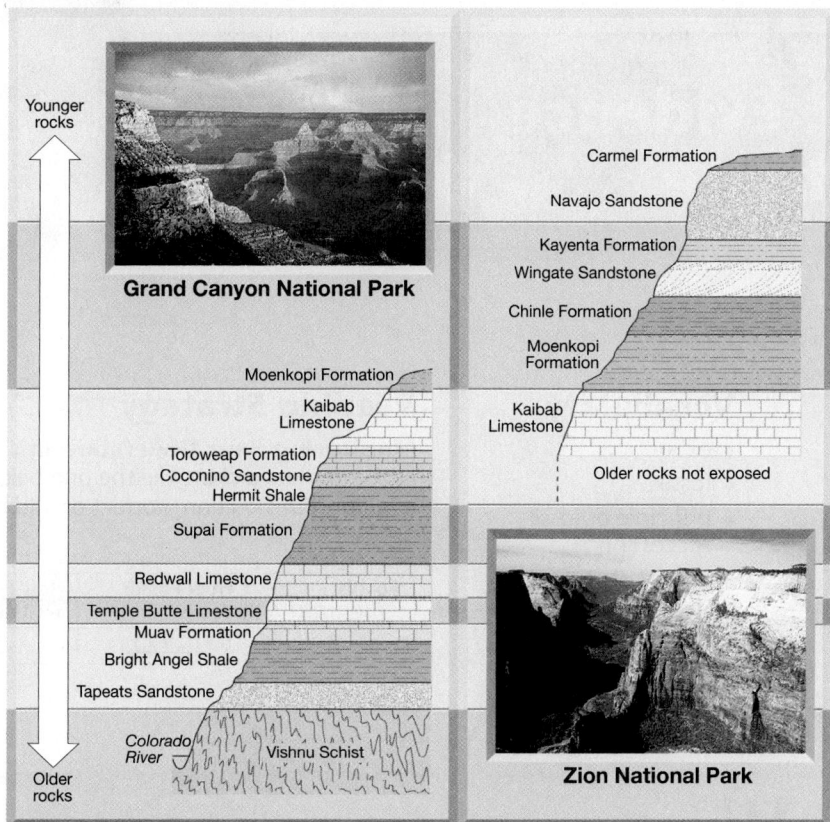

Figure 8 Correlation of rock layers at two locations on the Colorado Plateau: the Grand Canyon and Zion National Park. **Interpreting Diagrams** *Which rock layers are found in both canyons?*

By correlating the rocks from one place to another, it is possible to create a more complete view of the geologic history of a region. Figure 8, for example, shows the correlation of strata at two sites on the Colorado Plateau in southern Utah and northern Arizona. No single location contains the entire sequence. But correlation reveals a more complete picture of the sedimentary rock record.

Section 12.1 Assessment

Reviewing Concepts

1. 🔵 List three main ideas of the science of geology.
2. 🔵 List and briefly describe Steno's principles.
3. 🔵 In your own words, write definitions of inclusion, unconformity, and correlation.
4. What is the geologic column?

Critical Thinking

5. **Applying Concepts** How did the acceptance of uniformitarianism change the way scientists viewed Earth?
6. **Inferring** What can you infer about the age of sedimentary rock layers relative to the age of a sill intruded into those layers?

7. **Classifying** A geologist finds layers of sedimentary rocks immediately above an eroded anticline. What type of unconformity is this? Explain.
8. **Relating Cause and Effect** Why is the rock record for any given location on Earth incomplete?

Writing in Science

Descriptive Paragraph Imagine that you are hiking down into the Grand Canyon. Use some of Steno's principles to write a paragraph describing what you see, how old it all is, and how it was deposited.

12.2 Fossils: Evidence of Past Life

Reading Focus

Key Concepts

- What are the different types of fossils?
- What conditions help a fossil to form?
- What major developments helped scientists explain the fossil record?
- How do geologists interpret fossils and rocks?

Vocabulary

- extinct
- fossil
- principle of fossil succession
- theory of evolution
- natural selection
- adaptation
- index fossil

Reading Strategy

Monitoring Your Understanding Draw and complete a chart like the one below. After you finish this section, correct or add details as needed.

Fossils	How Fossils Form	How Fossils are Used
a. ___?___	b. ___?___	c. ___?___

Woolly mammoths once roamed the cold plains of northern Asia, North America, and Europe. Thousands of years ago, around the end of the last ice age, mammoths became extinct. An **extinct** organism is one that no longer exists on Earth. In the Arctic, scientists often find mammoth fossils, such as the huge tusks in Figure 1. A **fossil** is the remains or traces of an organism preserved from the geologic past.

Types of Fossils

Preserved remains, such as frozen mammoth fossils, are just one type of fossil. The different types of fossils include petrified fossils, molds and casts, carbon films, preserved remains, and trace fossils. Each type forms in a different way.

Figure 9 Preserved Remains The permafrost in Siberia preserved the frozen remains of this mammoth for thousands of years. Permafrost is a layer of ice that forms under land in the Arctic.

Petrified Fossils Fossils often form when an organism's remains become petrified, or "turned into stone." In this process, mineral-rich water soaks into the small cavities and pores of the original organism. The minerals precipitate from the water and fill the spaces. The petrified wood in Figure 10A formed in this way. Sometimes, minerals replace the cell walls or other solid material of an organism.

Molds and Casts Molds and casts are another common type of fossil. A fossil mold is created when a shell or other structure is buried in sediment and then dissolved by underground water. The mold reflects only the shape and surface markings of the organism. It doesn't reveal any information about its internal structure. Cast fossils (Figure 10B) are created if the hollow spaces of a mold are later filled with mineral matter.

Carbon Films Fossils called carbon films can preserve delicate details of leaves and animal parts. The formation of a carbon film begins when an organism is buried under fine sediment. Over time, pressure squeezes out liquids and gases and leaves behind a thin film of carbon, like that in Figure 10C. Black shale often contains carbon film fossils.

Sometimes, the carbon film itself is lost from a fossil. However, an impression of the fossil may remain. Impressions, like those of the fish in Figure 10D, often show fine details of an animal's structure.

Preserved Remains Sometimes, fossilization preserves all or part of an organism with relatively little change. The mammoth frozen in permafrost is one example. Another example is insects preserved in amber—the hardened resin, or sap, of ancient trees. The fly in Figure 10E was preserved after being trapped in a drop of sticky resin.

Fossils can also form when remains are preserved in tar. Tar is thick petroleum that collects in pools at the surface. The La Brea Tar Pits in Los Angeles, California, have yielded preserved remains of ice-age mammals such as mastodons and sabre-toothed cats.

Trace Fossils Trace fossils are indirect evidence of prehistoric life. Tracks, like those in Figure 10F, are animal footprints made of soft sediment that later changed to sedimentary rock. Burrows are holes made by an animal in sediment, wood, or rock that were later filled with mineral matter and preserved. Some of the oldest known fossils are believed to be worm burrows. Coprolites are fossils of dung and stomach contents. These can often provide useful information regarding the food habits of organisms. Gastroliths are highly polished stomach stones that were used in the grinding of food by some extinct reptiles.

Figure 10 Types of Fossilization
Six examples are shown here.
A Petrified wood in Petrified Forest National Park, Arizona **B** Natural casts of shelled organisms called ammonites **C** A fossil bee was preserved as a thin carbon film. **D** Impressions are common fossils and often show considerable detail. **E** An insect in amber **F** This dinosaur footprint was found in fine-grained limestone near Tuba City, Arizona.

For: Links on fossils in amber
Visit: PHSchool.com
Web Code: czd-4122

 **Reading Checkpoint** *What is a trace fossil?*

Conditions For Fossilization

All the fossils that geologists have found, arranged by their relative ages, make up the fossil record. But the fossil record includes only a fraction of the different kinds of organisms that have lived on Earth. Why? Some organisms are more likely than others to be preserved as fossils. **Two conditions that favor preservation of an organism as a fossil are rapid burial and the possession of hard parts.**

For a fossil to form, the remains of an organism must be buried quickly by sediment. Sediment protects the soft parts of a dead animal from being eaten by scavengers or decomposed by bacteria.

Organisms also have a better chance of being preserved if they have hard parts such as shells, bones, and teeth. Fossils of hard parts are more common than fossils of soft-bodied animals.

Fossils and the History of Life

During the 1700s and 1800s, some scientists thought that fossils might provide clues to the history of life on Earth. **Two major scientific developments helped scientists explain the fossil record: the principle of fossil succession and the theory of evolution.** According to the first, the fossil record showed that certain sets of organisms were characteristic of different periods in Earth's past. According to the second, living things had evolved, or changed, over time.

Fossil Succession The **principle of fossil succession** states that fossil organisms succeed one another in a definite and determinable order. Therefore, any time period can be recognized by its fossil content. This principle was developed by William Smith, an English engineer. Smith found that fossils weren't randomly distributed through rock layers. Instead, each layer contained a distinct assortment of fossils that did not occur in the layers above or below it. Smith's observations were confirmed by many geologists who followed.

Theory of Evolution Geologists had noticed that fossils from older rock layers were very different from the fossils in younger layers. English naturalist Charles Darwin developed a theory that helped to explain this fact.

In 1859, Darwin set forth the **theory of evolution**, which states that life forms have changed over time, or evolved, from simpler to more complex forms. To explain why evolution occurs, Darwin proposed the mechanism of natural selection. In **natural selection**, individuals that are better adapted to their environment are more likely to survive and reproduce than others of the same type. Organisms that are less well adapted are likely to become extinct.

Figure 11 This extinct water-dwelling mammal, *Ambulocetus natans*, evolved about 45 million years ago in south Asia. *Ambulocetus*, which means "walking whale," represents one stage in the evolution of modern whales from land animals.

Adaptation drives the process of evolution. Organisms possess certain traits, called **adaptations**, that affect their ability to survive and reproduce. Organisms that are well adapted to their environment survive. They pass on their traits to later generations. Thus, over time, one type of organism can evolve into a different type. For example, 50 million years ago, the ancestors of modern whales were land-dwelling mammals. The fossil record shows that, over millions of years, these mammals evolved adaptations for life in the oceans.

 **Reading Checkpoint** *What is an adaptation?*

Interpreting the Fossil Record

The principle of fossil succession and the theory of evolution helped geologists to interpret the fossil record. **Geologists used fossils to improve the correlation of rock layers and reconstruct past environments.**

Fossils and Correlation Geologists today use index fossils and groups of fossils to correlate rock layers. An **index fossil** is the fossil of an organism that was geographically widespread and abundant in the fossil record, but that existed for only a limited span of time. The presence of an index fossil in rock layers at different locations means that the layers are of roughly the same age.

Rock layers, however, do not always contain a specific index fossil. In this case, geologists can use groups of fossils to establish the relative age of the rock, as shown in Figure 12.

 Go **O**nline *active art*

For: Index fossil activity
Visit: www.PHSchool.com
Web Code: czp-4122

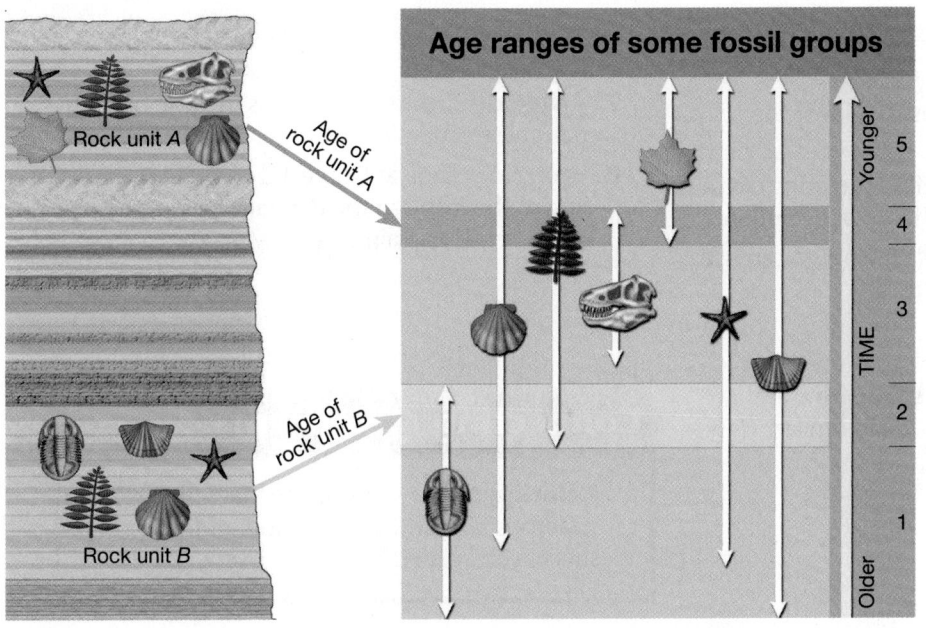

Figure 12 Correlating With Fossils Overlapping ranges of fossils help date rocks more exactly than using a single fossil. The fossils contained in rock unit A all have overlapping age ranges in time 4. The fossils in rock unit B have overlapping age ranges in time 2. Therefore, rock unit A was deposited in time 4, and rock unit B was deposited in time 2.

Figure 13 Fossil corals found in Texas limestone show this part of Texas was covered by a warm, tropical sea about 300 million years ago.

Fossils and Past Environments Fossils can also be used to reconstruct ancient environments. Because organisms evolve with adaptations suited to particular environments, fossils provide clues to the characteristics of those environments. For example, fossil teeth with flat surfaces suitable for grinding might be from an animal that ate grasses. If fossil pollen from grasses were abundant in the same rock layer, geologists could infer that the animal probably lived in a grassland.

Fossils can help geologists build an even more detailed picture of a past environment. Suppose geologists find fossil clam shells in limestone. They can infer that the region was once covered by a shallow sea. The geologists might also be able to conclude the approximate position of the ancient shoreline by observing the types and locations of fossils. For instance, fossil animals with thick shells capable of withstanding pounding waves must have lived near shorelines.

Fossils can also indicate the former temperature of the water. Certain present-day corals require warm and shallow tropical seas—like those around Florida and the Bahamas. When similar corals are found in ancient limestones, they indicate that a Florida-like marine environment must have existed when the corals were alive.

Section 12.2 Assessment

Reviewing Concepts

1. ◯ List the different types of fossils.
2. ◯ Describe the conditions that favor the formation of fossils.
3. ◯ In your own words, define the principle of fossil succession and the theory of evolution.
4. ◯ Describe two ways that geologists can use fossils to interpret Earth's history.

Critical Thinking

5. **Comparing and Contrasting** How are petrified fossils and carbon fossils similar? How are they different?

6. **Sequencing** Describe how a clam might become a fossil.
7. **Applying Concepts** What is the role of natural selection in evolution?
8. **Inferring** Look at Figure 12 on p. 345. Can any of the fossils in the diagram be used as an index fossil? Explain why or why not.

Connecting Concepts

Relating Ideas How are the law of superposition and the principle of fossil succession related?

12.3 Dating with Radioactivity

Early geologists like William Smith could only determine the relative ages of rock layers. They could not find exact dates for events in Earth's past. Today, geologists can determine the absolute age of a rock. A rock's absolute age is the approximate number of years before the present that the rock formed. For example, we know that Earth is about 4.56 billion years old and that the dinosaurs became extinct about 65 million years ago. To understand the method geologists used to arrive at these dates, you need first to understand radioactivity.

What Is Radioactivity?

Radioactivity is a process that involves the nucleus of the atom. Recall from Chapter 2 that each atom has a nucleus made up of protons and neutrons. The forces that bind protons and neutrons together in the nucleus are usually strong. However, in some atoms, the forces binding the protons and neutrons together are not strong enough, and the atoms are unstable. **During radioactive decay, unstable atomic nuclei spontaneously break apart, or decay, releasing energy.** The term for the process by which atoms decay is **radioactivity.** Figure 14 shows how radioactive decay releases energy in the form of three types of particles.

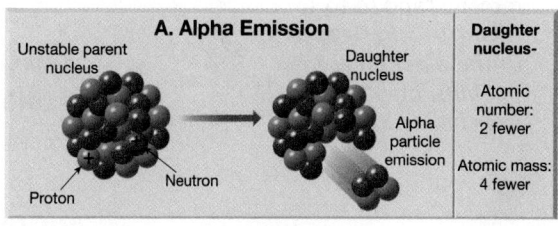

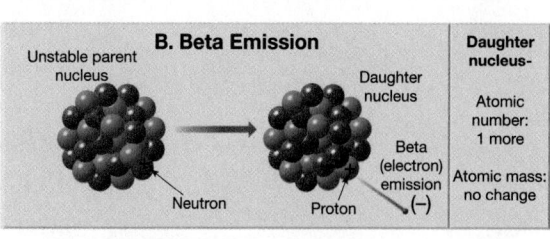

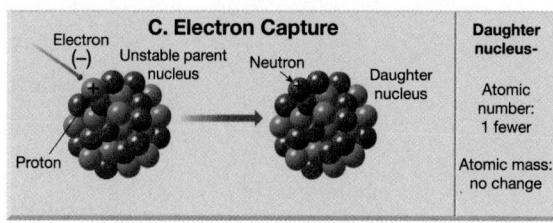

Figure 14 Radioactive Decay In each type of radioactive decay, the number of protons (atomic number) in the nucleus changes, thus producing a different element.

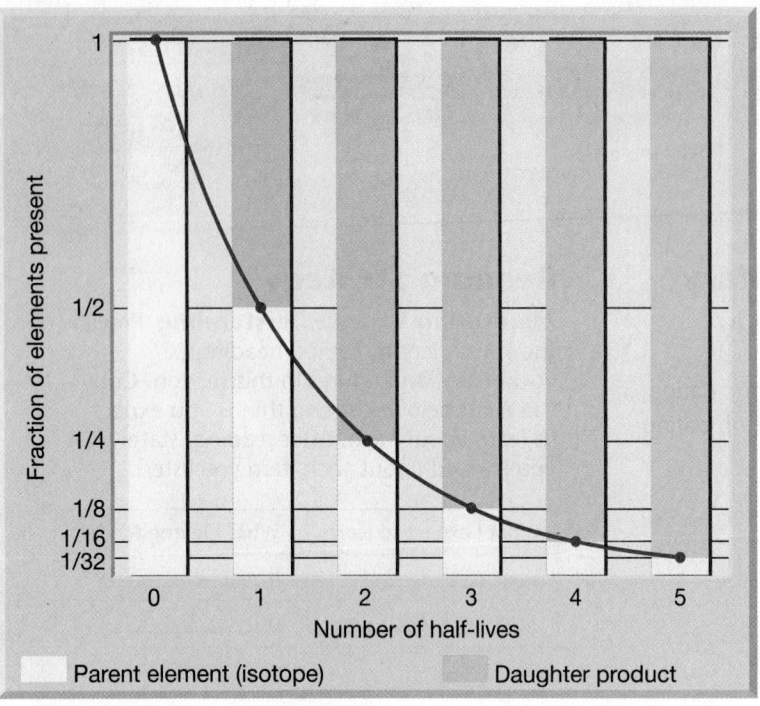

Parent element (isotope) **Daughter product**

Figure 15 The Half-Life Decay Curve The radioactive decay curve shows change that is exponential. Half of the radioactive parent remains after one half-life. After a second half-life, one quarter of the parent remains, and so forth. **Interpreting Graphs** *If $\frac{1}{32}$ of the parent material remains, how many half-lives have passed?*

Radioactive Isotopes Recall that the number of neutrons in the atoms of a given element can vary. These different forms of an element are called isotopes. An unstable, or radioactive, isotope of an element is called the parent. The isotopes that result from the decay of the parent are called the daughter products. What happens when unstable nuclei break apart? Radioactive decay continues until a stable or nonradioactive isotope is formed. For example, uranium-238 decays over time to form the stable isotope lead-206.

Half-Life A half-life is a common way of expressing the rate of radioactive decay. A **half-life** is the amount of time necessary for one half of the nuclei in a sample to decay to its stable isotope, as shown in Figure 15. If the half-life of a radioactive isotope is known and the parent/daughter ratio can be measured, the age of the sample can be calculated. For example, if the half-life of an unstable isotope is 1 million years, and $\frac{1}{16}$ of the parent isotope remains, this amount indicates that four half-lives have passed. The sample must be 4 million years old.

Radiometric Dating

Radiometric dating, also called radioactive decay dating, is a way of calculating the absolute ages of rocks and minerals that contain certain radioactive isotopes. **In radiometric dating, scientists measure the ratio between the radioactive parent isotope and the daughter products in a sample to be dated. The older the sample, the more daughter product it contains.**

How can a radioactive isotope serve as a reliable "clock"? The rates of decay for many isotopes have been precisely measured and do not vary under the physical conditions that exist in Earth's outer layers. Each radioactive isotope has been decaying at a constant rate since the formation of the rocks in which it occurs. The products of decay have also been accumulating at a constant rate. For example, when uranium is incorporated into a mineral that crystallizes from magma, lead isn't present from previous decay. The radiometric clock starts at this point. As the uranium decays, atoms of the daughter product (lead) are formed and begin to accumulate.

Of the many radioactive isotopes that exist in nature, five have proved particularly useful in providing radiometric ages for ancient rocks. The five radioactive isotopes are listed in Table 1.

Table 1 Radioactive Isotopes Frequently Used in Radiometric Dating

Radioactive Parent	Stable Daughter Product	Currently Accepted Half-Life Values
Uranium-238	Lead-206	4.5 billion years
Uranium-235	Lead-207	713 million years
Thorium-232	Lead-208	14.1 billion years
Rubidium-87	Strontium-87	47.0 billion years
Potassium-40	Argon-40	1.3 billion years

For igneous rock, radiometric dating establishes when minerals in the rock crystallized. For metamorphic rock, radiometric dating determines when heat and pressure caused new minerals to form in the rock or when daughter isotopes escaped from the minerals.

One frequently used type of radiometric dating is the potassium-argon method. In this method, geologists measure the ratio of radioactive potassium-40 atoms to stable argon atoms in a sample. Given the long half-life of potassium-40, this method can be used to date rocks that are hundreds of millions of years old. For example, geologists used potassium-argon dating to date lava from the Hawaiian islands.

An accurate radiometric date can be obtained only if the mineral remained in a closed system during the entire period since its formation. If the addition or loss of either parent or daughter isotopes occurs, then it is not possible to calculate a correct date. For example, an important limitation of the potassium-argon method stems from the fact that argon is a gas. Argon may leak from minerals and throw off measurements. Cross-checking of samples, using two different radiometric methods, is done whenever possible to ensure accuracy.

Although the basic principle of radiometric dating is simple, the actual procedure is complex. The analysis that determines the quantities of parent and daughter must be very precise. In addition, some radioactive materials do not decay directly into the stable daughter product. Uranium-238, for example, produces thirteen intermediate unstable daughter products before the fourteenth and final daughter product, the stable isotope lead-206, is produced.

 **Reading Checkpoint** *What is the potassium-argon method of radiometric dating?*

For: Links on radioactive dating
Visit: www.SciLinks.org
Web Code: cjn-4124

Dating with Carbon-14

To date organic materials, carbon-14 is used in a method called **radiocarbon dating.** Organic material is a substance that contains carbon and comes from a living thing. Carbon-14 is the radioactive isotope of carbon. Carbon-14 is continuously produced in the upper atmosphere. It quickly becomes incorporated into carbon dioxide, which circulates in the atmosphere and is absorbed by living matter. As a result, all organisms—including you—contain a small amount of carbon-14.

While an organism is alive, the decaying radiocarbon is continually replaced. Thus, the ratio of carbon-14 to carbon-12—the stable isotope of carbon—remains constant. **When an organism dies, the amount of carbon-14 gradually decreases as it decays. By comparing the ratio of carbon-14 to carbon-12 in a sample, radiocarbon dates can be determined.**

Because the half-life of carbon-14 is only 5730 years, it can be used to date recent geologic events up to about 75,000 years ago. The age of the object shown in Figure 16 was determined using radiocarbon dating. Carbon-14 has become a valuable tool for anthropologists, archaeologists, and historians, as well as for geologists who study recent Earth history.

Figure 16 Carbon-14 is used to date organic materials that formed up to about 75,000 years ago.

 Reading Checkpoint

What is compared when dating with carbon-14?

Radiometric Dating of Sedimentary Rock

Radiometric dating can rarely be used to date sedimentary rocks directly. Sedimentary rocks may contain particles that can be dated. But these particles are not the same age as the rocks in which they occur. The sediment from which the rock formed probably weathered from older rocks. Radiometric dating would not be accurate since the sedimentary rock is made up of so many older rock particles.

Geologists have developed an indirect method of dating sedimentary rocks. **To determine the age of sedimentary rock, geologists must relate the sedimentary rock to datable masses of igneous rock.** Applying Steno's principles, geologists identify two igneous rock masses. One rock mass must be relatively older than the sedimentary rock. The other rock mass must be younger. Then they use radiometric methods to date the two igneous rock masses. The age of the sedimentary rock must lie between the ages of the igneous rocks.

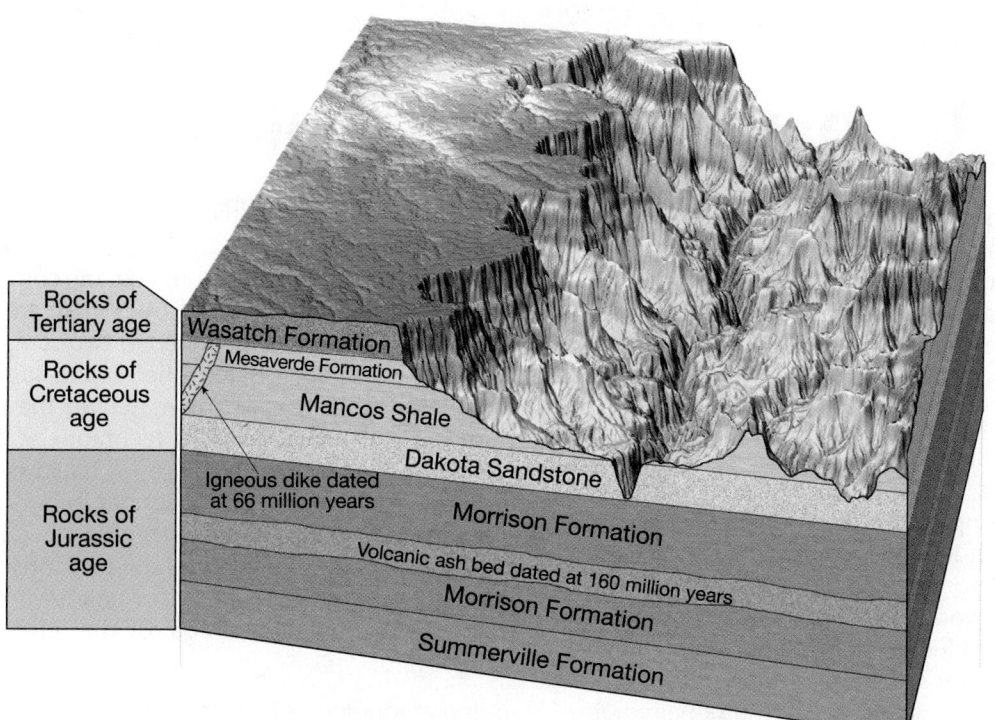

Look at Figure 17. Using the principle of superposition, you can tell that all the layers above the volcanic ash are younger than the ash. Using the principle of cross-cutting relationships, you can see that the dike is younger than the layers it cuts across. Therefore, the age of the sedimentary layers in between must lie between the ages of the two igneous features.

Figure 17 Sedimentary rock layers can be dated in relation to igneous rocks of known age—in this case, the volcanic ash bed and the igneous dike.
Inferring *What can you infer about the age of the Dakota sandstone?*

Section 12.3 Assessment

Reviewing Concepts

1. What happens to atoms that are radioactive?

2. What is the role of isotopes in radiometric dating?

3. Describe radiocarbon dating.

4. How do geologists use radiometric dating to date sedimentary rock layers indirectly?

Critical Thinking

5. **Applying Concepts** A geologist wants to use potassium-argon dating to date a granite rock found on the surface. What is a possible source of inaccuracy in dating the rock?

6. **Classifying** Which of the following could *not* be dated using radiocarbon dating: charcoal, wooden beam, clay pot, food in the clay pot? Explain.

7. **Interpreting Diagrams** Look at Figure 17 above. What can you infer about the absolute age of the Wasatch Formation in relation to the igneous dike?

Writing in Science

Descriptive Paragraph Discuss the use of radiocarbon dating in determining the age of an ancient civilization.

Dating With Tree Rings

The dating and study of annual rings in trees is called *dendrochronology*. Dendrochronology provides useful numerical dates for events in the historic and recent prehistoric past. Because tree rings are a storehouse of data, they are a valuable tool in the reconstruction of past environments.

If you look at the top of a tree stump or at the end of a log, you will see that it is made of a series of concentric rings, like those shown in Figure 18. Every year in temperate regions, trees add a layer of new wood under the bark. Each of these tree rings becomes larger in diameter outward from the center. During favorable environmental conditions, a wide ring is produced. During unfavorable environmental conditions, a narrow ring is produced. Trees growing at the same time in the same region show similar tree-ring patterns.

Because a single growth ring is usually added each year, you can determine the age of the tree by counting the rings. Cutting down a tree to count the rings is not necessary anymore. Scientists can use small, non-destructive core samples from living trees.

To make the most effective use of tree rings, extended patterns known as ring chronologies are established. They are produced by comparing the patterns of rings among trees in an area. If the same pattern can be identified in two samples, one of which has been dated, the second sample can be dated from the first by matching the ring pattern common to both. This technique, called cross dating, is illustrated in Figure 19. It allows the ages of tree remains that are no longer living to be dated. Tree-ring chronologies extending back for thousands of years have been established for some regions. To date a timber sample of unknown age, its ring pattern is matched against the reference chronology.

Tree-ring chronologies have important applications in such disciplines as climate, geology, ecology, and archaeology. For example, tree rings are used to reconstruct long-term climate variations within a certain region. Knowledge of such variations is of great value in studying and understanding the recent record of climate change.

Figure 18 Each year's growth for a tree can be seen as a ring. Because the amount of growth (thickness of a ring) depends upon precipitation and temperature, tree rings are useful records of past climates.

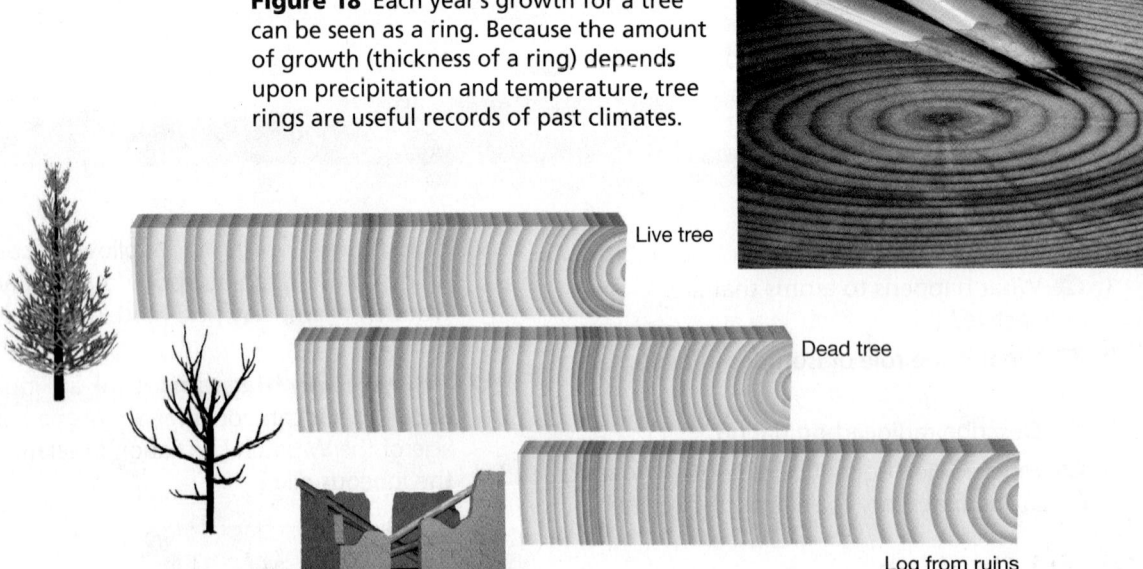

Live tree

Dead tree

Log from ruins

Figure 19 Using Tree Rings to Date Ancient Civilizations Cross dating is used to date an archaeological site by correlating tree-ring patterns using wood from trees of three different ages. First, a tree-ring chronology for the area is established using cores extracted from living trees. This chronology is extended further back in time by matching overlapping patterns from older, dead trees. Finally, cores taken from beams inside the ruin are dated using the chronology established from the other two sites.

12.4 The Geologic Time Scale

Reading Focus

Key Concepts

- What is the geologic time scale?
- How is the geologic time scale constructed?

Vocabulary

- geologic time scale
- eon
- Precambrian time
- era
- period
- epoch

Reading Strategy

Outlining As you read, make an outline of the important ideas in this section. Use the green headings as the main topics and fill in details from the remainder of the text.

The Geologic Time Scale
I. Structure of the Time Scale
A. _____?_____
B. _____?_____

You may have seen a timeline of major events in human history. Such a timeline might include events like the Industrial Revolution and the Apollo moon landings. Geologists have developed a timeline for events in Earth's history. The **geologic time** scale is a timeline that divides Earth's history into units representing specific intervals of time. **The geologic time scale is a record that includes both geologic events and major developments in the evolution of life.**

Geologists developed the geologic time scale during the 1800s. They used the fossil record to arrange Earth's rocks in chronological order by relative age. During the 1900s, radiometric dating enabled scientists to add dates to the geologic time scale. Today, geologists continue to revise the time scale as dating techniques improve and as new discoveries change their views of Earth's long history.

Structure of the Time Scale

The geologic time scale is divided into eons, eras, periods, and epochs. **Eons represent the longest intervals of geologic time. Eons are divided into eras. Each era is subdivided into periods. Finally, periods are divided into still smaller units called epochs.** Figure 21 shows the structure of the geologic time scale. In general, the breaks between units on the time scale mark major geologic events or changes in life forms, or both.

Figure 20 These cliffs on the coast of England are made of rock that formed about 200 million years ago. Over geologic time, forces in the crust slowly bent the rock's flat-lying layers into folds.

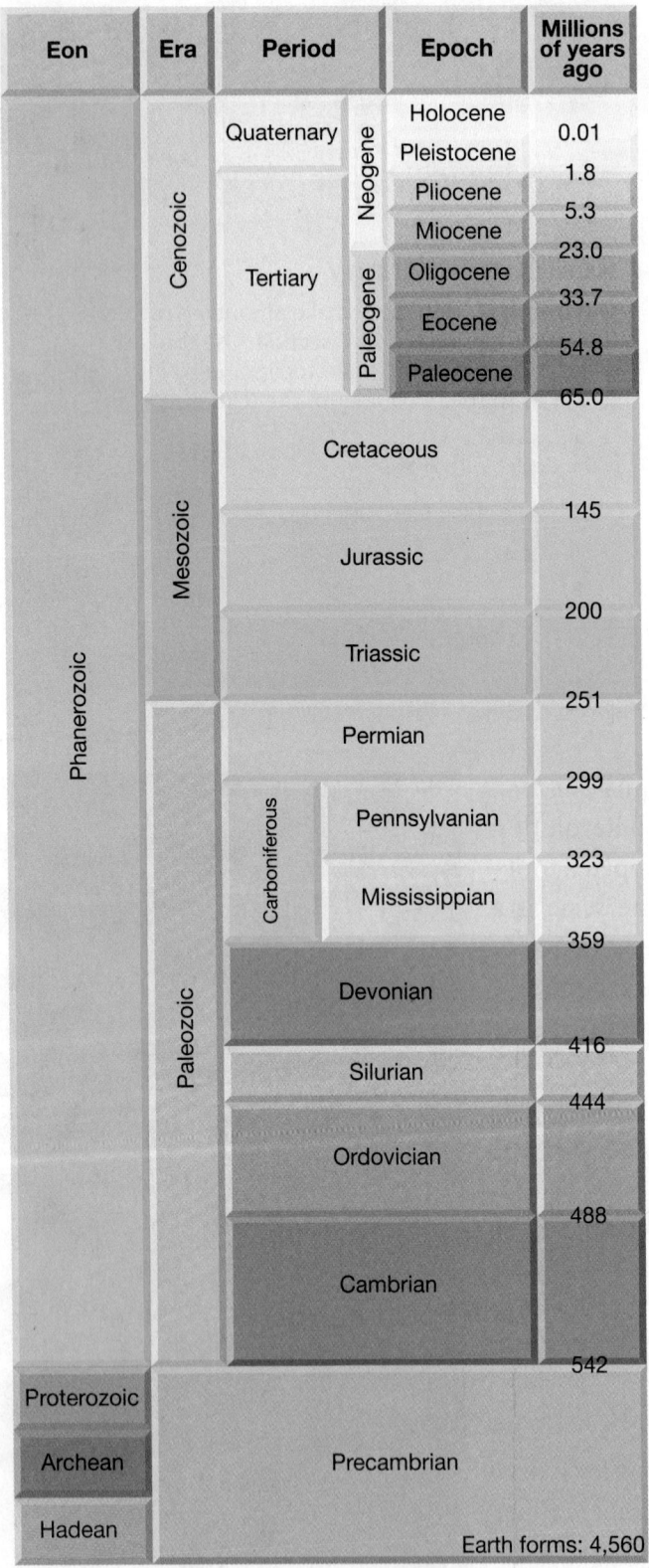

Eon	Era	Period		Epoch	Millions of years ago
Phanerozoic	Cenozoic	Quaternary	Neogene	Holocene	0.01
				Pleistocene	1.8
				Pliocene	5.3
		Tertiary		Miocene	23.0
			Paleogene	Oligocene	33.7
				Eocene	54.8
				Paleocene	65.0
	Mesozoic	Cretaceous			145
		Jurassic			200
		Triassic			251
	Paleozoic	Permian			299
		Carboniferous	Pennsylvanian		323
			Mississippian		359
		Devonian			416
		Silurian			444
		Ordovician			488
		Cambrian			542
Proterozoic		Precambrian			
Archean					
Hadean				Earth forms: 4,560	

Figure 21 The Geologic Time Scale The Phanerozoic eon is broken into more subdivisions than earlier eons. Yet the Phanerozoic makes up only about 12 percent of Earth's history. This figure is not drawn to scale.

Eons Geologists divide Earth's history into four long units called **eons**. About 88 percent of geologic time is made up of the first three of these eons—the Hadean, Archaean, and Proterozoic. During these eons, Earth formed, the atmosphere and oceans developed, and early life evolved.

Another term for this long time span is **Precambrian time**. Precambrian fossils are scarce. One reason for this is that there is very little Precambrian rock left at the surface. Over billions of years, most Precambrian rocks have been eroded or metamorphosed, destroying or altering fossils. In addition, for most of Earth's history life existed only as single-celled organisms, and these do not leave easily identifiable fossils. Only very late in the Precambrian did multi-celled organisms evolve in the oceans.

About 540 million years ago, the Phanerozoic eon began. The term *Phanerozoic* comes from the Greek words meaning "visible life." The term is appropriate because the rocks of this eon contain abundant fossils. These fossils document the evolution of more complex life forms.

Notice on the time scale the many subdivisions of the Phanerozoic. These subdivisions reflect the large amount of data that geologists have about the rocks and fossils of the Phanerozoic in comparison with data from earlier eons.

 **Reading Checkpoint** *What is Precambrian time?*

Eras There are three **eras** within the Phanerozoic eon: the Paleozoic, Mesozoic, and Cenozoic eras. The term *Paleozoic* comes from the Greek words for "ancient life." During the Paleozoic era, most of the major groups of organisms that live on Earth today evolved. For example, vertebrates (animals with backbones) and plants appeared.

The term *Mesozoic* means "middle life." During the Mesozoic era, forests developed on land and many types of reptiles, including dinosaurs, became abundant. Later in the Mesozoic, the first mammals evolved.

The term *Cenozoic* means "recent life." During the Cenozoic era, many different types of mammals and birds evolved, and flowering plants became abundant.

The fossil record shows that the Paleozoic and Mesozoic eras both ended with dramatic, worldwide changes in life forms. Many types of organisms became extinct, although others survived. The Cenozoic era continues today.

Periods and Epochs Each era is subdivided into **periods**. Different geologic events, environmental conditions, and life forms characterize each period. For example, the Carboniferous period is named for the large coal deposits that formed during that period. *Carboniferous* means "carbon bearing." Other geologic periods are named for the region where geologists first described the period's rocks and fossils. For example, Jurassic refers to the Jura Mountains of France and Switzerland.

Traditionally, geologists divided the Cenozoic era into two periods: the Tertiary and Quaternary. Today, most geologists divide the Cenozoic into the Paleogene and Neogene, as show in Figure 21. The periods of the Cenozoic are divided into still smaller units called **epochs**. For example, we live in the Holocene epoch of the Quaternary (or Neogene) period. The epochs of other periods, however are not usually referred to by specific names. Instead, the terms *early*, *middle*, and *late* are generally applied to the epochs of these earlier periods.

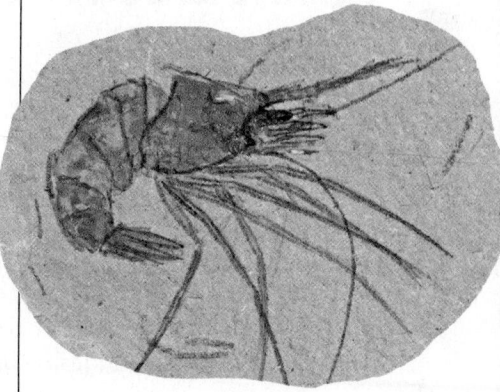

Figure 22 An imprint fossil preserves fine details of this shrimp from the Cretaceous period.

For: Links on the geologic time scale
Visit: www.SciLinks.org
Web Code: cjn-4125

Section 12.4 Assessment

Reviewing Concepts

1. What is the geologic time scale?
2. What subdivisions make up the geologic time scale?
3. How is the geologic time scale today different from the geologic time scale developed by geologists in the 1800s?
4. Why are there more subdivisions of the time scale for the Phanerozoic eon than for earlier eons?

Thinking Critically

5. **Interpreting Diagrams**   To which era does each of the following periods belong: Ordovician, Tertiary, Permian, Triassic?
6. **Calculating** What percentage of geologic time is made up of the Cenozoic era?

Writing in Science

Writing a Definition Research one of the periods of the geologic time scale. Write a definition of the period that includes the name of the era to which the period belongs, when the period began and ended, one major event from the period, and an explanation of the period's name.

Fossil Occurrence and the Age of Rocks

Groups of fossil organisms occur in the rock record for specific intervals of time. This time interval is called the fossil's range. Knowing the range of the fossils of specific organisms, or groups of organisms, can be used to find the relative age of rock layers. In this laboratory exercise, you will use such information to assign a date to a hypothetical unit of rock.

Problem
How can the occurrence of fossils and their known age ranges be used to date rocks?

Materials
- geologic time scale
- graph paper
- pencil

Skills
Interpreting Diagrams, Graphing, Hypothesizing, Inferring

Procedure

1. A section of rock made up of layers of limestone and shale has been studied and samples have been taken. A large variety of fossils were collected from the rock samples. Use a sheet of graph paper to make a bar graph using the information shown in the Fossil Data Table. Begin by listing the types of fossils on the horizontal axis. Use Figure A to list the units of the geologic time scale on the vertical axis.

2. Transfer the range data of each fossil onto your graph. Draw an X in each box, beginning at the oldest occurrence of the organism up to the youngest occurrence. Shade in the marked boxes. You will end up with bars depicting the geologic ranges of each of the fossils listed.

3. Examine your graph. Are there any time units that contain all of the fossils listed? Write this time period at the bottom of the graph.

	Type of Fossil	Oldest occurrence	Youngest occurrence
		Fossil Data Table	
1	Foraminifera	Silurian	Quaternary
2	Bryozoan	Silurian	Permian
3	Gastropod	Devonian	Pennsylvanian
4	Brachiopod	Silurian	Mississippian
5	Bivalve	Silurian	Permian
6	Gastropod	Ordovician	Devonian
7	Trilobite	Silurian	Devonian
8	Ostracod	Devonian	Tertiary
9	Brachiopod	Cambrian	Devonian

Analyze and Conclude

1. **Reading Graphs** What is the age of the hypothetical rock layer that these fossils were collected from?

2. **Inferring** Based on the age determined, do you think that this group of fossils could be considered index fossils? Why or why not?

3. **Inferring** Suppose that the particular trilobite listed in line 7 of the data table is limited to rocks of lower Devonian age and that these trilobite fossils are widespread throughout North America. Can this fossil be considered an index fossil? Why or why not?

4. **Connecting Concepts** The fossils in this group were collected from limestone and shale rocks. Based on what you have learned about the formation of these rock types, what type of environment did these organisms live in?

5. **Understanding Concepts** Shale often contains fossils of leaves. If the gastropods listed in line 3 and line 6 were collected from shale containing leaf fossils, could you use radiocarbon dating to assign a numerical date to this rock unit? Explain.

Go Further Use the library or Internet to research these fossils. Find out how some of them are used in the oil industry or the cosmetics industry.

Era	Period		Epoch	Millions of years ago
Cenozoic	Quaternary	Neogene	Holocene	0.01
			Pleistocene	1.8
	Tertiary		Pliocene	5.3
			Miocene	23.0
		Paleogene	Oligocene	33.7
			Eocene	54.8
			Paleocene	65.0
Mesozoic	Cretaceous			145
	Jurassic			200
	Triassic			251
Paleozoic	Permian			299
	Carboniferous	Pennsylvanian		323
		Mississippian		359
	Devonian			416
	Silurian			444
	Ordovician			488
	Cambrian			542
	Precambrian			

The Geologic Time Scale

12.1 Discovering Earth's History

Key Concepts

- In studying Earth's history, geologists make use of three main ideas:
  - the rock record provides evidence of geological events and life forms of the past;
  - processes observed on Earth in the present also acted in the past;
  - Earth is very old and has changed over geologic time.
- In relative dating, geologists follow several principles: the law of superposition, the principle of original horizontality, and the principle of cross-cutting relationships.
- Methods that geologists use to interpret the rock record include the study of inclusions and unconformities. Geologists also correlate rock layers at different locations.

Vocabulary

uniformitarianism, *p. 337;* relative dating, *p. 337;* law of superposition, *p. 338;* principle of original horizontality, *p. 338;* principle of cross-cutting relationships, *p. 339;* unconformity, *p. 340;* correlation, *p. 341*

12.2 Fossils: Evidence of Past Life

Key Concepts

- The different types of fossils include petrified fossils, molds and casts, carbon films, preserved remains, and trace fossils.
- Two conditions that favor preservation of an organism as a fossil are rapid burial and the possession of hard parts.
- Two major scientific developments helped scientists explain the fossil record: the principle of fossil succession and the theory of evolution.
- Geologists used fossils to improve the correlation of rock layers and reconstruct past environments.

Vocabulary

extinct, *p. 342;* fossil, *p. 342;* principle of fossil succession, *p. 344;* theory of evolution, *p. 344;* natural selection, *p. 344;* adaptation, *p. 345;* index fossil, *p. 345*

12.3 Dating with Radioactivity

Key Concepts

- During radioactive decay, unstable atomic nuclei spontaneously break apart, or decay, releasing energy.
- In radiometric dating, scientists measure the ratio between the radioactive parent isotope and the daughter products in a sample to be dated. The older the sample, the more daughter product it contains.
- When an organism dies, the amount of carbon-14 gradually decreases as it decays. By comparing the ratio of carbon-14 to carbon-12 in a sample, radiocarbon dates can be determined.
- To determine the age of sedimentary rock, geologists must relate the sedimentary rock to datable masses of igneous rock.

Vocabulary

radioactivity, *p. 347;* half-life, *p. 348;* radiometric dating, *p. 348;* radiocarbon dating, *p. 350*

12.4 The Geologic Time Scale

Key Concepts

- The geologic time scale is a record that includes both geologic events and major developments in the evolution of life.
- Eons represent the longest intervals of geologic time. Eons are divided into eras. Each era is subdivided into periods. Finally, periods are divided into still smaller units called epochs.

Vocabulary

geologic time scale, *p. 353;* eon, *p. 354;* Precambrian time, *p. 354;* era, *p. 355;* period, *p. 355;* epoch, *p. 355*

Reviewing Content

1. What principle states that the physical, chemical and biological laws that operate today have also operated in the geologic past?
   a. uniformitarianism
   b. theory of evolution
   c. principle of original horizontality
   d. law of superposition

2. What is the name of the process that matches up rocks of similar ages in different regions?
   a. indexing
   b. correlation
   c. succession
   d. superposition

3. What name is given to fossils that are widespread geographically, are abundant in number, and are limited to a short span of time?
   a. key
   b. succeeding
   c. relative
   d. index

4. What is the name of the process during which atomic nuclei decay?
   a. fusion
   b. correlation
   c. nucleation
   d. radioactivity

5. Which unit of geologic time is the greatest span of time?
   a. era
   b. eon
   c. period
   d. epoch

6. What are remains or traces of prehistoric life called?
   a. indicators
   b. replicas
   c. fossils
   d. fissures

7. What name is given to layers of tilted rocks that are overlain by younger, more flat-lying rock layers?
   a. disconformity
   b. angular unconformity
   c. nonconformity
   d. fault

8. What are atoms with the same atomic number but different mass numbers called?
   a. protons
   b. isotopes
   c. ions
   d. nucleotides

9. Which of Steno's principles states that most layers of sediments are deposited in flat-lying layers?
   a. original horizontality
   b. cross-cutting relationships
   c. fossil succession
   d. superposition

10. What name is given to pieces of rock that are contained within another, younger rock?
    a. intrusions
    b. interbeds
    c. hosts
    d. inclusions

11. About how old is Earth?
    a. 4,000 years
    b. 4.0 million years
    c. 5.8 million years
    d. 4.56 billion years

Understanding Concepts

12. How have the processes that affect Earth's surface changed through time?

13. Why does the law of superposition apply primarily to sedimentary rocks?

14. How are cross-cutting relationships used in relative dating?

15. How do unconformities form?

16. List and briefly describe three different types of fossils.

17. What two conditions increase an organism's chance of becoming a fossil?

18. What did Darwin propose as the mechanism of evolution? Explain.

19. Why can certain fossils, such as corals, be used to indicate former water temperature?

20. What is a half-life?

21. Explain how radioactivity and radiometric dating are related.

22. Why can't radiometric dating be used with accuracy on metamorphic rocks?

Critical Thinking

23. Comparing and Contrasting Compare the techniques of relative dating to those of radioactive decay dating.

24. Drawing Conclusions Why can't carbon-14 be used to date material that is older than 75,000 years?

25. Making Connections Why is it important to have a closed system when using radioactive decay dating?

26. Predicting An analysis of some sedimentary rocks suggests the environment was close to the shoreline where high energy waves hit the shore. Corals and shelled organisms lived here. Describe what their fossils would be like.

27. Applying Concepts Why is radioactive decay dating the most reliable method of dating the geologic past?

Analyzing Data

Refer to the diagram to answer Questions 28 and 29.

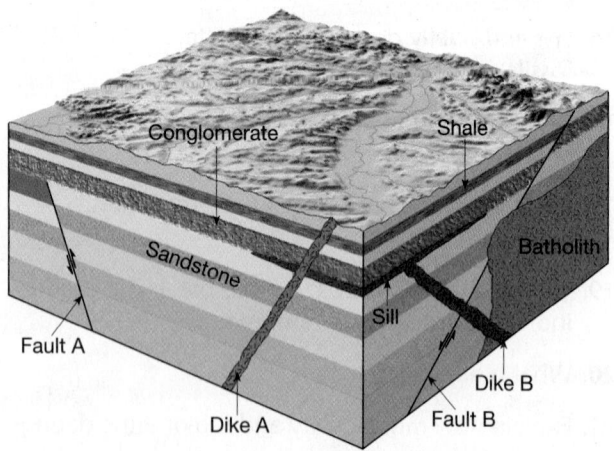

28. Which fault is older, A or B? Explain how you know.

29. Which dike is older, A or B? Explain how you know.

30. Calculating A sample of potassium-40 has a mass of 12.5 grams. If the sample originally had 50 grams of potassium-40 at the start of radioactive decay, how many half-lives have passed? The half-life of potassium-40 is 1.3 billion years. How old is the sample?

Concepts in Action

31. Applying Concepts Fossilized human remains are sometimes found in bogs in northwestern Europe. These bogs are wet, low-oxygen areas that contain decaying plant material. How would you go about dating such a fossil?

32. Comparing and Contrasting Apply the concept of uniformitarianism to explain how a particular sequence of rock layers could be interpreted as a former ocean coastline. (*Hint:* compare what you might see at a modern shoreline to what you would see in the rocks).

33. Predicting An organism evolves with certain adaptations for survival on a wet, tropical island. Over millions of years, plate movements shift the island into a cooler, drier climate. What might happen to this type of organism over time?

34. Calculating Nuclear power plants produce radioactive waste that must be stored properly until it is no longer harmful to life on Earth. Uranium-238 has a half-life of 4.5 billion years. If, in order to be safe, a uranium sample must decay to 1/64 of its original amount, for how many years must the waste be stored?

Performance-Based Assessment

Describing and Classifying Create a poster illustrating the different ways that fossils can form. Be sure to include altered and unaltered remains with examples of both. If possible, include samples of fossils that are found in your area.

Standardized Test Prep

Simplify the Diagram

When examining a diagram, it is important not to be confused by unnecessary information. It helps to identify only the features that relate to the question being asked. Reread the question with these features in mind and then answer the question. In the diagram below, you do not need to know what rock types are present.

How can you tell that dike C is older than fault H?

(A) The top of dike C is eroded.
(B) Dike C is broken by fault H.
(C) Fault H ends at the eroded layer E.
(D) Both dike C and fault H end at layer E.

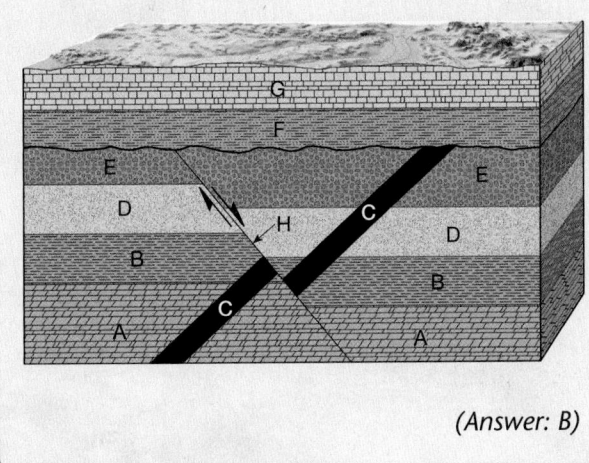

(Answer: B)

Choose the letter that best answers the question or completes the statement.

1. Who was the scientist that formulated the theory of uniformitarianism?
(A) Charles Darwin
(B) James Hutton
(C) William Smith
(D) Louis Agassiz

2. Using relative dating methods, which of the following are scientists able to do?
(A) Identify the order in which rock units formed.
(B) Assign a numerical date to each rock layer studied.
(C) Determine the age of the fossils within each layer.
(D) Identify what rock types are present.

Use the diagram below to answer Questions 3–5.

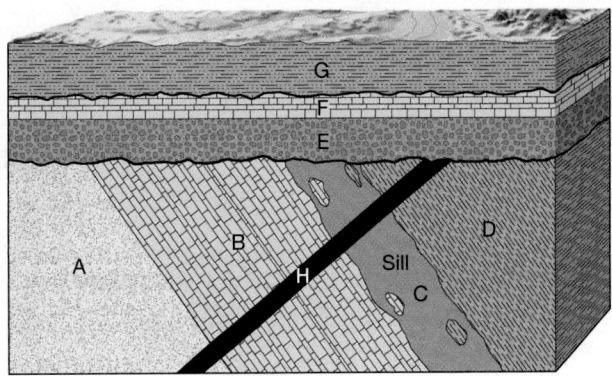

3. Which choice correctly lists the order in which rock layers A through D formed?
(A) A, B, C, D
(B) D, C, B, A
(C) B, C, D, A
(D) A, B, D, C

4. When were rock layers A through D uplifted and tilted?
(A) after deposition of layer G
(B) after deposition of layer F and before deposition of layer G
(C) after deposition of layer D and before deposition of layer E
(D) after deposition of layer A and before deposition of layer G

5. When was sill C intruded? Explain.

Answer the following in complete sentences.

6. Explain why decay rates can be used with confidence in radiometric dating.

7. Describe the relationship between uniformitarianism and time.

8. Explain the difference in fossilization between a mammoth frozen in ice and a seashell embedded in rock.

9. Explain why the time periods of the Paleozoic and Mesozoic are subdivided into early, middle, and late instead of named epochs, as they are in the Cenozoic.

This photograph shows petrified logs in the Rainbow Forest bed of Petrified Forest National Park in Arizona.

What caused the Permian mass extinction?

The Permian mass extinction was the most devastating event in the history of life on Earth. About 95 percent of all living species were destroyed. Scientists have several theories about how this occurred. In a work group, have each group member research the evidence in favor of one of the theories. In a presentation to the class, describe the time period, what species were common on Earth, and what groups survived the mass extinction. Then present the evidence for the theories in the form of a mock debate among group members. Have the class vote for the most likely theory, based on the evidence.

Quick Lab
Relative Dating

Exploration Lab
Modeling the Geologic Time Scale

 GEODe

Geologic Time
↳ Geologic Time Scale

Chapter Preview

Inquiry > Activity

What Are Fossils?

Procedure

1. Obtain and observe some examples of fossils. You may either find and collect examples of real fossils, get them from your teacher, or use pictures of fossils.

2. Share the fossils with your classmates so that you can observe several examples.

Think About It

1. **Observing** What kinds of organisms do the fossils show? What can you tell about the ancient organisms from these fossils?

2. **Inferring** How do you think these fossils were formed? What conditions were necessary for their formation?

13.1 Precambrian Time

Reading Focus

Key Concepts

- What were the major geologic developments during Precambrian time?

- What were the major developments in living things during Precambrian time?

Vocabulary

- shields
- photosynthesis
- stromatolites
- prokaryotes
- eukaryotes

Reading Strategy

Building Vocabulary Use the information about the vocabulary terms in this section to complete these phrases.

1. Shields are composed of a. __?__ ; are evidence of b. __?__ ; and are significant to Precambrian time because c. __?__ .

2. Stromatolites are composed of d. __?__ ; are evidence of e. __?__ ; and are significant to Precambrian time because f. __?__ .

Geologists travel to Isua, Greenland, to study some of Earth's oldest rocks. Radiometric dating shows that the rocks of the Isua greenstone belt are about 3.8 billion years old. Geologists think that Isua greenstone began as volcanic rock that formed under water. Over billions of years, heat and pressure changed the rock to greenstone, a metamorphic rock.

Traces of carbon in Isua greenstone rocks led some scientists to suggest that life existed as long as 3.8 billion years ago. But other scientists who studied these rocks concluded that the carbon probably was not from living things. It's very difficult to interpret the rock record of Earth's early history!

Figure 1 Isua Greenstone These metamorphic rocks found in Greenland are among the oldest known rocks on Earth.

Precambrian Earth

Geologists know little about early Precambrian time, when the Isua greenstone formed. Most rocks from this time have been eroded away, subducted, or greatly metamorphosed. Relative dating of Precambrian rocks is difficult because the rocks rarely contain fossils. Yet key geologic events occurred during Precambrian time. **Earth formed about 4.56 billion years ago. During Precambrian time, the atmosphere and oceans formed and plate tectonics began to build up continental landmasses.** You will learn how scientists determined the age of Earth and the solar system in Chapter 23.

Earth Forms Scientists hypothesize that Earth formed as gravity pulled together dust, rock, and ice in space. As Earth grew, its gravity increased, pulling in more of these materials. The high-velocity impact of rocks from space caused the planet to melt. Radioactive decay was also generating much more heat than at the present time. Melting permitted the most dense materials, such as iron and nickel, to sink toward Earth's center. Less dense materials, such as silicates, "floated," forming layers that became the mantle and crust. Over several hundred million years, the crust and mantle cooled and hardened, forming rock.

The Atmosphere Evolves Today, the air you breathe is a stable mixture of nitrogen, oxygen, a small amount of argon, and trace gases like carbon dioxide and water vapor. But our planet's original atmosphere, several billion years ago, was far different. Earth's original atmosphere was made up of gases similar to those released in volcanic eruptions—water vapor, carbon dioxide, nitrogen, and several trace gases, but no oxygen. Scientists think that as Earth's crust cooled, gases that had been dissolved in molten rock were gradually released.

Some of Earth's earliest life forms dramatically changed the makeup of Earth's atmosphere by using carbon dioxide and releasing oxygen. Slowly, the atmosphere's oxygen content increased. The Precambrian rock record suggests that much of this free oxygen combined with iron. Iron combines with oxygen to form iron oxides, or rust. Large deposits of iron-rich Precambrian sedimentary rocks, called banded iron formations, provide evidence of this process. Once the available iron finished reacting, about 2.5 billion years ago, oxygen began to accumulate in the atmosphere.

The Oceans Form Earth's oceans formed as the planet continued to cool. The water vapor condensed to form clouds, and great rains began. At first the rainwater evaporated in the hot air before reaching the ground or quickly boiled or evaporated when it did reach the ground. This evaporation sped up the cooling of Earth's surface. Torrential rains continued and slowly filled low areas, forming the oceans. This reduced not only the water vapor in the air but also the amount of carbon dioxide, which became dissolved in the water. A nitrogen-rich atmosphere remained.

Figure 2 Precambrian Time Precambrian time is made up of the Hadean, Archaean, and Proterozoic eons.
Reading Timelines *About how long ago did oxygen begin to build up in the atmosphere?*

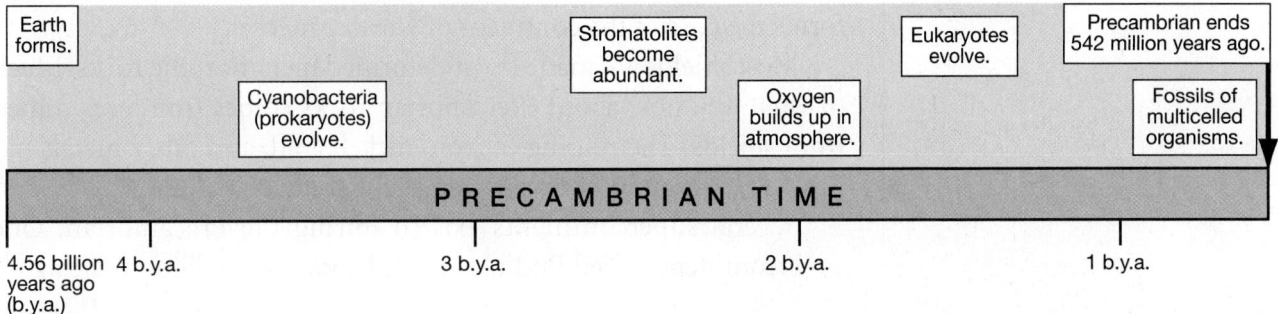

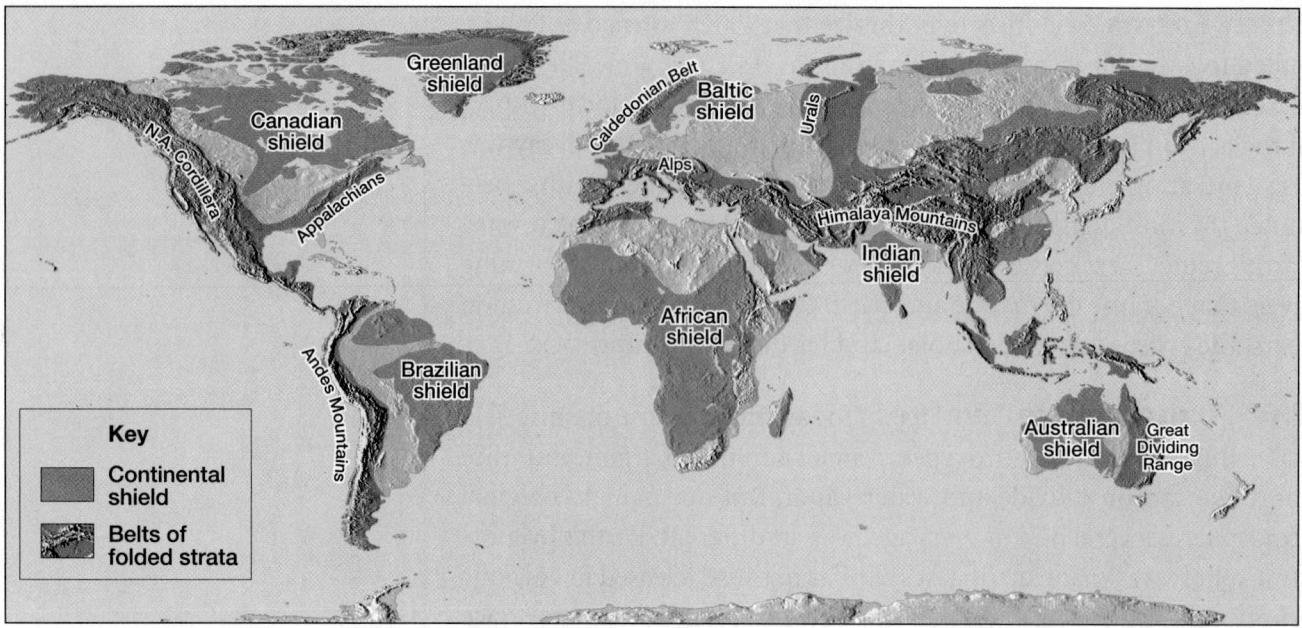

Figure 3 Remnants of Precambrian rocks are the continental shields. They are largely made up of metamorphosed igneous and sedimentary rocks.

Continents Develop Geologists think that small continents began to form about 500 million years after Earth's formation. As on Earth today, mantle convection drove the processes of plate tectonics. Tectonic forces caused early continents to grow by accretion and to split apart by rifting. For example, there is evidence that the Isua greenstone was accreted to Greenland's continental crust.

At the same time the rock cycle began. The early continents were made up of granitic igneous rock that was less dense than the volcanic rock of the oceanic crust. Weathering and erosion led to the formation of sedimentary rocks. Tectonic forces and volcanic activity in the crust helped to form metamorphic rocks.

Today, if you could view Earth from space, you would see relatively little Precambrian rock exposed at the surface. As you would expect from the Law of Superposition, most Precambrian rocks are buried beneath more recent rocks. But Precambrian rocks are exposed where younger rock layers are extensively eroded. Examples include the Grand Canyon and some mountain ranges. There are, however, large core areas of Precambrian rocks that make up the surface of some continents. These areas are called **shields** because they roughly resemble a warrior's shield in shape. The Canadian Shield, shown in Figure 3, forms the core of the continent of North America.

Most shields are made up of deformed metamorphic rocks. Much of what we know about Precambrian rocks comes from ores mined from shields. The mining of iron, nickel, gold, and other metals has provided Precambrian rock samples for study.

Several supercontinents existed during the Precambrian. One supercontinent, called Rodinia, existed about 800 million years ago.

Precambrian Life

Most Precambrian fossils are so small they are called microfossils. To study microfossils, geologists make very thin slices of rock that can be viewed under a microscope. Using microfossils and other evidence, geologists have begun to reconstruct life's early history. **The earliest life probably evolved in the oceans. Later, one-celled organisms evolved that used light energy to produce food through photosynthesis. These organisms consisted of simple cells called prokaryotes. Slowly, more complex cells, called eukaryotes, evolved. Late in the Precambrian, multi-celled organisms with soft bodies evolved.** As you read about the evolution of Precambrian life, remember that this process took nearly 4 billion years!

The Earliest Life Scientists do not know when life appeared on Earth or what it may have looked like. Because water is needed for most life processes of living things, the earliest life probably evolved in the oceans. Some scientists think that the first organisms might have resembled the bacteria found near hydrothermal vents in the deep ocean. You will learn more about these bacteria in Chapter 15.

Photosynthetic Organisms Precambrian rocks from about 3.5 billion years ago contain fossils of one-celled organisms. These organisms resemble modern cyanobacteria. Cyanobacteria are one-celled organisms that make their own food through photosynthesis. In **photosynthesis**, organisms use carbon dioxide and the energy of sunlight to make food in the form of carbohydrates. Photosynthesis releases oxygen into the environment.

Geologists have found trace fossils left by cyanobacteria from Precambrian time. The fossils are stromatolites, shown in Figure 4. **Stromatolites** are layered mounds of calcium carbonate deposited by cyanobacteria. Stromatolites closely resemble similar deposits made by modern bacteria. Today, stromatolites are relatively rare. They occur in warm, shallow water along sheltered coastlines. Geologists infer that Precambrian stromatolites formed in similar environments.

Figure 4 Stromatolites (left) are among the most common Precambrian fossils. These modern cyanobacteria (right) are similar to those that formed ancient stromatolites.

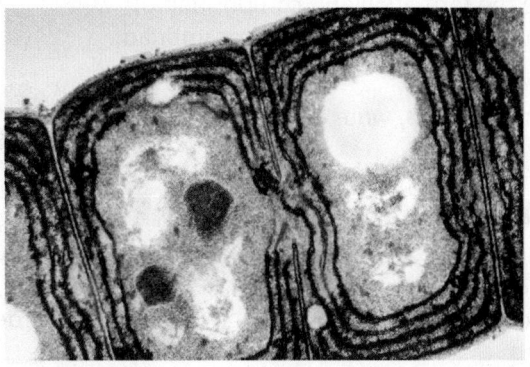

Prokaryotes and Eukaryotes During Precambrian time, two different groups of organisms evolved—prokaryotes and eukaryotes. Cyanobacteria belong to a group of simple one-celled organisms called prokaryotes. A **prokaryote** is a cell that lacks a nucleus. Earth's earliest organisms were prokaryotes.

About 1.8 billion years ago, cells evolved that were larger and more complex than prokaryotes. These cells, called **eukaryotes**, had nuclei. Geologists have found fossil eukaryotes—red and green algae that are about one billion years old. Many early eukaryotes were one-celled organisms. But unlike prokaryotes, eukaryotes can also be made up of many cells.

Multicelled Organisms The development of eukaryotes led to dramatic evolutionary change. Fossil evidence shows that the earliest animals had evolved by late in Precambrian time.

What did these early animals look like? In the 1940s, geologists found strange-looking fossils in the Ediacara Hills in southern Australia. The fossils were about 600 million years old. The Ediacaran fossils are molds and casts of soft-bodied animals. They resemble worms, jellyfish, and corals living in the oceans today. To be preserved as fossils, these animals must have been rapidly buried in fine sediment.

It's not known how, or if, Ediacaran animals are related to later organisms. Fossils of Ediacaran animals have since been found in many other parts of the world.

**Figure 5
Ediacaran Organisms**
Scientists have used 600-million-year-old Ediacaran fossils (left) to reconstruct what Earth's first multicelled organisms may have looked like (above).

Section 13.1 Assessment

Reviewing Concepts

1. 🕮 List the major geologic developments of the early Precambrian.
2. 🕮 Describe the major events in the history of life during the Precambrian.
3. Describe the formation and composition of Earth's atmosphere early in the Precambrian.
4. What is a shield?
5. In your own words, write a definition of *photosynthesis*.

Critical Thinking

6. **Relating Cause and Effect** How did the composition of the atmosphere change during the middle Precambrian? Explain.

7. **Applying Concepts** Why are stromatolites considered trace fossils?
8. **Comparing and Contrasting** How are prokaryotes and eukaryotes similar? How are they different?
9. **Inferring** Why are there relatively few fossils of late Precambrian animals?

Connecting Concepts

Earth's Early Eons Review the Geologic Time Scale in Chapter 12. Use library or Internet resources to research one of the eons of Precambrian time. Write a paragraph describing the major events of the eon.

13.2 Paleozoic Era: Life Explodes

Reading Focus

Key Concepts

- What kinds of environmental changes have affected the evolution of life?

- What were the major developments in Earth's geology and life forms during the Paleozoic era?

Vocabulary

- ◆ mass extinction
- ◆ Gondwana
- ◆ Laurasia
- ◆ amphibian
- ◆ reptile

Reading Strategy

Identifying Details Copy the table below. As you read, fill out the table with notes.

	Geologic Developments	Developments in Life Forms
Cambrian Period		
Ordovician Period		
Silurian Period		

What kind of organism formed the weird fossil in Figure 6? Scientists think that trilobites, which are now extinct, were related to insects and shrimp. Trilobites were among the first animals to have a hard outer covering. Throughout the Paleozoic era, there were major developments in the evolution of life. Many of these developments occurred in response to environmental change.

Each type, or species, of organism needs a certain environment in order to survive. If temperature, water, or food supply change too much, the species must evolve new adaptations or it will become extinct. **Environmental changes that have affected the course of evolution on Earth include the formation and breakup of continents, mountain building, volcanic activity, changes in climate, and changes in sea level.** Such changes have affected evolution throughout geologic time. Rapid change can lead to the extinction of many groups of organisms in a relatively short time, in an event called a **mass extinction.** But the fossil record shows that after each mass extinction, life rebounded as many new species evolved.

Cambrian Period

As during Precambrian time, life in the early Paleozoic was restricted to the seas. But the Cambrian period brought dramatic changes to Earth. **Many new groups of organisms evolved in a relatively short time in an event called the "Cambrian Explosion."**

Figure 6 Trilobite Fossil
Trilobites evolved early in the Paleozoic era.

Figure 7 From the Burgess shale fossils, scientists have reconstructed some of the animals of the Cambrian Explosion.

Figure 8 Paleozoic Era
During the Paleozoic, life forms evolved that could live on land.
Reading Timelines *During which period did the supercontinent Pangaea form?*

Cambrian Earth Geologic developments contributed to the Cambrian Explosion. The breakup of the supercontinent Rodinia formed many pieces of continents. New environments formed in the shallow seas between these pieces, some of which lay near the equator. Earth continued to warm after an ice age that had chilled the planet in the late Precambrian. This warming trend may have been a factor in the evolution of new living things.

Cambrian Life As a result of the Cambrian Explosion, the number of different kinds of organisms increased greatly in only 15 million years. Cambrian organisms are well known from the Burgess shale, a fossil-rich formation in the Canadian Rockies. Most Burgess shale fossils belong to several groups of invertebrates. An invertebrate is an animal that lacks a backbone. But the Burgess shale fossils also include early ancestors of vertebrates—animals with backbones. Figure 7 shows how scientists have reconstructed Burgess shale animals and their environment.

Cambrian animals were the first to evolve hard parts such as shells. The shells of mollusks, such as clams and snails, protected them. Shells also allowed body organs to function in a more controlled environment. Animals called arthropods evolved that had an external skeleton made of a protein called chitin. Modern arthropods include insects and crustaceans. One arthropod that evolved early in the Cambrian was the trilobite. A trilobite's exoskeleton permitted it to burrow through soft sediment in search of food. More than 600 types of these mud-burrowing scavengers evolved worldwide.

Geologists have found limestones from the Cambrian period that began as reefs in the oceans. A reef is deposited by living things or formed from their remains. Cambrian reefs were made up of the remains of sponges or mats of material produced by cyanobacteria.

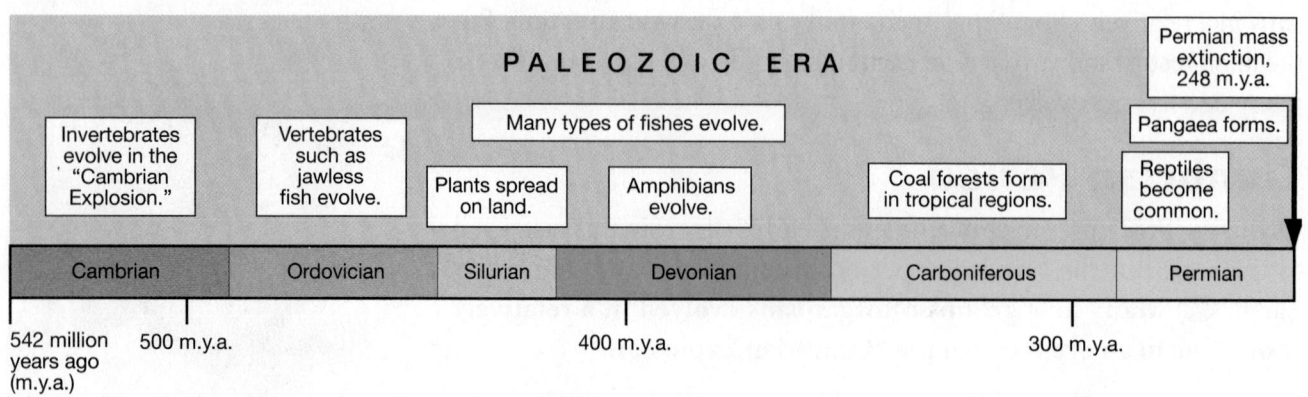

PALEOZOIC ERA

| | | | | | Permian mass extinction, 248 m.y.a. |

Invertebrates evolve in the "Cambrian Explosion."

Vertebrates such as jawless fish evolve.

Many types of fishes evolve.

Pangaea forms.

Plants spread on land.

Amphibians evolve.

Coal forests form in tropical regions.

Reptiles become common.

| Cambrian | Ordovician | Silurian | Devonian | Carboniferous | Permian |

542 million years ago (m.y.a.)   500 m.y.a.   400 m.y.a.   300 m.y.a.

Ordovician Period

 **During the Ordovician period, more complex communities of organisms developed in the oceans. The first land-dwelling plants evolved.** The period ended with a mass-extinction.

Ordovician Earth Plate movements pushed the huge landmass of **Gondwana** south during the Ordovician. Parts of five of today's continents made up Gondwana—South America, Africa, Australia, Antarctica, and parts of Asia. Collisions between landmasses near the equator led to mountain building in what is now eastern North America.

Ordovician Life During the Ordovician period, the diversity of organisms living in the oceans increased. For example, reef-building invertebrates called bryozoans evolved, along with early corals. Trilobites continued to be abundant, and shelled organisms called brachiopods became even more common. Brachiopods are among the most widespread Paleozoic fossils. Vertebrates became more common as jawless fishes evolved. Jawless fishes had a bony, external covering. They were the ancestors of later groups of fishes.

Another major development of the Ordovician was the evolution of land plants. These first plants resembled small, primitive plants such as liverworts. They lived in moist areas and reproduced through spores, not seeds. As plants multiplied on land, they added oxygen to the atmosphere.

Geologists think that an ice age caused a mass extinction at the end of the Ordovician. Volcanic eruptions may have contributed to this event.

Figure 9 Cephalopods, trilobites, brachiopods, snails, and corals inhabited the waters of the Ordovician period.

Reading Checkpoint *What is a brachiopod?*

Silurian Period

🔵 **The Silurian Period was a time of reef-building and continued evolution of fishes in the seas. By the end of the period, plants and animals were becoming widespread on land.**

Silurian Earth As you can see in Figure 11, the main part of Gondwana was centered on the South Pole during the Silurian period. In the tropics, shallow seas covered the vast plains of North America. Why did this occur? Parts of continents can rise or sink below sea level if plate motions upwarp or downwarp the crust. Also, several factors caused sea levels to rise, flooding low-lying parts of continents. Large barrier reefs formed in these shallow seas. The reefs restricted circulation between shallow marine basins and the open ocean. Water in these basins evaporated, depositing large quantities of rock salt and gypsum.

Silurian Life In the oceans, reef-building corals evolved during the Silurian period. Jawless fish survived, developing thick armor plates. The first jawed fish also evolved. Other ocean organisms of this period include strange-looking arthropods called eurypterids, shown in Figure 10.

On land, small plants similar to mosses spread over moist, lowland areas. During the Silurian, the first vascular plants evolved. The stem of a vascular plant contains thin tubes that carry liquids within the plant. These early plants were leafless spikes about the size of your index finger. There is also evidence from trace fossils that arthropods began to adapt to life on land during the Silurian period.

Figure 10 This eurypterid was a predator that lived in the ocean during the Silurian period.

Devonian Period

🔵**During the Devonian period, jawed fishes and sharks evolved in the seas. Plants continued to colonize the land, along with insects and other small arthropods. Later, amphibians evolved with adaptations for life on land.**

Devonian Earth A world map of Earth during the Devonian period would show two large continents. Gondwana still occupied a large part of the southern hemisphere. To the north, continental landmasses collided to form a new large continent, called **Laurasia**. Laurasia included what is now North America, Europe, and parts of Asia. As Europe and North America collided, mountains formed. Today, rocks from this mountain-building event make up part of the Appalachian Mountains.

Because Laurasia lay across the equator, western North America had a tropical climate. The interior of Laurasia would have been hot and dry.

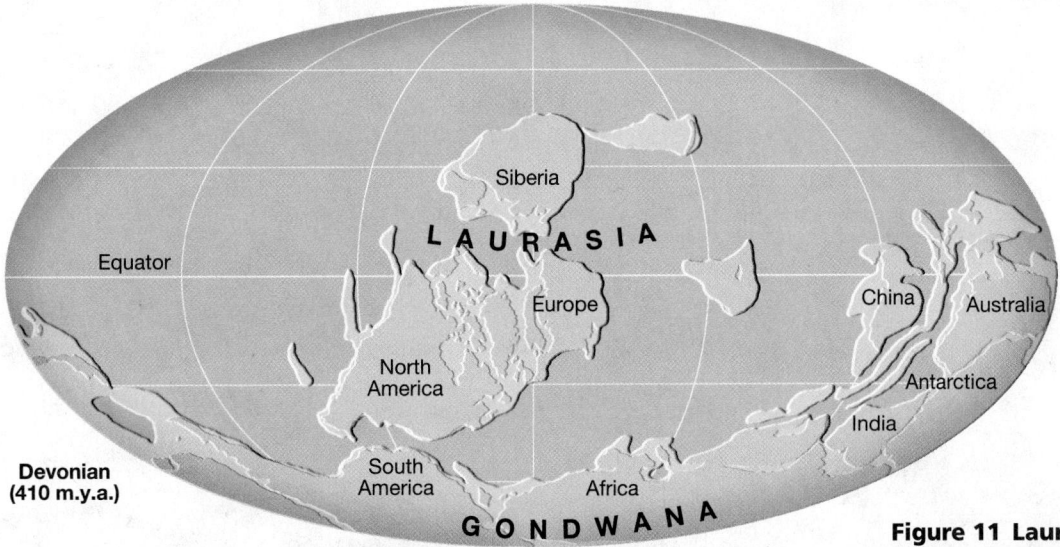

Devonian
(410 m.y.a.)

Figure 11 Laurasia and Gondwana The supercontinent Gondwana drifted toward the south pole during the Silurian. During the Devonian, Laurasia formed.

Devonian Life   Major developments in Devonian seas included the appearance of many new types of jawed fishes and the evolution of sharks. These jawed fishes had bony skeletons like those of present-day fishes. Sharks, in contrast, have skeletons made of softer material called cartilage. Reefs formed by sponges and new types of corals continued to form in tropical seas.

As land plants continued to evolve, the first forests developed. The Devonian forest was made up of large clubmosses, tree ferns, and twiglike plants called horsetails. Small fernlike plants covered the ground. There is fossil evidence that wingless insects, spiders, and centipedes lived in Devonian forests.

Toward the end of the Devonian, amphibians evolved from fishes. An **amphibian** is a four-legged animal, with lungs for breathing, that can live on land, but that lays its eggs in water. Frogs, toads, and salamanders are descended from early amphibians.

The fishes from which amphibians evolved probably lived in tidal flats or small ponds. They had primitive lungs as well as gills for breathing. They probably used their fins to push themselves along in soft mud. Eventually, these fishes evolved into true air-breathing amphibians with fishlike heads and tails, but with four legs. Many types of amphibians rapidly evolved because they had little competition from other land animals. Amphibians could eat the plants and insects that were already abundant on land.

Two mass extinctions struck Earth toward the end of the Devonian Period. The first affected mainly ocean organisms. For example, jawless and armored fishes became extinct.

Figure 12 Amphibians such as *Acanthostega* evolved during the Devonian period.

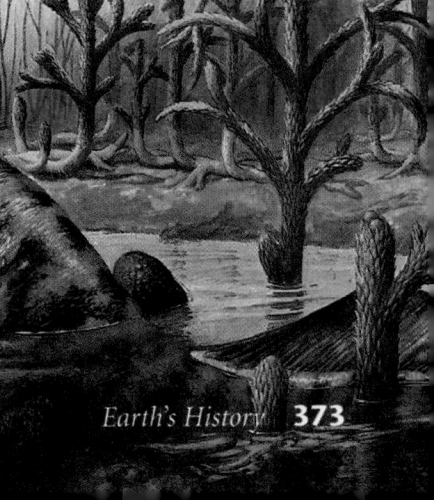

Reading Checkpoint   *What is an amphibian?*

Figure 13 Model of a Pennsylvanian Coal Swamp Shown are scale trees (left), seed ferns (lower left), and scouring rushes (right). Note the large dragonfly.

Carboniferous Period

The Carboniferous period saw the development of great "coal swamp forests" in wet, tropical regions. Amphibians and winged insects became common, and the first reptiles evolved. Geologists often divide the Carboniferous into two separate periods: the Mississippian and Pennsylvanian periods.

Carboniferous Earth During the Carboniferous Period, there was a series of collisions between Earth's major landmasses. For example, Africa collided with the eastern edge of North America. This event formed what is now the southern Appalachian mountains. By late in the period, landmasses began to merge to form the supercontinent Pangaea.

During the Carboniferous period, flat, low-lying parts of continents flooded again and again as sea levels rose and fell. In these areas, reef-building organisms laid down huge deposits of calcium carbonate. Today, these deposits form thick layers of limestone.

Carboniferous Life Among the animals that evolved during the Carboniferous period were the first **reptiles**. Reptiles are animals that lay leathery-shelled eggs that can survive out of water. Reptiles evolved from amphibians. Reptiles could live in drier areas where amphibians could not survive.

Vast swamps, called coal swamp forests, developed in wet, tropical regions during the Carboniferous, as shown in Figure 13. The amphibians and winged insects that had recently evolved lived in these forests.

When the plants and animals in the swamp died, their remains built up in thick layers. Over millions of years, pressure and heat changed these layers of sediment into deposits of coal. The Carboniferous takes its name from these coal deposits.

Not all plants of the Carboniferous lived in swamps. Seed-bearing plants evolved that were adapted to drier uplands. These plants included the first trees, a primitive type of conifer, or cone-bearing tree.

 **Reading Checkpoint** *How does coal form?*

Permian Period

As the Permian period began, Earth's continents were joined in the supercontinent Pangaea. The evolution of life during the period continued trends that began during the Carboniferous. But the Permian ended with the greatest mass extinction in geologic history.

Permian Earth The formation of Pangaea greatly changed global environments during the Permian period. Continental glaciers formed where Pangaea extended into the southern polar region. These ice ages in the southern hemisphere gradually ended when Pangaea drifted northward. This led to a warming trend. Deserts formed in the center of Pangaea, which was far from any source of moisture. Today, huge deposits of red sandstone provide evidence of these deserts.

As Earth's climate warmed, sea levels fell. Many of the shallow, continental seas dried up. As a result, there are few reefs dating to the later Permian. Reefs still flourished in a few small ocean basins, however. In what is now the southwestern United States, organic material from ocean organisms built up in the Permian basin. Over millions of years, these materials formed the oil deposits of West Texas and New Mexico.

Figure 14 *Mesosaurus* was a small freshwater reptile that lived during the Permian period.

Go **O**nline
active art

For: Continental Drift activity
Visit: www.SciLinks.org
Web Code: czp-4132

Figure 15 Pangaea During the Permian period, plate movements pushed together the major landmasses to form Pangaea.

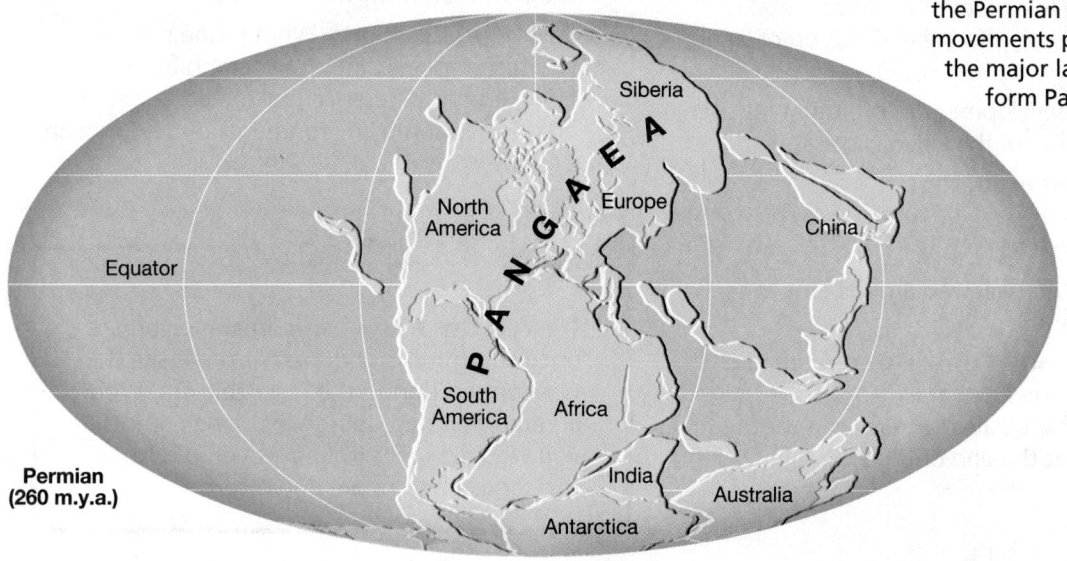

Siberia

North America

Europe

China

Equator

P A N G A E A

South America

Africa

India

Australia

Antarctica

Permian (260 m.y.a.)

Permian Life During the Permian period, life forms became more diverse on land and in the oceans. Conifers became abundant. New types of insects, amphibians, and reptiles evolved.

One group of early reptiles was the mammal-like reptiles. Fossils show that their legs, skulls, and jawbones were similar to those of a later group—the mammals. Some mammal-like reptiles had huge "sails" on their backs. These structures were formed from elongated spines covered with skin. Dimetrodon, shown in Figure 16, had a sail that may have helped regulate its body temperature.

The Permian Extinction Nearly 250 million years ago, a mass extinction ended the Permian period. Scientists think that the Permian extinction killed 96 percent of all species. Ocean organisms that became extinct included most brachiopods and bryozoans, and all trilobites. On land, most mammal-like reptiles died out, although a few survived.

Scientists aren't sure what caused the Permian extinction. One hypothesis is that huge volcanic eruptions in Siberia led to climate change. Another hypothesis is that the climate change resulted from an asteroid impact in Antarctica. Some scientists think that several factors led to environmental changes to which organisms could not adapt. One factor that might have affected ocean organisms was the loss of coastline as the continents collided to form Pangaea.

Figure 16 Early dinosaurs, such as the sail-backed *Dimetrodon,* evolved during the Permian period.

Section 13.2 Assessment

Reviewing Concepts

1. What are five types of environmental changes that can affect the evolution of living things?

2. List one development in evolution for each geologic period of the Paleozoic era.

3. What is a mass extinction?

Critical Thinking

4. **Inferring** What allowed amphibians to flourish on land?

5. **Comparing and Contrasting** Compare and contrast the life that existed at the beginning of the Paleozoic era with the life that existed at the end of the era.

6. **Applying Concepts** Explain how life made the transition from water to land.

7. **Applying Concepts** What is one main way in which reptiles differ from amphibians? How did this difference make reptiles better adapted to some environments of the Permian period?

Writing in Science

Descriptive Paragraph Imagine you are uncovering rocks and fossils from a site that was formed during the Paleozoic era. Write a paragraph describing what kinds of fossils you would expect to find as you dig from the surface and move downward.

13.3 Mesozoic Era: Age of Reptiles

Reading Focus

Key Concepts

- What were the major developments in Earth's geology and life forms during the periods of the Mesozoic era?

- How do scientists explain the mass extinction at the end of the Cretaceous period?

Vocabulary

- mammal
- gymnosperm

Reading Strategy

Summarizing List the blue headings from the section, leaving space to write after each heading. Use a bulleted list to write a brief summary of the text for each heading.

> **I. Triassic Period**
> - Triassic Earth
> - Triassic Life
> - _____?_____

After the Permian extinction, millions of years passed before the number and diversity of living things began to rise again. One group that became very successful and diverse was the ammonites. These extinct mollusks were related to squid and octopus. Ammonites have distinctive spiral-shaped shells, as shown in Figure 17. In each type of ammonite, the shell is slightly different from the shells of other types.

There were many changes in ocean environments during the Mesozoic era. As a result, many different types of ammonites evolved and became extinct after a few million years. For this reason, they make excellent index fossils. Ammonite index fossils help geologists date sedimentary rock layers from the different periods of the Mesozoic—the Triassic, Jurassic, and Cretaceous. You can see the main events of these periods in the timeline in Figure 17.

Figure 17 Mesozoic Era
The Mesozoic is called the "Age of Reptiles" because reptiles became so diverse during the era. Ammonites often serve as index fossils for the periods of this era.

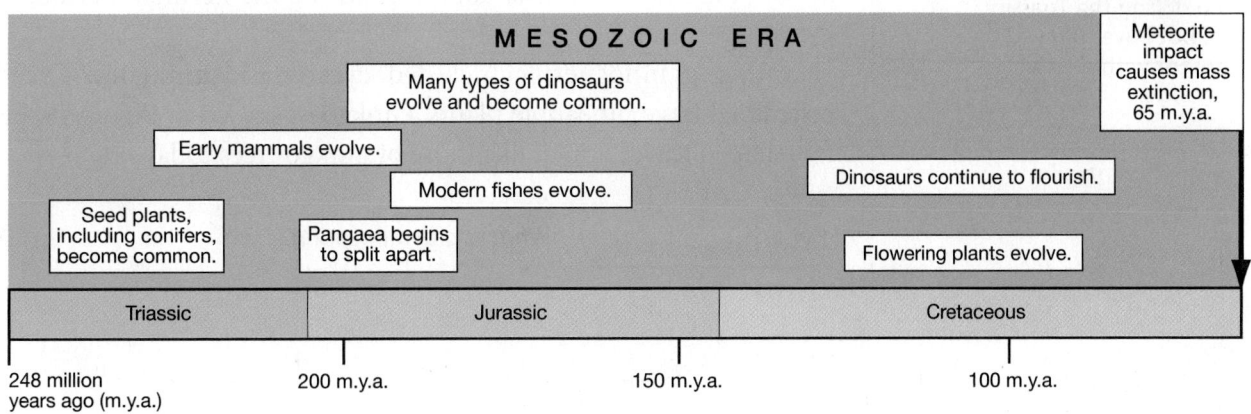

MESOZOIC ERA

Meteorite impact causes mass extinction, 65 m.y.a.

Many types of dinosaurs evolve and become common.

Early mammals evolve.

Modern fishes evolve.

Dinosaurs continue to flourish.

Seed plants, including conifers, become common.

Pangaea begins to split apart.

Flowering plants evolve.

| Triassic | Jurassic | Cretaceous |

248 million years ago (m.y.a.) | 200 m.y.a. | 150 m.y.a. | 100 m.y.a.

Triassic Period

Pangaea continued as a single, large landmass through most of the Triassic period. After a slow recovery from the Permian extinction, many kinds of reptiles evolved. Late in the period, the first mammals appeared.

Triassic Earth Most landmasses were fused together in the supercontinent Pangaea during the Triassic. A huge ocean, called *Panthalassa* (meaning "all sea") occupied the rest of Earth's surface.

In the interior of Pangaea, climates on land varied greatly from season to season. Pangaea had hot summers and cold winters, similar to those in the interior of North America or Asia today.

Toward the end of the Triassic, Pangaea began to split apart slowly. The split began as Africa pulled away from North and South America. You could say that the breakup of Pangaea continues today, about 200 million years later!

Triassic Life Several important new types of organisms evolved during the Triassic. For example, the first dinosaurs were among the many types of reptiles that evolved. Late in the Triassic, the first mammals evolved from a surviving group of mammal-like reptiles. Unlike reptiles, most mammals do not lay eggs. **Mammals** are warm-blooded animals that nourish their young with milk. Triassic mammals, such as *Megazostrodon,* were small, rodent-like animals.

The fossil record also shows that gymnosperms became common during the Triassic. **Gymnosperms** are a group of plants with seeds that lack a protective outer coat. Unlike spore-bearing plants, gymnosperms do not require standing water, such as dew, in their reproductive cycle. For this reason, they can use nutrients and occupy space in drier areas. Conifers, which first appeared during the Permian period, are gymnosperms.

Other gymnosperms included cycads and ginkgoes. Cycads resembled large pineapple plants. Ginkgoes, shown in Figure 19, had fan-shaped leaves, much like those of ginkgo trees today.

Figure 18 Ginkgo trees evolved during the Triassic period, but have survived to the present with relatively little change.

Reading Checkpoint *What is a gymnosperm?*

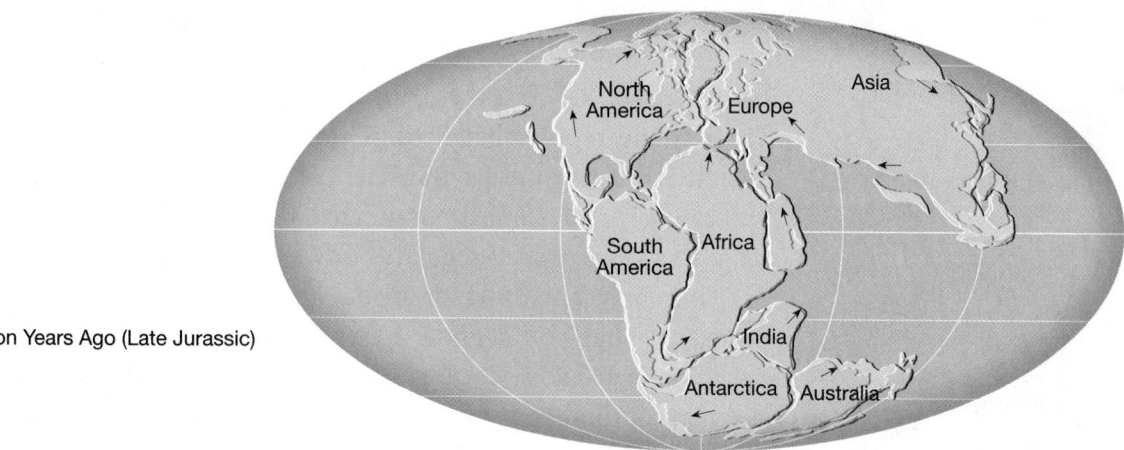

150 Million Years Ago (Late Jurassic)

Jurassic Period

Pangaea continued to split apart during the Jurassic period. Many kinds of dinosaurs evolved and became widely distributed.

Jurassic Earth

As rifts formed between parts of Pangaea, seas opened between the continents. At the same time, mountain building occurred in some areas, such as western North America. There, the North American plate moved west over an oceanic plate. Tectonic activity started a wave of deformation that moved inland along the entire western part of the continent.

The newly formed Jurassic seas helped to moderate the harsh climate conditions on Pangaea. Generally, climates were mild at all latitudes during the Jurassic. Warmer conditions contributed to the development of new life forms.

Jurassic Life

New developments occurred in the oceans, on land, and in the air during the Jurassic period. In the oceans, fishes with modern characteristics evolved. Their jaw structures, scales, skeletons, and fins were similar to those of most fishes living today.

Reptiles adapted to life in the oceans. Fish-eating plesiosaurs and ichthyosaurs became good swimmers but kept their reptilian teeth and breathed by means of lungs.

During the Jurassic period, dinosaurs developed into a varied and widespread group. Some dinosaurs, such as *Diplodocus*, *Brachiosaurus*, and *Stegosaurus*, were plant eaters. Meat-eating dinosaurs of the Jurassic included *Allosaurus*, shown in Figure 20.

Figure 19 By the late Jurassic period, an ocean began to form between North America and Africa as plate movements split Pangaea.
Reading Maps *Which landmass is the farthest from its present day location?*

Figure 20 Dinosaurs such as *Allosaurus* were fearsome predators. But there is evidence that many dinosaurs, including some meat-eaters, lived in groups, built nests, and cared for their young.

Evolution of Birds During the Jurassic, pterosaurs evolved. These flying reptiles had "wings" formed from membranes of skin attached to their forelegs. But scientists think that birds evolved from dinosaurs. In fact, some dinosaurs had feathers! The feathers may have served for display or to regulate body temperature.

The early ancestors of birds were probably small, feathered dinosaurs that could glide. Later, more birdlike animals such as *Archaeopteryx* evolved. As you can see in Figure 21, *Archaeopteryx* still had reptile-like teeth, claws on its wings, and a tail. It lacked the large breastbone that modern birds have to anchor flight muscles. But it could probably fly short distances.

 **Reading Checkpoint** *What was Archaeopteryx?*

Figure 21 Scientists think that animals similar to *Archaeopteryx* were probably the ancestors of modern birds.

Cretaceous Period

A greater diversity of life forms evolved during the Cretaceous period. Dinosaurs, birds, flowering plants, and small mammals all flourished. The period ended with a mass extinction that killed all dinosaurs and many other organisms.

Cretaceous Earth The landmasses that had made up Pangaea continued to move apart during the Cretaceous. At the same time, Earth's climates continued to be relatively warm.

Early in the Cretaceous, shallow seas invaded much of western North America. These shallow seas created great swamps like those of the Paleozoic era. The swamps formed the Cretaceous coal deposits of the western United States and Canada. In the seas near Europe, thick chalk deposits formed from the remains of one-celled ocean organisms.

Figure 22 Ankylosaurs were plant-eating dinosaurs that evolved tough "armored" plates as protection against predation.

Cretaceous Life Dinosaurs of the Cretaceous period evolved many different sizes, shapes, and ways of living. Large, slow-moving plant eaters waded on four legs in the shallows of swampy areas. Smaller, faster meat eaters ran on two hind legs. The Cretaceous was the time of the fierce *Tyrannosaurus rex,* the horned *Triceratops,* and gigantic plant eaters like *Apatosaurus.*

Other animal groups also appeared and flourished. Snakes evolved early in the Cretaceous. Mammals with more modern characteristics evolved.

Flowering plants, or angiosperms, also evolved during this period. **Angiosperms** are plants that produce flowers and seeds with an outer covering. Many modern angiosperms—including trees such as willow, birch, and sassafras—evolved and became common during the Cretaceous.

The Cretaceous Extinction

About 65 million years ago, the Cretaceous period ended in a mass extinction. The dinosaurs and most other large animals became extinct. Smaller reptiles, birds, and mammals were also affected, although some species of these animals survived. In the oceans, ammonites were among the species that became extinct.

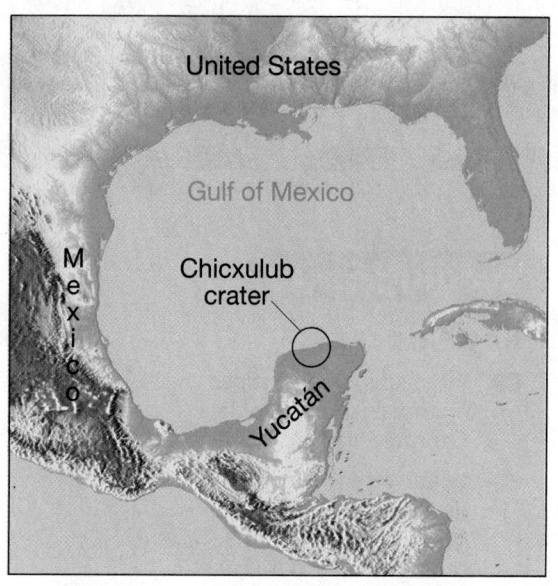

United States

Gulf of Mexico

Mexico

Chicxulub crater

Yucatán

Most scientists think that a large meteorite collided with Earth and caused the mass extinction at the end of the Cretaceous. The collision would have created huge quantities of dust that blocked out the sun, perhaps for years. This, in turn, would have caused plants to die. (Plants need sunlight for photosynthesis.) Without plants, plant-eating dinosaurs could not survive. Then, the meat-eating dinosaurs also starved and died out.

As shown in Figure 23, there is a meteorite impact crater of the correct age near the Yucatán peninsula in Mexico. Scientists have also found a thin, worldwide layer of sediment containing the element iridium. Iridium is a metal that is rare in Earth's crust, but that is found in stony meteorites.

Another hypothesis to explain the Cretaceous extinction is that huge volcanic eruptions in India led to climate changes. Some scientists think that disease may also have been a factor. As evidence, they point to a decline in dinosaur species even before the mass extinction. It is likely that several factors contributed to the Cretaceous extinction.

Figure 23 Cause of the Cretaceous Extinction? Some scientists think that the Chicxulub crater was formed by the meteoroid that may have caused the extinction of the dinosaurs.

Go Online
PLANETDIARY

For: Links on Cretaceous extinction
Visit: PHSchool.com
Web Code: czd-4133

Section 13.3 Assessment

Reviewing Concepts

1. List one development in evolution for each geologic period of the Mesozoic era.

2. Describe the causes of the mass extinction at the end of the Cretaceous period.

3. What is a mammal?

Critical Thinking

4. **Relating Cause and Effect** Would Pangaea's climate during the Triassic have favored amphibians or reptiles? Explain.

5. **Comparing and Contrasting** How do gymnosperms, such as conifers, differ from spore-bearing plants, such as ferns?

6. **Inferring** What can you infer about the environment of an organism if its fossil is found in limestone? If its fossil is found in coal? Explain.

7. **Predicting** How would you expect fossils to be different above and below the iridium layer deposited at the end of the Cretaceous?

Writing in Science

Explanatory Paragraph Use library or Internet resources to research a reptile of the Mesozoic era. Write a paragraph that explains where the fossils of this reptile have been found, the environment in which it lived, and the type of food it ate. Also state whether the reptile still exists or has become extinct.

13.4 Cenozoic Era: Age of Mammals

Reading Focus

Key Concepts

- What adaptations helped mammals succeed in the Cenozoic era?
- What were the major developments in Earth's geology and life forms during the periods of the Cenozoic era?

Vocabulary

- Milankovitch cycles

Reading Strategy

Monitoring Your Understanding Preview the Key Concepts, topic headings, vocabulary, and figures. List two things you expect to learn about each. After reading, state what you learned.

What I Expect to Learn	What I Learned

Figure 24 Cenozoic Era Mammals became abundant and diverse during the Cenozoic era. The saber-toothed cat (photo) became extinct about 10,000 years ago

If you could visit North America early in the Cenozoic era, you would notice differences from the present. For example, you would not see any grasses or large mammals. They evolved during the Cenozoic. The term *Cenozoic* means "recent life." Throughout this era, many life forms evolved that were similar to those of the present.

The Age of Mammals

If the Mesozoic was the "Age of Reptiles," the Cenozoic might be called the "Age of Mammals." During the Mesozoic, mammals were mainly small scavengers and plant-eaters. After the Cretaceous extinction, mammals began to adapt to environments and ways of getting a living once used by dinosaurs and other extinct reptiles.

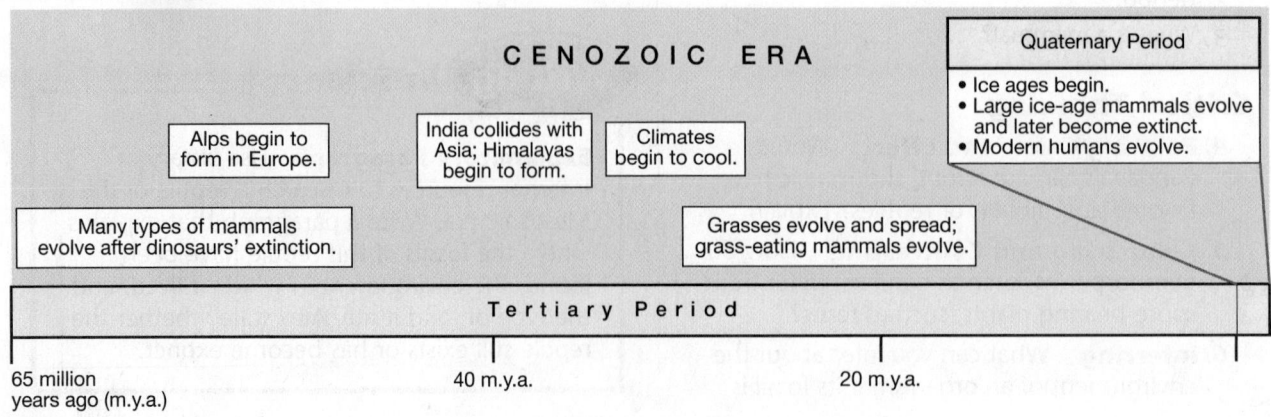

CENOZOIC ERA

Alps begin to form in Europe.

India collides with Asia; Himalayas begin to form.

Climates begin to cool.

Quaternary Period
- Ice ages begin.
- Large ice-age mammals evolve and later become extinct.
- Modern humans evolve.

Many types of mammals evolve after dinosaurs' extinction.

Grasses evolve and spread; grass-eating mammals evolve.

Tertiary Period

65 million years ago (m.y.a.)   40 m.y.a.   20 m.y.a.

Mammals succeeded during the Cenozoic because of adaptations that enabled them to out-compete the surviving reptiles. For example, because mammals are warm-blooded, they can survive in cold regions and search for food during any season or time of day. Other adaptations included more efficient hearts and lungs than reptiles, and the development of insulating body hair. These adaptations allowed mammals to lead more active lives than reptiles.

Tertiary Period

During the Tertiary period, mountain building and climate changes accompanied the breakup of Pangaea. Mammals became widespread and diverse worldwide.

Tertiary Earth   Major fragments of Pangaea became separate continents during the Tertiary. As you can see in Figure 25, seas separated South America from North America, and Europe from Africa. Plate movements led to major mountain building events in western North America (the Rockies), Europe (the Alps), and the Himalayas.

Generally, climates during the Tertiary were cooler than those of the Cretaceous. The mid-Tertiary had temperate, dry climates. Later in the period, Earth's climate cooled. This led to the development of continental glaciers in Antarctica about 10 million years ago.

Tertiary Life   The Tertiary saw the development of many new species, from songbirds to snakes. But the major development of the Tertiary was the evolution of many new types of mammals. Mammals evolved specialized limbs and teeth for life in particular environments. For example, meat eaters evolved sharp teeth for cutting and tearing. Rodents developed self-sharpening front teeth for gnawing. Plant eaters developed flat molars for chewing.

Some mammals evolved to take advantage of a rich new food source—grass. As the climate became cooler and drier, vast grasslands developed. Many types of grazing animals, including the ancestors of cattle and horses, evolved during the Tertiary.

Q *What are the La Brea tar pits?*

A The La Brea tar pits, located in downtown Los Angeles, contain fossils of ice-age mammals (including the saber-toothed cat in Figure 24) preserved in thick petroleum, or tar. Petroleum oozes to the surface in the tar pits. These organisms roamed southern California from 8,000 to 40,000 years ago. The fossils include 59 species of mammals and more than 130 species of birds.

Figure 25 Early in the Cenozoic, North America and South America were not connected, India had not collided with Asia, and Australia was still far south of where it is today.
Reading Maps *How did the distance between Antarctica and Australia change during the Cenozoic?*

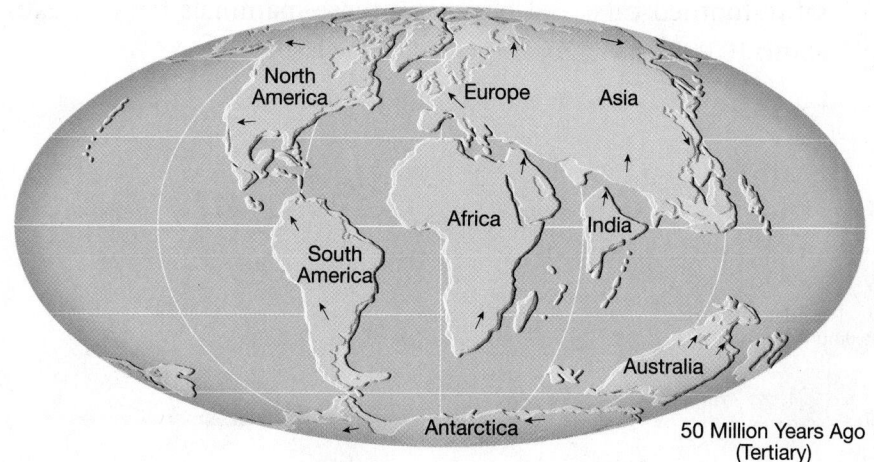

North America · Europe · Asia · Africa · India · South America · Australia · Antarctica

50 Million Years Ago (Tertiary)

Quaternary Period

🔑 **Two factors have greatly affected life on Earth during the Quaternary period: the advance and retreat of continental glaciers, which have formed and melted about 30 times in the last 3 million years, and the migration of _Homo sapiens_—modern humans—to every corner of Earth.**

Quaternary Earth A map showing Earth's physical features 2 million years ago would look much like a map of Earth today. But beginning in the late Tertiary, a series of ice ages covered large parts of the northern hemisphere with continental glaciers. What caused the ice ages? Because Earth is a complex system, many factors determine whether Earth's climate becomes cold enough for an ice age. These factors include ocean currents, the size of ice-covered areas, and the effects of living things on the atmosphere.

In the 1940s, astronomer Milutin Milankovitch proposed that three different cycles, related to Earth's movements, were the main cause of ice ages. These cycles are called **Milankovitch cycles**. For example, there is a 100,000-year cycle related to changes in the shape of Earth's orbit. You will learn more about these cycles in Chapter 21. Earth receives more or less energy from the sun depending on its position within each of the cycles. Milankovitch thought that ice ages occur when solar energy reaching Earth is at a minimum.

Scientists today think that Milankovitch cycles provide a partial explanation for recent ice ages, shown in Figure 26. But scientists are still looking for a more complete explanation.

Quaternary Life One trend in evolution during both the Tertiary and Quaternary periods was that some mammals became very large. During the ice ages, many large mammals lived on the cold grassland, or steppe, that bordered the ice-covered parts of North America, Europe, and Asia. These mammals included mastodons and mammoths, which were both huge relatives of the elephant. In North America, there were also giant beavers, ground sloths, wolves, bears, sabre-toothed cats, and bison. All these mammals became extinct about 10,000 years ago, at the end of the last ice age.

Figure 26 Scientists have determined that continental glaciers have advanced and then retreated at roughly 100,000-year intervals over the last 3 million years. **Inferring** _What can you infer about how the amount of solar energy reaching Earth changed between about 30,000 years ago and the present?_

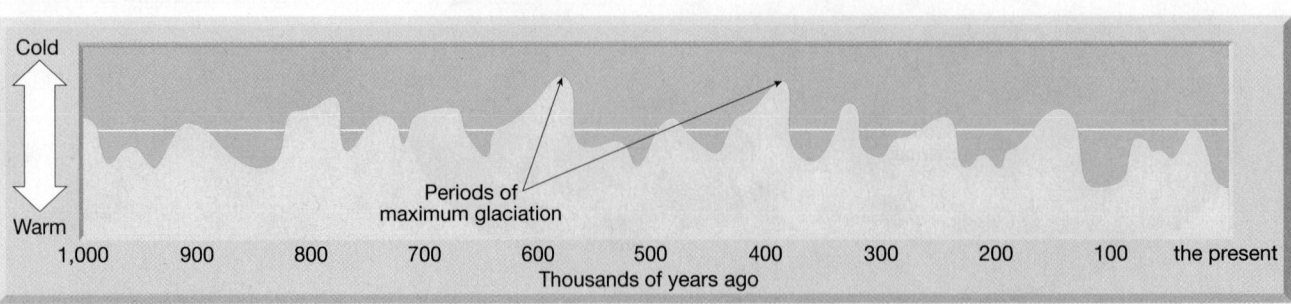

How can this extinction be explained? No single hypothesis provides a satisfactory explanation. Scientists have suggested disease or climate changes as possible explanations. Many other scientists have suggested that humans hunted the large ice-age mammals to extinction. But skeptics question whether small groups of humans could have caused so many different kinds of animals to become extinct over such a vast area.

Modern humans, *Homo sapiens,* evolved from ancestors in Africa more than 100,000 years ago. The fossil record shows that about 50,000 years ago early humans began to migrate out of Africa. Soon, the range of early humans extended from Europe, Africa, and Asia to Australia. Then, as sea level fell during the last ice age, a land bridge formed that connected Asia with North America. Scientists think that this land bridge enabled humans to migrate to the Americas about 14,000 years ago.

Today, humans inhabit every continent. Our species has become a powerful factor in changing Earth's environment. This in turn affects the other species with whom we share planet Earth.

Figure 27 Mammoths, related to modern elephants, were among the large mammals that became extinct at the close of the Ice Age.

 **Reading Checkpoint** *What hypotheses have been proposed to explain the extinction of large mammals about 10,000 years ago?*

Section 13.4 Assessment

Reviewing Concepts

1. Why did mammals become a successful group during the Cenozoic era?

2. List one major evolutionary development for each period of the Cenozoic era.

3. Describe plate movements and mountain building during the Tertiary period.

4. What are the Milankovitch cycles?

Critical Thinking

5. Inferring Which would have a better chance of surviving in a cold climate: a mammal or a reptile? Explain.

6. Predicting What characteristics would you expect an early mammal that lived in a grassland to have? Explain.

7. Relating Cause and Effect What caused the Alps and Himalayas to form during the Tertiary period?

Connecting Concepts

Earth's Changing Geography Scientists think that the Great Rift Valley in East Africa began to form during the late Tertiary and Quaternary periods. Review the formation of rift valleys in Chapter 9. Write a paragraph describing how the Great Rift Valley formed and what may happen to it in the future.

Modeling the Geologic Time Scale

Applying the techniques of geologic dating, the history of Earth has been subdivided into several different units that provide a meaningful time frame. The events that make up Earth's history can be arranged within this time frame to provide a clearer picture of the past. The span of a human life is like the blink of an eye compared to the age of Earth. Because of this, it can be difficult to comprehend the magnitude of geologic time.

Problem
How can the geologic time scale be represented in a way that allows a clearer visual understanding?

Materials
- strip of adding machine paper measuring 5 meters or longer
- meter stick or metric measuring tape
- pencil

Skills
Measuring, Calculating, Interpreting Diagrams

Procedure
1. Obtain a piece of adding machine paper slightly longer than 5 meters in length. Draw a line at one end of the paper and label it "Present."

2. Using the following scale, construct a timeline by completing Steps 3 and 4.

Scale

1 meter = 1 billion years

10 centimeters = 100 million years

1 centimeter = 10 million years

1 millimeter = 1 million years

3. Using the geologic time scale on page 387 as a reference, divide your timeline into the eons and eras of geologic time. Label each division with its name and indicate its absolute age.

4. Using the scale, plot and label the plant and animal events on your timeline that are listed on the geologic time scale.

Analyze and Conclude

1. **Calculating** What fraction or percent of geologic time is represented by the Precambrian eon?

2. **Explaining** Using your text and class notes as references, explain why the approximate time of 540 million years ago was selected to mark the end of the Precambrian time and the beginning of Phanerozoic eon.

3. **Inferring** Suggest one reason why the periods of the Cenozoic era have been further subdivided into several epochs with reasonably reliable accuracy.

4. **Analyzing Data** How many times longer is the whole of geologic time than the time represented by the 5,000 years of recorded history?

5. **Calculating** For what fraction or percent of geologic time have land plants been present on Earth?

Geologic Time Scale

Eon	Era	Millions of Years Ago
Phanerozoic	Cenozoic	65
	Mesozoic	251
	Paleozoic	542
Precambrian	Proterozoic — Late	900
	Proterozoic — Middle	1600
	Proterozoic — Early	2500
	Archean — Late	3000
	Archean — Middle	3400
	Archean — Early	3800
	Hadean	
	Earth forms: 4560	

Era	Period	Epoch	Development of Plants and Animals
Cenozoic	Quaternary (Neogene)	Holocene	Humans develop
		Pleistocene — 0.01	
		Pliocene — 1.8	"Age of Mammals"
		Miocene — 5.3	
	Tertiary (Paleogene)	Oligocene — 23.0	
		Eocene — 33.7	
		Paleocene — 54.8	Extinction of dinosaurs and many other species
		65.0	
Mesozoic	Cretaceous	"Age of Reptiles"	First flowering plants
	145		First birds
	Jurassic		
	200		Dinosaurs dominant
	Triassic		
	251		
Paleozoic	Permian	"Age of Amphibians"	Extinction of trilobites and many other marine animals
	299		First reptiles
	Carboniferous — Pennsylvanian		Large coal swamps
	323		
	Carboniferous — Mississippian		Amphibians abundant
	359		
	Devonian	"Age of Fishes"	First insect fossils
			Fishes dominant
	416		
	Silurian		First land plants
	444		First fishes
	Ordovician	"Age of Invertebrates"	
	488		Trilobites dominant
	Cambrian		
			First organisms with shells
	542		
	Precambrian		First multicelled organisms

13.1 Precambrian Time

Key Concepts

- Earth formed about 4.56 billion years ago. During Precambrian time, the atmosphere and oceans formed and plate tectonics began to build up continental landmasses.

- The earliest life probably evolved in the oceans. Later, one-celled organisms evolved that used light energy to produce food through photosynthesis. These organisms consisted of simple cells called prokaryotes. Slowly, more complex cells, called eukaryotes, evolved. Late in the Precambrian, multi-celled organisms with soft bodies evolved.

Vocabulary

shields, *p. 366;* photosynthesis, *p. 367;* stromatolites, *p. 367;* prokaryotes, *p. 368;* eukaryotes, *p. 368*

13.2 Paleozoic Era: Life Explodes

Key Concepts

- Environmental changes that have affected the course of evolution on Earth include the formation and breakup of continents, mountain building, volcanic activity, changes in climate, and changes in sea level.

- During the Cambrian period, many new groups of organisms evolved in a relatively short time in an event called the "Cambrian Explosion."

- During the Ordovician period, more complex communities of organisms developed in the oceans. The first land-dwelling plants evolved.

- The Silurian Period was a time of reef-building and continued evolution of fishes in the seas. By the end of the period, plants and animals were becoming widespread on land.

- During the Devonian period, jawed fishes and sharks evolved in the seas. Plants continued to colonize the land, along with insects and other small arthropods. Later, amphibians evolved with adaptations for life on land.

- The Carboniferous period saw the development of great "coal swamp forests" in wet, tropical regions. Amphibians and winged insects became common, and the first reptiles evolved.

- During the Permian period, the supercontinent Pangaea formed. The Permian ended with the greatest mass extinction in geologic history.

Vocabulary

mass extinction, *p. 369;* Gondwana, *p. 371;* Laurasia, *p. 373;* amphibian, *p. 373;* reptile, *p. 375*

13.3 Mesozoic Era: Age of Reptiles

Key Concepts

- Pangaea continued as a single, large landmass through most of the Triassic period. After a slow recovery from the Permian extinction, many kinds of reptiles evolved. Late in the period, the first mammals appeared.

- Pangaea continued to split apart during the Jurassic period. Many kinds of dinosaurs evolved and became widely distributed.

- A greater diversity of life forms evolved during the Cretaceous period. Dinosaurs, birds, flowering plants, and small mammals all flourished.

- Most scientists think that a large meteorite collided with Earth and caused the mass extinction at the end of the Cretaceous.

Vocabulary

mammal, *p. 378;* gymnosperm, *p. 378;* angiosperm, *p. 380*

13.4 Cenozoic Era: Age of Mammals

Key Concepts

- Mammals succeeded during the Cenozoic because of adaptations that enabled them to out-compete the surviving reptiles.

- During the Tertiary period, mountain building and climate changes accompanied the breakup of Pangaea. Mammals became widespread and diverse worldwide.

- Two factors have greatly affected life on Earth during the Quaternary period: the advance and retreat of continental glaciers and the migration of modern humans to every corner of Earth.

Vocabulary

Milankovitch cycles, *p. 384*

Assessment

Reviewing Content

Choose the letter that best answers the question or completes the statement.

1. Which era spans the least amount of time on the geologic scale?
   a. Cenozoic   **b.** Mesozoic
   c. Paleozoic   **d.** Precambrian

2. The most common Precambrian fossils are
   a. fish.
   b. stromatolites.
   c. trilobites.
   d. ferns.

3. Which era is known as the "age of reptiles"?
   a. Cenozoic   **b.** Mesozoic
   c. Paleozoic   **d.** Proterozoic

4. Modern squids descended from what type of early Paleozoic organisms?
   a. cephalopods   **b.** trilobites
   c. brachiopods   **d.** amphibians

5. Jawless fishes that evolved during the Devonian period were
   a. prokaryotes.
   b. amphibians.
   c. vertebrates.
   d. invertebrates.

6. Which adaptation allowed gymnosperm plants to out-compete spore-bearing plants?
   a. stems   **b.** seeds
   c. leaves   **d.** roots

7. Reptiles that were adapted to fly included the
   a. plesiosaurs.   **b.** pterosaurs.
   c. ichthyosaurs.   **d.** tyrannosaurs.

8. Humans first appeared during the
   a. Cretaceous period.
   b. Jurassic period.
   c. Quaternary period.
   d. Tertiary period.

9. Insulating body hair is a characteristic of
   a. mammals.
   b. amphibians.
   c. reptiles.
   d. invertebrates.

10. What development caused the emergence of animals that were grazing herbivores?
    a. seed plants
    b. grasses
    c. fruits
    d. carnivorous mammals

Understanding Concepts

11. How did plants help change Earth's early atmosphere?

12. What are shields? What kind of information is gained from shields?

Use the photograph below to answer Question 13.

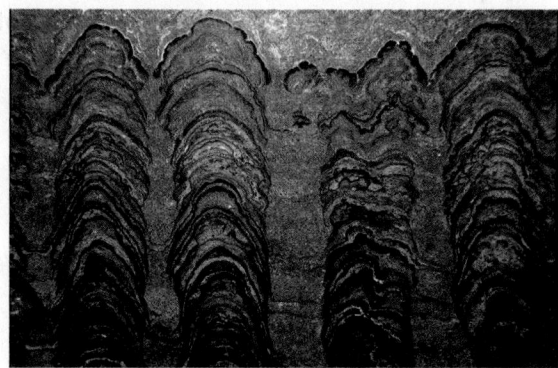

13. This photograph shows evidence of what kind of organism?

14. What significant tectonic activity occurred during the Mesozoic?

15. What present-day continents made up Gondwana?

16. To which large group of animals do trilobites belong?

17. Modern fishes and sharks both evolved from what type of ancient animals?

18. What development allowed mammals to adapt to different environments successfully?

Critical Thinking

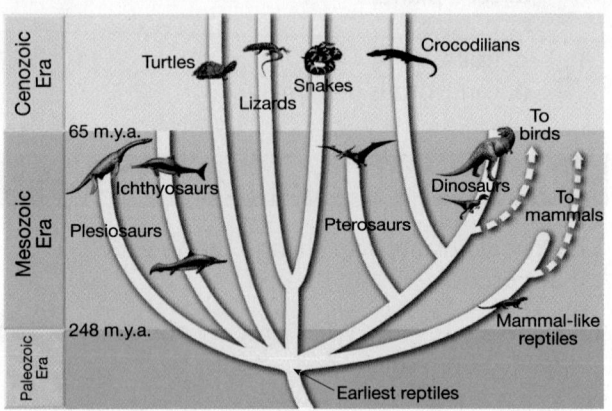

19. Interpreting Diagrams Examine the figure above, which shows the origin and development of reptile groups. Arrange these groups in relative chronological order from first appearance: crocodilians, lizards, plesiosaurs, and pterosaurs.

20. Interpreting Photographs Most of the vast North American coal resources located from Pennsylvania to Illinois began forming during the Pennsylvanian and Mississippian periods. Using Figure 7 on page 374, describe the climatic and biological conditions associated with this environment.

21. Inferring What role did plate tectonics play in determining the conditions that produced North America's coal reserves?

22. Making Generalizations Why is so little known about the Precambrian time?

23. Relating Cause and Effect What evidence do banded-iron formations provide about oxygen levels in the atmosphere during the early- to mid-Precambrian?

24. Inferring What is the major source of free oxygen in Earth's atmosphere?

25. Comparing and Contrasting Make a list of differences between amphibians and reptiles.

26. Developing Hypotheses The cougar, or mountain lion, evolved in North America. Today, its range extends throughout the mountains of South America as well. Write a hypothesis that explains the distribution of this species. Explain your answer. (*Hint:* Compare the map in Figure 25 on p. 383 with a map showing present-day positions of the continents.)

27. Applying Concepts Describe one main hypothesis that explains the cause of ice ages during the Quaternary period.

28. Relating Cause and Effect Why did large ice-age mammals become extinct about 10,000 years ago?

Concepts in Action

29. Classifying Match the following words and phrases to the most appropriate time span. Select among the following: Precambrian, early Paleozoic, late Paleozoic, Mesozoic, and Cenozoic.
   (a) Pangaea came into existence.
   (b) Encompasses the least amount of time
   (c) Shields
   (d) Age of dinosaurs
   (e) Triassic, Jurassic, and Cretaceous
   (f) Formation of most of the world's major iron-ore deposits
   (g) Age of fishes
   (h) Cambrian, Ordovician, and Silurian
   (i) Golden age of trilobites
   (j) Gymnosperms became abundant.

30. Writing in Science Write a paragraph explaining the relationship between the development and movement of plants, herbivore animals, and carnivore animals.

Performance-Based Assessment

Researching Research and select several different types of gymnosperm and angiosperm plants that are mentioned in the chapter. Also, research more primitive plants that existed before gymnosperms. Write a paragraph describing each plant, including information on its physical structure, reproduction, and characteristics that might cause it to be more successful in some eras than others.

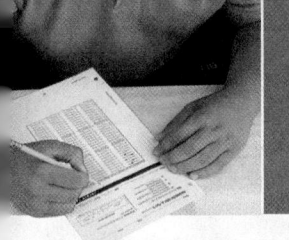

Standardized Test Prep

Choose the letter that best answers the question or completes the statement.

1. Which of the following modern-day continents was NOT a part of Gondwana?
(A) Africa
(B) North America
(C) South America
(D) Antarctica

2. Where did the water that makes up Earth's oceans originally come from?
(A) Water vapor as part of the original atmosphere
(B) Water vapor dissolved in molten rock
(C) Water vapor released by ancient plants during photosynthesis
(D) Liquid water settled into low areas of the surface

Use the diagram below to answer Questions 3 and 4.

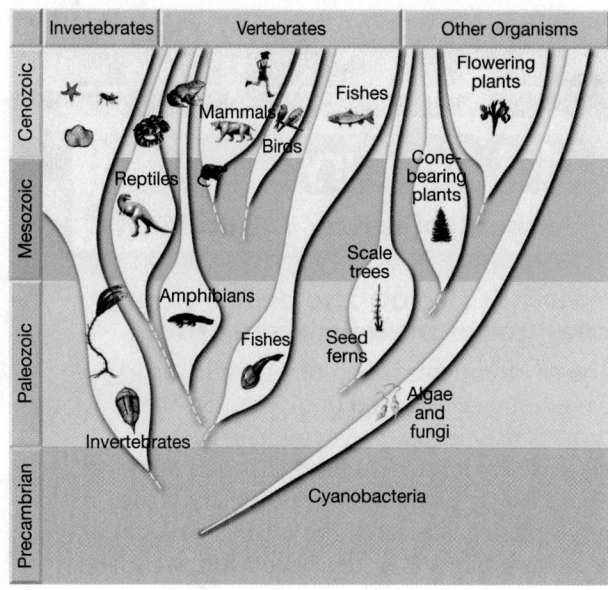

3. According to the diagram, which group of organisms appeared first?
(A) invertebrates
(B) flowering plants
(C) algae and fungi
(D) fishes

4. According to the diagram, when did the first mammals appear?
(A) Precambrian
(B) Paleozoic
(C) Mesozoic
(D) Cenozoic

Answer the following questions in complete sentences.

5. What are two hypotheses for the extinction of the dinosaurs and many other plant and animal groups at the end of the Mesozoic era?

6. Why is so little known about the Precambrian era?

7. List and describe four traits that separate mammals from reptiles.

21st Century Learning

Accountability and Adaptability

How has life on the ocean floor changed our views about life?

The environments found on ocean floors were not well explored until recently. The organisms scientists have found in these extreme environments have changed our ideas about life on Earth and the possibility of life on other planets. Research the organisms living in seafloor sediments or deep-sea hydrothermal vents. Find out how the discovery of some of these organisms has changed scientists' ideas about life on Earth or extraterrestrial life. Present what you discover to the class or post your findings in a class blog or wiki if available. Follow up with answers to your classmates' comments or questions.

Quick Lab
Evaporative Salts

Exploration Lab
Modeling Seafloor Depth Transects

 GEODe Oceans
↳ Floor of the Ocean

This photograph shows a view of ocean waves breaking on a beach.

OCEANOGRAPHY

Chapter Preview

Inquiry Activity

How Does Particle Size Affect Settling Rates?

Procedure

1. Fill two large transparent containers with water. Place two samples of sediment, one clay and one sand, on separate sheets of white paper. Examine the sediments with a hand lens. Determine which sediment sample has larger-sized particles. Record your observations.

2. Carefully measure 1 tbsp of the clay sample. Hold the spoon directly above the first container and pour the clay into the water. Using a stopwatch, time how long it takes for the entire clay sample to reach the bottom of the container and settle. Record the time.

3. Repeat Step 2 using the second container and the sand sample. Be sure to hold the spoon the same distance from the container as you did in the clay sample.

Think About It

1. **Drawing Conclusions** Which sample had smaller particles? Which sample took longer to settle in the water? Explain the general relationship between sediment size and settling rates.

2. **Predicting** Both of these sediments enter ocean water from rivers. Predict which type of sediment would be found closest to the coast. Which will be found father away? Explain.

14.1 The Vast World Ocean

Reading Focus

Key Concepts

- How much of Earth's surface is covered by water?
- How can the world ocean be divided?
- How does the topography of the ocean floor compare to that on land?
- What types of technology are used to study the ocean floor?

Vocabulary

- oceanography
- bathymetry
- sonar
- submersible

Reading Strategy

Building Vocabulary Draw a table similar to the one below that includes all the vocabulary terms listed for the section. As you read the section, define each term in your own words.

Vocabulary Term	Definition
oceanography	a. _____?_____
bathymetry	b. _____?_____
sonar	c. _____?_____
submersible	d. _____?_____

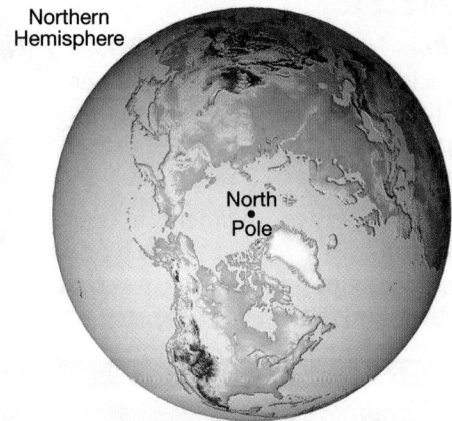

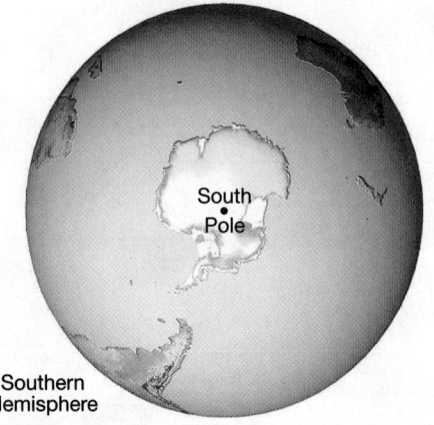

Figure 1 The World Ocean These views of Earth show that the planet is dominated by a single interconnected world ocean.

How deep is the ocean? How much of Earth is covered by the global ocean? What does the ocean floor look like? Humans have long been interested in finding answers to these questions. However, it was not until relatively recently that these simple questions could be answered. Suppose, for example, that all of the water were drained from the ocean. What would we see? Plains? Mountains? Canyons? Plateaus? You may be surprised to find that the ocean conceals all of these features, and more.

The Blue Planet

Look at Figure 1. You can see why the "blue planet" or the "water planet" are appropriate nicknames for Earth. **Nearly 71 percent of Earth's surface is covered by the global ocean.** Although the ocean makes up a much greater percentage of Earth's surface than the continents, it has only been since the late 1800s that the ocean became an important focus of study. New technologies have allowed scientists to collect large amounts of data about the oceans. As technology has advanced, the field of oceanography has grown. **Oceanography** is a science that draws on the methods and knowledge of geology, chemistry, physics, and biology to study all aspects of the world ocean.

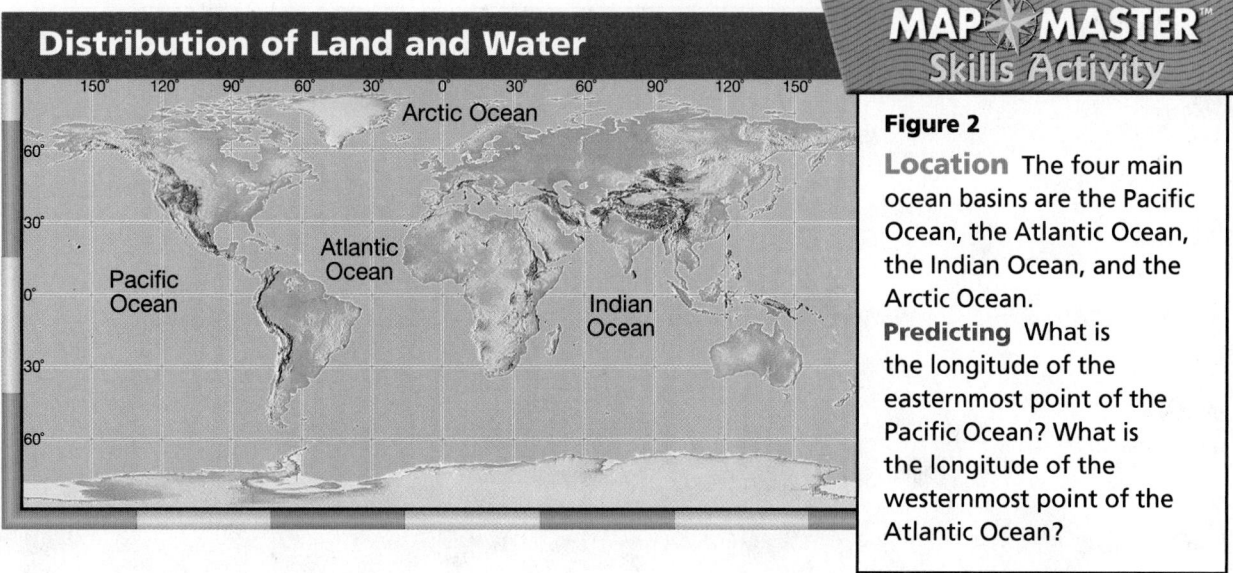

Distribution of Land and Water

MAP MASTER™
Skills Activity

Arctic Ocean

Pacific Ocean

Atlantic Ocean

Indian Ocean

Figure 2

Location The four main ocean basins are the Pacific Ocean, the Atlantic Ocean, the Indian Ocean, and the Arctic Ocean.
Predicting What is the longitude of the easternmost point of the Pacific Ocean? What is the longitude of the westernmost point of the Atlantic Ocean?

Geography of the Oceans

The area of Earth is about 510 million square kilometers. Of this total, approximately 360 million square kilometers, or 71 percent, is represented by oceans and smaller seas such as the Mediterranean Sea and the Caribbean Sea. Continents and islands comprise the remaining 29 percent, or 150 million square kilometers. **The world ocean can be divided into four main ocean basins—the Pacific Ocean, the Atlantic Ocean, the Indian Ocean, and the Arctic Ocean.** These ocean basins are shown in Figure 2.

The Pacific Ocean is the largest ocean. In fact, it is the largest single geographic feature on Earth. It covers more than half of the ocean surface area on Earth. It is also the world's deepest ocean, with an average depth of 3940 meters.

The Atlantic Ocean is about half the size of the Pacific Ocean, and is not quite as deep. It is a relatively narrow ocean compared to the Pacific. The Atlantic and Pacific Oceans are bounded to the east and west by continents.

The Indian Ocean is slightly smaller than the Atlantic Ocean, but it has about the same average depth. Unlike the Pacific and Atlantic oceans, the Indian Ocean is located almost entirely in the southern hemisphere.

The Arctic Ocean is about 7 percent of the size of the Pacific Ocean. It is only a little more than one-quarter as deep as the rest of the oceans.

 **Reading Checkpoint** *What are the four main ocean basins?*

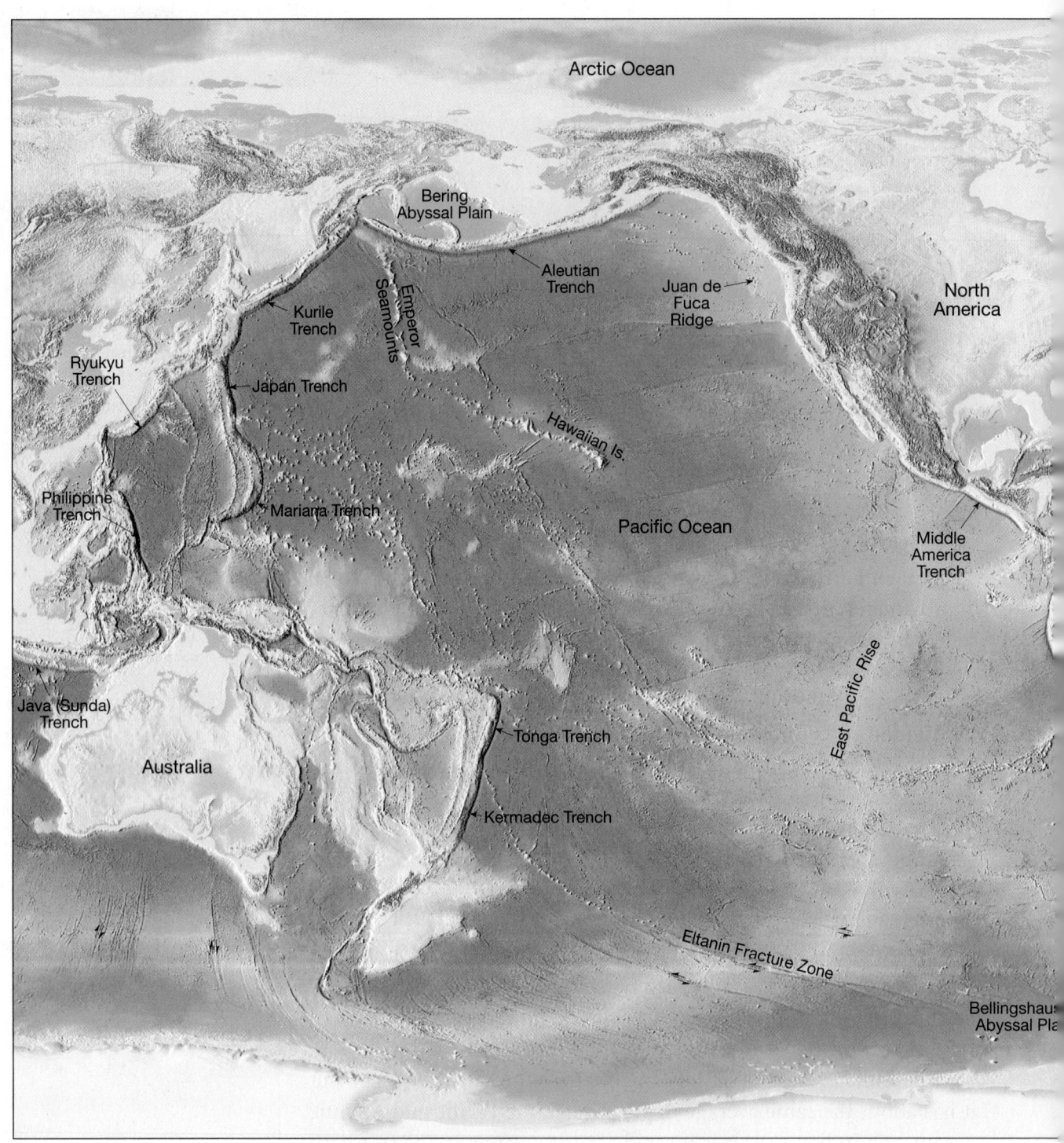

The map shows the topography of the Pacific Ocean floor and surrounding regions, labeled with the following features: Arctic Ocean, North America, Pacific Ocean, Australia, Bering Abyssal Plain, Aleutian Trench, Emperor Seamounts, Kurile Trench, Juan de Fuca Ridge, Ryukyu Trench, Japan Trench, Hawaiian Is., Philippine Trench, Mariana Trench, Middle America Trench, Java (Sunda) Trench, East Pacific Rise, Tonga Trench, Kermadec Trench, Eltanin Fracture Zone, Bellingshausen Abyssal Plain.

Figure 3 The topography of the ocean floor is as varied as the topography of the continents. The ocean floor contains mountain ranges, trenches, and flat regions called abyssal plains.
Interpreting Diagrams
List all of the features you can identify in the figure.

Mapping the Ocean Floor

If all the water were drained from the ocean basins, a variety of features would be seen. These features include chains of volcanoes, tall mountain ranges, trenches, and large submarine plateaus. **The topography of the ocean floor is as diverse as that of continents.** The topographic features of the ocean floor are shown in Figure 3.

An understanding of ocean-floor features came with the development of techniques to measure the depth of the oceans. **Bathymetry**

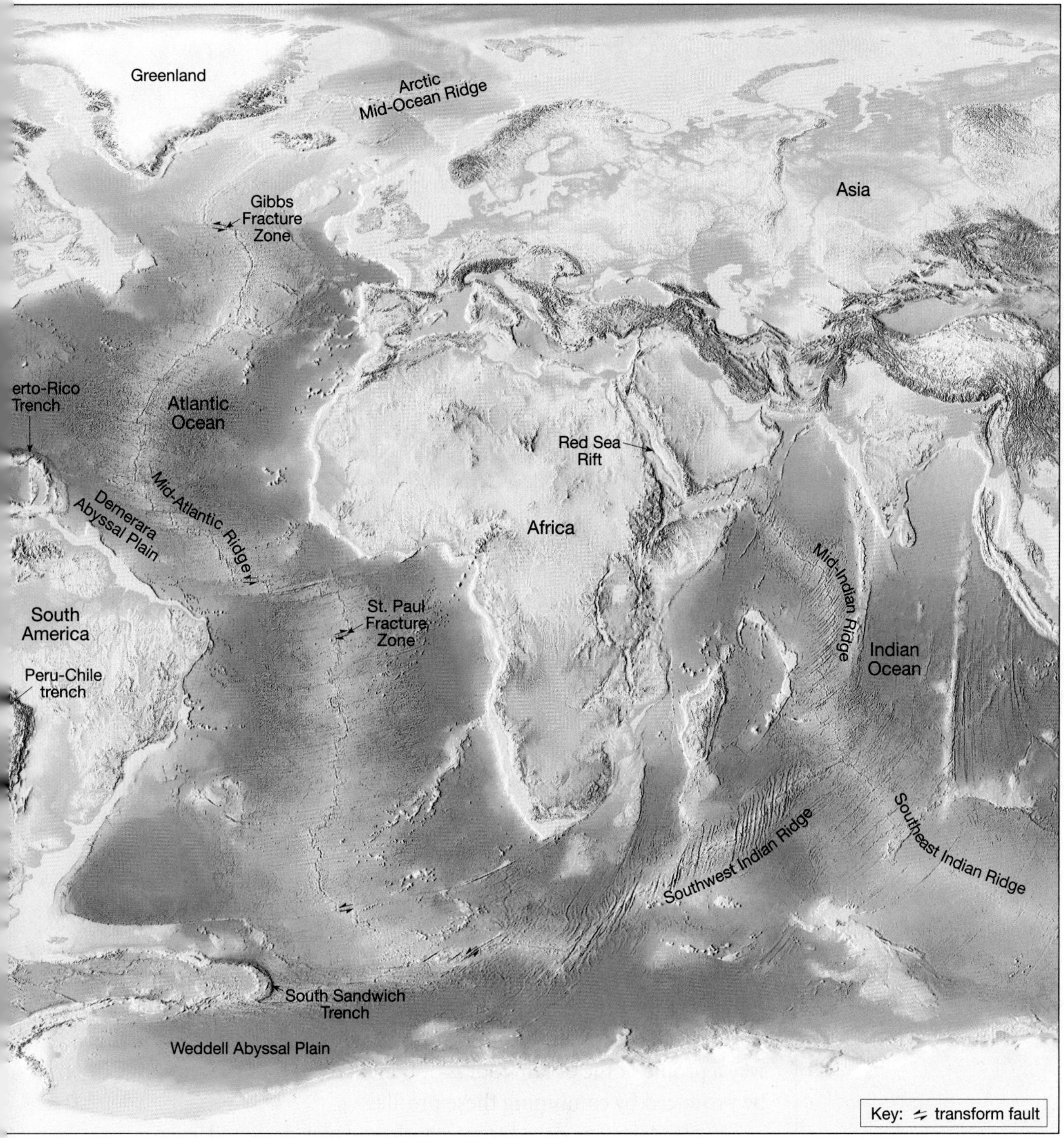

Greenland

Arctic
Mid-Ocean Ridge

Asia

Gibbs
Fracture
Zone

erto-Rico
Trench

Atlantic
Ocean

Red Sea
Rift

Demerara
Abyssal Plain

Mid-Atlantic Ridge

Africa

Mid-Indian Ridge

South
America

St. Paul
Fracture
Zone

Indian
Ocean

Peru-Chile
trench

Southwest Indian Ridge

Southeast Indian Ridge

South Sandwich
Trench

Weddell Abyssal Plain

Key: ⇌ transform fault

(*bathos* = depth, *metry* = measurement) is the measurement of ocean depths and the charting of the shape or topography of the ocean floor.

The first understanding of the ocean floor's varied topography did not unfold until the historic three-and-a-half-year voyage of the HMS *Challenger*. From December 1872 to May 1876, the *Challenger* expedition made the first—and perhaps still the most comprehensive—study of the global ocean ever attempted by one agency. The 127,500 kilometer trip took the ship and its crew of scientists to every ocean

Go Online

NSTA *SciLINKS*

For: Links on oceans
Visit: www.SciLinks.org
Web Code: cjn-5141

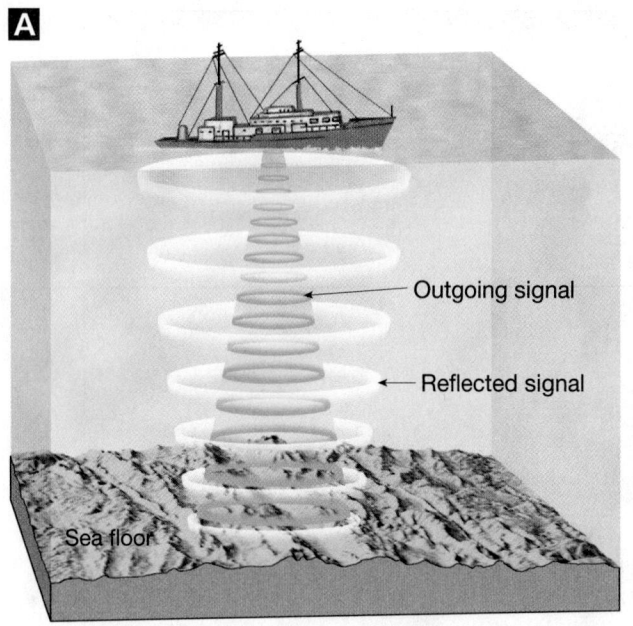
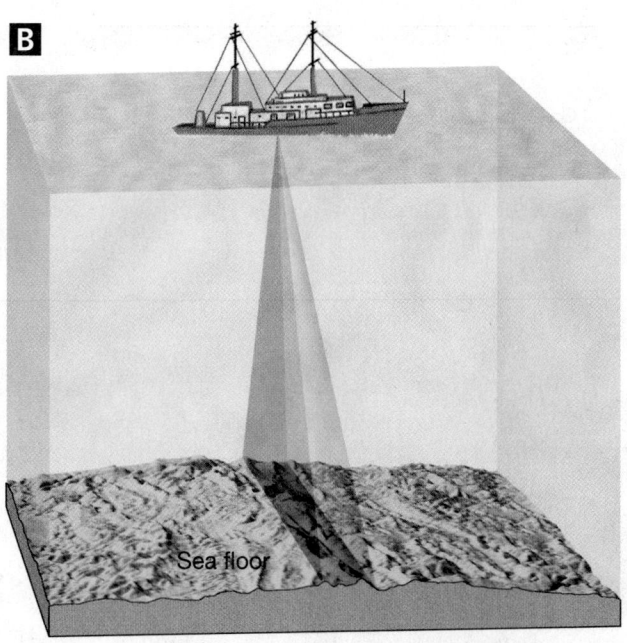

Figure 4 Sonar Methods
A By using sonar, oceanographers can determine the depth of the ocean floor in a particular area. **B** Modern multibeam sonar obtains a profile of a narrow swath of seafloor every few seconds.

except the Arctic. Throughout the voyage, they sampled various ocean properties. They measured water depth by lowering a long, weighted line overboard. **Today's technology—particularly sonar, satellites, and submersibles—allows scientists to study the ocean floor in a more efficient and precise manner than ever before.**

Sonar In the 1920s, a technological breakthrough occurred with the invention of sonar, a type of electronic depth-sounding equipment. Sonar is an acronym for **so**und **na**vigation **a**nd **r**anging. It is also referred to as echo sounding. Sonar works by transmitting sound waves toward the ocean bottom, as shown in Figure 4A. With simple sonar, a sensitive receiver intercepts the echo reflected from the bottom. Then a clock precisely measures the time interval to fractions of a second. Depth can be calculated from the speed of sound waves in water—about 1500 meters per second—and the time required for the energy pulse to reach the ocean floor and return. The depths determined from continuous monitoring of these echoes are plotted. In this way a profile of the ocean floor is obtained. A chart of the seafloor can be produced by combining these profiles.

In the last few decades, researchers have designed even more sophisticated sonar to map the ocean floor. In contrast to simple sonar, multibeam sonar uses more than one sound source and listening device. As you can see from Figure 4B, this technique obtains a profile of a narrow strip of ocean floor rather than obtaining the depth of a single point every few seconds. These profiles are recorded every few seconds as the research vessel advances. When a ship uses multibeam sonar to make a map of a section of ocean floor, the ship travels through the area in a regularly spaced back-and-forth pattern. Not surprisingly, this method is known as "mowing the lawn."

Satellites Measuring the shape of the ocean surface from space is another technological breakthrough that has led to a better understanding of the ocean floor. After compensating for waves, tides, currents, and atmospheric effects, scientists discovered that the ocean surface is not perfectly flat. This is because gravity attracts water toward regions where massive ocean floor features occur. Therefore, mountains and ridges produce elevated areas on the ocean surface. Features such as canyons and trenches cause slight depressions.

The differences in ocean-surface height caused by ocean floor features are not visible to the human eye. However, satellites are able to measure these small differences by bouncing microwaves off the ocean surface. Figure 5 shows how the outgoing radar pulses are reflected back to a satellite. The height of the ocean surface can be calculated by knowing the satellite's exact position. Devices on satellites can measure variations in sea-surface height as small as 3 to 6 centimeters. This type of data has added greatly to the knowledge of ocean-floor topography. Cross-checked with traditional sonar depth measurements, the data are used to produce detailed ocean-floor maps, such as the one previously shown in Figure 3.

 **Reading Checkpoint** *How do satellites help us learn about the shape of the seafloor?*

Go Online
PLANETDIARY

For: Links on mapping the ocean floor
Visit: PHSchool.com
Web Code: czd-5141

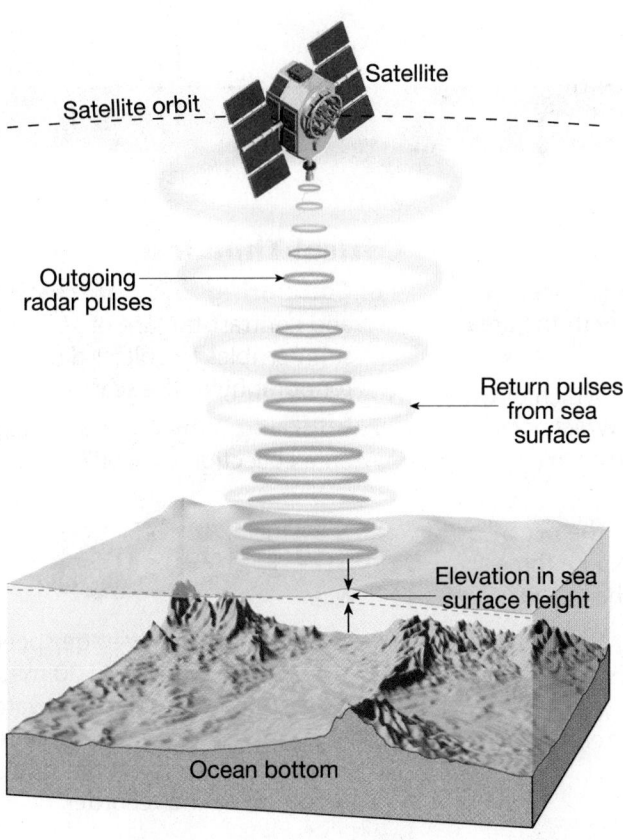

Satellite

Satellite orbit

Outgoing radar pulses

Return pulses from sea surface

Elevation in sea surface height

Ocean bottom

Figure 5 Satellite Method
Satellites can be used to measure sea-surface height. The data collected by satellites can be used to predict the location of large features on the seafloor. This method of data collection is much faster than using sonar.

The Ocean Floor **399**

Submersibles A **submersible** is a small underwater craft used for deep-sea research. Submersibles are used to collect data about areas of the ocean that were previously unreachable by humans. Submersibles are equipped with a number of instruments ranging from thermometers to cameras to pressure gauges. The operators of submersibles can record video and photos of previously unknown creatures that live in the abyss. They can collect water samples and sediment samples for analysis.

The first submersible was used in 1934 by William Beebe. He descended to a depth of 923 meters off of Bermuda in a steel sphere that was tethered to a ship. Since that time, submersibles have become more sophisticated. In 1960, Jacques Piccard descended in the untethered submersible *Trieste* to 10,912 meters below the ocean surface into the Mariana Trench. *Alvin* and *Sea Cliff II* are two other manned submersibles used for deep-sea research. *Alvin* can reach depths of 4000 meters, and *Sea Cliff II* can reach 6000 meters.

Today, many submersibles are unmanned and operated remotely by computers. These remotely operated vehicles (ROVs) can remain under water for long periods. They collect data, record video, use sonar, and collect sample organisms with remotely operated arms. Another type of submersible, the autonomous underwater vehicle (AUV), is under development. Its goal is to collect long-term data without interruption.

Section 14.1 Assessment

Reviewing Concepts

1. How does the area of Earth's surface covered by the oceans compare with the area covered by land?

2. Name the four ocean basins. Which of the four ocean basins is the largest? Which is located almost entirely in the southern hemisphere?

3. How does the topography of the ocean floor compare to that on land? Name three topographic features found on the ocean floor.

4. What types of technology are used to study the ocean floor?

5. Describe how sonar is used to determine seafloor depth.

Critical Thinking

6. **Comparing and Contrasting** Compare and contrast the use of satellites and submersibles to collect data about the topography of the seafloor.

7. **Inferring** Why is deep-sea exploration and data collection difficult?

Math Practice

8. Assuming the average speed of sound waves in water is 1500 meters per second, determine the water depth in meters if a sonar signal requires 4.5 seconds to hit the bottom and return to the recorder.

14.2 Ocean Floor Features

Reading Focus

Key Concepts

- What are the three main regions of the ocean floor?
- How do continental margins in the Atlantic Ocean differ from those in the Pacific Ocean?
- How are deep-ocean trenches formed?
- How are abyssal plains formed?
- What is formed at mid-ocean ridges?

Vocabulary

- ◆ continental margin
- ◆ continental shelf
- ◆ continental slope
- ◆ submarine canyon
- ◆ turbidity current
- ◆ continental rise
- ◆ ocean basin floor
- ◆ abyssal plains
- ◆ seamounts
- ◆ mid-ocean ridge
- ◆ seafloor spreading

Reading Strategy

Outlining Before you read, make an outline of this section. Use the green headings as the main topics and the blue headings as subtopics. As you read, add supporting details.

> I. Continental Margins
>
>   A. Continental Shelf
>
>   B. Continental Slope
>
>   C. _____ ?
>
> II. _____ ?
>
>   A. _____ ?

Oceanographers studying the topography of the ocean floor have divided it into three major regions. **The ocean floor regions are the continental margins, the ocean basin floor, and the mid-ocean ridge.** The map in Figure 6 outlines these regions for the North Atlantic Ocean. The profile at the bottom of the illustration shows the varied topography. Scientists have discovered that each of these regions has its own unique characteristics and features.

Figure 6 Topography of the North Atlantic Ocean Basin Beneath the map is a profile of the area between points A and B. The profile has been exaggerated 40 times to make the topographic features more distinct.

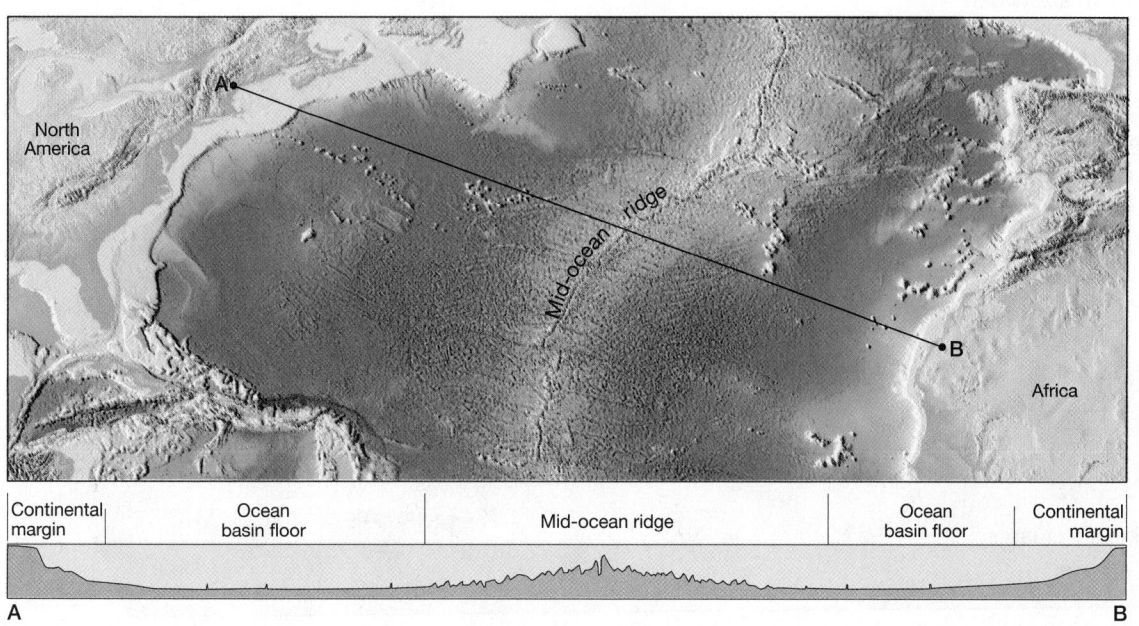

Continental margin	Ocean basin floor	Mid-ocean ridge	Ocean basin floor	Continental margin

A   B

Continental Margins

The zone of transition between a continent and the adjacent ocean basin floor is known as the **continental margin.** **In the Atlantic Ocean, thick layers of undisturbed sediment cover the continental margin. This region has very little volcanic or earthquake activity.** This is because the continental margins in the Atlantic Ocean are not associated with plate boundaries, unlike the continental margins of the Pacific Ocean. **In the Pacific Ocean, oceanic crust is plunging beneath continental crust. This force results in a narrow continental margin that experiences both volcanic activity and earthquakes.** Figure 7 shows the features of a continental margin found along the Atlantic coast.

Continental Shelf What if you were to begin an underwater journey eastward across the Atlantic Ocean? The first area of ocean floor you would encounter is the continental shelf. The **continental shelf** is the gently sloping submerged surface extending from the shoreline. The shelf is almost nonexistent along some coastlines. However, the shelf may extend seaward as far as 1500 kilometers along other coastlines. On average, the continental shelf is about 80 kilometers wide and 130 meters deep at its seaward edge. The average steepness of the shelf is equal to a drop of only about 2 meters per kilometer. The slope is so slight that to the human eye it appears to be a horizontal surface.

Continental shelves have economic and political significance. **Continental shelves contain important mineral deposits, large reservoirs of oil and natural gas, and huge sand and gravel deposits.** The waters of the continental shelf also contain important fishing grounds, which are significant sources of food.

Figure 7 Atlantic Continental Margin The continental margins in the Atlantic Ocean are wider than in the Pacific Ocean and are covered in a thick layer of sediment.
Explaining *Why are continental margins in the Pacific Ocean narrower and associated with earthquakes and volcanic activity?*

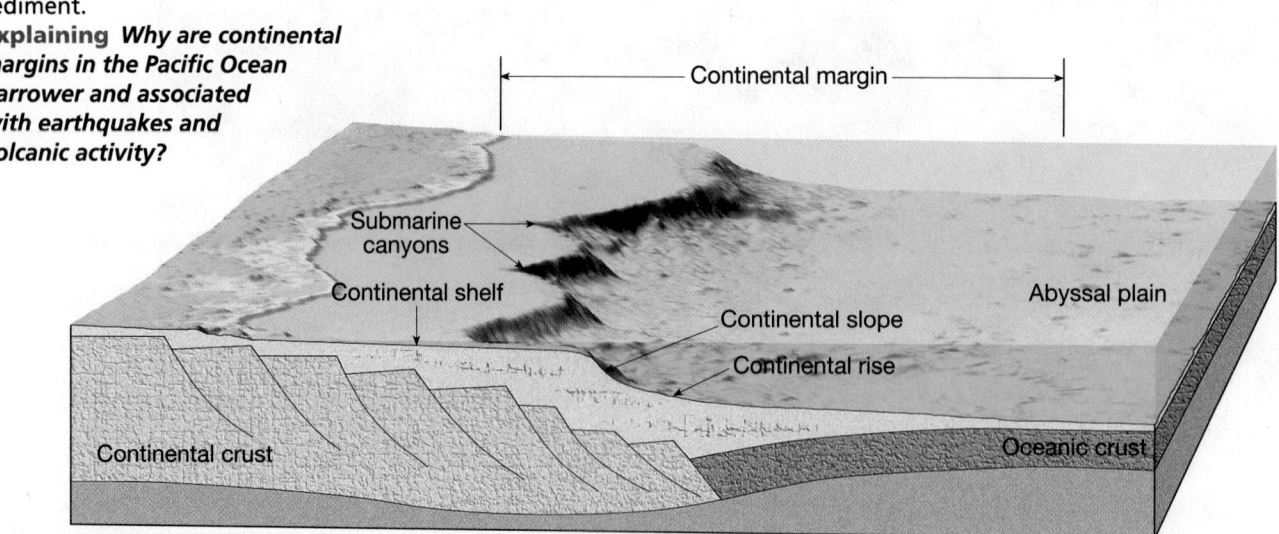

Continental Slope Marking the seaward edge of the continental shelf is the **continental slope.** This slope is steeper than the shelf, and it marks the boundary between continental crust and oceanic crust. The continental slope can be seen in Figure 7 on page 402. Although the steepness of the continental slope varies greatly from place to place, it averages about 5 degrees. In some places the slope may exceed 25 degrees. The continental slope is a relatively narrow feature, averaging only about 20 kilometers in width.

Deep, steep-sided valleys known as **submarine canyons** are cut into the continental slope. These canyons may extend to the ocean basin floor. Figure 8 shows how submarine canyons are formed. Most information suggests that submarine canyons have been eroded, at least in part, by turbidity currents. **Turbidity currents** are occasional movements of dense, sediment-rich water down the continental slope. They are created when sand and mud on the continental shelf and slope are disturbed—perhaps by an earthquake—and become suspended in the water. Because such muddy water is denser than normal seawater, it flows down the slope. As it flows down, it erodes and accumulates more sediment. Erosion from these muddy torrents is believed to be the major force in the formation of most submarine canyons. Narrow continental margins, such as the one located along the California coast, are marked with numerous submarine canyons.

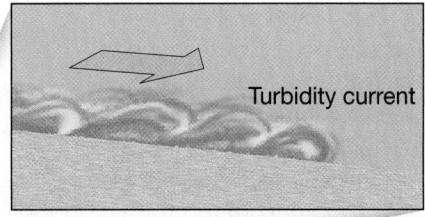

Submarine canyons

Turbidity current

Turbidity current

Figure 8 Submarine Canyons Most evidence suggests that submarine canyons probably formed as river valleys during periods of low sea level during recent ice ages. Turbidity currents continue to change the canyons.

Turbidity currents are known to be an important mechanism of sediment transport in the ocean. Turbidity currents erode submarine canyons and deposit sediments on the deep-ocean floor.

Continental Rise In regions where trenches do not exist, the steep continental slope merges into a more gradual incline known as the **continental rise.** Here the steepness of the slope drops to about 6 meters per kilometer. Whereas the width of the continental slope averages about 20 kilometers, the continental rise may be hundreds of kilometers wide.

 **Reading Checkpoint** *Compare and contrast the continental slope and continental rise.*

Go Online

NSTA SciLINKS

For: Links on ocean floor features
Visit: www.SciLinks.org
Web Code: cjn-5142

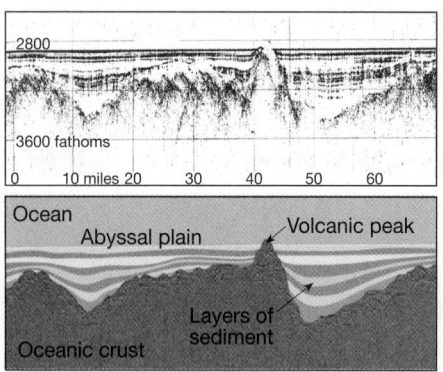

Figure 9 Abyssal Plain Cross Section This seismic cross section and matching sketch of a portion of the Madeira abyssal plain in the eastern Atlantic Ocean shows how the irregular oceanic crust is buried by sediments.

Ocean Basin Floor

Between the continental margin and mid-ocean ridge lies the **ocean basin floor.** The size of this region—almost 30 percent of Earth's surface—is comparable to the percentage of land above sea level. This region includes deep-ocean trenches, very flat areas known as abyssal plains, and tall volcanic peaks called seamounts and guyots.

Deep-Ocean Trenches Deep-ocean trenches are long, narrow creases in the ocean floor that form the deepest parts of the ocean. Most trenches are located along the margins of the Pacific Ocean, and many exceed 10,000 meters in depth. A portion of one trench—the Challenger Deep in the Mariana Trench—has been measured at a record 11,022 meters below sea level. It is the deepest known place on Earth. **Trenches form at sites of plate convergence where one moving plate descends beneath another and plunges back into the mantle.** Earthquakes and volcanic activity are associated with these regions. The large number of trenches and the volcanic activity along the margins of the Pacific Ocean give the region its nickname as the *Ring of Fire.*

Abyssal Plains **Abyssal plains** are deep, extremely flat features. In fact, these regions are possibly the most level places on Earth. Abyssal plains have thick accumulations of fine sediment that have buried an otherwise rugged ocean floor, as shown in Figure 9. **The sediments that make up abyssal plains are carried there by turbidity currents or deposited as a result of suspended sediments settling.** Abyssal plains are found in all oceans of the world. However, the Atlantic Ocean has the most extensive abyssal plains because it has few trenches to catch sediment carried down the continental slope.

Seamounts and Guyots The submerged volcanic peaks that dot the ocean floor are called **seamounts.** They are volcanoes that have not reached the ocean surface. These steep-sided cone-shaped peaks are found on the floors of all the oceans. However, the greatest number have been identified in the Pacific. Some seamounts form at volcanic hot spots. An example is the Hawaiian-Emperor Seamount chain, shown in Figure 3 on page 396. This chain stretches from the Hawaiian Islands to the Aleutian trench.

Once underwater volcanoes reach the surface, they form islands. Over time, running water and wave action erode these volcanic islands to near sea level. Over millions of years, the islands gradually sink and may disappear below the water surface. This process occurs as the moving plate slowly carries the islands away from the elevated oceanic ridge or hot spot where they originated. These once-active, now-submerged, flat-topped structures are called guyots.

Reading Checkpoint *What are abyssal plains?*

Mid-Ocean Ridges

The **mid-ocean ridge** is found near the center of most ocean basins. It is an interconnected system of underwater mountains that have developed on newly formed ocean crust. This system is the longest topographic feature on Earth's surface. It exceeds 70,000 kilometers in length. The mid-ocean ridge winds through all major oceans similar to the way a seam winds over the surface of a baseball.

The term *ridge* may be misleading because the mid-ocean ridge is not narrow. It has widths from 1000 to 4000 kilometers and may occupy as much as one half of the total area of the ocean floor. Another look at Figure 3 shows that the mid-ocean ridge is broken into segments. These are offset by large transform faults where plates slide past each other horizontally, resulting in shallow earthquakes.

Seafloor Spreading A high amount of volcanic activity takes place along the crest of the mid-ocean ridge. This activity is associated with seafloor spreading. **Seafloor spreading** occurs at divergent plate boundaries where two lithospheric plates are moving apart. ⬤**New ocean floor is formed at mid-ocean ridges as magma rises between the diverging plates and cools.**

Hydrothermal Vents Hydrothermal vents form along mid-ocean ridges. These are zones where mineral-rich water, heated by the hot, newly-formed oceanic crust, escapes through cracks in oceanic crust into the water. As the super-heated, mineral-rich water comes in contact with the surrounding cold water, minerals containing metals such as sulfur, iron, copper, and zinc precipitate out and are deposited.

Section 14.2 Assessment

Reviewing Concepts

1. ⬤ What are the three main regions of the ocean floor?

2. ⬤ How do continental margins in the Atlantic Ocean differ from those in the Pacific Ocean?

3. ⬤ What are trenches? How are deep-ocean trenches formed?

4. ⬤ What are abyssal plains? How are abyssal plains formed?

5. ⬤ What is formed at mid-ocean ridges?

Critical Thinking

6. **Comparing and Contrasting** Compare and contrast seamounts and guyots.

7. **Applying Concepts** Explain how turbidity currents are related to submarine canyons.

Writing in Science

Descriptive Paragraph Imagine you are about to take an underwater journey in a submersible across the Atlantic Ocean. Your journey begins at the coast, and you travel out toward the mid-ocean ridge. Write a paragraph describing the ocean floor features you will likely see on your journey.

Explaining Coral Atolls—
Darwin's Hypothesis

Coral atolls are ring-shaped structures that often extend several thousand meters below sea level. Corals are colonial animals about the size of an ant. They are related to jellyfish and feed with stinging tentacles. Most corals protect themselves by precipitating a hard external skeleton made of calcium carbonate. Coral reefs occur where corals reproduce and grow over many centuries. Their skeletons fuse into large structures called coral reefs.

The Problem with Corals

Corals require specific environmental conditions to grow. For example, reef-building corals grow best in waters with an average annual temperature of about 24°C. They cannot survive prolonged exposure to temperatures below 18°C or above 30°C. Reef-building corals also need clear sunlit water. As a result, the limiting depth of most active reef growth is only about 45 meters.

Gathering Data

How can corals—which require warm, shallow, sunlit water no deeper than a few dozen meters to live—create thick structures like coral atolls that extend into deep water? The naturalist Charles Darwin was one of the first to formulate a hypothesis on the origin of atolls. From 1831 to 1836, he sailed aboard the British ship HMS *Beagle* during its famous voyage around the world. In various places Darwin noticed a series of stages in coral-reef development. Development begins with a fringing reef, like the one shown in Figure 10A. The fringing reef forms along the sides of a volcanic island. As the volcanic island slowly sinks, the fringing reef becomes a barrier reef, as shown in Figure 10B. Figure 10C shows the final stage of development of the atoll. The volcano sinks completely underwater but the coral reef remains near the surface.

Darwin's Hypothesis

Figure 10 is a drawing that summarizes Darwin's hypothesis about atoll formation. As a volcanic island slowly sinks, the corals continue to build the reef upward. This explained how living coral reefs, which are restricted to shallow water, can build structures that now exist in much deeper water. The theory of plate tectonics supports Darwin's hypothesis. Plate tectonics explains how a volcanic island can become extinct and experience a change in elevation over long periods of time. As the hot ocean seafloor moves away from the mid-ocean ridge, it becomes denser and sinks. This is why islands also sink. Darwin's hypothesis is also supported by evidence from drilling that shows volcanic rock is beneath the oldest and deepest coral reef structures. Atolls owe their existence to the gradual sinking of volcanic islands containing coral reefs that build upward through time.

Figure 10 Formation of a Coral Atoll A A fringing coral reef forms around a volcanic island. **B** As the volcanic island sinks, the fringing reef slowly becomes a barrier reef. **C** Eventually, the volcano is completely underwater and a coral atoll remains.

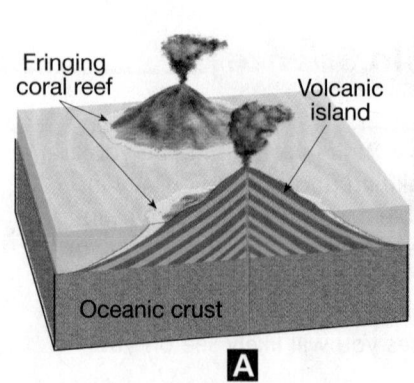

Fringing coral reef

Volcanic island

Oceanic crust

A

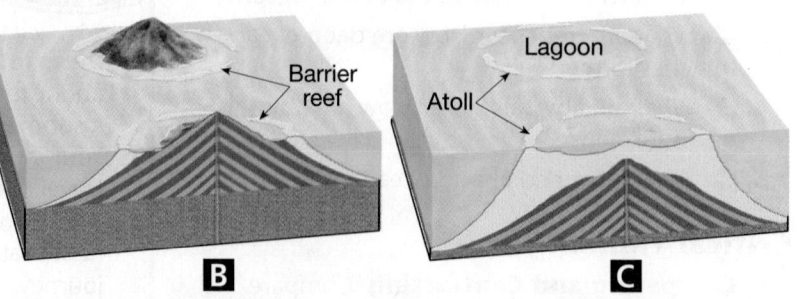

Barrier reef

B

Lagoon

Atoll

C

14.3 Seafloor Sediments

Reading Focus

Key Concepts

- What are the three types of ocean-floor sediments?
- What does terrigenous sediment consist of?
- What is the composition of biogenous sediment?
- How is hydrogenous sediment formed?

Vocabulary

- terrigenous sediment
- biogenous sediment
- calcareous ooze
- siliceous ooze
- hydrogenous sediment

Reading Strategy

Summarizing Make a table like the one below that includes all the headings for the section. Write a brief summary of the text for each heading.

Actions at Boundaries
I. Types of Seafloor Sediments
• Terrigenous sediments originated on land.
• Biogenous sediments are biological in origin.
• _____ ?

Except for steep areas of the continental slope and the crest of the mid-ocean ridge, most of the ocean floor is covered with sediment. Some of this sediment has been deposited by turbidity currents. The rest has slowly settled onto the seafloor from above. The thickness of ocean-floor sediments varies. Some trenches act as traps for sediment originating on the continental margin. The accumulation may approach 10 kilometers in thickness. In general, however, accumulations of sediment are much less—about 500 to 1000 meters.

Generally, coarser sediments, such as sand, cover the continental shelf and slope while finer sediments, such as clay, cover the deep-ocean floor. Figure 11 shows the distribution of the different types of ocean-floor sediments. Various types of sediment accumulate on nearly all areas of the ocean floor in the same way dust accumulates in all parts of your home. Even the deep-ocean floor, far from land, receives small amounts of windblown material and microscopic parts of organisms.

Figure 11 Distribution of Ocean-Floor Sediments Coarse-grained terrigenous deposits dominate continental margin areas. Fine-grained clay, or mud, is more common in the deepest areas of the ocean basins.
Infer _Why is it more common to find fine-grained sediments in the deepest areas of the ocean basins?_

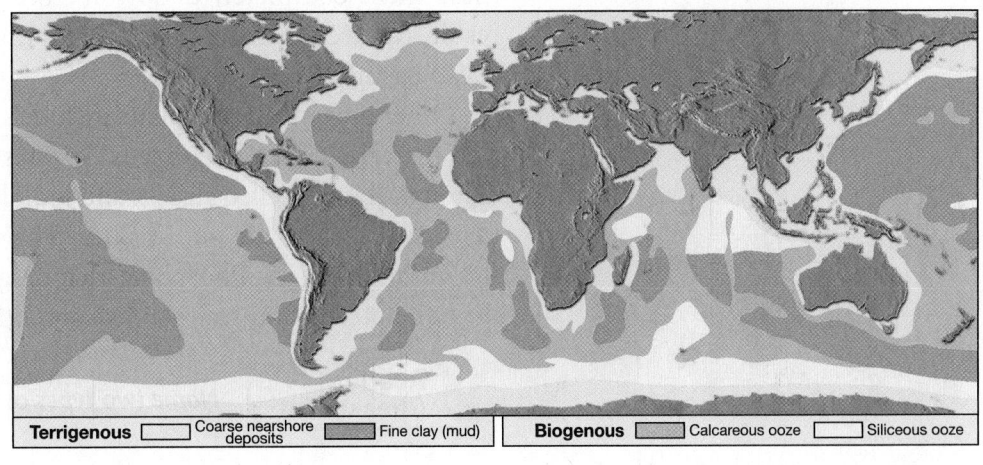

Terrigenous | Coarse nearshore deposits | Fine clay (mud)   Biogenous | Calcareous ooze | Siliceous ooze

Types of Seafloor Sediments

Ocean-floor sediments can be classified according to their origin into three broad categories: terrigenous sediments, biogenous sediments, and hydrogenous sediments. Ocean-floor sediments are usually mixtures of the various sediment types. Over millions of years, marine sediments such as sand or the shells and skeletons of ocean organisms can form sedimentary rock. For example, chalk is a form of limestone made up mostly of the tiny shells of one-celled ocean organisms.

Terrigenous Sediment Terrigenous sediment is sediment that originates on land. **Terrigenous sediments consist primarily of mineral grains that were eroded from continental rocks and transported to the ocean.** Larger particles such as gravel and sand usually settle rapidly near shore. Finer particles such as clay can take years to settle to the ocean floor and may be carried thousands of kilometers by ocean currents. Clay accumulates very slowly on the deep-ocean floor. To form a 1-centimeter abyssal clay layer, for example, requires as much as 50,000 years. In contrast, on the continental margins near the mouths of large rivers, terrigenous sediment accumulates rapidly and forms thick deposits. In the Gulf of Mexico, for instance, the sediment is many kilometers thick.

Biogenous Sediment Biogenous sediment is sediment that is biological in origin. **Biogenous sediments consist of shells and skeletons of marine animals and algae.** This debris is produced mostly by microscopic organisms living in surface waters. Once these organisms die, their hard shells sink, accumulating on the seafloor.

The most common biogenous sediment is calcareous ooze. **Calcareous ooze** is produced from the calcium carbonate shells of organisms. Calcareous ooze has the consistency of thick mud. When calcium carbonate shells slowly sink into deeper parts of the ocean, they begin to dissolve. In ocean water deeper than about 4500 meters, these shells completely dissolve before they reach the bottom. As a result, calcareous ooze does not accumulate in the deeper areas of ocean basins.

Other biogenous sediments include siliceous ooze and phosphate-rich material. **Siliceous ooze** is composed primarily of the shells of diatoms—single-celled algae—and radiolarians—single-celled animals that have shells made out of silica. The shells of these organisms are shown in Figure 12. Phosphate-rich biogenous sediments come from the bones, teeth, and scales of fish and other marine organisms.

 *Name two types of biogenous sediments.*

Hydrogenous Sediment 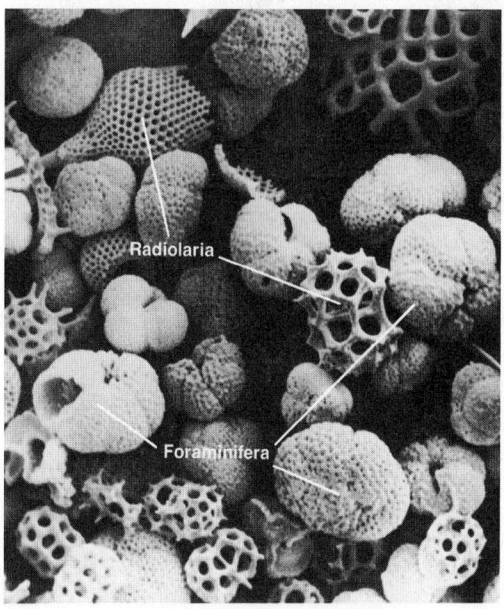 Hydrogenous sediment consists of minerals that crystallize directly from ocean water through various chemical reactions. Hydrogenous sediments make up only a small portion of the overall sediment in the ocean. They do, however, have many different compositions and are distributed in many different environments. Some of the most common types of hydrogenous sediment are listed below.

- Manganese nodules are rounded, hard lumps of manganese, iron, and other metals. These metals precipitate around an object such as a grain of sand. The nodules can be up to 20 centimeters in diameter and are often scattered across large areas of the deep ocean floor.
- Calcium carbonates form by precipitation directly from ocean water in warm climates. If this material is buried and hardens, a type of limestone forms. Most limestone, however, is composed of biogenous sediment.
- Evaporites form where evaporation rates are high and there is restricted open-ocean circulation. As water evaporates from such areas, the remaining ocean water becomes saturated with dissolved minerals that then begin to precipitate. Collectively termed "salts," some evaporite minerals do taste salty, such as halite, or common table salt. Other salts do not taste salty, such as the calcium sulfate minerals anhydrite ($CaSO_4$) and gypsum.

Figure 12 Biogenous Sediments The microscopic shells of radiolarians and foraminifers are examples of biogenous sediments. This photomicrograph has been enlarged hundreds of times.

Section 14.3 Assessment

Reviewing Concepts

1. What are the three types of ocean floor sediments?
2. What does terrigenous sediment consist of?
3. What is the composition of biogenous sediment?
4. How is hydrogenous sediment formed?

Critical Thinking

5. **Comparing and Contrasting** Compare and contrast calcareous ooze and siliceous ooze.
6. **Predicting** Would you expect to find more evaporites in an area of warm water that receives large amounts of sunlight such as the Red Sea or in an area of cold water that receives less sunlight such as the Greenland Sea?

Connecting Concepts

Origin of Sediments An oceanographer is studying sediment samples from the Bahama Banks. The sediments have a high amount of calcium carbonate. They are labeled biogenous but are later found to contain no shells from organisms that typically make up calcareous ooze. What other explanation is there for the origin of these sediments?

14.4 Resources from the Seafloor

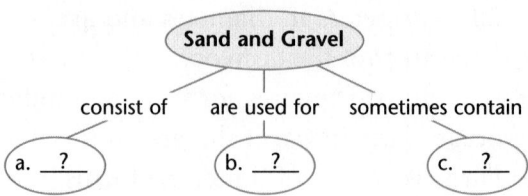

Reading Focus

Key Concepts

- Which ocean resources are used for energy production?
- How are gas hydrates formed?
- What other resources are derived from the ocean?

Vocabulary

♦ gas hydrates
♦ manganese nodule

Reading Strategy

Identifying Details Copy the concept map below. As you read, complete it to identify details about resources from the ocean.

Sand and Gravel

consist of   are used for   sometimes contain

a. ?   b. ?   c. ?

The ocean floor is rich in mineral and energy resources. Recovering them, however, often involves technological challenges and high costs. As technology improves we are able to access some of these resources more efficiently. However, other resources, such as manganese nodules, remain untouched.

Energy Resources

Most of the value of nonliving resources in the ocean comes from their use as energy products. **Oil and natural gas are the main energy products currently being obtained from the ocean floor.** Other resources have the potential to be used as a source of energy in the future.

Oil and Natural Gas The ancient remains of microscopic organisms are the source of today's deposits of oil and natural gas. These organisms were buried within marine sediments before they could decompose. After millions of years of exposure to heat from Earth's interior and pressure from overlying rock, the remains were transformed into oil and natural gas. The percentage of world oil produced from offshore regions has increased from trace amounts in the 1930s to more than 30 percent today. Part of this increase is due to advances in the technology of offshore drilling platforms such as the one shown in Figure 13.

Major offshore reserves exist in the Persian Gulf, in the Gulf of Mexico, off the coast of southern California, in the North Sea, and in the East Indies. Additional reserves are probably located off the north coast of Alaska and in the Canadian Arctic, Asian seas, Africa, and Brazil. One

Figure 13 Offshore drilling rigs tap the oil and natural gas reserves of the continental shelf. These platforms are near Santa Barbara, California.
Inferring *What changes to the marine environment may occur as a result of drilling for oil?*

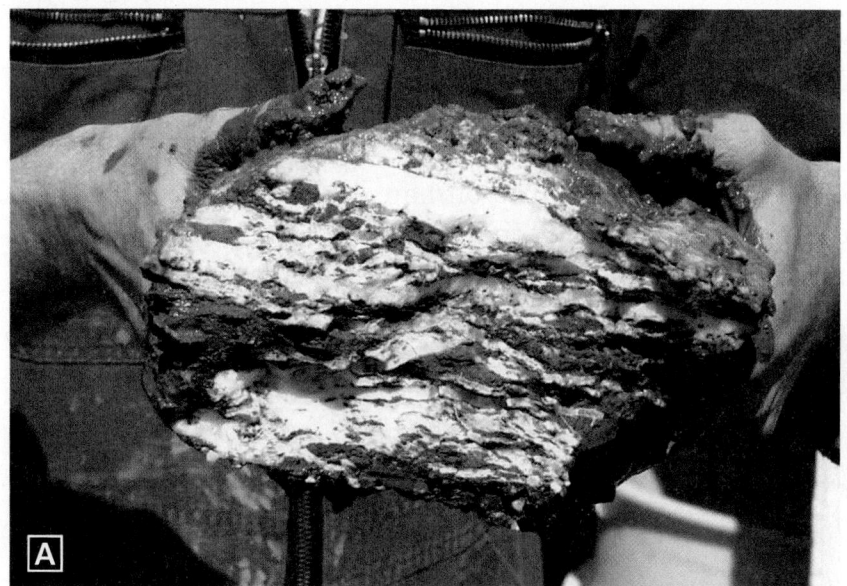

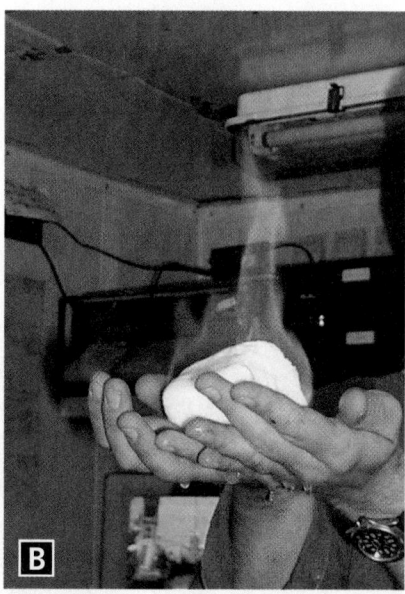

environmental concern about offshore petroleum exploration is the possibility of oil spills caused by accidental leaks during the drilling process.

Gas Hydrates **Gas hydrates** are compact chemical structures made of water and natural gas. The most common type of natural gas is methane, which produces methane hydrate. Gas hydrates occur beneath permafrost areas on land and under the ocean floor at depths below 525 meters.

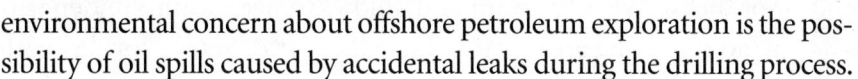 **Most oceanic gas hydrates are created when bacteria break down organic matter trapped in ocean-floor sediments.** The bacteria produce methane gas along with small amounts of ethane and propane. These gases combine with water in deep-ocean sediments in such a way that the gas is trapped inside a lattice-like cage of water molecules.

Vessels that have drilled into gas hydrates have brought up samples of mud mixed with chunks of gas hydrates like the one shown in Figure 14A. These chunks evaporate quickly when they are exposed to the relatively warm, low-pressure conditions at the ocean surface. Gas hydrates resemble chunks of ice but ignite when lit by a flame, as shown in Figure 14B. The hydrates burn because methane and other flammable gases are released as gas hydrates evaporate.

An estimated 20 quadrillion cubic meters of methane are locked up in sediments containing gas hydrates. This amount is double the amount of Earth's known coal, oil, and natural gas reserves combined. One drawback to using gas hydrates as an energy source is that they rapidly break down at surface temperatures and pressures. In the future, however, these ocean-floor reserves of energy may help provide our energy needs.

 **Reading Checkpoint** *What happens when gas hydrates are brought to the surface?*

Figure 14 Gas Hydrates
A A sample from the ocean floor has layers of white, ice-like gas hydrate mixed with mud.
B Gas hydrates evaporate when exposed to surface conditions, releasing natural gas that can be burned.

For: Links on ocean resources
Visit: www.SciLinks.org
Web Code: cjn-5144

Figure 15 These manganese nodules lie 5323 meters on the Pacific Ocean floor south of the island of Tahiti.
Applying Concepts *How do manganese nodules form?*

Other Resources

🔹 Other major resources from the ocean floor include sand and gravel, evaporative salts, and manganese nodules.

Sand and Gravel The offshore sand-and-gravel industry is second in economic value only to the petroleum industry. Sand and gravel, which include rock fragments that are washed out to sea and shells of marine organisms, are mined by offshore barges using suction devices. Sand and gravel are used for landfill, to fill in recreational beaches, and to make concrete.

In some cases, materials of high economic value are associated with offshore sand and gravel deposits. Gem-quality diamonds, for example, are recovered from gravels on the continental shelf offshore of South Africa and Australia. Sediments rich in tin have been mined from some offshore areas of Southeast Asia. Platinum and gold have been found in deposits in gold-mining areas throughout the world. Some Florida beach sands are rich in titanium.

Manganese Nodules As described earlier, **manganese nodules** are hard lumps of manganese and other metals that precipitate around a smaller object. Figure 15 shows manganese nodules on the deep-ocean floor. They contain high concentrations of manganese, iron, and smaller concentrations of copper,

☰Quick Lab

Evaporative Salts

Materials

400 mL beaker, table salt, tablespoon, balance, glass stirrer

Procedure

1. Place the empty beaker on the balance and add between 3 and 5 tablespoons of the salt. Measure the combined mass of the beaker and the salt. Record the measurement and remove the beaker from the balance.

2. Add 100 mL of water to the beaker and stir until the salt is dissolved.

3. Place the beaker in a warm, sunny area and allow the water to evaporate.

4. When all of the water has evaporated, place the beaker and its remaining contents on the balance and record the measurement.

Analyze and Conclude

1. **Comparing** How did the mass of the beaker and salt before the water was added compare to the mass of the beaker and salt after the water evaporated?

2. **Drawing Conclusions** What happened to the salt when the water evaporated?

3. **Predicting** How could the oceans be used as a source of salt?

nickel, and cobalt, all of which have a variety of economic uses. Cobalt, for example, is important because it is required to produce strong alloys with other metals. These alloys are used in high-speed cutting tools, powerful permanent magnets, and jet engine parts. With current technology, mining the deep-ocean floor for manganese nodules is possible but not economically profitable.

Manganese nodules are widely distributed along the ocean floor, but not all regions have the same potential for mining. Good locations for mining must have a large amount of nodules that contain an optimal mix of copper, nickel, and cobalt. Sites like this are limited. In addition, it is difficult to establish mining rights far from land. Also, there are environmental concerns about disturbing large portions of the deep-ocean floor.

Figure 16 Common table salt, or halite, is harvested from the salt left behind when ocean water evaporates. About 30 percent of the world's salt is produced by evaporating seawater.

Evaporative Salts When seawater evaporates, the salts increase in concentration until they can no longer remain dissolved. When the concentration becomes high enough, the salts precipitate out of solution and form salt deposits. These deposits can then be harvested, as shown in Figure 16. The most economically important salt is halite—common table salt. Halite is widely used for seasoning, curing, and preserving foods. It is also used in agriculture, in the clothing industry for dying fabric, and to de-ice roads.

Section 14.4 Assessment

Reviewing Concepts

1. What are the main energy resources from the ocean?
2. How are gas hydrates formed?
3. What drawbacks are associated with harvesting ocean resources for energy use?
4. What other resources are derived from the ocean?
5. What are the uses of evaporative salts?
6. What are manganese nodules? Why is it difficult to recover them from the ocean?

Critical Thinking

7. **Making Generalizations** How does technology influence the availability of resources from the ocean?

8. **Inferring** Near-shore mining of sand and gravel can result in large amounts of sediments being suspended in water. How might this affect marine organisms living in the area?

Connecting Concepts

Sand and Gravel Why are most sand and gravel deposits found on the continental shelf? What type of sediment is sand and gravel?

Modeling Seafloor Depth Transects

Oceanographers use a number of methods to determine the depth and topography of the ocean floor. Technology, such as sonar, satellites, and submersibles, have allowed scientists to produce detailed maps of the ocean floor in each ocean basin. In this lab, you will model a seafloor depth transect to determine the topography of an ocean basin created by your classmates.

Problem How can the topography of an ocean basin be determined?

Materials
- shoe box
- modeling clay
- aluminum foil
- pencil
- scalpel
- graph paper
- ruler

Skills Measuring, Graphing, Inferring, Drawing Conclusions

Procedure

Part A: Making a Model of the Seafloor

1. Reexamine Figure 3, Figure 7, and the figure below to determine which area of the ocean floor you will model. Be sure to identify the specific features that would be found in the area you choose to model. For example, if you were to model the continental margin you would want to include the continental shelf, continental slope, continental rise, and maybe some submarine canyons in your model. If you were to model the ocean basin floor you would want to include abyssal plains, trenches, seamounts, and guyots. Do not discuss the plan for your model with students outside your group.

2. Once you have determined which area of the ocean floor you will model, use the clay to make a contoured model of the seafloor inside the shoebox.

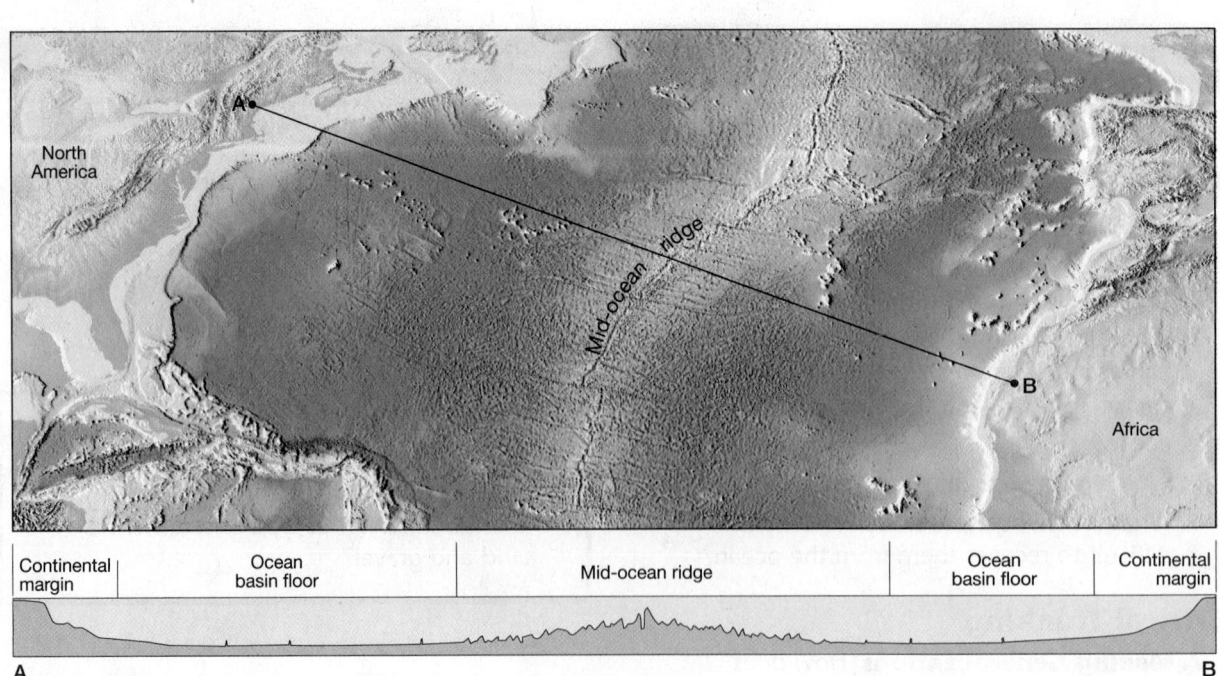

3. Cover the box with its top and exchange boxes with another group from your class. Do not remove the top of the box that you receive from another group.

Part B: Completing a Depth Transect

4. Obtain a piece of aluminum foil that is large enough to cover the top of the shoebox and fold over the sides of the box about an inch all the way around.

5. Spread the foil flat on your lab table. Place the ruler lengthwise on the foil, parallel to the edge of the foil. The ruler can be in the middle of the foil or off to the side. The line formed by the edge of the ruler will be your transect line.

6. Use a pencil to make tick marks on the foil piece every centimeter along the entire length of the foil.

7. Hold the foil in place over the top of the box. Quickly and carefully remove the top of the box and set the foil piece down in place of the top. Do not look in the box. Secure the foil in place on top of the box by turning down the foil over the sides of the box. Be sure the foil is taut across the top.

8. Label your graph paper. The *x*-axis will be "Distance along Transect Line" in centimeters, and the *y*-axis will be "Depth" in centimeters. Make tick marks along the *x*-axis once every centimeter. Make tick marks along the *y*-axis every half of a centimeter. **NOTE:** You may also use a computer to produce your graph.

9. Use the scalpel to carefully make a slit in the foil along the first centimeter mark. **CAUTION:** *The scalpel is extremely sharp. Handle it carefully.* After cutting the foil, gently place the ruler through the slit until it makes contact with the clay in the box. Be sure to hold the ruler straight and take the depth measurement. Record your data on the graph.

10. Repeat Step 9 for each point along the foil. When you are done, you should have a depth profile for the entire length of the box along your transect line.

11. Remove the foil from the box and examine the topography of the model.

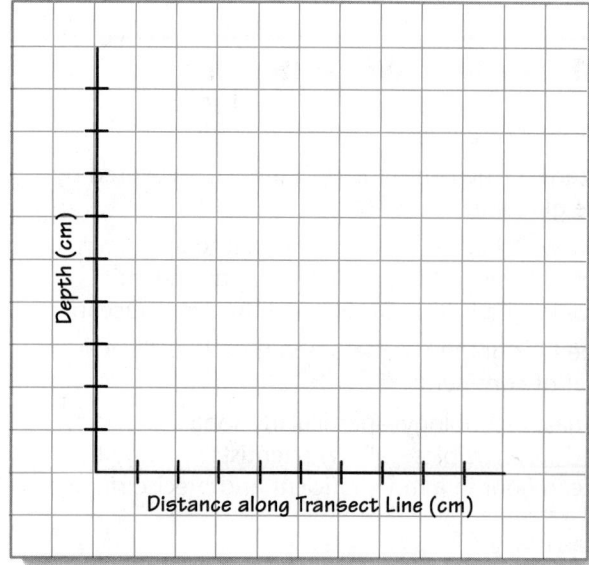

Depth (cm)

Distance along Transect Line (cm)

Analyze and Conclude

1. Inferring Based on your contour profile, what part of the ocean floor was being modeled? Check your answer with the group that created the model. Were you correct? Why or why not?

2. Comparing How does the profile on your graph compare with the contour of the model? Are there any major features in the model that did not appear on your graph? Why or why not?

3. Analyzing Data What could you have done to make your profile match the topography more accurately?

4. Explaining Before sonar was used to measure ocean depth, a less sophisticated method was used. A long line of rope with a lead weight on the end was tossed over the side of a ship and lowered until the weight hit the bottom. How is this method similar to what you did in the lab? How can the rope method lead to inaccuracies when trying to build an ocean floor profile?

14.1 The Vast World Ocean

Key Concepts

- Nearly 71 percent of Earth's surface is covered by the global ocean.

- The world ocean can be divided into four main ocean basins—the Pacific Ocean, the Atlantic Ocean, the Indian Ocean, and the Arctic Ocean.

- The topography of the ocean floor is as diverse as that of continents.

- Today, technology—particularly sonar, satellites, and submersibles—allows scientists to study the ocean floor in a more efficient and precise manner.

Vocabulary

oceanography, *p. 394*; bathymetry, *p. 396*; sonar, *p. 398*; submersible, *p. 400*

14.2 Ocean Floor Features

Key Concepts

- The ocean floor regions are the continental margins, the ocean basin floor, and the mid-ocean ridge.

- In the Atlantic Ocean thick layers of undisturbed sediment cover the continental margin. This region has very little volcanic or earthquake activity.

- In the Pacific Ocean oceanic crust is plunging beneath continental crust. This force results in a narrow continental margin that experiences both volcanic activity and earthquakes.

- Continental shelves contain important mineral deposits, large reservoirs of oil and natural gas, and huge sand and gravel deposits.

- Trenches form at sites of plate convergence where one moving plate descends beneath another and plunges back into the mantle.

- The sediments that make up abyssal plains are carried there by turbidity currents or are deposited as a result of suspended sediments settling.

- New ocean floor is formed at mid-ocean ridges as magma rises between the diverging plates and cools.

Vocabulary

continental margin, *p. 402*; continental shelf, *p. 402*; continental slope, *p. 403* submarine canyon, *p. 403*; turbidity current, *p. 403*; continental rise, *p. 403*; ocean basin floor, *p. 404*; abyssal plains, *p. 404*; seamounts, *p. 404*; mid-ocean ridge, *p. 405*; seafloor spreading, *p. 405*

14.3 Seafloor Sediments

Key Concepts

- Ocean-floor sediments can be classified according to their origin into three broad categories: terrigenous sediments, biogenous sediments, and hydrogenous sediments.

- Terrigenous sediments consist primarily of mineral grains that were eroded from continental rocks and transported to the ocean.

- Biogenous sediments consist of shells and skeletons of marine animals and algae.

- Hydrogenous sediments consist of minerals that crystallize directly from ocean water through various chemical reactions.

Vocabulary

terrigenous sediment, *p. 408*; biogenous sediment, *p. 408*; calcareous ooze, *p. 408*; siliceous ooze, *p. 408*; hydrogenous sediment, *p. 409*

14.4 Resources from the Seafloor

Key Concepts

- Oil and natural gas are the main energy products currently being obtained from the ocean floor.

- Most oceanic gas hydrates are created when bacteria break down organic matter trapped in ocean-floor sediments.

- Other major resources from the seafloor include sand and gravel, evaporative salts, and manganese nodules.

Vocabulary

gas hydrates, *p. 411*; manganese nodule, *p. 412*

Reviewing Content

Choose the letter that best answers the question or completes the statement.

1. Approximately what percentage of Earth's surface is covered by oceans?
   - **a.** 40
   - **b.** 50
   - **c.** 60
   - **d.** 70

2. Which ocean basin is the largest?
   - **a.** the Atlantic
   - **b.** the Indian
   - **c.** the Pacific
   - **d.** the Arctic

3. The use of sound waves to determine the depth of the ocean is called
   - **a.** submarine sounding.
   - **b.** sonar.
   - **c.** satellite altimetry.
   - **d.** submersible sounding.

4. The gently sloping submerged surface that extends from the shoreline toward the ocean basin floor is the continental
   - **a.** shelf.
   - **b.** slope.
   - **c.** rise.
   - **d.** margin.

5. Submarine canyons are believed to have been created by
   - **a.** rivers during the ice age.
   - **b.** earthquakes.
   - **c.** lost ships.
   - **d.** subduction.

6. Important mineral deposits, including large reservoirs of oil and natural gas, are associated with
   - **a.** the ocean basin floor.
   - **b.** the continental shelf.
   - **c.** abyssal plains.
   - **d.** the continental rise.

7. Calcareous ooze is an example of
   - **a.** terrigenous sediment.
   - **b.** biogenous sediment.
   - **c.** hydrogenous sediment.
   - **d.** a combination of hydrogenous and terrigenous sediment.

8. Sediments that consist of mineral grains that were eroded from continental rocks are called
   - **a.** terrigenous.
   - **b.** biogenous.
   - **c.** hydrogenous.
   - **d.** hydrates.

9. What could gas hydrates be used for?
   - **a.** as landfill
   - **b.** to make concrete
   - **c.** as a source of energy
   - **d.** as a source of cobalt and copper

10. Economically valuable materials such as diamonds, tin, and platinum are associated with which ocean floor resource?
    - **a.** oil and natural gas
    - **b.** sand and gravel
    - **c.** evaporative salts
    - **d.** manganese nodules

Understanding Concepts

11. Why is Earth called the "blue planet"?

12. What is bathymetry? What techniques do scientists use to discover more about the bathymetry of ocean basins?

13. Why is multibeam sonar more efficient than simple sonar at collecting data from the ocean floor?

14. Compare and contrast the size and topography of the Atlantic Ocean basin to that of the Pacific Ocean basin.

15. What is a continental shelf? What economic significance do continental shelves have?

16. Compare and contrast deep-ocean trenches and mid-oceanic ridges.

17. In which ocean basin are most trenches found? Why?

18. What is the difference between terrigenous sediments and biogenous sediments?

19. Explain the process by which hydrogenous sediments are formed.

20. Why is it uncommon to find calcareous ooze in deep-ocean basins?

21. From which area of the ocean basin are the resources of oil and natural gas harvested?

22. What current disadvantages exist to using gas hydrates as a form of energy?

23. What are the uses for sand and gravel harvested from the continental shelf?

The Ocean Floor **417**

Critical Thinking

24. **Interpreting Diagrams** Reexamine Figure 1. Why do you think that the Northern Hemisphere is called the "land hemisphere" and the Southern Hemisphere is called the "water hemisphere"?

25. **Making Generalizations** A friend says that because of gravity we can learn about the topography of the ocean floor. Explain why this is true.

26. **Inferring** The continental margin of the Atlantic Ocean is often referred to as a "passive" continental margin whereas Pacific Ocean continental margins are referred to as "active." Infer what the characteristics of passive and active continental margins would be.

27. **Inferring** There is usually very little sediment accumulation found at mid-ocean ridges. Why do you think this is true?

28. **Applying Concepts** Imagine you have been asked to invent a device that would be used to retrieve manganese nodules. What characteristics would the device have in order to successfully achieve this goal?

Math Skills

29. **Calculating** Assuming the average speed of sound waves in water is 1500 meters per second, determine, in seconds, how long it would take a sonar signal to hit the bottom and return to the recorder if the water depth is 7500 meters.

30. **Calculating** The rate of seafloor spreading in the Atlantic Ocean has been estimated to be about 2.5 centimeters per year. By how many centimeters will the Atlantic Ocean basin increase over a period of 7 years?

31. **Calculating** If the settling rate of very fine sand in the open ocean is 360 meters per day, how many days will it take for the sediment to reach the ocean floor at a depth of 4 kilometers?

Concepts in Action

Use the table below to answer Questions 32 and 33.

The table shows the kind of data that a simple sonar echo sounder would provide. The sonar is taken along a transect line in the Pacific Ocean. The stations are approximately 500 meters apart from each other.

Sonar Data			
Station Number	Depth (in meters)	Station Number	Depth (in meters)
1	5500	7	3110
2	5550	8	3285
3	4540	9	3490
4	4000	10	4000
5	3675	11	4675
6	3355	12	5000

32. **Making Graphs** Plot these points on a sheet of graph paper.

33. **Interpreting Data** The data recorded in the table was taken over a portion of the ocean basin floor in the Pacific Ocean. What ocean basin feature could be between stations 2 and 12?

Performance-Based Assessment

Researching Choose a resource that is harvested from the ocean. Research information about how the resource is formed, where in the ocean it is harvested, what methods and equipment are used in the harvesting of the resource, what it is used for, and if there are any negative impacts on the marine environment as a result of harvesting the resource. Present the results of your research to your class in the form of an oral presentation.

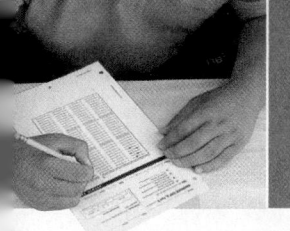

Standardized Test Prep

Test-Taking Tip

Avoiding Careless Mistakes

Students often make mistakes when they fail to examine a test question and possible answers thoroughly. Read the question carefully and underline key words that may change the meaning of the question, such as *not, except, excluding,* and so on. After choosing an answer, reread the question to check your selection.

Which of the following is NOT one of the four major topographic features of the ocean basin floor?

(A) deep-ocean trench
(B) abyssal plain
(C) submarine canyon
(D) seamount

(Answer: C)

Choose the letter that best answers the question or completes the statement.

1. Which of the following is NOT true of deep ocean trenches?
(A) They are long and narrow depressions in the ocean floor.
(B) They are sites where plates plunge back into the mantle.
(C) They are geologically very stable.
(D) They may act as sediment traps.

2. Movements of sediment-rich water down the continental slope are known as
(A) streaming currents.
(B) longshore currents.
(C) turbidity currents.
(D) avalanches.

Use the diagram below to answer Questions 3 and 4.

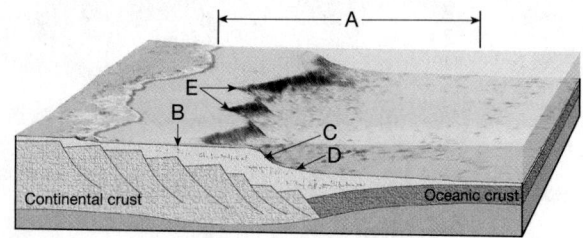

3. Which portion of the ocean floor is represented by the letter A? Describe its physical features.

4. Which ocean floor area is represented by the letter D? What are its characteristics?

5. What is the most economically important salt? Why is it important?

6. What are abyssal plains? What is underneath the plains, and how do they form?

Use the diagram below to answer Question 7.

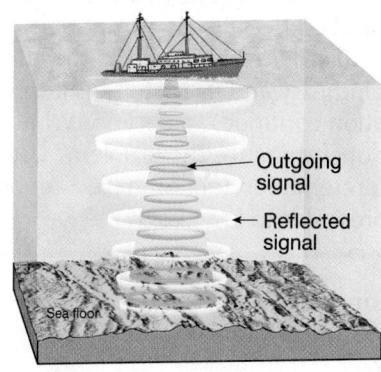

7. How is sonar used to determine the topography of ocean basins?

8. Sediment on the seafloor often leaves clues about various conditions that existed during deposition. What do the following layers in a seafloor sample tell about the environment in which each layer was deposited?
Layer 5 (top): Fine clay
Layer 4: Siliceous ooze
Layer 3: Calcareous ooze
Layer 2: Fragments of coral reef
Layer 1 (bottom): Volcanic rock

CHAPTER 15 Ocean Water and Ocean Life

The marine environment is a habitat for thousands of species of organisms, including the damselfish and corals shown here in the south Pacific near Fiji.

21st Century Learning

Economic Literacy

How can overfishing affect the economy?

The oceans provide fish and other seafood for large populations of people. However, as human populations have grown, so has the demand for seafood. This demand, along with improved fishing techniques, have caused a decline in the populations of many species of fish. Use the Web to research a declining population of a commercially important marine fish. Some examples include Atlantic salmon, swordfish, and cod. Learn how important this fish is economically. What might be the effects on the fish industry and its customers if the fish population continues to decline? What might be done to reduce the problem? Use a computer presentation tool to make a report and then present it to the class.

Exploration Lab
How Does Temperature Affect Water Density?

How the Earth Works
Ocean Life

OCEANOGRAPHY

Chapter Preview

15.1 The Composition of
Seawater

15.2 The Diversity of Ocean Life

15.3 Oceanic Productivity

Inquiry > Activity

How Does Salinity Affect the Density of Water?

Procedure

1. Fill a 500-mL graduated cylinder with 400 mL of fresh water. Fill a second 500-mL graduated cylinder with 400 mL of salt water. Precise measurement is important.

2. Gently place a small rubber ball or stopper in the fresh water. Record the new water level. Remove the object from the water and dry it off thoroughly.

3. Repeat Step 2 using the salt water. The object should float.

Think About It

1. **Calculating** What volume of fresh water was displaced by the object? What volume of salt water was displaced by the floating object?

2. **Drawing Conclusions** As the density of water increases, the volume of liquid displaced by an object decreases. Which water is more dense—fresh water or salt water?

3. **Drawing Conclusions** How does salinity affect the density of water?

15.1 The Composition of Seawater

Reading Focus

Key Concepts

- What units are used to express the salinity of ocean water?
- What are the sources of salt in ocean water?
- What factors affect the density of ocean water?
- What are the three main zones of the open ocean?

Vocabulary

- salinity
- thermocline
- density
- pycnocline
- mixed zone

Reading Strategy

Previewing Copy the table below. Before you read, preview the figures in this section and add three more questions to the table. As you read, write answers to your questions.

Questions About Seawater	Answers
What processes affect seawater salinity?	a. ___?___
b. _____?_____?	c. ___?___
d. _____?_____?	e. ___?___
f. _____?_____?	g. ___?___

Figure 1 Salts in Seawater This circle graph shows that 1000 grams of seawater with a salinity of 35‰ consists of 965 grams of water and 35 grams of various salts and other solids dissolved in the water.

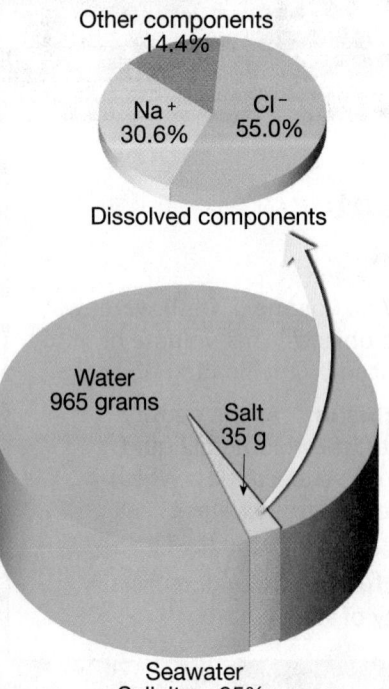

Other components 14.4%

Na⁺ 30.6%

Cl⁻ 55.0%

Dissolved components

Water 965 grams

Salt 35 g

Seawater Salinity = 35‰

What is the difference between pure water and seawater? One of the most obvious differences is that seawater contains dissolved substances that give it a salty taste. These dissolved substances include sodium chloride, other salts, metals, and even dissolved gases. In fact, every known naturally occurring element is found dissolved in at least trace amounts in seawater. The salt content of seawater makes it unsuitable for drinking or for irrigating most crops and causes it to be highly corrosive to many materials. However, many parts of the ocean are full of life adapted to this environment.

Water is the major component of nearly every life form on Earth. Our own body fluid chemistry is similar to the chemistry of seawater. Seawater consists of about 3.5 percent dissolved mineral substances that are collectively termed "salts." Although the percentage of dissolved components may seem small, the actual quantity is huge because the ocean is so vast.

Salinity

Salinity (*salinus* = salt) is the total amount of solid material dissolved in water. It is the ratio of the mass of dissolved substances to the mass of the water sample. Many common quantities are expressed in percent (%), which is parts per hundred. **Because the proportion of dissolved substances in seawater is such a small number, oceanographers typically express salinity in parts per thousand (‰).** The average salinity of seawater is 3.5% or 35‰. Figure 1 shows the principal elements that contribute to the ocean's salinity. **Most of the salt in seawater is sodium chloride, common table salt.**

Sources of Sea Salts What are the primary sources of dissolved substances in the ocean? ☞**Chemical weathering of rocks on the continents is one source of elements found in seawater.** These dissolved materials reach oceans through runoff from rivers and streams at an estimated rate of more than 2.3 billion metric tons per year. ☞**The second major source of elements found in seawater is from Earth's interior.** Through volcanic eruptions, large quantities of water vapor and other gases have been emitted into the atmosphere during much of geologic time. Scientists believe that this is the principal source of water in the oceans. About 4 billion years ago, as Earth's temperature cooled, the water vapor condensed and torrential rains filled the ocean basins with water. Certain elements—particularly chlorine, bromine, sulfur, and boron—were emitted along with the water. These elements exist in the ocean in much greater quantities than could be explained by weathering of rocks alone.

Processes Affecting Salinity Because the ocean is well mixed, the relative concentrations of the major components in seawater are essentially constant, no matter where the ocean is sampled. Surface salinity variation in the open ocean normally ranges from 33‰ to 38‰. Variations in salinity result from changes in the water content of the solution.

Figure 2 shows some of the different processes that affect the amount of water in seawater, thereby affecting salinity. Some processes add large amounts of fresh water to seawater, decreasing salinity. These processes include precipitation, runoff from land, icebergs melting, and sea ice melting.

Q *Is the ocean getting saltier?*

A Evidence suggests that the composition of seawater has been relatively stable for millions of years. Material is being removed just as rapidly as it is added by rivers and volcanic activity. Some dissolved components are removed from sea water by organisms as they build hard structures. Other components are lost when they chemically precipitate out of the water as sediment. Still others are exchanged at the oceanic ridge at hydrothermal vents. The net effect is that the overall makeup of seawater has remained relatively constant for a long time.

Icebergs

Sea ice

Runoff

Evaporation

Figure 2 Natural processes affect the salinity of seawater. **Applying Concepts** *Which processes decrease the salinity of seawater? Which processes increase it?*

Other processes remove large amounts of fresh water from seawater, increasing salinity. These processes include evaporation and the formation of sea ice. High salinities, for example, are found where evaporation rates are high, as is the case in the dry subtropical regions. In areas where large amounts of precipitation dilute ocean waters, as in the mid-latitudes and near the equator, salinity is lower. Both of these examples are shown on the graph in Figure 3.

Surface salinity in polar regions varies seasonally due to the formation and melting of sea ice. When seawater freezes in winter, salts do not become part of the ice. Therefore, the salinity of the remaining seawater increases. In summer when sea ice melts, the addition of relatively fresh water dilutes the solution and salinity decreases.

Ocean Temperature Variation

The ocean's surface water temperature varies with the amount of solar radiation received, which is primarily a function of latitude. The graph in Figure 3 shows this relationship. The intensity of solar radiation in high latitudes is much less than the intensity of solar radiation received in tropical latitudes. Therefore, lower sea surface temperatures are found in high-latitude regions. Higher sea surface temperatures are found in low-latitude regions.

Temperature Variation with Depth If you lowered a thermometer from the surface of the ocean into deeper water, what temperature pattern do you think you would find? Surface waters are warmed by the sun, so they generally have higher temperatures than deeper waters. However, the observed temperature pattern depends on the latitude.

Figure 4 on page 425 shows two graphs of temperature versus depth: one for low-latitude regions and one for high-latitude regions. The low-latitude curve begins with high temperature at the surface. However, the temperature decreases rapidly with depth because of the inability of the sun's rays to penetrate very far into the ocean. At a depth of about 1000 meters, the temperature remains just a few degrees above freezing and is relatively constant from this level down to the ocean floor. The **thermocline** (*thermo* = heat, *cline* = slope) is the layer of ocean water between about 300 meters and 1000 meters, where there is a rapid change of temperature with depth. The thermocline is a very important structure in the ocean because it creates a vertical barrier to many types of marine life.

Figure 3 This graph shows the variations in ocean surface temperature (top curve) and surface salinity (lower curve). **Interpreting Diagrams** *At which latitudes is sea surface temperature highest? Why?*

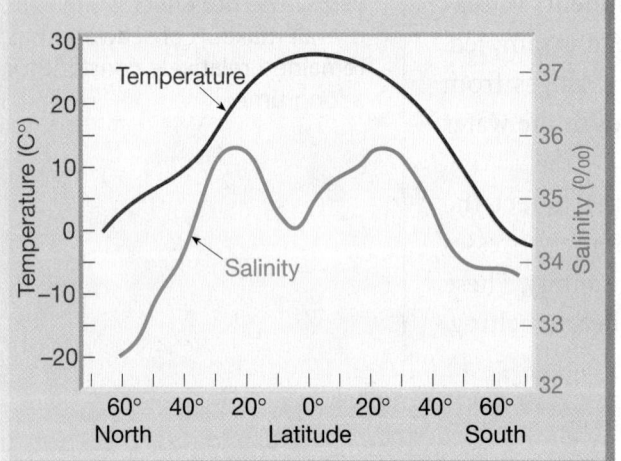

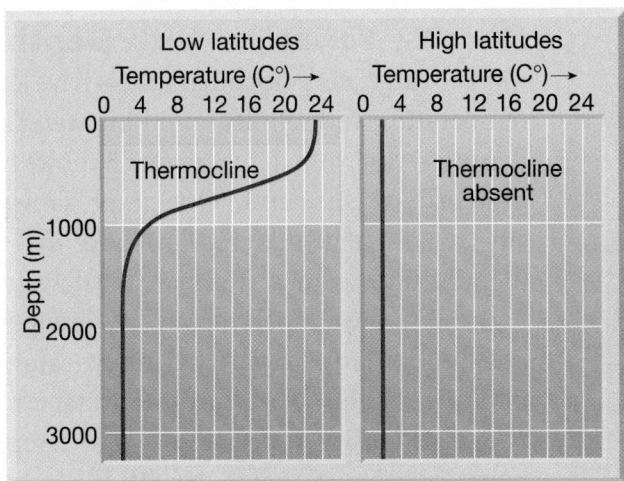

Figure 4 These graphs show the variations in ocean water temperature with depth for low-latitude and high-latitude regions. **Applying Concepts** *Why is the thermocline absent in the high latitudes?*

The high-latitude curve in Figure 4 shows a very different pattern from the low-latitude curve. Surface water temperatures in high latitudes are much cooler than in low latitudes, so the curve begins at the surface with a low temperature. Deeper in the ocean, the temperature of the water is similar to that at the surface, so the curve remains vertical. There is no rapid change of temperature with depth. A thermocline is not present in high latitudes. Instead, the water column is isothermal (*iso* = same, *thermo* = heat).

 **Reading Checkpoint** *What is the thermocline?*

Ocean Density Variation

Density is defined as mass per unit volume. It can be thought of as a measure of how heavy something is for its size. For example, an object that has low density is lightweight for its size, such as a dry sponge, foam packing, or a surfboard. An object that has high density, such as cement or most metals, is heavy for its size. Density is an important property of ocean water because it determines the water's vertical position in the ocean. Density differences cause large areas of ocean water to sink or float. When high-density seawater is added to low-density fresh water, the denser seawater sinks below the fresh water.

Factors Affecting Seawater Density Seawater density is influenced by two main factors: salinity and temperature. An increase in salinity adds dissolved substances and results in an increase in seawater density. An increase in temperature results in a decrease in seawater density. Temperature has the greatest influence on surface seawater density because variations in surface seawater temperature are greater than salinity variations. However, in the very cold, polar areas of the ocean, salinity affects density significantly. Cold water that also has high salinity is some of the highest-density water in the world.

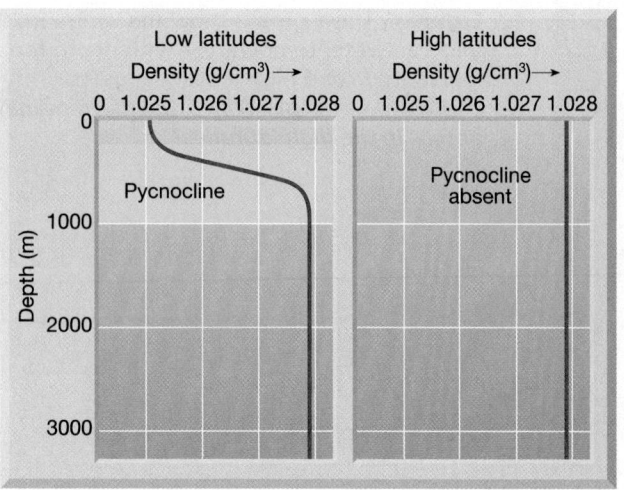

Low latitudes
Density (g/cm³) →
0 1.025 1.026 1.027 1.028

High latitudes
Density (g/cm³) →
0 1.025 1.026 1.027 1.028

Depth (m): 0, 1000, 2000, 3000

Pycnocline

Pycnocline absent

Figure 5 The graphs show variations in ocean water density with depth for low-latitude and high-latitude regions.
Interpreting Diagrams
What is the difference between the low-latitude graph and the high-latitude graph? Why does this difference occur?

Density Variation with Depth By sampling ocean waters, oceanographers have learned that temperature and salinity—and the water's resulting density—vary with depth. Figure 5 shows two graphs of density versus depth. One graph shows the density for low-latitude regions and the other for high-latitude regions. Compare the density curves in Figure 5 to the temperature curves in Figure 4. They are similar. This similarity demonstrates that temperature is the most important factor affecting seawater density. It also shows that temperature is inversely proportional to density. When two quantities are inversely proportional, they can be multiplied together to equal a constant. Therefore, if the value of one quantity increases, the value of the other quantity decreases proportionately. When water temperature increases, its density decreases.

 **Reading Checkpoint** *How does temperature affect the density of seawater?*

The **pycnocline** (*pycno* = density, *cline* = slope) is the layer of ocean water between about 300 meters and 1000 meters where there is a rapid change of density with depth. A pycnocline presents a significant barrier to mixing between low-density water above and high-density water below. A pycnocline is not present in high latitudes; instead, the water column is about the same density throughout.

Ocean Layering

The ocean, like Earth's interior, is layered according to density. Low-density water exists near the surface, and higher-density water occurs below. Except for some shallow inland seas with a high rate of evaporation, the highest-density water is found at the greatest ocean depths. Oceanographers generally recognize a three-layered structure in most parts of the open ocean: a shallow surface mixed zone, a transition zone, and a deep zone. These zones are shown in Figure 6.

Surface Zone Because solar energy is received at the ocean surface, it is here that water temperatures are warmest. The **mixed zone** is the area of the surface created by the mixing of water by waves, currents, and tides. The mixed zone has nearly uniform temperatures. The depth and temperature of this layer vary, depending on latitude and season. The zone usually extends to about 300 meters, but it may extend to a depth of 450 meters. The surface mixed zone accounts for only about 2 percent of ocean water.

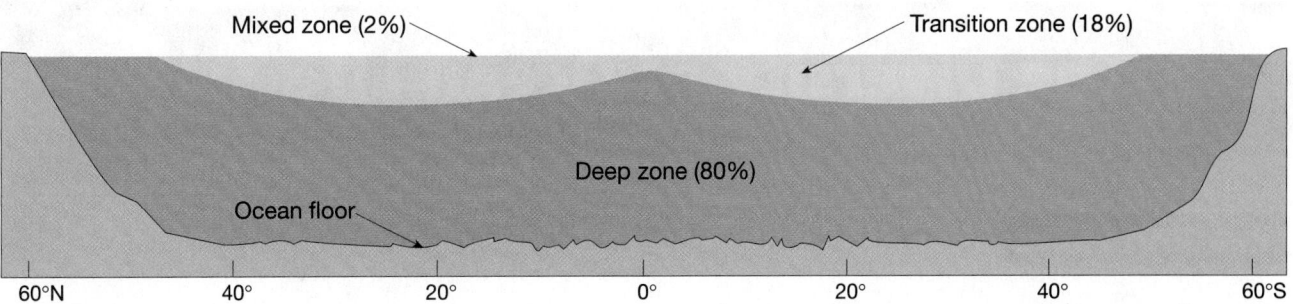

Mixed zone (2%) Transition zone (18%)

Deep zone (80%)

Ocean floor

60°N   40°   20°   0°   20°   40°   60°S

Transition Zone Below the sun-warmed zone of mixing, the temperature falls abruptly with depth as was seen in Figure 4. Here, a distinct layer called the transition zone exists between the warm surface layer above and the deep zone of cold water below. The transition zone includes a thermocline and associated pycnocline. This zone accounts for about 18 percent of ocean water.

Deep Zone Below the transition zone is the deep zone. Sunlight never reaches this zone, and water temperatures are just a few degrees above freezing. As a result, water density remains constant and high. The deep zone includes about 80 percent of ocean water.

In high latitudes, this three-layered structure of the open ocean does not exist as seen in Figure 6. The three layers do not exist because there is no rapid change in temperature or density with depth. Therefore, good vertical mixing between surface and deep waters can occur in high-latitude regions. Here, cold high-density water forms at the surface, sinks, and initiates deep-ocean currents, which are discussed in Chapter 16.

Figure 6 Ocean Zones
Oceanographers recognize three main zones of the ocean based on water density, which varies with temperature and salinity.

Section 15.1 Assessment

Reviewing Concepts

1. What is salinity?
2. What units are used to express the salinity of ocean water?
3. What are the sources of salt in ocean water?
4. Explain the relationship between latitude and sea surface temperature.
5. What factors affect the density of ocean water?
6. What are the three main zones of the open ocean?

Critical Thinking

7. **Inferring** Why does the salinity of seawater remain relatively constant over time?
8. **Summarizing** Explain the general pattern of temperature variation with depth in low-latitude oceans.

Writing in Science

Descriptive Paragraph Write a paragraph that describes the different characteristics of the three zones of the open ocean. Include an explanation of why polar regions do not exhibit the same pattern of water stratification.

15.2 The Diversity of Ocean Life

Reading Focus

Key Concepts
- How can marine organisms be classified?
- What is the difference between plankton and nekton?
- In which area of the ocean can most benthos organisms be found living?
- What factors are used to divide the ocean into marine life zones?

Vocabulary
- plankton
- phytoplankton
- zooplankton
- nekton
- benthos
- photic zone
- intertidal zone
- neritic zone
- oceanic zone
- pelagic zone
- benthic zone
- abyssal zone

Reading Strategy

Building Vocabulary Copy the table below. As you read, add definitions and examples to complete the table.

Definitions	Examples
Plankton: organisms that drift with ocean currents	bacteria
Phytoplankton: a. _____?_____	b. ___?___
Zooplankton: c. _____?_____	d. ___?___
Nekton: e. _____?_____	f. ___?___
Benthos: g. _____?_____	h. ___?___

A wide variety of organisms inhabit the marine environment. These organisms range in size from microscopic bacteria and algae to the largest organisms alive today—blue whales, which are as long as three buses lined up end to end. Marine biologists have identified over 250,000 marine species. This number is constantly increasing as new organisms are discovered.

Most marine organisms live within the sunlit surface waters. Strong sunlight supports photosynthesis by marine algae. Algae either directly or indirectly provide food for the majority of organisms. All marine algae live near the surface because they need sunlight to survive. Most marine animals also live near the surface because this is where they can find food.

Classification of Marine Organisms

Marine organisms can be classified according to where they live and how they move. They can be classified as either plankton (floaters) or nekton (swimmers). All other organisms are benthos, or bottom dwellers.

Plankton **Plankton** (*planktos* = wandering) **include all organisms—algae, animals, and bacteria—that drift with ocean currents.** Just because plankton drift does not mean they are unable to swim. Many plankton can swim but either move very weakly or move only vertically.

Figure 7 Plankton are organisms that drift with ocean currents. **A** This photo shows a variety of phytoplankton from the Atlantic Ocean. **B** The zooplankton shown here include copepods and the larval stages of other common marine organisms.

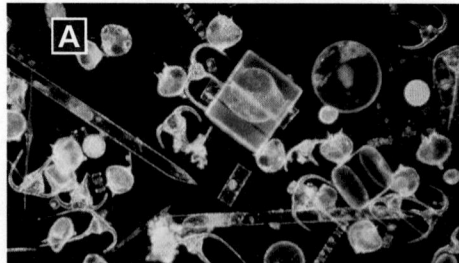

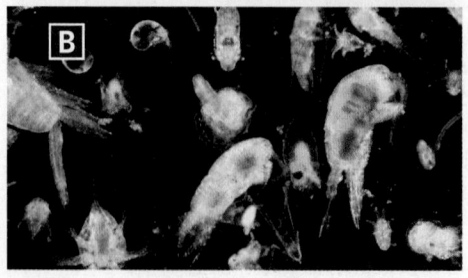

428 *Chapter 15*

Among plankton, the algae that undergo photosynthesis are called **phytoplankton.** Most phytoplankton, such as diatoms, are microscopic. Animal plankton, are called **zooplankton.** Zooplankton include the larval stages of many marine organisms such as fish, sea stars, lobsters, and crabs. Figure 7 shows members of each group.

Nekton

Nekton (*nektos* = swimming) **include all animals capable of moving independently of the ocean currents, by swimming or other means of propulsion.** Nekton are able to determine their position within the ocean and in many cases complete long migrations. Nekton include most adult fish and squid, marine mammals, and marine reptiles. Figure 8 shows examples of nekton.

Fish may appear to exist everywhere in the oceans, but they are more abundant near continents and islands and in colder waters. Some fish, such as salmon, swim upstream in fresh water rivers to spawn. Many eels do just the reverse, growing to maturity in fresh water and then swimming out of the streams to breed in the depths of the ocean.

Benthos

The term *benthos* (*benthos* = bottom) **describes organisms living on or in the ocean bottom.** Figure 9 shows some examples of benthos organisms. The shallow coastal ocean floor contains a wide variety of physical conditions and nutrient levels. Most benthos organisms can be found living in this area. Shallow coastal areas are the only locations where large marine algae, often called seaweeds, are found attached to the bottom. These are the only areas of the seafloor that receive enough sunlight for the algae to survive.

Throughout most of the deeper parts of the seafloor, animals live in perpetual darkness, where photosynthesis cannot occur. They must feed on each other or on whatever nutrients fall from the productive surface waters. The deep-sea bottom is an environment of coldness, stillness, and darkness. Under these conditions, life progresses slowly. Organisms that live in the deep sea usually are widely distributed because physical conditions vary little on the deep-ocean floor.

Figure 8 Nekton includes all animals capable of moving independently of ocean currents. **A** This squid can use propulsion to move through the water. **B** This school of grunts swims through the water with ease.
Inferring Why do you think some organisms, such as fish, are classified as plankton during some stages of their lives and nekton during other stages?

Figure 9 Benthos describes organisms living on or in the ocean bottom. **A** Sea star **B** Coral crab

Marine Life Zones

The distribution of marine organisms is affected by the chemistry, physics, and geology of the oceans. Marine organisms are influenced by a variety of physical factors. ⬤**Three factors are used to divide the ocean into distinct marine life zones: the availability of sunlight, the distance from shore, and the water depth.** Figure 10 shows the different zones in which marine life can be found.

Availability of Sunlight The upper part of the ocean into which sunlight penetrates is called the **photic zone** (*photos* = light). The clarity of seawater is affected by many factors, such as the amount of plankton, suspended sediment, and decaying organic particles in the water. In addition, the amount of sunlight varies with atmospheric conditions, time of day, season of the year, and latitude.

The euphotic zone is the portion of the photic zone near the surface where light is strong enough for photosynthesis to occur. In the open ocean, this zone can reach a depth of 100 meters, but the zone will be much shallower close to shore where water clarity is typically reduced. In the euphotic zone, phytoplankton use sunlight to produce food and become the basis of most oceanic food webs.

Although photosynthesis cannot occur much below 100 meters, there is enough light in the lower photic zone for marine animals to avoid predators, find food, recognize their species, and locate mates. Below this zone is the aphotic zone, where there is no sunlight.

Reading Checkpoint *What is the difference between the photic zone and the aphotic zone?*

Figure 10 Marine Life Zones
The ocean is divided into marine life zones, based on availability of light, distance from shore, and water depth. **Interpreting Diagrams** *Why are phytoplankton and larger algae found only in surface waters?*

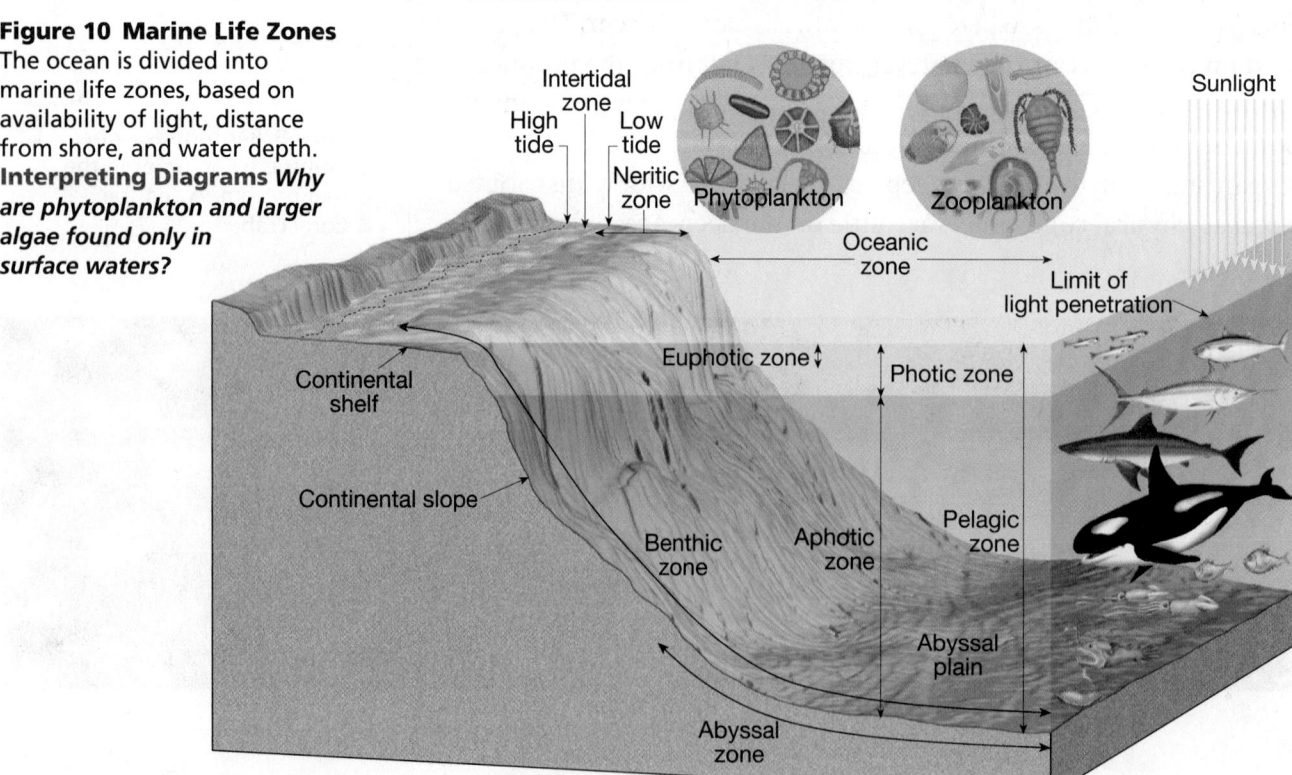

Distance from Shore Marine life zones can also be subdivided based on distance from shore. The area where the land and ocean meet and overlap is the **intertidal zone.** This narrow strip of land between high and low tides is alternately covered and uncovered by seawater with each tidal change. It appears to be a harsh place to live with crashing waves, periodic drying out, and rapid changes in temperature, salinity, and oxygen concentrations. However, the species that live here are well adapted to the constant environmental changes.

Seaward from the low-tide line is the **neritic zone.** This zone covers the gently sloping continental shelf. The neritic zone can be very narrow or may extend hundreds of kilometers from shore. It is often shallow enough for sunlight to reach all the way to the ocean floor, putting it entirely within the photic zone.

Although the neritic zone covers only about 5 percent of the world ocean, it is rich in both biomass and number of species. Many organisms find the conditions here ideal because photosynthesis occurs readily, nutrients wash in from the land, and the bottom provides shelter and habitat. This zone is so rich that it supports 90 percent of the world's commercial fisheries.

Beyond the continental shelf is the **oceanic zone.** The open ocean reaches great depths. As a result, surface waters typically have lower nutrient concentrations because nutrients tend to sink out of the photic zone to the deep-ocean floor. This low nutrient concentration usually results in smaller populations than the more productive neritic zone.

Water Depth A third method of classifying marine habitats is based on water depth. Open ocean of any depth is called the **pelagic zone.** Animals in this zone swim or float freely. The photic part of the pelagic zone is home to phytoplankton, zooplankton, and nekton, such as tuna, sea turtles, and dolphins. The aphotic part of this zone has giant squid and other species that are adapted to life in deep water.

Benthos organisms such as giant kelp, sponges, crabs, sea anemones, sea stars, and marine worms that attach to, crawl upon, or burrow into the seafloor occupy parts of the benthic zone. The **benthic zone** includes any sea-bottom surface regardless of its distance from shore and is mostly inhabited by benthos organisms.

The **abyssal zone** is a subdivision of the benthic zone. The abyssal zone includes the deep-ocean floor, such as abyssal plains. This zone is characterized by extremely high water pressure, consistently low temperature, no sunlight, and sparse life. Food sources at abyssal depths typically come from the surface. Some food is in the form of tiny decaying particles that steadily "rain" down from the surface. These particles provide food for filter-feeders, brittle stars, and burrowing worms. Other food arrives as large fragments or entire carcasses of organisms that sink from the surface. These pieces supply meals for actively searching fish, such as the grenadier, tripodfish, and hagfish.

Q *Do any deep-sea organisms produce light themselves?*

A Over half of deep-sea organisms—including fish, jellies, crustaceans, and deep-sea squid—can bioluminesce, which means they can produce light organically. These organisms produce light through a chemical reaction in specially designed structures or cells called photophores. Some of these cells contain luminescent bacteria that live symbiotically within the organism. In a world of darkness, the ability to produce light can be used to attract prey, define territory, communicate with others, or avoid predators.

Figure 11 When super-heated water meets cold seawater, minerals and metals precipitate out of the water to form this black smoker.

Hydrothermal Vents

Among the most unusual seafloor discoveries of the past 30 years have been the hydrothermal vents along the oceanic ridge. Here seawater seeps into the ocean floor through cracks in the crust.

The water becomes super-heated and saturated with minerals. Eventually the heated water escapes back into the ocean. When the hot water comes in contact with the surrounding cold water, the minerals precipitate out, giving the water the appearance of black smoke. These geysers of hot water are referred to as black smokers, like the one shown in Figure 11.

At some vents water temperatures of 100°C or higher support communities of organisms found nowhere else in the world. In fact, hundreds of new species have been discovered surrounding these deep-sea habitats since scientists found some vents along the Galápagos Rift in 1977. Chemicals from the vents become food for bacteria. The bacteria produce sugars and other foods that enable them and many other organisms to live in this very unusual and extreme environment. Look at Figure 12 for another example of organisms found along hydrothermal vents.

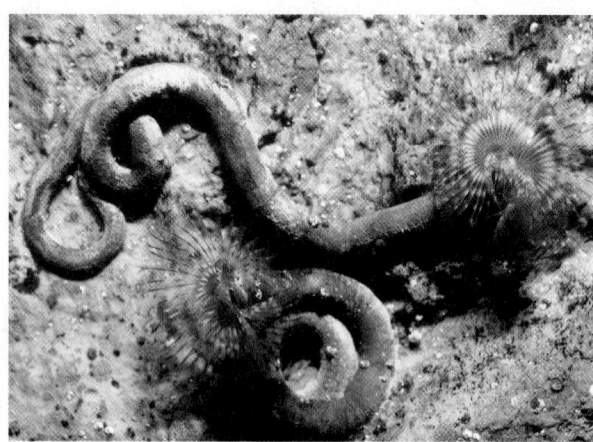

Figure 12 Tube worms up to 3 meters in length are among the organisms found along hydrothermal vents.

Section 15.2 Assessment

Reviewing Concepts

1. How can marine organisms be classified?
2. What is the difference between plankton and nekton?
3. In which area of the ocean do most benthos organisms live?
4. What factors are used to divide the ocean into marine life zones?
5. Why is the neritic zone rich in life?

Critical Thinking

6. **Inferring** Why do many fish in the abyssal zone locate food through chemical sensing?

7. **Inferring** Organisms that live in the intertidal zone must deal with harsh and changing conditions. What types of adaptations would benefit organisms living in this zone?

Writing in Science

Making Tables Make a table to organize the information about marine life zones presented in this section. Include the basis by which the zone is classified, any subdivisions of the zone, and the characteristics of each zone within the table.

15.3 Oceanic Productivity

Reading Focus

Key Concepts

- What factors influence a region's photosynthetic productivity?
- Describe the transfer efficiency between trophic levels.
- What advantage do organisms in a food web have over those in a food chain?

Vocabulary

- primary productivity
- photosynthesis
- chemosynthesis
- trophic level
- food chain
- food web

Reading Strategy

Identifying Main Ideas Copy the table below. As you read, write the main idea of each topic.

Topic	Main Idea
Productivity in polar oceans	a. ___?___
Productivity in tropical oceans	b. ___?___
Productivity in temperate oceans	c. ___?___

Like other ecosystems on Earth, organisms in the marine environment are interconnected through the web of food production and consumption. Marine producers include phytoplankton, larger algae such as seaweeds, and bacteria. Consumers include crabs, clams, sea stars, fish, dolphins, and whales. Why are some regions of the ocean teeming with life, while other areas seem barren? The answer is related to the amount of primary productivity in various parts of the ocean.

Primary Productivity

Primary productivity is the production of organic compounds from inorganic substances through photosynthesis or chemosynthesis. **Photosynthesis** is the use of light energy to convert water and carbon dioxide into energy-rich glucose molecules. **Chemosynthesis** is the process by which certain microorganisms create organic molecules from inorganic nutrients using chemical energy. Bacteria in hydrothermal vents use hydrogen sulfide as an energy source. Acting as producers, these bacteria support the hydrothermal vent communities.

Two factors influence a region's photosynthetic productivity: the availability of nutrients and the amount of solar radiation, or sunlight. Primary producers need nutrients such as nitrogen, phosphorus, and iron. Lack of nutrients can be a limiting factor in productivity. Thus, the most abundant marine life exists where there are ample nutrients and good sunlight. Oceanic productivity, however, varies dramatically because of the uneven distribution of nutrients throughout the photosynthetic zone and the availability of solar energy due to seasonal changes.

For: Links on photosynthesis in the oceans
Visit: PHSchool.com
Web Code: czd-5153

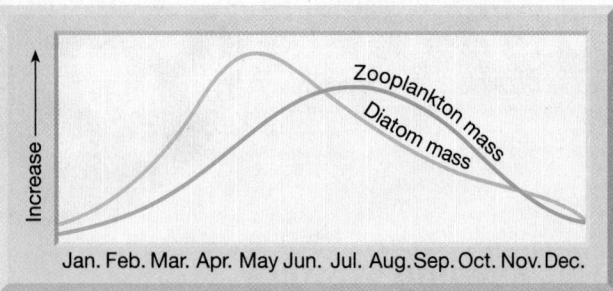

Figure 13 One example of productivity in polar oceans is illustrated by the Barents Sea. **Interpreting Diagrams** *Describe the relationship between the zooplankton and phytoplankton populations.*

Figure 14 Water Layers in the Tropics The permanent thermocline in tropical oceans prevents the mixing of surface and deep water masses. Productivity is limited by the amount of nutrients in surface waters.

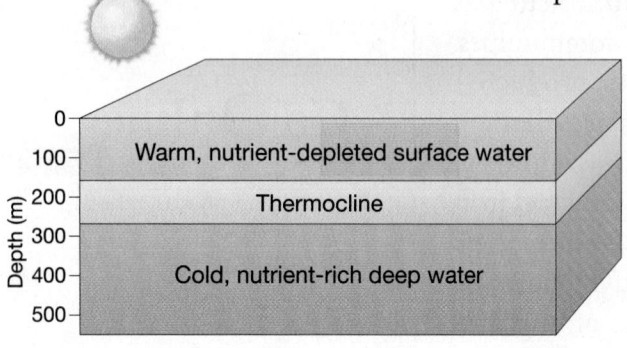

Productivity in Polar Oceans Polar regions such as the Arctic Ocean's Barents Sea, off the northern coast of Europe, experience continuous darkness for about three months of winter and continuous illumination for about three months during summer. Productivity of phytoplankton, mostly single-celled algae called diatoms, peaks there during May. This trend is shown in the graph in Figure 13. During May the sun rises high enough in the sky so that sunlight penetrates deep into the water. As soon as the diatoms develop, zooplankton begin feeding on them. As Figure 13 shows, the zooplankton biomass peaks in July and continues at a relatively high level until winter darkness begins in October.

Recall that density and temperature change very little with depth in polar regions and mixing occurs between surface waters and deeper, nutrient-rich waters. In the summer, however, melting ice creates a thin, low-salinity layer that does not readily mix with the deeper waters. This lack of mixing between water masses is crucial to summer production, because it helps prevent phytoplankton from being carried into deeper, darker waters. Instead, they are concentrated in the sunlit surface waters where they reproduce continuously.

Because of the constant supply of nutrients rising from deeper waters below, high-latitude surface waters typically have high nutrient concentrations. **The availability of solar energy, however, is what limits photosynthetic productivity in polar areas.**

Productivity in Tropical Oceans You may be surprised to learn that productivity is low in tropical regions of the open ocean. Because the sun is more directly overhead, light penetrates much deeper into tropical oceans than in temperate and polar waters. Solar energy also is available year-round. However, productivity is low because a permanent thermocline prevents mixing between surface waters and nutrient-rich deeper waters. Figure 14 shows how water masses are separated in the tropics. The thermocline is a barrier that cuts off the supply of nutrients from deeper waters below. **Productivity in tropical regions is limited by the lack of nutrients.** These areas have so few organisms that they are considered biological deserts.

Productivity in Temperate Oceans Productivity is limited by available sunlight in polar regions and by nutrient supply in the tropics. ●**In temperate regions, which are found at mid-latitudes, a combination of these two limiting factors, sunlight and nutrient supply, controls productivity.** These relationships are shown in Figure 15.

- **Winter** Productivity in temperate oceans is very low during winter, even though nutrient concentration is highest at this time. The reason is that solar energy is limited because days are short, and the sun angle is low. As a result, the depth at which photosynthesis can occur is so shallow that phytoplankton do not grow much.

- **Spring** The sun rises higher in the sky during spring, creating a greater depth at which photosynthesis can occur. A spring bloom of phytoplankton occurs because solar energy and nutrients are available, and a seasonal thermocline develops. The thermocline traps algae in the euphotic zone. This creates a tremendous demand for nutrients in the euphotic zone, so the supply is quickly depleted, causing productivity to decrease sharply. Even though the days are lengthening and sunlight is increasing, productivity during the spring bloom is limited by the lack of nutrients.

- **Summer** The sun rises even higher in the summer, so surface waters in temperate parts of the ocean continue to warm. A strong seasonal thermocline is created that prevents the mixing of surface and deeper waters. So nutrients depleted from surface waters cannot be replaced by those from deeper waters. Throughout summer, the phytoplankton population remains relatively low.

- **Fall** Solar radiation decreases in the fall as the sun moves lower in the sky. Surface temperatures drop and the summer thermocline breaks down. Nutrients return to the surface layer as increased wind strength mixes surface waters with deeper waters. These conditions create a fall bloom of phytoplankton, which is much less dramatic than the spring bloom. The fall bloom is very short-lived because sunlight becomes the limiting factor as winter approaches to repeat the seasonal cycle.

Figure 15 Productivity in Northern Hemisphere, Temperate Oceans The graph shows the relationship among phytoplankton, zooplankton, amount of sunshine, and nutrient levels for surface waters. **Analyzing** *What happens to phytoplankton in the spring and in the fall?*

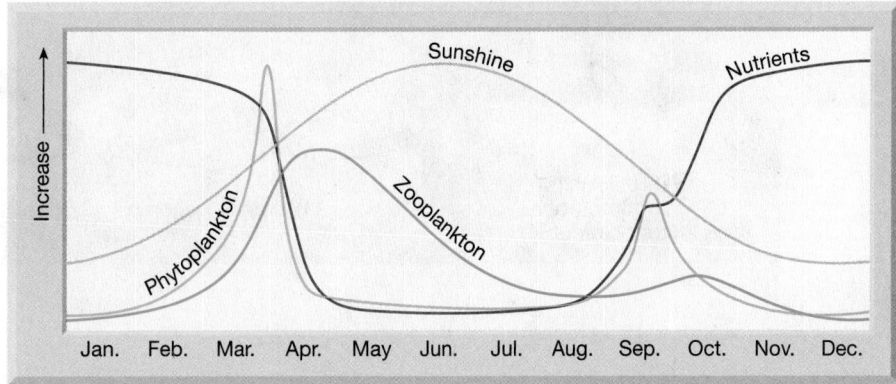

Oceanic Feeding Relationships

Marine algae, plants, bacteria, and bacteria-like organisms are the main oceanic producers. As producers make food available to the consuming animals of the ocean, energy passes from one feeding population to the next. Only a small percentage of the energy taken in at any level is passed on to the next because energy is consumed and lost at each level. As a result, the producers' biomass in the ocean is many times greater than the mass of top consumers, such as sharks or whales.

Trophic Levels Chemical energy stored in the mass of the ocean's algae is transferred to the animal community mostly through feeding. Zooplankton are herbivores (*herba* = grass, *vora* = eat), so they eat algae. Larger herbivores feed on the larger algae and marine plants that grow attached to the ocean bottom near shore. The herbivores are then eaten by carnivores (*carni* = meat, *vora* = eat). Smaller carnivores are eaten by another population of larger carnivores, and so on. Each of these feeding stages is called a **trophic level.**

Transfer Efficiency The transfer of energy between trophic levels is very inefficient. The efficiencies of different algal species vary, but the average is only about 2 percent. This means that 2 percent of the light energy absorbed by algae is ultimately changed into food and made available to herbivores. Figure 16 shows the passage of energy between trophic levels through an entire ecosystem—from the solar energy used by phytoplankton to a top-level carnivore, humans.

Figure 16 Energy Flow and Transfer Efficiency in an Ecosystem For every 500,000 units of radiant energy input available to the producers, only one unit of mass is added to the fifth trophic level.
Analyzing *What is the average transfer efficiency for phytoplankton? What is it for all of the other trophic levels?*

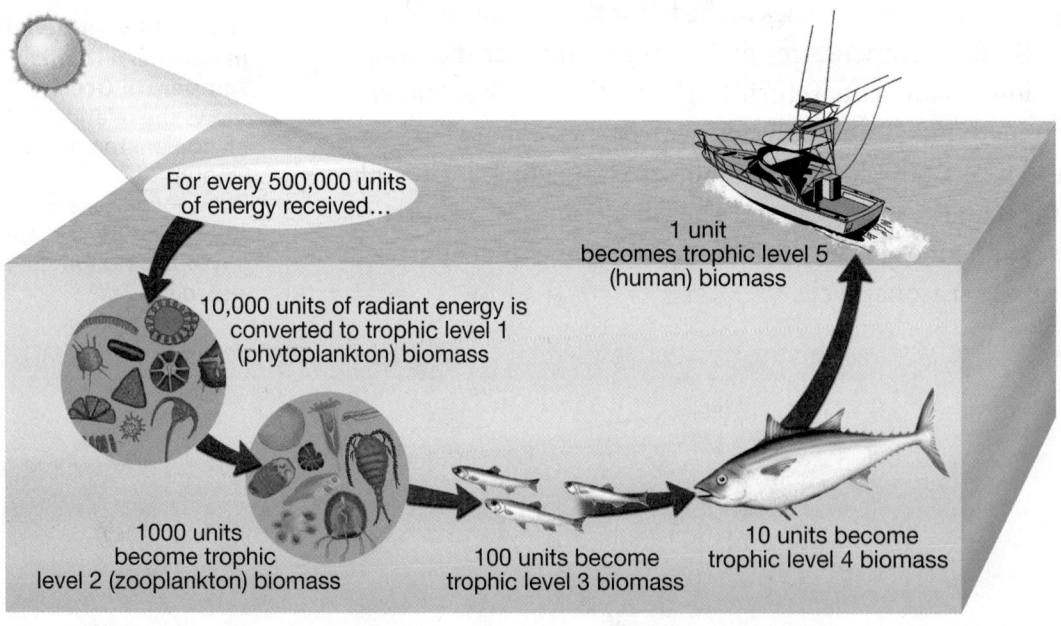

For every 500,000 units of energy received…

10,000 units of radiant energy is converted to trophic level 1 (phytoplankton) biomass

1000 units become trophic level 2 (zooplankton) biomass

100 units become trophic level 3 biomass

10 units become trophic level 4 biomass

1 unit becomes trophic level 5 (human) biomass

Food Chains and Food Webs

A **food chain** is a sequence of organisms through which energy is transferred, starting with the primary producer. A herbivore eats the producer, then one or more carnivores eats the herbivore. The chain finally culminates with the "top carnivore," which is not usually preyed upon by any other organism.

Figure 17A shows a simple food chain. Feeding relationships are rarely as simple as this food chain suggests. More often, top carnivores in a food chain feed on a number of different animals, each of which feeds on a variety of organisms. These feeding relationships form a **food web,** as shown in Figure 17B for North Sea herring.

Animals that feed through a food web rather than a food chain are more likely to survive because they have alternative foods to eat should one of their food sources diminish or disappear. Newfoundland herring, on the other hand, eat only copepods, so the disappearance of copepods would greatly affect their population.

A A food chain is the passage of energy along a single path.

B A food web is more complex with many organisms interacting and depending on each other.

Figure 17 A A food chain is the passage of energy along a single path. **B** A food web is a complex series of feeding relationships with many organisms interacting and depending on each other.

Go Online
active art

For: Ocean Food Web activity
Visit: PHSchool.com
Web Code: czp-5153

Section 15.3 Assessment

Reviewing Concepts

1. What factors influence a region's photosynthetic productivity?

2. Describe the transfer efficiency between trophic levels.

3. What advantage do organisms in a food web have over those in a food chain?

4. What limits primary productivity in tropical oceans? Why?

Critical Thinking

5. **Comparing and Contrasting** Compare and contrast photosynthesis and chemosynthesis. Give examples of organisms that undergo each process.

6. **Drawing Conclusions** Explain why producers are always the first tropic level in a food chain or food web.

Math **Practice**

7. If 700,000 energy units are received by phytoplankton in the ocean surface, how many energy units will reach a consumer that is on the fourth trophic level of a food chain?

How the Earth Works

Ocean Life

The world's oceans cover almost three quarters of the Earth's surface and are home to a vast array of life. Below the surface, the oceans become increasingly cold and dark. Even so, living things, ranging in size from giant whales to microscopic floating organisms called **plankton,** thrive at every depth. Some jellyfish and turtles float or swim near the surface. Whales and squid often live in the ocean's middepths. A whole host of strange-looking creatures swim or crawl around the darkest ocean depths.

Distribution of world's major oceans

ARCTIC OCEAN

NORTH AMERICA · EUROPE · ASIA
TROPIC OF CANCER
EQUATOR
AFRICA
PACIFIC OCEAN · ATLANTIC OCEAN
SOUTH AMERICA
INDIAN OCEAN
TROPIC OF CAPRICORN
AUSTRALIA
SOUTHERN OCEAN
ANTARCTICA

BIOLUMINESCENCE
Some fish have special organs called photophores that give off a glow. In this process, called **bioluminescence,** fish use the light to recognize members of their own species or as lures for attracting prey.

Elongate Fangjaw

VERTICAL ZONES
Oceanographers divide the oceans into zones based on depth. Each zone is home to living things that are adapted to survive at that depth. For example, deep-water animals cope with darkness, very cold temperatures, and pressures that would crush a human. Some creatures can survive in more than one zone.

A school of chromis swims among the coral off the coast of the Maldives in the Indian Ocean.

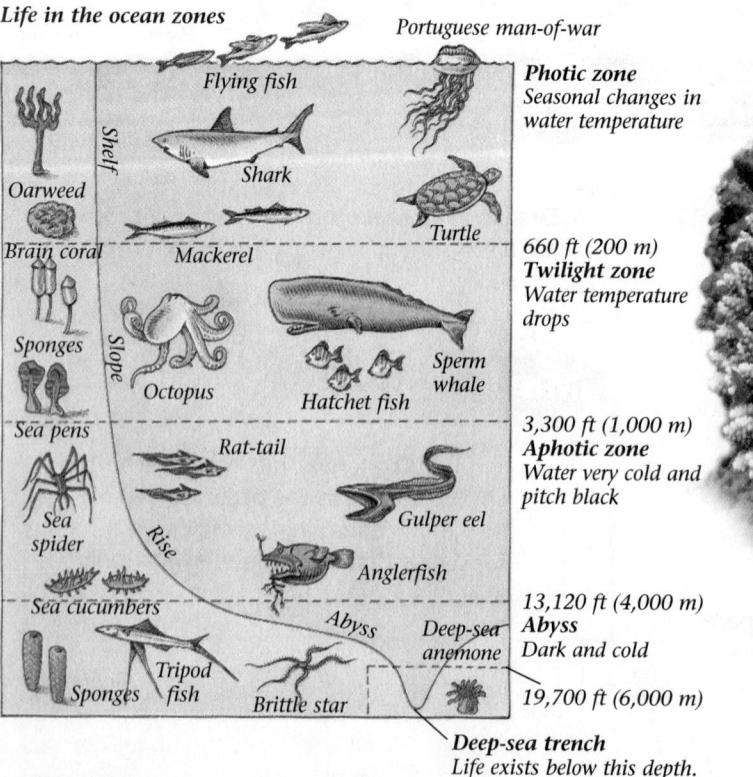

Life in the ocean zones

Portuguese man-of-war
Flying fish
Shelf
Oarweed
Shark
Brain coral
Mackerel
Turtle
Sponges
Slope
Octopus
Hatchet fish
Sperm whale
Sea pens
Rat-tail
Sea spider
Rise
Gulper eel
Anglerfish
Sea cucumbers
Abyss
Deep-sea anemone
Sponges
Tripod fish
Brittle star

Photic zone
Seasonal changes in water temperature

660 ft (200 m)
Twilight zone
Water temperature drops

3,300 ft (1,000 m)
Aphotic zone
Water very cold and pitch black

13,120 ft (4,000 m)
Abyss
Dark and cold

19,700 ft (6,000 m)
Deep-sea trench
Life exists below this depth.

CORAL REEFS

A coral is a tubular animal with tentacles. Most corals attach to a surface and build reefs that can rise above sea level around islands and continents. Other reefs are ring-shaped **atolls** around a lagoon of shallow water. Atolls grow over millions of years.

Growth of a coral atoll

1. Coral starts to grow around a volcanic island.

2. The island sinks. Sand collects on the growing coral reef and forms land.

3. The island disappears. Vegetation grows on the atoll that remains.

HYDROTHERMAL VENTS

On the deep ocean floor, hot, mineral-rich water gushes from cracks, called **hydrothermal vents.** Bacteria feed on chemicals in this water, forming the basis of a food chain that does not rely on sunlight and plants. Giant tube worms, clams, and blind white crabs live around these vents.

Worms and crabs live near a hydrothermal vent.

Australian sea lions are marine mammals that breathe air, feed at sea, and breed on land.

PHOTIC ZONE

Sunlight supports the growth of algae, sea grasses, and other plants on which some sea creatures feed. Marine mammals, squid, fish, and other animals have to be strong swimmers to move in the surface currents. Sea grasses and coral reefs provide food, shelter, and breeding sites for a variety of creatures.

Jellyfish can swim, but they are also influenced by ocean currents.

Forcepsfish

False eyespot

BRIGHT COLORS

Many fish have bright colors that attract mates and confuse predators. Complex coloration makes it hard to detect the outline of a fish. Some fish have eyespots, or false eyes. As a predator attacks the false head, the fish darts off in the opposite direction.

ASSESSMENT

1. **Key Terms** Define (a) plankton, (b) bioluminescence, (c) atoll, (d) hydrothermal vent.

2. **Ecosystems** Why does plant life grow near the ocean surface but not on the deep ocean floor?

3. **Physical Processes** How can the emergence of a volcano lead to the growth of coral and the formation of an atoll?

4. **Ecosystems** How are some fish specially adapted to attract prey or to escape predators?

5. **Critical Thinking** **Analyzing Processes** Suppose that changes in the environment cause a decline in the population of ocean plants and corals. How might that environmental change also cause damage to populations of fish, marine mammals, and other sea creatures?

Exploration Lab

How Does Temperature Affect Water Density?

Ocean water temperatures vary from equator to pole and change with depth. Temperature, like salinity, affects the density of seawater. However, the density of seawater is more sensitive to temperature fluctuations than salinity. Cool surface water, which has a greater density than warm surface water, forms in the polar regions, sinks, and moves toward the tropics.

Problem
How can you determine the effects of temperature on water density?

Materials
- 100 mL graduated cylinders (2)
- test tubes (2)
- beakers (2)
- food coloring or dye
- stirrer
- ice
- tap water
- graph paper
- colored pencils

Skills
Observing, Graphing, Inferring, Drawing Conclusions

Procedure

Part A

1. In a beaker, mix cold tap water with several ice cubes. Stir until the water and ice are well mixed.

2. Fill the graduated cylinder with 100 mL of the cold water from the beaker. The graduated cylinder should not contain any pieces of ice.

3. Put 2 to 3 drops of dye in a test tube and fill it 1/2 full with hot tap water.

4. Pour the contents of the test tube slowly into the graduated cylinder and record your observations.

5. Add a test tube full of cold tap water to a beaker. Mix in 2 to 3 drops of dye and a handful of ice to the beaker. Stir the solution thoroughly.

6. Fill the test tube 1/2 full of the solution from Step 5. Do not allow any ice into the test tube.

7. Fill the second graduated cylinder with 100 mL of hot tap water.

8. Pour the test tube of cold liquid slowly into the cylinder of hot water. Record your observations.

9. Clean the glassware and return it along with other materials to your teacher.

Part B

1. Photocopy the graph on the next page or copy it onto a separate sheet of graph paper.

2. Using the data in Table 1, plot a line on your graph for temperature. Using a different colored pencil, plot a line for density on the same graph.

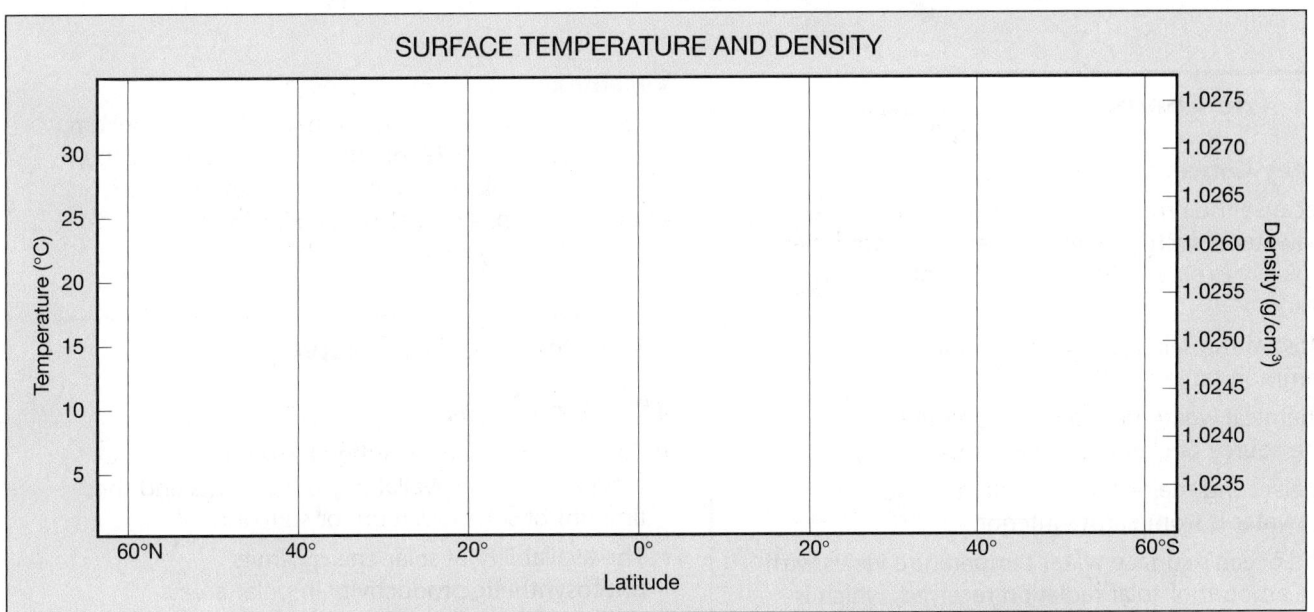

Table 1 Idealized Ocean Surface Water Temperatures and Densities at Various Latitudes		
Latitude	Surface Temperature (C°)	Surface Density (g/cm³)
60°N	5	1.0258
40°N	13	1.0259
20°N	24	1.0237
0°	27	1.0238
20°S	24	1.0241
40°S	15	1.0261
60°S	2	1.0272

Analyze and Conclude

1. **Observing** What differences did you observe in the behavior of the two water samples in Part A? Which water sample was the most dense in each experiment?

2. **Inferring** How does temperature affect the density of water?

3. **Drawing Conclusions** If two water samples of equal mass had equal salinities, which sample would be more dense: Water Sample A, which has a temperature of 25°C or water Sample B, which has a temperature of 14°C?

4. **Interpreting Diagrams** Describe the density and temperature characteristics of water in equatorial regions. Compare these characteristics to water found in polar regions.

5. **Inferring** What is the reason that higher average surface densities are found in the Southern Hemisphere?

6. **Communicating** Write a lab report describing your procedures in this experiment and how you reached your conclusions.

Study Guide

15.1 The Composition of Seawater

Key Concepts

- Because the proportion of dissolved substances in seawater is such a small number, oceanographers typically express salinity in parts per thousand (‰).
- Most of the salt in seawater is sodium chloride— common table salt.
- Chemical weathering of rocks on the continents is one source of elements found in seawater.
- The second major source of elements found in seawater is from Earth's interior.
- The ocean's surface water temperature varies with the amount of solar radiation received, which is primarily a function of latitude.
- Seawater density is influenced by two main factors: salinity and temperature.
- Oceanographers generally recognize a three-layered structure in most parts of the open ocean: a shallow surface mixed zone, a transition zone, and a deep zone.

Vocabulary

salinity, *p. 422*; thermocline, *p. 424*; density, *p. 425*; pycnocline, *p. 426*; mixed zone, *p. 426*

15.2 The Diversity of Ocean Life

Key Concepts

- Marine organisms can be classified according to where they live and how they move.
- Plankton include all organisms—algae, animals, and bacteria—that drift with ocean currents.
- Nekton include all animals capable of moving independently of the ocean currents, by swimming or other means of propulsion.
- The term *benthos* describes organisms living on or in the ocean bottom.
- Three factors are used to divide the ocean into distinct marine life zones: the availability of sunlight, the distance from shore, and the water depth.

Vocabulary

plankton, *p. 428*; phytoplankton, *p. 429*; zooplankton, *p. 429*; nekton, *p. 429*; benthos, *p. 429*; photic zone, *p. 430*; intertidal zone, *p. 431*; neritic zone, *p. 431*; oceanic zone, *p. 431*; pelagic zone, *p. 431*; benthic zone, *p. 431*; abyssal zone, *p. 431*

15.3 Oceanic Productivity

Key Concepts

- Two factors influence a region's photosynthetic productivity: the availability of nutrients and the amount of solar radiation, or sunlight.
- The availability of solar energy limits photosynthetic productivity in polar areas.
- Productivity in tropical regions is limited by the lack of nutrients.
- In temperate regions, which are found at mid-latitudes, a combination of these two limiting factors, sunlight and nutrient supply, controls productivity.
- The transfer of energy between trophic levels is very inefficient.
- Animals that feed through a food web rather than a food chain are more likely to survive because they have alternative foods to eat should one of their food sources diminish in quantity or even disappear.

Vocabulary

primary productivity, *p. 433*, photosynthesis, *p. 433*, chemosynthesis, *p. 433*, trophic level, *p. 436*, food chain, *p. 437*, food web, *p. 437*

Thinking Visually

Web Diagram Use the information in the chapter to complete the web diagram on marine life zones.

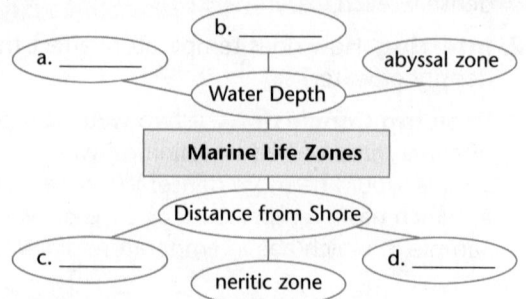

Reviewing Content

Choose the letter that best answers the question or completes the statement.

1. The most abundant salt in seawater is
   a. calcium chloride.
   b. magnesium chloride.
   c. sodium chloride.
   d. sodium fluoride.

2. Which process does NOT lead to a decrease in the salinity of seawater?
   a. runoff from land
   b. precipitation
   c. evaporation
   d. sea ice melting

3. Which term refers to the layer of water in which there is a rapid change of temperature with depth in the ocean?
   a. pycnocline
   b. abyssal zone
   c. thermocline
   d. isothermal line

4. Which is NOT a zone in the three-layered structure of the ocean according to density?
   a. mixed zone
   b. deep zone
   c. transition zone
   d. intertidal zone

5. Organisms that drift with ocean currents are
   a. nekton.
   b. plankton.
   c. neritic.
   d. pelagic.

6. Which term describes the upper part of the ocean into which sunlight penetrates?
   a. neritic zone
   b. intertidal zone
   c. oceanic zone
   d. photic zone

7. Phytoplankton are usually found in the
   a. benthic zone.
   b. photic zone.
   c. abyssal zone.
   d. aphotic zone.

8. The use of light energy by organisms to convert water and carbon dioxide into organic molecules is
   a. chemosynthesis.
   b. decomposition.
   c. photosynthesis.
   d. consumption.

9. During which season does primary productivity reach its peak in polar oceans?
   a. spring
   b. summer
   c. fall
   d. winter

10. In temperate oceans, primary productivity is limited by
    a. nutrients and oxygen concentration.
    b. nutrients and water temperature.
    c. sunlight and oxygen concentration.
    d. sunlight and nutrients.

Understanding Concepts

11. Why is salinity expressed in parts per thousand instead of percent?

12. What is the principal source of water in oceans? Why do scientists reach this conclusion?

13. Explain how the salinity of water in polar regions varies seasonally.

14. What is the range of salinity for surface waters in the open ocean?

15. Is there a thermocline present in high-latitude ocean waters? Why or why not?

16. Compare and contrast phytoplankton and zooplankton.

17. What factors may affect the depth of the photic zone in any given area of the ocean?

18. What is the oceanic zone? What limits the amount of production in the oceanic zone?

19. What is the difference between the pelagic zone and the benthic zone?

20. How does the permanent thermocline in tropical oceans affect primary productivity in those areas?

Copy the diagram onto a separate sheet of paper and use it to answer Questions 21 and 22.

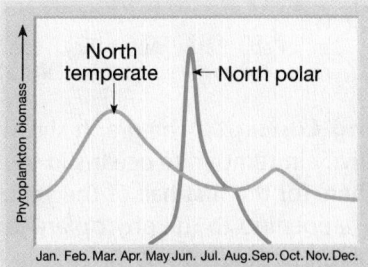

21. Draw a line on the graph that correctly represents the productivity of tropical oceans year-round.

22. Draw a line on the graph that represents the changes in zooplankton population in north temperate oceans throughout the course of a year.

23. What is the difference between a food chain and a food web?

Critical Thinking

24. Analyzing In the Red Sea, evaporation values are higher than the values of precipitation and river runoff, particularly in summer months. Do you think that the salinity of the water here is higher or lower than average ocean water salinity? Why?

25. Drawing Conclusions Water Mass A is 2°C with a salinity of 34.50‰. Water Mass B is 2°C with a salinity of 34.00‰. Water Mass C is 2°C with a salinity of 34.78‰. Order the water masses from lowest density to highest density. Which water mass will be nearest the surface? Which will be closest to the bottom?

26. Relating Cause and Effect Explain how the phytoplankton productivity in polar waters is related to the fact that density and temperature change very little with depth in polar waters.

Use the figure below to answer Questions 27–29.

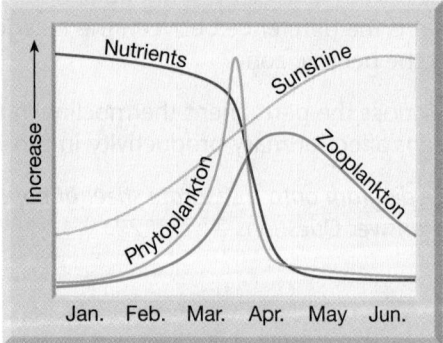

27. Applying Concepts The graph shows the productivity in temperate oceans in the northern hemisphere for the first half of the year. Describe what is happening to the phytoplankton and zooplankton populations in the graph. Explain what factors are affecting productivity.

28. Inferring Describe what the graph would look like if it were extended through December. How is it different than the January through June portion?

29. Drawing Conclusions How would this graph be different if it were for a temperate ocean in the southern hemisphere?

Concepts in Action

Use the table below to answer Questions 30 and 31.

Depth (m)	Temperature (°C)
0	23
200	22.5
400	20
600	14
800	8
1000	5
1200	4.5
1400	4.5
1600	4

30. Interpreting Data An oceanographer records the following temperature data for an area of ocean water. Graph the data on a sheet of graph paper. What feature exists between 400 and 1200 meters?

31. Applying Concepts For which area of the world oceans would this temperature variation with depth be present? What processes cause this to occur?

32. Formulating Hypotheses It has been observed that some species of zooplankton migrate vertically in ocean water. They spend the daylight hours at deeper depths of about 200 meters and at night move to the surface. Formulate a hypothesis that might explain this behavior.

Performance-Based Assessment

Designing Equipment Imagine you have been asked to collect marine plankton samples from surface waters near the coast. Recall that many plankton are microscopic or nearly so and that by definition, plankton drift with currents. Design a piece of equipment that will allow you to collect the plankton so that they can be brought to the lab and examined under a microscope. Include the materials you will use to construct the equipment, a drawing of it, and an explanation of how it should be used in the field.

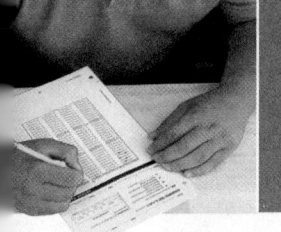

Standardized Test Prep

Test-Taking Tip

Watch for Qualifiers
The words *best*, *least*, and *greatest* are examples of qualifiers. If a question contains a qualifier, more than one answer will contain correct information. However, only one answer will be complete and correct for the question asked. Look at the question below. Eliminate any answers that are clearly incorrect. Then choose the remaining answer that offers the best explanation for the question asked.

Which factor has the *greatest* influence on the density of surface water in the ocean?

(A) temperature
(B) pressure
(C) salinity
(D) oxygen

(Answer: A)

Choose the letter that best answers the question or completes the statement.

1. The total amount of solid material dissolved in water is known as
(A) sediment load.
(B) salinity.
(C) total dissolved solids.
(D) density.

2. Thermoclines in oceans are *best* developed at
(A) lower latitudes.
(B) higher latitudes.
(C) both high and low latitudes.
(D) regions close to continents.

3. Which term describes a rapid change in density with depth?
(A) thermocline
(B) halocline
(C) isocline
(D) pycnocline

4. Animals capable of moving independently of ocean currents, by swimming or other means of propulsion are called
(A) benthos.
(B) plankton.
(C) nekton.
(D) pelagic.

5. During which season is productivity the *greatest* in temperate waters?
(A) spring
(B) summer
(C) fall
(D) winter

Use the diagram below to answer Questions 6 and 7.

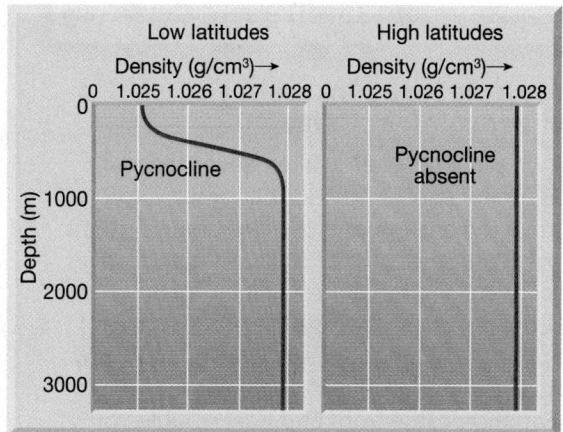

6. Explain what influences the formation of the pycnocline at low latitudes.

7. Why is the pycnocline absent at high latitudes?

8. What changes would occur to the food web below if the population of copepods was killed by a bacterial disease?

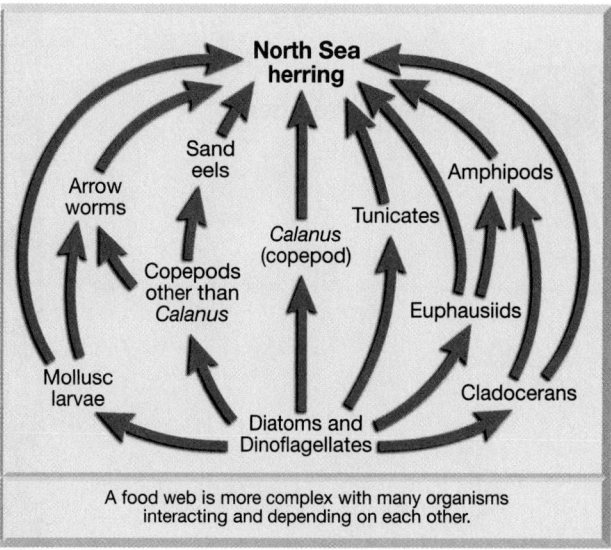

A food web is more complex with many organisms interacting and depending on each other.

16 The Dynamic Ocean

21st Century Learning
Creativity and Intellectual Curiosity

How can tides be used to generate electricity?

In the search for energy alternatives to fossil fuels, many people are looking for ways to harness the ocean's energy. Investigate systems for generating electricity using tides and waves. Prepare an electronic presentation for your class that details at least two systems that seem promising. Discuss how each works, and show illustrations if available. Discuss where your information came from and how reliable you think it is. For example, was the information provided by a company that would profit from the system, or another source? Discuss any disadvantages to the system. For example, is the system safe for wildlife, or does it interfere with other uses of the coastline?

Exploration Lab
Graphing Tidal Cycles

 GEODe Ocean
↳ Coastal Processes

Waves break along California's rocky Big Sur coast.

Chapter Preview

Inquiry > Activity

How Do Ocean Waves Form?

Procedure

1. Fill a rectangular, clear, plastic container with water to within about 3 cm of the top of the container.

2. Place a fan next to the container, aiming the flow of air toward the water. **CAUTION:** *Make sure the cord and the fan do not come in contact with the water in the container.*

3. Turn the fan on low power for 2–3 minutes. Observe what effect this has on the water in the container. Using a ruler, measure the size of the waves produced. Record your observations and data.

4. Turn the fan off and allow the water in the container to settle. Repeat Step 3 with the fan on high power.

Think About It

1. Inferring Where does the energy to produce most ocean waves come from?

2. Drawing Conclusions What is the relationship between the speed of the wind and the size of a wave?

16.1 Ocean Circulation

Reading Focus

Key Concepts

- How do surface currents develop?
- How do ocean currents affect climate?
- Why is upwelling important?
- How are density currents formed?

Vocabulary

- ♦ ocean current
- ♦ surface current
- ♦ gyre
- ♦ Coriolis effect
- ♦ upwelling
- ♦ density current

Reading Strategy

Identifying Main Ideas Copy and expand the table below. As you read, write the main idea of each topic.

Topic	Main Idea
Surface currents	a. _____?_____
Gyres	b. _____?_____
Ocean currents and climate	c. _____?_____
Upwelling	d. _____?_____

Figure 1 Wind not only creates waves, but it also provides the force that drives the ocean's surface circulation.

Ocean water is constantly in motion, powered by many different forces. Winds, for example, generate surface currents, which influence coastal climate. Winds also produce waves like the ones shown in Figure 1. Some waves carry energy from powerful storms to distant shores, where their impact erodes the land. In some areas, density differences create deep-ocean circulation. This circulation is important for ocean mixing and recycling nutrients.

Surface Circulation

Ocean currents are masses of ocean water that flow from one place to another. The amount of water can be large or small. Ocean currents can be at the surface or deep below. The creation of these currents can be simple or complex. In all cases, however, the currents that are generated involve water masses in motion.

Surface Currents Surface currents are movements of water that flow horizontally in the upper part of the ocean's surface. **Surface currents develop from friction between the ocean and the wind that blows across its surface.** Some of these currents do not last long, and they affect only small areas. Such water movements are responses to local or seasonal influences. Other surface currents are more permanent and extend over large portions of the oceans. These major horizontal movements of surface waters are closely related to the general circulation pattern of the atmosphere.

Ocean Surface Currents

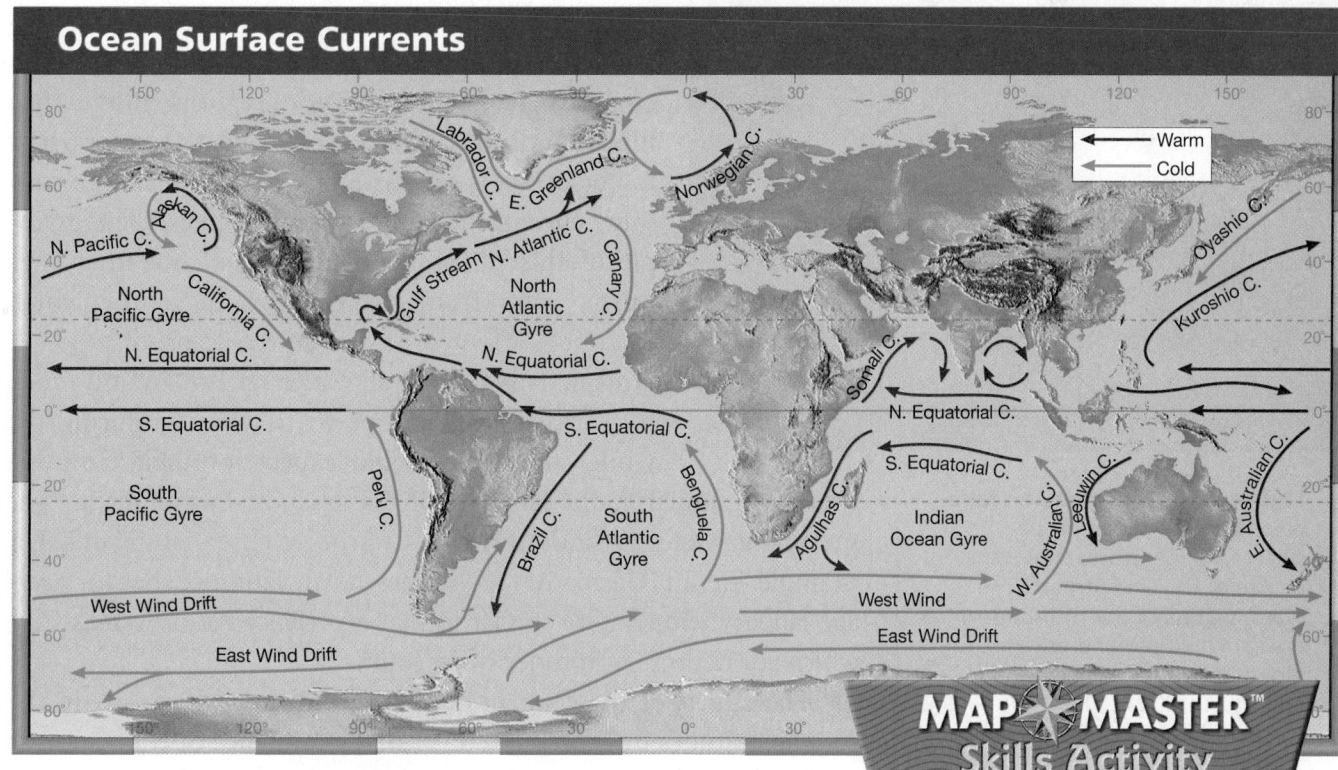

Gyres Huge circular-moving current systems dominate the surfaces of the oceans. These large whirls of water within an ocean basin are called **gyres** (gyros = a circle). There are five main ocean gyres: the North Pacific Gyre, the South Pacific Gyre, the North Atlantic Gyre, the South Atlantic Gyre, and the Indian Ocean Gyre.

Although wind is the force that generates surface currents, other factors also influence the movement of ocean waters. The most significant of these is the Coriolis effect. The **Coriolis effect** is the deflection of currents away from their original course as a result of Earth's rotation. **Because of Earth's rotation, currents are deflected to the right in the Northern Hemisphere and to the left in the Southern Hemisphere.** As a consequence, gyres flow in opposite directions in the two different hemispheres.

For example, trace the path of water in the North Atlantic Gyre in Figure 2. As water moves north from Florida in the Gulf Stream and North Atlantic Current, it is deflected to the right, or eastward. Water moving south in the Canary Current is deflected westward into the North Equatorial Current. This gyre moves in a clockwise direction.

Now look at the South Atlantic Gyre. Because the Coriolis effect deflects its current to the left, this gyre flows counterclockwise.

 **Reading Checkpoint** *What is a gyre?*

Figure 2
The ocean's circulation is organized into five major gyres, or circular current systems. The West Wind Drift flows around the continent of Antarctica.

Movement
Locate Which currents make up the Indian Ocean Gyre?
Locate Find the West Wind Drift on the map. Explain why the West Wind Drift is the only current that completely encircles Earth.
Drawing Conclusions Why is there not another comparable current that encircles Earth at the same latitude in the Northern Hemisphere?

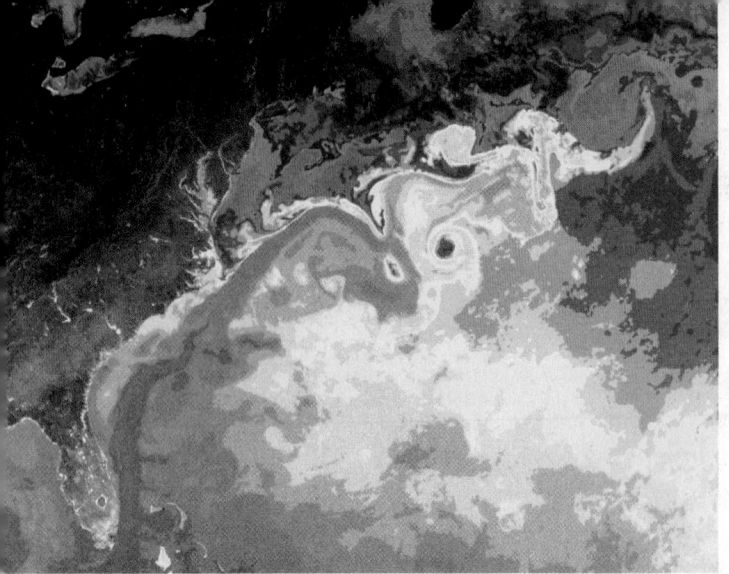

Figure 3 Gulf Stream This false-color satellite image of sea surface temperatures shows the course of the Gulf Stream. The warm waters of the Gulf Stream are shown in red and orange along the east coast of Florida and the Carolinas. The surrounding colder waters are shown in green, blue, and purple. Compare this image to the map of the Gulf Stream in Figure 2.

Ocean Currents and Climate Ocean currents have an important effect on climates. When **currents from low-latitude regions move into higher latitudes, they transfer heat from warmer to cooler areas on Earth.** The Gulf Stream, a warm water current shown in Figure 3, is an excellent example of this phenomenon. The Gulf Stream brings warm water from the equator up to the North Atlantic Current, which is an extension of the Gulf Stream. This current allows Great Britain and much of northwestern Europe to be warmer during the winter than one would expect for their latitudes, which are similar to the latitudes of Alaska and Newfoundland. The prevailing westerly winds carry this warming effect far inland. For example, Berlin, Germany (52 degrees north latitude), has an average January temperature similar to that experienced at New York City, which lies 12 degrees latitude farther south.

The effects of these warm ocean currents are felt mostly in the middle latitudes in winter. In contrast, the influence of cold currents is most felt in the tropics or during summer months in the middle latitudes. Cold currents begin in cold high-latitude regions. **As cold water currents travel toward the equator, they help moderate the warm temperatures of adjacent land areas.** Such is the case for the Benguela Current along western Africa, the Peru Current along the west coast of South America, and the California Current. These currents are shown in Figure 2.

Ocean currents also play a major role in maintaining Earth's heat balance. They do this by transferring heat from the tropics, where there is an excess of heat, to the polar regions, where less heat exists. Ocean water movement accounts for about a quarter of this heat transport. Winds transport the remaining three-quarters.

Upwelling In addition to producing surface currents, winds can also cause vertical water movements. **Upwelling** is the rising of cold water from deeper layers to replace warmer surface water. Upwelling is a common wind-induced vertical movement. One type of upwelling, called coastal upwelling, is most characteristic along the west coasts of continents, most notably along California, western South America, and West Africa.

Coastal upwelling occurs in these areas when winds blow toward the equator and parallel to the coast. Coastal winds combined with the Coriolis effect cause surface water to move away from shore. As the surface layer moves away from the coast, it is replaced by water that "upwells" from below the surface. This slow upward movement of water from depths of 50 to 300 meters brings water that is cooler than

For: Links on ocean currents
Visit: www.SciLinks.org
Web Code: cjn-5161

the original surface water and results in lower surface water temperatures near the shore.

 **Upwelling brings greater concentrations of dissolved nutrients, such as nitrates and phosphates, to the ocean surface.** These nutrient-enriched waters from below promote the growth of microscopic plankton, which in turn support extensive populations of fish and other marine organisms. Figure 4 is a satellite image that shows high productivity due to coastal upwelling off the southwest coast of Africa.

Reading Checkpoint *What is upwelling?*

Deep-Ocean Circulation

In contrast to the largely horizontal movements of surface currents, deep-ocean circulation has a significant vertical component. It accounts for the thorough mixing of deep-water masses.

Density Currents Density currents are vertical currents of ocean water that result from density differences among water masses. Denser water sinks and slowly spreads out beneath the surface. **An increase in seawater density can be caused by a decrease in temperature or an increase in salinity.** Processes that increase the salinity of water include evaporation and the formation of sea ice. Processes that decrease the salinity of water include precipitation, runoff from land, icebergs melting, and sea ice melting. Density changes due to salinity variations are important in very high latitudes, where water temperature remains low and relatively constant.

High Latitudes Most water involved in deep-ocean density currents begins in high latitudes at the surface. In these regions, surface water becomes cold, and its salinity increases as sea ice forms. When this water becomes dense enough, it sinks, initiating deep-ocean density currents. Once this water sinks, it is removed from the physical processes that increased its density in the first place. Its temperature and salinity remain largely unchanged during the time it is in the deep ocean. Because of this, oceanographers can track the movements of density currents in the deep ocean. By knowing the temperature, salinity, and density of a water mass, scientists are able to map the slow circulation of the water mass through the ocean.

Figure 4 Effects of Upwelling This image from the SeaStar satellite shows chlorophyll concentration along the southwest coast of Africa. High chlorophyll concentrations, in red, indicate high amounts of photosynthesis, which is linked to upwelling nutrients.

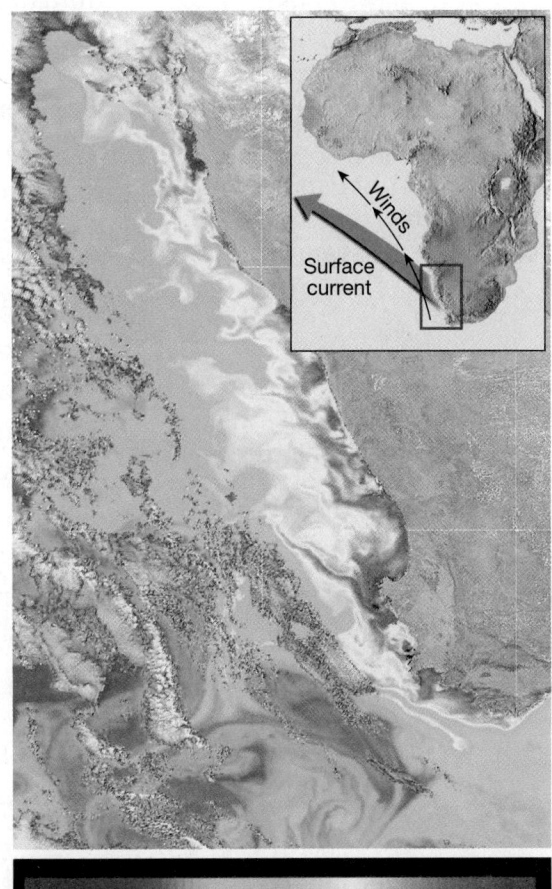

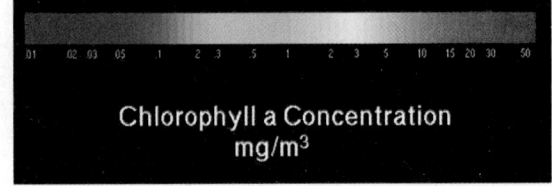

Chlorophyll a Concentration
mg/m³

Figure 5 Sea Ice in the Arctic Ocean When seawater freezes, sea salts do not become part of the ice, leading to an increase in the salinity of the surrounding water.
Drawing Conclusions *How does this process lead to the formation of a density current?*

Go Online
PLANETDIARY

For: Links on deep-ocean currents
Visit: PHSchool.com
Web Code: czd-5161

Figure 6 This cross section of the Atlantic Ocean shows the deep-water circulation of water masses formed by density currents.

Near Antarctica, surface conditions create the highest density water in the world. This cold, salty water slowly sinks to the sea floor, where it moves throughout the ocean basins in slow currents. After sinking from the surface of the ocean, deep waters will not reappear at the surface for an average of 500 to 2000 years.

Evaporation Density currents can also result from increased salinity of ocean water due to evaporation. In the Mediterranean Sea conditions exist that lead to the formation of a dense water mass at the surface that sinks and eventually flows into the Atlantic Ocean. Climate conditions in the eastern Mediterranean include a dry northwest wind and sunny days. These conditions lead to an annual excess of evaporation compared to the amount of precipitation. When seawater evaporates, salt is left behind, and the salinity of the remaining water increases. The surface waters of the eastern Mediterranean Sea have a salinity of about 38‰ (parts per thousand). In the winter months, this water flows out of the Mediterranean Sea into the Atlantic

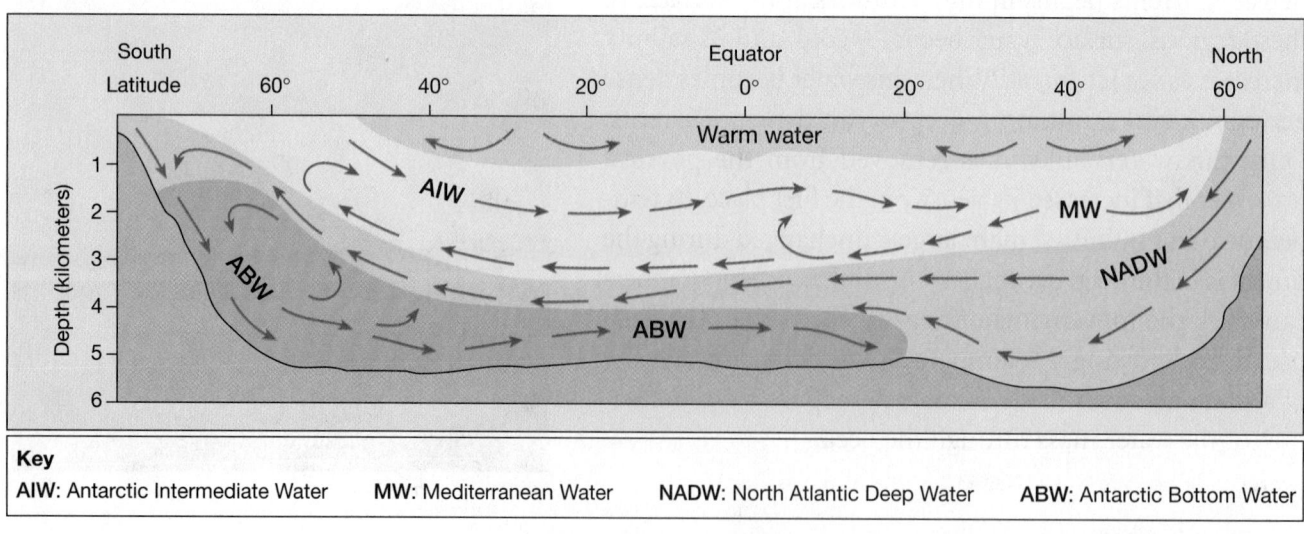

Key
AIW: Antarctic Intermediate Water   **MW:** Mediterranean Water   **NADW:** North Atlantic Deep Water   **ABW:** Antarctic Bottom Water

Ocean. At 38‰, this water is more dense than the Atlantic Ocean surface water at 35‰, so it sinks. This Mediterranean water mass can be tracked as far south as Antarctica. Figure 6 shows some of the different water masses created by density currents in the Atlantic Ocean.

A Conveyor Belt A simplified model of ocean circulation is similar to a conveyor belt that travels from the Atlantic Ocean through the Indian and Pacific oceans and back again. Figure 7 shows this conveyor belt model. In this model, warm water in the ocean's upper layers flows toward the poles. When the water reaches the poles, its temperature drops and salinity increases, making it more dense. Because the water is dense, it sinks and moves toward the equator. It returns to the equator as cold, deep water that eventually upwells to complete the circuit. As this "conveyor belt" moves around the globe, it influences global climate by converting warm water to cold water and releasing heat to the atmosphere.

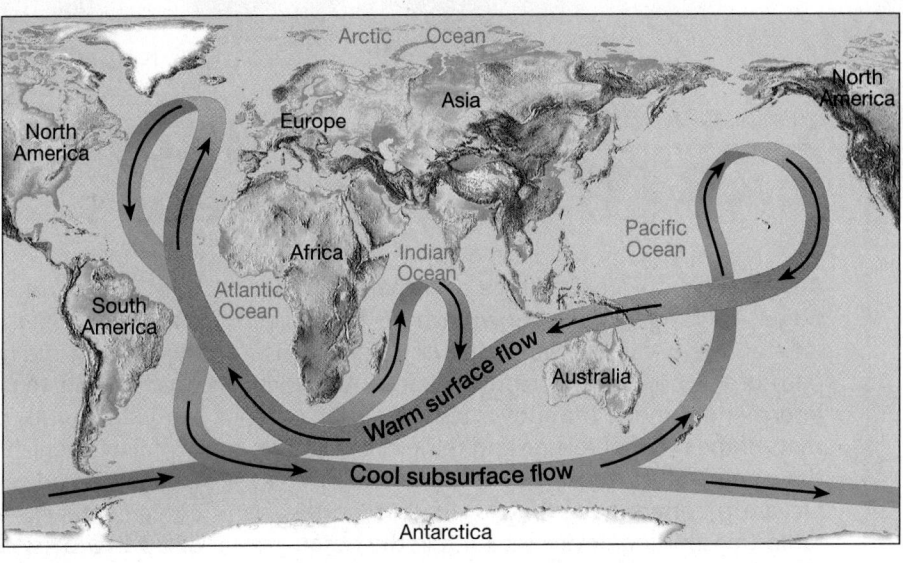

Figure 7 This "conveyor belt" model of ocean circulation shows a warm surface current with an underlying cool current.

Section 16.1 Assessment

Reviewing Concepts

1. How do surface currents develop?
2. What is the Coriolis effect? How does it influence the direction of surface currents flowing in the ocean?
3. How do ocean currents affect climate?
4. Why is upwelling important?
5. How are density currents formed?

Thinking Critically

6. **Applying Concepts** The average surface water temperature off of the coast of Ecuador is 21°C. The average surface water temperature off of the coast of Brazil at the same latitude is about 27°C. Explain why there is such a difference in water temperature between these areas at the same latitude.

7. **Inferring** During an El Niño event, the upwelling of cold, nutrient-rich water stops in areas off the coast of Peru. How might this affect the food web in this area?

Writing in Science

Explanatory Paragraph During the 1700s, mail ships sailed back and forth between England and America. It was noted that it took the ships two weeks longer to go from England to America than to travel the same route from America to England. It was determined that the Gulf Stream was delaying the ships. Write a paragraph explaining why this is true. Use Figure 2 to explain how sailors could avoid the Gulf Stream when sailing to America.

Shoes and Toys as Drift Meters

Any floating object can serve as a makeshift drift meter, as long as it is known where the object entered the ocean and where it was retrieved. The path of the object can then be inferred, providing information about the movement of surface currents. If the times of release and retrieval are known, the speed of currents can also be determined. Oceanographers have long used drift bottles—a radio-transmitting device set adrift in the ocean—to track the movement of currents and, more recently, to refine computer models of ocean circulation.

Many objects have accidentally become drift meters when ships have lost some (or all) of their cargo at sea. In this way, athletic shoes have helped oceanographers advance the understanding of surface circulation in the North Pacific Ocean. In May 1990, the container vessel *Hansa Carrier* was traveling from Korea to Seattle, Washington, when it encountered a severe North Pacific storm. During the storm the ship lost 21 deck containers overboard, including five that held athletic shoes. The shoes that were released from their containers floated and were carried east by the North Pacific Current. Within six months, thousands of the shoes began to wash up along the beaches of Alaska, Canada, Washington, and Oregon—over 2400 kilometers from the site of the spill. The inferred course of the shoes is shown in Figure 8. A few shoes were found on beaches in northern California, and over two years later shoes from the spill were even recovered from the north end of the main island of Hawaii.

With help from the beachcombing public and remotely based lighthouse operators, information on the location and number of shoes collected was compiled during the months following the spill. Serial numbers inside the shoes were traced to individual containers, which indicated that only four of the five containers had released their shoes. Most likely, one entire container sank without opening. A maximum of 30,910 pairs of shoes (61,820 individual shoes) were released. Before the shoe spill, the largest number of drift bottles purposefully released at one time by oceanographers was about 30,000. Although only 2.6 percent of the shoes were recovered, this compares favorably with the 2.4 percent recovery rate of drift bottles released by oceanographers conducting research.

In January 1992, another cargo ship lost 12 containers overboard during a storm to the north of where the shoes had previously spilled. One of these containers held 29,000 packages of small, floatable, colorful plastic bathtub toys in the shapes of blue turtles, yellow ducks, red beavers, and green frogs. Even though the toys were housed in plastic packaging glued to a cardboard backing, studies showed that after 24 hours in seawater, the glue deteriorated, thereby releasing over 100,000 individual floating toys.

The floating bathtub toys began to come ashore in southeast Alaska 10 months later, which verified computer models of North Pacific circulation. The models indicate that many of the bathtub toys will continue to be carried by the Alaska Current and will eventually disperse throughout the North Pacific Ocean.

Since 1992, oceanographers have continued to study ocean currents by tracking other floating items spilled from cargo ships, including 34,000 hockey gloves, 5 million plastic Lego pieces, and an unidentified number of small plastic doll parts.

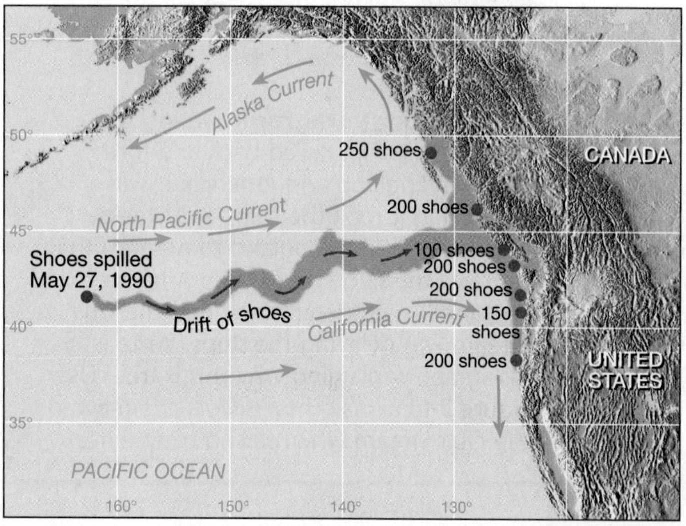

Figure 8 The map shows the path of drifting shoes and recovery locations from a spill in 1990.

16.2 Waves and Tides

Reading Focus

Key Concepts

- From where do ocean waves obtain their energy?
- What three factors affect the characteristics of a wave?
- How does energy move through a wave?
- What causes tides?

Vocabulary

- ◆ wave height
- ◆ wavelength
- ◆ wave period
- ◆ fetch
- ◆ tide
- ◆ tidal range
- ◆ spring tide
- ◆ neap tide

Reading Strategy

Building Vocabulary Copy the table below. As you read the section, define in your own words each vocabulary word listed in the table.

Vocabulary Term	Definition
Wave height	a. _____?_____
Wavelength	b. _____?_____
Wave period	c. _____?_____
Fetch	d. _____?_____

The movement of ocean water is a powerful thing. Waves created by storms release energy when they crash along the shoreline. Sometimes the energy of water movement can be harnessed and used to generate electricity.

Waves

Ocean waves are energy traveling along the boundary between ocean and atmosphere. Waves often transfer energy from a storm far out at sea over distances of several thousand kilometers. That's why even on calm days the ocean still has waves that travel across its surface. The power of waves is most noticeable along the shore, the area between land and sea where waves are constantly rolling in and breaking. Sometimes the waves are low and gentle. Other times waves, like the ones shown in Figure 9, are powerful as they pound the shore. If you make waves by tossing a pebble into a pond, or by splashing in a pool, or by blowing across the surface of a cup of coffee, you are giving energy to the water. The waves you see are just the visible evidence of the energy passing through the water. When observing ocean waves, remember that you are watching energy travel through a medium, in this case, water. In Chapter 24, you will study waves of the electromagnetic spectrum (which includes light). These waves transfer energy without matter as a medium.

Figure 9 The Force of Breaking Waves These waves are slamming into a seawall that has been built at Sea Bright, New Jersey, to protect the nearby electrical lines and houses from the force of the waves.

Q *Do waves always travel in the same directions as currents?*

A Not in all cases. Most surface waves travel in the same direction as the wind blows, but waves radiate outward in all directions from the disturbance that creates them. In addition, as waves move away from the sea area where they were generated, they enter areas where other currents exist. As a result, the direction of wave movement is often unrelated to that of currents. In fact, waves can even travel in a direction completely opposite to that of a current. A rip current, for example, moves away from the shoreline, opposite to the direction of incoming waves.

Go **Online**

For: Water Motion activity
Visit: PHSchool.com
Web Code: czp-5162

Wave Characteristics Most ocean waves obtain their energy and motion from the wind. When a breeze is less than 3 kilometers per hour, only small waves appear. At greater wind speeds, more stable waves gradually form and advance with the wind.

Characteristics of ocean waves are illustrated in Figure 10. The tops of the waves are the crests, which are separated by troughs. Halfway between the crests and troughs is the still water level, which is the level that the water would occupy if there were no waves. The vertical distance between trough and crest is called the **wave height.** The horizontal distance between two successive crests or two successive troughs is the **wavelength.** The time it takes one full wave—one wavelength—to pass a fixed position is the **wave period.**

The height, length, and period that are eventually achieved by a wave depend on three factors: (1) wind speed; (2) length of time the wind has blown; and (3) fetch. **Fetch** is the distance that the wind has traveled across open water. As the quantity of energy transferred from the wind to the water increases, both the height and steepness of the waves also increase. Eventually, a critical point is reached where waves grow so tall that they topple over, forming ocean breakers called whitecaps.

Wave Motion Waves can travel great distances across ocean basins. In one study, waves generated near Antarctica were tracked as they traveled through the Pacific Ocean basin. After more than 10,000 kilometers, the waves finally expended their energy a week later along the shoreline of the Aleutian Islands of Alaska. The water itself does not travel the entire distance, but the wave does. As a wave travels, the water particles pass the energy along by moving in a circle. This movement, shown in Figure 10, is called circular orbital motion.

Observations of a floating object reveals that it moves not only up and down but also slightly forward and backward with each successive wave.

Figure 10 Anatomy of a Wave
The diagram of a non-breaking wave shows the parts of a wave as well as the movement of particles at depth.

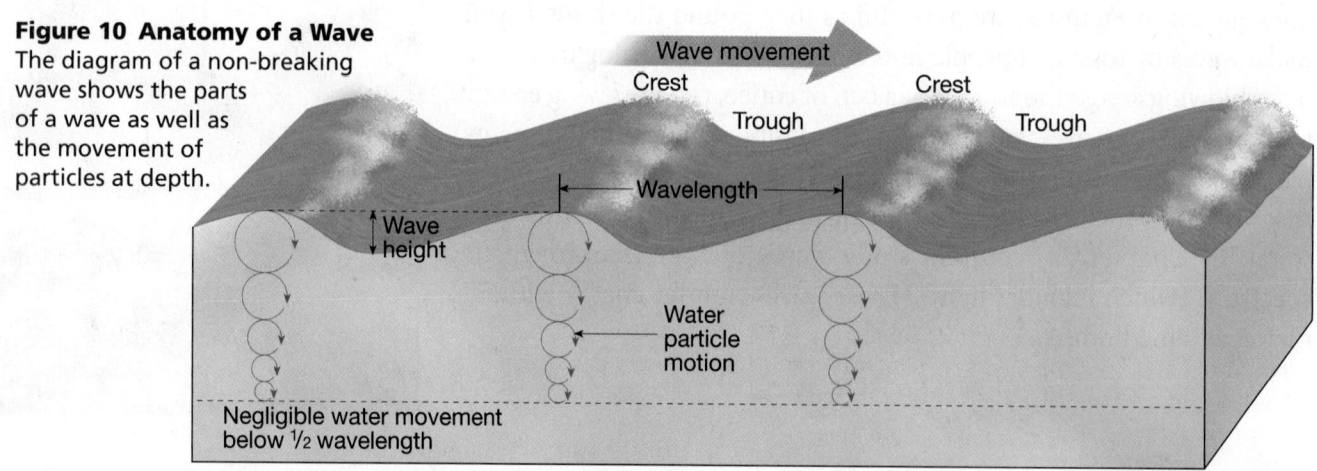

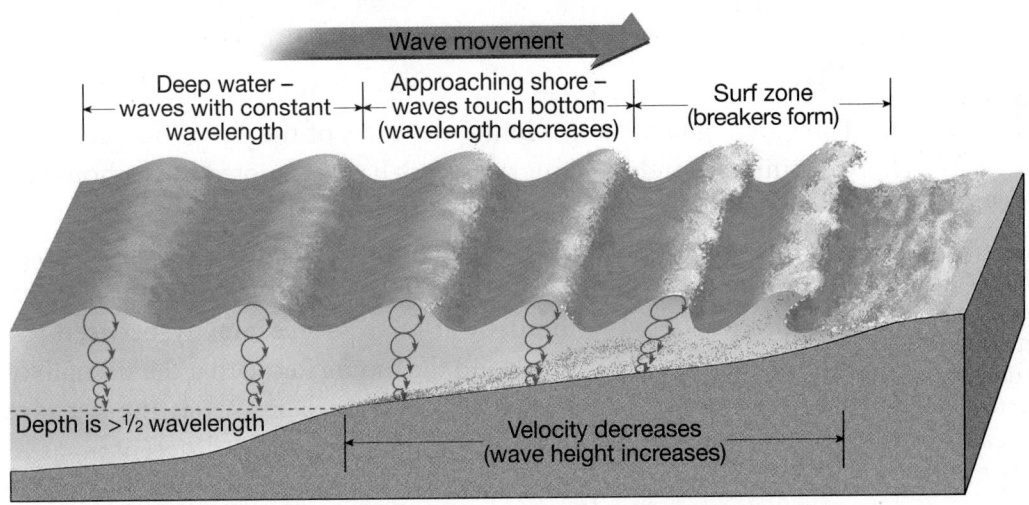

Deep water – waves with constant wavelength | Approaching shore – waves touch bottom (wavelength decreases) | Surf zone (breakers form)

Wave movement

Depth is >½ wavelength

Velocity decreases (wave height increases)

Figure 11 Breaking Waves Changes occur as a wave moves onto shore. As the waves touch bottom, wave speed decreases. The decrease in wave speed results in a decrease in wavelength and an increase in wave height.

This movement results in a circle that returns the object to essentially the same place in the water. ⬤ **Circular orbital motion allows energy to move forward through the water while the individual water particles that transmit the wave move around in a circle.**

The energy contributed by the wind to the water is transmitted not only along the surface of the sea but also downward. However, beneath the surface, the circular motion rapidly diminishes until—at a depth equal to one-half the wavelength measured from still water level—the movement of water particles becomes negligible. The dramatic decrease of wave energy with depth is shown by the rapidly decreasing diameters of water-particle orbits in Figure 10.

Breaking Waves

As long as a wave is in deep water, it is unaffected by water depth. However, when a wave approaches the shore, the water becomes shallower and influences wave behavior. The wave begins to "feel bottom" at a water depth equal to half of its wavelength. Such depths interfere with water movement at the base of the wave and slow its advance. Figure 11 shows the changes that occur as a wave moves onto shore.

As a wave advances toward the shore, the slightly faster waves farther out to sea catch up and decrease the wavelength. As the speed and length of the wave decrease, the wave steadily grows higher. Finally, a critical point is reached when the wave is too steep to support itself, and the wave front collapses, or breaks, causing water to advance up the shore.

The turbulent water created by breaking waves is called surf. On the landward margin of the surf zone, the turbulent sheet of water from collapsing breakers, called swash, moves up the slope of the beach. When the energy of the swash has been expended, the water flows back down the beach toward the surf zone as backwash.

 **Reading Checkpoint** *At what depth do the characteristics of a wave begin to change as it approaches the shore?*

For: Links on ocean waves
Visit: www.SciLinks.org
Web Code: cjn-5162

The Dynamic Ocean **457**

Tides

Tides are regular changes in the elevation of the ocean surface. Their rhythmic rise and fall along coastlines has been noted throughout history. Other than waves, they are the easiest ocean movements to observe. But the cause of tides was not well understood until Sir Isaac Newton applied the law of universal gravitation to them. Newton showed that there is a mutually attractive force, gravity, between any two bodies, as between Earth and the moon. Recall that the strength of the force of gravity between two objects decreases as the distance between the objects increases. At any given time, different areas of Earth's surface are different distances from the moon. The pull of the moon's gravity is greater at parts of Earth's surface that are closer to the moon and less at more distant locations. ◯**Ocean tides result from differences in the gravitational attraction exerted upon different parts of Earth's surface by the moon and, to a lesser extent, by the sun.**

The Cause of Tides The primary body that influences the tides is the moon, which makes one complete revolution around Earth every 29 and a half days. The sun, however, also influences the tides. It is far larger than the moon, but because it is much farther away, its effect is considerably less. In fact, the sun's tide-generating effect is only about 46 percent that of the moon's.

To illustrate how tides are produced, consider Earth as a rotating sphere covered to a uniform depth with water. Think about the gravitational forces in the Earth-moon system, ignoring the influence of the sun for now. This gravitational pull is strongest on the side of Earth closest to the moon and weakest on the far side of Earth from the moon. This difference causes Earth to be stretched slightly. The shape of the solid Earth is not affected much by this difference in pull. However, because water is a fluid, it can easily flow from location to location in response to differences in the pull of the moon's gravity.

Look at Figure 12. On the side of Earth closest to the moon, the pull of the moon's gravity on the oceans is greater than it is on the solid Earth. Ocean water flows toward this area, producing a tidal bulge, or high tide. On the side of Earth farthest from the moon, the pull of the moon's gravity on the oceans is weaker than it is on the solid Earth. As a result, water flows toward that area and a second, equally large tidal bulge forms on the side of Earth directly opposite the moon.

Figure 12 Tidal Bulges on Earth Caused by the Moon *Analyzing What force is involved in causing the tidal bulges?*

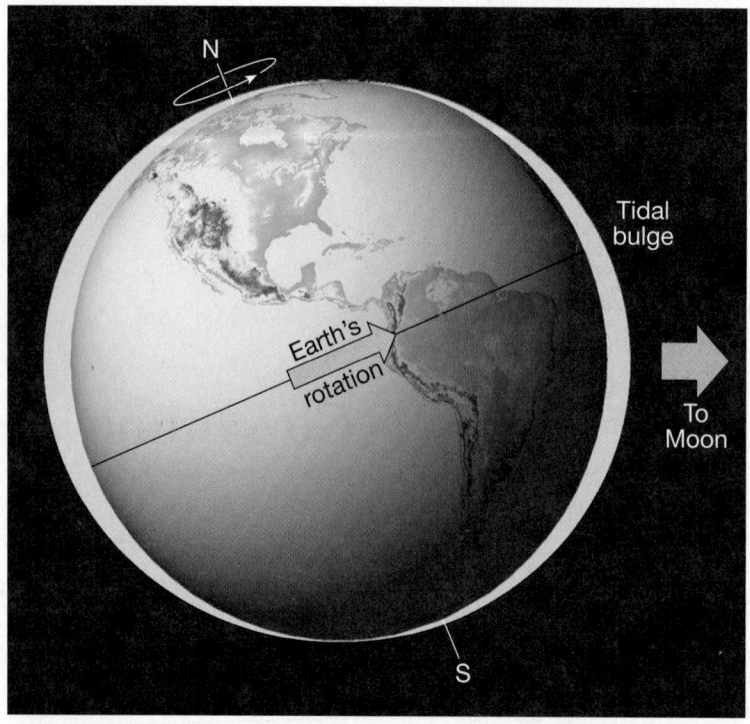

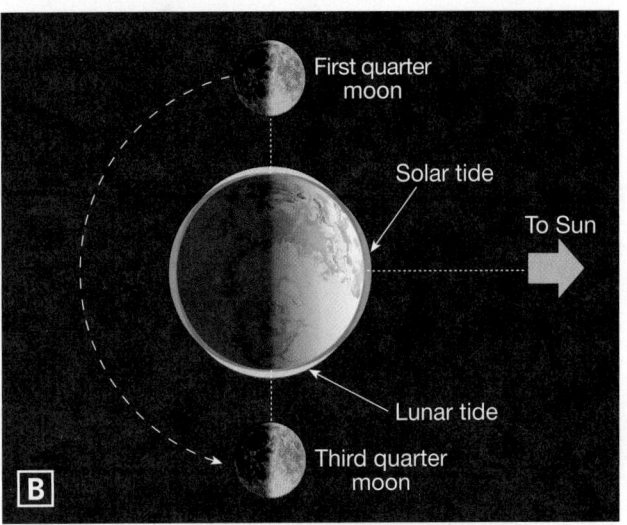

Because the position of the moon changes only moderately in a single day, the tidal bulges remain in place while Earth rotates "through" them. For this reason, if you stand on the seashore for 24 hours, Earth will rotate you through alternating areas of higher and lower water. As you are carried into each tidal bulge, the tide rises. As you are carried into the troughs between the tidal bulges, the tide falls. Most coastal locations experience two high tides and two low tides each day.

Tidal Cycle Although the sun is farther away from Earth than the moon, the gravitational attraction between the sun and Earth does play a role in producing tides. The sun's influence produces smaller tidal bulges on Earth. These tidal bulges are the result of the same forces involved in the bulges created by the moon. The influence of the sun on tides is most noticeable near the times of new and full moons. During these times, the sun and moon are aligned, and their forces are added together, as shown in Figure 13A. The combined gravity of these two tide-producing bodies causes larger tidal bulges (higher high tides) and larger tidal troughs (lower low tides). This combined gravity produces a large tidal range. The **tidal range** is the difference in height between successive high and low tides. **Spring tides** are tides that have the greatest tidal range due to the alignment of the Earth–moon–sun system. They are experienced during new and full moons. Conversely, at about the time of the first and third quarters of the moon, the gravitational forces of the moon and sun act on Earth at right angles. The sun and moon partially offset the influence of the other, as shown in Figure 13B. As a result, the daily tidal range is less. These tides are called **neap tides.** Each month there are two spring tides and two neap tides, each about one week apart.

 **Reading Checkpoint** *What is the tidal range?*

Figure 13 Earth-Moon-Sun Positions and the Tides
A When Earth, moon, and sun are aligned, spring tides are experienced. **B** When Earth, moon, and sun are at right angles to each other, neap tides are experienced.
Describing *How does the sun influence the formation of spring and neap tides?*

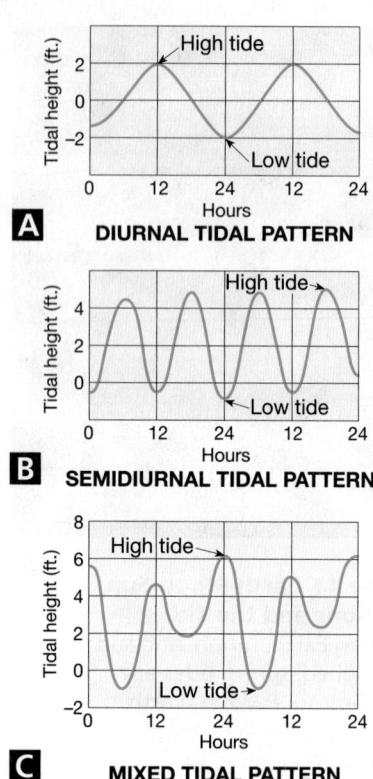

A DIURNAL TIDAL PATTERN

B SEMIDIURNAL TIDAL PATTERN

C MIXED TIDAL PATTERN

Figure 14 Tidal patterns

Tidal Patterns You now know the basic causes and types of tides. However, many factors—including the shape of the coastline, the configuration of ocean basins, and water depth—greatly influence the tides. Consequently, tides at various locations respond differently to the tide-producing forces. This being the case, the nature of the tide at any coastal location can be determined most accurately by actual observation. The predictions in tidal tables and tidal data on nautical charts are based on such observations.

⚷ **Three main tidal patterns exist worldwide: diurnal tides, semidiurnal tides, and mixed tides.** A diurnal tidal pattern is characterized by a single high tide and a single low tide each tidal day, as shown in the graph in Figure 14A. Tides of this type occur along the northern shore of the Gulf of Mexico.

A semidiurnal tidal pattern exhibits two high tides and two low tides each tidal day. The two highs are about the same height, and the two lows are about the same height. Figure 14B shows a semidiurnal tide pattern. This type of tidal pattern is common along the Atlantic Coast of the United States.

A mixed tidal pattern, shown in Figure 14C, is similar to a semidiurnal pattern except that it is characterized by a large inequality in high water heights, low water heights, or both. In this case, there are usually two high and two low tides each day. However, the high tides are of different heights, and the low tides are of different heights. Such tides are found along the Pacific Coast of the United States and in many other parts of the world.

Section 16.2 Assessment

Reviewing Concepts

1. ⚷ From where do ocean waves obtain their energy?

2. ⚷ What three quantities are used to describe a wave?

3. ⚷ How does energy move by means of a wave?

4. What changes occur in a wave as it approaches shore?

5. Which celestial bodies influence Earth tides?

6. ⚷ What force produces tides?

7. ⚷ What are the three types of tidal patterns?

Thinking Critically

8. **Inferring** Two waves have the same fetch and were created by winds of equal speed. Why might one wave be higher than the other?

9. **Relating Cause and Effect** Explain how the force of gravity leads to tides in Earth's oceans.

10. **Comparing and Contrasting** Compare and contrast spring tides and neap tides.

> ## Math ▶ Practice
>
> 11. **Calculating** Wavelength, wave period, and wave speed can be related to each other in the equation:
> $$\frac{\text{wavelength}}{\text{wave period}} = \text{wave speed}.$$
> If wavelength = 187 meters, and wave speed = 16.8 meters per second, what is the period of this wave?

16.3 Shoreline Processes and Features

Reading Focus

Key Concepts

- How are sediments along the shoreline moved?
- How does refraction affect wave action along the shore?
- What do longshore currents do?
- By which processes do shoreline features form?
- What structures can be built to protect a shoreline?
- What is beach nourishment?

Vocabulary

- beach
- wave refraction
- longshore current
- barrier islands

Reading Strategy

Summarizing Read the section on wave refraction. Then copy and complete the concept map below to organize what you know about refraction.

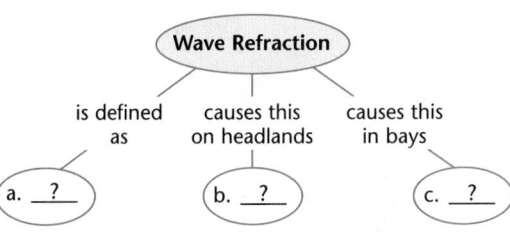

Beaches and shorelines are constantly undergoing changes as the force of waves and currents act on them. A **beach** is the accumulation of sediment found along the shore of a lake or ocean. Beaches are composed of whatever sediment is locally available. They may be made of mineral particles from the erosion of beach cliffs or nearby coastal mountains. This sediment may be relatively coarse in texture. Some beaches have a significant biological component. For example, most beaches in southern Florida are composed of shell fragments and the remains of organisms that live in coastal waters. Regardless of the composition, the sediment that makes up the beach does not stay in one place. The waves that crash along the shoreline are constantly moving it. Beaches can be thought of as material in transit along the shoreline.

Forces Acting on the Shoreline

Waves along the shoreline are constantly eroding, transporting, and depositing sediment. Many types of shoreline features can result from this activity.

Wave Impact During calm weather, wave action is minimal. During storms, however, waves are capable of causing much erosion. The impact of large, high-energy waves against the shore can be awesome in its violence. Each breaking wave may hurl thousands of tons of water against the land, sometimes causing the ground to tremble.

Figure 15 Erosion has undercut this sandstone cliff at Gabriola Island, British Columbia, Canada.

It is no wonder that cracks and crevices are quickly opened in cliffs, coastal structures, and anything else that is subjected to these enormous impacts. Water is forced into every opening, causing air in the cracks to become highly compressed by the thrust of crashing waves. When the wave subsides, the air expands rapidly. This expanding air dislodges rock fragments and enlarges and extends preexisting fractures.

Abrasion In addition to the erosion caused by wave impact and pressure, erosion caused by abrasion is also important. In fact, abrasion is probably more intense in the surf zone than in any other environment. Abrasion is the sawing and grinding action of rock fragments in the water. Smooth, rounded stones and pebbles along the shore are evidence of the continual grinding action of rock against rock in the surf zone. Such fragments are also used as "tools" by the waves as they cut horizontally into the land, like the sandstone shown in Figure 15. Waves are also very effective at breaking down rock material and supplying sand to beaches.

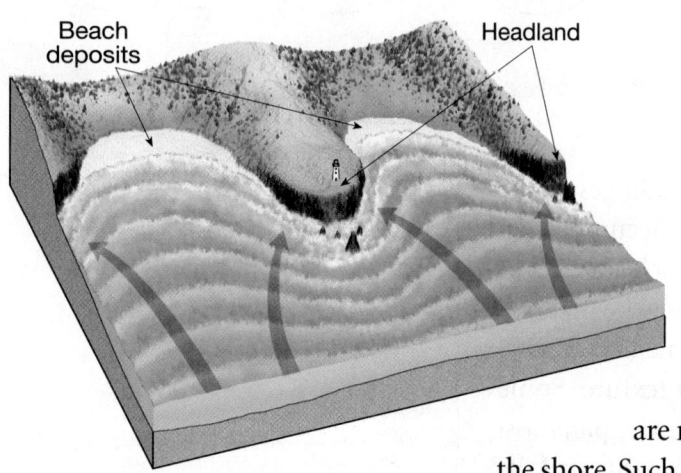

Figure 16 Wave Refraction
Waves are refracted as they come into shore. Wave energy is concentrated at the headlands and dispersed in the bays.
Inferring *What processes occur as a result of wave refraction on this shoreline?*

Wave Refraction Wave refraction is the bending of waves, and it plays an important part in shoreline processes. Wave refraction affects the distribution of energy along the shore. It strongly influences where and to what degree erosion, sediment transport, and deposition will take place.

Waves seldom approach the shore straight on. Rather, most waves move toward the shore at a slight angle. However, when they reach the shallow water of a smoothly sloping bottom, the wave crests are refracted, or bent, and tend to line up nearly parallel to the shore. Such bending occurs because the part of the wave nearest the shore touches bottom and slows first, whereas the part of the wave that is still in deep water continues forward at its full speed. The change in speed causes wave crests to become nearly parallel to the shore regardless of their original orientation.

Because of refraction, wave energy is concentrated against the sides and ends of headlands that project into the water, whereas wave action is weakened in bays. This type of wave action along irregular coastlines is illustrated in Figure 16. Waves reach the shallow water in front of the headland sooner than they do in adjacent bays. Therefore, wave energy is concentrated in this area, leading to erosion. By contrast, refraction in the bays causes waves to spread out and expend less energy. This refraction leads to deposition of sediments and the formation of sandy beaches.

What is wave refraction?

Longshore Transport Although waves are refracted, most still reach the shore at a slight angle. As a result, the uprush of water, or swash, from each breaking wave is at an oblique angle to the shoreline. These angled waves produce currents within the surf zone. The currents flow parallel to the shore and move large amounts of sediment along the shore. This type of current is called a **longshore current,** shown in Figure 17.

The water in the surf zone is turbulent. **Turbulence allows longshore currents to easily move the fine suspended sand and to roll larger sand and gravel particles along the bottom.** For a 10-year period at Oxnard, California, more than 1.4 million metric tons of sediment moved along the shore each year. Longshore currents can change direction because the direction that waves approach the beach changes with the seasons. Nevertheless, longshore currents generally flow southward along both the Atlantic and Pacific shores of the United States.

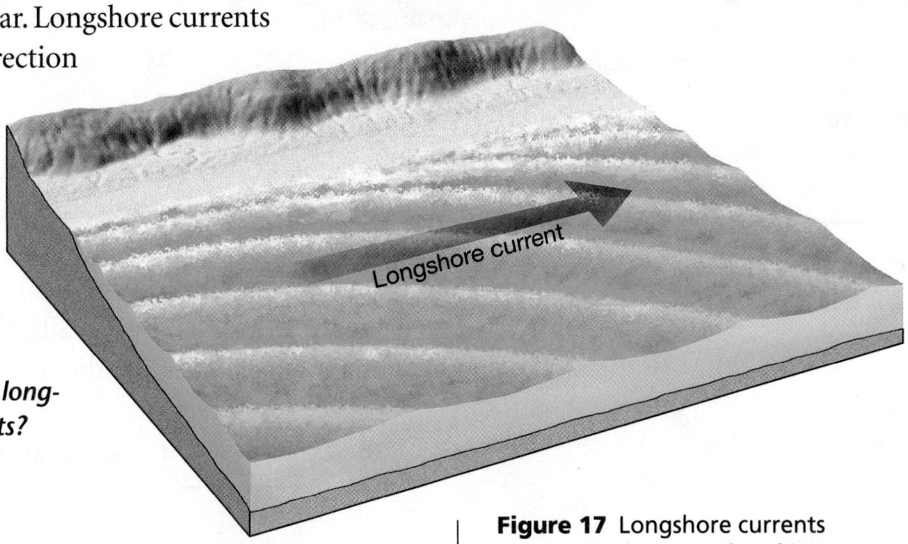

Reading Checkpoint *What causes longshore currents?*

Erosional Features

Shoreline features vary depending on the type of rocks exposed along the shore, the intensity of waves, the nature of coastal currents, and whether the coast is stable, sinking, or rising. **Shoreline features that originate primarily from the work of erosion are called erosional features. Sediment that is transported along the shore and deposited in areas where energy is low produce depositional features.**

Many coastal landforms owe their origin to erosional processes. Such erosional features are common along the rugged and irregular New England coast and along the steep shorelines of the West Coast of the United States.

Wave erosion is steadily wearing away the California coast. Where the coast is made up of sedimentary rock, average erosion is 15–30 centimeters per year. But where the coast consists of soil and sand, erosion can be as high as 2–3 meters per year. Coastal erosion is a hazard to structures built on cliffs and bluffs along the shore.

The cliffs along California's coast form as tectonic processes slowly uplift coastal land. At the same time, the energy of ocean waves undercuts the cliffs. Over time, this process produces features such as wave-cut cliffs and platforms, sea arches, and sea stacks.

Figure 17 Longshore currents are created by waves breaking at an angle.
Applying Concepts *Explain how longshore currents can change direction.*

Figure 18 In time, the sea arch will collapse and form a sea stack like the one on the left.

Wave-Cut Cliffs and Platforms Wave-cut cliffs, like the one shown in Figure 20C, result from the cutting action of the surf against the base of coastal land. As erosion progresses, rocks that overhang the notch at the base of the cliff crumble into the surf, and the cliff retreats. A relatively flat, benchlike surface, called a wave-cut platform, is left behind by the receding cliff. The platform broadens as the wave attack continues. Some debris produced by the breaking waves remains along the water's edge as sediment on the beach. The rest of the sediment is transported farther seaward.

Sea Arches and Sea Stacks Headlands that extend into the sea are vigorously attacked by waves because of refraction. The surf erodes the rock selectively and wears away the softer or more highly fractured rock at the fastest rate. At first, sea caves may form. When two caves on opposite sides of a headland unite, a sea arch like the one in Figure 18 results. Eventually, the arch falls in, leaving an isolated remnant, or sea stack, on the wave-cut platform.

✓ **Reading Checkpoint** *How does a sea arch form?*

Depositional Features

Recall that a beach is the shore of a body of water that is covered in sand, gravel, or other larger sediments. Sediment eroded from the beach is transported along the shore and deposited in areas where wave energy is low. Such processes produce a variety of depositional features.

Figure 19 This high-altitude image shows a baymouth bar along the coast of Martha's Vineyard, Massachusetts.

baymouth bar

Spits, Bars, and Tombolos Where longshore currents and other surf zone currents are active, several features related to the movement of sediment along the shore may develop. As shown in Figure 20B and C, a spit is an elongated ridge of sand that projects from the land into the mouth of an adjacent bay. Often the end in the water hooks landward in response to the dominant direction of the longshore current. The term baymouth bar is applied to a sandbar that completely crosses a bay, sealing it off from the open ocean. Find the baymouth bar in Figure 19. Such a feature tends to form across bays where currents are weak. The weak currents allow a spit to extend to the other side and form a baymouth bar. A tombolo is a ridge of sand that connects an island to the mainland or to another island. A tombolo forms in much the same way as a spit. Follow the formation of tombolos and other shoreline features in Figure 20.

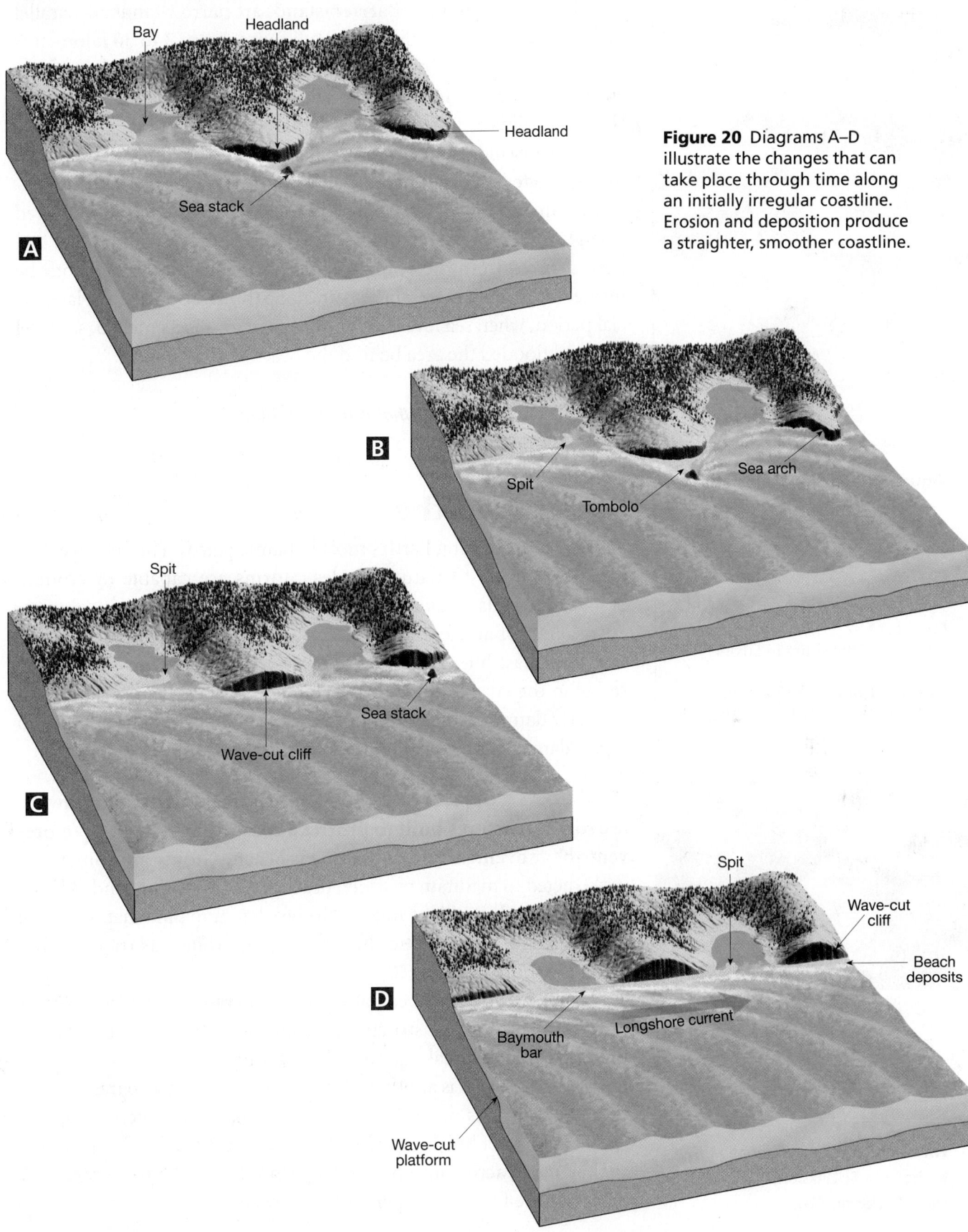

Figure 20 Diagrams A–D illustrate the changes that can take place through time along an initially irregular coastline. Erosion and deposition produce a straighter, smoother coastline.

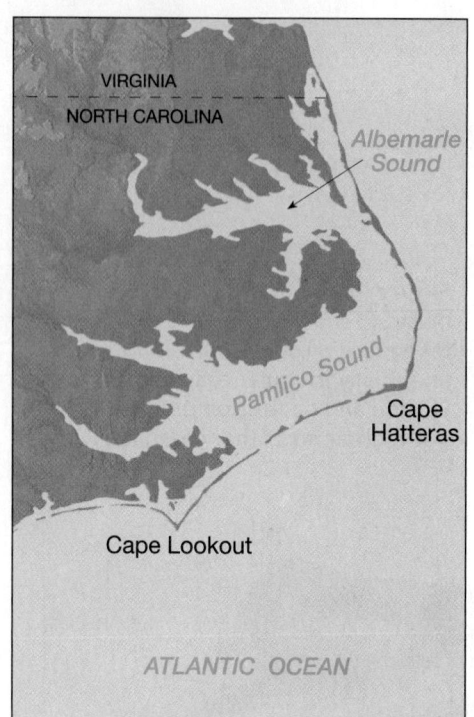

VIRGINIA
NORTH CAROLINA

Albemarle Sound

Pamlico Sound

Cape Hatteras

Cape Lookout

ATLANTIC OCEAN

Figure 21 The islands along the coast of North Carolina are examples of barrier islands.

Figure 22 A series of groins traps sand along the shore in Sussex, England.
Inferring *In which direction does the sand move along the coast in this photo? How do you know?*

Go Online

NSTA SciLINKS

For: Links on coastal changes
Visit: www.SciLinks.org
Web Code: cjn-5163

Barrier Islands The Atlantic and Gulf Coastal Plains are relatively flat and slope gently seaward. The shore zone in these areas is characterized by barrier islands. **Barrier islands** are narrow sandbars parallel to, but separated from, the coast at distances from 3 to 30 kilometers offshore. From Cape Cod, Massachusetts, to Padre Island, Texas, nearly 300 barrier islands rim the coast. The barrier islands along the coast of North Carolina are shown in Figure 21.

Barrier islands probably formed in several ways. Some began as spits that were later cut off from the mainland by wave erosion or by the general rise in sea level following the last glacial period. Others were created when turbulent waters in the line of breakers heaped up sand that had been scoured from the bottom. Finally, some barrier islands may be former sand-dune ridges that began along the shore during the last glacial period, when sea level was lower. As the ice sheets melted, sea level rose and flooded the area behind the beach-dune complex.

✓ **Reading Checkpoint** *What is a barrier island?*

Stabilizing the Shore

Shorelines are among Earth's most dynamic places. They change rapidly in response to natural forces. Storms are capable of eroding beaches and cliffs at rates that far exceed the long-term average erosion. Such bursts of accelerated erosion not only affect the natural evolution of a coast but can also have a profound impact on people who reside in the coastal zone. Erosion along the coast causes significant property damage. Huge sums of money are spent annually not only to repair damage but also to prevent or control erosion.

Protective Structures  **Groins, breakwaters, and seawalls are some structures built to protect a coast from erosion or to prevent the movement of sand along a beach.** Groins are sometimes constructed to maintain or widen beaches that are losing sand. A groin is a barrier built at a right angle to the beach to trap sand that is moving parallel to the shore. Notice how a series of groins has trapped sand along the shore in Figure 22.

Protective structures can also be built parallel to the shoreline. A breakwater is one such structure. Its purpose is to protect boats from the force of large breaking waves by creating a quiet water zone near the shore. A seawall is another protective structure built parallel to the shore. A seawall is designed to shield the coast and defend property from the force of breaking waves. Waves expend much of their energy as they move across an open beach. Seawalls reduce this process by reflecting the force of unspent waves seaward.

Protective structures often only offer temporary solutions to shoreline problems. The structures themselves interfere with the natural processes of erosion and deposition. Then more structures often need to be built in order to counteract the new problems that arise. Many scientists feel that using protective structures to divert the ocean's energy causes more harm than good.

Beach Nourishment 🐟**Beach nourishment is the addition of large quantities of sand to the beach system.** It is an attempt to stabilize shoreline sands without building protective structures. Examine the before and after photos shown in Figure 23. By building the beaches seaward, both beach quality and storm protection are improved. However, the same processes that removed the sand in the first place will eventually wash away the replacement sand as well.

Beach nourishment can be very expensive because huge volumes of sand must be transported to the beach from offshore areas, nearby rivers, or other source areas for sand. Beach nourishment can also have detrimental effects on local marine life. For example, beach nourishment at Waikiki Beach, Hawaii, involved replacing the natural coarse beach sand with softer, muddier sand. Destruction of the softer sand by breaking waves increased the water's turbidity, or "cloudiness," and killed offshore coral reefs.

Figure 23 Miami Beach
A Before beach nourishment
B After beach nourishment
Analyzing *What are the advantages and disadvantages of beach nourishment?*

Section 16.3 Assessment

Reviewing Concepts

1. 🐟 How are sediments along the shoreline moved?
2. What effect does wave impact have on shorelines?
3. 🐟 How does refraction affect wave action along the shore?
4. 🐟 What do longshore currents do?
5. 🐟 By which processes do shoreline features form?
6. Name three examples of shoreline features formed by erosion.
7. How do barrier islands form?
8. 🐟 What structures can be built to protect a shoreline?
9. 🐟 What is beach nourishment?

Thinking Critically

10. **Analyzing** How can beach nourishment be helpful? How can it be harmful?
11. **Comparing and Contrasting** Compare and contrast a tombolo and a barrier island.
12. **Relating Cause and Effect** A breakwater is built to reduce wave action in near-shore areas. How might the reduced wave action along the shore behind the breakwater affect sediment deposition? What problems might this cause?

Connecting ⊂ Concepts

Wave Refraction Relate the concept of wave refraction to the changes that occur as a wave enters shallow water and goes into shore.

Graphing Tidal Cycles

Tides are the cyclical rise and fall of sea level caused by the gravitational attraction of Earth to the moon and, to a lesser extent, to the sun. Gravitational pull creates a bulge in the ocean on the side of Earth nearest the moon. A similar bulge forms on the opposite side of Earth from the moon because the moon's pull is weaker on that side. Tides develop as the rotating Earth moves through these bulges, causing periods of high and low water. In this lab, you will make a graph of tidal data to determine whether an area has diurnal, semidiurnal, or mixed tides.

Problem
How can you determine the tidal pattern an area experiences?

Materials
- graph paper
- pencil

Skills
Graphing, Interpreting Data, Inferring, Drawing Conclusions

Procedure

1. Label the graph paper as below to make a graph of the tidal cycle. The x-axis should be in days, and the y-axis should be in feet. As shown below, place the x-axis at the top of the graph, rather than at the bottom.

2. Use the data in Table 1 to make a graph of the tidal cycle.

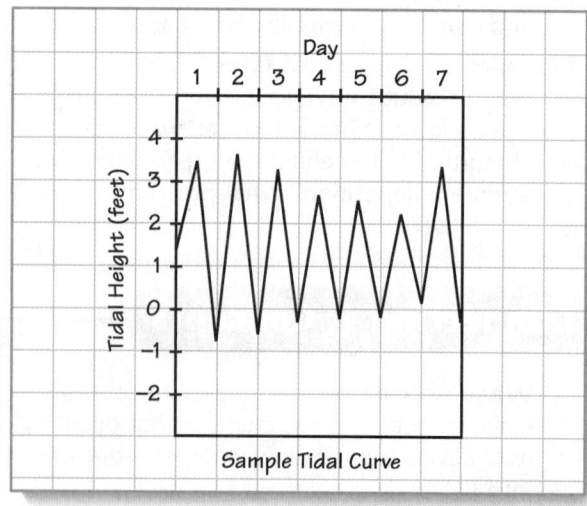

Sample Tidal Curve

High tide in Nova Scotia's Bay of Fundy

Low tide in the same area

Analyze and Conclude

1. **Applying Concepts** What tidal pattern does this area experience? Explain how you determined this.

2. **Calculating** What is the greatest tidal range for the data you graphed? What is the least tidal range? What types of tides correspond to each of these tidal ranges?

3. **Draw Conclusions** Based on your graph, identify the days when each moon phase could have occurred: new moon, first quarter moon, full moon, last quarter moon. How do you know this?

4. **Applying Concepts** On January 5th (Day 5 on the table) at 9:00 A.M., Jarred anchored his boat in about 4 feet of water at the beach. When he returned to his boat at 3:30 that afternoon, the boat was completely in the sand. What had happened? How long did Jarred have to wait to leave the area in his boat?

Table 1 Tidal Data for Long Beach, New York, January 2003

All times are listed in Local Standard Time (LST). All heights are in feet.

Day	Time	Height	Time	Height	Time	Height	Time	Height
1	05:45 A.M.	5.5	12:16 P.M.	−0.7	06:12 P.M.	4.4	——	—
2	12:18 A.M.	−0.5	06:35 A.M.	5.6	01:07 P.M.	−0.8	07:03 P.M.	4.4
3	01:10 A.M.	−0.5	07:23 A.M.	5.5	01:56 P.M.	−0.8	07:53 P.M.	4.4
4	01:59 A.M.	−0.4	08:11 A.M.	5.4	02:42 P.M.	−0.7	08:42 P.M.	4.3
5	02:45 A.M.	−0.2	08:59 A.M.	5.1	03:25 P.M.	−0.5	09:32 P.M.	4.2
6	03:30 A.M.	0.0	09:47 A.M.	4.8	04:07 P.M.	−0.3	10:23 P.M.	4.0
7	04:14 A.M.	0.3	10:35 A.M.	4.6	04:49 P.M.	−0.1	11:12 P.M.	3.9
8	05:01 A.M.	0.6	11:22 A.M.	4.3	05:32 P.M.	0.2	11:59 P.M.	3.9
9	05:54 A.M.	0.8	12:09 P.M.	4.0	06:18 P.M.	0.4	——	—
10	12:45 A.M.	3.9	06:56 A.M.	0.9	12:57 P.M.	3.7	07:10 P.M.	0.5
11	01:31 A.M.	3.9	07:59 A.M.	0.9	01:47 P.M.	3.5	08:02 P.M.	0.5
12	02:19 A.M.	4.0	08:57 A.M.	0.8	02:41 P.M.	3.4	08:53 P.M.	0.5
13	03:10 A.M.	4.1	09:50 A.M.	0.6	03:39 P.M.	3.5	09:41 P.M.	0.4
14	04:02 A.M.	4.3	10:38 A.M.	0.3	04:34 P.M.	3.6	10:28 P.M.	0.2
15	04:51 A.M.	4.6	11:26 A.M.	0.1	05:23 P.M.	3.7	11:15 P.M.	0.1
16	05:36 A.M.	4.8	12:12 P.M.	−0.1	06:08 P.M.	3.9	——	—
17	12:02 A.M.	−0.1	06:17 A.M.	5.0	12:57 P.M.	−0.3	06:51 P.M.	4.1
18	12:49 A.M.	−0.2	06:58 A.M.	5.1	01:40 P.M.	−0.5	07:32 P.M.	4.2
19	01:35 A.M.	−0.4	07:38 A.M.	5.2	02:22 P.M.	−0.6	08:15 P.M.	4.3
20	02:20 A.M.	−0.4	08:21 A.M.	5.2	03:30 P.M.	−0.7	09:01 P.M.	4.4
21	03:05 A.M.	−0.4	09:07 A.M.	5.1	03:44 P.M.	−0.7	09:51 P.M.	4.5
22	03:52 A.M.	−0.3	09:58 A.M.	4.9	04:27 P.M.	−0.6	10:44 P.M.	4.6
23	04:43 A.M.	−0.1	10:52 A.M.	4.7	05:13 P.M.	−0.4	11:37 P.M.	4.7
24	05:43 A.M.	0.1	11:48 A.M.	4.4	06:08 P.M.	−0.2	——	—
25	12:32 A.M.	4.7	06:53 A.M.	0.2	12:47 P.M.	4.2	07:11 P.M.	−0.1
26	01:30 A.M.	4.8	08:06 A.M.	0.2	01:50 P.M.	3.9	08:17 P.M.	0.0
27	02:31 A.M.	4.8	09:12 A.M.	0.1	02:57 P.M.	3.8	09:19 P.M.	0.0
28	03:35 A.M.	4.8	10:13 A.M.	−0.1	04:05 P.M.	3.9	10:17 P.M.	−0.1
29	04:37 A.M.	5.0	11:09 A.M.	−0.3	05:07 P.M.	4.0	11:13 P.M.	−0.2
30	05:33 A.M.	5.1	12:01 P.M.	−0.5	06:01 P.M.	4.2	——	—
31	12:06 A.M.	−0.3	06:22 A.M.	5.2	12:51 P.M.	−0.6	06:50 P.M.	4.3

Source: Center for Operational Oceanographic Products and Services, National Oceanographic and Atmospheric Association, National Ocean Service.

16.1 Ocean Circulation

Key Concepts

- Surface currents develop from friction between the ocean and the wind that blows across its surface.

- Because of Earth's rotation, currents are deflected to the right in the Northern Hemisphere and to the left in the Southern Hemisphere.

- When currents from low-latitude regions move into higher latitudes, they transfer heat from warmer to cooler areas on Earth.

- As cold water currents travel toward the equator, they help moderate the warm temperatures of adjacent land areas.

- Upwelling brings greater concentrations of dissolved nutrients, such as nitrates and phosphates, to the ocean surface.

- An increase in seawater density can be caused by a decrease in temperature or an increase in salinity.

Vocabulary

ocean current, *p. 448;* surface current, *p. 448;* gyre, *p. 449;* Coriolis effect, *p. 449;* upwelling, *p. 450;* density current, *p. 451*

16.2 Waves and Tides

Key Concepts

- Most ocean waves obtain their energy and motion from the wind.

- The height, length, and period that are eventually achieved by a wave depend on three factors: (1) wind speed; (2) length of time the wind has blown; and (3) fetch.

- Circular orbital motion allows energy to move forward through the water while the individual water particles that transmit the wave move around in a circle.

- Ocean tides result from differences in the gravitational attraction exerted upon different parts of Earth's surface by the moon and, to a lesser extent, by the sun.

- Three main tidal patterns exist worldwide: diurnal tides, semidiurnal tides, and mixed tides.

Vocabulary

wave height, *p. 456;* wavelength, *p. 456;* wave period, *p. 456;* fetch, *p. 456;* tide, *p. 458;* tidal range, *p. 459;* spring tide, *p. 459;* neap tide, *p. 459*

16.3 Shoreline Processes and Features

Key Concepts

- Waves are responsible for the movement of sediment along the shoreline.

- Because of refraction, wave energy is concentrated against the sides and ends of headlands that project into the water, whereas wave action is weakened in bays.

- Turbulence allows longshore currents to easily move the fine suspended sand and to roll larger sand and gravel particles along the bottom.

- Shoreline features that originate primarily from the work of erosion are called erosional features. Sediment is transported along the shore and deposited in areas where energy is low produce depositional features.

- Groins, breakwaters, and seawalls are some structures built to protect a coast from erosion or to prevent the movement of sand along a beach.

- Beach nourishment is the addition of large quantities of sand to the beach system.

Vocabulary

beach, *p. 461;* wave refraction, *p. 462;* longshore current, *p. 463;* barrier island, *p. 466*

Reviewing Content

Choose the letter that best answers the questions or completes the statement.

1. An ocean current moving from the equator toward a pole is
   a. cold.
   b. warm.
   c. cold in the Northern Hemisphere and warm in the Southern Hemisphere.
   d. warm in the Northern Hemisphere and cold in the Northern Hemisphere.

2. Because of the Coriolis effect, surface currents in the Southern Hemisphere are deflected
   a. to the left.   b. to the right.
   c. north.   d. south.

3. Which term describes the rising of cold water from deeper layers to replace warmer surface water?
   a. density current   b. downwelling
   c. surface current   d. upwelling

4. The energy and motion of most waves is derived from
   a. currents.   b. tides.
   c. wind.   d. gravity.

5. The five huge circular-moving systems of ocean surface currents are called
   a. density currents.   b. fetches.
   c. drifts.   d. gyres.

6. Daily changes in the elevation of the ocean surface are called
   a. surface currents.   b. tides.
   c. waves.   d. density currents.

7. Which of the following results from wave refraction?
   a. Wave energy is concentrated on headlands projecting into the water.
   b. Wave energy is concentrated in the recessed areas between headlands.
   c. Wave energy is largely dissipated before waves reach the shore.
   d. Headlands are enlarged because sediment is deposited on their seaward side.

8. The movement of water within the surf zone that parallels the shore is called
   a. tidal current.   b. density current.
   c. longshore current.   d. surface current.

9. Which describes a ridge of sand that connects an island to the mainland or another island?
   a. baymouth bar   b. sea arch
   c. sea stack   d. tombolo

10. Which is created through the process of erosion?
    a. baymouth bar   b. sea arch
    c. spit   d. tombolo

Understanding Concepts

11. Describe the influence that the Coriolis effect has on the movement of ocean waters.

12. Describe the effect that cold ocean currents have on the climates of adjacent land areas.

13. What role do ocean currents play in maintaining Earth's heat balance?

14. Describe coastal upwelling and the effect it has on fish populations.

15. Where and how is the densest water in all the oceans formed?

Use the figure below to answer Questions 16–18.

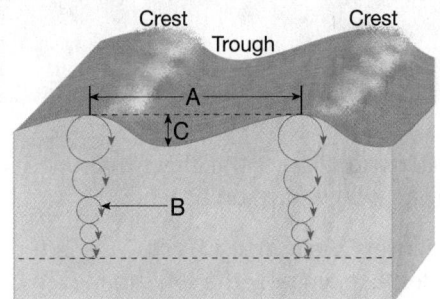

16. Identify which wave characteristics are represented by A and C.

17. Explain what B represents. What happens to a floating object as a wave passes through the water?

18. What factors can lead to an increase in the height of this wave?

The Dynamic Ocean   **471**

19. Compare and contrast a diurnal tidal pattern with a semidiurnal tidal pattern.

20. How does wave refraction result in sediment deposition in some shoreline areas?

21. How are a wave-cut cliff and wave-cut platforms related?

22. What are two types of protective structures used to stop erosion on beaches?

Critical Thinking

23. **Creating Models** Create a diagram that models the steps involved in the process of upwelling.

24. **Applying Concepts** The figure below shows the Earth–moon–sun system. What type of tide is experienced when Earth, the moon, and the sun are in these positions? What is the phase of the moon in the diagram?

Earth   Moon   To Sun

25. **Predicting** Predict the effect that the damming of rivers would have on beaches.

26. **Relating Cause and Effect** Discuss the origin of tides. Explain why the sun's influence on Earth's tides is only about half that of the moon's, even though the sun is much more massive than the moon.

Math Skills

27. **Calculating** As waves enter shallow water and decrease in speed, wave height increases and eventually a wave will break. The point at which a wave will break can be calculated using the formula for wave steepness: steepness = wave height/wavelength. When the steepness of a wave reaches 1/7, the wave will break. If the wavelength of a wave is 50 m, at what height will the wave break?

Concepts in Action

28. **Applying Concepts** Re-examine Figure 6. Describe the probable temperature and salinity characteristics for each water mass: Antarctic Bottom Water, North Atlantic Deep Water, and Mediterranean Water.

29. **Inferring** How do you think an increase in Earth's surface temperature would affect the "conveyor belt" model of currents in the ocean?

30. **Interpreting Diagrams** The graph below shows a tidal curve for Seattle, Washington. What type of tidal pattern does Seattle experience?

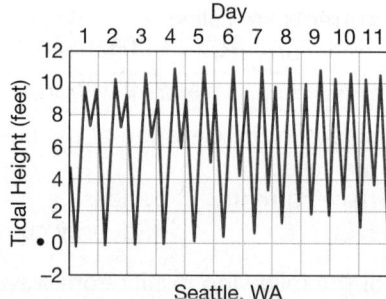

Seattle, WA

Performance-Based Assessment

Synthesizing Investigate the problems associated with shoreline development. Choose a coastal area that is experiencing problems with shoreline erosion. What actions have been taken to try to resolve the problems? Have the actions been effective? Why or why not? What are the advantages and disadvantages to different methods of preventing shoreline erosion? Offer a solution for the area you investigated.

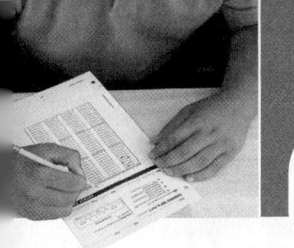

Standardized Test Prep

Anticipate the Answer
When answering a multiple-choice question, a useful strategy is to cover up the given answers and supply your own answer. Then compare your answer with those listed and select the one that most closely matches your answer.

Practice anticipating the answer in this question.

When waves reach shallow water, they are often bent and tend to become parallel to shore. This process is referred to as

(A) oscillation
(B) refraction
(C) reflection
(D) abrasion

(Answer: B)

Choose the letter that best answers the question or completes the statement.

1. Which of the following statements correctly explains a wave in the open ocean?
  (A) Water particles move in a circular path.
  (B) Waves continue to move without change, regardless of depth.
  (C) The waveform moves forward, and the water particles also advance.
  (D) A floating object does not move at all as a wave passes through the water.

2. A barrier built at a right angle to the beach to trap sand that is moving parallel to the shore is known as a
  (A) seawall.   (B) groin.
  (C) headland.   (D) sea stack.

3. In the open sea, the movement of water particles in a wave becomes negligible at a depth equal to
  (A) one-fourth the wavelength.
  (B) one-third the wavelength.
  (C) one-half the wavelength.
  (D) three-fourths the wavelength.

4. Which term refers to the time interval between the passage of successive wave crests?
  (A) wave height
  (B) wavelength
  (C) wave period
  (D) wave speed

5. What happens as a wave approaches the shore?
  (A) wavelength decreases and wave height increases
  (B) wavelength increases and wave height increases
  (C) wave speed decreases and wave height decreases
  (D) wave period decreases and wave height decreases

Answer the following questions in complete sentences.

Use the figure below to answer Question 6.

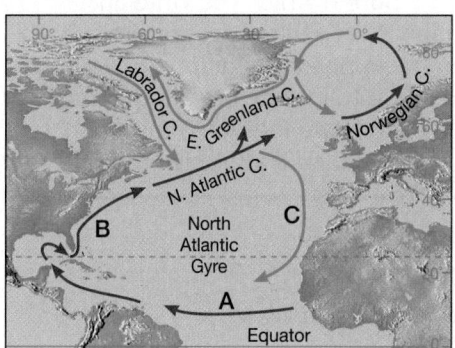

6. Identify the currents in the North Atlantic Gyre represented by A, B, and C. Specify whether each current is a warm water current or a cold water current. How does the North Atlantic Current affect weather in northwestern Europe?

7. What is the primary driving force of surface currents in the ocean? How do the distribution of continents on Earth and the Coriolis effect influence these currents?

17 The Atmosphere: Structure and Temperature

21st Century Learning
Global Awareness

How does latitude affect climate?

Several factors determine the climate where you live. Temperatures are affected by latitude, water bodies, altitude, geography, and prevailing winds. Look for a graph of the mean monthly temperatures for your town. Then find a graph for a town on another continent that is at the same latitude as your town. Prepare a report in which you write an explanation for any differences or similarities between the temperature graphs. In your report, be sure to include both of the graphs and maps of the two locations. Post your report to a class blog if available or wiki.

Exploration Lab

Heating Land and Water

How Earth Works

Earth's Atmosphere

GEODe

The Atmosphere
↳ Heating the Atmosphere

A bald eagle, found only in North America, soars over Mount Rainier National Park in Washington State.

Chapter Preview

Inquiry Activity

Modeling the Angle of the Sun

Procedure

1. Place a sheet of dark construction paper on a desk or table top. Hold a flashlight approximately 10 cm above the paper. The flashlight should be held at a 90° angle and pointed toward the paper.

2. Darken the room and turn on the flashlight. Have a partner trace the perimeter of the light on the paper.

3. Repeat step 2, but this time, tilt the flashlight so that it is at 45° to the paper. The end of the light should be 10 cm above the paper. Have a partner trace the perimeter of the light on the paper.

Think About It

1. **Observing** Describe the sizes and shapes of the light on the paper for steps 2 and 3.

2. **Modeling** Suppose the flashlight represents the sun, and the paper represents Earth's surface. Which angle gives more energy, per unit area, on the surface of Earth?

17.1 Atmosphere Characteristics

Reading Focus

Key Concepts

- How does weather differ from climate?

- Why do seasonal changes occur?

Vocabulary

- ◆ ozone
- ◆ troposphere
- ◆ stratosphere
- ◆ mesosphere
- ◆ thermosphere
- ◆ summer solstice
- ◆ winter solstice
- ◆ autumnal equinox
- ◆ spring equinox

Reading Strategy

Comparing and Contrasting Copy the Venn diagram below. As you read, complete the diagram by comparing and contrasting summer and winter solstices.

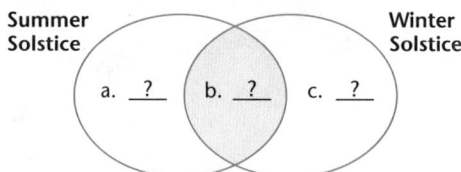

Summer Solstice   Winter Solstice

a. _?_   b. _?_   c. _?_

Earth's atmosphere is unique. No other planet in our solar system has an atmosphere with the exact mixture of gases or the moisture conditions and heat needed to sustain life as we know it. The gases that make up Earth's atmosphere and the controls to which they are subject are vital to our existence. In this chapter, you will begin to examine the ocean of air in which we live.

The state of the atmosphere at a given time and place is known as weather. The combination of Earth's motions and energy from the sun produce a variety of weather. As shown in Figure 1, weather strongly influences our everyday activities. **Weather is constantly changing, and it refers to the state of the atmosphere at any given time and place. Climate, however, is based on observations of weather that have been collected over many years. Climate helps describe a place or region.** Climate often is defined simply as "average weather," but this is not a complete description. For example, farmers need to know not only the average rainfall during a growing season, but they also need to know the frequency of extremely wet and extremely dry years. The most important measurable properties of weather and climate are air temperature, humidity, type and amount of precipitation, air pressure, and the speed and direction of the wind.

Figure 1 Buffalo, New York, was under a state of emergency in late December 2001 after receiving almost 2 meters of snow.

Reading Checkpoint   *How does weather differ from climate?*

Composition of the Atmosphere

The composition of the atmosphere has changed dramatically over Earth's nearly 4.6 billion year history. The atmosphere is thought to have started as gases that were emitted during volcanic eruptions. Evidence indicates that oxygen did not start to accumulate in the atmosphere until about 2.5 billion years ago. The atmosphere continues to exchange material with the oceans and life on Earth's surface.

Major Components Sometimes the term *air* is used as if it were a specific gas, which it is not. Air is a mixture of different gases and particles, each with its own physical properties. The composition of air varies from time to time and from place to place. However, if the water vapor, dust, and other variable components were removed from the atmosphere, its makeup would be very stable worldwide up to an altitude of about 80 kilometers.

Look at Figure 2. Two gases—nitrogen and oxygen—make up 99 percent of the volume of clean, dry air. Although these gases are the most common components of air, they don't affect the weather much. The remaining 1 percent of dry air is mostly the inert gas argon (0.93 percent) plus tiny quantities of a number of other gases. Carbon dioxide is present in only small amounts (approximately 0.039 percent), but it is an important component of air. Carbon dioxide is an active absorber of energy given off by Earth. Therefore, it plays a significant role in heating the atmosphere.

Variable Components Important materials that vary in the air from time to time and place to place include water vapor, dust particles, and ozone. These components also can have significant effects on weather and climate.

The amount of water vapor varies from almost none to about 4 percent by volume. Why is such a small quantity so significant? **Water vapor is the source of all clouds and precipitation. Like carbon dioxide, water vapor absorbs heat given off by Earth. It also absorbs some solar energy.**

Movements of the atmosphere allow a large quantity of solid and liquid particles to be suspended within it. Although visible dust sometimes clouds the sky, these relatively large particles are too heavy to stay in the air for very long. Still, many particles are microscopic and remain suspended for longer periods of time. These particles include sea salts from breaking waves, fine soil blown into the air, smoke and soot from fires, pollen and microorganisms lifted by the wind, and ash and dust from volcanic eruptions.

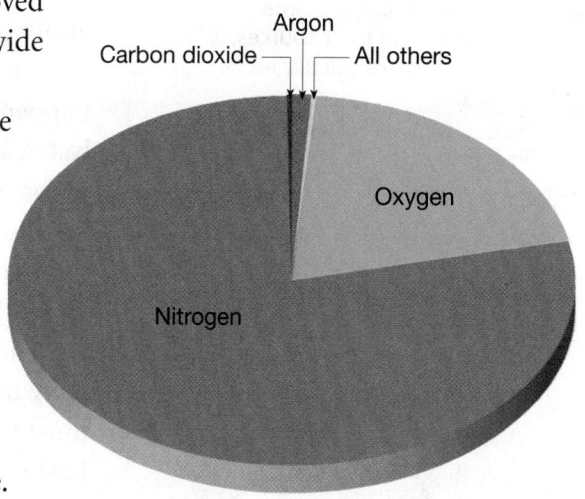

Figure 2 Volume of Clean, Dry Air Nitrogen and oxygen dominate the volume of gases composing dry air.

Primary Pollutants

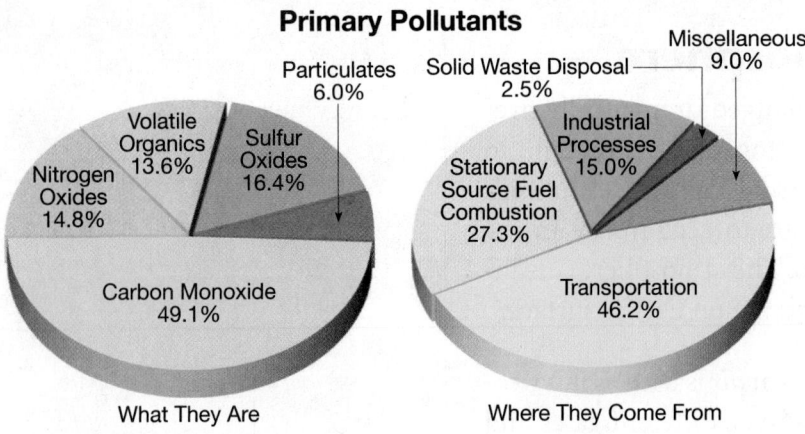

What They Are

Where They Come From

Figure 3 Primary Pollutants in the Atmosphere These circle graphs show major primary pollutants and their sources. Percentages are calculated by weight.

Source: U.S. Environmental Protection Agency.

For: Links on Atmosphere

Visit: PHSchool.com

Web Code: cuc-1171

Another important variable component of the atmosphere is ozone. **Ozone** is a form of oxygen that combines three oxygen atoms into each molecule (O_3). Ozone is not the same as the oxygen we breathe, which has two atoms per molecule (O_2). There is very little ozone in the atmosphere, and it is not distributed evenly. It is concentrated in a layer located between 10 and 50 kilometers above Earth's surface.

In this altitude range, oxygen molecules (O_2) are split into single atoms of oxygen (O) when they absorb ultraviolet (UV) radiation emitted by the sun. Ozone is then produced when a single atom of oxygen (O) and a molecule of oxygen (O_2) collide. This collision must happen in the presence of a third, neutral molecule that acts as a catalyst. A catalyst allows a reaction to take place without being consumed in the process. Ozone is concentrated 10 to 50 kilometers above Earth because the UV radiation from the sun is sufficient to produce single atoms of oxygen. In addition, there are enough gas molecules to bring about the required collisions.

The ozone layer is crucial to life on Earth. Ozone absorbs potentially harmful UV radiation from the Sun. **If ozone did not filter most UV radiation and all of the sun's UV rays reached the surface of Earth, our planet would be uninhabitable for many living organisms.**

Human Influence Air pollutants are airborne particles and gases that occur in concentrations large enough to endanger the health of organisms. Primary pollutants, shown in Figure 3, are emitted directly from identifiable sources. Emissions from transportation vehicles account for nearly half the primary pollutants by weight.

Secondary pollutants are not emitted directly into air. They form in the atmosphere when reactions take place among primary pollutants and other substances. For example, after the primary pollutant sulfur dioxide enters the atmosphere, it combines with oxygen to produce sulfur trioxide. Then the sulfur trioxide combines with water to create sulfuric acid, an irritating and corrosive substance.

Reactions triggered by strong sunlight are called photochemical reactions. For instance, when nitrogen oxides absorb solar radiation, a chain of complex reactions begins. If certain volatile organic compounds are present, secondary products form that are reactive, irritating, and toxic. This noxious mixture of gases and particles is called photochemical smog.

 *What are secondary pollutants?*

Height and Structure of the Atmosphere

Where does the atmosphere end and outer space begin? There is no sharp boundary. ⊜ **The atmosphere thins as you travel away from Earth until there are too few gas molecules to detect.**

Pressure Changes To understand the vertical extent of the atmosphere, examine Figure 4, which shows changes in atmospheric pressure with height. Atmospheric pressure is caused by the weight of the air above. At sea level, the average pressure is slightly more than 1000 millibars, or slightly more than 1 kilogram per square centimeter. One half of the atmosphere by mass lies below an altitude of 5.6 kilometers. Above 100 kilometers, only 0.00003 percent of all the gases making up the atmosphere exist.

Temperature Changes The pictures of snow-capped mountains rising above snow-free valleys shown in Figure 5 might remind you that Earth's atmosphere becomes colder as you climb higher. But not all layers of the atmosphere show this temperature pattern.

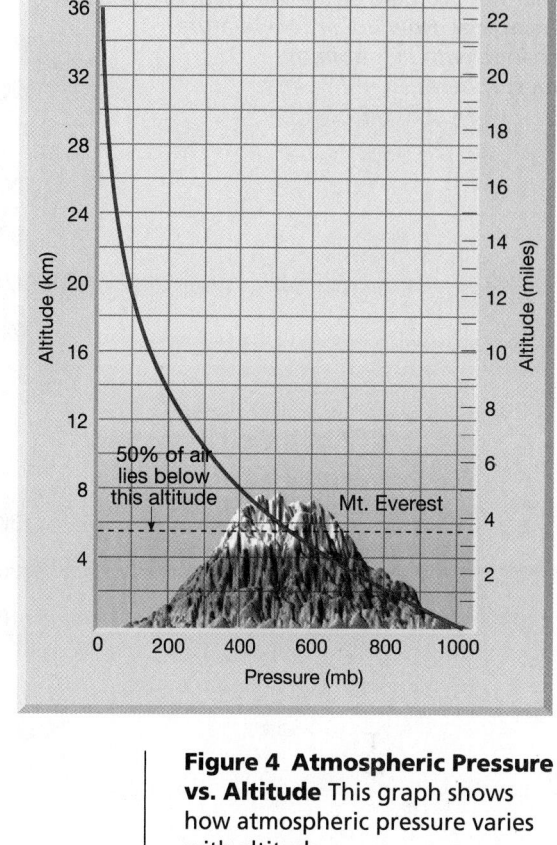

Figure 4 Atmospheric Pressure vs. Altitude This graph shows how atmospheric pressure varies with altitude.
Comparing *How do changes in air pressure at low altitudes compare with air pressure changes at high altitudes?*

Figure 5 In Jasper National Park in Alberta, Canada, snowy mountaintops contrast with warmer, snow-free lowlands below.

Figure 6 This diagram illustrates the thermal structure of the atmosphere. **Interpret** *How do air temperatures change with height in the mesosphere?*

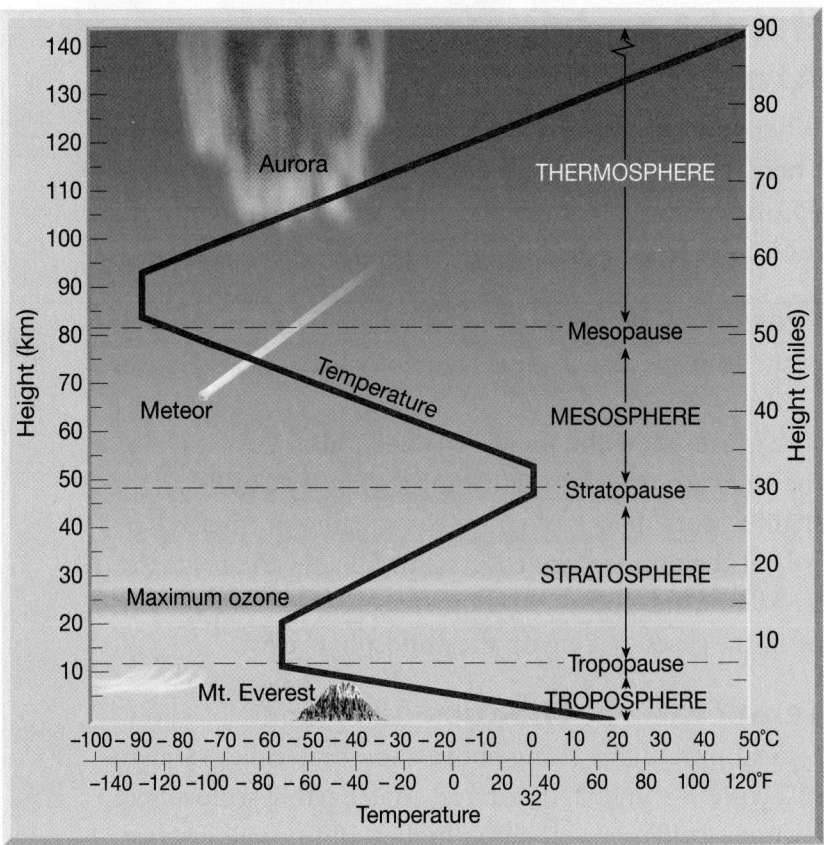

For: Links on the layers of the atmosphere
Visit: www.SciLinks.org
Web Code: cjn-6171

The atmosphere can be divided vertically into four layers based on temperature. Figure 6 illustrates these layers. The bottom layer, where temperature decreases with an increase in altitude, is the **troposphere.** It is in this layer that essentially all important weather phenomena occur. The thickness of the troposphere is not the same everywhere. It varies with latitude and the season. On average, the temperature drop continues to a height of about 12 kilometers, where the outer boundary of the troposphere, called the tropopause, is located.

Beyond the tropopause is the **stratosphere.** In the stratosphere, the temperature remains constant to a height of about 20 kilometers. It then begins a gradual increase in temperature that continues until the stratopause, at a height of nearly 50 kilometers above Earth's surface. Temperatures increase in the stratosphere because the atmosphere's ozone is concentrated here. Recall that ozone absorbs ultraviolet radiation from the sun. As a result, the stratosphere is heated.

In the third layer, the **mesosphere,** temperatures again decrease with height until the mesopause. The mesopause is more than 80 kilometers above the surface and the temperatures approach −90°C. The fourth layer extends outward from the mesopause and has no well-defined upper limit. It is the **thermosphere,** a layer that contains only a tiny fraction of the atmosphere's mass. Temperatures increase in the thermosphere because oxygen and nitrogen absorb short-wave, high-energy solar radiation.

Earth-Sun Relationships

Nearly all of the energy that drives Earth's variable weather and climate comes from the sun. Earth absorbs only a tiny percentage of the energy given off by the sun—less than one two-billionth. This may seem insignificant, but the amount is several hundred thousand times the electrical-generating capacity of the United States.

Solar energy is not distributed evenly over Earth's surface. The amount of energy received varies with latitude, time of day, and season. These variations in solar heating are caused by the motions of Earth relative to the sun and by variations in Earth's land and ocean surface. It is the unequal heating of Earth that creates winds and drives the ocean's currents. These movements transport heat from the tropics toward the poles, thus driving the phenomena we call weather.

Earth's Motions Earth has two principal motions—rotation and revolution. Rotation is the spinning of Earth about its axis. The axis is an imaginary line running through the north and south poles. Our planet rotates once every 24 hours, producing the daily cycle of daylight and darkness. Revolution is the movement of Earth in its orbit around the sun. Earth travels at nearly 113,000 kilometers per hour in an elliptical orbit about the sun.

Earth's Orientation We know that it is colder in the winter than in the summer. But why? Length of day and a gradual change in the angle of the noon sun above the horizon affect the amount of energy Earth receives. ● **Seasonal changes occur because Earth's position relative to the sun continually changes as it travels along its orbit.** Earth's axis is not perpendicular to the plane of its orbit around the sun. Instead it is tilted 23.5 degrees from the perpendicular, as shown in Figure 7. Because the axis remains pointed toward the North Star as Earth moves around the sun, the position of Earth's axis relative to the sun's rays is constantly changing. If the axis were not tilted, we would not have seasonal changes.

Sun's Apparent Path The changing orientation of Earth relative to the sun causes the sun's apparent path to vary with latitude and season. The angle of the noon sun can vary by up to 47 degrees (−23.5 degrees to +23.5 degrees) for many locations during the year. A mid-latitude city like New York, located about 40 degrees north latitude, has a maximum noon sun angle of 73.5 degrees when the sun's vertical rays reach their farthest northward location in June. Six months later, New York has a minimum noon sun angle of 26.5 degrees.

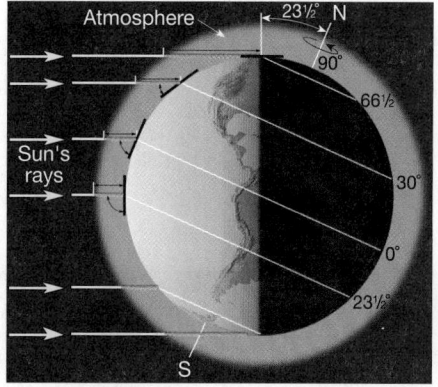

Figure 7 Tilt of Earth's Axis Earth's axis always points toward the North Star as it revolves around the sun.

In which direction does Earth's axis point?

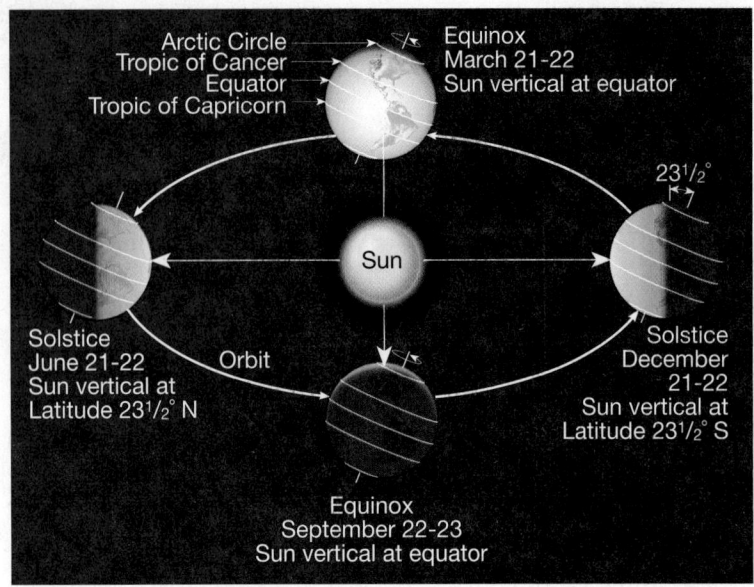

Figure 8 Solstices and equinoxes are important events in Earth's yearly seasonal cycle.

Labels in figure:
- Arctic Circle
- Tropic of Cancer
- Equator
- Tropic of Capricorn
- Equinox March 21-22 Sun vertical at equator
- $23\frac{1}{2}°$
- Sun
- Solstice June 21-22 Sun vertical at Latitude $23\frac{1}{2}°$ N
- Orbit
- Solstice December 21-22 Sun vertical at Latitude $23\frac{1}{2}°$ S
- Equinox September 22-23 Sun vertical at equator

Go **O**nline
active art

For: Seasons Activity
Visit: PHSchool.com
Web Code: czp-6171

The Seasons On June 21 or 22 each year the axis is such that the Northern Hemisphere is "leaning" 23.5 degrees toward the sun. This date, shown on the left side of Figure 8, is known as the **summer solstice,** or the first "official" day of summer. Six months later, in December, when Earth has moved to the opposite side of its orbit, the Northern Hemisphere leans 23.5 degrees away from the sun. December 21 or 22 is the **winter solstice,** the first day of winter. On days between these extremes, Earth's axis is leaning at amounts less than 23.5 degrees to the rays of the sun.

The equinoxes occur midway between the solstices. September 22 or 23 is the date of the **autumnal equinox** and the start of autumn in the Northern Hemisphere. March 21 or 22 is the date of the **spring equinox** and the start of spring for the Northern Hemisphere. On these dates, the vertical rays of the sun strike the equator (0 degrees latitude) because Earth is in a position in its orbit such that the axis is tilted neither toward nor away from the sun.

Length of Daylight The length of daylight compared to darkness also is determined by Earth's position in orbit. All latitudes receive 12 hours of daylight during the vernal and autumnal equinoxes (equal night). The length of daylight on the summer solstice in the Northern Hemisphere is greater than the length of darkness. The farther you are north of the equator on the summer solstice, the longer the period of daylight. When you reach the Arctic Circle, at 66.5 degrees north latitude, the length of daylight is 24 hours.

Section 17.1 Assessment

Reviewing Concepts

1. Compare and contrast weather and climate.
2. Why do seasonal changes occur?
3. How much of Earth's atmosphere is located below about 5.6 kilometers?
4. How do ozone molecules form in the stratosphere?
5. In which layers of the atmosphere does temperature increase with increasing height?

Critical Thinking

6. **Applying Concepts** Explain what would happen to air temperatures in the troposphere if carbon dioxide were removed from air.

Connecting Concepts

Connecting Concepts Using Figure 8, explain why solstices and equinoxes are opposite for the Northern and Southern hemispheres.

17.2 Heating the Atmosphere

Reading Focus

Key Concepts

- How are heat and temperature related?
- What are the three major mechanisms of heat transfer?
- How is the atmosphere affected by each of the heat transfer mechanisms?

Vocabulary

- ◆ heat
- ◆ temperature
- ◆ conduction
- ◆ convection
- ◆ radiation
- ◆ reflection
- ◆ scattering
- ◆ greenhouse effect

Reading Strategy

Using Prior Knowledge Before you read, copy the table below and write your definition for each vocabulary term. After you read, write the scientific definition of each term and compare it with your original definition.

Term	Your Definition	Scientific Definition
Heat	a. ___?___	b. ___?___
Temperature	c. ___?___	d. ___?___

The concepts of heat and temperature often are confused. The phrase "in the heat of the day" is one common expression in which the word "heat" is misused to describe the concept of temperature. **Heat is the energy transferred from one object to another because of a difference in their temperatures.** All matter is composed of atoms or molecules that possess kinetic energy, or the energy of motion. **Temperature** is a measure of the average kinetic energy of the individual atoms or molecules in a substance. When energy is transferred to the gas atoms and molecules in air, those particles move faster and air temperature rises. When air transfers energy to a cooler object, its particles move more slowly, and air temperature drops.

Energy Transfer as Heat

Three mechanisms of energy transfer as heat are conduction, convection, and radiation. All three processes, illustrated in Figure 9, happen simultaneously in the atmosphere. These mechanisms operate to transfer energy between Earth's surface (both land and water) and the atmosphere.

Conduction Anyone who has touched a metal spoon that was left in a hot pan has experienced the result of heat conducted through the spoon. **Conduction** is the transfer of heat through matter by molecular activity. The energy of molecules is transferred by collisions from one molecule to another. Heat flows from the higher temperature matter to the lower temperature matter.

Figure 9 Energy Transfer as Heat A pot of water on the campfire illustrates the three mechanisms of heat transfer.

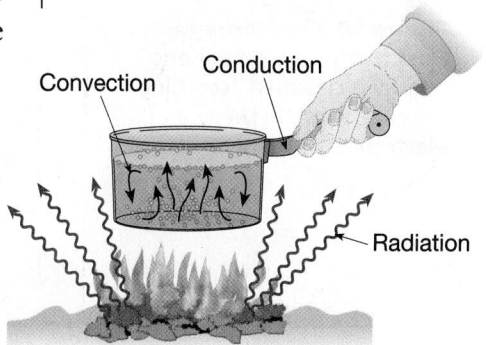

The ability of substances to conduct heat varies greatly. Metals are good conductors, as those of us who have touched hot metal have quickly learned. Air, however, is a very poor conductor of heat. Because air is a poor conductor, conduction is important only between Earth's surface and the air directly in contact with the surface. For the atmosphere as a whole, conduction is the least important mechanism of heat transfer.

Convection Much of the heat transfer that occurs in the atmosphere is carried on by convection. **Convection** is the transfer of heat by mass movement or circulation within a substance. It takes place in fluids, like the ocean and air, where the atoms and molecules are free to move about. Convection also takes place in solids, such as Earth's mantle, that behave like fluids over long periods of time.

The pan of water in Figure 9 shows circulation by convection. Radiation from the fire warms the bottom of the pan, which conducts heat to the water near the bottom of the container. As the water is heated, it expands and becomes less dense than the water above. The warmer water rises because of its buoyancy. At the same time, cooler, denser water near the top of the pan sinks to the bottom, where it becomes heated. As long as the water is heated unequally, it will continue to circulate. In much the same way, most of the heat acquired by radiation and conduction in the lowest layer of the atmosphere is transferred by convective flow.

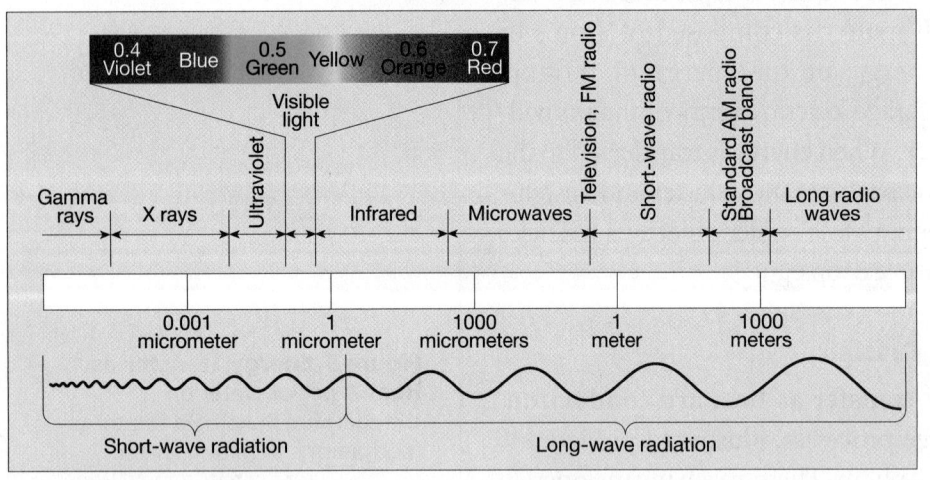

Figure 10 Electromagnetic Spectrum Electromagnetic energy is classified according to wavelength in the electromagnetic spectrum.

Electromagnetic Waves

The sun is the ultimate source of energy that causes our weather. Visible light, radiant heat energy, and ultraviolet rays from the sun are some of the forms of energy in the electromagnetic (EM) spectrum, shown in Figure 10. All of the radiation in this spectrum is carried by electromagnetic waves. Electromagnetic waves consist of changing electric and magnetic fields. The source of all electromagnetic waves is vibrating charges. Although different types of EM waves have different energies, they all travel through the vacuum of space at 300,000 kilometers per second. They travel only slightly slower through our atmosphere.

What is convection?

Imagine what happens when you toss a pebble into a pond. Ripples are made and move away from the location where the pebble hit the water's surface. Much like these ripples, electromagnetic waves move out from their source and come in various sizes. Electromagnetic waves are classified by their wavelength, or the distance from one crest to the next. Radio waves have the longest wavelengths, ranging to tens of kilometers. Gamma waves are the shortest, and are less than a billionth of a centimeter long.

Visible light is the only portion of the spectrum you can see. White light is really a mixture of colors. Each color corresponds to a specific wavelength, as shown in Figure 11.

Figure 11 Visible light consists of an array of colors commonly called the colors of the rainbow.

By using a prism, white light can be divided into the colors of the rainbow, from violet with the shortest wavelength—0.4 micrometer (1 micrometer is 0.0001 centimeter)—to red with the longest wavelength—0.7 micrometer.

Radiation The third mechanism of heat transfer is radiation. As shown in Figure 9, **radiation** travels out in all directions from its source. ⮕**Unlike conduction and convection, which need material to travel through, radiant energy can travel through the vacuum of space.** Solar energy reaches Earth by radiation.

To understand how the atmosphere is heated, it is useful to think about four laws governing radiation.

1. ⮕**All objects, at any temperature, emit radiant energy.** Not only hot objects like the sun but also Earth—including its polar ice caps—continually emit energy.

2. ⮕**Hotter objects radiate more total energy per unit area than colder objects do.**

3. ⮕**The hottest radiating bodies produce the shortest wavelengths of maximum radiation.** For example, the sun, with a surface temperature of nearly 6000°C, radiates maximum energy at 0.5 micrometers, which is in the visible range. The maximum radiation for Earth occurs at a wavelength of 10 micrometers, well within the infrared range.

4. ⮕**Objects that are good absorbers of radiation are good emitters as well.** Gases are selective absorbers and radiators. The atmosphere does not absorb certain wavelengths of radiation, but it is a good absorber of other wavelengths.

For: Links on conduction and convection
Visit: www.SciLinks.org
Web Code: cjn-6172

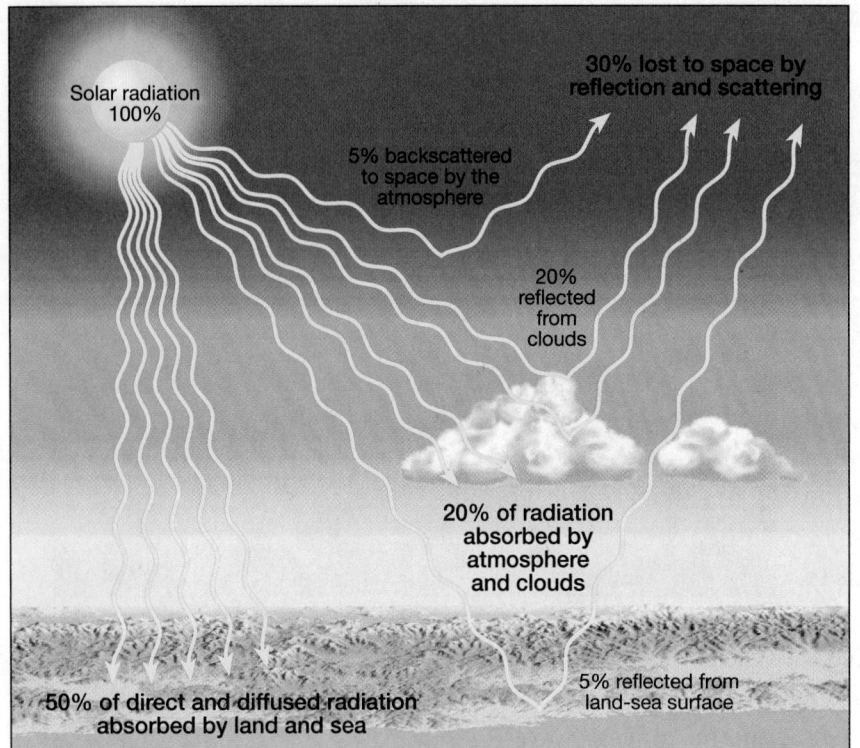

In the diagram:

Solar radiation 100%

30% lost to space by reflection and scattering

5% backscattered to space by the atmosphere

20% reflected from clouds

20% of radiation absorbed by atmosphere and clouds

50% of direct and diffused radiation absorbed by land and sea

5% reflected from land-sea surface

What Happens to Solar Radiation?

When radiation strikes an object, there usually are three different results.

1. **Some energy is absorbed by the object.** When radiant energy is absorbed, it is converted to heat and causes a temperature increase.

2. **Substances such as water and air are transparent to certain wavelengths of radiation.** These substances transmit the radiant energy. Radiation that is transmitted does not contribute energy to the object.

3. **Some radiation may bounce off the object without being absorbed or transmitted.** Figure 12 shows what happens to incoming solar radiation, averaged for the entire globe.

Figure 12 Solar Radiation This diagram shows what happens, on average, to incoming solar radiation by percentage.

Figure 13 Reflection vs. Scattering
A Reflected light bounces back with the same intensity.
B Scattering produces more light rays with a weaker intensity.

Reflection and Scattering Reflection occurs when an electromagnetic wave bounces off an object. The reflected radiation has the same intensity as the incident radiation. In contrast, **scattering** produces a larger number of weaker rays that travel in different directions. See Figure 13. Scattering disperses waves both forward and backward. However, more energy is dispersed in the forward direction. About 30 percent of the solar energy reaching the outer atmosphere is reflected back to space. This 30 percent also includes the amount of energy sent skyward by scattering. This energy is lost and does not heat Earth's atmosphere.

Small dust particles and gas molecules in the atmosphere scatter some incoming radiation in all directions. This explains how light reaches into the area beneath a shade tree, and how a room is lit in the absence of direct sunlight. Scattering also accounts for the brightness and even the blue color of the daytime sky. About half of the solar radiation that is absorbed at Earth's surface arrives as scattered radiation.

Absorption About 50 percent of the solar energy that strikes the top of the atmosphere reaches Earth's surface and is absorbed, as shown in Figure 12. Most of this energy is then reradiated skyward.

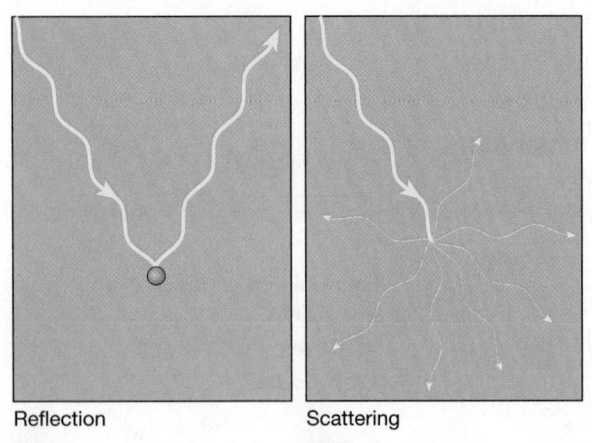

Reflection

Scattering

A   **B**

The atmosphere efficiently absorbs the longer wavelengths emitted by Earth. Water vapor and carbon dioxide are the major absorbing gases. When a gas molecule absorbs these waves, this energy is transformed into molecular motion that can be detected as a rise in temperature. Gases in the atmosphere eventually radiate some of this energy away. Some energy travels skyward, where it may be reabsorbed by other gas molecules. The rest travels earthward and is again absorbed. In this way, Earth's surface is continually supplied with heat from the atmosphere as well as from the sun.

Without these absorbing gases in our atmosphere, Earth would not be a suitable habitat for most types of living things on Earth today. This phenomenon has been termed the **greenhouse effect** because it was once thought that greenhouses were heated in a similar manner. (A more important factor in keeping a greenhouse warm is that the greenhouse itself prevents the mixing of air inside with cooler air outside.)

There is a balance of energy transfer into and out of Earth's atmosphere. Over time, incoming solar radiation is absorbed, reflected, or reradiated. As a result, the atmosphere's average temperature tends to remain constant from year to year. But the atmosphere's average temperature can and does change. It changes in response to factors that disturb its energy balance.

Photosynthesis Some incoming solar radiation is not absorbed and reradiated. Instead, it is absorbed by the chlorophyll in green plants. Plants use the energy from this radiation in photosynthesis. Thus solar energy is the main energy source for virtually all life on Earth.

Q *Isn't the greenhouse effect responsible for global warming?*

A It is important to note that the greenhouse effect and global warming *are not* the same thing. Without the greenhouse effect, Earth would be mostly uninhabitable. We do have mounting evidence that human activity (particularly the release of carbon dioxide into the atmosphere) is responsible for a rise in global temperatures. Thus, human activities seem to be enhancing an otherwise natural process (the greenhouse effect) to increase Earth's temperature. Nevertheless, to equate the greenhouse effect, which makes life possible, with undesirable changes to our atmosphere caused by human activity is incorrect.

Section 17.2 Assessment

Reviewing Concepts

1. How are heat and temperature related?
2. List and describe the three major mechanisms of heat transfer in the atmosphere.
3. How is the atmosphere affected by
   a. convection?
   b. conduction?
   c. radiation?
4. Describe what happens to solar radiation when it strikes an object.
5. Contrast reflection and scattering.

Critical Thinking

6. **Applying Concepts** Dark objects tend to absorb more radiation than light-colored objects. Explain whether dark objects or light objects on Earth's surface would be better radiators of heat.

Writing in Science

Descriptive Paragraph Write a paragraph that describes the four laws governing radiation discussed in this chapter. Make sure to use your own words. Use examples to reinforce concepts wherever possible.

17.3 Temperature Controls

Reading Focus

Key Concepts
- What is a temperature control?
- How do the heating of land and water differ?
- Why do some clouds reflect a portion of sunlight back to space?

Vocabulary
- ◆ albedo
- ◆ isotherm

Reading Strategy

Previewing Copy the table below. Before you read, use Figure 15 to describe the temperature variations for Vancouver and Winnipeg.

Temperature Variations	
Vancouver	a. _____?_____
Winnipeg	b. _____?_____

Figure 14 This modern instrument shelter contains an electrical thermometer called a thermistor.

Temperature is one of the basic elements of weather and climate. When someone asks what it is like outside, air temperature is often the first element we mention. At a weather station, the temperature is read on a regular basis from instruments mounted in an instrument shelter like the one in Figure 14. The shelter protects the instruments from direct sunlight and allows a free flow of air.

Why Temperatures Vary

A temperature control is any factor that causes temperature to vary from place to place and from time to time. Earlier in this chapter you examined the most important cause for temperature variations—differences in the receipt of solar radiation. Because variations in the angle of the sun's rays and length of daylight depend on latitude, they are responsible for warmer temperatures in the tropics and colder temperatures toward the poles. Seasonal temperature changes happen as the sun's vertical rays move toward and away from a particular latitude during the year. **Factors other than latitude that exert a strong influence on temperature include heating of land and water, altitude, geographic position, cloud cover, and ocean currents.**

Reading Checkpoint *List three factors that influence temperature.*

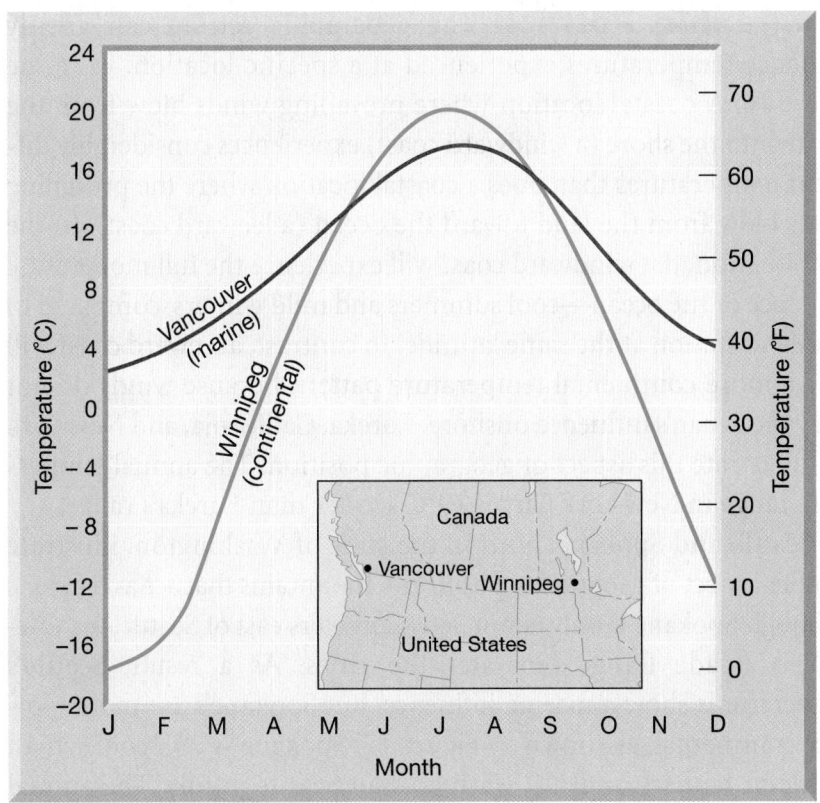

Figure 15 Mean Monthly Temperatures for Vancouver and Winnipeg Winnipeg illustrates the greater extremes associated with an interior location.
Calculating *How much lower is Winnipeg's January mean temperature than Vancouver's? Calculate the temperature to the nearest degree.*

Land and Water The heating of Earth's surface controls the temperature of the air above it. To understand variations in air temperature, we consider the characteristics of the surface. Different land surfaces absorb varying amounts of incoming solar energy. The largest contrast, however, is between land and water. **Land heats more rapidly and to higher temperatures than water. Land also cools more rapidly and to lower temperatures than water.** Temperature variations, therefore, are considerably greater over land than over water.

Monthly temperature data for two cities, shown in Figure 15, show the influence of a large body of water. Vancouver, British Columbia, is located along the windward Pacific coast. Winnipeg, Manitoba, is far from the influence of water. Both cities are at about the same latitude, so they experience similar lengths of daylight and angles of the sun's rays. Winnipeg, however, has much greater temperature extremes than Vancouver does. Vancouver's moderate year-round climate is due to its location by the Pacific Ocean.

Temperature variations in the Northern and Southern hemispheres are compared in Table 1. Water accounts for 61 percent of the Northern Hemisphere, and land accounts for the remaining 39 percent. In the Southern Hemisphere, 81 percent of the surface is water and only 19 percent of the surface is land. The Southern Hemisphere shows smaller annual temperature variations.

Table 1 Variation in Annual Mean Temperature Range (°C) with Latitude		
Latitude	Northern Hemisphere	Southern Hemisphere
0	0	0
15	3	4
30	13	7
45	23	6
60	30	11
75	32	26
90	40	31

Geographic Position The geographic setting can greatly influence temperatures experienced at a specific location. Examine Figure 16. A coastal location where prevailing winds blow from the ocean onto the shore (a windward coast) experiences considerably different temperatures than does a coastal location where the prevailing winds blow from the land toward the ocean (a leeward coast). In the first situation, the windward coast will experience the full moderating influence of the ocean—cool summers and mild winters, compared to an inland station at the same latitude. In contrast, a leeward coast will have a more continental temperature pattern because winds do not carry the ocean's influence onshore. Eureka, California, and New York City illustrate this aspect of geographic position. The annual temperature range in New York City is 19°C greater than Eureka's range.

Seattle and Spokane, both in the state of Washington, illustrate another aspect of geographic position—mountains that act as barriers. Although Spokane is only about 360 kilometers east of Seattle, the towering Cascade Range separates the cities. As a result, Seattle's temperatures show a marine influence, but Spokane's are more typically continental, as shown in Figure 17. Spokane is 7°C cooler than Seattle in January and 4°C warmer than Seattle in July. The annual range in Spokane is 11°C greater than in Seattle. The Cascade Range cuts Spokane off from the moderating influence of the Pacific Ocean.

Figure 16 Mean Monthly Temperatures for Eureka and New York City Eureka is strongly influenced by prevailing ocean winds, and New York City is not.

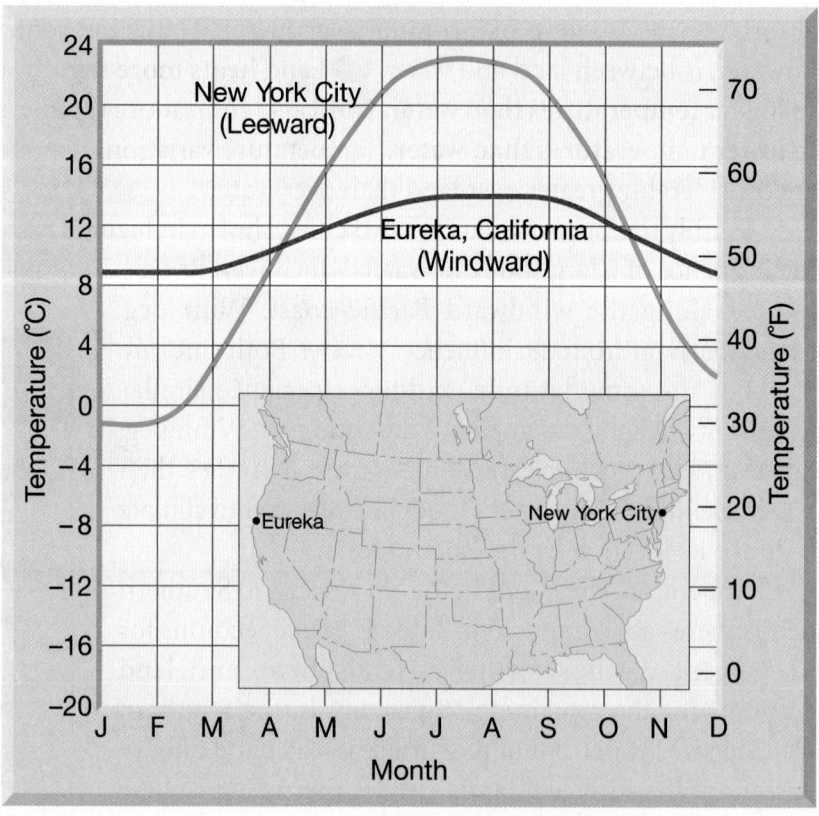

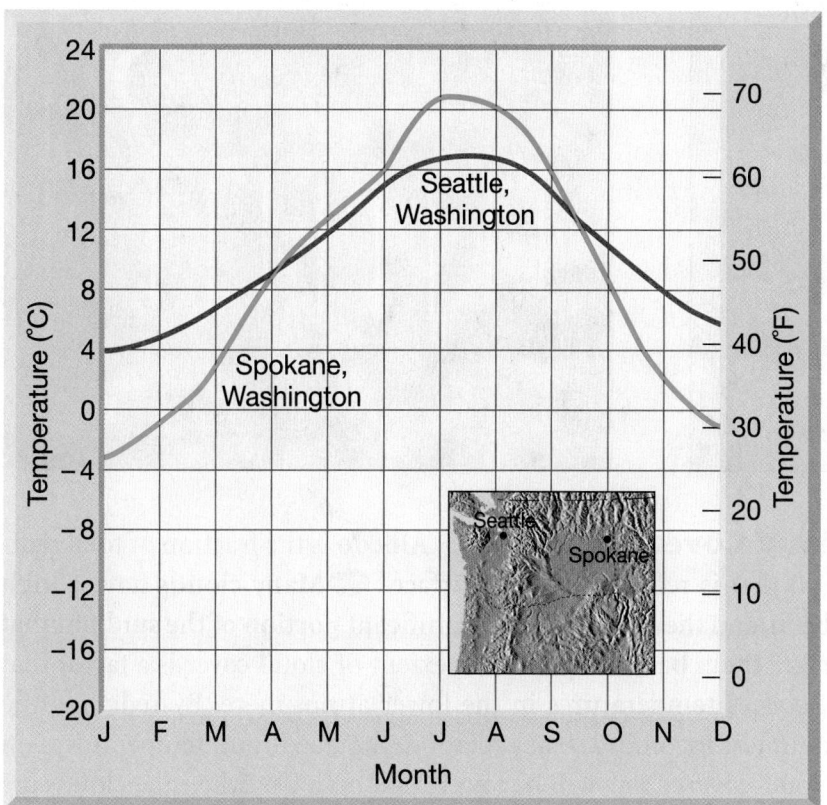

Figure 17 Mean Monthly Temperatures for Seattle and Spokane The Cascade Mountains cut off Spokane from the moderating influence of the Pacific Ocean. **Relating Cause and Effect** *How does this affect Spokane's annual temperature range?*

Figure 18 Mean Monthly Temperatures for Quito and Guayaquil Quito's altitude is much higher than Guayaquil's, causing Quito to experience cooler temperatures than Guayaquil.

Altitude Two cities in Ecuador, Quito and Guayaquil, demonstrate the influence of altitude on mean temperature. Both cities are near the equator and relatively close to one another, as shown in Figure 18. The annual mean temperature at Guayaquil is 25°C, compared to Quito's mean of 13°C. If you note these cities' elevations, you can understand the temperature difference. Guayaquil is only 12 meters above sea level, whereas Quito is high in the Andes Mountains at 2800 meters.

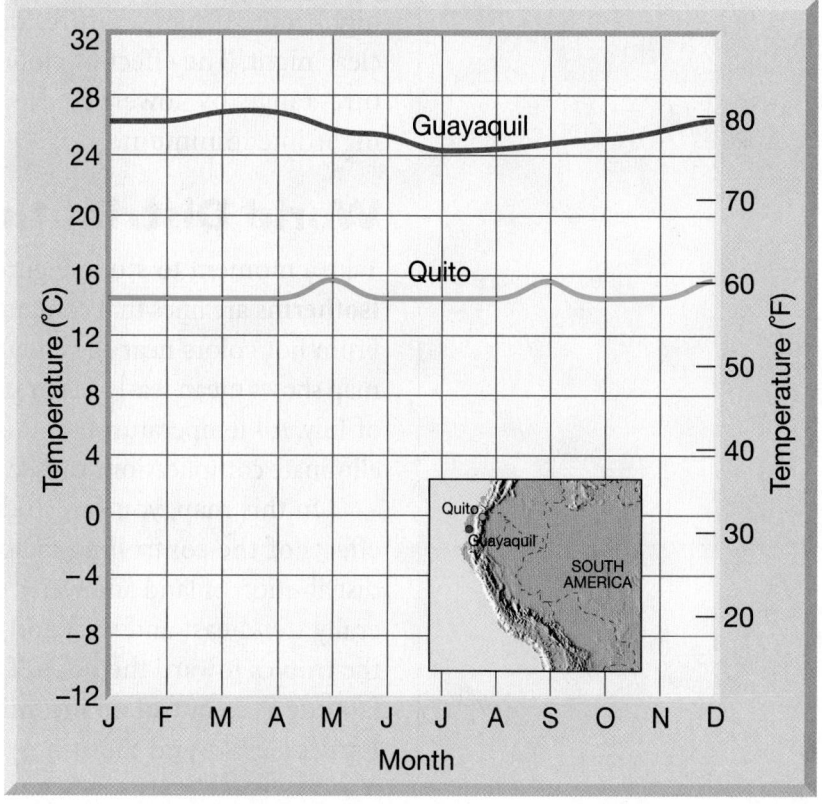

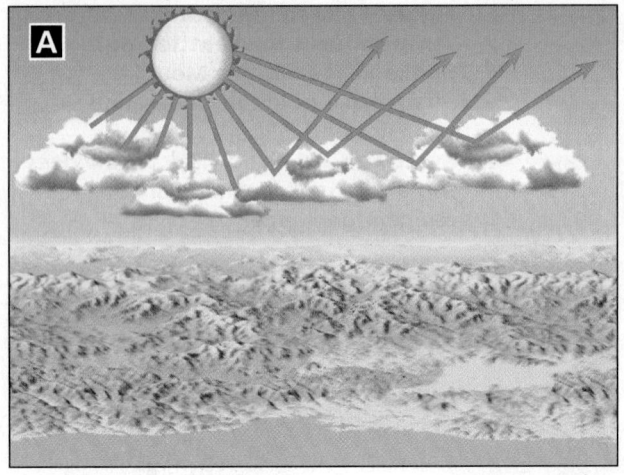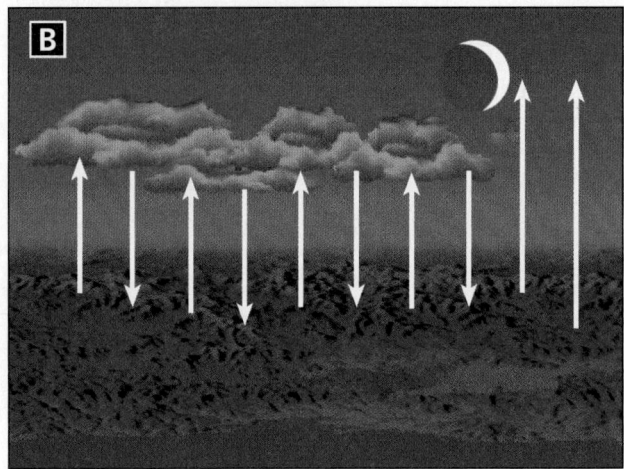

Figure 19 A During daylight hours, clouds reflect solar radiation back to space. **B** At night, clouds absorb radiation from the land and reradiate some of it back to Earth, increasing nighttime temperatures.

Cloud Cover and Albedo Albedo is the fraction of total radiation that is reflected by any surface. **Many clouds have a high albedo, and therefore reflect a significant portion of the sunlight that strikes them back to space.** The extent of cloud cover is a factor that influences temperatures in the lower atmosphere. By reducing the amount of incoming solar radiation, the maximum temperatures on a cloud-covered day will be lower than on a day when the clouds are absent and the sky is clear, as shown in Figure 19A.

At night, clouds have the opposite effect, as shown in Figure 19B. Clouds act as a blanket by absorbing outgoing radiation emitted by Earth and reradiating a portion of it back to the surface. Thus, cloudy nighttime air temperatures do not drop as low as they would on a clear night. The effect of cloud cover is to reduce the daily temperature range by lowering the daytime maximum and raising the nighttime minimum.

World Distribution of Temperature

Take a moment to study Figure 20, which is a world isothermal map. **Isotherms** are lines that connect points that have the same temperature. From hot colors near the equator to cool colors toward the poles, this map shows mean sea-level temperatures in the seasonally extreme month of July. All temperatures on this map have been reduced to sea level to eliminate complications caused by differences in altitude.

On this map, you can study global temperature patterns and the effects of the controlling factors of temperature, especially latitude, distribution of land and water, and ocean currents. The isotherms generally trend east and west and show a decrease in temperatures from the tropics toward the poles. This map emphasizes the importance of latitude as a control on incoming solar radiation, which in turn heats Earth's surface and the atmosphere above it.

World Isothermal Map

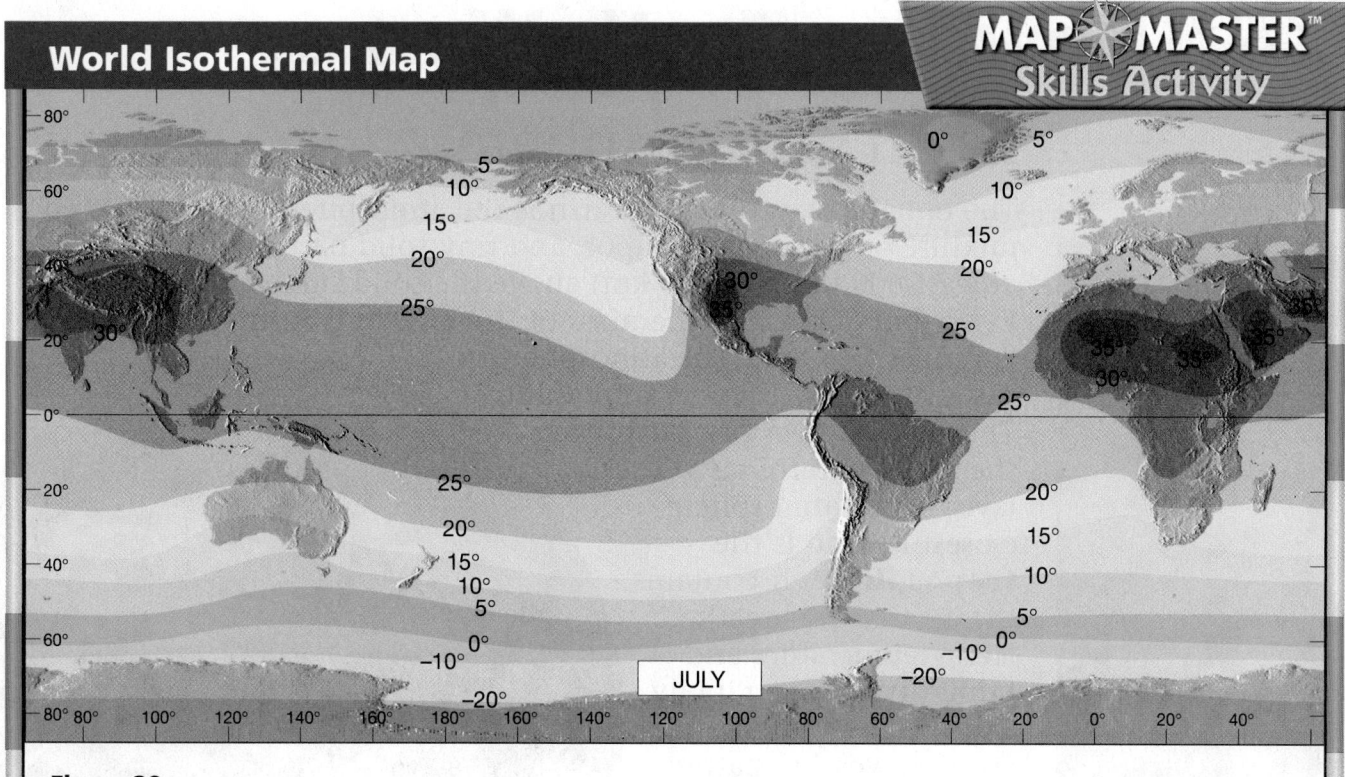

Figure 20

Regions The map shows the distribution of world mean sea-level temperatures averaged for the month of July.
Locating Estimate the latitude range for temperatures between 20 and 25 degrees Celsius in the Northern Hemisphere. Approximate to the nearest 5 degrees latitude for each extreme.
Predicting Do you expect the color of the temperature band to change near the equator for the month of January? Explain your prediction.

Section 17.3 Assessment

Reviewing Concepts

1. What is a temperature control?
2. How do the heating of land and water differ?
3. Why do many clouds reflect a significant amount of sunlight back to space?
4. Why do some coastal cities experience a moderation of temperature from water, while others do not?
5. List four specific controls of atmospheric temperature.

Critical Thinking

6. **Inferring** Look back at the graph in Figure 18. Why do the temperatures of these two cities stay within a limited range throughout the year?

Math ▸ Practice

7. Using the data in Table 1, determine the latitude that shows the greatest variation in average mean temperature between the Northern and Southern Hemispheres.

How the Earth Works

Earth's Atmosphere

The outermost part of the Earth is the atmosphere, a multilayered mixture of gases, water vapor, and tiny solid particles. It extends at least 600 miles (1,000 km) above the solid surface of the Earth, but about half the mass of these gases is in the lowest 3.5 miles (5.6 km). The atmosphere's gases support plant and animal life. They also protect the Earth from the sun's harmful rays. The layer of the atmosphere closest to land is the **troposphere.** It contains the air that we breathe. Here, temperature and humidity change rapidly, and the air is turbulent, creating weather patterns.

OXYGEN FROM PHOTOSYNTHESIS

Oxygen is a relative newcomer in the Earth's atmosphere. It has come from plants that, during **photosynthesis,** use carbon dioxide to make their food, while giving out oxygen. The earliest photosynthesizing plants, which probably looked like these algae, evolved about 3,500 million years ago.

THE ATMOSPHERE FROM SPACE

Viewed from space, Earth looks totally unlike other planets of our solar system. It is partly shrouded in white clouds, which swirl in patterns, making weather. **Clouds** are masses of tiny particles of water and dust floating in the atmosphere. A very low cloud is called fog.

OXYGEN CYCLE

A vast store of oxygen exists in oceans, rocks, and the atmosphere. Oxygen created by plant photosynthesis balances oxygen used by people and animals.

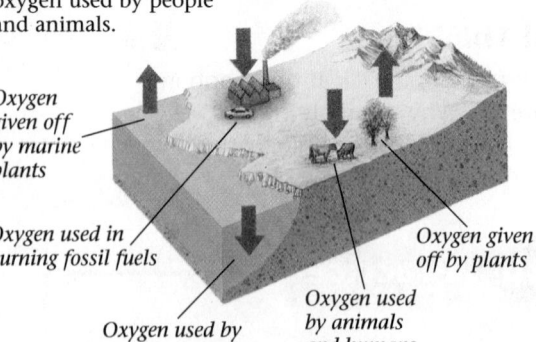

A large amount of oxygen is stored in the atmosphere

Oxygen given off by marine plants

Oxygen used in burning fossil fuels

Oxygen used by marine animals

Oxygen used by animals and humans

Oxygen given off by plants

FERTILE LAND

The atmosphere helps life to flourish on Earth. It offers protection from harmful radiations and provides nourishment for both plants and animals. Winds in the troposphere moderate daily and seasonal temperatures by distributing heat around the world.

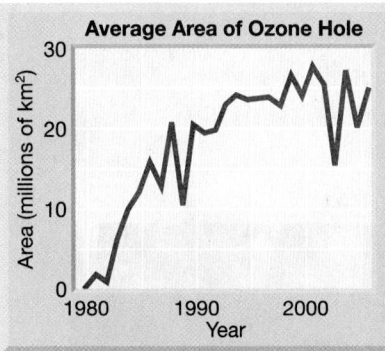

Average Area of Ozone Hole

SIZE OF OZONE HOLE
The ozone hole over Antarctica grew steadily during the 1980s. This correlated with the increased release of chlorofluorocarbon gases. By the mid-1990s, the winter hole was the size of North America. A ban on chlorofluorocarbons has halted the growth of the ozone hole.

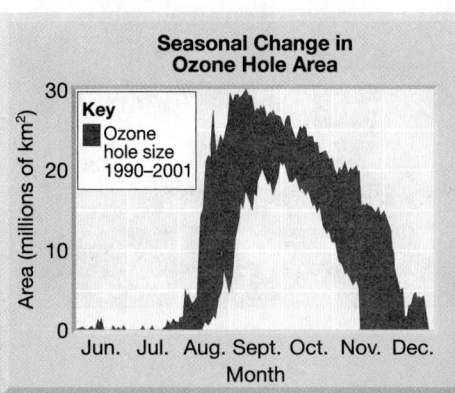

Seasonal Change in Ozone Hole Area

Key
■ Ozone hole size 1990–2001

YEARLY CHANGES IN OZONE HOLE
The ozone hole changes month-by-month as well as year-by-year. The formation of ozone requires sunlight, so no ozone is formed in the atmosphere above the South Pole during winter. As a result, the amount of ozone is lowest from September to November—spring in the Southern Hemisphere.

OZONE HOLE
The **ozone layer** is a region of ozone gas in the stratosphere that absorbs the sun's harmful ultraviolet rays. The ozone layer is vital for the survival of life on land. The thickness of the ozone layer varies naturally, affected by processes like volcanic eruptions. Beginning in the 1980s, human activities caused a hole in the ozone layer over Antarctica. The culprit was gases called chlorofluorocarbons, which are used in aerosols. These gases break down ozone in the stratosphere. As a result, the ozone layer got thinner each winter, and the hole got wider. At times, the ozone hole has grown large enough to threaten parts of South America.

VOLCANIC GASES
About 4 billion years ago, the Earth had no atmosphere and its surface was covered with erupting volcanoes. The Earth's atmosphere was formed mostly from gases spewed out by volcanoes.

ASSESSMENT

1. **Key Terms** Define **(a)** troposphere, **(b)** photosynthesis, **(c)** cloud, **(d)** ozone layer.

2. **Physical Processes** How was the earth's atmosphere formed?

3. **Natural Resources** How does carbon dioxide support life?

4. **Geographic Tools** How does the NASA satellite photograph display the growing problem of ozone holes?

5. **Critical Thinking Analyzing Processes** Study the diagram showing the oxygen cycle. **(a)** How would extensive deforestation affect the oxygen cycle? **(b)** Which part of the cycle can damage the ozone layer?

Heating Land and Water

In this lab you will model the difference in the heating of land and water when they are subjected to a source of radiation. You first will assemble simple tools. Then you will observe and record temperature data. Finally, you will explain the results of the experiment and how they relate to the moderating influence of water on air temperatures near Earth's surface.

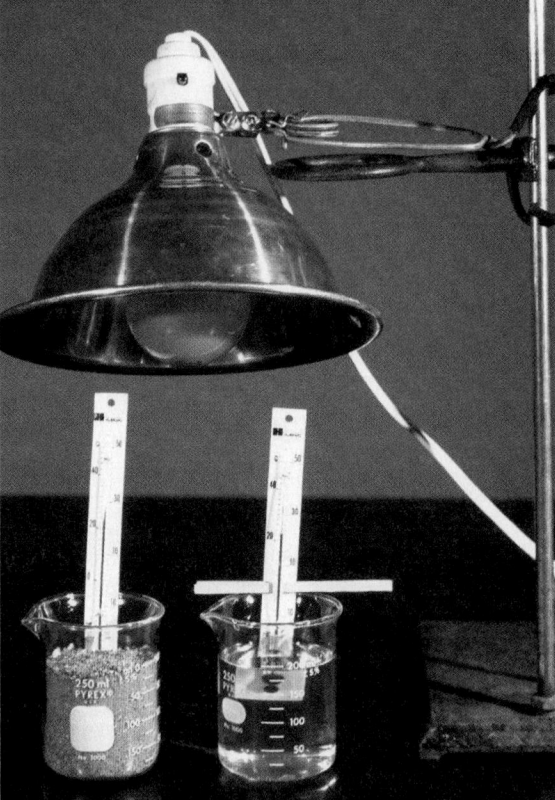

Problem How do the heating of land and water compare?

Materials
- 2 250-mL beakers
- dry sand
- tap water
- ring stand
- light source
- 2 flat wooden sticks
- 2 thermometers
- graph paper
- 3 colored pencils

Skills Modeling, Observing, Measuring, Analyzing Data

Procedure

Part A: Preparing for the Experiment

1. On a separate sheet of paper or on a computer spreadsheet, copy the data table shown.

2. Pour 200 mL of dry sand into one of the beakers. Pour 200 mL of water into the other beaker.

	Land and Water Heating Data Table										
	Starting Temperature	1 min	2 min	3 min	4 min	5 min	6 min	7 min	8 min	9 min	10 min
Water											
Dry sand											
Damp sand											

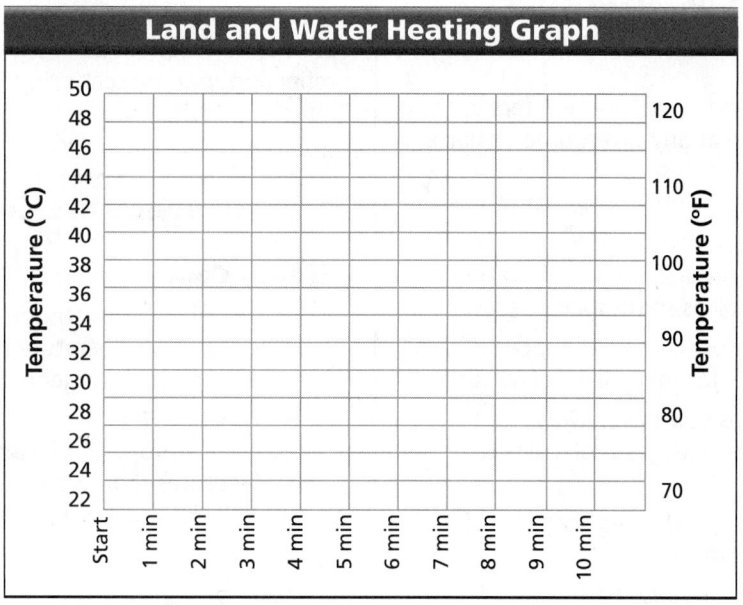

Land and Water Heating Graph

3. Hang a light source from a ring stand so that it is about 5 inches above the beaker of sand and the beaker of water. The light should be situated so that it is at the same height above both beakers.

4. Using the wooden sticks, suspend a thermometer in each beaker. The thermometer bulbs should be just barely below the surfaces of the sand and the water.

5. Record the starting temperatures for both the dry sand and the water in the data table.

Part B: Heating the Beakers

CAUTION *Do not touch the light source or the beakers without using thermal mitts.*

6. Turn on the light. Observe and record the temperatures in the data table at one-minute intervals for 10 minutes.

7. Turn off the light for several minutes. Dampen the sand with water and record the starting temperature for damp sand. Repeat step 6 for the damp sand.

Analyze and Conclude

1. Using Tables and Graphs Use a computer to graph the data you collected on a graph like the one above. Plot the temperatures for the water, dry sand, and damp sand. Use a different color line to connect the points for each material.

2. Comparing and Contrasting How does the changing temperature differ for dry sand and water when they are exposed to equal amounts of radiation?

3. Comparing and Contrasting How does the changing temperature differ for dry sand and damp sand when they are exposed to equal amounts of radiation?

4. Applying Locate Eureka, California, and Lafayette, Indiana, on a map. Infer which city would show the greatest annual temperature range. Explain your answer.

5. Communicating Write a lab report explaining your procedures and conclusions for this lab.

Study Guide

17.1 Atmosphere Characteristics

Key Concepts

- Weather is constantly changing, and it refers to the state of the atmosphere at any given time or place. Climate is the sum of all statistical weather information that helps describe a place or region.

- Water vapor is the source of all clouds and precipitation. Like carbon dioxide, it absorbs heat given off by Earth as well as some solar energy.

- If ozone did not filter most UV radiation, Earth would be uninhabitable for many living organisms.

- The atmosphere thins as you travel away from Earth, until there are too few gas molecules to detect.

- The atmosphere can be divided vertically into four layers based on temperature.

- Seasonal changes occur because Earth's position relative to the sun continually changes as it travels along its orbit.

Vocabulary

ozone, *p. 478;* troposphere, *p. 480;* stratosphere, *p. 480;* mesosphere, *p. 480;* thermosphere, *p. 480;* summer solstice, *p. 482;* winter solstice, *p. 482;* autumnal equinox, *p. 482;* spring equinox, *p. 482*

17.2 Heating the Atmosphere

Key Concepts

- Heat is the transfer of energy between two objects resulting from differences in their temperatures. Temperature is a measure of the average kinetic energy of individual particles.

- Three mechanisms of heat transfer are conduction, convection, and radiation. Unlike conduction and convection, radiant energy can travel through the vacuum of space.

- All objects, at any temperature, emit radiant energy. Hotter objects radiate more total energy per unit area than colder objects do. The hottest radiating bodies produce the shortest wavelengths of maximum radiation. Objects that are good absorbers of radiation are good emitters as well.

- Objects can absorb, transmit, scatter, or reflect radiation that strikes them.

Vocabulary

heat, *p. 483;* temperature, *p. 483;* conduction, *p. 483;* convection, *p. 484;* radiation, *p. 485;* reflection, *p. 486;* scattering, *p. 486;* greenhouse effect, *p. 487*

17.3 Temperature Controls

Key Concepts

- Factors other than latitude that exert a strong influence on temperature include heating of land and water, altitude, geographic position, cloud cover, and ocean currents.

- Land heats more rapidly and to higher temperatures than water. Land also cools more rapidly and to lower temperatures than water.

Vocabulary

albedo, *p. 492;* isotherm, *p. 492*

Thinking Visually

Concept Map Copy the concept map below onto a sheet of paper. Use information from the chapter to complete the concept map.

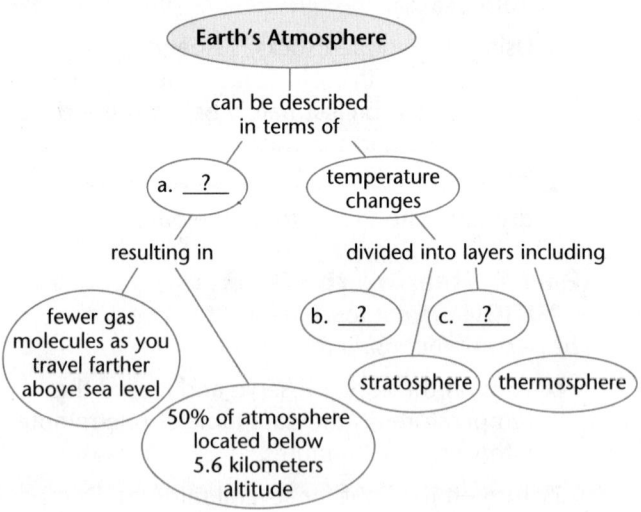

Reviewing Content

Choose the letter that best answers the question or completes the statement.

1. What is a description of atmospheric conditions over a long period of time?
   a. climate
   b. meteorology
   c. precipitation
   d. weather

2. The bottom layer of the atmosphere in which we live is called the
   a. mesosphere.
   b. stratosphere.
   c. thermosphere.
   d. troposphere.

3. Which form of radiation has the longest wavelength?
   a. blue light
   b. infrared
   c. radio waves
   d. ultraviolet

4. This layer of atmosphere contains ozone that filters UV radiation.
   a. mesosphere
   b. stratosphere
   c. thermosphere
   d. troposphere

5. The average kinetic energy of all the atoms and molecules that make up a substance is referred to as
   a. radiation.
   b. greenhouse effect.
   c. temperature.
   d. heat.

6. The two principle absorbers of radiation emitted by Earth's surface are carbon dioxide and
   a. nitrogen.
   b. oxygen.
   c. ozone.
   d. water vapor.

7. On a map showing temperature distributions, what are the lines connecting points of equal temperature?
   a. isobars
   b. isotemps
   c. isotherms
   d. equigrads

8. Which gas is most abundant in clean, dry air?
   a. argon
   b. carbon dioxide
   c. nitrogen
   d. oxygen

9. Select the best description of air.
   a. It is a compound.
   b. It is an element.
   c. It is a mixture.
   d. It is mainly oxygen and carbon dioxide.

10. Earth's atmosphere is thought to have become enriched in which gas about 2.5 billion years ago?
    a. argon
    b. carbon dioxide
    c. nitrogen
    d. oxygen

Understanding Concepts

11. Why are temperature variations greater over dry land than they are over water?

12. Describe how the ozone in the stratosphere forms.

13. Describe the three types of heat transfer in the atmosphere.

14. In what ways can geographic position be considered a temperature control?

15. Describe the two principle motions of Earth.

16. Explain why Earth's troposphere is mainly heated from the ground up.

17. Describe the effects of cloud cover on air temperature.

18. Why do temperatures increase in the stratosphere?

19. What causes the position of the noon sun to vary by as much as 47 degrees over a year's time?

Use the figure below to answer Question 20.

20. The illustration below shows two ways that radiation bounces off objects. Identify the process shown in each diagram. What clues in the illustration helped you identify these processes?

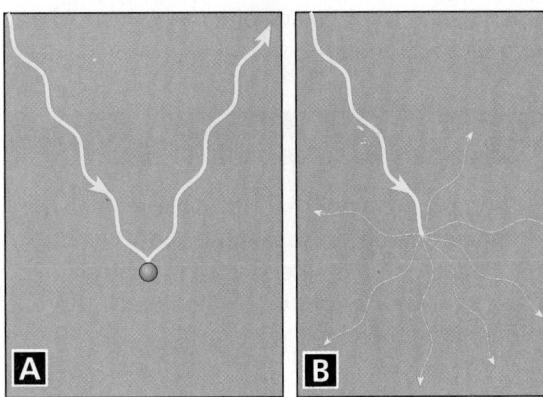

Assessment *continued*

Critical Thinking

Use the table below to answer Question 21.

Albedo of Various Surfaces	
Surface	**Percent Reflected**
Clouds, stratus	
< 150 meters thick	25–63
150–300 meters thick	45–75
300–600 meters thick	59–84
Average of all types	
and thicknesses	50–55
Concrete	17–27
Crops, green	5–25
Forest, green	5–10
Meadows, green	5–25
Ploughed field, moist	14–17
Road, blacktop	5–10
Sand, white	30–60
Snow, fresh-fallen	80–90
Snow, old	45–70
Soil, dark	5–15
Soil, light (or desert)	25–30
Water	8*

*Typical albedo value for a water surface. The albedo of a water surface varies greatly depending upon the sun angle.

21. Analyzing Data Using the data in the table, determine which types of surfaces have the highest average albedos.

22. Applying Concepts Determine the date after which the length of daylight gets progressively longer going south from the equator. Use Figure 8 to explain your answer.

23. Inferring Give an example of how the Earth system might be affected if Earth's axis were perpendicular to the plane of its orbit instead of being tilted 23.5 degrees.

Math Skills

24. Calculating Assume that the average rate of temperature decrease in the troposphere is 6.5°C/km. Using this rate, determine the air temperature at a height of 2 kilometers if the temperature at sea level were 23°C.

Concepts in Action

25. Inferring Yakutsk is located in Siberia at about 60 degrees north latitude. This Russian city has one of the highest average annual temperature ranges in the world: 62.2°C. Explain the reasons for the very high annual temperature range.

26. Making Generalizations Speculate on the changes in global temperatures that might occur if Earth had substantially more land area and less ocean area than it does at present. How might such changes influence the biosphere?

27. Applying Concepts Why are carbon dioxide and water vapor such important components in Earth's atmosphere? What would happen to life forms on Earth if these gases were no longer present in the atmosphere?

28. Generalizing State the relationship between the temperature of a radiating body and the wavelengths of radiation that it emits.

29. Interpreting Illustrations Refer to Figure 20. What can you determine about temperatures in regions where isotherms are closely spaced, compared with regions where isotherms are farther apart?

30. Writing in Science Write a paragraph that describes two environmental settings where you would expect the albedo of surfaces to be high. Your scenarios can describe any reasonable area on Earth's surface. Be sure to include as much detail as possible in your paragraph.

Performance-Based Assessment

Designing an Experiment Design and conduct an experiment that models how variations in color of an object can affect the amount of radiation it absorbs. As a first step, write a clear hypothesis statement. Then plan the materials you will need to design the experiment. Have your teacher approve your plan before you begin.

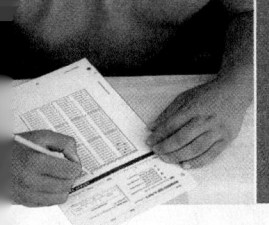

Standardized Test Prep

Choose the letter that best answers the question or completes the statement.

1. Which of these gases plays a more important role in weather processes than the others?
(A) argon
(B) carbon dioxide
(C) nitrogen
(D) oxygen

2. Practically all clouds and storms occur in this layer of the atmosphere.
(A) mesosphere
(B) stratosphere
(C) thermosphere
(D) troposphere

3. The primary wavelengths of radiation emitted by Earth's surface are
(A) longer than those emitted by the sun.
(B) shorter than those emitted by the sun.
(C) about the same as those emitted by the sun.
(D) about the same as UV radiation.

4. Which of the following is true about equinoxes?
(A) They occur in June and December.
(B) The sun's vertical rays are striking either the Tropic of Cancer or the Tropic of Capricorn.
(C) Lengths of daylight and darkness are equal everywhere.
(D) The length of daylight in the Arctic and Antarctic Circles is 24 hours.

Use the graph below to answer Questions 5 and 6.

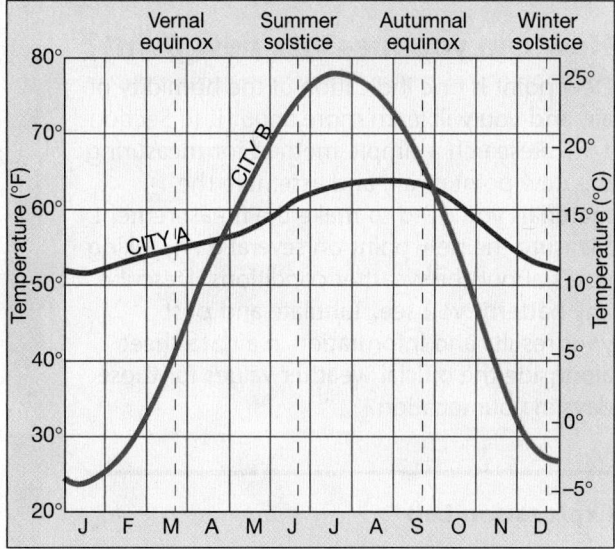

5. Determine the difference in December mean temperatures for cities A and B. Express your answer to the nearest degree C.

6. In which hemisphere are the cities located? Use information given in the graph to explain your answer.

18 Moisture, Clouds, and Precipitation

How can you measure dew point?

Dew point is one indication of the humidity of air, and you will learn more about it in Section 18.1. Research a simple method for measuring the dew point of air, and assemble the materials you need to make the measurement. Measure the dew point on several days, taking notes about the weather conditions. Describe any patterns you see. Tabulate and post your results and information in a data sheet alongside the official weather values for those days in your location.

Exploration Lab

Measuring Humidity

People and the Environment

Atmospheric Stability and Air Pollution

The Atmosphere
↳ Moisture and Cloud Formation

Sunrise colors stratocumulus clouds over the Sea of Cortez, Mexico.

Chapter Preview

Inquiry Activity

What Causes Condensation?

Procedure

1. Fill a 250-mL beaker about one-third full of tap water. Gradually add ice to the beaker. Gently stir the water-ice mixture with a thermometer.

2. Be sure to keep the thermometer in the water-ice mixture. Record the temperature at the moment water begins to form on the outside surface of the beaker.

Think About It

1. **Observing** At what temperature did water first appear on the outside of the beaker?

2. **Inferring** Where did the water that formed on the beaker's outer surface come from?

3. **Applying Concepts** Describe a process in nature that results from condensation with a change in temperature.

18.1 Water in the Atmosphere

Reading Focus

Key Concepts

- Which gas is most important for understanding atmospheric processes?
- What happens during a change of state?
- How do warm and cold air compare in their ability to hold water vapor?
- What is relative humidity?
- What can change the relative humidity of air?

Vocabulary

- precipitation
- latent heat
- evaporation
- condensation
- sublimation
- deposition
- humidity
- saturated
- relative humidity
- dew point
- hygrometer

Reading Strategy

Monitoring Your Understanding Before you read, copy the table. List what you know about water in the atmosphere and what you would like to learn. After you read, list what you have learned.

What I Know	What I Would Like to Learn	What I Have Learned
a. ___?___	b. ___?___	c. ___?___
d. ___?___	e. ___?___	f. ___?___

As you observe day-to-day weather changes, you can see the powerful role of water in the air. Water vapor is the source of all condensation and **precipitation,** which is any form of water that falls from a cloud. Look at Figure 1. Clouds and fog, as well as rain, snow, sleet, and hail, are examples of some of the more noticeable weather conditions. **When it comes to understanding atmospheric processes, water vapor is the most important gas in the atmosphere.** Water vapor makes up only a small fraction of the gases in the atmosphere, varying from nearly 0 to about 4 percent by volume. But the importance of water in the air greatly exceeds what these small percentages would indicate.

Water's Changes of State

The three states of matter are solid, liquid, and gas. Water can change from one state of matter to another—at temperatures and pressures experienced on Earth. This unique property allows water to freely leave the oceans as a gas and return again as a liquid, producing the water cycle. All water in the cycle must pass through the atmosphere as water vapor, even though the atmosphere only holds enough to make a global layer about 2 mm deep.

Figure 1 This downpour shows how precipitation can affect daily activities.

 **Reading Checkpoint** *What is the range in volume percent of water in the atmosphere?*

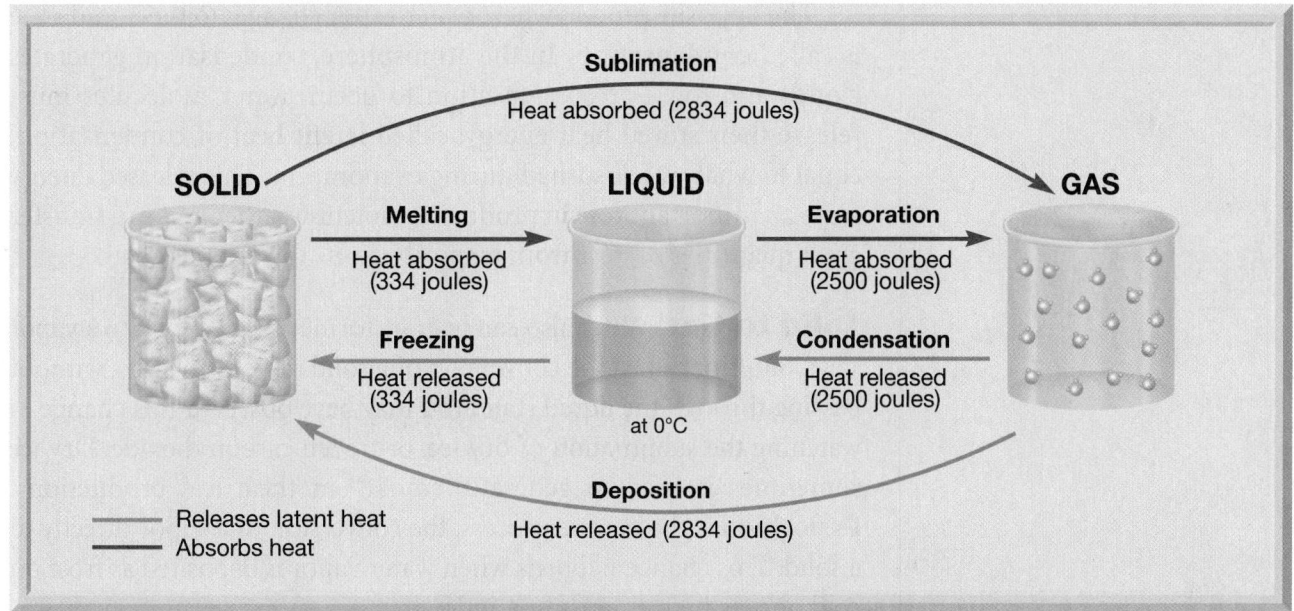

Figure 2 Changes of State The heat energy, in joules, is indicated for 1 gram of water.

Solid to Liquid 🔵 **The process of changing state requires that energy is transferred in the form of heat.** When heat is transferred to a glass of ice water, the temperature of the ice water remains a constant 0°C until all the ice has melted. If adding heat does not raise the temperature, then where does this energy go? In this case, the added heat breaks apart the crystal structure of the ice cubes. The bonds between water molecules in the ice crystals are broken forming the noncrystalline substance liquid water. You know this process as melting.

The heat used to melt ice does not produce a temperature change, so it is referred to as **latent heat.** *Latent* means "hidden," like the latent fingerprints hidden at a crime scene. This energy, measured in joules or calories, becomes stored in the liquid water and is not released as heat until the liquid returns to the solid state.

Latent heat plays a crucial role in many atmospheric processes. For example, the release of latent heat aids in forming the towering clouds often seen on warm summer days. It is the major source of energy for thunderstorms, tornadoes, and hurricanes.

Liquid to Gas The process of changing a liquid to a gas is called **evaporation.** You see in Figure 2 that it takes approximately 2500 joules of energy to convert 1 gram of liquid water to water vapor. The energy absorbed by the water molecules during evaporation gives them the motion needed to escape the surface of the liquid and become a gas. This energy is referred to as latent heat of vaporization.

You might have experienced a cooling effect when stepping dripping wet from a swimming pool or bathtub. This cooling results because it takes considerable energy to evaporate water. In this situation, the energy comes from your skin—hence the expression that "evaporation is a cooling process."

The opposite process where water vapor changes to the liquid state is called **condensation.** In the atmosphere, condensation generates clouds and fog. For condensation to occur, water molecules must release their stored heat energy, called latent heat of condensation, equal to what was absorbed during evaporation. This released energy plays an important role in producing violent weather and can transfer great quantities of heat from tropical oceans toward the poles.

Solid to Gas Water also can be transformed from a solid to a vapor state. **Sublimation** is the conversion of a solid directly to a gas, without passing through the liquid state. You may have observed this change in watching the sublimation of dry ice, or frozen carbon dioxide. Dry ice sometimes is used to generate "smoke" in theatrical productions. **Deposition** is the reverse process, the conversion of a vapor directly to a solid. This change happens when water vapor is deposited as frost on cold objects such as grass or windows.

Humidity

The general term for the amount of water vapor in air is **humidity.** Meteorologists use several methods to express the water-vapor content of the air. These include relative humidity and dew-point temperature.

Table 1 Water Vapor Needed for Saturation		
Temperature		Water Vapor Content at Saturation (g/kg)
°C	(°F)	
−40	(−40)	0.1
−30	(−22)	0.3
−20	(−4)	0.75
−10	(14)	2
0	(32)	3.5
5	(41)	5
10	(50)	7
15	(59)	10
20	(68)	14
25	(77)	20
30	(86)	26.5
35	(95)	35
40	(104)	47

Saturation Imagine a closed jar half full of water and half full of dry air. As the water begins to evaporate from the water surface, a small increase in pressure can be detected in the air above. This increase is the result of the motion of the water-vapor molecules that were added to the air through evaporation. As more and more molecules escape from the water surface, the pressure in the air above increases steadily. This forces more and more water molecules to return to the liquid. Eventually, the number of vapor molecules returning to the surface will balance the number leaving. At that point, the air is said to be **saturated.** The amount of water vapor required for saturation depends on temperature as shown in Table 1. **When saturated, warm air contains more water vapor than saturated cold air.**

Relative Humidity The most familiar and most misunderstood term used to describe the moisture content of air is relative humidity. **Relative humidity is a ratio of the air's actual water-vapor content compared with the amount of water vapor air can hold at that temperature and pressure.** Relative humidity indicates how near the air is to saturation, rather than the actual quantity of water vapor in the air.

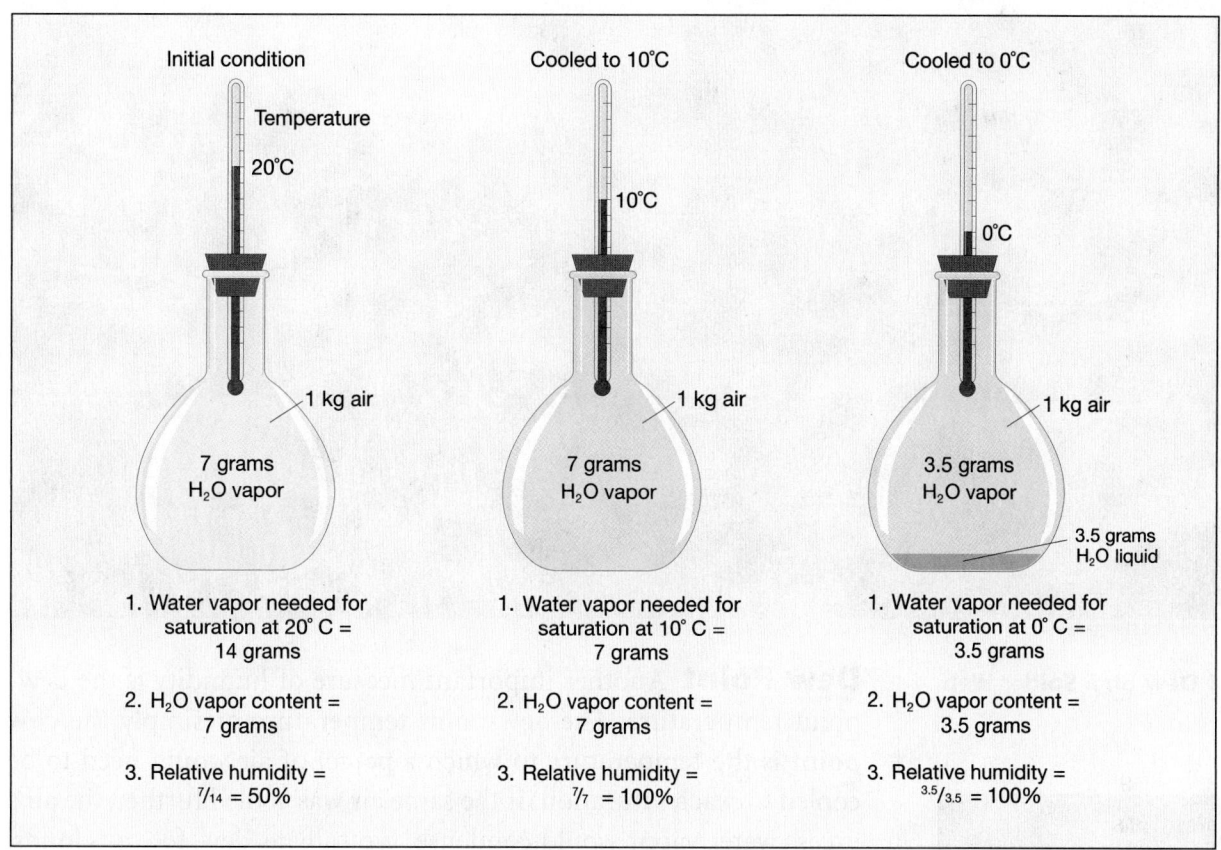

Initial condition	Cooled to 10°C	Cooled to 0°C

Temperature

20°C — 1 kg air — 7 grams H₂O vapor

10°C — 1 kg air — 7 grams H₂O vapor

0°C — 1 kg air — 3.5 grams H₂O vapor — 3.5 grams H₂O liquid

1. Water vapor needed for saturation at 20° C = 14 grams

2. H₂O vapor content = 7 grams

3. Relative humidity = $^7/_{14}$ = 50%

1. Water vapor needed for saturation at 10° C = 7 grams

2. H₂O vapor content = 7 grams

3. Relative humidity = $^7/_7$ = 100%

1. Water vapor needed for saturation at 0° C = 3.5 grams

2. H₂O vapor content = 3.5 grams

3. Relative humidity = $^{3.5}/_{3.5}$ = 100%

Relative humidity can be changed in two ways. First, it can be changed by adding or removing water vapor. In nature, moisture is added to air mainly by evaporation from the oceans and smaller bodies of water.

Second, because the amount of moisture needed for saturation depends on temperature, relative humidity varies with temperature. Notice in Figure 3 that when the flask is cooled from 20°C to 10°C, the relative humidity increases from 50 to 100 percent. However, once the air is saturated, further cooling does not change the relative humidity. Further cooling causes condensation, which keeps the air at its saturation level for the temperature. When air far above Earth's surface is cooled below its saturation level, some of the water vapor condenses to form clouds. Because clouds are made of liquid droplets, this moisture is no longer part of the water-vapor content of the air. **To summarize, when the water-vapor content of air remains constant, lowering air temperature causes an increase in relative humidity, and raising air temperature causes a decrease in relative humidity.**

Figure 3 Relative humidity varies with temperature.

For: Links on atmospheric moisture
Visit: www.SciLinks.org
Web Code: cjn-6181

Figure 4 Dew on a Spider Web

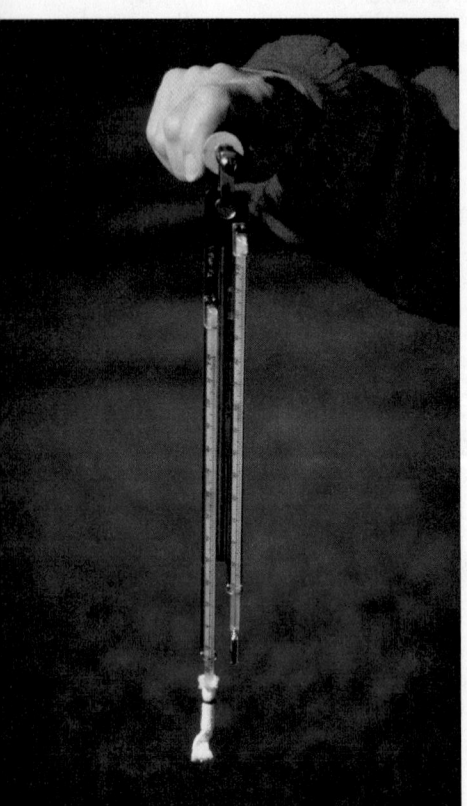

Figure 5 Sling Psychrometer
This psychrometer is used to measure both relative humidity and dew point.
Interpreting Photographs
Identify the wet bulb and the dry bulb in this photograph.

Dew Point Another important measure of humidity is the dew-point temperature. The dew-point temperature or simply the **dew point** is the temperature to which a parcel of air would need to be cooled to reach saturation. If the same air was cooled further, the air's excess water vapor would condense, typically as dew, fog, or clouds. During evening hours, objects near the ground often cool below the dew-point temperature and become coated with water. This is known as dew, shown on the spider web in Figure 4.

For every 10°C increase in temperature, the amount of water vapor needed for saturation doubles. Therefore, relatively cold saturated air at 0°C contains about half the water vapor of saturated air at a temperature of 10°C, and roughly one-fourth that of hot saturated air with a temperature of 20°C as shown in Table 1 on page 506. Because the dew point is the temperature at which saturation occurs, high dew-point temperatures indicate moist air, and low dew-point temperatures indicate dry air.

Measuring Humidity Relative humidity is commonly measured by using a **hygrometer.** One type of hygrometer, called a psychrometer, consists of two identical thermometers mounted side by side. See Figure 5. One thermometer, the dry-bulb thermometer, gives the present air temperature. The other, called the wet-bulb thermometer, has a thin cloth wick tied around the end.

To use the psychrometer, the cloth wick is saturated with water and air is continuously passed over the wick. This is done either by swinging the instrument freely in the air or by fanning air past it. Water evaporates from the wick, and the heat absorbed by the evaporating water makes the temperature of the wet bulb drop. The loss of heat that was required to evaporate water from the wet bulb lowers the thermometer reading. This temperature is referred to as the wet-bulb temperature.

The amount of cooling that takes place is directly proportional to the dryness of the air. The drier the air, the more moisture evaporates, and the lower is the temperature of the wet bulb. The larger the difference is between temperatures observed on the thermometers, the lower the relative humidity. If the air is saturated, no evaporation will occur, and the two thermometers will have identical readings. To determine the precise relative humidity and to calculate the dew point, standard tables are used.

A sling psychrometer would not be all that useful in a weather balloon used to monitor conditions in the upper atmosphere. A different type of hygrometer is used in instrument packages that transmit data back to a station on the ground. The electric hygrometer contains an electrical conductor coated with a chemical that absorbs moisture. The passage of current varies with the amount of moisture absorbed.

Q *Why is the air in buildings so dry in the winter?*

A If the water-vapor content of air stays constant, an increase in temperature lowers the relative humidity, and a drop in temperature raises the relative humidity. During winter months, outside air is comparatively cold. When this air is drawn into a building, it is heated to room temperature. This causes the relative humidity to drop, often to uncomfortably low levels of 10 percent or lower. Living with dry air can mean static electrical shocks, dry skin, sinus headaches, or even nosebleeds.

Section 18.1 Assessment

Reviewing Concepts

1. What is the most important gas for understanding atmospheric processes?

2. What happens to heat during a change of state?

3. How does the temperature of air influence its ability to hold water?

4. What does relative humidity describe about air?

5. List two ways that relative humidity can be changed.

6. What does a low dew point indicate about the moisture content of air?

Critical Thinking

7. **Interpreting Illustrations** Study Figure 2. For 1 gram of water, how do the energy requirements for melting and evaporation compare?

Math Practice

8. The air over Fort Myers, Florida, has a dew point of 25°C. Fort Myers has twice the water vapor content of the air over St. Louis, Missouri, and four times the water vapor content as air over Tucson, Arizona. Determine the dew points for St. Louis and Tucson.

18.2 Cloud Formation

Reading Focus

Key Concepts

- What happens to air when it is compressed or allowed to expand?
- List four mechanisms that can cause air to rise.
- Contrast movements of stable and unstable air.
- What conditions in air favor condensation of water?

Vocabulary

- dry adiabatic rate
- wet adiabatic rate
- orographic lifting
- front
- temperature inversion
- condensation nuclei

Reading Strategy

Identifying Main Ideas Copy the table. As you read, write the main idea for each topic.

Topic	Main Idea
Adiabatic temperature changes	a. _____?_____
Stability measurements	b. _____?_____
Degrees of stability	c. _____?_____

Figure 6 Clouds form when air is cooled to its dew point.

Recall that condensation occurs when water vapor changes to a liquid. Condensation may form dew, fog, or clouds. Although these three forms are different, all require saturated air to develop. Saturation occurs either when enough water vapor is added to air or, more commonly, when air is cooled to its dew point.

Near Earth's surface, heat is quickly exchanged between the ground and the air above. During evening hours, the surface radiates heat away, causing the surface and adjacent air to cool rapidly. This radiational cooling causes the formation of dew and some types of fog. In contrast, clouds, like those shown in Figure 6, often form during the warmest part of the day. Clearly, some other process must cool air enough to generate clouds.

Air Compression and Expansion

If you have pumped up a bicycle tire, you might have noticed that the pump barrel became warm. The increase in temperature you felt resulted from the work you did on the air to compress it. When air is compressed, the motion of gas molecules increases and the air temperature rises. The opposite happens when air is allowed to escape from a bicycle tire. The air expands and cools. The expanding air pushes on the surrounding air and cools by an amount equal to the energy used up.

Adiabatic Temperature Changes Temperature changes that happen even though heat isn't added or subtracted are called *adiabatic temperature changes*. They result when air is compressed or allowed to expand. **When air is allowed to expand, it cools, and when it is compressed, it warms.**

Expansion and Cooling As you travel from Earth's surface upward through the atmosphere, the atmospheric pressure decreases. This happens because there are fewer and fewer gas molecules. Any time a volume of air moves upward, it passes through regions of successively lower pressure. As a result, the ascending air expands and cools. Unsaturated air cools at the constant rate of 10°C for every 1000 meters of ascent. In contrast, descending air encounters higher pressures, compresses, and is heated 10°C for every 1000 meters it moves downward. This rate of cooling or heating applies only to unsaturated air and is called the **dry adiabatic rate.**

If a parcel of air rises high enough, it will eventually cool to its dew point. Here the process of condensation begins. From this point on as the air rises, latent heat of condensation stored in the water vapor will be released. Although the air will continue to cool after condensation begins, the released latent heat works against the adiabatic cooling process. This slower rate of cooling caused by the addition of latent heat is called the **wet adiabatic rate.** Because the amount of latent heat released depends on the quantity of moisture present in the air, the wet adiabatic rate varies from 5–9°C per 1000 meters.

Figure 7 shows the role of adiabatic cooling in the formation of clouds. Note that from the surface up to the condensation level the air cools at the dry adiabatic rate. The wet adiabatic rate begins at the condensation level.

 **Reading Checkpoint** *What happens to heat stored in water vapor when it is cooled to its dew point?*

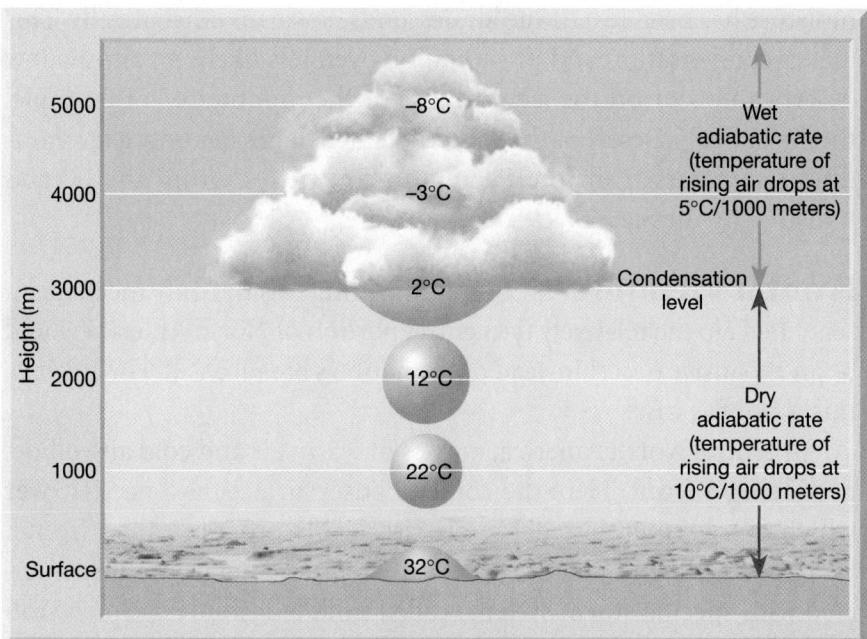

Figure 7 Cloud Formation by Adiabatic Cooling Rising air cools at the dry adiabatic rate of 10°C per 1000 meters, until the air reaches the dew point and condensation (cloud formation) begins. As air continues to rise, the latent heat released by condensation reduces the rate of cooling.
Interpreting Diagrams *Use this diagram to determine the approximate air temperature at 3500 m.*

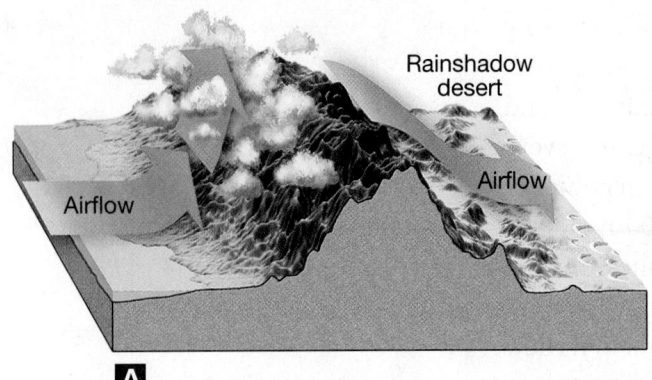

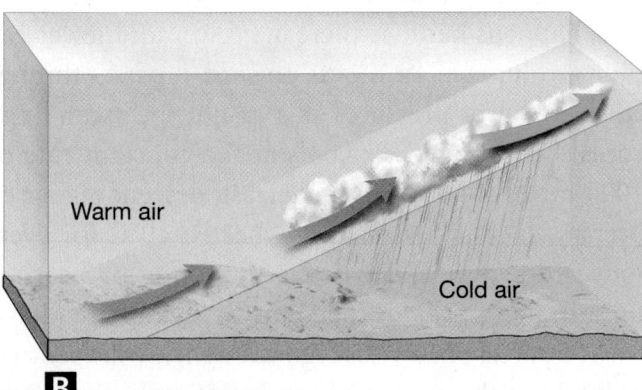

A

B

Figure 8 A Orographic Lifting
B Frontal Wedging
Relating Cause and Effect *Why does the warm air mass move upward over the cold air mass?*

For: Links on orographic lifting and rainfall
Visit: PHSchool.com
Web Code: czd-6182

Processes That Lift Air

In general, air resists vertical movement. Air located near the surface tends to stay near the surface. Air far above the surface tends to remain far above the surface. Some exceptions to this happen when conditions in the atmosphere make air buoyant enough to rise without the aid of outside forces. In other situations, clouds form because there is some mechanical process that forces air to rise. ◗ **Four mechanisms that can cause air to rise are orographic lifting, frontal wedging, convergence, and localized convective lifting.**

Orographic Lifting When elevated terrains, such as mountains, act as barriers to air flow, **orographic lifting** of air occurs. Look at Figure 8A. As air goes up a mountain slope, adiabatic cooling often generates clouds and precipitation. Many of the rainiest places on Earth are located on these windward mountain slopes.

By the time air reaches the leeward side of a mountain, much of its moisture has been lost. If the air descends, it warms adiabatically. This makes condensation and precipitation even less likely. A rain shadow desert can occur on the leeward side of the mountain. For example, the Great Basin Desert of the western United States lies only a few hundred kilometers from the Pacific Ocean, cut off from the ocean's moisture by the Sierra Nevada Mountains.

Frontal Wedging If orographic lifting was the only mechanism that lifted air, the relatively flat central portion of North America would be an expansive desert instead of the nation's breadbasket. Fortunately, this is not the case.

In central North America, masses of warm air and cold air collide, producing a **front.** Here the cooler, denser air acts as a barrier over which the warmer, less dense air rises. This process, called frontal wedging, is shown in Figure 8B. Weather-producing fronts are associated with specific storm systems called middle-latitude cyclones. You will study these in Chapter 20.

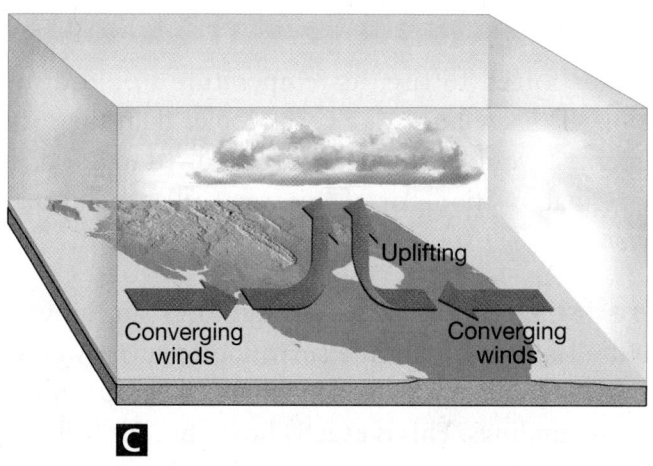

C

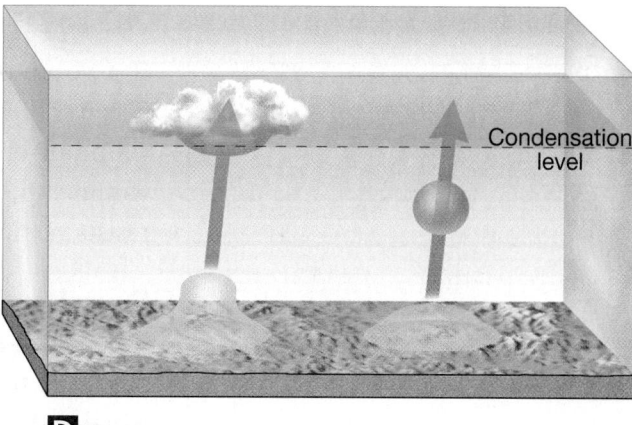

D

Convergence

Recall that the collision of contrasting air masses forces air to rise. In a more general sense, whenever air in the lower atmosphere flows together, lifting results. This is called convergence. When air flows in from more than one direction, it must go somewhere. Because it cannot go down, it goes up, as shown in Figure 8C. This leads to adiabatic cooling and possibly cloud formation.

The Florida peninsula provides an example of how convergence can cause cloud development and precipitation. On warm days, the airflow is from the ocean to the land along both coasts of Florida. This leads to a pileup of air along the coasts and general convergence over the peninsula. This pattern of air movement and the uplift that results is helped along by intense solar heating of the land. The result is that the peninsula of Florida experiences the greatest number of mid-afternoon thunderstorms in the United States.

Localized Convective Lifting

On warm summer days, unequal heating of Earth's surface may cause pockets of air to be warmed more than the surrounding air. For example, air above a paved parking lot will be warmed more than the air above an adjacent wooded park. Consequently, the parcel of air above the parking lot, which is warmer and less dense than the surrounding air, will move upward, as shown in Figure 8D. These rising parcels of warmer air are called thermals. The process that produces rising thermals is localized convective lifting. Birds such as hawks and eagles use these thermals to carry them to great heights where they can gaze down on unsuspecting prey. People have learned to use these warm parcels effectively for hang gliding. When warm parcels of air rise above the condensation level, clouds form. These clouds may produce mid-afternoon rain showers.

**Figure 8 C Convergence
D Localized Convective Lifting**

Reading Checkpoint

What are thermals?

Stability

If a volume of air was forced to rise, its temperature would drop because of expansion. If this volume of air was cooler than the surrounding environment, it would be denser, and if allowed to do so, it would sink to its original position. Air of this type, called stable air, resists vertical movement.

Density Differences If this imaginary volume of rising air was warmer and therefore less dense than the surrounding air, it would continue to rise until it reached an altitude where its temperature equaled that of its surroundings. This is exactly how a hot-air balloon works. The balloon rises as long as it is warmer and less dense than the surrounding air, as shown in Figure 9. This type of air is classified as unstable air. **Stable air tends to remain in its original position, while unstable air tends to rise.**

Stability Measurements Air stability is determined by measuring the temperature of the atmosphere at various heights. The rate of change of air temperature with height is called the environmental lapse rate. This rate is determined from observations made by aircraft and by radiosondes. A radiosonde is an instrument designed to collect weather data high in the atmosphere. Radiosondes are often carried into the air by balloons.

Degrees of Stability Air is stable when the temperature decreases gradually with increasing altitude. The most stable conditions happen when air temperature actually increases with height, called a **temperature inversion.** Temperature inversions frequently happen on clear nights as a result of radiation cooling off Earth's surface. The inversion is created because the ground and the air immediately above the ground will cool more rapidly than air higher above the ground. Under these conditions, there is very little vertical air movement. In contrast, air is considered unstable when the air close to the surface of Earth is significantly warmer than the air higher above the surface, indicating a large environmental lapse rate. Under these conditions, the air actually turns over, as the warm air below rises and is displaced by the colder air higher above the ground.

Figure 9 Hot-air balloons will rise as long as the air inside them is warmer than the air in the atmosphere surrounding them.

Stability and Daily Weather Recall that stable air resists vertical movement and that unstable air rises freely. But how do these facts apply to the daily weather?

Because stable air resists upward movement, you might conclude that clouds won't form when stable conditions are present in the atmosphere. Although this seems reasonable, remember that there are processes that force air above Earth's surface. These include orographic lifting, frontal wedging, and convergence. When stable air is forced above Earth's surface, the clouds that form are widespread and have little vertical thickness when compared to their horizontal dimension. Precipitation, if any, is light to moderate.

In contrast, clouds associated with the lifting of unstable air are towering and often generate thunderstorms and occasionally even a tornado. For this reason, on a dreary, overcast day with light drizzle, stable air has been forced above Earth's surface. During a day when cauliflower-shaped clouds appear to be growing as if bubbles of hot air are surging upward, the air moving up is unstable. Figure 10 shows cauliflower-shaped clouds caused by the rising of unstable air.

Figure 10 These clouds provide evidence of unstable conditions in the atmosphere.

 *What types of weather can result when stable air rises?*

Condensation

Recall that condensation happens when water vapor in the air changes to a liquid. This may be in the form of dew, fog, or clouds. **For any of these forms of condensation to occur, the air must be saturated.** Saturation occurs most commonly when air is cooled to its dew point, or less often when water vapor is added to the air.

Types of Surfaces Generally, there must be a surface for water vapor to condense on. When dew forms, objects at or near the ground, such as grass and car windows, serve this purpose. But when condensation occurs in the air above the ground, tiny bits of particulate matter, called **condensation nuclei,** serve as surfaces for water-vapor condensation. These nuclei are important because if they are absent, a relative humidity much above 100 percent is needed to produce clouds.

Condensation nuclei such as microscopic dust, smoke, and salt particles from the ocean are abundant in the lower atmosphere. Because of these plentiful particles, relative humidity rarely exceeds 100 percent. Some particles, such as ocean salt, are especially good nuclei because they absorb water. When condensation takes place, the initial growth rate of cloud droplets is rapid. It diminishes quickly because the excess water vapor is quickly absorbed by the numerous competing particles. This results in the formation of a cloud consisting of millions upon millions of tiny water droplets. These droplets are all so fine that they remain suspended in air. In the next section, you will examine types of clouds and the precipitation that forms from them.

Section 18.2 Assessment

Reviewing Concepts

1. Describe what happens to air temperature when work is done on the air to compress it.
2. What does stability mean in terms of air movement?
3. List four mechanisms that cause air to rise.
4. Describe conditions that cause condensation of liquid water in air.
5. What is a temperature inversion?
6. Which types of condensation nuclei are especially good for condensation to form?

Critical Thinking

7. **Hypothesizing** Study a world map. Hypothesize about other regions on Earth, other than the Florida peninsula, where convergence might cause cloud development and precipitation.

Connecting Concepts

Air Temperature Review the description of atmospheric temperature changes in Section 17.1. Then write a paragraph explaining how these differ from adiabatic temperature changes in parcels of air.

18.3 Cloud Types and Precipitation

Reading Focus

Key Concepts

- How are clouds classified?
- How are clouds and fogs similar and different?
- What must happen in order for precipitation to form?
- What controls the type of precipitation that reaches Earth's surface?

Vocabulary

- cirrus
- cumulus
- stratus
- Bergeron process
- supercooled water
- supersaturated air
- collision-coalescence process

Reading Strategy

Building Vocabulary Copy the table. As you read, add definitions.

Vocabulary Term	Definition
Cirrus	a. _____?_____
Cumulus	b. _____?_____
Stratus	c. _____?_____
Coalescence	d. _____?_____

Clouds are among the most striking and noticeable effects of the atmosphere and its weather. Clouds are a result of condensation best described as visible mixtures of tiny droplets of water or tiny crystals of ice. Clouds are of interest to meteorologists because clouds show what is going on in the atmosphere. If you try to recognize different types of clouds, you might find it hard to do. But, if you learn the basic classification scheme for clouds, recognizing cloud types will be easy.

Figure 11 Cirrus Clouds

Types of Clouds

Clouds are classified on the basis of their form and height. The three basic forms are: cirrus, cumulus, and stratus. All other clouds reflect one of these three basic forms or are combinations or modifications of them.

Cirrus (*cirrus* = a curl of hair) clouds are high, white, and thin. They can occur as patches or as delicate veil-like sheets or extended wispy fibers that often have a feathery appearance. An example of cirrus clouds is shown in Figure 11.

Cumulus (*cumulus* = a pile) clouds consist of rounded individual cloud masses. Refer to Figure 10 on page 515. Normally, they have a flat base and the appearance of rising domes or towers. These clouds are frequently described as having a cauliflower structure.

Stratus (*stratum* = a layer) clouds are best described as sheets or layers that cover much or all of the sky. While there may be minor breaks, there are no distinct individual cloud units.

There are three levels of cloud heights: high, middle, and low, as shown in Figure 12. High clouds normally have bases above 6000 meters. Middle clouds generally occupy heights from 2000 to 6000 meters. Low clouds form below 2000 meters. The altitudes listed for each height category are not hard and fast. There is some seasonal and latitudinal variation. For example, at high latitudes or during cold winter months in the mid-latitudes, high clouds often are found at lower altitudes.

High Clouds Three cloud types make up the family of high clouds: cirrus, cirrostratus, and cirrocumulus. Look at Figure 12. Cirrocumulus clouds consist of fluffy masses, while cirrostratus clouds are flat layers. All high clouds are thin and white and are often made up of ice crystals. This is because of the low temperatures and small quantities of water vapor present at high altitudes. These clouds are not considered precipitation makers. However, when cirrus clouds are followed by cirrocumulus or cirrostratus clouds and increased sky coverage, they may warn of approaching stormy weather.

Middle Clouds Clouds that appear in the middle range, from about 2000 to 6000 meters, have the prefix *alto-* as part of their name. Altocumulus clouds are composed of rounded masses that differ from

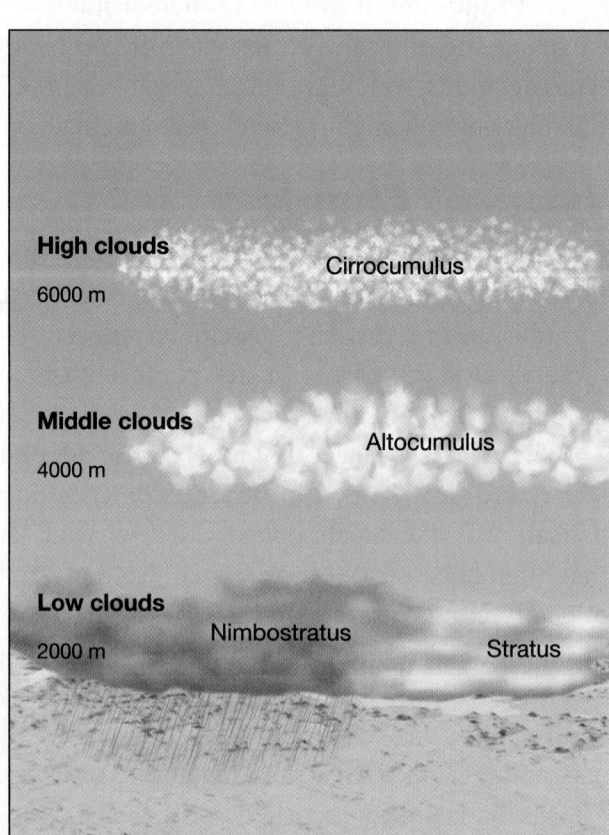

Figure 12 Cloud Classification
Clouds are classified according to form and height.
Interpreting Diagrams *Which cloud types are the chief precipitation makers?*

High clouds
6000 m
Cirrocumulus

Middle clouds
4000 m
Altocumulus

Low clouds
2000 m
Nimbostratus
Stratus

cirrocumulus clouds in that altocumulus clouds are larger and denser, as shown in Figure 12. Altostratus clouds create a uniform white to grayish sheet covering the sky with the sun or moon visible as a bright spot. Infrequent light snow or drizzle may accompany these clouds.

Low Clouds There are three members in the family of low clouds: stratus, stratocumulus, and nimbostratus. As illustrated in Figure 12, stratus clouds are a uniform, fog-like layer of clouds that frequently covers much of the sky. Occasionally, these clouds may produce light precipitation. When stratus clouds develop a scalloped bottom that appears as long parallel rolls or broken rounded patches, they are called stratocumulus clouds.

Nimbostratus clouds derive their name from the Latin word *nimbus,* which means "rainy cloud," and *stratus,* which means "to cover with a layer." As the name suggests, nimbostratus clouds are one of the main precipitation makers. Nimbostratus clouds form during stable conditions. You might not expect clouds to develop in stable air. But cloud growth of this type is common when air is forced upward, as occurs along a mountain range, a front, or where converging winds cause air to rise. Such a forced upward movement of stable air can result in a cloud layer that is largely horizontal compared to its depth.

 **Reading Checkpoint** **What does the Latin word stratus mean?**

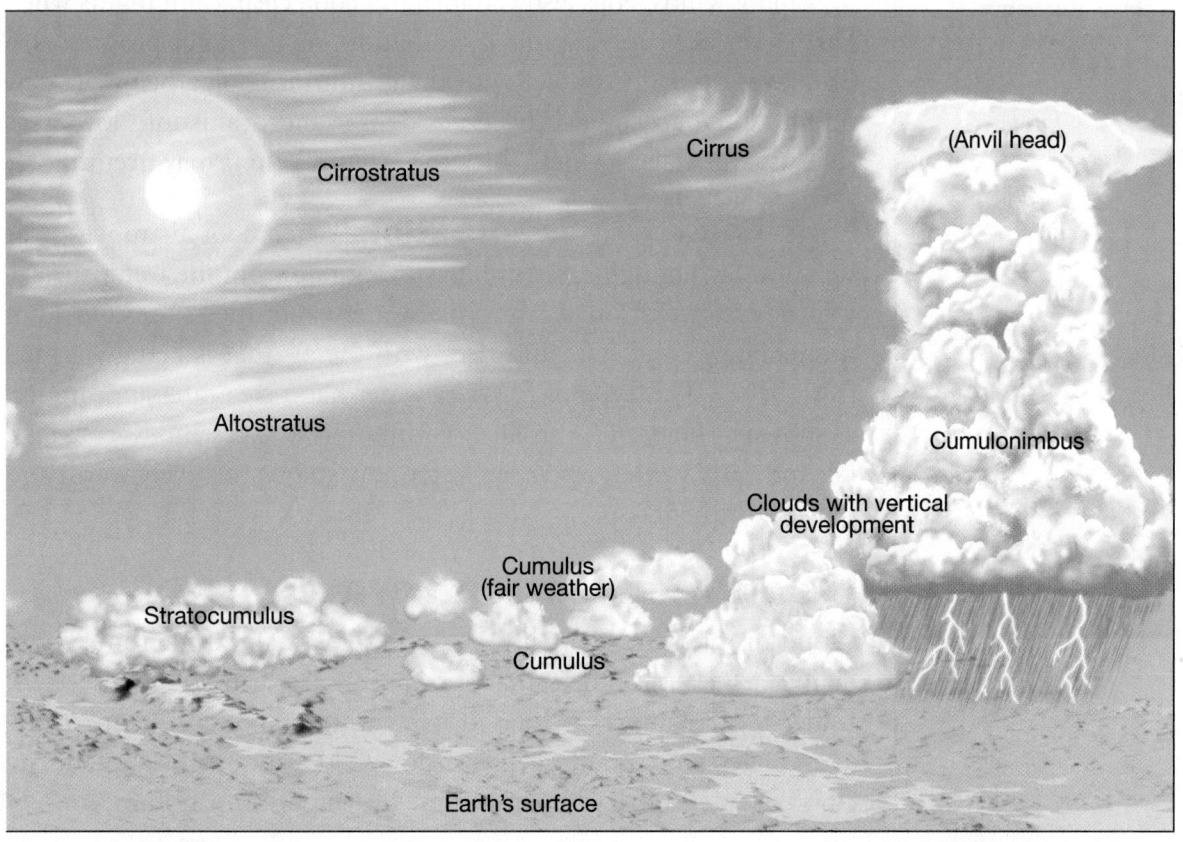

Figure 13 When water vapor rising from the warm lake water meets cold air, the water vapor condenses to form fog.

Clouds of Vertical Development Some clouds do not fit into any one of the three height categories mentioned. Such clouds have their bases in the low height range but often extend upward into the middle or high altitudes. They all are related to one another and are associated with unstable air. Although cumulus clouds are often connected with fair weather, they may grow dramatically under the proper circumstances. Once upward movement is triggered, acceleration is powerful, and clouds with great vertical range form. The end result often is a cumulonimbus cloud that may produce rain showers or a thunderstorm.

Fog

Physically, there is no difference between a fog and a cloud. Their appearance and structure are the same. The difference is the method and place of formation. Clouds result when air rises and cools adiabatically. Most fogs are the result of radiation cooling or the movement of air over a cold surface. Fogs also can form when enough water vapor is added to the air to bring about saturation. **Fog is defined as a cloud with its base at or very near the ground.** When fog is dense, visibility may be only a few dozen meters or less, making travel not only difficult but often dangerous.

Fogs Caused by Cooling A blanket of fog is produced in some West Coast locations when warm, moist air from the Pacific Ocean moves over the cold California Current and then is carried onshore by prevailing winds. Fogs also can form on cool, clear, calm nights when Earth's surface cools rapidly by radiation. As the night progresses, a thin layer of air in contact with the ground is cooled below its dew point. As the air cools, it becomes denser and drains into low areas such as river valleys, where thick fog accumulations may occur.

Fogs Caused by Evaporation When cool air moves over warm water, enough moisture may evaporate from the water surface to produce saturation. As the rising water vapor meets the cold air, it immediately condenses and rises with the air that is being warmed from below. This type of fog over water has a steaming appearance, as shown in Figure 13. It is fairly common over lakes and rivers in the fall and early winter, when the water may still be relatively warm and the air is rather crisp.

How Precipitation Forms

Cloud droplets are very tiny, averaging less than 20 micrometers in diameter. Because of their small size, the rate at which cloud droplets fall is incredibly slow. Most cloud droplets would evaporate before falling a few meters into unsaturated air below. **For precipitation to form, cloud droplets must grow in volume by roughly one million times.**

Cold Cloud Precipitation

The **Bergeron process,** shown in Figure 14, relies on two physical processes: supercooling and supersaturation. Cloud droplets do not freeze at 0°C as expected. In fact, pure water suspended in air does not freeze until it reaches a temperature of nearly −40°C. Water in the liquid state below 0°C is said to be **supercooled.** Supercooled water will readily freeze if it touches a solid object. Freezing nuclei are materials that have a crystal form that closely matches that of ice. Freezing nuclei can cause supercooled water to freeze.

When air is saturated (100% relative humidity) with respect to water, it is **supersaturated** with respect to ice (greater than 100% humidity). Ice crystals cannot coexist with water droplets in the air because the air "appears" supersaturated to the ice crystals. Any excess water vapor becomes ice that lowers the relative humidity near the surrounding droplets. Water droplets then evaporate to provide a continual source of water vapor for the growth of ice crystals.

Because the level of supersaturation with respect to ice can be quite high, the growth of ice crystals is rapid enough to produce crystals that are large enough to fall. As they fall the ice crystals contact cloud drops causing them to freeze. A chain reaction can occur and large crystals, called snowflakes, form. When the surface temperature is above 4°C, snowflakes usually melt before they reach the ground. Even on a hot summer day, a heavy downpour may have started as a snowstorm high in the clouds.

Warm Cloud Precipitation

Much rainfall can be associated with clouds located well below the freezing level, especially in the tropics. In warm clouds, the mechanism that forms raindrops is the **collision-coalescence process.** Some water-absorbing particles, such as salt, can remove water vapor from the air at relative humidities less than 100 percent, forming drops that are quite large. As these large droplets move through the cloud, they collide and coalesce (join together) with smaller, slower droplets.

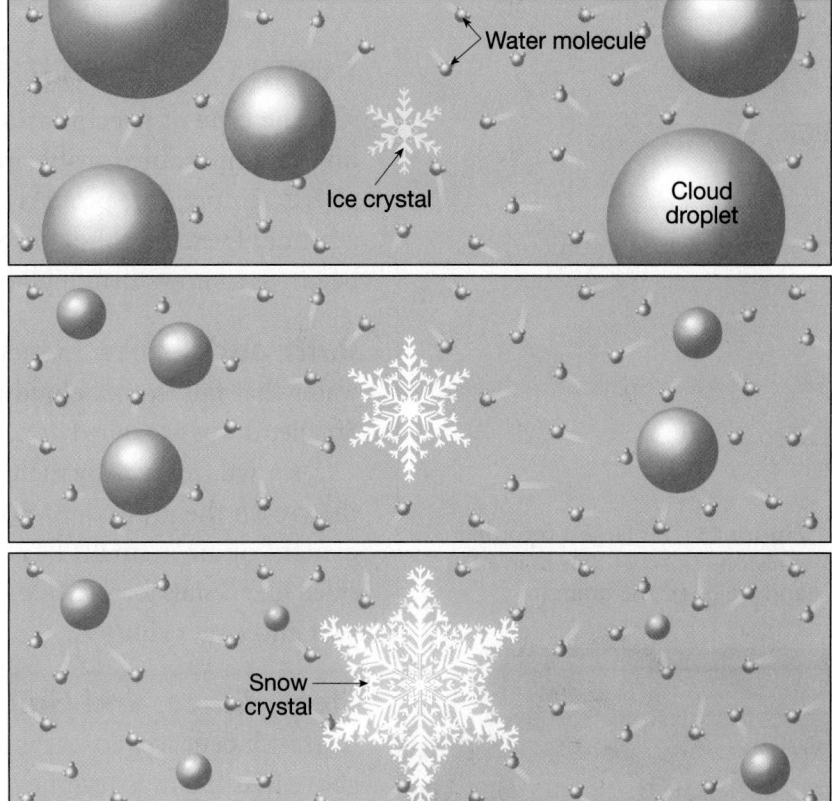

Figure 14 The Bergeron Process Ice crystals grow at the expense of cloud droplets until they are large enough to fall. The size of these particles has been greatly exaggerated.

For: Links on precipitation
Visit: www.SciLinks.org
Web Code: cjn-6184

Forms of Precipitation

The type of precipitation that reaches Earth's surface depends on the temperature profile in the lowest few kilometers of the atmosphere. Temperature profile is the way the air temperature changes with altitude. Even on a hot summer day, a heavy downpour may have begun as a snowstorm high in the clouds overhead.

Rain and Snow In meteorology, the term *rain* means drops of water that fall from a cloud and have a diameter of at least 0.5 mm. Smaller drops are called *drizzle*. When the surface temperature is above 4°C, snowflakes usually melt and continue their descent as rain before they reach the ground. At very low temperatures (when the moisture content of air is small) light, fluffy snow made up of individual six-sided ice crystals forms. At temperatures warmer than −5°C, ice crystals join into larger clumps.

Sleet, Glaze, and Hail Sleet is the fall of small particles of clear-to-translucent ice. For sleet to form, a layer of air with temperatures above freezing must overlie a subfreezing layer near the ground. Glaze, also known as freezing rain, results when raindrops become super-cooled (below 0°C) as they fall through subfreezing air near the ground and turn to ice when they impact objects.

Hail is produced in cumulonimbus clouds. Hailstones begin as small ice pellets that grow by collecting supercooled water droplets as they fall through a cloud. If the ice pellets encounter a strong updraft, they may be carried upward and begin the downward journey once more. Each trip through the supercooled portion of the cloud may be represented by another layer of ice, as shown in Figure 15.

Figure 15 This largest recorded hailstone fell over Kansas in 1970 and weighed 766 grams.

Section 18.3 Assessment

Reviewing Concepts

1. How are clouds classified?
2. Compare and contrast clouds and fogs.
3. What must happen in order for precipitation to form?
4. Describe how the temperature profile of air near Earth's surface controls the type of precipitation that falls to the ground.

Critical Thinking

5. **Predicting** What type of precipitation would fall to Earth's surface if a thick layer of air near the ground was −8°C?

6. **Classifying** Identify the following cloud types as producers of heavy, light, or generally no precipitation.

   a. cirrocumulus   b. cumulonimbus
   c. stratus   d. nimbostratus

Writing in Science

Compare-Contrast Paragraph Write a paragraph comparing the Bergeron and collision-coalescence processes. Relate each to the type(s) of precipitation that can result.

people and the ENVIRONMENT

Atmospheric Stability and Air Pollution

Air quality is closely linked to the atmosphere's ability to scatter pollutants. Perhaps you've heard "Dilution is the solution to pollution." To a large degree, this is true. If the air into which pollution is released is not dispersed, the air will become more toxic. Two of the most important atmospheric conditions affecting the distribution of pollutants are wind strength and air stability.

When winds are weak or calm, the concentration of pollutants is higher than when winds are strong. High wind speeds mix polluted air into a larger volume of surrounding air, causing the pollution to be more diluted. When winds are light, there is less turbulence and mixing, so the concentration of pollutants is higher.

Atmospheric stability affects vertical movements of air. In general, the larger the extent of vertical mixing, the better the air quality is. During a temperature inversion, the atmosphere is very stable and it does not move much vertically. Warm air overlying cooler air acts as a lid and prevents upward

movement, which leaves pollutants trapped near the ground, as shown in Figure 16.

Some inversions form near the ground, while others form higher above the ground. A surface inversion develops close to the ground on clear and relatively calm nights because the ground is a better radiator of heat than the air above it. Radiation from the ground to the clear night sky causes more rapid cooling at the surface than higher in the atmosphere. The result is that the air close to the ground is cooled more than the air above, yielding a temperature profile similar to the one shown in Figure 17. After sunrise, the ground is heated and the inversion disappears.

Although surface inversions usually are shallow, they may be thick in regions where the land surface is uneven. Because cold air is denser than warm air, the chilled air near the surface gradually drains from slopes into adjacent lowlands and valleys. As might be expected, these thicker surface inversions will not spread out as quickly after sunrise.

Figure 16 Air Pollution in Downtown Los Angeles Temperatures inversions act as lids to trap pollutants below.

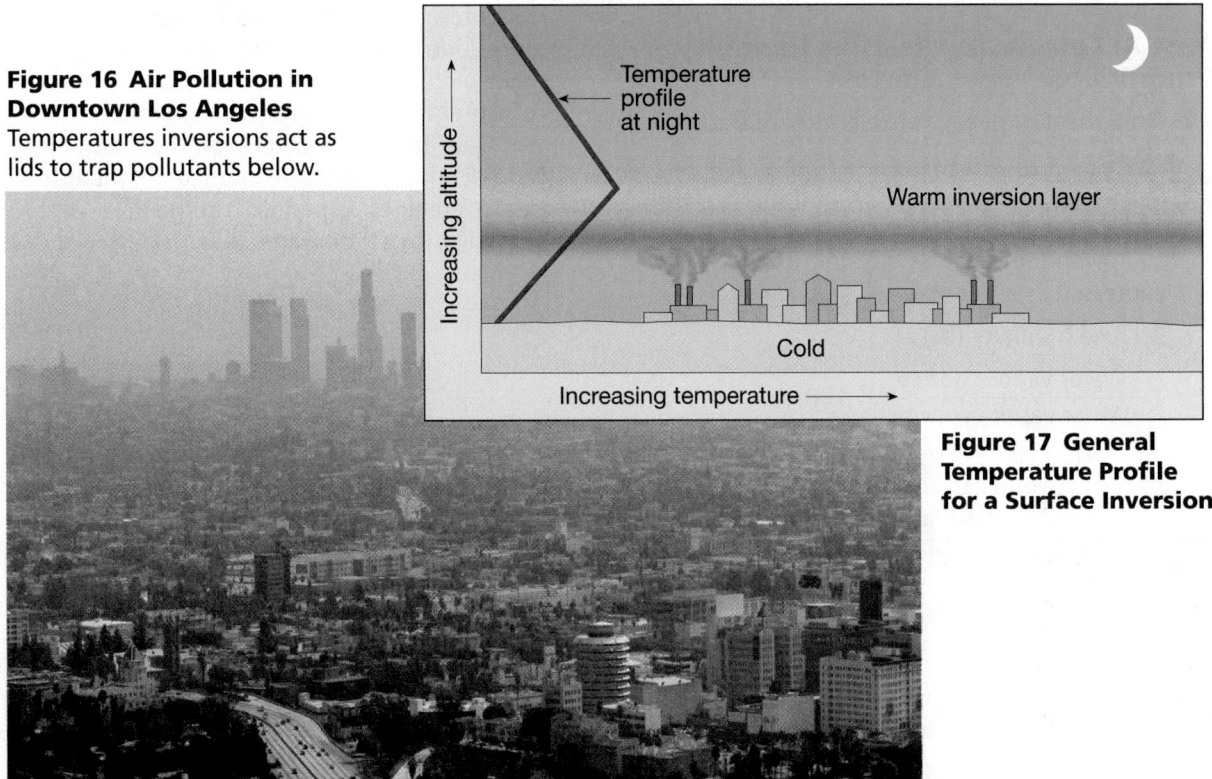

Temperature profile at night

Warm inversion layer

Increasing altitude

Cold

Increasing temperature

Figure 17 General Temperature Profile for a Surface Inversion

Measuring Humidity

Relative humidity is a measurement used to describe water vapor in the air. In general, it expresses how close the air is to saturation. In this lab, you will use a psychrometer and a data table to determine the relative humidity of air.

Problem How can relative humidity be determined?

Materials
- calculator
- water at room temperature
- psychrometer

Alternative materials for psychrometer:
- 2 thermometers
- cotton gauze
- paper fan
- string

Skills Observing, Measuring, Analyzing Data, Calculating

Procedure

Part A: Calculating Relative Humidity From Water Vapor Content

1. On a sheet of paper, make a copy of Data Table 1.

2. Relative humidity is the ratio of the air's water vapor content to its water vapor capacity at a given temperature. Relative humidity is expressed as a percent.

Relative humidity (%) =

$$\frac{\text{Water vapor content}}{\text{Water vapor capacity}} \times 100$$

3. At 25°C, the water vapor capacity is 20 g/kg. Use this information to complete Data Table 1.

Part B: Determining Relative Humidity Using a Psychrometer

4. A psychrometer consists of two thermometers. The wet-bulb thermometer has a cloth wick that is wet with water and spun for about 1 minute. Relative humidity is determined from the difference in temperature reading between the dry-bulb temperature and the wet-bulb temperature, by using Data Table 2. For example, suppose a dry-bulb temperature is measured as 20°C, and a wet-bulb temperature is 14°C. Read the relative humidity from Data Table 2.

5. If a psychrometer is not available, construct a wet-bulb thermometer by tying a piece of cotton gauze around the end of a thermometer. Wet it with room-temperature water and fan it until the temperature stops changing.

6. Make wet-bulb and dry-bulb temperature measurements for air in your classroom and air outside. On a separate sheet of paper, make a copy of Data Table 3. Record your measurements. Use your measurements and Data Table 2 to determine the relative humidity inside and outside. You might also need to refer to Appendix F in the Relative Humidity Chart, on page 747.

Data Table 1 Relative Humidity Determination Based on Water Vapor Content			
Air Temperature (°C)	Water Vapor Content (g/kg)	Water Vapor Capacity (g/kg)	Relative Humidity (%)
25	5	20	25
25	12		
25	18		

Data Table 2 Relative Humidity (percent)

Dry-bulb Temperature (°C)	Depression of Wet-bulb Temperature (Dry-bulb Temperature − Wet-bulb Temperature = Depression of the Wet Bulb)																					
	1	2	3	4	5	6	7	8	9	10	11	12	13	14	15	16	17	18	19	20	21	22
−20	28																					
−18	40																					
−16	48	0																				
−14	55	11																				
−12	61	23																				
−10	66	33	0																			
−8	71	41	13																			
−6	73	48	20	0																		
−4	77	54	43	11																		
−2	79	58	37	20	1																	
0	81	63	45	28	11																	
2	83	67	51	36	20	6																
4	85	70	56	42	27	14																
6	86	72	59	46	35	22	10	0														
8	87	74	62	51	39	28	17	6														
10	88	76	65	54	43	33	24	13	4													
12	88	78	67	57	48	38	28	19	10	2												
14	89	79	69	60	50	41	33	25	16	8	1											
16	90	80	71	62	54	45	37	29	21	14	7	1										
18	91	81	72	64	56	48	40	33	26	19	12	6	0									
20	91	82	74	66	58	51	44	36	30	23	17	11	5	0								
22	92	83	75	68	60	53	46	40	33	27	21	15	10	4	0							
24	92	84	76	69	62	55	49	42	36	30	25	20	14	9	4	0						
26	92	85	77	70	64	57	51	45	39	34	28	23	18	13	9	5						
28	93	86	78	71	65	59	53	47	42	36	31	26	21	17	12	8	2					
30	93	86	79	72	66	61	55	49	44	39	34	29	25	20	16	12	8	4				
32	93	86	80	73	68	62	56	51	46	41	36	32	27	22	19	14	11	8	4			
34	93	86	81	74	69	63	58	52	48	43	38	34	30	26	22	18	14	11	8	5		
36	94	87	81	75	69	64	59	54	50	44	40	36	32	28	24	21	17	13	10	7	4	
38	94	87	82	76	70	66	60	55	51	46	42	38	34	30	26	23	20	16	13	10	7	5
40	94	89	82	76	71	67	61	57	52	48	44	40	36	33	29	25	22	19	16	13	10	7

Relative Humidity Values

Data Table 3 Relative Humidity Determinations Using Dry- and Wet-Bulb Thermometers

	Inside	Outside
Dry-bulb temperature (°C)		
Wet-bulb temperature (°C)		
Difference between dry-bulb and wet-bulb temperatures (°C)		
Relative humidity (%)		

Analyze and Conclude

1. **Comparing and Contrasting** How do the relative humidity measurements for inside and outside compare? Why are your determinations similar or different?

2. **Applying Concepts** Explain the principle behind using a psychrometer to determine relative humidity.

3. **Applying Concepts** Suppose you hear on the radio that the relative humidity is 90 percent on a winter day. Can you conclude that this air contains more moisture than air on a summer day with a 40 percent relative humidity? Explain why or why not.

4. **Applying Concepts** Why is a cool basement often damp in the summer?

18.1 Water in the Atmosphere

Key Concepts

- Water vapor is the most important gas in the atmosphere for understanding atmospheric processes.
- The process of changing state requires that energy is transferred in the form of heat.
- When saturated, warm air contains more water vapor than cold air.
- Relative humidity is a ratio of the air's actual water-vapor content compared with the amount of water vapor needed for saturation at that temperature and pressure.
- When the water-vapor content of air remains constant, lowering air temperature causes an increase in relative humidity, and raising air temperature causes a decrease in relative humidity.

Vocabulary

precipitation, *p. 504;* latent heat, *p. 505;* evaporation, *p. 505;* condensation, *p. 506;* sublimation, *p. 506;* deposition, *p. 506;* humidity, *p. 506;* saturated, *p. 506;* relative humidity, *p. 506;* dew point, *p. 508;* hygrometer, *p. 508*

18.2 Cloud Formation

Key Concepts

- When air is allowed to expand, it cools, and when it is compressed, it warms.
- Four mechanisms that can cause air to rise are orographic lifting, frontal wedging, convergence, and localized convective lifting.
- Stable air tends to remain in its original position, while unstable air tends to rise.
- For condensation of water to occur, the air must be saturated.

Vocabulary

dry adiabatic rate, *p. 511;* wet adiabatic rate, *p. 511;* orographic lifting, *p. 512;* front, *p. 512;* temperature inversion, *p. 514;* condensation nuclei, *p. 516*

18.3 Cloud Types and Precipitation

Key Concepts

- Clouds are classified on the basis of their form and height.
- Fog is a cloud with its base at or very near the ground.
- In order for precipitation to form, cloud droplets must grow in volume by roughly one million times.
- The type of precipitation that reaches Earth's surface depends on the temperature profile in the lowest few kilometers of the atmosphere.

Vocabulary

cirrus, *p. 517;* cumulus, *p. 517;* stratus, *p. 518;* Bergeron process, *p. 521;* supercooled water, *p. 521;* supersaturated air, *p. 521;* collision-coalescence process, *p. 521*

Thinking Visually

Concept Map Copy the concept map below onto a sheet of paper. Use information from the chapter to complete the concept map.

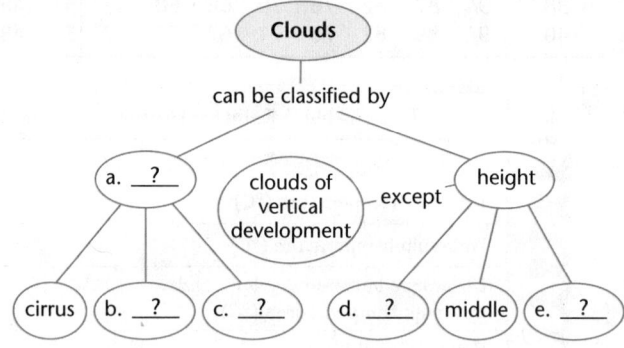

Reviewing Content

Choose the letter that best answers the question or completes the statement.

1. What is the general term for water vapor in air?
   a. capacity
   b. condensation
   c. humidity
   d. saturation

2. During which process does water vapor change to the liquid state?
   a. condensation
   b. deposition
   c. melting
   d. sublimation

3. The ratio of air's actual water-vapor content to the amount of water needed for saturation is the
   a. adiabatic rate.
   b. dew point.
   c. relative humidity.
   d. water capacity.

4. What are visible mixtures of tiny water droplets or ice crystals suspended in air?
   a. clouds
   b. dew
   c. hail
   d. sleet

5. Air that has a 100 percent relative humidity is said to be
   a. dry.
   b. saturated.
   c. stable.
   d. unstable.

6. Compared to clouds, fogs are
   a. a different composition.
   b. at lower altitudes.
   c. colder.
   d. thicker.

7. Which of the following clouds are high, white, and thin?
   a. cirrus
   b. cumulus
   c. nimbostratus
   d. stratus

8. Which of the following words means "rainy cloud"?
   a. cirrus
   b. cumulus
   c. nimbus
   d. stratus

9. Which of the following substances changes from one state of matter to another at temperatures and pressures experienced at Earth's surface?
   a. carbon dioxide
   b. nitrogen
   c. oxygen
   d. water

10. Which of the following forms when supercooled raindrops freeze on contact with solid objects near Earth's surface?
    a. freezing rain
    b. hail
    c. sleet
    d. snow

Understanding Concepts

11. What happens when unstable air is forced to rise?

12. Describe the conditions that might cause convergence.

13. As you drink an ice-cold beverage on a hot day, the outside of the glass becomes wet. Explain why this happens.

14. What is the difference between condensation and precipitation?

15. Why does air cool when it rises through the atmosphere? What is this type of cooling known as?

16. Write a general statement relating air temperature and the amount of water vapor needed to saturate the air.

17. Describe the difference between clouds and water vapor.

18. List two changes of state for water that cause latent heat to be released.

Use the figure below to answer Questions 19 and 20.

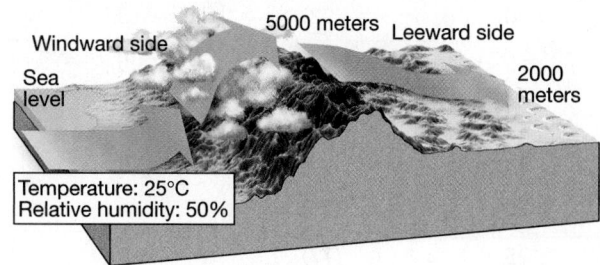

19. Which air-lifting mechanism is shown?

20. Use the dry adiabatic rate of 10°C per kilometer to determine the air temperature on the windward side of the mountains at an altitude of 500 meters.

Critical Thinking

21. Applying Concepts What is the physical property of thermals that helps birds of prey? Describe how this physical property helps these birds.

22. Applying Concepts Explain how urban areas contribute to localized convective lifting.

23. Identifying Cause and Effect Describe how atmospheric stability affects daily weather. Include specific examples.

24. Applying Concepts In general, when traveling in foggy conditions, what types of topography should you be most cautious of?

Math Skills

Use the table below to answer Questions 25–27.

Water Vapor Needed for Saturation

Temperature		Mass of water vapor per kg of air (g/kg)
°C	(°F)	
−40	(−40)	0.1
−30	(−22)	0.3
−20	(−4)	0.75
−10	(14)	2
0	(32)	3.5
5	(41)	5
10	(50)	7
15	(59)	10
20	(68)	14
25	(77)	20
30	(86)	26.5
35	(95)	35
40	(104)	47

25. Analyzing Data According to the table, how much water vapor is required to saturate a kilogram of air at each of the following temperatures?
    a. 40°C
    b. 0°C
    c. −10°C

26. Calculating How does the amount of water vapor required to saturate 1 kilogram of air change when it is cooled from 10°C to 0°C?

27. Calculating Use the table to determine the relative humidity of air at 15°C when its water vapor content is 7 g/kg.

Concepts in Action

28. Inferring Mount Waialeale, Hawaii, is located on a windward mountain slope. A weather station there records the highest average annual rainfall at 1234 cm. Explain what processes could contribute to this extreme rainfall.

29. Interpreting Illustrations After studying Figure 2, summarize the processes by which water changes from one state of matter to another. For each case, point out whether heat energy is absorbed or released.

30. Writing in Science The amount of precipitation that falls at any particular place and time is controlled by the quantity of moisture in the air and many other factors, which may include (1) an increase in the elevation of the land, (2) a decrease in the area covered by forests and other types of vegetation, and (3) an increase in the percentage of time that the winds blow from an adjacent body of water. Write a paragraph explaining how each of these factors might change the precipitation at a particular location.

Performance-Based Assessment

Designing an Experiment Design and conduct an experiment that explores daily variations in temperature and relative humidity. As a first step, write a clear hypothesis statement. Then plan and design the experiment. Include sample data tables in your plan. Have your teacher approve your plan before you begin.

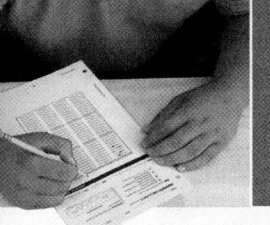

Standardized Test Prep

Test-Taking Tip

When answering a question with a graph, keep these tips in mind:

- Read the question thoroughly to identify what the question is asking.
- Study the title of the graph. This may help you identify what information is available from the graph.
- Examine the graph and note the axes labels.
- Identify the scale of the axes.
- Recall information, equations, definitions, relationship, and so forth that may be required to interpret the graph.
- Once you have chosen your answer, check it against the graph.

Graph 1 Temperature and Relative Humidity

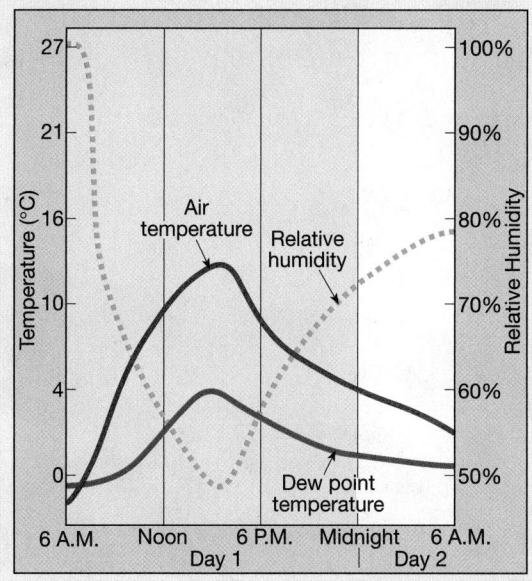

The graph above depicts variations in temperature and relative humidity on a spring day. Which of the following statements is true?

(A) When temperature increases, relative humidity increases.

(B) When temperature decreases, relative humidity decreases.

(C) When temperature increases, relative humidity decreases.

(D) Temperature and relative humidity are not related.

(Answer: C)

Choose the letter that best answers the question or completes the statement.

1. The dew point is the temperature at which
   (A) cumulus clouds change to cirrus clouds.
   (B) hailstones are formed.
   (C) liquid water changes to vapor.
   (D) air becomes saturated with water vapor.

2. Which process is most important for cloud formation?
   (A) cooling by compression of air
   (B) cooling by contact with a cold surface
   (C) cooling by expansion of air
   (D) cooling by radiation from Earth's surface

3. The process by which water vapor changes directly to a solid is
   (A) condensation.
   (B) deposition
   (C) evaporation.
   (D) sublimation.

Use the graph below to answer Questions 4–5.

Graph 2 Temperature and Relative Humidity

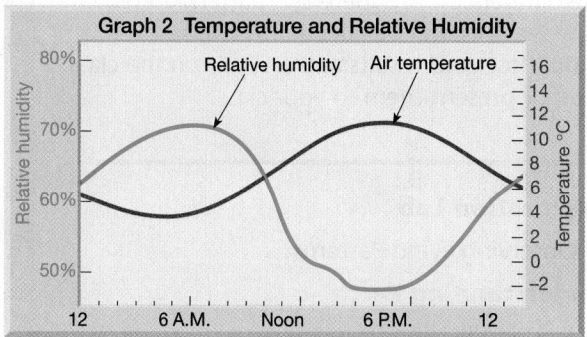

4. According to this graph, when is relative humidity at its maximum?

5. When does the lowest relative humidity occur?

CHAPTER 19 Air Pressure and Wind

21st Century Learning

Problem Identification, Formulation, and Solution

What effects has El Niño had on your weather?

El Niño affects winter weather in North America and occurs roughly every 2 to 7 years. The winters of 1972–73, 1982–83, and 1997–98 had extreme El Niños. Use the Internet to find out how El Niño may have affected the winter weather where you live. First look up the average monthly winter temperatures and precipitation during two of the El Niño years listed above. Then look up the same data for four non- El Niño years. Make a table to show the differences. Are there any patterns? Predict how weather will be affected by the next El Niño. Post your results and analysis on the class blog or present them to your class.

Exploration Lab

Observing Wind Patterns

Understanding Earth

Tracking El Niño from Space

GEODe Earth Science

The Atmosphere
↳ Air Pressure and Wind

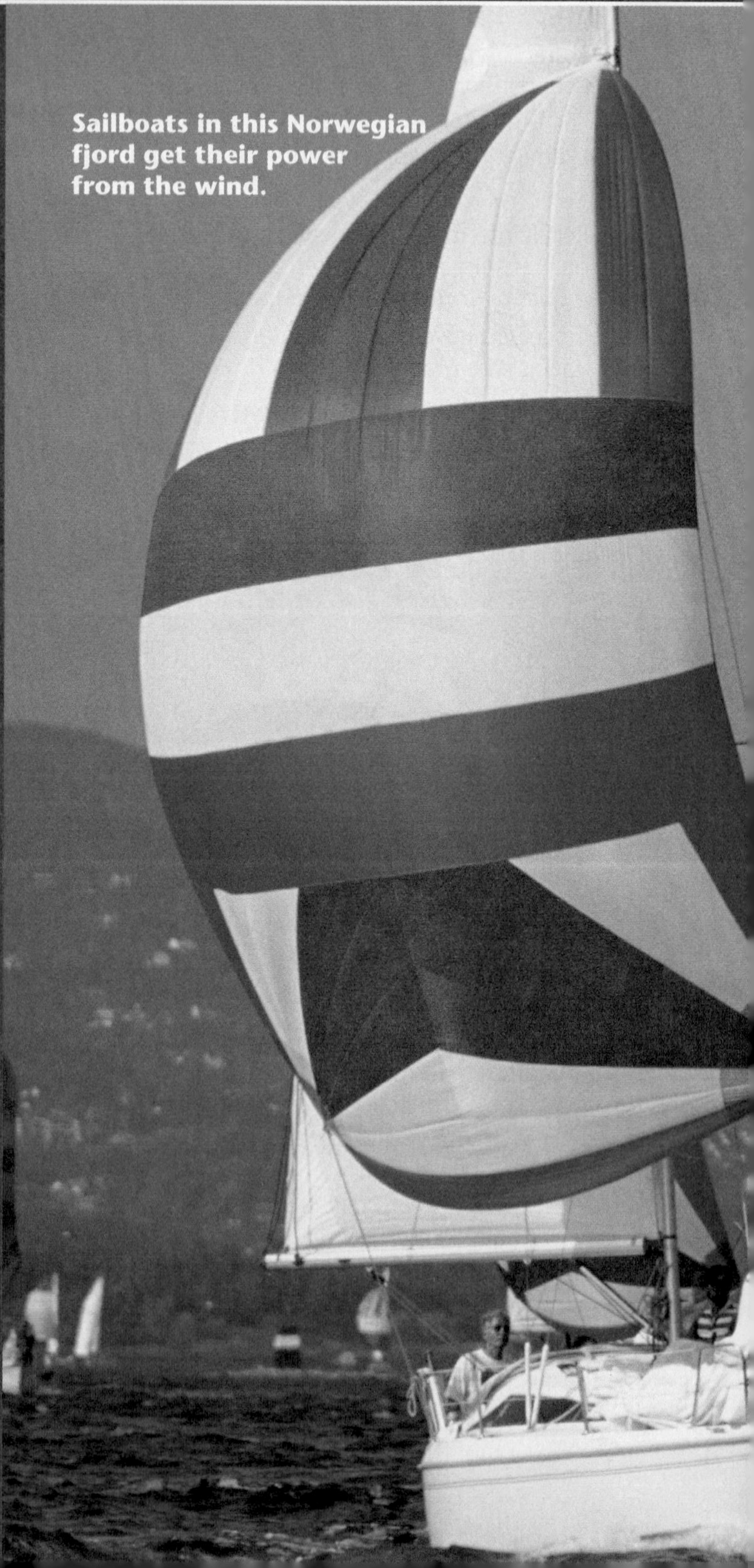

Sailboats in this Norwegian fjord get their power from the wind.

Chapter Preview

Inquiry Activity

How Do Gradients Influence Speed?

Procedure

1. Build a steep ramp using textbooks, wood blocks, or other items in your classroom. Roll a tennis ball down the ramp.

2. Now build another ramp. This ramp should have a slope, or gradient, that is much less steep. Keep the length of the ramp the same as in step 1.

3. Roll the tennis ball down the second ramp. Compare the speeds of the ball for both ramps.

Think About It

1. **Observing** Which ramp setup caused the ball to roll the fastest?

2. **Applying Concepts** Like the ramps you built, air pressure also forms gradients. Wind is air that flows down the "slopes" of air pressure gradients. What air pressure conditions do you think would favor faster wind speeds?

19.1 Understanding Air Pressure

Reading Focus

Key Concepts

- Describe how air pressure is exerted on objects.
- What happens to the mercury column of a barometer when air pressure changes?
- What is the ultimate energy source for wind?
- How does the Coriolis effect influence free-moving objects?

Vocabulary

- ◆ air pressure
- ◆ barometer
- ◆ pressure gradient
- ◆ Coriolis effect
- ◆ jet stream

Reading Strategy

Identifying Main Ideas Copy the table below. As you read, write the main ideas for each topic.

Topic	Main Ideas
Air Pressure Defined	Air pressure is the weight of air above. It is exerted in all directions.
Measuring Air Pressure	a. ____?____
Factors Affecting Wind	b. ____?____

Figure 1 These palm trees in Corpus Christi, Texas, are buffeted by hurricane-force winds.

For: Measuring Air Pressure Activity
Visit: PHSchool.com
Web Code: czp-6191

Of the various elements of weather and climate, changes in air pressure are the least noticeable. When you listen to a weather report, you probably focus on precipitation, temperature, and humidity. Most people don't wonder about air pressure. Although you might not perceive hour-to-hour and day-to-day variations in air pressure, they are very important in producing changes in our weather. For example, variations in air pressure from place to place can generate winds like those shown in Figure 1. The winds, in turn, bring change in temperature and humidity. Air pressure is one of the basic weather elements and is an important factor in weather forecasting. Air pressure is closely tied to the other elements of weather in a cause-and-effect relationship.

Air Pressure Defined

Air pressure is simply the pressure exerted by the weight of air above. Average air pressure at sea level is about 1 kilogram per square centimeter. This pressure is roughly the same pressure that is produced by a column of water 10 meters in height. You can calculate that the air pressure exerted on the top of a 50-centimeter-by-100-centimeter school desk exceeds 5000 kilograms, which is about the mass of a 50-passenger school bus. Why doesn't the desk collapse under the weight of the air above it? **Air pressure is exerted in all directions—down, up, and sideways. The air pressure pushing down on an object balances the air pressure pushing up on the object.**

Reading Checkpoint *What is average air pressure at sea level?*

Imagine a tall aquarium that has the same dimensions as the desktop in the previous example. When this aquarium is filled to a height of 10 meters, the water pressure at the bottom equals 1 atmosphere, or 1 kilogram per square centimeter. Now imagine what will happen if this aquarium is placed on top of a student desk so that all the force is directed downward. The desk collapses because the pressure downward is greater than the pressure exerted in the other directions. When the desk is placed inside the aquarium and allowed to sink to the bottom, however, the desk does not collapse in the water because the water pressure is exerted in all directions, not just downward. The desk, like your body, is built to withstand the pressure of 1 atmosphere.

Measuring Air Pressure

When meteorologists measure atmospheric pressure, they use a unit called the millibar. Standard sea-level pressure is 1013.2 millibars. You might have heard the phrase "inches of mercury," which is used by the media to describe atmospheric pressure. This expression dates from 1643, when Torricelli, a student of the famous Italian scientist Galileo, invented the mercury barometer. A **barometer** is a device used for measuring air pressure (*bar* = pressure, *metron* = measuring instrument).

Torricelli correctly described the atmosphere as a vast ocean of air that exerts pressure on us and all objects around us. To measure this force, he filled a glass tube, closed at one end, with mercury. He then put the tube upside down into a dish of mercury, as shown in Figure 2A. The mercury flowed out of the tube until the weight of the column was balanced by the pressure that the atmosphere exerted on the surface of the mercury in the dish. In other words, the weight of mercury in the column (tube) equaled the weight of the same size column of air that extended from the ground to the top of the atmosphere.

When air pressure increases, the mercury in the tube rises. When air pressure decreases, so does the height of the mercury column. With some improvements, the mercury barometer is still the standard instrument used today for measuring air pressure.

The need for a smaller and more portable instrument for measuring air pressure led to the development of the aneroid barometer. The aneroid barometer uses a metal chamber with some air removed. This partially emptied chamber is extremely sensitive to variations in air pressure. It changes shape and compresses as the air pressure increases, and it expands as the pressure decreases. One advantage of the aneroid barometer is that it can be easily connected to a recording device, shown in Figure 2B. The device provides a continuous record of pressure changes with the passage of time.

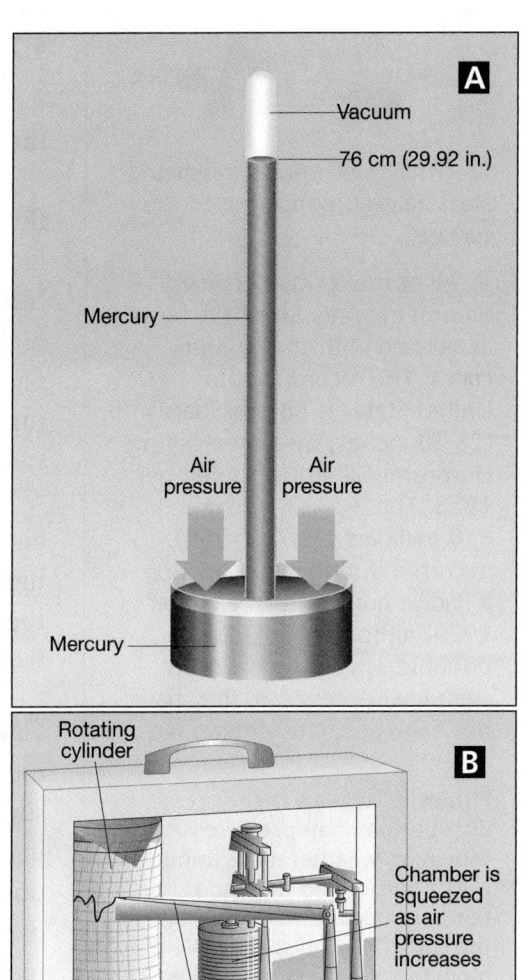

Figure 2 **A Mercury Barometer** Standard atmospheric pressure at sea level is 29.92 inches of mercury. **B Aneroid Barometer** The recording mechanism provides a continuous record of pressure changes over time. **Applying Concepts** *Why would a continuous record help weather forecasters?*

For: Links on atmospheric pressure
Visit: www.SciLinks.org
Web Code: cjn-6191

Q *What is the lowest barometric pressure ever recorded at Earth's surface?*

A All of the lowest recorded barometric pressures have been associated with strong hurricanes. The record for the United States is 888 millibars (26.20 inches) measured during Hurricane Gilbert in September 1988. The world's record, 870 millibars (25.70 inches), occurred during Typhoon Tip, a Pacific hurricane, in October 1979. Although tornadoes undoubtedly have produced even lower pressures, they have not been accurately measured.

Figure 3 Isobars The distribution of air pressure is shown on weather maps using isobar lines. Wind flags and feathers indicate wind speed (ff is the code for wind speed). Winds blow toward the station circles. **Interpreting Visuals** *Use the data on this map to explain which pressure cell, high or low, has the fastest wind speeds.*

Factors Affecting Wind

As important as vertical motion is, far more air moves horizontally, the phenomenon we call wind. What causes wind?

Wind is the result of horizontal differences in air pressure. Air flows from areas of higher pressure to areas of lower pressure. You may have experienced this flow of air when opening a vacuum-packed can of coffee or tennis balls. The noise you hear is caused by air rushing from the higher pressure outside the can to the lower pressure inside. Wind is nature's way of balancing such inequalities in air pressure. **The unequal heating of Earth's surface generates pressure differences. Solar radiation is the ultimate energy source for most wind.**

If Earth did not rotate, and if there were no friction between moving air and Earth's surface, air would flow in a straight line from areas of higher pressure to areas of lower pressure. But both factors do exist, so the flow of air is not that simple. **Three factors combine to control wind: pressure differences, the Coriolis effect, and friction.**

Pressure Differences Wind is created by differences in pressure—the greater these differences are, the greater the wind speed is. Over Earth's surface, variations in air pressure are determined from barometric readings taken at hundreds of weather stations. These pressure data are shown on a weather map, like the one in Figure 3, using isobars. Isobars are lines on a map that connect places of equal air pressure. The spacing of isobars indicates the amount of pressure change occurring over a given distance. These pressure changes are expressed as the **pressure gradient**.

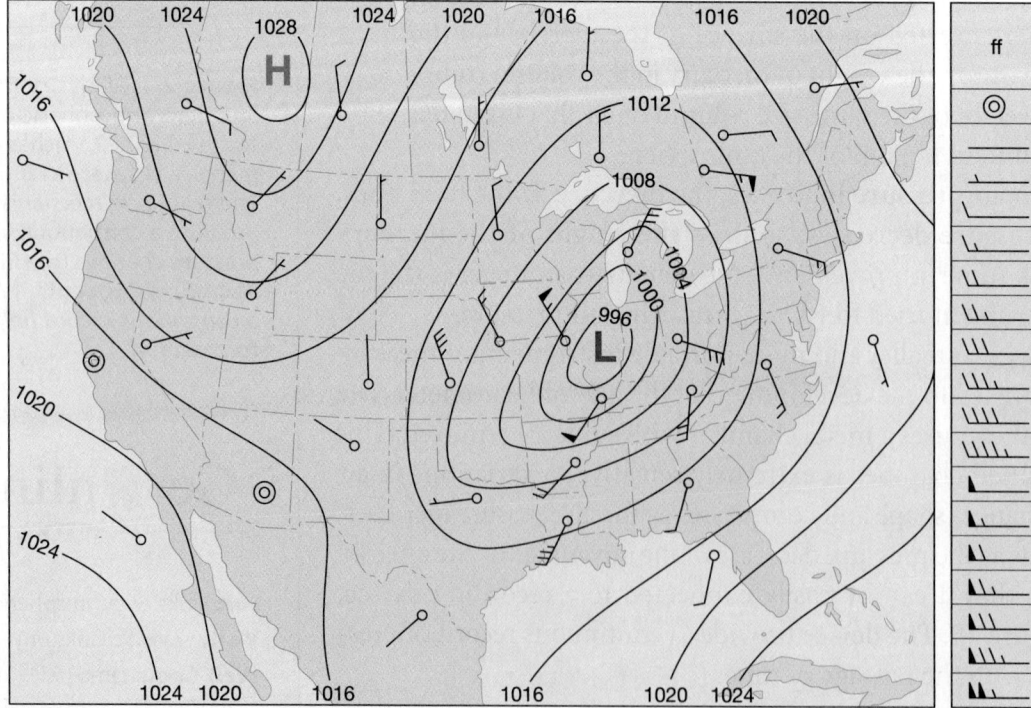

ff	Miles per hour
◎	Calm
⎯	1–2
⎬	3–8
⎬	9–14
⎬	15–20
⎬	21–25
⎬	26–31
⎬	32–37
⎬	38–43
⎬	44–49
⎬	50–54
⎬	55–60
⎬	61–66
⎬	67–71
⎬	72–77
⎬	78–83
⎬	84–89
⎬	119–123

A steep pressure gradient, like a steep hill, causes greater acceleration of a parcel of air. A less steep pressure gradient causes a slower acceleration. ⬤**Closely spaced isobars indicate a steep pressure gradient and high winds. Widely spaced isobars indicate a weak pressure gradient and light winds.** The pressure gradient is the driving force of wind. The pressure gradient has both magnitude and direction. Its magnitude is reflected in the spacing of isobars. The direction of force is always from areas of higher pressure to areas of lower pressure and at right angles to the isobars. Friction affects wind speed and direction. The Coriolis effect affects wind direction only.

Coriolis Effect The weather map in Figure 3 shows typical air movements associated with high- and low-pressure systems. Air moves out of the regions of higher pressure and into the regions of lower pressure. However, the wind does not cross the isobars at right angles as you would expect based solely on the pressure gradient. This change in movement results from Earth's rotation and has been named the Coriolis effect.

⬤**The Coriolis effect describes how Earth's rotation affects moving objects. All free-moving objects or fluids, including the wind, are deflected to the right of their path of motion in the Northern Hemisphere. In the Southern Hemisphere, they are deflected to the left.** The reason for this deflection is illustrated in Figure 4. Imagine the path of a rocket launched from the North Pole toward a target located on the equator. The true path of this rocket is straight, and the path would appear to be straight to someone out in space looking down at Earth. However, to someone standing on Earth, it would look as if the rocket swerved off its path and landed 15 degrees to the west of its target.

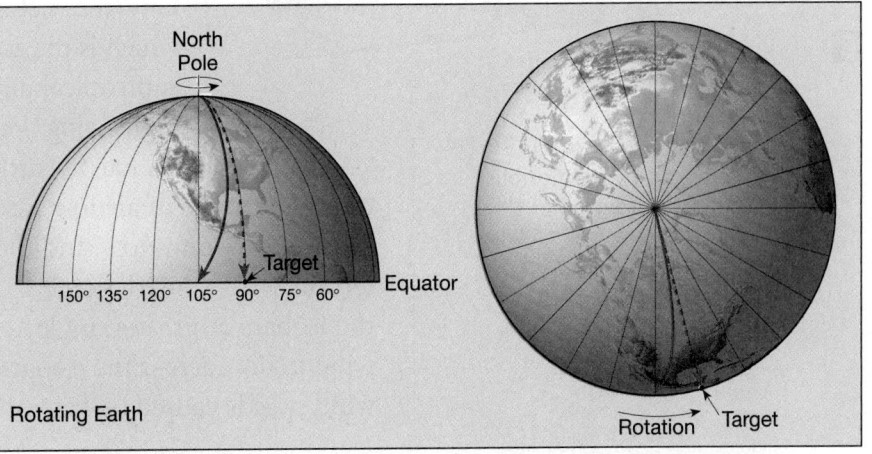

This slight change in direction happens because Earth would have rotated 15 degrees to the east under the rocket during a one-hour flight. The counterclockwise rotation of the Northern Hemisphere causes path deflection to the right. In the Southern Hemisphere, the clockwise rotation produces a similar deflection, but to the left of the path of motion.

The apparent shift in wind direction is attributed to the Coriolis effect. This deflection: 1) is always directed at right angles to the direction of airflow; 2) affects only wind direction and not wind speed; 3) is affected by wind speed—the stronger the wind, the greater the deflection; and 4) is strongest at the poles and weakens toward the equator, becoming nonexistent at the equator.

Figure 4 The Coriolis Effect Because Earth rotates 15° each hour, the rocket's path is curved and veers to the right from the North Pole to the equator. **Calculating** *How many degrees does Earth rotate in one day?*

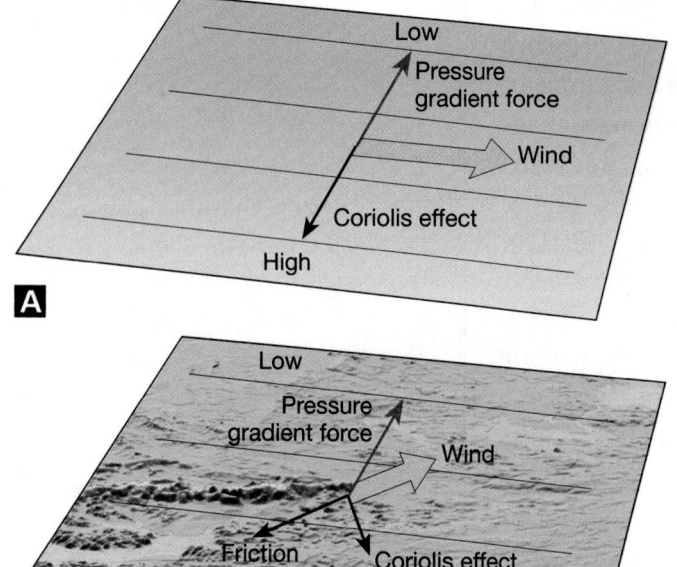

A

B

Figure 5 A Upper-level wind flow is balanced by the Coriolis effect and pressure gradient forces. **B** Friction causes surface winds to cross isobars and move toward lower pressure areas.

Friction The effect of friction on wind is important only within a few kilometers of Earth's surface. Friction acts to slow air movement, which changes wind direction. To illustrate friction's effect on wind direction, first think about a situation in which friction does not play a role in wind's direction.

When air is above the friction layer, the pressure gradient causes air to move across the isobars. As soon as air starts to move, the Coriolis effect acts at right angles to this motion. The faster the wind speed, the greater the deflection is. The pressure gradient and Coriolis effect balance in high-altitude air, and wind generally flows parallel to isobars, as shown in Figure 5A. The most prominent features of airflow high above the friction layer are the jet streams. **Jet streams** are fast-moving rivers of air near the tropopause that travel between 120 and 240 kilometers per hour in a west-to-east direction. One such jet stream is situated over the polar front, which is the zone separating cool polar air from warm subtropical air. Jet streams were first encountered by high-flying bombers during World War II.

For air close to Earth's surface, the roughness of the terrain determines the angle of airflow across the isobars. Over the smooth ocean surface, friction is low, and the angle of airflow is small. Over rugged terrain, where the friction is higher, winds move more slowly and cross the isobars at greater angles. As shown in Figure 5B, friction causes wind to flow across the isobars at angles as great as 45 degrees. Slower wind speeds caused by friction decrease the Coriolis effect.

Section 19.1 Assessment

Reviewing Concepts

1. Why don't objects such as a table collapse under the weight of air above them?

2. Suppose the height of a column in a mercury barometer is decreasing. What is happening?

3. What is the ultimate energy source for most wind?

4. How does the Coriolis effect influence motion of free-moving objects?

5. Why do jet streams flow parallel to isobars?

Critical Thinking

6. **Interpreting Illustrations** Study Figures 5A and 5B. Why are the wind arrows drawn to different lengths in these figures?

Connecting ⊂ Concepts

Solar Radiation Review section 17.3. Describe examples of unequal heating of Earth's atmosphere that could lead to air pressure differences that ultimately influence wind.

19.2 Pressure Centers and Winds

Reading Focus

Key Concepts

- Describe how winds blow around pressure centers in the Northern and Southern Hemispheres.

- What are the air pressure patterns within cyclones and anticyclones?

- How does friction control net flow of air around a cyclone and an anticylone?

- How does the atmosphere attempt to balance the unequal heating of Earth's surface?

Vocabulary

- cyclone
- anticyclone
- trade winds
- westerlies
- polar easterlies
- polar front
- monsoon

Reading Strategy

Comparing and Contrasting Copy the table below. As you read about pressure centers and winds, fill in the table indicating to which hemisphere the concept applies. Use N for Northern Hemisphere, S for Southern Hemisphere, and B for both.

Cyclones rotate counterclockwise.	a. _____?_____
Net flow of air is inward around a cyclone.	b. _____?_____
Anticyclones rotate counterclockwise.	c. _____?_____
Coriolis effect deflects winds to the right.	d. _____?_____

Pressure centers are among the most common features on any weather map. By knowing just a few basic facts about centers of high and low pressure, you can increase your understanding of present and forthcoming weather. You can make some weather generalizations based on pressure centers. For example, centers of low pressure are frequently associated with cloudy conditions and precipitation. By contrast, clear skies and fair weather may be expected when an area is under the influence of high pressure, as shown in Figure 6.

Figure 6 These sunbathers at Cape Henlopen, Delaware, are enjoying weather associated with a high-pressure center.

Highs and Lows

Lows, or **cyclones** (*kyklon* = moving in a circle) are centers of low pressure. Highs, or **anticyclones,** are centers of high pressure. **In cyclones, the pressure decreases from the outer isobars toward the center. In anticyclones, just the opposite is the case—the values of the isobars increase from the outside toward the center.**

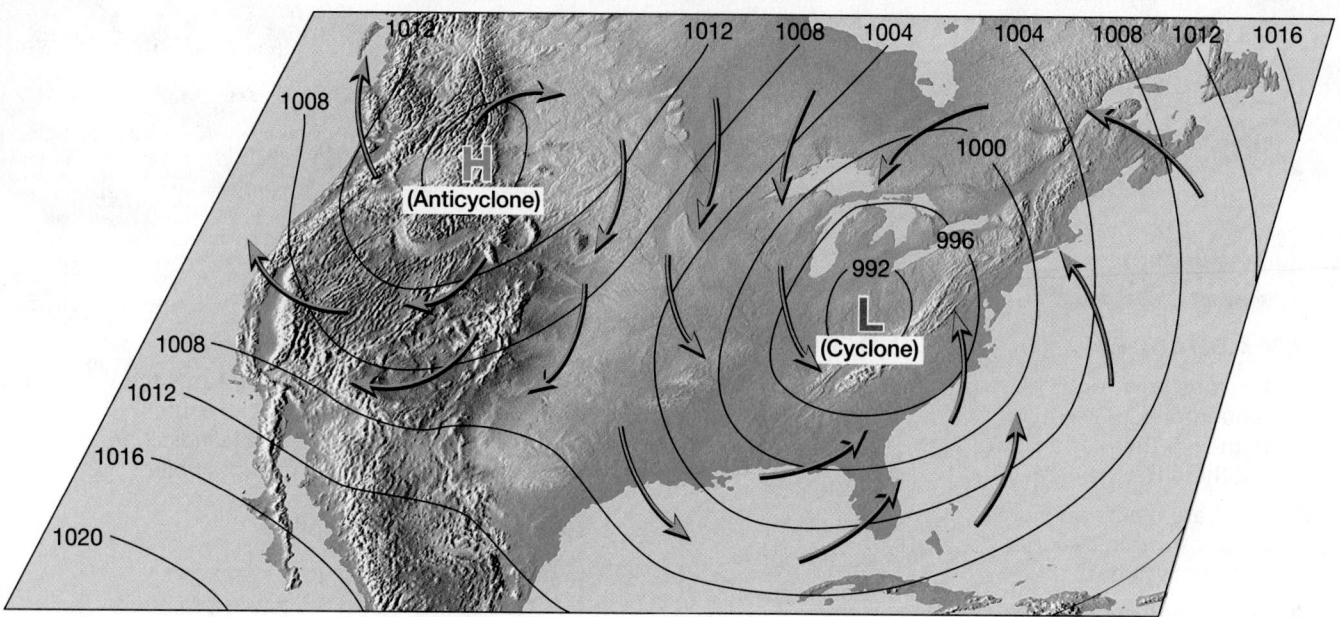

Figure 7 This map shows cyclonic and anticyclonic winds in the Northern Hemisphere. Pressure is measured in millibars.

Cyclonic and Anticyclonic Winds You learned that the two most significant factors that affect wind are the pressure gradient and the Coriolis effect. Winds move from higher pressure to lower pressure and are deflected to the right or left by Earth's rotation. **When the pressure gradient and the Coriolis effect are applied to pressure centers in the Northern Hemisphere, winds blow counterclockwise around a low. Around a high, they blow clockwise.** Notice the wind directions in Figure 7.

In the Southern Hemisphere, the Coriolis effect deflects the winds to the left. Therefore, winds around a low move clockwise. Winds around a high move counterclockwise. **In either hemisphere, friction causes a net flow of air inward around a cyclone and a net flow of air outward around an anticyclone.**

Weather and Air Pressure Rising air is associated with cloud formation and precipitation, whereas sinking air produces clear skies.

Imagine a surface low-pressure system where the air is spiraling inward. Here the net inward movement of air causes the area occupied by the air mass to shrink—a process called horizontal convergence. Whenever air converges (or comes together) horizontally, it must increase in height to allow for the decreased area it now occupies. This increase in height produces a taller and heavier air column. A surface low can exist only as long as the column of air above it exerts less pressure than does the air in surrounding regions. This seems to be a paradox—a low-pressure center causes a net accumulation of air, which increases its pressure.

Reading Checkpoint *With what type of weather is rising air associated?*

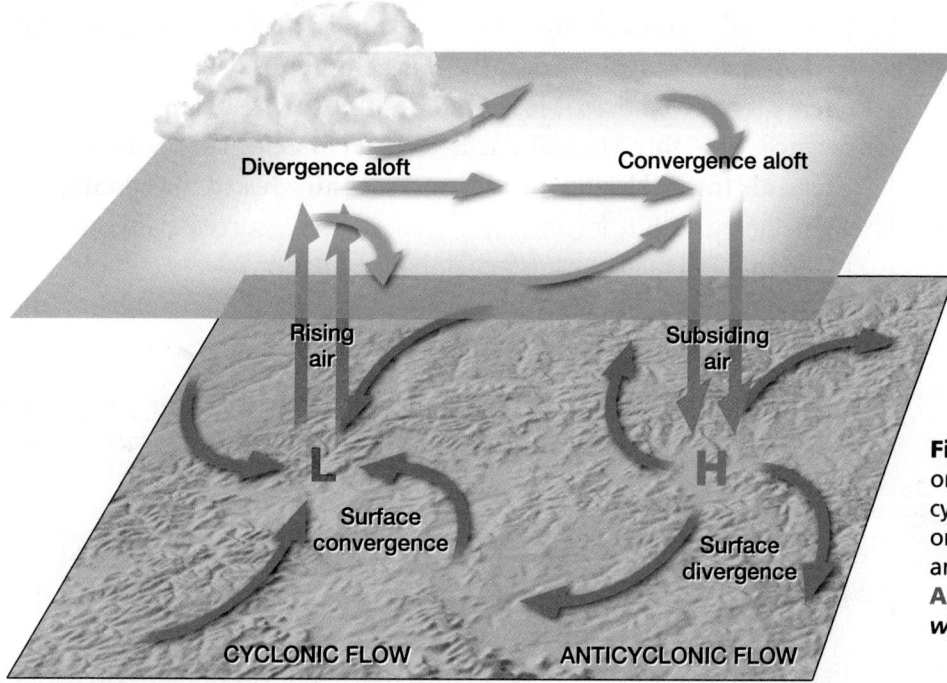

Figure 8 Air spreads out, or diverges, above surface cyclones, and comes together, or converges, above surface anticyclones.
Applying Concepts *Why is fair weather associated with a high?*

In order for a surface low to exist for very long, converging air at the surface must be balanced by outflows aloft. For example, surface convergence could be maintained if divergence, or the spreading out of air, occurred above the low at a rate equal to the inflow below. Figure 8 shows the relationship between surface convergence (inflow) and divergence (outflow) needed to maintain a low-pressure center. Surface convergence around a cyclone causes a net upward movement. Because rising air often results in cloud formation and precipitation, a low-pressure center is generally related to unstable conditions and stormy weather.

Like cyclones, anticyclones also must be maintained from above. Outflow near the surface is accompanied by convergence in the air above and a general sinking of the air column, as shown in Figure 8.

Weather Forecasting Now you can see why weather reports emphasize the locations and possible paths of cyclones and anticyclones. The villain in these reports is always the low-pressure center, which can produce bad weather in any season. Lows move in roughly a west-to-east direction across the United States, and they require a few days, and sometimes more than a week, for the journey. Their paths can be somewhat unpredictable, making accurate estimation of their movement difficult. Because surface conditions are linked to the conditions of the air above, it is important to understand total atmospheric circulation.

For: Links on weather forecasting
Visit: PHSchool.com
Web Code: czd-6192

Global Winds

The underlying cause of wind is the unequal heating of Earth's surface. In tropical regions, more solar radiation is received than is radiated back to space. In regions near the poles the opposite is true—less solar energy is received than is lost. ⊙ **The atmosphere balances these differences by acting as a giant heat-transfer system. This system moves warm air toward high latitudes and cool air toward the equator.** On a smaller scale, but for the same reason, ocean currents also contribute to this global heat transfer. Global circulation is very complex, but you can begin to understand it by first thinking about circulation that would occur on a non-rotating Earth.

 *How does the atmosphere balance the unequal heating of Earth's surface?*

Non-Rotating Earth Model On a hypothetical non-rotating planet with a smooth surface of either all land or all water, two large thermally produced cells would form, as shown in Figure 9. The heated air at the equator would rise until it reached the tropopause—the boundary between the troposphere and the stratosphere. The tropopause, acting like a lid, would deflect this air toward the poles. Eventually, the upper-level airflow would reach the poles, sink, spread out in all directions at the surface, and move back toward the equator. Once at the equator, it would be reheated and begin its journey over again. This hypothetical circulation system has upper-level air flowing toward the pole and surface air flowing toward the equator.

Rotating Earth Model If the effect of rotation were added to the global circulation model, the two-cell convection system would break down into smaller cells. Figure 10 illustrates the three pairs of cells that would carry on the task of redistributing heat on Earth. The polar and tropical cells retain the characteristics of the thermally generated convection described earlier. The nature of circulation at the middle latitudes, however, is more complex.

Near the equator, rising air produces a pressure zone known as the equatorial low—a region characterized by abundant precipitation. As shown in Figure 10, the upper-level flow from the equatorial low reaches 20 to 30 degrees, north or south latitude, and then sinks back toward the surface. This sinking of air and its associated heating due

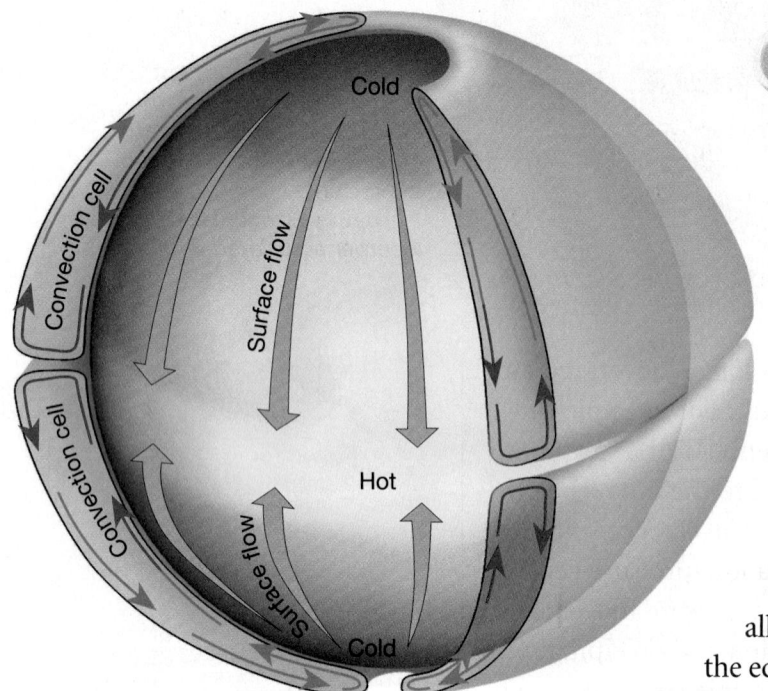

Figure 9 Circulation on a Non-Rotating Earth A simple convection system is produced by unequal heating of the atmosphere.
Relating Cause and Effect *Why would air sink after reaching the poles?*

to compression produce hot, arid conditions. The center of this zone of sinking dry air is the subtropical high, which encircles the globe near 30 degrees north and south latitude. The great deserts of Australia, Arabia, and the Sahara in North Africa exist because of the stable dry conditions associated with the subtropical highs.

At the surface, airflow moves outward from the center of the subtropical high. Some of the air travels toward the equator and is deflected by the Coriolis effect, producing the trade winds. **Trade winds** are two belts of winds that blow almost constantly from easterly directions. The trade winds are located between the subtropical highs and the equator. The remainder of the air travels toward the poles and is deflected, generating the prevailing **westerlies** of the middle latitudes. The westerlies make up the dominant west-to-east motion of the atmosphere that characterizes the regions on the poleward side of the subtropical highs. As the westerlies move toward the poles, they encounter the cool polar easterlies in the region of the subpolar low. The **polar easterlies** are winds that blow from the polar high toward the subpolar low. These winds are not constant winds like the trade winds. In the polar region, cold polar air sinks and spreads toward the equator. The interaction of these warm and cool air masses produces the stormy belt in the middle latitudes known as the **polar front.**

This simplified global circulation is dominated by four pressure zones. The subtropical and polar highs are areas of dry subsiding (sinking) air that flows outward at the surface, producing the prevailing winds. The low-pressure zones of the equatorial and subpolar regions are associated with inward and upward airflow accompanied by clouds and precipitation.

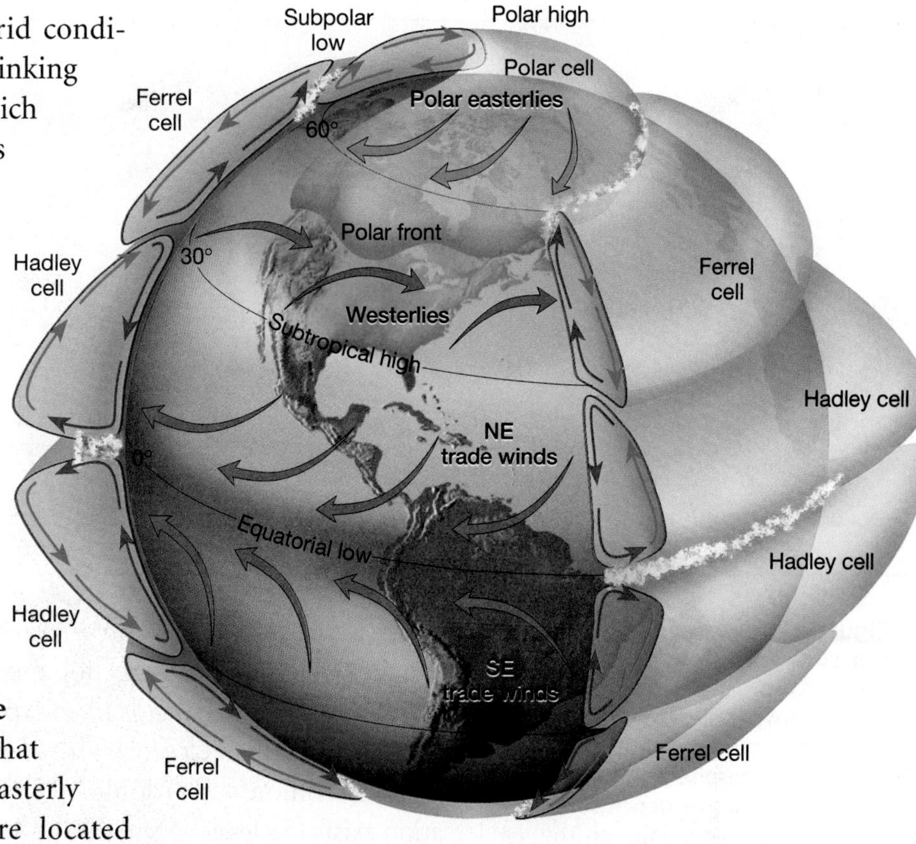

 **Reading Checkpoint** *What is the polar front?*

Figure 10 Circulation on a Rotating Earth This model of global air circulation proposes three pairs of cells.
Interpreting Diagrams *Describe the patterns of air circulation at the equatorial and subpolar lows.*

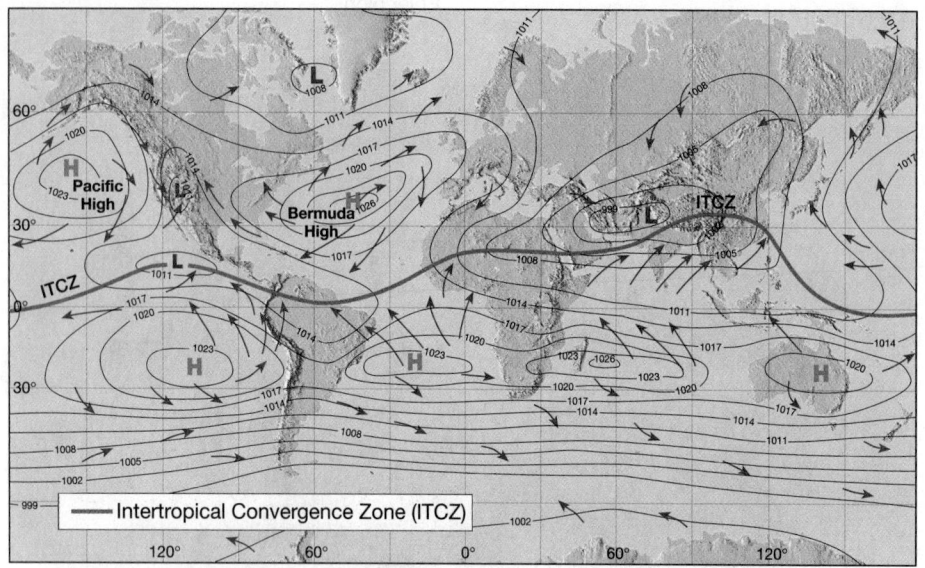

Figure 11 Average Surface Pressure and Global Circulation, July
In July, low-pressure cells develop over the continents in the Northern Hemisphere. Also, the Intertropical Convergence Zone moves north of the equator. The ITCZ is a zone of unstable air that forms along the equator where the northeast and southeast tradewinds converge.

Influence of Continents

Where landmasses break up the ocean surface, large seasonal temperature differences disrupt the global pattern of pressure zones in the atmosphere. Large landmasses, particularly in the Northern Hemisphere, become cold in the winter when a seasonal high-pressure system develops. From this high-pressure system, surface airflow is directed off the land. In the summer, landmasses are heated and develop low-pressure cells, which permit air to flow onto the land as shown in Figure 11. These seasonal changes in wind direction are known as the **monsoons.** During warm months, areas such as India experience a flow of warm, water-laden air from the Indian Ocean, which produces the rainy summer monsoon. The winter monsoon is dominated by dry continental air. A similar situation exists to a lesser extent during summer over North America. Rising, unstable air along the western side of the Bermuda High brings rain to the East Coast. At the same time, thunderstorms occur in the Southwest as moist air streams into the region from the Gulf of Mexico and the Gulf of California.

Section 19.2 Assessment

Reviewing Concepts

1. Describe how winds blow around pressure centers in the Northern Hemisphere.

2. Compare the air pressure for a cyclone with an anticyclone.

3. How does friction control the net flow of air around a cyclone and an anticyclone?

4. Describe how the atmosphere balances the unequal heating of Earth's surface.

5. What is the only truly continuous pressure belt? Why is it continuous?

6. In general, what type of weather can you expect if a low-pressure system is moving into your area?

Critical Thinking

7. **Identifying Cause and Effect** What must happen in the air above for divergence at the surface to be maintained? What type of pressure center accompanies surface divergence?

Math Practice

8. Examine Figure 7. What is the approximate range of barometric pressure indicated by the isobars on the map? What is the pressure interval between adjacent isobars?

19.3 Regional Wind Systems

Reading Focus

Key Concepts

- What causes local winds?
- Describe the general movement of weather in the United States.
- What happens when unusually strong, warm ocean currents flow along the coasts of Ecuador and Peru?
- How is a La Niña event triggered?

Vocabulary

- prevailing wind
- anemometer
- El Niño

Reading Strategy

Previewing Copy the table below. Before you read, use Figure 17 to locate examples of the driest and wettest regions on Earth. After you read, identify the dominant wind system for each location.

Precipitation	Location	Dominant Wind System
Extremely low	a. _____?_____	b. _____?_____
Extremely high	c. _____?_____	d. _____?_____

$\mathbf{C}$irculation in the middle latitudes is complex and does not fit the convection system described for the tropics. Between about 30 and 60 degrees latitude, the general west-to-east flow, known as the westerlies, is interrupted by migrating cyclones and anticyclones. In the Northern Hemisphere, these pressure cells move from west to east around the globe.

Local Winds

Small-scale winds produced by a locally generated pressure gradient are known as local winds. **The local winds are caused either by topographic effects or by variations in surface composition—land and water—in the immediate area.**

Land and Sea Breezes In coastal areas during the warm summer months, the land surface is heated more intensely during the daylight hours than an adjacent body of water is heated. As a result, the air above the land surface heats, expands, and rises, creating an area of lower pressure. As shown in Figure 12, a sea breeze then develops because cooler air over the water at higher pressure moves toward the warmer land and low pressure air. The breeze starts developing shortly before noon and generally reaches its greatest intensity during the mid- to late afternoon. These relatively cool winds can be a moderating influence on afternoon temperatures in coastal areas.

Figure 12 Sea Breeze During daylight hours, the air above land heats and rises, creating a local zone of lower air pressure. Pressure is measured in millibars (mb).

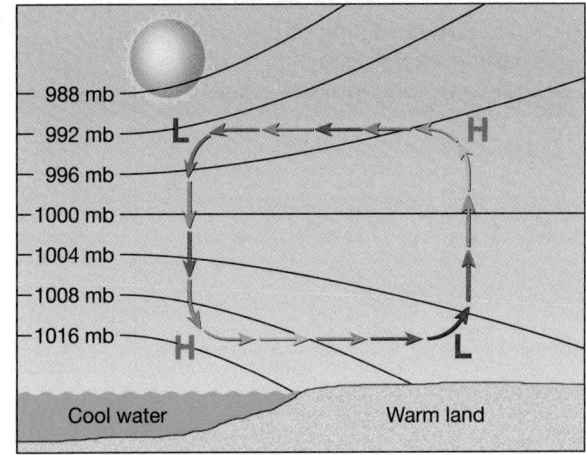

988 mb
992 mb
996 mb
1000 mb
1004 mb
1008 mb
1016 mb

Cool water — Warm land

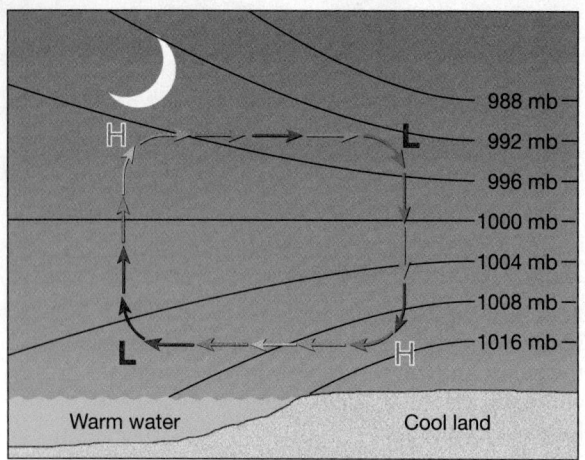

Warm water   Cool land

Figure 13 Land Breeze At night, the land cools more rapidly than the sea, generating an offshore flow called a land breeze.
Inferring *How would the isobar lines be oriented if there was no air pressure change across the land–water boundary?*

	988 mb
	992 mb
	996 mb
	1000 mb
	1004 mb
	1008 mb
	1016 mb

At night, the reverse may take place. The land cools more rapidly than the sea, and a land breeze develops, as shown in Figure 13. The cooler air at higher pressures over the land moves to the sea, where the air is warmer and at lower pressures. Small-scale sea breezes also can develop along the shores of large lakes. People who live in a city near the Great Lakes, such as Chicago, recognize this lake effect, especially in the summer. They are reminded daily by weather reports of the cool temperatures near the lake as compared to warmer outlying areas.

Valley and Mountain Breezes A daily wind similar to land and sea breezes occurs in many mountainous regions. During daylight hours, the air along the slopes of the mountains is heated more intensely than the air at the same elevation over the valley floor. Because this warmer air on the mountain slopes is less dense, it glides up along the slope and generates a valley breeze, as shown in Figure 14A. The occurrence of these daytime upslope breezes can often be identified by the cumulus clouds that develop on adjacent mountain peaks.

 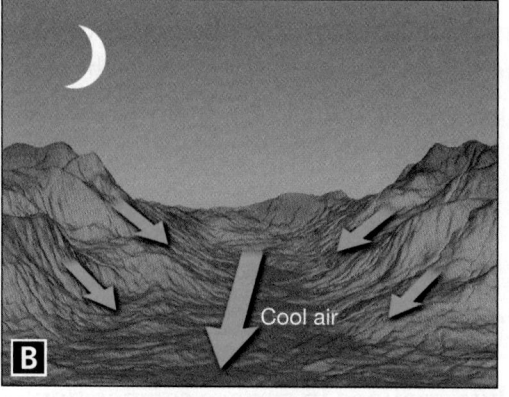

Warm air

Cool air

Figure 14 A Valley Breeze Heating during the day generates warm air that rises from the valley floor. **B Mountain Breeze** After sunset, cooling of the air near mountain slopes can result in cool air moving into the valley.

After sunset, the pattern may reverse. The rapid cooling of the air along the mountain slopes produces a layer of cooler air next to the ground. Because cool air is denser than warm air, it moves downslope into the valley. Such a movement of air, illustrated in Figure 14B, is called a mountain breeze. In the Grand Canyon at night, the sound of cold air rushing down the sides of the canyon can be louder than the sound of the Colorado River below.

The same type of cool air drainage can occur in places that have very modest slopes. The result is that the coldest pockets of air are usually found in the lowest spots. Like many other winds, mountain and valley breezes have seasonal preferences. Although valley breezes are most common during the warm season when solar heating is most intense, mountain breezes tend to be more dominant in the cold season.

 Reading Checkpoint) *What type of local wind can form in the Grand Canyon at night?*

How Wind Is Measured

Two basic wind measurements—direction and speed—are particularly important to the weather observer. Winds are always labeled by the direction from which they blow. A north wind blows from the north toward the south. An east wind blows from the east toward the west. The instrument most commonly used to determine wind direction is the wind vane, shown in the upper right of Figure 15. Wind vanes commonly are located on buildings, and they always point into the wind. The wind direction is often shown on a dial connected to the wind vane. The dial indicates wind direction, either by points of the compass—N, NE, E, SE, etc.—or by a scale of 0° to 360°. On the degree scale, 0° or 360° are north, 90° is east, 180° is south, and 270° is west.

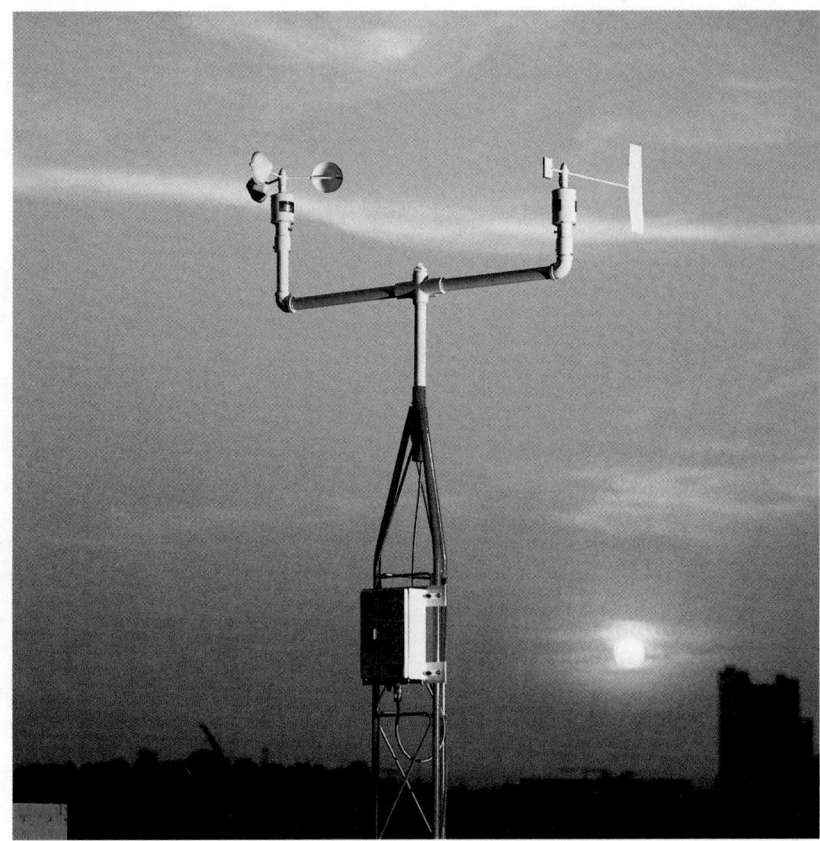

Figure 15 Wind Vane and Cup Anemometer
Interpreting Photographs *How does the position of a wind vane tell you which direction the wind is blowing?*

 **Reading Checkpoint** *Toward which direction does a SE wind blow?*

Wind Direction When the wind consistently blows more often from one direction than from any other, it is called a **prevailing wind.** Recall the prevailing westerlies that dominate circulation in the middle latitudes. **In the United States, the westerlies consistently move weather from west to east across the continent.** Along within this general eastward flow are cells of high and low pressure with the characteristic clockwise and counterclockwise flows. As a result, the winds associated with the westerlies, as measured at the surface, often vary considerably from day to day and from place to place. In contrast, the direction of airflow associated with the trade winds is much more consistent.

Wind Speed Shown in the upper left of Figure 15, a cup **anemometer** (*anemo* = wind, *metron* = measuring instrument) is commonly used to measure wind speed. The wind speed is read from a dial much like the speedometer of an automobile. Places where winds are steady and speeds are relatively high are potential sites for tapping wind energy.

For: Links on winds
Visit: www.SciLinks.org
Web Code: cjn-6193

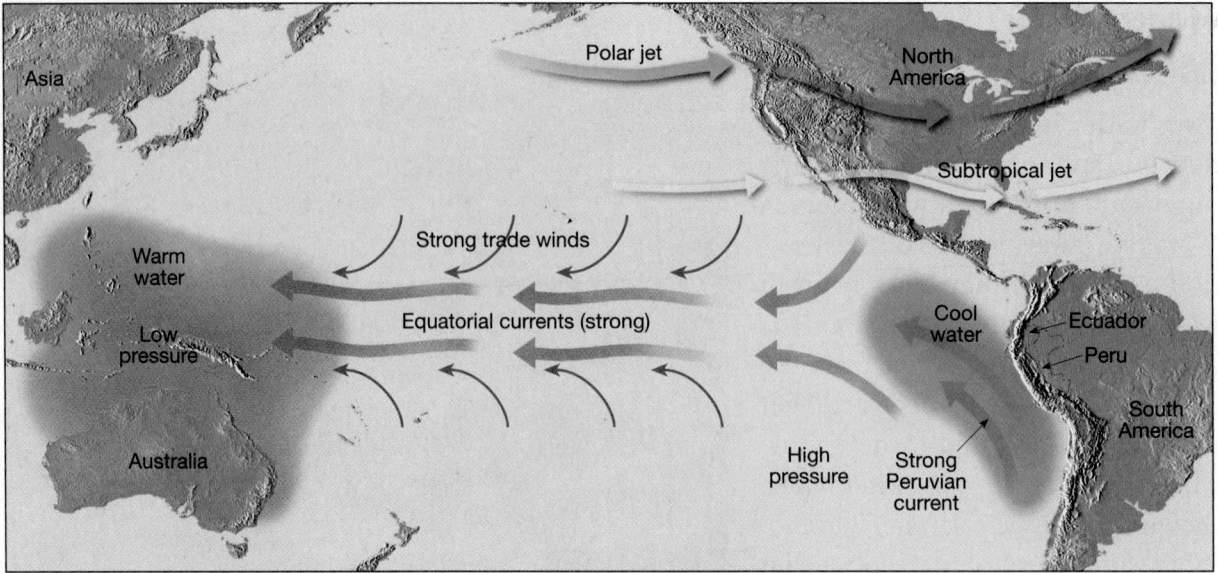

Figure 16 Normal Conditions
Trade winds and strong equatorial ocean currents flow toward the west.

El Niño and La Niña

Look at Figure 16. The cold Peruvian current flows toward the equator along the coasts of Ecuador and Peru. This flow encourages upwelling of cold nutrient-filled waters that contain the food source for millions of fish, particularly anchovies. Near the end of the year, however, a warm current that flows southward along the coasts of Ecuador and Peru replaces the cold Peruvian current. During the nineteenth century, the local residents named this warm current El Niño ("the child") after the Christ child because it usually appeared during the Christmas season. Normally, these warm countercurrents last for a few weeks and then give way to the cold Peruvian flow again.

El Niño At irregular intervals of three to seven years, these warm countercurrents become unusually strong and replace normally cold offshore waters with warm equatorial waters. Scientists use the term **El Niño** for these episodes of ocean warming that affect the eastern tropical Pacific.

The onset of El Niño is marked by abnormal weather patterns that drastically affect the economies of Ecuador and Peru. As shown in Figure 17, these unusually strong countercurrents accumulate large quantities of warm water that block the upwelling of colder, nutrient-filled water. As a result, the anchovies starve, devastating the local fishing industry. At the same time, some inland areas that are normally arid receive an abnormal amount of rain. Here, pastures and cotton fields have yields far above the average. These climatic fluctuations have been known for years, but they were originally considered local phenomena. It now is understood that El Niño is part of the global circulation and that it affects the weather at great distances from Peru and Ecuador.

When an El Niño began in the summer of 1997, forecasters predicted that the pool of warm water over the Pacific would displace the

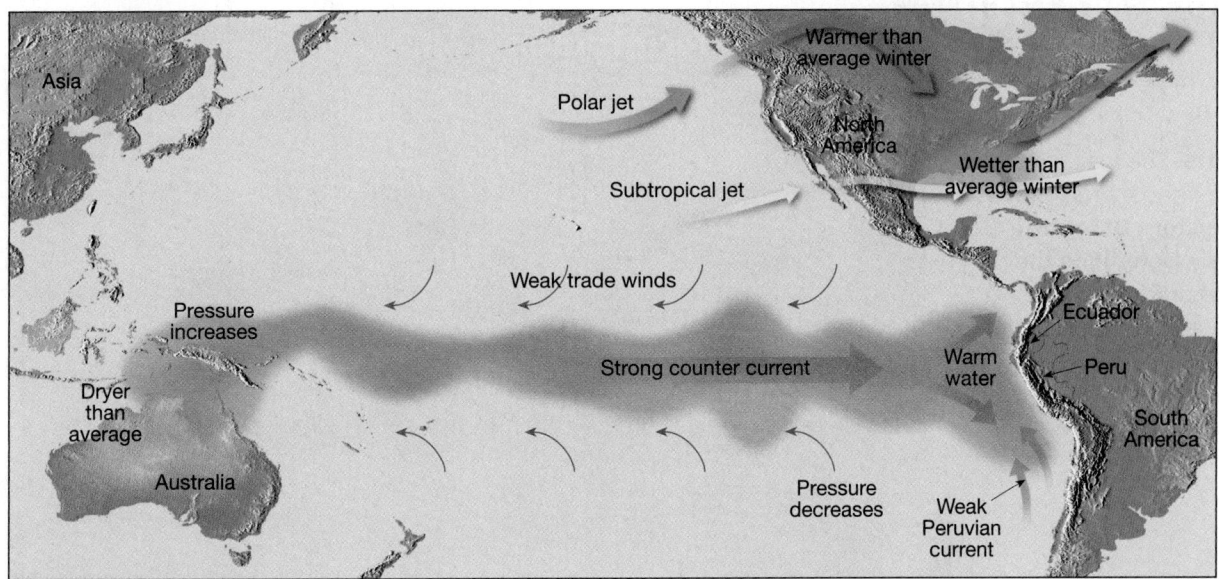

Asia

Warmer than average winter

Polar jet

North America

Subtropical jet

Wetter than average winter

Weak trade winds

Pressure increases

Ecuador

Strong counter current

Warm water

Peru

Dryer than average

South America

Australia

Pressure decreases

Weak Peruvian current

paths of both the subtropical and midlatitude jet streams, as shown in Figure 17. The jet streams steer weather systems across North America. As predicted, the subtropical jet brought rain to the Gulf Coast. Tampa, Florida, received more than three times its normal winter precipitation. The mid-latitude jet pumped warm air far north into the continent. As a result, winter temperatures west of the Rocky Mountains were significantly above normal.

Figure 17 El Niño Warm countercurrents cause reversal of pressure patterns in the western and eastern Pacific.

 **Reading Checkpoint** *What is an El Niño and what effect does it have on weather?*

La Niña The opposite of El Niño is an atmospheric phenomenon known as La Niña. Once thought to be the normal conditions that occur between two El Niño events, meteorologists now consider La Niña an important atmospheric phenomenon in its own right. **Researchers have come to recognize that when surface temperatures in the eastern Pacific are colder than average, a La Niña event is triggered that has a distinctive set of weather patterns.** A typical La Niña winter blows colder than normal air over the Pacific Northwest and the northern Great Plains. At the same time, it warms much of the rest of the United States. The Northwest also experiences greater precipitation during this time. During the La Niña winter of 1998–99, a world-record snowfall for one season occurred in Washington State. La Niña impact can also increase hurricane activity. A recent study concluded that the cost of hurricane damages in the United States is 20 times greater in La Niña years as compared to El Niño years.

The effects of both El Niño and La Niña on world climate are widespread and vary greatly. These phenomena remind us that the air and ocean conditions of the tropical Pacific influence the state of weather almost everywhere.

Go Online

NSTA *SciLINKS*

For: Links on La Niña and El Niño
Visit: www.SciLinks.org
Web Code: cjn-6211

Global Precipitation

Figure 18

Regions The map shows average annual precipitation in millimeters. **Using the Map Key** Determine the range of precipitation that dominates Northern Africa. **Identify Causes** Which weather pattern influences precipitation in this area?

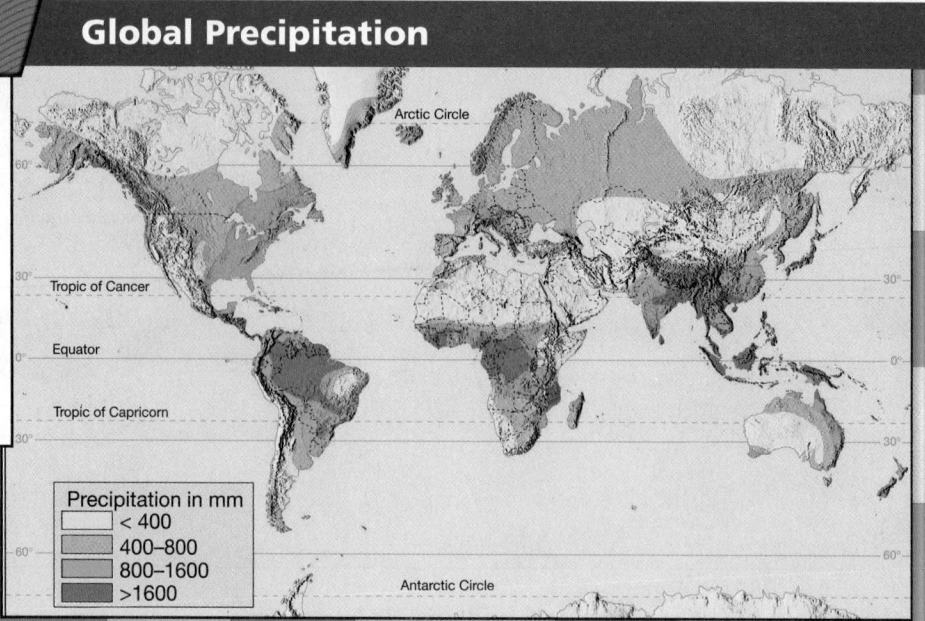

Precipitation in mm
	< 400
	400–800
	800–1600
	>1600

Global Distribution of Precipitation

Figure 18 shows that the tropical region dominated by the equatorial low is the rainiest region on Earth. It includes the rain forests of the Amazon basin in South America and the Congo basin in Africa. In these areas, the warm, humid trade winds converge to yield abundant rainfall throughout the year. In contrast, areas dominated by the subtropical high-pressure cells are regions of extensive deserts. Variables other than pressure and wind complicate the pattern. For example, the interiors of large land masses commonly experience decreased precipitation. However, you can explain a lot about global precipitation if you apply your knowledge of global winds and pressure systems.

Section 19.3 Assessment

Reviewing Concepts

1. What are local winds, and how are they caused?

2. Describe the general movement of weather in the United States.

3. What happens when strong, warm countercurrents flow along the coasts of Ecuador and Peru?

4. How is a La Niña event recognized?

5. What two factors mainly influence global precipitation?

Critical Thinking

6. **Interpreting illustrations** Study Figure 17. How could air pressure changes influence weather patterns in this region?

Writing in Science

Compare-Contrast Paragraph Write a paragraph comparing the features and effects of El Niño and La Niña. Include specific weather patterns associated with each phenomenon.

Tracking El Niño from Space

The images in Figure 19 show the progression of the 1997–98 El Niño. They were derived from data collected by the satellite TOPEX/Poseidon.* This satellite bounces radar signals off the ocean surface to precisely measure the distance between the satellite and the sea surface. When combined with high-precision data from the Global Positioning System (GPS) of satellites, maps of sea-surface topography like these can be produced. These maps show the topography of the sea surface. The presence of hills indicates warmer-than-average water, and the areas of low topography, or valleys, indicate cooler-than-normal water. Using water topography, scientists can determine the speed and direction of surface ocean currents.

The colors in these images show sea-level height relative to the average. When you focus on the images, remember that hills are warm colors and valleys are cool colors. The white and red areas indicate places of higher-than-normal sea-surface heights. In the white areas, the sea surface is between 14 and 32 centimeters above normal. In the red areas, sea level is elevated by about 10 centimeters. Green areas indicate average conditions, whereas purple shows zones that are at least 18 centimeters below average sea level.

The images show the progression of the large warm-water mass from west to east across the equatorial Pacific Ocean. At its peak in November 1997, the surface area covered by the warm water mass was about one and one half times the size of the 48 contiguous United States. The amount of warm water added to the eastern Pacific with a temperature between 21°C and 30°C was about 30 times the combined volume of the water in all of the United States Great Lakes.

*Source: NASA's Goddard Space Flight Center

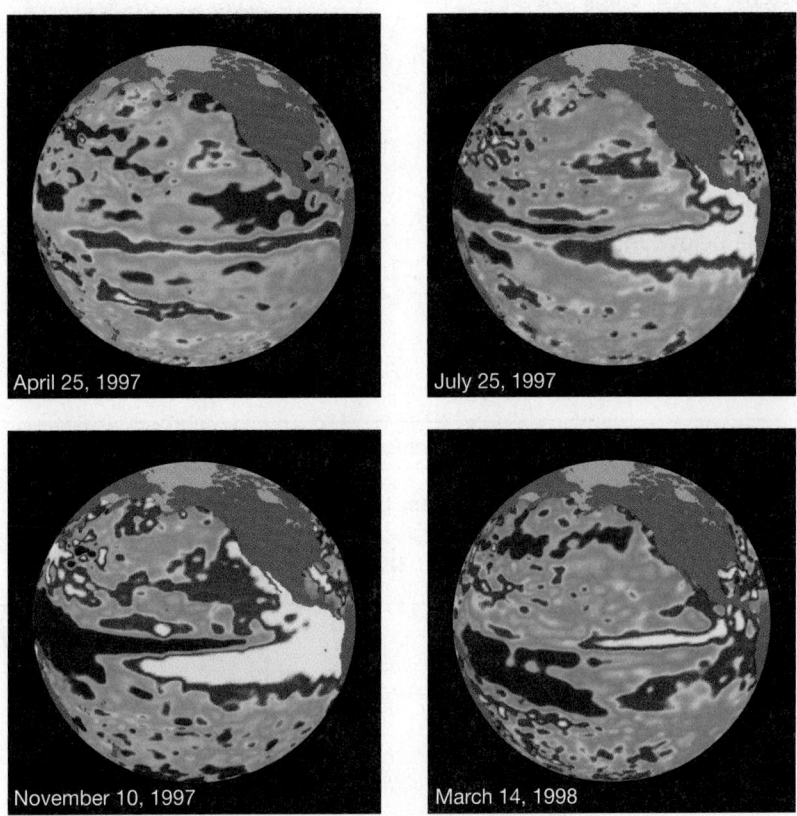

April 25, 1997

July 25, 1997

November 10, 1997

March 14, 1998

Figure 19 Progression of the 1997–98 El Niño

Observing Wind Patterns

Atmospheric pressure and wind are two elements of weather that are closely interrelated. Most people don't usually pay close attention to the pressure given in a weather report. However, pressure differences in the atmosphere drive the winds that often bring changes in temperature and moisture.

Problem
How can surface barometric pressure maps be interpreted?

Materials
- 1 copy each of Figure 1 and Figure 2
- paper
- pencil

Skills
Observing, Analyzing Data, Calculating

Procedure

1. Look at Figure 2. This map shows surface global wind patterns and average global barometric pressure for the month of January.

2. Examine the individual pressure cells in Figure 2. Then complete the diagrams in your copy of Figure 1. Label the isobars with appropriate pressures, and use arrows to indicate the surface air movement in each pressure cell.

3. Copy the data table below. Indicate the movements of air in high and low pressure cells by completing the table.

Northern Hemisphere

HIGH

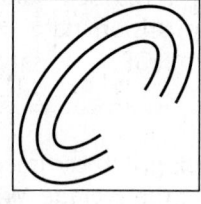
LOW

Southern Hemisphere

HIGH

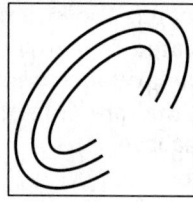
LOW

Figure 1

Air Movement in Pressure Cells Data Table				
Air Movement	N. Hem. High	N. Hem. Low	S. Hem High	S. Hem. Low
into/out of				
rises/sinks				
rotates CW/CCW*				

* CW = clockwise; CCW = counterclockwise

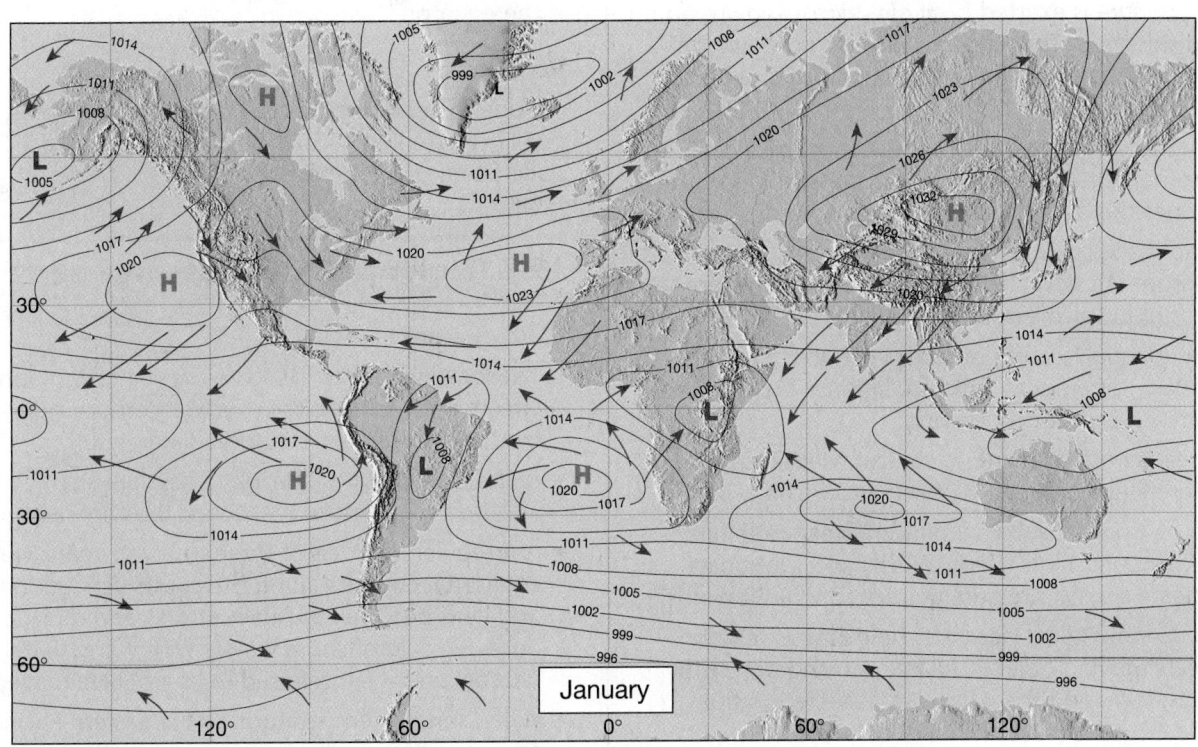

Figure 2

Analyze and Conclude

1. **Comparing and Contrasting** Summarize the differences and similarities in surface air movement between a Northern Hemisphere cyclone and a Southern Hemisphere cyclone.

2. **Interpreting Illustrations** Use your textbook as a reference to locate and write the name of each global wind belt at the appropriate location on your copy of the map in Figure 2. Also indicate the region of the polar front.

3. **Applying** Label areas on your copy of Figure 2 where you would expect high wind speeds to occur.

4. **Applying** Label an area on your copy of Figure 2 where circulation is most like the idealized global wind model for a rotating Earth. Explain why this region on Earth is so much like the model.

Study Guide

19.1 Understanding Air Pressure

Key Concepts

- Air pressure is exerted in all directions—down, up, and sideways. The air pressure pushing down on an object balances the air pressure pushing up on the object.

- When air pressure increases, the mercury in the barometric tube rises. When air pressure decreases, so does the height of the mercury column.

- Wind is the result of horizontal differences in air pressure. Air flows from areas of higher pressure to areas of lower pressure.

- The unequal heating of Earth's surface generates pressure differences. Solar radiation is the ultimate energy source for most wind.

- Three factors combine to control wind: pressure differences, the Coriolis effect, and friction.

- Closely spaced isobars indicate a steep pressure gradient and high winds. Widely spaced isobars indicate a weak pressure gradient and light winds.

- The Coriolis effect describes how Earth's rotation affects moving objects. All free-moving objects or fluids, including the wind, are deflected to the right of their path of motion in the Northern Hemisphere. In the Southern Hemisphere, they are deflected to the left.

Vocabulary

air pressure, *p. 532;* barometer *p. 533;* pressure gradient, *p. 534;* Coriolis effect, *p. 535;* jet stream, *p. 536*

19.2 Pressure Centers and Winds

Key Concepts

- In the Northern Hemisphere, winds blow inward and counterclockwise around a low. Around a high, they blow outward and clockwise.

- In cyclones, the pressure decreases from the outer isobars toward the center. In anticyclones, just the opposite is the case—the values of the isobars increase from the outside toward the center.

- In either hemisphere, pressure difference, the Coriolis effect, and friction causes a net flow of air inward around a cyclone and a net flow of air outward around an anticyclone.

- The atmosphere balances differences in solar radiation in the tropics and the poles by acting as a giant heat-transfer system. This system moves warm air toward high latitudes and cool air toward the equator.

Vocabulary

cyclone, *p. 538;* anticyclone, *p. 538;* trade winds, *p. 541;* westerlies, *p. 541;* polar easterlies, *p. 541;* polar front, *p. 541;* monsoon, *p. 542*

19.3 Regional Wind Systems

Key Concepts

- The local winds are caused either by topographic effects or by variations in surface composition— land and water—in the immediate area.

- In the United States, the westerlies consistently move weather from west to east across the continent.

- At irregular intervals of three to seven years, warm equatorial currents along the coasts of Ecuador and Peru become unusually strong and replace normally cold offshore waters with warm waters. This occurrence is referred to as an El Niño event.

- When surface temperatures in the eastern Pacific are colder than average, a La Niña event is triggered that has a distinctive set of weather patterns.

Vocabulary

prevailing wind, *p. 545;* anemometer, *p. 545;* El Niño, *p. 546;* La Niña, *p. 547*

Thinking Visually

Concept Map Copy the concept map below onto a sheet of paper. Use information from the chapter to complete the concept map.

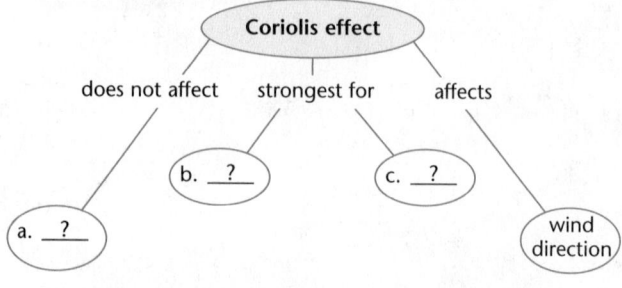

Reviewing Content

Choose the letter that best answers the question or completes the statement.

1. The mercurial barometer was invented by
   a. Galileo. **b.** Newton.
   c. Torricelli. **d.** Watt.

2. The force exerted by the air above is called
   a. air pressure. **b.** convergence.
   c. divergence. **d.** the Coriolis effect.

3. What are centers of low pressure called?
   a. air masses **b.** anticyclones
   c. cyclones **d.** jet streams

4. Variations in air pressure from place to place are the principal cause of
   a. clouds. **b.** lows.
   c. hail. **d.** wind.

5. In the winter, large landmasses often develop a seasonal
   a. high-pressure system.
   b. low-pressure system.
   c. typhoon.
   d. trade wind.

6. A sea breeze is most intense
   a. during mid- to late afternoon.
   b. in the late morning.
   c. late in the evening.
   d. at sunrise.

7. What is the pressure zone that is associated with rising air near the equator?
   a. equatorial low **b.** equatorial high
   c. subtropical low **d.** subtropical high

8. What are high-altitude, high-velocity winds?
   a. cyclonic currents **b.** isobars
   c. jet streams **d.** pressure gradients

9. Where is deflection of wind due to the Coriolis effect the strongest?
   a. near the equator **b.** in the midlatitudes
   c. near the poles **d.** near the westerlies

10. In what stormy region do the westerlies and polar easterlies converge?
    a. equatorial low **b.** subpolar high
    c. polar front **d.** subtropical front

Understanding Concepts

11. Describe how an aneroid barometer works.

12. Write a general statement relating the spacing of isobars to wind speed.

13. Describe the weather that usually accompanies a
    a. drop in barometric pressure.
    b. rise in barometric pressure.

14. How does the Coriolis effect modify air movement in the Southern Hemisphere?

15. The trade winds originate from which pressure zone?

16. List and briefly describe three examples of local winds.

17. On a wind vane with a degree scale, which type of wind is indicated by 90 degrees?

Use the figure below to answer Questions 18–20.

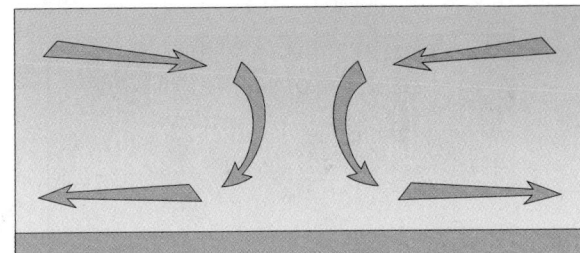

A

B

18. In diagram A, what type of surface air flow is shown?

19. What type of surface pressure system is illustrated in diagram B?

20. Select the diagram in which air at the surface first begins to pile up.

Critical Thinking

21. **Predicting** If you are in the Northern Hemisphere and are directly west of the center of a cyclone, what most likely will be the wind direction? What will the wind direction be if you are west of an anticyclone in the Northern Hemisphere?

22. **Applying Concepts** If you were looking for a location to place a wind turbine to generate electricity, how would you use the spacing of isobars in making your decision?

23. **Hypothesizing** What differences in the biosphere would you predict for areas dominated by low-pressure systems compared to those dominated by high-pressure systems?

Math Skills

Use the illustration below to answer Questions 24–26.

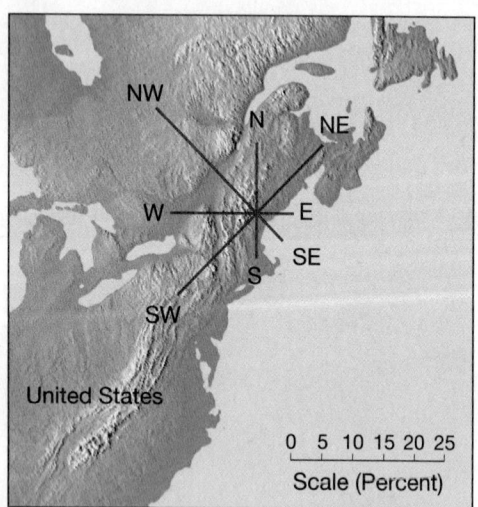

United States

0 5 10 15 20 25
Scale (Percent)

24. **Analyzing Data** According to the map, which winds dominate this region?

25. **Measuring** About what percent of the time do winds blow from the east?

26. **Calculating** Determine the approximate percent of time that winds blow from either the west or the northwest in this area.

Concepts in Action

27. **Predicting** How might a La Niña event impact the weather in your area?

28. **Applying Concepts** Mercury is 13 times heavier than water. If you built a barometer using water rather than mercury, how tall would it have to be to record standard sea-level pressure? Express your answer in centimeters. (Hint: How many centimeters of mercury represent standard sea-level pressure?)

29. **Interpreting Illustrations** After studying Figure 16, explain the relationship between water temperature and the type of air pressure system that develops.

Performance-Based Assessment

Observing For two weeks, keep a daily air pressure, wind, and precipitation log in your science notebook. Be sure to note any changes, and note if any of the changes occur over the course of a single day. At the end of two weeks, organize your information into a data table. Prepare a short summary that includes any patterns you determine among these variables. Report the results orally to your class.

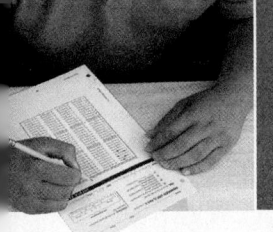

Standardized Test Prep

Choose the letter that best answers the question or completes the statement.

1. The Sahara in North Africa and the Australian desert, as well as others, are associated with which pressure zone?
 (A) equatorial low
 (B) polar high
 (C) subpolar low
 (D) subtropical high

2. What does a steep air pressure gradient cause?
 (A) high winds
 (B) light winds
 (C) variable winds
 (D) north winds

3. Low-pressure systems are usually associated with
 (A) descending air.
 (B) diverging surface winds.
 (C) clear weather.
 (D) precipitation.

4. A sea breeze usually originates during the
 (A) evening and flows toward the land.
 (B) day and flows toward the land.
 (C) evening and flows toward the water.
 (D) day and flows toward the water.

Use the illustration below to answer Questions 5 and 6.

5. Using this scale, determine the standard sea level pressure in millibars and inches of mercury. Express your answers to the nearest millibar and to the nearest hundredth of an inch.

6. What is the corresponding pressure, in millibars, for a pressure measurement of 30.30 inches of mercury?

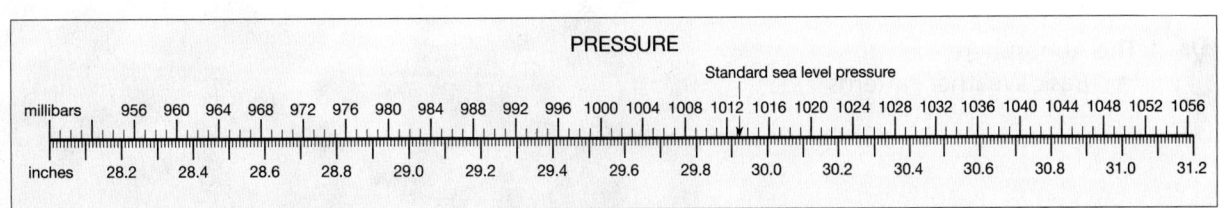

PRESSURE
Standard sea level pressure

millibars   956 960 964 968 972 976 980 984 988 992 996 1000 1004 1008 1012 1016 1020 1024 1028 1032 1036 1040 1044 1048 1052 1056

inches   28.2   28.4   28.6   28.8   29.0   29.2   29.4   29.6   29.8   30.0   30.2   30.4   30.6   30.8   31.0   31.2

CHAPTER 20

Weather Patterns and Severe Storms

21st Century Learning

Problem Identification, Formulation, and Solution

What are the hazards of severe weather?

Severe weather can cause injury, damage to property, and even loss of human life. Use the Internet to research which type of weather-related events caused the greatest number of injuries and deaths last year in your state. Then find out what the citizens of your state can do to protect themselves when severe weather strikes. Present to the class your data and conclusions.

Application Lab

Middle-Latitude Cyclones

How the Earth Works

Winds and Storms

GEODe EARTH SCIENCE

The Atmosphere
↳ Basic Weather Patterns

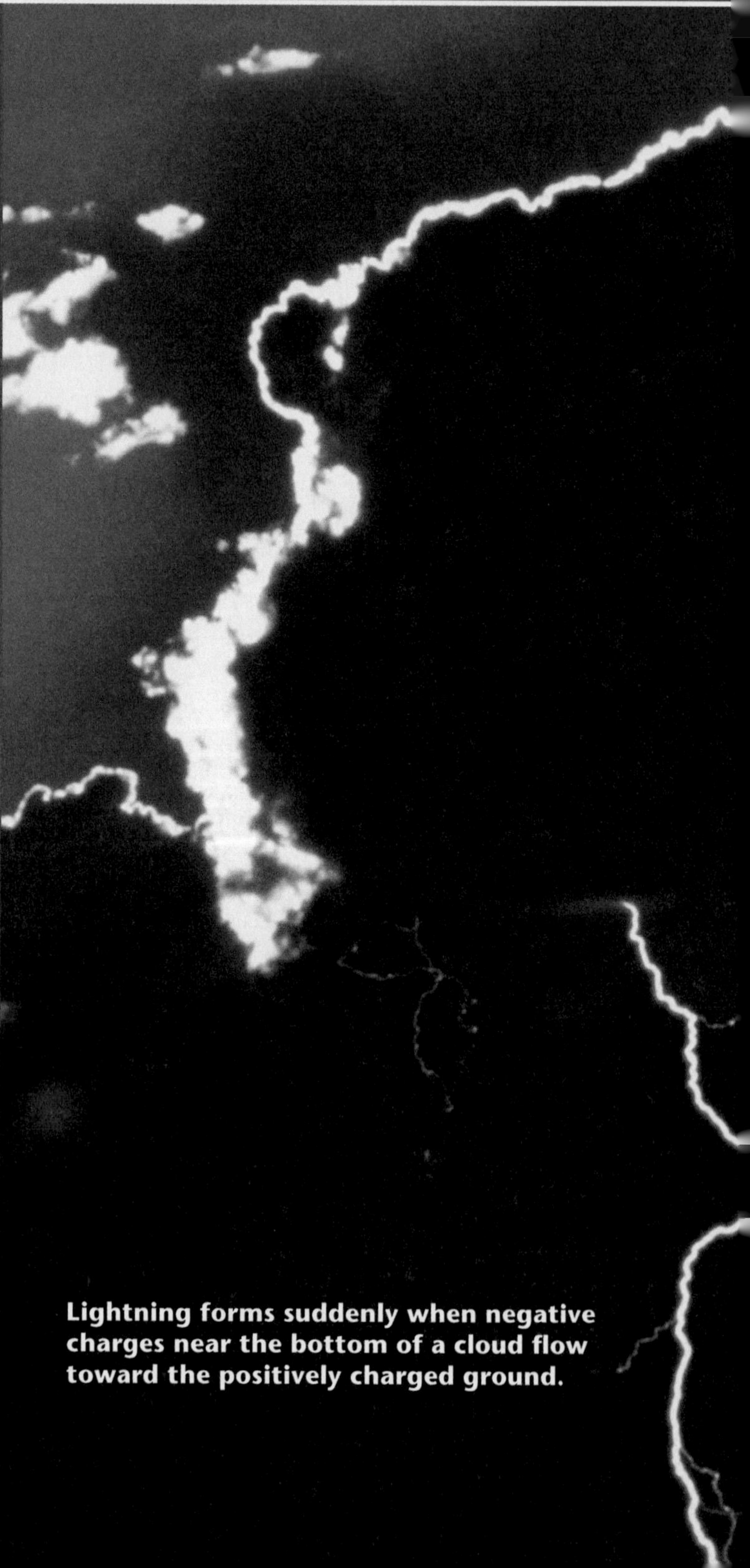

Lightning forms suddenly when negative charges near the bottom of a cloud flow toward the positively charged ground.

Chapter Preview

Inquiry Activity

How Can You Model the Movement of Air in a Tornado?

Procedure

1. Pour tap water into a 1-L plastic bottle until it is about two-thirds full. Wipe off any water from the outside of the bottle as well as from the opening.

2. Without getting any of either substance on the outside of the bottle, add about 30 mL of liquid dishwashing soap and a spoonful of glitter to the water in the bottle.

3. Center a washer on the mouth of the bottle.

4. Invert another 1-L empty bottle and place its mouth over the washer.

5. Wrap about 10 cm of duct tape around the mouths of the bottles to seal them. Be careful not to move the washer as you do this.

6. Quickly invert the bottles so that the bottle holding the water is on top. Then, while holding the top bottle, swirl the bottles in a counterclockwise direction.

7. Observe your mini-tornado.

Think About It

1. **Observing** How did the water move in the bottle?

2. **Modeling** What might the glitter represent?

3. **Formulating Hypotheses** What kinds of forces do you think acted on the water to make it move as it did?

20.1 Air Masses

Reading Focus

Key Concepts

- What is an air mass?
- What happens as an air mass moves over an area?
- How are air masses classified?
- Which air masses influence much of the weather in North America?
- Why do continental tropical air masses have little effect on weather in North America?

Vocabulary

- air mass

Reading Strategy

Building Vocabulary Copy the table. As you read this section, write a definition for each of the terms in the table. Refer to the table as you read the rest of the chapter.

Term	Definition
Air mass	a. _____?_____
Source region	b. _____?_____
Polar air mass	c. _____?_____
Tropical air mass	d. _____?_____
Continental air mass	e. _____?_____
Maritime air mass	f. _____?_____

Figure 1 Tornado Damage in Kansas The force of the wind during a tornado was strong enough to drive a piece of metal into the utility pole.

Severe storms are among nature's most destructive forces. Every spring and summer, for example, newspapers and newscasts report the damage caused by tornadoes, which are short but violent windstorms that move quickly over land. The forces associated with these storms can be incredibly strong, as you can see from the damage shown in Figure 1. During late summer and early fall, you have probably heard reports about severe storms known as hurricanes. Unlike tornadoes, hurricanes form over Earth's tropical oceans. As they move toward land, the strong winds and heavy rains produced by these storms produce tremendous destruction along their paths. You are probably most familiar with a type of severe storm known as a thunderstorm. Thunderstorms are a type of severe weather that produces heavy rains, loud noises you know as thunder, and flashes of light called lightning. Before learning more about these different types of violent weather, you will learn about the atmospheric conditions that most often affect the day-to-day weather.

Air Masses and Weather

For the many people who live in the middle latitudes, which include much of the United States, summer heat waves and winter cold spells are familiar experiences. During summer heat waves, several days of high temperatures and high humidity often end when a series of storms pass through the area. This stormy weather is followed by a few days of relatively cool weather. By contrast, winter cold spells are often characterized by periods of frigid temperatures under clear skies. These bitter cold periods are usually followed by cloudy, snowy, relatively warm days that seem mild when compared to those just a day earlier. In both of these situations, periods of fairly constant weather conditions are followed by a short period of changes in the weather. What do you think causes these changes?

Air Masses The weather patterns just described result from movements of large bodies of air called air masses. **An air mass is an immense body of air that is characterized by similar temperatures and amounts of moisture at any given altitude.** An air mass can be 1600 kilometers or more across and several kilometers thick. Because of its size, it may take several days for an air mass to move over an area. This causes the area to experience fairly constant weather, a situation often called air-mass weather. Some day-to-day variations may occur, but the events will be very unlike those in an adjacent air mass.

Movement of Air Masses When an air mass moves out of the region over which it formed, it carries its temperature and moisture conditions with it. An example of the influence of a moving air mass is shown in Figure 2. A cold, dry air mass from northern Canada is shown moving southward. The initial temperature of the air mass is −46°C. It warms 13 degrees by the time it reaches Winnipeg. The air mass continues to warm as it moves southward through the Great Plains and into Mexico. Throughout its southward journey, the air mass becomes warmer. But it also brings some of the coldest weather of the winter to the places in its path. **As it moves, the characteristics of an air mass change and so does the weather in the area over which the air mass moves.**

 **Reading Checkpoint** *What is an air mass, and what happens as it moves over an area?*

Go Online
PLANETDIARY

For: Links on Tornadoes
Visit: PHSchool.com
Web Code: cuc-1200

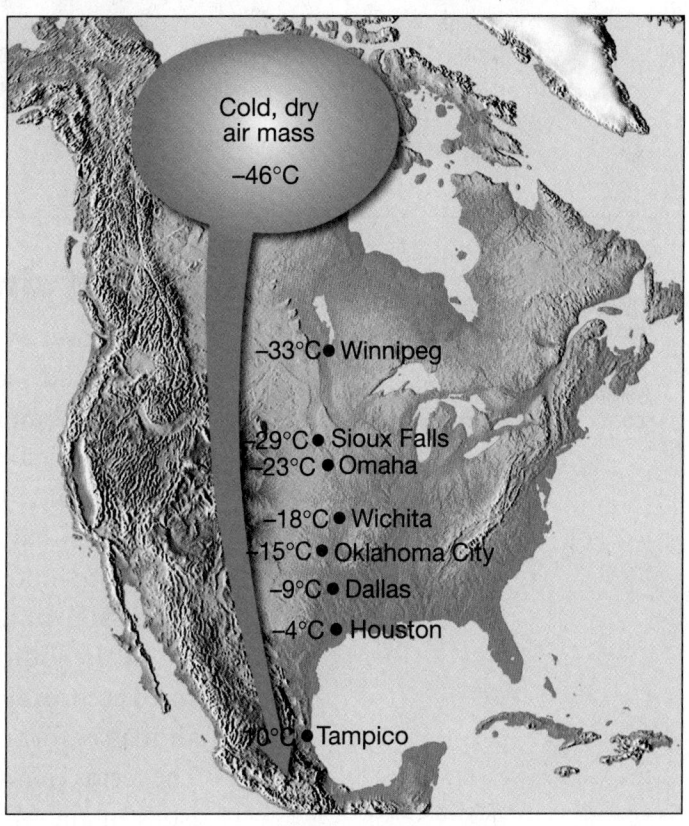

Figure 2 As a frigid Canadian air mass moves southward, it brings colder weather to the area over which it moves.
Computing *How much warmer was the air mass when it reached Tampico, Mexico, than when it formed?*

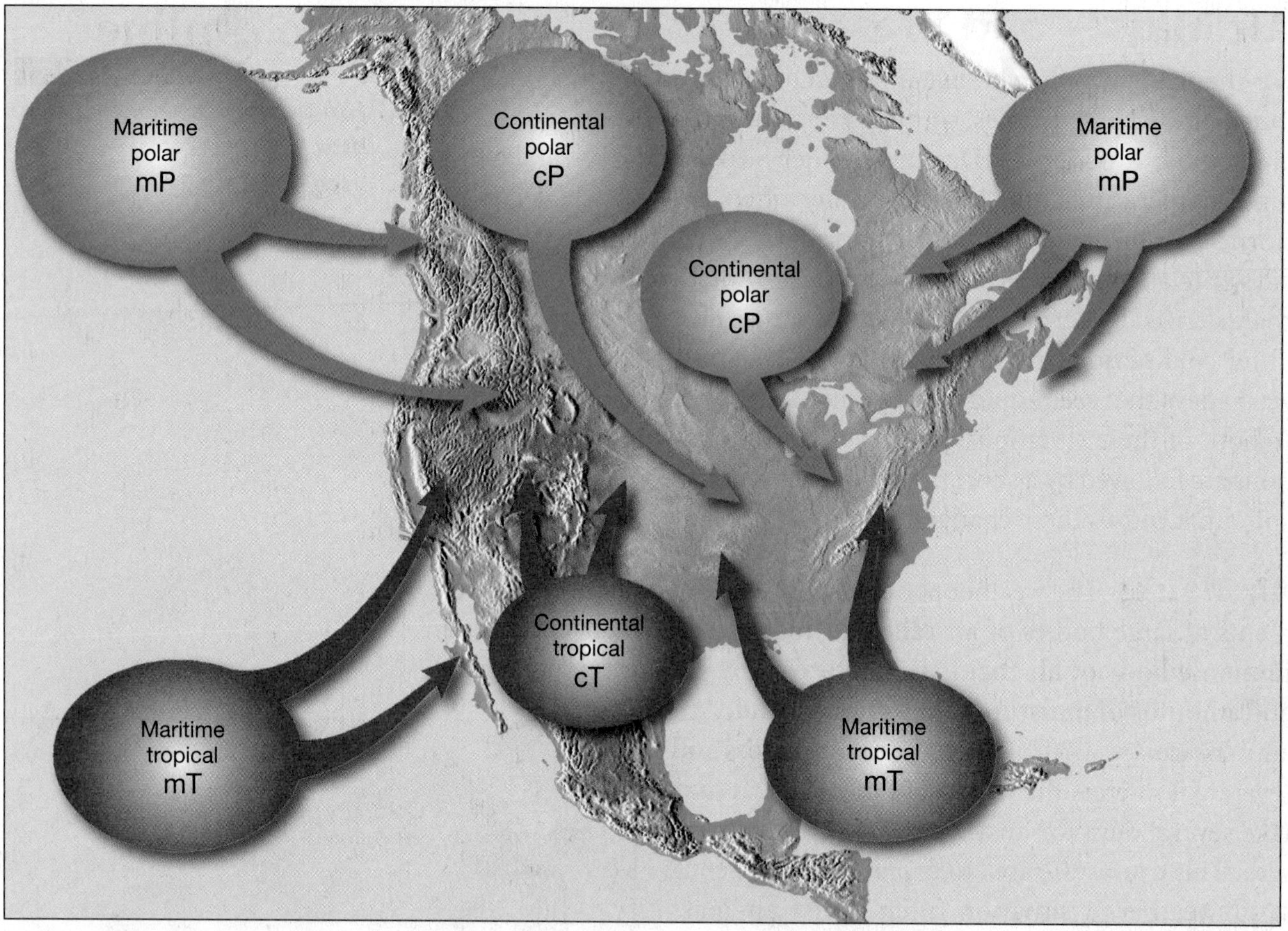

The figure shows a relief map of North America with labeled air masses and arrows indicating their movement:

- Maritime polar mP (upper left, over the Pacific)
- Continental polar cP (upper center, over Canada)
- Continental polar cP (center)
- Maritime polar mP (upper right, over the Atlantic)
- Maritime tropical mT (lower left, over the Pacific)
- Continental tropical cT (lower center, over Mexico/southwest)
- Maritime tropical mT (lower center-right, over the Gulf/Atlantic)

Figure 3 Air masses are classified by the region over which they form. **Interpreting Maps** *What kinds of air masses influence the weather patterns along the west coast of the United States?*

Go Online

NSTA *sci*LINKS

For: Links on air masses
Visit: www.SciLinks.org
Web Code: cjn-6201

Classifying Air Masses

The area over which an air mass gets its characteristic properties of temperature and moisture is called its source region. The source regions that produce air masses that influence the weather in North America are shown in Figure 3. Air masses are named according to their source region. Polar (P) air masses form at high latitudes toward Earth's poles. Air masses that form at low latitudes are tropical (T) air masses. The terms *polar* and *tropical* describe the temperature characteristics of an air mass. Polar air masses are cold, while tropical air masses are warm.

 In addition to their overall temperature, air masses are classified according to the surface over which they form. Continental (c) air masses form over land. Maritime (m) air masses form over water. The terms *continental* and *maritime* describe the moisture characteristics of the air mass. Continental air masses are likely to be dry. Maritime air masses are humid.

Using this classification scheme, there are four basic types of air masses. A continental polar (cP) air mass is dry and cool. A continental tropical (cT) air mass is dry and warm or hot. Maritime polar (mP) and maritime tropical (mT) air masses both form over water. But a maritime polar air mass is much colder than a maritime tropical air mass.

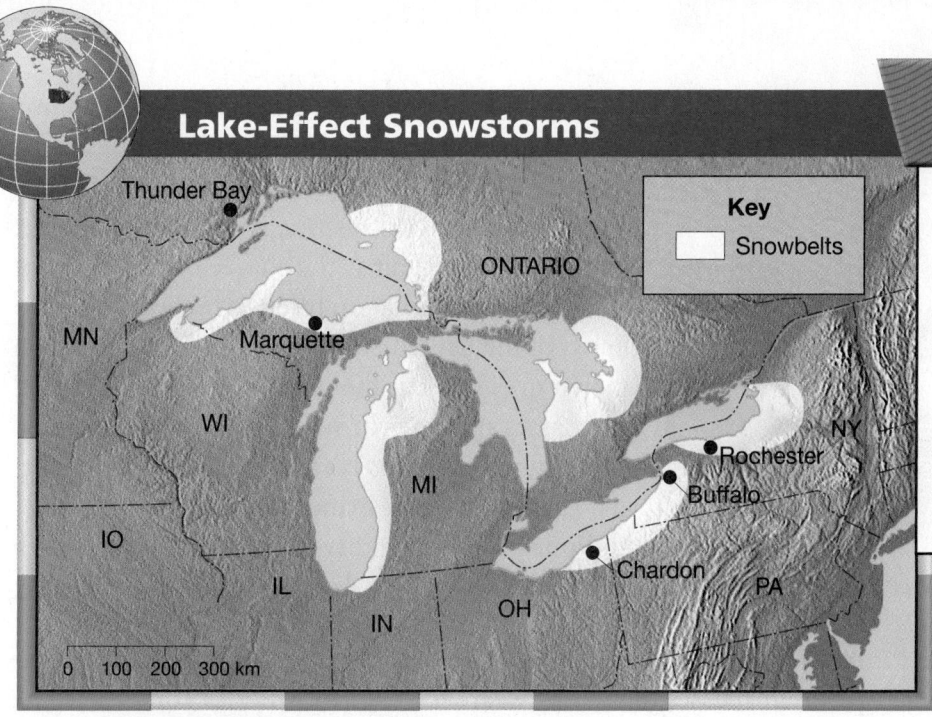

MAP MASTER™
Skills Activity

ONTARIO

Thunder Bay

MN

Marquette

WI

MI

IO

IL

IN

OH

Chardon

PA

NY

Rochester

Buffalo

Key
Snowbelts

0 100 200 300 km

Figure 4

Location Marquette, Michigan, is southeast of Thunder Bay, Ontario.
Identify What type of air mass influences the weather of these two cities?
Infer Which of these cities receives more snow in an average winter? Why?

Weather in North America

Much of the weather in North America, especially weather east of the Rocky Mountains, is influenced by continental polar (cP) and maritime tropical (mT) air masses. The cP air masses begin in northern Canada, the interior of Alaska, and the Arctic areas. The mT air masses most often begin over the warm waters of the Gulf of Mexico, the Caribbean Sea, or the adjacent Atlantic Ocean.

Continental Polar Air Masses
Continental polar air masses are uniformly cold and dry in winter and cool and dry in summer. In summer, cP air masses may bring a few days of relatively cooler weather. In winter, this continental polar air brings the clear skies and cold temperatures you associate with a cold wave.

Continental polar air masses are not, as a rule, associated with heavy precipitation. However, those that cross the Great Lakes during late autumn and winter sometimes bring snow to the leeward shores, as shown in Figure 4. These localized storms, which are known as lake-effect snows, make Buffalo and Rochester, New York, among the snowiest cities in the United States. What causes lake-effect snow? During late autumn and early winter, the difference in temperature between the lakes and adjacent land areas can be large. The temperature contrast can be especially great when a very cold cP air mass pushes southward across the lakes. When this occurs, the air gets large quantities of heat and moisture from the relatively warm lake surface. By the time it reaches the opposite shore, the air mass is humid and unstable. Heavy snow, like that shown in Figure 5, is possible.

Figure 5 A six-day lake-effect snowstorm in November 1996 dropped a record 175 cm (69 in.) of snow on Chardon, Ohio.

 **Reading Checkpoint** *What causes large amounts of snow to fall on the southern and eastern shores of the Great Lakes?*

Maritime Tropical Air Masses

Maritime tropical air masses also play a dominant role in the weather of North America. These air masses are warm, loaded with moisture, and usually unstable. Maritime tropical air is the source of much, if not most, of the precipitation received in the eastern two thirds of the United States. The heavy precipitation shown in Figure 6 is the result of maritime tropical air masses moving through the area. In summer, when an mT air mass invades the central and eastern United States, it brings the high temperatures and oppressive humidity typically associated with its source region.

Figure 6 Rain Storm over Florida Bay in the Florida Keys

Maritime Polar Air Masses

During the winter, maritime polar air masses that affect weather in North America come from the North Pacific. Such air masses often begin as cP air masses in Siberia. The cold, dry continental polar air changes into relatively mild, humid, unstable maritime polar air during its long journey across the North Pacific, as shown in Figure 7. As this maritime polar air arrives at the western shore of North America, it is often accompanied by low clouds and showers. When this maritime polar air advances inland against the western mountains, uplift of the air produces heavy rain or snow on the windward slopes of the mountains.

Maritime polar air masses also originate in the North Atlantic off the coast of eastern Canada. These air masses influence the weather of the northeastern United States. In winter, when New England is on the northern or northwestern side of a passing low-pressure center, the counterclockwise winds draw in maritime polar air. The result is a storm characterized by snow and cold temperatures, known locally as a nor'easter.

Figure 7 During winter, maritime polar (mP) air masses in the northern Pacific Ocean usually begin as continental polar (cP) air masses in Siberia.
Inferring *What happens to the mP air masses as they cross the Pacific?*

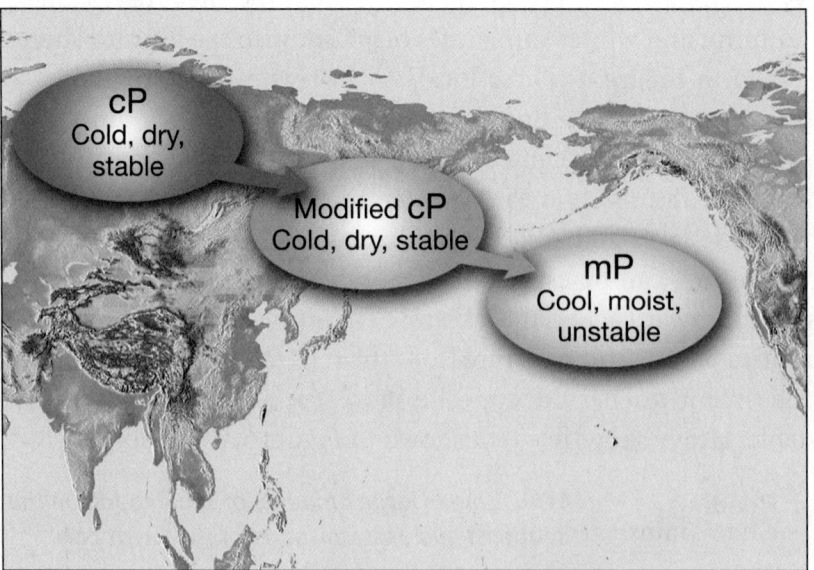

cP
Cold, dry, stable

Modified cP
Cold, dry, stable

mP
Cool, moist, unstable

Continental Tropical Air Masses Continental tropical air masses have the least influence on the weather of North America. These hot, dry air masses begin in the southwestern United States and Mexico during the summer. **Only occasionally do cT air masses affect the weather outside their source regions.** However, when a cT air mass does move from its source region, it can cause extremely hot, droughtlike conditions in the Great Plains in the summer. Movement of such air masses in the fall results in mild weather in the Great Lakes region, often called Indian summer. Conditions during Indian summer are unseasonably warm and mild, as shown in Figure 8.

Figure 8 A cT air mass produces a few days of warm weather amid the cool days of fall in the Great Lakes region.

Go Online
PLANETDIARY

For: Links on Tropical Storms
Visit: PHSchool.com
Web Code: cuc-1201

Section 20.1 Assessment

Reviewing Concepts

1. What is an air mass?
2. What happens as an air mass moves over an area?
3. How are air masses classified?
4. Which types of air masses have the greatest effect on weather in North America?
5. Why do continental tropical air masses have little effect on weather in North America?

Critical Thinking

6. **Comparing and Contrasting** Compare and contrast the four types of air masses.
7. **Explaining** Explain which type of air mass could offer relief from a scorching summer to the Midwestern United States. Justify your choice.

8. **Applying Concepts** How can continental polar air be responsible for lake-effect snowstorms in the Great Lakes region?
9. **Identifying** Look again at Figure 3. What kinds of air masses influence the weather patterns over Florida?
10. **Synthesizing** What kind of weather could be expected in southern Canada if an mT air mass was to invade the region in mid-July?

Writing in Science

Explanatory Paragraph Pick one of the air masses shown in Figure 3 that affects the weather in your area. Write a paragraph that explains the weather typically associated with the air mass in both the summer and the winter.

20.2 Fronts

Key Concepts

- What happens when two air masses meet?
- How is a warm front produced?
- What is a cold front?
- What is a stationary front?
- What are the stages in the formation of an occluded front?
- What is a middle-latitude cyclone?
- What fuels a middle-latitude cyclone?

Vocabulary

- ◆ front
- ◆ warm front
- ◆ cold front
- ◆ stationary front
- ◆ occluded front

Reading Strategy

Outlining As you read, make an outline like the one below. Include information about how each of the weather fronts discussed in this section forms and the weather associated with each.

Fronts
I. Warm front
A. _____ ?
B. _____ ?
II. Cold front
A. _____ ?
B. _____ ?

Formation of Fronts

Recall that air masses have different temperatures and amounts of moisture, depending on their source regions. Recall also that these properties can change as an air mass moves over a region. What do you think happens when two air masses meet? **When two air masses meet, they form a front, which is a boundary that separates two air masses of different properties.** Fronts can form between any two contrasting air masses. Fronts are often associated with some form of precipitation, such as that shown in Figure 9.

In contrast to the vast sizes of air masses, fronts are narrow. Most weather fronts are between about 15 and 200 km wide. Above Earth's surface, the frontal surface slopes at a low angle so that warmer, less dense air overlies cooler, denser air. Occasionally, the air masses on both sides of a front move in the same direction and at the same speed. When this happens, the front acts simply as a barrier that travels with the air masses. In most cases, however, the distribution of pressure across a front causes one air mass to move faster than the other. When this happens, one air mass advances into another, and some mixing of air occurs.

Figure 9 Precipitation from a Storm in South Africa Storms often form at fronts.

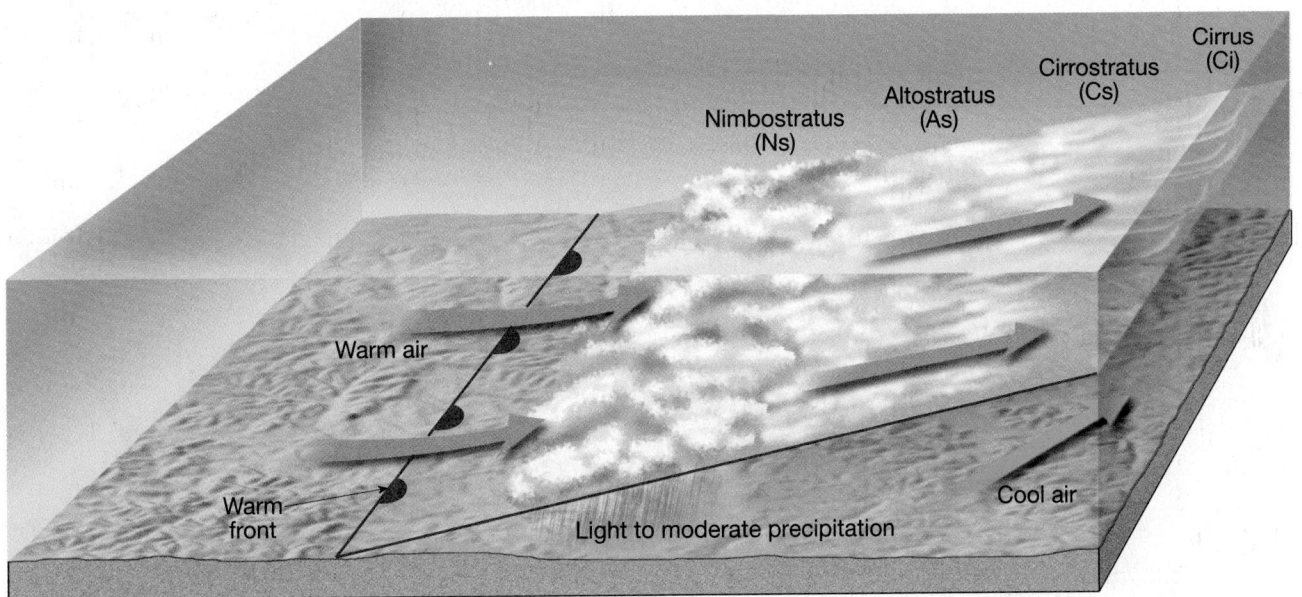

Types of Fronts

Fronts are often classified according to the temperature of the advancing front. There are four types of fronts: warm fronts, cold fronts, stationary fronts, and occluded fronts.

Warm Fronts  **A warm front forms when warm air moves into an area formerly covered by cooler air.** On a weather map, the surface position of a warm front is shown by a red line with red semicircles that point toward the cooler air.

The slope of the warm front is very gradual, as shown in Figure 10. As warm air rises, it cools to produce clouds, and frequently precipitation. The sequence of clouds shown in Figure 10 typically comes before a warm front. The first sign of the approaching warm front is the appearance of cirrus clouds. As the front nears, cirrus clouds change into cirrostratus clouds, which blend into denser sheets of altostratus clouds. About 300 kilometers ahead of the front, thicker stratus and nimbostratus clouds appear, and rain or snow begins.

Because of their slow rate of movement and very low slope, warm fronts usually produce light-to-moderate precipitation over a large area for an extended period. A gradual increase in temperature occurs with the passage of a warm front. The increase is most apparent when a large temperature difference exists between adjacent air masses. Also, a wind shift from the east to the southwest is associated with a warm front.

 *What causes a warm front to form?*

Figure 10 Formation of a Warm Front A warm front forms when warm air glides up over a cold, dense air mass. The affected area has warmer temperatures, and light to moderate precipitation.

Go Online
active art

For: Weather Fronts activity
Visit: PHSchool.com
Web Code: czp-6202

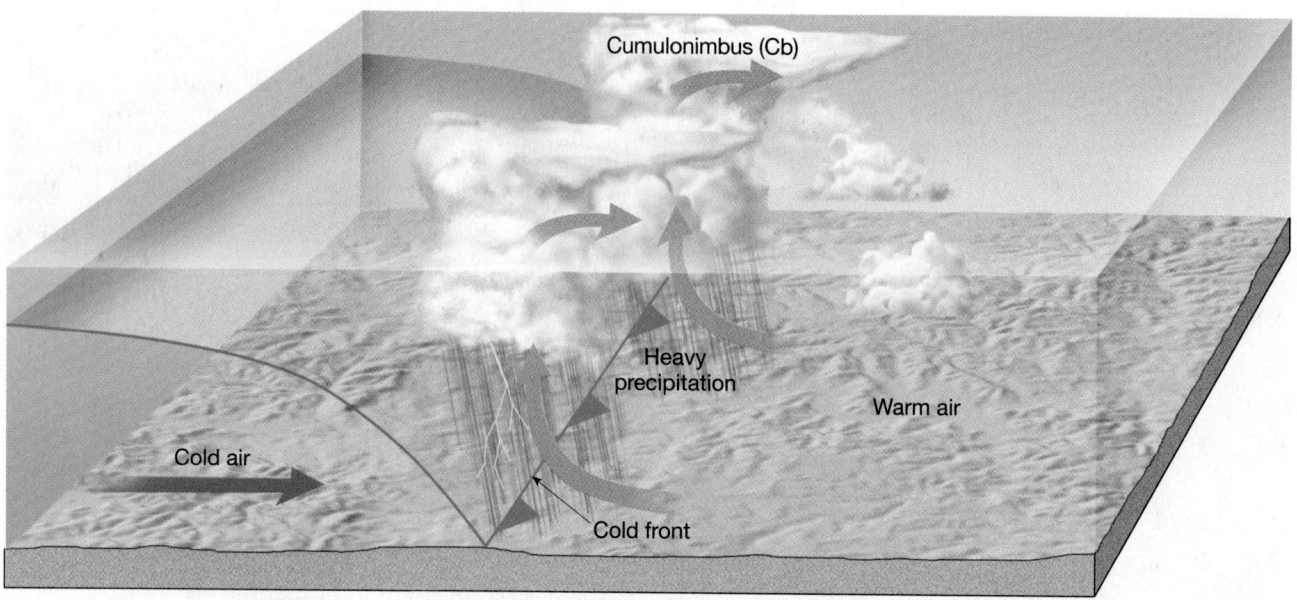

Labels in figure: Cumulonimbus (Cb), Heavy precipitation, Warm air, Cold air, Cold front

Figure 11 Formation of a Cold Front A cold front forms when cold air moves into an area occupied by warmer air. The affected area experiences thunderstorms if the warm air is unstable.

Cold Fronts **A cold front forms when cold, dense air moves into a region occupied by warmer air.** On a weather map, the surface position of a cold front is shown by a blue line edged with blue triangles that point toward the warmer air mass.

Figure 11 shows how a cold front develops. As this cold front moves, it becomes steeper. On average, cold fronts are about twice as steep as warm fronts and advance more rapidly than warm fronts do. These two differences—rate of movement and steepness of slope—account for the more violent weather associated with a cold front.

The forceful lifting of air along a cold front can lead to heavy downpours and gusty winds. As a cold front approaches, towering clouds often can be seen in the distance. Once the cold front has passed, temperatures drop and wind shifts. The weather behind a cold front is dominated by a cold air mass. So, weather clears soon after a cold front passes. When a cold front moves over a warm area, low cumulus or stratocumulus clouds may form behind the front.

Stationary Fronts Occasionally, the flow of air on either side of a front is neither toward the cold air mass nor toward the warm air mass, but almost parallel to the line of the front. **In such cases, the surface position of the front does not move, and a stationary front forms.** On a weather map, stationary fronts are shown by blue triangles on one side of the front and red semicircles on the other. Sometimes, gentle to moderate precipitation occurs along a stationary front.

Reading Checkpoint *How are cold fronts different from warm fronts?*

Occluded Fronts 🔑 **When a cold front overtakes a warm front, an occluded front forms.** As you can see in Figure 12, an occluded front develops as the advancing cold air wedges the warm front upward. The weather associated with an occluded front is generally complex. Most precipitation is associated with the warm air's being forced upward. When conditions are suitable, however, the newly formed front is capable of making light precipitation of its own.

It is important to note that the descriptions of weather associated with fronts are general descriptions. The weather along any individual front may or may not conform to the idealized descriptions you've read about. Fronts, like all aspects of nature, do not always behave as we would expect.

Middle-Latitude Cyclones

Now that you know about air masses and what happens when they meet, you're ready to apply this information to understanding weather patterns in the United States. The main weather producers in the country are middle-latitude cyclones. On weather maps, these low-pressure areas are shown by the letter L.

🔑 **Middle-latitude cyclones are large centers of low pressure that generally travel from west to east and cause stormy weather.** The air in these weather systems moves in a counterclockwise direction and in toward the center of the low. Most middle-latitude cyclones have a cold front, and frequently a warm front, extending from the central area. Forceful lifting causes the formation of clouds that drop abundant precipitation.

How do cyclones form? The first stage is the development of a stationary front, which is shown in Figure 14A on page 569. The front forms as two air masses with different temperatures move in opposite directions. Over time, the front takes on a wave shape, as shown in Figure 14B. The wave is usually hundreds of kilometers long.

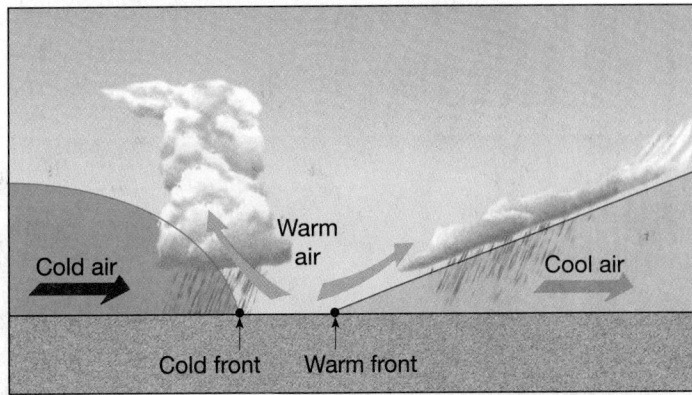

A A cold front moves toward a warm front, forcing warm air aloft.

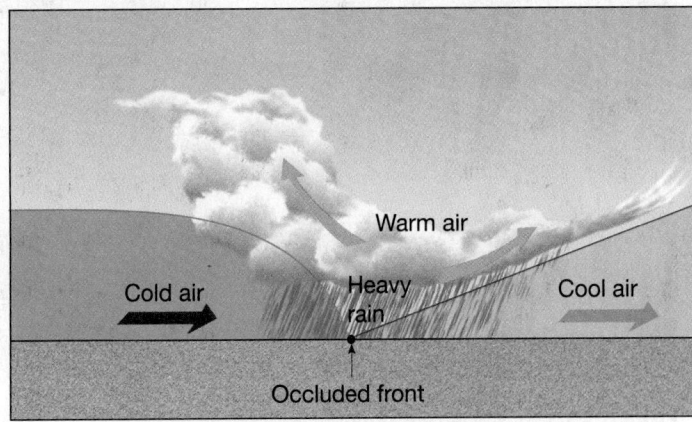

B A cold front merges with the warm front to form an occluded front that drops heavy rains.

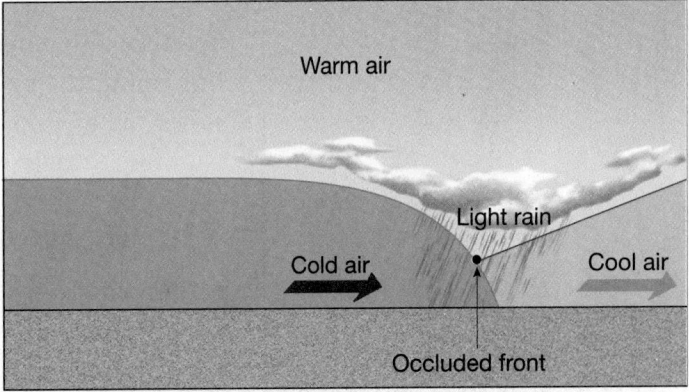

C Because occluded fronts often move slowly, light precipitation can fall for several days.

Figure 12 An occluded front forms when a cold front overtakes a warm front, producing a complex weather pattern.

As the wave develops, warm air moves towards Earth's poles. There it invades the area formerly occupied by colder air. Meanwhile, cold air moves toward the equator. This change in airflow near the surface is accompanied by a change in pressure. The result is a counterclockwise airflow in the Northern Hemisphere, as Figure 14C shows.

Recall that a cold front advances faster than a warm front. When this occurs in the development of a middle-latitude cyclone, the cold front closes in and eventually lifts the warm front, as Figure 14D shows. This process, which is known as occlusion, forms the occluded front shown in Figure 14E. As occlusion begins, the storm often gets stronger. Pressure at the storm's center falls, and wind speeds increase. In the winter, heavy snowfalls and blizzard-like conditions are possible during this phase of the storm's evolution. Figure 13 shows this phase of a mature cyclone.

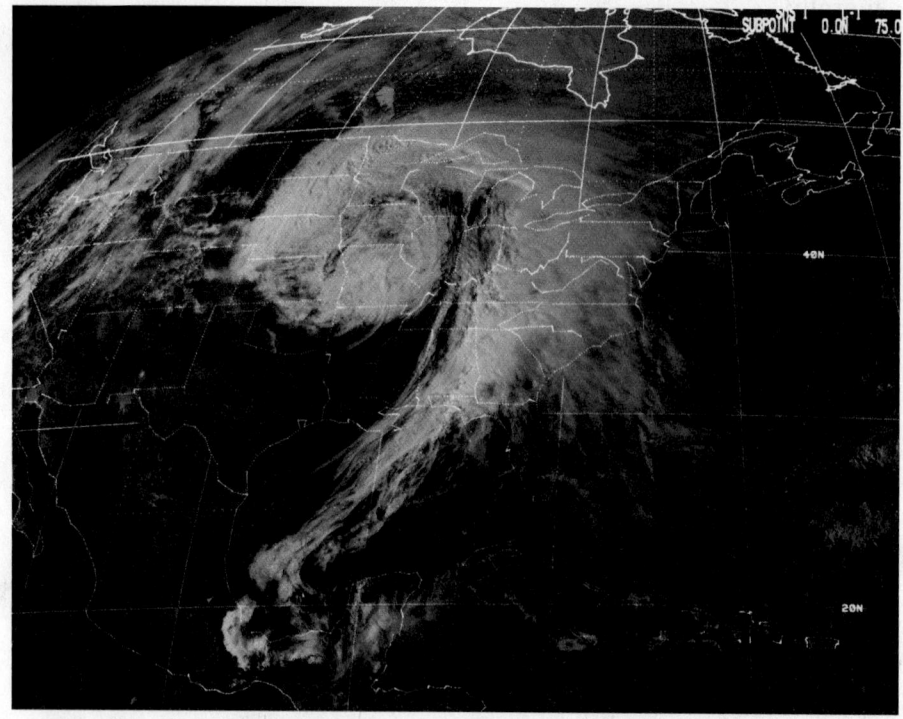

Figure 13 This is a satellite view of a mature cyclone over the eastern United States.

As more of the warm air is forced to rise, the amount of pressure change weakens. In a day or two, the entire warm area is displaced. Only cold air surrounds the cyclone at low levels. The horizontal temperature difference that existed between the two air masses is gone. At this point, the cyclone has exhausted its source of energy. Friction slows the airflow near the surface, and the once highly organized counterclockwise flow fades away (Figure 14F).

The Role of Airflow Aloft

Airflow aloft plays an important role in maintaining cyclonic and anticyclonic circulation. In fact, these rotating surface wind systems are actually generated by upper-level flow.

Cyclones often exist for a week or longer. For this to happen, surface convergence must be offset by outflow somewhere higher in the atmosphere. As long as the spreading out of air high up is equal to or greater than the surface inflow, the low-pressure system can be sustained. **More often than not, air high up in the atmosphere fuels a middle-latitude cyclone.**

 **Reading Checkpoint** *How do middle-latitude cyclones form and develop?*

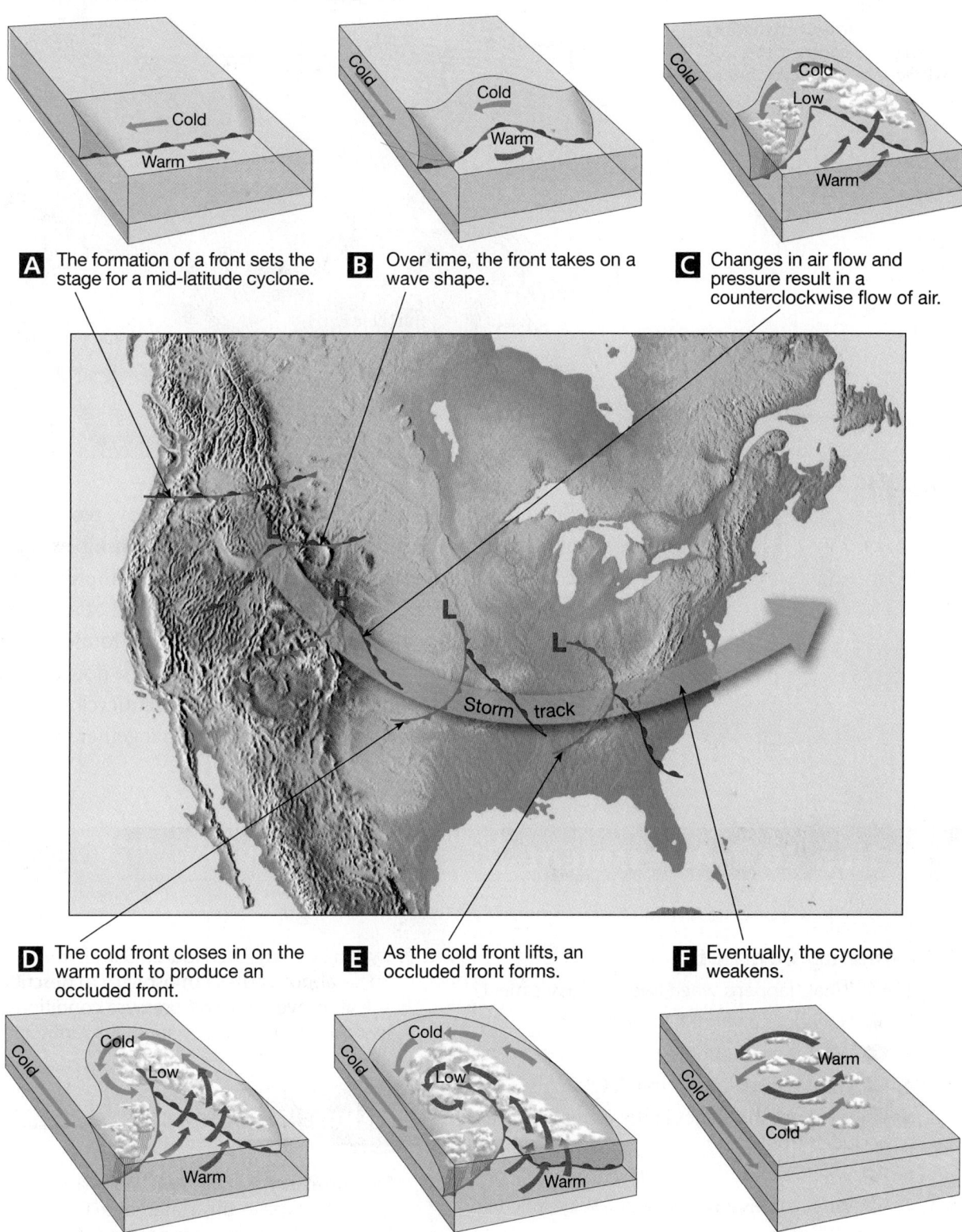

A The formation of a front sets the stage for a mid-latitude cyclone.

B Over time, the front takes on a wave shape.

C Changes in air flow and pressure result in a counterclockwise flow of air.

D The cold front closes in on the warm front to produce an occluded front.

E As the cold front lifts, an occluded front forms.

F Eventually, the cyclone weakens.

Figure 14 Cyclones have a fairly predictable life cycle.

Figure 15 Movements of air high in the atmosphere fuel the cyclones and anticyclones near Earth's surface.
Comparing and Contrasting *Compare and contrast the movement of air in cyclones and anticyclones.*

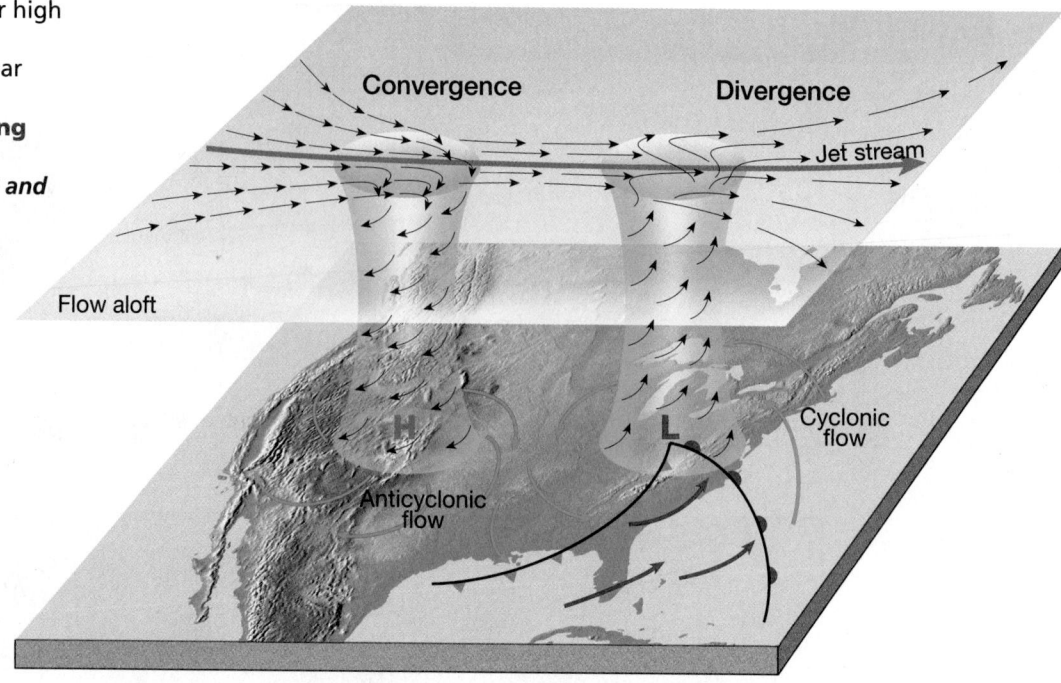

Because cyclones bring stormy weather, they have received far more attention than anticyclones. However, a close relationship exists between these two pressure systems. As shown in Figure 15, the surface air that feeds a cyclone generally originates as air flowing out of an anticyclone. As a result, cyclones and anticyclones typically are found next to each other. Like a cyclone, an anticyclone depends on the flow of air high in the atmosphere to maintain its circulation. In an anticyclone, air spreading out at the surface is balanced by air coming together from high up.

Section 20.2 Assessment

Reviewing Concepts

1. What happens when two air masses meet?
2. How does a warm front form?
3. What is a cold front?
4. What is a stationary front?
5. What are the stages in the formation of an occluded front?
6. What is a middle-latitude cyclone?
7. What causes a middle-latitude cyclone to sustain itself?

Critical Thinking

8. **Comparing and Contrasting** Compare and contrast warm fronts and cold fronts.

9. **Synthesizing** Use Figure 15 and what you know about Earth's atmosphere to describe the air movement and pressure conditions associated with both cyclones and anticyclones.

Writing in Science

Explanatory Paragraph Write a paragraph to explain this statement: The formation of an occluded front marks the beginning of the end of a middle-latitude cyclone.

20.3 Severe Storms

Reading Focus

Key Concepts
- What is a thunderstorm?
- What causes a thunderstorm to form?
- What is a tornado?
- How does a tornado form?
- What is a hurricane?
- How does a hurricane form?

Vocabulary
- thunderstorm
- tornado
- hurricane
- eye wall
- eye
- storm surge

Reading Strategy

Identifying Cause and Effect Copy the table and complete it as you read this section.

Severe Storms		
	Causes	Effects
Thunderstorms	a. ___?___	b. ___?___
Tornadoes	c. ___?___	d. ___?___
Hurricanes	e. ___?___	f. ___?___

Severe weather has a fascination that everyday weather does not provide. For example, a thunderstorm with its jagged lightning and booming thunder can be an awesome sight. The damage and destruction caused by these storms, as well as other severe weather, can also be frightening. A single severe storm can cause billions of dollars in property damage as well as many deaths. This section discusses three types of severe storms and their causes.

Thunderstorms

Have you ever seen a small whirlwind carry dust or leaves upward on a hot day? Have you observed a bird glide effortlessly skyward on an invisible updraft of hot air? If so, you have observed the effects of the vertical movements of relatively warm, unstable air. These examples are caused by a similar thermal instability that occurs during the development of a thunderstorm. **A thunderstorm is a storm that generates lightning and thunder. Thunderstorms frequently produce gusty winds, heavy rain, and hail.** A thunderstorm may be produced by a single cumulonimbus cloud and influence only a small area. Or it may be associated with clusters of cumulonimbus clouds that stretch for kilometers along a cold front.

Figure 16 Lightning is a spectacular and potentially dangerous feature of a thunderstorm.

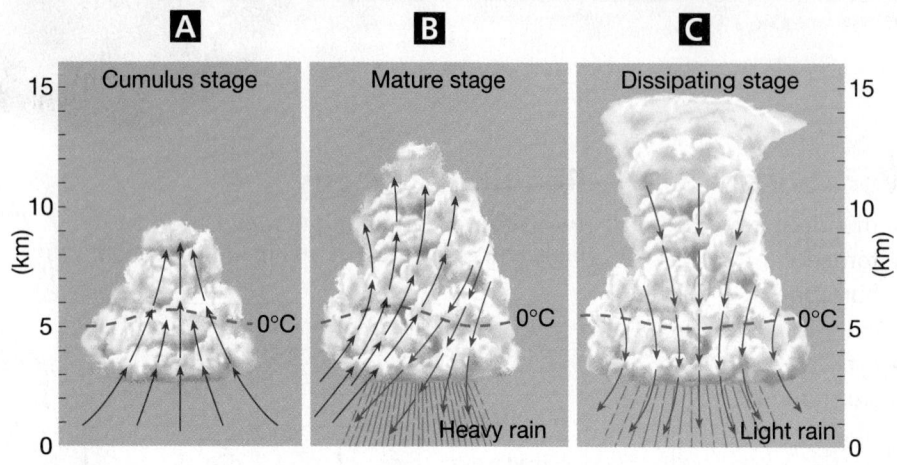

Figure 17 A During the cumulus stage, warm, moist air is supplied to the cloud. **B** Heavy precipitation falls during the mature stage. **C** The cloud begins to evaporate during the dissipating stage. **Observing** *How do the clouds involved in the development of a thunderstorm vary?*

For: Links on Severe Storms
Visit: PHSchool.com
Web Code: cuc-1204

Occurrence of Thunder-storms How common are thunderstorms? Consider these numbers. At any given time, there are an estimated 2000 thunderstorms in progress on Earth. As you might expect, the greatest number occurs in the tropics where warmth, plentiful moisture, and instability are common atmospheric conditions. About 45,000 thunderstorms take place each day. More than 16 million occur annually around the world. The United States experiences about 100,000 thunderstorms each year, most frequently in Florida and the eastern Gulf Coast region. Most parts of the country have from 30 to 100 storms each year. The western margin of the United States has little thunderstorm activity because warm, moist, unstable maritime tropical air seldom penetrates this region.

Development of Thunderstorms Thunderstorms form when warm, humid air rises in an unstable environment. The development of a thunderstorm generally involves three stages. During the cumulus stage, shown in Figure 17A, strong updrafts, or upward movements of air, supply moist air. Each new surge of warm air rises higher than the last and causes the cloud to grow vertically.

Usually within an hour of the initial updraft, the mature stage begins, as shown in Figure 17B. At this point in the development of the thunderstorm, the amount and size of the precipitation is too great for the updrafts to support. So, heavy precipitation is released from the cloud. The mature stage is the most active stage of a thunderstorm. Gusty winds, lightning, heavy precipitation, and sometimes hail are produced during this stage.

Eventually, downdrafts, or downward movements of air, dominate throughout the cloud, as shown in Figure 17C. This final stage is called the dissipating stage. During this stage, the cooling effect of the falling precipitation and the flowing in of colder air from high above cause the storm to die down.

The life span of a single cumulonimbus cell within a thunderstorm is only about an hour or two. As the storm moves, however, fresh supplies of warm, humid air generate new cells to replace those that are scattering.

Reading Checkpoint *Describe the stages in the development of a thunderstorm.*

Tornadoes

🔹 **Tornadoes are violent windstorms that take the form of a rotating column of air called a vortex. The vortex extends downward from a cumulonimbus cloud all the way to the ground.** Some tornadoes consist of a single vortex. But within many stronger tornadoes, smaller vortexes rotate within the main funnel. These smaller vortexes have diameters of only about 10 meters and rotate very rapidly. Smaller vortexes explain occasional observations of tornado damage in which one building is totally destroyed, while another one, just 10 or 20 meters away, suffers little damage.

Occurrence and Development of Tornadoes

In the United States, about 770 tornadoes are reported each year. These severe storms can occur at any time during the year. However, the frequency of tornadoes is greatest from April through June. In December and January, tornadoes are far less frequent.

🔹 **Most tornadoes form in association with severe thunderstorms.** An important process in the formation of many tornadoes is the development of a mesocyclone. A mesocyclone is a vertical cylinder of rotating air that develops in the updraft of a thunderstorm. The formation of this large vortex begins as strong winds high up in the atmosphere cause winds lower in the atmosphere to roll, as shown in Figure 18A. In Figure 18B, you can see that strong thunderstorm updrafts cause this rolling air to tilt. Once the air is completely vertical (Figure 18C), the mesocyclone is well established. The formation of a mesocyclone does not necessarily mean that a tornado will follow. Few mesocyclones produce tornadoes like the one shown in Figure 19 on page 574.

For: Links on fronts and severe weather
Visit: www.SciLinks.org
Web Code: cjn-6203

Q *What is the most destructive tornado on record?*

A The Tri-State Tornado, which occurred on March 18, 1925, started in southeastern Missouri and remained on the ground over a distance of 352 kilometers, until it reached Indiana. Casualties included 695 people dead and 2027 injured. Property losses were also great, with several small towns almost totally destroyed.

Formation of a Mesocyclone

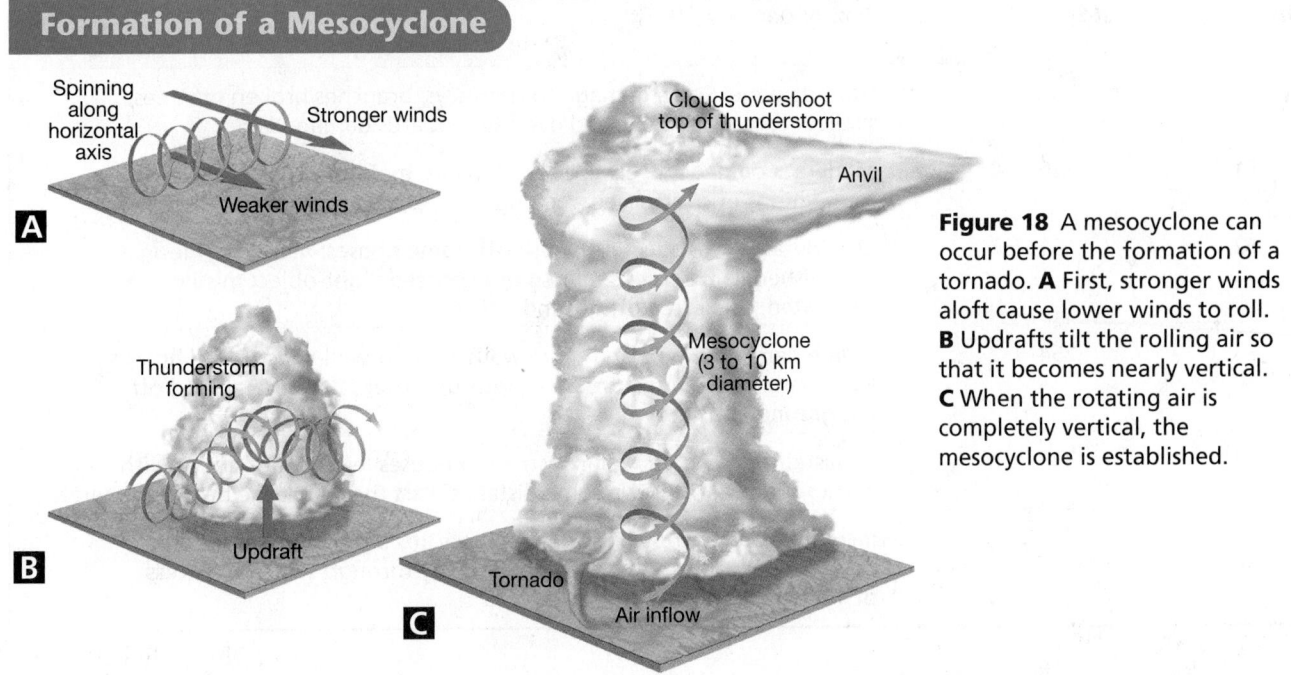

Figure 18 A mesocyclone can occur before the formation of a tornado. **A** First, stronger winds aloft cause lower winds to roll. **B** Updrafts tilt the rolling air so that it becomes nearly vertical. **C** When the rotating air is completely vertical, the mesocyclone is established.

Figure 19 The tornado shown here descended from the lower portion of a mesocyclone in the Texas Panhandle in May 1996.

Tornado Intensity Pressures within some tornadoes have been estimated to be as much as 10 percent lower than pressures immediately outside the storm. The low pressure within a tornado causes air near the ground to rush into a tornado from all directions. As the air streams inward, it spirals upward around the core. Eventually, the air merges with the airflow of the cumulonimbus cloud that formed the storm. Because of the tremendous amount of pressure change associated with a strong tornado, maximum winds can sometimes approach 480 kilometers per hour. One scale used to estimate tornado intensity is the Fujita tornado intensity scale, shown in Table 1. Because tornado winds are difficult to measure directly, a rating on this scale is usually determined by assessing the worst damage produced by a storm.

Tornado Safety The Storm Prediction Center (SPC) located in Norman, Oklahoma, monitors different kinds of severe weather. The SPC's mission is to provide timely and accurate forecasts and watches for severe thunderstorms and tornadoes. Tornado watches alert people to the possibility of tornadoes in a specified area for a particular time period. A tornado warning is issued when a tornado has actually been sighted in an area or is indicated by weather radar.

Table 1 Fujita Tornado Intensity Scale		
Intensity	**Wind Speed Estimates (kph)**	**Typical Damage**
F0	< 116	Light damage. Some damage to chimneys; branches broken off trees; shallow-rooted trees pushed over; sign boards damaged.
F1	116–180	Moderate damage. Peels surface off roofs; mobile homes pushed off foundations or overturned; moving cars blown off roads.
F2	181–253	Considerable damage. Roofs torn off frame houses; mobile homes demolished; large trees snapped or uprooted; light-object missiles generated; cars lifted off ground.
F3	254–332	Severe damage. Roofs and some walls torn off well-constructed houses; trains overturned; most trees in forest uprooted; heavy cars lifted off the ground and thrown.
F4	333–419	Devastating damage. Well-constructed houses leveled; structures with weak foundations blown some distance; cars thrown; large missiles generated.
F5	> 419	Incredible damage. Strong frame houses lifted off foundations and carried away; automobile-sized missiles fly through the air in excess of 100 m; bark torn off trees.

Hurricanes

If you've ever been to the tropics or seen photographs of these regions, you know that warm breezes, steady temperatures, and heavy but brief tropical showers are the norm. It is ironic that these tranquil regions sometimes produce the most violent storms on Earth. **Whirling tropical cyclones that produce sustained winds of at least 119 kilometers per hour are known in the United States as hurricanes.** In other parts of the world, these severe tropical storms are called typhoons, cyclones, and tropical cyclones.

Regardless of the name used to describe them, hurricanes are the most powerful storms on Earth. At sea, they can generate 15-meter waves capable of destruction hundreds of kilometers away. If a hurricane hits land, strong winds and extensive flooding can cause billions of dollars in damage and great loss of life. Hurricane Katrina, which is shown in a satellite image in Figure 20, was one such storm. In August 2005, Katrina brought flooding rains and high winds to Louisiana and Mississippi. It caused a storm surge that devastated cities, towns, and islands along the coast. Katrina also damaged the levees separating New Orleans from Lake Pontchartrain, flooding much of the city for many weeks. It was the costliest natural disaster in United States history, and the deadliest U.S. hurricane since 1928.

Hurricanes are becoming a growing threat because more and more people are living and working near coasts. At the start of the twenty-first century, more than 50 percent of the U.S. population lived within 75 kilometers of a coast. This number is expected to increase even more in the early decades of this century.

Q *Why are hurricanes given names, and who picks the names?*

A Actually, the names are given once the storms reach tropical-storm status (winds between 61–119 kilometers per hour). Tropical storms are named to provide ease of communication between forecasters and the general public regarding forecasts, watches, and warnings. Tropical storms and hurricanes can last a week or longer, and two or more storms can be occurring in the same region at the same time. Thus, names can reduce the confusion about what storm is being described.

The World Meteorological Organization creates the lists of names. The names for Atlantic storms are used again at the end of a six-year cycle unless a hurricane was particularly destructive or otherwise noteworthy. Such names are retired to prevent confusion when the storms are discussed in future years.

Figure 20 This satellite image of Hurricane Katrina shows its position in the Gulf of Mexico a day before the hurricane moved onto land. Katrina eventually made landfall near the Louisiana-Mississippi border.

For: Links on Hurricanes, Cyclones, and Typhoons

Visit: PHSchool.com

Web Code: cuc-1203

Occurrence of Hurricanes Most hurricanes form between about 5 and 20 degrees north and south latitude. The North Pacific has the greatest number of hurricanes, averaging 20 per year. The coastal regions of the southern and eastern United States experience fewer than five hurricanes, on average, per year. Although many tropical disturbances develop each year, only a few reach hurricane status. A storm is a hurricane if the spiraling air has sustained winds of at least 119 kilometers per hour.

Development of Hurricanes A hurricane is a heat engine that is fueled by the energy given off when huge quantities of water vapor condense. ◯►**Hurricanes develop most often in the late summer when water temperatures are warm enough to provide the necessary heat and moisture to the air.** A hurricane begins as a tropical disturbance that consists of disorganized clouds and thunderstorms. Low pressures and little or no rotation are characteristic of these storms.

Occasionally, tropical disturbances become hurricanes. Figure 21 shows a cross section of a well-developed hurricane. An inward rush of warm, moist surface air moves toward the core of the storm. The air then turns upward and rises in a ring of cumulonimbus clouds. This doughnut-shaped wall that surrounds the center of the storm is the **eye wall.** Here the greatest wind speeds and heaviest rainfall occur. Surrounding the eye wall are curved bands of clouds that trail away from the center of the storm. Notice that near the top of the hurricane, the rising air is carried away from the storm center. This outflow provides room for more inward flow at the surface.

At the very center of the storm is the **eye** of the hurricane. This well-known feature is a zone where precipitation ceases and winds subside. The air within the eye gradually descends and heats by compression, making it the warmest part of the storm.

Figure 21 Cross Section of a Hurricane The eye of the hurricane is a zone of relative calm, unlike the eye wall region where winds and rain are most intense.
Describing *Describe the airflow in different parts of a hurricane.*

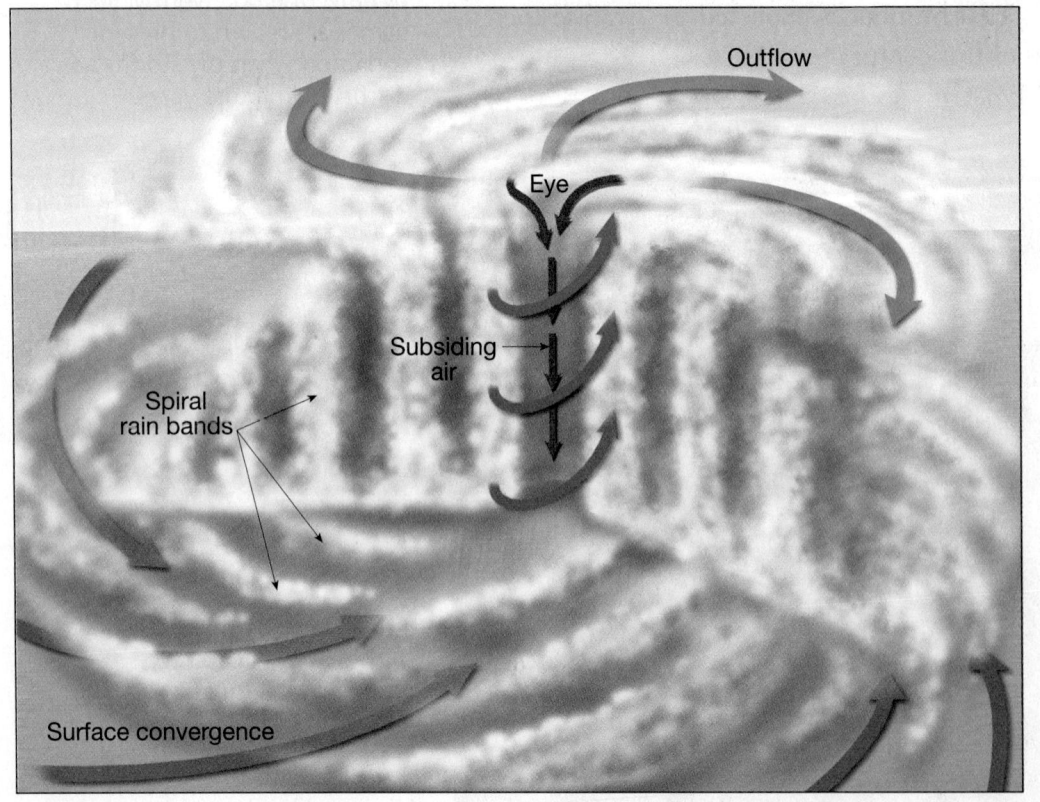

Hurricane Intensity The intensity of a hurricane is described using the Saffir-Simpson scale shown in Table 2. The most devastating damage from a hurricane is caused by storm surges. A **storm surge** is a dome of water about 65 to 80 kilometers wide that sweeps across the coast where a hurricane's eye moves onto land.

A hurricane weakens when it moves over cool ocean waters that cannot supply adequate heat and moisture. Intensity also drops when storms move over land because there is not sufficient moisture. In addition, friction with the rough land surface causes winds to subside. Finally, if a hurricane reaches a location where the airflow aloft is unfavorable, it will die out.

Table 2 Saffir-Simpson Hurricane Scale		
Category	Sustained Wind Speeds (kph)	Typical Damage
1	119–153	Storm surge 1.2–1.5 meters; some damage to unanchored mobile homes, shrubbery, and trees; some coastal flooding; minor pier damage.
2	154–177	Storm surge 1.6–2.4 meters; some damage to buildings' roofs, doors, and windows; considerable damage to mobile homes and piers; moderate coastal flooding.
3	178–209	Storm surge 2.5–3.6 meters; some structural damage to small buildings; some large trees blown over; mobile homes destroyed; some coastal and inland flooding.
4	210–249	Storm surge 3.7–5.4 meters; severe damage to trees and signs; complete destruction of mobile homes; extensive damage to doors and windows; severe flooding inland.
5	> 249	Storm surge >5.4 meters; complete roof failure on many buildings; some complete building failure; all trees and signs blown away; major inland flooding.

Section 20.3 Assessment

Reviewing Concepts

1. 🌐 What is a thunderstorm?
2. 🌐 What causes a thunderstorm?
3. 🌐 What is a tornado?
4. 🌐 How does a tornado form?
5. 🌐 What is a hurricane?
6. 🌐 How does a hurricane form?

Critical Thinking

7. **Formulating Hypotheses** What kind of front is associated with the formation of tornadoes? Explain.

8. **Synthesizing** Explain why a hurricane quickly loses its strength as the storm moves onto land.

Writing in Science

Explanatory Paragraph Examine Tables 1 and 2 to contrast the damage caused by tornadoes and hurricanes. Use the data to explain why even though hurricanes have lower wind speeds, they often cause more damage than tornadoes do.

 # How the Earth Works

Winds and Storms

The world's atmosphere is forever on the move. **Wind,** or air in motion, occurs because solar radiation heats up some parts of the sea and land more than others. Air above these hot spots becomes warmer and less dense than the surrounding air and therefore rises. Elsewhere, cool air sinks because it is more dense. Winds blow because air squeezed out by sinking, cold air is sucked in under rising, warm air. Wind may move slowly as in a gentle breeze. In extreme weather, wind moves rapidly, creating terrifyingly destructive storms.

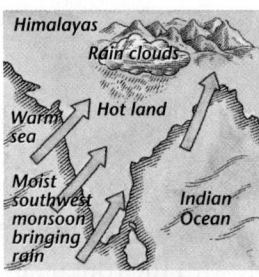

Southwest Monsoon
During the early summer, the hot, dry lands of Asia draw in cooler, moist air from the Indian Ocean.

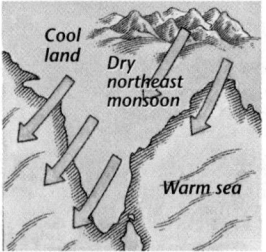

Northeast Monsoon
The cold, dry winter air from Central Asia brings chilly, dusty conditions to South Asia.

MONSOONS
Seasonal winds called monsoons affect large areas of the tropics and subtropics. They occur in South Asia, southern North America, eastern Australia, and other regions of the world. In South Asia, southwest monsoons generally bring desperately needed rain from May until October.

THUNDERSTORMS
Thunderclouds are formed by powerful updrafts of air that occur along cold fronts or over ground heated very strongly by the sun. Ice crystals and water droplets high in the cloud are torn apart and smashed together with such ferocity that they become charged with electricity. Thunderstorms can unleash thunder, lightning, wind, rain, and hail.

LIGHTNING AND THUNDER
Electricity is discharged from a thundercloud in the form of lightning. A bolt of lightning can heat the air around it to a temperature four times as hot as the sun's surface. The heated air expands violently and sends out a rumbling shock wave that we hear as thunder.

TORNADOES

Tornadoes may strike wherever thunderstorms occur. A **tornado** begins when a column of strongly rising warm air is set spinning by high winds at a cloud's top. A funnel is formed and may touch the ground. With winds that can rise above 419 kph, tornadoes can lift people, cars, and buildings high into the air and then smash them back to the ground.

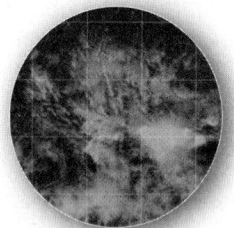

BLIZZARDS

In a **blizzard,** heavy snowfall and strong winds often make it impossible to see. Winds pile up huge drifts of snow. Travel and communication can grind to a halt.

HOW TROPICAL STORMS DEVELOP

Tropical storms begin when water evaporates over an ocean in a hot tropical region to produce huge clouds and thunderstorms. When the storms cluster together and whirl around a low-pressure center, they form a **tropical cyclone.** Tropical cyclones with winds of at least 119 kph are called hurricanes in some regions and **typhoons** in other regions. The sequence below shows satellite images of an Atlantic hurricane.

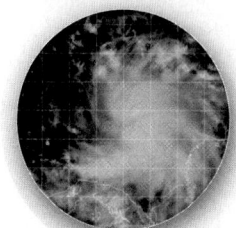

Stage 1: Thunderstorms develop over the ocean.

IMPACT OF TROPICAL STORMS

Tropical storms are often devastating. The strongest winds, with gusts sometimes more than 249 kph, occur at the storm's center, or eye. When a tropical storm strikes land, raging winds can uproot trees and destroy buildings. Vast areas may be swamped by torrential rain, and coastal regions may be overwhelmed by a **storm surge,** a wall of water up to 8 m high sucked up by the storm's eye.

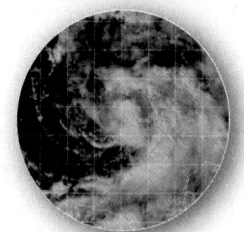

Stage 2: Storms group to form a swirl of cloud.

These women wade through the streets of Dhaka, Bangladesh, flooded by a tropical cyclone. In 1991, a cyclone killed more than 130,000 Bangladeshis.

A Pacific typhoon struck this ship off the coast of Taiwan in November 2000.

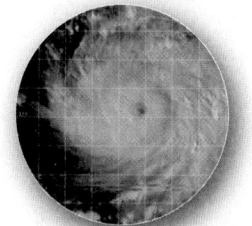

Stage 3: Winds grow and a distinct center forms in the cloud swirl.

Stage 4: Eye forms. The hurricane is now at its most dangerous.

ASSESSMENT

1. **Key Terms** Define **(a)** wind, **(b)** tornado, **(c)** blizzard, **(d)** tropical cyclone, **(e)** typhoon, **(f)** storm surge.

2. **Physical Processes** How do thunderstorms come into being?

3. **Economic Activities** **(a)** How can storms have a negative impact on economic activities? **(b)** How can monsoons benefit economic activities?

4. **Natural Hazards** How can a tropical cyclone result in the loss of thousands of lives?

5. **Critical Thinking Developing a Hypothesis** Since 1991, the Bangladeshi government has constructed hundreds of concrete storm shelters in coastal regions of the country. **(a)** Why do you think the government decided on this policy? **(b)** How do you think the policy has benefited the country?

Stage 5: Eye passes over land. The hurricane starts to weaken.

Middle-Latitude Cyclones

You've learned that much of the day-to-day weather in the United States is caused by middle-latitude cyclones. In this lab, you will identify some of the atmospheric conditions associated with a middle-latitude cyclone. Then you will use what you know about Earth's atmosphere and weather to predict how the movement of the low-pressure system affects weather in the area.

Problem
How do middle-latitude cyclones affect weather patterns?

Materials
- tracing paper
- sharp pencil
- paper clips or removable tape
- metric ruler
- colored pencils

Skills
Observing, Comparing and Contrasting, Predicting

Procedure
1. Use the paper clips or removable tape to secure the tracing paper over the map on the facing page.
2. Carefully trace all of the features and boundaries on the map. Be sure to include the isobars—the lines that show atmospheric pressure. Use the ruler to trace lines EA and GF.
3. Remove the tracing paper. Place it next to the map.
4. Transfer all of the letters and numbers on the map to your tracing.
5. Use the colored pencils to color the cold air, cool air, and warm air areas on the tracing. Also color the symbols used to designate the fronts.
6. Identify and label the cold front, warm front, and occluded front on your tracing.
7. Draw arrows that show the direction of surface winds at points A, C, E, F, and G.

Analyze and Conclude
1. **Describing** In which direction are the surface winds moving?
2. **Identifying** At which stage of formation is the cyclone? Explain your answer. Refer to Figure 14 if necessary.
3. **Explaining** Is the air in the center of the cyclone rising or falling? What effect does this have on the potential for condensation and precipitation?
4. **Inferring** Find the center of the low, which is marked with the letter L. What type of front has formed here? What happens to the maritime tropical air in this type of front?

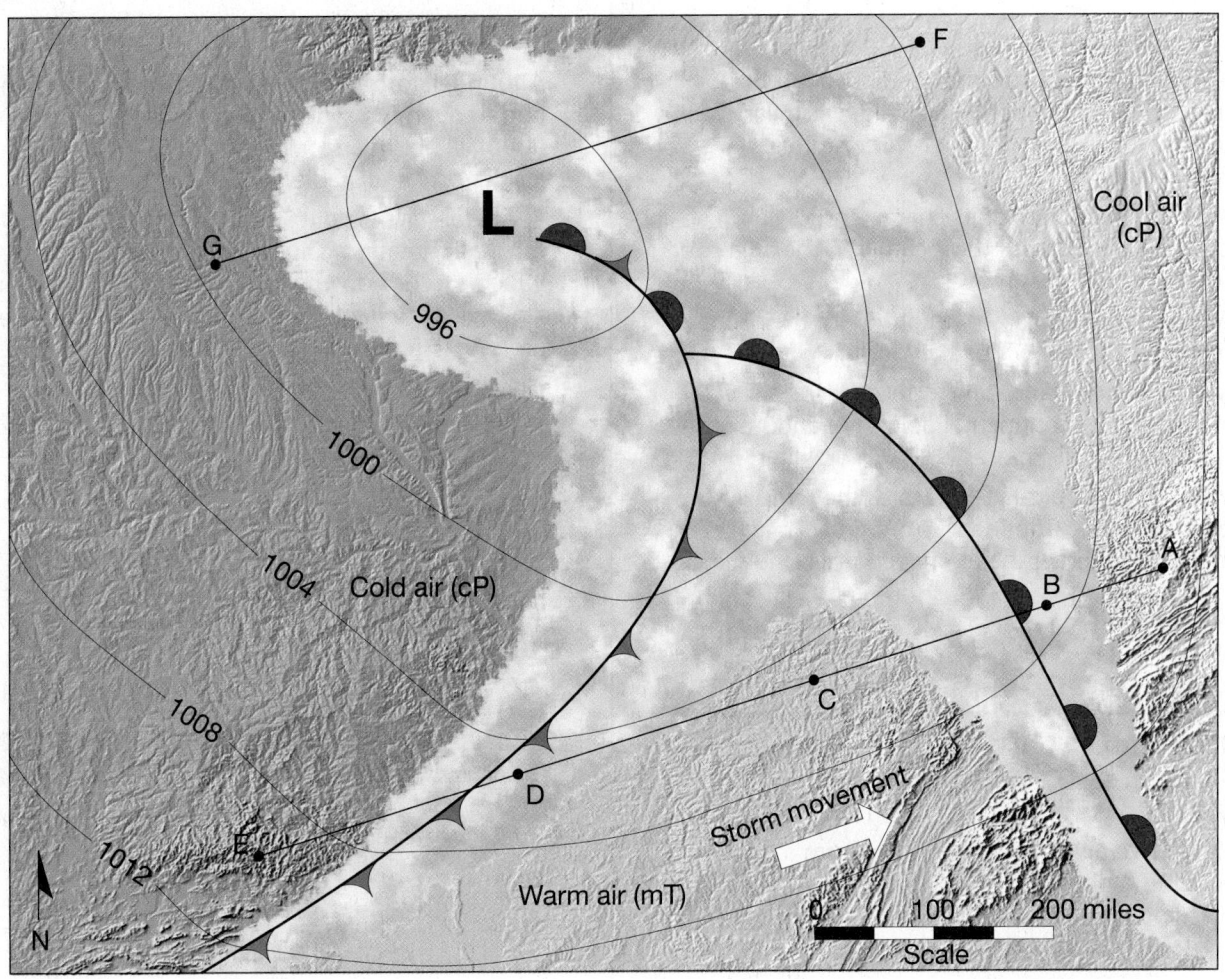

5. **Predicting** Once the warm front passes, in which direction will the wind at point B blow?

6. **Synthesizing** Describe the changes in wind direction and moisture in the air that will likely occur at point D after the cold front passes.

7. **Synthesizing** Describe the wind directions, humidity, and precipitation expected for a city as the cyclone moves and the city's relative position changes from point A to B, point C, point D, and finally from point D to E.

Go Further Find out and explain how subpolar lows affect middle-latitude cyclones over the United States in winter.

Study Guide

20.1 Air Masses

Key Concepts

- An air mass is an immense body of air in the troposphere that is characterized by similar temperatures and amounts of moisture at any given altitude.
- As an air mass moves, its characteristics can change, and so does the weather in the area over which the air mass moves.
- Air masses are classified according to their source region, the place where they form.
- Much of the weather in North America is influenced by continental polar (cP) and maritime tropical (mT) air masses.
- Polar (P) or tropical (T) indicates the temperature of an air mass. Continental (c) or maritime (m) indicates whether the air mass is dry or humid.

Vocabulary

air mass, p. 559

20.2 Fronts

Key Concepts

- When two air masses meet, they form a front, which is a boundary that separates two contrasting air masses.
- A warm front forms when warm air moves into an area formerly covered by cooler air.
- A cold front forms when cold, dense air moves into a region occupied by warmer air.
- A stationary front forms when the surface position between two air masses does not move.
- An occluded front forms when a cold front overtakes a warm front, producing a complex weather pattern.
- A middle-latitude cyclone is a large center of low pressure that generally travels from west to east and causes stormy weather.

Vocabulary

front, p. 564; warm front, p. 565; cold front, p. 566; stationary front, p. 566; occluded front, p. 567

20.3 Severe Storms

Key Concepts

- A thunderstorm generates thunder and lightning and frequently produces gusty winds, heavy rain, and hail. Thunderstorms form when warm, humid air rises in an unstable environment.
- Tornadoes are violent windstorms that take the form of a rotating column of air called a vortex, which extends downward from a cumulonimbus cloud all the way to the ground. Most tornadoes are associated with severe thunderstorms.
- Hurricanes are whirling tropical cyclones with sustained high winds that sometimes develop over the ocean when water temperatures are warm enough to provide the necessary heat and moisture to fuel the storms.

Vocabulary

thunderstorm, p. 571; tornado, p. 573; hurricane, p. 575; eye wall, p. 576; eye, p. 576; storm surge, p. 577

Thinking Visually

Concept Map Use what you know about fronts and air masses to complete this concept map.

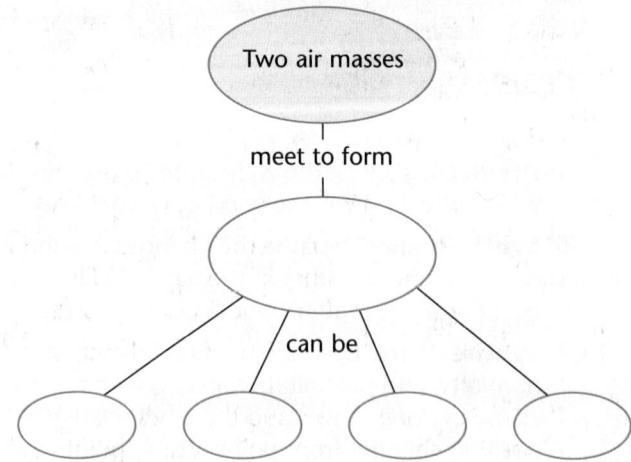

Reviewing Content

Choose the letter that best answers the question or completes the statement.

1. If an area is experiencing consecutive days of constant weather, this weather is called
   a. air-mass weather.
   b. warm-front weather.
   c. cold-front weather.
   d. occluded-front weather.

2. An air mass that forms over the Gulf of Mexico is a(n)
   a. cP air mass.　　b. mP air mass.
   c. cT air mass.　　d. mT air mass.

3. Air masses that have the greatest influence on weather in the midwestern United States are
   a. mT and cT air masses.
   b. cP and mT air masses.
   c. mP and cP air masses.
   d. cT and cP air masses.

4. Lake-effect snow is associated with a(n)
   a. mP air mass.　　b. mT air mass.
   c. cP air mass.　　d. cT air mass.

5. "Rain long foretold, long last; short notice, soon past." The first five words of this weather proverb refer to a(n)
   a. warm front.　　b. cold front.
   c. anticyclone.　　d. tornado.

6. Which front often produces hours of moderate-to-light precipitation over a large area?
   a. polar　　b. maritime
   c. cold　　d. warm

7. A thunderstorm is most intense during its
   a. cumulus stage.　　b. wave stage.
   c. mature stage.　　d. dissipating stage.

8. When a hurricane reaches land, its intensity decreases as the result of
   a. increase in pressure and temperature.
   b. lack of cold, dry air to fuel the storm.
   c. successive updrafts into the eye wall.
   d. friction and the lack of warm, moist air.

9. The eye of a hurricane
   a. has the greatest wind speeds.
   b. is warmer than the rest of the storm.
   c. experiences high pressures.
   d. is responsible for heavy precipitation.

Understanding Concepts

10. What kinds of changes occur as an air mass moves over an area?

11. Describe the effects of cP and mT air masses on much of the weather in the United States.

12. Describe weather associated with a warm front.

13. What kind of weather is associated with a cold front while it is over an area and once it passes?

14. What is a stationary front?

15. Sequence the steps that lead to the formation of an occluded front.

16. Describe the stages involved in the development of a middle-latitude cyclone.

17. How are cyclones and anticyclones related?

18. Describe the formation of a thunderstorm.

19. What is a mesocyclone and how does it form?

20. Describe the different parts of a hurricane.

Use this map to answer Questions 21–24.

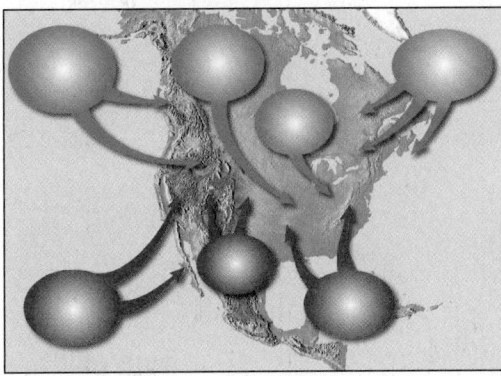

21. Name the three red air masses and identify the source region of each.

22. Identify the cold air masses, starting with the air mass farthest west and moving eastward.

23. Which air masses would supply the largest amount of precipitation to the area east of the Rocky Mountains?

24. Which of the air masses has the greatest influence on weather along the northwest coast?

Assessment *continued*

Critical Thinking

25. Comparing and Contrasting Compare and contrast polar air masses with tropical air masses.

26. Synthesizing What type of air mass is responsible for most of the warm fronts east of the Rocky Mountains?

27. Inferring What kinds of weather conditions would you expect in regions north of a middle-latitude cyclone during winter?

28. Comparing and Contrasting Compare and contrast tornadoes and hurricanes.

29. Identifying Cause and Effect Great damage and significant loss of life can take place a day or more after a hurricane has moved ashore and weakened. Explain why this might happen.

Map Skills

Use the map to answer Questions 30–34.

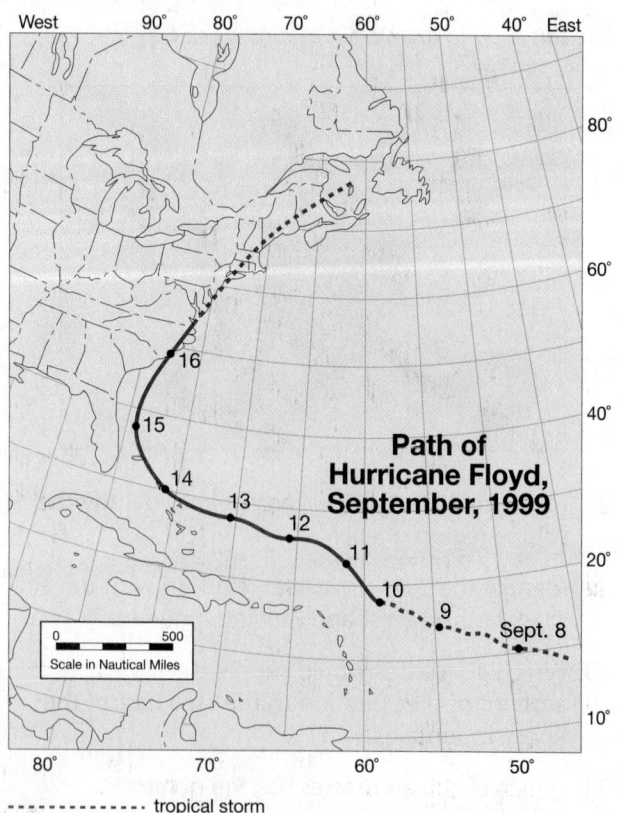

Path of Hurricane Floyd, September, 1999

West 90° 80° 70° 60° 50° 40° East

80°
60°
16
15
40°
14
13
12
11 20°
10
9   Sept. 8
10°

0   500
Scale in Nautical Miles

80° 70° 60° 50°

- - - - - - - tropical storm
————— hurricane

30. Reading Maps Over which ocean did Hurricane Floyd develop and move?

31. Interpreting Graphs On which days was Floyd a tropical storm?

32. Describing Describe the path of Hurricane Floyd from September 10 through September 16.

33. Inferring When was Hurricane Floyd most intense? Explain.

34. Reading Maps When and where did Hurricane Floyd move onto land?

Concepts in Action

35. Synthesizing Describe weather conditions that you would observe if the center of a middle-latitude cyclone passed north of you.

36. Applying Concepts What kinds of negative effects might a hurricane have on coastal ecosystems?

37. Writing in Science Use what you know about weather patterns to write a paragraph to explain which parts of the Earth system interact to produce the high snowfall in the Great Lakes region of North America.

Performance-Based Assessment

Applying Concepts Find out about precautions people should take during any of the three types of severe storms discussed in this chapter. Summarize your findings in three separate posters.

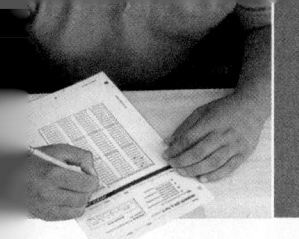

Standardized Test Prep

Using Maps
Most maps in Earth science are used to show geographic features such as mountains and bodies of water, tectonic features such as plate boundaries, and different types of rocks. Maps, like those shown below, can also be used to show statistical information. When using such maps to answer questions, be sure you understand what each map is showing before you try to answer the questions.

Use the maps below and what you know about thunderstorms and tornadoes to answer the questions on this page.

Choose the letter that best answers the question or completes the statement.

1. What part of Texas experiences the greatest average number of days with thunderstorms per year?
   (A) the southernmost tip
   (B) the southwestern portion of the state
   (C) the northern panhandle
   (D) the easternmost portion of the state

2. The part of Texas that experiences the greatest average number of tornadoes per year 26,000 km^2 is the area colored
   (A) tan.
   (B) green.
   (C) yellow.
   (D) dark red.

3. How many tornadoes on average are experienced per year in the area referred to in Question 2?
   (A) 1.0–2.0
   (B) 2.0–3.0
   (C) 5.0–7.0
   (D) 7.0–9.0

Answer the following question in complete sentences.

4. Does there appear to be a relationship between the number of days with thunderstorms and the average number of tornadoes in Texas? Explain.

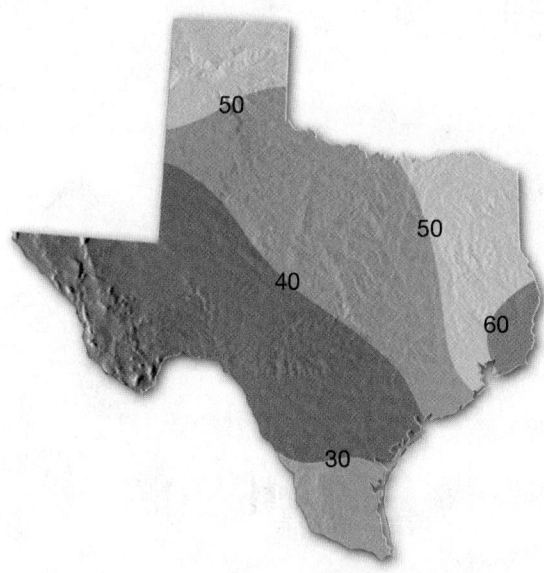

Average Number of Days/Year
with Thunderstorms

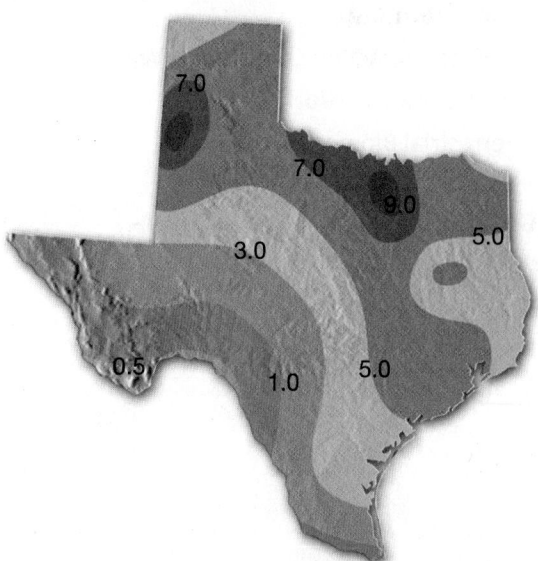

Average Number of Tornadoes per Year
per 26,000 km^2

This forest in Denali Park, Alaska, includes coniferous forest and tundra vegetation.

Chapter Preview

Inquiry > Activity

Global Warming: What Is Causing It?

Global warming is one of the most hotly debated environmental issues. The world is getting warmer. Do we need to worry about it? How much warming is due to human activities? In this activity, you will gather the evidence to decide for yourself.

Procedure

1. Gather information on the topic using the Internet. Focus your search to answer questions 1 through 4 under Think About It.

2. Now evaluate opposing points of view on this topic from credible sources. Search the Internet to find three articles that present the view that the damaging consequences of global warming are due to an increase in carbon dioxide from human activities. Find three articles that suggest that global warming is due to natural causes.

3. Print each article and analyze the information by completing items 5 and 6.

4. Formulate your own opinion on the global warming issue based on your research. Complete items 7 and 8.

Think About It

1. What is the greenhouse effect?

2. List three greenhouse gases.

3. List three facts about global warming.

4. List three uncertainties about global warming.

5. Use a marker to highlight the facts in each article that are supported by data.

6. Use a marker of another color to highlight claims that are not well supported.

7. What did you decide? Is global warming due to human activity, or is it the result of natural fluctuations in climate?

8. Write a letter in which you attempt to persuade your state senator to agree with your position. Support your stance with facts based on your research.

21.1 Factors That Affect Climate

Reading Focus

Key Concepts

- How does latitude affect climate?
- How does elevation affect climate?
- What effect does a mountain range have on climate?
- How do large bodies of water affect climate?
- What effect do global winds have on climate?
- How does vegetation affect climate?

Vocabulary

- tropical zone
- temperate zone
- polar zone

Reading Strategy

Summarizing Information Copy the table. As you read, summarize the effect(s) each factor has on climate.

Factor	Effect(s) on Climate
1. Latitude	a. ____?____
2. Elevation	b. ____?____
3. Topography	c. ____?____
4. Water bodies	d. ____?____
5. Global wind	e. ____?____
6. Vegetation	f. ____?____

Figure 1 Maroon Bells Area, Colorado All of Earth's spheres interact to affect climate.
Identifying *In the photograph, identify at least two components of each of the spheres shown.*

Recall from Chapter 17 that climate includes not only the average weather conditions of an area, but also any variations from those norms. In this section, you will learn that climate involves more than just the atmosphere. Powered by the sun, the climate system is a complex exchange of energy and moisture among Earth's different spheres, all of which are shown in Figure 1.

Factors That Affect Climate

The varied nature of Earth's surface and the many interactions that occur among Earth's spheres give every location a distinctive climate. You will now find out how latitude, elevation, topography, large bodies of water, global winds, and vegetation affect the two most important elements of climate—temperature and precipitation.

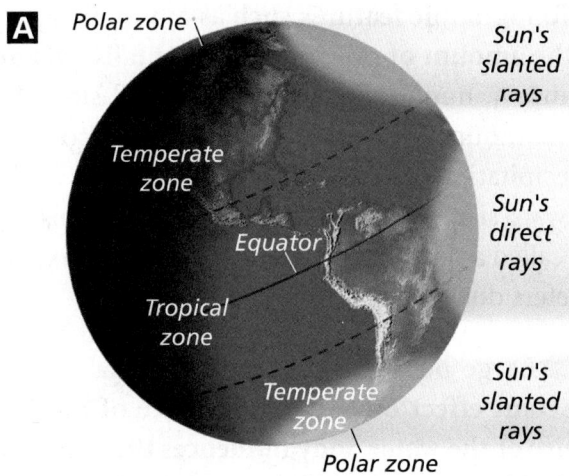

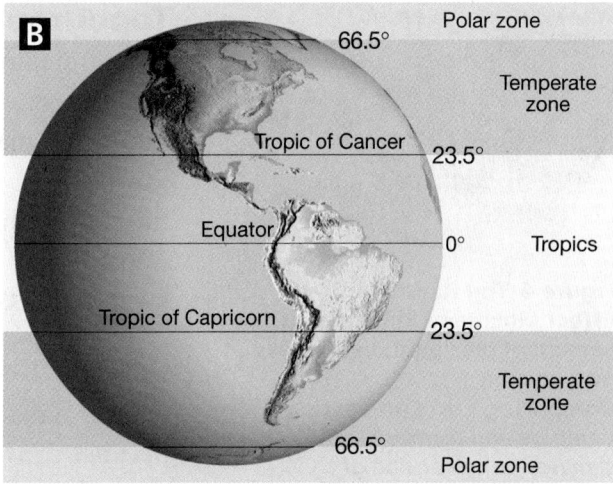

Latitude Latitude is the distance north or south of the equator. As latitude increases, the average intensity of solar energy decreases. Can you explain why? Study Figures 2A and 2B. Notice that near the equator, the sun's energy strikes the planet at nearly right angles. Therefore, in this region, between about 23.5° north (Tropic of Cancer) and 23.5° south (Tropic of Capricorn) of the equator, the sun's rays are most intense. This region is called the **tropical zones,** or the tropics. Temperatures in the tropical zones are generally warm year-round. In the **temperate zones,** which are between about 23.5° and 66.5° north and south of the equator, the sun's energy strikes Earth at a smaller angle than near the equator. This causes solar energy to be spread out over a larger area. In addition, the length of daylight in the summer is much greater than in the winter. As a result, temperate zones have hot summers and rather cold winters. In the **polar zones,** which are between 66.5° north and south latitudes and the poles, the energy strikes at an even smaller angle, causing the light and heat to spread out over an even larger area. Therefore, the polar regions experience very cold temperatures, even in the summer.

Because of the effect of latitude, less solar energy per unit of area is transferred into the atmosphere in the polar regions than in the tropics. This difference in energy affects weather and climate from the equator to the poles. Differences in energy lead to the pressure differences that produce winds. Differences in energy affect evaporation rates and the formation of clouds, air masses, and storms. Over time, energy differences on a global scale also determine climate.

Elevation Elevation, or height above sea level, affects an area's climate. Air temperature decreases with elevation by an average of about 6.5°C every 1000 meters. The higher the elevation is, the colder the climate. The elevation of an area also determines the amount of precipitation it receives. Figure 3 shows how the climates of two cities at roughly the same latitude are affected by their height above sea level.

Figure 2 Earth's Major Climate Zones A Solar energy striking Earth's surface near the poles is less intense than radiation striking near the equator. **B** Earth can be divided into three zones based on these differences in incoming solar radiation.

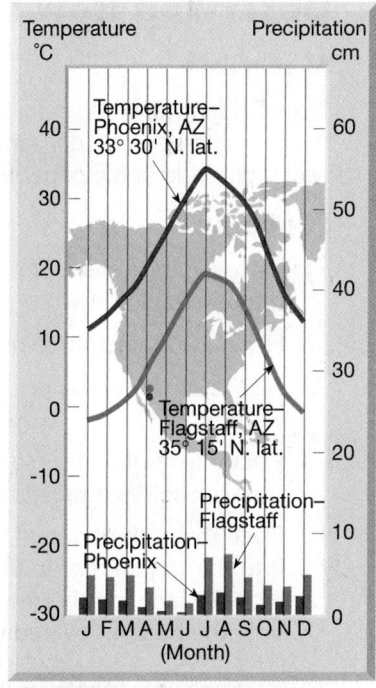

Figure 3 Climate Data for Two Cities This climate graph shows data for two cities in Arizona. Phoenix has an elevation of 338 m. Flagstaff has an elevation of 2134 m.
Interpreting Graphs *How does elevation affect annual temperatures and precipitation?*

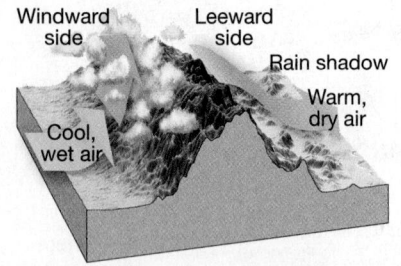

Windward side Leeward side

Rain shadow

Warm, dry air

Cool, wet air

Figure 4 The Rain Shadow Effect Mountains influence the amount of precipitation that falls over an area.
Comparing and Contrasting *Compare and contrast the climates on either side of a mountain.*

Topography Topographic features such as mountains play an important role in the amount of precipitation that falls over an area. As shown in Figure 4, humid air on the windward side of a mountain moves up the mountain's slopes and eventually cools to form clouds. Heavy precipitation often falls from these clouds. By the time air reaches the leeward side of a mountain, much of the moisture is lost. This dry area is called a rain shadow. Rain shadows can extend for hundreds of kilometers downwind of a mountain range.

Water Bodies Large bodies of water such as lakes and oceans have an important effect on the temperature of an area because the temperature of the water body influences the temperature of the air above it. Places downwind of a large body of water generally have cooler summers and milder winters than places at the same latitude that are farther inland. In the Quick Lab below, you can observe how a body of water can influence climate.

Observing How Land and Water Absorb and Release Energy

Materials

2 small, identical containers; 2 laboratory thermometers; water; dry sand; masking tape; watch or clock; book; paper towels or rags for spills

Procedure

1. On a separate sheet of paper, make a copy of the data table shown.

2. Fill one container three-quarters full of dry sand.

3. Fill the other container three-quarters full of water.

4. Place the containers in a sunny area on a flat surface such as a tabletop or a lab bench.

5. Place the bulb of one of the thermometers into the sand. Prop up the thermometer with a book. Tape the thermometer in place so that only the bulb is covered with sand.

6. Repeat Step 5 with the water.

7. Record the initial temperature of each substance in your data table.

8. Record the temperature of each thermometer every 5 minutes for about 20 minutes.

9. Remove the containers from the sunny area.

10. Record the temperature of each thermometer for another 20 minutes.

Analyze and Conclude

1. **Comparing and Contrasting** Which substance heated faster? Which substance cooled faster?

2. **Drawing Conclusions** How does a large body of water affect the temperature of nearby areas?

	Heat Absorption and Retention of Water and Sand						
	Time	Temp H_2O	Temp Sand		Time	Temp H_2O	Temp Sand
Sunny Area	0			Shady Area	0		
	5				5		
	10				10		
	15				15		
	20				20		

Atmospheric Circulation

🔑 **Global winds are another factor that influences climate because they distribute heat and moisture around Earth.** Recall from Chapter 19 that winds constantly move warm air toward the poles and cool air toward the equator. The low-pressure zones at the equator and in the middle latitudes lead to the formation of clouds that drop precipitation as rain or snow.

Vegetation

You probably already know that the types of plants that grow in a region depend on climate, as shown in Figures 5A and 5B. But did you know that vegetation affects climate? 🔑 **Vegetation can affect both temperature and the precipitation patterns in an area.** Vegetation influences how much of the sun's energy is absorbed and how quickly this energy is released. This affects temperature. During a process called transpiration, plants release water vapor from their leaves into the air. So, transpiration influences precipitation. Studies also indicate that some vegetation releases particles that act as cloud seeds. This increase in particles such as pollen promotes the formation of clouds, which also influences regional precipitation patterns.

Figure 5 Arizona Vegetation
A Cacti and scrub are common types of vegetation in the hot, dry climate of Phoenix, Arizona.
B The vegetation in the highlands of Flagstaff, Arizona, is much different.
Formulating Hypotheses
Which of these areas would receive more precipitation? Why?

Section 21.1 Assessment

Reviewing Concepts

1. 🔑 How does latitude affect climate?
2. 🔑 How does elevation affect climate?
3. 🔑 How does a mountain range affect climate?
4. 🔑 How do large bodies of water affect climate?
5. 🔑 What effect do global winds have on climate?
6. 🔑 Describe different ways in which vegetation affects climate.

Critical Thinking

7. **Comparing and Contrasting** Compare and contrast tropical zones, temperate zones, and polar zones in terms of location and the intensity of solar radiation that each receives.

8. **Explaining** Explain why deserts are common on the leeward sides of mountain ranges.
9. **Applying Concepts** Look again at Figures 3 and 5. What two factors contribute to the average annual temperature in both areas?

Writing in Science

Explanatory Paragraph Write a paragraph to explain how three of the factors discussed in this section affect the climate of your area.

21.2 World Climates

Reading Focus

Key Concepts

- What is the Köppen climate classification system?
- What are humid tropical climates?
- Contrast the different types of humid mid-latitude climates.
- What are the characteristics of dry climates?
- What are the characteristics of polar climates?
- How do highland climates compare with nearby lowlands?

Vocabulary

- Köppen climate classification system
- wet tropical climate
- tropical wet and dry climate
- humid subtropical climate
- marine west coast climate
- dry-summer subtropical climate
- subarctic climate

Reading Strategy

Outlining Copy and continue the outline for each climate type discussed in this section. Include temperature and precipitation information for each climate type, as well as at least one location with that climate type.

I. **World Climates**
  A. Humid tropical
    1. Wet tropics
    2. _____?_____
  B. Humid mid-latitude
    1. _____?_____
    2. _____?_____
  C. Dry
    1. _____?_____
    2. _____?_____

Figure 6 An ice cap climate is a polar climate in which the average monthly temperature is always below freezing.

If you were to travel around the world, you would find an incredible variety of climates. So many, in fact, that it might be hard to believe they could all occur on the same planet! Despite the diversity, climates can be classified according to average temperatures and amount of precipitation. In this section, you will learn about the Köppen climate classification system, which is commonly used to group climates.

The Köppen Climate Classification System

Many classification systems have been used to group climates. Perhaps the best-known and most commonly used system is the Köppen climate classification system. **The Köppen climate classification system uses mean monthly and annual values of temperature and precipitation to classify climates.** This system is often used because it classifies the world into climatic regions in a realistic way.

The Köppen system has five principal groups: humid tropical climates, dry climates, humid mid-latitude climates, polar climates, and highland climates. An example of a polar climate is shown in Figure 6. All of these groups, except climates classified as dry, are defined on the basis of temperature. Dry climates are classified partly according to the amount of precipitation that falls over an area. Each of the five major groups is further subdivided. See Figure 9 on page 594.

Figure 7 Rain Forest in Malaysia The vegetation in the tropical rain forest is the most luxuriant found anywhere on Earth.

Humid Tropical Climates

🔑 **Humid tropical climates are climates without winters. Every month in such a climate has a mean temperature above 18°C. The amount of precipitation can exceed 200 cm per year.** There are two types of humid tropical climates: wet tropical climates and tropical wet and dry climates.

Wet Tropical The tropical rain forest shown in Figure 7 is typical of a **wet tropical climate.** Wet tropical climates have high temperatures and much annual precipitation. Why? Recall what you've learned about how latitude affects climate. The intensity of the sun's rays in the tropics is consistently high. Because the sun is directly overhead much of the time, changes in the length of daylight throughout the year are slight. The winds that blow over the tropics cause the warm, humid, unstable air to rise, cool, condense, and fall as precipitation. Look at Figure 9 on pages 594 and 595. Notice that regions with humid tropical climates form a belt on either side of the equator.

Tropical Wet and Dry

Refer again to Figure 9. Bordering the wet tropics are climates classified as tropical wet and dry climates. **Tropical wet and dry climates** have temperatures and total precipitation similar to those in the wet tropics, but experience distinct periods of low precipitation. Savannas, which are tropical grasslands with drought-resistant trees, are typical of tropical wet and dry climates. A savanna in Africa is shown in Figure 8.

Figure 8 African Savanna Drought-resistant trees and tall grasses are typical vegetation of a savanna.

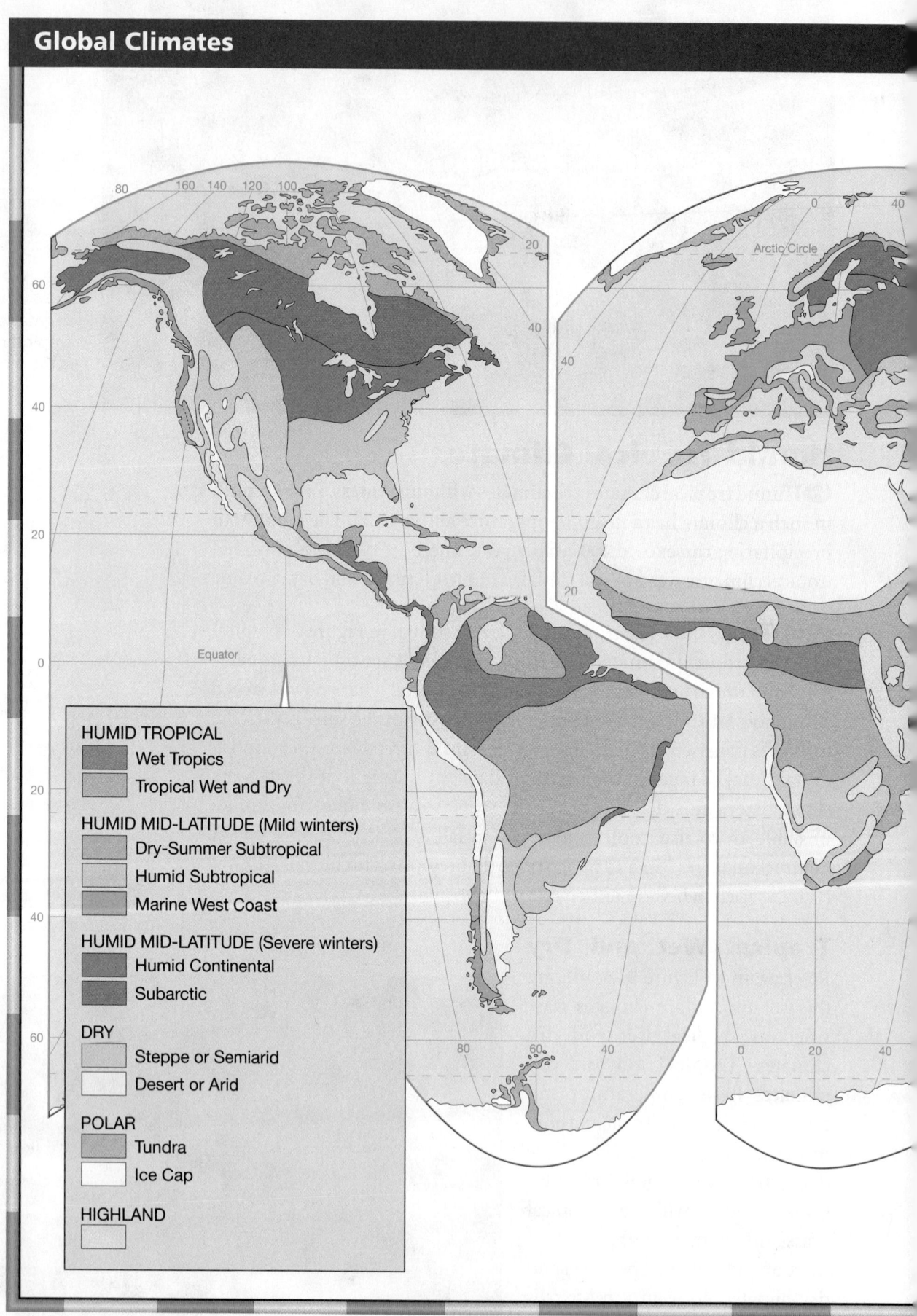

HUMID TROPICAL
- Wet Tropics
- Tropical Wet and Dry

HUMID MID-LATITUDE (Mild winters)
- Dry-Summer Subtropical
- Humid Subtropical
- Marine West Coast

HUMID MID-LATITUDE (Severe winters)
- Humid Continental
- Subarctic

DRY
- Steppe or Semiarid
- Desert or Arid

POLAR
- Tundra
- Ice Cap

HIGHLAND

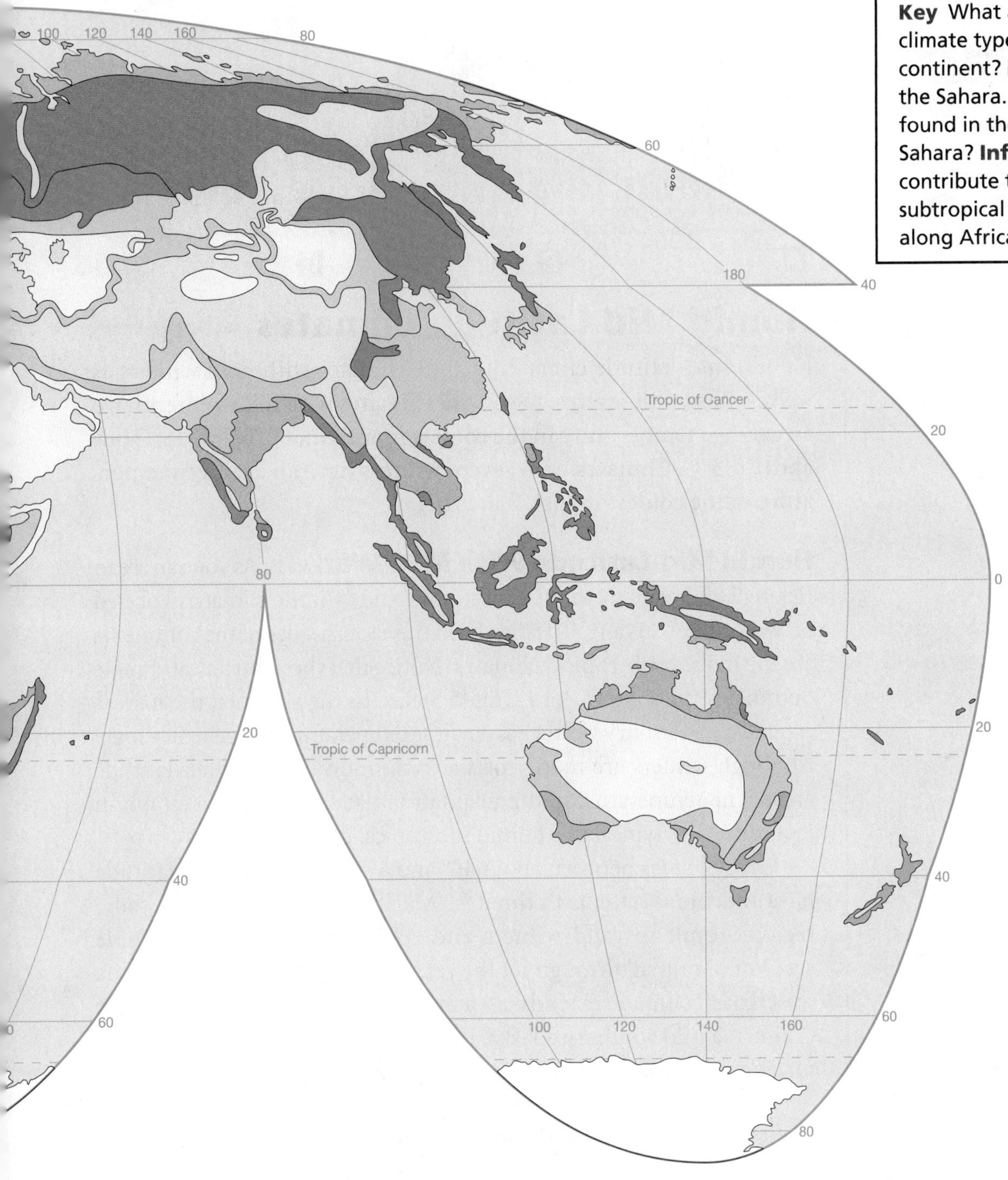
100
120
140
160
80
60
180
40
Tropic of Cancer
20
0
80
20
Tropic of Capricorn
20
40
40
60
100
120
140
160
60
80

MAP MASTER™ Skills Activity

Figure 9

Regions Find Africa on the map. **Use the Map Key** What are the major climate types of this continent? **Locate** Locate the Sahara. What climate is found in the region of the Sahara? **Infer** What may contribute to the subtropical marine climate along Africa's southern tip?

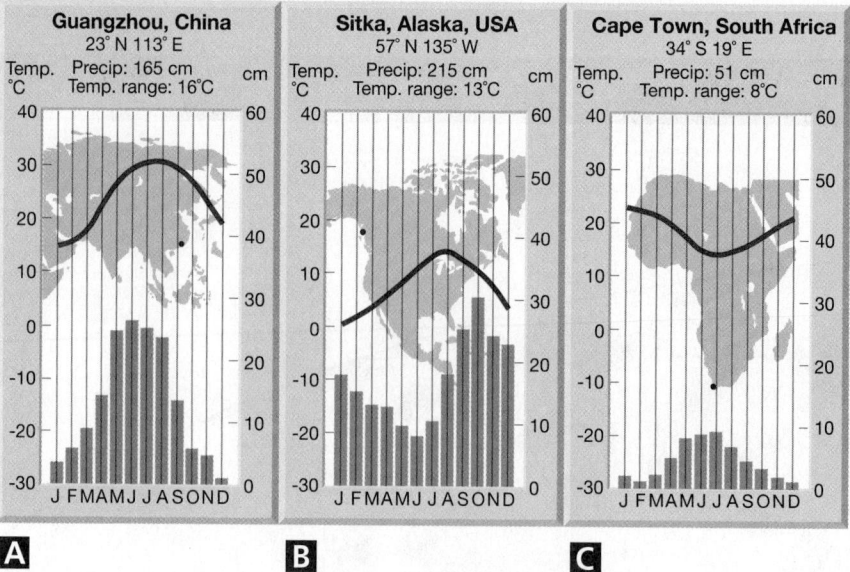

A **B** **C**

Figure 10 Each of these graphs shows typical climate data of the mid-latitude climates with mild winters. Graph **A** shows a humid subtropical climate. Graph **B** shows a marine west coast climate. Graph **C** shows a dry-summer subtropical climate.

Humid Mid-Latitude Climates

Humid mid-latitude climates include climates with mild winters as well as those with severe winters. ○━ **Climates with mild winters have an average temperature in the coldest month that is below 18°C but above −3°C. Climates with severe winters have an average temperature in the coldest month that is below −3°C.**

Humid Mid-Latitude With Mild Winters As you can see in Figure 9, there are three types of humid mid-latitude climates. Located between about 25° and 40° latitude on the eastern sides of the continents are the **humid subtropical climates.** Notice that the subtropical climate dominates the southeastern United States. In the summer, these areas experience hot, sultry weather as daytime temperatures are generally high. Although winters are mild, frosts are common in the higher-latitude areas. The temperature and precipitation data shown in the graph in Figure 10A are typical of a humid subtropical climate.

Coastal areas between about 40° and 65° north and south latitude have **marine west coast climates.** Maritime air masses over these regions result in mild winters and cool summers with an ample amount of rainfall throughout the year. In North America, the marine west coast climate extends as a narrow belt from northernmost California into southern Alaska. The data in Figure 10B are typical of marine west coast climates.

As you can see in Figure 9, regions with **dry-summer subtropical climates** are located between about 30° and 45° latitude. These climatic regions are unique because they are the only humid climate that has a strong winter rainfall maximum, as shown in Figure 10C. In the United States, dry-summer subtropical climate is found only in California. It is sometimes referred to as a mediterranean climate.

For: Links on Drought
Visit: PHSchool.com
Web Code: cuc-1212

 Reading Checkpoint   *Describe the conditions typical of a humid subtropical climate.*

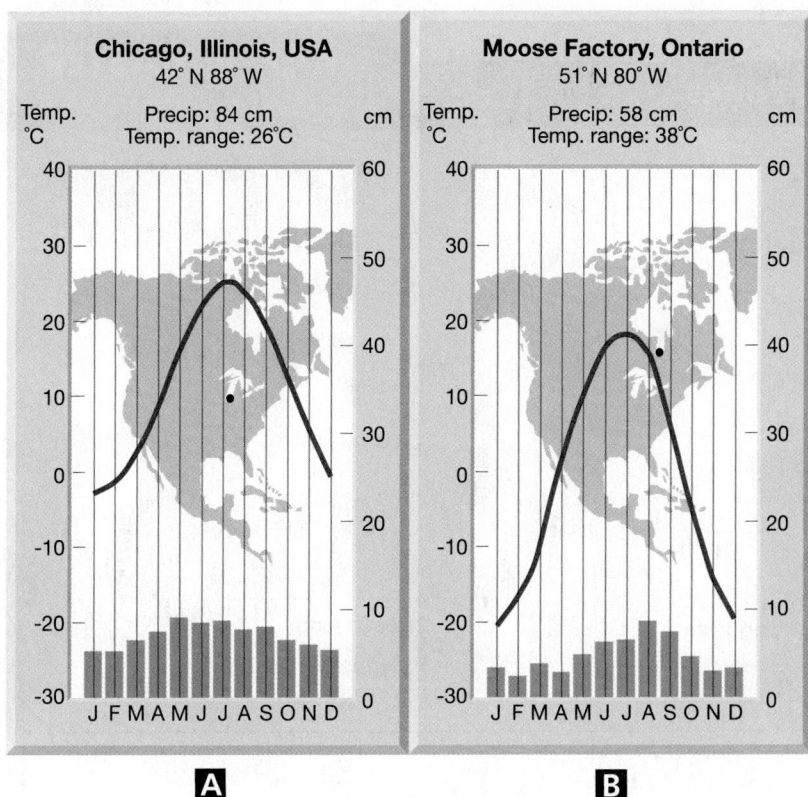

Chicago, Illinois, USA
42° N 88° W

Temp. °C   Precip: 84 cm
            Temp. range: 26°C   cm

Moose Factory, Ontario
51° N 80° W

Temp. °C   Precip: 58 cm
            Temp. range: 38°C   cm

A   **B**

Figure 11 Graph **A** displays data typical of a humid continental climate. The trends shown in graph **B** are typical of a subarctic climate.
Interpreting Graphs *What are the typical temperatures and amounts of precipitation for Chicago, Illinois, in May and June?*

Humid Mid-Latitude With Severe Winters

Humid Mid-Latitude With Severe Winters There are two types of humid mid-latitude climates with severe winters: the humid continental climates and the subarctic climates. Continental landmasses strongly influence both of these climates. As a result, such climates are absent in the Southern Hemisphere. There, oceans dominate the middle-latitude zone. Locate the regions having a humid continental climate, which are shown in blue, on Figure 9. Note that areas with such climates lie between approximately 40° and 50° north latitude. As you can see in Figure 11A the winters are severe, while the summers are typically quite warm. Note, too, that precipitation is generally greater in summer than in winter.

North of the humid continental climate and south of the tundra is an extensive **subarctic climate** region. From Figure 9, you can see that this climate zone covers a broad expanse. Such climates stretch from western Alaska to Newfoundland in North America, and from Norway to the Pacific coast of Russia in Eurasia. Winters in these regions are long and bitterly cold. By contrast, summers in the subarctic are remarkably warm but very short. The extremely cold winters and relatively warm summers combine to produce the highest annual temperature ranges on Earth.

 **Reading Checkpoint**   *Compare and contrast two types of humid mid-latitude climates with severe winters.*

Extent of Dry Climate Zones

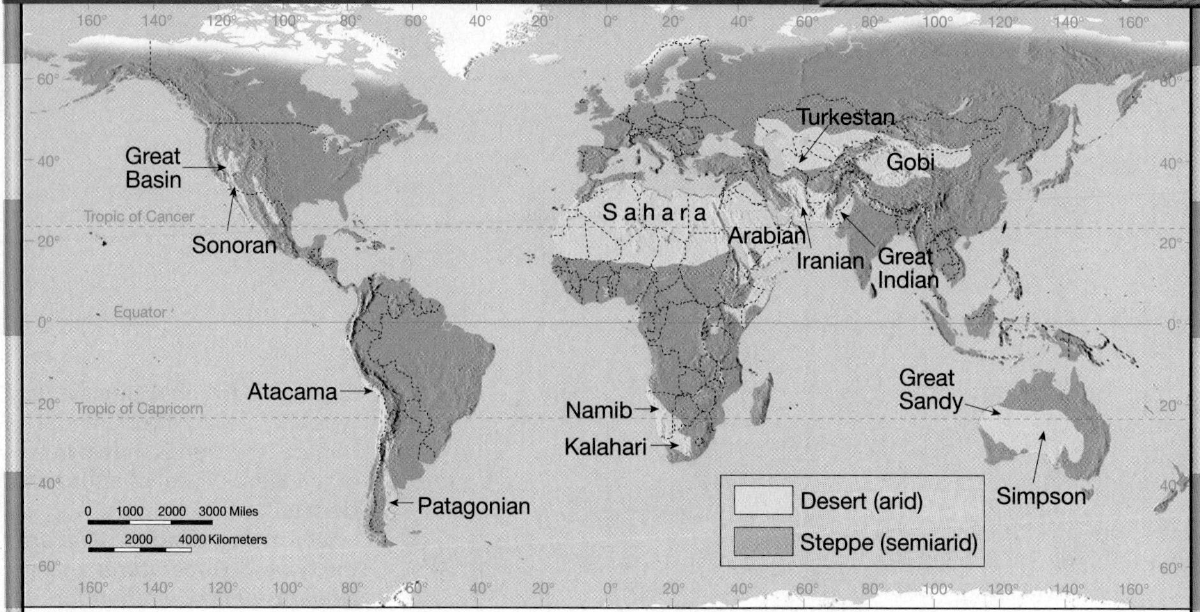

Figure 12

Location Locate each of the places listed.
Identify Identify the desert(s) in each place or region.
1. Chile
2. southwestern United States
3. central Australia
4. northwestern India
5. southern Africa

Describe About how much of Australia has a desert climate?

Q *Are deserts always hot?*

A Deserts can certainly be hot places. The record high temperature for the United States, 57°C, was set at Death Valley, California. However, deserts also experience very cold temperatures. The average daily minimum in January in Phoenix, Arizona, is 1.7°C, a temperature just barely above freezing. At Ulan Bator in Mongolia's Gobi Desert, the average high temperature in January is only −19°C!

Dry Climates

A dry climate is one in which the yearly precipitation is not as great as the potential loss of water by evaporation. In other words, dryness is not only related to annual rainfall, but is also a function of evaporation. Evaporation, in turn, is closely dependent upon temperature. There are two types of dry climates: arid, or desert, and semi-arid, or steppe, as shown in Figure 12. Arid and semi-arid climates have many features in common. In fact, the difference between them is slight. The steppe is a marginal and more humid variant of the desert. The steppe represents a transition zone that surrounds the desert and separates it from humid climates.

Dry climates exist as the result of the global distribution of air pressure and winds. In regions near the tropics of Cancer and Capricorn, air is subsiding. When air sinks, it is compressed and warmed. Such conditions are opposite of those needed for clouds to form precipitation. As a result, regions with dry climates experience mostly clear, sunny skies and dry climates. Other dry areas including the Great Basin in North America and the Gobi Desert of Eurasia occur where prevailing winds meet mountain barriers. These arid regions are called rain shadow deserts.

Some of Earth's driest desert climates occur where a cold ocean current affects the west coast of a continent. A cold current cools the air above it. This strengthens the sinking of air in the warm, dry air-masses that cause deserts. The Namib desert in Africa and the Atacama desert in Peru are examples of this type of extremely dry coastal desert.

Polar Climates

Polar climates are those in which the mean temperature of the warmest month is below 10°C. Polar winters are periods of perpetual night, or nearly so, making temperatures extremely cold. During the summer, temperatures remain cool despite the long hours of daylight. Very little precipitation falls in polar regions.

There are two types of polar climates. The tundra climate, shown in Figure 13, is a treeless region found almost exclusively in the Northern Hemisphere. The ice cap climate does not have a single monthly mean above 0°C. The landscape is covered by permanent ice and snow. Ice cap climates occur in high mountain areas and in Greenland and Antarctica.

Highland Climates

Highland climates are localized. This means that they are much different from climates in surrounding areas. Conditions of highland climates often vary abruptly from one place to another. For example, south-facing slopes are warmer than north-facing slopes, and air on the windward sides of mountains is wetter than air on the leeward sides. In general, highland climates are cooler and wetter than nearby areas at lower elevations. Locate the highland climate regions on Figure 9. What do they all have in common?

Figure 13 Tundra North of Nome, Alaska Tundra plant life includes mostly mosses, shrubs, and flowering herbs.

Go Online

NSTA SciLINKS

For: Links on climates of the world
Visit: www.SciLinks.org
Web Code: cjn-6212

Section 21.2 Assessment

Reviewing Concepts

1. What is the Köppen climate classification system?
2. Describe the characteristics of humid tropical climates.
3. What are some characteristics of humid mid-latitude climates?
4. What defines a dry climate?
5. What are the characteristics of polar climates?
6. How do highland climates compare with nearby lowlands?

Critical Thinking

7. **Identifying** Use Figure 9 to identify the climate type of your city. Describe some characteristics of your city's climate type.
8. **Formulating Conclusions** Can tundra climates exist at low latitudes? Explain.

Writing in Science

Explanatory Paragraph Write a paragraph in which you explain why Antarctica can be classified as a desert.

21.3 Climate Changes

Reading Focus

Key Concepts

- Describe natural processes that can cause changes in climate.
- What is the greenhouse effect?
- What is global warming?
- What are some of the consequences of global warming?

Vocabulary

- greenhouse effect
- global warming

Reading Strategy

Identifying Cause and Effect Copy the table, then complete the table as you read.

Climate Changes	
Causes	Effects
a. ___?___	b. ___?___
c. ___?___	d. ___?___
e. ___?___	f. ___?___

Figure 14 Effect of El Niño
In 1998, bad weather conditions and flooding in Alabama were attributed to El Niño.

Climate is always changing. Some of these changes are short-term. Others occur over long periods of geologic time. Some climate changes are the result of natural processes, such as the flood caused by El Niño, shown in Figure 14. Others are related to human activities.

Natural Processes That Change Climate

Many different natural processes can cause climates to change. Some act over very long time scales, and some over much shorter time scales. All occur together, making climate change a very complex process.

Plate Tectonics Geographic changes in Earth's land and oceans due to plate tectonics cause changes in climate over very long time scales. Oceans open and close, changing ocean circulation patterns. Large supercontinents like Pangaea develop monsoon climates, as in Asia. But most important, mountain building cools global climates by removing carbon dioxide from the atmosphere. For example, Earth has been cooling over the past 50 million years because of the collision of India and Asia that created the Himalayas. In this process, mountains weather and erode quickly, and the sediments wash down rivers and into the ocean where they form carbonate rocks such as limestone. The carbon in limestone begins as carbon dioxide in the atmosphere. Weathering removes carbon dioxide from the atmosphere and buries it on the sea floor. Before India collided with Asia, there was three times as much carbon dioxide in the atmosphere as there is now.

Earth's Orbital Motions Changes in the shape of Earth's orbit and the tilt of Earth's axis of rotation affect global climates over intermediate time scales. Earth's orbit is always elliptical. But over 100,000–400,000 year periods, the path becomes more and then less elliptical. This change in shape brings Earth closer to and then farther from the sun. This affects global climates: Earth is warmer when it is closer to the sun. The tilt of Earth's orbit also changes with respect to the rest of the solar system, with a 100,000 year period. The tilt and direction of Earth's axis of rotation change over periods of about 20,000–40,000 years. The tilt of Earth's axis changes by about 3 degrees. This affects the severity of the seasons. When Earth's axis is less tilted, the temperature difference between summer and winter is less.

Ocean Circulation Recall from Chapter 19 that El Niño is a change in ocean circulation that causes parts of the eastern tropical Pacific Ocean to become warmer than usual. These changes in ocean circulation also can result in short-term climate fluctuations. For example, some areas that are normally arid receive large amounts of rain during El Niño. Also, some regions that receive abundant precipitation may experience dry periods when the ocean circulation patterns change.

Solar Activity In general, the sun has been giving off increasing amounts of energy over its lifetime. Over short time scales, fluctuations in the amount of solar radiation can change global climates. An increase in sunspots appears to correspond with warm periods in Europe and North America. Fewer sunspots seem to be correlated with cooler periods. For example, the "Little Ice Age" in Europe during the 1600s occurred when there were very few sunspots. This process is not understood and is still being investigated.

Volcanic Eruptions As you can see in Figure 15, volcanic eruptions can emit large volumes of ash and dust into Earth's atmosphere. Volcanic eruptions also send minute particles containing sulfur into the air. If the volume of these very fine particles called aerosols is great enough, it can cause short-term changes in Earth's surface temperature. Volcanic ash, dust, and sulfur-based aerosols in the air increase the amount of solar radiation that is reflected back into space. This causes Earth's lower atmosphere to cool. But over longer time scales, volcanic eruptions can raise global temperatures by adding gases like carbon dioxide to the atmosphere, increasing the greenhouse effect.

 **Reading Checkpoint** *Identify five natural processes that cause climate changes.*

Figure 15 Mount Pinatubo in the Philippines ejected volcanic ash into the atmosphere when it erupted in 1991.

Human Impact on Climate Changes

Natural processes have certainly contributed to many climatic changes throughout Earth's 4.6-billion year history. These processes will also cause some of the future shifts in Earth's climates. But human activities have contributed and will contribute to global climatic change.

The Greenhouse Effect The greenhouse effect is a natural warming of both Earth's lower atmosphere and Earth's surface. The major gases involved in the greenhouse effect are water vapor, carbon dioxide, and methane. These greenhouse gases, as they are often called, are transparent to solar radiation, and therefore much of this energy reaches Earth's surface. Most of this energy is then reradiated skyward. The greenhouse gases are good absorbers of Earth's radiation. These gases maintain warm temperatures in the lower atmosphere, making Earth habitable for living things. Without the greenhouse effect, Earth would be much too cold to support most types of life presently living on Earth. But an increase in the greenhouse effect could prove devastating.

Studies indicate that human activities for the past 200 or so years have strengthened the greenhouse effect. As you can see in Figure 16, carbon dioxide levels in the air have risen at a rapid pace since about 1850. Much of this greenhouse gas has been added by the burning of fossil fuels. The clearing of forests also contributes to an increase in carbon dioxide because this gas is released when vegetation is burned or when it decays.

Global Warming As a result of increases in carbon dioxide levels, as well as other greenhouse gases, global temperatures have increased. This increase is called global warming. Figure 17 shows that during the twentieth century, Earth's average surface temperatures increased about 1.0°C. Scientists predict that by the year 2100, temperatures could increase by more than another 5°C.

Figure 16 Change in CO₂ Levels
The rapid increase in carbon dioxide concentration since 1850 has closely followed the increase in carbon dioxide emissions from burning fossil fuels. The concentration is measured in parts per million (ppm).
Inferring *What do you think initiated this increase in carbon dioxide levels?*

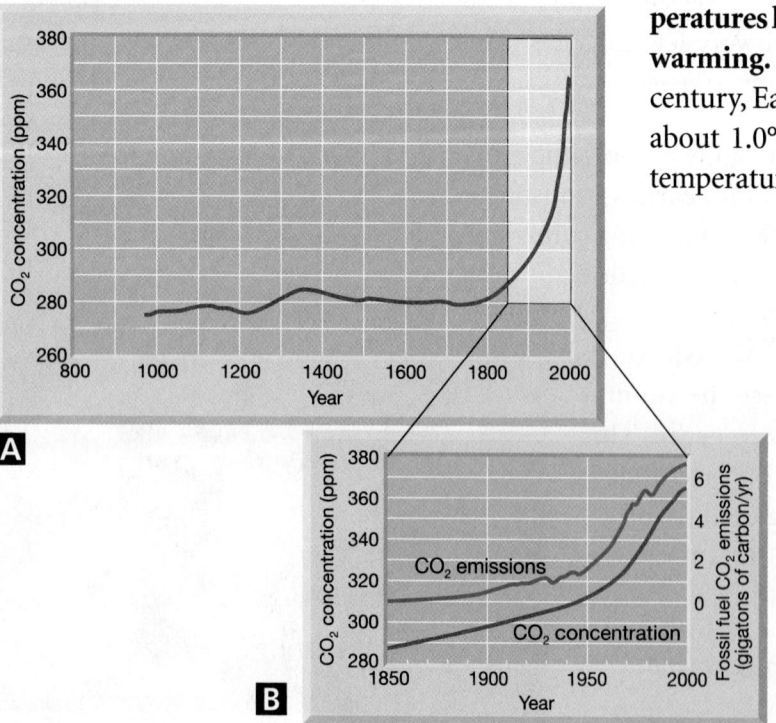

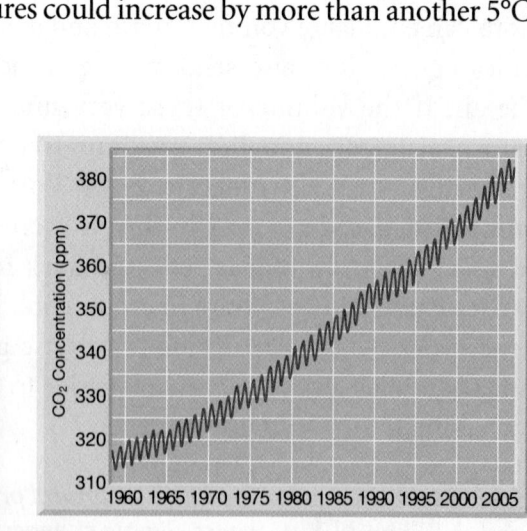

Scientists base their predictions about global warming on computer models of change in Earth's atmosphere called climate models. Climate models are complex computer programs. These models involve huge amounts of data on temperature, precipitation, and other variables. But climate models cannot describe Earth's atmosphere completely. For this reason, the results from a model are always an approximation. What follows is one prediction of how temperature increases could affect Earth.

Warmer surface temperatures increase evaporation rates. This, in turn, increases the amount of water vapor in the atmosphere. Water vapor is an even more powerful absorber of radiation emitted by Earth than is carbon dioxide. Therefore, more water vapor in the air will magnify the effect of carbon dioxide and other gases.

Temperature increases will also cause sea ice to melt. Ice reflects more incoming solar radiation than liquid water does. The melting of the ice will cause a substantial increase in the solar energy absorbed at the surface. This, in turn, will magnify the temperature increase created by higher levels of greenhouse gases. The melting of sea ice and ice sheets will also cause a global rise in sea level. This will lead to shoreline erosion and coastal flooding. Warmer oceans could also lead to stronger and more frequent storms, including hurricanes.

Scientists also expect that weather patterns will change as a result of the projected global warming. More intense heat waves and droughts in some regions and fewer such events in other places are also predicted. Hotter, more arid conditions have already led to more forest fires in the western United States.

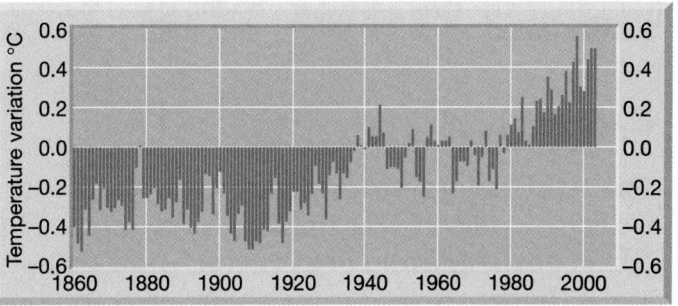

Figure 17 Global Warming
Increases in the levels of greenhouse gases have caused changes in Earth's average surface temperatures.
Interpreting Graphs *What year was the warmest to date?*

For: Links on the carbon cycle/global warming
Visit: www.SciLinks.org
Web Code: cjn-6213

Section 21.3 Assessment

Reviewing Concepts

1. ⬤ Describe five natural processes that can cause climate change.
2. ⬤ What is the greenhouse effect?
3. ⬤ What is global warming?
4. ⬤ What are some of the possible effects of global warming?

Critical Thinking

5. **Formulating Hypotheses** Which would have a longer effect on climate changes— volcanic ash and dust or the same volume of sulfur-based aerosols? Why?

6. **Predicting** How might cloud cover change as the result of global warming?
7. **Synthesizing** How might global warming affect Earth's inhabitants, including humans?

Writing in Science

Persuasive Paragraphs Write at least two paragraphs to persuade your friends and family to reduce their consumption of fossil fuels. Be sure to explain why the usage of such energy sources should be reduced.

How the Earth Works

Coniferous Forests

The world's largest forests extend across the far north, where winters can last for eight months. These dense **coniferous forests** consist of spruces, pines, and other trees that carry their seeds in cones. They are particularly suited for coping with cold conditions. Animals in northern forests find plentiful food during the long days of summer, but the season is brief and cold weather soon returns. To survive the harsh winter, many animals migrate south, while others hibernate.

Distribution of northern coniferous forests

FORESTS AND LAKES
Coniferous forests often grow on land once covered by ice age glaciers. These glaciers scoured the ground, scraping away soil and creating rounded hills and hollows. When the glaciers melted, the hills became covered with trees and the hollows turned into lakes.

CONIFER LEAVES
Most conifers have small evergreen leaves that are tough enough to withstand the coldest winters. A narrow shape helps the leaves to cope with strong winds.

White spruce

Waterlogged soil beneath trees is acidic and infertile.

Bobcat

PREDATORS
Mammals are relatively scarce in northern forests, so the **predators** that feed upon other animals sometimes have to cover vast distances to find food. Bobcats may roam many miles searching for small prey. Wolves hunt in packs for deer and other large mammals.

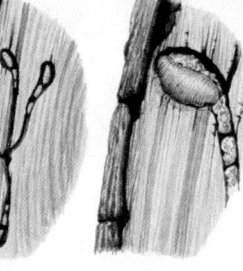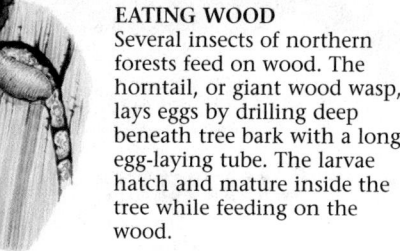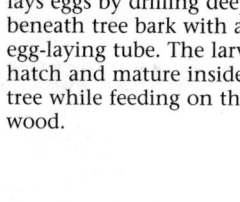

EATING WOOD

Several insects of northern forests feed on wood. The horntail, or giant wood wasp, lays eggs by drilling deep beneath tree bark with a long egg-laying tube. The larvae hatch and mature inside the tree while feeding on the wood.

1. A horntail lays eggs deep in a tree trunk.

2. Young larvae bore away from the drill-hole.

3. Each larva matures inside a chamber near the bark of the tree.

Red crossbill

SEED EATERS

Some birds rely on conifer seeds for food. Crossbill finches have unique bills that are crossed at the tips. This helps them remove seeds from cones. Clark's nutcracker, a member of the crow family, hides 20,000 or more seeds each fall. It is able to remember the locations of many of these seeds for up to nine months.

Spruce cone

Cold lake water contains few nutrients but is often rich in oxygen.

Caribou

ADAPTED FOR TRAVEL

To help them walk across thick layers of snow without sinking, caribou and elk have hooves with broadly splayed toes that help to distribute their weight. Lynx and snowshoe hares have similar adaptations.

Caribou hooves act as snowshoes.

COPING WITH COLD

To avoid extreme winter temperatures, bears, woodchucks, and other mammals hibernate. During the fall, they build up a store of fat in their bodies that will last until spring. They then go into **hibernation,** which slows their bodily functions to a minimum.

Woodchuck

ASSESSMENT

1. **Key Terms** Define **(a)** coniferous forest, **(b)** predator, **(c)** hibernation.

2. **Climates** Describe the climatic conditions that are generally found in northern coniferous forests.

3. **Ecosystems** How do trees serve as a food source for birds and insects?

4. **Ecosystems** How are mammals of northern coniferous forests well suited for survival in their natural environment?

5. **Critical Thinking Developing a Hypothesis** Deforestation has not reduced northern coniferous forests to the same degree that it has reduced mid-latitude deciduous forests. Why do you think that northern coniferous forests have fared better than deciduous forests to the south?

605

Human Impact on Climate and Weather

Scientists are now closely monitoring how daily human activity is changing microclimates. There is concern that changing microclimates can have an effect on global climates. In this investigation, you will explore some of the ways that human activities are changing the atmosphere.

Problem
How do we know that human activity is changing Earth's climates?

Materials
- paper
- pen or pencil

Skills
Calculating, Measuring, Using Tables, Analyzing Data

Procedure

1. Table 1 lists many of the types, sources, and amounts of primary pollutants. Use this table to answer items 1, 2, 3, and 4 under Analyze and Conclude.

2. Look at Figure A. The pollutants listed are linked to a wide variety of negative health effects such as eye irritation, heart damage, and lung damage. The pollutants shown are also linked to reduced visibility, reduced crop yields, and damage to ecosystems. Study the figure and answer items 5, 6, and 7.

3. Look at Figure B. Scientists have noted the increasing levels of carbon dioxide in the atmosphere. Research continues to determine whether these increasing levels are affecting global climates. Use Figure B to answer item 8.

4. Look at Table 2. This table presents data on the effects of large cities on their surrounding microclimates. Temperatures in cities can be higher than the surrounding countryside. Meteorologists call this effect "the urban heat island." Study the data in the table and answer items 9, 10, and 11.

Analyze and Conclude

1. **Interpreting Data** What is the leading source (by weight) of primary pollutants? How many metric tons of this pollutant are added to the atmosphere each year?

2. **Interpreting Data** Which of the following is the most abundant primary pollutant?
   a. carbon monoxide
   b. sulfur oxides

3. **Calculating** Your answer for item 2 is what percentage of all primary pollutants?
   a. 25%   b. 50%   c. 75%

4. **Calculating** What is the approximate total weight (in million metric tons) of all primary pollutants added to the atmosphere?

Table 1 Estimated Nationwide Emissions (millions of metric tons/year)						
Source	Carbon Monoxide	Partic- ulates	Sulfur Oxides	Volatile Organics	Nitrogen Oxides	Total
Transportation	43.5	1.6	1.0	5.1	7.3	58.5
Stationary Source Fuel Combustion	4.7	1.9	16.6	0.7	10.6	34.5
Industrial Processes	4.7	2.6	3.2	7.9	0.6	19.0
Solid Waste Disposal	2.1	0.3	0.0	0.7	0.1	3.2
Miscellaneous	7.2	1.2	0.0	2.8	0.2	11.4
Total	62.2	7.6	20.8	17.2	18.8	126.6

Source: U.S. Environmental Protection Agency

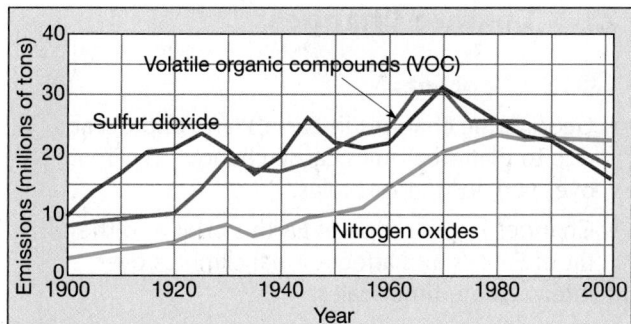

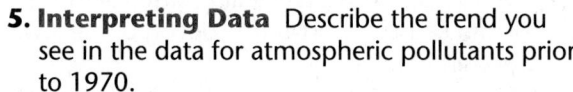

Figure A

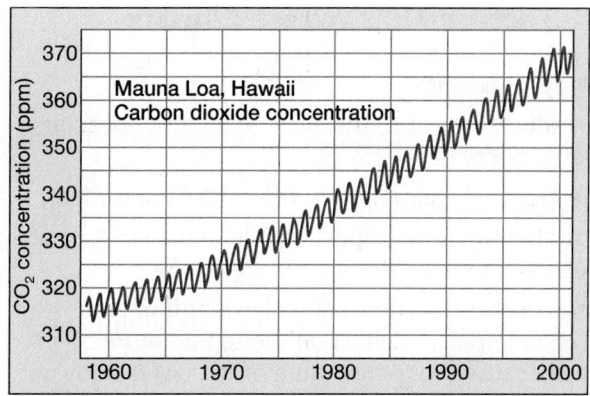

Figure B

5. Interpreting Data Describe the trend you see in the data for atmospheric pollutants prior to 1970.

6. Interpreting Data Describe the trend you see in the data for atmospheric pollutants since 1970.

7. Inferring Suggest a reason for the changing trend.

8. Calculating What has been the approximate percentage increase in atmospheric carbon dioxide near Mauna Loa since 1958?

9. Interpreting Data Compared to rural areas, which factors are increased by urbanization? Which factors are decreased?

10. Interpreting Data Of all of the factors shown, which shows the greatest increase due to urbanization?

11. Predicting Suggest a possible reason for each of the following effects on the weather that is influenced by a city.
   a. increased frequency of thunderstorms
   b. lower wind speed
   c. increased precipitation

Go Further Use the internet to search for climate data for your region. What trends do you see in the data since 1970? Suggest a hypothesis that could be used to test your conclusions.

Table 2 Average Climatic Changes Produced by Cities	
Element	**Comparison with Rural Areas**
Particulate matter	10 times more
Temperature	
Annual mean	0.5–1.5°C higher
Winter	1–2°C higher
Solar radiation	15–30% less
Ultraviolet, winter	30% less
Ultraviolet, summer	5% less
Precipitation	5–15% more
Thunderstorm frequency	16% more
Winter	5% more
Summer	29% more
Relative humidity	6% lower
Winter	2% lower
Summer	8% lower
Cloudiness (frequency)	5–10% more
Fog (frequency)	60% more
Winter	100% more
Summer	30% more
Wind speed	25% lower
Calms	5–20% more

Source: After Landsberg, Changnon, and others.

21.1 Factors That Affect Climate

🌐 Key Concepts

- As latitude increases, the average intensity of solar energy decreases.
- The higher the elevation is, the colder the climate.
- Mountains play an important role in the amount of precipitation that falls over an area.
- Large bodies of water such as lakes and oceans have an important effect on the temperature of an area because the temperature of the water body influences the temperature of the air above it.
- Global winds affect climate because they distribute heat and moisture around Earth.
- Vegetation can affect both temperature and the precipitation patterns in an area.

Vocabulary

tropical zone, *p. 589;* temperate zone, *p. 589;* polar zone, *p. 589*

21.2 World Climates

🌐 Key Concepts

- The Köppen climate classification system uses mean values of temperature and precipitation to classify climates.
- Humid tropical climates have no winters.
- Humid mid-latitude climates with mild winters have an average temperature in the coldest month that is below 18°C but above −3°C. In areas with severe winters, average temperatures in the coldest month are below −3°C.
- In dry climates, yearly precipitation is less than the potential loss of water by evaporation.
- Polar climates have a mean temperature in the warmest month that is below 10°C.
- Highland climates are generally cooler and wetter than nearby areas at lower elevations.

Vocabulary

Köppen climate classification system, *p. 592;* wet tropical climate, *p. 593;* tropical wet and dry climate, *p. 593;* humid subtropical climate, *p. 596;* marine west coast climate, *p. 596;* dry-summer subtropical climate, *p. 596;* subarctic climate, *p. 597*

21.3 Climate Changes

🌐 Key Concepts

- Geographic changes in Earth's land and oceans due to plate tectonics cause changes in climate over very long time scales.
- Changes in the shape of Earth's orbit and the tilt of Earth's axis affect global climates over intermediate time scales.
- Changes in ocean circulation can result in short-term climate fluctuations.
- Over short time scales, fluctuations in the amount of solar radiation can change global climates.
- Volcanic ash, dust, and sulfur-based aerosols in the air can cause a short-term cooling of the lower atmosphere.
- The greenhouse effect is a natural warming of Earth's lower atmosphere and Earth's surface.
- As a result of increases in carbon dioxide levels, as well as other greenhouse gases, global temperatures have increased to cause global warming.
- Global warming causes changes in sea level.

Vocabulary

greenhouse effect, *p. 602;* global warming, *p. 602*

Thinking Visually

Identifying Causes and Effects Copy the table below onto a sheet of paper. Use the information in the chapter to complete the table.

Some Factors That Influence Climate	
Causes	**Effects**
1. Increase in latitude	1. _____?_____
2. _____?_____	2. Highland climate
3. Increase in greenhouse gases	3. _____?_____
4. _____?_____	4. More coastal erosion
5. Large volcanic eruption	5. _____?_____
6. Nearby lake	6. _____?_____

Reviewing Content

Choose the letter that best answers the question or completes the statement.

1. Which of the following is true?
   a. Climates at high latitudes are very warm.
   b. A nearby lake causes a climate to be colder.
   c. Vegetation can increase the amount of precipitation that falls over an area.
   d. Places at lower elevations generally have lower temperatures.

2. Humid tropical climates always experience
   a. severe winters.   b. dry summers.
   c. low humidity.   d. warm temperatures.

3. In a dry climate, yearly precipitation is
   a. less than the potential rate of evaporation.
   b. greater than the rate of evaporation.
   c. greater in a desert than a steppe.
   d. less than that in a polar climate.

4. The greenhouse effect is best described as
   a. solely an increase in Earth's surface temperature.
   b. a natural warming effect of the atmosphere.
   c. a result of global warming.
   d. any short-term change in climate.

5. Recent global warming appears to be the result of
   a. changes in global wind patterns.
   b. a decrease in the greenhouse effect.
   c. increases in greenhouse gases in the air.
   d. changes in Earth's revolution around the sun.

6. Melting ice caps can result in which of the following?
   a. a rise in sea level
   b. a fall in sea level
   c. colder temperatures
   d. less precipitation

7. An increase in ocean temperatures can cause
   a. melting of sea ice.
   b. most forms of ocean life to flourish.
   c. a decrease in sea level.
   d. global wind patterns to stabilize.

Understanding Concepts

Use this map to answer Questions 8–10.

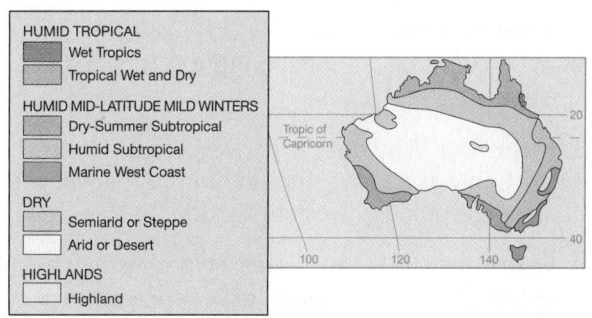

8. Describe the dominant climate in Australia.

9. Identify the type of climate found on the other parts of the continent.

10. What causes much of the east-southeastern part of the country to experience warm, humid, and marine west coast climates?

11. What powers Earth's climate system, and which of Earth's spheres are involved in this system?

12. Name the three major climate zones, and explain why their overall temperatures differ.

13. Why can two places at the same latitude have different climates?

14. What climate data are needed in order to classify a climate using the Köppen climate classification system?

15. Describe the characteristics of a wet tropical climate.

16. Describe the characteristics of a humid continental climate, and give one example of a place with such a climate.

17. Explain the greenhouse effect caused by Earth's atmosphere.

18. How have humans contributed to the increase in the levels of carbon dioxide in the atmosphere?

19. What is global warming?

20. How might global warming affect global precipitation?

Assessment *continued*

Critical Thinking

21. Synthesizing Can a region at low latitudes have snow? Explain.

22. Applying Concepts How does elevation affect the amount of precipitation that falls over an area?

23. Inferring Why do marine west coast climates exist only as narrow strips in North America, yet are widespread in western Europe?

24. Formulating Hypotheses Hypothesize why rain shadow deserts rarely experience fog.

Using Graphs

Use the graph below to answer Questions 25–29.

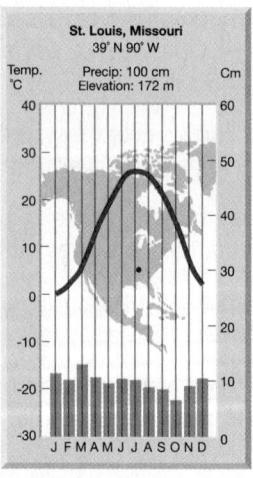

St. Louis, Missouri
39° N 90° W
Temp. °C — Precip: 100 cm — Elevation: 172 m — Cm

25. Reading Graphs What is the highest average annual temperature, and during which month does it occur?

26. Reading Graphs What is the lowest annual temperature, and during which month does it occur?

27. Calculating What is the average annual temperature range for St. Louis?

28. Inferring What is the wettest season of the year in St. Louis?

29. Classifying Classify the climate of St. Louis using the Köppen climate classification system.

Concepts in Action

30. Synthesizing Cities are referred to as urban heat islands. Use what you know about factors that affect climate to explain this statement.

31. Applying Concepts What do you think can be done to reduce the steady increase in global carbon dioxide levels?

32. Writing in Science Suppose you're a writer for the school newspaper. You are doing a story on how global warming might affect your area. Write an article that explains at least three effects that an increase in Earth's surface temperature might have on the climate of your area.

Performance-Based Assessment

Applying Concepts Make flyers with catchy slogans to suggest ways to reduce your community's use of fossil fuels. Get permission to post the flyers in grocery stores, community halls, shopping malls, and other common areas.

Standardized Test Prep

Test-Taking Tip

Using More Than One Visual
Sometimes an answer to a test question requires that you use or interpret more than one visual. When this occurs, carefully study the visuals before you read the questions pertaining to them. Look for similarities and differences between the visuals. Refer to the visuals again as you read each of the questions associated with the visuals.

Choose the letter that best answers the question or completes the statement. Use the graphs to answer the questions on this page.

1. Earth's temperatures were similar to the temperatures on our planet today
 (A) about 150,000 years ago.
 (B) about 135,000 years ago.
 (C) about 50,000 years ago.
 (D) about 25,000 years ago.

2. When do you think Earth was covered with more ice than is on our planet today?
 (A) between 150,000 and 140,000 years ago
 (B) between 140,000 and 120,000 years ago
 (C) between 135,000 and 20,000 years ago
 (D) between 20,000 and 10,000 years ago

3. Which part of the temperature graph shows the global warming trend discussed in the chapter?
 (A) the time from about 170,000 to 140,000 years ago
 (B) the time from about 120,000 to 100,000 years ago
 (C) the time from about 70,000 to 60,000 years ago
 (D) the time from about 100 years ago to the present

4. When during the past 160,000 years were carbon dioxide concentrations the highest?
 (A) about 150,000 years ago
 (B) about 120,000 years ago
 (C) about 40,000 years ago
 (D) about 1000 years ago

5. What were the carbon dioxide levels in the atmosphere during Earth's coldest period in the past 160,000 years?
 (A) between about 190 and 200 ppm
 (B) between about 220 and 240 ppm
 (C) between about 240 and 260 ppm
 (D) between about 260 and 280 ppm

Write one or two complete sentences to answer each of the following questions.

6. Describe the trends shown on the graphs.

7. Based on what you know about global warming and the data shown in these graphs, do you think the current global warming trends are natural changes or are they only the result of human activities? Support your answer with reasons.

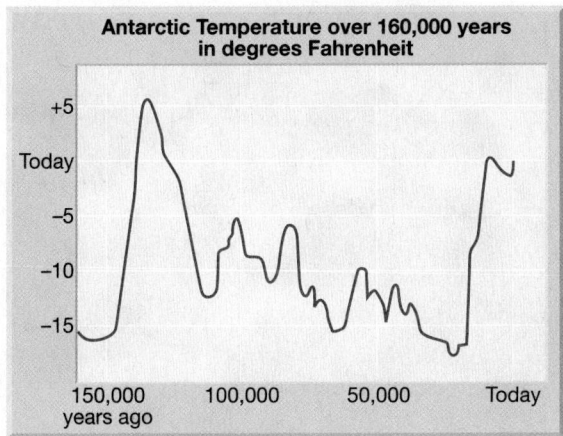

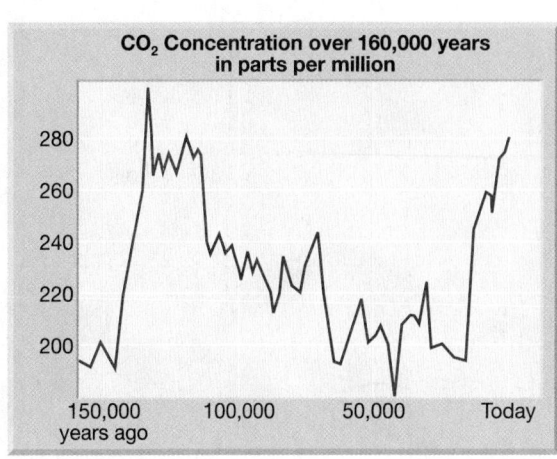

CHAPTER

22

Origin of Modern Astronomy

21st Century Learning

Information and Media Literacy

What is the origin of the Moon?

Current scientific opinion mostly supports the "giant impact" hypothesis of the origin of Earth's moon. However, there are several other hypotheses and not all of the key evidence is available. Investigate this topic on the Web and find two articles that discuss competing hypotheses about the origin of the Moon. One of the articles should be from a reliable source, and the other from a less reliable source. Discuss what makes each article reliable or unreliable on a blog or in your notes. Include the links to the two articles.

Exploration Lab

Modeling Synodic and Sidereal Months

GEODe   Astronomy
└▸ Earth's Moon

Chapter Preview

Inquiry Activity

How Do Impact Craters Form?

Procedure

1. Fill a large, plastic container with sand to a depth of about 3 cm. Flatten the surface of the sand with a wooden ruler.

2. One at a time, drop each of the different-sized balls from heights of 0.5 m, 1 m, and 2 m into the container. Make sure to smooth the surface of the sand between each drop.

3. Measure the diameter and height of the crater produced each time. Record your measurements in a data table.

Think About It

1. **Making Graphs** Identify your dependent and independent variables. Then plot your data on a line graph.

2. **Controlling Variables** Which of the variables is directly related to the velocity of the falling objects?

3. **Drawing Conclusions** Examine your data closely. What can you conclude about the general relationships between crater size and the size, mass, and velocity of the object that produced the crater?

22.1 Early Astronomy

Reading Focus

Key Concepts

- How does the geocentric model of the solar system differ from the heliocentric model?
- What were the accomplishments of early astronomers?

Vocabulary

- astronomy
- geocentric
- orbit
- heliocentric
- retrograde motion
- ellipse
- astronomical unit (AU)

Reading Strategy

Comparing and Contrasting Copy the table below. As you read about the geocentric and heliocentric models of the solar system, fill in the table.

	Location of Earth	Location of Sun	Supporters of Model
Geocentric Model	center of universe	a. ___?___	b. ___?___
Heliocentric Model	c. ___?___	d. ___?___	e. ___?___

Earth is one of the planets and many smaller bodies that orbit the sun. The sun is part of a much larger family of perhaps 400 billion stars that make up our galaxy, the Milky Way. There are billions of galaxies in the universe. A few hundred years ago scientists thought that Earth was the center of the universe. In this chapter, you will explore some events that changed the view of Earth's place in space. You will also examine Earth's moon.

Figure 1 Early astronomers often used instruments called astrolabes to track the positions of the sun and stars.

Ancient Greeks

Astronomy is the science that studies the universe. It deals with the properties of objects in space and the laws under which the universe operates. The "Golden Age" of early astronomy (600 B.C.–A.D. 150) was centered in Greece. The early Greeks used philosophical arguments to explain natural events. However, they also relied on observations. The Greeks used instruments such as the astrolabe in Figure 1 to find the positions of the sun and stars. The Greeks developed the basics of geometry and trigonometry. Using mathematics, they measured the sizes and distances of the sun and the moon.

The famous Greek philosopher Aristotle (384–322 B.C.) concluded that Earth is round because it always casts a curved shadow on the moon when it passes between the sun and the moon. Aristotle's belief that Earth is round was largely abandoned in the Middle Ages.

The first successful attempt to establish the size of Earth is credited to Eratosthenes (276–194 B.C.). As shown in Figure 2, he observed the angles of the noonday sun in two Egyptian cities—Syene (now Aswan) and Alexandria. Finding that the angles differed by 7 degrees, or 1/50 of a circle, he concluded that the circumference of Earth must be 50 times the distance between these two cities. The cities were 5000 stadia apart, giving him a measurement of 250,000 stadia. Many historians believe the stadia was 157.6 meters. This would make Eratosthenes' calculation of Earth's circumference—about 39,400 kilometers—a measurement very close to the modern circumference of 40,075 kilometers.

Probably the greatest of the early Greek astronomers was Hipparchus (second century B.C.), best known for his star catalog. Hipparchus determined the location of almost 850 stars, which he divided into six groups according to their brightness.

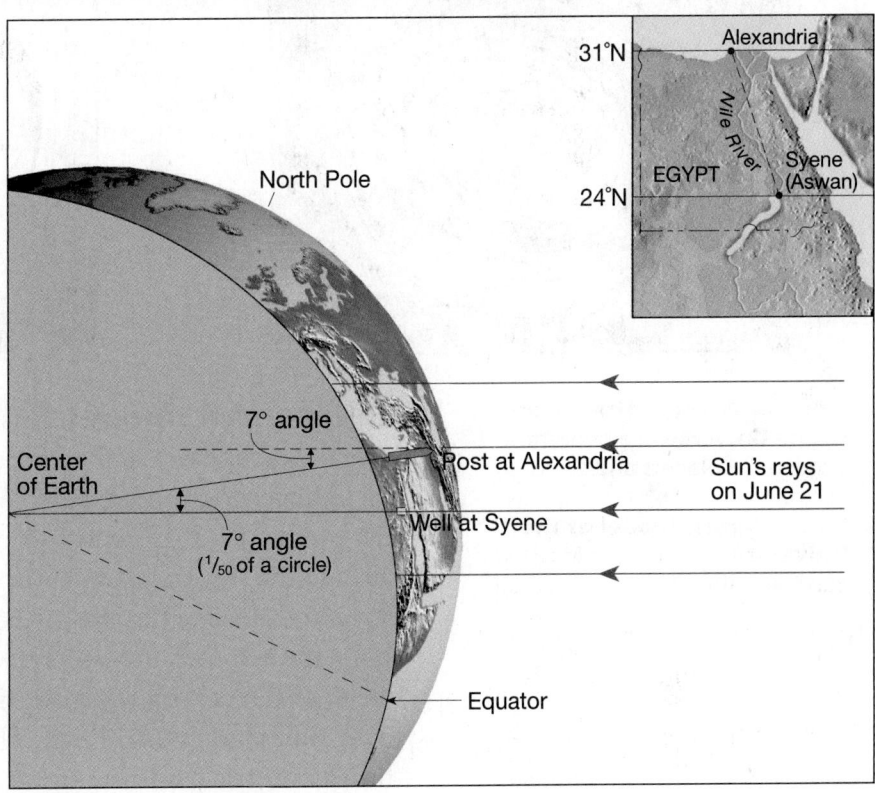

Calculating Earth's Circumference

Figure 2 This diagram shows the orientation of the sun's rays at Syene (Aswan) and Alexandria in Egypt on June 21 when Eratosthenes calculated Earth's circumference.

Geocentric Model

The Greeks believed in a **geocentric** universe, in which Earth was a sphere that stayed motionless at the center. **In the geocentric model, the moon, sun, and the known planets—Mercury, Venus, Mars, and Jupiter—go around Earth.** The path of an object as it goes around another object in space is called an **orbit**. Beyond the planets was a transparent, hollow sphere on which the stars traveled daily around Earth. This was called the celestial sphere. To the Greeks, all of the heavenly bodies, except seven, appeared to remain in the same relative position to one another. These seven wanderers included the sun, the moon, Mercury, Venus, Mars, Jupiter, and Saturn. Each was thought to have a circular orbit around Earth. The Greeks were able to explain the apparent movements of all celestial bodies in space by using this model. Although the Greeks' model of the universe was not correct, astronomers today still use the concept of the celestial sphere to describe the motion of objects in the sky as seen from Earth. Figure 3A on page 616 illustrates the geocentric model.

For: Links on early astronomers
Visit: www.SciLinks.org
Web Code: cjn-7221

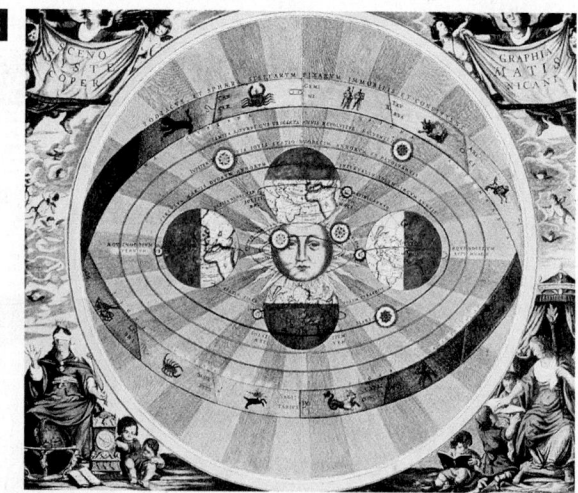

Figure 3 A Geocentric Model of the Universe In a geocentric system, the planets and sun orbit Earth.
B Heliocentric Model of the Universe In a heliocentric system, Earth and the other planets orbit the sun.

Heliocentric Model

Aristarchus (312–230 B.C.) was the first Greek to propose a sun-centered, or **heliocentric,** universe. **In the heliocentric model, Earth and the other planets orbit the sun.** Aristarchus used geometry to calculate the relative distances from Earth to the sun and from Earth to the moon. He later used these distances to calculate the size of the sun and the moon. But Aristarchus came up with measurements that were much too small. However, he did learn that the sun was many times more distant than the moon and many times larger than Earth. Though there was evidence to support the heliocentric model, as shown in Figure 3B, the Earth-centered view dominated Western thought for nearly 2000 years.

Ptolemaic System

Much of our knowledge of Greek astronomy comes from Claudius Ptolemy. In A.D. 141, Ptolemy presented a model of the universe that was called the Ptolemaic system. The precision with which his theory was able to predict the motion of the planets allowed it to go unchallenged for nearly 13 centuries.

Just like the Greek model, Ptolemy's model had the planets moving in circular orbits around a motionless Earth. However, the motion of the planets against the background of stars seemed odd. Each planet, if watched night after night, moves slightly eastward among the stars. But periodically, each planet appears to stop, reverse direction for a time, and then resume an eastward motion. The apparent westward drift is called **retrograde motion** and is illustrated in Figure 4. This rather odd apparent motion results from the combination of the motion of Earth and the planet's own motion around the sun. Ptolemy explained retrograde motion by saying that planets moved along smaller circles, which in turn moved along their orbits around Earth. He called these smaller circles *epicycles.*

Ptolemy's theory was wrong—the planets do not orbit Earth. Yet his theory was able to account for the planets' apparent motions.

For: Links on astronomy
Visit: PHSchool.com
Web Code: cuc-1221

What is retrograde motion?

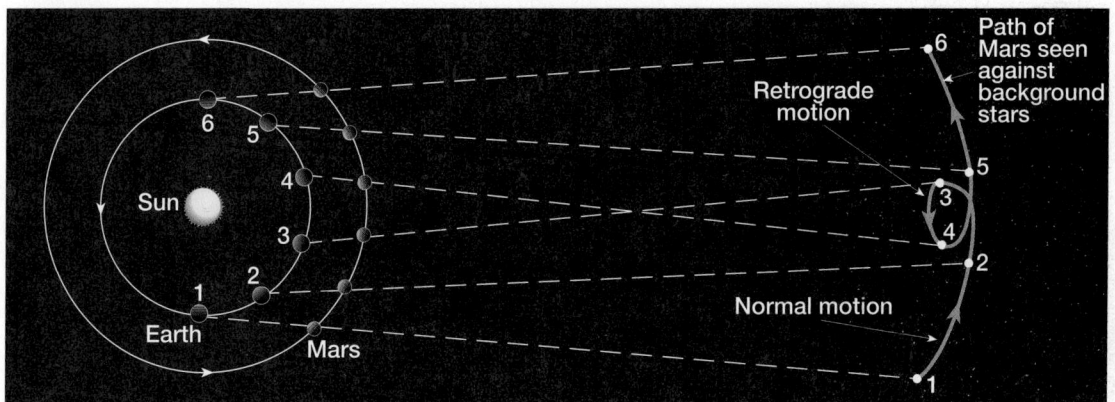

The Birth of Modern Astronomy

The development of modern astronomy involved a break from previous philosophical and religious views. Scientists began to discover a universe governed by natural laws. We will examine the work of five noted scientists: Nicolaus Copernicus, Tycho Brahe, Johannes Kepler, Galileo Galilei, and Sir Isaac Newton.

Nicolaus Copernicus For almost 13 centuries after the time of Ptolemy, very few astronomical advances were made in Europe. The first great astronomer to emerge after the Middle Ages was Nicolaus Copernicus (1473–1543) from Poland. Copernicus became convinced that Earth is a planet, just like the other five planets that were known. To him, it made more sense that Earth, rather than the entire sky, rotated once every day.

⚫ **Copernicus concluded that Earth is a planet. He proposed a model of the solar system with the sun at the center.** This was a major break from the ancient idea that a motionless Earth lies at the center. Copernicus used circles, which were considered to be the perfect geometric shape, to represent the orbits of the planets. However, the planets seemed to stray from their predicted positions.

Tycho Brahe Tycho Brahe (1546–1601) was born of Danish nobility three years after the death of Copernicus. Brahe became interested in astronomy while viewing a solar eclipse that had been predicted by astronomers. He persuaded King Frederick II to build an observatory near Copenhagen. The telescope had not yet been invented. At the observatory, Brahe designed and built instruments, such as the angle-measuring device shown in Figure 5. He used these instruments for 20 years to measure the locations of the heavenly bodies. ⚫ **Brahe's observations, especially of Mars, were far more precise than any made previously.** In the last year of his life, Brahe found an able assistant, Johannes Kepler. Kepler kept most of Brahe's observations and put them to exceptional use.

Figure 4 Retrograde Motion When viewed from Earth, Mars moves eastward among the stars each day. Then periodically it appears to stop and reverse direction. This apparent movement, called retrograde motion, occurs because Earth has a faster orbital speed than Mars and overtakes it.

Figure 5 Tycho Brahe in His Observatory Brahe (central figure) is painted on the wall within the arc of a sighting instrument called a quadrant.

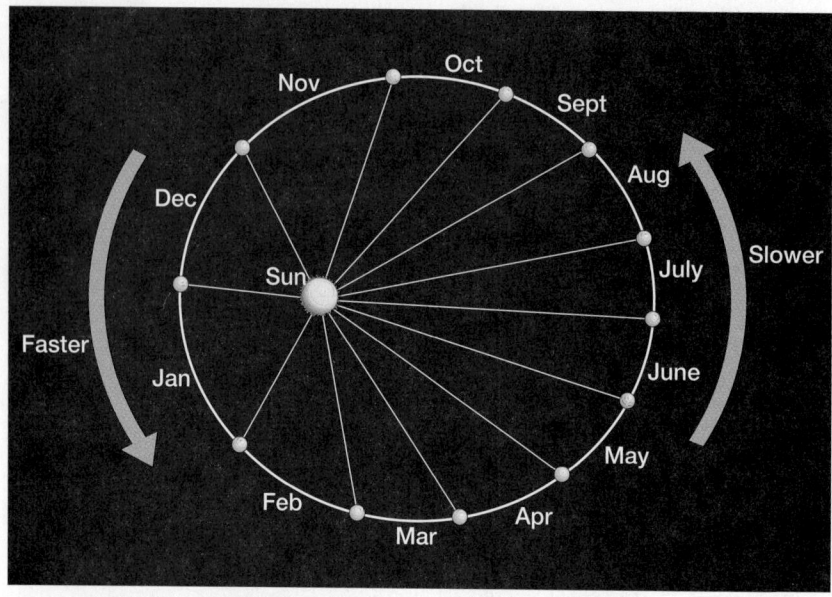

Figure 6 Planet Revolution
A line connecting a planet to the sun would move in such a manner that equal areas are swept out in equal times. Thus, planets revolve slower when they are farther from the sun and faster when they are closer.

Johannes Kepler Johannes Kepler (1571–1630) had a good mathematical mind and a strong belief in the accuracy of Brahe's work. ◗**Kepler discovered three laws of planetary motion.** The first two laws resulted from his inability to fit Brahe's observations of Mars to a circular orbit. Kepler discovered that the orbit of Mars around the sun is not a perfect circle. Instead, it is an oval-shaped path. The oval is called an **ellipse.** Two points inside the ellipse, each called a *focus*, help to determine the shape of the ellipse. The further apart the foci, the more stretched out the ellipse. About the same time, Kepler realized that the speed of Mars in its orbit changes in a predictable way. As Mars approaches the sun, it speeds up. As it moves away from the sun, it slows down.

Kepler summarized three laws of planetary motion:

1. The path of each planet around the sun is an ellipse, with the sun at one focus. The other focus is symmetrically located at the opposite end of the ellipse.

2. Each planet revolves so that an imaginary line connecting it to the sun sweeps over equal areas in equal time intervals, as shown in Figure 6. If a planet is to sweep equal areas in the same amount of time, it must travel more rapidly when it is nearer the sun and more slowly when it is farther from the sun.

3. The square of the length of time it takes a planet to orbit the sun (orbital period) is proportional to the cube of its mean distance to the sun.

In its simplest form, the orbital period of revolution is measured in Earth years. The planet's distance to the sun is expressed in astronomical units. The **astronomical unit (AU)** is the average distance between Earth and the sun. It is about 150 million kilometers.

Using these units, Kepler's third law states that the planet's orbital period squared is equal to its mean solar distance cubed ($T^2 = d^3$). Therefore, the solar distances of the planets can be calculated when their periods of revolution are known. For example, Mars has a period of 1.88 years, which squared equals 3.54. The cube root of 3.54 is 1.52, and that is the distance to Mars in astronomical units shown in Table 1.

Table 1 Period of Revolution and Solar Distances of Planets		
Planet	Solar Distance (*d*) (AU)*	Period (*T*) (Earth years)
Mercury	0.39	0.24
Venus	0.72	0.62
Earth	1.00	1.00
Mars	1.52	1.88
Jupiter	5.20	11.86
Saturn	9.54	29.46
Uranus	19.18	84.01
Neptune	30.06	164.80
Pluto**	39.44	247.70

*AU = astronomical unit. **As of 2007, Pluto is a dwarf planet.

Galileo Galilei Galileo Galilei (1564–1642) was the greatest Italian scientist of the Renaissance. 🔑 **Galileo's most important contributions were his descriptions of the behavior of moving objects.** All astronomical discoveries before his time were made without the aid of a telescope. In 1609, Galileo heard that a Dutch lens maker had devised a system of lenses that magnified objects. Galileo constructed his own telescope and used it to study the sky. It magnified distant objects to three times the size seen by the unaided eye.

Using the telescope, Galileo was able to view the universe in a new way. He made many important discoveries that supported Copernicus's view of the universe, such as the following:

1. *The discovery of four satellites, or moons, orbiting Jupiter.* This proved that the old idea of Earth being the only center of motion in the universe was wrong. Here, plainly visible, was another center of motion—Jupiter. People who opposed the sun-centered system said that the moon would be left behind if Earth really revolved around the sun. Galileo's discovery disproved this argument.

2. *The discovery that the planets are circular disks, not just points of light, as was previously thought.* This showed that the planets were not stars.

3. *The discovery that Venus has phases just like the moon.* So Venus orbits its source of light—the sun. Galileo saw that Venus appears smallest when it is in full phase and therefore farthest from Earth, as shown in Figure 7.

4. *The discovery that the moon's surface was not smooth.* Galileo saw mountains, craters, and plains. Before Galileo, people thought that the objects in the sky were smooth and perfect.

5. *The discovery that the sun had sunspots, or dark regions.* These blemishes on the sun showed that the sun was not perfect. Galileo tracked the movement of these spots and estimated the rotational period of the sun as just under a month.

The Solar System Model Evolves

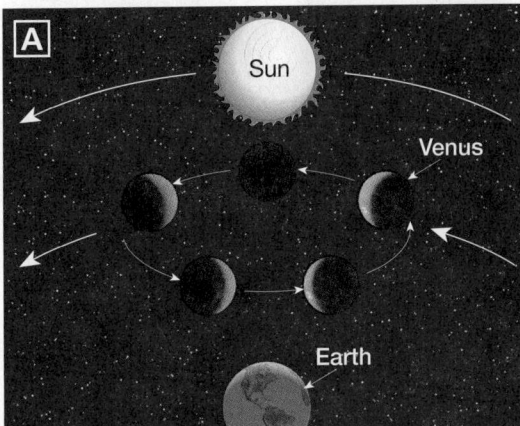

In the Ptolemaic system, the orbit of Venus lies between the sun and Earth.

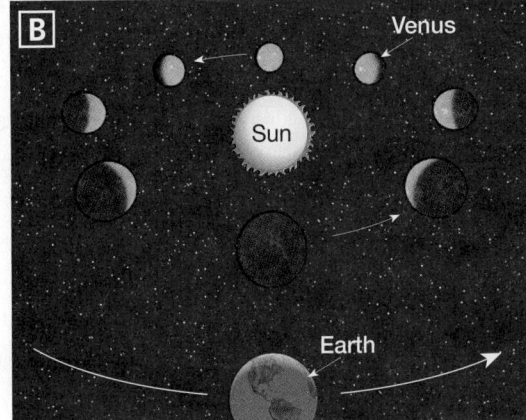

In the Copernican system, Venus orbits the sun and more of its phases are visible from Earth.

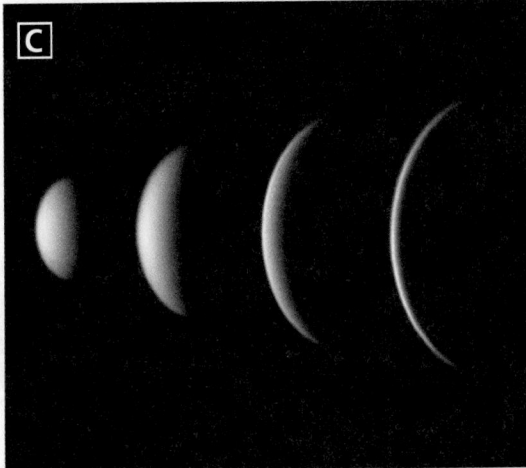

As Galileo observed, Venus goes through phases similar to the moon.

Figure 7
Relating Cause and Effect *In the geocentric model, which phase of Venus would be visible from Earth?*

Figure 8 Sir Isaac Newton explained that the force of gravity kept the planets in their orbits.

Sir Isaac Newton Sir Isaac Newton (1642–1727), shown in Figure 8, was born in the year of Galileo's death. Many scientists had attempted to explain the forces involved in planetary motion. Kepler believed that some force pushed the planets along in their orbits. Galileo correctly reasoned that no force is required to keep an object in motion. And he proposed that a moving object will continue to move at a constant speed and in a straight line. This concept is called inertia.

The problem, then, was not to explain the force that keeps the planets moving but rather to determine the force that keeps them from going in a straight line out into space. Newton described a force that holds the moon in orbit around Earth. **Although others had theorized the existence of such a force, Newton was the first to formulate and test the law of universal gravitation.**

Universal Gravitation According to Newton, every body in the universe attracts every other body with a force that is directly proportional to their masses and inversely proportional to the square of the distance between their centers of mass. The mass of an object is a measure of the total amount of matter it contains.

The gravitational force decreases with distance, so that two objects 3 kilometers apart have 3^2, or 9, times less gravitational attraction than if the same objects were 1 kilometer apart.

The law of universal gravitation also states that the greater the mass of the object, the greater is its gravitational force. For example, the mass of the moon creates a gravitational force strong enough to cause ocean tides on Earth. But the tiny mass of an artificial satellite has no measurable effect on Earth.

Weight is not the same as mass. Weight is the force of gravity acting upon an object. Therefore, weight varies when gravitational forces change, even if mass is constant. Weight is properly expressed in newtons (N). See Figure 9.

Figure 9 Weight is the force of gravity acting on an object. **A** An astronaut with a mass of 88 kg weighs 863 N on Earth. **B** An astronaut with a mass of 88 kg weighs 141 N on the moon.

A Astronaut on Earth
Mass = 88.0 kg; Weight = 863 N

B Astronaut on Moon
Mass = 88.0 kg; Weight = 141 N

Newton proved that the force of gravity, combined with the tendency of a planet to remain in straight-line motion, results in the elliptical orbits that Kepler discovered. Earth, for example, moves forward in its orbit about 30 kilometers each second. During the same second, the force of gravity pulls it toward the sun about 0.5 centimeter. Newton concluded that it is the combination of Earth's forward motion and its "falling"

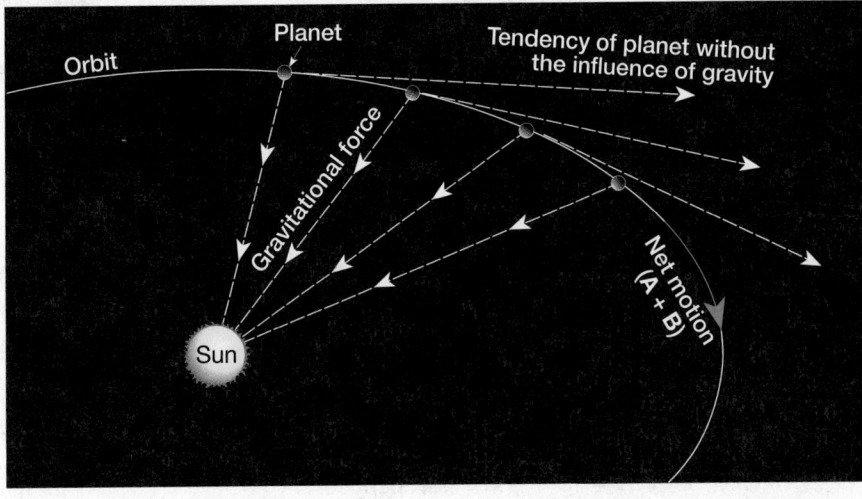

Figure 10 Without the influence of gravity, planets would move in a straight line out into space.

motion that defines its orbit. As Figure 10 shows, if gravity were somehow eliminated, Earth would move in a straight line out into space. If Earth's forward motion suddenly stopped, gravity would pull it directly toward the sun.

Newton used the law of universal gravitation to redefine Kepler's third law, which states the relationship between the orbital periods of the planets and their solar distances. When restated, Kepler's third law takes into account the masses of the bodies involved and provides a method for determining the mass of a body when the orbit of one of its satellites is known.

Section 22.1 Assessment

Reviewing Concepts

1. 🔵 Compare and contrast the geocentric and heliocentric models of the universe.

2. What produces the retrograde motion of Mars?

3. 🔵 What geometric arrangements did Ptolemy use to explain retrograde motion?

4. 🔵 What major change did Copernicus make in the Ptolemaic system? Why was this change significant?

Critical Thinking

5. **Applying Concepts** What role did the telescope play in Galileo's contributions to science?

6. **Summarizing** In your own words, summarize Kepler's three laws of planetary motion.

Math Practice

7. Use Kepler's third law to show that the distance of a planet whose period is 5 years is 2.9 AU from the sun. Do the same for a planet with a period of 10 years at 4.6 AU from the sun, and a planet with a period of 10 days at 0.09 AU from the sun.

22.2 The Earth-Moon-Sun System

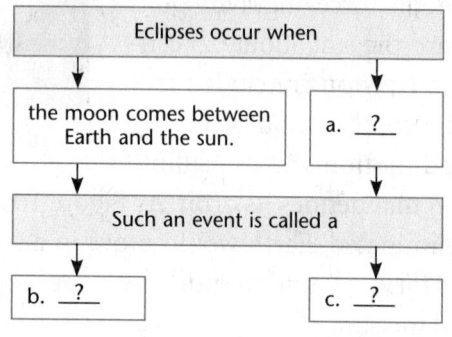

Reading Focus

Key Concepts

- In what ways does Earth move?
- What causes the phases of the moon?
- Why are eclipses relatively rare events?

Vocabulary

- rotation
- revolution
- precession
- perihelion
- aphelion
- perigee
- apogee
- phases of the moon
- solar eclipse
- lunar eclipse

Reading Strategy

Monitoring Your Understanding Copy and complete the flowchart below.

Eclipses occur when

the moon comes between Earth and the sun.	a. ?

Such an event is called a

b. ?	c. ?

Figure 11 On the summer solstice, the sun can be observed rising above the heel stone of Stonehenge, an ancient observatory in England.

If you gaze away from the city lights on a clear night, it will seem that the stars produce a spherical shell surrounding Earth. This impression seems so real that it is easy to understand why many early Greeks regarded the stars as being fixed to a solid, celestial sphere. The sun and moon, on the other hand, constantly changed their positions against the stars. Prehistoric people built observatories to chart their motions. The structure known as Stonehenge, shown in Figure 11, was probably an attempt at better solar predictions. At the beginning of summer in the Northern Hemisphere (the summer solstice on June 21 or 22), the rising sun comes up directly above the heel stone of Stonehenge. Besides keeping this calendar, Stonehenge may also have provided a method of determining eclipses. In this section, you'll learn more about the movements of bodies in space that cause events such as eclipses.

Motions of Earth

The two main motions of Earth are rotation and revolution. **Rotation** is the turning, or spinning, of a body on its axis. **Revolution** is the motion of a body, such as a planet or moon, along its orbit around some point in space. For example, Earth revolves around the sun, and the moon revolves around Earth. Earth also has another very slow motion known as **precession,** which is the slight movement, over a period of 26,000 years, of Earth's axis.

Rotation The main results of Earth's rotation are day and night. Earth's rotation has become a standard method of measuring time because it is so dependable and easy to use. Each rotation of Earth around its axis equals about 24 hours. You may be surprised to learn that we can measure Earth's day in two ways. Most familiar is the apparent solar day, the time interval from one noon to the next, which is, on average, about 24 hours. Noon is when the sun has reached its highest point in the sky for that day.

The sidereal day, on the other hand, is the time it takes for Earth to make one complete rotation (360 degrees) with respect to a star other than our sun. The sidereal day is measured by the time required for a star to reappear at the identical position in the sky where it was observed the day before. The sidereal day has a period of 23 hours, 56 minutes, and 4 seconds (measured in mean solar time), which is almost 4 minutes shorter than the mean solar day. This difference results because the direction to distant stars barely changes because of Earth's slow revolution along its orbit. The direction to the sun, on the other hand, changes by almost 1 degree each day. This difference is shown in Figure 12.

Why do we use the mean solar day instead of the sidereal day as a measurement of our day? In sidereal time, "noon" occurs four minutes earlier each day. Therefore, after six months, "noon" occurs at "midnight." Astronomers use sidereal time because the stars appear in the same position in the sky every 24 sidereal hours.

 **Reading Checkpoint** *How is the solar day measured?*

Figure 12 Sidereal Day It takes Earth 23 hours and 56 minutes to make one rotation with respect to the stars (sidereal day). However, after Earth has completed one sidereal day, point Y has not yet returned to the "noon position" with respect to the sun. Earth has to rotate another 4 minutes to complete the solar day.

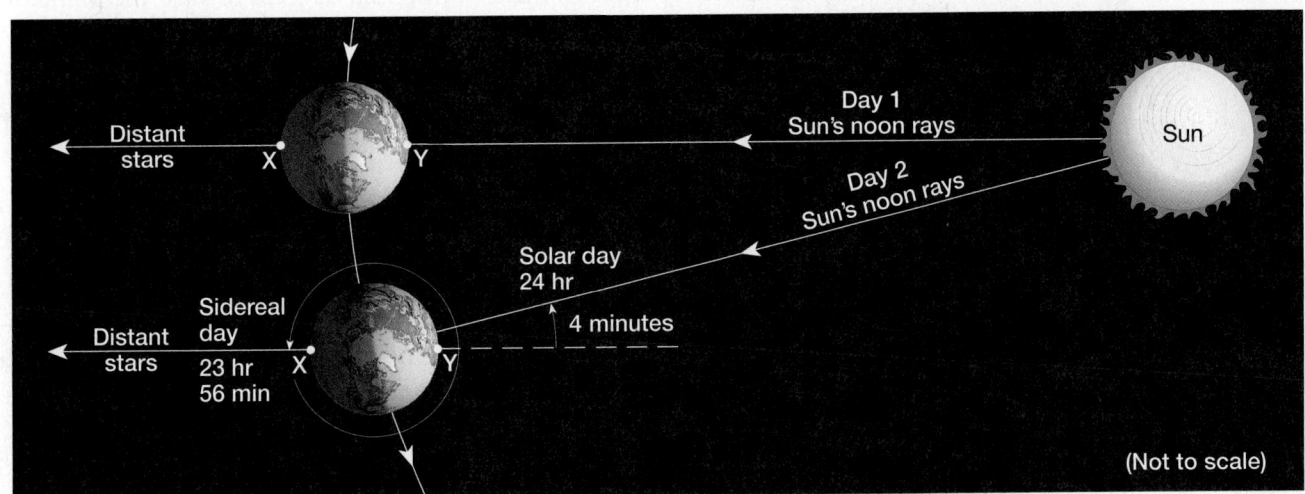

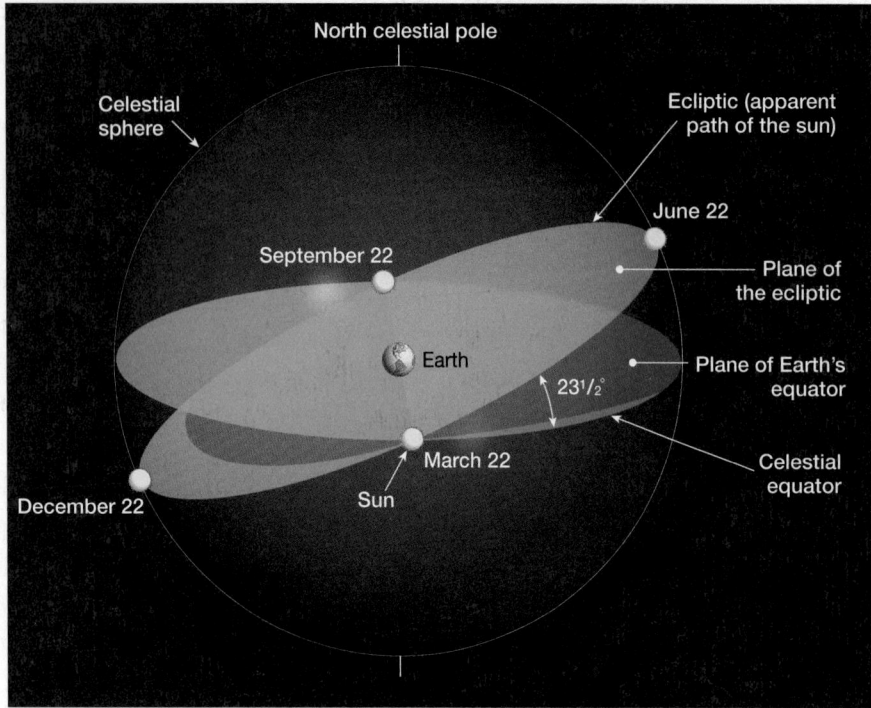

Figure 13 The Celestial Sphere
Earth's orbital motion causes the apparent position of the sun to shift about 1 degree each day on the celestial sphere.

Revolution Earth revolves around the sun in an elliptical orbit at an average speed of 107,000 kilometers per hour. Its average distance from the sun is 150 million kilometers. But because its orbit is an ellipse, Earth's distance from the sun varies. At **perihelion,** Earth is closest to the sun—about 147 million kilometers away. Perihelion occurs about January 3 each year. At **aphelion,** Earth is farthest from the sun—about 152 million kilometers away. Aphelion occurs about July 4. So Earth is farthest from the sun in July and closest to the sun in January.

Because of Earth's annual movement around the sun, each day the sun appears to move among the constellations. The apparent annual path of the sun against the backdrop of the celestial sphere is called the ecliptic, as shown in Figure 13. Generally, the planets and the moon travel in nearly the same plane as Earth. So their paths on the celestial sphere lie near the ecliptic.

Earth's Axis and Seasons The imaginary plane that connects Earth's orbit with the celestial sphere is called the plane of the ecliptic. The projection of Earth's equator onto the sky is the celestial equator. Earth's axis of rotation is tilted about 23.5 degrees toward the plane of the ecliptic. Because of Earth's tilt, the apparent path of the sun and the celestial equator intersect each other at an angle of 23.5 degrees. This angle is very important to Earth's inhabitants. Because of the inclination of Earth's axis to the plane of the ecliptic, Earth has its yearly cycle of seasons.

When the apparent position of the sun is plotted on the celestial sphere over a period of a year's time, its path intersects the celestial equator at two points. From a Northern Hemisphere point of view, these intersections are called the spring equinox (March 20 or 21) and autumn equinox (September 22 or 23). On June 21 or 22, the date of the summer solstice, the sun appears 23.5 degrees north of the celestial equator. Six months later, on December 21–22, the date of the winter solstice, the sun appears 23.5 degrees south of the celestial equator.

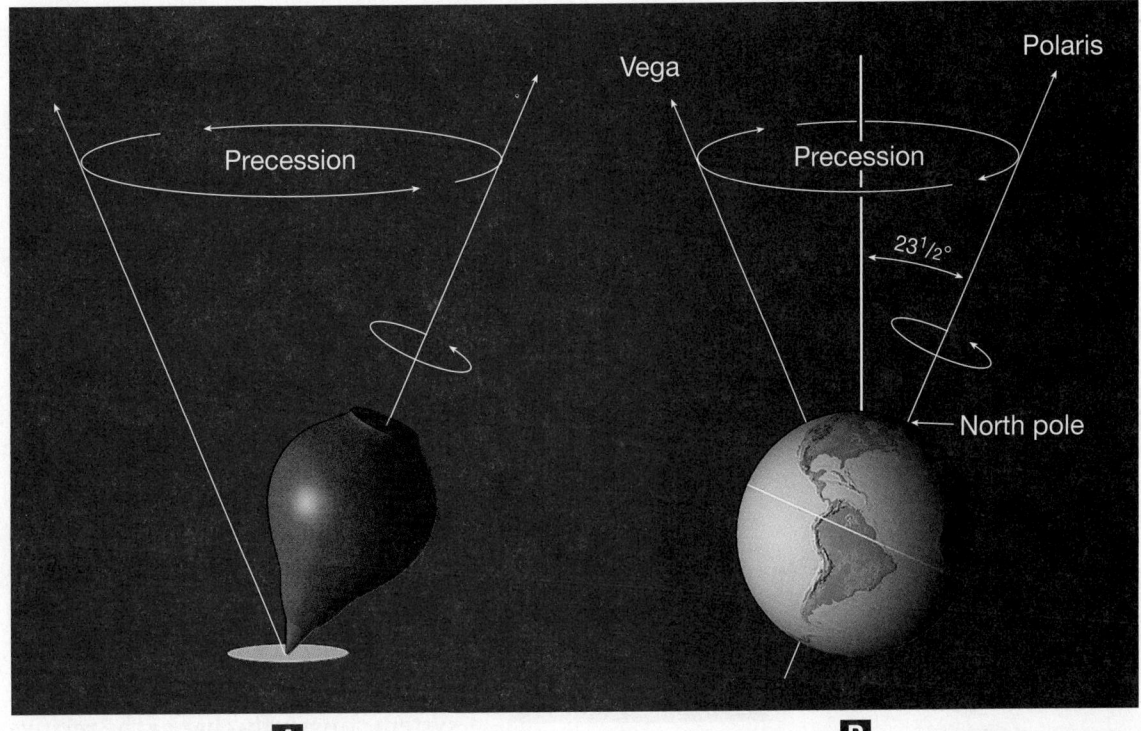

A **B**

Precession A slow movement of Earth, called **precession**, is the motion of Earth's axis as it traces out a circle on the sky. Earth's axis varies in tilt between 21.5° and 24.5° with a repeating period of 41,000 years. As discussed in Chapter 21, this is important in affecting climate change. In addition, the direction in which the axis points continually changes. This movement is very similar to the wobble of a spinning top, as shown in Figure 14A. At the present time, the axis points toward the bright star Polaris. In about 13,000 years, it will point toward the bright star Vega, which will then become the North Star, as shown in Figure 14B. The period of precession, or the amount of time for the axis to complete one circle, is 26,000 years. By the year 28,000, Polaris will once again be the North Star.

Earth-Sun Motion In addition to its own movements, Earth accompanies the sun as the entire solar system speeds in the direction of the bright star Vega at 20 kilometers per second. Also, the sun, like other nearby stars, revolves around the Milky Way Galaxy. This trip takes 230 million years to traverse at speeds approaching 250 kilometers per second. The galaxies themselves are also in motion. The Milky Way Galaxy is presently approaching one of its nearest galactic neighbors, the Andromeda Galaxy. The motions of Earth are many and complex, and its speed in space is very great.

 **What is precession?**

Figure 14 Precession
A Precession is similar to a spinning top. It causes the North Pole to point at different parts of the sky during a 26,000-year cycle. **B** Today, the North Pole points to Polaris.
Interpreting Illustrations *What star will the North Pole point to in about 13,000 years?*

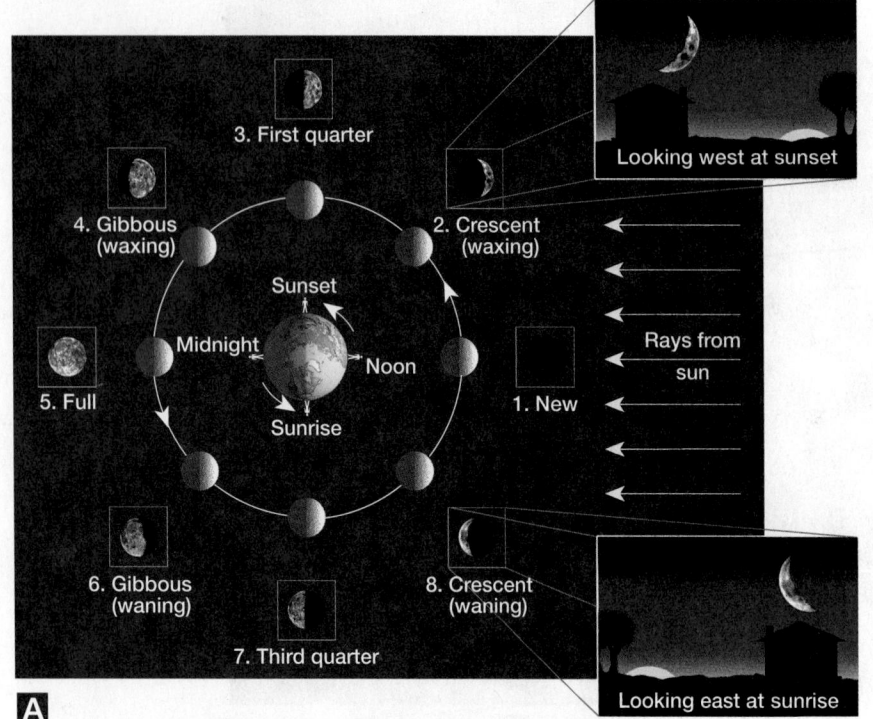

A

Motions of the Earth-Moon System

Earth has one natural satellite, the moon. In addition to accompanying Earth in its annual trip around the sun, our moon orbits Earth within a period of about one month. When viewed from above the North Pole, the direction of this motion is counterclockwise. Because the moon's orbit is elliptical, its distance to Earth varies by about 6 percent, averaging 384,401 kilometers. At a point known as **perigee,** the moon is closest to Earth. At a point known as **apogee,** the moon is farthest from Earth.

The motions of the Earth-moon system constantly change the relative positions of the sun, Earth, and moon. This results in changes in the appearance of the moon, as you'll read about next.

Phases of the Moon The first astronomical event to be understood was the regular cycle of the phases of the moon. On a monthly basis, we observe the **phases of the moon** as a change in the amount of the moon that appears lit. Look at the new moon shown in Figure 15A. About two days after the new moon, a thin sliver (crescent phase) appears low in the western sky just after sunset. During the following week, the lighted portion of the moon visible from Earth increases (waxing) to a half circle (first-quarter phase) and can be seen from about noon to midnight. In another week, the complete disk (full-moon phase) can be seen rising in the east as the sun is sinking in the west. During the next two weeks, the percentage of the moon that can be seen steadily declines (waning), until the moon disappears altogether (new-moon phase). The cycle soon begins again with the reappearance of the crescent moon.

🌑 **Lunar phases are caused by the changes in how much of the sunlit side of the moon faces Earth.** See Figure 15B. Half of the moon is illuminated at all times. But to an observer on Earth, the percentage of the bright side that is visible depends on the location of the moon with respect to the sun and Earth. When the moon lies between the sun and Earth, none of its bright side faces Earth.

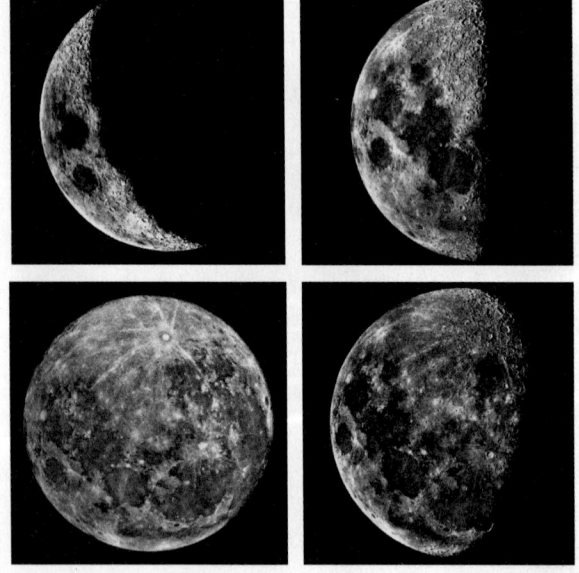

B

Figure 15 Phases of the Moon
A The outer figures show the phases as seen from Earth's Northern Hemisphere.
B Compare these photographs with the diagram. Clockwise from the top left, they show four phases: waning crescent, third quarter, waning gibbous , and full.

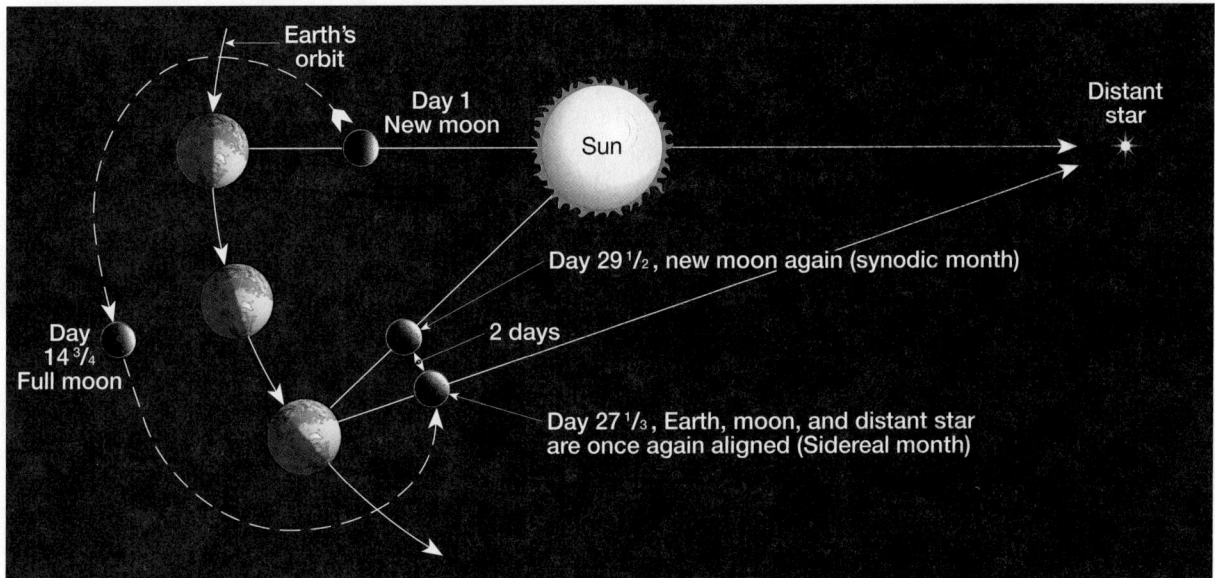

When the moon lies on the side of Earth opposite the sun, all of its lighted side faces Earth. So we see the full moon. At all positions between the new moon and the full moon, a part of the moon's lit side is visible from Earth.

Lunar Motions The cycle of the moon through its phases requires 29 1/2 days, a time span called the synodic month. This cycle was the basis for the first Roman calendar. However, this is the apparent period of the moon's revolution around Earth and not the true period, which takes only 27 1/3 days and is known as the sidereal month. The reason for the difference of nearly two days each cycle is shown in Figure 16. Note that as the moon orbits Earth, the Earth-moon system also moves in an orbit around the sun. Even after the moon has made a complete revolution around Earth, it has not yet reached its starting position, which was directly between the sun and Earth (new-moon phase). The additional motion to reach the starting point takes another two days.

An interesting fact about the motions of the moon is that the moon's period of rotation about its axis and its revolution around Earth are the same. They are both 27 1/3 days. Because of this, the same side of the moon always faces Earth. Only orbiting satellites and astronauts have seen the "back," or far side, of the moon. The far side of the moon appears much more densely cratered than the side we see.

Because the moon rotates on its axis only once every 27 1/3 days, any location on its surface experiences periods of daylight and darkness lasting about two weeks. This, along with the absence of an atmosphere, accounts for the high surface temperature of 127°C on the day side of the moon and the low surface temperature of −173°C on its night side.

 **Reading Checkpoint** *Why does the same side of the moon always face Earth?*

Figure 16 Lunar Motion As the moon orbits Earth, the Earth-moon system also moves in orbit around the sun. Thus, even after the moon makes one revolution around Earth, it has not yet reached its starting point in relation to the stars.

Q *Why do we sometimes see the moon in daytime?*

A During phases of the lunar cycle other than the full moon, the moon and sun are not directly opposite each other. This makes it possible to see the moon during daylight hours.

For: Phases of the Moon activity
Visit: PHSchool.com
Web Code: czp-7222

Origin of Modern Astronomy **627**

Eclipses

Along with understanding the moon's phases, the early Greeks also realized that eclipses are simply shadow effects. When the moon moves in a line directly between Earth and the sun, it casts a dark shadow on Earth. This produces a **solar eclipse.** This situation occurs during new-moon phases. The moon is eclipsed when it moves within Earth's shadow, producing a **lunar eclipse.** This situation occurs during full-moon phases. Figure 17 illustrates solar and lunar eclipses.

Why doesn't a solar eclipse occur with every new moon and a lunar eclipse with every full moon? They would if the orbit of the moon lay exactly along the plane of Earth's orbit. However, the moon's orbit is inclined about 5 degrees to the plane that contains Earth and the sun. During most new-moon phases, the shadow of the moon misses Earth (passes above or below). During most full-moon phases, the shadow of Earth misses the moon. ◖**During a new-moon or full-moon phase, the moon's orbit must cross the plane of the ecliptic for an eclipse to take place.** Because these conditions are normally met only twice a year, the usual number of eclipses is four. These occur as a set of one solar and one lunar eclipse, followed six months later with another set. Occasionally, the alignment can result in additional eclipses. However, the total number of eclipses in one year isn't more than seven.

Figure 17 A Observers in the umbra see a total solar eclipse. Those in the penumbra see a partial eclipse. The path of the solar eclipse moves eastward across the globe. The figure shows a total solar eclipse.
B During a total lunar eclipse, the moon's orbit carries it into Earth's umbra. During a partial eclipse, only a portion of the moon enters the umbra.

Solar and Lunar Eclipse

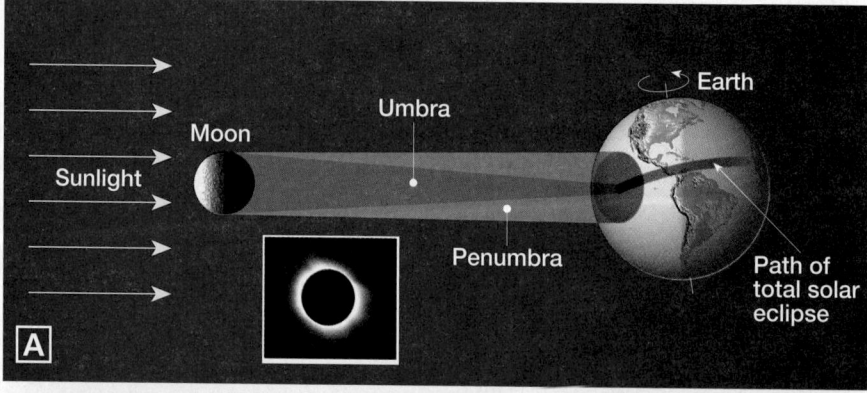

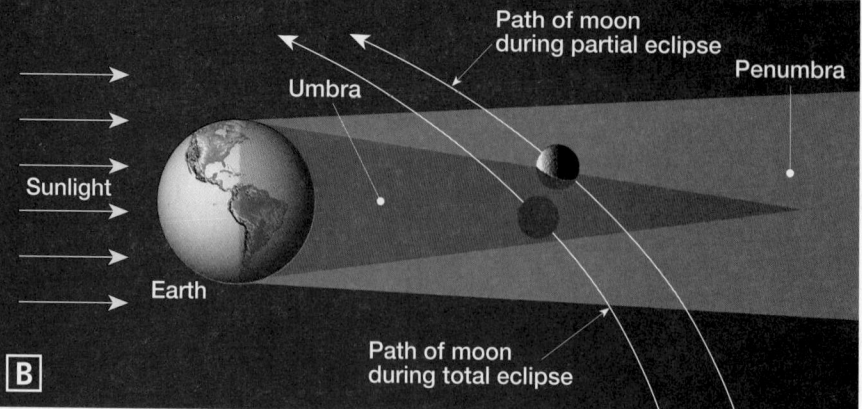

During a total lunar eclipse, Earth's circular shadow can be seen moving slowly across the disk of the full moon. When totally eclipsed, the moon is completely within Earth's shadow, but it is still visible as a coppery disk. This happens because Earth's atmosphere bends and transmits some long-wavelength light (red) into its shadow. A total eclipse of the moon can last up to four hours and is visible to anyone on the side of Earth facing the moon.

During a total solar eclipse, the moon casts a circular shadow that is never wider than 275 kilometers, about the length of South Carolina. Anyone observing in this region will see the moon slowly block the sun from view and the sky darken. When the eclipse is almost complete, the temperature sharply drops a few degrees. The solar disk is completely blocked for seven minutes at the most. This happens because the moon's shadow is so small. Then one edge of the solar disk reappears.

When the eclipse is complete, the dark moon is seen covering the complete solar disk. Only the sun's brilliant white outer atmosphere is visible. Total solar eclipses are visible only to people in the dark part of the moon's shadow known as the umbra. A partial eclipse is seen by those in the light portion of the shadow, known as the penumbra.

A total solar eclipse is a rare event at any location. The next one that will be visible from the United States will take place on August 21, 2017. It will sweep southeast across the country from Oregon to South Carolina.

Section 22.2. Assessment

Reviewing Concepts

1. 🗨 In what ways does Earth move?
2. What phenomena result from Earth's rotation and revolution?
3. 🗨 What causes the phases of the moon?
4. How does the crescent phase that precedes the new moon differ from the crescent phase that follows the new moon?
5. 🗨 Why don't eclipses occur during every full-moon or new-moon phase?
6. Describe the locations of the sun, moon, and Earth during a solar eclipse and during a lunar eclipse.

Critical Thinking

7. **Predicting** Currently, Earth is closest to the sun in January (perihelion) and farthest from the sun in July (aphelion). However, 13,000 years from now, precession will cause perihelion to occur in July and aphelion to occur in January. Assuming no other changes, how might this affect average summer temperatures for your location? What about average winter temperatures?

Writing in Science

Firsthand Account Imagine you are an assistant for one of the ancient astronomers. You are present when the astronomer makes an important discovery. Write a firsthand account describing the discovery and its impact on science.

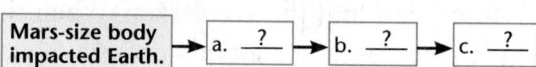

Key Concepts

- What processes created surface features on the moon?
- How did the moon form?

Vocabulary

- ◆ crater
- ◆ ray
- ◆ mare
- ◆ rille
- ◆ lunar regolith

Reading Strategy

Sequencing Copy Copy the flowchart below. As you read, fill in the stages leading to the formation of the moon.

| Mars-size body impacted Earth. | → | a. ___?___ | → | b. ___?___ | → | c. ___?___ |

Figure 18 This is what the moon's surface looks like from Earth when viewed through a telescope.

Mare Imbrium (Sea of Rains)

Mare Tranquillitatus (Sea of Tranquility)

Copernicus crater

Kepler crater

Lunar Highlands

Earth now has hundreds of satellites. Only one natural satellite, the moon, accompanies us on our annual journey around the sun. Other planets also have moons. But our planet-satellite system is unusual in the solar system, because Earth's moon is large compared to its parent planet. The diameter of the moon is 3475 kilometers, about one-fourth of Earth's diameter of 12,756 kilometers.

Much of what we know about the moon, shown in Figure 18, comes from data gathered by the *Apollo* moon missions. Six *Apollo* spacecraft landed on the moon between 1969 and 1972. Uncrewed spacecraft such as the *Lunar Prospector* have also explored the moon's surface. From calculation of the moon's mass, we know that its density is 3.3 times that of water. This density is comparable to that of mantle rocks on Earth. But it is considerably less than Earth's average density, which is 5.5 times that of water. Geologists have suggested that this difference can be accounted for if the moon's iron core is small. The gravitational attraction at the lunar surface is one-sixth of that experienced on Earth's surface. (A 150-pound person on Earth weighs only 25 pounds on the moon). This difference allows an astronaut to carry a heavy life-support system easily. An astronaut on the moon could jump six times higher than on Earth.

The Lunar Surface

When Galileo first pointed his telescope toward the moon, he saw two different types of landscape— dark lowlands and bright highlands. Because the dark regions resembled seas on Earth, they were later named maria, which comes from the Latin word for *sea*. Today we know that the moon has no atmosphere or liquid water. Therefore, the moon doesn't have the weathering and erosion that continually change Earth's surface. Also, tectonic forces aren't active on the moon, therefore volcanic eruptions no longer occur. However, because the moon is unprotected by an atmosphere, a different kind of erosion occurs. Tiny particles from space continually bombard its surface and gradually smooth out the landscape. Even so, it is unlikely that the moon has changed very much in the last 3 billion years, except for the formation of a few craters.

Craters The most obvious features of the lunar surface are **craters,** which are round depressions in the surface of the moon. There are many craters on the moon. The larger craters are about 250 kilometers in diameter, about the width of Indiana. **Most craters were produced by the impact of rapidly moving debris or meteoroids.**

By contrast, Earth has only about a dozen easily recognized impact craters. Friction with Earth's atmosphere burns up small debris before it reaches the ground. Evidence for most of the craters that formed in Earth's history has been destroyed by erosion, deposition, or tectonic processes.

The formation of an impact crater is modeled in Figure 19. Upon impact, the colliding object compresses the material it strikes. This process is similar to the splash that occurs when a rock is dropped into water. In larger meteor craters, a central peak forms after the impact.

Most of the ejected material lands near the crater, building a rim around it. The heat generated by the impact is enough to melt rock. Astronauts have brought back samples of glass and rock formed when fragments and dust were welded together by the impact.

Formation of a Crater

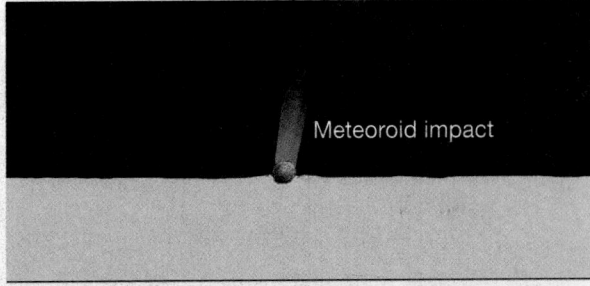

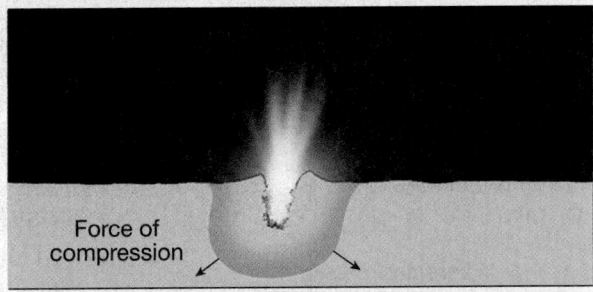

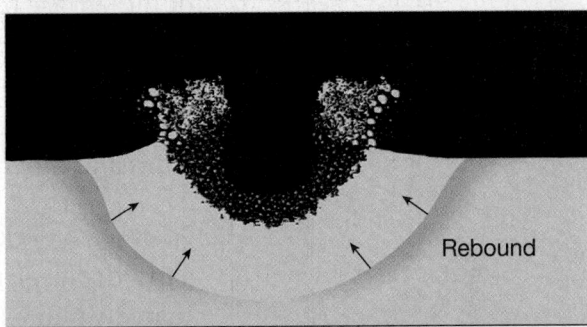

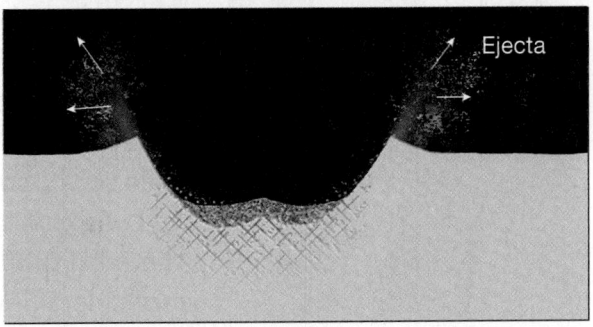

Figure 19 The energy of the rapidly moving meteoroid is transformed into heat energy. Rock compresses and then quickly rebounds. The rebounding rock causes debris to be ejected from the crater.

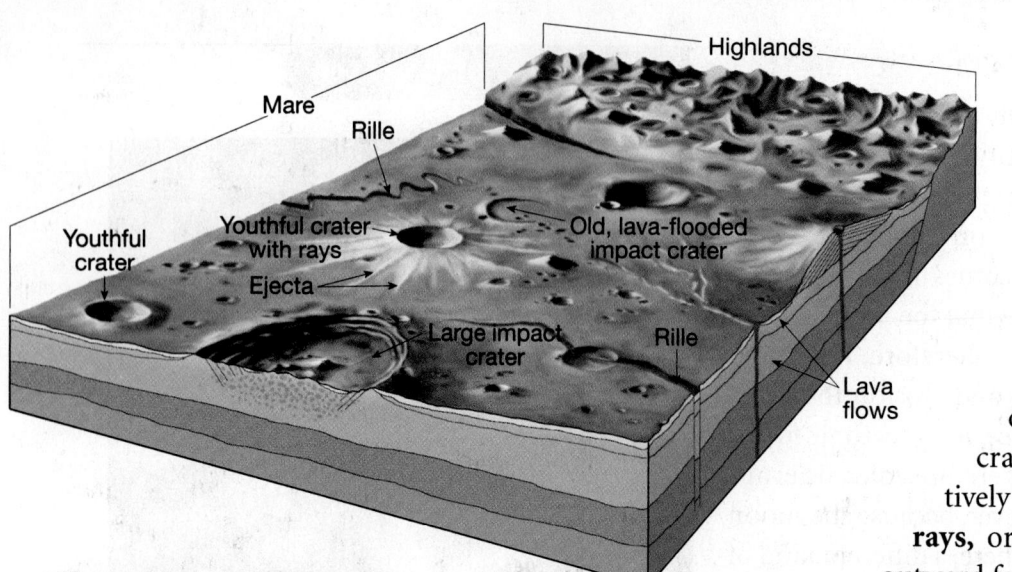

Figure 20 Major topographic features on the moon's surface include craters, maria, and highlands.
Identifying *Where are rilles located?*

Labels in figure: Mare, Rille, Youthful crater, Youthful crater with rays, Highlands, Old, lava-flooded impact crater, Ejecta, Large impact crater, Rille, Lava flows

A meteoroid only 3 meters in diameter can blast out a 150-meter-wide crater. A few of the large craters, such as those named Kepler and Copernicus, formed from the impact of bodies 1 kilometer or more in diameter. These two large craters are thought to be relatively young because of the bright **rays,** or splash marks that radiate outward for hundreds of kilometers.

Highlands

Most of the lunar surface is made up of densely pitted, light-colored areas known as highlands. In fact, highlands cover most of the surface of the far side of the moon. The same side of the moon always faces Earth. Within the highland regions are mountain ranges. The highest lunar peaks reach elevations of almost 8 kilometers. This is only 1 kilometer lower than Mount Everest. Figure 20 shows highlands and other features of the moon.

Maria

A dark, relatively smooth area on the moon's surface is called a **mare** (plural: maria). **Maria, ancient beds of basaltic lava, originated when asteroids punctured the lunar surface, letting magma "bleed" out.** Apparently, the craters were flooded with layer upon layer of very fluid basaltic lava somewhat resembling the Columbia Plateau in the northwestern United States. The lava flows are often over 30 meters thick. The total thickness of the material that fills the maria could reach thousands of meters.

Long channels called **rilles** are associated with maria. Rilles look somewhat similar to valleys or trenches. Rilles may be the remnants of ancient lava flows. Some rilles could be graben-like structures.

Regolith

All lunar terrains are mantled with a layer of gray debris derived from a few billion years of bombardment from meteorites. This soil-like layer, called **lunar regolith,** is composed of igneous rocks, glass beads, and fine lunar dust. In the maria that have been explored by *Apollo* astronauts, the lunar regolith is just over 3 meters thick.

 **Reading Checkpoint** *What is lunar regolith?*

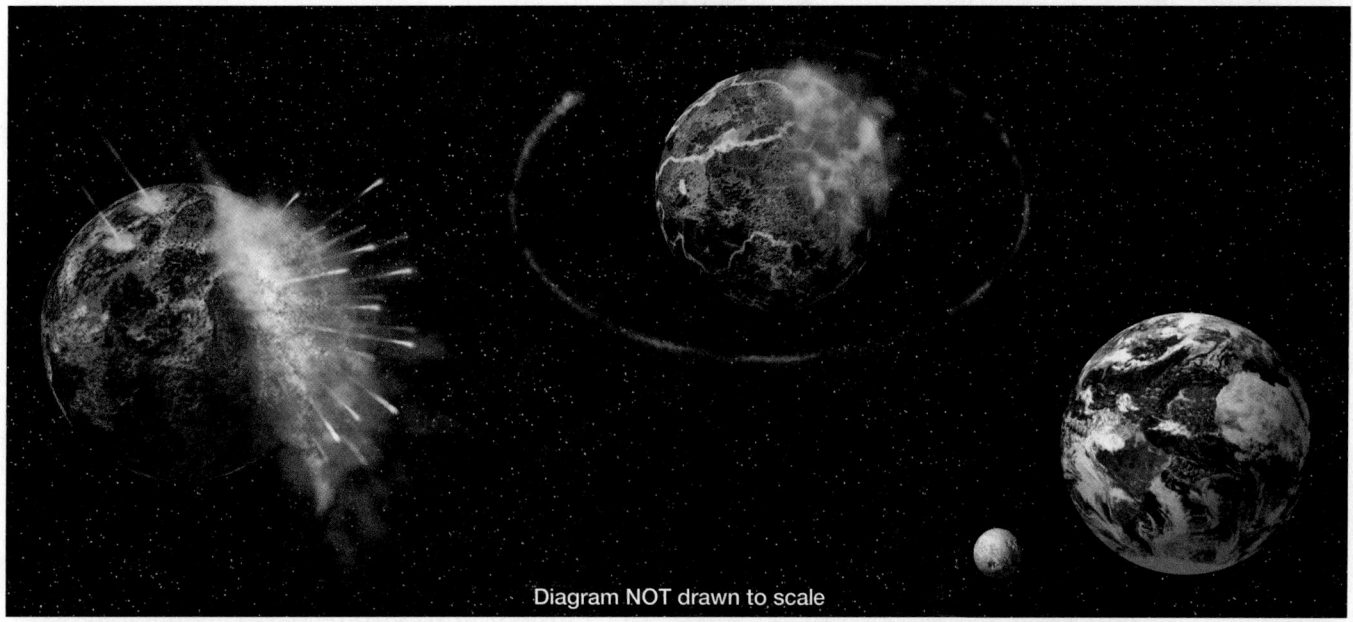
Diagram NOT drawn to scale

Lunar History

The moon is our nearest planetary neighbor. Although astronauts have walked on its surface, much is still unknown about its origin. The most widely accepted model for the origin of the moon is that when the solar system was forming, a body the size of Mars impacted Earth. The impact, shown in Figure 21, would have liquefied Earth's surface and ejected huge quantities of crustal and mantle rock from an infant Earth. A portion of this ejected debris would have entered an orbit around Earth where it combined to form the moon.

The giant-impact hypothesis is consistent with other facts known about the moon. The ejected material would have been mostly iron-poor mantle and crustal rocks. These would account for the lack of a sizable iron core on the moon. The ejected material would have remained in orbit long enough to have lost the water that the moon lacks. Despite this supporting evidence, some questions remain unanswered.

Geologists have worked out the basic details of the moon's later history. One of their methods is to observe variations in crater density (the number of craters per unit area). The greater the crater density, the older the surface must be. From such evidence, scientists concluded that the moon evolved in three phases—the original crust (highlands), maria basins, and rayed craters.

During its early history, the moon was continually impacted as it swept up debris. This continuous attack, combined with radioactive decay, generated enough heat to melt the moon's outer shell and possibly the interior as well. Remnants of this original crust occupy the densely cratered highlands. These highlands have been estimated to be as much as 4.5 billion years old, about the same age as Earth.

Figure 21 The moon may have formed when a large object collided with Earth. The resulting debris was ejected into space. The debris began orbiting around Earth and eventually united to form the moon.

One important event in the moon's evolution was the formation of maria basins. Radiometric dating of the maria basalts puts their age between 3.2 billion and 3.8 billion years, about a billion years younger than the initial crust. In places, the lava flows overlap the highlands, which also explains the younger age of the maria deposits.

The last prominent features to form were the rayed craters. Material ejected from these young depressions is clearly seen covering the surface of the maria and many older rayless craters. Even a relatively young crater like Copernicus, shown in Figure 22, must be millions of years old. If it had formed on Earth, erosional forces would have erased it long ago. If photographs of the moon taken several hundreds of millions of years ago were available, they would show that the moon has changed little. The moon is an inactive body wandering through space and time.

Figure 22 Rayed craters such as Copernicus were the last major features to form on the moon.

Section 22.3 Assessment

Reviewing Concepts

1. How did most lunar craters form?
2. How did maria originate?
3. How did the moon form?

Critical Thinking

4. **Identifying** On Earth, the four major spheres (atmosphere, hydrosphere, geosphere, and biosphere) interact as a system. Which of these spheres are absent, or nearly absent, on the moon? Based on your answer, identify at least five processes that operate on Earth but not on the moon.

5. **Inferring** Why are craters more common on the moon than on Earth, even though the moon is a much smaller target?

Connecting Concepts

Scientific Evidence Write a paragraph explaining what evidence scientists use to reconstruct the history of the moon.

Foucault's Experiment

Earth rotates on its axis once each day to produce periods of daylight and darkness. However, day and night and the apparent motions of the stars can be accounted for equally well by a sun and celestial sphere that revolve around a stationary Earth.

Copernicus realized that a rotating Earth greatly simplified the existing model of the universe. He was unable, however, to prove that Earth rotates. The first real proof was presented 300 years after his death by the French physicist Jean Foucault.

The Swinging Pendulum

In 1851, Foucault used a free-swinging pendulum to demonstrate that Earth does, in fact, turn on its axis. To picture Foucault's experiment, imagine a large pendulum swinging over the North Pole, as shown in the illustration on this page. Keep in mind that once a pendulum is put into motion, it continues swinging in the same plane unless acted upon by some outside force. Assume that a sharp point is attached to the bottom of this pendulum, marking the snow as it swings. If we were to observe the marks made by the point, we would see that the pendulum is slowly but continually changing position. At the end of 24 hours, the pendulum would have returned to its starting position.

Evidence of Earth's Rotation

No outside force acted on the pendulum to change its position. So what we observed must have been Earth rotating beneath the pendulum. Foucault conducted a similar experiment when he suspended a long pendulum from the dome of the Pantheon in Paris. Today, Foucault pendulums can be found in some museums to re-create this famous scientific experiment.

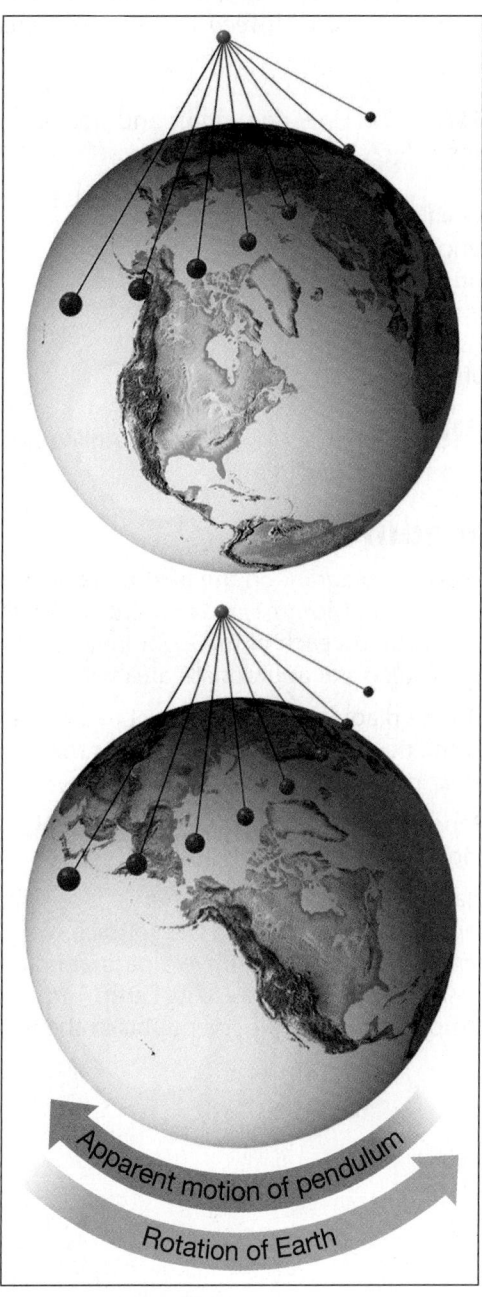

Apparent motion of pendulum

Rotation of Earth

Modeling Synodic and Sidereal Months

The time interval required for the moon to complete a full cycle of phases is 29.5 days, or one synodic month. The true period of the moon's revolution around Earth, however, is only 27.3 days and is known as the sidereal month. In this lab, you will model the differences between synodic and sidereal months.

Problem How do synodic and sidereal months differ?

Materials
- pencil
- paper
- lamp
- basketball
- softball

Skills Observing, Using Models, Analyzing Data, Drawing Conclusions

Procedure

1. Copy the diagram on the next page on a piece of paper. In Month 1, indicate the dark half of the moon on each of the eight lunar positions by shading the appropriate area with a pencil.

2. On the diagram of Month 1, label the position of the new moon. Do the same for the other lunar phases.

3. Repeat Steps 1 and 2 for the diagram of Month 2.

4. Place the lamp on a desk or table. The lamp represents the sun. Hold the softball, which represents the moon. Have a partner hold the basketball, which represents Earth. Turn on the lamp and turn off all other lights in the room.

5. Stand so that the "moon" is in the position of the new-moon phase in Month 1, relative to "Earth" and the "sun." Revolve the moon around Earth while at the same time moving both Earth and the moon to Month 2. Stop at the same numbered position at which you began. Use the diagrams to guide your movements.

Analyze and Conclude

1. **Using Models** After one complete revolution beginning at the new-moon phase in Month 1, in what position is the moon located in Month 2?

2. **Interpreting Data** Based on your answer to the previous question, does this position occur before or after the moon has completed one full cycle of phases?

3. **Identifying** In Month 2, what position represents the new-moon phase? When the moon reaches this position, will it have completed a synodic or sidereal month?

4. **Summarizing** In your own words, explain the difference between a sidereal and synodic month.

Go Further With your partner's help, use the lamp, softball, and basketball to model the positions of the sun, Earth, and moon during a lunar eclipse and a solar eclipse. On your diagram, label the position of the moon during each eclipse.

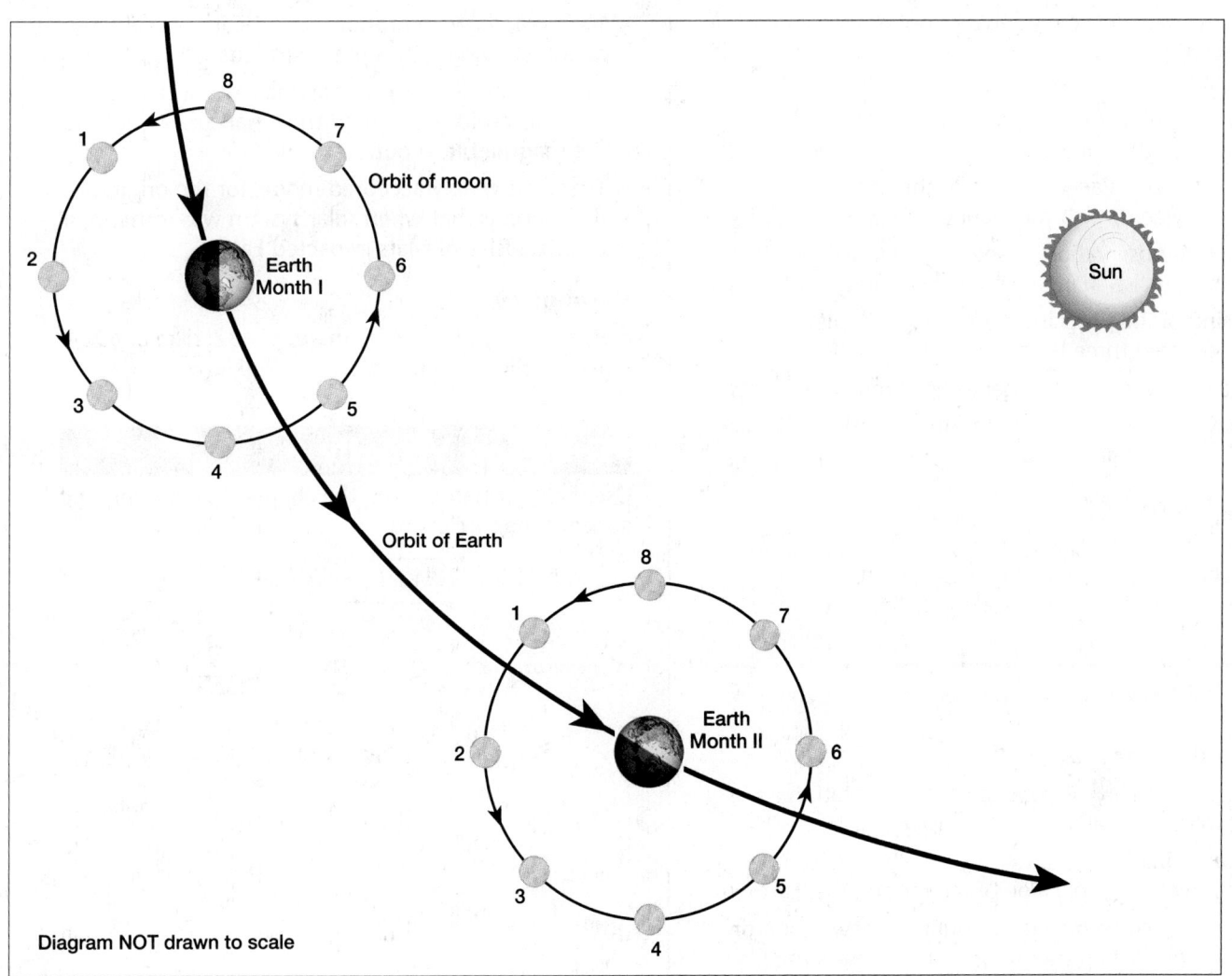

Orbit of moon

Earth
Month I

Sun

Orbit of Earth

Earth
Month II

Diagram NOT drawn to scale

Study Guide

22.1 Early Astronomy

Key Concepts

- In the geocentric model, the moon, sun, and the known planets—Mercury, Venus, Mars, and Jupiter—orbit Earth.
- In the heliocentric model, Earth and the other planets orbit the sun.
- Copernicus placed the sun at the center of the solar system, with the planets orbiting around it.
- Brahe's observations, especially of Mars, were far more precise than any made previously.
- Using Brahe's precise observations, Kepler discovered three laws of planetary motion.
- Galileo described the behavior of moving objects.
- Newton was the first to formulate and test the law of universal gravitation.

Vocabulary

astronomy, *p. 614;* geocentric, *p. 615;* orbit, *p. 615;* heliocentric, *p. 616;* retrograde motion, *p. 616;* ellipse, *p. 618;* astronomical unit (AU), *p. 618*

22.2 The Earth-Moon-Sun System

Key Concepts

- The two main motions of Earth are rotation and revolution.
- Lunar phases are caused by the changes in how much of the sunlit side of the moon faces Earth.
- An eclipse can only occur during a new moon or full moon when the moon's orbit crosses the plane of the ecliptic.

Vocabulary

rotation, *p. 622;* revolution, *p. 622;* precession, *p. 622;* perihelion, *p. 624;* aphelion, *p. 624;* perigee, *p. 626;* apogee, *p. 626;* phases of the moon, *p. 626;* solar eclipse, *p. 628;* lunar eclipse, *p. 628*

22.3 Earth's Moon

Key Concepts

- Most craters were produced by the impact of rapidly moving debris or meteoroids.
- Mare, an ancient bed of basaltic lava, originated when asteroids punctured the lunar surface, letting the magma bleed out.
- The most widely accepted model for the origin of the moon is that when solar system was forming, a body the size of Mars impacted Earth.

Vocabulary

crater, *p. 631;* ray, *p. 632;* mare, *p. 632;* rille, *p. 632;* lunar regolith, *p. 632*

Thinking Visually

Use the information from the chapter to complete the concept map below.

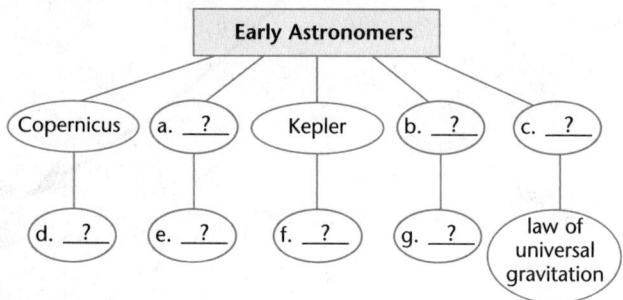

Reviewing Content

Choose the letter that best answers the question or completes the statement.

1. Who first proposed that the sun was the center of the universe?
   a. Aristotle
   b. Aristarchus
   c. Anaxogoras
   d. Hipparchus

2. One astronomical unit averages about
   a. 93 million kilometers.
   b. 150 million kilometers.
   c. 210 million kilometers.
   d. 300 million kilometers.

3. During which month is Earth farthest from the sun?
   a. January
   b. April
   c. July
   d. October

4. In 13,000 years, Earth's axis will point toward
   a. Polaris.
   b. Vega.
   c. the sun.
   d. the moon.

5. At what point is the moon nearest to Earth during its orbit?
   a. at apogee
   b. at perihelion
   c. during an eclipse
   d. at perigee

6. What type of eclipse occurs when the moon casts its shadow on Earth?
   a. lunar
   b. sidereal
   c. solar
   d. synodic

7. During the period that the moon's phases are changing from new to full, the moon is always
   a. waning.
   b. approaching Earth.
   c. waxing.
   d. receding from Earth.

8. The large, dark regions on the moon are called
   a. highlands.
   b. craters.
   c. mountains.
   d. maria.

9. Rilles are associated with which of the following lunar features?
   a. craters
   b. maria
   c. rays
   d. highlands

10. The oldest lunar features are
    a. highlands.
    b. rayed craters.
    c. rilles.
    d. maria.

Understanding Concepts

11. List three accomplishments of Hipparchus.

12. Describe how Eratosthenes measured the size of Earth.

13. What was Tycho Brahe's contribution to science?

14. Use Kepler's third law ($T^2 = d^3$) to determine the period of a planet whose solar distance is 10 AU.

15. What is an astronomical unit?

16. Newton learned that the orbits of planets are the results of what two forces?

17. Explain the difference between the mean solar day and the sidereal day.

18. What is the approximate length of the cycle of the phases of the moon?

19. What phase of the moon occurs approximately one week after the new moon?

20. How many eclipses normally occur each year?

21. How long can a total eclipse of the moon last? A total eclipse of the sun?

22. Describe three features found on the moon's surface.

23. Briefly outline the history of the moon.

Critical Thinking

24. Drawing Conclusions Does Earth move faster in its orbit near perihelion (January) or near aphelion (July)? Based on your answer, is the solar day longest in January or July?

25. Predicting The moon rotates very slowly on its axis. Predict how this affects the lunar surface temperature.

26. Applying Concepts Solar eclipses are slightly more common than lunar eclipses. Why then is it more likely that your region of the country will experience a lunar eclipse?

27. Making Generalizations In what ways do the interactions between Earth and its moon influence the Earth-moon system? If Earth did not have a moon, would the atmosphere, hydrosphere, geosphere, and biosphere be any different? Explain.

Analyzing Data

Use the photograph below to answer Questions 28–30.

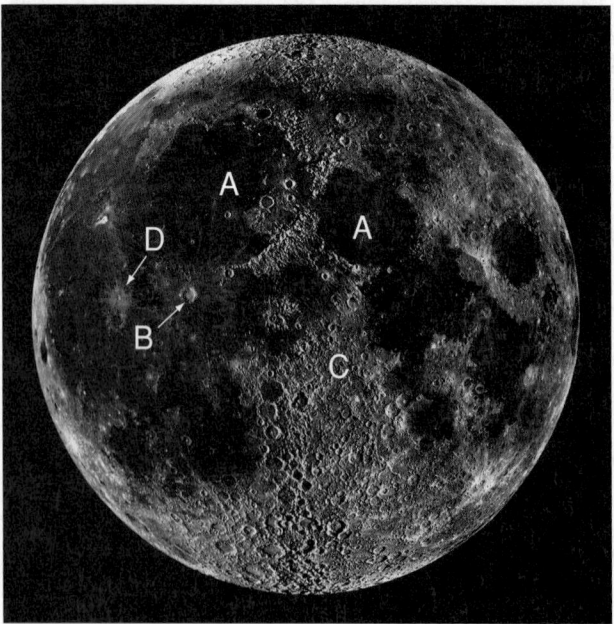

28. Interpreting Data What feature exists at point A? How did this feature likely form?

29. Identifying Which point represents a ray? Which point represents highlands?

30. Inferring What is the oldest feature in the photograph? How do you know?

Concepts in Action

31. Relating Cause and Effect How does the fact that Venus appears full when it is smallest support Copernicus's view rather than the Ptolemaic system?

32. Explaining Explain how Galileo's discovery of Jupiter's moons supported the heliocentric model.

33. Identifying What is the result of the moon's period of rotation and revolution being the same?

34. Applying Concepts How is crater density used in the relative dating of features on the moon?

Performance-Based Assessment

Observing Record at least four observations of the moon over the next two weeks. Sketch the moon at each observation. Use shading to show the phase you see. Note the date and time of each observation. Afterwards, write a paragraph describing how the size and shape of the lit portion of the moon changed over the length of your observations.

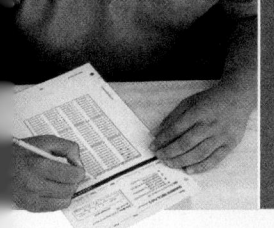

Standardized Test Prep

Test-Taking Tip

Eliminating Unreasonable Answers
When you answer a multiple-choice question, you can often eliminate at least one answer because it is clearly incorrect. If you eliminate one or more choices, you increase your odds of choosing the correct answer. In the question below, you can immediately eliminate choice A because the moon does not have rivers on its surface. Clearly, choices B and D cannot both be true because they relate to the same phenomenon. You can eliminate both of these choices because volcanic activity is not currently occurring on the moon. The remaining choice, C, must be the correct answer.

The most important forces currently modifying the moon's surface are

(A) rivers.
(B) lava flows.
(C) tiny particles from space.
(D) volcanoes.

1. The Ptolemy system proposed that
   (A) Earth revolved around the sun.
   (B) the sun was the center of the universe.
   (C) Earth was a wanderer.
   (D) Earth was the center of the universe.

2. What is the shape of a planet's orbit?
   (A) circular
   (B) irregular
   (C) elliptical
   (D) constantly changing

3. Explain why Mars appears to have retrograde motion.

4. List and describe four motions that Earth continuously experiences.

5. Compare and contrast an umbra and a penumbra.

Use the diagram below to answer Questions 6 and 7.

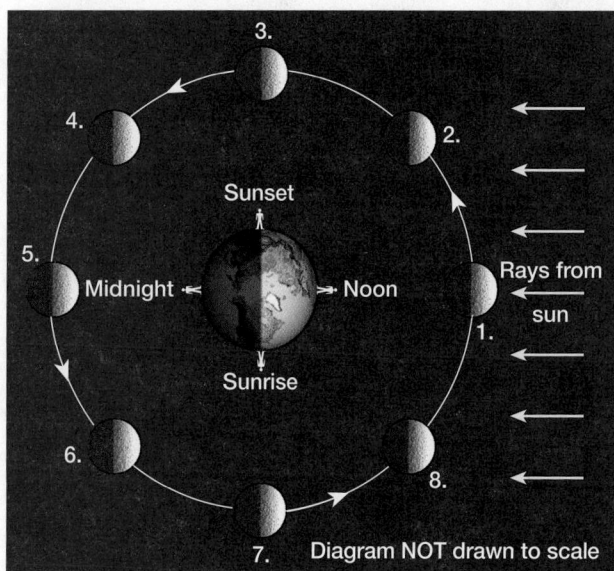

6. Select the number that illustrates the moon's position in its orbit for each of the following phases: full, third quarter, waxing crescent, new, waning.

7. What number represents the position of the moon during a lunar eclipse? A solar eclipse?

CHAPTER 23

Touring Our Solar System

21st Century Learning

Communication Skills

Where in the Solar System have we probed and why?

Humans have sent out numerous probes into our solar system. Research these missions and learn where they went and why. Find out where they are now if the mission is ongoing. Use a paper or computer graphic diagram of the solar system to create a graphic to illustrate these solar-system missions. Draw out the track of each of the solar system missions, showing where the mission visited, halted, or where it is now. Create a legend that contains each mission's name, purpose, dates, and other relevant information.

Exploration Lab

Modeling the Solar System

Earth as A System

Is Earth on a Collision Course?

GEODe EARTH SCIENCE

Astronomy
→ The Planets: An Overview
Calculating Your Age and Weight on Other Planets

Earth's Moon
A Brief Tour of the Planets

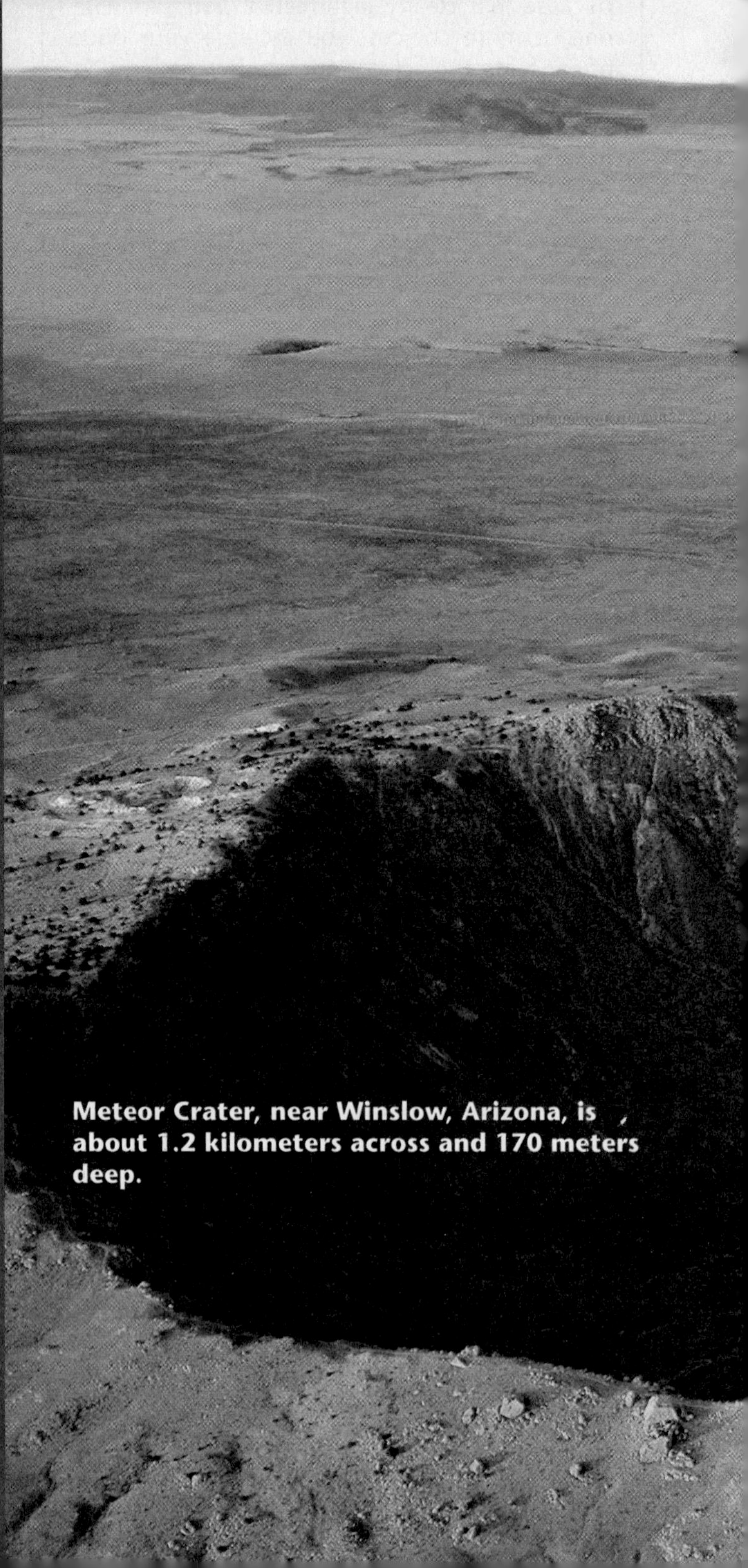

Meteor Crater, near Winslow, Arizona, is about 1.2 kilometers across and 170 meters deep.

Chapter Preview

Inquiry Activity

What Is the Shape of a Planetary Orbit?

Procedure

1. Place a piece of cardboard about 20 cm square on a flat surface. Place two push pins into the cardboard about 3 cm apart.

2. Tie the ends of a piece of string together. Loop the string around the pushpins.

3. Using a pencil to keep the string taut, trace around the pins.

4. Repeat steps 1 through 3, varying the distance between the two pins.

Think About It

1. **Observing** What type of shape did you draw?

2. **Observing** What happened when the pins were moved farther apart?

3. **Comparing** How do your drawings compare with the shapes you see in Figure 1 on the next page?

23.1 The Solar System

Key Concepts

- How do terrestrial planets differ from Jovian planets?
- How did the solar system form?

Vocabulary

- terrestrial planet
- Jovian planet
- nebula
- planetesimal

Reading Strategy

Relating Text and Diagrams As you read, refer to Figure 3 to complete the flowchart on the formation of the solar system.

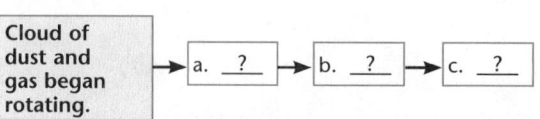

The sun is the hub of a huge rotating system of planets, their satellites, and numerous smaller bodies. An estimated 99.85 percent of the mass of our solar system is contained within the sun. The planets collectively make up most of the remaining 0.15 percent. As Figure 1 shows, the planets, traveling outward from the sun, are Mercury, Venus, Earth, Mars, Jupiter, Saturn, Uranus, and Neptune.

Guided by the sun's gravitational force, each planet moves in an elliptical orbit, and all travel in the same direction. The nearest planet to the sun—Mercury—has the fastest orbital motion at 48 kilometers per second, and it has the shortest period of revolution. By contrast, the most distant planet, Neptune, has an orbital speed of 5 kilometers per second, and it requires 165 Earth-years to complete one revolution.

Imagine a planet's orbit drawn on a flat sheet of paper. The paper represents the planet's orbital plane. The orbital planes of seven planets lie within 3 degrees of the plane of the sun's equator. Mercury's orbit is inclined by 7 degrees.

Figure 1 Orbits of the Planets and Pluto The positions of the planets and Pluto are shown to scale along the bottom of the diagram.

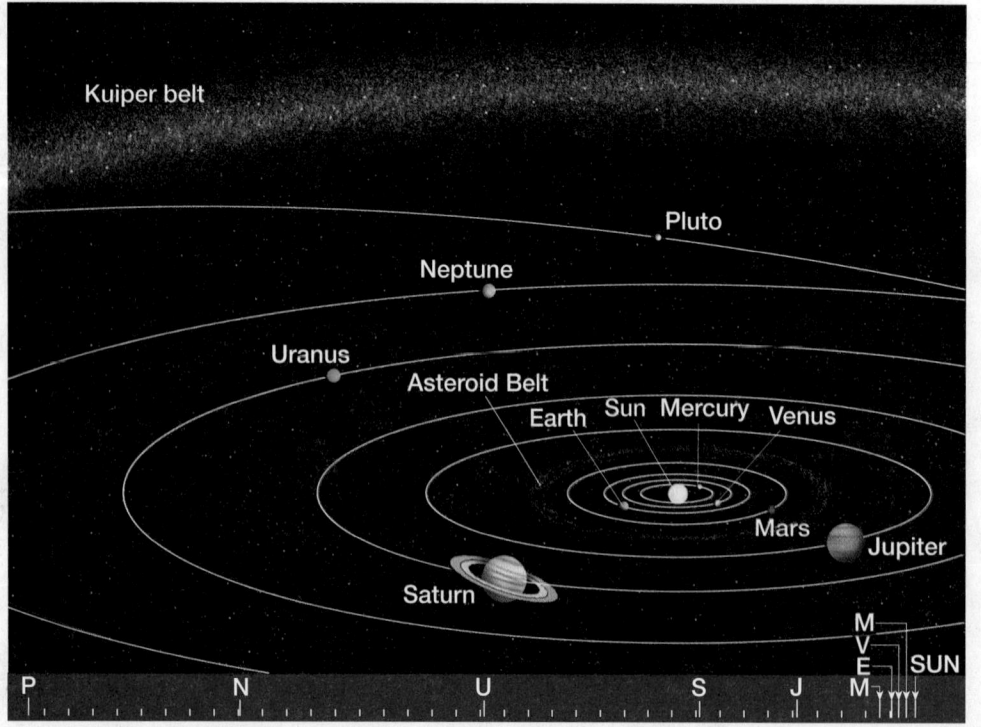

The Planets: An Overview

Careful examination of Table 1 shows that the planets fall quite nicely into two groups. The **terrestrial planets**—Mercury, Venus, Earth, and Mars—are relatively small and rocky. (*Terrestrial* = Earth-like.)The **Jovian planets**—Jupiter, Saturn, Uranus, and Neptune—are huge gas giants. (*Jovian* = Jupiter-like.)

 **Size is the most obvious difference between the terrestrial and the Jovian planets.** The diameter of the largest terrestrial planet, Earth, is only one-quarter the diameter of the smallest Jovian planet, Neptune. Also, Earth's mass is only 1/17 as great as Neptune's. Hence, the Jovian planets are often called giants. Because of their distant locations from the sun, the four Jovian planets are also called the outer planets. The terrestrial planets are closer to the sun and are called the inner planets. As we shall see, there appears to be a correlation between the positions of these planets and their sizes.

 **Density, chemical makeup, and rate of rotation are other ways in which the two groups of planets differ.** The densities of the terrestrial planets average about five times the density of water. The Jovian planets, however, have densities that average only 1.5 times the density of water. One of the outer planets, Saturn, has a density only 0.7 times that of water, which means that Saturn would float if placed in a large enough water tank. The different chemical compositions of the planets are largely responsible for these density differences.

Reading Checkpoint *Compare the densities of terrestrial planets and Jovian planets.*

Go Online
active art

For: Solar System activity
Visit: PHSchool.com
Web Code: czp-7231

Table 1 Planetary Data

Planet	Average Distance from Sun AU	Average Distance from Sun Millions of km	Period of Revolution	Orbital Velocity km/s	Period of Rotation	Diameter (km)	Relative Mass (Earth = 1)	Average Density (g/cm^3)	Number of Known Satellites*
Mercury	0.39	58	88^d	47.5	59^d	4878	0.06	5.4	0
Venus	0.72	108	225^d	35.0	244^d	12,104	0.82	5.2	0
Earth	1.00	150	365.25^d	29.8	23^h 56^m 04^s	12,756	1.00	5.5	1
Mars	1.52	228	687^d	24.1	24^h 37^m 23^s	6794	0.11	3.9	2
Jupiter	5.20	778	12^{yr}	13.1	9^h 50^m	143,884	317.87	1.3	63
Saturn	9.54	1427	29.5^{yr}	9.6	10^h 14^m	120,536	95.14	0.7	56
Uranus	19.18	2870	84^{yr}	6.8	17^h 14^m	51,118	14.56	1.2	27
Neptune	30.06	4497	165^{yr}	5.3	16^h 03^m	50,530	17.21	1.7	13
Pluto**	39.44	5900	248^{yr}	4.7	6.4^d	approx. 2300	0.002	1.8	3

*Includes all satellites discovered as of December 2006.

**Pluto is included for purposes of comparison.

Mercury

Venus

Earth

Mars

Sun

Jupiter

Saturn

Uranus

Neptune

Pluto

Figure 2 The planets and Pluto are drawn to scale.
Interpreting Diagrams *How do the sizes of the terrestrial planets compare with the sizes of the Jovian planets?*

The Interiors of the Planets

The planets (and Pluto) are shown to scale in Figure 2. The substances that make up the planets are divided into three groups: gases, rocks, and ices. The classification of these substances is based on their melting points.

1. The gases—hydrogen and helium—are those with melting points near absolute zero (−273°C or 0 kelvin).
2. The rocks are mainly silicate minerals and metallic iron, which have melting points above 700°C.
3. The ices include ammonia (NH_3), methane (CH_4), carbon dioxide (CO_2), and water (H_2O). They have intermediate melting points. For example, H_2O has a melting point of 0°C.

The terrestrial planets are dense, consisting mostly of rocky and metallic substances, and only minor amounts of gases and ices. The Jovian planets, on the other hand, contain large amounts of gases (hydrogen and helium) and ices (mostly water, ammonia, and methane). This accounts for their low densities. The outer planets also contain substantial amounts of rocky and metallic materials, which are concentrated in their cores.

The Atmospheres of the Planets

The Jovian planets have very thick atmospheres of hydrogen, helium, methane, and ammonia. By contrast, the terrestrial planets, including Earth, have meager atmospheres at best. A planet's ability to retain an atmosphere depends on its mass and temperature, which accounts for the difference between Jovian and terrestrial planets.

Simply stated, a gas molecule can escape from a planet if it reaches a speed known as the escape velocity. For Earth, this velocity is 11 kilometers per second. Any material, including a rocket, must reach this speed before it can escape Earth's gravity and go into space.

A comparatively warm body with a small surface gravity, such as our moon, cannot hold even heavy gases, like carbon dioxide and radon. Thus, the moon lacks an atmosphere. The more massive terrestrial planets of Earth, Venus, and Mars retain some heavy gases. Still, their atmospheres make up only a very small portion of their total mass.

In contrast, the Jovian planets have much greater surface gravities. This gives them escape velocities of 21 to 60 kilometers per second—much higher than the terrestrial planets. Consequently, it is more difficult for gases to escape from their gravitational pulls. Also, because the molecular motion of a gas depends upon temperature, at the low temperatures of the Jovian planets even the lightest gases are unlikely to acquire the speed needed to escape.

Formation of the Solar System

Between stars is "the vacuum of space." However, it is not a pure vacuum because it is populated with regions of dispersed dust and gases. A cloud of dust and gas in space is called a **nebula** (*nebula* = cloud; plural: *nebulae*). A nebula, shown in Figure 3A, often consists of 92 percent hydrogen, 7 percent helium, and less than 1 percent of the remaining heavier elements. For some reason not yet fully understood, these thin gaseous clouds begin to rotate slowly and contract gravitationally. As the clouds contract, they spin faster. For an analogy, think of ice skaters—their speed increases as they bring their arms near their bodies.

Nebular Theory Scientific studies of nebulae have led to a theory concerning the origin of our solar system. ⟵**According to the nebular theory, the sun and planets formed from a rotating disk of dust and gases.** As the speed of rotation increased, the center of the disk began to flatten out, as shown in Figure 3B. Matter became more concentrated in this center, where the sun eventually formed.

Figure 3 Formation of the Solar System A According to the nebular theory, the solar system formed from a rotating cloud of dust and gas. **B** The sun formed at the center of the rotating disk. **C** Planetesimals collided, eventually gaining enough mass to be planets.

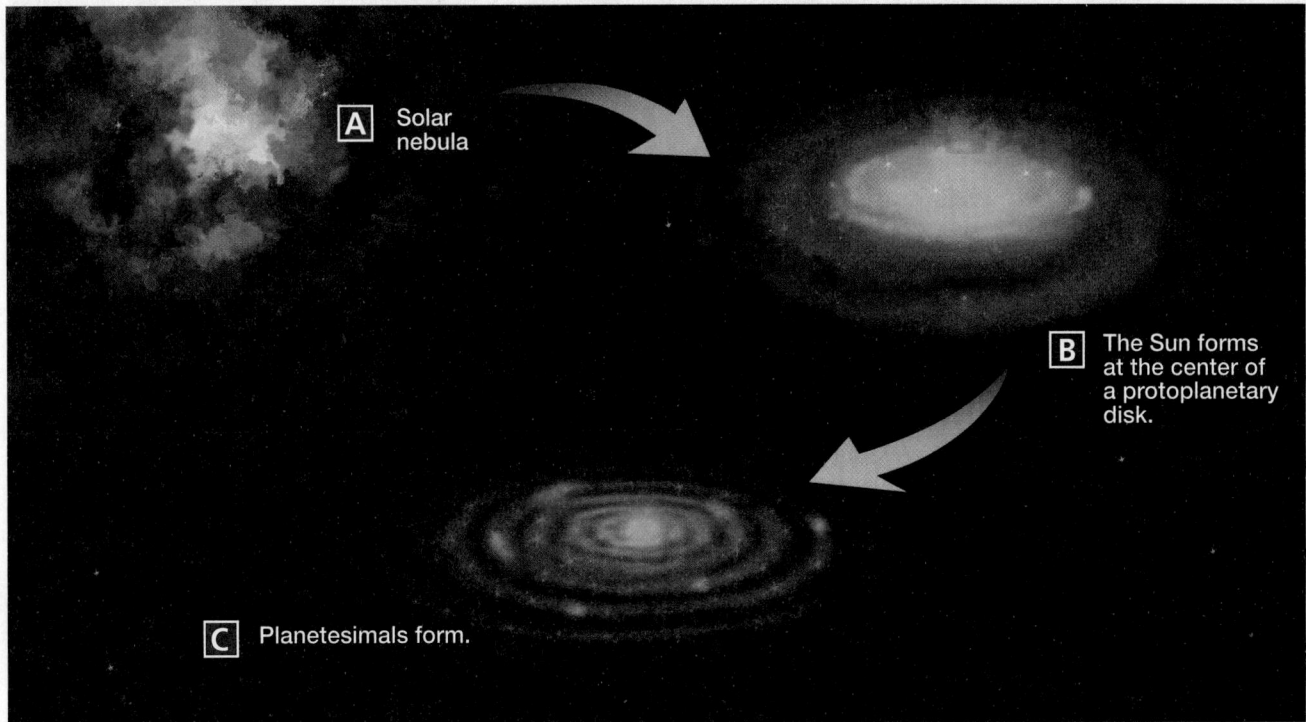

A Solar nebula

B The Sun forms at the center of a protoplanetary disk.

C Planetesimals form.

Planetesimals The growth of planets began as solid bits of matter began to collide and clump together through a process known as accretion. The colliding matter formed small, irregularly shaped bodies called **planetesimals.** As the collisions continued, the planetesimals grew larger, as shown in Figure 3C on page 647. They acquired enough mass to exert a gravitational pull on surrounding objects. In this way, they added still more mass and grew into true planets.

In the inner solar system, close to the sun, temperatures were so high that only metals and silicate minerals could form solid grains. It was too hot for ices of water, carbon dioxide, and methane to form. As shown in Figure 4, the inner planets grew mainly from substances with high melting points.

In the frigid outer reaches of the solar system, on the other hand, it was cold enough for ices of water and other substances to form. Consequently, the Jovian planets grew not only from accumulations of solid bits of material but also from large quantities of ices. Eventually, the Jovian planets became large enough to gravitationally capture even the lightest gases, such as hydrogen and helium. This enabled them to grow into giants.

Figure 4 The terrestrial planets formed mainly from silicate minerals and metallic iron that have high melting points. The Jovian planets formed from large quantities of gases and ices.

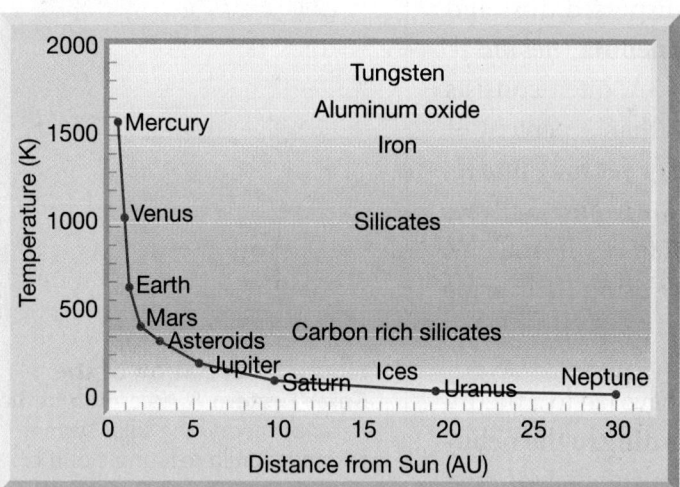

Section 23.1 Assessment

Reviewing Concepts

1. Which planets are classified as terrestrial? Which planets are classified as Jovian?

2. List the planets in order, beginning with the planet closest to the sun.

3. ⊙ How do the terrestrial planets differ from the Jovian planets?

4. What is a nebula?

5. ⊙ How did distance from the sun affect the size and composition of the planets?

Critical Thinking

6. ⊙ **Summarizing** Summarize the nebular theory of the formation of the solar system.

7. **Inferring** Among the planets in our solar system, Earth is unique because water exists in all three states—solid, liquid, and gas—on its surface. How would Earth's water cycle be different if its orbit was outside the orbit of Mars?

Math ◆ Practice

8. Jupiter is 6.3×10^8 (630 million kilometers) from Earth. Calculate how long it would take to reach Jupiter if you traveled at
   1) 100 km/h (freeway speed);
   2) 1,000 km/h (jetliner speed);
   3) 40,000 km/h (rocket speed); and
   4) 3.0×10^8 km/s (speed of light).

23.2 The Terrestrial Planets

Reading Focus

Key Concepts

- What are the distinguishing characteristics of each terrestrial planet?

Reading Strategy

Using Prior Knowledge Copy the web diagram below. Before you read, add properties that you already know about Mars. Then add details about each property as you read. Make a similar web diagram for the other terrestrial planets.

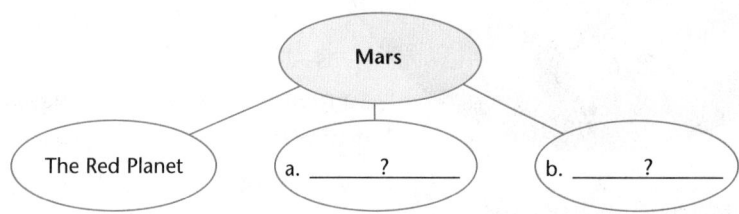

In January 2004, the space rover, *Spirit,* bounced onto the rocky surface of Mars, known as the Red Planet. Shown in Figure 5, *Spirit* and its companion rover, *Opportunity,* were on the Red Planet to study minerals and geological processes, both past and present. They also searched for signs of the liquid water—such as eroded rocks or dry stream channels on Mars's surface. For the next few months, the rovers sent back to Earth numerous images and chemical analysis of Mars's surface. Much of what we learn about the planets has been gathered by rovers, such as *Spirit,* or space probes that travel to the far reaches of the solar system, such as *Voyager.* In this section, we'll explore three terrestrial planets—Mercury, Venus, and Mars—and see how they compare with Earth.

Mercury: The Innermost Planet

Mercury, the innermost and smallest planet, is hardly larger than Earth's moon and is smaller than three other moons in the solar system. Like our own moon, it absorbs most of the sunlight that strikes it and reflects only 6 percent of sunlight back into space. This low percentage of reflection is characteristic of terrestrial bodies that have no atmosphere. Earth, on the other hand, reflects about 30 percent of the light that strikes it. Most of this reflection is from clouds.

Figure 5 *Spirit* roved the surface of Mars and gathered data about the Red Planet's geologic past and present.

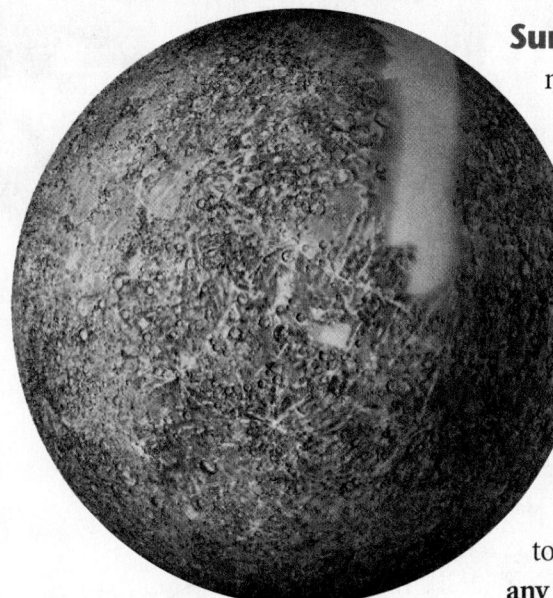

Figure 6 Mercury's surface looks somewhat similar to the far side of Earth's moon.

Figure 7 Venus This global view of the surface of Venus is computer generated from two years of Magellan Project radar mapping. The twisting bright features that cross the planet are highly fractured mountains and canyons of the eastern Aphrodite highland.

For: Links on extraterrestrial volcanoes
Visit: www.SciLinks.org
Web Code: cjn-7232

Surface Features Mercury has cratered highlands, much like the moon, and some smooth terrains that resemble maria. Unlike the moon, however, Mercury is a very dense planet, which implies that it contains a large iron core for its size. Also, Mercury has very long scarps (deep slopes) that cut across the plains and craters alike. These scarps may have resulted from crustal changes as the planet cooled and shrank.

Surface Temperature Mercury, shown in Figure 6, revolves around the sun quickly, but it rotates slowly. One full day-night cycle on Earth takes 24 hours. On Mercury, one rotation requires 59 Earth-days. Nighttime temperatures drop as low as −173°C, and noontime temperatures exceed 427°C—hot enough to melt lead. **Mercury has the greatest temperature extremes of any planet.** The odds of life as we know it existing on Mercury are almost nonexistent.

 **Reading Checkpoint** *How does Mercury's period of rotation compare with Earth's?*

Venus: The Veiled Planet

Venus is second only to the moon in brilliance in the night sky. It orbits the sun once every 255 Earth-days. Venus is similar to Earth in size, density, mass, and location in the solar system. Thus, it has been referred to as "Earth's twin." Because of these similarities, it is hoped that a detailed study of Venus will provide geologists with a better understanding of Earth's history.

Surface Features Venus is covered in thick clouds that hide its surface from view. Nevertheless, radar mapping by the uncrewed *Magellan* spacecraft and by instruments on Earth have revealed a varied topography with features somewhat between those of Earth and Mars, as shown in Figure 7. To map Venus, radar pulses are sent toward the planet's surface, and the heights of plateaus and mountains are measured by timing the return of the radar echo. **Data have confirmed that basaltic volcanism and tectonic activity shape Venus's surface. Based on the low density of impact craters, these forces must have been very active during the recent geologic past.**

About 80 percent of Venus's surface consists of plains covered by volcanic flows. Some lava channels extend hundreds of kilometers—one is 6800 kilometers long. Scientists have identified thousands of now inactive volcanic structures. Most are small shield volcanoes, although more than 1500 volcanoes greater than 20 kilometers across have been mapped. Figure 8 shows two of these volcanoes—one is Sapas Mons, 400 kilometers across and 1.5 kilometers high. Flows from this volcano mostly erupted from its flanks rather than its summit, in the manner of Hawaiian shield volcanoes.

Only 8 percent of Venus's surface consists of highlands that may be similar to continental areas on Earth. Tectonic activity on Venus seems to be driven by upwelling and downwelling of material in the planet's interior.

Surface Temperature On Venus, the greenhouse effect has heated the planet's atmosphere to 475°C. That's hot enough to melt lead! Several factors contribute to what scientists have called Venus's *runaway* greenhouse effect.

The main reason for the runaway greenhouse effect on Venus is that its atmosphere is 97 percent carbon dioxide, a greenhouse gas. Venus lacks oceans in which carbon dioxide gas could dissolve, thus removing it from the atmosphere. Scientists think that oceans on Venus may have evaporated early in its history. Water vapor in the atmosphere then accelerated the greenhouse effect. But the atmosphere eventually lost most of its water vapor. The sun's ultraviolet radiation broke down water molecules into hydrogen and oxygen. These gases then escaped into space.

 *Describe the composition of Venus's atmosphere.*

Figure 8 Sapas Mons and Maat Mons In this computer-generated image from Venus, Maat Mons, a large volcano, is near the horizon. Sapas Mons is the bright feature in the foreground.
Comparing and Contrasting *What features on Venus are similar to those on Earth? What features are different?*

Mars: The Red Planet

Mars has evoked great interest throughout history. Mars is easy to observe, which may explain why so many people are fascinated by it. Mars is known as the Red Planet because it appears as a reddish ball when viewed through a telescope. Mars also has some dark regions that change intensity during the Martian year. The most prominent telescopic features of Mars are its brilliant white polar caps.

Figure 9 Many parts of Mars's landscape resemble desert areas on Earth.

Figure 10 Valles Marineris
Mars's Valles Marineris canyon system is more than 5000 kilometers long and up to 8 kilometers deep. The dark spots on the left edge of the image are huge volcanoes.

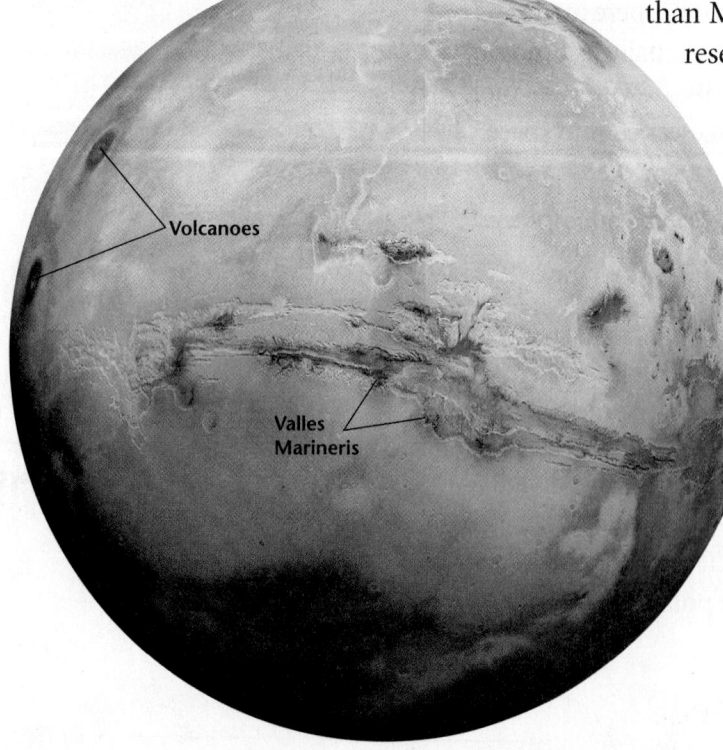

Volcanoes

Valles Marineris

The Martian Atmosphere The Martian atmosphere has only 1 percent the density of Earth's. It is made up primarily of carbon dioxide with tiny amounts of water vapor. Data from Mars probes confirm that the polar caps of Mars are made of water ice, covered by a thin layer of frozen carbon dioxide. As winter nears in either hemisphere, temperatures drop to −125°C, and additional carbon dioxide is deposited. **Although the atmosphere of Mars is very thin, extensive dust storms occur and may cause the color changes observed from Earth. Hurricane-force winds up to 270 kilometers per hour can persist for weeks.** The composition of Mars's atmosphere is similar to that of Venus. But Mars is very cold. Why doesn't the greenhouse effect warm Mars's atmosphere? The reason is that Mars's atmosphere is extremely thin compared with the atmosphere of Venus (or Earth). Scientists think that, early in its history, Mars had a thick atmosphere warmed by the greenhouse effect. But Mars's gravity was too low for the planet to keep its atmosphere. Most of the gases escaped into space, and the planet cooled.

Surface Features *Mariner 9,* the first spacecraft to orbit another planet, reached Mars in 1971 amid a raging dust storm. When the dust cleared, images of Mars' northern hemisphere revealed numerous large inactive volcanoes. The biggest, Olympus Mons, is the size of Ohio and is 23 kilometers high—over two and a half times higher than Mount Everest. This gigantic volcano and others resemble Hawaiian shield volcanoes on Earth.

Most Martian surface features are old by Earth standards. The highly cratered southern hemisphere is probably 3.5 billion to 4.5 billion years old. Even the relatively "fresh" volcanic features of the northern hemisphere may be older than 1 billion years.

Another surprising find made by *Mariner 9* was the existence of several canyons that are much larger than Earth's Grand Canyon. The largest, Valles Marineris, is shown in Figure 10. It is thought to have formed by slippage of material along huge faults in the crustal layer.

Water on Mars Some areas of Mars exhibit drainage patterns similar to those created by streams on Earth. The rover *Opportunity,* for example, found evidence of evaporite minerals and geologic formations associated with liquid water, as shown in Figure 11. In addition, *Viking* images have revealed ancient islands in what is now a dry streambed. When these streamlike channels were first discovered, some observers speculated that a thick water-laden atmosphere capable of generating torrential downpours once existed on Mars. If so, what happened to this water? The present Martian atmosphere contains only traces of water.

Images from the *Mars Global Surveyor* indicate that groundwater has recently migrated to the surface. These spring-like seeps have created gullies where they emerge from valley and crater walls. Some of the escaping water may have initially frozen due to the average Martian temperatures that range between −70°C and −100°C. Eventually, however, it seeped out as a slurry of sediment, ice, and liquid that formed the gullies.

Many scientists do not accept the theory that Mars once had an active water cycle similar to Earth's. Rather, they believe that most of the large stream-like valleys were created by the collapse of surface material caused by the slow melting of subsurface ice. Data from *Opportunity,* however, indicate that some areas were "drenched" in water. It will take scientists many months, if not years, to analyze the data gathered by the latest Mars mission. Because water is an essential ingredient for life, scientists and nonscientists alike are enthusiastic about exploring this phenomenon.

Figure 11 These channels show that liquid water once flowed on the surface of Mars.

Section 23.2 Assessment

Reviewing Concepts

1. ⬤ Which inner planet is smallest?
2. ⬤ How does Venus compare with Earth?
3. ⬤ Identify one distinguishing characteristic of each inner planet.
4. ⬤ What surface features does Mars have that are also common on Earth?

Critical Thinking

5. **Making Judgments** Besides Earth, which inner planet may have been most able to support life? Explain your answer.
6. **Relating Cause and Effect** Why are surface temperatures so high on Venus?

Writing in Science

Editorial A space mission to the moon or Mars often costs millions of dollars. Yet, it is hoped that space exploration can give us valuable knowledge about the solar system. Consider the pros and cons of space exploration. Then write an editorial stating whether or not you believe the costs are worth the potential benefits.

23.3 The Outer Planets (and Pluto)

Reading Focus

Key Concepts

- What characteristics distinguish each outer planet?
- Why is Pluto not considered a planet?

Vocabulary

- dwarf planet

Reading Strategy

Summarizing Make a table like the one shown that includes a row for each outer planet. Write a brief summary of the characteristics of each planet.

Outer Planets	Characteristics
Jupiter	largest; most mass, Great Red Spot
a. ___?___	b. ___?___
c. ___?___	d. ___?___

Figure 12 This artist's rendition shows *Cassini* approaching Saturn.

In 2004, the space probe *Cassini*, launched seven years earlier, finally reached the planet Saturn. The mission of *Cassini*, shown in Figure 12, was to explore Saturn's stunning ring system and its moons, including the unique moon Titan. In 2005, the *Huygens* probe, carried into space by the Cassini orbiter, descended to Titan's surface for further studies. In this section, we'll take a clue from *Cassini* and explore the outer planets—Jupiter, Saturn, Uranus, and Neptune.

Jupiter: Giant Among Planets

Jupiter is only 1/800 as massive as the sun. Still, it is the largest planet by far. **Jupiter has a mass that is 2 1/2 times greater than the mass of all the other planets and moons combined.** In fact, had Jupiter been about 10 times larger, it would have evolved into a small star. Jupiter rotates more rapidly than any other planet, completing one rotation in slightly less than 10 Earth-hours.

When viewed through a telescope or binoculars, Jupiter appears to be covered with alternating bands of multicolored clouds that run parallel to its equator. The most striking feature is the Great Red Spot in the southern hemisphere, shown in Figure 13A. The Great Red Spot was first discovered more than three centuries ago by two astronomers, Giovanni Cassini (for whom the space probe was named) and Robert Hooke. When *Pioneer 11* moved within 42,000 kilometers of Jupiter's cloud tops, images from the orbiter indicated that the Great Red Spot is a cyclonic storm.

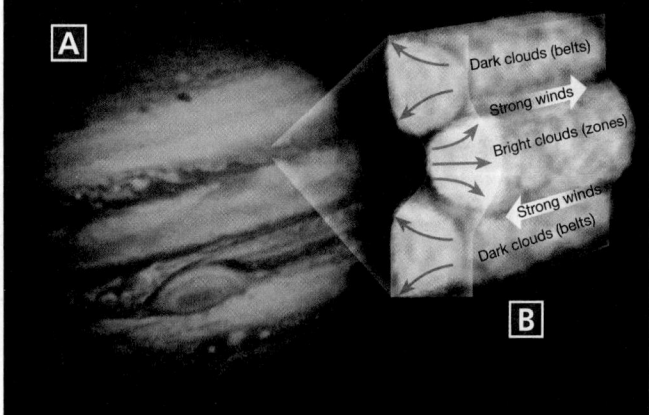

Figure 13 A When photographed by *Voyager 2*, the Great Red Spot was the size of two Earth-size circles placed side by side. **B** The dark clouds are regions where gases are sinking and cooling. The convection currents and the rapid rotation of the planet generate high-speed winds.

Structure of Jupiter Although Jupiter is called a gas giant, it is not simply a ball of gas. At 1000 kilometers below the clouds, the pressure is great enough to compress hydrogen gas into a liquid. Consequently, Jupiter is thought to be a gigantic ocean of liquid hydrogen. Less than halfway into Jupiter's interior, extreme pressures cause the liquid hydrogen to turn into liquid metallic hydrogen. Jupiter is also believed to have a rocky and metallic central core.

Jupiter's hydrogen-helium atmosphere is very active. It contains small amounts of methane, ammonia, water, and sulfur compounds. The wind systems, shown in Figure 13B, generate the light- and dark-colored bands that encircle this giant. Unlike the winds on Earth, which are driven by solar energy, Jupiter itself gives off nearly twice as much heat as it receives from the sun. Thus, the interior heat from Jupiter produces huge convection currents in the atmosphere.

Jupiter's Moons Jupiter's satellite system, consisting of 63 moons discovered so far, resembles a miniature solar system. The four largest moons, Io, Europa, Ganymede, and Callisto, were discovered by Galileo in 1610. Each of the four Galilean satellites is a unique geological world. The moons are shown in Figure 14. The innermost of the Galilean moons, Io, is one of four known volcanically active bodies in our solar system. The other volcanically active bodies are Earth, Saturn's moon Enceladus, and Neptune's moon Triton. The heat source for volcanic activity on Io is thought to be tidal energy generated by a relentless "tug of war" between Jupiter and the other Galilean moons. The gravitational power of Jupiter and nearby moons pulls and pushes on Io's tidal bulge as its orbit takes it alternately closer to and farther from Jupiter. This gravitational flexing of Io is transformed into frictional heat energy and results in Io's volcanic eruptions.

Go Online

NSTA SciLINKS

For: Links on the outer planets
Visit: www.SciLinks.org
Web Code: cjn-7233

Figure 14 Jupiter's Moons
A Io is the innermost moon and is one of only four volcanically active bodies in the solar system. **B** Europa—the smallest of the Galilean moons—has an icy surface that is crossed by many linear features. **C** Ganymede is the largest Jovian moon, and it contains cratered areas, smooth regions, and areas covered by numerous parallel grooves. **D** Callisto—the outermost of the Galilean moons—is densely cratered, much like Earth's moon.

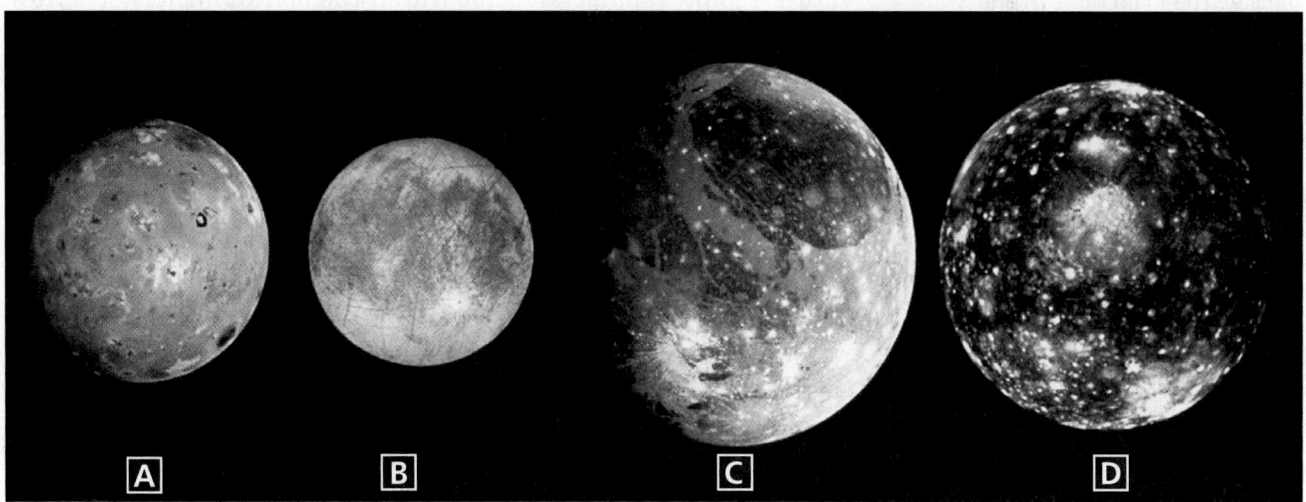

Jupiter's Rings Jupiter's ring system was one of the most unexpected discoveries made by *Voyager 1*. By analyzing how these rings scatter light, researchers concluded that the rings are composed of fine, dark particles, similar in size to smoke particles. The faint nature of the rings also indicates that these minute fragments are widely dispersed. The particles are thought to be fragments blasted by meteorite impacts from the surfaces of Metis and Adrastea, two small moons of Jupiter.

 *Which Galilean moon is volcanically active?*

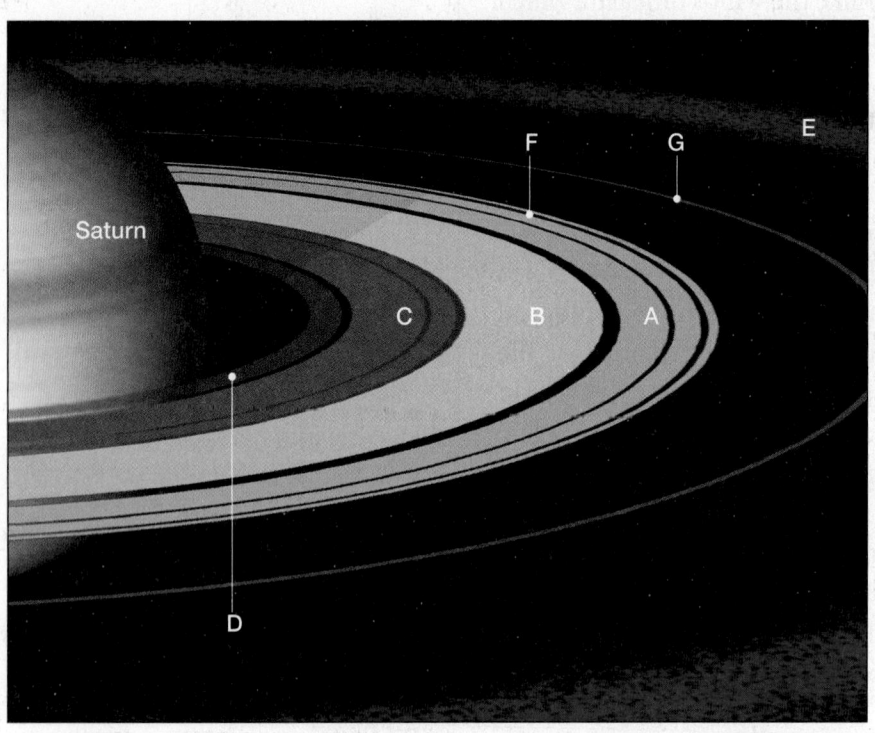

Figure 15 Saturn's Rings
Saturn's rings fall into two categories based on particle density. The main rings (A and B) are densely packed. In contrast, the outer rings are composed of widely dispersed particles.

Saturn: The Elegant Planet

Requiring 29.46 Earth-years to make one revolution, Saturn is almost twice as far from the sun as Jupiter. However, its atmosphere, composition, and internal structure are thought to be remarkably similar to Jupiter's. **The most prominent feature of Saturn is its system of rings, shown in Figure 15.** In 1610, Galileo used a primitive telescope and first saw the structures that were later found to be the rings. They appeared as two small bodies adjacent to the planet. Their ring nature was explained 50 years later by the Dutch astronomer Christian Huygens.

Features of Saturn In 1980 and 1981, flyby missions of the *Voyagers 1* and *2* spacecraft came within 100,000 kilometers of Saturn. More information was gained in a few days than had been acquired since Galileo first viewed this elegant planet.

1. Saturn's atmosphere is very active, with winds roaring at up to 1500 kilometers per hour.
2. Large cyclonic "storms" similar to Jupiter's Great Red Spot, although smaller, occur in Saturn's atmosphere.
3. Eleven additional moons were discovered.
4. The rings of Saturn were found to be more complex than expected.

More recently, observations from ground-based telescopes, the Hubble Space Telescope, and *Cassini* have added to our knowledge of Saturn's ring and moon system. When the positions of Earth and Saturn allowed the rings to be viewed edge-on—thereby reducing the glare from the main rings—Saturn's faintest rings and satellites became visible.

Figure 16 Saturn's Moons This image of Saturn shows several of its moons.

Saturn's Rings Until the discovery that Jupiter, Uranus, and Neptune also have ring systems, this phenomenon was thought to be unique to Saturn. Although the four known ring systems differ in detail, they share many attributes. They all consist of multiple concentric rings separated by gaps of various widths. In addition, each ring is composed of individual particles—"moonlets" of ice and rock—that circle the planet while regularly impacting one another.

Most rings fall into one of two categories based on particle density. Saturn's main rings, designated A and B in Figure 15, and the bright rings of Uranus are tightly packed and contain "moonlets" that range in size from a few centimeters to several meters. These particles are thought to collide frequently as they orbit the parent planet. Despite the fact that Saturn's dense rings stretch across several hundred kilometers, they are very thin, perhaps less than 100 meters from top to bottom.

At the other extreme, the faintest rings, such as Jupiter's ring system and Saturn's outermost rings, are composed of very fine particles that are widely dispersed. Saturn's outermost rings are designated E in Figure 15. In addition to having very low particle densities, these rings tend to be thicker than Saturn's bright rings.

Saturn's Moons Saturn's satellite system consists of 56 moons, some of which are shown in Figure 16. Titan is the largest moon and is bigger than Mercury. It is covered with rivers and oceans of liquid hydrocarbons. Titan and Neptune's Triton are the only moons in the solar system known to have substantial atmospheres. Because of its dense gaseous cover, the atmospheric pressure at Titan's surface is about 1.5 times that at Earth's surface. Another moon, Enceladus, is one of four known volcanically active bodies in our solar system. In 2006, the *Cassini* space probe discovered liquid water geysers in the moon's south polar region.

 **Reading Checkpoint** *How many moons of Saturn have been discovered thus far?*

Uranus: The Sideways Planet

A unique feature of Uranus, shown in Figure 17, is that it rotates "on its side."  **Instead of being generally perpendicular to the plane of its orbit like the other planets, Uranus's axis of rotation lies nearly parallel with the plane of its orbit.** Its rotational motion, therefore, has the appearance of rolling, rather than the top-like spinning of the other planets. Uranus's spin may have been altered by a giant impact.

A surprise discovery in 1977 revealed that Uranus has a ring system. This find occurred as Uranus passed in front of a distant star and blocked its view. Observers saw the star "wink" briefly both before and after Uranus passed by. Later studies indicate that Uranus has at least nine distinct ring belts.

The five largest moons of Uranus show varied terrain. Some of the moons have long, deep canyons and linear scars, whereas others possess large, smooth areas on otherwise crater-riddled surfaces. Miranda, the innermost of the five largest moons, has a greater variety of landforms than any body yet examined in the solar system.

Reading Checkpoint *What is unique about Uranus's axis of rotation?*

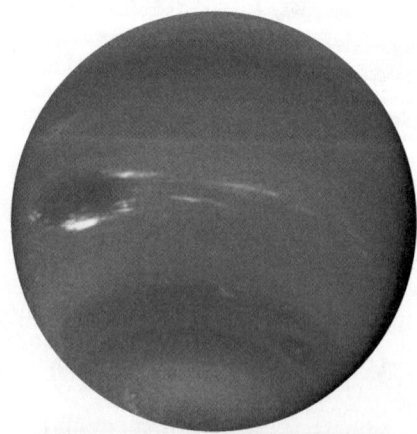

Figure 17 The axis of rotation of Uranus is nearly parallel with the plane of its orbit. This photo also shows the planet's ring system.

Neptune: The Windy Planet

As shown in Figure 18, Neptune has a dynamic atmosphere, much like those of Jupiter and Saturn. **Winds exceeding 1000 kilometers per hour encircle Neptune, making it one of the windiest places in the solar system.** It also had an Earth-size blemish called the Great Dark Spot that was reminiscent of Jupiter's Great Red Spot. The Great Dark Spot was assumed to be a large rotating storm. About five years after the Great Dark Spot was discovered, it vanished, only to be replaced by another dark spot in the planet's northern hemisphere, which also vanished within a few years.

Neptune has many surprising features. Perhaps most surprising are the cirrus-like clouds that occupy a layer about 50 kilometers above the main cloud deck. The clouds are most likely frozen methane. *Voyager* images revealed that the bluish planet also has a ring system.

Neptune has 13 known moons. Triton, Neptune's largest moon, is nearly the size of Earth's moon. Triton is the only large moon in the solar system that exhibits retrograde motion. This motion indicates that Triton formed independently of Neptune and was gravitationally captured.

Triton also has the lowest surface temperature yet measured on any body in the solar system at −200°C. Its atmosphere is mostly nitrogen with a little methane. Despite low surface temperatures, Triton displays volcanic-like activity.

Figure 18 The Great Dark Spot of Neptune (photographed by *Voyager 2* in 1989) is visible in the center of the left of the image. Bright cirrus-like clouds that travel at high speeds around the planet are also visible.
Identifying *What was the Great Dark Spot?*

Pluto: Dwarf Planet

Until 2006, Pluto was considered to be one of the nine planets. But in August of 2006, the International Astronomical Union (IAU) redefined the word "planet" in a way that excluded Pluto. **Pluto is not considered a planet, because it has not cleared the neighborhood around its orbit.**

Because Pluto was no longer a planet, the IAU also created a new term to describe it. A **dwarf planet** is a round object that orbits the sun but has not cleared the neighborhood around its orbit. A planet's gravity is strong enough for it to pull in smaller nearby bodies, thus clearing its orbital path. But a dwarf planet's gravity is too weak to attract all the debris nearby. Therefore, a dwarf planet orbits in a zone along with other small solar system bodies.

Pluto is the most well known of the dwarf planets. However, it is neither the largest nor the first to be discovered. The dwarf planet Ceres, which is in the asteroid belt, was discovered in 1801. And the dwarf planet Eris, just discovered in 2005, is slightly larger than Pluto. All dwarf planets likely contain a mixture of rock and ice, but can be found in very different parts of the solar system. Pluto is unusual in that it has a moon, Charon, which is more than half its size and may be considered a dwarf planet on its own. It is not yet known how many objects in the solar system will be considered dwarf planets. As new discoveries are made, this definition may be revisited.

Figure 19 This Hubble image shows Pluto and its moon Charon.

Section 23.3 Assessment

Reviewing Concepts

1. What is the largest planet? What is the smallest?

2. What is Jupiter's Great Red Spot?

3. Identify one distinguishing characteristic of each outer planet and Pluto.

4. How are Saturn's moon Titan and Neptune's Triton similar?

5. In what way is Io similar to Earth? What other body shows this similarity?

Critical Thinking

6. **Relating Cause and Effect** What may have caused Uranus's unique axis of rotation?

7. **Making Judgments** Should Pluto have been reclassified as a dwarf planet? Explain your answer.

Connecting Concepts

Convection Currents Write a brief paragraph comparing and contrasting atmospheric convection currents on Jupiter and Earth.

23.4 Minor Members of the Solar System

Reading Focus

Key Concepts

- Where are most asteroids located?
- What is the structure of a comet?
- What is the origin of most meteoroids?

Vocabulary

- ◆ asteroid
- ◆ comet
- ◆ coma
- ◆ meteoroid
- ◆ meteor
- ◆ meteorite

Reading Strategy

Building Vocabulary Copy the table below. Then as you read the section, write a definition for each vocabulary term in your own words.

Vocabulary	Definition
asteroid	a. ___?___
b. ___?___	c. ___?___
d. ___?___	e. ___?___

I n February 2001 an American spacecraft, *NEAR Shoemaker*, finished its mission in spectacular fashion—it became the first visitor to an asteroid. This historic accomplishment was not part of *NEAR Shoemaker's* original goal, which was to orbit the asteroid, taking images and gathering data about these objects in space. With this mission accomplished, however, NASA engineers wanted to see if they could actually land a spacecraft on an asteroid. The data they would gather would be priceless. As an added benefit, NASA would gain valuable experience that might help in the future to deflect an asteroid on a collision course with Earth.

Although it was not designed for landing, *NEAR Shoemaker*—shown in Figure 20—successfully touched down on the asteroid, Eros. It generated information that has planetary geologists both intrigued and perplexed. The spacecraft drifted toward the surface of Eros at the rate of 6 kilometers per hour. The images obtained revealed a barren, rocky surface composed of particles ranging in size from fine dust to boulders up to 8 meters across. Researchers unexpectedly discovered that fine debris is concentrated in the low areas that form flat deposits resembling ponds. Surrounding the low areas, the landscape is marked by an abundance of large boulders.

Seismic shaking is one of several hypotheses being considered as an explanation for the boulder-laden topography. This shaking would move the boulders upward. The larger materials rise to the top while the smaller materials settle to the bottom, which is similar to what happens when a can of mixed nuts is shaken.

Figure 20 This artist's rendition shows *NEAR Shoemaker* touching down on the asteroid Eros.

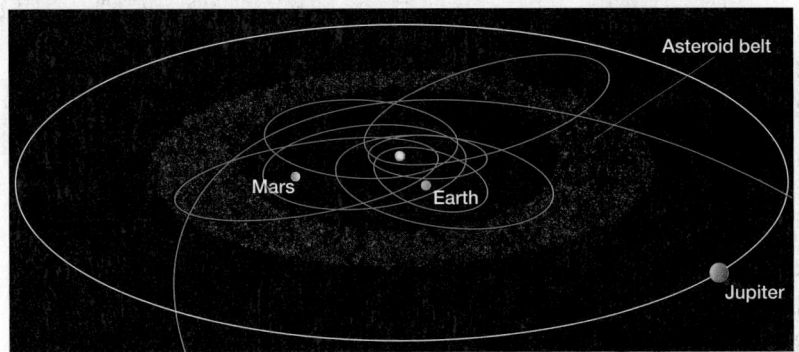

Figure 21 The orbits of most asteroids lie between Mars and Jupiter. Also shown are the orbits of a few near-Earth asteroids. Perhaps a thousand or more asteroids pass close to Earth. Luckily, only a few dozen of these are thought to be larger than 1 kilometer in diameter.

Asteroids

Asteroids are small rocky bodies that orbit the sun. The largest, the dwarf planet Ceres, is about 1000 kilometers in diameter, but more than a million are greater than 1 kilometer across. By definition, asteroids are larger than 10 meters in diameter. **Most asteroids lie in the asteroid belt between the orbits of Mars and Jupiter. They have orbital periods of three to six years.** Some asteroids have very elongated orbits and travel very near the sun, and a few larger ones regularly pass close to Earth and the moon as shown in Figure 21. Many of the most recent impact craters on the moon and Earth were probably caused by collisions with asteroids. Inevitably, future Earth–asteroid collisions will occur.

Many asteroids have irregular shapes, as shown in Figure 22. Because of this, planetary geologists first speculated that they might be fragments of a broken planet that once orbited between Mars and Jupiter. However, the total mass of the asteroids is estimated to be only 1/1000 that of Earth, which itself is not a large planet. What happened to the remainder of the original planet? Others have hypothesized that several larger bodies once coexisted in close proximity, and their collisions produced numerous smaller ones. The existence of several families of asteroids has been used to support this explanation. However, no conclusive evidence has been found for either hypothesis.

 **Reading Checkpoint** *What is an asteroid?*

Figure 22 Asteroid 951, also called Gaspra, is probably the fragment of a larger body that was torn apart by a collision.

Comets

Comets are among the most interesting and unpredictable bodies in the solar system. **Comets** are pieces of rocky and metallic materials held together by frozen water, ammonia, methane, carbon dioxide, and carbon monoxide. Many comets travel in very elongated orbits that carry them far beyond Pluto. These comets take hundreds of thousands of years to complete a single orbit around the sun. However, a few have orbital periods of less than 200 years and make regular encounters with the inner solar system.

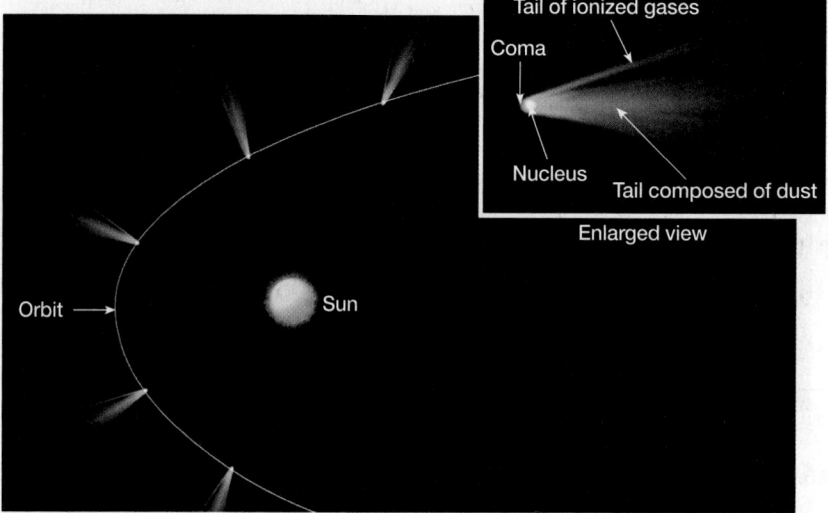

Figure 23 A comet's tail always points away from the sun.

Tail of ionized gases
Coma
Nucleus
Tail composed of dust
Enlarged view
Orbit
Sun

Coma When first observed, a comet appears very small. But as it approaches the sun, solar energy begins to vaporize the frozen gases. This produces a glowing head called the **coma,** shown in Figure 23.  **A small glowing nucleus with a diameter of only a few kilometers can sometimes be detected within a coma. As comets approach the sun, some, but not all, develop a tail that extends for millions of kilometers.**

The fact that the tail of a comet points away from the sun in a slightly curved manner led early astronomers to propose that the sun has a repulsive force that pushes the particles of the coma away, thus forming the tail. Today, two solar forces are known to contribute to this formation. One, radiation pressure, pushes dust particles away from the coma. The second, known as solar wind, is responsible for moving the ionized gases, particularly carbon monoxide. You'll learn more about solar wind in the next chapter. Sometimes a single tail composed of both dust and ionized gases is produced, but often two tails are observed.

As a comet moves away from the sun, the gases forming the coma recondense, the tail disappears, and the comet returns to cold storage. Material that was blown from the coma to form the tail is lost from the comet forever. Therefore it is believed that most comets cannot survive more than a few hundred close orbits of the sun. Once all the gases are expelled, the remaining material—a swarm of tiny metallic and stony particles—continues the orbit without a coma or a tail.

Kuiper Belt Comets apparently originate in two regions of the outer solar system. Those with short orbital periods are thought to orbit beyond Neptune in a region called the Kuiper belt. Like the asteroids in the inner solar system, most Kuiper belt comets move in nearly circular orbits that lie roughly in the same plane as the planets. A chance collision between two Kuiper belt comets, or the gravitational influence of one of the Jovian planets, may occasionally alter the orbit of a comet enough to send it to the inner solar system, and into our view.

✔ **Reading Checkpoint** *In which direction does the tail of a comet point?*

Oort Cloud Unlike Kuiper belt comets, comets with long orbital periods aren't confined to the plane of the solar system. These comets appear to be distributed in all directions from the sun, forming a spherical shell around the solar system called the Oort cloud. The gravitational effect of another object in space is thought to send an occasional Oort cloud comet into a highly eccentric orbit that carries it toward the sun. However, only a tiny portion of the Oort cloud comets pass into the inner solar system.

Halley's Comet The most famous short-period comet is Halley's comet, shown in Figure 24. Its orbital period averages 76 years. When it passed near Earth in 1910, Halley's comet had developed a tail nearly 1.6 million kilometers long and was visible during the daylight hours.

In March 1986, the European probe *Giotto* approached to within 600 kilometers of the nucleus of Halley's comet and obtained the first images of this elusive structure. We now know that the nucleus is potato-shaped, 16 kilometers by 8 kilometers. The surface is irregular and full of craterlike pits. Gases and dust that vaporize from the nucleus to form the coma and tail appear to gush from parts of its surface as bright jets or streams.

Figure 24 Halley's Comet will return to the inner solar system in 2061.

Meteoroids

Nearly everyone has seen a "shooting star." This streak of light occurs when a meteoroid enters Earth's atmosphere. A **meteoroid** is a small solid particle that travels through space. **Most meteoroids originate from any one of the following three sources: (1) interplanetary debris that was not gravitationally swept up by the planets during the formation of the solar system, (2) material from the asteroid belt, or (3) the solid remains of comets that once traveled near Earth's orbit.** A few meteoroids are believed to be fragments of the moon, or possibly Mars, that were ejected when an asteroid impacted these bodies.

Some meteoroids are as large as asteroids. Most, however, are the size of sand grains. Consequently, they vaporize before reaching Earth's surface. Meteoroids that enter Earth's atmosphere and burn up are called **meteors.** The light that we see is caused by friction between the particle and the air, which produces heat.

Occasionally, meteor sightings can reach 60 or more per hour. These displays, called meteor showers, result when Earth encounters a swarm of meteoroids traveling in the same direction and at nearly the same speed as Earth. As shown in Table 2, some meteor showers are closely associated with the orbits of some comets, strongly suggesting that they are material lost by these comets. The Perseid meteor shower, which occurs each year around August 12, may be the remains of Comet 1862 III.

Go Online
PLANETDIARY

For: Links on comets and meteor showers
Visit: PHSchool.com
Web Code: czd-7234

Table 2 Major Meteor Showers		
Shower	Approximate Dates Each Year	Associated Comet
Quadrantids	Jan. 4–6	
Lyrids	Apr. 20–23	Comet 1861 I
Eta Aquarids	May 3–5	Halley's comet
Delta Aquarids	July 30	
Perseids	Aug. 12	Comet 1862 III
Draconids	Oct. 7–10	Comet Giacobini-Zinner
Orionids	Oct. 20	Halley's comet
Taurids	Nov. 3–13	Comet Encke
Andromedids	Nov. 14	Comet Biela
Leonids	Nov. 18	Comet 1866 I
Geminids	Dec. 4–16	

A meteoroid that actually reaches Earth's surface is called a **meteorite.** A few very large meteorites have blasted out craters on Earth's surface, similar to those on the moon. The most famous is Meteor Crater in Arizona. Prior to moon rocks brought back by astronauts, meteorites such as the one in Figure 25 were the only extraterrestrial materials that could be directly examined.

Meteorites and the Age of the Solar System

How did scientists determine the age of the solar system? They used evidence from meteorites, moon rocks, and Earth rocks. Radiometric dating of meteorites found on Earth shows that the oldest meteorites formed more than 4.57 billion years ago. These meteorites are the oldest-known materials in the solar system. Some are made mostly of iron. Others, called stony meteorites, contain silicates. Scientists think that the composition of meteorites is similar to the composition of other materials in the inner solar system during its formation.

Moon rocks from the lunar highlands have a composition similar to that of stony meteorites. These moon rocks date to about 4.5 billion years ago, almost as old as the oldest meteorites. From these facts, scientists infer that the moon must be just slightly younger than the formation of the solar system, which occured 4.567 billion years ago.

The ages of the oldest known Earth rocks are consistent with this conclusion. Scientists have dated rocks found in northwestern Canada at about 4 billion years old. These are the oldest rocks found on Earth so far. In addition, some tiny crystals of the mineral zircon found in sedimentary rocks in Australia are 4.4 billion years old.

Figure 25 This meteorite is made up mostly of iron.

Section 23.4 Assessment

Reviewing Concepts

1. ⬤ Where are most asteroids located?
2. ⬤ Describe the structure of a comet.
3. Where do short-period comets come from? What about long-period comets?
4. ⬤ Meteoroids originate from what three sources?

Critical Thinking

5. **Comparing and Contrasting** Compare and contrast a meteoroid, meteor, and meteorite.
6. **Predicting** What do you think would happen if Earth passed through the tail of a comet?

Math ⬥ **Practice**

7. It has been estimated that Halley's comet has a mass of 1×10^{11} metric tons. This comet is estimated to lose 1×10^8 metric tons of material each time its orbit brings it close to the sun. With an orbital period of 76 years, what is the maximum remaining life span of Halley's comet?

Is Earth on a Collision Course?

The solar system is cluttered with meteoroids, asteroids, active comets, and extinct comets. These fragments travel at great speeds and can strike Earth with the explosive force of a powerful nuclear weapon.

Ancient Collisions

During the last few decades, it has become increasingly clear that comets and asteroids have collided with Earth far more frequently than was previously known. The evidence for these collisions is giant impact structures. See Figure 26. More than 100 impact structures have been identified as shown on the map in Figure 27. Most are so old that they no longer resemble impact craters. However, evidence of their intense impact remains. One notable exception is a very fresh-looking crater near Winslow, Arizona, known as Meteor Crater.

Evidence is mounting that about 65 million years ago a large asteroid about 10 kilometers in diameter collided with Earth. This impact may have caused the extinction of the dinosaurs, as well as nearly 50 percent of all plant and animal species.

Close Calls

More recently, a spectacular explosion has been linked to the collision of our planet with a comet or asteroid. In 1908, in a remote region of Siberia, a "fireball" that appeared more brilliant than the sun exploded with a violent force. The shock waves rattled windows and triggered reverberations heard up to 1000 kilometers away. The "Tunguska event," as it is called, scorched, de-limbed, and flattened trees up to 30 kilometers from the epicenter. However, expeditions to the area did not find any evidence of an impact crater or metallic fragments. It is believed that the explosion—which equaled at least a 10-megaton nuclear bomb—occurred a few kilometers above the surface. It was most likely the end of a comet or perhaps a stony asteroid. The reason it exploded prior to impact remains unclear.

A reminder of the dangers of living with these small but deadly objects from space came in 1989 when an asteroid—nearly 1 kilometer across—shot past Earth. The asteroid came close to Earth, passing it by only twice the distance to the moon. It traveled at a speed of 70,000 kilometers per hour, and it could have made an impact crater 10 kilometers in diameter and perhaps 2 kilometers deep.

Figure 26
Manicouagan, Quebec, is a 200-million-year-old eroded impact structure. The lake outlines the crater remnant.

Figure 27 Major Impact Structures

• Impact structures

Modeling the Solar System

An examination of any scale model of the solar system reveals that the distances from the sun and the spacing between the planets appear to follow a regular pattern. The best way to examine this pattern is to build an actual scale model of the solar system.

Problem How can you model distances among the planets and their distances from the sun?

Materials
- meter stick
- colored pencils
- calculator
- 6-meter length of adding machine paper

Skills Calculating, Using Models

Procedure

Note: Figure A on page 667 may help you model the solar system.

1. Place the 6-meter length of adding machine paper on the floor.

2. Draw an "X" about 10 centimeters from one end of the adding machine paper. Label this mark "sun."

Table 3			
Planet	Distance from Sun		Diameter (km)
	AU	Millions of km	
Mercury	0.39	58	4878
Venus	0.72	108	12,104
Earth	1.00	150	12,756
Mars	1.52	228	6794
Jupiter	5.20	778	143,884
Saturn	9.54	1427	120,536
Uranus	19.18	2870	51,118
Neptune	30.06	4497	50,530
Pluto*	39.44	5900	2300

*Pluto is a dwarf planet.

3. Table 3 shows the mean distances of the planets and Pluto from the sun, as well as their diameters. Use the table and the following scale to calculate the proper scale distance of each object from the sun:

   1 millimeter = 1 million kilometers

   1 centimeter = 10 million kilometers

   1 meter = 1000 million kilometers

4. After calculating the scale distances, draw a small circle for each object at its proper scale distance from the sun. Use a different-colored pencil for the inner and outer planets and for Pluto. Write the name of each object next to its position.

Analyze and Conclude

1. **Using Models** Where is Earth located on your model? Where are the rest of the planets located? Where is Pluto located?

2. **Observing** What pattern of spacing do you observe? Summarize the pattern for both the inner and outer planets.

3. **Interpreting Data** Which object or objects vary most from the general pattern of spacing?

Go Further Determine how to expand your model to include the scale sizes of the planets. Refer to the table for the diameters of each planet (Table 3). Develop a scale, and then calculate the proper scale size of the planets. Draw the planets to scale on your model.

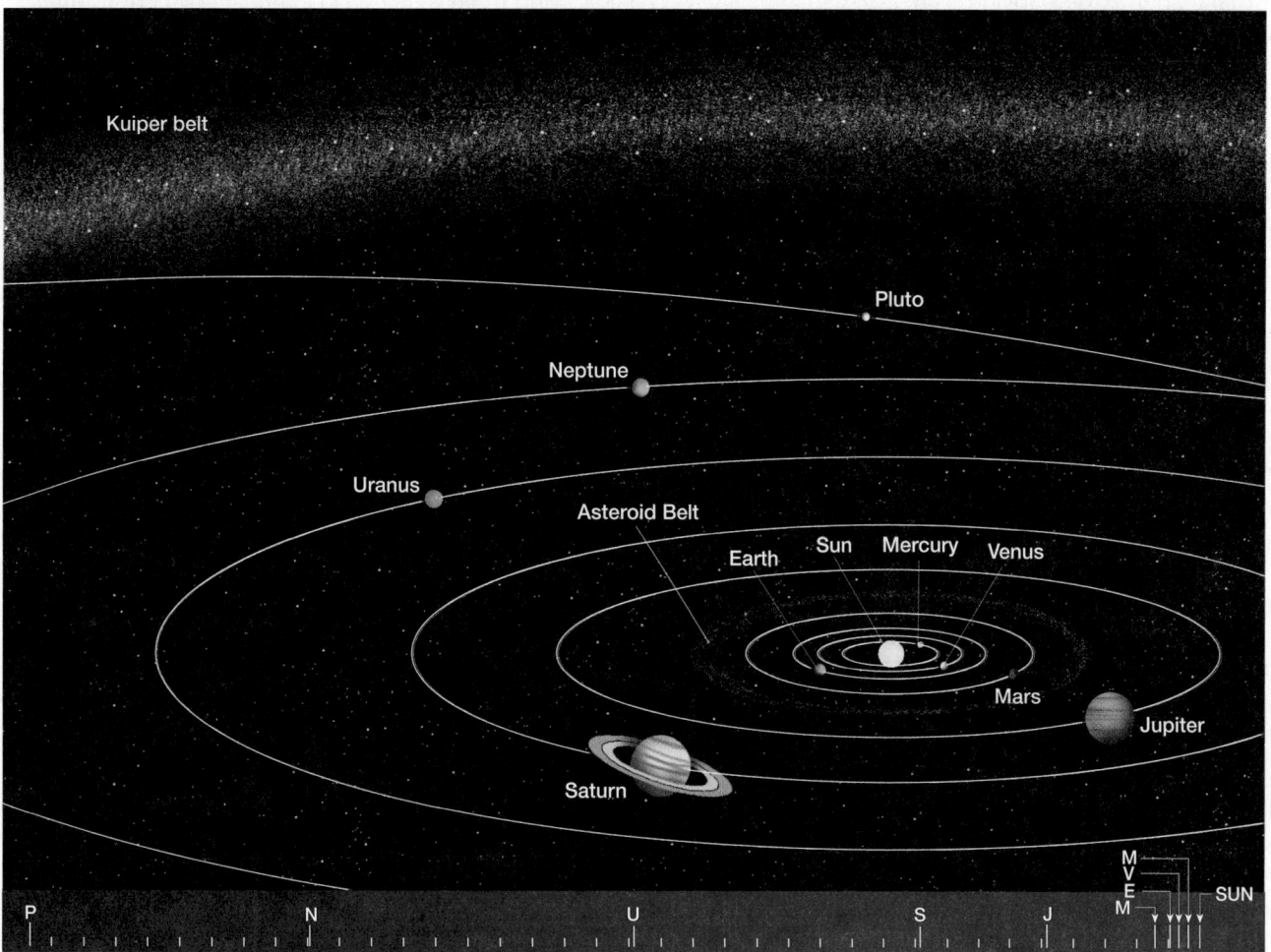

Figure A

23.1 The Solar System

Key Concepts

- Size is the most obvious difference between the terrestrial and the Jovian planets.
- Density, chemical makeup, and rate of rotation are other ways in which the two groups of planets differ.
- According to the nebular theory, the sun and planets formed from a rotating disk of dust and gases.

Vocabulary

terrestrial planet, *p. 645;* Jovian planet, *p. 645;* nebula, *p. 647;* planetesimal, *p. 648*

23.2 The Terrestrial Planets

Key Concepts

- Mercury has the greatest temperature extremes of any planet.
- The surface temperature of Venus reaches 475°C, and its atmosphere is 97 percent carbon dioxide.
- Some areas of Mars exhibit drainage patterns similar to those created by streams on Earth.

23.3 The Outer Planets (and Pluto)

Key Concepts

- Jupiter has a mass that is 2 1/2 times greater than the mass of all the other planets and moons combined.
- The most prominent feature of Saturn is its system of rings.
- Instead of being generally perpendicular to the plane of its orbit like the other planets, Uranus's axis of rotation lies nearly parallel with the plane of its orbit.
- Winds exceeding 1000 kilometers per hour encircle Neptune, making it one of the windiest places in the solar system.
- Pluto is not considered a planet because it has not cleared the neighborhood around its orbit.

Vocabulary

dwarf planet, *p. 659*

23.4 Minor Members of the Solar System

Key Concepts

- Most asteroids lie between the orbits of Mars and Jupiter. They have orbital periods of three to six years.
- A small glowing nucleus with a diameter of only a few kilometers can sometimes be detected within a coma. As comets approach the sun, some, but not all, develop a tail that extends for millions of kilometers.
- Most meteoroids originate from any one of the following three sources: (1) interplanetary debris that was not gravitationally swept up by the planets during the formation of the solar system, (2) material from the asteroid belt, or (3) the solid remains of comets that once traveled near Earth's orbit.

Vocabulary

asteroid, *p. 661;* comet, *p. 661;* coma, *p. 662;* meteoroid, *p. 663;* meteor, *p. 663;* meteorite, *p. 664*

Thinking Visually

Copy and complete the table below comparing and contrasting the inner and outer planets. Include information about each planet's diameter, distance from the sun, composition, and number of moons.

Inner and Outer Planets		
Inner Planets		
	Diameter	**Distance from Sun**
Mercury	4878 km	0.39 AU
a. ___?___		
b. ___?___		
c. ___?___		
Outer Planets		
	Diameter	**Distance from Sun**
Jupiter	143,884 km	5.3 AU
d. ___?___		
e. ___?___		
f. ___?___		

Reviewing Content

Choose the letter that best answers the question or completes the statement.

1. Which of these planets is not a terrestrial planet?
   a. Earth **b.** Mercury
   c. Venus **d.** Uranus

2. What theory describes the formation of the solar system from a huge cloud of dust and gases?
   a. protoplanet theory
   b. nebular theory
   c. planetesimal theory
   d. solar theory

3. Which of the following is NOT a characteristic of Jovian planets?
   a. large size
   b. composed mostly of gases and ice
   c. lack of moons
   d. located beyond the orbit of Mars

4. Which planet was explored by the rovers *Spirit* and *Opportunity?*
   a. Mercury **b.** Jupiter
   c. Mars **d.** Venus

5. Which two planets are most alike?
   a. Jupiter and Mercury
   b. Earth and Mercury
   c. Mars and Uranus
   d. Uranus and Venus

6. Which of the following is NOT true of Jupiter?
   a. It is more massive than all the other planets and moons combined.
   b. It has huge rotating storms.
   c. It has a thin ring system.
   d. It has a solid surface.

7. Which moon is known to have active volcanism?
   a. Io **b.** Phobos
   c. Europa **d.** Titan

8. What bodies in the solar system orbit between Mars and Jupiter?
   a. comets
   b. stars
   c. asteroids
   d. meteorites

9. A comet's tail always points
   a. away from the sun.
   b. toward the sun.
   c. up.
   d. down.

10. Meteoroids that strike Earth are called
    a. asteroids.
    b. comets.
    c. meteors.
    d. meteorites.

Understanding Concepts

11. What objects are found in the solar system?

12. What substances make up most of the solar system? Classify them as gas, rock, or ice.

13. Describe general characteristics and location of the terrestrial planets.

14. What is Olympus Mons? Where is it found?

15. Why has Mars been the planet most studied by telescopes?

16. Why is life unlikely to exist on Venus?

17. Which planets have ring systems?

18. What four bodies in the solar system exhibit volcanic activity?

19. What are moonlets?

20. How are Uranus and Neptune similar?

21. Why isn't Pluto classified as either a terrestrial planet or a Jovian planet?

22. How big is the largest asteroid?

23. Which minor members of the solar system are thought to have formed beyond the orbit of Pluto?

24. What is the bright glowing head of a comet called?

25. What evidence indicates that our solar system is about 4.6 billion years old?

Critical Thinking

26. **Analyzing Data** What evidence supports the theory that liquid water may have existed on Mars? What evidence refutes the possibility of a wet Martian climate?

27. **Drawing Conclusions** Mercury is closer to the sun than Venus. Venus, however, is hotter. Why?

28. **Classifying** Suppose a new object is discovered in the Kuiper belt. If this new object is roughly the size of Earth's moon, how would you classify it? Why?

29. **Making Generalizations** Why is it more difficult for gases to escape from the Jovian planets than from the terrestrial planets?

30. **Applying Concepts** Why would it be difficult to verify that an impact may have altered Uranus's axis of rotation?

Analyzing Data

Use the table in the right column to answer Questions 31–34.

31. **Identifying** Which two terrestrial planets have similar atmospheric compositions?

32. **Interpreting Data** What makes these two planets' atmospheres very different?

33. **Inferring** What gas is present in Earth's atmosphere, but nearly absent in the atmospheres of Venus and Mars? What do you think explains its presence on Earth? (*Hint:* What does Earth have that Venus and Mars both lack?)

34. **Analyzing Data** Based on the data in the table, how would you describe the effect of increasing atmospheric pressure on surface temperature?

Concepts in Action

35. **Relating Cause and Effect** Weight is a function of the gravitational attraction of an object on your mass. On which planet would you expect to weigh the least? Explain your answer.

36. **Calculating** Refer to Table 1 on page 645. Using the table, determine how old you are in Jupiter-years.

37. **Identifying** Which features on Earth offer clear evidence that comets and asteroids have struck its surface?

Performance-Based Assessment

Using Models Use a fan, a Styrofoam ball, several pushpins, and several pieces of ribbon to create a model of a comet. Explain what each part of the model represents. Work with a partner to demonstrate the orbit of your model. Make sure that the "tail" points in the proper direction.

Comparison of the Atmospheres and Surface Temperatures of Mercury, Venus, Earth, Mars					
Planet or Body	Gases (% by volume)			Surface Temperature (range)	Surface Atmospheric Pressure (bars)
	N_2	O_2	CO_2		
Mercury	0	trace	0	−173° to 427°C	10^{-15}
Venus	3.5	< 0.01	96.5	475°C (small range)	92
Earth	78.01	20.95	0.03	−40° to 75°C	1.014
Mars	2.7	1.3	95.32	−120° to 25°C	0.008

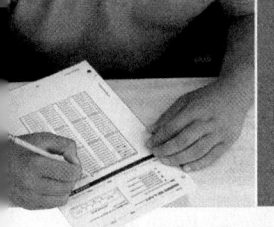

Standardized Test Prep

Test-Taking Tip

Questions with NOT

Questions containing absolute negative qualifiers, such as NOT, can be tricky. If the question lists statements, it helps to look at each statement and add NOT just before the verb. For example, rephrase statement A below as "Mars does NOT have moons." Then try to think of one example that disproves this statement. Mars and Earth are the only two terrestrial planets that have moons. Thus, the statement is not true. Repeat this process for each choice until you find one that is true in all cases.

Which of the following is NOT true of Mars?

(A) Mars has moons.
(B) Mars has rings.
(C) Mars is often called the Red Planet.
(D) Mars has volcanoes.

(Answer: B)

1. Which is NOT the most obvious difference between the terrestrial and Jovian planets?
   (A) mass
   (B) color
   (C) density
   (D) chemical makeup

2. Which planet does NOT have a density that is greater than water?
   (A) Mercury
   (B) Mars
   (C) Venus
   (D) Saturn

3. Why was Mercury unable to retain an atmosphere during its formation?
   (A) Mercury has a high surface temperature and has a low mass.
   (B) Mercury is the largest planet.
   (C) Mercury is the farthest planet from the sun.
   (D) Mercury revolves slowly.

4. What causes the bright streak in the sky known as a meteor?

Use the photograph below to answer Questions 5 and 6.

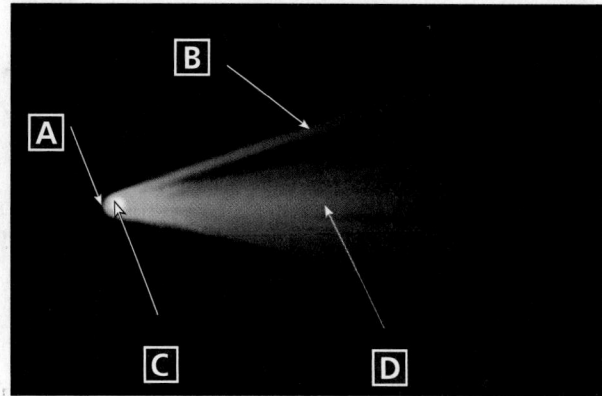

5. What features do labels B and D represent? What forces produce these features?

6. What are features A and C? How do they differ?

24 Studying the Sun

21st Century Learning

Health Literacy

How does Earth protect humans from dangerous radiation?

Life on Earth depends on solar radiation, but some forms of radiation can be dangerous for humans. Research the kinds of radiation that are dangerous to human life, and the problems this radiation can cause. Also, research the natural protection that Earth provides against radiation damage. Create a blog entry that explains the types of solar radiation and the problems you have discovered. Describe the protection that Earth provides and explain what might happen without it.

Exploration Lab

Tracking Sunspots

Earth as a System

Solar Activity and Climatic Change

This photograph shows Kitt Peak National Observatory near Tucson, Arizona.

Chapter Preview

Inquiry Activity

How Does the Position of the Setting Sun Change?

Procedure

1. Several minutes before sunset, estimate where the sun will set on the western horizon. Draw prominent features, such as buildings and trees, to the north and south of the sun's setting position.

2. As the sun sets, draw its position relative to the fixed features on the horizon. **CAUTION** *Never look directly at the sun; eye damage may result.*

3. Note the date and time of your observation.

4. Return to the same position several days later. Repeat the activity and record the results. Wait several more days and then do the activity one more time.

Think About It

1. **Observing** How did the sun's position at sunset change over the course of your observations?

2. **Predicting** Based on your observations, predict where the sun might set in several weeks time. Sketch the sun on your drawing relative to the fixed features on the horizon.

24.1 The Study of Light

Key Concepts

- What types of radiation make up the electromagnetic spectrum?
- What can scientists learn about a star by studying its spectrum?
- How can astronomers determine whether a star is moving toward or away from Earth?

Vocabulary

- ◆ electromagnetic spectrum
- ◆ photon
- ◆ spectroscopy
- ◆ continuous spectrum
- ◆ absorption spectrum
- ◆ emission spectrum
- ◆ Doppler effect

Reading Strategy

Predicting Copy the table. Before you read, predict the meaning of the term *electromagnetic spectrum*. After you read, revise your definition if it was incorrect.

Vocabulary Term	Before You Read	After You Read
electromagnetic spectrum	a. ___?___	b. ___?___

Astronomers study light. Almost everything that is known about the universe beyond Earth comes by analyzing light from distant sources. Consequently, an understanding of the nature of light is basic to modern astronomy. This chapter describes light and the tools used by astronomers to gather light in order to probe the universe. In addition, we will examine the nearest source of light, our sun. By understanding how the sun works, astronomers can better grasp the nature of more distant objects in space.

Electromagnetic Radiation

Stars and other bodies in space emit light that can be used to study them. Although visible light is most familiar to us, it makes up only a small part of the different types of energy known as electromagnetic radiation. ●**Electromagnetic radiation includes gamma rays, X-rays, ultraviolet light, visible light, infrared radiation, microwaves, and radio waves.** The arrangement of these waves according to their wavelengths and frequencies is called the **electromagnetic spectrum.** Figure 1 shows the electromagnetic spectrum. All energy, regardless of wavelength, travels through the vacuum of space at the speed of light, or 300,000 kilometers per second. Over a 24-hour day, this equals a staggering 26 billion kilometers. Nothing is faster than the speed light in a vacuum. In addition, the speed of light is the same to all observers, whether or not they are moving with respect to the light.

Figure 1 Electromagnetic Spectrum The electromagnetic spectrum classifies radiation according to wavelength and frequency.
Interpreting Diagrams *Which type of radiation has the shortest wavelength?*

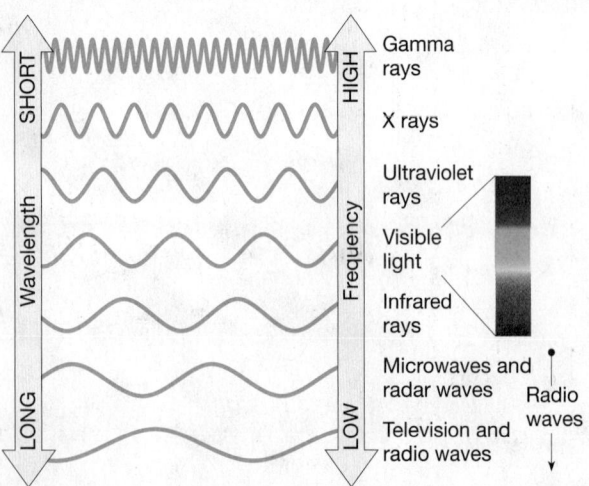

Nature of Light Experiments have shown that light can be described in two ways. In some instances light behaves like waves, and in others like particles. In the wave sense, light can be thought of as swells in the ocean. This motion is characterized by a property known as wavelength, which is the distance from one wave crest to the next. Wavelengths vary from several kilometers for radio waves to less than a billionth of a centimeter for gamma rays, as shown in Figure 1. Most of these waves are either too long or too short for our eyes to see.

The narrow band of electromagnetic radiation we can see is sometimes called visible light. However, visible light consists of a range of waves with various wavelengths. This fact is easily demonstrated with a prism, as shown in Figure 2. As visible light passes through a prism, the color with the shortest wavelength, violet, is bent more than blue, which is bent more than green, and so forth. Thus, visible light can be separated into its component colors in the order of their wavelengths, producing the familiar rainbow of colors.

Table 1 Colors and Corresponding Wavelengths	
Color	Wavelength (nanometers*)
Violet	380–440
Blue	440–500
Green	500–560
Yellow	560–590
Orange	590–640
Red	640–750

*One nanometer is 10^{-9} meter.

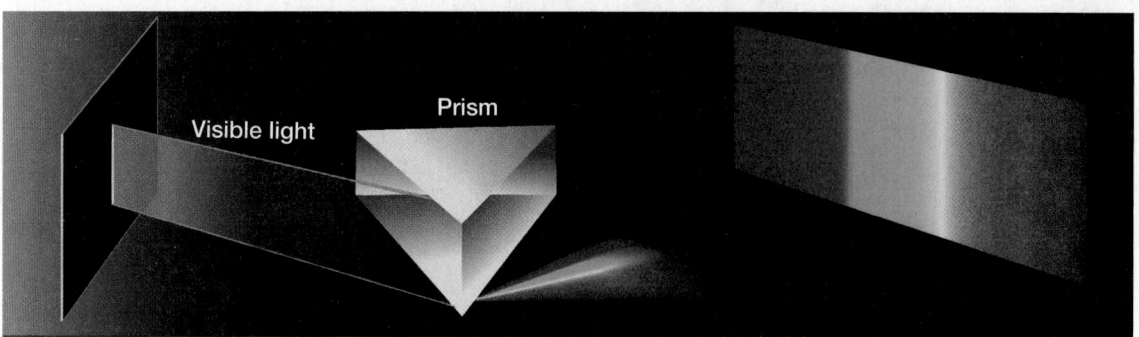

Visible light | Prism

Photons Wave theory, however, cannot explain some effects of light. In some cases, light acts like a stream of particles called **photons.** Photons can be thought of as extremely small bullets fired from a machine gun. They can push on matter. The force they exert is called radiation pressure. Photons from the sun are responsible for pushing material away from a comet to produce its tail. Each photon has a specific amount of energy, which is related to its wavelength in a simple way: Shorter wavelengths have more energetic photons. Thus, blue light has more energetic photons than does red light.

Which theory of light—the wave theory or the particle theory—is correct? Both, because each will predict the behavior of light for certain phenomena. As George Abell, a well-known astronomer, stated about all scientific laws, "The mistake is only to apply them to situations that are outside their range of validity."

 **Reading Checkpoint** *What are photons?*

Figure 2 Spectrum A spectrum is produced when sunlight or visible light is passed through a prism, which bends each wavelength at different angles.

For: Links on the electromagnetic spectrum
Visit: www.SciLinks.org
Web Code: cjn-7441

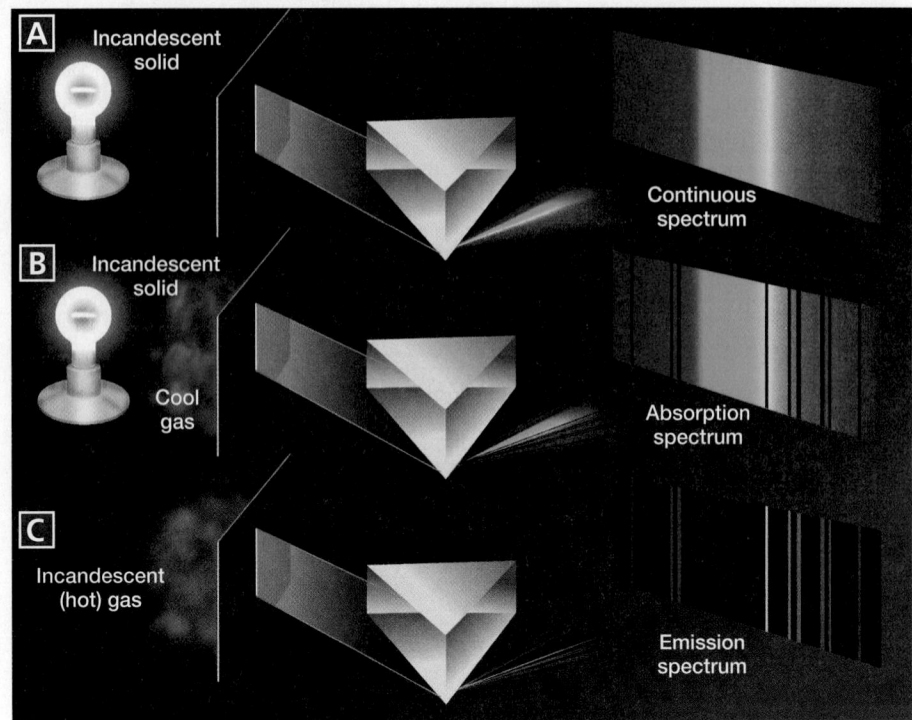

Figure 3 Formation of Spectra
A A continuous spectrum consists of a band of uninterrupted color. **B** An absorption spectrum contains dark lines. **C** An emission spectrum contains bright lines.

Labels within figure:
A Incandescent solid — Continuous spectrum
B Incandescent solid — Cool gas — Absorption spectrum
C Incandescent (hot) gas — Emission spectrum

Spectroscopy

When Sir Isaac Newton used a prism to disperse visible light into its component colors, he unknowingly introduced the field of spectroscopy. **Spectroscopy** is the study of the properties of light that depend on wavelength. The rainbow of colors Newton produced included all wavelengths of visible light. It was later learned that two other types of spectra exist. Each is generated under somewhat different conditions.

Continuous Spectrum

A **continuous spectrum** is produced by an incandescent solid, liquid, or gas under high pressure. (*Incandescent* means "to emit light when hot.") The spectrum consists of an uninterrupted band of color, as shown in Figure 3A. One example would be visible light generated by a common light bulb. This is the type of spectrum Newton produced.

Absorption Spectrum

An **absorption spectrum** is produced when visible light is passed through a relatively cool gas under low pressure. The gas absorbs selected wavelengths of light. So the spectrum appears continuous, but with a series of dark lines running through it, as shown in Figure 3B.

Emission Spectrum

An **emission spectrum** is produced by a hot gas under low pressure. It is a series of bright lines of particular wavelengths, depending on the gas that produces them. As shown in Figure 3C, these bright lines appear in the exact location as the dark lines that are produced by the same gas in an absorption spectrum.

The spectra of most stars are of the dark-line, or absorption, type. The importance of these spectra is that each element or compound in its gaseous form produces a unique set of spectral lines. **When the spectrum of a star is studied, the spectral lines act as "fingerprints." These lines identify the elements present and thus the star's chemical composition.** The spectrum of the sun contains thousands of dark lines. More than 60 elements have been identified by matching these lines with those of elements known on Earth.

 **Reading Checkpoint**   *What is spectroscopy?*

The Doppler Effect

When an ambulance approaches, the siren seems to have a higher-than-normal pitch. When it is moving away, the pitch sounds lower. This effect, which occurs for both sound and light waves, is called the Doppler effect. The **Doppler effect** refers to the perceived change in wavelength of a wave that is emitted from a source that is moving away or toward an object. It takes time for the wave to be emitted. If the source is moving away from you, the beginning of the wave is emitted nearer to you than the end. From the listener's perspective the wave appears to be stretched. The opposite is true for a wave moving toward you.

The visible light from a source that is moving away from an observer appears redder because its waves are lengthened. This effect is only noticeable to the human eye at velocities approaching the speed of light. Objects moving toward an object have their light waves shifted toward the blue, or shorter, wavelength. In addition, the amount of shift is related to the rate of movement. Thus, if a source of red light moved toward you, it could actually appear blue. The same effect would be produced if you moved and the light source was stationary.

In astronomy, the Doppler effect is used to determine whether a star or other body in space is moving away from or toward Earth. Larger Doppler shifts indicate higher speeds; smaller Doppler shifts indicate slower speeds. Doppler shifts are generally measured from the dark lines in the spectra of stars by comparing them with a standard spectrum produced in the laboratory.

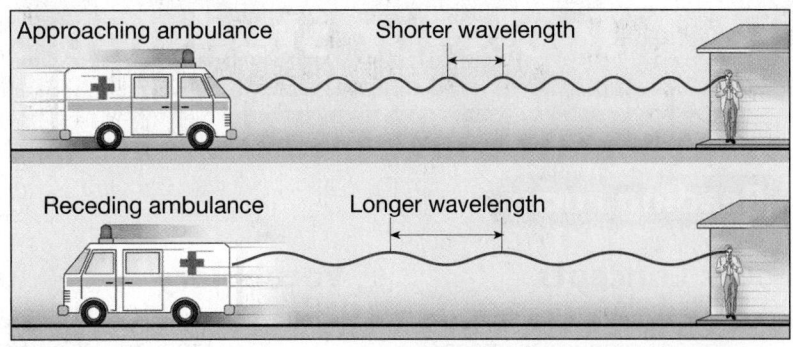

Figure 4 The Doppler Effect
The wavelength of the sound of an approaching ambulance is compressed as it approaches an observer. For a receding ambulance, the wavelength is stretched out and the observer notes a lower-pitched sound. When this effect is applied to light, a shorter wavelength is noted for an approaching object and is seen as blue light. A longer wavelength is noted for a receding object, which is seen as red light.

Section 24.1 Assessment

Reviewing Concepts

1. What types of radiation make up the electromagnetic spectrum?

2. Compare and contrast the three different types of spectra.

3. How do scientists determine the elements present in a star?

4. How can scientists determine whether a star is moving toward or away from Earth?

Critical Thinking

5. **Sequencing** Sequence the components of visible light according to wavelength, beginning with the shortest wavelength.

6. **Applying Concepts** Based on what you know about prisms and visible light, how do you think rainbows form in Earth's atmosphere?

Writing in Science

List of Questions Make a list of questions that you would like to ask a scientist about the nature of light. Your questions should cover both the wave theory and the particle theory of light.

24.2 Tools for Studying Space

Reading Focus

Key Concepts

- How does a refracting telescope produce an image?
- Why are most large telescopes reflecting telescopes?
- How does a radio telescope gather data?
- What advantages do space telescopes have over Earth-based telescopes?

Vocabulary

- ◆ refracting telescope
- ◆ chromatic aberration
- ◆ reflecting telescope
- ◆ radio telescope

Reading Strategy

Comparing and Contrasting Copy the Venn diagram. As you read, complete it to show the differences between refracting and reflecting telescopes.

Refracting Telescopes   Reflecting Telescopes

a. ___?___   light-gathering, resolving, and magnifying power   b. ___?___

Figure 5 Yerkes Telescope The telescope at Yerkes Observatory is the largest refracting telescope in the world.

Now that we've examined the nature of light, let's turn our attention to the tools astronomers use to intercept and study the energy emitted by distant objects in the universe. Because the basic principles of detecting radiation were originally developed through visual observations, the astronomical tools we'll explore first will be optical telescopes. An example is shown in Figure 5. To create an image that is a great distance away, a telescope must collect as much light as possible. Optical telescopes contain mirrors, lenses, or both to accomplish this task.

Today optical telescopes are most often located in observatories on mountaintops. Above the densest part of the atmosphere, there is less air to scatter, dim, and distort the incoming light. Also, there is less water vapor to absorb infrared radiation.

Refracting Telescopes

Galileo is considered to be the first person to have used telescopes for astronomical observations. Having learned about the newly invented instrument, Galileo built one of his own that was capable of magnifying objects 30 times. Because this early instrument, like its modern counterparts, used a lens to bend or refract light, it is known as a **refracting telescope.**

Focus  The most important lens in a refracting telescope, the objective lens, produces an image by bending light from a distant object so that the light converges at an area called the focus (*focus* = central point). A star appears as a point of light. For nearby objects, the image appears inverted.

You can easily demonstrate the latter case by holding a lens in one hand and, with the other hand, placing a white card behind the lens. Now vary the distance between them until an image from a window appears on the card. The distance between the focus (where the image appears) and the lens is called the focal length of the lens.

Astronomers usually study an image from a telescope by first photographing the image. However, if a telescope is used to examine an image directly, a second lens, called an eyepiece, is required. The eyepiece magnifies the image produced by the objective lens. In this respect, it is similar to a magnifying glass. The objective lens produces a very small, bright image of an object, and the eyepiece enlarges the image so that details can be seen. Figure 6 shows the parts of a refracting telescope.

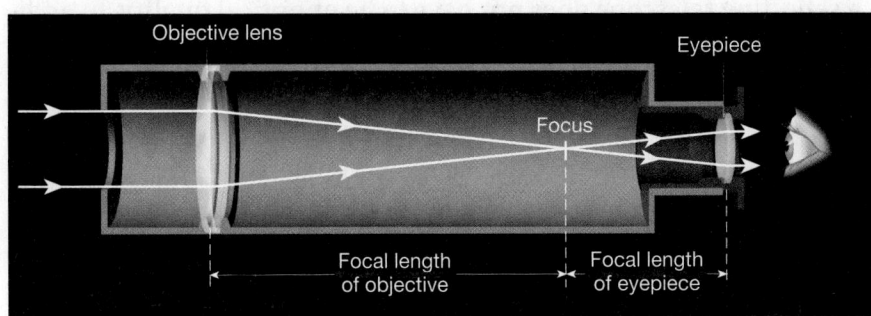

Figure 6 Simple Refracting Telescope A refracting telescope uses a lens to bend light.

Chromatic Aberration Although used extensively in the nineteenth century, refracting telescopes suffer a major optical defect. A lens, like a prism, bends the shorter wavelengths of light more than the longer ones. Consequently, when a refracting telescope is in focus for red light, blue and violet light are out of focus. The troublesome effect, known as **chromatic** (*chroma* = color) **aberration** (*aberrare* = to go astray), weakens the image and produces a halo of color around it. When blue light is in focus, a reddish halo appears. When red light is in focus, a bluish halo appears. Although this effect cannot be eliminated completely, it is reduced by using a second lens made of a different type of glass.

✓ **Reading Checkpoint** *What is chromatic aberration?*

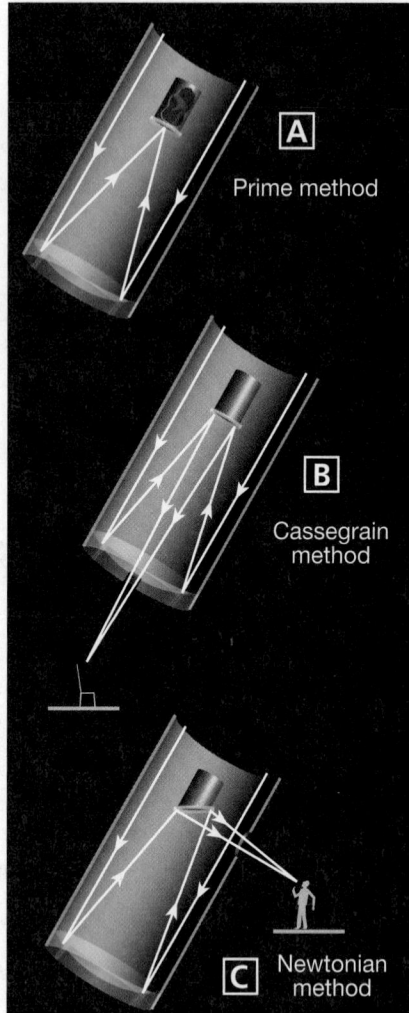

**Figure 7 Viewing Methods
With Reflecting Telescopes**
A The prime method is only used
with very large telescopes.
B The Cassegrain method is most
commonly used. Note that a small
hole in the center of the mirror
allows light to pass through.
C This figure shows the
Newtonian method.

For: Links on telescopes
Visit: www.SciLinks.org
Web Code: cjn-7242

Reflecting Telescopes

Newton was bothered by chromatic aberration so he built telescopes that reflected light from a shiny surface—a mirror. Because reflected light is not dispersed into its component colors, the chromatic aberration is avoided. **Reflecting telescopes** use a concave mirror that focuses the light in front of a mirror, rather than behind it, like a lens. The mirror, called the objective, is generally made of glass that is finely ground and coated with a highly reflective material, usually an aluminum compound.

Because the focus of a reflecting telescope is in front of the mirror, an observer must be able to view the image without blocking too much incoming light. Figure 7A shows a viewing cage for the observer within the telescope. Figures 7B and 7C show how secondary mirrors can be used to view the image from outside the telescope.

Advantages of Reflecting Telescopes

As you might guess, it's a huge task to produce a large piece of high-quality, bubble-free glass for refracting telescopes. **Most large optical telescopes are reflectors. Light does not pass through a mirror so the glass for a reflecting telescope does not have to be of optical quality.** In addition, a lens can be supported only around the edge, so it sags. But mirrors can be supported fully from behind. One disadvantage of most reflecting telescopes is that the secondary mirror blocks some light entering the telescope. Thus, a reflecting telescope with a 10-inch opening will not collect as much light as a 10-inch refractor.

Properties of Optical Telescopes

Both refracting and reflecting telescopes have three properties that aid astronomers in their work: 1) light-gathering power, 2) resolving power, and 3) magnifying power. Light-gathering power refers to the telescope's ability to intercept more light from distant objects, thereby producing brighter images. Telescopes with large lenses or mirrors "see" farther into space than do those with small ones.

Another advantage of telescopes with large objectives is their greater resolving power, which allows for sharper images and finer detail. For example, with the naked eye, the Milky Way appears as a vague band of light in the night sky. But even a small telescope is capable of resolving, or separating it into, individual stars. Lastly, telescopes have magnifying power, which is the ability to make an image larger. Magnification is calculated by dividing the focal length of the objective by the focal length of the eyepiece. Thus, the magnification of a telescope can be changed by simply changing the eyepiece.

 **Reading Checkpoint** *What is light-gathering power?*

A

B

Detecting Invisible Radiation

As you learned earlier, sunlight is made up of more than just the radiation that is visible to our eyes. Gamma rays, X-rays, ultraviolet radiation, infrared radiation, and radio waves are also produced by stars. Photographic film that is sensitive to ultraviolet and infrared radiation has been developed. This extends the limits of our vision. However, most of this radiation cannot penetrate our atmosphere, so balloons, rockets, and satellites must transport cameras "above" the atmosphere to record it.

A narrow band of radio waves is able to penetrate the atmosphere. Measurement of this radiation is important because we can map the galactic distribution of hydrogen. Hydrogen is the main material from which stars are made.

Radio Telescopes The detection of radio waves is accomplished by big dishes called **radio telescopes,** shown in Figure 8A. In principle, the dish of one of these telescopes operates in the same manner as the mirror of an optical telescope. **A radio telescope focuses the incoming radio waves on an antenna, which absorbs and transmits these waves to an amplifier, just like a radio antenna.**

Because radio waves are about 100,000 times longer than visible radiation, the surface of the dish doesn't need to be as smooth as a mirror. Except for the shortest radio waves, a wire mesh is a good reflector. However, because radio signals from celestial sources are very weak, large dishes are necessary to intercept an adequate signal.

Radio telescopes have poor resolution, making it difficult to pinpoint the radio source. Pairs or groups of telescopes reduce this problem. When several radio telescopes are wired together, as shown in Figure 8B, the resulting network is called a radio interferometer.

Figure 8 A The 43-meter Radio Telescope at Green Bank, West Virginia The dish acts like the mirror of a reflecting telescope, focusing radio waves onto the antenna. **B The Very Large Array Near Socorro, New Mexico** Twenty-seven identical antennas operate together to form this radio network. **Identifying** *What is a network of radio telescopes called?*

Q *Why do astronomers build observatories on mountaintops?*

A Observatories are most often located on mountaintops because sites above the densest part of the atmosphere provide better conditions for "seeing."

Advantages of Radio Telescopes Radio telescopes have some advantages over optical telescopes. They are much less affected by turbulence in the atmosphere, clouds, and the weather. No protective dome is required, which reduces the cost of construction. "Viewing" is possible 24 hours a day. More important, radio telescopes can "see" through interstellar dust clouds that obscure visible wavelengths. Radio telescopes can also detect clouds of gases too cool to emit visible light. These cold gas clouds are important because they are the sites of star formation.

Radio telescopes are, however, hindered by human-made radio interference. While optical telescopes are placed on remote mountaintops to reduce interference from city lights, radio telescopes are often hidden in valleys to block human-made radio interference.

Radio telescopes have revealed such spectacular events as the collision of two galaxies. They also discovered intense and distant radio sources called quasars.

 **Reading Checkpoint** *Why can radio telescopes be used 24 hours a day?*

Space Telescopes

Have you ever seen a blurring effect caused by the movement of air on a hot summer day? That blurring effect also distorts the images produced by most telescopes on Earth. On a night when the stars twinkle, viewing a star clearly through a telescope is difficult because the air is moving rapidly. This causes the image to move about and blur.

One way to get around the distorting effects of Earth's atmosphere—send telescopes into space. **Space telescopes orbit above Earth's atmosphere and thus produce clearer images than Earth-based telescopes.**

Hubble Space Telescope

The first space telescope, built by NASA, was the Hubble Space Telescope, shown in Figure 9. Hubble was put into orbit around Earth in April 1990. This 2.4-meter space telescope has 10 billion times more light-gathering power than the human eye. Hubble has given us many spectacular images. It has provided data about planets that orbit other stars, the birth of stars, objects known as black holes, and the age of the universe.

Hubble and many Earth-based telescopes have detected more than 140 extrasolar planets. An extrasolar planet is a planet in orbit around a star other than the sun. How do astronomers detect an extrasolar planet? A planet's gravity causes a Doppler shift in light emitted by the planet's star. By measuring the Doppler shift in the star's emission spectrum, astronomers can infer that a planet is present. Most known extrasolar planets are thought to be gas giants larger than Jupiter.

Figure 9 Hubble Space Telescope Hubble was deployed into Earth orbit by the space shuttle *Discovery*.

Special Purpose Telescopes

Space telescopes have been designed for a variety of special purposes. Like radio telescopes, these space telescopes often reveal surprising features of the objects they study. They are often designed to observe objects in space at wavelengths outside the visible spectrum. Data from space telescopes enable astronomers to classify these objects. They can also study the processes that formed the objects.

Several space telescopes have been designed for special purposes. To study X-rays, NASA uses the Chandra X-Ray Observatory. One of Chandra's main missions is to gather data about black holes— objects whose gravity is so strong that visible light cannot escape them. Another space telescope, the Compton Gamma-Ray Observatory, was used to study both visible light and gamma rays emitted by black holes and other objects in space. For example, it observed exploding stars that give off powerful bursts of gamma radiation. In 2013, NASA plans to launch the James Webb Space Telescope to study infrared radiation. This telescope will be able to detect infrared radiation from stars and galaxies that formed early in the history of the universe.

Figure 10 The Milky Way Galaxy Different types of telescopes have observed the Milky Way at different parts of the spectrum, including visible light, X-ray, gamma ray, and infrared.

Section 24.2 Assessment

Reviewing Concepts

1. 🔵 How does a refracting telescope work?
2. How does a reflecting telescope differ from a refracting telescope?
3. 🔵 Why are most large optical telescopes reflecting telescopes?
4. 🔵 How do radio telescopes gather data?
5. 🔵 Why do space telescopes obtain clearer images than Earth-based telescopes?

Critical Thinking

6. **Calculating** If a telescope has an objective with a focal length of 50 centimeters and an eyepiece with a focal length of 25 millimeter, what will be the magnification?

7. **Applying Concepts** Using the numbers from the previous question, would an eyepiece with a greater focal length increase or decrease magnification? Explain.

Connecting C Concepts

Electromagnetic Radiation Recall the different types of electromagnetic radiation. Based on what you've learned in this section, would you recommend sending a telescope into space to study radio waves? Why or why not?

24.3 The Sun

Reading Focus

Key Concepts

- What is the structure of the sun?
- What are the characteristics of features on the sun?
- How does the sun produce energy?

Vocabulary

- photosphere
- chromosphere
- corona
- solar wind
- sunspot
- prominence
- solar flare
- aurora
- nuclear fusion

Reading Strategy

Monitoring Your Understanding Preview the Key Concepts, topic headings, vocabulary, and figures in this section. Copy the table below, listing two things you expect to learn. After reading, fill in the table below, stating what you have learned about each item you listed.

What I Expect to Learn	What I Learned
a. _____?_____	b. _____?_____
c. _____?_____	d. _____?_____

The sun is one of the 400 billion stars that make up the Milky Way galaxy. It is Earth's primary source of energy. Everything—from the fossil fuels we burn in our automobiles to the food that we eat—is ultimately derived from solar energy. The sun is also important to astronomers, since until just a few years ago it was the only star whose surface we could study. Even with the largest telescopes, most other stars appear only as points of light.

Because of the sun's brightness and its damaging radiation, it is not safe to observe it directly. However, a telescope can project its image on a piece of cardboard held behind the telescope's eyepiece. In this manner, the sun can be studied safely. This basic method is used in several telescopes around the world. One of the finest is at the Kitt Peak National Observatory in southern Arizona, shown in Figure 11. It consists of an enclosure with moving mirrors that direct sunlight to an underground mirror. From the mirror, an image of the sun is projected to an observing room, where it is studied.

Compared to other stars, the sun is an average star. However, on the scale of our solar system, it is truly gigantic. Its diameter is equal to 109 Earth diameters, or 1.35 million kilometers. Its volume is 1.25 million times as great as Earth's. Its mass is 332,000 times the mass of Earth and its density is only one quarter that of solid Earth.

Figure 11 The McMath-Pierce Solar Telescope at Kitt Peak Near Tucson, Arizona Movable mirrors at the top follow the sun, reflecting its light down the sloping tunnel.

Structure of the Sun

Because the sun is made of gas, no sharp boundaries exist between its various layers. 🔑 **Keeping this in mind, we can divide the sun into four parts: the solar interior; the visible surface, or photosphere; and two atmospheric layers, the chromosphere and corona.** These parts are shown in Figure 12. The sun's interior makes up all but a tiny fraction of the solar mass. Unlike the outer three layers, the solar interior cannot be directly observed. Let's discuss the visible layers first.

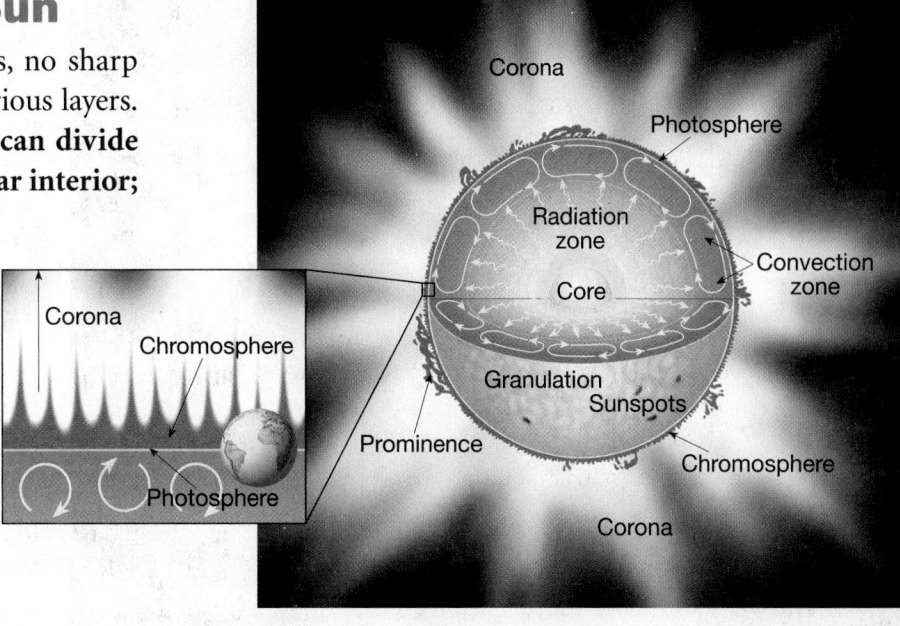

Photosphere The **photosphere** (*photos* = light, *sphere* = a ball) radiates most of the sunlight we see and can be thought of as the visible "surface" of the sun. The photosphere consists of a layer of gas less than 500 kilometers thick. It is neither smooth nor uniformly bright, as the ancients had imagined.

When viewed through a telescope, the photosphere's grainy texture is apparent. This is the result of numerous relatively small, bright markings called granules, which are surrounded by narrow, dark regions, as shown in Figure 13. Granules are typically the size of Texas, and they owe their brightness to hotter gases that are rising from below. As this gas spreads, cooling causes it to darken and sink back into the interior. Each granule survives only 10 to 20 minutes. The combined motion of new granules replacing old ones gives the photosphere the appearance of boiling. This up-and-down movement of gas is called convection. Besides producing the grainy appearance of the photosphere, convection is believed to be responsible for the transfer of energy in the uppermost part of the sun's interior.

The composition of the photosphere is revealed by the dark lines of its absorption spectrum. Studies reveal that 90 percent of the sun's surface atoms are hydrogen, almost 10 percent are helium, and only minor amounts of the other detectable elements are present. Other stars also have high proportions of these two lightest elements, a fact we shall discuss later.

Figure 12 Structure of the Sun
The sun can be divided into four parts: the solar interior, the photosphere, the chromosphere, and the corona.

Figure 13 Granules Granules are the yellowish-orange patches on the photosphere.
Describing *Describe the movement of gases in the convection zone.*

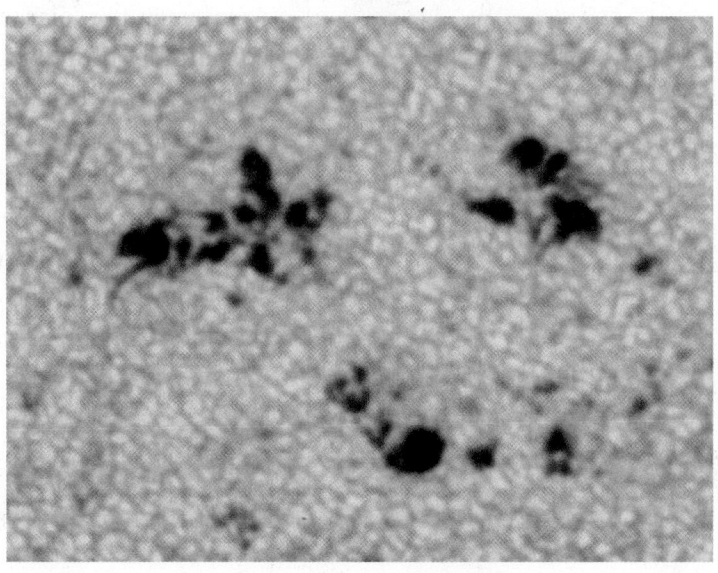

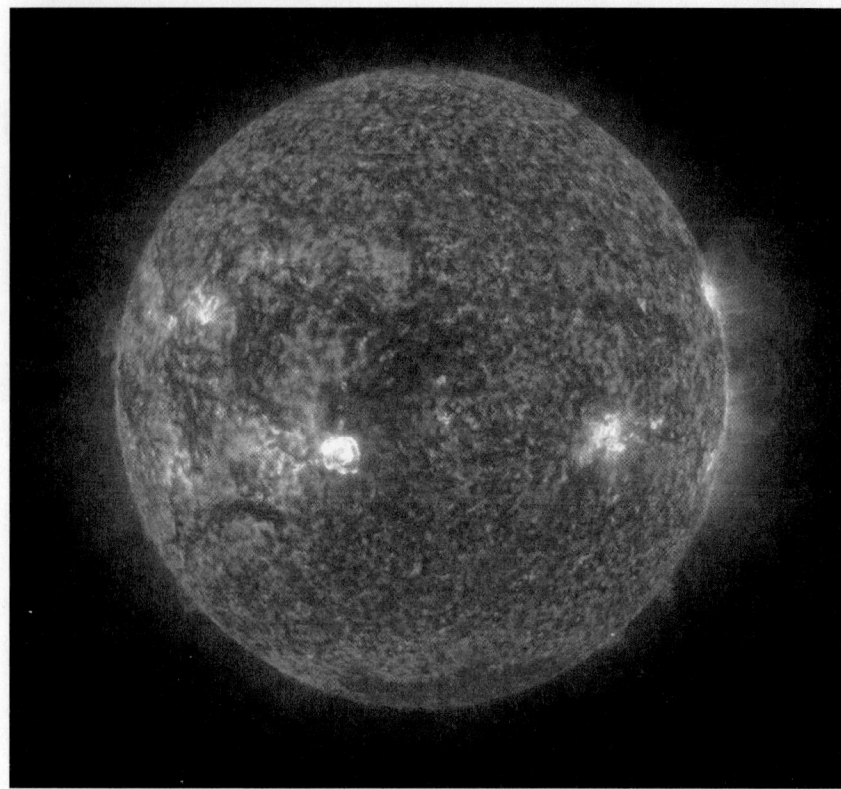

Chromosphere Just above the photosphere lies the **chromosphere,** a relatively thin layer of hot gases a few thousand kilometers thick. Astronomers can observe the chromosphere for a few moments during a total solar eclipse or by using a special instrument that blocks out the light from the photosphere. Under such conditions, it appears as a thin red rim around the sun. Because the chromosphere consists of hot, incandescent gases under low pressure, it produces an emission spectrum that is nearly the reverse of the absorption spectrum of the photosphere. One of the bright lines of hydrogen contributes a good portion of its total light and accounts for this sphere's red color.

Figure 14 Chromosphere The chromosphere is a thin layer of hot gases that appears as a red rim around the sun when photographed through a special filter.

Corona The outermost portion of the solar atmosphere, the **corona** (*corona* = crown) is visible only when the brilliant photosphere is covered. This envelope of ionized gases normally extends a million kilometers from the surface of the sun and produces a glow about half as bright as the full moon.

At the outer fringe of the corona, the ionized gases have speeds great enough to escape the gravitational pull of the sun. The streams of protons and electrons that flow from the corona constitute the **solar wind.** This wind travels outward through the solar system at speeds up to 800 kilometers per second and eventually is lost to space. During its journey, the solar wind interacts with the bodies of the solar system, continually bombarding lunar rocks and altering their appearance. Although Earth's magnetic field prevents the solar winds from reaching our surface, these winds do affect our atmosphere, as we'll discuss later.

Studies of the energy emitted from the photosphere indicate that its temperature averages about 6000 K. Upward from the photosphere, the temperature increases, exceeding 1 million K at the top of the corona. Although the corona temperature is much higher than that of the photosphere, it radiates much less energy because of its very low density.

 **Reading Checkpoint** *What is the solar wind?*

The Active Sun

The most conspicuous features on the surface of the sun are the dark regions. They were occasionally observed before the advent of the telescope, but were generally regarded as objects located somewhere between the sun and Earth. In 1610, Galileo concluded that these regions were part of the solar surface. From their motion, he deduced that the sun rotates on its axis about once a month. Later observations indicated that not all parts of the sun rotate at the same speed. The sun's equator rotates once in 25 days, while a location 70 degrees from the solar equator, whether north or south, requires 33 days for one rotation. Imagine if Earth rotated in a similar manner! The sun's nonuniform rotation is evidence of its gaseous nature.

Sunspots What are those dark areas Galileo observed? The dark regions on the surface of the photosphere are called **sunspots.** As Figure 15 shows, an individual spot contains a black center rimmed by a lighter region. **Sunspots appear dark because of their temperature, which is about 1500 K less than that of the surrounding solar surface.** If these dark spots could be observed away from the sun, they would appear many times brighter than the full moon.

In the nineteenth century, an accurate record of sunspot occurrences was kept. The sunspot data revealed that the number of sunspots observable varies in an 11-year cycle. First, the number of sunspots increases to a maximum, with perhaps a hundred or more visible at a given time. Then their numbers gradually decline to a minimum, when only a few or even none are visible.

Go Online
PLANETDIARY

For: Links on sunspots and weather
Visit: PHSchool.com
Web Code: czd-7243

Figure 15 Sunspots A Sunspots often appear as groups of dark areas on the sun. **B** A close-up of an individual sunspot shows a black center surrounded by a lighter region.

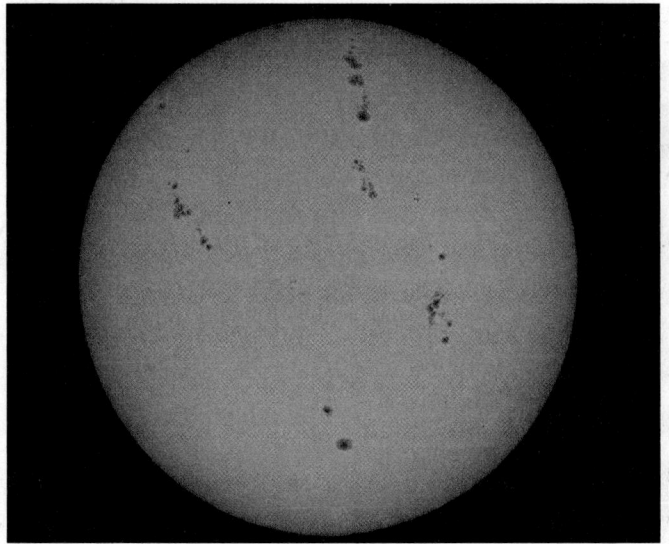

A

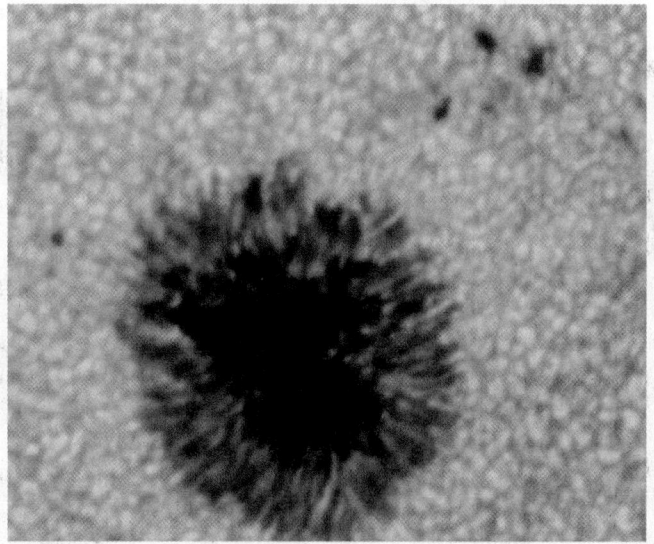

B

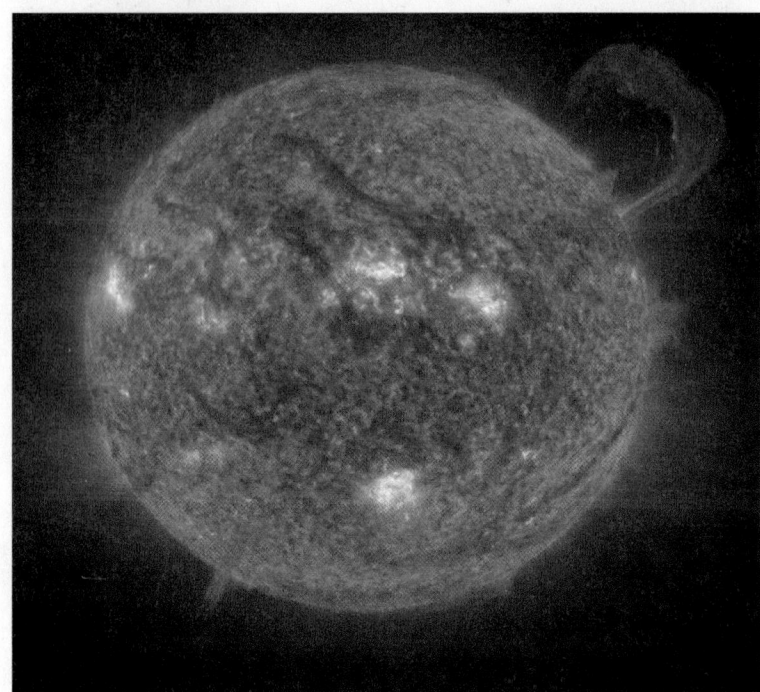

Figure 16 Solar Prominence
Solar prominences are huge, arched structures, best observed when they are on the edge of the sun.

Figure 17 Aurora Borealis or Northern Lights in Alaska
The same phenomenon occurs toward the south pole, where it is called the aurora australis or southern lights.

Prominences Among the more spectacular features of the active sun are prominences (*prominere* = to jut out). **Prominences** are huge cloudlike structures consisting of chromospheric gases. They often appear as great arches that extend well into the corona. Many prominences have the appearance of a fine tapestry and seem to hang motionless for days at a time. Others rise almost explosively away from the sun. These eruptive prominences reach speeds up to 1000 kilometers per second and may leave the sun entirely. **Prominences are ionized gases trapped by magnetic fields that extend from regions of intense solar activity.** Refer to Figure 16.

Solar Flares The most explosive events associated with sunspots are solar flares. **Solar flares** are brief outbursts that normally last about an hour and appear as a sudden brightening of the region above a sunspot cluster. **During their existence, solar flares release enormous amounts of energy, much of it in the form of ultraviolet, radio, and X-ray radiation.** At the same time, fast-moving atomic particles are ejected, causing the solar wind to intensify. Although a major flare could conceivably endanger the crew of a space flight, they are relatively rare. About a day after a large outburst, the ejected particles reach Earth, where they can affect long-distance radio communications.

The most spectacular effects of solar flares, however, are the **auroras,** also called the northern and southern lights. Following a strong solar flare, Earth's upper atmosphere near its magnetic poles is set aglow for several nights. The auroras appear in a wide variety of forms, one of which is shown in Figure 17. Sometimes the display looks like colorful ribbons moving with the breeze. At other times, the auroras appear as a series of luminous arcs or as a foglike glow. Auroral displays, like other solar activities, vary in intensity with the 11-year sunspot cycle.

 *What are solar flares?*

The Solar Interior

The interior of the sun cannot be observed directly. For that reason, all we know about it is based on information acquired from the energy it radiates and from theoretical studies. The source of the sun's energy was not discovered until the late 1930s.

Nuclear Fusion Deep in its interior, the sun produces energy by a process known as **nuclear fusion.** This nuclear reaction converts four hydrogen nuclei into the nucleus of a helium atom. Tremendous energy is released. **During nuclear fusion, energy is released because some matter is actually converted to energy, as shown in Figure 18.** How does this process work? Consider that four hydrogen atoms have a combined atomic mass of 4.032 atomic mass units (4 × 1.008) whereas the atomic mass of helium is 4.003 atomic mass units, or 0.029 less than the combined mass of the hydrogen. The tiny missing mass is emitted as energy according to Einstein's equation:

$$E = mc^2$$

E equals energy, *m* equals mass, and *c* equals the speed of light. Because the speed of light is very great (300,000 km/s), the amount of energy released from even a small amount of mass is enormous.

The conversion of just one pinhead's worth of hydrogen to helium generates more energy than burning thousands of tons of coal. Most of this energy is in the form of high-energy photons that work their way toward the solar surface. The photons are absorbed and reemitted many times until they reach a layer just below the photosphere. Here, convection currents help transport this energy to the solar surface, where it radiates through the transparent chromosphere and corona.

Only a small percentage of the hydrogen in the nuclear reaction is actually converted to energy. Nevertheless, the sun is consuming an estimated 600 million tons of hydrogen each second; about 4 million tons are converted to energy. As hydrogen is consumed, the product of this reaction—helium—forms the solar core, which continually grows in size.

Reading Checkpoint *What happens during the process of nuclear fusion?*

Go Online
NSTA *SciLINKS*

For: Links on nuclear fusion in the sun
Visit: www.SciLinks.org
Web Code: cjn-7243

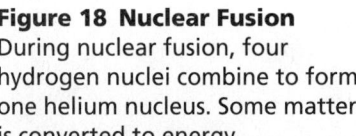

Figure 18 Nuclear Fusion
During nuclear fusion, four hydrogen nuclei combine to form one helium nucleus. Some matter is converted to energy.

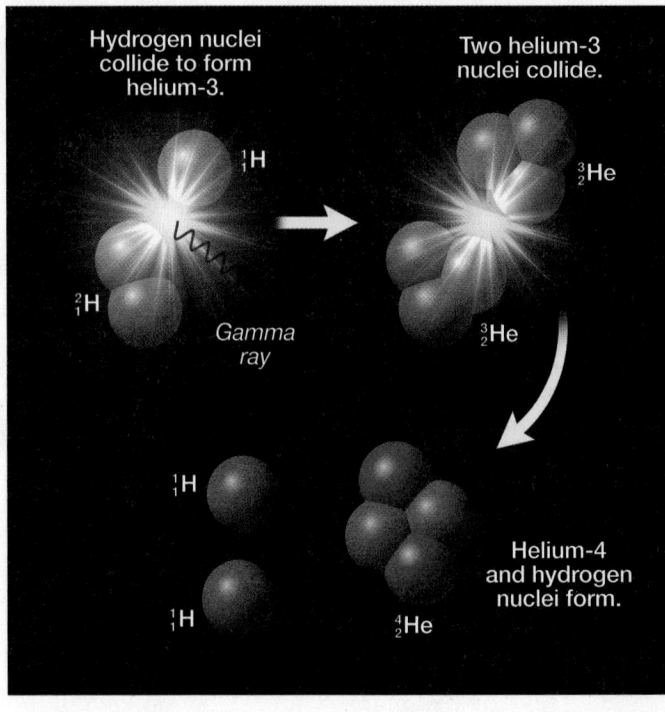

Hydrogen nuclei collide to form helium-3.

^1_1H

^2_1H

Gamma ray

Two helium-3 nuclei collide.

^3_2He

^3_2He

^1_1H

^1_1H

Helium-4 and hydrogen nuclei form.

^4_2He

Figure 19 The sun is the source of more than 99 percent of all energy on Earth.

Just how long can the sun produce energy at its present rate before all of its hydrogen fuel is consumed? Even at the enormous rate of consumption, the sun, shown in Figure 19, has enough fuel to last easily another 100 billion years. However, evidence from other stars indicates that the sun will grow dramatically and engulf Earth long before all of its hydrogen is gone. It is thought that a star the size of the sun can exist in its present stable state for 10 billion years. As the sun is already 4.5 billion years old, it is "middle-aged."

For nuclear fusion to occur, the sun's internal temperature must have reached several million degrees. But what caused this increase in temperature? The solar system is believed to have formed from an enormous compressed cloud of dust and gases—mostly hydrogen. When gases are compressed, their temperature increases due to the higher pressure. All of the bodies in the solar system were compressed. However, the sun was the only one, because of its size, that became hot enough for nuclear fusion to occur. Astronomers currently estimate its internal temperature at 15 million K.

The planet Jupiter is basically a hydrogen-rich ball; if it were about 10 times more massive, it too might have become a star. The idea of one star orbiting another may seem odd, but recent evidence indicates that about 50 percent of the stars in the universe probably occur in pairs or multiples.

Section 24.3 Assessment

Reviewing Concepts

1. What is the structure of the sun?
2. Which layer of the sun can be thought of as its surface?
3. Describe some characteristics of features on the sun.
4. Are the same number of sunspots always present on the sun? Explain.
5. How does the sun produce energy?
6. How much longer will the sun likely exist in its present state?

Critical Thinking

7. **Relating Cause and Effect** Why do sunspots appear dark?
8. **Applying Concepts** What is the effect on Earth's atmosphere of a strong solar flare?

Math Practice

9. Of the 6×10^8 tons of hydrogen the sun consumes each second, about 4×10^6 tons are converted to energy. What percentage of the total energy consumed per second is converted to energy?

Solar Activity and Climatic Change

Some people believe that changes in solar activity relate to climatic change. The effect of such changes would seem direct and easily understood: Increases in solar output would cause the atmosphere to warm, and reductions would result in cooling. This notion is appealing because it can be used to explain climatic changes of any length or intensity.

Still, there is at least one major drawback: No major long-term variations in the total intensity of solar radiation have yet been measured. Such measurements were not even possible until satellite technology became available. Now that it is possible, we will need many years of records before we begin to sense how variable the sun really is.

Sunspot Cycles

Several theories for climatic change based on a variable sun relate to sunspot cycles. The most recognizable features on the surface of the sun are the dark regions called sunspots. See Figure 20. The number of sunspots seems to increase and decrease over a cycle of about 11 years. The graph in Figure 21 below shows the annual number of sunspots, beginning in the early 1700s. However, this pattern is not always regular.

There have been long periods when sunspots have been absent or nearly absent. These events correspond closely with cold periods in Europe and North America. In contrast, periods of high sunspot activity have been associated with warmer times in these regions.

Conflicting Evidence

Because of these data, some scientists have suggested that changes in solar activity are an important cause of climatic change. But other scientists seriously question this notion. Their hesitation stems in part from investigations using different climatic

records from around the world that failed to find a significant relationship between solar activity and climate. Even more troubling is that there is no way to test the relationship.

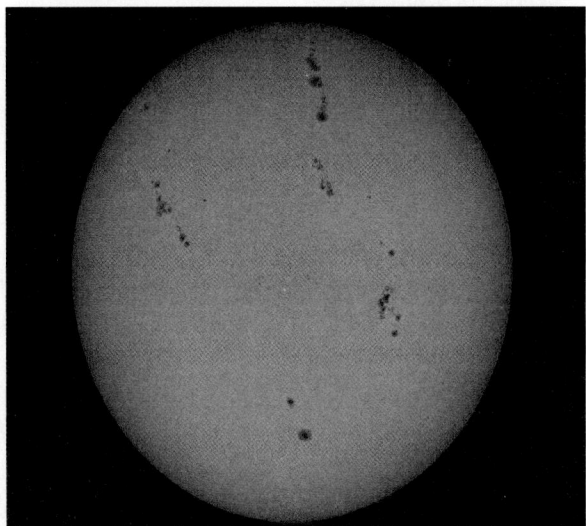

Figure 20 Dark regions on the surface of the sun are called sunspots.

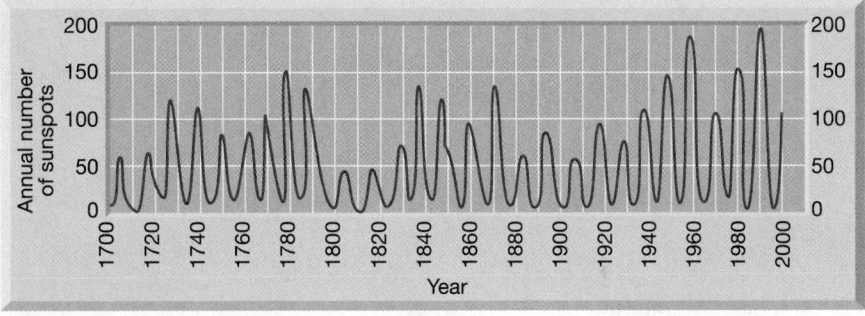

Figure 21 Mean Annual Sunspot Numbers

Tracking Sunspots

Sunspots begin as small areas about 1600 kilometers in diameter. Most last for only a few hours. However, some grow into dark regions many times larger than Earth and last for a month or more. In this lab you will count the number of sunspots over the course of several days.

Problem
How can you use a telescope to safely view and count the number of sunspots on the sun's surface?

Materials
- telescope
- small cardboard box
- large cardboard box
- piece of white paper
- metric ruler
- pencil
- tape

Skills
Observing, Interpreting Data, Making and Using Graphs

Procedure

1. Position a telescope on a tripod outside in a sunny spot away from trees and other obstacles. The eyepiece should face away from the sun. ⚠**CAUTION** *Never look at the sun directly. Do not view the sun through the telescope. These actions could cause eye damage.*

2. Place the large cardboard box on the ground about 15 centimeters in front of the telescope's eyepiece.

3. Use the pencil to punch a hole in one side of the small cardboard box. Tape a sheet of white paper inside the opposite end of the box, as shown in the illustration on this page.

4. Place the small box on top of the large box so that its front is open for viewing. The hole in the small box should face the eyepiece of the telescope. Adjust the telescope so that the eyepiece, the hole, and the white paper are aligned.

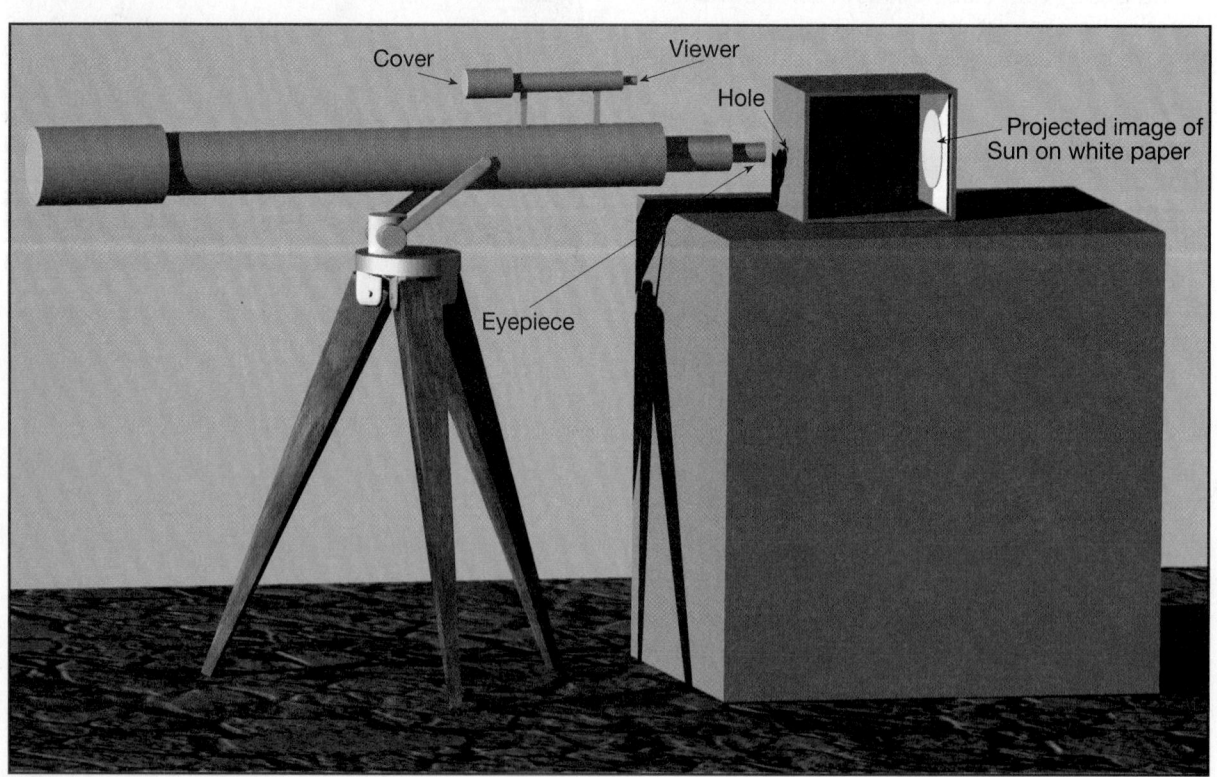

Cover

Viewer

Hole

Projected image of Sun on white paper

Eyepiece

5. Adjust the small box until you see an image of the sun projected onto the paper. You may adjust the telescope to obtain a clearer image, but do not look through the viewer to accomplish this. You may also vary the distance between the box and the telescope to obtain better images.

6. Record the number of sunspots that you observe in a data table similar to the one below. Trace the outlines of sunspots on the paper. Shade in the sunspots and use the ruler to measure their size.

7. As weather permits, make several more viewings of sunspots over the course of the next few days. During each viewing, repeat steps 1–6. Be sure to note the movement of the sunspots.

Analyze and Conclude

1. **Making Graphs** How many sunspots did you observe? Make a line graph of your data using your data table.

2. **Observing** How did the number of sunspots vary over the course of your observations?

3. **Interpreting Data** Why did the sunspots move?

4. **Interpreting Data** Based on your observations, could you detect any pattern in the statistical variability in the number of sunspots? Why or why not?

5. **Designing Experiments** A scientist hypothesizes that sunspots affect weather and climate on Earth. Can a valid experiment be designed to test the hypothesis? Explain.

Go Further The diameter of the sun is approximately 1.35 million kilometers. Use this number to develop a scale to estimate the sizes of the sunspots.

Sample Data Table		
Day	Number of Sunspots	Movement?
1		
2		
3		
4		
5		

Study Guide

24.1 The Study of Light

🌐 Key Concepts

- Electromagnetic radiation includes gamma rays, X-rays, ultraviolet light, visible light, infrared radiation, microwaves, and radio waves.

- When the spectrum of a star is studied, the spectral lines act as "fingerprints." These lines identify the elements present and thus the star's chemical composition.

- In astronomy, the Doppler effect is used to determine whether a star or other body in space is moving away from or toward Earth.

Vocabulary

electromagnetic spectrum, *p. 674;* photon, *p. 675;* spectroscopy, *p. 676;* continuous spectrum, *p. 676;* absorption spectrum, *p. 676;* emission spectrum, *p. 676;* Doppler effect, *p. 677*

24.2 Tools for Studying Space

🌐 Key Concepts

- In a refracting telescope, the objective lens produces an image by bending light from a distant object in such a way that the light converges at an area called the focus.

- Most large optical telescopes are reflectors. Light does not pass through a mirror so the glass for a reflecting telescope does not have to be of optical quality. This means chromatic aberration is not a problem.

- A radio telescope focuses the incoming radio waves on an antenna, which absorbs and transmits these waves to an amplifier, just like any radio antenna.

- Space telescopes orbit above Earth's atmosphere and thus produce clearer images than Earth-based telescopes.

Vocabulary

refracting telescope, *p. 678;* chromatic aberration, *p. 679;* reflecting telescope, *p. 680;* radio telescope, *p. 681*

24.3 The Sun

🌐 Key Concepts

- The sun can be divided into four parts: the solar interior; the visible surface, or photosphere; and two atmospheric layers, the chromosphere and corona.

- Sunspots appear dark because of their temperature, which is about 1500 K less than that of the surrounding solar surface.

- Prominences are ionized gases trapped by magnetic fields that extend from regions of intense solar activity.

- Solar flares release enormous amounts of energy, much of it in the form of ultraviolet, radio, and X-ray radiation.

- During nuclear fusion, energy is released because some matter is converted to energy.

Vocabulary

photosphere, *p. 685;* chromosphere, *p. 686;* corona, *p. 686;* solar wind, *p. 686;* sunspot, *p. 687;* prominence, *p. 688;* solar flare, *p. 688;* aurora, *p. 688;* nuclear fusion, *p. 689*

Thinking Visually

Concept Map Use information from the chapter to complete the concept map below.

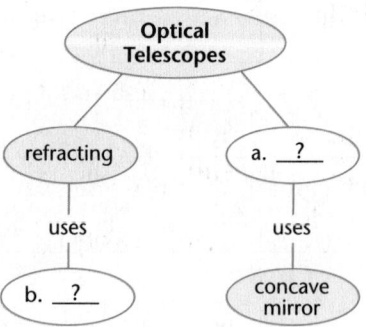

Assessment

Interactive textbook with assessment at PHSchool.com

Reviewing Content

Choose the letter that best answers the question or completes the statement.

1. Which type of radiation has the shortest wavelength?
   a. gamma rays　　b. X-rays
   c. visible light　　d. radio waves

2. The energy of a photon is related to its
   a. size.　　b. mass.
   c. density.　　d. wavelength.

3. As light passes through a prism, which color will bend the most?
   a. red　　b. violet
   c. yellow　　d. blue

4. Which type of telescope uses a concave mirror?
   a. refracting　　b. reflecting
   c. ultraviolet　　d. infrared

5. Which of the following is not a property of optical telescopes?
   a. resolving power
   b. magnifying power
   c. reflecting power
   d. light-gathering power

6. When several radio telescopes are wired together, the resulting network is called a radio
   a. receiver.
   b. interferometer.
   c. tuner.
   d. antenna.

7. The numerous, relatively small bright markings on the sun's photosphere are called
   a. auroras.　　b. sunspots.
   c. granules.　　d. prominences.

8. The thin, red rim seen around the sun during a total solar eclipse is the
   a. chromosphere.　　b. corona.
   c. solar wind.　　d. photosphere.

9. Which features of the sun look like huge cloudlike arches?
   a. solar flares　　b. sunspots
   c. auroras　　d. prominences

10. What is the source of the sun's energy?
    a. magnetism
    b. nuclear fission
    c. nuclear fusion
    d. radiation pressure

Understanding Concepts

11. What two factors determine how radiation is arranged on the electromagnetic spectrum?

12. Which color has the longest wavelength? The shortest?

13. Compare and contrast the wave theory and the particle theory of light.

14. Describe a continuous spectrum. Give an example of a natural phenomenon that exhibits a continuous spectrum.

15. Which type of spectrum do most stars have?

16. What optical defect is associated with refracting telescopes?

17. What three properties do optical telescopes have that aid astronomers?

18. What are some advantages of radio telescopes over optical telescopes?

19. List three space telescopes and describe the type of radiation studied by each.

20. Compare the diameter of the sun to that of Earth.

21. What is solar wind?

22. What "fuel" does the sun consume?

23. What happens to the matter that is consumed in nuclear fusion?

Critical Thinking

24. Summarizing Briefly summarize the relationship between Doppler shift and the speed of a moving object.

25. Inferring Why would the moon make a good site for an optical observatory?

26. Relating Cause and Effect The photosphere has a boiling appearance. Why?

27. Drawing Conclusions Can the solar wind be thought of as evidence for the particle theory of light? Explain your answer.

Analyzing Data

Use the graph to answer Questions 28–31.

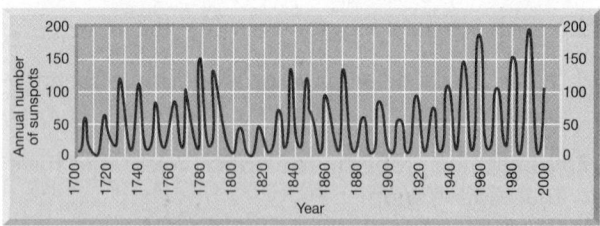

28. Identifying Which years had the lowest number of sunspots? The highest?

29. Interpreting Data Describe any patterns in the data.

30. Predicting When will the next period of maximum sunspot activity occur?

31. Analyzing Data Based on the data alone, is it possible to predict how many sunspots will occur during the next peak? Why or why not?

Concepts in Action

32. Inferring What can you infer about a star that exhibits a red shift in its spectra?

33. Explaining Why do astronomers seek to design telescopes with larger and larger objectives?

34. Relating Cause and Effect What could you infer about solar activity if you spotted an aurora that lasted several nights?

Performance-Based Assessment

Oral Presentation The sun is Earth's main source of energy. Work in a group to develop a presentation describing what might happen if the sun's energy increased by 10 percent. Discuss the effects on global temperatures, ocean shorelines, and polar caps. Be sure to consider changes in the amount of surface vegetation, and the impact of these changes on levels of atmospheric carbon dioxide.

Standardized Test Prep

Choose the letter that best answers the question or completes the statement.

1. Which of the following is NOT considered a form of electromagnetic radiation?
(A) radio waves
(B) gravity
(C) gamma rays
(D) visible light

2. The sun produces energy by converting
(A) oxygen nuclei to carbon dioxide.
(B) oxygen nuclei to nitrogen nuclei.
(C) hydrogen nuclei to helium nuclei.
(D) helium nuclei to hydrogen nuclei.

Answer the following questions in complete sentences.

3. What happens to the temperature of a gas when it is compressed?

4. Describe the composition of the sun's surface and compare it with that of other stars.

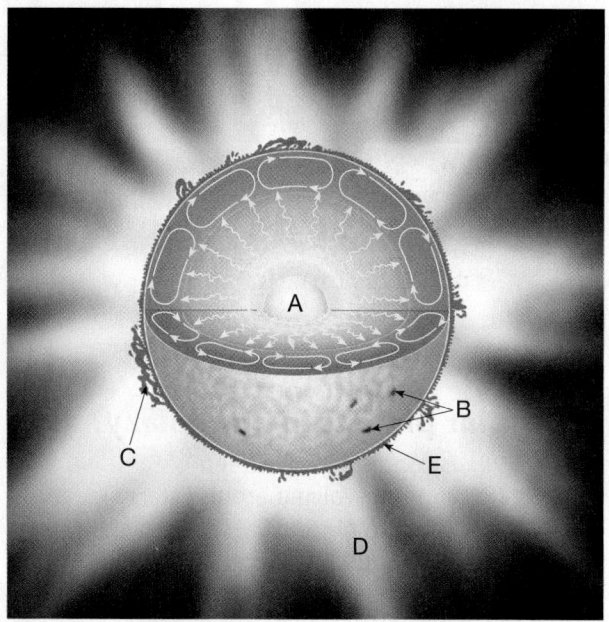

Use the diagram above to answer Questions 5 and 6.

5. What is the innermost layer of the sun called? What is the outermost layer?

6. What letters represent features found on the sun's photosphere? Identify each feature.

21st Century Learning

Problem Identification, Formulation, and Solution

What can you find out about extrasolar planets in our galaxy?

Since 1992, astronomers have been discovering planets revolving around stars other than the sun in our galaxy. These planets are called extrasolar planets because they are outside our solar system. Research the currently known extrasolar planets. Find the planets around the three stars closest to the sun and create a data table with information about the stars and their orbiting planets. Present the data in class or on the class blog. Provide any other interesting facts that you discover about these stars or planets. Do additional research to answer your classmates' questions.

Exploration Lab

Observing Stars

Dust and gases produce colorful nebulae.

Chapter Preview

Inquiry Activity

How Do Astronomers Measure Distances to Nearby Stars?

Procedure

1. Close your left eye. With your index finger in a vertical position, use your right eye to line up your finger with a distant object, such as a tree.

2. Without moving your finger, view the object with your left eye opened and your right eye closed.

Think About It

1. **Observing** What happened to the position of your finger when you observed it with your left eye?

2. **Predicting** What might happen if you repeated the activity, holding your finger farther from your eyes? Test your prediction.

25.1 Properties of Stars

Reading Focus

Key Concepts

- What can we learn by studying star properties?
- How does distance affect parallax?
- What factors determine a star's apparent magnitude?
- What relationship is shown on a Hertzsprung-Russell diagram?

Vocabulary

- ◆ constellation
- ◆ parallax
- ◆ binary star
- ◆ light-year
- ◆ apparent magnitude
- ◆ absolute magnitude
- ◆ main-sequence star
- ◆ red giant
- ◆ supergiant
- ◆ Cepheid variable
- ◆ nova
- ◆ nebulae

Reading Strategy

Previewing Copy the table below. Before you read, write two questions about the Hertzsprung-Russell diagram on page 704. As you read, write answers to your questions.

Questions about the Hertzsprung-Russell Diagram	
Question	Answer
a. _____?_____	b. _____?_____
c. _____?_____	d. _____?_____

The star Proxima Centauri is about 100 million times farther away from Earth than the moon. Yet, besides the sun, it is the closest star to Earth. The universe is incomprehensibly large. What is the nature of this vast universe? Do stars move, or do they remain in one place? Does the universe extend infinitely in all directions, or does it have boundaries? This chapter will answer these questions by examining the universe and the most numerous objects in the night sky—the stars.

As early as 5000 years ago, people became fascinated with the star-studded skies and began to name the patterns they saw. These patterns of stars were named in honor of mythological characters or great heroes, such as Orion, shown in Figure 1.

Although the stars that make up a pattern all appear to be the same distance from Earth, some are many times farther away than others.

The word **constellation** is used to designate an area of the sky that contains a specific pattern of stars. A star in any one of these areas is considered part of the constellation, even if that star is not part of the pattern. The sky is divided into 88 constellations, just as the United States is divided into states. Therefore, constellations can be used as a "map" of the night sky.

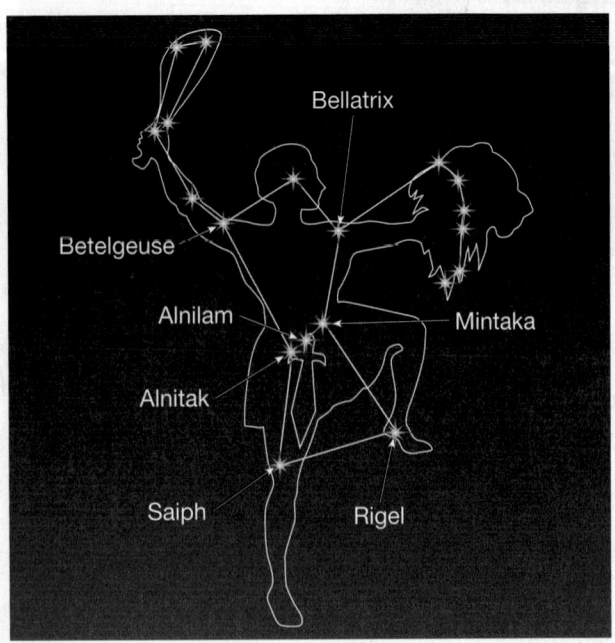

Figure 1 Orion The constellation Orion was named for a hunter.

Characteristics of Stars

A great deal is known about the universe beyond our solar system. This knowledge hinges on the fact that stars, and even gases in the "empty" space between stars, radiate electromagnetic energy in all directions into space. The key to understanding the universe is to collect this radiation and unravel the secrets it holds. Astronomers have devised many ways to do just that. We will begin by examining some properties of stars, such as color, temperature, and mass.

Figure 2 Stars of Orion This time-lapse photograph shows stars as streaks across the night sky as Earth rotates. The streaks clearly show different star colors.

Star Color and Temperature All objects, including stars and planets, emit and absorb radiation. We can see planets because they reflect some of the light that hits them. Stars, on the other hand, are blackbody radiators. A blackbody absorbs all of the electromagnetic radiation that strikes it. It also gives off the maximum amount of radiation possible at a given temperature. The energy of radiation given off by stars depends on their temperatures. Study the stars in Figure 2 and note their color. ⚿**Color is a clue to a star's temperature.** Very hot stars with surface temperatures above 30,000 K emit most of their energy in the form of short-wavelength light and therefore appear blue. Red stars are much cooler, and most of their energy is emitted as longer-wavelength red light. Stars with temperatures between 5000 and 6000 K appear yellow, like the sun.

Binary Stars and Stellar Mass In the early nineteenth century, astronomers discovered that many stars orbit each other. These pairs of stars, pulled toward each other by gravity, are called **binary stars.** More than 50 percent of the stars in the universe may occur in pairs or multiples.

⚿**Binary stars are used to determine the star property most difficult to calculate—its mass.** The mass of a body can be calculated if it is attached by gravity to a partner. As shown in Figure 3, binary stars orbit each other around a common point called the center of mass. For stars of equal mass, the center of mass lies exactly halfway between them. If one star is more massive than its partner, their common center will be closer to the more massive one. If the sizes of their orbits are known, the stars' masses can be determined.

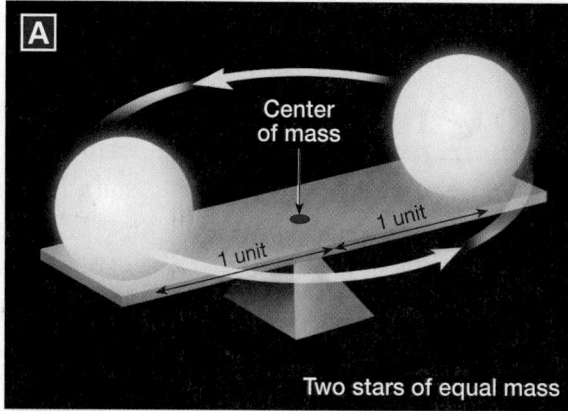

A

Center of mass

1 unit

1 unit

Two stars of equal mass

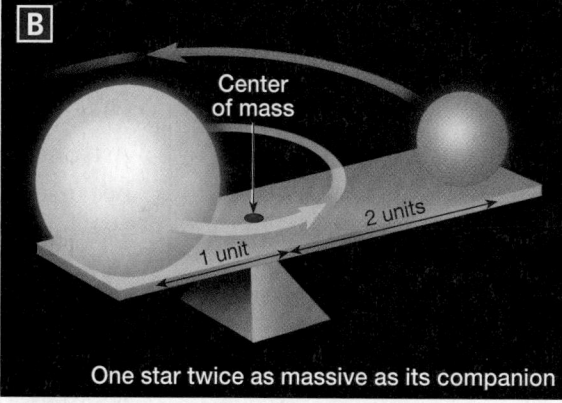

B

Center of mass

1 unit

2 units

One star twice as massive as its companion

Figure 3 Common Center of Mass
A For stars of equal mass, the center of mass lies in the middle. **B** A star twice as massive as its partner is twice as close to the center of mass. It therefore has a smaller orbit than its less massive partner.

Reading Checkpoint   *What is a binary star system?*

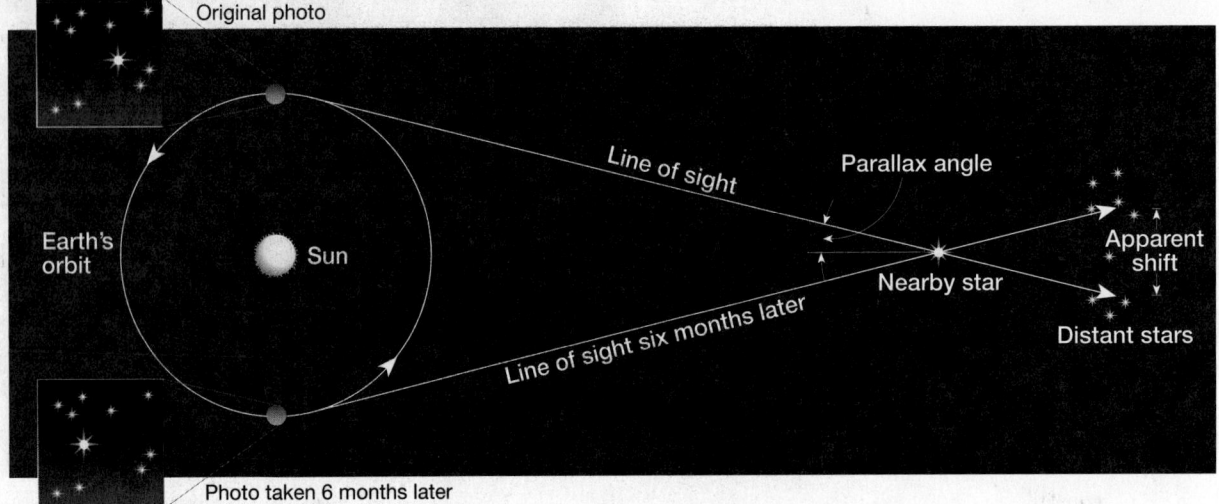

Original photo

Line of sight

Parallax angle

Earth's orbit

Sun

Line of sight six months later

Nearby star

Apparent shift

Distant stars

Photo taken 6 months later

Figure 4 Parallax The parallax angle shown here is exaggerated to illustrate the principle. Because the distances to even the nearest stars are huge, astronomers work with very small angles.
Relating Cause and Effect *What caused the star to appear to shift?*

Go Online
PLANETDIARY

For: Links on Earth's orbit and parallax
Visit: PHSchool.com
Web Code: czd-7251

Measuring Distances to Stars

Although measuring the distance to a star is very difficult, astronomers have developed some methods of determining stellar distances.

Parallax The most basic way to measure star distance is parallax. **Parallax** is the slight shifting in the apparent position of a nearby star due to the orbital motion of Earth. Parallax is determined by photographing a nearby star against the background of distant stars. Then, six months later, when Earth has moved halfway around its orbit, a second photograph is taken. When these photographs are compared, the position of the nearby star appears to have shifted with respect to the background stars. Figure 4 shows this shift and the resulting parallax angle.

🔑 **The nearest stars have the largest parallax angles, while those of distant stars are too small to measure.** In fact, all parallax angles are very small. The parallax angle to the nearest star (besides the sun), Proxima Centauri, is less than 1 second of arc, which equals 1/3600 of a degree. To put this in perspective, fully extend your arm and raise your little finger. Your finger is roughly 1 degree wide. Now imagine tracking a movement that is only 1/3600 as wide as your finger.

Before the invention of precise instruments for measuring parallax, astronomers did not understand the scale of the universe. Astronomers once inferred that the planets were closer than the stars because the planets could be seen to pass in front of the stars. They knew the principle of parallax, but the parallax angles of the stars were too small to be measured. It was not until 1673 that Gian Domenico Cassini used parallax to measure the distance between Earth and Mars. Later, in 1838, Friedrich Bessel and two other astronomers used parallax to determine the distances to several stars.

Light-Year Distances to stars are so large that units such as kilometers or astronomical units are often too hard to use. A better unit to express stellar distance is the **light-year,** which is the distance light travels in one year—about 9.5×10^{12} or 9.5 trillion kilometers. Proxima Centauri is about 4.3 light-years away from the sun.

Stellar Brightness

The measure of a star's brightness is its magnitude. The stars in the night sky have an assortment of sizes, temperatures, and distances, so their brightnesses vary widely.

Apparent Magnitude Some stars may appear dimmer than others only because they are farther away. A star's brightness as it appears from Earth is called its **apparent magnitude.** ⬡ **Three factors control the apparent brightness of a star as seen from Earth: how big it is, how hot it is, and how far away it is.**

Astronomers use numbers to rank apparent magnitude. The larger the number is, the dimmer the star. Just as we can compare the brightness of a 50-watt bulb to that of a 100-watt bulb, we can compare the brightness of stars having different magnitudes. A first-magnitude star is about 100 times brighter than a sixth-magnitude star. Therefore, two stars that differ by 5 magnitudes have a ratio in brightness of 100 to 1. It follows, then, that the brightness ratio of two stars differing by only one magnitude is about 2.5. A star of the first magnitude is about 2.5 times brighter than a star of the second magnitude.

 **Reading Checkpoint** *What is apparent magnitude?*

Absolute Magnitude Astronomers are also interested in how bright a star actually is, or its **absolute magnitude.** Two stars of the same absolute magnitude usually do not have the same apparent magnitude because one may be much farther from us than the other. The one that is farther away will appear dimmer. To compare their absolute brightness, astronomers determine what magnitude the stars would have if they were at a standard distance of about 32.6 light-years. For example, the sun, which has an apparent magnitude of −26.7, would, if located at a distance of 32.6 light-years, have an absolute magnitude of about 5. Stars with absolute magnitude values lower than 5 are actually brighter than the sun. Because of their distance, however, they appear much dimmer. Table 1 lists the absolute and apparent magnitudes of some stars as well as their distances from Earth.

Table 1 Distance, Apparent Magnitude, and Absolute Magnitude of Some Stars			
Name	**Distance (light-years)**	**Apparent Magnitude***	**Absolute Magnitude***
Sun	NA	−26.7	5.0
Alpha Centauri	4.27	0.0	4.4
Sirius	8.70	−1.4	1.5
Arcturus	36	−0.1	−0.3
Betelgeuse	520	0.8	−5.5
Deneb	1600	1.3	−6.9

*The more negative, the brighter; the more positive, the dimmer.

 **Reading Checkpoint** *What is absolute magnitude?*

Hertzsprung-Russell Diagram

Early in the twentieth century, Einar Hertzsprung and Henry Russell independently developed a graph used to study stars. It is now called a Hertzsprung-Russell diagram (H-R diagram). **A Hertzsprung-Russell diagram shows the relationship between the absolute magnitude and temperature of stars.** By studying H-R diagrams, we learn a great deal about the sizes, colors, and temperatures of stars.

In the H-R diagram shown in Figure 5, notice that the stars are not uniformly distributed. About 90 percent are **main-sequence stars** that fall along a band that runs from the upper-left corner to the lower-right corner of the diagram. As you can see, the hottest main-sequence stars are the brightest, and the coolest main-sequence stars are the dimmest.

The brightness of the main-sequence stars is also related to their mass. The hottest blue stars are about 50 times more massive than the sun, while the coolest red stars are only 1/10 as massive. Therefore, on the H-R diagram, the main-sequence stars appear in decreasing order, from hotter, more massive blue stars to cooler, less massive red stars.

Above and to the right of the main sequence in the H-R diagram lies a group of very bright stars called **red giants.** The size of these giants can be estimated by comparing them with stars of known size that have the same surface temperature. Objects with equal surface temperatures radiate the same amount of energy per unit area. Therefore, any difference in the brightness of two stars having the same surface temperature is due to their relative sizes. Some stars are so large that they are called **supergiants.** Betelgeuse, a bright red supergiant in the constellation Orion, has a radius about 800 times that of the sun.

Stars in the lower-central part of the H-R diagram are much fainter than main-sequence stars of the same temperature. Some probably are no bigger than Earth. This group is called white dwarfs, although not all are white.

Figure 5 Hertzsprung-Russell Diagram In this idealized chart, stars are plotted according to temperature and absolute magnitude.

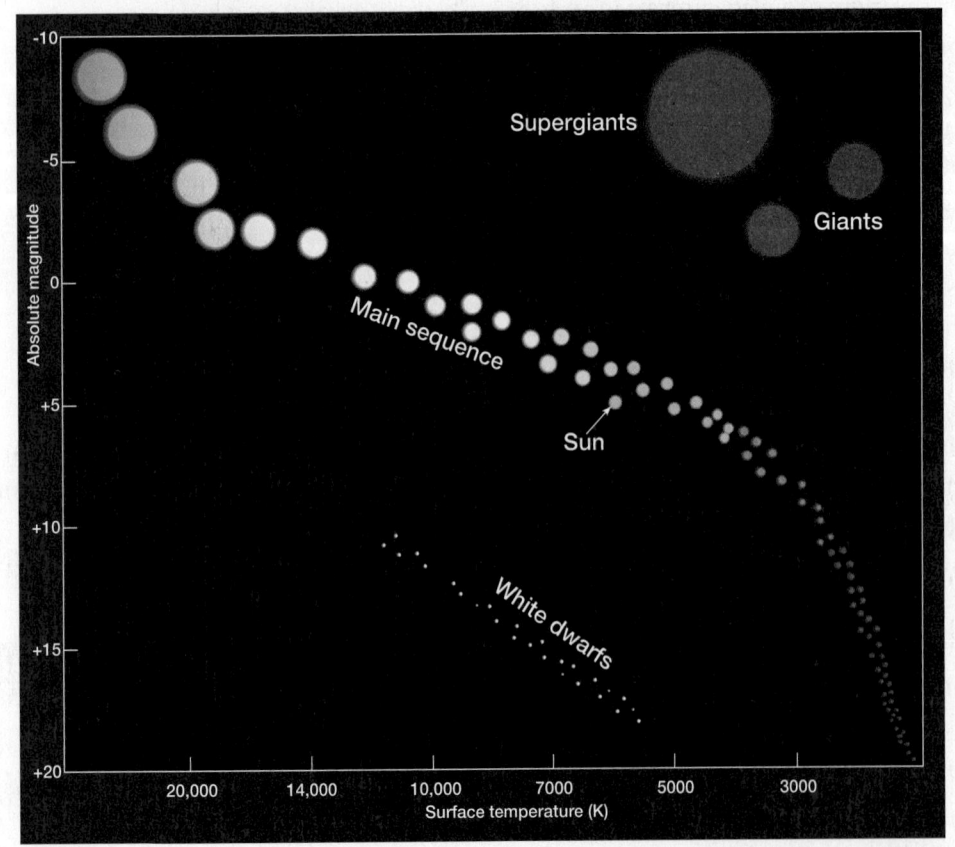

Soon after the first H-R diagrams were developed, astronomers realized their importance in interpreting stellar evolution. Just as with living things, a star is born, ages, and dies.

Variable Stars Stars may fluctuate in brightness. **Cepheid variables** are stars that get brighter and fainter in a regular pattern. The interval between two successive occurrences of maximum brightness is called a light period. In general, the longer the light period of a Cepheid, the greater its absolute magnitude is. Once the absolute magnitude is known, it can be compared to the apparent magnitude of the Cepheid. Based on this comparison, astronomers can figure out how far away the Cepheid is. Measuring Cepheid variable periods is an important means of determining distances within our universe.

A different type of variable is associated with a **nova,** or sudden brightening of a star. During a nova eruption, the outer layer of the star is ejected at high speed. A nova, shown in Figure 6, generally reaches maximum brightness in a few days, remains bright for only a few weeks, then slowly returns in a year or so to its original brightness. Only a small amount of its mass is lost during the flare-up. Some stars have experienced more than one such event. In fact, the process probably occurs repeatedly.

Scientists think that most novas occur in binary systems consisting of an expanding red giant and a nearby hot white dwarf. Hydrogen-rich gas from the oversized giant is transferred by gravity to the white dwarf. Eventually, the added gas causes the dwarf to ignite explosively. Such a reaction rapidly heats and expands the outer layer of the hot dwarf to produce a nova. In a relatively short time, the white dwarf returns to its prenova state, where it remains inactive until the next buildup occurs.

Figure 6 Nova These photographs, taken two months apart, show the decrease in brightness that follows a nova flare-up.

Interstellar Matter Between existing stars is "the vacuum of space." However, it is not a pure vacuum, for there are clouds of dust and gases known as **nebulae.** If this interstellar matter is close to a very hot star, it will glow and is called a bright nebula. The two main types of bright nebulae are emission nebulae and reflection nebulae.

Emission nebulae consist largely of hydrogen. They absorb ultraviolet radiation emitted by a nearby hot star. Because these gases are under very low pressure, they emit this energy as visible light. This conversion of ultraviolet light to visible light is known as fluorescence. You can see this effect in fluorescent lights. Reflection nebulae, as the name implies, merely reflect the light of nearby stars. Reflection nebulae are thought to be composed of dense clouds of large particles called interstellar dust.

Figure 7 Dark Nebula The Horsehead Nebula is found in the constellation Orion.

Some nebulae are not close enough to a bright star to be lit up. They are called dark nebulae. Dark nebulae, such as the one shown in Figure 7, can easily be seen as starless regions when viewing the Milky Way.

Although nebulae appear very dense, they actually consist of thinly scattered matter. Because of their enormous size, however, their total mass may be many times that of the sun. Astronomers study nebulae because stars and planets form from this interstellar matter.

Section 25.1 Assessment

Reviewing Concepts

1. ⊕ What can astronomers learn by studying a star's color?

2. Binary stars can be used to establish what property of stars?

3. ⊕ How does distance affect parallax?

4. ⊕ What factors determine a star's apparent magnitude?

5. ⊕ The H-R diagram shows the relationship between what two factors?

Critical Thinking

6. **Problem Solving** How many times brighter is a star with an absolute magnitude of 7 than a star with an absolute magnitude of 12?

7. **Inferring** Scientists think that only a small amount of a star's mass is lost during a nova. Based on what you have learned about novas, infer what evidence scientists use to support this theory.

Writing in Science

Web Site Make an educational Web site about the H-R diagram for younger students. Use Figure 5 as a guide. Include a color key and other elements to help clarify concepts such as star temperature, the Kelvin scale, and absolute magnitude.

25.2 Stellar Evolution

Reading Focus

Key Concepts

- What stage marks the birth of a star?
- Why do all stars eventually die?
- What stages make up the sun's life cycle?

Vocabulary

- protostar
- supernova
- white dwarf
- neutron star
- pulsar
- black hole

Reading Strategy

Sequencing Copy the flowchart below. As you read, complete it to show how the sun evolves. Expand the chart to show the evolution of low-mass and high-mass stars.

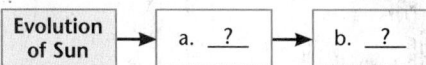

Determining how stars are born, age, and then die was difficult because the life of a star can span billions of years. However, by studying stars of different ages, astronomers have been able to piece together the evolution of a star. Imagine that an alien from outer space lands on Earth. This alien wants to study the stages of human life. By examining a large number of humans, the alien observes the birth of babies, the activities of children and adults, and the death of elderly people. From this information, the alien then attempts to put the stages of human development into proper sequence. Based on the number of humans in each stage of development, the alien would conclude that humans spend more of their lives as adults than as children. In a similar way, astronomers have pieced together the story of stars.

Star Birth

The birthplaces of stars are dark, cool interstellar clouds, such as the one in Figure 8. These nebulae are made up of dust and gases. In the Milky Way, nebulae consist of 92 percent hydrogen, 7 percent helium, and less than 1 percent of the remaining heavier elements. For some reason not yet fully understood, some nebulae become dense enough to begin to contract. A shock wave from an explosion of a nearby star may trigger the contraction. Once the process begins, gravity squeezes particles in the nebula, pulling every particle toward the center. As the nebula shrinks, gravitational energy is converted into heat energy.

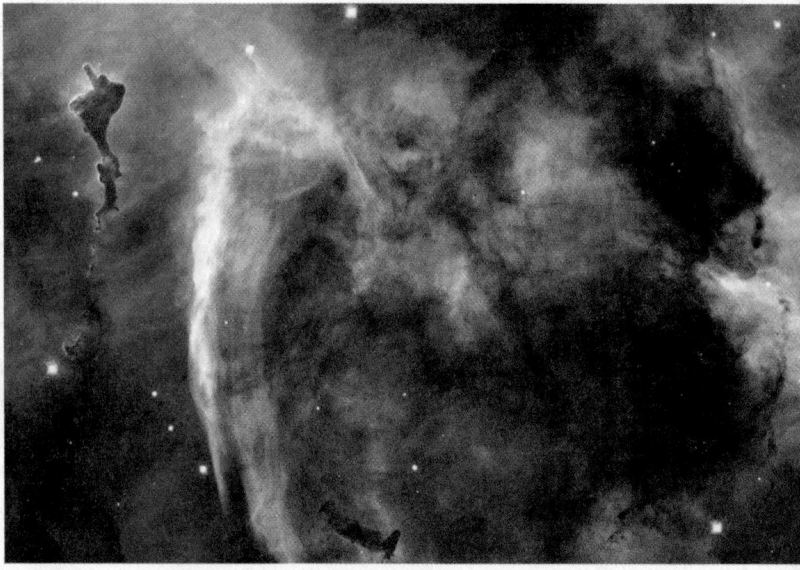

Figure 8 Nebula Dark, cool clouds full of interstellar matter are the birthplace of stars.

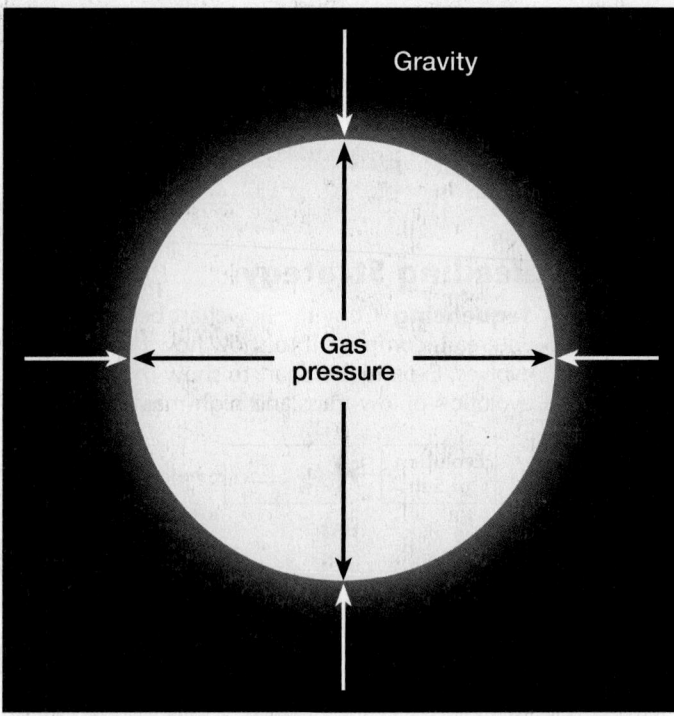

Figure 9 Balanced Forces A main-sequence star is balanced between gravity, which is trying to squeeze it, and gas pressure, which is trying to expand it.

Protostar Stage The initial contraction spans a million years or so. As time passes, the temperature of this gaseous body slowly rises until it is hot enough to radiate energy from its surface in the form of long-wavelength red light. This large red object is called a protostar. A **protostar** is a developing star not yet hot enough to engage in nuclear fusion.

During the protostar stage, gravitational contraction continues—slowly at first, then much more rapidly. This collapse causes the core of the protostar to heat much more intensely than the outer layer. **When the core of a protostar has reached about 10 million K, pressure within is so great that nuclear fusion of hydrogen begins, and a star is born.**

Heat from hydrogen fusion causes the gases to increase their motion. This in turn causes an increase in the outward gas pressure. At some point, this outward pressure exactly balances the inward force of gravity, as shown in Figure 9. When this balance is reached, the star becomes a stable main-sequence star. Stated another way, a stable main-sequence star is balanced between two forces: gravity, which is trying to squeeze it into a smaller sphere, and gas pressure, which is trying to expand it.

Main-Sequence Stage From this point in the evolution of a main-sequence star until its death, the internal gas pressure struggles to offset the unyielding force of gravity. Typically, hydrogen fusion continues for a few billion years and provides the outward pressure required to support the star from gravitational collapse.

Different stars age at different rates. Hot, massive blue stars radiate energy at such an enormous rate that they deplete their hydrogen fuel in only a few million years. By contrast, the least massive main-sequence stars may remain stable for hundreds of billions of years. A yellow star, such as the sun, remains a main-sequence star for about 10 billion years.

An average star spends 90 percent of its life as a hydrogen-burning, main-sequence star. Once the hydrogen fuel in the star's core is depleted, it evolves rapidly and dies. However, with the exception of the least-massive red stars, a star can delay its death by fusing heavier elements and becoming a giant.

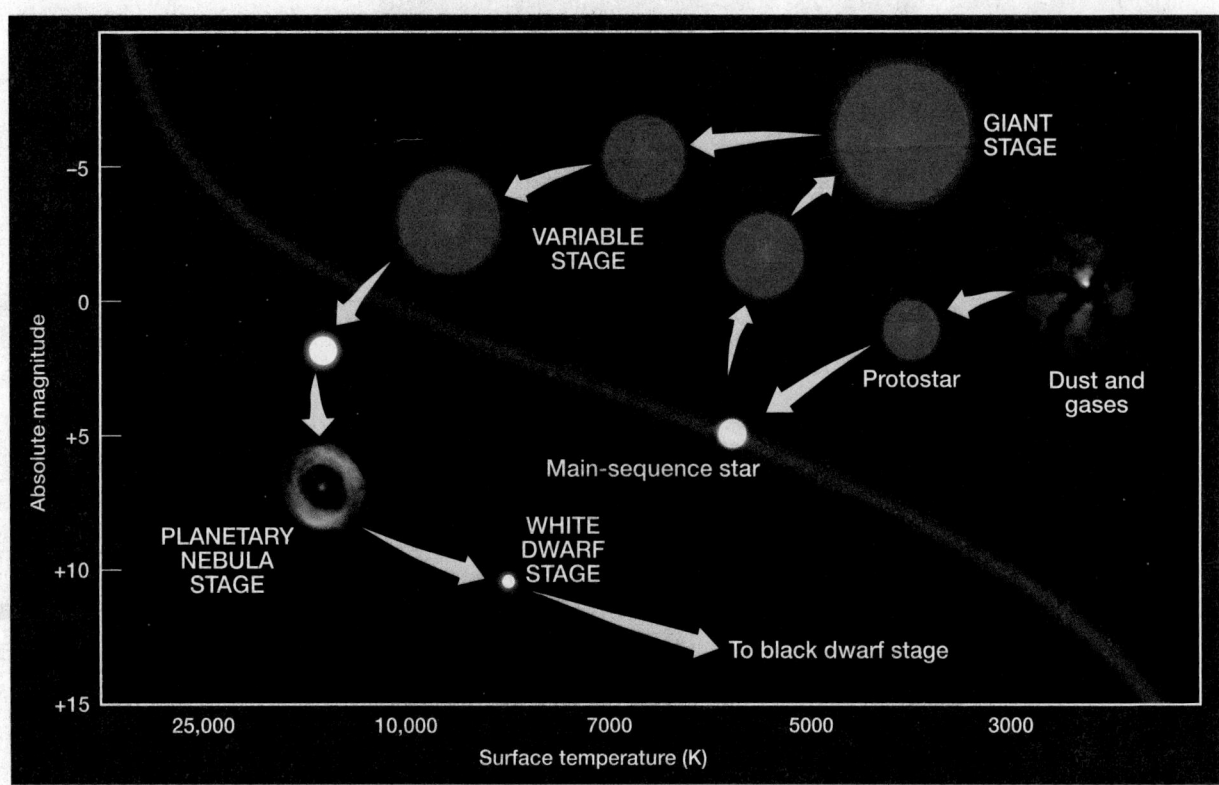

Figure 10 Life Cycle of a Sunlike Star A medium-mass star, similar to the sun, will evolve along the path shown here. **Interpreting Diagrams** *What is the first stage in the formation of the star? What is the last stage?*

Red-Giant Stage The red-giant stage occurs because the zone of hydrogen fusion continually moves outward, leaving behind a helium core. Eventually, all the hydrogen in the star's core is consumed. While hydrogen fusion is still progressing in the star's outer shell, no fusion is taking place in the core. Without a source of energy, the core no longer has enough pressure to support itself against the inward force of gravity. As a result, the core begins to contract.

As the core contracts, it grows hotter by converting gravitational energy into heat energy. Some of this energy is radiated outward, increasing hydrogen fusion in the star's outer shell. This energy in turn heats and expands the star's outer layer. The result is a giant body hundreds to thousands of times its main-sequence size, as shown in Figure 10.

As the star expands, its surface cools, which explains the star's reddish appearance. During expansion, the core continues to collapse and heat until it reaches 100 million K. At this temperature, it is hot enough to convert helium to carbon. So, a red giant consumes both hydrogen and helium to produce energy.

Eventually, all the usable nuclear fuel in these giants will be consumed. The sun, for example, will spend less than a billion years as a giant. More massive stars will pass through this stage even more rapidly. The force of gravity will again control the star's destiny as it squeezes the star into a much smaller, denser piece of matter.

For: Lives of Stars activity
Visit: PHSchool.com
Web Code: czp-7252

 **Reading Checkpoint** *Why do red giants have a reddish appearance?*

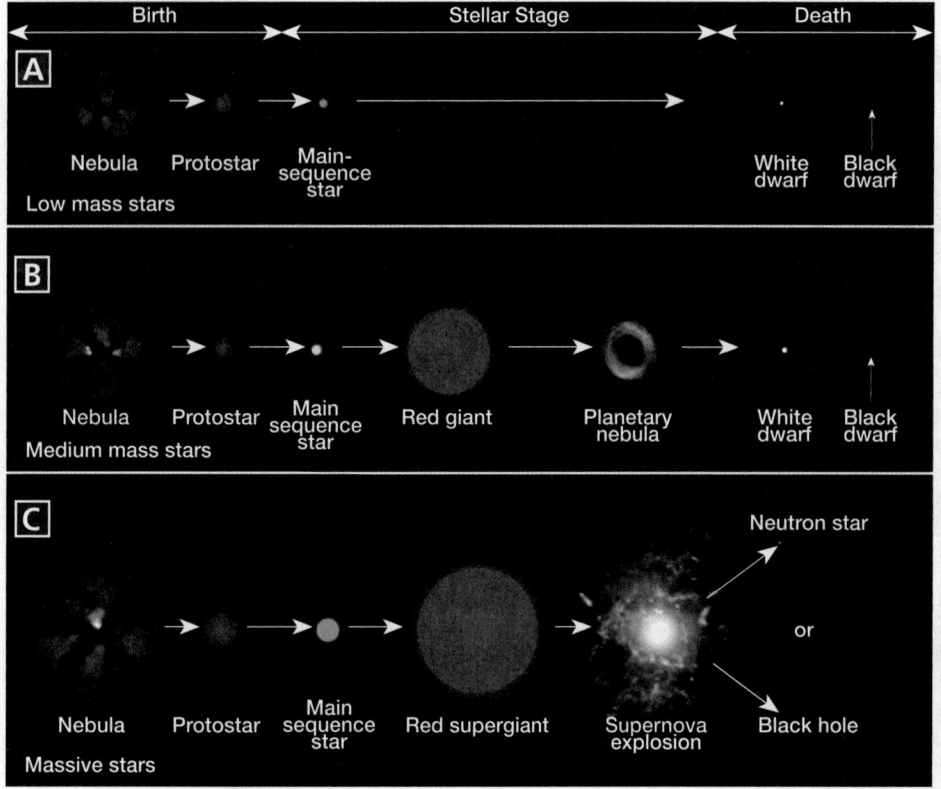

Birth | Stellar Stage | Death

A Low mass stars

Nebula → Protostar → Main-sequence star → ... → White dwarf → Black dwarf

B Medium mass stars

Nebula → Protostar → Main sequence star → Red giant → Planetary nebula → White dwarf → Black dwarf

C Massive stars

Nebula → Protostar → Main sequence star → Red supergiant → Supernova explosion → Neutron star *or* Black hole

Figure 11 Stellar Evolution
A A low-mass star uses fuel at a low rate and has a long life span. **B** Like a low-mass star, a medium-mass star ends as a black dwarf. **C** Massive stars end in huge explosions, then become either neutron stars or black holes.

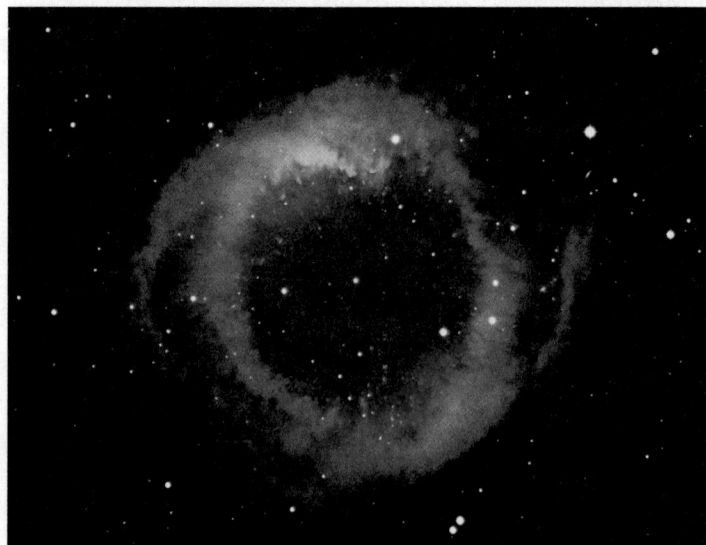

Figure 12 Planetary Nebula
During its collapse from a red giant to a white dwarf, a medium-mass star ejects its outer layer, forming a round cloud of gas.

Burnout and Death

Most of the events of stellar evolution discussed so far are well documented. What happens next is based more on theory. 🔑 **We do know that all stars, regardless of their size, eventually run out of fuel and collapse due to gravity.** With this in mind, let's consider the final stages of stars of different masses.

Death of Low-Mass Stars As shown in Figure 11A, stars less than one half the mass of the sun consume their fuel at a fairly slow rate. Consequently, these small, cool red stars may remain on the main sequence for up to 100 billion years. Because the interior of a low-mass star never reaches high enough temperatures and pressures to fuse helium, its only energy source is hydrogen. So, low-mass stars never evolve into red giants. Instead, they remain as stable main-sequence stars until they consume their hydrogen fuel and collapse into a white dwarf, which you will learn more about later.

Death of Medium-Mass Stars As shown in Figure 11B, stars with masses similar to the sun evolve in essentially the same way. During their giant phase, sunlike stars fuse hydrogen and helium fuel at a fast rate. Once this fuel is exhausted, these stars also collapse into white dwarfs.

During their collapse from red giants to white dwarfs, medium-mass stars are thought to cast off their bloated outer layer, creating an expanding round cloud of gas. The remaining hot, central white dwarf heats the gas cloud, causing it to glow. These often beautiful, gleaming spherical clouds are called planetary nebulae. An example of a planetary nebula is shown in Figure 12.

Death of Massive Stars

In contrast to sunlike stars, stars with masses four times that of the sun have relatively short life spans, as shown in Figure 11C. These stars end in a brilliant explosion called a **supernova.** During a supernova, a star becomes millions of times brighter than its prenova stage. If one of the nearest stars to Earth produced such an outburst, it would be brighter than the sun. Supernovae are rare. None have been observed in our galaxy since the invention of the telescope, although Tycho Brahe and Galileo each recorded one about 30 years apart. An even larger supernova was recorded in 1054 by the Chinese. Today, the remnant of this great outburst is the Crab Nebula, shown in Figure 13.

A supernova event is thought to be triggered when a massive star consumes most of its nuclear fuel. Without a heat engine to generate the gas pressure required to balance its immense gravitational field, the star collapses. This implosion, or bursting inward, is huge, resulting in a shock wave that moves out from the star's interior. This energetic shock wave destroys the star and blasts the outer shell into space, generating the supernova event.

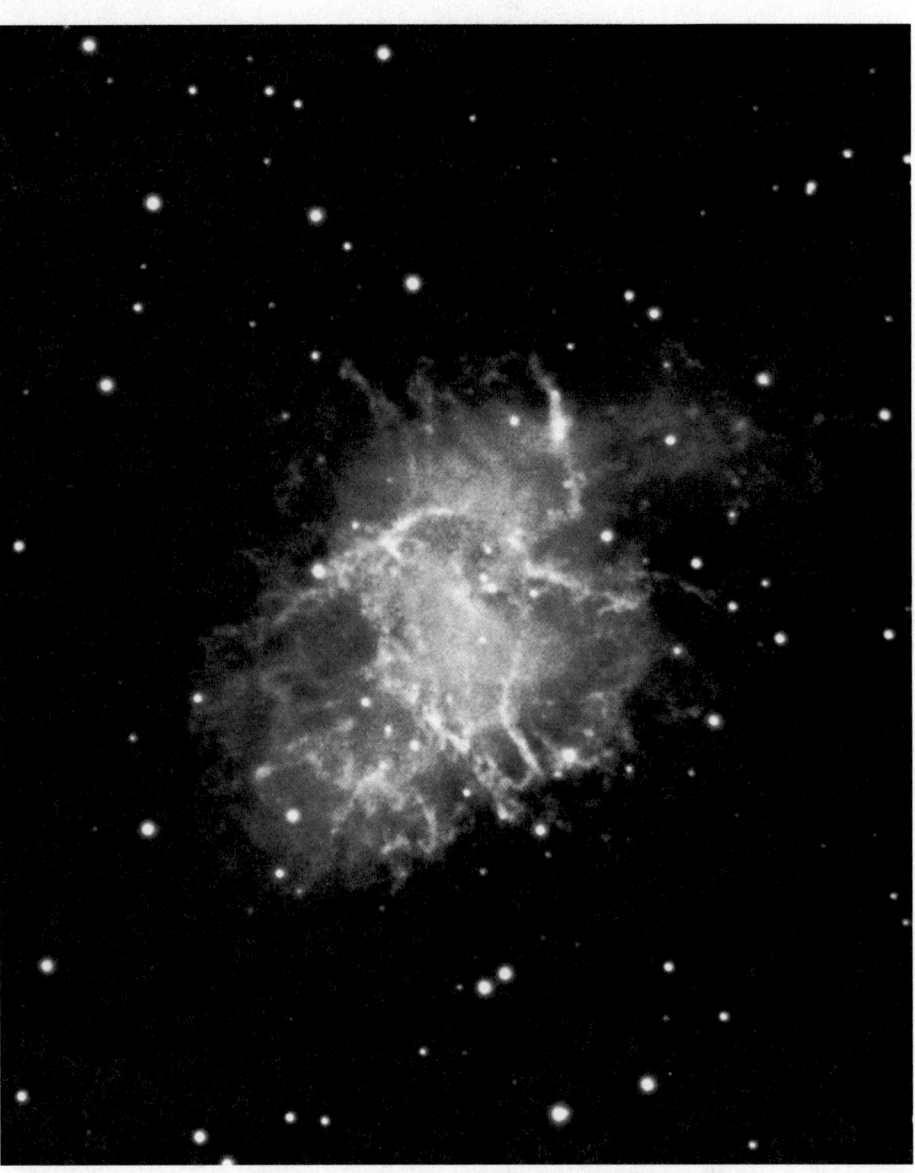

Figure 13 Crab Nebula
This nebula, found in the constellation Taurus, is the remains of a supernova that took place in 1054.

 **Reading Checkpoint** *What is a supernova?*

H-R Diagrams and Stellar Evolution

Hertzsprung-Russell diagrams have been helpful in formulating and testing models of stellar evolution. They are also useful for illustrating the changes that take place in an individual star during its life span. Refer back to Figure 10, which shows the evolution of a star about the size of the sun. Keep in mind that the star does not physically move along this path. Its position on the H-R diagram represents the color and absolute magnitude of the star at various stages in its evolution.

Nucleosynthesis

Nucleosynthesis A dying star can be a factory where new elements form. Stars produce all the naturally occurring chemical elements beyond helium in the periodic table. The process that produces chemical elements inside stars is called nucleosynthesis.

Nucleosynthesis starts with the fusion of hydrogen nuclei to form helium. Over time, the helium nuclei begin to fuse, forming nuclei of heavier elements. These heavier elements may also fuse. Elements between lithium and iron in the periodic table form in this way. Certain elements heavier than iron form as iron nuclei absorb neutrons released during fusion. The rarest heavy elements form at temperatures up to 1 billion degrees Celsius when a star explodes in a supernova. The explosion scatters the star's elements across space. There, they are available to form new stars and planets.

The mass of a star determines the highest atomic number of the elements it can produce. Only the most massive stars produce elements heavier than iron. The sun cannot produce elements heavier than oxygen.

Stellar Remnants

Eventually, all stars consume their nuclear fuel and collapse into one of three states—white dwarf, neutron star, or black hole. Although different in some ways, these small, compact objects are all composed of incomprehensibly dense material and all have extreme surface gravity.

White Dwarfs White dwarfs are the remains of low-mass and medium-mass stars. They are extremely small stars with densities greater than any known material on Earth. Although some white dwarfs are no larger than Earth, the mass of such a dwarf can equal 1.4 times that of the sun. A spoonful of such matter would weigh several tons. Densities this great are possible only when electrons are displaced inward from their regular orbits, around an atom's nucleus, allowing the atoms to take up less than the "normal" amount of space.

As a star contracts into a white dwarf, its surface becomes very hot, sometimes exceeding 25,000 K. Even so, without a source of energy, it can only become cooler and dimmer. Table 2 summarizes the evolution of stars of various masses. **The sun began as a nebula, will spend much of its life as a main-sequence star, and then will become a red giant, planetary nebula, white dwarf, and finally, a black dwarf.**

Table 2 Summary of Evolution for Stars of Various Masses				
Initial Mass of Interstellar Cloud (Sun = 1)	Main-Sequence Stage	Giant Phase	Evolution After Giant Phase	Final Stage
1–3	Yellow	Yes	Planetary nebula	White dwarf
6	White	Yes	Supernova	Neutron star
20	Blue	Yes (Supergiant)	Supernova	Black hole

Neutron Stars After studying white dwarfs, scientists made what might at first appear to be a surprising conclusion. The smallest white dwarfs are the most massive, and the largest are the least massive. The explanation for this is that a more massive star, because of its greater gravitational force, is able to squeeze itself into a smaller, more densely packed object than can a less massive star. So, the smaller white dwarfs were produced from the collapse of larger, more massive stars than were the larger white dwarfs.

This conclusion led to the prediction that stars smaller and more massive than white dwarfs must exist. These objects, called **neutron stars,** are thought to be the remnants of supernova events. In a white dwarf, the electrons in the atoms are pushed close to the nucleus, while in a neutron star, the electrons are forced to combine with protons to produce neutrons. If Earth were to collapse to the density of a neutron star, it would have a diameter equal to the length of a football field. A pea-size sample of this matter would weigh 100 million tons. This is approximately the density of an atomic nucleus. Neutron stars can be thought of as large atomic nuclei.

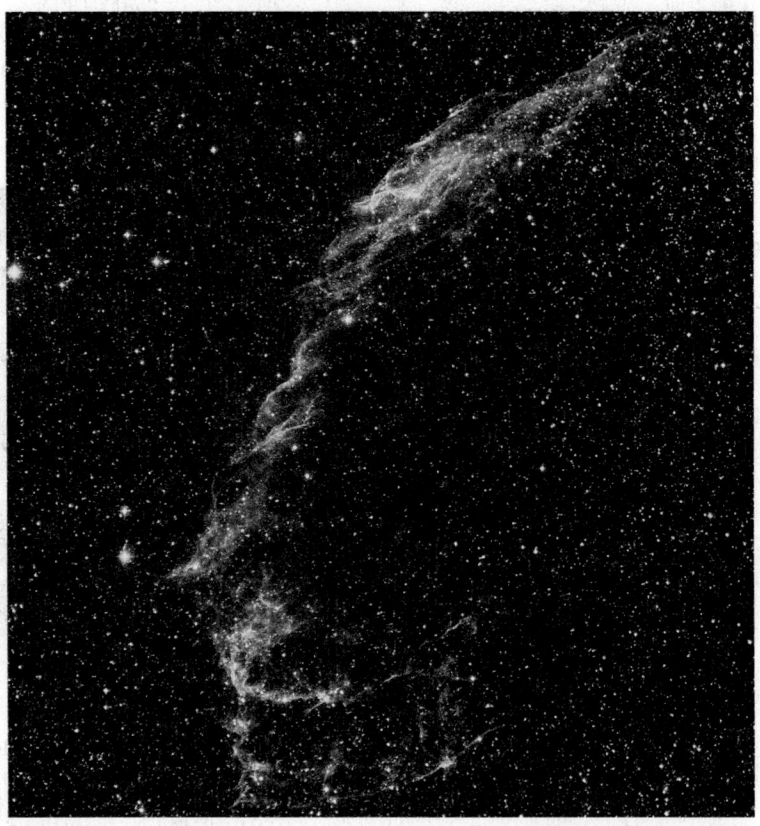

Figure 14 Veil Nebula Located in the constellation Cygnus, this nebula is the remnant of an ancient supernova.

Supernovae During a supernova, the outer layer of the star is ejected, while the core collapses into an extremely hot neutron star about 20 kilometers in diameter. Although neutron stars have high surface temperatures, their small size would greatly limit their brightness. Finding one with a telescope would be extremely difficult.

However, astronomers think that a neutron star would have a very strong magnetic field. Further, as a star collapses, it will rotate faster, for the same reason ice skaters rotate faster as they pull in their arms. Radio waves generated by these rotating stars would be concentrated into two narrow zones that would align with the star's magnetic poles. Consequently, these stars would resemble a rapidly rotating beacon emitting strong radio waves. If Earth happened to be in the path of these beacons, the star would appear to blink on and off, or pulsate, as the waves swept past. A spinning neutron star that appears to give off pulses of radio waves is called a **pulsar.**

In the early 1970s, a pulsar was discovered in the Crab Nebula. This pulsar is undoubtedly the remains of the supernova of 1054.

Black Holes Are neutron stars made of the most dense materials possible? No. During a supernova event, remnants of stars at least 20 times more massive than the sun apparently collapse into objects even smaller and denser than neutron stars. Dense objects with gravity so strong that not even light can escape their surface are called **black holes**. Anything that moves too near a black hole would be swept in by its gravity and lost forever.

How can astronomers find an object whose gravitational field prevents the escape of all matter and energy? One strategy is to find evidence of matter being rapidly swept into a region of apparent nothingness. Scientists think that as matter is pulled into a black hole, it should become very hot and emit a flood of X-rays before being pulled in. Because isolated black holes would not have a source of matter to swallow up, astronomers first looked at binary-star systems.

A likely candidate for a black hole is Cygnus X-1, a strong X-ray source in the constellation Cygnus. In this case, the X-ray source can be observed orbiting a supergiant companion with a period of 5.6 days. It appears that gases are pulled from this companion and spiral into the disk-shaped structure around the black hole. An artist's impression of this is shown in Figure 15. Some scientists also think that there are supermassive black holes in the centers of many galaxies. Our own galaxy may have a black hole in the center with a mass of 1 to 2 billion suns.

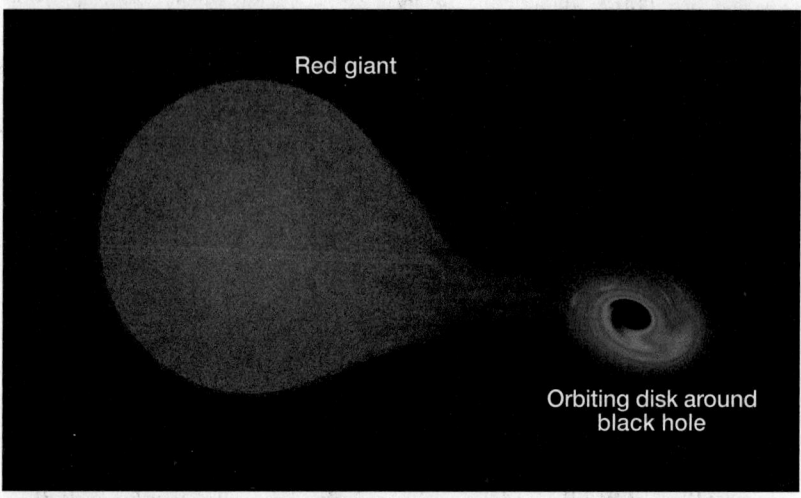

Red giant

Orbiting disk around black hole

Figure 15 Black Hole Gases from the red giant spiral into the black hole.

Go **O**nline

NSTA *SciLINKS*

For: Links on black holes
Visit: www.SciLinks.org
Web Code: cjn-7252

Section 25.2 Assessment

Reviewing Concepts

1. What is a protostar?
2. At what point is a star born?
3. What causes a star to die?
4. Describe the life cycle of the sun.

Critical Thinking

5. **Inferring** Why are less massive stars thought to age more slowly than more massive stars, even though less massive stars have much less "fuel"?

6. **Relating Cause and Effect** Why is interstellar matter important to stellar evolution?

Connecting Concepts

Supernova If a supernova explosion were to occur near our solar system, what might be some possible consequences of the intense X-ray radiation that would reach Earth?

25.3 The Universe

On a clear and moonless night away from city lights, you can see a truly marvelous sight—our own Milky Way Galaxy, as shown in Figure 16. **Galaxies** are large groups of stars, dust, and gases held together by gravity. There may be 400 billion stars in the Milky Way Galaxy alone. Our galaxy looks milky because the solar system is located within a flat disk—the galactic disk. We view it from the inside and see stars in every direction.

The Milky Way Galaxy

Imagine that you are hiking in an enormous forest. You look around and see equal numbers of trees in every direction. Are you in the center of the forest? Not necessarily. Because the trees block your view, almost anywhere in the forest will seem to be the center. When astronomers began to survey the stars located along the plane of the Milky Way, it appeared that equal numbers of stars lay in every direction. Was Earth at the center of the galaxy? The stars made it look like Earth was at the center. But that is not actually the case.

Figure 16 Milky Way Galaxy
Notice the dark band caused by interstellar dark nebulae.

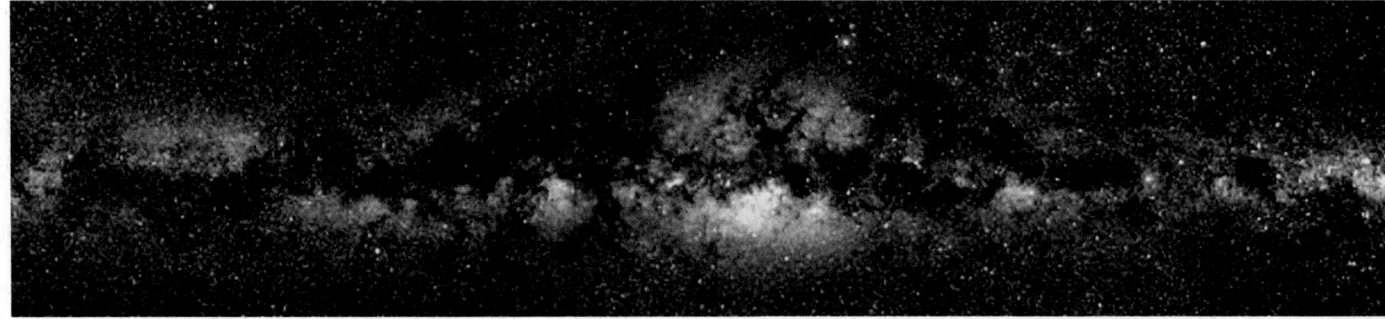

Overhead view

A Arms

Nucleus

Sun

←————— 100,000 light-years —————→

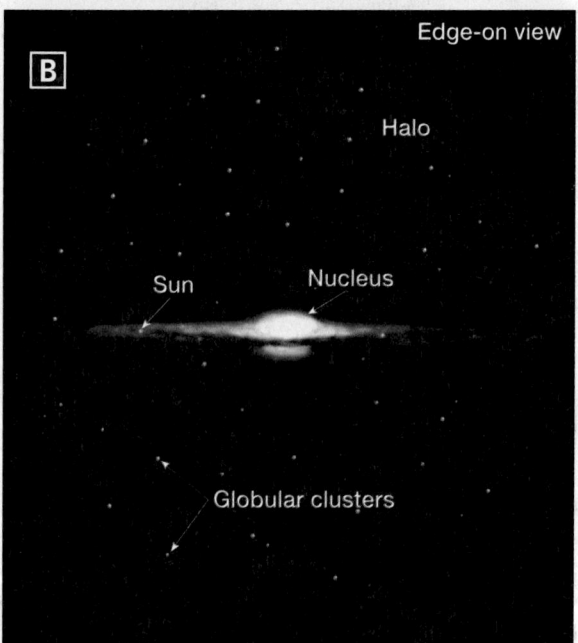

Edge-on view

B Halo

Sun Nucleus

Globular clusters

Figure 17 Structure of the Milky Way A The spiral arms are clearly visible in the overhead view of our galaxy. **B** Our solar system is located about 30,000 light-years from the galactic nucleus.

Size of the Milky Way

Size of the Milky Way It's hard to study the Milky Way Galaxy with optical telescopes because large quantities of interstellar matter block our vision. With the aid of radio telescopes, scientists have partly determined the structure of our galaxy. ◯**The Milky Way is a large spiral galaxy whose disk is about 100,000 light-years wide and about 10,000 light-years thick at the nucleus.** As viewed from Earth, the center of the galaxy lies beyond the constellation Sagittarius. Figure 17 shows the structure of the Milky Way.

How big is the Milky Way Galaxy?

Structure of the Milky Way Radio telescopes reveal that the Milky Way has at least three distinct spiral arms, with some signs of splintering. The sun is positioned in one of these arms about two thirds of the way from the center, or galactic nucleus, at a distance of about 30,000 light-years. The stars in the arms of the Milky Way rotate around the galactic nucleus. The most outward arms move the slowest, and the ends of the arms appear to trail. Our solar system orbits the galactic nucleus about every 230 million years.

Surrounding the galactic disk is a nearly round halo made of thin gas and numerous clusters of stars. These star clusters do not participate in the rotating motion of the arms but have their own orbits that carry them through the disk. Although some clusters are very dense, they pass among the stars of the arms with plenty of room to spare.

Where is our solar system located within the Milky Way Galaxy?

Types of Galaxies

In the mid-1700s, German philosopher Immanuel Kant proposed that the fuzzy patches of light scattered among the stars were actually distant galaxies like the Milky Way. Today we know that the universe includes hundreds of billions of galaxies, each containing hundreds of billions of stars. From these hundreds of billions of galaxies, scientists have identified several basic types.

Spiral Galaxies As shown in Figure 18A, spiral galaxies are usually disk-shaped, with a somewhat greater concentration of stars near their centers. There are numerous variations, though. Viewed broadside, the arms are often seen extending from the central nucleus and sweeping gracefully away. The outermost stars of these arms rotate most slowly, giving the galaxy the appearance of a pinwheel.

One type of spiral galaxy, however, has its stars arranged in the shape of a bar, which rotates as a rigid system. Attached to each end of these bars are curved spiral arms. These have become known as barred spiral galaxies, as shown in Figure 18B. Recent evidence indicates that the Milky Way may be a barred spiral galaxy. Spiral galaxies are generally quite large. About 10 percent of all galaxies are thought to be barred spirals, and another 20 percent are regular spiral galaxies.

Elliptical Galaxies About 60 percent of galaxies are classified as elliptical galaxies. Elliptical galaxies range in shape from round to oval. Although most are small, the very largest known galaxies—200,000 light-years in diameter—are elliptical. This type of galaxy, shown in Figure 19, does not have spiral arms.

Irregular Galaxies Only 10 percent of the known galaxies have irregular shapes and are classified as irregular galaxies. The best-known irregular galaxies, the Large and Small Magellanic Clouds, are easily visible from the Southern Hemisphere with the unaided eye. These galaxies were named after the explorer Ferdinand Magellan, who observed them when he sailed around Earth in 1520. They are our nearest galactic neighbors—only 150,000 light-years away. An irregular galaxy is shown in Figure 20.

🔵 **In addition to shape and size, one of the major differences among different types of galaxies is the age of their stars.** Irregular galaxies are composed mostly of young stars, while elliptical galaxies contain old stars. The Milky Way and other spiral galaxies have both young and old stars, with the youngest located in the arms.

Figure 18 Spiral Galaxies
A A spiral galaxy looks somewhat like a pinwheel. **B** A barred spiral galaxy has a bar through its center, with arms extending outward from the bar.

Figure 19 Elliptical Galaxy Most galaxies are classified as elliptical with shapes ranging from round to oval.

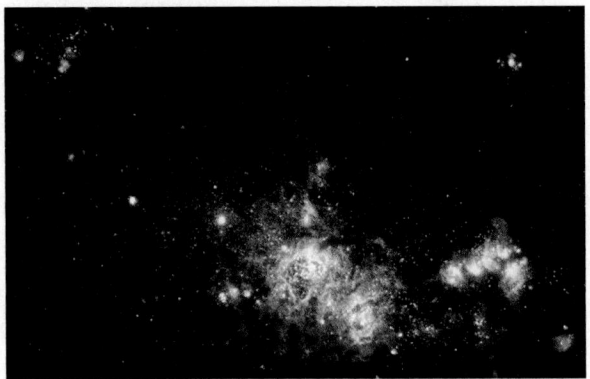

Figure 20 Irregular Galaxy Irregular galaxies have a variety of shapes.
Describing *What type of stars would you find in an irregular galaxy?*

Figure 21 Galaxy Cluster This cluster of galaxies is located about 1 million light-years from Earth.

Galaxy Clusters Once astronomers discovered that stars were found in groups, they wondered whether galaxies also were grouped or just randomly distributed throughout the universe. They found that, like stars, galaxies are grouped in **clusters.** One such cluster is shown in Figure 21. Some clusters may contain thousands of galaxies. Our own cluster, called the Local Group, contains at least 28 galaxies. Of these, three are spirals, 11 are irregulars, and 14 are ellipticals. Galaxy clusters also make up huge groups called superclusters, which make up vast thread-like structures called filaments, the largest known structures in the universe.

Quasars In the 1960s, astronomers discovered objects that were very bright and very far away. They called them quasi-stellar objects, or quasars, since they looked like stars. Because it takes their light billions of years to reach Earth, quasars must have existed when the universe was very young. Quasars must emit huge amounts of radiation, or they would be too dim for us to detect. The leading theory is that they are massive black holes in the center of very young galaxies.

The Expanding Universe

Recall the Doppler effect from Chapter 24. Remember that when a source is moving away, its light appears redder than it actually is, because its waves appear lengthened. Objects approaching have their light waves shifted toward the blue or shorter wavelengths. Therefore, the Doppler effect reveals whether a star or other body in space is moving away from Earth or toward Earth. The amount of shift allows us to calculate the rate of this relative movement. Large Doppler shifts indicate higher speeds; smaller Doppler shifts indicate lower speeds.

Red Shifts One of the most important discoveries of modern astronomy was made in 1929 by Edwin Hubble. Observations completed several years earlier revealed that most galaxies have Doppler shifts toward the red end of the spectrum. The red shift occurs because the light waves are "stretched," which shows that Earth and the source are moving away from each other. Hubble set out to explain this red shift phenomenon.

Hubble realized that dimmer galaxies were probably farther away than were brighter galaxies. He tried to determine whether a relationship existed between the distances to galaxies and their red shifts. Hubble used estimated distances based on relative brightness and Doppler red shifts to discover that galaxies that exhibit the greatest red shifts are the most distant.

Hubble's Law A consequence of the universal red shift is that it predicts that most galaxies—except for a few nearby—are moving away from us. Recall that the amount of Doppler red shift depends on the speed at which the object is moving away. Greater red shifts indicate faster speeds. Because more distant galaxies have greater red shifts, Hubble concluded that they must be retreating from us at greater speeds. This idea is currently termed **Hubble's law.** It states that galaxies are retreating from us at a speed that is proportional to their distance.

Hubble was surprised at this discovery because it implied that the most distant galaxies are moving away from us many times faster than those nearby. What does this mean? ●**The red shifts of distant galaxies indicate that the universe is expanding.**

To help visualize the nature of this expanding universe, imagine a loaf of raisin bread dough that has been set out to rise for a few hours. As shown in Figure 22, as the dough doubles in size, so does the distance between all of the raisins. However, the raisins that were originally farther apart traveled a greater distance in the same time span than those located closer together. We therefore conclude that in an expanding universe, as in the raisin bread dough analogy, those objects located farther apart move away from each other more rapidly.

Another feature of the expanding universe can be demonstrated. No matter which raisin you select, it will move away from all the other raisins. Likewise, no matter where one is located in the universe, every other galaxy—again, except those in the same cluster—will be moving away. Hubble had indeed advanced our understanding of the universe. The Hubble Space Telescope is named in his honor.

✓ **Reading Checkpoint** *What is Hubble's law?*

2 cm 5 cm

Raisin bread dough before it rises.

A

6 cm 15 cm

Raisin bread dough a few hours later.

B

Figure 22 Raisin Dough Analogy As the dough rises, raisins that were farther apart travel a greater distance in the same time as those that were closer together. Like galaxies in an expanding universe, the distant raisins move away from one another more rapidly than those that are near one another.

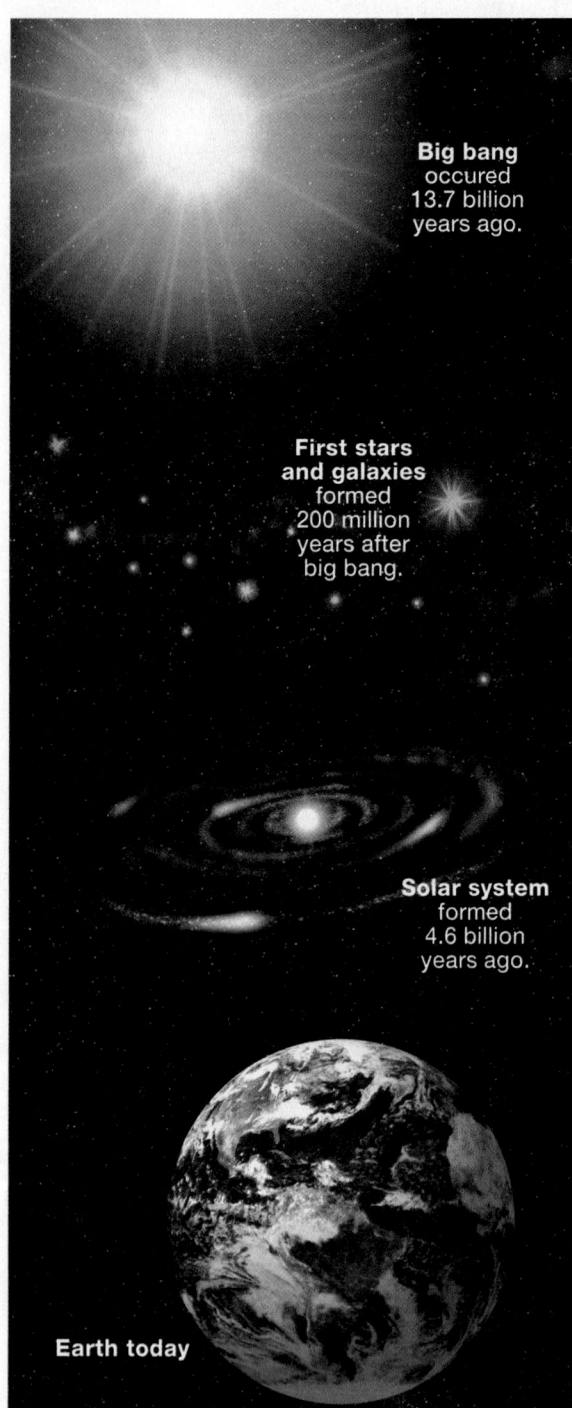

Big bang
occured
13.7 billion
years ago.

**First stars
and galaxies**
formed
200 million
years after
big bang.

Solar system
formed
4.6 billion
years ago.

Earth today

Figure 23 The Big Bang
According to the big bang theory,
the universe began 13.7 billion
years ago. Two hundred million
years later, the first stars and
galaxies began to form.

The Big Bang

How did the universe begin? Any theory about the origin of the universe must account for the fact that all distant galaxies are moving away from us. Although all galaxies appear to be moving away from Earth, it seems unlikely that our planet is the center of the universe.

A more probable explanation exists. Imagine a balloon with paper-punch dots glued to its surface. When the balloon is inflated, each dot spreads apart from every other dot. Similarly, if the universe is expanding, every galaxy would be moving away from every other galaxy.

This concept of an expanding universe led to the widely accepted big bang theory. According to the **big bang theory,** the universe began as a violent explosion from which the universe continues to expand, evolve, and cool. **The big bang theory states that at one time, the entire universe was confined to a dense, hot, supermassive ball. Then, about 13.7 billion years ago, a violent explosion occurred, hurling this material in all directions.** The big bang, as shown in Figure 23, marks the beginning of the universe. All matter and space were created at that instant.

Recall that protons, neutrons, and electrons are some of the subatomic particles that make up all matter. Scientists think that these particles formed within a few seconds from the energy of the big bang. Scientists can model conditions in the early universe, using machines called particle accelerators. These devices smash subatomic particles together at very high speeds. The collision produces other particles that may exist for only a few billionths of a second. But they give scientists a brief glimpse of matter in the early universe. After several hundred thousand years, the universe became cool enough for atoms to form. Gases in the universe continued to cool and condense. They eventually formed the stars and galaxies.

Supporting Evidence Scientists have gathered substantial evidence that supports the big bang theory. For example, the red shift of galaxies that you read about earlier indicates that the universe is still expanding. Scientists discovered a type of energy called cosmic microwave background radiation. This energy was detected as faint radio signals coming from every direction in space. Scientists think that this radiation was produced during the big bang.

 **Reading Checkpoint** *What evidence supports the big bang?*

The Big Crunch? If the universe began with a big bang, how will it end? One view is that the universe will last forever. In this scenario, the stars will slowly burn out, being replaced by an invisible form of matter and black holes that will travel outward through an endless, dark, cold universe. The other possibility is that the outward flight of the galaxies will slow and eventually stop. Gravitational contraction would follow, causing the galaxies to collapse into the high-energy, high-density mass from which the universe began. This scenario, the big bang operating in reverse, has been called the "big crunch."

Material called "dark matter" could affect the rate at which the universe expands. Dark matter is matter that cannot be directly observed because it does not give off radiation. Galaxies contain most of the visible mass of the universe, but there is evidence that what we see makes up less than one-tenth its total mass. Measurements of galactic rotation suggest that dark matter accounts for the rest of the universe's mass.

Whether the universe will expand forever or collapse upon itself depends on its average density. If the average density of the universe is more than its critical density—about one atom for every cubic meter—the gravitational field is enough to stop the outward expansion and cause the universe to contract. But, if the density of the universe is less than the critical value, it will expand forever. Current estimates place the density of the universe below the critical density, which predicts an ever-expanding, or open, universe. However, the universe is expanding even faster now than in the past. This may be due to a theoretical new force that astronomers have named "dark energy." The view currently favored by most scientists is that we live in an expanding universe with no ending point.

Section 25.3 Assessment

Reviewing Concepts

1. What is a galaxy?
2. Describe the size and structure of the Milky Way Galaxy.
3. How do galaxies differ?
4. What evidence indicates that the universe is expanding?
5. What is the big bang theory?

Critical Thinking

6. **Comparing and Contrasting** Compare and contrast the three types of galaxies.
7. **Inferring** If the universe is an open universe, what can you infer about its average density?

Writing in Science

Descriptive Paragraph Scientists are continuously searching the Milky Way Galaxy for other stars that may have planets. What types of stars would most likely have a planet or planets suitable for life as we know it? Write a paragraph describing these stars.

Astrology—Forerunner of Astronomy

Many people confuse astrology and astronomy to the point of believing these terms to be synonymous. Nothing can be further from the truth. Astronomy is a scientific investigation of the universe to discover the properties of celestial objects and the laws under which the universe operates. Astrology, on the other hand, is based on ancient superstitions that a person's actions and personality are based on the positions of the planets and stars now, and at the person's birth. Scientists do not accept astrology, regarding it as a pseudoscience ("false science"). Most people who read horoscopes do so only as a pastime and do not let them influence their daily living.

Figure 24 The Constellations of the Zodiac Earth is shown in its autumn (September) position in orbit, from which the sun is seen against the background of the constellation Virgo.

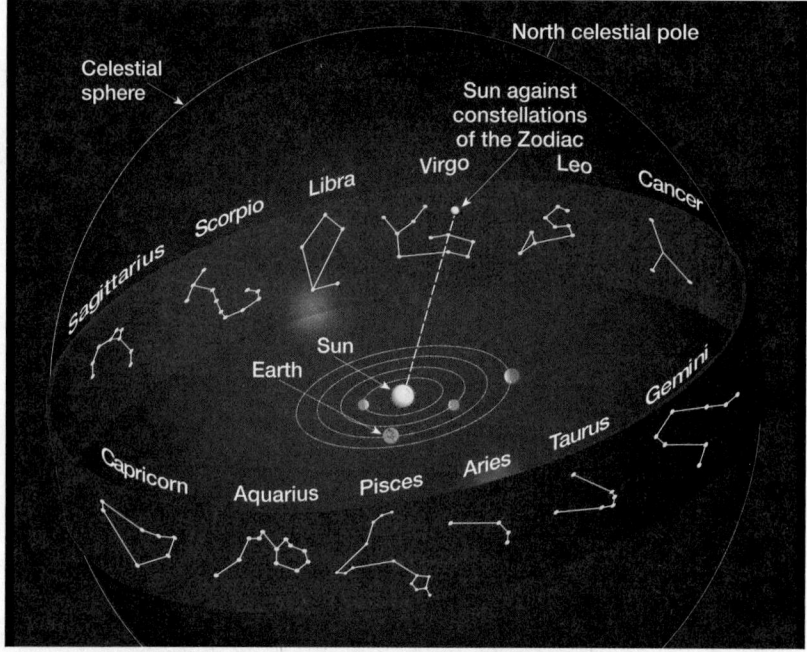

Astrology began more than 3000 years ago when the positions of the planets were plotted as they regularly migrated against the background of the "fixed" stars. Because the solar system is "flat," like a whirling Frisbee, the planets orbit the sun along nearly the same plane. Therefore, the planets, sun, and moon all appear to move along a band around the sky known as the zodiac. Because Earth's moon cycles through its phases about 12 times each year, the Babylonians divided the zodiac into 12 constellations, as shown in Figure 24. Thus, each successive full moon can be seen against the backdrop of the next constellation.

When the zodiac was first established, the vernal equinox (first day of spring) occurred when the sun was viewed against the constellation Aries. However, during each succeeding vernal equinox, the position of the sun shifts very slightly against the background of stars. Now, over 2000 years later, the vernal equinox occurs when the sun is in Pisces. In several years, the vernal equinox will occur when the sun appears against Aquarius.

Although astrology is not a science and has no basis in fact, it did contribute to the science of astronomy. The positions of the moon, sun, and planets at the time of a person's birth (sign of the zodiac) were considered to have great influence on that person's life. Even the great astronomer Kepler was required to make horoscopes part of his duties. To make horoscopes for the future, astrologers tried to predict the future positions of the celestial bodies. Thus, some of the improvements in astronomical instruments were made because of the desire for more accurate predictions of events such as eclipses, which were considered highly significant in a person's life.

Observing Stars

Throughout history, people have been recording the nightly movement of stars that results from Earth's rotation, as well as the seasonal changes in the constellations as Earth revolves around the sun. Early astronomers offered many explanations for the changes before the true nature of the motions was understood in the seventeenth century. In this lab, you'll observe and identify stars.

Problem How can you use star charts to identify constellations and track star movements?

Materials
- star charts (in the Appendix)
- penlight
- notebook

Skills Observing, Summarizing, Interpreting Data

Procedure

1. On a clear, moonless night as far from street lights as possible, go outside and observe the stars.

2. In a data table like the one below, make a list of the different colors of stars that you see.

3. Select one star that is overhead or nearly so. Observe and record its movement over a period of one hour. Also note the direction of its movement (eastward, westward).

4. Select a star chart suitable for your location and season. Locate several constellations. Sketch and label the constellations in your notebook.

5. Locate the North Star (Polaris) in the night sky. Observe the motion of stars that surround the North Star.

6. Repeat your observations several weeks later at the exact location.

Analyze and Conclude

1. **Observing** How many different colors of stars did you observe? How do these colors relate to star temperature?

2. **Interpreting Data** In which direction did the star that you observed appear to move? How is this movement related to the direction of Earth's rotation?

3. **Summarizing** Write a brief summary of the motion of the stars that surround the North Star. Be sure to include any changes you observed during your second viewing.

Go Further Find the Big Dipper, which is part of the constellation Ursa Minor. A binary star system makes up the stars of the Big Dipper. Locate the star pair and sketch them in their proper location in the Big Dipper.

Data Table				
Date	Star Colors	Star Movement	Constellations	Motions of Stars Around North Star

25.1 Properties of Stars

Key Concepts

- Color is a clue to a star's temperature.
- Binary stars can be used to determine stellar mass.
- The nearest stars have the largest parallax angles, while those of distant stars are too small to measure.
- Three factors control the apparent brightness of a star as seen from Earth: how big it is, how hot it is, and how far away it is.
- A Hertzsprung-Russell diagram shows the relationship between the absolute magnitude and temperature of stars.

Vocabulary

constellation, *p. 700;* binary star, *p. 701;* parallax, *p. 702;* light-year, *p. 702;* apparent magnitude, *p. 703;* absolute magnitude, *p. 703;* main-sequence star, *p. 704;* red giant, *p. 704;* supergiant, *p. 704;* Cepheid variable, *p. 705;* nova, *p. 705;* nebulae, *p. 706*

25.2 Stellar Evolution

Key Concepts

- When the core of a protostar has reached at least 10 million K, pressure within is so great that nuclear fusion of hydrogen begins, and a star is born.
- All stars, regardless of their size, eventually run out of fuel and collapse due to gravity.
- Stars like the sun begin as a nebula, spend much of their lives as main-sequence stars, become red giants, planetary nebulae, white dwarfs, and finally, black dwarfs.

Vocabulary

protostar, *p. 708;* supernova, *p. 711;* white dwarf, *p. 712;* neutron star, *p. 713;* pulsar, *p. 713;* black hole, *p. 714*

25.3 The Universe

Key Concepts

- The Milky Way is a large spiral galaxy whose disk is about 100,000 light-years wide and about 10,000 light-years thick at the nucleus.
- In addition to shape and size, one of the major differences among different types of galaxies is the age of their stars.
- The red shifts of distant galaxies indicate that the universe is expanding.
- The big bang theory states that at one time, the entire universe was confined to a dense, hot, supermassive ball. Then, about 13.7 billion years ago, a violent explosion occurred, hurling this material in all directions.

Vocabulary

galaxy, *p. 715;* cluster, *p. 718;* Hubble's law, *p. 719;* big bang theory, *p. 720*

Thinking Visually

Concept Map Use information from the chapter to complete the concept map below.

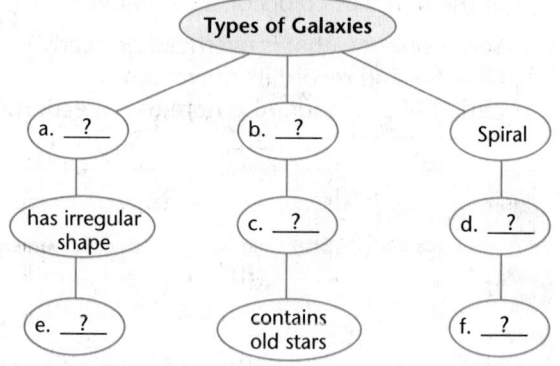

Reviewing Content

Choose the letter that best answers the question or completes the statement.

1. Distances to stars are usually expressed in units called
   - **a.** miles.
   - **b.** kilometers.
   - **c.** light-years.
   - **d.** astronomical units.

2. The measure of a star's brightness is called its
   - **a.** parallax.
   - **b.** color index.
   - **c.** visual binary.
   - **d.** magnitude.

3. Distances to nearby stars can be determined from
   - **a.** fluorescence.
   - **b.** stellar parallax.
   - **c.** stellar mass.
   - **d.** emission nebulae.

4. Which color stars have the highest surface temperature?
   - **a.** red
   - **b.** orange
   - **c.** yellow
   - **d.** blue

5. Which type of star is the sun?
   - **a.** black hole
   - **b.** black dwarf
   - **c.** main sequence
   - **d.** red giant

6. What happens to a sun-like star after it has used up all the fuel in its core?
   - **a.** supernova
   - **b.** neutron star
   - **c.** red giant
   - **d.** nebula

7. Which object has such a strong surface gravity that light cannot escape it?
   - **a.** black hole
   - **b.** black dwarf
   - **c.** red giant
   - **d.** white dwarf

8. Stars that are composed of matter in which electrons have combined with protons are called
   - **a.** black holes.
   - **b.** neutron stars.
   - **c.** red giants.
   - **d.** white dwarfs.

9. Hubble's law states that galaxies are retreating from Earth at a speed that is proportional to their
   - **a.** distance from Earth.
   - **b.** volume.
   - **c.** mass.
   - **d.** temperature.

10. What theory states that the universe began in a violent explosion?
    - **a.** the big crunch
    - **b.** the Doppler effect
    - **c.** Hubble's law
    - **d.** the big bang

Understanding Concepts

11. Which property of a star can be determined by its color?

12. About how many stars in our galaxy are estimated to occur in pairs or multiples?

13. What is parallax?

14. Compare and contrast apparent magnitude and absolute magnitude.

15. What color is the most massive type of main-sequence star? The least massive?

16. At what temperature does nuclear fusion begin?

17. A stable main-sequence star is balanced between which two forces?

18. What element is the main fuel for main-sequence stars? For red giants?

19. What type of stars end their lives as supernovae?

20. What is a pulsar?

21. How long does it take our solar system to orbit the Milky Way Galaxy?

22. More distant galaxies have greater red shifts. What does this indicate about the universe?

23. What is cosmic microwave background radiation?

Critical Thinking

24. **Explaining** Why are radio telescopes instead of optical telescopes used to determine the structure of the Milky Way Galaxy?

25. **Drawing Conclusions** Imagine that you are a scientist studying the birth of stars in a spiral galaxy. Which part of the galaxy would you study? Explain your answer.

Analyzing Data

Use the diagram below to answer Questions 26–28.

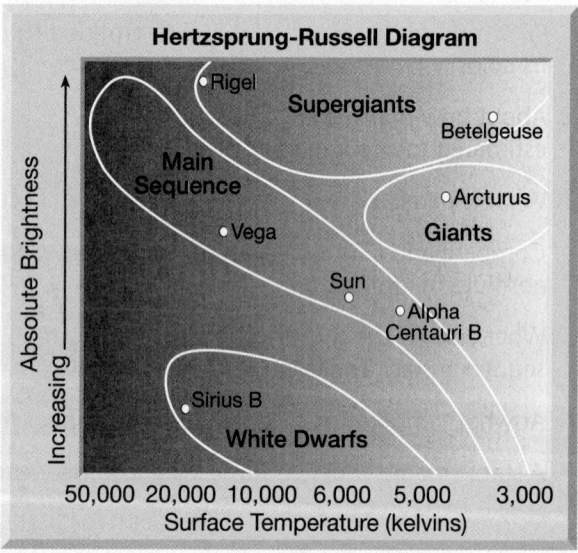

Hertzsprung-Russell Diagram

26. **Interpreting Graphs** What is the brightest star in the diagram? The hottest?

27. **Analyzing Data** How does the absolute brightness of white dwarfs compare with that of supergiants?

28. **Summarizing** What is the relationship between absolute brightness and temperature for a main-sequence star?

Concepts in Action

29. **Explaining** How can a binary star system be used to determine a star's mass?

30. **Inferring** Would you use parallax to determine the distance to a faraway star? Why or why not?

31. **Calculating** The closest star to the sun, Proxima Centauri, is 4.3 light-years away. How many kilometers from the sun is Proxima Centauri?

Performance-Based Assessment

Using Models Use materials provided by your teacher to construct a scale model of the Milky Way Galaxy. Before you begin, be sure to develop a workable scale for your model.

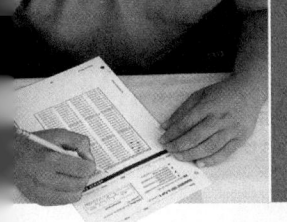

Standardized Test Prep

Sequencing a Series of Events
When a test question requires you to sequence a series of events, first try to predict the correct sequence before looking at the answer choices. Then compare your sequence to those listed. Be sure to pay attention to qualifiers in the question, such as *first, earliest, increasing,* or *decreasing,* as these may help you eliminate choices.

Which sequence of events describes the big bang theory? Begin with the earliest event.

(A) Explosion; atoms form; stars form; all matter concentrated at a single point.
(B) All matter concentrated at a single point; explosion; atoms form; stars form.
(C) Explosion; stars form; all matter concentrated at a single point; atoms form.
(D) Stars form; atoms form; all matter concentrated at a single point; explosion.

(Answer: B)

Choose the letter that best answers the question or completes the statement.

1. What can you estimate about a Cepheid variable if you know its absolute magnitude and apparent magnitude?
(A) mass
(B) distance
(C) temperature
(D) volume

2. Based on the red shifts of distant galaxies, astronomers conclude that
(A) Earth is in the center of the universe.
(B) the universe is contracting.
(C) the universe is expanding.
(D) new galaxies are continually being added to the universe.

Answer the following questions in complete sentences.

3. What types of stars are thought to be the remnants of supernova explosions?

4. How do the lives of the most massive stars end? What are the two possible products of this event?

Use the illustration below to answer Questions 5 and 6.

5. Sequence the steps in the evolution of a medium-mass star, such as the sun.

6. At which stage in its evolution is the star the hottest? The brightest?

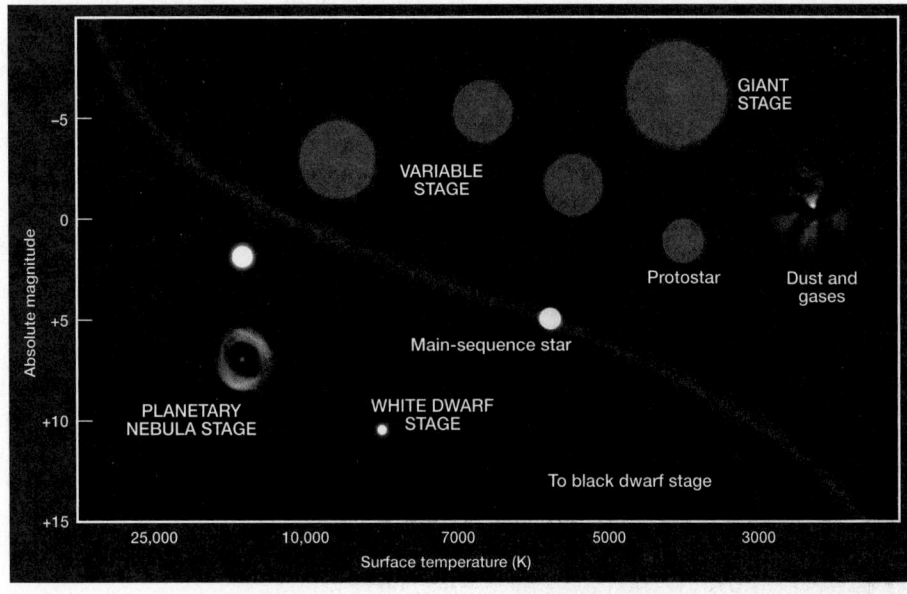

Basic Process Skills

During a science course, you often carry out some short lab activities as well as more detailed experiments. Here are some skills that you will use as you work.

Observing

In every science activity, you make a variety of observations. **Observing** is using one or more of the five senses to gather information. Many observations involve the senses of sight, hearing, touch, and smell.

Sometimes you will use tools that increase the power of your senses or make observations more precise. For example, hand lenses enable you to see things in greater detail. Tools may help you eliminate personal opinions or preferences.

In science it is customary to record your observations at the time they are made, usually by writing or drawing in a notebook. You may occasionally make records by using computers, cameras, videotapes, and other tools. As a rule, scientists keep complete accounts of their observations, often using tables to help organize their observations in a regular way.

Inferring

In science as in everyday life, observations are usually followed by inferences. **Inferring** is interpreting an observation or statement based on prior knowledge. For example, you can make several observations using the strobe photograph below. You can observe that the

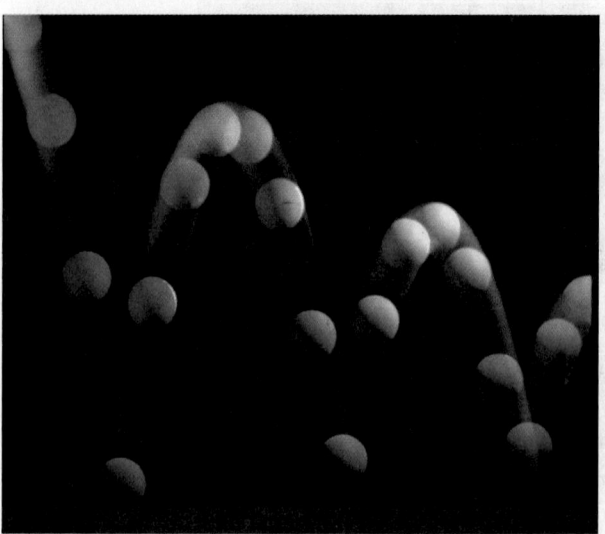

ball is moving. Based on the motion of the ball, you might infer that the ball was thrown downward at an angle by an experimenter. In making that inference, you would use your knowledge about the motion of projectiles. Someone who knew more about projectile motion might infer that the ball loses energy with each bounce. That is why the height decreases with each bounce.

Notice that an inference is an act of reasoning, not a fact. That means an inference may be logical but not true. It is often necessary to gather further information before you can be confident that an inference is correct. For scientists, that information may come from further observations or from research into the work done by others.

Comparing Observations and Inferences	
Sample Observation	**Sample Inference**
The ball moves less and less vertical distance in the time between each flash of the strobe light.	Gravity is slowing down the ball's upward motion.
The ball moves the same distance to the right in the time between each flash of the strobe light.	Air resistance is so small that it does not slow down the ball's horizontal motion.

Predicting

People often make predictions, but their statements about the future could be either guesses or inferences. In science, a **prediction** is an inference about a future event based on evidence, experience, or knowledge. For example, you can say, *On the first day next month, it will be sunny all day.* If your statement is based on evidence of weather patterns in the area, then the prediction is scientific. If the statement was made without considering any evidence, it's just a guess.

Predictions play a major role in science because they offer scientists a way to test ideas. If scientists understand an event or the properties of a particular object, they should be able to make accurate predictions about that event or object. Some predictions can be tested simply by making observations. For others, carefully designed experiments are needed.

Measuring

Measurements are important in science because they provide specific information and help observers avoid bias. **Measuring** is comparing an object or process to a standard. Scientists use a common set of standards, called the International System of Units, abbreviated as SI (for its French name, *Système International d'Unités*).

What distance does the ball travel in each time interval in the strobe photograph? You can make measurements on the photograph to make more precise statements about the ball's motion.

Calculating

Once scientists have made measurements, calculations are a very important part of analyzing data. How fast is a ball moving? You could directly measure the speed of a ball using probeware such as a motion sensor. But you can also calculate the speed using distance and time measurements. **Calculating** is a process in which a person uses mathematical operations to manipulate numbers and symbols.

Classifying

Classifying is grouping items according to some organizing idea or system. Classifying occurs in every branch of science but it's especially important in chemistry because there are so many different ways that elements can combine to form compounds.

Sometimes you place objects into groups using an established system. Other times you create a system by observing a variety of objects and identifying their properties. For example, you could group household cleaners into those that are abrasive and those that are not. Or you could categorize cleaners as toxic or non-toxic. Ammonia is toxic, whereas vinegar is not.

Using Tables and Graphs

Scientists represent and organize data in tables and graphs as part of experiments and other activities. Organizing data in tables and graphs makes it easier to see patterns in data. Scientists analyze and interpret data tables and graphs to determine the relationship of one variable to another and to make predictions based on the data.

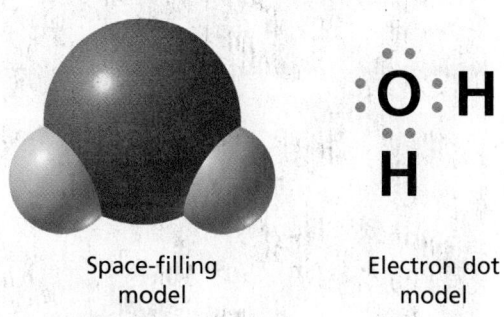

Space-filling model   Electron dot model

Using Models

Some cities refuse to approve new tall buildings if they would cast shadows on existing parks. As architects plan buildings in such locations, they use models to show where a proposed building's shadow will fall at any time of day at any season of the year. A **model** is a mental or physical representation of an object, process, or event. In science, models are usually made to help people understand natural objects and the processes that affect these objects.

Models can be varied. Mental models, such as mathematical equations, can represent some kinds of ideas or processes. For example, the equation for the surface area of a sphere can model the surface of Earth, enabling scientists to determine its size. Models can be two-dimensional (flat) or three-dimensional (having depth). In chemistry, for example, there are several ways to model the arrangement of atoms in a molecule. Two models for a water molecule are shown above. The electron dot model is two-dimensional. It has the advantage of clearly showing how electrons are shared among atoms in the molecule. The space-filling model cannot show the number of electrons inside the atoms or between atoms, but it does show the arrangement of atoms in space.

Experimental Methods

A science experiment is a procedure designed so that there is only one logical explanation for the results. Some types of experiments are fairly simple to design. Others may require ingenious problem solving.

Posing Questions

As a gardener harvested corn in her vegetable garden, she noticed that on one side of the garden the plants produced very few ears of corn. The gardener wondered, *Why didn't the plants on one side of the garden produce as much corn?*

An experiment may begin when someone like the gardener asks a specific question or wants to solve a particular problem. Sometimes the original question leads directly to an experiment, but often researchers need to restate the problem before they can design an appropriate experiment. The gardener's question about the corn, for example, is too broad to be tested by an experiment, since there are so many possible different answers. To narrow the topic, the gardener might think about several related questions: *Were the seeds the same on both sides of the garden? Was the sunlight the same? Is there something different about the soil?*

Formulating Hypotheses

In science, a question about an event is answered by developing a possible explanation called a **hypothesis**. The hypothesis may be developed after long thought and research or come to a scientist "in a flash." To be useful, a hypothesis must lead to predictions that can be tested.

In this case, the gardener decided to focus on the quality of the soil on each side of her garden. She did some tests and discovered that the soil had a lower pH on the side where the plants did not produce well. That led her to propose this hypothesis: *If the pH of the soil is too low, the plants will produce less corn.* The next step is to make a prediction based on the hypothesis, for example, *If the pH of the soil is increased using lime, the plants will yield more corn.* Notice that the prediction suggests the basic idea for an experiment.

Designing Experiments

A carefully designed experiment can test a prediction in a reliable way, ruling out other possible explanations. As scientists plan their experimental procedures, they pay particular attention to the variables that must be controlled and the procedures that must be defined.

The gardener decided to study three groups of plants:

Group 1—20 plants on the side of the garden with a low pH;

Group 2—20 plants on the side of the garden with a low pH, but with lime added; and

Group 3—20 plants on the side of the garden with a high pH.

Controlling Variables

As researchers design an experiment, they identify the **variables**, factors that can change. Some common variables include mass, volume, time, temperature, light, and the presence or absence of specific materials. An experiment involves three categories of variables. The factor that scientists purposely change is called the **manipulated variable**. The factor that may change because of the manipulated variable and that scientists want to observe is called the **responding variable**. And the factors that scientists purposely keep the same are called the **controlled variables**. Controlling variables helps make researchers confident that the observed changes in the responding variable are due to changes in the manipulated variable.

For the gardener, the manipulated variable is the pH of the soil. The responding variable is the number of ears of corn produced by the plants. Among the variables that must be controlled are the amount of sunlight received each day, the time of year when seeds are planted, and the amount of water the plants receive.

When you read about certain experiments, you may come across references to a control group (or "a control") and the experimental groups. All of the groups in an experiment are treated exactly the same except for the manipulated variable. In an experimental group, the manipulated variable is being changed. The control group is used as a standard of comparison. It may consist of objects that are not changed in any way or objects that are being treated in the usual way. For example, in the gardener's experiment, Group 1 is the control group, because for these plants nothing is done to change the low pH of the soil.

Forming Operational Definitions

In an experiment, it is often necessary to define one or more variables explicitly so that any researcher could measure or control the variable in exactly the same way. An **operational definition** describes how a particular variable is to be measured or how a term is to be defined. In this context, the term operational means "describing what to do."

The gardener, for example, has to decide exactly how much lime to add to the soil. Can lime be added after the seeds are planted or only before planting? At what pH should no more lime be added to the soil? In this case, the gardener decided to add lime only before planting, and to add enough lime to make the pH equal in Groups 2 and 3.

Analyzing Data

The observations and measurements that are made in an experiment are called **data**. Scientists customarily record data in an orderly way. When an experiment is done, the researcher analyzes the data for trends or patterns, often by doing calculations or making graphs, to determine whether the results support the hypothesis.

For example, the gardener regularly measured and recorded data such as the soil moisture, daily sunlight, and pH of the soil. She found that the soil pH in Groups 2 and 3 started the same, but after two months the soil pH for Group 3 was a little higher than the soil pH for Group 2.

After harvesting the corn, the gardener recorded the numbers of ears of corn produced by each plant. She totaled the number of ears for each group. Her results were the following.

Group 1: 67 ears of corn

Group 2: 102 ears of corn

Group 3: 126 ears of corn

The overall trend was clear: The gardener's prediction was correct.

Drawing Conclusions

Based on whether the results confirm or refute the hypothesis, researchers make a final statement that summarizes the experiment. That final statement is called the **conclusion**. For example, the gardener's conclusion was, *Adding lime to soil with a low pH will improve the production of corn plants.*

Communicating Results

When an experiment has been completed, one or more events may follow. Researchers may repeat the experiment to verify the results. They may publish the experiment so that others can evaluate and replicate their procedures. They may compare their conclusion with the discoveries made by other scientists. And they may raise new questions that lead to new experiments. For example, *Why does the pH level decrease over time when soil is treated with lime?*

Evaluating and Revising

Scientists must be flexible about the conclusions drawn from an experiment. Further research may help confirm the results of the experiment or make it necessary to revise the initial conclusions. For example, a new experiment may show that lime can be effective only when certain microbes are present in the soil. Scientists continuously evaluate and revise experiments based on the findings in new research.

Science Safety

Laboratory work can be exciting, but it can be dangerous if you don't follow safety rules. Ask your teacher to explain any rules you don't understand. Always pay attention to safety symbols and **CAUTION** statements.

General Safety Rules and First Aid

1. Read all directions for an experiment several times. Follow the directions exactly as they are written. If you are in doubt, ask your teacher for assistance.
2. Never perform unauthorized or unsupervised labs, or handle equipment without specific permission.
3. When you design an experiment, do not start until your teacher has approved your plan.
4. If a lab includes physical activity, use caution to avoid injuring yourself or others. Tell your teacher if there is a reason that you should not participate.
5. Never eat, drink, or bring food into the laboratory.
6. Report all accidents to your teacher immediately.
7. Learn the correct ways to deal with a burn, a cut, and acid splashed in your eyes or on your skin.
8. Be aware of the location of the first-aid kit. Your teacher should administer any required first aid.
9. Report any fire to your teacher immediately. Find out the location of the fire extinguisher, the fire alarm, and the phone where emergency numbers are listed.

Dress Code

10. Always wear safety goggles to protect your eyes when working in the lab. Avoid wearing contact lenses. If you must wear contact lenses, ask your teacher what precautions you should take.
11. Wear a laboratory apron to protect your skin and clothing from harmful chemicals or hot materials.
12. Wear disposable plastic gloves to protect yourself from contact with chemicals that can be harmful. Keep your hands away from your face. Dispose of gloves according to your teacher's instructions.
13. Tie back long hair and loose clothing. Remove any jewelry that could contact chemicals or flames.

Heating and Fire Safety

14. Hot plates, hot water, and hot glassware can cause burns. Never touch hot objects with your bare hands. Use an oven mitt or other hand protection.
15. Use a clamp or tongs to hold hot objects. Test an object by first holding the back of your hand near it. If you feel heat on the back of your hand, the object may be too hot to handle.
16. Tie back long hair and loose clothing, and put on safety goggles before using a burner. Follow instructions from your teacher for lighting and extinguishing burners. If the flame leaps out of a burner as you are lighting it, turn the gas off. Never leave a flame unattended or reach across a flame. Make sure your work area is not cluttered with materials.
17. If flammable materials are present, make sure there are no flames, sparks, or exposed sources of heat.
18. Never heat a chemical without your teacher's permission. Chemicals that are harmless when cool can be dangerous when heated. When heating a test tube, point the opening away from you and others in case the contents splash or boil out of the test tube.
19. Never heat a closed container. Expanding hot gases may cause the container to explode.

Using Electricity Safely

20. To avoid an electric shock, never use electrical equipment near water, or when the equipment or your hands are wet. Use ground fault circuit interrupter (GFCI) outlets if you or your equipment may come into contact with moisture.
21. Use only sockets that accept a three-prong plug. Never use two-prong extension cords or adapters. When removing an electrical plug from a socket or extension cord, grasp the plug, not the cord.
22. Disconnect equipment that is not in use. Be sure cords are untangled and cannot trip anyone.
23. Do not use damaged electrical equipment. Look for dangerous conditions such as bare wires or frayed cords. Report damaged equipment immediately.

Using Glassware Safely

24. Handle fragile glassware, such as thermometers, test tubes, and beakers, with care. Do not touch broken glass. Notify your teacher if glassware breaks. Never use chipped or cracked glassware.
25. Never force glass tubing into a stopper. Your teacher will demonstrate the proper methods.
26. Never heat glassware that is not thoroughly dry. Use a wire screen to protect glassware from flames.
27. Hot glassware may not appear hot. Never pick up glassware without first checking to see if it is hot.
28. Never eat or drink from laboratory glassware.

Using Chemicals Safely

29. Do not let any corrosive or poisonous chemicals get on your skin or clothing, or in your eyes. When working with poisonous or irritating vapors, work in a well-ventilated area and wash your hands thoroughly after completing the activity.
30. Never test for an odor unless instructed by your teacher. Avoid inhaling a vapor directly. Use a wafting motion to direct vapor toward your nose.
31. Never mix chemicals "for the fun of it." You might produce a dangerous, possibly explosive substance.
32. Never touch, taste, or smell a chemical that you do not know for certain to be harmless.
33. Use only those chemicals listed in an investigation. Keep the lids on the containers when chemicals are not being used. To avoid contamination, never return chemicals to their original containers.
34. Take extreme care not to spill any chemicals. If a spill occurs, immediately ask your teacher about the proper cleanup procedure. Dispose of all chemicals as instructed by your teacher.
35. Be careful when working with acids or bases. Pour these chemicals over the sink, not over your workbench. If an acid or base gets on your skin or clothing, rinse it off with plenty of cold water. Immediately notify your teacher about an acid or base spill.
36. When diluting an acid, pour the acid into water. Never pour water into the acid.

Using Sharp Instruments

37. Use sharp instruments only as directed. Scissors, scalpels, pins, and knives are sharp and can cut or puncture your skin. Always direct sharp edges and points away from yourself and others.
38. Notify your teacher immediately if you cut yourself when in the laboratory.

End-of-Experiment Rules

39. All chemicals and any other materials used in the laboratory must be disposed of safely. Follow your teacher's instructions.
40. Clean up your work area and return all equipment to its proper place. Thoroughly clean glassware before putting it away.
41. Wash your hands thoroughly with soap, or detergent, and warm water. Lather both sides of your hands and between your fingers. Rinse well.
42. Check that all burners are off and the gas supply for the burners is turned off.

Safety Symbols

 General Safety Awareness
Follow all safety instructions.

 Physical Safety
Use caution in physical activities.

 Safety Goggles
Always wear goggles in the laboratory.

 Lab Apron
Always wear a lab apron in the laboratory.

 Plastic Gloves
Protect your hands from unsafe chemicals.

 Heating
Be careful using sources of heat.

 Heat-Resistant Gloves
Do not touch hot objects with bare hands.

 Flames
Work carefully around open flames.

 No Flames
Flammable materials may be present.

 Electric Shock
Take precautions to avoid electric shock.

 Fragile Glassware
Handle glassware carefully.

 Corrosive Chemical
Work carefully with corrosive chemicals.

 Poison
Avoid contact with poisonous chemicals.

 Fumes
Avoid inhaling dangerous vapors.

 Sharp Object
Use caution with sharp or pointed tools.

 Disposal
Follow instructions for disposal.

 Hand Washing
Wash your hands before leaving the lab.

Reading and Study Skills

At the beginning of each section, you will find a reading strategy to help you study. Each strategy uses a graphic organizer to help you stay organized. The following strategies and graphic organizers are used throughout the text.

Reading Strategies

Using Prior Knowledge

This strategy helps you think about your own experience before you read a section. Research has shown that you learn new material better if you can relate it to something you already know.

Previewing

Previewing a lesson can give you a sense of how the textbook is organized and what lies ahead. One technique is to look at the section topics (in green and blue type). You also can preview by reading captions. Sometimes previewing helps you simply because you find out a topic isn't as hard as you thought it might be.

Predicting

You can preview a section and then make a prediction. For example, you might predict the meaning of an important concept. Then, as you read, check to see if your prediction was correct. Often you find out that you knew more about a topic than you realized.

Building Vocabulary

Start building new vocabulary by previewing a section and listing boldface terms you don't recognize. Then look for each term as you read. Writing a sentence with a term, and defining a term in your own words are two techniques that will help you remember definitions.

Identifying the Main Idea

The key symbols next to boldface sentences identify the main ideas in a section. You can use topic sentences to find the main idea in a paragraph. Often, a topic sentence is the first or second sentence in a paragraph.

Identifying Cause and Effect

Cause-and-effect relationships are very important in science. A flowchart will help you identify cause-and-effect relationships as you read about a process.

Comparing and Contrasting

Comparing and contrasting can help you understand how concepts are related. Comparing is identifying both similarities and differences, while contrasting focuses on the differences. Compare-and-contrast tables and Venn diagrams work best with this strategy.

Sequencing

When you sequence events, it helps you to visualize the steps in a process and to remember the order in which they occur. Sequences often involve cause-and-effect relationships. Use flowcharts for linear sequences and cycle diagrams for repeating sequences.

Relating Text and Figures

You can use diagrams and photographs to focus on the essential concepts in a section. Then find text that extends the information in the figures. You can also reinforce concepts by comparing different figures.

Summarizing

Summarizing requires you to identify key ideas and state them briefly in your own words. You will remember the content of an entire section better even if you summarize only a portion of the section.

Outlining

You can quickly organize an outline by writing down the green and blue headings in a section. Then add phrases or sentences from the boldface sentences to expand the outline with the most important concepts.

Monitoring Your Understanding

You can evaluate your progress with graphic organizers such as a Know-Write-Learn (KWL) table. To make a KWL table, construct a table with three columns, labeled K, W, and L. Before you read, write what you already know in the first column (K). In the middle column, write what you want to learn (W). After you read, write what you learned (L).

Graphic Organizers

Concept Maps and Web Diagrams

A **concept map** is a diagram that contains concept words in ovals and connects the ovals with linking words. Often the most general concept is placed at the top of the map. The content of the other ovals becomes more specific as you move away from the main concept. Linking words are written on a line between two ovals.

A **web diagram** is a type of concept map that shows how several ideas relate to one central idea. Each subtopic may also link to subtopics, creating the visual effect of a spider web. Linking words are usually not included.

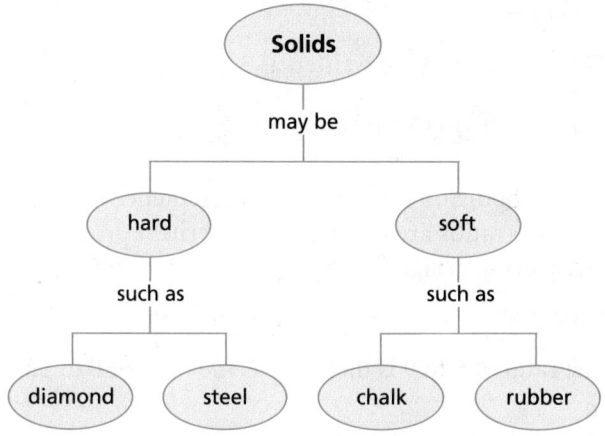

Compare-and-Contrast Tables

A **compare-and-contrast table** is a way of showing the similarities and differences between two or more objects or processes. The table provides an organized framework for making comparisons based on specific characteristics.

The items to be compared are usually column headings across the top of the table. Characteristics for comparison are listed in the first column. You complete the table by filling in information for each item.

Compare-and-Contrast Table		
Contents	**Book**	**CD-ROM**
Paper pages	Yes	No
Photographs	Yes	Yes
Videos	No	Yes

Venn Diagrams

A **Venn diagram** consists of two or more ovals that overlap. Each oval represents a particular object or idea. Unique characteristics are shown in the part of each oval that does not overlap. Shared characteristics are shown in the area of overlap.

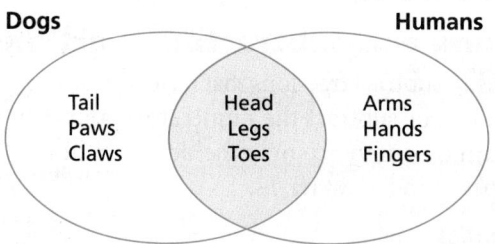

Flowcharts

A **flowchart** is used to represent the order in which a set of events occurs. Each step in the sequence is described in a box. Each box is linked to the next box with an arrow. The flowchart shows a sequence from beginning to end.

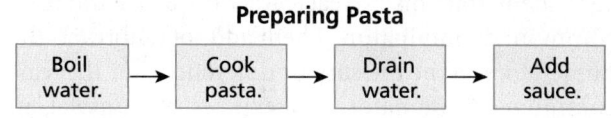

Cycle Diagrams

A **cycle diagram** shows boxes representing a cyclical sequence of events. As in a flowchart, boxes are linked with arrows, but the sequence does not have a beginning or end. The boxes are usually arranged in a clockwise circle.

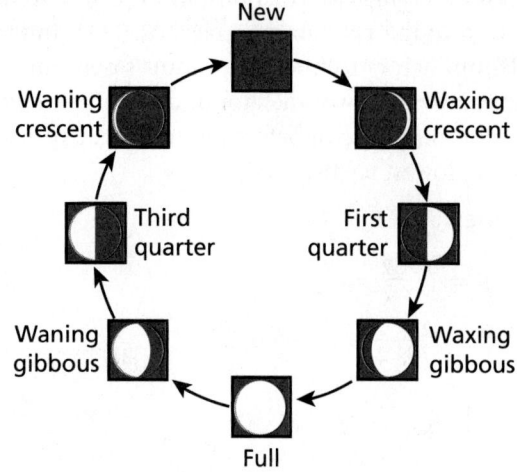

Throughout your study of science, you will often need to solve math problems. This appendix is designed to help you quickly review the basic math skills you will use most often.

Fractions

Adding and Subtracting Fractions

To add or subtract fractions that have the same denominator, add or subtract the numerators, and then write the sum or difference over the denominator. Express the answer in lowest terms.

Examples

$$\frac{3}{10} + \frac{1}{10} = \frac{3+1}{10} = \frac{4}{10} = \frac{2}{5}$$

$$\frac{5}{7} - \frac{2}{7} = \frac{5-2}{7} = \frac{3}{7}$$

To add or subtract fractions with different denominators, find the least common denominator. Write an equivalent fraction for each fraction using the least common denominator. Then add or subtract the numerators. Write the sum or difference over the least common denominator and express the answer in lowest terms.

Examples

$$\frac{1}{3} + \frac{3}{5} = \frac{5}{15} + \frac{9}{15} = \frac{5+9}{15} = \frac{14}{15}$$

$$\frac{7}{8} - \frac{1}{4} = \frac{7}{8} - \frac{2}{8} = \frac{7-2}{8} = \frac{5}{8}$$

Multiplying Fractions

When multiplying two fractions, multiply the numerators to find the product's numerator. Then multiply the denominators to find the product's denominator. It helps to divide any numerator or denominator by the greatest common factor before multiplying. Express the answer in lowest terms.

Examples

$$\frac{3}{5} \times \frac{2}{7} = \frac{3 \times 2}{5 \times 7} = \frac{6}{35}$$

$$\frac{4}{14} \times \frac{6}{9} = \frac{2 \times 2}{7 \times 2} \times \frac{2 \times 3}{3 \times 3} = \frac{2 \times 2}{7 \times 3} = \frac{4}{21}$$

Dividing Fractions

To divide one fraction by another, invert and multiply. Express the answer in lowest terms.

Examples

$$\frac{2}{5} \div \frac{3}{4} = \frac{2}{5} \times \frac{4}{3} = \frac{2 \times 4}{5 \times 3} = \frac{8}{15}$$

$$\frac{9}{16} \div \frac{5}{8} = \frac{9}{16} \times \frac{8}{5} = \frac{9 \times 1}{2 \times 5} = \frac{9}{10}$$

Ratios and Proportions

A ratio compares two numbers or quantities. A ratio is often written as a fraction expressed in lowest terms. A ratio also may be written with a colon.

Examples

The ratio of 3 to 4 is written as 3 to 4, $\frac{3}{4}$, or 3 : 4.

The ratio of 10 to 5 is written as $\frac{10}{5} = \frac{2}{1}$, or 2 : 1.

A proportion is a mathematical sentence that states that two ratios are equivalent. To write a proportion, place an equal sign between the two equivalent ratios.

Examples

The ratio of 6 to 9 is the same as the ratio of 8 to 12.

$$\frac{6}{9} = \frac{8}{12}$$

The ratio of 2 to 4 is the same as the ratio of 7 to 14.

$$\frac{2}{4} = \frac{7}{14}$$

You can set up a proportion to determine an unknown quantity. Use x to represent the unknown. To find the value of x, cross multiply and then divide both sides of the equation by the number that comes before x.

Example

Two out of five students have blue notebooks. If this same ratio exists in a class of twenty students, how many students in the class have blue notebooks?

$$\frac{2}{5} = \frac{x}{20} \qquad \leftarrow \textbf{Cross multiply.}$$

$$2 \times 20 = 5x \qquad \leftarrow \textbf{Divide.}$$

$$8 = x$$

Percents and Decimals

To convert a percent to a decimal value, write the number without the percent sign and move the decimal point two places to the left. Add a zero before the decimal point.

Examples

$$38\% = 0.38$$
$$13.92\% = 0.1392$$

You can convert a decimal value to a percent value by moving the decimal point two places to the right and adding the percent sign.

Examples

$$0.46 = 46\%$$
$$0.8215 = 82.15\%$$

Exponents

A base is a number that is used as a factor. An exponent is a number that tells how many times the base is to be used as a factor.

Example

$$2^5 = 2 \times 2 \times 2 \times 2 \times 2 = 32$$

A power is any number that can be expressed as a product in which all of the factors are the same. Any number raised to the zero power is 1. Any number raised to the first power is that number. The only exception is the number 0, which is zero regardless of the power it is raised to.

Exponents	
Powers of 2	**Powers of 10**
$2^2 = 4$	$10^2 = 100$
$2^1 = 2$	$10^1 = 10$
$2^0 = 1$	$10^0 = 1$
$2^{-1} = \frac{1}{2}$	$10^{-1} = \frac{1}{10}$
$2^{-2} = \frac{1}{4}$	$10^{-2} = \frac{1}{100}$

Multiplying Exponents

To multiply exponential expressions with the same base, add the exponents. The general expression for exponents with the same base is $x^a \times x^b = x^{a+b}$.

Example

$$3^2 \times 3^4 = (3 \times 3) \times (3 \times 3 \times 3 \times 3) = 3^6 = 729$$

To raise a power to a power, keep the base and multiply the exponents. The general expression is $(x^a)^b = x^{ab}$.

Example

$$(3^2)^3 = (3^2) \times (3^2) \times (3^2) = 3^6 = 729$$

To raise a product to a power, raise each factor to the power. The general expression is $(xy)^n = x^n y^n$.

Example

$$(3 \times 9)^2 = 3^2 \times 9^2 = 9 \times 81 = 729$$

Dividing Exponents

To divide exponential expressions with the same base, keep the base and subtract the exponents. The general expression is:

$$\frac{x^a}{x^b} = x^{a-b}$$

Example

$$\frac{5^6}{5^4} = 5^{6-4} = 5^2 = 25$$

When the exponent of the denominator is greater than the exponent of the numerator, the exponent of the result is negative. A negative exponent follows the general expression:

$$x^{-n} = \frac{1}{x^n}$$

Example

$$2^3 \div 2^5 = 2^{3-5} = 2^{-2} = \frac{1}{2^2} = \frac{1}{4}$$

Math Skills

Scientific Notation

Scientific notation is used to express very large numbers or very small numbers. To convert a large number to scientific notation, move the decimal point to the left until it is located to the right of the first nonzero number. The number of places that you move the decimal point becomes the positive exponent of 10.

Example

$18{,}930{,}000 = 1.893 \times 10^7$

To write a number less than 1 in scientific notation, move the decimal point to the right of the first nonzero number. Use the number of places you moved the decimal point as the negative exponent of 10.

Example

$0.0027 = \dfrac{2.7}{10 \times 10 \times 10} = 2.7 \times 10^{-3}$

Adding and Subtracting

To add or subtract numbers in scientific notation, the exponents must be the same. If they are different, rewrite one of the numbers to make the exponents the same. Then write the answer so that only one number is to the left of the decimal point.

Example

$3.20 \times 10^3 + 5.1 \times 10^2$

$\quad = 32.0 \times 10^2 + 5.1 \times 10^2$
$\quad = 37.1 \times 10^2$
$\quad = 3.71 \times 10^3$

Multiplying and Dividing

To multiply or divide numbers in scientific notation, the exponents are added or subtracted.

Examples

$(1.2 \times 10^3) \times (3.4 \times 10^4) = (4.1 \times 10^{3+4})$
$\qquad\qquad\qquad\qquad\qquad = 4.1 \times 10^7$

$(5.0 \times 10^9) \div (2.5 \times 10^6) = (2.0 \times 10^{9-6})$
$\qquad\qquad\qquad\qquad\qquad = 2.0 \times 10^3$

Significant Figures

When measurements are combined in calculations, the uncertainty of each measurement must be correctly reflected in the final result. The digits that are accurate in the answer are called significant figures. When the result of a calculation has more significant figures than needed, the result must be rounded off. If the first digit after the last significant digit is less than 5, round down. If the first digit after the last significant digit is 5 or more, round up.

Examples

1577 rounded to three significant figures is 1580.
1574 rounded to three significant figures is 1570.
2.458462 rounded to three significant figures is 2.46.
2.458462 rounded to four significant figures is 2.458.

Adding and Subtracting

In addition and subtraction, the number of significant figures in the answer depends on the number with the largest uncertainty.

Example

$$
\begin{array}{r}
25.34 \text{ g} \\
152 \text{ g} \\
+ \quad 4.009 \text{ g} \\
\hline
181 \text{ g}
\end{array}
$$

The measurement with the largest uncertainty is 152 g and it is measured to the nearest gram. Therefore, the answer is given to the nearest gram.

Multiplying and Dividing

In multiplication and division, the measurement with the smallest number of significant figures determines the number of significant figures in the answer.

Example

$\text{Density} = \dfrac{\text{Mass}}{\text{Volume}}$

$\qquad\quad = \dfrac{20.79 \text{ g}}{5.5 \text{ mL}}$

$\qquad\quad = 3.8 \text{ g/mL}$

Because 5.5 mL has only two significant figures, the answer must be rounded to two significant figures.

Formulas and Equations

An equation is a mathematical sentence that contains one or more variables and one or more mathematical operators (such as $+$, $-$, $\div$, $\times$, and $=$). An equation expresses a relationship between two or more quantities.

A formula is a special kind of equation. A formula such as $V = l \times w \times h$ states the relationship between unknown quantities represented by the variables V, l, w, and h. The formula means that volume (of a rectangular solid) equals length times width times height. Some formulas have numbers that do not vary, such as the formula for the perimeter of a square: $P = 4s$. In this formula, the number 4 is a constant.

To solve for a quantity in an equation or formula, substitute known values for the variables. Be sure to include units.

Example

An airplane travels in a straight line at a speed of 600 km/h. How far does it fly in 3.5 hours?

Write the formula that relates speed, distance, and time.

$$\text{Speed} = \frac{\text{Distance}}{\text{Time}}$$
$$v = \frac{d}{t}$$

To solve for distance, multiply both sides of the equation by t.

$$v = \frac{d}{t}$$
$$v \times t = \frac{d}{t} \times t$$
$$v \times t = d$$

Substitute in the known values.

$$600 \text{ km/h} \times 3.5 \text{ h} = d$$
$$d = 2100 \text{ km}$$

Conversion Factors

Many problems involve converting measurements from one unit to another. You can convert units by using an equation that shows how units are related. For example, 1 in. $= 2.54$ cm relates inches and centimeters.

To write a conversion factor, divide both sides of the equation by 1 in.

$$\frac{1 \text{ in.}}{1 \text{ in.}} = \frac{2.54 \text{ cm}}{1 \text{ in.}}$$
$$1 = 2.54 \text{ cm/in.}$$

Because the conversion factor is equal to 1, you can multiply one side of an equation by it and preserve equality. You can make a second conversion factor by dividing both sides of the equation by 2.54 cm.

$$\frac{1 \text{ in.}}{2.54 \text{ cm}} = \frac{2.54 \text{ cm}}{2.54 \text{ cm}} = 1$$

One conversion factor converts inches to centimeters and the other converts centimeters to inches. Choose the conversion factor that cancels out the unit that you have a measurement for.

Example

Convert 25 inches to centimeters. Use d to represent the unknown number of centimeters.

$$d = 25 \text{ in.} \times \frac{2.54 \text{ cm}}{1 \text{ in.}}$$
$$= 64 \text{ cm}$$

Some conversions are more complicated and require multiple steps.

Example

Convert 23°F to a Celsius temperature.

The conversion formula is
$$°F = \left(\frac{9}{5} \times °C\right) + 32°F$$

Substitute in 23°F:

$$23°F = \left(\frac{9}{5} \times °C\right) + 32°F$$
$$23°F - 32°F = \frac{9}{5} \times °C$$
$$-9°F = \frac{9}{5} \times °C$$
$$-9°F \times \frac{5}{9} = -5°C$$

Data Tables

Data tables help to organize data and make it easier to see patterns in data. If you plan data tables before doing an experiment, they will help you record observations in an orderly fashion.

The data table below shows United States immigration data for the year 2001. Always include units of measurement so people can understand the data.

Immigration to the United States, 2001	
Place of Origin	**Number of Legal Immigrants**
Africa	53,948
Asia	349,776
Europe	175,371
North America	407,888
South America	68,888

Bar Graphs

To make a bar graph, begin by placing category labels along the bottom axis. Add an overall label for the axis *Place of Origin*. Decide on a scale for the vertical axis. An appropriate scale for the data in the table is 0 to 500,000. Label the vertical axis *Number of People*. For each continent, draw a bar whose height corresponds to the number of immigrants. You will need to round off the values. For example, the bar for Africa should correspond to 54,000 people. Add a graph title to make it clear what the graph shows.

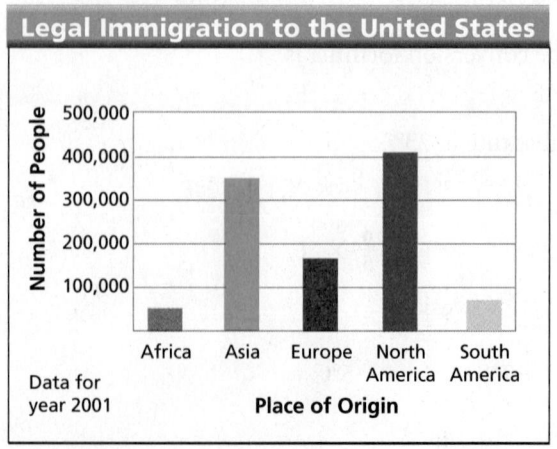

Circle Graphs

Use the total number to calculate percentages. For example, the percentage of immigrants from Africa in 2001 was 53,948 ÷ 1,061,984 = 0.051 ≈ 5%. Multiply each percent by 360° to find the central angle of each wedge. For Africa, the central angle is 18°. Use a protractor to draw each central angle. Color and label the wedges and finish your graph with a title.

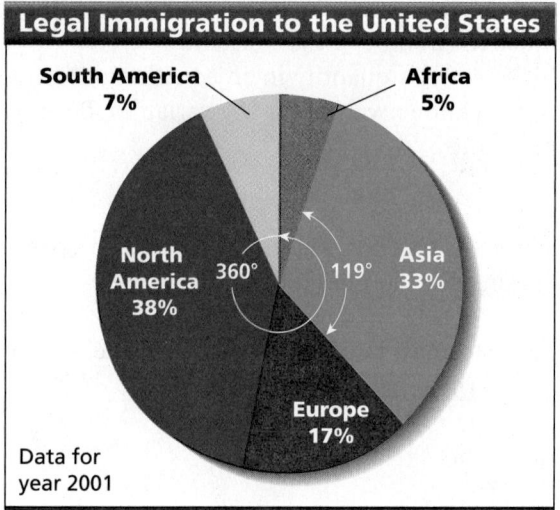

Line Graphs

The slope of a straight-line graph equals the "rise over the run." The rise is the change in the y values and the run is the change in the x values. Using points A and B on the graph below gives

$$\text{Slope} = \frac{\text{Rise}}{\text{Run}} = \frac{5-3}{9-3} = \frac{2}{6} = 0.33$$

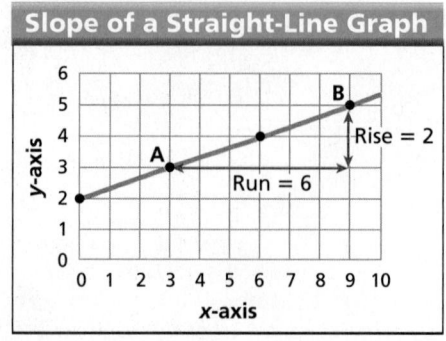

Appendix A | SI Units

SI *(Système International d'Unités)* is a revised version of the metric system, which was originally developed in France in 1791. SI units of measurement are used by scientists throughout the world. The system is based on multiples of ten. Each unit is ten times larger or ten times smaller than the next unit. The most commonly used SI units are given below.

You can use conversion factors to convert between SI and non-SI units. Try the following conversions. How tall are you in meters? What is your weight in newtons? What is your normal body temperature in degrees Celsius?

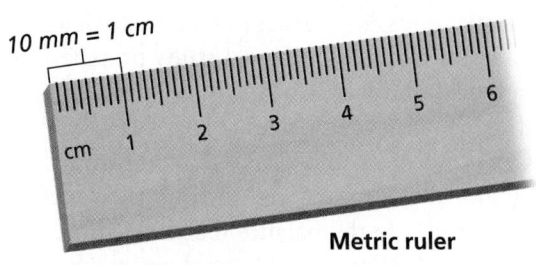

Metric ruler

Commonly Used Metric Units

Length	The distance from one point to another
meter (m)	A meter is slightly longer than a yard. 1 meter = 1000 millimeters (mm) 1 meter = 100 centimeters (cm) 1000 meters = 1 kilometer (km)

Volume	The amount of space an object takes up
liter (L)	A liter is slightly more than a quart. 1 liter = 1000 milliliters (mL)

Mass	The amount of matter in an object
gram (g)	A gram has a mass equal to about one paper clip. 1000 grams = 1 kilogram (kg)

Temperature	The measure of hotness or coldness
degrees Celsius (°C)	0°C = freezing point of water at sea level 100°C = boiling point of water at sea level

Riders Beams

Triple-Beam Balance

Metric–Customary Equivalents

2.54 centimeters (cm) = 1 inch (in.)
1 meter (m) = 39.37 inches (in.)
1 kilometer (km) = 0.62 miles (mi)
1 liter (L) = 1.06 quarts (qt)
250 milliliters (mL) = 1 cup (c)
9.8 newtons (N) = 2.2 pounds (lb)
$°C = 5/9 × (°F – 32)$

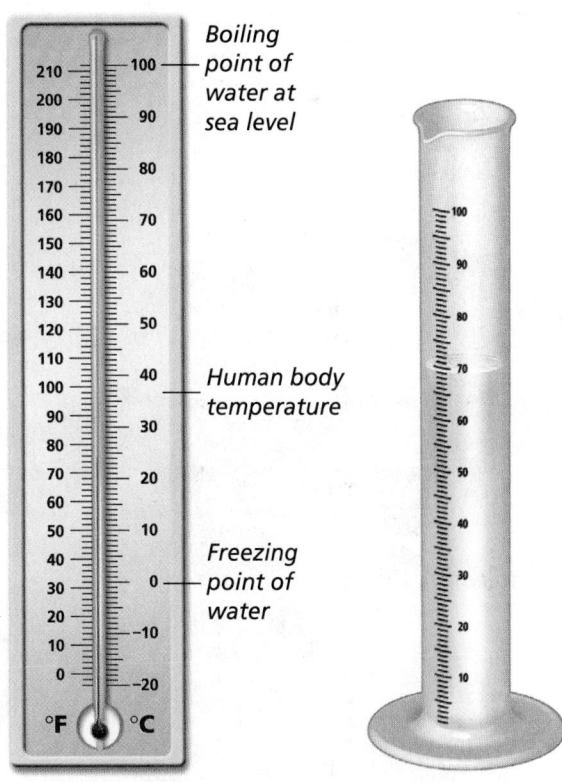

Boiling point of water at sea level

Human body temperature

Freezing point of water

Thermometer

Graduated cylinder

The laboratory balance is an important tool in scientific investigations. You can use a balance to determine the masses of materials that you study or experiment with in the laboratory.

Different kinds of balances are used in the laboratory. One kind of balance is the triple-beam balance. The balance that you may use in your science class is probably similar to the balance illustrated. To use the balance properly, you should learn the name, location, and function of each part of the balance you are using.

The Triple-Beam Balance

The triple-beam balance is a single-pan balance with three beams The back, or 100-gram, beam is divided into ten units of 10 grams. The middle, or 500-gram, beam is divided into five units of 100 grams. The front, or 10-gram, beam is divided into ten major units, each of which is 1 gram. Each 1-gram unit is further divided into units of 0.1 gram. What is the largest mass you could measure with a triple-beam balance?

The following procedure can be used to find the mass of an object with a triple-beam balance.

1. When no object is on the pan, and the riders are at zero, make sure the pointer is at zero. If it is not, use the adjustment screw to zero the balance.
2. Place the object on the pan.
3. Move the rider on the middle beam notch by notch until the horizontal pointer drops below zero. Move the rider back one notch.
4. Move the rider on the back beam notch by notch until the pointer again drops below zero. Move the rider back one notch.
5. Slowly slide the rider along the front beam until the pointer stops at zero. The mass of the object is the sum of the readings on the three beams.

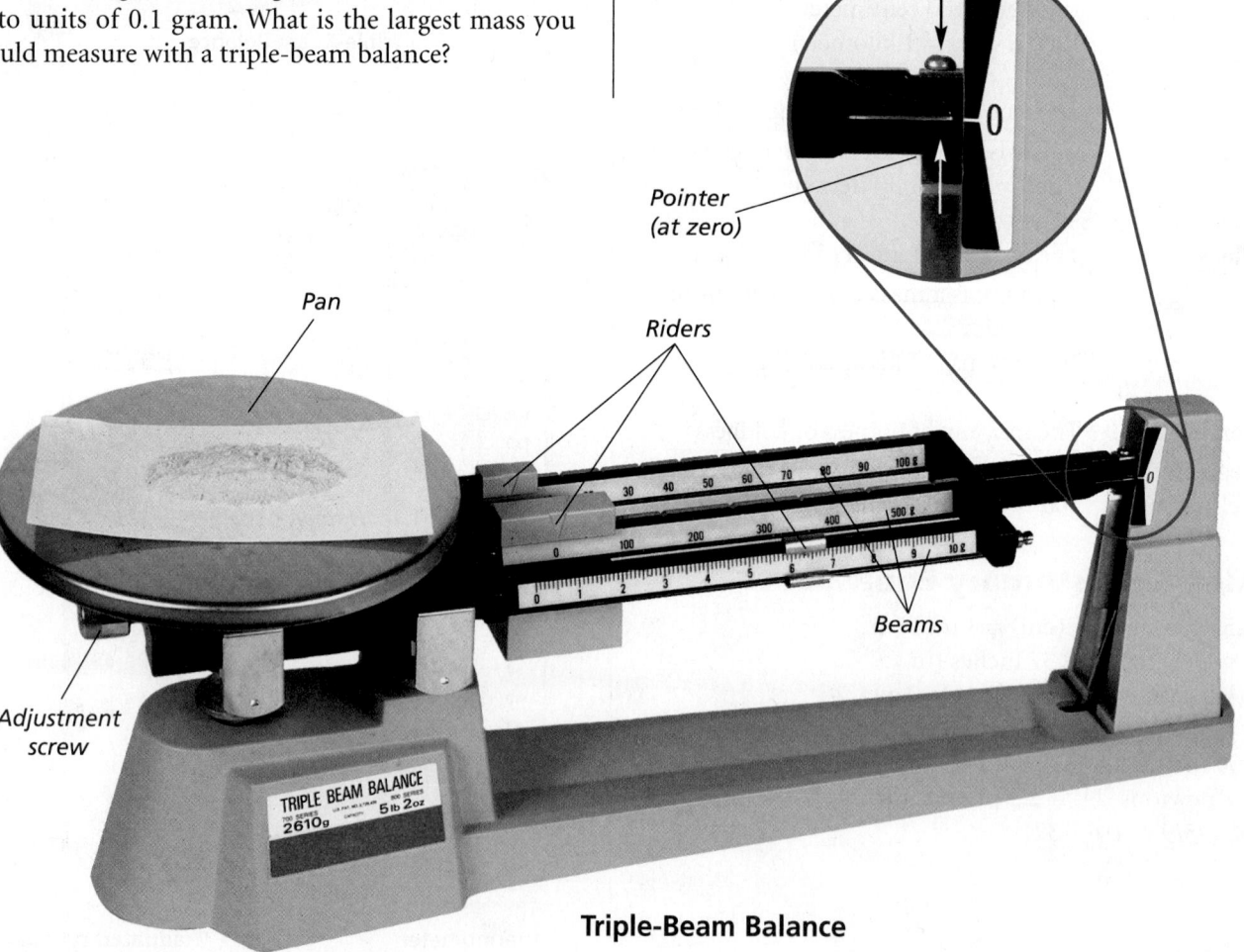

Pointer (at zero)

Pan *Riders*

Beams

Adjustment screw

TRIPLE BEAM BALANCE
2610g   5 lb 2 oz

Triple-Beam Balance

Element	Symbol	Atomic Number	Atomic Mass[†]	Element	Symbol	Atomic Number	Atomic Mass[†]
Actinium	Ac	89	(277)	Neodymium	Nd	60	144.24
Aluminum	Al	13	26.982	Neon	Ne	10	20.179
Americium	Am	95	(243)	Neptunium	Np	93	(237)
Antimony	Sb	51	121.75	Nickel	Ni	28	58.71
Argon	Ar	18	39.948	Niobium	Nb	41	92.906
Arsenic	As	33	74.922	Nitrogen	N	7	14.007
Astatine	At	85	(210)	Nobelium	No	102	(259)
Barium	Ba	56	137.33	Osmium	Os	76	190.2
Berkelium	Bk	97	(247)	Oxygen	O	8	15.999
Beryllium	Be	4	9.0122	Palladium	Pd	46	106.4
Bismuth	Bi	83	208.98	Phosphorus	P	15	30.974
Bohrium	Bh	107	(264)	Platinum	Pt	78	195.09
Boron	B	5	10.81	Plutonium	Pu	94	(244)
Bromine	Br	35	79.904	Polonium	Po	84	(209)
Cadmium	Cd	48	112.41	Potassium	K	19	39.098
Calcium	Ca	20	40.08	Praseodymium	Pr	59	140.91
Californium	Cf	98	(251)	Promethium	Pm	61	(145)
Carbon	C	6	12.011	Protactinium	Pa	91	231.04
Cerium	Ce	58	140.12	Radium	Ra	88	(226)
Cesium	Cs	55	132.91	Radon	Rn	86	(222)
Chlorine	Cl	17	35.453	Rhenium	Re	75	186.21
Chromium	Cr	24	51.996	Rhodium	Rh	45	102.91
Cobalt	Co	27	58.933	Roentgenium	Rg	111	(272)
Copernicium	Cn	112	(277)	Rubidium	Rb	37	85.468
Copper	Cu	29	63.546	Ruthenium	Ru	44	101.07
Curium	Cm	96	(247)	Rutherfordium	Rf	104	(261)
Darmstadtium	Ds	110	(269)	Samarium	Sm	62	150.4
Dubnium	Db	105	(262)	Scandium	Sc	21	44.956
Dysprosium	Dy	66	162.50	Seaborgium	Sg	106	(263)
Einsteinium	Es	99	(252)	Selenium	Se	34	78.96
Erbium	Er	68	167.26	Silicon	Si	14	28.086
Europium	Eu	63	151.96	Silver	Ag	47	107.87
Fermium	Fm	100	(257)	Sodium	Na	11	22.990
Fluorine	F	9	18.998	Strontium	Sr	38	87.62
Francium	Fr	87	(223)	Sulfur	S	16	32.06
Gadolinium	Gd	64	157.25	Tantalum	Ta	73	180.95
Gallium	Ga	31	69.72	Technetium	Tc	43	(98)
Germanium	Ge	32	72.59	Tellurium	Te	52	127.60
Gold	Au	79	196.97	Terbium	Tb	65	158.93
Hafnium	Hf	72	178.49	Thallium	Tl	81	204.37
Hassium	Hs	108	(265)	Thorium	Th	90	232.04
Helium	He	2	4.0026	Thulium	Tm	69	168.93
Holmium	Ho	67	164.93	Tin	Sn	50	118.69
Hydrogen	H	1	1.0079	Titanium	Ti	22	47.90
Indium	In	49	114.82	Tungsten	W	74	183.85
Iodine	I	53	126.90	Ununhexium	Uuh	116	(293)
Iridium	Ir	77	192.22	Ununoctium	*Uuo	117	(299)
Iron	Fe	26	55.847	Ununpentium	*Uup	115	(288)
Krypton	Kr	36	83.80	Ununquadium	*Uuq	114	(289)
Lanthanum	La	57	138.91	Ununtrium	*Uuz	113	(284)
Lawrencium	Lr	103	(262)	Uranium	U	92	238.03
Lead	Pb	82	207.2	Vanadium	V	23	50.941
Lithium	Li	3	6.941	Xenon	Xe	54	131.30
Lutetium	Lu	71	174.97	Ytterbium	Yb	70	173.04
Magnesium	Mg	12	24.305	Yttrium	Y	39	88.906
Manganese	Mn	25	54.938	Zinc	Zn	30	65.38
Meitnerium	Mt	109	(268)	Zirconium	Zr	40	91.22
Mendelevium	Md	101	(258)				
Mercury	Hg	80	200.59				
Molybdenum	Mo	42	95.94				

[†] Number in parentheses gives the mass number of the most stable isotope.

*Name not officially assigned.

Appendices

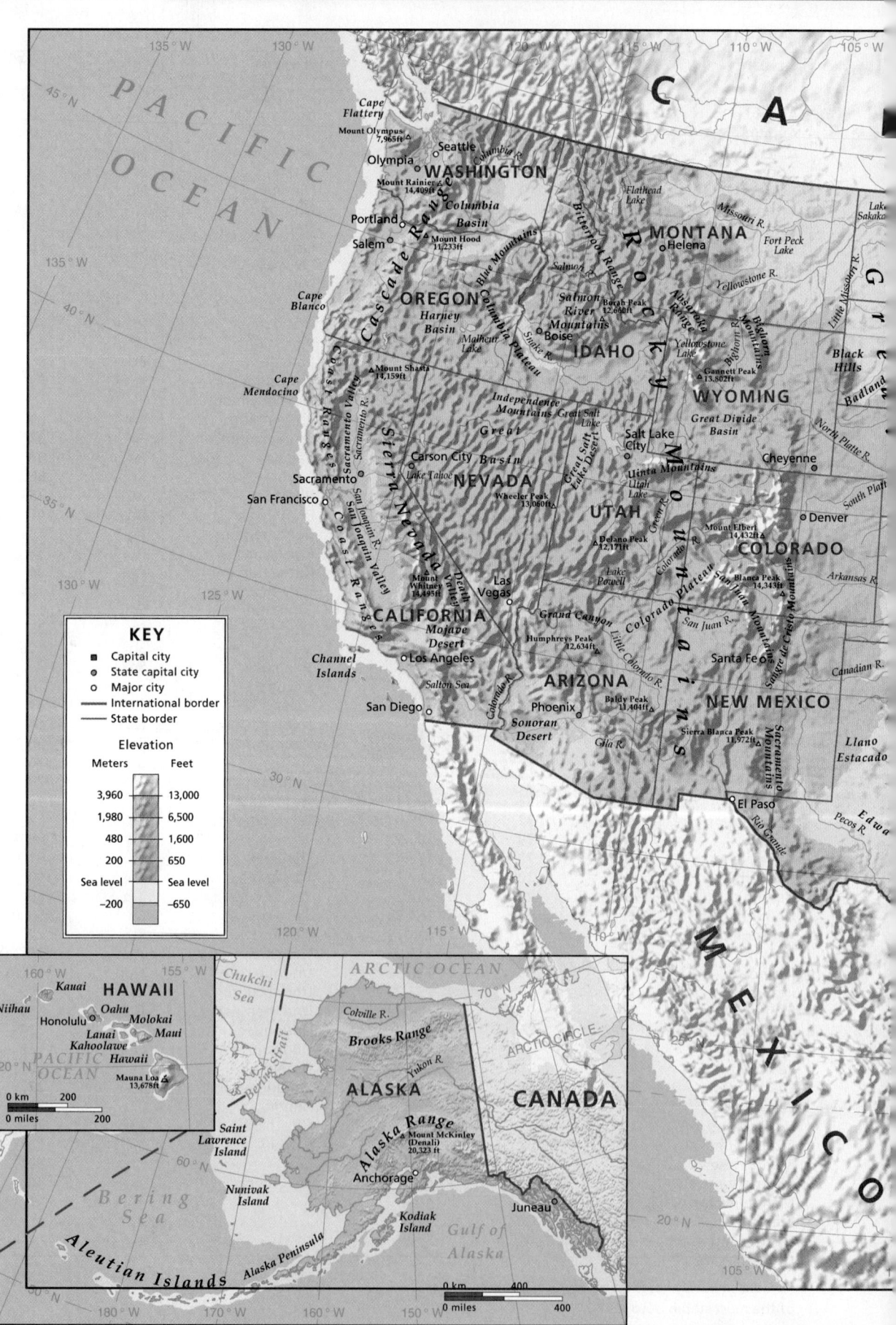

Appendices

This weather map shows data collected from many weather stations. Below the map is an explanation of what the symbols mean.

Weather Map

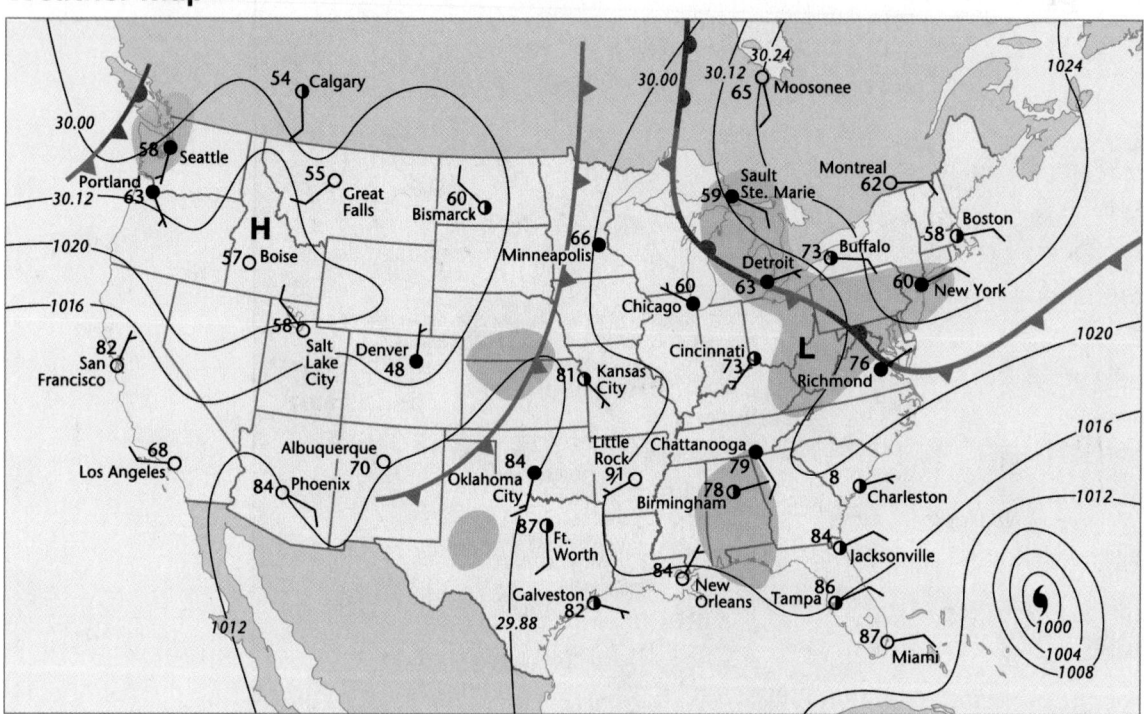

Explanation of Fronts

Cold Front
Boundary between a cold air mass and a warm air mass. Brings brief storms and cooler weather.

Warm Front
Boundary between a warm air mass and a cold air mass. Usually accompanied by precipitation.

Stationary Front
Boundary between warm and cold air masses when no movement occurs. Long periods of precipitation.

Occluded Front
Boundary on which a warm front has been overtaken by a cold front. Brings precipitation.

Weather	Symbol
Drizzle	
Fog	
Hail	
Haze	
Rain	
Shower	
Sleet	
Smoke	
Snow	
Thunderstorm	
Hurricane	

Wind Speed (mph)	Symbol
1–2	
3–8	
9–14	
15–20	
21–25	
26–31	
32–37	
38–43	
44–49	
50–54	
55–60	
61–66	
67–71	
72–77	

Cloud Cover (%)	Symbol
0	
10	
20–30	
40	
50	
60	
70–80	
90	
100	

How Symbols Are Used on a Weather Map

Amount of cloud cover (100%)

Atmospheric pressure (millibars)

Temperature (°F)

38 1018

Wind direction (from the southwest)

Wind speed (21–25 mph)

To find the relative humidity, measure the wet-bulb and dry-bulb temperatures with a sling psychrometer. Find the dry-bulb reading in the left column and the difference between readings at the top of the table. The number where these readings intersect is the relative humidity in percent.

Relative Humidity (percent)														
Dry-Bulb Reading (°C)	Difference Between Wet-Bulb and Dry-Bulb Readings (°C)													
	1	2	3	4	5	6	7	8	9	10	11	12	13	14
5	86	72	58	45	33	20	7							
6	86	73	60	48	35	24	11							
7	87	74	62	50	38	26	15							
8	87	75	63	51	40	29	19	8						
9	88	76	64	53	42	32	22	12						
10	88	77	66	55	44	34	24	15	6					
11	89	78	67	56	46	36	27	18	9					
12	89	78	68	58	48	39	29	21	12					
13	89	79	69	59	50	41	32	23	15	7				
14	90	79	70	60	51	42	34	26	18	10				
15	90	80	71	61	53	44	36	27	20	13	6			
16	90	81	71	63	54	46	38	30	23	15	8			
17	90	81	72	64	55	47	40	32	25	18	11			
18	91	82	73	65	57	49	41	34	27	20	14	7		
19	91	82	74	65	58	50	43	36	29	22	16	10		
20	91	83	74	66	59	51	44	37	31	24	18	12	6	
21	91	83	75	67	60	53	46	39	32	26	20	14	9	
22	92	83	76	68	61	54	47	40	34	28	22	17	11	6
23	92	84	76	69	62	55	48	42	36	30	24	19	13	8
24	92	84	77	69	62	56	49	43	37	31	26	20	15	10
25	92	84	77	70	63	57	50	44	39	33	28	22	17	12
26	92	85	78	71	64	58	51	46	40	34	29	24	19	14
27	92	85	78	71	65	58	52	47	41	36	31	26	21	16
28	93	85	78	72	65	59	53	48	42	37	32	27	22	18
29	93	86	79	72	66	60	54	49	43	38	33	28	24	19
30	93	86	79	73	67	61	55	50	44	39	35	30	25	21

Autumn Sky

To use this chart, hold it up in front of you and turn it so the direction you are facing is at the bottom of the chart. The chart works best at 35° N latitude, but it can be used at other latitudes. It works best at the following dates and times: September 1 at 10:00 P.M., October 1 at 8 P.M., and November 1 at 6 P.M.

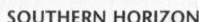

Winter Sky

To use this chart, hold it up in front of you and turn it so the direction you are facing is at the bottom of the chart. The chart works best at 35° N latitude, but it can be used at other latitudes. It works best at the following dates and times: December 1 at 10:00 P.M., January 1 at 8 P.M., and February 1 at 6 P.M.

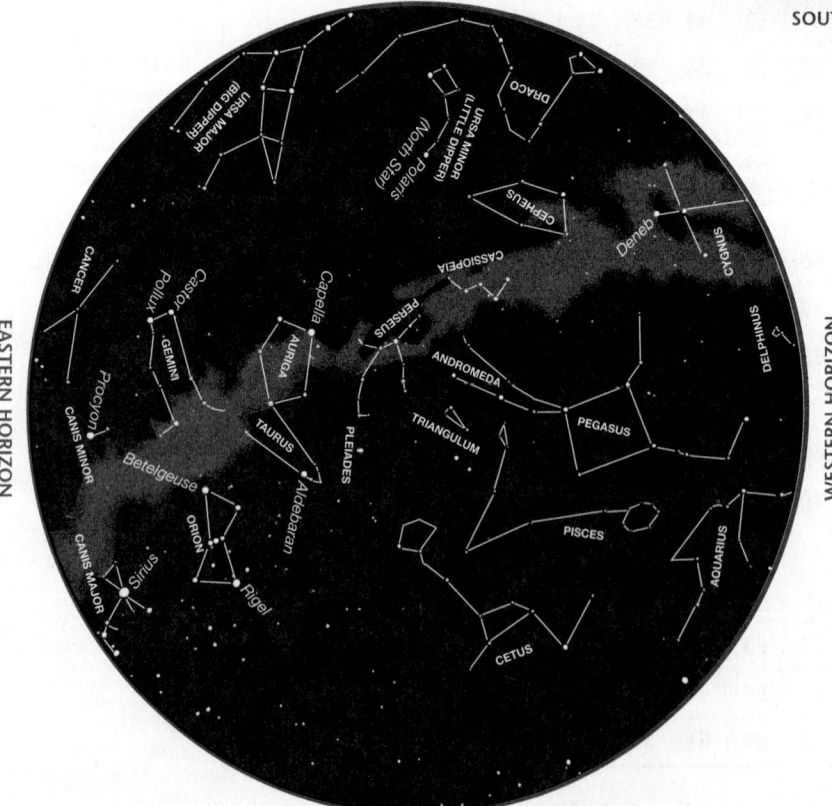

Spring Sky

To use this chart, hold it up in front of you and turn it so the direction you are facing is at the bottom of the chart. The chart works best at 35° N latitude, but it can be used at other latitudes. It works best at the following dates and times: March 1 at 10:00 P.M. and April 1 at 8 P.M.

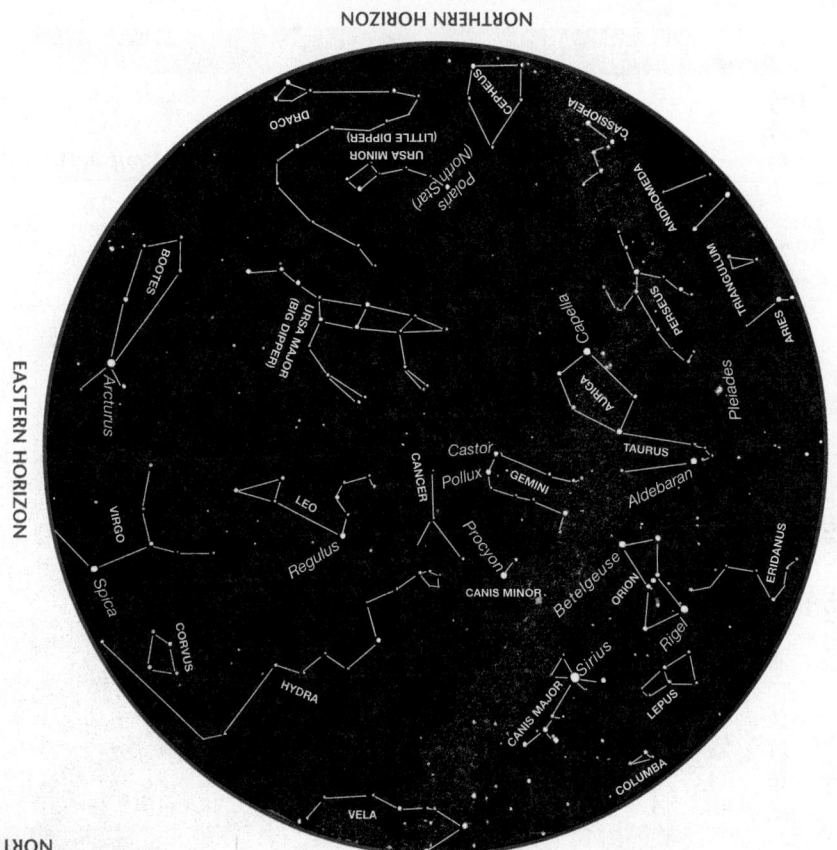

Summer Sky

To use this chart, hold it up in front of you and turn it so the direction you are facing is at the bottom of the chart. The chart works best at 35° N latitude, but it can be used at other latitudes. It works best at the following dates and times: May 15 at 11:00 P.M. and June 15 at 9 P.M.

Dew-point temperature (°C)

Dry bulb (°C)

(Dry-Bulb Temperature Minus Wet-Bulb Temperature = Depression of the Wet Bulb)

Dry-Bulb (Air) Temperature

Dew-Point Values

Dry bulb	1	2	3	4	5	6	7	8	9	10	11	12	13	14	15	16	17	18	19	20	21	22
−20	−33																					
−18	−28																					
−16	−24																					
−14	−21	−36																				
−12	−18	−28																				
−10	−14	−22																				
−8	−12	−18	−29																			
−6	−10	−14	−22																			
−4	−7	−12	−17	−29																		
−2	−5	−8	−13	−20																		
0	−3	−6	−9	−15	−24																	
2	−1	−3	−6	−11	−17																	
4	1	−1	−4	−7	−11	−19																
6	4	1	−1	−4	−7	−13	−21															
8	6	3	1	2	−5	−9	−14															
10	8	6	4	1	−2	−5	−9	−14	−18													
12	10	8	6	4	1	−2	−5	−9	−16													
14	12	11	9	6	4	1	−2	−5	−10	−17												
16	14	13	11	9	7	4	1	−1	−6	−10	−17											
18	16	15	13	11	9	7	4	2	−2	5	10	−19										
20	19	17	15	14	12	10	7	4	2	−2	−5	−10	−19									
22	21	19	17	16	74	12	10	8	5	3	−1	−5	−10	−19								
24	23	21	20	18	16	14	12	10	8	6	2	−1	−5	−10	−18							
26	25	23	22	20	18	17	15	13	11	9	6	3	0	−4	−9	−18						
28	27	25	24	22	27	19	17	16	14	11	9	7	4	1	−3	−9	16					
30	29	27	26	24	23	21	19	18	16	14	12	70	8	5	1	−2	−8	−15				
32	31	29	28	27	25	24	22	21	19	17	15	13	11	8	5	2	−2	−7	−14			
34	33	31	30	29	27	26	24	23	21	20	18	16	14	12	9	6	3	−1	−5	−12	−29	
36	35	33	32	31	29	28	27	25	24	22	20	19	17	15	13	10	7	4	0	−4	−10	
38	37	35	34	33	32	30	29	28	26	25	23	21	19	17	15	13	11	8	5	1	−3	9
40	39	37	36	35	34	32	31	30	28	27	25	24	22	20	18	16	14	12	9	6	2	−2

Appendix I — World Soils

The map on the next page shows the generalized pattern of global soil orders according to the *Comprehensive Soil Classification System* (CSCS). It should be examined in conjunction with the table below, which briefly describes each of the soil orders depicted on the map. To avoid subjective decisions as to classification (a problem that plagued earlier systems), the CSCS defined its classes strictly in terms of soil characterisitics. That is, it is based on features that can be observed or inferred.

The CSCS uses a hierarchy of six categories, or levels. The system recognizes 10 major global *orders* that can be further subdivided into *suborders, great groups, subgroups, families,* and *series*. Note, however, that on the scale of a world map, only the largest units (soil orders) can be shown and then only in an extremely generalized way. Although the distribution pattern of major soil orders is more complex than can be shown, the major distinguishing regional properties of world soils are depicted.

World Soil Orders

Entisols	Youngest soils on the Earth. Just beginning to develop in response to the weathering phenomena in the environment. Do not display natural horizons. Found in all climates. They weather slowly over thousands of years; consequently, volcanic ash deposits or sand deposits form the basis for entisols.
Vertisols	Soils containing large amounts of clay, which shrink upon drying and swell with the addition of water. Found in subhumid to arid climates, provided that adequate supplies of water are available to saturate the soil after periods of drought. Soil expansion and contraction exert stresses on human structures.
Inceptisols	Young soils that reveal developmental characteristics (horizons) in response to climate and vegetation. Exist from the Arctic to the tropics on young land surfaces. Common in alpine areas, on river floodplains, in stables and dune areas, and in areas once glaciated.
Aridsols	Soils that develop in dry places, such as the desert, where water—precipitation and groundwater—is insufficient to remove soluble minerals. Frequently irrigated for intensive agricultural production, although salt accumulation poses a problem.
Mollisols	Dark, soft soils that have developed under grass vegetation, generally found in prairie areas. Soil fertility is excellent because potential evaporation generally exceeds precipitation. Also found in hardwood forests with significant earthworm activity. Climatic range is boreal or alpine to tropical. Dry seasons are normal.
Spodosols	Soils found only in humid regions on sandy material. Range from the boreal coniferous forests into tropical forests. Beneath the dark upper horizon of weathered organic material lies a light-colored horizon of leached material, the distinctive property of this soil.
Alfisols	Mineral soils that form under boreal forests or broadleaf deciduous forests, rich in iron and aluminum. Clay particles accumulate in a subsurface layer in response to leaching in moist environments. Fertile, productive soils, because they are neither too wet nor too dry.
Ultisols	Soils that represent the products of long periods of weathering. Water percolating through the soil concentrates clay particles in the lower horizons (argillic horizons). Restricted to humid climates in the temperate regions and the tropics where the growing season is long. Abundant water and a long frost-free period contribute to extensive leaching, hence poorer soil quality.
Oxisols	Soils that occur on old land surfaces unless parent materials were strongly weathered before they were deposited. Generally found in the tropics and subtropical regions. Rich in iron and aluminum oxides, oxisols are heavily leached; hence are poor soils for agricultural activity. Few, if any, exist in the United States.
Histosols	Organic soils with little or no climatic implications. Can be found in any climate where organic debris can accumulate to form a bog soil. Dark, partially decomposed organic material commonly referred to as *peat*.

Source: Robert E. Norris et al., *Geography: An Introductory Perspective*, Columbus, Ohio: Merrill, 1982.

Appendices

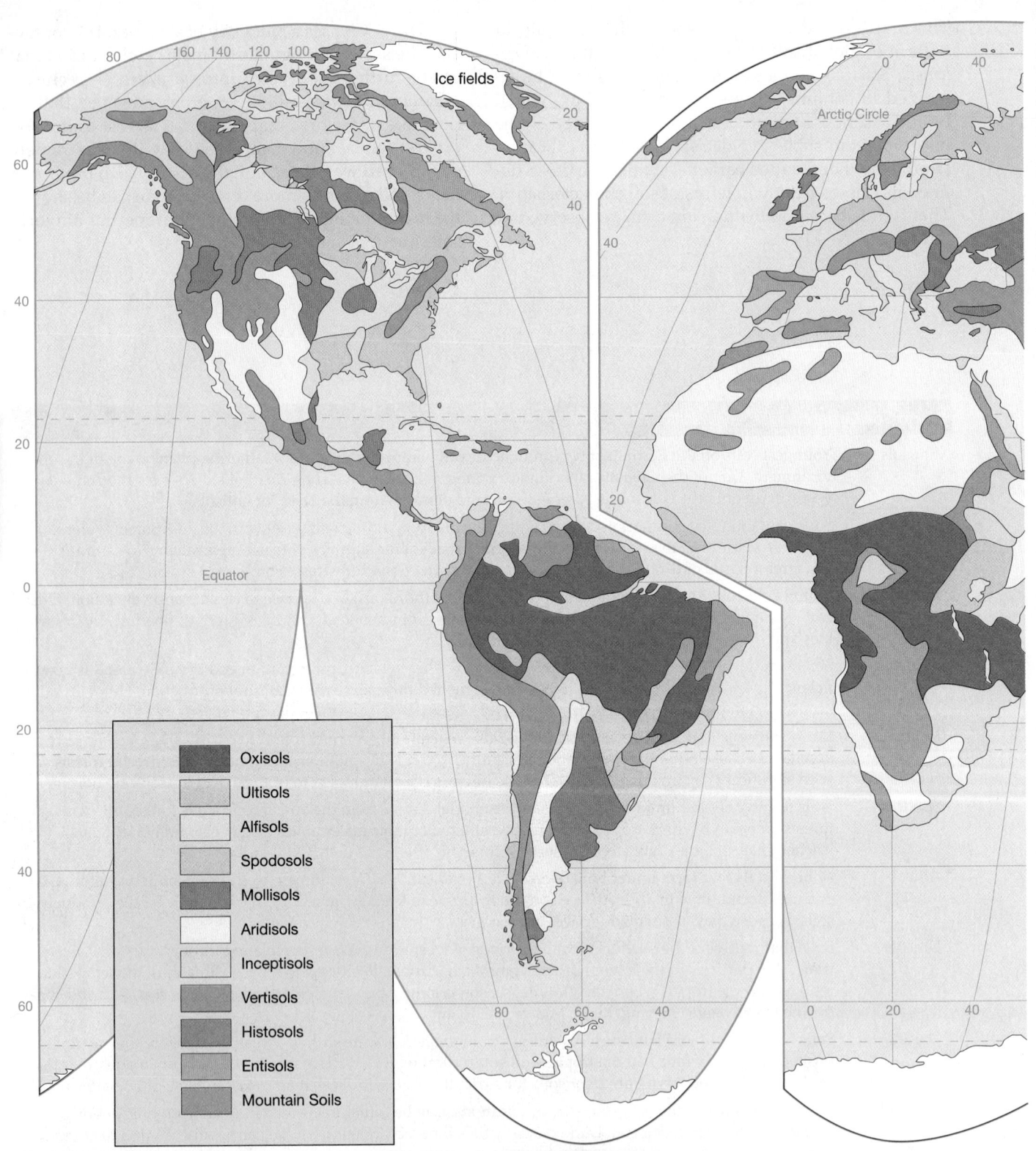

Ice fields

Arctic Circle

Equator

Legend:
- Oxisols
- Ultisols
- Alfisols
- Spodosols
- Mollisols
- Aridisols
- Inceptisols
- Vertisols
- Histosols
- Entisols
- Mountain Soils

Soil distribution. The pattern of global soil orders is remarkably similar to the pattern of major climates. Soil classification is from the *Comprehensive Soil Classification System.*

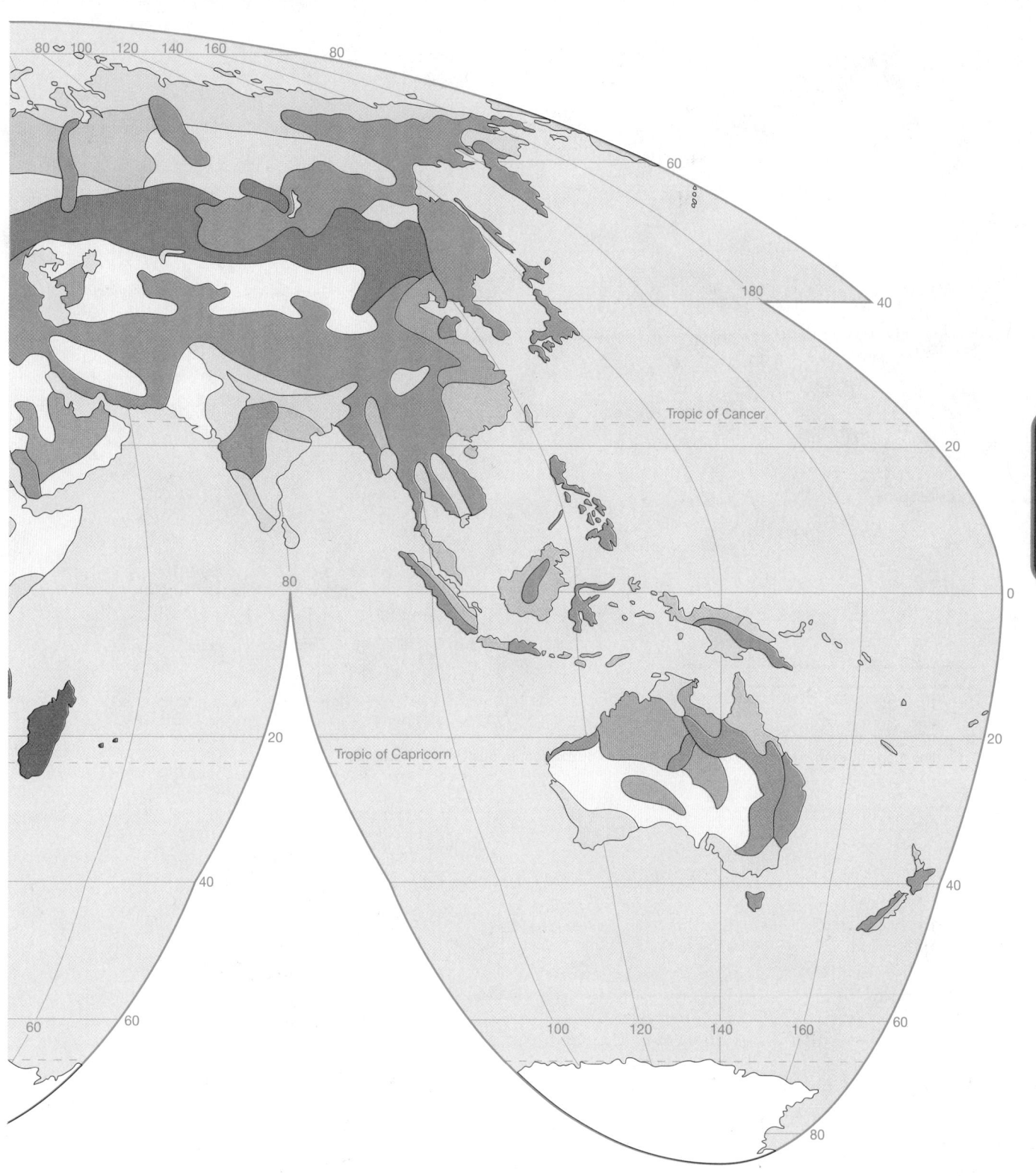

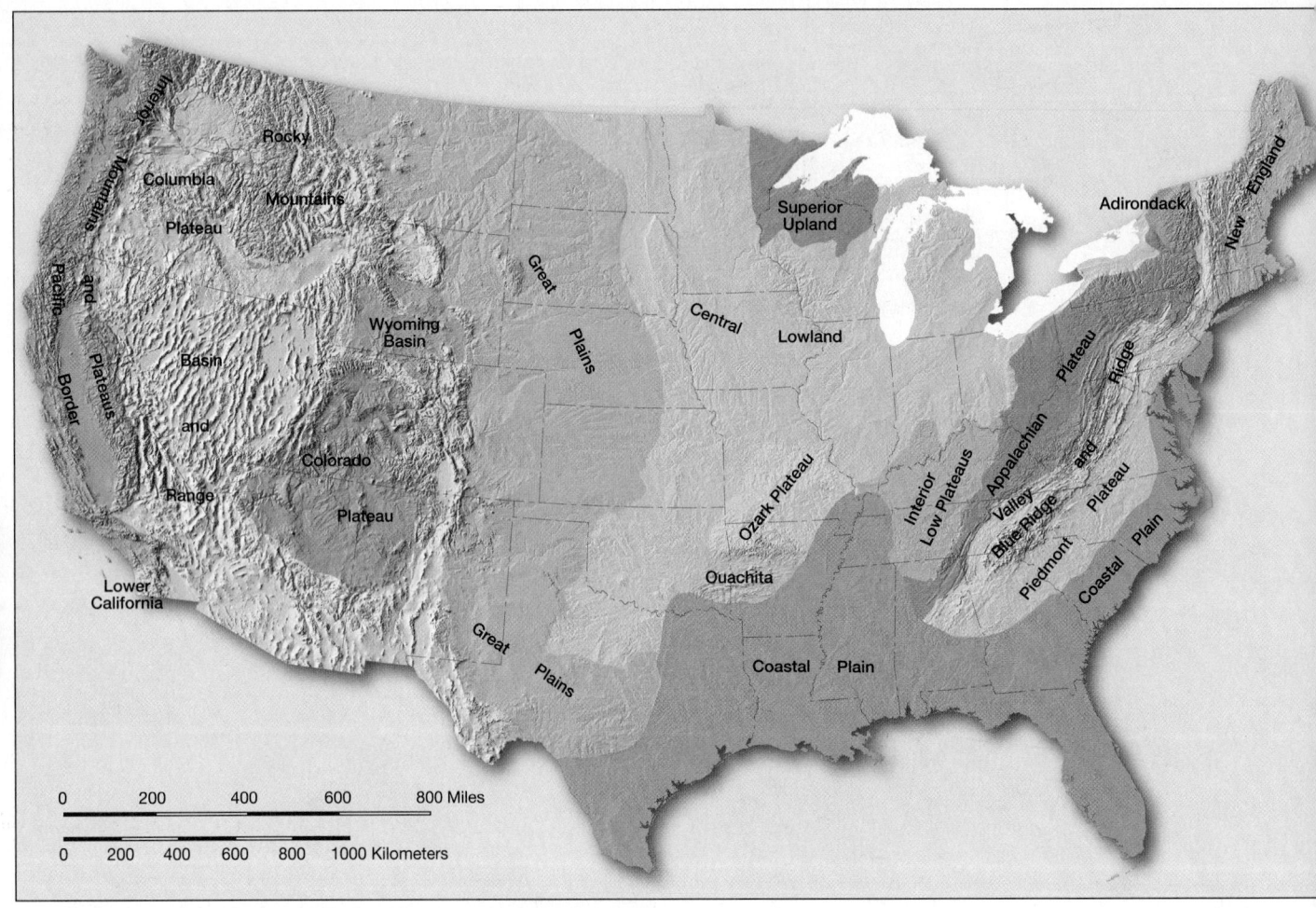

Outline map showing major physiographic provinces of the contiguous United States.

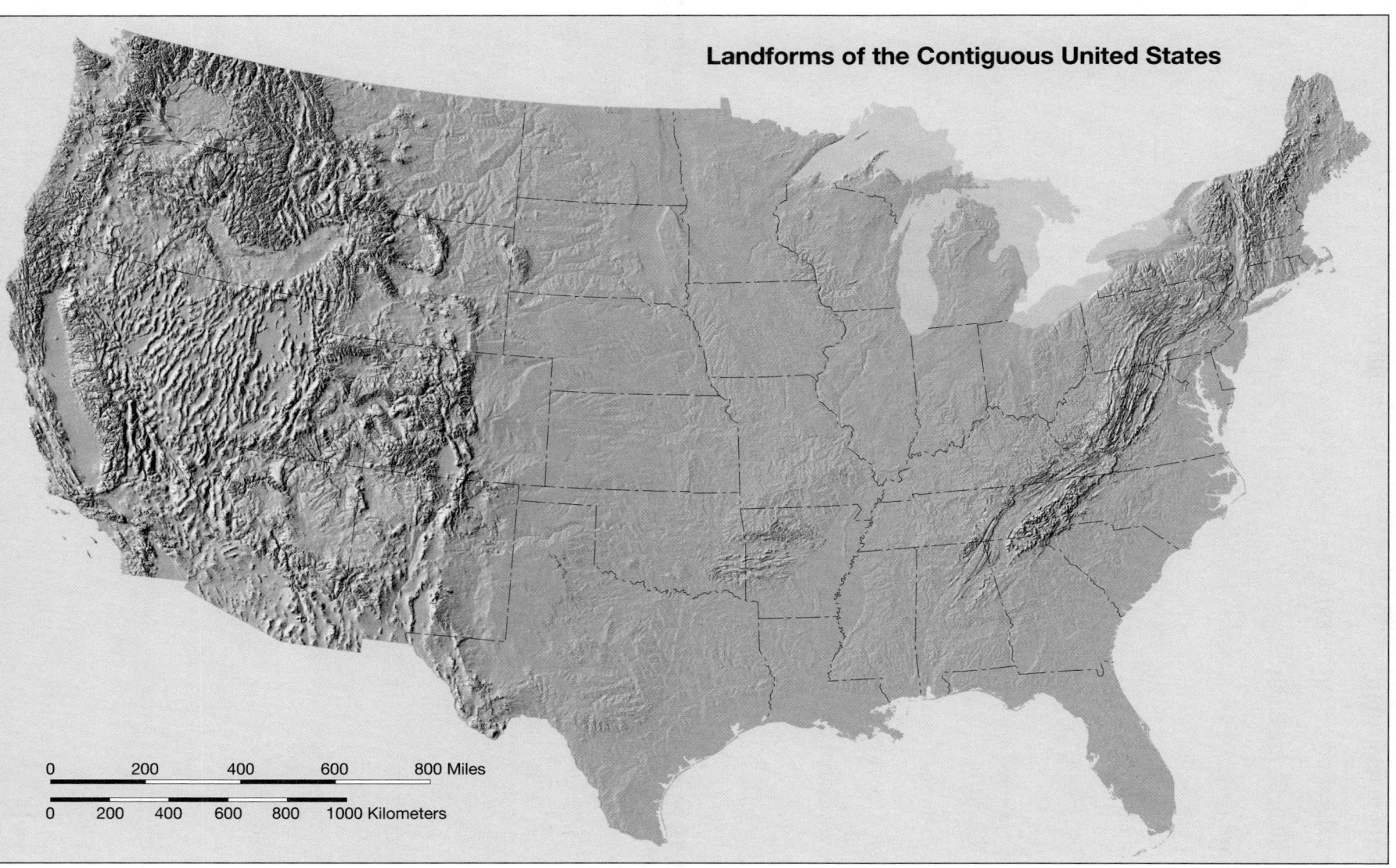

Landforms of the Contiguous United States

| 0 | 200 | 400 | 600 | 800 Miles |

| 0 | 200 | 400 | 600 | 800 | 1000 Kilometers |

Digital shaded relief landform map of the United States. (Data provided by the U.S. Geological Survey)

Speed of light in a vacuum	3.00×10^8 m/s
Free fall acceleration of Earth's surface	9.81 m/s^2
Moment of inertia for Earth	8.03×10^{31} kg•m^2
Mass of Earth	5.98×10^{24} kg
Radius of Earth	6.37×10^6 m
Mass of the Moon	7.35×10^{22} kg
Radius of the Moon	1.74×10^6 m
Mass of the Sun	1.99×10^{30} kg
Radius of the Sun	6.96×10^5 km
Earth-Sun distance (mean)	1.496×10^8 km
Earth-Moon distance (mean)	3.84×10^5 km
Earth's gravitational constant	6.67×10^{11} N•m^2/kg^2

Some SI Derived Units

Quantity	Unit name	Abbreviation
Force	newton	N
Energy and work	joule	J
Power	watt	W
Pressure	pascal	Pa

Glossary

A

absolute magnitude the apparent brightness of a star if it were viewed from a distance of 32.6 light-years; used to compare the true brightness of stars (p. 703)

absolute magnitude/magnitud absoluta luminosidad aparente de una estrella si se observara a una distancia de 32.6 años luz; usada para comparar la luminosidad real de las estrellas (pág. 703)

absorption spectrum a continuous spectrum produced when white light is passed through a cool gas under low pressure; The gas absorbs selected wavelengths of light, and the spectrum looks like it has dark lines superimposed. (p. 676)

absorption spectrum/espectro de absorción espectro continuo producido cuando pasa luz blanca a través de un gas frío a presión baja; El gas absorbe determinadas longitudes de onda de luz y el espectro pareciera tener líneas oscuras superpuestas. (pág. 676)

abyssal plain very level area of the deep-ocean floor, usually lying at the foot of the continental rise (p. 404)

abyssal plain/planicie abisal área muy nivelada del fondo oceánico profundo, que se encuentra por lo general en la base del pie continental (pág. 404)

abyssal zone a subdivision of the benthic zone characterized by extremely high pressures, low temperatures, low oxygen, few nutrients, and no sunlight (p. 431)

abyssal zone/zona abisal subdivisión de la zona bentónica caracterizada por tener presiones extremadamente altas, bajas temperaturas, poco oxígeno, pocas sustancias nutrientes y ausencia de luz solar (pág. 431)

accretion process that occurs when crustal fragments collide with and stay connected to a continental plate (p. 324)

accretion/acreción proceso que ocurre cuando los fragmentos corticales chocan con una placa continental y permanecen conectados a ella (pág. 324)

accretionary wedge a large wedge-shaped mass of sediment that accumulates in subduction zones; Here sediment is scraped from the subducting oceanic plate and accreted to the overriding crustal block. (p. 321)

accretionary wedge/prisma acrecionario masa grande de sedimento en forma de prisma que se acumula en las zonas de subducción; El sedimento es raspado de la placa oceánica de subducción y acrecentado al bloque cortical preponderante. (pág. 321)

adaptation a trait that helps an organism survive and reproduce (p. 344)

adaptation/adaptación rasgo que ayuda a sobrevivir y a reproducirse a un organismo (pág. 344)

aftershock a small earthquake that follows the main earthquake (p. 221)

aftershock/replica terremoto pequeño que sigue al terremoto mayor (pág. 221)

air mass a large body of air that is characterized by similar temperatures and amounts of moisture at any given altitude (p. 559)

air mass/masa de aire cuerpo grande de aire que se caracteriza por tener temperatura y humedad similares a cualquier altitud dada (pág. 559)

air pressure the force exerted by the weight of a column of air above a given point (p. 532)

air pressure/ presión de aire fuerza ejercida por el peso de una columna de aire sobre un punto dado (pág. 532)

albedo the fraction of total radiation that is reflected back by a surface (p. 492)

albedo/albedo fracción de la radiación total que es reflejada por una superficie (pág. 492)

alluvial fan a fan-shaped deposit of sediment formed when a stream's slope is abruptly reduced (p. 201)

alluvial fan/abanico aluvial depósito de sedimentos en forma de abanico, formado cuando la vertiente de una corriente de agua se reduce abruptamente (pág. 201)

amphibian a vertebrate that lives part of its life on land and part of its life in water (p. 373)

amphibian/anfibio vertebrado que vive parte de su vida en la tierra y parte en el agua (pág. 373)

Glossary

andesitic composition the composition of igneous rocks lying between felsic and mafic (p. 73)

andesitic composition/composición andesítica composición de rocas ígneas que se encuentra entre las rocas félsicas y máficas (pág. 73)

anemometer an instrument used to determine wind speed (p. 545)

anemometer/anemómetro instrumento usado para determinar la velocidad del viento (pág. 545)

angiosperm flowering plant that produces seeds within a fruit (p. 380)

angiosperm/angiosperma planta que da flores y produce semillas dentro de una fruta (pág. 380)

anticline a fold in sedimentary strata resembling an arch (p. 312)

anticline/anticlinal pliegue en el estrato sedimentario que parece un arco (pág. 312)

anticyclone a high-pressure center characterized by a clockwise flow of air in the Northern Hemisphere (p. 538)

anticyclon/anticiclón centro de alta presión en el hemisferio norte que se caracteriza por una masa de aire que se mueve en dirección de las agujas del reloj (pág. 538)

aphelion the place in the orbit of a planet where the planet is farthest from the sun (p. 624)

aphelion/afelio punto en la órbita de un planeta en el que éste se encuentra más alejado del Sol (pág. 624)

apogee the point where the moon is farthest from Earth (p. 626)

apogee/apogeo punto donde la Luna se encuentra más alejada de la Tierra (pág. 626)

apparent magnitude the brightness of a star when viewed from Earth (p. 703)

apparent magnitude/magnitud aparente luminosidad de una estrella vista desde la Tierra (pág. 703)

aquifer rock or soil through which groundwater moves easily (p. 171)

aquifer/acuífero roca o tierra a través de la cual el agua subterránea se mueve fácilmente (pág. 172)

artesian well a well in which the water naturally rises above the level of the water table (p. 173)

artesian well/pozo artesiano pozo en el cual el agua sube naturalmente por encima del nivel freático (pág. 173)

asteroid a small, rocky body, which can range in size from a few hundred kilometers to less than a kilometer; The asteroids' orbits lie mainly between those of Mars and Jupiter. (p. 661)

asteroid/asteroide cuerpo rocoso y pequeño, cuyo tamaño puede variar entre cientos de kilómetros a menos de un kilómetro; Las órbitas de los asteroides se encuentran principalmente entre las órbitas de Marte y Júpiter. (pág. 661)

asthenosphere a weak plastic layer of the mantle situated below the lithosphere; The rock within this zone is easily deformed. (p. 235)

asthenosphere/astenosfera capa plástica y débil del manto situada debajo de la litosfera; La roca en esta zona se deforma fácilmente. (pág. 235)

astronomical unit (AU) average distance from Earth to the sun; 1.5×10^8, or 150 million kilometers (p. 618)

astronomical unit (AU)/unidad astronómica (UA) distancia promedio de la Tierra al Sol; 1.5×10^8, ó 150 millones de kilómetros (pág. 618)

astronomy the scientific study of the universe; It includes the observation and interpretation of celestial bodies and phenomena. (p. 3)

astronomy/astronomía estudio científico del universo; incluye la observación y la interpretación de cuerpos y fenómenos celestes (pág. 3)

atmosphere the gaseous portion of a planet; the planet's envelope of air; one of the traditional subdivisions of Earth's physical environment (p. 7)

atmosphere/atmósfera porción gaseosa de un planeta; envoltura de aire del planeta; una de las subdivisiones tradicionales del medio ambiente físico de la Tierra (pág. 7)

atomic number the number of protons in the nucleus of an atom (p. 35)

atomic number/número atómico número de protones en el núcleo de un átomo (pág. 35)

aurora a bright display of ever-changing light caused by solar radiation interacting with the upper atmosphere in the region of the poles (p. 688)

aurora/aurora polar luz brillante en constante movimiento causada por la radiación solar que interactúa con la parte superior de la atmósfera en la región de los polos (pág. 688)

autumnal equinox the equinox that occurs on September 22 or 23 in the Northern Hemisphere and on March 21 or 22 in the Southern Hemisphere (p. 482)

autummal equinox/equinoccio de otoño equinoccio que ocurre el 22 ó 23 de septiembre en el hemisferio norte y el 21 ó 22 de marzo en el hemisferio sur (pág. 482)

B

barometer an instrument that measures atmospheric pressure (p. 533)

barometer/barómetro instrumento que mide la presión atmosférica (pág. 533)

barrier island a low, elongated ridge of sand that parallels the coast (p. 466)

barrier island/isla barrera lomo de arena bajo y alargado que se encuentra paralelo a la costa (pág. 466)

basaltic composition a compositional group of igneous rocks indicating that the rock contains substantial dark silicate minerals and calcium-rich plagioclase feldspar (p. 73)

basaltic composition/composición basáltica grupo composicional de rocas ígneas que indica que la roca contiene cantidades sustanciales de minerales de silicato oscuros y feldespato de plagioclasa rico en calcio (pág. 73)

batholith a large mass of igneous rock that formed when magma intruded at depth, became crystallized, and subsequently was exposed by erosion; Batholiths have a surface exposure greater than 100 square kilometers. (p. 297)

batholith/batolito masa grande de roca ígnea que se forma cuando el magma penetra en la profundidad, se cristaliza y luego queda expuesta debido a la erosión; los batolitos tienen una superficie expuesta mayor a los 100 kilómetros cuadrados (pág. 297)

bathymetry the measurement of ocean depths and the charting of the shape or topography of the ocean floor (p. 396)

bathymetry/batimetría medición de las profundidades marinas y trazado de la forma o topografía del fondo marino (pág. 396)

beach the accumulation of sediment found along the shore of a lake or an ocean (p. 461)

beach/playa acumulación de sedimento que se encuentra a lo largo de la costa de un lago u océano (pág. 461)

bed load sediment that is carried by a stream along the bottom of its channel (p. 165)

bed load/carga del lecho sedimento arrastrado por una corriente de agua a lo largo del fondo de su canal (pág. 165)

benthic zone 0the marine-life zone that includes any sea-bottom surface regardless of its distance from shore (p. 431)

benthic zone/zona béntica zona de vida marina que incluye cualquier superficie del fondo del mar sin importar su distancia de la costa (pág. 431)

benthos the forms of marine life that live on or in the ocean bottom; includes marine algae, sea stars, and crabs (p. 429)

benthos/bentos organismos marinos que viven en el fondo marino; incluyen algas marinas, estrellas de mar y cangrejos (pág. 429)

Bergeron process a theory that relates the formation of precipitation to supercooled clouds, freezing nuclei, and the different saturation levels of ice and liquid water (p. 521)

Bergeron process/proceso de Bergeron teoría que relaciona la formación de precipitación con nubes sobreenfriadas, núcleos congelados y los diferentes niveles de saturación del agua helada y el agua líquida (pág. 521)

big bang theory the theory that proposes that the universe originated as a single mass, which subsequently exploded (p. 720)

big bang theory/teoría del Big Bang teoría que propone que el universo se originó como una masa única, la cual estalló posteriormente (pág. 720)

binary star one of two stars revolving around a common center of mass under their mutual gravitational attraction (p. 701)

Glossary

binary star/estrella binaria una de dos estrellas que giran alrededor de un centro de masa común atraídas por su fuerza gravitacional mutua (pág. 701)

biogenous sediment seafloor sediment of biological origin, such as shells and skeletons of marine life (p. 408)

biogenous sediment/sedimento biogénico sedimento del fondo marino de origen biológico, como conchas y esqueletos de organismos marinos (pág. 408)

biosphere all life on Earth; the parts of the solid Earth, hydrosphere, and atmosphere in which living organisms can be found (p. 7)

biosphere/biosfera toda la vida en la Tierra; partes de la Tierra sólida, la hidrosfera y la atmósfera en las que se encuentran los organismos vivos (pág. 7)

black hole a massive star that has collapsed to such a small volume that its gravity prevents the escape of everything, including light (p. 714)

black hole/agujero negro estrella masiva que se ha reducido a un volumen tan pequeño que su fuerza de gravedad no permite que nada se escape, incluyendo la luz (pág. 714)

C

calcareous ooze thick, common biogenous sediment produced by dissolving calcium carbonate shells (p. 408)

calcareous ooze/fango calcáreo sedimento biógeno común y grueso, producido por la disolución de conchas de carbonato de calcio (pág. 408)

caldera a large depression typically caused by collapse or ejection of the summit area of a volcano (p. 292)

caldera/caldera depresión grande causada típicamente por el colapso o la expulsión de la cima de un volcán (pág. 292)

capacity the total amount of sediment a stream is able to transport (p. 165)

capacity/capacidad cantidad total de sedimento que puede transportar una corriente de agua (pág. 165)

cavern a naturally formed underground chamber or series of chambers most commonly produced by solution activity in limestone (p. 176)

cavern/caverna cámara subterráneas o serie de cámaras subterráneas formadas naturalmente y producidas comúnmente por actividad de solución sobre piedra caliza (pág. 176)

cementation solidification of sediments by the deposition of dissolved minerals in the tiny spaces between the sedimentary particles (p. 76)

cementation/cementación solidificación de sedimentos por el depósito de minerales disueltos en los espacios diminutos entre las partículas sedimentarias (pág. 76)

Cepheid variable a star whose brightness varies periodically because it expands and contracts; a type of pulsating star (p. 705)

Cepheid variable/variable Cefeida estrella cuya luminosidad varía periódicamente porque se expande y se contrae; tipo de estrella púlsar (pág. 705)

chemical bond a force that holds together atoms that form a compound (p. 38)

chemical bond/enlace químico fuerza que une los átomos que forman un compuesto (pág. 38)

chemical sedimentary rock sedimentary rock consisting of material that was precipitated from water by either inorganic or organic means (p. 77)

chemical sedimentary rock/roca sedimentaria química roca sedimentaria formada de material precipitado del agua por medios inorgánicos u orgánicos (pág. 77)

chemical weathering the processes by which the internal structure of a mineral is altered by the removal and/or addition of elements (p. 129)

chemical weathering/meteorización química proceso mediante el cual la estructura interna de un mineral es alterada por la extracción y/o la suma de elementos (pág. 129)

chemosynthesis the process by which certain microorganisms use chemical energy to produce food (p. 433)

chemosynthesis/quimiosíntesis proceso por el cual ciertos microorganismos usan energía química para producir alimento (pág. 433)

chromatic aberration the property of a lens whereby light of different colors is focused at different places (p. 679)

chromatic aberration/aberración cromática propiedad de una lente en la cual se enfoca luz de diferentes colores en distintos lugares (pág. 679)

chromosphere the first layer of the solar atmosphere found directly above the photosphere (p. 686)

chromosphere/cromosfera primera capa de la atmósfera solar que se encuentra directamente por encima de la fotosfera (pág. 686)

cinder cone a small volcano built primarily of pyroclastic material ejected from a single vent (p. 290)

cinder cone/cono de escoria volcán pequeño formado principalmente de material piroclástico expulsado por una sola abertura (pág. 290)

cirque an amphitheater-shaped basin at the head of a glaciated valley produced by frost wedging and plucking (p. 193)

cirque/circo cuenca en forma de anfiteatro en la cabecera de un valle glaciar producida por la erosión de hielo (pág. 193)

cirrus one of three basic cloud forms; also one of the three high cloud types; They are thin, delicate ice-crystal clouds often appearing as veil-like patches or thin, wispy fibers. (p. 517)

cirrus/cirro una de las tres formaciones básicas de las nubes; también uno de los tres tipos de nubes altas; son nubes cristalinas delicadas que parecen retazos de velo o fibras tenues y finas (pág. 517)

clastic sedimentary rock a sedimentary rock made of broken fragments of preexisting rock (p. 77)

clastic sedimentary rock/roca sedimentaria clástica roca sedimentaria hecha de fragmentos rotos de roca preexistente (pág. 77)

cleavage the tendency of a mineral to break along planes of weak bonding (p. 52)

cleavage/clivaje tendencia de un mineral a fracturarse a lo largo de planos de enlace débiles (pág. 52)

cold front a front along which a cold air mass thrusts beneath a warmer air mass (p. 566)

cold front/frente frío frente en el que una masa de aire frío avanza bajo una masa de aire caliente (pág. 566)

collision-coalescence process a theory of raindrop formation in warm clouds (above 0°C) in which large cloud droplets collide and join together with smaller droplets to form a raindrop; Opposite electrical charges may bind the cloud droplets together. (p. 521)

collision-coalescence process/proceso de coalescencia y colisión teoría sobre la formación de gotas de agua en nubes cálidas (por encima de los 0 °C), en la cual las gotas grandes de agua en una nube chocan y se unen con gotitas más pequeñas para formar una gota de mayor tamaño; Las corrientes eléctricas opuestas pueden unir las gotitas. (pág. 521)

coma the fuzzy, gaseous component of a comet's head (p. 662)

coma/coma componente gaseoso y difuso que rodea el núcleo de un cometa (pág. 662)

comet a small body made of rocky and metallic pieces held together by frozen gases; Comets generally revolve about the sun in an elongated orbit. (p. 661)

comet/cometa cuerpo pequeño formado por materiales rocosos y metálicos unidos por medio de gases congelados; Los cometas generalmente giran alrededor del Sol en una órbita alargada. (pág. 661)

compaction process by which sediments are squeezed together by the weight of overlying materials driving out water (p. 76)

compaction/compactación proceso por el cual los sedimentos se unen y expulsan agua debido al peso de los materiales que los cubren (pág. 76)

composite cone a volcano composed of both lava flows and pyroclastic material (p. 291)

composite cone/estratovolcán volcán compuesto de flujos de lava y material piroclástico (pág. 291)

compost partly decomposed organic material that is used as fertilizer (p. 115)

compost/compost material orgánico parcialmente descompuesto que se usa como fertilizante (pág. 115)

compound a substance formed by the chemical combination of two or more elements in definite proportions and usually having properties different from those of its constituent elements (p. 37)

compound/compuesto sustancia formada por la combinación química de dos o más elementos en proporciones definidas y que tiene usualmente propiedades diferentes a las de los elementos que la componen (pág. 37)

condensation the change of state from a gas to a liquid (p. 506)

condensation/condensación cambio de estado de un gas a un líquido (pág. 506)

condensation nuclei tiny bits of particulate matter that serve as surfaces on which water vapor condenses (p. 516)

condensation nuclei/núcleos de condensación partículas muy pequeñas de materia que sirven como superficies para que se condense el vapor (pág. 516)

conduction the transfer of heat through matter by molecular activity; Energy is transferred through collisions from one molecule to another. (p. 483)

conduction/conducción transferencia de calor a través de la materia por actividad molecular; la energía se transfiere a través de choques de una molécula contra otra (pág. 483)

conservation the careful use of resources (p. 113)

conservation/conservación uso cuidadoso de los recursos (pág. 113)

constellation an apparent group of stars originally named for mythical characters; The sky is presently divided into 88 constellations. (p. 700)

constellation/constelación grupo aparente de estrellas nombrado originalmente a partir de personajes míticos; el cielo se encuentra en la actualidad dividido en 88 constelaciones (pág. 700)

contact metamorphism changes in rock caused by the heat from a nearby magma body (p. 81)

contact metamorphism/metamorfismo de contacto cambios en una roca causados por el calor de una masa de magma cercano (pág. 81)

continental drift a hypothesis that originally proposed that the continents had once been joined to form a single supercontinent; The supercontinent broke into pieces, which drifted into their present-day positions. (p. 248)

continental drift/deriva continental hipótesis que propuso originalmente que los continentes

estuvieron unidos formando un solo supercontinente; El supercontinente se quebró en pedazos, los cuales se desplazaron hasta sus posiciones actuales. (pág. 248)

continental glacier a very large, thick mass of glacial ice that covers a large region and flows outward in all directions from one or more accumulation centers; also called a continental ice sheet (p. 189)

continental glacier/glaciar continental masa muy grande y gruesa de hielo glacial que cubre una región grande y fluye hacia afuera en todas direcciones desde uno o más centros de acumulación; también se le llama capa de hielo continental (pág. 189)

continental margin that portion of the seafloor adjacent to the continents; It may include the continental shelf, continental slope, and continental rise. (p. 402)

continental margin/margen continental porción del suelo marino adyacente a los continentes; puede incluir la plataforma continental, el talud continental y el pie continental (pág. 402)

continental rise the gently sloping surface at the base of the continental slope (p. 403)

continental rise/pie continental superficie que se encuentra levemente en declive en la base del talud continental (pág. 403)

continental shelf the gently sloping submerged portion of the continental margin, extending from the shoreline to the continental slope (p. 402)

continental shelf/plataforma continental porción sumergida y levemente en declive del margen continental, que se extiende desde la costa hasta el talud continental (pág. 402)

continental slope the steep gradient that leads to the deep-ocean floor and marks the seaward edge of the continental shelf (p. 403)

continental slope/talud continental pendiente empinada que conduce al suelo marino profundo y marca el límite de la plataforma continental que da al mar (pág. 403)

continental volcanic arc mountains formed in part by volcanic activity caused by the subduction of oceanic lithosphere beneath a continent (p. 265)

continental volcanic arc/arco volcánico continental montañas formadas en parte por actividad volcánica causada por la subducción de la litosfera volcánica debajo de un continente (pág. 265)

continuous spectrum an uninterrupted band of light emitted by an incandescent solid, liquid, or gas under pressure (p. 676)

continuos spectrum/espectro continuo banda de luz continua emitida por un sólido, un líquido o un gas incandescente bajo presión (pág. 676)

contour interval on a topographic map, tells the distance in elevation between adjacent contour lines (p. 14)

contour interval/intervalo entre curvas de nivel en un mapa topográfico, indica la diferencia de altitud entre dos curvas de nivel adyacentes (pág. 14)

contour line line on a topographic map that indicates an elevation; Every point along a contour line has the same elevation. (p. 14)

contour line/curva de nivel línea en un mapa topográfico que indica una altitud; Todos los puntos a lo largo de una curva de nivel tienen la misma altitud. (pág. 14)

convection the transfer of heat by the movement of a mass or substance; It can take place only in fluids. (p. 484)

convection/convección transferencia de calor por el movimiento de una masa o sustancia; puede ocurrir sólo en líquidos (pág. 484)

convection current the motion of matter resulting from changes in temperature; The convective flow of material in the mantle is due to Earth's unequal heating and causes the tectonic plates to move. (p. 269)

convection current/corriente de convección movimiento de materia resultante de cambios en la temperatura; El flujo convectivo de material en el manto se debe al calentamiento desigual de la tierra y hace que las placas tectónicas se muevan. (pág. 269)

convergent boundary a boundary in which two plates move together (p. 262)

convergent boundary/límite convergente límite en el cual dos placas se muevan juntas (pág. 262)

core the innermost layer of Earth, located beneath the mantle; The core is divided into an outer core and an inner core. (p. 8)

core/núcleo capa más interna de la tierra, ubicada debajo del manto; El núcleo está dividido en un núcleo exterior y un núcleo interior. (pág. 8)

Coriolis effect the apparent deflective force of Earth's rotation on all free-moving objects, including the atmosphere and oceans; Deflection is to the right in the Northern Hemisphere and to the left in the Southern Hemisphere. (p. 449)

Coriolis effect/efecto de Coriolis aparente fuerza desviadora que la rotación de la Tierra ejerce sobre todos los objetos que están en movimiento libre, incluyendo la atmósfera y los océanos; El desvío es hacia la derecha en el hemisferio norte y hacia la izquierda en el hemisferio sur. (pág. 449)

corona the outer weak layer of the solar atmosphere (p. 686)

corona/corona solar débil capa exterior de la atmósfera solar (pág. 686)

correlation establishing the equivalence of rocks of similar age in different areas (p. 340)

correlation/correlación establecimiento de la equivalencia de rocas de edades similares en diferentes áreas (pág. 340)

covalent bond a bond that forms when atoms share electrons (p. 39)

covalent bond/enlace covalente enlace que se forma cuando los átomos comparten electrones (pág. 39)

crater the depression at the summit of a volcano or that which is produced by a meteorite impact (p. 289)

crater/cráter depresión en la cumbre de un volcán o la que se produce por el impacto de un meteorito (pág. 289)

creep the slow downhill movement of soil and regolith (p. 147)

creep/reptación movimiento lento cuesta abajo de tierra y regolitos (pág. 147)

crevasse a deep crack in the brittle surface of a glacier (p. 190)

crevasse/hendidura grieta profunda en la superficie frágil de un glaciar (pág. 190)

Glossary

cross-cutting relationships, principle of a principle of relative dating; A rock or fault is younger than any rock or fault through which it cuts. (p. 339)

cross-cutting relationships, principle of/relaciones de corte transversal, principio de principio de datación relativa; Una roca o falla es más joven que cualquier roca o falla que atraviesa. (pág. 339)

crust the thin, rocky outer layer of Earth (p. 8)

crust/corteza capa exterior fina y rocosa de la tierra (pág. 8)

crystal form the external appearance of a mineral as determined by its internal arrangement of atoms (p. 49)

crystal form/forma cristalina apariencia externa de un mineral determinada según la distribución interna de los átomos (pág. 49)

cumulus one of three basic cloud forms; also the name given to one of the clouds of vertical development; They are billowy individual cloud masses that often have flat bases. (p. 517)

cumulus/cúmulo una de las tres formas básicas de las nubes; nombre dado también a una de las nubes de desarrollo vertical; son masas de nubes individuales ondulantes que tienen a menudo bases planas (pág. 517)

cyclone a low-pressure center characterized by a counterclockwise flow of air in the Northern Hemisphere (p. 538)

cyclone/ciclón centro de baja presión en el hemisferio norte caracterizado por una corriente de aire que corre en sentido contrario a las manecillas del reloj (pág. 538)

D

decompression melting melting due to a drop in confining pressure that occurs as rock rises (p. 281)

decompression melting/fusión por descompresión fusión debida a una disminución de la presión restrictiva que ocurre a medida que una roca va subiendo (pág. 281)

deflation the lifting and removal of loose material by wind (p. 203)

deflation/deflación levantamiento y remoción de material suelto por el viento (pág. 203)

deformation general term for the processes of folding, faulting, shearing, compression, or extension of rocks as the result of various natural forces (p. 308)

deformation/deformación término general para los procesos de plegamiento, formación de fallas, partición, comprensión o extensión en rocas, como resultado de diferentes fuerzas naturales (pág. 308)

delta an accumulation of sediment formed where a stream enters a lake or an ocean (p. 166)

delta/delta acumulación de sedimento que se forma donde una corriente de agua entra a un lago u océano (pág. 166)

density mass per unit volume of a substance, usually expressed as grams per cubic centimeter (p. 53)

density/densidad masa por unidad de volumen de una sustancia, expresada por lo general en gramos por centímetro cúbico (pág. 53)

density current current of ocean water that results from density differences among water masses (p. 451)

density current/corriente de densidad corriente de agua oceánica que resulta de las diferencias de densidad entre las masas de agua (pág. 451)

deposition the process by which an agent of erosion loses energy and drops the sediment it is carrying; also the process by which water vapor is changed directly to a solid without passing through the liquid state (p. 76, p. 506)

desposition/deposición proceso por el cual un agente de erosión pierde energía y deja caer el sedimento que arrastra; también es el proceso por el cual el vapor de agua pasa al estado sólido sin pasar por el estado líquido (pág. 76, pág. 506)

desert pavement a layer of coarse pebbles and gravel created when wind removed the finer material (p. 204)

desert pavement/pavimento desértico capa de guijarros gruesos y grava que se forma cuando el viento remueve el material más fino (pág. 204)

dew point the temperature to which air has to be cooled in order to reach saturation (p. 508)

dew point/punto de condensación temperatura a la cual se tiene que enfriar el aire para que alcance la saturación (pág. 508)

dike a tabular-shaped intrusive igneous feature that occurs when magma is injected into fractures in the surrounding rock, cutting across preexisting rock layers (p. 296)

dike/dique masa intrusiva de magma solidificado de forma tabular que se forma cuando el magma es inyectado en las fracturas de la roca circundante, penetrando transversalmente las capas de rocas preexistentes (pág. 296)

dinosaur land-dwelling reptile of the Mesozoic era (p. 377)

dinosaur/dinosaurio reptil de tierra de la era Mesozoica (pág. 377)

discharge the quantity of water in a stream that passes a given point in a period of time (p. 161)

discharge/caudal cantidad de agua en una corriente que pasa por un punto determinado en un período (pág. 161)

divergent boundary a region where the rigid plates are moving apart, typified by the oceanic ridges (p. 262)

divergent boundary/límite divergente zona donde las placas tectónicas se separan, tipificada por las dorsales oceánicas (pág. 262)

divide an imaginary line that separates the drainage of two streams; often found along a ridge (p. 169)

divide/divisoria de aguas línea imaginaria que separa el drenaje de dos corrientes de agua; frecuentemente se encuentra a lo largo de una elevación (pág. 169)

Doppler effect the apparent change in frequency of electromagnetic or sound waves caused by the relative motions of the source and the observer (p. 677)

Doppler effect/efecto Doppler variación aparente en la frecuencia de una onda sonora o electromagnética debido al movimiento relativo entre la fuente de la onda y el observador (pág. 677)

drainage basin the land area that contributes water to a stream (p. 169)

drainage basin/cuenca de avenamiento área de tierra que aporta agua a un arroyo (pág. 169)

drumlin a streamlined asymmetrical hill composed of glacial till; The steep side of the hill faces the direction from which the ice advanced. (p. 196)

drumlin/drumlin colina asimétrica compuesta de tilita glacial; El lado empinado de la colina mira hacia la dirección desde la cual avanzó el hielo. (pág. 196)

dry adiabatic rate the rate of adiabatic cooling or warming in unsaturated air; The rate of temperature change is 1°C per 100 meters. (p. 511)

dry adiabatic rate/tasa adiabática seca tasa de enfriamiento o calentamiento adiabático en el aire no saturado; la tasa de cambio en la temperatura es de 1 °C por cada 100 metros (pág. 511)

dry-summer subtropical climate a climate located on the west sides of continents between 30° and 45° latitude; It is the only humid climate with a strong winter precipitation maximum. (p. 596)

dry-summer subtropical climate/clima subtropical de veranos secos clima que se encuentra en el occidente de los continentes entre los 30° y 45° de latitud; es el único clima húmedo que tiene una precipitación máxima elevada en invierno (pág. 596)

dune a hill or ridge of wind-deposited sand (p. 204)

dune/duna colina o elevación formada por arena depositada por el viento (pág. 204)

dwarf planet a round object that orbits the sun but has not cleared the neighborhood around its orbit (p. 659)

dwarf planet/planeta enano un cuerpo esférico que está en órbita alrededor del Sol, pero no ha limpiado la vecindad de su órbita (pág. 659)

E

earthflow slow-moving downslope movement of water-saturated, clay-rich sediment, most characteristic of humid regions (p. 146)

earthflow/deslizamiento de tierra movimiento lento y descendente de sedimento saturado con agua, rico en arcilla, muy característico de las regiones húmedas (pág. 146)

earthquake the vibration of Earth produced by the rapid release of energy (p. 218)

Glossary

earthquake/terremoto vibración de la Tierra producida por una liberación rápida de energía (pág. 218)

Earth science the name for all the sciences that collectively seek to understand Earth; It includes geology, oceanography, meteorology, and astronomy. (p. 2)

Earth science/ciencias de la Tierra nombre dado a todas las ciencias que colectivamente estudian la Tierra; incluye la geología, la oceanografía, la meteorología y la astronomía (pág. 2)

elastic rebound tendency for deformed rock along a fault to spring back to its original shape after an earthquake (p. 220)

elastic rebound/rebote elástico tendencia de la roca deformada a lo largo de una falla geológica a volver a su configuración original después de un sismo (pág. 220)

electromagnetic spectrum the arrangement of electromagnetic radiation according to wavelength (p. 674)

electromagnetic spectrum/espectro electromagnético orden de la radiación electromagnética según la longitud de onda (pág. 674)

element a substance that cannot be broken down into simpler substances by ordinary chemical or physical means (p. 34)

element/elemento sustancia que no puede ser descompuesta en sustancias más sencillas a través de métodos químicos o físicos comunes (pág. 34)

ellipse an oval (p. 618)

ellipse/elipse óvalo (pág. 618)

El Niño the name given to the periodic warming of the ocean that occurs in the central and eastern Pacific; A major El Niño episode can cause extreme weather in many parts of the world. (p. 546)

El Niño/El Niño nombre dado al calentamiento periódico que ocurre en las regiones central y oriental del océano Pacífico; Un episodio intenso de El Niño puede causar fenómenos climáticos extremos en muchas partes del mundo. (pág. 546)

emission spectrum a series of bright lines of particular wavelengths produced by a hot gas under low pressure (p. 676)

emission spectrum/espectro de emisión serie de luces brillantes con longitudes de onda específicas, producidas por un gas caliente sometido a bajas presiones (pág. 676)

energy level one of several distinct regions around the nucleus of an atom where electrons are located (p. 35)

energy level/nivel de energía una de varias regiones específicas que rodea el núcleo de un átomo y en donde se ubican los electrones (pág. 35)

eon the largest time unit on the geologic time scale, next in order of magnitude above era (p. 354)

eon/eón unidad de mayor intervalo en la escala geocronológica, mayor que una era (pág. 354)

epicenter the location on Earth's surface directly above the focus, or origin, of an earthquake (p. 219)

epicenter/epicentro punto en la superficie de la Tierra que está justo sobre el foco, u origen, de un terremoto (pág. 219)

epoch a unit of the geologic time scale that is a subdivision of a period (p. 355)

epoch/época unidad de la escala geocronológica, que es una subdivisión de un período (pág. 355)

era a major division on the geologic time scale; Eras are divided into shorter units called periods. (p. 354)

era/era una de las grandes divisiones de la escala geocronológica; Las eras se dividen en unidades más pequeñas llamadas períodos. (pág. 354)

erosion the incorporation and transportation of material by a mobile agent, such as water, wind, or ice (p. 76)

erosion/erosión incorporación y transporte de un material por un agente móvil, como el agua, el viento o el hielo (pág. 76)

esker sinuous ridge composed largely of sand and gravel deposited by a stream flowing in a tunnel beneath a glacier near its terminus (p. 197)

esker/esker elevación alargada y sinuosa, compuesta por arena y grava que han sido depositadas por un arroyo que fluye por el túnel de un glaciar, cerca de su punta. (pág. 197)

eukaryote an organism whose cells contain nuclei (p. 368)

eukaryote/eucariota organismo cuyas células contienen núcleos (pág. 368)

evaporation the process of converting a liquid to a gas (p. 505)

evaporation/evaporación proceso mediante el cual un líquido se convierte en gas (pág. 505)

evolution, theory of theory developed by Charles Darwin stating that all the different kinds of living things have changed over time (p. 345)

evolution, theory of/evolución, teoría de la teoría elaborada por Charles Darwin que sostiene que todos los seres vivos se han transformado a través del tiempo (pág. 345)

exfoliation type of weathering caused by reducing pressure on a rock surface, allowing slabs of outer rock to break off in layers (p. 128)

exfoliation/exfoliación tipo de meteorización causada por la disminución de la presión en una superficie rocosa, lo que permite que los estratos externos de la roca se desprendan en láminas (pág. 128)

extinct term used to describe a type of organism that no longer exists anywhere on Earth (p. 342)

extinct/extinto describe un tipo de organismo que ya no existe en la Tierra (pág. 342)

extrusive igneous rock igneous rock that has formed on Earth's surface (p. 71)

extrusive igneous rock/roca ígnea extrusiva roca ígnea que ha sido formada en la superficie de la Tierra (pág. 71)

eye a zone of scattered clouds and calm averaging about 20 kilometers in diameter at the center of a hurricane (p. 576)

eye/ojo zona de calma, con pocas nubes, que en promedio mide 20 kilómetros de diámetro y que se encuentra en el centro de un huracán (pág. 576)

eye wall the doughnut-shaped area of intense cumulonimbus development and very strong winds that surrounds the eye of a hurricane (p. 576)

eye wall/pared del ojo zona en forma de rosquilla con gran intensidad de cumulonimbos y fuertes vientos, que rodea el ojo de un huracán (pág. 576)

F

fault a fracture in Earth along which movement has occurred (p. 218)

fault/falla fractura en la Tierra en la cual ha habido movimiento (pág. 218)

fault-block mountain a mountain formed when large blocks of crust are tilted, uplifted, or dropped between large normal faults (p. 317)

fault block mountain/montaña de bloque de falla montaña formada cuando los bloques grandes de corteza terrestre se inclinan, se elevan o caen entre fallas grandes (pág. 317)

fetch the distance that the wind has traveled across open water (p. 456)

fetch/alcance del viento distancia que ha recorrido el viento sobre aguas abiertas (pág. 456)

firn coarse grains of ice resulting from recrystallization of compressed snow (p. 189)

firn/neviza granos gruesos de hielo formados cuando la nieve comprimida se vuelve a cristalizar (pág. 189)

flood occurs when the discharge of a stream becomes so great that it exceeds the carrying capacity of its channel and overflows its banks (p. 168)

flood/inundación ocurre cuando el caudal de una corriente de agua es tan grande que sobrepasa la capacidad de su canal y se desborda por sus riberas (pág. 168)

floodplain the flat, low-lying portion of a stream valley subject to periodic flooding (p. 167)

floodplain/planicie aluvial parte plana y baja del valle de un arroyo que está expuesta a inundaciones periódicas (pág. 167)

focus the point within Earth where an earthquake originates (p. 218)

focus/foco punto dentro de la Tierra en el cual se origina un terremoto (pág. 218)

folded mountain a mountain created primarily by compressional stresses, which create folds in the rock layers (p. 316)

folded mountain/montaña de pliegues montaña que ha sido creada principalmente por esfuerzos de compresión, los caules causan pliegues en los estratos de roca (pág. 316)

Glossary

foliated metamorphic rock a metamorphic rock with a texture that gives the rock a layered appearance (p. 83)

foliated metamorphic rock/roca metamórfica esquistosa roca metamórfica que tiene una textura que le da una apariencia de capas (pág. 83)

food chain a succession of organisms through which food energy is transferred, starting with primary producers (p. 437)

food chain/cadena alimentaria serie de organismos a través de los cuales se transfiere la energía de los alimentos y que empieza por los productores primarios (pág. 437)

food web a group of interrelated food chains (p. 437)

food web/red alimentaria grupo de cadenas alimentarias interrelacionadas (pág. 437)

foreshock a small earthquake that often precedes a major earthquake (p. 221)

foreshock/sismo premonitor pequeño terremoto que generalmente precede a un terremoto mayor (pág. 221)

fossil the remains or traces of an organism preserved from the geologic past (p. 342)

fossil/fósil remanentes o vestigios de un organismo que ha sido preservado del pasado geológico (pág. 342)

fossil fuel general term for any hydrocarbon that may be used as a fuel, including coal, oil, and natural gas (p. 95)

fossil fuel/combustible fósil término general usado para describir los hidrocarburos que se utilizan como combustible, entre los cuales están el carbón mineral, el petróleo y el gas natural (pág. 95)

fossil succession, principle of geologic principle stating that fossil organisms succeed one another in a definite order in the rock record (p. 344)

fossil succession, principle of/sucesión faunística, principio de la principio geológico que sostiene que los fósiles indican el orden particular de la formación de las rocas (pág. 344)

fracture any break or rupture in rock along which no appreciable movement has taken place (p. 53)

fracture/fractura discontinuidad en una roca en la cual no se manifiesta que haya ocurrido movimiento alguno (pág. 53)

front the boundary between two adjoining air masses having contrasting characteristics (p. 512)

front/frente límite entre dos masas de aire adyacentes que tienen características que contrastan (pág. 512)

frost wedging the mechanical breakup of rock caused by the expansion of freezing water in cracks and crevices (p. 127)

frost wedging/gelifracción fragmentación mecánica de una roca, causada por la expansión tras la congelación del agua en sus grietas y poros (pág. 127)

G

galaxy a group of stars, dust, and gases held together by gravity (p. 715)

galaxy/galaxia grupo de estrellas, polvo y gas unidos por la gravedad (pág. 715)

galaxy cluster a system of galaxies containing from several to thousands of member galaxies (p. 718)

galaxy cluster/cúmulo de galaxias sistema que puede contener hasta miles de galaxias (pág. 718)

gas hydrate a gas, such as methane, trapped in a lattice-like structure of water molecules (p. 411)

gas hydrate/hidrato de gas un gas, por ejemplo el metano, que queda atrapado en una red de moléculas de agua (pág. 411)

geocentric describes the concept of an Earth-centered universe (p. 615)

geocentric/geocéntrico describe un universo cuyo centro es la Tierra (pág. 615)

geologic time scale the division of Earth history into blocks of time—eons, eras, periods, and epochs; The time scale was created using relative dating principles. (p. 353)

geologic time scale/escala geocronológica división de la historia de la Tierra en bloques de tiempo: eones, eras, períodos y épocas; La escala cronológica fue creada usando los principios de datación relativa. (pág. 353)

geology the science that examines Earth, its form and composition, and the changes it has undergone and is undergoing (p. 2)

geology/geología ciencia que estudia la Tierra, su forma, su composición y los cambios que ha tenido y que continúa teniendo (pág. 2)

geosphere layer of Earth under both the atmosphere and the oceans; It is composed of the core, the mantle, and the crust. (p. 7)

geosphere/geosfera estrato de la Tierra que se encuentra bajo la atmósfera y los océanos; está compuesta por el núcleo, el manto y la corteza (pág. 7)

geothermal energy energy that can be extracted from Earth's internal heat, for example, natural steam used for power generation (p. 105)

geothermal energy/energía geotérmica energía que puede extraerse del calor interno de la Tierra; por ejemplo, el vapor natural que se usa para generar electricidad (pág. 105)

geothermal gradient the gradual increase in temperature with depth in the crust; The average is 30°C per kilometer in the upper crust. (p. 291)

geothermal gradient/gradiente geotérmico aumento gradual de la temperatura a medida que se penetra en la corteza; La media es 30 °C por kilómetro en la corteza superior. (pág. 291)

geyser a hot spring or fountain that ejects water at various intervals (p. 172)

geyser/géiser manantial o fuente de agua caliente que expele agua a intervalos (pág. 172)

glacial erratic an ice-transported rock not derived from bedrock near its present site (p. 194)

glacial erratic/bloque errático roca transportada por el hielo y que no se originó del lecho rocoso donde se encuentra (pág. 194)

glacier a thick mass of ice originating on land from the compaction and recrystallization of snow that shows evidence of past or present flow (p. 188)

glacier/glaciar masa gruesa de hielo que se origina en la superficie terrestre por compactación y recristalización de la nieve, mostrando evidencias de flujo en el pasado o en la actualidad (pág. 188)

global warming the increase in average temperatures of Earth and the atmosphere due in part to increased carbon dioxide levels (p. 110)

global warming/calentamiento global aumento de la temperatura media de la Tierra y de la atmósfera causado en parte por el aumento en los niveles de dióxido de carbono (pág. 110)

Gondwana late Paleozoic continent that formed the southern portion of Pangaea, consisting of all or parts of present-day South America, Africa, Australia, India, and Antarctica (p. 370)

Gondwana/Gondwana continente de finales del paleozoico, que formaba la porción austral de Pangea y que abarcaba lo que hoy en día son América del Sur, África, Australia, India y la Antártida (pág. 370)

graben a valley formed by the downward displacement of a fault-bounded block (p. 317)

graben/fosa tectónica valle formado por el desplazamiento descendente de un bloque rodeado de fallas (pág. 317)

gradient the slope of a stream over a certain distance (p. 161)

gradient/gradiente pendiente de un arroyo a lo largo de una distancia determinada (pág. 161)

granitic composition a compositional group of igneous rocks that indicate a rock is composed almost entirely of light-colored silicates, mainly quartz and feldspar (p. 73)

granitic composition/composición de granito grupo estructural de rocas ígneas que indica que una roca está compuesta casi enteramente de silicatos de color claro, principalmente cuarzo y feldespato (pág. 73)

greenhouse effect the heating of Earth's surface and atmosphere from solar radiation being absorbed and emitted by the atmosphere, mainly by water vapor and carbon dioxide (p. 487)

greenhouse effect/efecto invernadero calentamiento de la superficie y la atmósfera de la Tierra debido a la absorción y emisión de radiación solar por la atmósfera, principalmente por el vapor de agua y el dióxido de carbono (pág. 487)

groundwater water underground in the zone of saturation (p. 171)

groundwater/agua subterránea agua que se encuentra bajo la tierra, en las zonas de saturación (pág. 171)

gymnosperm seed-bearing plant that bears its seeds on the surfaces of cones (p. 378)

gymnosperm/gimnosperma planta cuyas semillas se encuentran en las superficies de los conos (pág. 378)

gyre the large circular surface current pattern found in each ocean (p. 449)

gyre/giro patrón de corriente circular grande que se encuentra en todos los océanos (pág. 449)

H

half-life the time required for one half of the atoms of a radioactive substance to decay (p. 348)

half-life/vida media tiempo requerido para que se desintegre la mitad de los átomos de una sustancia radiactiva (pág. 348)

hardness the resistance a mineral offers to scratching (p. 52)

hardness/dureza resistencia que ofrece un mineral a ser rayado (pág. 52)

heliocentric describes the view that the sun is at the center of the solar system (p. 616)

heliocentric/heliocéntrico describe la idea de que el Sol es el centro del sistema solar (pág. 616)

heat thermal energy transferred from one object to another (p. 483)

heat/calor energía térmica que se transfiere de un objeto a otro (pág. 483)

Hertzsprung-Russell diagram *See* H-R diagram

Hertzsprung-Russell diagram/diagrama Hertzprung-Russell *ver* diagrama HR

horst an elongated, uplifted block of crust bounded by faults (p. 317)

horst/pilar tectónico bloque de corteza alargado que ha sido empujado hacia arriba y se encuentra rodeado de fallas (pág. 317)

hot spot a concentration of heat in the mantle capable of producing magma, which rises to Earth's surface; The Pacific plate moves over a hot spot, producing the Hawaiian Islands. (p. 285)

hot spot/punto caliente concentración de calor en el manto capaz de producir magma, la cual sube a la superficie terrestre; la placa tectónica del Pacífico se mueve sobre un punto caliente que formó las islas hawaianas (pág. 285)

H-R diagram a plot of stars according to their absolute magnitudes and temperatures (p. 704)

H-R diagram/diagrama HR diagrama de estrellas basado en las temperaturas y magnitudes absolutas de las mismas (pág. 704)

Hubble's law a law that states that the galaxies are retreating from the Milky Way at a speed that is proportional to their distance (p. 719)

Hubble's law/ley de Hubble ley que establece que las galaxias se alejan de la vía láctea a una velocidad proporcional a sus distancias (pág. 719)

humidity a general term referring to water vapor in the air but not to liquid droplets of fog, cloud, or rain (p. 506)

humidity/humedad término general que se refiere al vapor de agua en el aire, excluyendo las gotas líquidas de niebla, nubes o lluvia (pág. 506)

humid subtropical climate a climate generally located on the eastern side of a continent and characterized by hot, sultry summers and cool winters (p. 596)

humid subtropical climate/clima subtropical húmedo clima que generalmente se encuentra en la parte oriental de un continente y que se caracteriza por tener veranos calientes y sofocantes, e inviernos templados (pág. 596)

hurricane a tropical cyclonic storm having winds in excess of 119 kilometers per hour (p. 575)

hurricane/huracán tormenta tropical ciclónica con vientos cuyas velocidades exceden los 119 kilómetros por hora (pág. 575)

hydroelectric power the power generated by falling water (p. 105)

hydroelectric power/energía hidroeléctrica energía generada por el agua en movimiento (pág. 105)

hydrogenous sediment seafloor sediment consisting of minerals that crystallize from seawater; An important example is manganese nodules. (p. 409)

hydrogenous sediment/sedimento hidrogenado sedimento del fondo oceánico, formado por minerales que se han cristalizado a partir del agua marina; Un ejemplo importante son los nódulos de manganeso. (pág. 409)

hydrosphere the water portion of Earth; one of the traditional subdivisions of Earth's physical environment (p. 7)

hydrosphere/hidrosfera parte acuática de la Tierra; una de las divisiones tradicionales del medio ambiente físico de la Tierra (pág. 7)

hydrothermal solution the hot, watery solution that escapes from a mass of magma during the later stages of crystallization; Such solutions may alter the surrounding rock. (p. 83)

hydrothermal solution/solución hidrotérmica solución acuosa y caliente que sale del magma durante las últimas fases de la cristalización; Estas soluciones pueden alterar las rocas que las rodean. (pág. 83)

hygrometer an instrument designed to measure relative humidity (p. 508)

hygrometer/higrómetro instrumento diseñado para medir la humedad relativa (pág. 508)

hypothesis a tentative explanation that is tested to determine if it is valid (p. 23)

hypothesis/hipótesis explicación tentativa cuya validez es sometida a prueba (pág. 23)

I

ice age a period of time when much of Earth's land is covered by glaciers (p. 88)

ice age/era glacial período en el que gran parte de la Tierra estaba cubierta por glaciares (pág. 88)

igneous rock a rock formed by the crystallization of molten magma (p. 66)

igneous rock/roca ígnea roca formada por la cristalización de magma líquido (pág. 66)

index fossil a fossil that is associated with a particular span of geologic time (p. 346)

index fossil/fósil índice fósil asociado a un período específico en la escala geocronológica (pág. 346)

infiltration the movement of surface water into rock or soil through cracks and pore spaces (p. 159)

infiltration/infiltración movimiento del agua desde la superficie hacia las rocas o la tierra a través de grietas y aperturas porosas (pág. 159)

inner core the solid innermost layer of Earth, about 1220 kilometers in radius (p. 235)

inner core/núcleo interno estrato sólido más profundo de la Tierra; tiene un radio de 1220 kilómetros (pág. 235)

intertidal zone the area where land and sea meet and overlap; the zone between high and low tides (p. 431)

intertidal zone/zona intermareal área donde se encuentran y se solapan la tierra y el mar; zona entre la marea alta y la marea baja (pág. 431)

intraplate volcanism igneous activity that occurs within a tectonic plate away from plate boundaries (p. 285)

intraplate volcanism/vulcanismo de placa actividad ígnea que ocurre en una placa tectónica lejos de sus límites (pág. 285)

intrusive igneous rock igneous rock that formed below Earth's surface (p. 71)

intrusive igneous rock/roca ígnea intrusiva roca ígnea formada bajo la superficie de la Tierra (pág. 71)

ion an atom or a molecule that possesses an electrical charge (p. 37)

ion/ion átomo o molécula que tiene una carga eléctrica (pág. 37)

ionic bond a bond that forms between negative and positive ions (p. 38)

ionic bond/enlace iónico enlace que se forma entre iones negativos e iones positivos (pág. 38)

isostasy the concept that Earth's crust is floating in gravitational balance upon the material of the mantle (p. 310)

isostasy/isostasia concepto que explica que la corteza terrestre está flotando sobre el material del manto gracias a un equilibrio gravitacional (pág. 310)

isostatic adjustment process of establishing a new level of gravitational equilibrium (p. 310)

isostatic adjustment/ajuste isostático proceso en el cual se establece un nuevo nivel de equilibrio gravitacional (pág. 310)

isotherm a line connecting points of equal temperature (p. 492)

isotherm/isoterma línea que conecta puntos que tienen temperaturas idénticas (pág. 492)

isotope an atom with the same number of protons but different numbers of neutrons for a given element; An isotope's mass number is different from that of the given element. (p. 36)

isotope/isótopo para cualquier elemento, es un átomo con igual número de protones pero distinto número de neutrones; el número de masa de un isótopo es distinto al de ese elemento (pág. 36)

J

jet stream swift (120–240 kilometers per hour), high-altitude winds (p. 536)

jet stream/corriente de chorro vientos de alta velocidad (120–240 kilómetros por hora) que se encuentran a grandes altitudes (pág. 536)

Jovian planet the Jupiter-like planets: Jupiter, Saturn, Uranus, and Neptune; These planets have relatively low densities and are huge gas giants. (p. 645)

Jovian planet/planeta joviano cualquier planeta de la familia de Júpiter: Júpiter, Saturno, Urano y Neptuno; Estos planetas tienen densidades relativamente bajas y están compuestos principalmente de gas. (pág. 645)

K

karst topography an area that has a land surface or topography with numerous depressions called sinkholes (p. 178)

karst topography/relieve kárstico zona cuya superficie o topografía presenta numerosas depresiones llamadas dolinas (pág. 178)

kettle depression created when a block of ice became lodged in glacial deposits and subsequently melted (p. 196)

kettle/marmita depresión creada cuando se derrite un bloque de hielo que se había alojado en un depósito glacial (pág. 196)

Köppen climate classification system a system for classifying climates that is based on mean monthly and annual values of temperature and precipitation (p. 592)

Köppen climate classification system/sistema de clasificación de climas de Köppen sistema para clasificar los climas en base a los valores promedio de las temperaturas y de las precipitaciones mensuales y anuales (pág. 592)

L

laccolith a massive igneous body intruded between preexisting strata (p. 296)

laccolith/lacolito cuerpo ígneo gigantesco que ha penetrado entre dos estratos preexistentes (pág. 296)

lahar mudflow made up of water-soaked volcanic ash and rock (p. 294)

lahar/lahar, el colada de barro formado por ceniza volcánica y roca saturadas de agua (pág. 294)

latent heat the energy absorbed or released during a change in state (p. 505)

latent heat/calor latente energía absorbida o desprendida durante un cambio de estado físico (pág. 505)

laterite a red, highly leached soil type found in the tropics that is rich in oxides of iron and aluminum (p. 139)

laterite/laterita suelo rojizo y altamente lixiviado de las regiones tropicales, rico en óxidos de hierro y aluminio (pág. 139)

latitude the distance north or south of the equator, measured in degrees (p. 11)

latitude/latitud distancia al norte o al sur del ecuador, que se mide en grados (pág. 11)

Laurasia the continental mass that formed the northern portion of Pangaea, consisting of present-day North America and Eurasia (p. 372)

Laurasia/Laurasia masa continental que se formó en la parte norte de Pangea, y que abarcaba lo que hoy en día son América del Norte y Eurasia (pág. 372)

lava magma that reaches Earth's surface (p. 67)

lava/lava magma que ha llegado a la superficie de la Tierra (pág. 67)

lava plateau landform produced by repeated eruptions of fluid basaltic magma that builds up in thick layers (p. 293)

lava plateau/llanura de lava formación producida por sucesivas erupciones volcánicas y la acumulación de magma basáltica en capas gruesas (pág. 293)

light-year the distance light travels in a year, about 9.5 trillion kilometers (p. 702)

light-year/año luz distancia recorrida por la luz en un año o aproximadamente 9.5 billones de kilómetros (pág. 702)

liquefaction a phenomenon, sometimes associated with earthquakes, in which soils and other unconsolidated materials saturated with water are turned into a liquid that is not able to support buildings (p. 229)

liquefaction/licuefacción fenómeno, a veces asociado con los terremotos, en el cual la tierra, junto con otros materiales no consolidados saturados con agua, se convierten en un líquido que no es capaz de sostener los edificios (pág. 229)

lithosphere the rigid outer layer of Earth, including the crust and upper mantle (p. 235)

lithosphere/litosfera capa externa y rígida de la Tierra, que incluye la corteza y el manto superior (pág. 235)

loess deposits of windblown silt, lacking visible layers, generally light yellow, and capable of maintaining a nearly vertical cliff (p. 204)

loess/loes depósitos de limo transportado por el viento, generalmente amarillos y sin estratos visibles, y que son capaces de crear precipicios casi verticales (pág. 204)

longitude the distance east or west of the prime meridian, measure in degrees (p. 11)

longitude/longitud distancia hacia el este o el oeste del Primer meridiano; se mide en grados (pág. 11)

longshore current a near-shore current that flows parallel to the shore (p. 463)

longshore current/corriente litoral corriente que está cerca de la costa y que fluye paralela a la misma (pág. 463)

lunar eclipse an eclipse of the moon; A lunar eclipse occurs when the moon passes through Earth's shadow. (p. 628)

lunar eclipse/eclipse lunar eclipse de la Luna; ocurre cuando la Luna pasa a través de la sombra de la Tierra (pág. 628)

lunar regolith a thin, gray layer on the surface of the moon, consisting of loosely compacted, fragmented material believed to have been formed by repeated impacts of meteorites (p. 632)

lunar regolith/regolito lunar capa gris y delgada sobre la superficie lunar compuesta de material fragmentado y ligeramente compactado, el cual se cree que fue formado por los impactos repetidos de meteoritos (pág. 632)

luster the appearance or quality of light reflected from the surface of a mineral (p. 49)

luster/brillo apariencia o calidad de la luz que es reflejada por la superficie de un mineral (pág. 49)

M

magma a body of molten rock found at depth, including any dissolved gases and crystals (p. 67)

magma/magma roca fundida que se encuentra en las profundidades de la Tierra; puede contener gas y cristales disueltos (pág. 67)

main-sequence star a star that falls into the main sequence category on the H-R diagram; This category contains the majority of stars and runs diagonally from the upper left to the lower right on the H-R diagram. (p. 704)

main-sequence star/estrella de secuencia principal estrella que pertenece a la categoría de Secuencia Principal en el diagrama HR; esta categoría contiene la mayoría de las estrellas y pasa diagonalmente de la esquina superior izquierda a la esquina inferior derecha en el diagrama HR (pág. 704)

mammal animal that bears live young and maintains a steady body temperature (p. 378)

mammal/mamífero animal que da a luz y es capaz de regular su temperatura corporal (pág. 378)

manganese nodule rounded lump of hydrogenous sediment scattered on the ocean floor, consisting mainly of manganese and iron and usually containing small amounts of copper, nickel, and cobalt (p. 412)

manganese nodule/nódulo de manganeso masa redonda de sedimento hidrogenado que se encuentra esparcida por el fondo oceánico; está formado principalmente por manganeso y hierro, y generalmente tiene pequeñas cantidades de cobre, níquel y cobalto (pág. 412)

mantle the 2890-kilometer-thick layer of Earth located below the crust (p. 8)

Glossary

mantle/manto estrato de la Tierra que se encuentra justo por debajo de la corteza; tiene 2890 kilómetros de profundidad (pág. 8)

mantle plume a mass of hotter-than-normal mantle material that ascends toward the surface, where it may lead to igneous activity (p. 269)

mantle plume/pluma eruptiva masa de material del manto caliente que sube hacia la superficie, donde puede desencadenar una actividad ígnea (pág. 269)

mare (*plural* maria) the Latin name for the smooth areas of the moon formerly thought to be seas (p. 632)

mare/mare (plural: maria) nombre en Latín para las zonas lisas de la Luna que antiguamente se pensaba eran mares (pág. 632)

marine west coast climate a climate found on windward coasts from latitudes 40° to 65° and dominated by maritime air masses; Winters are mild, and summers are cool. (p. 596)

marine west coast climate/clima marítimo de la costa oeste clima de las costas expuestas al viento que se encuentran entre las latitudes 40° y 65°; En este clima predominan los aires marinos, los inviernos son templados y los veranos son frescos. (pág. 596)

mass extinction when many types of living things become extinct at the same time (p. 369)

mass extinction/extinción en masa cuando muchos tipos de seres vivos se extinguen al mismo tiempo (pág. 369)

mass movement the downslope movement of rock, regolith, and soil under the direct influence of gravity (p. 143)

mass movement/movimiento de masas movimiento descendente de rocas, regolito y tierra por influencia directa de la gravedad (pág. 143)

mass number the number of neutrons and protons in the nucleus of an atom (p. 36)

mass number/número de masa número de neutrones y protones en el núcleo de un átomo (pág. 36)

meander a looplike bend in the course of a stream (p. 163)

meander/meandro sinuosidad en el recorrido de un arroyo (pág. 163)

mechanical weathering the physical disintegration of rock, resulting in smaller fragments (p. 126)

mechanical weathering/meteorización mecánica desintegración física de las rocas que produce fragmentos más pequeños (pág. 126)

mesosphere the layer of the atmosphere immediately above the stratosphere and characterized by decreasing temperatures with height (p. 480)

mesosphere/mesosfera estrato de la atmósfera que se encuentra inmediatamente por encima de la estratosfera y está caracterizada por el descenso de la temperatura con el aumento de la altura (pág. 480)

metallic bond a bond that forms when electrons are shared by metal ions (p. 39)

metallic bond/enlace metálico enlace que se forma cuando los iones metálicos comparten electrones (pág. 39)

metamorphic rock rock formed by the alteration of preexisting rock deep within Earth (but still in the solid state) by heat, pressure, and/or chemically active fluids (p. 66)

metamorphic rock/roca metamórfica roca formada por la alteración de una roca preexistente en las profundidades de la Tierra (pero todavía en estado sólido) debido al calor, la presión o líquidos químicamente activos (pág. 66)

metamorphism the changes in mineral composition and texture of a rock subjected to high temperature and pressure within Earth (p. 80)

metamorphism/metamorfismo cambios en la composición mineral y la textura de una roca sometida a temperaturas y presiones elevadas dentro de la Tierra (pág. 80)

meteor the luminous phenomenon observed when a meteoroid enters Earth's atmosphere and burns up, popularly called a shooting star (p. 663)

meteor/meteoro fenómeno luminoso que se observa cuando un meteoroide entra a la atmósfera de la Tierra y se desintegra, conocido popularmente como estrella fugaz (pág. 663)

meteorite any portion of a meteoroid that reaches Earth's surface (p. 664)

meteorite/meteorito cualquier fragmento de un meteoroide que llega a la superficie terrestre (pág. 664)

meteoroid a small, solid particle that travels through space (p. 663)

meteoroid/meteoroide partícula sólida y pequeña que viaja a través del espacio (pág. 663)

meteorology the scientific study of the atmosphere and atmospheric phenomena; the study of weather and climate (p. 3)

meteorology/meteorología estudio científico de la atmósfera y los fenómenos que ocurren en ella; estudio del estado del tiempo y el clima (pág. 3)

mid-ocean ridge a continuous elevated zone on the floor of all the major ocean basins and varying in width from 1000 to 4000 kilometers; The rifts at the crests of ridges represent divergent plate boundaries. (p. 255)

mid-ocean ridge/dorsal oceánica zona de elevación continua en el fondo de todas las cuencas de los océanos, cuya anchura varía entre 1000 y 4000 kilómetros; las grietas en las cimas de las elevaciones representan límites divergentes de las placas tectónicas (pág. 255)

Milankovitch cycles cycles related to Earth's movements, such as its orbit around the sun, that scientists think may help to cause ice ages (p. 384)

Milankovitch cycles/ciclos de Milankovitch ciclos relacionados a los movimientos de la Tierra, tales como el cambio de su órbita alrededor del Sol, que los científicos creen influencian períodos glaciales (pág. 384)

mineral a naturally occurring, inorganic crystalline material with a unique chemical composition (p. 43)

mineral/mineral material cristalino inorgánico que ocurre de manera natural y que tiene una composición química única (pág. 43)

mixed zone an area of the ocean surface with uniform temperatures created by the mixing of water by waves, currents, and tides (p. 426)

mixed zone/zona mixta área de la superficie del océano que tiene una temperatura uniforme mantenida por la mezcla de aguas por el viento, las corrientes y las mareas (pág. 426)

Moho the Mohorovičić discontinuity, which is shortened to Moho; It is the boundary separating the crust from the mantle, discernible by an increase in the velocity of seismic waves. (p. 236)

Moho/Moho la discontinuidad de Mohorovičić, abreviada Moho; es el límite que separa la corteza del manto y que se distingue por un aumento en la velocidad de las ondas sísmicas (pág. 236)

Mohs scale a series of 10 minerals used as a standard in determining hardness (p. 52)

Mohs scale/escala de Mohs serie de 10 minerales usados como guía para determinar la dureza (pág. 52)

moment magnitude a more precise measure of earthquake magnitude than the Richter scale, which is derived from the amount of displacement that occurs along a fault zone and estimates the energy released by an earthquake (p. 225)

moment magnitude/magnitud de momento medida más exacta para la magnitud de un terremoto que la escala de Richter, que se deriva del desplazamiento que ocurre a lo largo de una zona de falla y estima la energía que libera un terremoto (pág. 225)

monocline a large steplike fold in otherwise horizontal sedimentary strata (p. 313)

monocline/pliegue monoclinal pliegue grande en forma de escalón en un estrato horizontal de sedimento (pág. 313)

monsoon seasonal reversal of wind direction associated with large continents, especially Asia; In winter, the wind blows from land to sea. In summer, the wind blows from sea to land. (p. 542)

monsoon/monzón cambio estacional en la dirección del viento asociado con los grandes continentes, particularmente Asia; En invierno, el viento sopla de la tierra al mar y en verano, sopla del mar a la tierra. (pág. 542)

moraine a ridge of unsorted sediment left by a glacier (p. 194)

moraine/morrena loma de sedimento mixto depositado por un glaciar (pág. 194)

mudflow quickly moving downhill flow of soil and rock fragments containing a large amount of water (p. 146)

mudflow/corriente de barro movimiento descendente y rápido de tierra y fragmentos de roca que contienen gran cantidad de agua (pág. 146)

N

natural levee an elevated landform that parallels a stream and acts to confine its waters, except during floodstage (p. 167)

natural levee/terraplén natural formación de tierra elevada paralela a un arroyo y que sirve para contener sus aguas, excepto durante una etapa de inundación (pág. 167)

natural selection process by which characteristics that make an individual better suited to its environment become more common in a species (p. 345)

natural selection/selección natural proceso por el cual las características que permiten a un individuo adaptarse mejor a su medio ambiente se hacen más comunes en una especie (pág. 345)

neap tide lowest tidal range, occurring near the times of the first-quarter and third-quarter phases of the moon (p. 459)

neap tide/marea muerta menor rango entre mareas, que ocurre aproximadamente cuando la Luna está en cuarto creciente y en cuarto menguante (pág. 459)

nebula a cloud of gas and/or dust in space (p. 647)

nebula/nébula nube de gas y/o polvo en el espacio (pág. 647)

nekton organisms that can move independently of ocean currents by swimming or other means of propulsion; includes most adult fish and squid, marine mammals, and marine reptiles (p. 429)

nekton/necton grupo de organismos que pueden moverse independientemente de las corrientes del océano, nadando o mediante otros medios de propulsión; incluye la mayoría de los peces y calamares adultos, y los mamíferos y reptiles marinos (pág. 429)

neritic zone the marine-life zone that extends from the low-tide line out to the shelf break (p. 431)

neritic zone/zona nerítica zona con vida marítima que se extiende desde la línea de marea baja hasta el talud continental (pág. 431)

neutron star a star of extremely high density composed entirely of neutrons (p. 713)

neutron star/estrella de neutrones estrella de gran densidad, compuesta enteramente de neutrones (pág. 713)

nonfoliated metamorphic rock metamorphic rock that does not exhibit a banded or layered appearance (p. 83)

nonfoliated metamorphic rock/roca metamórfica no esquistosa roca metamórfica que no tiene una apariencia estratificada (pág. 83)

nonpoint source pollution water pollution that does not have a specific point of origin (p. 109)

nonpoint source pollution/contaminación no localizada contaminación del agua que no tiene un origen determinado (pág. 109)

nonrenewable resource resource that takes millions of years to form (p. 94)

nonrenewable resource/recurso no renovable recurso que toma millones de años en formarse (pág. 94)

normal fault a fault in which the rock above the fault plane has moved down relative to the rock below (p. 314)

normal fault/falla normal falla en la que la roca que está por encima del plano de la falla se desplaza hacia abajo, en relación a la roca que está por debajo (pág. 314)

normal polarity a magnetic field that is the same as that which exists at present (p. 258)

normal polarity/polaridad normal campo magnético igual al que existe en el presente (pág. 258)

nova a star that explosively increases in brightness (p. 705)

nova/nova estrella cuyo brillo aumenta repentinamente (pág. 705)

nuclear fusion the way in which the sun produces energy; Nuclear fusion occurs when less massive nuclei combine into more massive nuclei, releasing tremendous amounts of energy. (p. 689)

nuclear fusion/fusión nuclear proceso mediante el cual el Sol genera energía; La fusión nuclear ocurre cuando los núcleos menos masivos se unen para formar núcleos más masivos y desprenden enormes cantidades de energía en el proceso. (pág. 689)

O

occluded front a front formed when a cold front overtakes a warm front; It marks the beginning of the end of a middle-latitude cyclone. (p. 567)

occluded front/frente ocluido frente que se forma cuando un frente frío alcanza a un frente cálido; indica el principio del fin de un ciclón de las latitudes medias (pág. 567)

ocean basin floor area of the deep-ocean floor between the continental margin and the oceanic ridge (p. 404)

ocean basin floor/cuenca del fondo oceánico zona del fondo de los océanos profundos, ubicada entre el margen continental y la elevación oceánica (pág. 404)

ocean current mass of ocean water that flows from one place to another (p. 448)

ocean current/corriente oceánica masa de agua oceánica que fluye de un lugar a otro (pág. 448)

oceanic zone the marine-life zone beyond the continental shelf (p. 431)

oceanic zone/zona oceánica zona con vida marina que se encuentra más allá de la plataforma continental (pág. 431)

oceanography the scientific study of the oceans and oceanic phenomena (p. 3)

oceanography/oceanografía estudio científico de los océanos y sus fenómenos (pág. 3)

ore a material from which a useful mineral or minerals can be mined at a profit (p. 98)

ore/mena material a partir del cual se pueden explotar minerales útiles para obtener un beneficio económico (pág. 98)

original horizontality, principle of a principle of relative dating; Layers of sediments are generally deposited in a horizontal or nearly horizontal position. (p. 338)

original horizontality, principle of/horizontalidad

original, principio de la principio de la datación relativa; Los estratos de sedimentos generalmente son depositadas en posición horizontal o casi horizontal. (pág. 338)

orogenesis the processes that collectively result in the formation of mountains (p. 316)

orogenesis/orogénesis aquellos procesos que en colectivo resultan en la formación de las montañas (pág. 316)

orographic lifting mountains acting as barriers to the flow of air, forcing the air to ascend; The air cools adiabatically, and clouds and precipitation may result. (p. 512)

orographic lifting/elevación orográfica montaña o montañas que forman una barrera para el flujo del aire, empujando el aire hacia arriba; El aire se enfría de manera adiabática, lo cual causa la formación de nubes y precipitación. (pág. 512)

outer core a layer beneath the mantle about 2260 kilometers thick; The outer core contains liquid iron and generates Earth's magnetic field. (p. 235)

outer core/núcleo exterior estrato que se encuentra por debajo del manto, con un grosor de aproximadamente 2260 kilómetros; El núcleo exterior contiene hierro líquido y genera el campo magnético de la Tierra. (pág. 235)

outwash plain a relatively flat, gently sloping plain consisting of materials deposited by meltwater streams in front of the margin of an ice sheet (p. 196)

outwash plain/llanura aluvial llanura relativamente plana y con leves inclinaciones formada por materiales depositados por los arroyos de aguanieve al borde de un helero (pág. 196)

ozone a molecule of oxygen containing three oxygen atoms (p. 478)

ozone/ozono molécula de oxígeno que contiene tres átomos de oxígeno (pág. 478)

P

P wave earthquake wave that pushes and pulls rocks in the direction of the wave; also known as a compression wave (p. 222)

P wave/onda P onda sísmica que empuja y atrae las rocas; también se llama onda de compresión (pág. 222)

paleomagnetism The study of changes in Earth's magnetic field, as shown by patterns of magnetism in rocks that have formed over time. (p. 258)

paleomagnetism/paleomagnetismo El estudio de los cambios en el campo magnético de la Tierra, según lo muestran los patrones de magnetismo en las rocas que se han formado a través del tiempo. (pág. 258)

Pangaea the proposed supercontinent that 200 million years ago began to break apart and form the present landmasses (p. 248)

Pangaea/Pangea supercontinente que hace 200 millones de años comenzó a fragmentarse y a formar las masas de tierra actuales (pág. 248)

pedalfer soil of humid regions characterized by the accumulation of iron oxides and aluminum-rich clays in the B horizon (p. 139)

pedalfer/pedalfer suelo de las regiones húmedas que se caracteriza por la acumulación de óxidos de hierro y de arcillas ricas en aluminio en el horizonte B (pág. 139)

pedocal soil associated with drier regions and characterized by an accumulation of calcium carbonate in the upper horizons (p. 139)

pedocal/pedocal suelo asociado con las regiones más secas y que se caracteriza por una acumulación de carbonato de calcio en los horizontes superiores (pág. 139)

pelagic zone open ocean of any depth; Animals in this zone swim or float freely. (p. 431)

pelagic zone/zona pelágica océano abierto de cualquier profundidad; Los animales de esta zona nadan o flotan libremente. (pág. 431)

perigee the point at which the moon is closest to Earth (p. 626)

perigee/perigeo el punto en el que la Luna está más cerca de la Tierra (pág. 626)

perihelion the point in the orbit of a planet where it is closest to the sun (p. 624)

perihelion/perihelio el punto en la órbita de un planeta en el que éste está más cerca del Sol (pág. 624)

period a basic unit of the geologic time scale that is a subdivision of an era; Periods may be divided into smaller units called epochs. (p. 355)

period/período unidad básica de la escala geocronológica que es una subdivisión de una era; los períodos pueden dividirse en unidades más pequeñas llamadas épocas (pág. 355)

permeability a measure of a material's ability to transmit fluids (p. 171)

permeability/permeabilidad la capacidad de un material para transmitir fluidos (pág. 171)

phases of the moon the progression of changes in the moon's appearance during the month (p. 626)

phases of the moon/fases de la Luna la progresión de los cambios de la apariencia de la Luna a lo largo del mes (pág. 626)

photic zone the upper part of the ocean into which sunlight penetrates (p. 430)

photic zone/zona fótica parte superior del océano en la que penetra la luz solar (pág. 430)

photon a small packet of light energy (p. 675)

photon/fotón partícula de energía luminosa (pág. 675)

photosphere the region of the sun that radiates energy to space; visible surface of the sun (p. 685)

photosphere/fotosfera región del Sol que irradia energía al espacio; la superficie visible del Sol (pág. 685)

photosynthesis the process by which plants, algae, and certain prokaryotes use light energy to convert water and carbon dioxide into energy-rich glucose molecules (p. 367, 433)

photosynthesis/fotosíntesis proceso mediante el cual plantas, algas y ciertos procariotas usan la energía luminosa para convertir agua y dióxido de carbono en moléculas de glucosa ricas en energía (pág. 367, 433)

phytoplankton algal plankton, which are the most important community of primary producers in the ocean (p. 429)

phytoplankton/fitoplancton plancton algal, que es la comunidad más importante de productores primarios del océano (pág. 429)

planetesimal small, irregularly shaped body formed by colliding matter (p. 648)

planetesimal/planetésimo cuerpo pequeño, de forma irregular, formado por materia en colisión (pág. 648)

plankton passively drifting or weakly swimming organisms that cannot move independently of ocean currents; includes microscopic algae, protozoa, jellyfish, and larval forms of many animals (p. 428)

plankton/plancton organismos que flotan pasivamente o nadan débilmente, que no se pueden mover independientemente de corrientes oceánicas; incluyen algas microscópicas, protozoos, medusas y formas larvales de muchos animales (pág. 428)

plate one of numerous rigid sections of the lithosphere that moves as a unit over the material of the asthenosphere (p. 254)

plate/placa una de las numerosas secciones rígidas de la litosfera que se mueve como unidad sobre la materia de la astenosfera (pág. 254)

plate tectonics the theory that proposes that Earth's outer shell consists of individual plates that interact in various ways and thereby produce earthquakes, volcanoes, mountains, and the crust itself (p. 254)

plate tectonics/tectónica de placas teoría que propone que la capa exterior de la Tierra se compone de placas individuales que interactúan de varias maneras y producen como resultado terremotos, volcanes, montañas y la corteza en sí (pág. 254)

playa lake a flat area on the floor of an undrained desert basin (playa) that fills and becomes a lake after heavy rain (p. 201)

playa lake/salar superficie plana en el suelo de una cuenca desértica sin drenaje que se llena y se convierte en un lago tras lluvias fuertes (pág. 201)

pluton an intrusive igneous structure that results from the cooling and hardening of magma beneath the surface of Earth (p. 295)

pluton/plutón estructura intrusiva ígnea que resulta del enfriamiento y endurecimiento del magma bajo la superficie de la Tierra (pág. 295)

point source pollution water pollution that comes from a known and specific location (p. 108)

point source pollution/contaminación de fuentes localizadas contaminación acuática que procede de una fuente conocida y específica (pág. 108)

polar easterlies in the global pattern of prevailing winds, winds that blow from the polar high toward the subpolar low; These winds, however, should not be thought of as persistent winds, such as the trade winds. (p. 541)

polar easterlies/vientos polares del este en el patrón global de vientos dominantes, los vientos que soplan desde la zona polar de alta presión a la zona subpolar de baja presión; Sin embargo, estos vientos no deben considerarse como vientos persistentes, como por ejemplo los vientos alisios. (pág. 541)

polar front the stormy frontal zone separating cold air masses of polar origin from warm air masses of tropical origin (p. 541)

polar front/frente polar la zona frontal tormentosa que separa masas de aire frío de origen polar de masas de aire cálido de origen tropical (pág. 541)

polar zone the region between 66.5° north and south latitudes and the poles; The sun's rays strike at a very small angle in the polar zone. (p. 589)

polar zone/zona polar la región entre los 66.5° de latitud y los polos; Los rayos del Sol llegan a la zona polar en un ángulo muy pequeño. (pág. 589)

porosity the volume of open spaces in rock or soil (p. 171)

porosity/porosidad el volumen de espacios abiertos en una roca o suelo (pág. 171)

porphyritic texture an igneous texture consisting of large crystals embedded in a matrix of much smaller crystals (p. 72)

porphyritic texture/textura porfirítica textura ígnea formada por grandes cristales incrustados en una matriz de cristales mucho más pequeños (pág. 72)

Precambrian time the long time span from Earth's formation to the beginning of the Cambrian period; made up of the Hadean, Archaean, and Proterozoic eons (p. 354)

Precambrian time/tiempo Precámbrico el lapso de tiempo desde la formación de la Tierra hasta el comienzo del período Cámbrico; comformado por los eones Hadeico, Arcaico y Proterozoico (pág. 354)

precession a slow motion of Earth's axis that traces out a cone over a period of 26,000 years (p. 622)

Glossary

precession/precesión movimiento lento del eje de la Tierra que traza un cono a lo largo de un período de 26,000 años (pág. 622)

precipitation any form of water that falls from a cloud (p. 504)

precipitation/precipitación cualquier forma de agua que cae de una nube (pág. 504)

pressure gradient the amount of pressure change occurring over a given distance (p. 534)

pressure gradient/gradiente de presión medida del cambio de presión que ocurre a lo largo de una distancia dada (pág. 534)

prevailing wind a wind that consistently blows from one direction more than from another (p. 545)

prevailing wind/viento dominante un viento que sopla constantemente de una dirección más que de otra (pág. 545)

primary productivity the production of organic matter from inorganic substances through photosynthesis or chemosynthesis (p. 433)

primary productivity/productividad primaria la producción de materia orgánica a partir de sustancias inorgánicas a través de la fotosíntesis o quimiosíntesis (pág. 433)

prokaryote organism whose cells lack a nucleus and some other cell structures (p. 368)

prokaryote/procariota organismo cuyas células carecen de núcleo y otras estructuras celulares (pág. 368)

prominence a concentration of gases above the solar surface that appears as a bright archlike structure (p. 688)

prominence/prominencia concentración de gases sobre la superficie solar que aparece como una estructura brillante en forma de arco (pág. 688)

protostar a collapsing cloud of gas and dust destined to become a star; a developing star not yet hot enough to engage in nuclear fusion (p. 708)

protostar/protoestrella nube de gas y polvo en colapso destinada a convertirse en una estrella; una estrella en desarrollo que todavía no está lo suficientemente caliente para iniciar la fusión nuclear (pág. 708)

pulsar a variable radio source of small size that emits radio pulses in very regular periods (p. 713)

pulsar/púlsar fuente de radio variable de tamaño pequeño que emite pulsaciones de radio en períodos muy regulares (pág. 713)

pycnocline a layer of water in which there is a rapid change of density with depth (p. 426)

pycnocline/picnoclina capa de agua en la que se produce un rápido cambio de densidad con la profundidad (pág. 426)

pyroclastic material the volcanic rock ejected during an eruption, including ash, bombs, and blocks (p. 289)

pyroclastic material/material piroclástico roca volcánica expulsada durante una erupción, incluyendo cenizas, bombas y bloques (pág. 289)

R

radiation the transfer of energy (heat) through space by electromagnetic waves (p. 485)

radiation/radiación transferencia de energía (calor) a través del espacio mediante ondas electromagnéticas (pág. 485)

radioactivity the spontaneous decay of certain unstable atomic nuclei (p. 347)

radioactivity/radiactividad desintegración espontánea de ciertos núcleos atómicos inestables (pág. 347)

radiocarbon (carbon-14) dating method for determining age by comparing the amount of carbon-14 to the amount of carbon-12 in a sample (p. 350)

radiocarbon (carbon-14) dating/datación por radiocarbono (carbono-14) método para determinar la edad mediante la comparación de la cantidad de carbono-14 con la cantidad de carbono-12 en una muestra (pág. 350)

radiometric dating the procedure of calculating the absolute ages of rocks and minerals that contain radioactive isotopes (p. 348)

radiometric dating/datación radiométrica procedimiento para calcular las edades absolutas de rocas y minerales que contienen isótopos radiactivos (pág. 348)

radio telescope a telescope designed to make observations in radio wavelengths (p. 681)

radio telescope/radiotelescopio telescopio diseñado para hacer observaciones en longitud de ondas de radio (pág. 681)

ray any of a system of bright elongated streaks, sometimes associated with a crater on the moon (p. 632)

ray/rayo cualquiera de los sistemas de haces alargados luminosos, a veces asociados con un cráter en la Luna (pág. 632)

recycling the collecting and processing of used items so they can be made into new products (p. 116)

recycling/reciclaje recolección y procesamiento de objetos usados para que puedan convertirse en nuevos productos (pág. 116)

red giant a large, cool star of high luminosity; a star occupying the upper-right portion of the H-R diagram (p. 704)

red giant/gigante roja estrella grande, fría, de gran luminosidad; estrella que ocupa la parte superior derecha del diagrama HR (pág. 704)

reflecting telescope a telescope that concentrates light from distant objects by using a concave mirror (p. 680)

reflecting telescope/telescopio reflector telescopio que concentra la luz de objetos distantes usando un espejo cóncavo (pág. 680)

reflection the process whereby light bounces back from an object at the same angle at which it encounters a surface and with the same intensity (p. 486)

reflection/reflexión proceso por el cual la luz rebota de un objeto en el mismo ángulo en el que llega a su superficie y con la misma intensidad (pág. 486)

refracting telescope a telescope that uses a lens to bend and concentrate the light from distant objects (p. 678)

refracting telescope/telescopio refractor telescopio que usa una lente para doblar y concentrar la luz de objetos distantes (pág. 678)

refraction *See* wave refraction.

refraction/refracción *Ver* onda de refracción.

regional metamorphism metamorphism associated with large-scale mountain-building processes (p. 81)

regional metamorphism/metamorfismo regional metamorfismo asociado con procesos de formación de montañas a gran escala (pág. 81)

regolith the layer of rock and mineral fragments that nearly everywhere covers Earth's surface (p. 133)

regolith/regolito manto de fragmentos de rocas y minerales que cubre casi toda la superficie de la Tierra (pág. 133)

rejuvenation a change in the base level of a stream, often caused by regional uplift (p. 163)

rejuvenation/rejuvenecimiento cambio en el nivel bajo de un arroyo, a menudo causado por levantamiento regional (pág. 163)

relative dating process by which rocks are placed in their proper sequence or order; Only the chronological order of events is determined, not the absolute age in years. (p. 337)

relative dating/datación relativa proceso por el que las rocas se colocan en su propia secuencia u orden; Sólo se determina el orden cronológico de los sucesos, no la edad absoluta en años. (pág. 337)

relative humidity the ratio of the air's water-vapor content to its water-vapor capacity (p. 506)

relative humidity/humedad relativa la proporción del contenido de vapor de agua en el aire y su capacidad de vapor de agua (pág. 506)

renewable resource a resource that is virtually inexhaustible or that can be replenished over relatively short time spans (p. 94)

renewable resource/recurso renovable recurso que virtualmente no se puede agotar o que se puede renovar en un lapso relativamente corto (pág. 94)

reptile vertebrate with scaly skin that lays eggs with tough, leathery shells (p. 375)

reptile/reptil vertebrado con piel de escamas que pone huevos de cascarón duro y correoso (pág. 375)

retrograde motion the apparent westward motion of the planets with respect to the stars (p. 616)

retrograde motion/movimiento retrógrado el aparente movimiento hacia el oeste de los planetas con respecto a las estrellas (pág. 616)

Glossary

reverse fault a fault in which the material above the fault plane moves up in relation to the material below (p. 314)

reverse fault/falla inversa falla en la que el material sobre el plano de la falla se desliza hacia arriba en relación con el material de abajo (pág. 314)

reverse polarity a magnetic field opposite to that which exists at present (p. 258)

reverse polarity/polaridad inversa campo magnético opuesto al que existe en el momento (pág. 258)

revolution the motion of one body about another, as Earth about the sun (p. 622)

revolution/revolución o traslación movimiento de un cuerpo alrededor de otro, como el de la Tierra alrededor del Sol (pág. 622)

ridge-push a mechanism that may contribute to plate motion; It involves the oceanic lithosphere sliding down the oceanic ridge under the pull of gravity. (p. 270)

ridge-push/empuje de dorsal mecanismo que puede contribuir al movimiento de placas; implica que la litosfera oceánica se desliza hacia abajo por la dorsal oceánica bajo la atracción de la gravedad (pág. 270)

rift valley deep faulted structure found along the axes of divergent plate boundaries; Rift valleys can develop on the seafloor or on land. (p. 255)

rift valley/valle de rift estructura de fallas profundas que se encuentra a lo largo de los ejes de los límites de placas divergentes; Los valles de rift pueden formarse en el suelo marino o en la tierra. (pág. 255)

rille long channel associated with lunar maria; A rille looks similar to a valley or a trench. (p. 632)

rille/rille canal alargado asociado con los maria lunares; Un rille es parecido a un valle o una fosa. (pág. 632)

Ring of Fire volcano belt that rims the Pacific Ocean (p. 284)

Ring of Fire/Cinturón de Fuego gran cadena de volcanes que rodea el océano Pacifico (pág. 284)

rock a consolidated mixture of minerals (p. 66)

rock/roca mezcla de minerales consolidados (pág. 66)

rock cycle a model that illustrates the origin of the three basic rock types and the interrelatedness of Earth materials and processes (p. 67)

rock cycle/ciclo de la roca modelo que ilustra el origen de los tres tipos básicos de rocas y la interrelación de materiales y procesos de la Tierra (pág. 67)

rockfall occurs when rocks or rock fragments fall freely through the air; common on steep slopes (p. 145)

rockfall/desprendimiento de rocas ocurre cuando rocas o fragmentos de roca caen libremente por el aire; son comunes en pendientes pronunciadas (pág. 145)

rockslide occurs when a mass of rock slides rapidly downslope along planes of weakness (p. 145)

rockslide/deslizamiento de rocas ocurre cuando una masa de rocas se desliza rápidamente pendiente a lo largo de taludes inestables (pág. 145)

rotation the spinning of a body, such as Earth, about its axis (p. 622)

rotation/rotación el giro de un cuerpo, como la Tierra, alrededor de su eje (pág. 622)

runoff water that flows over the land surface rather than seeping into the ground (p. 109)

runoff/escorrentía agua que fluye sobre la superficie del suelo, en lugar de filtrarse en ella (pág. 109)

S

S wave a seismic wave that shakes particles perpendicular to the direction the wave is traveling (p. 222)

S wave/onda S onda sísmica que sacude partículas perpendiculares a la dirección en que viaja la onda (pág. 222)

salinity the proportion of dissolved salts to pure water, usually expressed in parts per thousand (‰) (p. 422)

salinity/salinidad la proporción de sales disueltas en agua pura, generalmente expresada en partes por miles (‰) (pág. 422)

saturated the state of air that contains the maximum quantity of water vapor that it can hold at any given temperature and pressure (p. 506)

saturated/saturado el estado del aire que contiene la máxima cantidad de vapor de agua que puede retener a una temperatura y presión determinadas (pág. 506)

scattering the redirecting (in all directions) of light by small particles and gas molecules in the atmosphere; The result is more light rays with weaker intensity. (p. 486)

scattering/dispersión la redirección (en todas direcciones) de luz por pequeñas partículas y moléculas de gas en la atmósfera; El resultado es más rayos de luz con menos intensidad. (pág. 486)

seafloor spreading the process by which plate tectonics produces new oceanic lithosphere at ocean ridges (p. 259)

seafloor spreading/expansión de los suelos oceánicos proceso por el cual la tectónica de placas produce una nueva litosfera oceánica en las dorsales oceánicas (pág. 259)

seamount an isolated volcanic peak that rises at least 1000 meters above the deep-ocean floor (p. 404)

seamount/monte marino pico volcánico aislado que se eleva al menos 1000 metros sobre el suelo oceánico (pág. 404)

sediment loose particles created by the weathering and erosion of rock, by chemical precipitation from solution in water, or from the secretions of organisms and transported by water, wind, or glaciers (p. 68)

sediment/sedimento partículas sueltas formadas por la meteorización y la erosión de una roca, por la precipitación química de una solución en agua o por las secreciones de organismos, y transportadas por el agua, el viento o los glaciares (pág. 68)

sedimentary rock rock formed from the weathered products of preexisting rocks that have been transported, deposited, compacted, and cemented (p. 66)

sedimentary rock/roca sedimentaria roca formada a partir de productos erosionados de rocas anteriores que han sido transportados, depositados, endurecidos y cimentados (pág. 66)

seismic gap an area along a fault where there has not been any earthquake activity for a long period of time (p. 231)

seismic gap/brecha sísmica área a lo largo de una falla donde no ha habido actividad sísmica durante un largo período (pág. 231)

seismic waves vibrations that travel through Earth carrying the energy released during an earthquake (p. 218)

seismic waves/ondas sismicas vibraciones que se desplazan por la Tierra, llevando la energia liberada durante un terremoto (pág. 218)

seismogram the record made by a seismograph (p. 214)

seismogram/sismograma registro hecho por un sismógrafo (pág. 214)

seismograph an instrument that records seismic waves (p. 214)

seismograph/sismógrafo instrumento que registra ondas sísmicas (pág. 214)

shield A large, relatively flat expanse of ancient metamorphic rock within the stable continental interior (p. 365)

shield/escudo extensión grande y relativamente plana de roca metamórfica antigua dentro del interior continental estable (pág. 365)

shield volcano a broad, gently sloping volcano built from fluid basaltic lavas (p. 290)

shield volcano/volcán en escudo volcán ancho, de laderas poco inclinadas, formado por el fluido de lavas basálticas (pág. 290)

silicate any one of numerous minerals that have the oxygen and silicon tetrahedron as their basic structure (p. 45)

silicate/silicato cualquiera de los numerosos minerales que tienen como su estructura básica el tetraedro de oxígeno y silicio (pág. 45)

siliceous ooze biogenous sediment composed of the silica-based shells of single-celled animals and algae (p. 408)

siliceous ooze/fango silíceo sedimento biógeno compuesto de esqueletos de sílice de animales unicelulares y algas (pág. 408)

silicon-oxygen tetrahedron a structure composed of four oxygen atoms surrounding a silicon atom, which constitutes the basic building block of silicate minerals (p. 45)

silicon-oxygen tetrahedron/tetraedro de oxígeno y silicio estructura compuesta de cuatro átomos de oxígeno que rodean un átomo de silicio, que constituye la pieza clave para formar los silicatos (pág. 45)

sill a tabular igneous body formed when magma is injected along sedimentary bedding surfaces (p. 296)

sill/sill cuerpo tabular ígneo que se forma cuando el magma es inyectado a lo largo de superficies de lechos sedimentarios (pág. 296)

sinkhole a depression produced in a region where soluble rock has been removed by groundwater (p. 178)

sinkhole/dolina depresión que se produce en una región cuando el agua subterránea disuelve la roca soluble (pág. 178)

slab-pull a mechanism that contributes to plate motion in which cool, dense oceanic crust sinks into the mantle and "pulls" the trailing lithosphere along (p. 270)

slab-pull/subducción de placa mecanismo que contribuye al movimiento de placas en el cual la corteza oceánica, densa y fría se hunde en el manto, arrastrando consigo la listosfera (pág. 270)

slump the downward slipping of a mass of rock or unconsolidated material moving as a unit along a curved surface (p. 146)

slump/desprendimienro el movimiento hacia abajo de una masa de rocas o material no consolidado que se mueve como unidad a lo largo de una superficie curva (pág. 146)

snowline lowest elevation in a particular area that remains covered in snow all year (p. 188)

snowline/línea de nieve elevación más baja en un área concreta que queda cubierta por la nieve todo el año (pág. 188)

soil a combination of mineral and organic matter, water, and air; that portion of the regolith that supports plant growth (p. 133)

soil/suelo combinación de materia mineral y orgánica, agua y aire; parte del regolito que permite el crecimiento de plantas (pág. 138)

soil horizon a layer of soil that has identifiable characteristics produced by chemical weathering and other soil-forming processes (p. 138)

soil horizon/horizonte capa del suelo que tiene unas características identificables producidas por alteraciones químicas y otros procesos de formación del suelo (p. 138)

soil profile a vertical section through a soil showing its succession of horizons and the underlying parent material (p. 138)

soil profile/perfil del suelo sección vertical de un suelo que muestra la sucesión de horizontes y los materiales litológicos subyacentes (pág. 138)

solar eclipse an eclipse of the sun; A solar eclipse occurs when the moon moves in a line directly between Earth and the sun, casting a shadow on Earth. (p. 628)

solar eclipse/eclipse solar eclipse del Sol; Un eclipse solar ocurre cuando la Luna se mueve en línea directa entre la Tierra y el Sol, formando una sombra sobre la Tierra. (pág. 268)

solar flare a sudden and tremendous eruption in the solar chromosphere (p. 688)

solar flare/destello solar gran erupción de energía repentina en la cromosfera solar (pág. 688)

solar wind streams of protons and electrons ejected at high speed from the solar corona (p. 686)

solar wind/viento solar ráfagas de protones y electrones lanzadas a alta velocidad desde la corona solar (pág. 686)

sonar An electronic depth-sounding mechanism; Sonar is an acronym for sound navigation and ranging. Sonar calculates ocean depth by recording the time it takes for an energy pulse to reach the ocean floor and return. (p. 254)

sonar/sonar mecanismo electrónico de sonido de profundidad; *Sonar* es un acrónimo en inglés para *Sound Navigation and Ranging* (navegación y rango de sonido); un sonar calcula la profundidad del océano al registrar el tiempo que tarda una pulsación de energía en llegar al suelo oceánico y volver. (pág. 254)

spectroscopy the study of the properties of light that depend on wavelength (p. 676)

spectroscopy/espectroscopia estudio de las propiedades de la luz que depende de la longitud de onda (pág. 676)

spring a flow of groundwater that emerges naturally at the ground surface (p. 171)

spring/manantial fuente de agua subterránea que emerge de forma natural en la superficie de la tierra (pág. 171)

spring equinox the equinox that occurs on March 21 or 22 in the Northern Hemisphere (p. 482)

spring equinox/equinoccio de primavera el equinoccio que tiene lugar el 21 ó 22 de marzo en el hemisferio norte (pág. 482)

spring tide highest tidal range that occurs due to the alignment of Earth, the moon, and the sun (p. 459)

spring tide/marea viva rango de marea más alto que ocurre debido a la alineación de la Tierra, la Luna y el Sol (pág. 459)

stalactite an icicle-like structure that hangs from the ceiling of a cavern (p. 177)

stalactite/estalactita estructura en forma de carámbano que cuelga del techo de una caverna (pág. 177)

stalagmite a columnlike form that grows upward from the floor of a cavern (p. 177)

stalagmite/estalagmita estructura en forma de columna que crece hacia arriba desde el suelo de una caverna (pág. 177)

stationary front a situation in which the surface position of a front does not move; The flow on either side of such a boundary is nearly parallel to the position of the front. (p. 566)

stationary front/frente estacionario situación en la que la posición de la superficie de un frente no se mueve; El movimiento a cada lado de ese límite es casi paralelo a la posición del frente. (pág. 566)

storm surge the abnormal rise of the sea along a shore as a result of strong winds (p. 577)

storm surge/marea de tempestad la subida anormal del mar a lo largo de la costa como resultado de fuertes vientos (pág. 577)

strain the change in shape or volume of a body of rock as a result of stress (p. 308)

strain/deformación el cambio en la forma o el volumen de un cuerpo rocoso como resultado del esfuerzo (pág. 308)

stratosphere the layer of the atmosphere immediately above the troposphere, characterized by increasing temperatures with height, due to the concentration of ozone (p. 480)

stratosphere/estratosfera la capa de la atmósfera inmediatamente por encima de la troposfera, que se caracteriza por el aumento de la temperatura con la altura, debido a la concentración de ozono (pág. 480)

stratus one of three basic cloud forms; They are sheets or layers that cover much or all of the sky. (p. 518)

stratus/estrato una de las tres formas básicas de las nubes; son como sábanas o capas que cubren todo o casi todo el cielo (pág. 518)

streak the color of a mineral in powdered form (p. 51)

streak/raya el color de un mineral en forma pulverizada (pág. 51)

stream channel the course that the water in a stream follows (p. 161)

stream channel/cauce el curso que sigue el agua de una corriente (pág. 161)

stress the force per unit area acting on a solid (p. 308)

stress/esfuerzo la fuerza por unidad de área que actúa sobre un sólido (pág. 308)

strike-slip fault a fault along which the movement is horizontal and parallel to the trend of the fault (p. 315)

strike-slip fault/falla de desgarre falla a lo largo de la cual el movimiento es horizontal y paralelo a la tendencia de la falla (pág. 315)

stromatolite structure produced by algae trapping sediment and forming layered mounds of calcium carbonate (p. 368)

stromatolite/estromatolito estructura producida por algas atrapadas en sedimento que forma pilas estratificadas de carbonato de calcio (pág. 368)

subarctic climate a climate found north of the humid continental climate and south of the polar climate; characterized by bitterly cold winters and short cool summers; Places within this climatic realm experience the highest annual temperature ranges on Earth. (p. 597)

Glossary

subartic climate/clima subártico clima que prevalece al norte del clima húmedo continental y al sur del clima polar; se caracteriza por inviernos fríos rigurosos y veranos frescos y cortos; Los lugares que se hallan en este ambiente tienen el rango de temperaturas más elevado de la Tierra. (pág. 597)

subduction the process by which oceanic crust sinks beneath a trench and back into the mantle at a colliding plate boundary (p. 256)

subduction/subducción proceso mediante el cual la corteza oceánica se hunde debajo de una fosa y vuelve al manto por el borde de una placa convergente (pág. 256)

sublimation the conversion of a solid directly to a gas without passing through the liquid state (p. 506)

sublimation/sublimación conversión de un sólido directamente a gas sin pasar por estado líquido (pág. 506)

submarine canyon a seaward extension of a valley that was cut on the continental shelf during a time when sea level was lower; a canyon carved into the outer continental shelf, slope, and rise by turbidity currents (p. 403)

submarine canyon/cañón submarino extensión de un valle hacia el mar que se cortó en la plataforma continental durante una era en la que el nivel del mar era más bajo; un cañón cavado en la parte exterior de la plataforma continental, el talud continental y el pie continental por corrientes de turbidez (pág. 403)

submersible a small underwater craft used for deep-sea research (p. 400)

submersible/sumergible nave submarina pequeña que se usa en la investigación oceánica (pág. 400)

summer solstice the solstice that occurs on June 21 or 22 in the Northern Hemisphere and on December 21 or 22 in the Southern Hemisphere (p. 482)

summer solstice/solsticio de verano solsticio que tiene lugar el 21 ó 22 de junio en el hemisferio norte y el 21 ó 22 de diciembre en el hemisferio sur (pág. 482)

sunspot a dark spot on the sun, which is cool by contrast to the surrounding photosphere (p. 687)

sunspot/mancha solar área oscura del Sol que está más fría que la fotosfera que la rodea (pág. 687)

supercooled water the condition of water droplets that remain in the liquid state at temperatures well below 0°C (p. 521)

supercooled water/agua subenfriada condición en que las gotas de agua permanecen en estado líquido a temperaturas inferiores a 0°C (pág. 521)

supergiant a very large, very bright red giant star

supergiant/supergigante estrella roja muy grande y muy brillante (pág. 704)

supernova an exploding star that increases in brightness many thousands of times (p. 711)

supernova/supernova estrella en explosión que aumenta su brillo muchos miles de veces (pág. 711)

superposition, law of a law that states that in any undeformed sequence of sedimentary rocks, each bed is older than the layers above and younger than the layers below. (p. 338)

superposition, law of/ley de superposición ley que enuncia que en cualquier secuencia no deformada de rocas sedimentarias, cada capa es más antigua que los estratos de arriba y más joven que los estratos de abajo (pág. 338)

supersaturated air the condition of air that is more highly concentrated than is normally possible under given temperature and pressure conditions; When describing humidity, it refers to a relative humidity that is greater than 100 percent. (p. 521)

supersaturated air/aire sobresaturado condición del aire con un nivel de concentración mucho más alto de lo que es normalmente posible bajo ciertas condiciones de temperatura y presión; al describir la humedad, se refiere a una humedad relativa que es mayor que el 100 por ciento (pág. 521)

surface current movement of water that flows horizontally in the upper part of the ocean's surface (p. 448)

surface current/corriente superficial movimiento de agua que fluye horizontalmente en la parte superior de la superficie oceánica (pág. 448)

surface wave a seismic wave that travels along the surface of Earth (p. 223)

surface wave/onda superficial onda sísmica que viaja a lo largo de la superficie de la Tierra

syncline a linear downfold in sedimentary strata; the opposite of anticline (p. 312)

syncline/sinclinal pliegue lineal en el estrato sedimentario; lo opuesto de anticlinal (pág. 312)

system any size group of interacting parts that form a complex whole (p. 18)

system/sistema grupo de cualquier tamaño de partes relacionadas que forman un conjunto complejo (pág. 18)

T

talus an accumulation of rock debris at the base of a cliff (p. 127)

talus/talud acumulación de restos de roca al pie de un acantilado (pág. 127)

temperate zone region located between 23.5° and 66.5° north and south of the equator; The sun's rays strike Earth at a smaller angle in the temperate zone than near the equator. (p. 589)

temperate zone/zona templada región situada entre 23.5° y 66.5° norte y sur del ecuador; Los rayos de Sol llegan a la Tierra formando un ángulo más pequeño en la zona templada que en el ecuador. (pág. 589)

temperature a measure of the average kinetic energy of individual atoms or molecules in a substance (p. 483)

temperature/temperatura medición de la energía cinética promedio de los átomos o moléculas individuales en una sustancia (pág. 483)

temperature inversion a layer of limited depth in the atmosphere of limited depth where the temperature increases rather than decreases with height (p. 514)

temperature inversion/inversión de temperatura capa de poca densidad en la atmósfera de poca densidad donde la temperatura aumenta con la altura en vez de descender (pág. 514)

terrane a crustal block bounded by faults, whose geologic history is distinct from the histories of adjoining crustal blocks (p. 324)

terrane/terreno formación de rocas de la corteza rodeada de fallas, cuya historia geológica es distinta a la historias de las formaciones de rocas lindantes (pág. 324)

terrestrial planet any of the Earth-like planets, including Mercury, Venus, Mars, and Earth

terrestrial planet/planeta terrestre cualquiera de los planetas similares a la Tierra, como Mercurio, Venus, Marte y Tierra (pág. 645)

terrigenous sediment seafloor sediment derived from eroded rocks on land (p. 408)

terrigenous sediment/sedimento terrígeno sedimento en el fondo oceánico que se deriva de la erosión de rocas en la tierra (pág. 408)

theory a well-tested and widely accepted view that explains certain observable facts (p. 24)

theory/teoría perspectiva comprobada y generalmente aceptada que explica ciertos hechos observables (pág. 24)

thermocline a layer of water in which there is a rapid change in temperature with depth (p. 424)

thermocline/termoclina capa de agua en la cual se observa un rápido cambio de temperatura con la profundidad (pág. 424)

thermosphere the region of the atmosphere immediately above the mesosphere and characterized by increasing temperatures due to absorption of very short-wave solar energy by oxygen (p. 480)

thermosphere/termosfera capa de la atmósfera inmediatamente superior a la mesosfera y que se caracteriza por un aumento de temperatura causado por la absorción de energía solar de ondas muy cortas por el oxígeno (pág. 480)

thrust fault a reverse fault with a dip less than 45°, normally about 10–15° (p. 314)

thrust fault/falla de empuje falla inversa con una depresión de menos de 45°, normalmente entre 10°y 15° (pág. 314)

thunderstorm a storm produced by a cumulonimbus cloud and always accompanied by lightning and thunder; It is of relatively short duration and usually accompanied by strong wind gusts, heavy rain, and sometimes hail.

thunderstorm/tormenta eléctrica tormenta causada por una nube cumulonimbo y siempre acompañada de relámpagos y truenos; es de duración relativamente corta y va generalmente acompañada de fuertes ráfagas de viento, precipitaciones y a veces granizo (pág. 571)

tidal range the difference in height between successive high and low tides (p. 459)

tidal range/rango de marea diferencia en altura entre sucesivas mareas altas y bajas (pág. 459)

tide daily change in the elevation of the ocean surface (p. 458)

tide/marea cambios diarios en el ascenso de la superficie oceánica (pág. 458)

till sediment of different sizes deposited directly by a glacier (p. 194)

till/tillita sedimentos de diferentes tamaños depositados directamente por un glaciar

topographic map a map that represents Earth's surface in three dimensions; It shows elevation, distance, directions, and slope angles. (p. 14)

topographic map/mapa topográfico mapa que representa la superficie de la Tierra en tres dimensiones; muestra elevación, distancia, direcciones y ángulos de inclinación (pág. 14)

tornado a small, very intense cyclonic storm with exceedingly high winds, most often produced along cold fronts in conjunction with severe thunderstorms (p. 573)

tornado/tornado pequeña tormenta ciclónica pero sumamente intensa, con vientos de gran velocidad, que a menudo ocurre a lo largo de frentes fríos acompañados de poderosas tormentas eléctricas (pág. 573)

trade winds two belts of winds that blow almost constantly from easterly directions and are located on the north and south sides of the subtropical highs (p. 541)

trade winds/vientos alisios dos cinturones de viento que soplan casi constantemente desde la dirección del este y que se encuentran al norte y al sur de los centros de las altas presiones subtropicales (pág. 541)

transform fault boundary a boundary in which two plates slide past each other without creating or destroying lithosphere (p. 263)

transform fault boundary/límite de falla de transformación límite en el que dos placas se deslizan a lo largo de la falla sin generar o destruir litosfera (pág. 263)

travertine a form of limestone that is deposited by hot springs or as a cave deposit (p. 177)

travertine/travertino tipo de piedra caliza que es depositada por fuentes termales o que forma parte del depósito de cuevas (pág. 177)

trench a surface feature in the seafloor produced by the descending plate during subduction

trench/fosa depresión en el fondo oceánico causada por la placa descediente durante la subducción (pág. 255)

tributary a stream that empties itself into another stream (p. 162)

tributary/afluente corriente de agua que desemboca en otra corriente (pág. 162)

trophic level a nourishment level in a food chain; Plant and algae producers constitute the lowest level, followed by herbivores and a series of carnivores at progressively higher levels. (p. 436)

trophic level/nivel trófico nivel de alimentación en la cadena alimenticia; los productores como las plantas y las algas forman parte del nivel más bajo, seguidos de herbívoros y una serie de carnívoros en los niveles superiores progresivos

tropical wet and dry climate a climate that is transitional between the wet tropics and the subtropical steppes (p. 593)

tropical wet and dry climate/clima tropical seco y húmedo clima de transición entre los húmedos trópicos y las estepas subtropicales (pág. 593)

tropical zone region between 23.5° north (the tropic of Cancer) and 23.5° south (the tropic of Capricorn) of the equator; The sun's rays are most intense and the temperatures are always warm. (p. 589)

tropical zone/zona tropical región entre 23.5° norte (trópico de Cáncer) y 23.5° sur (trópico de Capricornio) del ecuador; los rayos solares son de mayor intensidad y la temperatura es siempre cálida (pág. 589)

troposphere the lowermost layer of the atmosphere; It is generally characterized by a decrease in temperature with height. (p. 480)

troposphere/troposfera capa más inferior de la atmósfera; generalmente se caracteriza por un decrecimiento de la temperatura con la altura (pág. 480)

tsunami the Japanese word for a seismic sea wave

tsunami/tsunami palabra japonesa con la que se denomina a una ola sísmica marina (pág. 230)

turbidity current a downslope movement of dense, sediment-laden water created when sand and mud on the continental shelf and slope are dislodged and thrown into suspension (p. 403)

turbidity current/corriente de turbidez movimiento descendente de una densa masa de agua cargada de sedimentos que ocurre cuando la arena y el barro de la plataforma y el talud continental se desplazan y quedan en suspensión

U

ultramafic igneous rock composed mainly of iron and magnesium-rich minerals (p. 73)

ultramafic/ultramáfica roca ígnea compuesta principalmente de hierro y minerales ricos en magnesio (pág. 73)

unconformity a surface that represents a break in the rock record, caused by erosion or lack of deposition (p. 340)

unconformity/discordancia superficie que representa una interrupción en la evolución de la roca, causada por erosión o por falta de deposición (pág. 340)

uniformitarianism the concept that processes that have shaped Earth in the past are essentially the same as those operating today (p. 337)

uniformitarianism/uniformismo principio que dice que los procesos que dieron forma a la Tierra en el pasado geológico son esencialmente los mismos que ocurren en la actualidad (pág. 337)

uplifted mountain a circular or an elongated structure formed by uplifting of the underlying basement rock (p. 316)

uplifted mountain/montaña formada por elevación estructura circular o elongada formada por el levantamiento de rocas subyacentes del basamento (pág. 316)

upwelling the rising of cold water from deeper layers to replace warmer surface water that has been moved away (p. 450)

upwelling/afloramiento movimiento ascendente de aguas frías desde las profundidades del mar para reemplazar las aguas más calidas de la superficie que han sido desplazadas (pág. 450)

V

valley glacier a glacier confined to a mountain valley, which in most instances had previously been a stream valley; also known as an alpine glacier (p. 189)

valley glacier/glaciar de valle glaciar localizado en un valle de montaña, que en varias etapas anteriores había sido un valle fluvial; también conocido como glaciar alpino (pág. 189)

vent an opening in the surface of Earth through which molten rock and gases are released (p. 287)

vent/chimenea abertura en la superficie de la Tierra a través de la cual salen roca derretida y gases (pág. 287)

ventifact a cobble or pebble polished and shaped by the sandblasting effect of wind (p. 204)

ventifact/ventifacto canto o guijarro pulido y esculpido por el efecto abrasivo del viento

viscosity a measure of a fluid's resistance to flow

viscosity/viscosidad una medida que indica la resistencia de un líquido al fluir (pág. 287)

volcanic island arc a chain of volcanic islands generally located a few hundred kilometers from a trench where subduction of one oceanic slab beneath another is occurring (p. 266)

volcanic island arc/arco de islas volcánicas una cadena de islas volcánicas generalmente ubicada a unos cientos de kilómetros de una fosa donde está ocurriendo la subducción de una placa océanica debajo de otra (pág. 266)

volcanic neck hardened magma in a volcano's pipe (p. 293)

volcanic neck/cuello volcánico desposito de magma solidificada en la chimenea de un volcán

volcano a mountain formed of lava and/or pyroclastic material (p. 289)

volcano/volcán montaña formada de lava y/o material piroclástico (pág. 289)

W

warm front a front along which a warm air mass overrides a retreating mass of cooler air (p. 565)

Glossary

warm front/frente cálido zona frontal de una masa de aire cálido que avanza para reemplazar una masa de aire frío que retrocede (pág. 656)

water cycle the constant movement of water among the oceans, the atmosphere, geosphere, and the biosphere (p. 158)

water cycle/ciclo del agua movimiento constante del agua en los océanos, la atmósfera, la geosfera y la biosfera (pág. 158)

water table the upper level of the saturated zone of groundwater (p. 171)

water table/nivel freático nivel superior de la zona de saturación de las aguas subterráneas (pág. 171)

wave height the vertical distance between the trough and crest of a wave (p. 456)

wave height/altura de la ola distancia vertical entre el valle y la cresta de una ola (pág. 456)

wavelength the horizontal distance separating successive crests or troughs (p. 456)

wavelength/longitud de la ola distancia horizontal que separa crestas o valles sucesivos (pág. 456)

wave period the time interval between the passage of successive crests at a stationary point (p. 456)

wave period/período de la ola el intervalo entre el paso de crestas sucesivas por un mismo punto

wave refraction the process by which the portion of a wave in shallow water slows, causing the wave to bend and tend to align itself with the underwater contours (p. 462)

wave refraction/refracción de la ola proceso en que la porción de una ola en aguas poco profundas disminuye su velocidad, lo cual causa que la ola se rompa y tienda a alinearse con las curvas de la superficie submarina (pág. 462)

weathering the disintegration and decomposition of rock at or near Earth's surface (p. 68)

weathering/meteorización la desintegración y descomposición de una roca en o cerca de la superficie de la Tierra (pág. 68)

well an opening bored into the zone of saturation

well/pozo abertura excavada dentro de la zona de saturación (pág. 173)

westerlies the dominant west-to-east motion of the atmosphere that characterizes the regions on the poleward side of the subtropical highs (p. 541)

westerlies/vientos del oeste el movimiento dominante de oeste a este de la atmósfera que caracteriza las regiones en el lado polar de las zonas de alta presión subtropicales (pág. 541)

wet adiabatic rate the rate of adiabatic temperature change in saturated air; The rate of temperature change is variable, but it is always less than the dry adiabatic rate. (p. 511)

wet adiabatic rate/tasa adiabática húmeda la tasa del cambio de temperatura adiabática en el aire saturado; La tasa de cambio de temperatura es variable, pero siempre es menor que la tasa adiabática seca. (pág. 511)

wet tropical climate a climate with high temperatures and high annual precipitation

wet tropical climate/clima tropical húmedo clima de altas temperaturas y alta precipitación anual (pág. 593)

white dwarf a star that has exhausted most or all of its nuclear fuel and has collapsed to a very small size, believed to be near its final stage of evolution (p. 712)

white dwarf/enana blanca estrella que ha agotado todo o casi todo su combustible nuclear y que se desvanece hasta alcanzar un tamaño pequeño, que se considera el estado final de su evolución

winter solstice the solstice that occurs on December 21 or 22 in the Northern Hemisphere and on June 21 or 22 in the Southern Hemisphere (p. 482)

winter solstice/solsticio de invierno el solsticio que tiene lugar el 21 ó 22 de diciembre en el hemisferio norte, y el 21 ó 22 de junio en el hemisferio sur (pág. 482)

Z

zone of saturation zone where all open spaces in sediment and rock are completely filled with water (p. 171)

zone of saturation/zona de saturación zona donde todos los espacios abiertos en el sedimento y la roca están completamente llenos de agua (pág. 171)

zooplankton animal plankton (p. 429)

zooplankton/zooplancton plancton animal

Index

Index

Index

Index

Index

Index

Acknowledgments

Editorial development, design, and production
Navta Associates, Inc.

Pages 148–149, **Soil** Taken from *Dictionary of the Earth,* published by Dorling Kindersley Limited. © Dorling Kindersley Limited, 1994, pp. 130–132; *Ecology* published by Dorling Kindersley Limited. © Dorling Kindersley Limited, 2000, pp. 22–23; *Earth,* published by Dorling Kindersley Limited. © Dorling Kindersley Limited, 2000, pp. 52–53. Pages 208–209, **Erosion** Taken from *Earth,* published by Dorling Kindersley Limited. © Dorling Kindersley Limited, 2000, pp. 54–55; *Dictionary of the Earth,* published by Dorling Kindersley Limited. © Dorling Kindersley Limited, 1994, pp. 112–113, 123. Pages 238–239, **Effects of Earthquakes** Taken from *Volcano & Earthquake,* published by Dorling Kindersley Limited. © Dorling Kindersley Limited, 2000, pp.46–47, 56–57. Pages 298–299, **Effects of Volcanoes** Taken from *Volcano & Earthquake,* published by Dorling Kindersley Limited. © Dorling Kindersley Limited, 2000, pp. 14–15, 22, 34–35, 39, 40–41. Pages 438–439, **Ocean Life** Taken from *Nature Encyclopedia,* published by Dorling Kindersley Limited. © Dorling Kindersley Limited, 1998, pp. 68–69, 72–73, 188. Pages 494–495, **Earth's Atmosphere** Taken from *Earth,* published by Dorling Kindersley Limited. © Dorling Kindersley Limited, 2000, pp. 10–11. Pages 578–579, **Winds and Storms** Taken from *Weather,* published by Dorling Kindersley Limited. © Dorling Kindersley Limited, 2000, pp. 38–39, 44–45. Pages 604–605, **Coniferous Forests** Taken from *Nature Encyclopedia,* published by Dorling Kindersley Limited. © Dorling Kindersley Limited, 1998, pp. 78–79.

Illustration
All illustrations by Dennis Tasa

Photographs
Every effort has been made to secure permission and provide appropriate credit for photographic material. The publisher deeply regrets any omission and pledges to correct errors called to its attention in subsequent editions.

Unless otherwise acknowledged, all photographs are the property of Pearson Education, Inc.

Photo locators denoted as follows: Top (T), Center (C), Bottom (B), Left (L), Right (R), Background (Bkgd)

Cover
Jim Lopes/Shutterstock

Front Matter
iv Art Wolfe Inc.; vi (T) Dennis Tasa/Tasa Graphic Arts, Inc., (CL, BL) E. J. Tarbuck, (TL) GeoScience Resources/American Geological Institute; vii Carl Purcell/Photo Researchers, Inc.; viii (B) Stephen Studd/Getty Images; ix (T) Laura Crossey, Ph.D./University of New Mexico Department of Earth and Planetary Sciences; (B) Francois Gohier/Photo Researchers, Inc.; x Seapics; xi Kent Wood/Photo Researchers, Inc.; xii (C) NASA/Science Source/Photo Researchers, Inc.; xiii SPL/Photo Researchers, Inc.; xv (T) Bettman/Corbis, (M) ©David Butow/Corbis, (B) Lawrence Lawry/Photo Researchers, Inc.; xx (B) David Frazier/Photo Researchers, Inc., (C) Reuters/Corbis, (T) SPL/Photo Researchers, Inc.; xxi (C) Fernanda Preto/Getty Images, (TR) Bojan Brecelj/Corbis, (B) King-Holmes/SPL/Photo Researchers, Inc., (TL) Hagai Nativ/PhotoStock-Israel/Alamy, (CL) Pat Lanza-Field/Bruce Coleman, Inc./Photoshot

Chapter 1
1 (C) Art Wolfe Inc.; 2 (TR) Art Wolfe Inc., (BL) James L. Amos/Corbis; 3 (CR) Randy M. Ury/Corbis; 6 (T) Art Wolfe Inc.; 7 (TR) Art Wolfe Inc., (CL) NASA, (CR) NASA/Science Source/Photo Researchers, Inc.; 11 (TR) Art Wolfe Inc.; 15 (C) ©David Butow/Corbis; 16 (T) NASA; 18 (TR) Art Wolfe Inc.; 19 (CR) Jack Dykinga Photography; 20 (CL) Roger Wood/Corbis; 22 (TL) Guy Vanderelst/Getty images, (C) Reuters/Corbis; 23 (TR) Art Wolfe Inc.; 25 (T) Art Wolfe Inc., (C) NASA

Chapter 2
32 (C) Jeffrey A. Scovil; 34 (TR) Jeffrey A. Scovil; 41 (BL) Tom Pantages; 42 (T, CL) Dennis Tasa/Tasa Graphic Arts, Inc.; 43 (CR) Nicholas Rigg/Getty Images; 44 (L) MarcelClemens/Shutterstock, (TR) Jeffrey A. Scovil, (BL) Thom Lang/Corbis; 45 (TBR, CR) E. J. Tarbuck, (TR, CR) GeoScience Resources/American Geological Institute; 46 (B) Dennis Tasa/Tasa Graphic Arts, Inc., (TR) GeoScience Resources/American Geological Institute, (TL) Martin Zwick/AGE fotostock/SuperStock; 47 (BR) Breck P. Kent Natural History Photography; 49 (TR, CR) GeoScience Resources/American Geological Institute; 50 (B) Fred Ward/Black

Star, (TR) Jeffrey A. Scovil; 51 (TL, TC) E. J. Tarbuck, (BR) Herve Berthoule/Photo Researchers, Inc.; 53 (TR) ©Chip Clark/Smithsonian Institution, (CR) E. J. Tarbuck; 54 (BL) Paul Silverman/Fundamental Photographs; 56 (BR) ©DK Images, (T) Jeffrey A. Scovil, (BL) Lawrence Lawry/Photo Researchers, Inc.; 57 (T) Jeffrey A. Scovil, (TR) Rosemary Weller/Getty Images; 58 Dennis Tasa/Tasa Graphic Arts, Inc.; 60 Dennis Tasa/Tasa Graphic Arts, Inc.

Chapter 3
64 (C) Regien Paassen/Shutterstock; 66 (TR) Regien Paassen/Shutterstock, (CL, BL) GeoScience Resources/American Geological Institute; 68 ©Christophe Testi/Shutterstock; 69 (TR) E. J. Tarbuck; 70 (B) Martin Rietze/Stocktrek Images/Alamy, (TR) Regien Paassen/Shutterstock; 71 (TR, TL) E. J. Tarbuck; 72 (BL) E. J. Tarbuck; 73 (CR) Hubert Stadler/Corbis; 75 (B) ©John R. McNair/Shutterstock, (TR) Regien Paassen/Shutterstock; 76 (TL, BL) E. J. Tarbuck; 77 (R, L) E. J. Tarbuck; 78 (TL) E. J. Tarbuck, (BR) Sinclair Stammers/Photo Researchers, Inc.; 80 (TR) Regien Paassen/Shutterstock, (BL) Michael Collier; 81 (TR) Andrew Ward/Life File/Getty Images; 82 (CL) ©Philip Dombrowski; 83 (BR) Breck P. Kent Natural History Photography, (TR) E. J. Tarbuck; 85 (T) Regien Paassen/Shutterstock; 86 (T) E. J. Tarbuck; 87 (TR, BR, CL) E. J. Tarbuck; 90 E. J. Tarbuck; 91 (TR, TL, BR, BL) E. J. Tarbuck, (BR) GeoScience Resources/American Geological Institute

Chapter 4
92 (C) Bettmann/Corbis; 94 (TR) Bettmann/Corbis; 99 (B) Fred Lutgens; 100 ©Bettmann/Corbis; 102 (TR) Bettmann/Corbis, (B) Thomas Del Brase Photography; 103 (TR) Martin Bond/Photo Researchers, Inc.; 104 (BL) J.Mead/Photo Researchers, Inc.; 105 Michael Collier; 106 Ted J. Clutter/Photo Researchers Inc.; 108 (TR) Bettmann/Corbis; 109 (TR) Janis Burger/Bruce Coleman, Inc./Photoshot; 110 (TL) Stefan Zaklin/Stringer/Getty Images; 111 R. Ian Lloyd/Masterfile Corporation; 113 (TR) Bettmann/Corbis, (BR) Steve Starr/Corbis; 114 (BL) SuperStock; 116 (TL) Monty Rakusen/Photolibrary Group, Inc.; 117 (C) Bettmann/Corbis, (C) Michael Collier

Chapter 5
124 (C) Katrina Brown/Shutterstock; 126 (L) Katrina Brown/Shutterstock, (BL) Jane Hallin/Alamy; 127 (BL) Susan Rayfield/Photo Researchers, Inc.; 128 (T) Breck P. Kent Natural History Photography; 129 (L) ©Egmont Strigl/AGE Fotostock, (BR, BC) E. J. Tarbuck; 130 (TL) Doug Plummer/Photo Researchers, Inc.; 131 (TR) E. J. Tarbuck; 132 (TL) Art Wolfe Inc.; 133 (TR) Katrina Brown/Shutterstock; 138 ©Kenneth W. Fink/Photo Researchers, Inc.; 139 R. Ian Lloyd Productions; 140 (B) U.S. Department of Agriculture, (TL) Wayne Lawler/Photo Researchers, Inc.; 141 Carl Purcell/Photo Researchers, Inc.; 143 (TR) Katrina Brown/Shutterstock; 144 ©YURI CORTEZ/AFP/Getty Images; 145 U.S. Geological Society; 146 (T) Chuck Place Photography, (B) E. J. Tarbuck; 147 (R) ©Daniel Goodchild/Alamy Images; 148 (CL) Andrew Green/©DK Images, (B) Georg Gerster/Photo Researchers, Inc.; 149 (TL) ©DK Images, (C) Clive Streeter/DK Images, (BR) Mike Saunders/©DK Images

Chapter 6
156 (C) Jochen Schlenker/Robert Harding; 158 (TR) Jochen Schlenker/Robert Harding; 163 (R, L) Michael Collier; 164 (TR) Jochen Schlenker/Robert Harding; 165 AP Photo/Mark Lyons 167 Art Wolfe Inc.; 168 (B) GeoEye Inc. Satellite Image; 171 (TR) Jochen Schlenker/Robert Harding; 172 (L) Ken Hamblin; 175 U.S. Geological Survey; 176 (B) F. Rossotto/Corbis, (C) Roy Morsch/Corbis; 177 ©Michael Nichols/Getty Images, Mark Lyons/©AP Images; 178 Martin Zwick/age fotostock/Superstock; 179 (TR) St. Petersburg Times; 180 (T) Jochen Schlenker/Robert Harding

Chapter 7
186 (C) Mark Conlin/Getty Images; 188 (B) Ron Niebrugge/Alamy, (TR) Mark Conlin/Getty Images; 190 (T) Bill Stevenson/Alamy; 191 (T) Steve Allen/Getty Images; 192 Kevin Schafer/Alamy; 194 (C, B) E. J. Tarbuck, (T) Marli Bryant Miller; 195 John Schwieder/Alamy; 199 (B) Michael Melford/National Geographic/Getty Images, (TR) Mark Conlin/Getty Images; 200 (T) E. J. Tarbuck; 201 (TL) Michael Collier; 202 (L) Guy Edwardes/Getty Images, (R) Terry Donnelly/Getty Images; 203 (CR) State Historical Society of North Dakota, (TR) Mark Conlin/Getty Images; 204 (TR) Dave Hamman/Getty Images, (B) Fred Lutgens; 205 (TR) Don W Fawcett/Getty Images, (TL) Michael Collier; 208 (CR) James Stevenson/©DK Images, (T) Jack Sharpe/Shutterstock, (B) Andrzej Gibasiewicz/Shutterstock; 209 (BC) ©DK Images, (TR) Ken Hamblin, (TL, CL) Mike Saunders/©DK Images, (BR) SPL E285/022/Photo Researchers, Inc., (TR) Tetra Images/Alamy Images

Chapter 8

216 (C) Yann Arthus-Bertrand "Earth From Above"/Altitude/Peter Arnold, Inc.; 218 (TR) Yann Arthus-Bertrand "Earth From Above"/Altitude/Peter Arnold, Inc.; 219 Bettmann/Corbis; 222 (TR) Yann Arthus-Bertrand "Earth From Above"/Altitude/Peter Arnold, Inc.; 228 (B) Matthew McDermott/Polaris Images, (TR) Yann Arthus-Bertrand "Earth From Above"/Altitude/Peter Arnold, Inc.; 229 (BR) La Prensa Grafica/©AP Images, (BL) NOAA; 232 FLETCHER & BAYLIS/Getty Images; 233 (TR) Yann Arthus-Bertrand "Earth From Above"/Altitude/Peter Arnold, Inc.; 238 (T) ©The Granger Collection, NY, (B) Jorge Silva/Corbis; 239 (BR) Andrew Green/©DK Images, (TR, TC) Andrew S. Dalsimer/Photoshot, (BL) Bettmann/Corbis, (TL) Lenny Ignelzi/©AP Images

Chapter 9

246 (C) WorldSat International Inc.; 248 (T) WorldSat International Inc.; 252 Thomas Barrat/Shutterstock; 254 (BL) Verena Tunnicliffe/University of Victoria, BC, CA, (T) WorldSat International Inc.; 256 NASA; 261 (T) WorldSat International Inc.; 269 (T) WorldSat International Inc.; 270 (T) WorldSat International Inc.

Chapter 10

278 (C) Art Wolfe Inc.; 280 (TR) Art Wolfe Inc., (B) Dolores Ochoa R./©AP Images; 286 (TR) Art Wolfe Inc., (BR, BL) U.S. Geological Survey; 288 (L) Philippe Bourseiller/Getty Images, (R) U.S. Geological Survey; 290 (T) Greg Vaughn Photography, (BR) Michael Collier; 291 Diane N. Ennis/Shutterstock; 292 (B) Kevin Ebi/Alamy; 293 (T) ©Bob Stefko/Getty Images, (CR) University of Washington Libraries, Special Collections Division, John Shelton Collection, KC 6673; 295 (TR) Art Wolfe Inc., (BR) Laura Crossey, Ph.D./University of New Mexico Department of Earth and Planetary Sciences; 296 (TR) E. J. Tarbuck; 297 (TR) Art Wolfe Inc.; 298 (BL) Vulkanette/Shutterstock, (C) Andrey Lebedev/Shutterstock, (C) Phyllis Picardi/Imagestate Media, (TL) Rapho Agence/Photo Researchers, Inc.; 299 (CR, BR) ©DK Images, (CC) ©dalish/Shutterstock

Chapter 11

306 (C) Art Wolfe Inc.; 308 (TR, BL) Art Wolfe Inc.; 312 (TR) Art Wolfe Inc., (B) Darwin Wiggett/Corbis; 313 (B) Stephen Studd/Getty Images; 314 Fletcher & Baylis/Photo Researchers, Inc.; 316 (BR) Chris Noble/Getty Images; 317 (BL) Michael Collier; 320 (TR) Art Wolfe Inc., (BL) Terry Donnelly/Alamy Images; 332 (T) Art Wolfe Inc.; 333 (T) Art Wolfe Inc., (CR) U.S. Geological Survey

Chapter 12

334 (C) Bryan Busovicki/Shutterstock; 336 (TR) Bryan Busovicki/Shutterstock, (CL, BL) U.S. Geological Survey; 338 (TL) E. J. Tarbuck, (B) Francois Gohier/Photo Researchers, Inc.; 339 (B) E. J. Tarbuck; 341 (T, C) E. J. Tarbuck; 342 (TR) Bryan Busovicki/Shutterstock, (CL) Reuters/Corbis; 343 (TL) Patrick Poendl/Shutterstock, (BC) Breck P. Kent Natural History Photography, (TC, BL) E. J. Tarbuck, (TR) Florissant Fossil Beds National Monuments/US National Park Service/Herb Meyer; 344 Carl Buell; 346 Colin Keates/Getty Images; 347 (TR) Bryan Busovicki/Shutterstock; 350 Reuters/Corbis; 352 All Canada Photos/SuperStock, (T) Bryan Busovicki/Shutterstock; 353 (TR) Bryan Busovicki/Shutterstock, (BR) Martin Bond/Photo Researchers, Inc.; 355 Ed Reschke/Photolibrary Group, Inc.

Chapter 13

362 (C) Clara/Shutterstock; 364 (TR) Clara/Shutterstock, (BL) James L. Amos/Corbis; 367 (BR) Biophoto Associates/Photo Researchers, Inc., (BL) SPL/Photo Researchers, Inc.; 368 (T) Chase Studio/Photo Researchers, Inc., (B) Sinclair Stammers/Photo Researchers, Inc.; 369 (TR) Clara/Shutterstock, (BR) GeoScience Resources/American Geological Institute; 370 (TL) Publiphoto/Photo Researchers, Inc.; 371 Neg #GEO 80820C/©The Field Museum of Natural History, Chicago; 372 Kaj R. Svensson/Photo Researchers, Inc.; 373 (BR) Publiphoto/Photo Researchers, Inc.; 374 Neg #GEO85637C/©The Field Museum of Natural History, Chicago; 375 Arnold Newman/Peter Arnold, Inc.; 376 Francois Gohier/Photo Researchers, Inc.; 377 (TR) Clara/Shutterstock, (B) Sinclair Stammers/Photo Researchers, Inc.; 378 Biophoto Associates/Photo Researchers, Inc.; 379 (B) Chris Butler/Photo Researchers, Inc.; 380 (BL) Francois Gohier/Photo Researchers, Inc.; 382 (TR) Clara/Shutterstock, (B) Topham/The Image Works, Inc.; 385 Photo Researchers, Inc.; 389 SPL/Photo Researchers, Inc.

Chapter 14

392 (C) Galyna Andrushko/Shutterstock; 394 (TR) Galyna Andrushko/Shutterstock; 401 (TR) Galyna Andrushko/Shutterstock; 406 (T) Galyna Andrushko/Shutterstock; 407 (TR) Galyna Andrushko/Shutterstock; 409 Deep Sea Drilling Project/Scripps Institution of Oceanography; 410 (BL) Greg Ochocki/Photo Researchers, Inc., (TR) Galyna Andrushko/Shutterstock; 411 (TR, TL) ©IFM-GEOMAR; 412 Institute of Oceanographic Sciences/NERC/Photo Researchers, Inc.; 413 W. Townsend, Jr./Photo Researchers, Inc.

Chapter 15

420 (C) Seapics; 422 (TR) Seapics; 423 (TR) Eastcott Momatiuk/Getty Images, (BL) NASA, (BR) Paul Steel/Corbis, (TL) Steve Allen/Getty Images; 428 (C, B) Norman T Nicoll/Natural Visions, (TR) Seapics; 429 (BL) David Hall/Photo Researchers, Inc., (BR) Images&Stories/Alamy, (T) Tom McHugh/Photo Researchers, Inc.; 432 (T) Dudley Foster/©Woods Hole Oceanographic Institution; 433 (TR) Seapics; 438 (TR, BL) ©DK Images, (C) Helmut Corneli/Alamy; 439 (BR) blickwinkel/Schmidbauer/Alamy, (TR) Kelvin Aitken/Peter Arnold, Inc., (TL) Malcolm McGregor/©DK Images, (CR) Ronald Sefton/Photoshot; 440 E. J. Tarbuck

Chapter 16

446 (C) Jeffrey Murray/Getty Images; 448 (B) sergioboccardo/Shutterstock, (TR) Jeffrey Murray/Getty Images; 450 (L) Rosenstiel School of Marine and Atmospheric Science; 451 (BR) NASA; 452 (T) British Antarctic Survey/Photo Researchers, Inc.; 454 (T) Jeffrey Murray/Getty Images; 455 (TR) Jeffrey Murray/Getty Images, (BR) Rafael Macia/Photo Researchers, Inc.; 461 (TR) Jeffrey Murray/Getty Images, (BR) W.K. Fletcher/Photo Researchers, Inc.; 464 (T) Sinclair Stammers/Photo Researchers, Inc., (B) U.S. Department of Agriculture; 466 (B) Skyscan/Corbis; 467 (T, B) Courtesy U. S. Army Corps of Engineers, (B) Nova Scotia Department of Tourism, Culture & Heritage; 468 (T) Nova Scotia Department of Tourism, Culture & Heritage

Chapter 17

474 (C) Stone/Getty Images; 476 (BL) Mike Groll/Stringer/Getty Images, (TR) Stone/Getty Images; 479 (B) Natalia Bratslavsky/Shutterstock; 483 (TR) Stone/Getty Images; 485 Gary Yeowell/Getty Images; 488 (CL) Bobbe Z. Christopherson, (TR) Stone/Getty Images; 494 (TR) Johnson Space Center/NASA Image Exchange, (BL) Nicholas Hall/©DK Images, (BL) SPL E540/072/Photo Researchers, Inc., (TL) Wayne Lawler/Photo Researchers, Inc.; 495 (TR) NASA Image Exchange, (TL, BL) Stephen Bull/©DK Images; 496 E. J. Tarbuck

Chapter 18

502 Dina Calvarese/Shutterstock; 508 (T) Jacek Chabraszewski/Shutterstock, (B) E. J. Tarbuck; 510 E. J. Tarbuck; 515 Tuna/iStockphoto 517 (B) E. J. Tarbuck; 520 Ales Liska/Shutterstock; 522 NOAA; 523 (B) ©David Butow/Corbis

Chapter 19

530 (C) Terje Rakke/Getty Images; 532 (B) Annie Griffiths Belt/Getty Images, (TR) Terje Rakke/Getty Images; 537 (B) Jake Rajs/Getty Images, (TR) Terje Rakke/Getty Images; 543 (TR) Terje Rakke/Getty Images; 545 (TR) Belfort Instrument Company; 549 (B) NASA, (T) Terje Rakke/Getty Images

Chapter 20

556 (C) Kent Wood/Photo Researchers, Inc.; 557 (TR) National Gallery of Art, Washington, DC; 558 (TR) Kent Wood/Photo Researchers, Inc., (B) NOAA; 561 (B) Tony Dejak/©AP Images; 562 (T) Tony Arruza/Corbis; 563 Layne Kennedy/Corbis; 564 (B) Kenneth Garrett/National Geographic Image Collection, (TR) Kent Wood/Photo Researchers, Inc.; 568 NOAA; 571 (TR) Kent Wood/Photo Researchers, Inc.; 574 Warren Faidley/Weatherstock®; 575 NOAA; 578 (TR) ©DK Images, (BL) 1989 - Warren Faidley/Weatherstock®; 579 (TL) 1996 - Warren Faidley/Weatherstock®, (BL) AFP PHOTO/Jewel SAMAD/Getty Images, (C) JOHNSON LIU/AFP/Getty Images, (R) Naval Research Laboratory, (TR) Richard Corey/Getty Images

Chapter 21

586 (C) Yva Momatiuk and John Eastcott/Photo Researchers, Inc.; 588 (B) Pete Saloutos/Corbis, (TR) Yva Momatiuk and John Eastcott/Photo Researchers, Inc.; 591 (L) Charlie Ott Photography/Photo Researchers, Inc., (R) iStockphoto/Thinkstock; 592 (B) David Keaton/Corbis, (TR) Yva Momatiuk and John Eastcott/Photo Researchers, Inc.; 593 (T) Art Wolfe/Photo Researchers, Inc., (B) Stan Osolinski/Dembinsky Photo Associates; 599 (T) Natalie Fobes/Corbis; 600 (TR) Yva Momatiuk and John Eastcott/Photo Researchers, Inc.; 601 StockTrek/Getty Images; 604 (BC) ©DK Images, (CR) Matthew Ward/©DK Images, (BL) Winfried Wisniewski/Corbis; 605 (CR) ©DK Images, (CC) Cyril Laubscher/©DK Images, (BR) Joe McDonal/Corbis, (TR) Johnny Johnson/Stone/Getty Images, (TL) Malcolm McGregor/©DK Images, (CC) Peter Chadwick/©DK Images; 606 (BC) ©DK Images, (CR) Matthew Ward/©DK Images, (BL) Winfried Wisniewski/Corbis

Chapter 22

612 PhotoPlus Magazine/Getty Images; 614 (B) David Lees/Corbis; 616 (R) Bettman/Corbis, (L) Stapleton Collection/Corbis; 617 (BR) Royal Ontario Museum; 619 (B) SSPL/Getty Images; 620 (BR) NASA, (T) Yerkes Observatory Photograph; 622 (B) SPL/Photo Researchers, Inc.; 626 (CR, CL, BR, BL) Lick Observatory; 628 (Inset) alnilam/iStockphoto; 630 (B) Lick Observatory; 634 NASA; 635 (T) PhotoPlus Magazine/Getty Images, (L) Museum of Science and Industry; 640 (B) Lick Observatory

Chapter 23
642 (C) Michael Collier; **644** (T) Michael Collier; **649** (T) Michael Collier, (B) NASA; **650** (T, B) NASA; **651** SPL/Photo Researchers, Inc.; **652** (T) NASA, (B) U.S. Geological Survey; **653** NASA; **654** (T) Michael Collier; **655** Nasa/National Geographic Image Collection; **657** NASA; **658** (T) California Association for Research in Astronomy/Photo Researchers, Inc., (B) NASA; **659** NASA; **660** (T) Michael Collier; **661** (B) NASA; **663** Jerry Lodriguss/Photo Researchers, Inc.; **664** James P. Mandaville/Aramco World Magazine; **665** (T) Michael Collier, (C) U.S. Geological Survey

Chapter 24
672 (C) SPL/Photo Researchers, Inc.; **674** (TR) SPL/Photo Researchers, Inc.; **678** (TR) SPL/Photo Researchers, Inc., (B) Yerkes Observatory Photograph; **681** (L) David Parker/SPL/Photo Researchers, Inc., (R) National Radio Astronomy Observatory; **682** NASA; **683** NASA; **684** (TR) SPL/Photo Researchers, Inc. (B) Kent Wood/Photo Researchers; **685** (B) National Solar Observatory/NOAO/AURA/NSF; **686** NASA; **687** (R) National Solar Observatory/NOAO/AURA/NSF; **688** (B) Pi-Lens/Shutterstock; **690** Péter Gudella/Shutterstock; **691** (T) SPL/Photo Researchers, Inc.

Chapter 25
698 (C) SPL/Photo Researchers, Inc.; **700** (TR) SPL/Photo Researchers, Inc.; **701** (T) NOAO/AURA/NSF; **705** (T, B) Lick Observatory; **706** Anglo-Australian Observatory; **707** (B) NASA, (TR) SPL/Photo Researchers, Inc.; **710** (BL) Anglo-Australian Observatory; **711** Lick Observatory; **713** (TR) California Institute of Technology/Palomar Observatory; **715** (B) Dr. Axel Mellinger, (TR) SPL/Photo Researchers, Inc.; **717** (T) Anglo-Australian Observatory, (CR) California Institute of Technology/Palomar Observatory, (BL) ESO Education & Public Relations, (BR) NASA; **718** (BL) NASA; **722** Fundamental Photographs, (T) SPL/Photo Researchers, Inc.

Skill and Reference Handbook
729 (B) Russ Lappa; **730** Benjamin Volant/Alamy Images; **731** Martin Shields/Getty Images; **742** (C) Russ Lappa.